ANCIENT ISRAEL
Myths and Legends

LILITH AND THE ANGELS

From an original painting by F. H. Amshewitz, R.B.A.

Page 78

ANCIENT ISRAEL
Myths and Legends

3 Volumes in 1

ANGELO S. RAPPOPORT

Ph.D.

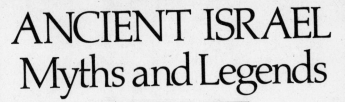

With Illustrations by
J.H. Amshewitz

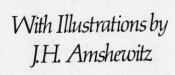

THE MYSTIC PRESS
LONDON

Previously published by The Gresham Publishing
Company Ltd

This edition published 1987 by The Mystic Press
a division of Bestseller Publications Ltd
Princess House, 50 Eastcastle Street, London W1

FOREWORD

To the average person myth and legend are things from the distant past, a time when people still believed that day and night were the result of the sun being pulled across the sky by a chariot, that if you sailed too close to the edge of the world you might fall off into the jaws of hungry serpents, and that with the help of the philosopher's stone it was possible to turn lead into gold.

Yet whether or not we wish to acknowledge them, myths and legends still abound today. Maybe not in the classical form of gods who pull the strings of the universe—although the Allah of the Moslem religion or the figurehead of Buddhism are myths to worshipers of the Judeo-Christian God, and vice versa—but certainly in the stereotypes, beliefs, and apocryphal wisdom to which all societies cling that set them apart from other cultures and give them identity within the history of their people.

The impulse to create myths has never been extinguished and no doubt never will be. Dictionaries tell us that a myth is a historical story that embodies a cultural or world view, and that a legend is a more secular expression of a myth, a historical tale that cannot be substantiated. But these definitions fail to emphasize that both are a natural expression of the human need to put the unknowable or inexplicable into some kind of easily recognizable order. To the Greeks and Romans, that might have meant anthropomorphizing the unpredictability of natural disasters by endowing these events with the same personalities they saw bringing about the orderly and regular change of seasons. From our twentieth-century perspective, that may seem like a rather primitive way of looking at the natural world. Yet in modern science, nuclear physicists are postulating the existence of sub-atomic particles that defy all natural laws as we know them, that are unobservable, and yet must be present from the effect they appear to have on observable phenomena. Who is to say that centuries from now, this will seem any less absurd than a religious culture that attributed the coming of winter to Persephone's unwilling return to the underworld? The history of knowledge is the history of discarded myths.

The myths and legends of a particular culture usually provide more of an insight into that culture than standard history texts. They express matters larger than everyday life—what a society most fears, most reveres, most hopes for and most wants to believe—but which significantly affect everyday life. The myths and legends of ancient Israel are no exception. The Hebrew culture, whose identity is more bound up with its religion (a sort of intermediary between myth and history) than most, is an example. Reading the numerous legends and variants that Angelo S. Rappoport has gathered in *Ancient Israel: Myths and Legends*, one cannot help but ask questions about the people that produced them. What kind of authority did they seek in a divinity who would smite cedars for their pride and make them weep? Presumably the same unquestionable kind of authority which God would later use to discipline man for the same offense. Who can leave the heroic treatments of David, Moses, and Isaac without coming to the conclusion that these men were role models for their culture.

Rappoport reminds us that the myths and legends of ancient Israel were always concerned with the manifestation of divine will and that they had a moral purpose. That these allegories had a didactic function is undeniable, but it should also be kept in mind that, even in their "un-reality," they are admirably practical. When one wants to know why something is, and how it came to be that way, one has only to turn to myth to find the shortest distance between the two points. To note that after the divine will created the earth—but before it created man—it "called into being the Divine Throne, the Holy Law, Repentance, Paradise, Hell, the Holy Temple, and the name of the Messiah; in a word, all the conditions which represent Divine Providence, Law and Order, Good Deeds, Reward and Punishment, Prayer and Redemption," is to learn that man came into a world of predetermined rules that were subject neither to interpretation nor abrogation. Why must man follow these rules? Because they were ordained before his creation. In a world where the black and white of moral and ethical values constantly threatens to turn gray, myth provides a spiritual compass with which the individual can always find true north.

A serious discussion of a society's myths risks giving them more weight than even their creators would. No group fashions its culture from myths; rather, myth, like any other art, is an artifact of the culture. (It should be remembered that myths and legends spring from the same oral tradition that eventually gave rise to literature.) Readers should come to *Ancient Israel: Myths and Legends* to find out something more about the ancient Hebrew culture than he already knows, perhaps by comparing its myths with the myths of his own nationality, or balancing different myths that have arisen over the same theme within the Hebrew culture. That these stories sometimes clash with each other in no way diminishes their value. Myths are not right or wrong. They simply are there, because mankind needs them and has the imagination to create them.

—Richard Michaels

ANCIENT ISRAEL
Myths and Legends

Volume 1

Contents

Plates

VOLUME ONE

PREFACE

The times when the myths and legends, fables and parables contained in Jewish post-Biblical literature, in the *Talmud* and in the *Midrashim*, were taken literally and quoted for the purpose of throwing ridicule upon the people of Israel are behind us. The science of folk-lore now looks upon myths and legends as congenial products of the popular mind and of the soul of the people. Such products Jewish mythical and legendary lore may claim to be. All myths and legends owe their origin and existence to the conceptions of the people and their traditions. They are manifesting the characteristics of each race, mirroring its soul, its dreams and hopes, its joys and sorrows.

Jewish myths and legends are therefore of interest to us because they reveal the soul of a people, of a peculiar people. All through Jewish myth and legend there is an echo of sadness, but also of hope. The present may be gloomy, but the Lord never forsakes those who put their trust in Him. Jewish myths and legends also possess a particular attraction for us, be we Christians or Jews, because they all centre round Biblical personages and the episodes related in the Bible, which is the book *par excellence*, and which for centuries has exercised a cultural influence upon humanity. They cluster round personages with whom we have been familiar since our earliest childhood.

In Western modern prose and poetry Biblical personages are usually depicted and represented in such a way as to convey to us a wrong impression. They often strike us as caricatures, so strange as to offend our religious and æsthetic feelings. Such is not the case in the legendary lore of the Hebrews, which is an eastern product. Here the personages with whom we are familiar are painted in their original and natural colours. However much they may be surrounded by imaginary descriptions, it is always done in a Biblical spirit, in a spirit congenial to that of the Testament. Monologues and dialogues taking place in heaven or upon earth, angels descending at the express command of God and taking part in the actions of men, do not at all shock us. The Rabbis and mythographers of Judaism gave a full expression to the beliefs and traditions of the people, to the floating myths and legends, but they invested this legendary lore with a beautiful symbolism.[1] They made use of this branch of post-Biblical lore as a means of expression for speculative thought and profound spiritual teaching.

A study of Jewish myth and legend is almost necessary if one wishes to understand and appreciate the ethical background of Jewish life and literature, of the people who were the first to fuse life, literature, economics, and politics into one with ethics and religion (as has been done by the Prophets and continued by the gentle Rabbi of Nazareth). More than any other branch of Jewish literature, perhaps, the legendary lore shows us the outlook of the Jews upon life and the world. In order, however, to appreciate these myths and legends, fables, tales, and parables, at their full value, the reader should bear in mind the social surroundings under which they developed. He should read these myths and legends without European prejudices, and not look at them with European eyes.

> "Wer den Dichter will verstehen,
>   Muss in des Dichters Lande gehen,"
> says Heine.

---

[1] That dealer in curiosities, Isaac D'Israeli, entirely misunderstood the symbolism of Jewish legendary lore (see *Curiosities of Literature*, 1835, Vol. I, pp. 100–5).

The myths and legends of Israel deal with the creation of the world, the mysteries of creation, angels and demons, Paradise and Hell, with the creation of Man, with Patriarchs, Prophets, and Priests, with kings and popular heroes. Their origin lies not so much in a desire to invent as in that of explaining Holy Writ and human destiny. Long after the Biblical canon had been closed and Israel had left its national soil, the Jews continued to weave legends round Biblical personages and Biblical episodes, and this poetic activity extended over ten centuries. Its tendency was to supplement by phantasy, imagination, legend, and exposition, what appeared incomprehensible in Holy Scripture. In our opinion Jewish myths and legends are *not* the " first and primitive material out of which evolved and developed the Bible ". We are not looking for myth and legend in the Bible.

We deal in the Introduction with the influence which India, Egypt, Babylonia, and Persia have exercised upon Jewish myth and legend, and also with the influence which Jewish legendary lore has, in its turn, exercised upon mediæval folk-lore. Throughout this volume (and the following) we have also referred to Mohammedan tradition, and the reader is offered a survey of the legends of Islam clustering round Biblical characters.

This work is intended for the general reader who may have heard of the myths and legends clustering round Biblical characters and episodes, but who has no opportunity of reading them, the sources being inaccessible to him. We hope, however, that even the scholar will peruse these volumes with interest and to some advantage, whilst the Biblical student may find therein points to interest him. We have read almost all the sources available and referred to them in our notes and in the appended bibliography. Not only Hebrew and Aramaic sources, but also Hellenistic have been consulted, and we have made an effort to bring together as many myths and legends

as time and space would permit us. The scattered threads
of all these myths, and especially legends, we have woven
together in such a way as to form a continuous narrative.
We hope, therefore, that our readers will peruse with interest
and enjoyment the myths, legends, and tales contained in the
following chapters.

ANGELO S. RAPPOPORT.

INTRODUCTION

I

The Characteristics of Jewish Myth and Legend

Jewish myths have this in common with the myths of other nations, that they are the offspring of phantasy and imagination, without any basis of reality. All the powers of nature are placed under the control and rule of a higher will. Like the myths of other nations, the myths of Israel, too, are mostly allegories describing the origin and development of some power of nature.

Jewish myths, however, differ considerably in many of their characteristics from the myths of other peoples. The nations of antiquity looked upon the personified powers and manifestations of nature as upon so many independent and self-sufficing beings. For them, nature was a conglomeration of numerous manifestations of wills. Jewish myths differ in this respect, for Jewish thought is based upon the idea of *one* unique will, manifesting itself in the Universe. The invisible rulers of all natural manifestations are therefore the servants and representatives of this one and unique power ruling the Universe.

Another characteristic trait distinguishing Jewish myths from the myths of other nations is the following: The higher beings manifesting themselves in corporeal shape and form, and who, in the mythologies of other nations, take an interest and a part in human actions, do so *without any moral purpose*. Jewish myths, on the contrary, are always based upon a moral and ethical idea. The Most High, the Supreme Ruler of the Universe, is the source of moral perfection and the moral being *par excellence*, His sole aim and constant desire being the happiness, prosperity, and welfare of His creatures. He vouchsafes unto men as unto all the creatures His benevolence and mercy. Only when the latter abandon the right path and act contrary to morality, does He wax wroth with them, often punishing them severely. His punishment, however, is not the result of revenge, but serves a moral purpose, for His punishment and His chastisements are intended to make the sinners repent, turn back, and mend their ways. He is thus once more acting in accordance with the principles of morality. And just as the Supreme Being, the Most High, so all His representatives, the superior beings who serve to execute His commands, are highly moral beings, their slightest transgressions being punished severely. In the mythologies of other nations myth and religion are closely interwoven. Among the Greeks, for instance, the numerous gods and semigods, and even the heroes, had their separate cults and enjoyed divine worship and honour. Not so among the Jews. Myth among the Jews is only in so far related to religion as it endeavours to proclaim and to lay stress upon the omnipotence of the Creator, one and unique, and to glorify the Lord of the Universe, all His representatives serving to increase His power. They enjoy no divine worship whatever, they themselves, on the contrary, being engaged in proclaiming the power and majesty of the One God, glorifying His name and singing hymns in His praise.

A further characteristic trait which distinguishes Jewish myths from the myths of other nations concerns the plastic arts. Among the nations of antiquity, and particularly among the Greeks, myths were from the very beginning closely related to and interwoven with the plastic arts. Every product of imagination and phantasy, however grotesque and bizarre, was made manifest to the people and was impressed upon their minds by an artistic representation in colour and line, painted on canvas or carved in marble and stone. Wherever the eye turned, in temples, upon public places, and in private houses, it met the artistic representation of some national myth which thus impressed itself upon the mind of the nation and became part of the national spirit.

Not so among the Jews. The Mosaic Code rigorously forbids the plastic imitation of all natural phenomena and of the manifestations of the powers of nature. Myths, therefore, could not for long take root in the popular mind of the Jews, and only remained the patrimony of the cultured and educated, of the scribes, the scholars and teachers. According to their own conceptions and philosophies, their *Weltanschauungen* and the schools of thought to which they belonged, these learned men extended and elaborated the myths, but always with a view to ethical teachings and moral lessons to be drawn from the respective myths. Thus Jewish myth does not always remain in a sphere accessible to the uncultured mind, but lives and moves and has its being on the Pisgah heights of thought which are only attained by a developed intellectuality. From the domain of popular imagination Jewish myth has, therefore, for the most part, passed into the realm of metaphysics.

Jewish myths may be lacking the attractiveness and *joie de vivre* of Greece, but they are distinguished by their innate moral basis.

The majority of Jewish myths and legends came into existence towards the end of the Jewish national life, and bear the traces of Persian or Græco-Roman influence. But everywhere these influences were adapted to Jewish monotheistic conceptions and were modified accordingly. Persian dualism, the struggle between Ormuzd and Ahriman, did not suit Jewish monotheism, and the principle of evil and darkness was imagined not as an equal power with the principle of good, and as an independent creator, but as a rebel against his master, as the winged Seraph Sammael, who, as a punishment for his arrogance, was hurled from regions celestial into those of darkness. Jewish myth further shows another characteristic distinguishing it from the myths of Greece. Both sexes, masculine and feminine, are admitted into the heaven of Greece. Both males and females exercise with equal arbitrariness their unlimited powers, benevolent or pernicious, controlling the destinies of man. Gods and goddesses in the Greek Pantheon have their serving spirits representing both sexes. In Jewish myths, on the contrary, the feminine sex is entirely excluded from celestial regions, to which women, in a truly Oriental way, are not admitted. On the other hand, the female beings abound in the realm of darkness. There are no female angels but numerous female demons in Jewish myths, a circumstance due to Oriental influences.

And yet, man and woman are equally admitted into Paradise. Serah, the daughter of Asher, entered Paradise alive, and there were prophetesses in Israel upon whom the Divine Spirit descended.

Jewish myths deal with all parts of the Universe. They extend to heaven and to earth, water and air, angels and demons, Paradise and Hell.

Just as the myths of other nations, the myth of ancient Israel is the graceful, light-winged child of phantasy, the foster-child of the two wonderful twin sisters Religion and Language which, from the very beginning of civilization, have raised savage man from the depths of animal instinct to a higher spiritual level. The ethical purpose of Jewish myths and legends is to explain the course of the Universe and the destinies of man. They endeavour to show that all creatures are guilty and should strive to expiate their guilt. Whilst, however, the mythographers of other nations turned to nature, the Jews turned to the Bible, and the majority of their myths and legends are based upon passages of the Holy Writ, endeavouring to explain them so as to appeal to the people. Jewish myths and legends, therefore, mostly deal with Old Testament history, and with Old Testament characters, and it was in the direction of the Bible that Jewish imagination, the imagination of the mythographers of Judaism, took its flight. These myths and legends were based upon and woven round the Biblical episodes of the Creation of World and Man, of the Garden of Eden, the Creation and Fall of Adam, the Fallen Angels, the stories about the Patriarchs, Prophets, and Priests, of the Kings and Heroes.

It was natural, however, that pagan elements should penetrate into these myths and legends. Round the Biblical stories were woven legends and myths not only about the Only God, but about a host of angels, demons, and spirits who are the mediators between Jehovah and Israel. The Jews are a wander-nation, and so is their lore. In the course of their peregrinations the Jews adopted many ideas and conceptions from their neighbours with whom they came into contact. The Jewish lore, which originated in the ruins of Palestine, was carried to and continued in Babylonia and Africa, and the river which issued forth from the Holy Land was later on swelled by the stream of mysticism which discharged its waters upon the intellectual productions of the Jews and fertilized the field of their imagination.

II

Foreign Influence upon Jewish Myth and Legend

Jewish myths and legends, although a product of the national Jewish spirit, are subject to many foreign influences. Palestine was from the beginning a thoroughfare where East and West met and mingled, and, from a political point of view, it was, perhaps, unfortunate that Moses should have chosen a spot where the eastern and western legions were destined constantly to meet. From an intellectual point of view, however, the Promised Land had the advantage of becoming, to a certain extent, the melting-pot of different civilizations and *Weltanschauungen*. Foreign civilizations, Egyptian, Persian, Babylonian, and Indian, have left their traces upon Judaism, and especially upon the Jewish myths and legends which, side by side with the Law, were developed among the nation, handed down from generation to generation, and penetrated into the oral law and its Haggadic portions.

Both the *Talmud* and the *Midrashim* distinctly show traces of foreign influence in their Haggadic portions, i.e. in the myths, legends, tales, and parables. Often these influences are diametrically opposed to the spirit of Judaism, whilst on other occasions they are changed and adapted so as to suit the ethical exigencies of Judaism.

It was especially during the Hellenistic period that foreign myths and legends penetrated into Judaism and gained citizen rights. The Hellenistic Jews, who wrote in Greek, were not eclectic, but thoroughly syncretistic and easily accessible to foreign influences. The description of the death of Adam and of Eve, where angels came to bury them, the description of the death of Moses, where we read that the Creator Himself came to take his soul and that the three ministering angels, Michael, Gabriel, and Zagsagel were present, preparing the Prophet's couch and spreading out a sheet of fine linen, are reminiscent of Egyptian mythology.   Amsath, Huphy, Daumatuf, and Quabah Sanuf, the four Egyptian geniuses of death, are supposed to remain near the soulless body, and separate gods watch over every limb.[1] Egyptian and Phœnician myths and legends of gods and heroes are introduced into Jewish popular lore. They are changed, altered, and adapted, so as to suit the spirit of monotheism, but never can they deny their foreign origin. Myths and legends relating to the mysteries of creation, of life and death, to the birth of the child, to the cradle and the death-bed, to the domains of theogony and apotheosis, enter *en masse* from Egypt, Phœnicia, and Greece, and later on from Babylonia, Persia, and India, and are re-echoed in Talmud and Midrash. Thus, in the pages of this volume, we have told many legends relating to the angels, the creation of the world, the death of Adam and Abraham, and generally the angel of death.

From the Jews this conception of the four angels being present at the death of man was taken over by Christianity and gnosticism.

The legends relating to Eve often remind us of the Egyptian goddess Isis, those relating to Adam of Yima or Yemshid, whilst the legends about Joseph (as related in the second volume of this work) distinctly resemble those of Osiris and the Egyptian myths about this divinity. The death of Joseph and the finding of his coffin by Moses, as related in Jewish legend, bear a striking resemblance to the myth about Osiris. Typhon, we read in Plutarch,[2] had once, by a ruse, prevailed upon his brother Osiris to lie down in a box. Thereupon Typhon closed the box, nailed it up, poured molten lead over

---

[1] See Güdemann, in *Monatsschrift*, Vol. XXV, p. 227.
[2] Plutarch, *De Is. et Os.*, 22, 13.

it, and threw it into the Nile. Isis, informed of this deed, wandered about, searching for the body of her son. She was at last informed by children, to whom the gift of prophecy had been vouchsafed, in which direction the coffin had been carried away by the waters of the Nile. She found the coffin and buried it. It is Isis in Egyptian mythology who finds the coffin, whilst it is Serah in the Jewish legend. Güdemann[1] rightly remarks that the name of Serah's father, Asser or Asher, may have some connection with the Egyptian name of Osiris, which is Assar. It has also been pointed out that the legends relating to Crœsus and his wealth had penetrated into the Talmud, where they centre round the name of Eliezer ben Charsum, who was immensely wealthy, and on the day of whose death Belshazzar was born.[2]

Of the Greek legend of Ariadne and her thread, we are reminded by a legend in *Midrash Shir-Hashirim*[3] and in *Midrash Koheleth*.[4] There was once a vast palace with numerous entrance doors, and whoever entered the palace lost his way therein. A wise man, one day, fastened a reel of reed at the entrance, and the people were thus able to find their way in the labyrinth without losing themselves. That the *Haggadah*, which contains the essential parts of Jewish myths and legends, has borrowed from Hellenism, is undeniable, although it is not always easy to trace the sources. The story of the bed of Procrustes is found in *Sanhedrin*,[5] where it is told of the Sodomites.

Not only Greece, Egypt, and Phœnicia, but Persia, Babylonia, and even distant India exercised their influence upon the myths and legends of Israel as they have come down to us in Talmud and Midrash. The Indian work *Pantshatantra*, which was destined to be translated during the later Middle Ages by a Jew, was, no doubt, known to the Rabbis of the

---

[1] *Monatsschrift*, Vol. XXV, p. 231.
[2] *Yoma*, 9a; 35b; *Midrash Koheleth*, 4 8; see also Perles, in *Monatsschrift*, Vol. XXI, pp. 268–70.   [3] 1, 1.   [4] 2, 12.   [5] 109b.

Talmud and the Haggadists of the Midrash. The story of Nahum Ish Gimso [1] reminds us of an Indian story in the *Pantshatantra*.[2]

The legend about the creation of Eve which explains the reasons why woman was created from the rib of man is explained as follows in the Midrash. Eve was not created from the head of Adam, lest she should be vain, nor from his eyes, lest she should be wanton, nor from his mouth, lest she should be given to gossiping, nor from his ears, lest she should be an eavesdropper, nor from his hands, lest she should be meddlesome, nor from his feet, lest she should be a gadabout, nor from his heart, lest she should be jealous. She was drawn from man's rib, which is a hidden part, so that she might be modest and retiring. And yet, notwithstanding all the precautions taken by the Creator, woman has all the faults God wished to guard her against.[3]

This passage finds a parallel in the following Indian legend:

When the Creator had made up His mind to fashion woman, He suddenly noticed that the matter at His disposal had already been entirely used up in the creation of Adam. What did He do? He took the undulations of the serpent, the clinging faculty of the creepers, the trembling of the blade of grass, the erect stature of the reed, the velvet of the flower, the lightness of the leaf, the look of the gazelle, the cheerfulness of the sun-ray, the tears of the clouds, the inconstancy of the wind, the softness of down, the sweetness of honey, the cruelty of the tiger, the burning heat of fire, the freezing effect of ice, and the chattering of the magpie, mixed all these elements together and created woman.[4]

The legends and myths about Adam, as contained in Jewish sources, in Talmud and Midrash, also bear traces of Persian influence. The influence of Parsism, if not upon

---

[1] *Taanit*, 21a. [2] Th. Benfey, *Pantshatantra*, I, 129. [3] *Genesis Rabba*, 18.
[4] Cf. August Wunsche, in *Wissenschaftliche Beilage der Leipziger Zeitung*, 1905, No. 67; see also Daehnhardt, *Natursagen*, Vol. I, p. 123, note.

the Bible, as some scholars pretend,[1] is paramount when we
come to Jewish myths as contained in the Midrashim and the
Haggadic portions of the Talmud. The majority of legends
relating to Adam which we have told in the pages of this book
bear a striking resemblance to the stories of Yima or Yemshid
and of Meshia, although, of course, it is difficult to draw the
line and to prove to what an extent the Jews influenced their
Persian neighbours, and to what an extent they were influenced
by the latter.

Jewish demonology has also been influenced by the
Persians, although some scholars are of opinion that it is un-
wise to draw hasty comparisons between Jewish and Persian
demonology.[2] It must, however, be admitted that the Adam
legends and those of Yima and Meshia have much in common.
The reader will find many of the legends of Adam from
Talmud and Midrash quoted in the following pages.

Jewish mythographers drew largely and borrowed from
their Persian neighbours not only because the latter were
already a highly civilized nation, but also because the Persians
were opposed to the image cult. Persian was also the vernacular
of the Jews dwelling in the country, as we are informed in the
Talmud.[3] In the *Vendidad* we read that Yima is called the
Brilliant One, because (as explained by a commentator) light
emanated from him. He was destined to live eternally, but,
in consequence of his sin, he was condemned to death. Like
Adam, who fasted 130 years and kept away from Eve,[4] Yima,
too, after his fault, repented.[5]

Of Indian origin may be the story of King Solomon and
Asmodeus who usurped the King's place, whilst the King was
wandering about in distant lands, begging from door to door. The
legend was taken over by the Mohammedans and brought to

[1] Erik Stave, *Ueber den Einfluss des Parsismus auf das Judentum*, Haarlem, 1898.
[2] See *Revue des Etudes Juives*, Vol. VIII, p. 202.
[3] *Sotah*, 49b.   [4] *Erubin*, 18b.
[5] Kohut, in *Z.D.M.G.*, Vol. XXV, pp. 59–94.

Europe, where it appeared at first in the *Gesta Romanorum*, and was told of the Emperor Jovinianus.[1]

Of Indian origin may also be the legend of Abraham and Nimrod. Terah, the father of Abraham, had handed over his son to the terrible Nimrod that he might punish him for his iconoclasm.

" If," said Nimrod, " thou wilt not worship the God of thy father, then worship at least fire."

" Why," said Abraham, " should we worship fire rather than water? Is not water stronger than fire which it has the power to quench?"

" Well then," replied Nimrod, " prostrate thyself before water and worship it."

" Clouds," said Abraham, " are greater than water, for they contain in themselves this element."

" Well then, adore the clouds," said Nimrod.

" The wind," again said Abraham, " is more powerful than the clouds, for it disperses them. Why should we not worship the wind?"

" Then, worship the wind," replied Nimrod, growing impatient.

" Man," said Abraham imperturbably, " is even stronger than wind, for he can fight against it. Why should we not worship man?"

Nimrod's patience was now at an end, and he gave orders that Abraham be thrown into the fiery furnace.[2]

Jewish legend also relates that when the Egyptians were about to seize the new-born Jewish babes with the intention of killing them, the earth opened her mouth and swallowed them up, thus protecting them until they had grown up, when

[1] See, however, against Varnhagen, *Ein indisches Märchen auf seiner Wanderung*, Berlin, 1882, the refutation in *Revue des Etudes Juives*, Vol. XVII, pp. 58–65.

[2] See *Genesis Rabba*, 38; Benfey, *loc. cit.*, 376–7; see also Koehler, *Germania*, Vol. II, pp. 481–5, where several mediæval fables containing the same idea are mentioned; see also A. C. M. Robert, *Fables Inédites*, Paris, 1825, Vol. I, p. ccxvii, and compare the fable by La Fontaine, *La Souris métamorphosée en Fille*.

they returned to their respective homes.[1] In the same tractate of the Talmud it is also related that when Moses was born, the house was filled with light, and parallels to this legend are found not only in the life of Buddha, who cast a light upon his surroundings when he was still in his mother's womb,[2] but also in those of Aesculapius and Servius Tullius. It is further related[3] that, when the Israelites had passed the Red Sea, the sucklings began to sing hymns in praise of the Lord. The Indian Prithu, Buddha, the Greek Apollo, all spoke immediately after their birth, whilst Bacchus sang in his mother's womb.[4]

III

Jewish Influence upon Mediæval Folk-lore

If Jewish myths and legends bear the traces of Egyptian, Indian, Persian, Babylonian, or Greek influence, Jewish legendary lore has, on the other hand, penetrated into European literature and affected the fables, parables, and heroic tales of other nations. To a great extent the folk-literature of the Middle Ages owes its dissemination to the Jews. They carried the precious merchandise from East to West and back again from West to East. The Jews have ever been famous as commercial travellers, but they have not always limited their sphere of action to material goods. They have also hawked about the intellectual and poetical wares and products of humanity: Religion, Philosophy, Poetry, and Folk-lore. St. Paul may be said to have been the first and most famous traveller of this kind. He introduced to the Aryan world the best products of Judea: The Prophets and Christianity. Medi-

---

[1] *Sotah,* 12b.
[2] P. Toldo in *Studien zur vergleichenden Litteraturgeschichte,* 1901, p. 339.
[3] *Sotah,* 30b.   [4] Toldo, *loc. cit.,* p. 340.

ators of the spiritual and intellectual life of distant lands and of a
remote past, the Jews brought to Europe intellectual treasures
and enriched mediæval literature with the wealth of an apocryphal and legendary lore. Hellenistic and Roman, French
and German, Italian, or English culture has affected the Jews,
but they, too, have influenced the peoples among whom it has
been their destiny to dwell. Although not all popular tales,
myths, or legends mentioned also in Jewish sources can be
directly attributed to the Jews—for they may have been derived
from third and earlier sources—a good many myths, legends,
tales, and fables were brought to Europe by the Jews and found
citizen rights in European literature. It would, for instance,
be going too far to ascribe all beast-fables to the Talmud, for
a good many of them may owe their origin to India and Egypt,
but there is no doubt that they were brought to Europe by the
Jews. It is, however, no exaggeration to say that most myths
and legends about Creation and the Old Testament characters
found in mediæval and modern literature may directly be
traced to the Talmud and the Midrashim. The Jews transmitted
these legends and tales to their neighbours. During the Middle
Ages they were, perhaps, the best translators;[1] they took up the
spade and dug the gold from the rich mines, bringing it speedily
into circulation. Through their translations they acquainted
Europe with the mythical and legendary lore of the East.
Three converted Jews produced the most favourite popular
works during the Middle Ages. They were: Petrus Alphonsus,
author of the *Disciplina Clericalis*; John of Capua, who translated
into Latin *Kalila and Dimna*, or the *Fables of Bidpai*, from the
Hebrew of a certain Rabbi Joel;[2] and finally Pauli, author of
Schimpf and Ernst. We must further mention the *Mishle Sendebar*,
and Ibn Chisdai's *Prince and Dervish* (*Barlaam and Josaphat*).
The latter work was not translated from Hebrew into any

---

[1] See M. Steinschneider, *Die Hebräischen Uebersetzungen des Mittelalters und die Juden als Dolmetscher*, 2 Vols., Berlin, 1893.
[2] See M. Gaster, in *Monatsschrift*, 1880, p. 36.

other language till the end of last century, but it may still have influenced European literature.

Jewish influence upon Christianity and Christian legends has been admitted by many Christian scholars.[1] Several legends contained in the little book *Hibbur Yafeh*, written by Rabbi Nissim,[2] have evidently been translated or utilized by Rudolf von Ems (*Der gute Gerhard*).[3] The legends about Adam, Joseph, and Moses in Christian sources may be traced to Jewish influences.

Unfortunately, many tales of which no trace is to be found in either Talmud or Midrash are attributed to the Jews, the Talmud being given as their source. During the sixteenth century, when Reuchlin and Pfefferkorn waged their famous war for and against the Talmud, many pamphlets appeared wherein, as is usually the case, passages from the Talmud were consciously and purposely represented in an unfavourable light. Comparative mythology was yet unknown in those days, and what now appears merely an allegory or a legend was taken literally.

Thus it is interesting to notice that, in a poem dating from the year 1557, Hans Sachs[4] relates the following story.

The Creator had taken a rib from Adam, intending to shape woman out of it. He put it aside and was busy removing the blood from His hands, when a dog, passing by, caught up the rib and ran off with it. An angel caught the dog by his tail and tore it off. Out of the dog's tail the Lord made woman, long-haired, and beautiful of figure. Woman possesses now two qualities which are due to her dog-tail origin. Like the dog, who wags his tail when he is anxious to get something, woman flatters and caresses man when she wishes to get something

---

[1] H. Gunter, *Die christliche Legende des Avendlandes*, Heidelberg, 1910.

[2] See Zunz, *Gottesdienstliche Vorträge*, p. 133.

[3] See Gaster, *Germania*, Vol. XXV, pp. 274–84.

[4] *Fabeln und Schwänke*, ed. Gotze, I, 522, No. 182; see also Daehnhardt, *loc. cit.*, pp. 19–20. Of Jewish origin are also the two poems by Hans Sachs, *The Monk with the Capon*, and *The Gold in the Stick of Cydias* (Cf., however, *Zeitschrift für vergl. Litteraturgesch.*, Vol. XI, pp. 38–59).

out of him. She barks like a dog when she does not get her will.
Now this legend is found in the folk-lore of the Bulgarians,
Hungarians, Lettonians, Ukrainians, &c.[1] Hans Sachs, however, attributed this story to the Talmud, just as another story
in Hermann Schraders' *Bilder-Schmuck der deutschen Sprache*
is attributed to the Talmud. There is, of course, nothing of
the kind either in the Talmud or in the Midrashim.

A similar error was made by Thomas Moore, who wrote
a poem based on the legend that Adam was created with a
tail and that out of this tail God made Eve, giving as its
origin Rabbinic Lore. It is entitled: *The Rabbinical Origin of
Woman*, and was printed in the edition of 1826 on page 467.
It runs as follows:

> They tell us that woman was made of a rib
> Just picked from a corner so snug in the side;
> But the Rabbins swear to you that this is a fib,
> And 't was not so at all that the sex was supplied.
>
> And old Adam was fashioned, the first of his kind,
> With a tail like a monkey, full yard and a span,
> And when nature cut off this appendage behind,
> Why, then woman was made of the tail of the man.
>
> If such is the tie between women and men,
> The ninny who weds is a pitiful elf,
> For he takes to his tail, like an idiot, again,
> And makes a most damnable ape of himself.
>
> Yet, if we may judge, as the fashion prevails,
> Every husband remembers the original plan,
> And knowing his wife is no more than his tail,
> Why, he leaves her behind him as much as he can.

The legend, however, that Adam was created as an andro-
gyne, and that Eve had been cut off from his body, is of

---

[1] See Daehnhardt, *Natursagen*, Vol. I, pp. 115–24.

rabbinic origin, and has found its way into Arabic and Christian literature.

The Jewish legend according to which God took for the creation of Adam dust from the four corners of the world, red, black, white, and brown,[1] is not only found in Arabic and Syriac literature, but has also a parallel in Slavonic literature.[2]

In the *Dialogue between Saturn and Solomon* it is stated that Adam's body was made from earth, his red blood out of fire, his breath out of the wind, his inconstancy of mind from the clouds, his eyes out of flowers, his sweat out of dew, and his tears out of salt.[3] This legend is also found in a different version in Russian folk-lore.[4]

We are referring in this volume to Lilith, who, according to rabbinic legend, was the first wife of Adam. The influence of this legend may be traced, as it seems to us, in Russian folk-lore, where it is said that woman had been made out of a dough and placed in the sun to dry. A dog swallowed her up, and the Lord created another woman out of Adam's rib.[5]

The story of Noah, Satan, and the planting of the vine, related in the pages of this volume from the *Midrash Tanchuma* (*Gen.* 9, 20), may be of Indian origin, as the four qualities of the vine are described in a collection of anecdotes and sayings of Indian sages. Wine has four qualities which it communicates to those who drink it; they are the qualities and characteristics of the peacock, the ape, the lion, and the pig.[6] Anyhow, this legend, which, in a different version, is also related in *Genesis Rabba*, 36, and is referred to in *Yalkut* I, § 61, not only occurs in Arabic but has penetrated into European literature. Damiri tells this story of Adam.[7] It is found in the

---

[1] See Ch. 13.   [2] Daehnhardt, *loc. cit.*, p. 112.
[3] See R. Koehler, *Kleinere Schriften*, Berlin, 1900, Vol. II, p. 2.
[4] Daehnhardt, *loc. cit.*, p. 111.   [5] *Ibid.*, p. 116.
[6] See *Z.D.M.G.*, Vol. XL, pp. 412, 425; Daehnhardt, *loc. cit.*, p. 308.
[7] See Goldziher in *Z.D.M.G.*, Vol. XXIV, p. 209, note 2; Grünbaum, *Neue Beiträge zur semitischen Sagenkunde*, p. 435.

Gesta Romanorum,[1] is mentioned by Pauli in his *Schimpf and Ernst*,[2] in a German poem of the fourteenth century, and in a poem by Hans Sachs.[3]

A modern Greek legend (where Satan is not one of the dramatis personæ), which reminds us of the journey of Dionysius to Naxos, relates the following story. When Saint Dionysius (who takes the place of the pagan God) was still young, he travelled through Hellas to Naxia. He saw a small plant which was very beautiful and took it with him. Afraid lest it would dry up under the scorching sun before he reached Naxia, he found the bone of a bird and stuck the plant into it. It grew, however, so fast that its roots soon traversed the bone. The Saint, therefore, stuck the bone of the bird into the bone of a lion, and this again, when the plant still continued to grow, into the bone of an ass. When he arrived at Naxia and found that the roots of the plant were entangled with the bones of the bird, of the lion, and of the ass, he planted it just as it was. Wonderful grapes grew up, out of which Dionysius pressed wine. And lo! when men drank of it they acquired all the characteristic traits of birds, lions, and asses. When a man drinks one cup he sings like a bird, he is as strong as a lion when he drinks more, and makes an ass of himself when he has had too much wine.[4]

The story of Noah and the planting of the vine, and especially the four qualities of wine, is also found in various Slavonic tales and legends, in a German poem by Joh. Martin Usteri, and in Victor Hugo's *Les Misérables*.[5] Daehnhardt also mentions an Indian tale which relates how opium came into existence, and this story bears a striking resemblance, if not to the part

---

[1] Ed. Oesterley, p. 539.   [2] Ed. Oesterley, p. 161.

[3] See Daehnhardt, *loc. cit.*, p. 303; *Revue des Traditions Populaires*, IV, p. 411; R. Koehler, Vol. I, p. 577; Tendlau, *Das Buch der Sagen*, p. 181; see also Grünbaum, *Jüdisch-Deutsche Chrestomathie*, p. 184.

[4] See Hahn, *Griechische und albanische Maerchen*, II, 76; Daehnhardt. *loc. cit.*, p. 308; Grünbaum, *Neue Beiträge zur semitischen Sagenkunde*, p. 440.

[5] Book VI, Ch. 9; cf. Koehler, *loc. cit.*, Vol. I, p. 577.

which Satan is supposed to have taken in the planting of the
vine, at least to the qualities wine is said to possess.

A Rishi once changed a mouse into a cat, a dog, an ape,
a pig, an elephant, and a maiden. The maiden becomes queen,
but one day falls into a well and is drowned. At the advice of
the Rishi she is left there, and the well is stopped. From her
body grows the plant out of which opium is made. The smoker
of opium acquires all the characteristic traits of the animals
into which the mouse had been changed. He is frolicsome
like the mouse, loves milk like the cat, is quarrelsome like the
dog, dirty like the ape, wild like the wild pig, and proud like
a queen.[1]

The Midrash relates that Abraham, after imagining that
either the moon or the sun had created the world and were the
rulers of the Universe, came to the conclusion, when he saw
them disappear from the sky, that they were only servants of
the Creator and dependent upon a higher will. He broke the
idols of his father, and was brought before Nimrod and thrown
into a burning furnace, but, whilst the servants of Nimrod who
approached the fire were immediately consumed, Abraham
walked about unmolested in the midst of the flames.[2] The
entire legend from the Midrash is found (as Mr. Israel Levi
has already discovered before us) in the works of St. Atha-
nasius,[3] where it is told of Melchizedec, a brother of Melchi,
and a son of Queen Salem and of her husband, an infidel
Greek whose name was also Melchi. The Christian author
bases his story upon a passage in the *Epistle to the Hebrews*,
7, 3, where it is said: " He is without father or mother. . . ."

Many stories found in the Midrash about the cruelty of
Sodom and the sentences of its judges we have related in the
pages of this volume. The story about the long and short
beds reminds us of the bed of Procrustes, whilst Benfey[4] calls

---

[1] Daehnhardt, *loc. cit.*, pp. 299–300.   [2] See Ch. 19.
[3] Migne, *Patrologia Graeca*, Vol. XXVIII, col. 523–9.   [4] *Loc. cit.*, p. 402

attention to a tale by Lutfullah in which the judge follows
the method of the judges of Sodom.

In the third century of the Hegira there lived in Cairo
a judge of the name of Mansur ben Musia. A soldier had
borrowed money from a Jew and given the latter a bill wherein
he promised him a pound of his flesh, should he be unable
to pay. When the day of payment arrived, the soldier found
himself unable to pay his debt; the Jew wanted to drag him
before the judge, and the soldier escaped. In his flight he
jostles a pregnant woman whom he knocks down so that she
miscarries, runs against a rider, gives his horse a blow and
knocks out the latter's eye. He runs on, climbs up upon a hut,
falls through the roof and kills a man. The Jew, the cousin
of the pregnant woman, the rider, and the son of the man
who had been killed, catch the soldier and bring him before
the judge. In front of the latter's house they see a drunken
man, whilst another man, still alive, is being buried. The
judge now pronounces the following sentences: With regard
to the Jew, he decides in the Shakespearian fashion, namely:

> Therefore prepare thee to cut off the flesh.
> Shed thou no blood, nor cut thou less nor more,
> But just a pound of flesh; if thou cut'st more
>
> .   .   .   .
>
> Thou diest, and all thy goods are confiscate.[1]

As for the rider, who was asking half the price of his horse
which he valued at 200 gold pieces, the judge decrees that
the horse be cut lengthwise into two equal halves, the un-
damaged half being kept by the owner, whilst the damaged
be given to the soldier, who, however, should pay 100 gold
pieces to the rider. With regard to the woman, the soldier
is to live so long with her until she has another child. As for
the son whose father the soldier had killed, the son is to get
upon the roof of the hut, fall down upon the soldier and thus

---

[1] *The Merchant of Venice*, Act IV, Scene 1.

kill him. Naturally, all the plaintiffs withdraw their claims. When the judge is asked who the drunken man is, he replies that he is the taster, drinks being often mixed with poison. As for the man who was being buried alive, two witnesses had testified that he had died, but he had now returned. As the two witnesses confirmed their statement that the man had really died, it could not be his real self but a ghost, and in order to put an end to the discussion, the judge had ordered the man to be buried.[1]

Numerous stories about demons and devils in mediæval literature are traceable to the East, and especially to Jewish literature. They have been imported into Europe by the Crusaders, the Moors of Spain, and especially by the Jews. The story of the wood-cutter and the Spirit in *Thousand and One Nights* reminds us of the famous tale of Belfegor as related by Machiavel, where a certain peasant makes his fortune by curing noble persons possessed by Belfegor. Belfegor had been sent down to earth to find out whether there was any truth in the complaints of many souls brought to hell that their predicament was due to their wives. Belfegor, in order to find out the truth, married a lady of birth, and settled in Florence under the name of Roderic de Castile. His wife being somewhat of a scold, he was glad to escape from her and to keep in hiding by possessing certain noble ladies. In the case of the daughter of the King of France, he refused to leave her, in spite of the entreaties of the peasant to whom he owed a debt of gratitude. The peasant at last used a stratagem and approaching the possessed princess exclaimed: " Roderic, your wife is coming in search of you." Scarcely had Belfegor heard these words than he leaped out of the princess and descended straight to hell, where he confirmed the statement the truth of which he had been commissioned to find out.[2]

---

[1] See Benfey, *loc. cit.*, pp. 402–3; see also Gaster, in *Monatsschrift*, 1880, pp. 115–17.
[2] See Dunlop, *History of Prose Fiction*, Vol. I, pp. 186–8; Benfey, *loc. cit.*, pp. 525–6.

Now this tale, which also spread in various Slavonic countries, may be traced in the Talmud,[1] where it is told of the demon Ben-Temalion who entered the daughter of the Emperor of Rome and was expelled by Rabbi Simon ben Yohai. One day the Rabbi and several other men went as a deputation to Rome with a view to asking the Emperor to revoke certain edicts against the Jews. Ben-Temalion meeting them on the way, offered them his services. He would enter the royal princess and consent to leave her only when the Rabbi was asked to cure her of her madness. Ben-Temalion kept his word. As the princess was constantly calling for Rabbi Simon, he was summoned into the Imperial presence and undertook to cure the princess. He whispered into her ear the name of Ben-Temalion, and the demon immediately left the possessed maiden. As a reward for his cure, Rabbi Simon obtained from the Emperor the repeal of the laws hostile to the Jews. Such is the Jewish legend as given in the Talmud, in Rashi, and in the *Tefillat R. Simon ben Yohai*.[2]

It has, however, been pointed out by some scholars that during the first centuries of our era the legends about holy men and saints exorcising devils and curing possessed men and women were particular only to the Christian literature. Some have, therefore, seen in the story of Ben-Temalion an historical background, referring to a Roman Senator who was friendly disposed to the Jews,[3] whilst Mr. Israel Levi[4] maintains that the story of Ben-Temalion (or Ben Talmion) is a Christian legend about the apostle Bartholomew which found entrance into the Talmud.[5] We see, however, no reason for these theories. The Jewish legend may be traced to an Indian source[6] and the Christian legend is based upon the Talmud. It

---

[1] *Meilah*, 17b.
[2] Jellinek, *Beth-Hamidrash*, Vol. IV, pp. 117–8; see also *ibid.*, Vol. VI, pp. 128–30.
[3] See Geiger's *Zeitschrift*, Vol. II, pp. 273–8.
[4] *Revue des Etudes Juives*, Vol. VIII, pp. 200–2; Vol. X, pp. 68–93.
[5] See Fabricius, *Codex Novi Test.*, p. 674; Migne, *Dictionnaire des Apocryphes*, II, col. 153–7.   [6] See Benfey, *loc. cit.*, I, p. 520.

is more probable that the friendly demon is turned into a Saint than vice versa.

In the *Çuka Saptati* the following story is told.

In the town of Vatsaman there once lived a Brahman who was wise but very poor. His wife, Karagara, was such a shrew that a friendly demon, dwelling in a tree near the house, escaped to the desert on account of her bad temper. Soon afterwards the Brahman himself, unable to stand any longer the temper of his wife, left his house. He met the demon who thus addressed him: " Fear not, O Brahman, I was an inmate of thy house and I will do thee a good turn. Go thou to the town of Mrigavati where the King of Madana lives. I will enter the body of his daughter and only consent to leave her at thy command. The Brahman went to Mrigavati and everything happened as the demon had arranged. Thereupon the demon entered the body of another princess, but when the Brahman was called and asked to cure her, the demon refused to leave his new abode, in spite of the Brahman's adjurations. When, however, the latter suddenly exclaimed: " Here cometh my wife Karagara," the demon took fright and fled.[1]

The story of King Solomon and the finding of the Shamir finds parallels in Arabic and European literature. An Arabic tale based upon the Talmud story[2] runs as follows. One day King Solomon summoned the Ifrits or Afrits, demons and jinns, and commanded them to bring before him the demon Sahr. " O Prophet of God," said the Ifrits, " Allah has given unto this Sahr so much strength that all the demons together are unable to do anything against him. There is only *one* way by which this Sahr may be brought into our power. Every month he visits a source situated upon an island where he drinks his fill. It is now our advice to empty this source and

---

[1] See *Çuka Saptati*, transl. by R. Schmidt, Kiel, 1894, pp. 66–7 (46th night); Benfey, *loc. cit.*, I, pp. 519–20; *Revue des Etudes Juives*, Vol. X, pp. 68–9; *Z.D.M.G.*, Vol. XXXI, p. 332.   [2] *Gittin*, 68b.

fill it with wine. When Sahr comes to visit the source and does not find any water, he will drink the wine, get intoxicated, and fall asleep. We shall then be able to seize him and bring him before thee." Solomon commanded them to act accordingly. The jinns emptied the source of water, filled it with wine, and hid themselves near by behind trees. Soon Sahr appeared, and smelling the wine, exclaimed: " O wine, thou art delicious, but thou dost deprive one of intelligence, makest stupid the wise, and causest regret." He left the source without having drunk out of it. On the third day, being tormented by thirst, he returned. " I cannot escape," he exclaimed, " the fate which God has decided to bring upon me." He drank his fill, made a few steps, but fell down. From all sides the Ifrits hurried to the spot and carried him away, whilst flames were issuing forth from his mouth and nostrils. When Sahr appeared before Solomon and beheld his signet ring, his strength left him, and humbly prostrating himself before the king, he called out: " How great is thy power, O Prophet of God, but it will leave thee one day and nothing but remembrance will remain!" " Thou speakest the truth," said Solomon.[1]

That Solomon required the Shamir wherewith to cut the stones for the Temple is also related by Kazwini. The diamond is a stone which cuts all other stones. Now when King Solomon began to build the Temple, he commanded the demons to hew stones. They caused such a noise that the people complained. The king thereupon summoned the most wily among the jinns into his presence and asked them whether there existed a means how to hew the stones without making any noise. " We, O Prophet," replied the Ifrits, " know not of such a means, but there is a demon named Sahr who is not in thy service; he may know of it." Solomon commanded the Ifrits to bring this demon into his presence, and when he

---

[1] Alkisai, quoted by Grünbaum, in *Neue Beiträge zur semitischen Sagenkunde*, pp. 227–8.

came he put the same question to him. " I know of a stone, O Prophet of God," replied Sahr, " with which thou mayest cut stones without causing any noise, but I know not where the stone may be found. I will tell thee, however, how to find out where this stone is. Visit an eagle's nest." Solomon commanded the Ifrits to find an eagle's nest. The eagle was just away, and they placed a glass globe over his young. When the eagle came and saw his young imprisoned under the glass globe, he flew away. He returned on the following morning holding a stone in his beak, and with this stone he cut the glass. When Solomon heard this, he summoned the eagle into his presence. " Tell me, where didst thou find the stone with which thou didst cut the glass globe?" " The stone, O Prophet of God," replied the eagle, " I found upon a mountain in the west, the *Samur* mountain." When Solomon heard this, he had stones brought from the Samur mountain with which the stones for the Temple were cut.[1]

The story of King Solomon and the finding of the Shamir is mentioned not only by Petrus Comestor in his famous work (*Historia Scholastica*), but also by Garnerius, bishop of Langres (1195), and is related in the poem *Das Lob Salomons*, a German epic dating from the eighth century.[2] The author of this poem has evidently borrowed from the Babylonian Talmud his reference to the " Worm on the Lebanon ".

" King Solomon," says the author, " made up his mind to catch a dragon (Ashmedai), and in order to do so, he emptied all the water wells of Jerusalem, and filled one of them with wine and hydromel. The dragon drank and, being intoxicated, was easily caught and sent to King Solomon. Thereupon the dragon thus addressed the king: ' Sire, if thou releasest me I will teach thee how to build the Temple in one year.' Thereupon the dragon told the king of a worm on the Lebanon

---

[1] Grünbaum, *loc. cit.*, pp. 229–30.
[2] See K. Mullenhoff und Scherer, *Denkmäler deutscher Poesie und Prosa aus dem 8–12 Jahrhundert*, 3rd ed., Berlin, 1892, I, pp. 124–41.

out of the sinews of which he advised him to make a cord wherewith to saw stones. King Solomon gave orders for the worm to be caught on the Lebanon, and out of its sinews a cord was made, so that the king could build the Temple without making use of any iron tools, in accordance with the instructions he had received." [1]

The Shamir is mentioned by Grimm in his *Deutsche Mythologie*, and by A. Kuhn, in his *Herabholung des Feuers*.

" The spring wurzel," writes Grimm, " is a herb that can be procured in the following manner: The nest of a green or black woodpecker, while she has chicks, is closed tight with a wooden bung; the bird, on becoming aware of this, flies away, knowing where to find a wonderful root which men would seek in vain. She comes carrying it in her bill and holds it before the bung, which immediately flies out as if driven by a powerful blow. Now, if you are in hiding and raise a great clamour on the woodpecker's arrival, she is frightened and lets the root fall." [2] Grimm then relates the story of the rock-splitting Shamir as found in the Talmud. [3]

The Shamir is either a worm or a stone, and was one of the ten marvels created in the evening twilight of the sixth day or the first Friday. [4]

In Jewish tradition, the Shamir is an insect rather than a stone. In some non-Jewish works, on the other hand, a plant is described to which the power of splitting stone is attributed. This reminds us of the story of Rabbi Simon, who had nailed up the nest of the hoopæ (the bird Dukhiphath). The latter brought a plant and placed it upon the nail which was at once destroyed. This story has passed to the Greeks, [5] and is incorporated in the *Gesta Romanorum* where it is told of the Emperor Diocletianus.

[1] *Kings*, 6, 7; see Leo Landau, *Hebrew-German Romances*, Teutonia, Leipzig, 1912, XXI, p. 16.
[2] Grimm, *Teutonic Mythology*, London, 1883, Vol. III, p. 973.
[3] See *ibid.*, Vol. IV, p. 1598, note.   [4] *Abot*, V, 6.
[5] See Aelian., *Histor. animal.*, III, 26.

In a learned article, Israel Levi pointed out the resemblance of the story of Ashmedai, especially in the first part where the demon is performing certain actions which strike Benajah as strange, with the story of the *Hermit and the Angel*.[1] We are referring to this comparison in Vol. II, where we venture to differ from the eminent authority. The story of Asmodeus and Benajah only in so far resembles that of the Angel and the Hermit that in both we see a being endowed with supernatural powers, committing certain acts which strike his companion as strange, but which are justified by deeper reasons known to him alone. Here, however, it is the question of the Shamir that interests us, and no mention whatever of this worm or stone is made in the story of the Angel and the Hermit. The story of the Shamir is also found in the *Historical Mirror* by Vincent de Beauvais, and is related by Gervasius of Tilbury.[2] As for the tale relating Solomon's exile and return, we again find parallels not only in the *Gesta Romanorum*, but also in English and German mediæval poetry. (*Robert of Cysilie*, and *Der nackte König*).[3]

The story of the fox and the weasel,[4] which we have related in this volume and which is taken from the *Alphabetam Siracidis*, finds a parallel in *Yalkut* I, § 182, and in Berechya Ha-Nakdan's *Fox-fables*, No. 105. An exactly similar story is found in Benfey's *Pantshatantra*, and in the Syr. translation of Bickell (Leipzig, 1876), where it is related of the turtle.[5]

Rabbinic myths, legends, and tales have entered Moslem literature, and Mohammed and his commentators have largely drawn from Jewish sources, especially from the Haggadah, as the pages of this volume will show. Such, for instance, is

---

[1] See *Revue des Etudes Juives*, Vol. VIII, pp. 64–73; Gaston Paris, *La Poésie du Moyen Age*, pp. 151–87.

[2] *Otia Imperialia*; see also Cassel, in *Denkschriften der Königl. Akad. der Wissenschaften*, Erfurt, 1854.

[3] See F. H. von der Hagen, *Gesammtabenteuer*, 1850, Vol. III, p. cxv and p. 409.

[4] See Ch. 14.

[5] See Benfey, *loc. cit.*, I, pp. 475–8; Gaster, in *Monatsschrift*, 1880, pp. 475–8.

the myth of Shemhazai and Azael, a tale of Jewish origin which, in Mohammedan literature, is told of Harut and Marut.[1] The Jews themselves, however, may have borrowed this myth from Babylonia. Estira, who rejected the advances of the fallen angel, is Ishtar, or Istahar, goddess of love and passion, worshipped in Syria and Palestine under the name of Ashtoreth, who played an important part in the mythology of the Assyrians and Babylonians. She is supposed to have fallen in love with the hero named Gilgamesh who, however, refused to yield to her charms and rejected her advances. When Istahar asked him to kiss her and be her bridegroom, Gilgamesh reminded her of the sad fate incurred by her previous lovers who were driven forth from her embrace and encountered many misfortunes. Enraged at such an insult, Istahar, who was the daughter of the god Anu, went up to heaven and asked her father to avenge her.[2]

The story of Sunda and Upasunda in the *Mahabharata* also bears a striking resemblance to the myth of Shemhazai and Azael and of Harut and Marut. Sunda and Upasunda were so austere that they acquired much merit for themselves and ultimately sovereignty over heaven and earth. Brahma, jealous of them, created a lovely maiden named Tilottamâ whom he sent as a gift to the brothers. Both brothers desiring to have her as wife, hate sprang up in their hearts, and they slew each other. The maiden returned to Brahma, who was delighted at her achievement. He blessed her and said: " Thou shalt circle all over the world where the sun shines, and no one shall be able to gaze at thee on account of thy brilliancy."[3] The Jews may have borrowed the tale of Shemhazai and Azael from Babylonia, but there is no doubt that Mohammed derived it from a Jewish source.

---

[1] See Ch. 6.
[2] See M. Jastrow, *Religion of Babylonia and Assyria*, 1898; P. Haupt, *Das babylonische Nimrodepos*, Leipzig, 1884–91; see also Tisdal, *The Original Sources of the Quran*, 1905, pp. 101–2. [3] See Tisdal, *loc. cit.*, p. 103

Jewish legends and tales have also penetrated into *Thousand and One Nights*. Although according to Benfey, " the substance of all the fables may be entirely traced to India," [1] the Talmud may also be considered as one of the sources of *Thousand and One Nights*.

The story of the pious man who refused to commit the sin of adultery, and to whom a ruby, taken from the throne he was to occupy in Paradise, was sent down from heaven, is to be found literally in the Talmud (*Taanith*, 24b–25a), where it is told of the pious Rabbi Chanina ben Dosa whose poverty was proverbial. The tale of the Sultan of Yemen and his three sons, who were exceedingly sharp and intelligent, and could guess the truth from the most insignificant details which would escape the eye of the ordinary observer, is to be found literally in the Talmud[2] and in *Midrash Echa*, where the stories are told of the inhabitants of Jerusalem, renowned for their cleverness and logical deductions of which a modern Sherlock Holmes might have been proud. Not only into *Thousand and One Nights* but also into European literature have these tales found entrance, and some are mentioned in the collection *Cento novelle antiche* (thirteenth century) and in Voltaire's *Zadig*. The story of the *Wandering Jew* seems to us to be a development of the legends clustering round the Prophet Elijah, and Chidhr of the Moslems, whilst the Faust legend has many analogies with the story of Solomon and Ashmedai.[3]

The story of the blind and the lame joint-gardeners of a rich man who stole the fruit of the garden, the lame getting upon the shoulders of the blind man, is based upon the conversation between the Emperor Antonine and Rabbi Jehuda. This tale has been incorporated in the *Gesta Romanorum*.[4]

[1] *Loc. cit.*, I, p. 117.   [2] *Sanhedrin*, 104.
[3] See for reference notes, Vols. II and III of this work.
[4] Cf. Perles, in *Monatsschrift*, 1873, p. 14 ff.

IV

The Sources of Jewish Myth and Legend

Jewish myths and legends have come down to us in the rich and abundant storehouse of post-Biblical literature. They are scattered all over the *Talmud*, " the vast sea of the Talmud ", and over the *Midrashim*, or the so-called expository literature. Much material is also found in the *Targumim*, or Biblical translations and paraphrases, in the *Apocrypha* and in the *Apocalypses*, and above all in the *Pseudoepigraphical* literature. The works of Philo and Josephus, of Demetrius and Artapanus, the commentaries of the Pentateuch and the works of the later mystics, are also sources which we have consulted for the present and the following volumes. In the Talmud the myths and legends are to be found in the *Haggadah* (*Agada*), that is, in the Haggadic portions of the Talmud. And here it will be necessary, for the benefit of the general reader, to explain the meaning and nature of the Haggadah.

Originally Haggadah meant recitation of the teaching of Scripture, and, in a narrower sense, the exegetic amplification of Biblical passages, especially of the non-legal portions. Gradually the word was applied to Biblical exegesis and interpretation in general. It explained the Law from both the religious and the ethical standpoints, expressing religious and philosophical, ethical, and mystical thoughts, but always with a view to bringing near to man Him at whose word the world came into being. Its purpose was that of inducing man to walk in the ways of the Lord.[1]

The Haggadah, or narrative, was the popular branch of the expository literature, for, instead of dealing with ritual

[1] See Sifri, *Deuteron.*, 11, 22.

and legal matters, as does the *Halachah*, it concerned itself
with old traditions, customs, and beliefs, myths and legends,
parables and allegories, in a word, with all that enters not
only into the domain of mythology but also into that of folk-
lore. Whilst the Halachah concerned itself with the legal
portions of the Bible, the Haggadah drew its material from the
narrative portions and the poetical passages of the Old Testament. The Haggadah is thus the more cheerful sister of the
serious Halachah. Her office is to *say* and to relate, and, in
order to be able to do so effectively, one of the characteristics
of the Haggadah had to be freedom. It had its origin in human
reflection, but also in freedom of thought and in subjective
conceptions, and it is therefore a product of the times and of
the ideas prevalent, subject to the social surroundings under
which the Haggadists lived and moved. Foreign influences,
Indian, Egyptian, Babylonian, Persian, and Hellenistic, left
their traces upon the Haggadah which did not come to an
end with the conclusion of the Talmud towards the close of
the fifth century (A.D.), but continued for many centuries.
Anthropomorphism and superstitions, which are foreign to the
spirit of Judaism, thus crept in and gained citizen rights in
the Haggadah.[1]

Zunz has defined the Haggadah as follows.

" It is intended both to bring heaven down to the community and to lift man up to heaven. Its aim is both to glorify
God and to comfort Israel. The Haggadah, therefore, contains not only myths, legends, fables, and tales, but also religious truths and moral maxims, legends from Jewish history
which attest Israel's past greatness and its nationality, and
comforting reflections which are calculated to give new courage
to the people in exile. It kept aloof, at first, from mysticism,
and refrained from entering the domain of metaphysics, but
following the example of the East, the Haggadah, where it

---

[1] See E. Schürer, *Geschichte der jüd. Litteratur*, Vol. II, pp. 349–50.

treats of the creation of the world and the hosts of angels, often allowed itself to indulge in an even exaggerated anthropomorphism." [1] The Haggadah is thus a sister of the Halachah, or the legal post-Biblical literature, and, like the latter, it bases itself on Holy Scripture, confining itself only to the historical and ethical parts. Often, however, it not only draws ideas from the text, but also tries to introduce new ideas into the text, endeavouring to justify such ideas by Biblical quotations, so as to impress the people. [2]

Some scholars, however, reject this division of post-Biblical lore, especially Talmudic, into Halachah and Haggadah. They define Haggadah as the " primitive literature of Israel, out of which issued the collection of the myths and legends of the Bible ", and which also contains those myths and legends which had been eliminated from the Biblical canon. [3] But even Goldziher, who sees in the Bible the principal source of Jewish myth, admits the importance and value of the Haggadah as a source of Jewish mythology. [4]

During centuries the Haggadah or Haggadic lore, as contained in the sources enumerated above, flourished and developed as a branch of popular poetry, but the Rabbis and teachers in the schoolhouses took hold of the popular traditions and made use of them for their own ethical purposes. The Haggadah thus became an enchanted realm of poetry upon whose flower-gardens generations laboured with loving care. These flower-gardens open before the student's gaze, every flower wafting to him the perfume of the East. [5]

Heine compared the Haggadah to the mild light of the moon, and the hanging gardens of Babylonia. [6] Mild and dreamy, peaceful and soothing indeed is the Haggadah, pro-

[1] Zunz, *Gottesdienstliche Vorträge*, 1892, pp. 362–3.
[2] See Hamburger, *Real-Encyclopædie*, s.v. *Agada* and *Agadisches Schrifttum*.
[3] See Ch. Harari, *La Tradition littéraire Hébraïque*, Genève, 1918, pp. 170 and 280.
[4] J. Goldziher, *Der Mythos bei den Hebräern*, 1876, p. 35; see also Schürer, *loc. cit.*; Güdemann in *Revue des Etudes Juives*, Vol. IX.
[5] See Karpeles, *Geschichte der jüd. Litteratur*, p. 127.
[6] *Romanzero, Rabbi Jehuda ben Halevi*.

ducing the effect of the poetic twilight, and like the gardens
of Babylonia which are said to have been laid out by the king
of Babylon in order to remind Semiramis, his queen, of the
hills in her native land, so the Haggadah wafts to Israel in
exile the perfume of its native soil.[1]

The Haggadah has also been compared to those angels
whose existence is a fleeting one. They emerge from the fiery
river, *Nehar di Nur*, sing a hymn of praise in honour of the
Creator, and disappear.[2] Its purpose was to attract the hearers
and to cheer them up. The Haggadah is a mosaic in both
senses of the word. It is *mosaic*, because it is based upon the
Books of Moses, and it is mosaic because its construction
resembles that oriental invention which is called *mosaic*.[3]

It contains the elements of the myths and legends of other
nations, it deals with solar myths and lunar myths, with cosmic
myths and zoological myths, with the attributes of God, with
angels and demons and all creation, but everything is derived
from and substantiated by the Bible. Angels and demons
people and poetically personify nature, yet it is not the nature
of the Aryans and of the Slavs, but that of the monotheistic
Semites and of the Bible-respecting Hebrews.

To a certain extent we may apply to the Haggadah the
words by which Matthew Arnold defined poetry, namely,
" a criticism of life ". The Haggadah invented new tales and
legends, adjusted old ones, but infused them with an ethical,
philosophical, and even political purpose. The floating myths
of the Jews were collected by the Rabbis of the Talmud and
by the Haggadists of post-Talmudic times. They made a
critical selection of existing material and systematized it so
as to suit the needs of the people, but always for the purpose
of explaining and *criticizing* life and human actions.

[1] See Grünbaum, *Neue Beiträge zur semitischen Sagenkunde*, p. 3; see also Josephus, *Contra Ap.*, I, 19, 20.
[2] See De Rossi, *Meor Enaim*, ed. Mantua, p. 77.
[3] See Grünbaum, *Gesammelte Aufsätze*, p. 4.

MYTH AND LEGEND OF ANCIENT ISRAEL

VOLUME I

CHAPTER I

Mysteries of Creation

The God of Israel—Difference between Indian, Persian, Egyptian, Greek, and Jewish myths—Manifestation of the God of Israel—He manifests Himself unto Moses—The High-Priest Ishmael ben Elisha blesses the Lord—The abode of God—He fills the whole universe—Clad in clouds, He visits His worlds—The daily occupations of the Creator—Certain missions are not entrusted to angels—God Himself changes the flames into a garden of roses and saves Abraham—Creation of the world—God produces a fine subtle matter, the *Hylé* of the Greeks—Tohu and Bohu—The four elements—Premundane Creation—The Torah, or Divine Wisdom—The counsel of the Torah—The Throne of Glory—The heavenly court of justice—The cosmos an animated being—The plurality of the worlds—Many worlds created and destroyed—Nine hundred and seventy-four generations existed before the creation of the world.

UNLIKE the myths of other nations—the myths of India, Egypt, Persia, and Greece—Jewish myth deals but little with the origin of God. He was there before the mountains were born, before the world was created, and from the beginning of time to the end of days He exists and is God.[1] Since time immemorial His throne is established.[2] Jewish myth-makers, according to the advice of Ben Sira, refrain from inquiring into the mysteries of Divinity. " So far thou hast permission to speak; thenceforward thou hast not permission to speak. For thus it is written in the Book of Ben Sira: Seek not out

[1] *Ps.* 90, 2. [2] *Ibid.*, 93, 2.

1

the things that are too hard for thee, and into the things that are hidden from thee inquire thou not. In what is permitted to thee instruct thyself; thou hast no business with secret things." [1] God was, has been, and is, and that was sufficient even for those who indulged in creating and fashioning the myths of Israel. Therein consists the difference between the myths of Israel and those of other nations who relate the birth of their respective Gods.

If, however, Jewish myth is silent as to the origin of God, it dwells frequently upon the fantastic descriptions of His essence, His abode, His actions, and His daily occupations. Like the myths of other nations, Jewish myth, too, imagines the Creator of the Universe as a perfect being resembling man, who was created in His image. His attributes are omnipotence, omniscience, benevolence, and loving-kindness.

On certain, although rare, occasions, this ruler of the Universe takes the shape of man in order to manifest Himself to His creatures. Thus Jewish myth relates that one of the three strangers, whom Abraham so hospitably received in his tent in the plain of Mamre, was God Himself who had appeared in human shape to His perfect servant, the son of Terah.[2] It was God Himself who frequently manifested Himself to Moses, and in the shape of an old man He appeared to Sennacherib, King of Assyria.[3]

One day, Jewish myth relates, the High-Priest Ishmael, the son of Elisha, upon entering the Holy of Holies, perceived the Almighty sitting upon a throne and asking the priest for a blessing. "Mayest Thou," promptly said the High-Priest, "never be swayed by wrath against Thy creatures, and may it be Thy will to treat them with mercy and loving-kindness."[4] The Almighty nodded His head in approval. We find a parallel in Greek myth, when we read of Jupiter

---

[1] *Hagigah*, 13a.　　[2] *Pirke de Rabbi Eliezer*, Ch. 29.　　[3] *Sanhedrin*, 95b.　　[4] *Berachoth*, 7a.

who nodded his head when Thetis interceded for her son Achilles.[1]

The abode of God is frequently dealt with in Jewish myth. The wonderful starlit vault above us is the seat of the Almighty. Here He dwells surrounded by His heavenly hosts. The myth makers of post-exilic Judaism were, however, not satisfied with *one* Heaven and imagined seven, placing the seat of the Creator in the seventh or the highest. But this abode, the seventh Heaven, is only the preferred and favourite dwelling place of the God of Jewish myth. He is everywhere and fills the whole universe. Basing themselves upon the words of the Psalmist, Jewish mythographers imagine the omnipresence of the Creator.[2]

The soul fills the body, just as the Divine presence fills the Universe.[3] Frequently, the God of Jewish myth leaves this abode in Heaven and descends upon earth to pay a visit to His creatures. Herein, however, Jewish myth once more differs considerably from the myths of other nations. Jupiter harnesses his iron-shod, golden-maned horses, and, arrayed in golden garments, seated in his chariot, visits the world.[4] The God of Jewish myth is clad in clouds and visits His worlds upon the wings of the wind. He is seated upon the Throne of Glory and His chariots are upon the Ophanim. He rideth upon a swift cloud and upon the wings of the wind, for it is said: " And he rode upon a cherub, and did fly; yea, he flew upon the wings of the wind." [5]

Whilst the Gods of pagan antiquity are like ordinary mortals, sharing their passions and even their vices, the God of Israel, even of Jewish myth, where anthropomorphistic conceptions play such an important rôle, is a perfect ethical being, whose superiority and Divine attributes are manifested even in moments of wrath and anger.[6] His Divine attributes

[1] *Iliad* I, 524. [2] *Ps.* 139, 8–10; *Is.* 6, 3. [3] *Berachoth*, 10a. [4] *Iliad* VIII, 41. [5] *Ps.* 18, 10; *Pirke de Rabbi Eliezer*, Ch. 4. [6] *Pesachim*, 87b.

describe His high perfection, for which human language can find no adequate description.[1]

Largely does Jewish myth dwell upon the minute description of the daily occupations of Divinity. The day consists of twelve hours, and during the first four hours the Creator explains to His heavenly hosts the precepts of the Divine law. During the next four hours He is seated on the throne of judgment, judging the actions of his creatures. During the last four hours He is again busy ordaining the sustenance and protection of his creatures.[2] But whilst the God of Jewish myth usually commissions His ministering angels to execute His commands, He often reserves unto Himself certain missions which He, in His loving-kindness and mercy, executes Himself. Such are the birth of the child, the distribution of rain, and the resuscitation of the dead.[3] These missions are not entrusted to any angel, but are directly executed by the God of Jewish myth Himself. Marriages, too, are, according to Jewish myth, concluded in Heaven under the direction of God Himself.[4]

Very frequently, according to Jewish myth, God refuses to allow one of His ministering angels to interfere in the affairs of man, but Himself condescends to vouchsafe His assistance and His help to His beloved creatures, and especially to His faithful and perfect servants. Thus, when Abraham was thrown into the furnace, by order of the terrible Nimrod, the angel Gabriel was ready to hasten to Abraham's assistance, but the Creator waved him back, and Himself changed the flames into a bed of roses upon which the son of Terah went to sleep, to the amazement of the servants of Nimrod.[5]

The angel of death is also never allowed to take the souls of perfect men and to separate them from their bodies. It is God Himself, according to Jewish myth, who bids the souls

[1] *Berachoth*, 33b.   [2] *Abodah Zarah*. 3b.   [3] *Taanith*, 2a.
[4] *Moed Katon*, 18b; *Leviticus Rabba*, 8.   [5] *Pesachim*, 118a.

of these perfect favourites of Divinity to leave their earthly prison-houses, sparing them the agonies of death.[1]

THE CREATION OF THE WORLD

God and the world are, according to Jewish myth, two inseparable conceptions, standing to each other in the relation of cause and effect. The world came into existence by the will of God, because He wished creation and especially man to glorify and sanctify His name, and to proclaim His glory.[2] The world and man were created for the purpose of giving God an opportunity to manifest His glory, His omnipotence and His benevolence.[3] He created the world by the word of His mouth. In Indian myth we read that Brahma, by the word of His mouth, called into being all the creatures of the visible world. But Jewish myth differs from the myth of India, for none of the Jewish myths in either pre-talmudic or post-talmudic times speak of any pre-existing matter out of which the world was called into being. It was created out of nothing, and thus Jewish myth is in strict accordance with Holy Writ.

From absolute nothingness All-Father, the Creator, first produced a fine subtle matter, which had no consistence whatever, but possessed the potential power to receive the imprint of form. This was the first matter, or what the Greeks called *Hylé*.

From this first matter, which was *Tohu*, the Creator produced all things. He then clothed it in form which is *Bohu*. First matter, which the Creator extracted from nothing, at first resembled one point, which was the stone of foundation of creation. This stone of foundation God shaped in four different forms which are fire, water, earth, and air. These four elements envelop each other. Water surrounds earth; air surrounds water; fire surrounds air. When this point or

---

[1] *Baba Batra*, 17a.   [2] *Pirke de Rabbi Eliezer*, Ch. 3.   [3] *Genesis Rabba*, 1.

stone of foundation had taken these four forms, it became
luminous, " and it was light ". The world was created.[1]

At the moment of creation, say other mythographers,
the four cardinal points were united to the four elements:
fire, air, water, and earth. Out of the amalgamation of these
God fashioned Adam. His body was the union of two worlds,
the world above and the world below. The four elements are
the first mystery of everything, for they are the progenitors
and the fathers of all the worlds. From them issued gold,
silver, iron, and copper, and from the mixture of these four
other metals issue. Fire, water, air, and earth are the first
roots of the worlds above and of the worlds below, for all the
created worlds are based upon them.

But before creating the Universe, relates Jewish myth,
before God called into being the visible world, He established the conditions under which the world He had decided
to create could endure for ever. The world could not exist,
said the Almighty, if there were not first laws and conditions
necessary for its continued existence. Such conditions were,
according to Jewish myth, Divine Providence, the Law,
Repentance, Punishment and Reward, Prayer and Freewill.

God, therefore, before fashioning Heaven and Earth,
and the whole visible world, man and the other creatures,
called into being the Divine Throne, the Holy Law, Repentance, Paradise, Hell, the Holy Temple, and the name of
the Messiah; in a word, all the conditions which represent
Divine Providence, Law and Order, Good Deeds, Reward
and Punishment, Prayer and Redemption.[2]

Thus, before the world was created, the Maker of the
Universe existed alone with His name. It entered His mind
to create the world, and he drew the plan of the world, but
it would not stand. He traced the foundations of the world,

---

[1] Nachmanides, *Commentary to the Pentateuch.*
[2] *Pirke de Rabbi Eliezer*, Ch. 3; *Nedarim*, 39b; *Pesachim*, 54a.

that is He drew its plans, after which the world was to be created. He is likened unto an architect who draws the plans before building a palace.

The *Torah*, which is wisdom, was with the Creator prior to Creation, and He took counsel with her concerning the creation of the world. The Torah, or wisdom, advised Him to create the world and she said: " Lord and Sovereign of the Universe! Thou art the Sovereign and the King, but there is no host over whom Thou canst rule; there is also no people who could pay honour unto Thee and glorify Thy name." And the Creator listened unto the counsel of the Torah, which is wisdom, for it pleased Him greatly.[1] The pre-existent emanation of the Torah, or the Law, from God, thus occupies the place of the *Logos*.

As for the Throne of Glory, it is suspended in the air high above, and the Divine Glory hath the appearance of the colour of amber. One half is fire and the other is hail, being the two attributes of love and justice. Life is at His right hand and death at His left.[2] A sceptre of fire is in His hand and a veil separates the Divine Glory from the ministering angels, only seven angels being allowed to minister within the veil which is called *Pargod*.[3]

The footstool of the Creator is like unto fire and hail, and represents Justice and Love. And the foundations of the throne, round which fire is continually flashing, are righteousness and justice by which He rules the world.

But none of the ministering angels, neither the *Chajjoth*, nor the *Ophanim* know the place of His Glory. All stand in awe and dread, in trembling and fear. And although standing near the place of Glory, *at* the side of the throne, the ministering angels know not the place of His Glory. Therefore, they only respond: " Blessed be the Glory of the Lord from His place." [4]

[1] *Pirke de Rabbi Eliezer*, Ch. 3.
[2] *Ibid*, ch. 4; see also Jellinek, *Beth-Hamidrash*, Vol. II, p. 41.
[3] *Hagigah*, 5a, 15a; *Yoma*, 77; *Berachoth*, 18b.   [4] *Ezek.* 3, 17.

Throughout Jewish myth, dealing with cosmogony and creation, there also runs the old Oriental idea that everything that exists upon earth has its counterpart in heaven.

This idea is even older than the Platonic doctrine of Ideas. The Rabbis of the Talmud teach that the realm of earth corresponds to the celestial realm. Rabbi Abahu, who lived in the third century of our era, says that all that is above exists also below. You will find that everything that the Eternal created above He also created below.[1]

But in retaining the old Oriental conception Jewish myths and legends always presuppose the idea of an omniscient, all-wise Creator who created everything according to a wise plan.

Herein lies the whole conception of Jewish myth with regard to cosmogony.[2]

Thus, the prototype of the earthly garden of Eden is the celestial Eden or Paradise. The prototype of the earthly court of justice is the celestial one, presided over by the Creator himself. This heavenly court holds its sittings in the highest heaven, in the vicinity of the Throne of Glory. The secret scribe and vice-president of this celestial court of justice is Metatron. He is assisted by the angels Jophiel and Suriel, whilst the angel Enphiel is the keeper of the seal, and the angels Achseriel and Rasiel are the heralds. The archangels Michael, Gabriel, Raphael and Uriel (also Nuriel) are the assessors. In this celestial court two seats of glory exist, one for justice and the other for mercy. The Jewish legends speak not only of the celestial court of justice but also of a heavenly academy, and relate that many of the just and pious Rabbis were allowed to be present in this heavenly academy whither they were carried up and down in their chairs by ministering angels.[3]

The Rabbis of the Talmud also go so far as to imagine

---

[1] *Exodus Rabba*, 33.   [2] E. Bischoff, *Babylonisch-Astrales*, p. 21.   [3] *Baba Mezia*, 85b.

the cosmos as an animated being. And just as man is endowed with a living soul, so the whole universe is singing the praises of and is rendering homage to the living Creator. The sun, the moon and the stars, in a word, the entire cosmos is a living being endowed with a soul. The entire visible world is a being endowed with life. Man is the crown of creation, and everything that God created in man He also created in the cosmos.[1]

This conception of the cosmos as a living being is also met with in the Babylonian myth, where Marduk, after his victory over the goddess Tiamat, creates the world out of her body. Here, as Bischoff rightly remarks,[2] we have the doctrine of modern philosophers who teach a psycho-physical monism. The soul of the world is an idea common to Plato, the Neoplatonists, Paracelsus, and others.[3]

The present world, however, is neither the first nor the only world in existence. Before the world was created there existed already many others. The Eternal created many worlds and destroyed them until He produced the present cosmos. And He spake: " The other worlds did not please me, but this one does please me."[4] The pre-existing worlds were preparations for the present one. In this mythical conception lies the idea of an organic progress. When the pre-existing worlds had fulfilled their purpose they disappeared. Not only the worlds, however, but also all their inhabitants had been created and destroyed; they came and went.[5] Nine hundred and seventy-four generations had existed before the creation of this world, but they were swept away because they were wicked and did not please the Lord of the Universe.[6]

Thus many worlds preceded the creation of the present

Abot de Rabbi Nathan, Ed. Schechter, p. 46a; W. Bacher, Die Agada der Tanaiten, Vol. I, p. 365; Midrash Tehillim, Ps. 19, 2.   [2] Loc. cit., p. 108.
[3] Paulsen, Einleitung in die Philosophie, 1893, pp. 91–116, 239–251; Midrash Tehillim, Ps. 19, 2; Koheleth Rabba, 1, 4.
[4] Genesis Rabba, 3; see also W. Bacher Die Agada der Palästinensischen Amoräer, Vol. II, p. 138.   [5] Midrash Tehillim, Ps. 90, 5.   [6] Hagigah, 13b–14a.

one, worlds came and disappeared. In this mythical conception one may already trace the modern evolutionary idea. Jewish myth and legend further speak of a plurality of worlds. Apart from our own cosmos, there are numerous other cosmic systems. God, teach the Rabbis, has many cosmic worlds, and, carried upon the wings of the Cherubim, He manifests His presence in all of them.[1]

[1] *Abodah Zarah*, 3b.

CHAPTER II

The Story of Creation

The six days of creation—The lump of snow—The stone of foundation
—The arrogant waters—The trees of Bashan and the mountain of iron—
The light of the Divine garment—The four corners of the world—The
incompleted corner facing north—The waters and the sand—The creation
of Light—The two luminaries—Sun and moon—Two Kings with one crown
—The complaint of the moon and its punishment—The chariot of the sun
—The habitation of the moon—Worship of the moon—Astarte, Urania,
and Isis—Leviathan and Behemoth—The story of creation in the Slavonic
Book of Enoch—The stone Advel—The substance called Arkas—Things
created on eve of Sabbath.

THE story of the six days of creation is related differently
in various sources. On the first day the Creator took a lump
of snow from underneath the throne of His Glory and threw
it upon the surface of the waters, and it became earth. And
then He took a stone of foundation and threw it upon the
place where once the Temple was to stand, and the world was
founded upon it. And He called to the earth and commanded
it to stand still and not to toss about like a ship upon the waves
of the sea.

On the second day the Creator said there should be a dam
or *rakia* in the midst of the waters, that is the waters were
commanded to divide themselves, one portion ascending
and the other descending. But the waters were arrogant and
rebelled against the command of the Creator, and all ascended.
And the Creator said: " I commanded you to divide, one portion to ascend and the other to descend," but the waters were

11

obstinate and refused to obey the command of the Creator of the Universe. Then the Creator stretched out His little finger and tore the waters into twain, and the lower portion descended suddenly.

And on the third day all the trees and timber in the garden of Eden were created, and all the trees and fruit trees upon earth. And when the cedars of Lebanon and the trees of Bashan saw that they had been created first, they raised their heads and were proud. But the Creator said: " I hate pride and arrogance," and He forthwith created iron to cut down the proud trees. When the trees saw that the Lord of the Universe had created a mountain of iron, they wept bitterly, and some of them are known as weeping trees. When the Creator heard them weeping, He asked them why they cried. " We thought," replied the trees, " that no one is like unto us in the world, who are the tallest in creation; but now Thou hast created iron to destroy us." " You will furnish the handle for the axe, and you will rule over the iron as the iron will rule over you," replied the Creator, and thus He made peace between them.[1]

On the fourth day He took fire and sealed it, and fashioned the sun out of it. It is called *Shamesh*,[2] because it serves the world. And He took light and sealed it and fashioned the moon out of it. And both luminaries were alike. But the moon grew jealous and complained to the Creator. It was punished and its light was diminished. Thereupon the moon pleaded and said: " Lord of the Universe, I have only spoken one word and so great is my punishment." But the Creator replied: " In days to come thy light will once more be as the light of the sun."[3]

On the fifth day He created out of light and water the Leviathan and all the fishes in the sea. On the sixth day He

[1] *Genesis Rabba*, 5.
[2] *Shamesh*, to minister, wait upon; see Jastrow, *Dictionary of the Targumim, s.v.*
[3] *Hullin*, 60b; *Genesis Rabba*, 6; *Midrash Agadah*, ed. Buber, p. 3.

took water and dust and light and created all the animals, and the wild beasts and the domestic animals, and the birds and the creeping worms.[1]

The book called *Pirke de Rabbi Eliezer* describes the story of the creation as follows: The heavens He created from the light of His garment. He took His garment and stretched it out and the heavens extended farther and farther, until the Creator cried unto them to stop. " Be stayed," He said, " it is sufficient," and they stopped. And then the Creator took the snow from beneath His throne of glory and scattered it upon the waters, and the waters became congealed and the earth was formed. And thus the snow became earth. The hooks of the heavens He fixed in the waters of the ocean which flow between the ends of the heavens and the ends of the earth. He created four corners or directions in the world, facing east, south, west, and north. From the corner facing east there goeth forth to the world light, whilst the dews and rains of blessing descend upon the world from the corner facing south. The treasuries of snow and hail are stored up in the corner facing west, and from there cold and rain and heat descend upon the world. But the corner facing north was not completed, for the Creator said: " Let anyone come and finish this corner and then the world will know that he is a God." This corner is the abode of lightning and thunder, of winds and of earthquakes; here also dwell the demons and spirits, for it is from the northern corner that evil breaks forth and comes upon the world.[2]

On the second day the Creator of the Universe called into existence the firmament, the angels, and the fire of Gehenna, for on the second day the Creator did not say " and it was good ". The firmament which He created on the second day divides the waters above from the waters below, and

[1] *Midrash Konen*, Jellinek, *Beth-Hamidrash*, Vol. II, pp. 24–27.
[2] *Jeremiah*, 1, 14; *Pirke de Rabbi Eliezer*, Ch. 3.

were it not for that firmament the world would be engulfed by the waters above it and below it.

On the third day the earth was as flat as a plain, the waters covering the entire surface of the whole earth. At the word of the Creator the waters gathered and were rolled into the valleys, and the hills and mountains appeared. The waters then became proud and arrogant, rose tumultuously to a great height, covered the face of the earth, and threatened to over-run and drown the whole earth. But the Creator rebuked them, subduing them and placing them beneath the hollow of His feet, making the sand the boundary and fence of the sea. And when the mighty waters saw the sand-grains, how small and insignificant they were, they laughed at them and mocked them. " We are not afraid of you," they said, " for the smallest wave will destroy you and swallow you up." The sand-grains appointed to fight against the waves of the sea were frightened, but the biggest of the sand-grains said: " My brothers, do not be afraid. We are powerless and in-significant as long as we are separate, and the slightest breeze can blow us away. If, however, we stick together we are a great power, and able to oppose the inrush of the arrogant waters." And from all corners of the earth the sand-grains came and united into one compact mass, so that the arrogant waters were frightened and drew back. And when the waters rise and see the sand, they recede and return to their place. They neither diminish nor increase because God has measured them in the palm of his hand.[1]

On the fourth day He created the sun and the moon. And the two luminaries were created both equal, one was not greater than the other, for they were both equal in shape and form and height, and they illumined the world equally. But soon rivalry arose between them, and they quarrelled.

---

[1] *Midrash Tehillim*, Ps. 93; *Pirke de Rabbi Eliezer*, Ch. 3; *Baba Batra*, 74b. See also *Monatsschrift für Geschichte und Wissenschaft d. Judent.*, 1912, p. 148.

The moon was not satisfied, for she envied the illuminating powers of the sun. And she appeared before the Father of All, and thus she spake: " Thou didst create the heavens and the earth, but the heavens are greater than the earth; Thou also didst create fire and water, but water is stronger than fire, for it has the power to extinguish fire. Now Thou didst create the sun and the moon who are both equal and are alike unto two kings with one crown." And the Father of All rebuked the moon and thus He spake: " As thou didst obstinately refuse to do my will, and didst harbour evil intentions against thy colleague the sun, thou shalt be made smaller. Sixty times will I diminish thy size, and thy brightness shall be sixty times smaller than the brightness of the sun." And thus the greater light was set to rule the day, and the lesser light, that is the moon, to rule the night.[1]

The sun is led and accompanied by ministering angels both during the day and during the night. Crowned as a bridegroom, the sun rides forth every day in a chariot. In summer his rays look down upon the earth and would consume it with fire, but every night he takes a cooling bath in the ice above so as to temper the inner heat.[2] The Divine Glory resides in the west, and the sun, having risen in the east and set in the west, enters in the presence of Divine Glory, and bowing low thus he speaks: " Lord of the Universe! I have fulfilled all Thy commands." [3]

The moon inhabits a place between the clouds and the thick darkness, which are like two dishes one above the other. These clouds form the clothing or covering of the moon who travels between them, peeping out from between the two in the form of a little horn until the middle of the month, when it is full moon. From the middle to the end of the month, the moon is being gradually covered by the clouds between which she travels,

---

[1] Hullin, 60b.   [2] Genesis Rabba, 6.
[3] M. Gaster, The Chronicles of Jerahmeel, p. 11 (3, 5).

until the end of the month when she is entirely covered.[1]

The worship of the moon was very extensive among the Orientals, and Holy Scripture bids the Israelites to be very careful when they see the sun, the moon, the stars, and the entire host of heaven and not to pay them worship, for they are only creations of the only God and appointed for the service of the nations on earth.[2] " If I beheld the sun when it shined," says Job, " or the moon walking in brightness, and my heart has been secretly enticed, or my mouth hath kissed my hand." [3] The moon was worshipped in Asia under the name of Meni, of Astarte, the Goddess of the Groves, the Queen of Heaven. She is Urania and Coelestis in Syria, the Isis of Egypt, and Alilat of Arabia. She is the Diana, Bellona, Minerva of the Greeks; sacrifices were offered unto her, in the highways and upon roofs of houses. Even human sacrifices were offered unto the moon according to Strabo and Lucian. The Jewish myth-makers, among whom monotheism always struggled against Asiatic heathen polytheism, have therefore woven many myths and legends about the moon. All these myths, however, have, as has been pointed out, an ethical setting.

On the fifth day the waters, at the command of the Creator, brought forth all kinds of animals, and Leviathan, the flying-serpent whose dwelling is in the deepest waters.

On the sixth day the Creator brought forth all kinds of animals from the earth. And He also called forth from the earth the Behemoth which stretches its limbs upon a thousand hills and seeks its daily food upon a thousand hills.[4] It drinks the waters of the Jordan which encompass the land of Israel, half of them flowing above the earth and half below the earth. And the day of the great Messianic banquet prepared for the righteous, this beast will be sacrificed and served.[5]

---

[1] M. Gaster, *The Chronicles of Jerahmeel*, p. 11 (3, 5).
[2] *Deuteron.* 4, 19; 17, 3.   [3] *Job*, 31, 26, 27.   [4] *Ps.* 1, 10; *Job*, 40, 15.
[5] *Pirke de Rabbi Eliezer*, Ch. 11; see also *Baba Batra*, 75a; *Genesis Rabba*, 7; *Midrash Agadah*, edit. Buber, p. 3.

The Slavonic *Book of Enoch* describes the story of creation as follows: Before everything visible was, the All-Father wandered about among the invisible like the sun which is wandering from east to west and from west to east. But whilst the sun has rest in itself, He, the Creator, had none, because He was the All-Father and Creator. And He decided to lay the foundations and to produce the visible Creation. And he commanded that the visible issue and descend from the invisible.

And there came forth a very big stone called *Advel*, and He, the Creator, saw it and lo, Advel had in its body a big light. And He said: " Burst asunder, Advel, thou fiery stone, and let the visible issue forth from thee." And Advel, the fiery stone, burst asunder and out of it broke forth an immense light and forth came an immense æon which revealed the whole creation as it had been conceived and designed by the Creator, the All-Father. And out of it He made His own throne and sat upon it.

And He said unto the light: " Rise higher and be fixed above the throne and become the foundation of all celestial things." And for the second time All-Father called to the invisible deep and caused to come forth a substance called *Arkas*, firm and heavy and red. And He spoke unto Arkas, the substance heavy and very red: " Burst asunder, Arkas, and let issue forth out of thee the creation of all things below." And when Arkas was divided there issued forth from it an æon, dark and immense, bearing in itself the creation of all things below. And the Creator spake unto it: " Go down and be fixed below and become the foundation of the creation of all things below and there should be nothing beneath the darkness." And there is nothing beneath the darkness, as there is nothing above the light which is the foundation of all celestial things. And He commanded that a portion of the light and of the darkness should mix, and out of this mixture of light and darkness issued forth a thick substance which was firm. This was water. And the Creator spread it out above the darkness which is below and underneath the light which is above, and thus the waters were spread out in both directions. And He surrounded the waters with light and made seven circles within, fashioning them like crystal, moist and dry, that is like glass, and having the appearance of ice. And these were the seven heavens, and He showed unto each its place and its way. And thus He made firm the circle of heaven and He also made firm the great stone of foundation. Thereupon He commanded the waters under the heavens to assemble. And the waves of the waters below the heavens were turned into stone, firm and immense, out of which stones earth was fashioned, which was called dry land. In the midst of the earth He placed the abyss.[1] And He gathered the sea in one place and bound it as with a yoke, and thus He spake unto the sea: " I set a limit unto thee and thou wilt not trespass and separate from thy elements."

On the eve of the Sabbath, that is in the twilight of the sixth day, ten things were created, and these were: the mouth of the earth,[2] the mouth of the well;[3] the mouth of the ass;[4] the rainbow;[5] the Manna;[6] the Shamir;[7] the shape of the alphabet, the writing, the tables of the Law, and the ram which Abraham sacrificed in the place of Isaac.[8]

---

[1] R. H. Charles and Morfill, *The Secrets of Enoch*.   [2] *Numbers*, 16, 32.
[3] Well of Hagar, *Gen.* 21, 19; and *Numbers*, 21, 16.   [4] *Numbers*, 22, 28.
[5] *Genesis*, 9, 13.   [6] *Exodus*, 16, 15.   [7] *I Kings*, 6, 7.
[8] *Pesachim*, 54a; *Pirke de Rabbi Eliezer*, Ch. 19; see also *Palest. Targum* to Numbers, 22, 28.

CHAPTER III

The Seven Heavens or Firmaments
and the Seven Underworlds

Description of the seven heavens—Villon, Rekia, Shekhakim, Szebhul, Maon, Makhon, and Araboth—The unborn souls—Enoch visits the seven heavens—The rebellious angels—Paradise—The gates of the sun—The watchers—The seven underworlds—Eretz hatachtonah—Adamah, Arka, Ge, Neshia, Zija, Tebel—The two rulers of Arka—Ephrira and Kastimon —The ten unholy, gruesome spheres—Thomiel, Goiel, Sairiel—The hurling raven—The sphere of Sammael.

THE SEVEN HEAVENS

THE number of firmaments is already discussed in Talmudic myth. One Rabbi is of opinion that there are two firmaments, but others maintain that there are seven. It has been rightly pointed out that this number seven is due to Babylonian influences, where we read of a sevenfold division of the Lower World. When *Ishtar* descends to Hades she has to pass through seven gateways in order to reach the interior of the infernal city.[1] The doctrine of the seven heavens is also found among the Parsees. The Slavonic *Enoch* and the *Testament of the Twelve Patriarchs*[2] also speak of the seven heavens.

In the *Testament of Levi*,[3] the third son of Jacob, we read of a vision which Levi had, beholding the seven heavens.

The *Chronicles of Jerahmeel* also speak of the seven heavens. The Lord then opened the seven doors of the seven

---

[1] R. H. Charles, *Expository Times*, Nov.–Dec., 1895.
[2] See R. H. Charles, *The Testament of the Twelve Patriarchs*, 1917, and article in Hastings' *Dict. of the Bible.*   [3] *Ibid*, pp. 36–37.

heavens, and revealed himself unto Israel, face to face in His glory and with His crown.[1]

According to Jewish myth, both in the Talmud, the Midrashim, the *Pseudapigraphia* and later sources, there are thus seven heavens: the *Villon* (Vellum), in which there is the sun; the *Rekia*, in which the sun shines, and the moon, stars, and planets are fixed; the *Shekhakim*, in which the millstones are kept to make the *manna* for the pious; *Szebhul*, in which are the upper Jerusalem and the Temple and the Altar, and in which Michael, the chief angel-prince, offers sacrifices; the *Maon*, in which the angels of the Ministry dwell, they sing by night and are silent by day (for the sake of the honour of Israel); *Makhon*, in which are the treasures of snow and hail, the chambers of noxious dews, the receptacles of water, the chambers of wind, and the cave of mist; their doors are of fire.

The last heaven is *Araboth*. Here justice, judgment, and righteousness dwell. Here also are the treasures of life, peace and blessing; here the souls of the just and righteous dwell together with the souls of those who are to be born in future; here also is the dew by which the dead are once to be raised. In Araboth also are the *Ophanim* and *Seraphim*, and living creatures and ministering angels, and the Throne of Glory, and over it is enthroned the Great King.[2]

With regard to the souls yet unborn, Jewish myth places them in the seventh heaven.

In the beginning of things God the All-Father also created a great number of souls destined one day to inhabit a human body. There is a treasure or storehouse in Heaven where these souls are kept until the moment arrives for each of them to descend upon earth and be united to " mortal coil ". According to some myths these souls are hidden beneath the

---

[1] Gaster, *The Chronicles of Jerahmeel*, p. 148 (52, 11).
[2] *Hagigah*, 12b; *Pirke de Rabbi Eliezer*, Ch. 4.

throne of All-Father, whilst in other places it is maintained
that the souls yet unborn walk freely in the celestial fields
in company of the souls of the pious who have already passed
through a body.[1] All these souls inhabit the seventh heaven
where all the treasures of life and blessing are kept. The
Redeemer will only come when all these souls created at the
beginning of things will have sojourned upon earth and
" shuffled off mortal coil ".[2]

Some souls are spirits sent down upon earth and ordered
to inhabit a human body as a punishment for faults committed.
For others it is a test and an opportunity to show their strength.
In the struggle of the soul, the celestial inmate, against the
passions and instincts inherent in matter, the soul has an
opportunity to show its worth and remain faithful to its celestial origin or to betray it.[3]

The *Midrash of the Ten Commandments* gives the following
description of the seven heavens: He further created the
seven heavens or *rakiim*. The lowest of the seven heavens
is called *Villon* and is like a curtain drawn before the houses,
so that those who are inside can see all that happens outside,
but those who are outside cannot perceive those who are
within. And there are windows in the Villon, through which
the ministering angels can see the children of men and all
the mortals and their doings, whether they are walking on
the path of righteousness or not. And above the Villon is
the second heaven called *Rakia*. In it are fixed the stars and
planets and constellations, and in it there are twelve windows
corresponding to the twelve hours of day and night. And
three hundred and sixty-five angels minister and are set to
serve the sun and to lead it from window to window whilst
it turns round the world. In the night they lead the moon
before these windows.

And above the Rakia is the third heaven called *Shekhakim*,

---

[1] *Hagigah*, 12b.   [2] *Niddah*, 13b; *Yebamoth*, 62a.   [3] *Genesis Rabba*, 9.

or clouds. Above the Shekhakim is the Szebhul, and above the Szebhul is the *Makhon* or the fifth heaven. It contains the treasuries of snow and hail, and the apartments of dew, and the chambers of storm and wind. And all are closed behind doors of fire. And above the Makhon is the sixth heaven which is *Maon*, and where dwell hosts of angels who sing hymns of praise during the night. It also contains the treasuries of blessing. Above Maon is *Araboth*, which is the abode of right and justice, and of the dew of life and of blessing. It is the abode of the souls of the just and the pious, and here is the Throne of Glory and here dwell the holy Seraphim and Cherubim, who glorify and sanctify the Creator.[1]

The seven heavens are also described in the Slavonic *Enoch*: The angels thereupon carried Enoch to Heaven. In the first heaven he saw a great sea, which was greater than the earthly sea and where the rulers of the stars were dwelling. There were also the treasuries of snow and ice, and dread angels were guarding them. In the second heaven Enoch saw prisoners suspended and awaiting eternal judgment. They were the angels who had rebelled against God, and they begged Enoch to intercede for them and obtain the mercy of the Most High. But Enoch replied: " I am but a mortal man who knoweth not whither he goeth or what awaiteth him, and I am not worthy to pray for angels." In the third heaven Enoch saw a garden, full of trees of beautiful colour, bearing fruit, ripe and fragrant. There was also the tree of life on which rests the glory of God, when the Lord of the Universe comes to visit Paradise. This place, said the angels accompanying Enoch, is prepared for those who feed the hungry, clothe the naked, and raise the fallen; who accomplish righteous judgment and walk without blame before the Lord. In the northern region of this third heaven Enoch further saw a place very terrible to behold. It was full of gloom and

---

[1] *Midrash of the Ten Commandments*, Jellinek, *Beth-Hamidrash*, Vol. I, p. 64.

impenetrable darkness, surrounded on all sides by fire, cold
and ice. " This place," said the angels accompanying Enoch,
" is prepared for those who commit deeds of wickedness on
earth; who are guilty of lying and stealing, of murder and
theft, of envy and calumny; who oppress the poor and harbour
evil thoughts."

From the third heaven Enoch was conducted to the fourth,
and here he was shown the courses of the sun and of the
moon.

He also witnessed the phœnixes and the *chalkadri* who
had heads of crocodiles and feet and tails of lions. Nine
hundred measures was their size, and their appearance of
purple colour like the rainbow. They attended the chariot
of the sun upon which it rides forth to shine upon the world,
and each had twelve wings. There he also saw the eastern
and western gates of the sun. In the fifth heaven Enoch saw
the watchers who had rebelled against God, and whose brethren
had already been confined in torment in the second heaven.
Thereupon Enoch was carried to the sixth heaven, and here
he saw the angels who record the deeds of man, regulate the
courses of the stars and all the powers of nature. At last he
was raised to the seventh heaven. And there he saw the Throne
of Glory and hosts of angels sitting on the steps of the Throne.
And Enoch fell down and worshipped. Thereupon the archangel Michael divested him of his earthly robes, and anointed
him with the oil from the tree of mercy, and clothed him in
the raiment of God's glory, and he became like one of the
glorious inhabitants of the celestial regions.[1]

The Seven Underworlds

And just as there are seven heavens so there are also seven
planets of the earth; surrounded, like seven globes, by heavens.
The seven earths are one beneath the other, and counting

[1] Charles and Morfill, *The Secrets of Enoch.*

upwards their names are as follows: the nethermost world (*Eretz hatachtonah*), *Adamah*, *Arka*, *Ge*, *Neshia*, *Zija*, and *Tebel*. The last is the uppermost of the worlds or earths, and is situated under the source of life.

It is related that when Adam was expelled from the Garden of Eden, he was sent to the nethermost earth, that is the *Eretz hatachtonah* which is a place of perdition, where nothing grows, and where there is no light, but utter darkness, for the heaven which is called Villon is dark. And when Adam entered this place a great fear seized him, and the flaming sword was turning round in the utter darkness and he knew not where to hide himself. And thus he remained for twenty-four hours and repented of his sins. The Creator had mercy upon him, and brought him to the second earth called Adamah. On this earth there is light from the stars and planets, and it is inhabited by demons and spirits.

Upon Arka there is a light shed by the sun, and it is inhabited by men, some of whom are giants, whilst others belong to a race of pigmies, and they are not endowed with reason such as the inhabitants of the earth planet called Tebel.

Sometimes they are just, but sometimes they are wicked and evil, endeavouring to cause harm to those who inhabit the upper earth which is Tebel, that is our own planet.

In Arka, which is the land of light and darkness, two rulers reign, one over light and the other over darkness.

And there was strife between them. They made peace only when Cain, who had slain his brother Abel, came down to them. They are named Ephrira and Kastimon. One of them has the face of a bull, and the other that of an eagle, but when they are in darkness they change into serpents and creep on their bellies. And when they pass the place where Aza and Azael are chained, the two chained demons awake and cry aloud and begin to rove about between the mountains of darkness, in their fear that the Creator will now call them

to judgment. Ephrira and Kastimon swim over the seas and
rove about in the world, and when they perceive Naamah [1]
they follow her and endeavour to seize her, but she leaps sixty
thousand miles and appears to men in different shapes, trying
to seduce the race of men. Ephrira and Kastimon return once
more to Arka, their abode in the netherworlds.

Gia or Ge is a vast place and is the length of the Gehinnom,
or hell. Gia is near the element of fire, and its inmates possess
wealth and precious stones. They make gifts to all those
who come down to them either in consequence of the transmigration of souls, or driven by avarice and cupidity. Gia
is situated in the midst of the seven worlds, and its inhabitants
are well versed in witchcraft, but they also possess other wisdom.

And the fifth world is called *Neshia* (which is derived
from the word *Neshia*, forgetfulness) and it is inhabited by
a race of pigmies who have no memory whatever.

The sixth world is called *Zija*, and it is very dry and
peopled by a race of very handsome men. They are always
searching after sources or streams and often enter the waters
and thus swim up to Tebel, the planet which is inhabited by
the race of men. There is more faith in them than among
other men.

Zones resembling in their nature the seven different worlds
are to be found upon the earth which we inhabit, namely
Tebel, containing races of men resembling in their appearance and nature those mentioned above.[2]

There are also ten unholy dark and gruesome spheres,
spheres of darkness as counterparts to the spheres of light.

The first sphere of darkness is called *Thomiel*, derived from
the word *Thomim* which means twins, for this dark sphere
is the twin sister of the highest celestial region.

---

[1] Naamah, the sister of Tubal Cain, who is supposed to have been the wife of Shamdon
and the mother of Asmodeus.

[2] *Emek hamelekh*, fol. 179, col. 4; 180, col. 1; *Yalkut Rubeni, Genesis*; see also Eisenmenger,
Entdecktes Judenthum, Vol. I, p. 459; M. Bin Gorion, *Die Sagen der Juden*, Vol. I, pp. 330–
334.

And, just as there is a ruler in the region of light, there is
one also in the region of darkness. (Here again we evidently
have the influence of Persian dualism.)

The second sphere is called *Goiel*—derived from the word
goah, to bleat—for from that sphere there continually issues
forth a bleating intended to disturb the Divine harmony and
radiance and the order reigning in the Universe.

The third sphere is named *Sairiel*—derived from *sair*,
hairy—which is the mother of everything wicked and evil.
All evil deeds and wicked unholy powers, also venomous
speech issue forth from this unholy sphere.

The fourth sphere makes the world tremble, and is constantly endeavouring to annihilate and destroy it. It drives out
peace from the Garden of Eden and from the world, and is
anxious to rout out all lovely plants.

The fifth sphere is the beginning of a tangible world, but
still invisible to the human eye. The throne of the ruler of
this sphere is made of living flame. And were it not for the
mercy and loving-kindness of the Creator, the evil hosts and
inmates of this sphere would have long ago destroyed all
living creatures in one instant. From this terrible and unholy
sphere issue forth sin and evil inclinations and spread in the
world. It is also the abode of the angel of death who dwells
in this unholy sphere.

The sixth sphere is constantly at war with omnipotent
Providence. At certain moments it rebels against and declares
war to the Ruler of the Universe. And then the world trembles
in its foundations, harmony is disturbed, and terrible events
occur and weigh heavily upon the upper and netherworlds.

The seventh sphere is called the hurling raven. For, as
the cruel raven throws away its brat, so the ruler of this
unholy sphere is constantly endeavouring to throw away and
scatter the holy seed guarded in the treasury of the world's
foundation.

The eighth sphere is the sphere of *Sammael*. It is responsible for strife and discomfort which exist in the world. For the ruler of this sphere roves all over the world and destroys the treasures of all other spheres. The inhabitants of this sphere know not the truth, and appear in different shapes. But they are always *red*. Their banner is red, their armies are red, their clothes are red, and the ground beneath them is *red*. The prince of the ninth sphere is called Gamliel. His servants change into serpents and spread horror among all those who behold them. The tenth sphere is called Lilith, and its prince is called Sariel; he is the great king of the demons who rule over the air.[1]

[1] *Yalkut Rubeni, Genesis*; Bin Gorion, *loc. cit.*, pp. 335–337.

CHAPTER IV

The Heavenly Hosts

Difference between Jewish and other myths—Divine messengers—Belief in higher beings—Angelology of the Old Testament—Jewish folklore—Conflict between monotheism and polytheism—The angelology of the Talmud—Persian and Babylonian influence—The hierarchy of the angels—The Ascension of Moses—He meets numerous angels—The Erelim—Nogah and Maadim—The Ishim—The angel Dinah or Jephephiah—The functions of the angels—Akatriel and Sandalphon—Rahab, prince of the sea—Ridja, lord of rain—Ben Nez, prince of storm—Tutelary angels—The creation of the angels—Created on second or fifth day—Creation of angels discussed by Fathers of Christian Church—St. Augustine, and Origen—Dionysius the Areopagite.

THE ANGELS

WITH regard to angels Jewish myth differs considerably from the myths of other nations.

In the various mythologies of both eastern and western nations all the phenomena of nature, all universal and local occurrences are looked upon as the manifestations of separate independent divinities. The gods of Greece and India are many and various. They recognize, it is true, a superior God, a chief, but they, too, enjoy divine honours and dignities.

Jewish myth differs in this respect as in many others from such conceptions. Here, all natural manifestations, all universal and local events are the result of the will of *one* perfect Being, the Eternal and Creator, from whom everything emanates and to whom everything is subject.

Even Jewish myth, steeped as it was in monotheism, would not tolerate an idea bordering on duality or plurality of gods.

The ministering angels, therefore, peopling the Pantheon created by Jewish myth, are not at all independent agents with Divine power, independence, and free will. They enjoy no will of their own, but are the obedient and willing messengers and agents of a Divine Providence whose bidding they are bound to do. God Himself being often too exalted and too high to interfere in the affairs of the world, excepting certain rare occasions, charges these angels to execute His decrees.

The Rabbis of the Talmud, and the exponents of pre-talmudic and post-talmudic Jewish myth and legend, were so anxious to avoid any idea that could give rise to the conception of duality and, above all, plurality, that they distinctly repeated the teaching that the angels were created either on the second or on the fifth day. Premundane creation was limited to abstract ideas, to wisdom, reward, and punishment.

The belief in higher beings, more perfect than man, is common to antiquity and especially to the Orient. Not only were the heavens and the whole universe peopled with angels and demons, that is to say, with good and evil spirits, but primitive man, and especially the Orientals, believed in the influence which these higher and more perfect beings or spirits exercised upon the sublunar world. The angels also served as intermediaries between man and Divinity. The mythologies of antiquity are full of such spirits, partly good, partly evil, and arranged in a perfect hierarchy. The Old Testament knows almost nothing of such spirits, for whenever the mention of angels is made they are used in the sense of agencies of the Divine power. In the Old Testament, the appearance of angels is nothing else but the manifestation of the activity of Divinity in the world of the senses. They are messengers,[1] or the impersonal acts of Divine Providence.

---

[1] Malachim, ἄγγελοι.

Side by side, however, with the Old Testament, folklore and popular imagination gave rise to a number of myths and legends, which the Rabbis and masters of the Cabbala, or Hebrew mysticism, subsequently utilized for allegorical and ethical purposes. Jewish angelology and the myths and legends about angels and demons passed through many phases before they arrived to pure mysticism.

The angelology of the Jews has always been the result of the conflict constantly waged between monotheism and the polytheism of the Oriental past, which never ceased and still lingered on in the imagination of the people. Before the Babylonian captivity the struggle was one between the One God—Unique and Universal, the God of the Hebrew prophets—and the national, local Gods of Oriental antiquity. Constantly the Jewish people showed a hankering for the polytheism of Egypt and Canaan; constantly the people forgot the worship of the One God and prostrated themselves before the altars of the many gods of antiquity. Angelology became a compromise between pure monotheism and polytheism. Whilst, however, the Bible looks upon angels only as personifications of the acts of the One God, the Babylonian captivity was responsible for a considerable change. No angel is mentioned by name in Holy Scripture. The Jews had no angelology before the Babylonian captivity, and the Talmud Jerushalmi remarks that the names of the angels were brought from Babylon.[1] In Persia and Babylonia the Jews came into contact with a new polytheism, and with an elaborate angelology, rich and varied, the angelology of the Babylonians, and especially of the Persians. The ancient Oriental polytheism still lingered in the popular mind, and the people eagerly grasped the ideas which gave such scope to their imagination and satisfied their polytheistic inclinations. Monotheism, how-

---

[1] *Jer, Rosh-ha-Shanah*, I, 2; see Grünbaum in *Z.D.M.G.*, Vol. XXXI, p. 25*f*; *Genesis Rabba*, 48; see also Bacher, *Die Agada der Palästinensischen Amoräer*, I, p. 412.

ever, was still deeply rooted in the Jewish mind, and the Unique and only God was often considered too sacred and too holy to weave myths and legends round Him.

Under the influence of Parsism and the teaching of Zarathustra, angels begin to appear in Jewish lore in human shape and form, receive separate names, and are arranged in an hierarchy like the servants and courtiers of a king. The heads and chiefs are called princes, and the Jewish myths know of six or seven such angel-princes. The influence of the teaching of Zarathustra upon the angel—and demon—myths of ancient Israel is quite comprehensible. The period during which the Jews lived in Persia and Media, whither they had been exiled by Nebuchadnezzar, coincides with the time of the highest development of the Zend cult. It was here in Persia that Israel acquired the popular Persian beliefs in Paradise and Hell, in angels, demons, and genii. But these myths and legends received at the hands of the Jewish nation a monotheistic colouring, and were made use of by the Rabbis of the Talmud and the masters of the Cabbala to teach monotheism, to extol the majesty, omnipresence and omnipotence of the Creator, and to draw moral and ethical lessons.

The first to mention an angel by name is *Tobit*, where we read that the angel Raphael conducted Tobias into Media.[1] Daniel, who lived at Babylon, already mentions the angels Michael and Gabriel.[2] The second book of *Esdras* mentions Uriel.[3]

Jewish angelology, however, was developed after the return of the Jews from Babylonian captivity, and the myths and legends gathering round the angels and demons are scattered through the Talmud, the Midrashim, and the works of the Cabbalists. Popular imagination ascribes to some of the angels the function of teaching Adam, Noah, the Patriarchs, Moses, and the later heroes of Jewish history. In fact, a whole

---

[1] *The Book of Tobit*, 3, 17; 11, 2. [2] *Daniel*, 8, 16; 9, 21; 10, 21. [3] 4, 36.

mass of myth and legend has been woven into the heroic history of Israel. The names of the angels are always a composition of the name of God and the special commission entrusted to them. And thus the name of each ministering angel depends upon his message and often varies with it.[1] On his breast each angel has a tablet, in which the name of God and that of the angel is combined.[2]

Numerous were the angels whom Moses beheld when he ascended to Heaven. This is described in the book called *The Ascension of Moses* (or *Gedullath Moshe*). Moses was carried up to Heaven by the angel Metatron, accompanied by fifteen thousand angels on the right hand and fifteen thousand angels on the left hand. In the first heaven he saw many windows at each of which stood an angel. And Metatron explained to him that these windows were the windows of life and of death, of prayers and supplication, of peace and war, of joy and tears, of sin and repentance, of life and death. In the second heaven he saw one angel three hundred parasangs long, accompanied by myriads of other angels who, as Metatron explained to him, were placed over the clouds and rain. In the third heaven Moses saw an angel whose length is a journey of five hundred years, accompanied by myriads of other ministering angels, placed over corn, trees, and fruits. They were called *Erelim*, and the angel presiding over them had seventy thousand heads and seventy thousand mouths in each head, and seventy thousand tongues in each mouth. In the fourth heaven he saw the Temple built of red, green, and white fire, of gems and carbuncle. And there he also saw the angels placed over the sun and the moon, over the stars and the planets. He further saw there the two stars called *Nogah* and *Maadim*, one standing above the sun to cool its intense heat in summer, and the other standing above the moon to protect the world against the cold of the moon.

[1] *Exodus Rabba*, 29; *Genesis Rabba*, 78.　　[2] *Yalkut*, Vol. II, § 797; see W. Bacher, *loc. cit.*

In the fifth heaven Moses saw angels who were half of fire
and half of snow, and although the snow was above the fire
it did not extinguish it. They belonged to the angel-group
called *Ishim*. In the sixth heaven Moses saw an angel whose
length was a journey of five hundred years and who was
entirely of ice, and myriads of angels belonging to the group
of the *holy watchers* stood by his side and praised the Lord.
And in the seventh heaven Moses saw the angel of wrath
and the angel of anger, and also the angel of death. The angels
of wrath and anger were wholly of fire and fastened with
chains of dark and red fire. The angel of death was full of
fiery eyes, so that anyone who looked at him fell down in dread.
In this heaven, which is called *Araboth*, Moses also saw an
angel called *Dina* who is teaching the souls created by God
and placed in Paradise. His name is also Jephephiah.[1]

And thus, the heavenly hosts, the ministering angels, are
represented in post - exilic Jewish myths and legends somewhat resembling the retinue of an Oriental ruler, whom even
the foremost courtiers are not allowed to see in his secret
and very private apartments. From behind a curtain (the
Pargod) He issues His commands.[2] The ministering angels,
or the *Malachei Hashareth*, are not only the agents of Providence, the messengers of Divine commissions, but they also
have the function of singing hymns in praise of the Creator
and of protecting mankind, in particular the virtuous and
pious. The host of angels, whose function it is to sing hymns
in praise of the Creator, are being daily created. They are
called forth by the breath of Almighty from the rivers of
liquid fire flowing under the throne of the Eternal. We thus
find in Jewish literature, under the influence of the Persian
religious system, a veritable Pantheon which could have
easily become dangerous to Jewish monotheism. But Judaism

[1] *Gedullath Moshe*, Amsterdam, 1754; see also Gaster in *Journal of the Royal Asiatic Society*, 1893, pp. 572–620.
[2] *Berachoth*, 18b; *Sanhedrin*, 89b; *Yoma*, 77a. See also The Koran, *Sura*, 42, 50.

utilized these elements for the purpose of concentrating the plurality of Divine powers and manifestations in the power of the One God. There is no trace whatever in Jewish myth of any idea of either a plurality of Divinities or even of a dualism. Like the sun, the moon, and the stars, the angels are supernatural powers, obeying the command of the Creator and doing His bidding. They are all the servants of the Almighty, and even the angels of destruction only obey the command of God and execute His decrees.[1]

As the angels are vastly superior to men, in capacities and dignities, so popular imagination, in order to make them in some degree comprehensible to human understanding, invested them with a nature, offices, and occupations similar to those which occur among men. They are thus represented as servants and attendants of All-Father, the King of the Universe, who is surrounded by a court of angels like a great king. They are the courtiers and ministers, the attendants and councillors of the Divine King.

The Prophets had already spoken poetically of the angels as the host of heaven standing round the throne of the Lord of the Universe, and frequently sent to the lower world to execute His decrees. Thus we read in Job: " There was a day when the sons of God came to present themselves before the Lord." [2] " I saw the Lord sitting on His throne, and all the hosts of heaven standing by Him, on His right hand and on His left." [3]

The angels were thus supposed to be dwelling in Heaven, in the regions of light, and myth and legend became busy, describing how they are clothed in garments of light, radiance, and glory, standing before the throne of the Creator.

Innumerable are the functions of the angels. Some are appointed for celestial service, whilst others are attached to the earth and especially to man. Others again are continually

[1] E. Bischoff, *Babylonisch-Astrales*, p. 139.　　[2] *Job*, 1, 6.　　[3] *I Kings*, 22, 19.

travelling between Heaven and earth. To every thought and
to every action of man, either for good or for evil, there corresponds in Heaven or upon earth, in the netherworlds and
in space, a group of angels (or demons). The Jewish myths
and legends in the Talmud and in the Midrashim mention
the names of a number of such angels. *Akatriel* is specially
appointed to carry swiftly on his wings the words and innermost thoughts of man to the celestial regions and before the
throne of God, whilst *Sandalphon*, who surpasses in height
all his heavenly colleagues, passes his time in weaving crowns
of glory for his Creator.[1] There is another class of angels
whom the Creator calls into existence for a very short span
of time. They arise from the river of fire, sing a hymn to His
glory, and then disappear.[2]

Every day the angels pass before the throne of the Eternal,
and then take up their places and their functions.

Whenever a soul, after its sojourn upon earth, in the
prison house of the body, rejoins its heavenly abode, a joyous
tremor passes through the hosts of Heaven. The news is
passed on from one group of the celestials to another, and
all of them utter a shout of joy, giving thanks to the Master
who has brought back to them one of their companions.

And just as the planets influence the course of nature,
so the angels, too, preside over natural occurrences. Thus
Michael is the prince of snow, Gabriel the prince of fire,
Jorkami prince of hail, Rahab is the prince of the sea,[3] Ridja
the prince of rain.[4]

Rashi,[5] in his commentary to the passage in *Yoma*, 21*a*,
quotes *Taanith*, 25*b*, where it is said that Ridja resembles a calf
and stands midway between the upper and the nether waters.

It should be borne in mind that the planet of rain in the
Pleiades is in the sign of the bull.

---

[1] *Hagigah*, 13*b*.   [2] *Hagigah*, 14*a*; *Genesis Rabba*, 78.   [3] *Baba Batra*, 74*b*.   [4] *Taanith*, 25*b*.
[5] Solomon bar Isaac, French Commentator on Bible and Talmud (1040–1105).

Ben Nez is the prince of the storm.[1] Numerous other angels are mentioned in later Jewish Midrashic lore, such as Galgaliel, Ophaniel, Barakiel (lightning), Lailahel (night), Raashiel (earthquake), Shalgiel (snow), &c.

The choir of celestial singers consists of six hundred and ninety-four myriads of angels, who daily pronounce and praise the Holy name, saying: " Blessed be the name of Thy heavenly glory from sunrise to sunset."[2]

The angels have another function and that is to accompany man and watch over him. Every pious and virtuous act accomplished by man produces a tutelary angel. The tutelary angels also have the function of pleading the cause of the just and pious before the Throne of the Eternal. Whenever one of the heroes or pious men of Israel meets with a calamity, or is in great distress, they intercede before the Throne of Glory. Thus, when Abraham raised his hand to sacrifice his son Isaac, when Pharaoh intended to kill Moses, hosts of ministering angels prostrated themselves before the Throne of the Eternal, and pleaded until the Creator saved them.[3]

With regard to the creation of the angels opinions differ. Some say that the angels were created either on the second or on the fifth day of Creation,[4] and that God consulted with them when He said: " Let us make man in our image, after our likeness." Others, however, are of opinion that the angels were created long before the world came into existence.

Apart, however, from the ministering angels created at the beginning of the world, the creation of these winged messengers is still being continued, for to execute every behest of God a new angel is created who passeth away as soon as he has executed the command of the Holy One.

[1] *Baba Batra*, 25a.
[2] *Pirke de Rabbi Eliezer*, Ch. 12; see also Kohut, in *Abhandlungen für die Kunde des Morgenlandes*, Vol. IV, p. 19.
[3] *Genesis Rabba*, 65; *Pirke de Rabbi Eliezer*, Ch. 32; see also *Hagigah*, 5a.
[4] *Genesis Rabba* 1 and 3; see also G. Friedlaender's Transl. of *Pirke de Rabbi Eliezer*, p. 20, note 3.

Some of the ministering angels have only a very fleeting existence. They are created every day, and after having uttered the praises of the Eternal pass away into the river of fire, called Nehar di Nur, whence they issued. Companies of angels are thus being created daily, some of whom continue their existence, whilst others, issuing from the fiery river and created only for the daily service of the Eternal and for the purpose of executing His commands, pass away.[1]

Very frequently we also find in Rabbinic and Midrashic folklore, that the phenomena and powers of nature are hypostatized into angels. Sea and wind, hail and rain, life and death, health and disease, wealth and poverty are supposed to be presided over by a special angel.

The question of the creation of angels is discussed not only in Jewish lore but also in the works of the Christian Fathers of the Church. St. Augustine is of opinion that the angels were created on the first day and that they are included in the name of *Light*,[2] whilst Origen [3] writes that the angels were created long before the world. Some authors base themselves upon the passage in *Job*: " Where wast thou when I laid the foundation of the earth; and all the Sons of God shouted for joy?" [4]

Both the Rabbis of the Talmud and the Fathers of the Christian Church frequently refer to angels as appropriated to persons, nations, empires, countries, and cities. But already Daniel refers to Michael as the protector of Israel, and to the angel protector of Persia, when he makes the angel Gabriel say that " the prince of the kingdom of Persia withstood him one and twenty days ".[5] The idea of the tutelary angels of the various nations is supposed to have its foundation in the passage of the *Septuaginta*, " God had set the bounds of the peoples according to the number of the *angels* of Israel ".[6]

[1] *Hagigah*, 14a; *Book of Enoch*, 14, 19; 70, 1.
[2] St. Augustine, *Lib. I de Genesi ad litt.*, Cap. 9.   [3] Origen, *Hom. I in Genes.*
[4] *Job*, 38, 4, 7.   [5] *Daniel*, 10, 21.   [6] *Deuteron.* 32, 8.

This passage is supposed to mean the government of each particular country and nation with which God had entrusted His angels. The belief that guardian angels were commissioned to attend individuals, to take care of and to protect them, was shared by heathens and Jews alike, and is shared by the Fathers of the Church. Plato speaks of the two demons or genii who accompany every man, one prompting him to good, the other to evil, and Hesiod speaks of the aerial spirits designed to be the guardians of mankind.[1] In the *Vita Adami*, Adam refers to the guardian angels set to guard Eve and himself. It was during their absence that the enemy came to Eve and caused her to sin.

The celestial hierarchy is also the subject of many discussions in Jewish lore, parallels to which are found in the works of other nations. Many of the Fathers of the Church have discussed the question, and Dionysius the Areopagite, devotes an entire treatise to the question of the hierarchy of angels.

The precedence of the angels, their different names, according to their degrees of power and knowledge, all constitute so much material for numerous myths and legends. "We are not to be surprised," writes a Christian author, "at these visions fabricated by the Jews, for if they be compared with those of many Christian authors, who have settled a ceremonial and rules for precedency among angels, the Jews would appear not more blamable in this point than some Christians."[2]

---

[1] Hesiod, *Works and Days*, I, Vers. 121.
[2] Basnage, *Histoire des Juifs*, Vol. IV, Chap. 9; see also Calmet, *Dictionary of the Bible*, Vol. I, p. 128.

CHAPTER V

The Angel-Princes, or Archangels

The seven archangels: Michael, Gabriel, Uriel, Raphael, Metatron, Sandalphon, Rediyao (Ridia)—The four national angels of Israel—Uza the guardian angel of Egypt—The functions of the angels—The two angels of death, Gabriel and Sammael—The angel Rediyao—The story of Metatron —Metatron and Mithra—The Prince of the Presence—Sar Haolam—He teaches Moses—Elisha ben Abuyah meets Metatron—A Jewish Faust—The punishment of Metatron—The two Metatrons—Enoch-Metatron—Enoch is translated to Heaven where he becomes Metatron—Protest of the angels against Enoch-Metatron—Great honour shown to Enoch-Metatron—Thirty thousand gates of wisdom are opened to him—The mysteries of the Law and the secrets of Nature are revealed to Enoch-Metatron—He bears witness against the sinful generation of the Flood—The jealousy of the angels— Moses meets the angel Kemmuel, the guardian of Heaven, and Hadarniel —The fire of Sandalphon—The fiery river Rigyon—Gallizur, or Rasiel— The angels pay homage to Moses—Jephephiah hands over the Holy Law to Moses.

THE ANGEL-PRINCES

Apart from the ministering angels there are the angel-princes, four of whom surround the throne of the Creator. They are Michael, Raphael, Gabriel, and Uriel.

These angel-princes enjoy the privilege of being within the *Pargod*, or the veil, whilst all the others only hear Divine commands from behind the veil or curtain.[1]

The seven angel-princes, or archangels, in Jewish myth, correspond to the seven *Amshaspands* of Persia which are influenced by the seven Babylonian gods of the planets. The names of these angels are often changed in accordance with their particular functions,[2] and it is interesting to notice that

---

[1] *Hagigah*, 5b; *Pirke de Rabbi Eliezer*, Ch. 4.   [2] *Genesis Rabba*, 78.

when the star of Marduk is in the zenith, he is called Ninib.[1]

The seven angel - princes are: Michael, Gabriel, Uriel, Raphael, Metatron, Sandalphon, and Rediyao. They are above all others in rank and dignity, and are allowed in the vicinity of the Divine throne of light. Michael, which name means " Who is like God ", is to the right; Gabriel, which means " Strength of God ", is to the left; Uriel, which means " Splendour of God ", is in front of the Throne; and Raphael, which means " Healing from God ", is behind the Throne.[2] They are the four national angels, that is the angels of Israel, and hence their Hebrew names. They are the watchers of Israel. Michael's principal qualities are: mercy, loving - kindness, and peace.[3] He constantly pleads the cause of Israel and defends it before the Throne of the Eternal.

Thus, when the Almighty said to Michael, this tutelary angel of Israel: " Thy nation has sinned," the angel pleaded: " Lord of the Universe! There are many pious individuals who ought to outweigh the sin of the collectivity." [4] But all the other nations, too, have each their tutelary angels. The tutelary angel of Egypt is Uza, and when the children of Israel were led out of Egypt, Uza complained and clamoured for justice before the Throne of the Eternal. " The nation Thou art taking out of Egypt I have a right upon," argued Uza. But Michael, the defender of Israel, appeared and soon crushed all the arguments of Uza.[5]

Michael, the angel-prince, is the harbinger and messenger bringing and announcing good tidings. He is also the prince of peace, and as such is often called the high-priest, ministering in Heaven.[6]

In the *Book of Enoch* frequent mention is made of the angel of peace.

Gabriel, who is next to Michael, is the strength of the

---

[1] Jeremias, *Das alte Testament*, p. 78.　　　[2] *Numbers Rabba*, 2.　　　[3] *Yalkut*, § 186.
[4] *Yoma*, 77a.　　[5] *Midrash Abkir*, quoted in *Yalkut*, § 241.　　[6] *Hagigah*, 12b; *Zebachim*, 62a.

Lord. He manifests the Divine justice and punishment of the wicked, and only for the latter he is terrible, being mild with regard to the just. Divine justice is thus identified with Gabriel. He is to the left of the Creator, and represents not only the avenging and punishing power of the Almighty against Israel, but also against the hostile elements which arise in the midst of Israel or against other nations. He is the personification of justice and not, as imagined in the traditions of the Mohammedans, the enemy of Israel. Michael is made of snow, Gabriel of fire, but they live peacefully together without the fire of the one injuring the snow of the other.[1]

According to Moslem tradition, Gabriel is the national angel and the angel of revelation of the Moslems and is placed to the right of the Creator.

In Jewish legend, it was Gabriel who punished the Egyptian servant when she refused to fetch Moses out of the waters.[2] It was he who was busy in the destruction of Sodom,[3] but it was also Gabriel who marked the fronts of the wicked with a letter in blood, and those of the pious and just with a letter in ink, so that the angels of destruction should not harm them.[4]

Girt with his sword of justice ever since the six days of creation, Gabriel exercises justice in wars and on the battle-fields, punishing the traitors and helping the just.[5]

He also acts as angel of death. For there are two angels of death, one for the inhabitants of the Holy Land of Palestine, who is Gabriel, and the other, who is Sammael, for the rest of the world. Both Gabriel and Sammael receive their orders from Metatron who is the president of this triumvirate of death. Metatron issues his orders to Gabriel, Gabriel to Sammael, and the latter again to the ministering serving messengers of death who bring the departed souls to their senders.[6]

---

[1] *Debarim Rabba*, 5'; see also *Shir-Hashirim Rabba*.   [2] *Sotah*, 12b; *Exodus Rabba*, 1.
[3] *Pirke de Rabbi Eliezer*, Ch. 25; *Genesis Rabba*, 50; *Baba Mezia*, 86b.
[4] *Sabbath*, 55a.   [5] *Sanhedrin*, 26a.   [6] *Yalkut Rubeni*, § 13; *Yalkut Chadash*, § 44.

Gabriel is fire, not only fire that consumes dry and even wet matter, but fire that drives away fire.[1]

Uriel personifies the radiance emanating from the Divine nature, and Raphael personifies the Divine power of healing. He heals and banishes disease, and is consequently known also under the name of Suriel, the angel who calls back or causes to disappear every disease.[2] He is mentioned in the *Book of Enoch* under the name of Surjan.

The angel Sandalphon stands upon the earth, whilst his head reaches the heavens. He is supposed to stand behind the chariot and to weave crowns for the Creator.[3]

The angel Rediyao, who has been compared to the Persian Ardvi-Cüra, is the angel of rain, the genius of water, both of the celestial and the earthly waters. His terrible voice resounds continually throughout the world. And some of the Rabbis relate in the folkloristic tales of the Talmud, that Rediyao resembles a calf. He stands midst between the upper and the lower water floods, or the *Tehomoth*. He cries unto the upper floods: " Let flow thy waters;" and unto the lower Tehomoth he commands: " Let arise thy floods." [4]

THE STORY OF METATRON

The myths and legends of ancient Jewish angelology are particularly busy with the angel-prince who is known as Metatron. It has been suggested that the idea of Metatron has been borrowed from the Persian Mithra, and that the very name of this angel, like all the other names of the angels, has come from Persia.[5] It seems to me that this is quite a plausible theory, although the majority of authors derive the name of Metatron from the Greek $\mu\epsilon\tau\alpha\delta\rho\acute{o}\nu o\varsigma$ (or $\delta\rho\acute{o}\nu o\nu$).[6]

Metatron is the prince of the Presence, the prince of the

---

[1] *Yoma*, 21b; see Kohut, *loc. cit.*, p. 33. [2] *Berachoth*, 51a.
[3] *Hagigah*, 13b; *Exodus Rabba*, 21. [4] *Taanith*, 25b. [5] Kohut, *loc. cit.*
[6] A. Franck, *La Kabbale*; Graetz, *Gnosticismus*; Hirschfeld, *Frankels' Zeitschrift*, 1846, p. 353; Edersheim, *The Life and Times of Jesus the Messiah*, 1883, Vol. I, p. 47, note.

face, the prince of the world. Into the innermost chamber of the Divine Presence he is allowed to penetrate, whilst other angels only receive his commands from behind the veil.[1]

He is the angel of God who spoke to Moses in the name of the Lord of the Universe, and who received the mission to lead the Children of Israel into the Holy Land. He is severe and revengeful against all those who forsake the name of the Lord.[2]

But Metatron is also the protector of the world, its superintendent into whose hands the world is given and who is therefore called the *Sar ha-Olam*, the prince of the world.[3]

In early Jewish myth and legend Metatron is represented as the vicegerent of the Creator. It is he who transmits the orders of the Eternal to Moses. He also instructs infants who have died without knowledge.[4] He is called the prince of the universe, charged by God, the All-Father, to create the world.

We thus find in the myth of Metatron the influence of the idea of the demi-ourgos. Judaism, however, could not allow this gnostic doctrine, and those who taught it were excommunicated.

Metatron is also the preserver and guardian of the law and of the Holy Writ, and it was he who afterwards became the teacher and instructor of Moses. Kohut suggested that Sagsagel, who is mentioned in Rabbinic legend as the teacher of Moses and as being present at the latter's death, is only another epithet for Metatron.[5] Metatron is thus the greatest of all angels. He is the representative of God, the angel of the face; he speaks in the name of God.

But Jewish monotheism strongly opposed the idea that Metatron had either the power to forgive sins, or was to be

[1] *Hagigah*, 5a, 15a, 16a.   [2] *Sanhedrin*, 38b.
[3] *Hullin*, 66a; *Sanhedrin*, 94a; *Yebamot*, 16b.   [4] *Abodah Zarah*, 3b.
[5] Kohut, *loc. cit.*, p. 42.

adored or regarded as a mediator between man and his Maker.

Of Elisha ben Abuyah it is told that one day he saw Metatron sitting in Heaven and would have inferred that there were two supreme powers.

The Story of Elisha ben Abuyah and Metatron

A Jewish Faust

And it came to pass that one day the Rabbi Elisha, the son of Abuyah, was allowed to pry into Paradise, and he perceived the angel Metatron, the recording angel, sitting on a seat, and registering the merits of the Children of Israel. At this sight the Rabbi was struck with astonishment, and would have inferred that there were two supreme powers in Heaven.

He exclaimed: " Is it not laid down that there is no sitting in Heaven and no shortsightedness?" And in order to prove the angel's inferiority, Metatron was ordered by the heavenly court to receive sixty fiery lashes from another angel. Metatron then asked and obtained leave to cancel all the past merits of the apostate Rabbi who was henceforth known by the name of *Akher* (another). And one day, which happened to be a Sabbath, and the day of atonement, the Rabbi was riding along when he heard from Heaven: " Return all the backsliding children, but Akher alone abide thou in thy sin." [1]

According to some sources, however, Metatron is supposed to be none other than Enoch, the son of Jared, after his translation to Heaven. The Enoch legend, in Jewish lore, gradually underwent a change. In the earlier Haggadah Enoch is not identical with Metatron.

In the Slavonic *Book of Enoch*, the son of Jared is described as a very wise man whom God loved and received, enabling

[1] *Hagigah,* 15*a.*

him to see the heavenly abodes, kingdoms of the wise, great, and never-changing God. Two angels, therefore, appeared to Enoch and bade him make ready to ascend to Heaven. Enoch thereupon admonished his sons to walk before the face of the Lord and to keep His judgments, and, furthermore, not to seek for him till he was brought back to them. Carried aloft through the air by the two angels he visited the seven heavens.

And when God had communicated to Enoch the secrets of Creation, and how he created the visible out of the invisible, he commanded him to return to earth for thirty days, there to teach his sons during that time. And Enoch did as the Lord had commanded him. He told his sons what he had seen, and admonished them and instructed them. He described unto them the courses of the sun and of the moon, thunder and lightning, Hell and Paradise, and impressed upon them the necessity of fearing God. But whilst fearing God they should never revile man, for man being made in the image of God, he who reviles man really reviles God. Enoch further admonished his sons not to swear, either by Heaven or by earth, to live in meekness, refrain from revenge, and to be open-handed and generous to the needy.

When the thirty days elapse, Enoch once more addresses his sons and the people who assemble at Achuzan to listen to his words and to take leave of him. He addresses them on various topics, bids them be faithful, and announces a time when there will be neither labour nor sickness, neither suffering nor sorrow, neither night nor darkness. He is then carried off to the highest heaven.

In the later Haggadah, however, Enoch, the son of Jared, becomes identical with Metatron.

He, Enoch, served before the Lord in truth, and was not among the inhabitants of the earth, for he was translated above into the firmament, through the word of the Lord;

and He called him by the name of Metatron, that is the great scribe.

Enoch himself related the story of his ascension to Heaven to Rabbi Ishmael, who spoke to him and asked him the reason of his great honour, and why he was greater than any prince, and higher than any angel.

And Enoch told the Rabbi as follows:

" I was in reality Enoch, the son of Jared. And when the generation of the Flood had sinned before the Lord and did not walk in the path of righteousness, the Lord took me from that sinful generation into the highest heaven, that I might be a witness against that generation. The Eternal, blessed be His name, removed me from earth, that I should stand before the Throne of Glory and the seat of His majesty, and before the wheels of His chariot, there to accomplish the requirements of the Most High. Thereupon my flesh became flame, and my arteries fire; my eyeballs became torches of fire, and the light of my eyes the flashing of lightning. My body became burning fire, my limbs fiery, burning wings, and the hair of my head was a flame. Flames were cleft asunder by my right hand. A wind, a storm and a tempest blew around me, and the voice of a mighty earthquake was before and behind me. I was carried to Heaven in a fiery chariot, by horses of fire. And when I entered into the presence of God, the sacred Chajjoth, Seraphim, Ophanim, Cherubim, all the fiery ministering angels recoiled five thousand three hundred and eighty miles at the smell of me, crying aloud: ' What a smell hath come among us from the son of woman. Why is he admitted into Heaven?' But the Almighty replied: ' Cherubim and Seraphim, ye, my servants all, know that I have exalted the son of Jared to be chief among the angels of Heaven. All my sons upon earth have rejected My sovereignty and are adoring idols, but the son of Jared alone hath remained faithful unto Me. In reward therefore for his virtue I exalt him.' " And the height of Enoch-Metatron is very great, for it would take a man five hundred years to walk from his heel to the crown of his head.[1]

Metatron is further described in Jewish myth as follows: Enoch-Metatron had seventy names, corresponding to the seventy languages of the world and to the seventy Kings of Kings. He was greater than all the princes of Heaven and earth, more beloved than all the ministering angels, and more powerful than all the mighty ones. He was Enoch the son of Jared. When the generation of the Flood walked in the path of evil and did evil deeds, the Creator took him, and he ascended to Heaven. And here he bore witness against the sinful generation of the Flood.

The Creator sent for him the heavenly prince Anphiel, and he took Enoch, he who was Metatron, before the very eyes of men and brought him in a fiery chariot, drawn by fiery horses up to Heaven. And ministering angels announced his ascent and brought him into the spheres of splendour. But the fiery Seraphim and Cherubim knew of his coming even when he was still sixty-five thousand three hundred miles away. And they murmured and said:

" What is the worth of this man born of woman, and who is he that he should come among us who are fashioned of liquid fire?" But the voice of the Creator resounded from one end of the world unto the other and proclaimed: " Do not murmur, ye my ministering angels, Cherubim and Seraphim. The race of men has become wicked, and the sons of men have done evil deeds. They have served and prostrated themselves before strange gods and idols. Enoch alone, the son of Jared, walked in the path of righteousness, and excelled in justice and virtue and faith. And this is his reward." And Enoch, the son of Jared, who was called henceforth Metatron,

---

[1] Menachem Recanati, *Commentary to the Five Books of Moses*; see also *Sepher Hekhalot*, in Jellinek, *Beth-Hamidrash*, Vol. V, pp. 172–175.

was carried upon the wings of splendour into the highest of
heavenly spheres, into the midst of a great palace in Araboth,
the seventh heaven.

And here, surrounded by fiery ministering angels, Cherubim
and Seraphim who do the bidding of the Creator of the Universe, between flaming Seraphim and radiant *Hashmalim*,
Enoch-Metatron became the chief of the hosts of ministering
angels.

And the Creator opened before Enoch-Metatron the
thirty thousand gates of wisdom, and the thirty thousand
gates of reason and intelligence. He also opened unto him
the gates of life and peace, of power and courage, of benevolence and generosity, of love and law, and of mercy, humility,
and fear of the Lord. And Enoch-Metatron received the
heavenly gifts of wisdom and knowledge, of reason and intelligence, of life and love, of mercy and courage, of power
and grace, of radiance, beauty and pride. And after he had
been endowed with these heavenly gifts, the Creator blessed
Enoch-Metatron with three hundred and sixty-five thousand
blessings, and he became great and glorified throughout the
Universe. And the Creator gave unto Enoch-Metatron seventy-
two wings, thirty-six to his right and thirty-six to his left.
And He also gave unto him three hundred and sixty-five
thousand eyes, and every eye is like unto the great heavenly
light.

He was endowed with all the splendour and beauty and
radiance that exist in the Universe. And Enoch-Metatron
is seated upon a throne of splendour, and a canopy of radiance,
light, and beauty is above him, for all the splendour and all
the light of the world are woven into it.

And a voice announced from Heaven to Heaven and all
over the earth, saying: "The Lord of the World, the Creator of
the Universe, has raised Enoch-Metatron, His faithful servant,
above all the princes in Heaven and upon earth, and made him

the mightiest angel of the Presence. And all supplications to the Creator of the Universe are henceforth to be addressed through Enoch-Metatron, for he is endowed with wisdom and knowledge, with reason and understanding beyond all other angels. And the mysteries of the upper worlds and of the netherworlds are open unto Enoch-Metatron."

And all the mysteries of the law and the depths of piety were revealed unto Enoch-Metatron. The innermost thoughts of all the creatures are open to him, and all the riddles of the Universe and the mysteries of creation are known to him.

Clad in a radiant garment of light, and wearing a crown set with forty-nine precious stones that are more resplendent than the sun, his radiance sheds its light in all the four corners of Araboth and in the seven heavens, and in the four corners of the earth.

And with a flaming finger the Creator of the Universe engraved upon the crown of Enoch-Metatron all the signs by which were created heaven and earth, the seas and rivers, the mountains and the hills, the stars, planets, thunder and lightning, snow and hail, storm and wind, all the elements of the Universe, its harmony and order.

And when Enoch-Metatron placed the radiant crown upon his head, all the princes and angels of the heavenly host trembled and were filled with awe. And the angels of fire and of lightning, of storm and wind, of wrath and fury, of hail and snow and rain, of day and night, of the sun, the moon, the stars, and planets, all those who are set over the destinies of the world, they quaked and trembled before Enoch-Metatron.

Blinded by the glory and radiance emanating from the countenance of this prince of angels and leader of the heavenly host, they fell upon their faces and did homage to him.

He bears witness against the sinful generation of men who were destroyed in the great flood. For when men dare

to assail the benevolence and mercy of the Creator who wiped
out the generation of the Flood and all their wives and children
and their cattle and beasts, Enoch-Metatron, who was chosen
from among them and ascended to Heaven, bears witness to
the justice and mercy of All-Father who punishes the wicked
and rewards the just and virtuous.[1]

The Jealousy of the Angels

The angels are often supposed to be jealous of man and
particularly of Israel, to whom the Eternal has vouchsafed
His loving-kindness. Thus, when Moses ascended to Heaven
to receive the Law, the angels raised a protest and plotted to
destroy him. And it came to pass that when the son of Amram
was carried in a cloud to the celestial regions he was met by
the angel Kemuel, the gatekeeper of the abode of the angels,
who commands the host of twelve thousand angels of destruction, keeping watch at the gates of *Rakia*. He barred the
way to Moses and thus he spoke: " How darest thou approach
the seat of the fiery inhabitants of Heaven, son of Amram?
Return to earth, lest I destroy thee with my fiery breath."
But the son of Amram boldly replied: " I come not of my
own will, but with the permission of the Most High, blessed
be His name, who commanded me, His servant, to appear
before the Throne of Glory there to receive the Holy Law."
And Moses wrestled with Kemuel and conquered him. Thereupon the son of Amram continued his way when he met the
angel Hadarniel. This angel is taller and more terrible than
the other celestial inhabitants, and at every word that he
speaketh thousands of flashes of lightning issue from his
mouth. Hadarniel raised his terrible voice which sent fear
into the heart of Moses and caused him to quake. " How
darest thou approach the seat of the Holy of Holies, O son of

---

[1] Jellinek, *Beth-Hamidrash*, Vol. V, pp. 172–176; see *ibid*, Vol. II, pp. 114–116; see also
The Book of Yashar, Migne, *Dictionnaire des Apocryphes*, Vol. II.

Amram," he cried. But a voice from the Throne of Glory was heard which bade Hadarniel be silent. And thus spake the voice from the Throne of Glory. " Ever since you have been created by the word of My mouth, you have been jealous of man and have sought him quarrel. At the beginning of things, when it was My design to create man, many among you raised a protest and cried, ' What is man that Thou shouldst remember him.' [1] But I destroyed many hosts of these angels with My little finger,[2] and I created man in My own image. And now you seek quarrel with My faithful servant, the son of Amram, whom I have commanded to ascend to these heavenly regions to receive the Holy Law." Thus spake the voice from the Throne of Glory.

When Hadarniel heard these words he hastened before the throne of the Eternal, blessed be His name, and thus he pleaded: " Lord of the Universe! It is known unto Thee that I was unaware of Thy command to the son of Amram or that it was Thy sovereign will that he should appear in these celestial regions. And now I will be his guide and attendant, ministering unto him and obeying him even as a pupil does obey his master." Thereupon, Hadarniel, who is taller than his companions and from whose mouth issue forth flashes of lightning, bent low before the son of Amram and went before him, even as a pupil goes before his master. And when they reached the fire of Sandalphon, Hadarniel turned unto Moses and thus he spake: " O son of Amram! Turn back now, for I cannot bear the fire of Sandalphon, lest it will destroy me." When Moses perceived Sandalphon he was frightened in his heart, and prayed unto the Lord of the Universe to protect him from the fire of this mighty angel. The Lord had pity upon Moses and protected him with His boundless love, until he had passed the fire of Sandalphon. Of Sandalphon it is said that he is taller than his companions,

---

[1] *Ps.* 8, 6.　　　[2] *Sanhedrin,* 38*b.*

and that his place is behind the celestial chariot (the Merkaba), weaving crowns of glory for the Creator.

When Moses had passed the fire of Sandalphon he met the angel Rigyon who is really a fiery river issuing forth from underneath the Throne of Glory.[1] In this fiery stream the angels bathe every morning. Whenever the ministering angels appear before the Throne of Glory to be judged by the Lord of the Universe, they plunge into the fiery river of Rigyon and are rejuvenated. When the son of Amram had passed the fiery river of Rigyon, he met the angel Gallizur, who is also called Rasiel. It is he who listens to what is being proclaimed behind the veil before the Throne of Glory, and makes it known unto the world. And the prophet Elijah, standing upon the mount of Horeb, hears the words proclaimed by the angel and announces the message to the world and to humanity.

Gallizur, he who is Rasiel, also stands before the Throne of Glory, and spreading out his wings intercepts the breath of the *Chajjoth*, for otherwise the ministering angels would all be burnt to death through the fiery breath of the Chajjoth. And when Moses, the son of Amram, perceived the angel Gallizur, he who is called Rasiel, he trembled mightily and quaked, but the Holy One, blessed be His name, protected him. Thereupon a host of angels of destruction who are hovering in the celestial regions, doing the bidding of the Lord of the Universe, met the son of Amram.

Jealous of the honour vouchsafed to the son of man, they made ready to destroy him with the fire of their breath, but the Holy One, blessed be His name, spread out over Moses the radiance from the Throne of Glory and saved him from the jealousy of the ministering angels.

And when the moment arrived for Moses to descend upon earth, trembling and terror seized him once more. But the Holy One, blessed be His name, called the angel Jephephiah,

---

[1] *Daniel*, 7, 10; *Threni*, 3, 23.

the prince of the law, of learning, and of knowledge, and commanded him to hand over the Holy Law to the son of Amram. When the ministering angels saw the honour done unto Moses, the faithful servant of the Lord of the Universe, they became his friends and taught him many secrets. And even the angel of death and Metatron, the prince of the Presence, taught him secrets.[1]

SANDALPHON

Have you read in the Talmud of old,
In the legends the Rabbins have told
　　Of the limitless realms of the air,—
Have you read it—the marvellous story
Of Sandalphon, the angel of glory,
　　Sandalphon, the angel of prayer?

How, erect, at the outermost gates
Of the City Celestial he waits,
　　With his feet on the ladder of light,
That crowded with angels unnumbered,
By Jacob was seen, as he slumbered
　　Alone in the desert at night.

The angels of wind and of fire
Chant only one hymn, and expire
　　With the song's irresistible stress;
Expire in their rapture and wonder,
As harp-strings are broken asunder
　　By music they throb to express.

But serene in the rapturous throng,
Unmoved by the rush of the song,
　　With eyes unimpassioned and slow,
Among the dead angels, the deathless
Sandalphon stands listening breathless
　　To the sounds that ascend from below,

<hr />

[1] *Journal of Royal Asiatic Society*, 1893, pp. 588–590; see also Jellinek, *Beth-Hamidrash*, Vol. II, pp. 43–45; Wertheimer, *Batte Midrashot*, Vol. IV, pp. 22–30; Gaster, *The Chronicles of Jerahmeel*, pp. 144–146.

From the spirits on earth that adore,
From the souls that entreat and implore
  In the fervour and passion of prayer;
From the hearts that are broken with losses,
And weary with dragging the crosses
  Too heavy for mortals to bear.

And he gathers the prayers as he stands,
And they change into flowers in his hands,
  Into garlands of purple and red;
And beneath the great arch of the portal,
Through the streets of the City Immortal
  Is wafted the fragrance they shed.

It is but a legend, I know,
A fable, a phantom, a show,
  Of the ancient Rabbinical lore;
Yet the old mediæval tradition,
The beautiful strange superstition,
  But haunts me and holds me the more.

When I look from my window at night,
And the welkin above is all white,
  All throbbing and panting with stars,
Among them majestic is standing
Sandalphon, the angel, expanding
  His pinions in nebulous bars.

And the legend, I feel, is a part
Of the hunger and thirst of the heart,
  The frenzy and fire of the brain,
That grasps at the fruitage forbidden,
The golden pomegranates of Eden,
  To quiet its fever and pain.

H. W. Longfellow.

CHAPTER VI

The War in Heaven and the Fallen Angels

The revolt of the angels—Sammael, known also as Satan—His jealousy of first man—He struggles with the archangel Michael—Michael's song of triumph—Sammael is appointed angel of death—He often takes the shape of an angel of light—His function to tempt and accuse men—Sammael, called Iblis, in Mohammedan legend—The fallen angels, Shemhazai and Azael—The virtuous maiden—Shemhazai and Istahar or Estirah—The dream of Heyya and Aheyya—Shemhazai suspends himself between Heaven and earth—Istahar and Astarte—Aza and Azael—The pilgrimage of the magicians to the dark mountains, the abode of Aza and Azael—The fallen angels in the *Book of Enoch*—The plot of the angels on Mount Ardis—The fallen angels and the giants—The corruption of man—The story of Harut and Marut—Idris (Enoch) intercedes on their behalf—The punishment of Harut and Marut in Babylon—The angel of death—Moses and the angel of death—Michael refuses to take the soul of Abraham—The disappointment of the angel of death—He appears in his real, terrific form and frightens the servants of Abraham.

ALTHOUGH all the angels called into being by the Father of all were pure and holy, some of them allowed themselves to be swayed by pride. They dared to imagine themselves as powerful and as great as the Creator Himself, the Lord of the Universe. In their rebellion and subsequent fall, they dragged down with them a number of the celestial inmates. At the head of the rebels was he who is now known as Sammael or Satan. First of the Seraphim and the greatest of all created beings, he headed the rebels. He at first recognized only as his superior the Creator Himself, but soon a mad ambition entered his heart, and he wished to seat himself upon a throne as high as that of the Creator Himself. A terrible war was waged between the hosts headed by Sammael and those led by Michael, and Sammael was defeated.

Sammael, who is also known as Satan, was one of the Seraphim, with twelve wings, and a regent of the planet Mars, which, by the way, he still rules. Jealous of the Creator, he brooded rebellion. He desired to be as great as God and said in his heart: " I will ascend into Heaven, I will exalt my throne above the stars of God; I will sit also upon the mount of the Congregation in the sides of the North; I will ascend above the heights of the clouds; I will be like the Most High." [1] Sammael's jealousy knew no bounds, especially when he saw the favourite position of the first man. He refused to worship Adam and pay him homage, but, on the contrary, plotted with other angels to bring about the fall of man. Against the express command of the Creator he excited the passions of Adam and of Eve, who committed the first sin and were expelled from Eden. Sammael himself, however, after having led Adam and Eve into sin, had to suffer eternal punishment. Driven out of Heaven and from among his companions of light, the Seraphim, he and his hosts were precipitated out of the place of bliss, weighed down by the curse of the Creator. The Seraph did not submit without a struggle, and there was a war between Sammael and his hosts, on one side, and the angels who obeyed the will of God, on the other. It was the angel Michael especially who struggled with Sammael, the chief of the rebels. In his struggle the latter caught the wings of Michael and tried to drag him down with him in his fall, but the Eternal saved Michael, whence he has derived his name of the *Plethi*, or the Rescued.[2] Michael, on obtaining his great victory, sang a song of triumph to God.

" Glory to our God!" he sang; " praise to His Holy Name;

---

[1] *Isaiah*, 14, 13-14; *Yalkut Rubeni*, § 3.

[2] Rabbi Behai (Bahya), *Commentary on the Books of Moses*, section *Achare Moth*; see also Eisenmenger, *Entdecktes Judentum*, Vol. I, p. 831.

for He is our God, and glory be to Him. He is our Lord, and His be the triumph. His right hand He hath stretched forth and hath manifested His power. He hath cast down our adversary. Mad indeed are those who resist Him, and accursed are those who depart from His commandments! He knoweth all things and never can err! All that He wills is just and good, and His advice is holy. He is Supreme Intelligence and cannot be deceived, and His perfect being cannot will what is evil. Nothing is above that which is supreme, and nothing is better than that which is perfect. None is worthy beside Him, but those whom He hath made worthy. Above all things He must be loved, and adored as the Eternal King. Ye, who have abandoned your God, revolted against Him, and desired to be Gods yourselves, have now fallen from your high estates, and gone down like a fallen stone. Acknowledge now that God is great, that His works are perfect, and that His judgments are just. From eternity to eternity, through all the ages glory be to God, and praises of joy for all His works." [1]

And as it was Sammael who had been the cause of the penalty of death being decreed against the human race, for had Adam not sinned death would have been unknown, Sammael was appointed as the executioner of the human race, or the angel of death. He was cast down from Heaven as a punishment of his pride and jealousy, and fell down with all his company. By his envy and malice, death, with all other evils, came into the world. And by the permission of the Creator, Sammael still exercises an influence and has a government over his subordinates, who are fallen angels like himself. To test good men, and chastise bad ones, the Creator often makes use of Sammael or Satan. He seduces men and leads them upon the path of wickedness, for he or his subordinates often torment, obsess, or possess men and inspire them with wicked

---

[1] Fabricius, *Codex Pseudoepigraphus, Vet. Test.*, 1722, Vol. I, p. 21.

designs and evil intentions. Like a roaring lion he now roves about in the world, full of rage, intent upon destroying and betraying men and trying to involve them in guilt, wickedness and evil deeds.

His power and his malice, however, luckily for men, are restrained, and kept under control by the Creator, who has set a limit to Sammael's power.

Sometimes he can transform himself into an angel of light. He is the great enemy, the seducer, the slanderer, the accuser of man, the mischief-maker, and tempter. He is at once the evil instinct in man's heart and an evil agent external to man and real. He is the envious and malicious opponent of man. But he is not, as has been maintained,[1] a stupid hater, envious only of man and not a rebel, an enemy of God and of the principle of goodness. In Rabbinic demonology the spiritual element is not at all entirely eliminated. Very frequently Satan appears in Rabbinic literature as the personification of the principle of evil.

He is represented as the servant of God, whose function it is to tempt and accuse man, and often to punish. But he is also represented in Jewish legend as the rebel, not the equal and dual principle, but the unfaithful, disloyal, rebellious subject.

The apostate angel and chief of the rebels would have been condemned to utter destruction and consumed entirely by the little finger of the Almighty; but he was a necessary factor in the scheme of things.[2] In order that men may receive their reward or punishment for their actions, the Creator gave them freedom of will. By the exercise of their free will they either obey or transgress the commands of God. Men have the freedom to choose good or evil. Sammael's function is now to lead them astray and to induce them to commit sins. When he has succeeded he then appears as prosecutor

---

[1] Edersheim, *loc. cit.*, Vol. II, p. 753.   [2] *Yoma*, 69b.

before the heavenly tribunal. He is thus, seducer, tempter, accuser, and executioner.[1] His name is Sammael, either from the word *simme*, meaning to deceive or to blind, or from *semol*, meaning left, because he stands on the left side of men. Others derive the name of Sammael from *sam*, poison, and *El*, God, or the venom of God, since he is also identical with the Angel of Death.[2]

And ever since his fall, Sammael, who is also known as Satan, the old Serpent, or the Unclean Spirit, endeavours to enlarge his kingdom of darkness and to increase his sway over man. Formerly chief among the angels of God, he is now the prince of the realm of darkness, and ruler of the devils. Cast out from Heaven, he still seeks to exalt himself into the place of the Creator, trying to lead men away from the worship of the true God, and then appearing before the throne of the Eternal to accuse them.

In Mohammedan tradition, the fall of the angels and the rebellion of Sammael, or of Iblis, is supposed to have taken place after the creation of man. When God made man, He thus addressed the angels: " Bow and adore him, for I have breathed a part of My spirit in him." And all the angels of Heaven, of every degree and form, adored man, and fell down before him. Iblis alone refused to obey. Out of pride and envy he refused to do the bidding of the Lord, and disobeyed Him. Thereupon he was cursed by the Creator, and cast out of Heaven and the realms of delight. The Koran also says that " all the angels adored Adam, but Satan or Iblis refused to do so ". " I will not adore Adam," he said, " for I am better than he. He is made of earth, but I am made of fire." God thereupon cursed Iblis, for his pride, vanity, and disobedience, and gave him the form of a devil. [3]

---

[1] *Baba Batra*, 16a.
[2] *Targum Jerushalmi, Genesis*, 3, 6; see also article *Sammael* in *Jewish Encyclopædia*.
[3] Zotenberg, *Chronique de Tabari*, 1867, I, Ch. 27.

The Story of Shemhazai and Azael

Among the followers of Sammael were other angels, and notably two known as Aza and Azael or Shemhazai and Azael, of whom the following myth is related.

When the generation of the Flood transgressed the commands of the Creator, sinned and served idols, the Lord of the Universe was greatly concerned, and grieved that He had created man. Then two angels, Shemhazai and Azael, appeared before the Lord, and thus they spake: " Lord of the Universe! When Thou didst create man did we not say: ' What is man that Thou shouldst remember him '. We would have taken the place of man to cultivate the earth, people and inhabit the world."

" Had you taken the place of man, and lived in the earthly world," replied the Creator, " you would have been worse than man, for swayed by passion you would have committed sins, more heinous sins than those committed by man. You would have been even more stubborn." " Give us Thy sanction, O Lord of the Universe, to dwell among the children of man and inhabit the earth, and we will sanctify Thy name." And the Creator gave sanction unto Shemhazai and Azael to descend upon earth and there to dwell. But the two angels, who had descended upon earth and mixed with the children of man, soon sinned and transgressed.

Shemhazai cast his eyes upon a handsome maid called Istahar or Estirah, and a mighty love for her was kindled in his heart. " Listen to my request," he pleaded, but she refused to lend an ear to his pleadings. " I will not lend an ear to thy pleadings until thou teachest me the name of the Creator by the mention of which thou art enabled to ascend to Heaven." And Shemhazai, swayed by his passion for Istahar, yielded to her request and taught her the secret name of the Creator. Istahar thereupon uttered the name, and in virtue of its power she ascended to Heaven and was saved from perdition. And because she had avoided sin and had remained pure, she was placed among the seven constellations or Pleiades where she shines brightly.[1] And when Shemhazai and Azael saw this they hardened their hearts, and chose wives from among the daughters of men, and married them and begat children. Shemhazai had two daughters whose names were Heyya and Aheyya, or Hiwwa and Hijja. And they led men into sin and transgression. Thereupon a messenger came from Heaven and announced unto Shemhazai and Azael that the world would soon be destroyed and the inhabitants all perish in a great flood. And Shemhazai was grieved in his heart and wept aloud. And Hiwwa and Hijja had a dream which greatly troubled them. For they saw angels with axes in their hands, cutting down all the trees in a great garden. And Shemhazai was sore troubled in his heart, and repented of his sins. He suspended himself between Heaven and earth, with head downwards, and thus he still remains, because he durst not appear before God. But Azael did not repent of his sins and continued to lead the children of men into transgression.[2]

In this legend we evidently have the influence of Chaldean mysticism, elaborated by the Jewish imagination in a Jewish spirit. Istahar is none other but Ishtar, or Astarte, the Venus of the Phœnicians, who alone fills the entire Phœnician Olympus. But in Jewish legend the Phœnician element is changed. Astarte is no longer the goddess of sin, but is rehabilitated by her contact with the angels. She resists temptation, pronounces the tetragrammaton by virtue of which she ascends to Heaven and receives an honourable place in the Pleiades.

[1] Istahar is evidently the Assyro-Babylonian goddess Ishtar, goddess of love and war.
[2] Jellinek, *Beth-Hamidrash*, Vol. IV, pp. 127–128; Gaster, *Chronicles of Jerahmeel*, p. 52; see also *Midrash Abkir*, quoted in *Yalkut*, § 44; Reymundus Martinus, *Pugio Fidei*, ed. Leipzig, p. 937; Geiger, *Was hat Mohammed aus dem Judentum genommen*, p. 107; Barto-locci, *Bibliotheca Magna Rabbinica*, I, p. 259; see for comparative literature, M. Grünbaum in *Z.D.M.G.*, Vol. XXXI, pp. 225–231.

Another version of this legend relates that Aza and Azael now live in the dark mountains, and that they are visited by the magicians who travel to them to learn wisdom. And as soon as the traveller is perceived by the two demons, they at once call aloud, and big and fiery serpents gather round and surround them. The travelling magician in the meantime waits at the entrance to the dark mountains. Then Aza and Azael send out to him a spirit or demon in the shape of a small animal resembling a cat. Its head is like the head of a serpent, and it has two tails. And when the magician perceives the little animal he covers his face. He holds in his hand a basin containing the ashes of a burnt white cock, which he throws into the face of the animal, that leads him to the place in the dark mountains where Aza and Azael are chained. Three times he steps upon the chain until he is addressed and spoken to by Aza and Azael. Closing his eyes he falls upon his knees and worships the fallen angels. And because he has burned incense before them, they teach him the art of magic and witchcraft. Thus he remains in the dark mountains for fifty days. And when the day arrives for his return into the world, he is led out of the dark mountains by the little animal which resembles a cat and by a fiery serpent.[1]

They are the self-same Aza and Azael who afterwards taught Solomon, the King of Israel, all secrets. Every day he mounted an eagle who bore him to the dark mountains where he learned wisdom from the mouth of Aza and Azael.[2]

The same legend is related in the *Book of Enoch*, although the tendency there is somewhat different. And in those days it happened that the sons of men had multiplied, and unto them were born daughters, both elegant and beautiful. And it came to pass that the sons of Heaven, that is the fallen angels, beheld the daughters of men and became enamoured of them.

---

[1] *Emek hamelekh*, p. 108b; Bin Gorion, *Die Sagen der Juden*, Vol. I, p. 319–321.
[2] *Emek hamelekh*, p. 5d; see also Jellinek, *Beth-Hamidrash*, Vol. II, p. 86.

And the sons of Heaven said to each other: " Come, let us select wives for ourselves from the offspring of men." But their leader named Samyaza (or Shemhaza) spoke unto them and said: " I fear that you will perhaps not be courageous enough to perform such an enterprise, and that I alone shall suffer for so grievous a crime." But all the sons of Heaven, when they heard the words of Shemhaza (Samyaza), swore and bound themselves by mutual execrations to execute the projected undertaking. Now their number was two hundred, and they all descended upon Ardis, which is the top of Mount Armon. The mountain they called Armon because they had sworn upon it, and had bound themselves by mutual execrations. And the names of the chiefs of the sons of Heaven who had thus sworn to take wives from among the daughters of man, were: Samyaza, Urakabarameel, Akibeel, Tamiel, Ramuel, Danel, Azkeel, Sarakuyal, Asael, Armers, Batraal, Anane, Zavebe, Samsaveel, Ertael, Turel, Yomyael, Azazyal, eighteen in all who were the prefects of the two hundred with Samyaza as their chief. And all these sons of Heaven took wives from among the daughters of men, and they taught their wives sorcery, incantations and the divining of roots. They begat children, and the women brought forth giants, whose stature was each three hundred cubits. These giants were a curse to men, for they devoured all that the labour of men had produced, until it became impossible to feed them. The giants injured beasts and birds, fishes and reptiles, ate their flesh and drank their blood.

And Azazyal taught men how to make swords, knives, shields, breastplates, the fabrication of mirrors, making them see that which was behind them. He also taught them the workmanship of bracelets and of ornaments, and also the use of paint, and how to beautify the eyebrows. He further taught them the use of valuable stones of all kinds, and the use of all sorts of dyes, and the world thus became greatly

altered. It became corrupted in many ways. And the other
sons of Heaven and the giants turned against men and destroyed
them. And they cried out and their voice reached to Heaven.
Then Michael, Gabriel, Raphael, Suryal, and Uriel, looking
down from their celestial abode, saw the quantity of blood
which was being shed upon earth and all the iniquity which
was being done upon it, and said one to the other: " The
earth deprived of her children has cried to God, and the cry
has reached the gate of Heaven." And they turned to God,
and thus they spake: " Thou art the Lord and King of all.
Thou art the Lord of Lords, King of Kings and God of Gods.
The throne of Thy glory is for ever and ever, and for ever and
ever is Thy name sanctified and glorified. Thou possessest
power over all things, and Thou hast seen what Azazyal hath
done. Verily he hath taught every species of iniquity upon
earth, and Samyaza hath taught sorcery, and the whole earth
hath been filled with iniquity. And now the groaning of those
who are dead is ascending to the gates of Heaven."

Thereupon the Creator of all sent out a messenger to the
son of Lamech, commanding him to conceal himself, for all
the earth would soon perish.[1]

A parallel to this legend is found in Moslem myth and
legend, where it runs as follows: Harut and Marut were two
angels who were chastised in Babylon. And it came to pass
when Adam had been driven out of Paradise, that there were
some among the angels who took pity upon him, and pleaded
on his behalf before the throne of the Lord of the Universe.

But many more were those who hurled words of menace
upon our first parent, because he had transgressed the command of the Eternal. And among those who heaped words
of menace and insult upon Adam were the two angels Harut
and Marut. But Adam thus addressed them: " O ministering
angels of my Lord, have pity upon me and do not insult me

---

[1] *The Book of Enoch*, trans. by R. H. Charles, Chap. 6–7.

and hurl words of menace at me. For what has happened unto me was only by the will of the Lord of the Universe." And the Maker of the Universe tried the two angels, and they rebelled against Him and were expelled from Heaven. And it came to pass that in the days of Idris (Enoch) they approached the latter and begged him to intercede on their behalf before the King of the Universe, perchance He would forgive them. Said Idris (Enoch): " How am I to know that the Lord has forgiven you?" And they made answer: " Intercede on our behalf and pray for us to the Lord of the Universe, and if thou dost behold us and see us before thee, then thou wilt know that thy prayer has been heard and we have been forgiven. But if thou wilt not see us then surely it is a sign that we are doomed to perdition." And Idris listened to their words and prayed for them to the Eternal. But when he turned round he could nowhere behold them, and he knew that they were doomed. And it was given to Harut and Marut to choose between a punishment upon earth and a punishment in the world to come, but they preferred to suffer punishment upon earth. Thereupon they were exiled to Babylon, where they are tortured in a pit and will thus remain until the day of resurrection.

And Ibn Amr relates that when the ministering angels looked down from their celestial abode upon earth and saw how the sons of men were sinning and transgressing the commands of the Eternal, they accused them before the Creator. And the Father of the Universe said: " Had you been in man's place you would have been equally wicked."

But the angels exclaimed: " Lord of the Universe! Had we been in man's place we would have proclaimed Thy glory and praised Thee continually." And the Father of the Universe replied: " Choose among you two angels; " and they chose Harut and Marut who were sent down upon earth, and the desires and passions of man were put into them.

And very soon they sinned against the Lord of the Universe and transgressed his commands.

It was given to them to choose between punishment in this world and punishment in the next, but they preferred to suffer in this world, for it is only for a time, whilst suffering in the next is eternal. Such is the story of the two angels Harut and Marut who are punished at Babylon.[1]

The Angel of Death

The legends about the angel of death are to be found in the literature of many nations.

The angel of death, whom the Creator commissions to separate the soul from the body, is to be found in the myths and legends of the Arabians, Persians, Turks, and other nations.

He is called Azrael by the Arabians, and Mordad by the Persians. Popular imagination has woven many legends round the angel of death, and given rise to many superstitions.

When he has killed a man, we read in Jewish legendary lore, the angel of death washes his sword in the water of the house, thus communicating a mortal quality to it, and therefore the water is thrown away.[2]

Thus the angel of death is supposed to be seated on the grave of the person who dies, where he causes the wicked to suffer a second death. As soon as the dead is buried, the soul returns to the body and it becomes alive. Then the angel of death takes an iron chain, half of which is cold as ice and half burning hot. He strikes the body with it three times, separating its members, removing its bones, and reducing the whole to ashes. The good angels then come and gather and reunite all the parts, and re-

---

[1] Kazwini, *Cosmography*, Ethe's translation (1868), p. 126.
[2] See on angel of death *Abodah Zarah*, 20b.

THE WAR IN HEAVEN

place the body in the grave. Such is the punishment of those who have sinned; but the pious, especially those who have liberally given alms, are exempt from such punishment.[1]

The legends in Talmud and Midrash of the angel of death relate of his disappointments when coming to separate from the body the soul of a pious man, one of the heroic and saintly personages of Israel.

The Midrash *Petirat Moshe* (Death of Moses)[2] relates the following legend:

When the day arrived for Moses to die, the Creator decided not to allow the angel of death to interfere. He at first required the angel Gabriel to command the soul of the son of Amram out of the latter's body. But the angel Gabriel excused himself, whilst the angel Michael likewise desired to be dispensed with in this particular case. The Creator then required the angel Zagziel to fetch the soul of Moses, but this angel said that having been the preceptor of Moses he could not take away his life. The Creator then sent Sammael (who is at once Satan and the angel of death). Sammael advanced toward Moses, determined to force the soul out of the body of the leader of the Children of Israel. Struck, however, with the radiance of the countenance of Moses and by the virtue of the name of God written on the rod with which Moses performed his miracles, Sammael was compelled to retire. It was the Creator Himself who subsequently condescended to call forth the soul of Moses from his body.[3] A similar disappointment had awaited Sammael when he came to take the soul of Abraham. The angel Michael having replied that he could not take the soul of Abraham, the Lord of the Universe summoned Azazel (Sammael) the angel of death, the terrible

---

[1] Elia Levita, *Tishbi*; see also Eisenmenger, *loc. cit.*; Buxtorf, *Synagoga Judaica*, I, 35.
[2] See Jellinek, *Beth-Hamidrash*, Vol. I, p. 21; Zunz, *Gottesdienstliche Vorträge*, p. 146.
[3] Jellinek, *Beth-Hamidrash*, Vol. I, p. 129; see also *A Legend on the Death of Moses*, by A. Löwy, in *Proceedings of the Society of Biblical Archæology*, Vol. IX (Dec., 1886), pp. 40-47.

and many eyed, he who carries the bitter cup of death, and who is therefore called Sammael, and bade him go and take the soul of Abraham.

" Cast aside," said the Lord of the Universe, to the angel of death, " cast aside thy terrific aspect and thy impurity and assume the radiant and lovely form of a shining angel. In the garb of a bright and beautiful angel of light, in the shape and form of a handsome youth, exhaling the beauty of regions celestial, go and appear to Abraham, and take away his soul with all gentleness." Thus spake the Ruler of the Universe, and Sammael gladly accepted the mission to take away the soul of Abraham. In the shape of a beautiful youth, radiant and sunlike in his splendour, he appeared before the son of Terah, in the plain of Mamre.

Abraham rose to meet his guest, and Sammael thus addressed the old man: " Peace unto thee, thou friend of the Most High." " And who art thou?" asked Abraham, " whence dost thou come and which is thy destination?" " I am the bitter cup of death," replied Sammael, " and I have come to take thy soul, for thy days have come to an end." " And dost thou appear to all men in such beautiful and radiant form?" asked Abraham. " No," said Sammael. " To the sinners and ungodly I appear in a terrible form. I am many eyed and serpent-headed, and I carry in my hand the bitter cup of poison, a drop of which I cast into the mouth of the sinner who is about to die. But to the just I appear with a crown of light upon my head, like a divine messenger of peace."

Thereupon Abraham, desirous of beholding the real shape of the angel of death, spoke the holy name of God and asked Sammael to appear in his true and terrific form. " Present to me," he said, " thy terrible and terrific form, and thy terror-inspiring shape that I may behold thee." And lo, the angel of death showed himself in all his ugliness, cruelty, and bitterness. He put on his most awful and terrible form, and appeared with seven dragon heads and fourteen faces.

Some of his heads had the face of serpents and others were breathing flames of fire, and the sight was so terrible that seven thousand servants, male and female, of Abraham's household died, and Abraham himself fainted. He soon, however, regained consciousness, interceded for his servants, and prayed for them who had died before their time, and the angel Michael brought them to life again.

" Resume now thy former beautiful form," said Abraham, " for I cannot bear thy terrible real shape." And Sammael resumed the shape of a beautiful angel, but refused to leave Abraham, following him wherever he went. Abraham, however, refused to give up his soul to Sammael.

At the command of the Almighty, the angel Michael came and lured away the soul of Abraham as if in a dream. A host of angels at once descended from Heaven, and taking the soul of the old man, received it in heaven-spun garments like snow, and bore it away on a fiery chariot.[1]

[1] *The Testament of Abraham*, published in Robinson's Texts and Studies, II, 2, Cambridge 1892.

CHAPTER VII

The Demons

WE have seen that the angels are divided into two groups, angels of good and angels of evil, that is angels of light and angels of darkness, or fallen angels.

Real Judaism does not admit the existence of a principle of evil, *per se*; such a principle has no place in the absolute, and consequently this dualism of powers is practically opposed to Judaism.

The popular imagination, however, eagerly took hold of the idea that evil is independent of human action, and that there exist beings who are not only the incarnation of evil but also at war with the Creator himself. This is a concession made by Judaism to foreign ideas and influences.

Besides the fallen angels, Jewish myth also knows of demons, or evil spirits.

The demonology of the Talmud and of Rabbinic folklore has been influenced not by the Babylonian cult of Marduk-Bel, but by that of Ormuzd and Ahriman. The Persian devas, the devas of Ahriman, have invaded Jewish folklore and acquired citizen right in Jewish myth and legend.

The demons of the Jews, like the devas of Ahriman, male and female, fill the world, and in hosts of tens of thousands surround man in all shapes and forms, spreading disease and suffering among mortals. From birth to death these devas, demons who multiply continually, lay siege to men and give them no respite.

Persian influence is thus noticeable in the Jewish legends about evil spirits. Cunning and malicious, they are dangerous to man, but they are not always absolutely evil. Sometimes they are, like the sprites of fairy tales, like the elves, hobgoblins and gnomes, even serviceable and kind, and may be made not only innocuous but obedient to man.

They are divided into *Shedim*, *Roukhin*, *Mazikin*, and *Lilin*. They propagate themselves, and their number is unlimited. In three things they resemble man, whilst in three they are like angels. Like man they take nourishment, propagate themselves, and die. But like angels they have wings, pass through space unhindered, and know the future.

" For six things have been said about demons: they are like angels in three particulars, but resemble men in three others. Like angels they have wings, are able to fly from one end of the world to the other, and know the future. Whilst, however, the angels have the future revealed to them, they learn it by listening behind the veil. Like men, however, the demons eat and drink, marry and beget children and increase and ultimately die." [1]

They assume either the form of human beings or any

[1] *Hagigah*, 16a; see S. Louis, in *Proceedings of the Society of Biblical Archæology*, Vol. IX (June, 1881), pp. 217–228.

other form. They lodge in trees, caper bushes, in gardens, vineyards, in ruined and desolate houses, and dirty places.

To go alone into such places is dangerous, and the eves of Wednesday and Saturday were considered dangerous times.[1] The evil spirits and demons, the Shedim, Roukhin, Mazikin, and Lilin, can be mischievous, but they can never create anything themselves.

The demons have no power over anything that is sealed, counted, measured or tied up.[2] The pronouncing of the " Ineffable Name " (the *Shem hameforash*) has a paramount influence over them, and by it they can always be conquered.

Thus King Solomon conquered Ashmedai by the power and the virtue of the Ineffable Name.

These evil spirits are supposed to lurk everywhere around man. They crowd the academies and are to be found by the side of the bride. They are said to be found in the crumbs we throw on the floor, *in the water we drink, in the diseases which attack us*, in the oil, in the vessels, in the air, in the room, at every moment of day and night. No mortal could survive it, if he saw their number, for they are like the earth that is thrown up around a bed that is sown.[3]

Here, it may be pointed out, *en passant*, we have some trace of the idea of microbes and of the first indications of microbiology of which modern science is so proud.

The Shedim, Roukhin, Mazikin, and Lilin, are both male and female spirits. The hurtful spirits are known as *Malakhe Khabalah*, or angels of destruction; they exercise their power either by day or by night and are divided into different classes. They are called: *Zaphrire*, morning spirits; *Tihare*, midday spirits; *Telane*, evening spirits; and *Lilin*, night spirits, according to the time during which they are active.

With regard to myths and legends about demons, genii,

---

[1] *Pesachim*, 112b.   [2] *Hullin*, 105b.   [3] *Berachoth*, 6a.

and evil spirits, pre-exilian Judaism knows but little about them. Judaism, as represented in the Old Testament, knows no evil principle. The spirit of darkness and wickedness which rebels against and opposes the omnipotent Creator according, to the Scriptures is not the result of a necessary emanation, but is the voluntary act of an omnipotent Creator. The tempter, the principle of evil, is not a power equal to and waging war against the omnipotent Creator, but a created being and a rebel.[1]

Thoroughly monotheistic, pre-exilian Judaism could not tolerate any idea harbouring upon polytheism. Thus Satan, or Sammael, is, unlike in the dual religion of Persia, not an independent original power waging war against Divinity, but a created being, a personification of the principle of evil, created for the purpose of testing the moral strength of man.[2]

In consequence of Babylonian and Persian influences the old Oriental beliefs, against which monotheism had fought and still continues to do so, received a new impetus.

Angels and demons acquired citizen rights in Jewish folklore, in Jewish myths and legends. The Psalmists and prophets who shared the exile may have protested against the invasion of foreign elements, and repeatedly declared themselves against any dual principles. But popular imagination and folklore seized upon the elements which were to some extent related to the old Oriental beliefs lingering among the people, and interwove them into Jewish myths and legends with a strongly monotheistic background.

And just as the angels in Jewish myth and legend are not independent beings but executors of the will of the One God, His messengers and ministering spirits, so also are their opposites. The spirits and demons, the inhabitants of the realm of darkness and destruction, of negation, of morally-evil, the

---

[1] *Targum, Ps.* 121, 6; *Targum Pseudo-Jonathan, Deuteron.,* 32, 24; *Targum Canticles,* 4, 6.   [2] E. Bischoff, *Elemente der Kabbalah,* p. 224.

devils and demons, are the servants of the One God, doing His bidding. Unlike the devas of Persia, whence the Jewish demonology has been derived (although sufficient elements existed in Judaism to develop it independently) who are to some extent independent beings and opponents of Ormuzd, so the Shedim are servants of the Creator, submissive and obedient subjects.

And as the Shedim in Jewish myth are not opponents of the will of the Creator, and not in constant fight with the inhabitants of the realms of light, like the Persian devas, they are not so badly treated as are the Persian devas.

In Jewish myth and legend the Shedim, too, serve to glorify the One Creator and to testify to His omnipotence.[1]

Various theories are expounded in Jewish literature with regard to the origin of demons and evil spirits. According to some mythographers, the demons are the living souls which the Lord of the Universe created in addition to the beasts of the earth, the cattle and creeping things. Every day He created several things: Heaven, earth, and light on the first day; the firmaments, hell, and the ministering angels on the second; trees, herbs, and rivers on the third; sun, moon, and stars on the fourth day; the fishes, Leviathan, and the birds on the fifth day. But on the sixth day He had to produce twice as many creatures, doing the work also of the seventh day, which is the Sabbath and a day of rest. On the sixth day He created Adam and Eve and many creatures. He also produced many other souls for new creatures, but was interrupted by the arrival of the Sabbath and these creatures remained unfinished and incomplete.

These beings are the demons and spirits. The Lord had created their souls, but their bodies were not completed on account of the Sabbath on which the Lord of the Universe rested, and so they remained souls without bodies.[2]

---

[1] *Talmud Jerushalmi, Berachoth; Yalkut, Leviticus,* § 665.   [2] *Genesis Rabba,* 7.

In other sources, however, we read that the demons were created long before man came into existence. They were the inhabitants of the earth and its masters. Dry land and sea were alike full of demons who lived happily for æons in peace and tranquillity, for the whole planet was their domain. They were obedient and did the bidding of the Lord. But a day came when wickedness and evil deeds increased among the demons, and they ignored the commandments of the Creator, and earth was full of their iniquity, and it cried to the Lord. And the Creator decided to put an end to the reign of the demons. He sent down a host of angels who waged a terrible war against the wicked and evil-doing demons and drove them from the face of the earth. Many of these demons the angels took captive, and among the latter was also Sammael, the chief leader, the curse and enemy of man. He was a youth in those days and knew not to distinguish between good and evil.

But he learned the way of the angels who spread over the planet and peopled it, and he acquired much wisdom and in time became the chief and leader of the angels. But the reign of the angels also came to an end, for in His great wisdom the Creator decided to send man and the sons of man to inhabit and people the earth. But the angels who were then the masters and rulers of the earth refused to leave it, for they were very happy there. And thus they spoke: " O Lord of the Universe! Thou dost intend to place upon earth man, as lord of creation, who will one day commit wicked deeds, do much evil and shed innocent blood. He will take our place and follow in the ways of the demons and the children of Satan. We are praising Thy holy name every day, and are proclaiming Thy glory in the upper and netherworlds." But the Creator carried out His purpose, and created man.[1]

---

[1] Kalonymos ben Kalonymos, *Iggeret baale Hayyim* (on the animals); see Julius Landsberger, *Abhandlung über die Thiere*, 1882.

According to the Ethiopic *Book of Enoch* the demons proceeded from the giants, the offspring of the fallen angels who lusted after the daughters of men. They now accomplish man's moral ruin, and their power will last until the day of final judgment.

There is not one Satan in the *Book of Enoch*, but many Satans, and Jequn was the first to lead astray all the children of the angels, bring them down to the earth and lead them astray through the daughters of men.

Fanuel, one of the four angels of the Presence, prevents the Satans from appearing before the Lord of Spirits to accuse man. They are all members of a kingdom of evil, in opposition to God, of a realm of darkness which is ruled under the name of Satan. This kingdom of evil existed already before the angels fell by corrupting themselves with the daughters of man.

On the great day of judgment the four angels Michael, Gabriel, Rufael, and Fanuel will take hold of these Satans, and cast them into a burning furnace, so that the Lord of Spirits may take vengeance on them for their unrighteousness in becoming subjects to Satan and leading astray those who dwell on the earth.[1]

The Satans thus have a right of access to Heaven, where they appear before the Throne of Glory to accuse men.

They are at once tempters, accusers, and punishers or executioners. The view of the *Book of Enoch* to a certain extent coincides with the views expressed in the Talmud and in the Midrashim.[2] Satan or Sammael, who was jealous of Adam and of Eve and caused the serpent to seduce the woman, coalesce into one personality. The supreme ruler of the evil spirits and demons, as of all the fallen angels, is thus Sammael, although there are other princes and kings of demons.

[1] R. H. Charles, *The Book of Enoch*, 54, 6.
[2] See Whitehouse, article *Satan* in Hastings' *Dictionary of the Bible*, Vol. IV, p. 409.

Legions innumerable of Shedim and Roukhin, of demons and spirits, obey their commands. For the spirits of evil who surround man are legion. They are hostile both to his body and to his soul, and constantly seek to do him harm. From the very birth of man, they lurk in the shadow, watching for an opportunity to undo him. These demons are even responsible for the terrible phantoms which appear to man and the evil thoughts which crowd his brain. They are everywhere, and no man could bear the sight of all the demons who surround him. They are everywhere on land and in the water, and every drop of water we drink contains numerous evil spirits.

They are very powerful, for they are more numerous than mankind. At every moment a war is being constantly waged between the demons and the angels, who are appointed to protect man against the evil influence of the demons.

The Story of Lilith

Queen of the demons is Lilith, long-haired and winged.[1] She is supposed to have been the first wife of Adam. She had been one of the wives of Sammael, but of a wild, heroic and passionate nature she left her spouse and joined Adam. From their union issued the demons or Shedim, who rove about in the world as wicked spirits, persecute and plague men, and bring upon them illness, disease, and other sufferings.

Lilith, like Adam, had been created from the dust (Adamah) of the earth. But as soon as she had joined Adam they began to quarrel, each refusing to be subservient and submissive to the other. " I am your lord and master," spoke Adam, " and it is your duty to obey me." But Lilith replied: " We are both equal, for we are both issued from dust (Adamah), and I will not be submissive to you." And thus they quarrelled and none would give in. And when Lilith saw this she spoke

---

[1] *Niddah*, 16b; *Erubin*, 100b

the Ineffable Name of the Creator and soared up into the air. Thereupon Adam stood in prayer before the Creator and thus he spake: " O Lord of the Universe, the woman Thou hast given me has fled from me."

And the Holy One, blessed be His name, sent at once three angels whose names were Senoi, Sansenoi, and Sammangelof, to fetch and bring Lilith back to Adam. He ordered them to tell her to return, and if she refused to obey then a hundred of her offspring would die daily. The three aforementioned angels followed Lilith, and they found her in the midst of the sea, on the mighty waves (which were once to drown the Egyptians).

They communicated to her the command of the Eternal, but she refused to return. And the angels spake to this rebel, this she-demon: " We will drown thee in the sea." But she made answer: " Know ye not that I have been created for the purpose of weakening and punishing little children, infants and babes. I have power over them from the day they are born until they are eight days old if they are boys, and until the twentieth day if they are girls." And when the three angels heard her speech they wished to drown her by force, but she begged them to let her live, and they gave in. She swore to them in the name of the living God that whenever she came and saw the names or images or faces of these three angels, Senoi, Sansenoi, and Sammangelof, upon an amulet or cameo in the room where there was an infant, she would not touch it. But because she did not return to Adam, every day a hundred of her own children or spirits and demons die.

The legend of Lilith and the message of the three angels is found in several sources of Rabbinical lore in some of which it is quoted from the *Alphabetum Siracidis*.[1]

---

[1] *Alphabetum Siracidis (Sepher Ben Sira)*, edit. Steinschneider, 1858. See on Lilith. Gaster, in *Monatsschrift für Gesch. u. Wissenschaft d. Judent.*, Vol. XXIX (1880), pp. 553–555,

The book known as the *Sefer Rasiel* describes the formula to be written upon amulets or cameos and to be placed in the rooms where there are new-born babes. It refers to Lilith as the *first Eve*, and conjures her in the name of the three angels and the angel of the sea to whom she had sworn not to harm the babes in whose rooms she found written on paper the names of the three angels.[1]

Lilith is thus a female night demon, and is also known under the name of *Meyalleleth*, or the howling one.

The she-demon *Makhlath* (the dancer) and her daughter *Agrath*[2] are two female demons who live in strife with Lilith. Lilith is accompanied by four hundred and eighty hosts of evil spirits and destroying angels, and she is constantly howling. Makhlath is accompanied by four hundred and seventy-eight hosts of evil spirits. She and her daughter Agrath, from the Zend word *Agra* = beating, are in constant enmity with Lilith.

Constant war is waged between them, and they meet on the day of atonement. Whilst they are thus engaged in quarrel and strife, the prayers of Israel ascend to Heaven, whilst the accusers are absent, being otherwise engaged.[3]

Agrath commands hosts of evil spirits and demons, and rides in a big chariot. Her power is paramount on Wednesdays and Saturdays, for on these days Agrath, the daughter of Makhlath, roves about in the air accompanied by eighteen myriads of evil spirits.[4]

The Story of Ashmedai

King of the demons is Ashmedai or Asmodaeus. The name of Ashmedai is never mentioned in the Talmud of Jerusalem nor in the older Palestinian sources.

He is very cunning and malignant. Of immense strength

---

[1] Elia Levita, *Tishbi*, s.v. *Lilith*.   [2] *Pesachim*, 112b; *Numbers Rabba*, 12.
[3] *Yalkut Chadash*, s.v. *Keshaphim*, No. 56.   [4] *Pesachim*, 112b.

and very powerful, he is intent upon doing harm to man.
And yet he is frequently ready to perform deeds of kindness.
Ashmedai fore-knows the future, and by the use of the Ineffable Name he can be made serviceable unto man and compelled to do what is bidden by those who pronounce the
Ineffable Name. Thus, by the power and in virtue of his
signet ring on which was engraven the Ineffable Name, King
Solomon gained power over Ashmedai and made him do his
bidding. The legend of King Solomon and Ashmedai runs
as follows:

King Solomon, the son of David, was about to build the
Temple of the Lord. " And the house, when it was in building,
was built of stone made ready before it was brought thither." [1]

Now before the operation was begun King Solomon
consulted with the Rabbis and asked them: " How shall I
accomplish this without using tools of iron?" as no iron was
to be used in the construction of the Temple. And the Rabbis
remembered that an insect existed since the creation of the
world which possessed the power of cutting stones, for even
the hardest substance could not resist the power of this insect.
The Rabbis therefore replied to the King: " There is an
insect called *Shamir* with which Moses once cut the precious
stones of the *Ephod*." [2] Hearing these words the King asked:
" And where may this Shamir be found?" To which the
Rabbis made answer as follows: " Conjure up a male and
a female demon and coerce them; perchance they know where
the Shamir is now to be found and they will reveal the secret
unto thee." And the King did as they had counselled him.
He conjured up into his presence a male and a female demon,
and when they refused to reveal unto him the whereabouts of
the Shamir he gave orders to torture them.

But all this was in vain, for the male and the female demon
both declared that not knowing the whereabouts of the Shamir

[1] *I Kings*, 6, 7.   [2] *Leviticus*, 8, 7.

they could not reveal the secret to King Solomon. " But perhaps," they continued, " Ashmedai, the king of the demons, knows the hiding-place and will reveal the secret to the King."

The King thereupon urged them to tell him where Ashmedai might be found. And the male and female demon answered as follows: " Ashmedai's residence is on a high mountain, where he has dug a deep pit which serves him as a cistern. This he has filled with water. Every morning before ascending to Heaven, to study in the school of wisdom there and to listen to the decrees of the Upper Assembly, he covers his cistern over with a stone and seals it with his own seal. Every day when he returns from his celestial visit, he carefully examines the seal, and on finding that it has not been broken, he drinks, quenches his thirst and finally covers it again with the stone, seals the stone with his own seal and takes his departure." Thus spoke the male and female demon, and King Solomon decided to test the truth of their assertions.

He thereupon sent his trusty servant Benaiah, the son of Jehoiada, and enjoined him to capture Ashmedai, the king of the demons. Benaiah armed himself with a magic chain and a ring upon which the Ineffable Name was engraved, and went out to execute the command of King Solomon. He also provided himself with skins of wine and a fleece of wool.

When he arrived at the mountain where Ashmedai had his abode, Benaiah at once cunningly set to work. He first dug a pit below that of Ashmedai, and into it he drained off the water from the pit of the demon, and plugged the hole with the fleece he had brought. He then dug another pit higher up, and in it he made a channel through which he filled the emptied pit of Ashmedai with the wine from the skins he had brought. He thereupon levelled the ground so as not to arouse the suspicion of the demon king, and withdrew to a tree nearby, where he waited for the return of Ashmedai, and for an opportunity to seize him.

And when he had waited a little while, he heard a noise in the air as of the beating of gigantic wings. Benaiah soon perceived Ashmedai, who was descending from Heaven whither he had gone to study in the school of wisdom and to listen to the decrees of the Upper Assembly. The demon king examined his seal, and seeing that it had not been tampered with, raised the stone. But lo! to his surprise he found the cistern filled with wine. Now Ashmedai, like all other demons, hates wine, and usually abstains from drinking it. He was therefore unwilling to drink from the cistern, muttering to himself that " wine is a mocker; strong drink is raging, and whosoever is deceived thereby is not wise ". At last, however, being thirsty, the demon king could not resist the temptation to drink and proceeded to quench his thirst. When he had drunk his fill, Ashmedai, demon king though he was, became intoxicated and lay down to sleep. Thereupon Benaiah quickly came forth from his hiding-place and stealthily approached the sleeping demon. He took up the magic chain he had brought with him and upon which was engraved the Ineffable Name of God, and fastened it round the neck of the sleeping demon. At last Ashmedai awoke from his sleep. He was mightily wroth and roared like a lion in his fury, when he saw himself bound and fettered.

He seized the chain to break it, but Benaiah called out to him and warned him: " The name of the Lord is upon thee." Ashmedai, cowed and conquered, desisted. And thus Benaiah, the trusty servant of King Solomon, secured the king of the demons, and made him prisoner. He thereupon proceeded on his return journey, leading the demon king with him. As they travelled along they passed a palm tree and Ashmedai rubbed himself against it, but by so doing uprooted the tree and threw it down. Walking a little farther they drew near to the hut of a poor widow; she came out and implored the demon not to rub himself against her hut as he might uproot it. Ashmedai complied with the request of the poor woman, and as he was bending back rather quickly, he broke a bone in his body, whereupon he said: " This is that which is written: ' And a gentle answer breaketh the bone '." Proceeding farther on their way they saw a blind man straying out of his way, whereupon the demon king hailed him and directed him aright. When a little farther he descried a drunken man who was in a similar difficulty, he again showed him the road. A wedding party then passed along, rejoicing and making merry, but at the sight of the merry-makers Ashmedai wept. And when a little farther on he heard a man ordering at a shoemaker's a pair of shoes that would last him seven years, he burst out into a peal of uncontrollable laughter. He shrieked and jeered and muttered words of scorn when he saw a magician at his tricks. Benaiah wondered greatly and asked the demon king to explain unto him the reason of his strange and almost incomprehensible conduct. " Why didst thou so promptly help the blind man, guiding him and putting him aright when he strayed?" asked Benaiah. And Ashmedai made answer: " Because I heard it proclaimed in Heaven that this blind man was perfectly righteous and would inherit the world to come, and that whosoever rendered him a service would also earn a claim to a place in the world of the future." " And why," queried Benaiah, " didst thou put right the man who, overcome with drink, was wandering out of his way?" " Because," replied Ashmedai, " I have heard it proclaimed in Heaven that this man was wholly and entirely bad and wicked, and so I rendered him a good service so that he might not lose all, but, at least, receive some good in the world that now is."

" And why," continued Benaiah to question his prisoner, " why didst thou weep when thou didst see the rejoicing wedding party pass?" " The bridegroom of that wedding party," replied Ashmedai, " is destined to die within thirty days, and his newly wedded wife will soon be a widow and will needs wait thirteen years for her husband's brother who is now only an infant.[1]" "And why didst thou laugh when thou didst hear the man ordering a pair of shoes that should last him seven years?" again queried Benaiah. "Because," Ashmedai replied, "the man was not sure of even living seven days." "And why thy jeers and scorn when thou sawest the magician at his works?" "Because," was the answer of the demon king, "at that very moment the magician was sitting upon a vast treasure hidden in the soil underneath him, and yet he knew it not, although he pretended that he could foretell the future and unravel mysteries."

And when the demon king was brought into the royal city, he was kept three days before being led into the presence of the King of Israel. "Why am I not being led into the presence of the King?" he queried. And the answer was that the King had drunk too much wine and could not receive him, as the wine had overpowered him. Thereupon Ashmedai took up a brick and placed it upon the top of another brick. When this action of the demon was in due course communicated to the King of Israel, the latter said: "By this action Ashmedai meant: if the wine has overpowered him, go and make him drunk again."

On the following day the demon king once more asked: "And why am I not being led to-day into the presence of the King?" And the answer was that the King had eaten too much and was resting. Thereupon the demon went and removed the brick he had placed on the top of the other. And when in due course this action of the demon was again reported to the King, he replied: "By this action Ashmedai meant: if he has eaten too much let him keep diet, be stinted in his food for a day."

At last, on the third day, the demon king was introduced

---

[1] *Deuteron.* 25, 5–10.

to the King of Israel. Ashmedai then measured off four cubits upon the floor with a stick, and thus he spoke to King Solomon: "When thou diest, thou wilt rest in thy grave and possess in this world not more than four cubits of earth. But now, although thou hast conquered the world, thou art not yet content and must needs overcome me, too, and make me prisoner." To which the King of Israel made reply: "I have made thee prisoner because I wish to build the Temple, and, as I am not allowed to use iron tools, I must have the Shamir by virtue of which I can have the stones split. I have made thee prisoner so that thou mayest reveal to me the place where the Shamir is to be found." Thus spake the King.

But Ashmedai answered: "I do not have the Shamir in my possession, for it has not been committed to my charge. Know then, O King, that the Shamir was committed to the charge of the Prince of the Sea who entrusted it to the moor-cock; and the moor-cock has promised upon oath that he would return it again to the Prince of the Sea." Thus spoke Ashmedai, and the King of Israel, marvelling greatly, asked: "And what does the moor-cock do with the Shamir?" "The moor-cock," replied the demon, "carries the Shamir to some bleak rocky mountain which he cleaves asunder by means of the Shamir, to which, as thou well knowest, no substance however hard can resist. And into the cleft thus formed the moor-cock carries verdant grass, herbs, and seeds of various plants and trees. Thus when the valley is clothed with grass and green it becomes a place fit for habitation."

Thereupon King Solomon sent out his servants to search for the nest of the moor-cock. At last Benaiah found the nest, and saw that it contained a young brood. Covering the nest with a glass globe, he awaited the return of the moor-cock.

When the bird came and saw its young but was unable to get at them, the nest being impenetrably covered with the glass globe, he went and fetched the Shamir so as to apply it to the glass and break it. At the very moment when the moor-cock was about to apply the Shamir to the glass in order to cut it, Benaiah gave a shout, and the moor-cock was so frightened that in his agitation he dropped the Shamir.

Snatching it up Benaiah went off with it. The moor-cock, however, finding that he was now unable to keep his oath, according to which he was bound to return the Shamir to the Prince of the Sea, went and strangled himself.

And now Ashmedai remained in the power of Solomon, who detained him until the building of the Temple was completed. Once, however, Ashmedai got the better of Solomon.

One day, when Ashmedai was alone in the presence of the King, the latter said: " Thou seest now that the demons are but little superior to men, and have no power over them, for I have conquered thee and made thee prisoner." To this Ashmedai replied: " If thou wilt take this chain from my neck and give me for a while thy signet ring I will show thee my superiority." Foolishly, Solomon decided to put Ashmedai to the test, took off the chain from his neck and handed him the signet ring; but no sooner had he done this when he had cause to regret his rash action.

Snatching him up, Ashmedai swallowed the King, then he stretched out his wings, so that one touched Heaven and the other the earth, and vomited out the King of Israel in a distant land, four hundred miles away. Ashmedai then gave himself out as King Solomon and took his place, whilst the King himself was far away in a strange country and obliged to beg his bread from door to door. Thus Solomon wandered for many years until he came back to Jerusalem. He went to the house of the Sanhedrin and said: " I, the preacher, was King over Israel in Jerusalem," but the members of the Sanhedrin thought that he was mad, and would not believe him.

When, however, he came every day repeating the same thing, they began to reason and to ask themselves what he really meant by his words. They accordingly sent for Benaiah, King Solomon's trusted servant, and asked him: " Does the King ask thee now into his presence?" to which Benaiah replied that he had not been asked into the King's presence for some time. The members of the Sanhedrin thereupon made inquiries whether he who, according to the stranger, had taken the King's place, ever visited the royal harem. And when the ladies of the harem replied that he did visit the harem, the members of the Sanhedrin sent instructions that they should watch his feet, and see whether his feet were like those of a cock.

But the answer came back that the King visited his harem in stockinged feet and wearing slippers. Thereupon the Rabbis felt sure that the stranger had spoken the truth and that Ashmedai had taken the place of Solomon, the son of David, King of Israel. They escorted the King to the palace, and here restored unto him the chain and the ring on both of which the name of God was engraven. Then Solomon straightaway advanced into the presence-chamber, where Ashmedai, arrayed in Solomon's royal garments, was sitting on the throne. No sooner did he see Solomon enter than he took fright, and uttering a terrible shriek he raised his wings and flew away into space.[1]

[1] *Gittin*, 68*b*; Jellinek, *Beth-Hamidrash*, Vol. II, pp. 86–87; see also *Sotah*, 48*b*.

CHAPTER VIII

The Spirits of the Air

The demon Ornias and the foreman's little boy—The archangel Michael and the signet ring—The capture of Ornias—He is condemned to hew stones for the Temple—The angel Uriel and the big whales—Beelzeboul, prince of the demons—The female demons—The she-demon Onoskelis—The arrogant reply of Asmodeus—The liver and gall of the fish *Glanos*—Asmodeus is condemned to prepare the clay for the Temple—The son of Beelzeboul who is dwelling in the Red Sea—Beelzeboul is condemned to saw Theban marbles—The cloud of dust—The spirit of ashes—The seven female spirits—The headless demon who is wholly voice—The big hound Rabdos—He leads the King's servant to a mine of green beryl—The headless demon is condemned to cast a light on the artisans at work—The roaring lion.

NOT only Ashmedai, however, but all the spirits of the air, on the earth, and under the earth, and all the demons were controlled by King Solomon, and it was with their help that he was able to build the Temple.[1] It happened, when King Solomon was building the Temple, that the demon named Ornias came every day at sunset among the artificers. He took away half of the pay of the foreman's (*proto maistros*) little son and also half of his food. He then sucked away the life blood of the boy by sucking the thumb of his right hand, so that the child grew thinner every day and began to pine away. And when King Solomon, who loved the boy, inquired after the reason of his thinness and his ailment, the boy thus spake: "O mighty King! an evil demon named Ornias takes

---

[1] The following legends are related in the *Testament of Solomon*. See F. F. Fleck, *Wissenschaftliche Reise*, II, 3; Bornemann in *Zeitschrift für Historische Theologie*, 1844 (Germ. transl.); and Conybeare in *Jewish Quarterly Review*, Vol. XI, pp. 1–45; see also Fabricius, *loc. cit.*, I, p. 1047; Migne, *Patrologia Graeco-Latina*, Vol. CXX, col. 1315–1362.

away every day at sunset half of my food and he also sucks the thumb of my right hand."

When King Solomon heard these words he was very grieved, and prayed to the Lord of Hosts that he might deliver into his hands and give him authority over the evil demon Ornias. The prayer of the King was heard, for soon the angel Michael appeared to him and brought him a signet ring with a seal upon which the Ineffable Name was engraved.

And the archangel Michael thus addressed King Solomon: "Take this ring, O King, which is a gift sent to thee by the Lord of Hosts. The engraving of the seal consists of five *A's* interlaced; and as long as thou wilt wear this ring thou wilt have great power over all the demons in the air, upon the earth, and under the earth, be they male or female." When the King heard these words spoken by the archangel Michael, and saw the ring sent to him as a gift by the Lord of Hosts, he rejoiced in his heart and gave thanks to the Creator, glorifying His name. Thereupon King Solomon called the boy who was the son of the foreman of the artificers, and thus he spake unto him: "Take this ring, my child, and when at sunset the fierce demon comes to visit thee, *throw* the ring at his chest and command him to appear in my presence. And thus thou shalt speak unto him: 'In the name of God, the Lord of the Universe, King Solomon calls thee hither.' When thou wilt have spoken these words thou wilt at once run and come to me and not be afraid of the demon whatever he may say." Thus spake King Solomon. And the boy took the ring and did as the King had commanded him. When at sunset Ornias descended upon him and prepared to take away his pay and his food, he threw the ring at the demon's chest, and commanded him in the name of God to appear before King Solomon. Thereupon he went off and ran to the King. When the demon heard the words of the boy and the command of the King, he was greatly perturbed and begged the child to take off the ring, and not to lead him before the King, promising him as a reward all the gold of the earth. But the boy, remembering the instructions he had received, would not listen to Ornias. And thus, greatly rejoicing, he brought the demon before the gates of the royal palace. When the King heard what had happened he was greatly rejoiced. He rose up from his throne and went out into the court of his palace where he beheld the demon Ornias greatly troubled and trembling. And the King thus spake unto Ornias: "Tell me, O demon, who art thou, what is thy name and to what sign of the Zodiac dost thou belong and art subject?" To this the demon made answer: "My name is Ornias, and I am subject to the Zodiacal sign of the waterpourer." He further informed the King of Israel that he often took the shape of a comely female leading man into temptation, and that he also metamorphosed himself into a lion, when he served and helped other demons to carry out their designs. "And whose offspring art thou?" queried the King. To which Ornias replied: "I am the offspring of the archangel Uriel." When Solomon heard these words from the mouth of the demon named Ornias, he glorified the Lord of Hosts, the God of Heaven and of earth, and greatly rejoiced in his heart.

He thereupon sealed the demon and set him down to hew stones for the Temple, all the stones which had been brought to Jerusalem by the sea of Arabia, and were lying along the shore. But Ornias was loth to be subject to King Solomon, and being fearful of iron, as all demons are, implored the King of Israel to let him go free, which request, however, King Solomon would not grant. Thereupon the King prayed unto the archangel Uriel to come down and help him subdue the rebellious demon. And the archangel Uriel descended from the heavens and appeared before King Solomon. He informed the latter that all the angels and demons had their destinies, for from all eternity it is written down and destined

what powers they may exercise and what acts they are to perform and to whom they are to be subject. He (the archangel
Uriel) thereupon commanded all the big whales of the sea to
come out of the deep, and having cast the destiny of Ornias
upon the ground, he announced that it had been destined from
all eternity that the demon Ornias should be subject to King
Solomon and do his bidding. Thereupon the angel Uriel
commanded the demon Ornias to obey the commands of
the King of Israel and to hew the stones for the Temple,
the huge stones which had been brought from Arabia by
sea, and were lying along the shore.

And the King of Israel, to whom Ornias was subject,
even according to his destiny, thus spake unto the demon:
" I command thee to take this ring and to hie thee to the
prince of all the demons and to bring him hither." Whereupon Ornias took the signet ring of the King, and taking to
his wings sped away to the prince of the demons whose name
is Beelzeboul. To him he spoke: " Hie thee to King Solomon
for he bids thee appear in his presence." And when the prince
of demons refused to obey the summons, Ornias, as he had
been instructed, threw the signet ring at his chest and repeated: " In the name of God, King Solomon commands
thee to appear before him." Beelzeboul uttered a cry of
rage, and from his mouth issued a burning flame and a veritable river of fire; but he was bound to obey the command,
and he followed Ornias before King Solomon. When this
mighty prince of demons appeared before the King of Israel,
the latter praised the Lord and glorified Him, giving thanks
to the Creator who had subjected unto His servant all the
spirits of the air and all the demons upon earth and under
the earth.

Then King Solomon addressed the prince of the demons,
and thus he spake unto him: " O mighty demon, tell me,
who am King of Israel, who art thou and what is thy name?"

To this the prince of the demons made answer: " I am Beelzeboul, and *exarch* of the demons. It is I who have the power to make appear before thee all my subject spirits." He then promised to the King to make manifest the apparition of all the demons of the air and upon earth, and to make them subject to the King.

Thereupon the King inquired of Beelzeboul whether there were many female demons, to which Beelzeboul made answer that there were many more females among the demons than males. The King, therefore, expressed the wish to behold one of these female demons. Beelzeboul at once took to his wings and hied himself to distant regions, but soon he returned bringing with him a fair and comely she-demon, fair of skin and lovely of countenance. And when King Solomon beheld this female demon he asked her: " Who art thou?" to which she replied that her name was Onoskelis, and that in the shape of a beautiful woman she worked mischief among men, leading them into temptation. She was born of an echo in a wood, and her dwelling-places were ravines, caves, and precipices.

And when King Solomon asked her to name the angel who usually frustrated her evil designs, she replied: " The angel who frustrates my designs is dwelling in thee, O King."

When the King heard these words he thought that Onoskelis was mocking him and he waxed angry, and ordered one of his soldiers to strike her. But Onoskelis assured the King that it was even so. " Be assured," she cried, " that by the wisdom of God given unto thee, I am subject to thy will, O Solomon, son of David." Thereupon King Solomon sealed and bound the female demon named Onoskelis, and commanded her to spin the hemp for the ropes to be used in the Temple.

And night and day she stood there and did the bidding of the King, spinning the hemp. Thereupon King Solomon commanded that another demon be brought to him. And immediately the demon named Asmodeus was brought before him. Asmodeus was bound and looked furious and enraged. " Who art thou?" queried the King of Israel. " And who art thou?" asked Asmodeus by way of a reply. " This is an arrogant reply," said the King. But Asmodeus said: " How shall I answer thee? Art thou not a son of man? I, Asmodeus, am the offspring of an angel out of his marriage with a daughter of man. Any answer which I, Asmodeus, who am of celestial origin, may choose to make to one earthborn can never be called arrogant. Is not my star bright in heaven, the star which some men call the dragon's child? Do not, therefore, O Solomon, son of David, ask me too many questions, for thy glory is only of short duration. After a little time thy kingdom will be destroyed and thy tyranny over us demons will be short. And then we shall once more have a free field among men, who will revere us as if we were gods, ignorant as they are of the names of the angels who command us and frustrate our designs." Thus spake Asmodeus, and his glance was full of anger.

And when King Solomon heard this speech he bade his soldiers to bind the demon even more carefully, and to flog him with thongs of leather (ox-hide). He then commanded the demon to be more humble in his speech and to tell him now what was his name and what his business. To which the demon made answer: " Among mortals I am called Asmodeus, and it is my business to estrange the hearts of newly-wedded couples and to alienate their affections. I waste away the beauty of young women and estrange the hearts of men." " And is this thy only business?" queried the King. " No," replied the demon. " My business is also to lead men who are wedded into temptation, to make them abandon their lawful wives and seek out the wives of other men, to commit grievous sins and even murderous deeds."

And when King Solomon heard these words, he said unto Asmodeus: " I command thee, Asmodeus, to tell me the name of the angel who has the power to subdue thee and to bring to nought thy designs." Whereupon Asmodeus replied: " The name of the archangel who has the power to frustrate my designs is Raphael, he who stands before the Throne of Glory." He then told the King that the liver and gall of a fish called the *Glanos*, when smoked over the coals of a tamarisk, would put him to flight. But the King queried still further: " Art thou sure, Asmodeus, that thou hast spoken the whole truth and that thou didst hide nothing from me?" Whereupon the demon cried out and said: " Whatever I have told thee, O King of Israel, is true, and the power of God, which hath bound me with indissoluble bonds, knoweth this full well. And now, O King, I pray thee not to condemn me to work in or upon water." But the King only smiled and said: " Thou shalt carry the iron, but also prepare the clay for the construction of the Temple, tread it with thy feet and carry the water for it." And he ordered his servants to give to Asmodeus ten water jars wherein to fetch and carry the water for the clay. And he also burned over Asmodeus the liver and the gall of the fish *Glanos*, and thus the malice and unbearable rage of the demon were frustrated. And groaning loudly the demon carried out the commands of the King.

Thereupon King Solomon once more summoned before him Beelzeboul, the prince of the demons, and seating himself upon a magnificent throne, he thus addressed the chief of the demons: " Tell me, O Beelzeboul, why art thou alone prince of demons?" To this Beelzeboul made answer: " Because I alone am left of all the angels of Heaven who came down upon earth. I was the first angel in the first heaven, my name being Beelzeboul; and now I am the prince and ruler of all those who are bound in Tartarus. I also have a child whose abode is the Red Sea. He is subject unto me, and at certain times he comes up, revealing unto me all he has done, and I give him new courage." "And what is thy business?" queried the King. "I," replied Beelzeboul, "am the ally of foreign tyrants; and furthermore, I excite evil desires and wicked inclinations in the hearts of the chosen servants of God. They commit grievous sins, and I thus lead them to destruction. It is I, too, who place envy and wicked thoughts in the hearts of men, and am the cause of envy, murderous deeds, and wars. Thus, I destroy the world, and all those who contribute to the destruction of this world are my servants and act thus because I have inspired them."

Thereupon the King said unto Beelzeboul: "Bring before me thy son who dwelleth in the Red Sea." The prince of the demons then replied: "I will not bring my son before thee, but another demon shall come to me, a demon whose name is Ephippas. Him thou mayest bind and he may bring up my son from the depth of the sea." "And how comes it," queried the King, "that thy son can live in the depth of the sea, and what is his name?" The prince of demons replied: "Ask me not, O King, for thou wilt not learn it from me, but by my command my son will come to thee and he will tell thee."

Thereupon the King set Beelzeboul to saw Theban marbles, and when the other demons beheld their chief sawing Theban marbles they howled aloud in their joy.

The King then commanded another demon to present himself before him. And lo! there appeared one who carried his head high up, whilst the remaining part of that spirit was curled up like a snake. Breaking through the few soldiers, this demon raised up a fearful cloud of dust which he hurled upwards and downwards so as to frighten the King.

But Solomon stood up and spat on the ground right in that spot where the cloud of dust was raised, and sealed the spot with the ring he had received from the archangel.

Thereupon the dust wind at once ceased. The King then asked the spirit: " Who art thou and what is thy name?" The demon once more raised a dust, and answered: " What is thy desire, O King?" " Tell me thy name, so that I may ask thee a question," replied the King. " Tell me also thy employment and pursuit." And the demon replied: " I am the spirit of ashes: I set fire to fields and destroy houses; and my principal occupation is during the summer, when I am particularly busy." " And under whose authority," asked the King, " dost thou do harm?" " Under the authority of the archangel Azael," replied the demon; whereupon the King summoned Azael and set a seal upon the demon. He then commanded the demon to seize huge stones and throw them up to the work people on the top of the structure. And the demon was compelled to do the King's bidding.

Thereupon King Solomon ordered another demon to come before him. And lo! there appeared seven female spirits, fair and comely to behold and beautiful in appearance. And the King questioned them as to their names and their employment. " We are of the thirty three elements of the ruler of darkness," they answered all at once. But the King questioned them one by one, beginning with the first and ending with the seventh.

And the first of these seven female spirits said: " I am Deception. I deceive and excite evil inclinations, but my designs are frustrated by the angel Lamechalal." And the second female spirit said: " I am Strife, the strife of strifes; but the angel who frustrates me is called Barnchiachel." And the third spirit said: " I am called Klathon, that is battle, and my business consists in causing honourable and decent people to quarrel and to attack one another; and Marmarath is the name of the angel who frustrates all my designs." The fourth spirit then said: " I am Jealousy; I cause men to lose their reason, I divide them and make them hostile to one another, and whenever Strife follows me I even alienate husband and wife, estrange parents and children, and tear brothers from sisters. Alas, however, I have an angel who frustrates my designs and his name is Balthial." And the fifth female spirit said: " I am Power; I raise up tyrants, I sweep kings out of the way by power. I also lend power to rebels, but the angel who is opposed to me is Asteraoth." And the sixth spirit said: " I am Error (Seduction). I induce men into error, and I will induce thee, too, into error, O King Solomon, as I have already done once when at my inspiration thou didst slay thine own brother. I also lead men into error, so that they pry into graves. I also instruct the thieves, and I lead men away from piety, and I do many other evil things, but I have an angel who frustrates me and his name is Uriel."

" I am the worst of all," said the seventh female spirit. " I can make even thee worse than thou art. Our stars are in heaven and we live together and we change our places together. We live together, sometimes in Lydia, sometimes in Olympus, and sometimes in a high mountain." The King heard these words of the female spirits and wondered greatly. Thereupon he sealed them with his ring, and because they were many he set them to dig the foundations of the Temple, which was two hundred and fifty cubits in length. He ordered them to be very industrious, and although they grumbled and protested they immediately started to perform the task set to them.

The King then bade another demon come to him.

And lo! there was brought before him a demon who had the limbs of a man but no head. And when the King beheld him he said to him: " Who art thou?" " I am a demon," replied the headless spirit. " I am called Envy, and it is my delight to swallow heads so that I may secure one for myself. But I am anxious to have such an head as thou hast, King Solomon." And when the King heard these words he swiftly stretched out his hand against the demon's chest and sealed him. Whereupon the headless spirit threw himself upon the ground and exclaimed: " Woe unto me, whither have I come through the traitor Ornias?" The King then asked him: " How dost thou manage to see, and how dost thou manage to speak, having no head, no eyes, and no tongue?" But the spirit, whose voice nevertheless came up to the King, made answer: " I am able to see by means of my feelings, and manage to speak because I am wholly voice, having inherited the voices of many men. I smash the heads of many, and when I en-counter some at the crossways I seize their heads, cutting them off with my hands as if with a sword. Then I put these heads upon myself, but the fire that is in me comes up through my neck and devours them." " Tell me now," queried the King, " the name of the angel by whom thou art frustrated?" To which the headless demon replied: " He is the fiery flash of lightning."

Thereupon the King bade another demon to appear in his presence. And lo! there came a big hound and spoke with a loud and powerful voice: " Hail thee, O King Solomon, son of David!" The King was greatly astounded and even frightened, and he asked the hound: " Who art thou, O hound?" To which the demon, in the shape of a hound, made answer: " Alas, I do appear to thee to be a hound, but even before thou wast, O King Solomon, I was a man, committing many evil deeds in the world. I was greatly learned in letters and even dared to hold back the stars of heaven, and to accomplish other divine works." " And what is thy name," queried the King, " and thy pursuit?" " My name," replied the demon, " is *Rabdos* (staff)." And he proceeded: " If thou, O King, wilt send thy servant with me I will lead him to a spot in the mountains and there he will find a mine of green beryl, which thou canst take away, so that thou mayest adorn the Temple with it." When the King heard these words, he bade his servant to accompany the hound to the spot in the mountains. " Take

this signet ring," he added, " and whoever will show thee
the green stone, him shalt thou at once seal with this signet
ring. Mark with great care the spot and bring the demon
back with thee." And the servant set off, accompanied by
the hound, who showed him the spot where there was a mine
of green stones. When the servant returned with the huge
hound, the King bound both the headless demon and the
hound, and set the latter to keep guard over the headless
fiery spirit, so that the light emitted by him through his maw
by day and night be cast on the artisans at work in the Temple
of God. Thereupon the King took two hundred shekels
from the treasure of the mine for the supports of the altar,
and then closed the treasure of the mine. He then commanded
the demons to cut marble for the Temple.

King Solomon thereupon bade another demon to appear
before him, and there came one in the shape of a roaring
lion. And the spirit thus addressed the King: " I am a spirit.
O King, incapable of being perceived, although it is my business to enfeeble men who are lying sick. I am, however, also
able to cast out demons, legions of them being under my
control." " What is thy name," asked the King, " and what
is the name of the angel by whom thou art frustrated?" " My
name," replied the spirit in the form of a roaring lion, " is
Lion-bearer, but I cannot tell thee the name of the angel
who frustrates me, for in so doing I would bind not only myself but also the legions of demons who are under my control."
But the King adjured him in the name of God to tell him the
name of the angel by whom he was frustrated, and the spirit
answered: " I am bound by him who is the greatest among
men and whose name is the figure 644." The King thereupon set all the legions under his control to carry wood from
the forest, but the roaring lion himself he bade saw the wood
into small pieces with his teeth, for burning it in the furnace,
for the construction of the Temple.

CHAPTER IX

King Solomon and the Serving Demons

The three-headed dragon—The treasure at the entrance of the Temple —Obizuth, the she-demon with invisible limbs—The winged dragon with the face of a man—Enepsigos, the she-demon with three heads—The demon who is half horse and half fish—The thirty-six spirits—The old workman and his son—The prediction of Ornias—The demons are able to foretell the future—The weakness and fall of demons—Adares, King of Arabia—His message to the King of Israel—The demon in the shape of a fierce wind—The capture of the demon by means of the signet ring and a leather flask—The demon Ephippas lifts the huge stone—Abezithibod, the demon dwelling in the Red Sea.

AND it came to pass that King Solomon bade another demon appear before him, and one day there came forward a terrible three-headed dragon. " I am a most terrible spirit," he said, " for I blind children in their mother's womb and make them deaf and mute. I also cause men to fall down and to grind their teeth and to foam." And he further said: " At the entrance of the Temple which thou hast begun to build, O King, there lieth hidden a treasure of gold; dig it up, O Solomon, son of David, and carry it off." Thus spake the three-headed dragon, and the King ordered his servants to dig up the treasure at the entrance of the Temple, and they found much gold, even as the demon had said. The King then sealed him with his signet ring, and bade him make bricks for the construction of the Temple.

Thereupon there came before the King another demon

100

who had the form of a woman. She had a head, and her hair was dishevelled, but her limbs were invisible.

And the King said unto this spirit: "Who art thou, and what is thy name?" To this the she-demon replied: "And who art thou and why art thou anxious to know all concerning me? As I am here, bound before thee, I will, however, tell thee, O King, and thou shalt learn who I am. I am called Obizuth, and I never sleep, for I roam about in the world, visiting women in childbirth. Not a single night am I idle, for if I am not successful in one place I visit another and strangle the newly-born babes. I roam about everywhere, east and west, and I have many names and many shapes and forms. Although I am standing before thee thou canst not command me, for my sole employment is the destruction of new-born babes."

And the King marvelled greatly at the appearance of this female demon, for, although the head of the spirit was that of a woman, the countenance bright and greeny, and the hair dishevelled like that of a dragon, the limbs and the body remained invisible. " Tell me," queried the King, " what is the name of the angel by whom thou art frustrated?" To which the female demon replied: " The name of the angel by whom I am frustrated is Apharoph, which is Raphael. And if any man knoweth his name and doth write it over a woman in childbirth, then I am not able to approach or harm her." The King then commanded that the hair of the female demon be bound, and that she be hung up in front of the Temple of God, so that everybody might see and praise the Lord, who had vouchsafed wisdom and power to the King of Israel through the signet ring.

And there appeared again before King Solomon a spirit which had the appearance of a dragon, but his face and feet were those of a man; and he also had wings on his back. " I am the winged dragon," said the spirit, " and alas, I have been subdued by thy ring and the wisdom which has been vouchsafed unto thee, O King." And when the demon said this the breath issuing from his mouth set fire to the wood of the frankincense tree, and burned and consumed all the wood collected, and placed in the Temple. And the King, seeing what this demon had done, marvelled greatly, and asked him to tell him the name of the angel by whom he was frustrated. The winged dragon made answer: " I am frustrated by the great angel who dwelleth in the second heaven called Bazazath." Thereupon the King invoked this angel, and by means of his signet ring he bound the winged dragon and condemned him to saw up blocks of marble for the construction of the Temple. He then bade another demon to appear before him. And lo! there appeared one that had the shape of a woman, but on her shoulders she carried two other heads with hands. " Who art thou?" queried King Solomon. " I am Enepsigos, but I have numerous other names." " And what is the name of the angel who subdues thee?" asked the King. " Why dost thou ask, what seekest thou?" said the spirit, by way of reply, " my shapes are numerous; like the goddess that I am called, I undergo changes and assume different shapes. Seek not, therefore, to know all about me. But this much thou mayest know, so hearken unto my words: I dwell in the moon and therefore possess three forms. I am sometimes invoked by the wise as *Kronos*, but at other times I come down and appear in another shape, whilst at others I appear in the form as thou seest me now. The angel to whom I am subjected sits in the third heaven and his name is Rathanael." The King at once invoked the angel Rathanael and bound the spirit with a triple chain.

Thereupon there came before the King another spirit who had in front the shape and form of a horse but behind that of a fish. " I am a mighty and fierce demon of the sea," he called in a loud and terrible voice, " and I seek to seize gold and silver. Changing myself into waves I am busy over the wide expanses of the sea and of the waters, where I whirl ships round and round, destroying them and throwing men into the sea. I get hold of men and money. The money I take to the bottom of the sea, but the bodies of the men I cast out upon the shore. And I came up from the depth of the sea to take counsel with Beelzeboul who is the ruler of the spirits in the air, upon the earth, and under the earth, but he bound me and delivered me into thy hands, O King. But in two or three days I shall no longer be able to converse with thee, because I shall have no water which is my element. Jameth is the angel who frustrates my designs." Thus spake the spirit of the sea. Thereupon King Solomon commanded that the demon of the sea be thrown into a phial containing sea-water, to seal this phial with marbles and asphalt and pitch, and to deposit it in the Temple.

And there appeared again another demon in the shape of a man with bright, gleaming eyes, carrying a blade in his hand. " I am the descendant of a giant who was killed during the massacre of the giants," said he, " I often dwell among the tombs and assume the form of the dead, destroying with my sword all those whom I manage to catch." And when the King had shut up this demon there appeared before him thirty-six spirits with ugly, shapeless heads, but human in form. There were some who had the faces of oxen, some those of asses, and others the faces of birds. Marvelling greatly, the King asked them who they were. To this they made answer: " We are the thirty-six elements, the rulers of darkness, and we have come before thee, O King, because the Lord of the Universe has given thee authority over all the spirits in the air, on the earth, and likewise under the earth." And the first of them said: " I am the first leader of the Zodiacal sign and am called the *ram*." And all these thirty-six spirits King Solomon caused to be bound, setting them to fetch

water for the Temple. Some of the demons he condemned
to drudgery and heavy work in the Temple, whilst others
were shut up in prisons, so that they were made harmless.

And it came to pass that one day an old workman appeared
before the King and complained against his only son who
did insult and ill-treat him. He beseeched the King to avenge
him and to condemn the son to die, as was the law.[1] And
just as the King was about to pronounce sentence in this matter,
the demon Ornias laughed aloud. The King thereupon commanded the demon to be brought before him, and he thus
addressed him: " Accursed demon, how didst thou dare to
laugh at me and in my royal presence?"

To this the demon Ornias made answer: " Be not angry,
O mighty King. I did not laugh at thee or because of thee,
but because of the old man and his wretched son. The old
man is anxious to have his son condemned to death, but in
three days the boy will anyhow die an untimely death." And
the King marvelled greatly at the words of the demon, and
asked: " Is this so? dost thou speak the truth?" " It is true,
O King," replied the demon Ornias. " And how dost thou
know this?" queried the King. " We demons," replied Ornias,
" often ascend into the firmaments; there we fly about among
the angels and the stars, and we hear the sentences which are
proclaimed, and which go forth upon the souls of men."
" And how can you demons ascend to Heaven and intermingle
with the holy angels and the stars?" further queried the King.
To this the demon replied: " Whatever happens in Heaven
also occurs upon earth. We demons fly about in the air beneath
the lower firmament, where we contemplate all the heavenly
powers and hear their voices and the voices of all the heavenly
beings. But we have nowhere to alight and rest, and thus we
lose our strength and grow tired, and on account of our weakness, finding nowhere anything to lay hold of, we fall down

[1] *Deuteron.*, 21, 18–21.

like lightning in the depth of night, or like leaves from the trees. People seeing us fall down imagine that stars are falling, but it is not so, O great King. The stars having firm foundations in the firmaments do not fall, but it is only one of us demons falling from on high. We fall and set on fire cities and fields." Thus spake the demon, and the King marvelled greatly. The King, therefore, sent the old man home, commanding him to appear once more in his presence in five days. And when five days had passed, the King sent again for the old man. The latter appeared with sad face and in a great grief. " Alas, great King," wailed the old man, " I am childless and sit in despair by the grave of my boy who died two days ago." The King on hearing these words, knew that Ornias had spoken the truth and that demons are in reality able to foretell the future.

The power of Solomon over the demons became so great that he could subdue even the fiercest among them. Thus one day, Adares, the King of the Arabians, sent a message to King Solomon, of whose wisdom and power over all the spirits of the air he had heard, begging him to deliver Arabia from a terrible demon, who, in the shape of a fierce wind, blew over the country from early dawn until the third hour. " Its blast," wrote the King of Arabia, " is so terrible and so harsh that neither man nor beast can withstand it but are slain." The King of Arabia, therefore, begged the King of Israel to send a man and capture this terrible demon, promising in return for this act of righteousness, that he and his people and all his land would serve King Solomon, and that Arabia would live in peace with him.

Thereupon King Solomon called one of his trusted servants, and ordered him to take a camel and also a leather flask, and to betake himself to Arabia where the evil spirit, fierce and terrible, was blowing. Solomon also gave his trusted servant

his signet ring and thus he spoke: " When thou wilt reach
Arabia and the place where the evil spirit bloweth so fiercely,
place the signet ring in front of the mouth of the leather flask,
and hold both of them towards the great and terrible blast
of the spirit. When thou wilt see that the flask is blown out
then hastily tie up its mouth, for the demon will be in it.
Then thou wilt seal the flask with the seal-ring very securely,
and placing it upon thy camel bring it hither. On the way,
no doubt, the demon will offer thee gold and silver and much
treasure to let him go free. Take heed not to be persuaded,
but try to find out from the demon and make him point out
the places where there are treasures and gold and silver. Now,
fare thee well, and bring the demon from Arabia hither without fail." Thus spake King Solomon, and his trusted servant
did as he had been bidden, and set off into Arabia to the place
where, fierce and terrible, the demon was blowing and blasting.

And when he arrived into this region of Arabia he waited
till dawn, when the fierce and evil spirit began his daily blast.
Facing the demon's blast, the messenger from King Solomon
placed the leather flask upon the ground and held the ring on
the mouth of the flask, so that the demon blew through the
finger ring into the flask and blew it out. And when the
servant of King Solomon saw that the flask was blown out,
he knew that the demon was in it, and he promptly drew
tight the opening of the flask in the name of the Lord God.
He then sealed the flask securely with the seal ring, even
as his master had bidden him do, but he tarried three days
in the country to make trial. And lo! the fierce and
terrible wind had ceased, for the demon now shut up in the
leather flask no longer did blow against the city. And the
Arabs marvelled greatly and praised the Lord God who had
given such wisdom and power to King Solomon.

They then heaped gifts upon the servant of King Solomon,
and sent him away with much honour. And when the messenger

returned to Jerusalem he placed the leather flask containing the demon of Arabia in the Temple.

Now it came to pass that just at this moment King Solomon was in great distress. The Temple was being completed, but there was an immense corner stone which had still to be placed on the pinnacle of the Temple, and this work neither workmen nor demons had as yet been able to accomplish. Work as they might, they were not strong enough to stir it and lift it up to put it in its allotted place. Now on the next morning, after the return of his messenger from Arabia, the King went into the Temple and sat in deep distress, thinking about the heavy stone which neither workmen nor demons had been able to stir from its place. And lo! the flask containing the fierce demon from Arabia stood up, walked around seven steps, then fell down and did homage to King Solomon. The latter commanded the demon in the flask to stand up and tell him his name and employment. King Solomon then said to the demon: "Who art thou and by what angel art thou frustrated?" And the demon replied: "I am the demon called Ephippas and I am able to remove mountains and to overthrow them." "Canst thou raise this stone," asked King Solomon, "and lay it in its place?" "Verily," said the demon, "I can do this, and with the help of the demon who presides over the Red Sea, I can bring up a pillar of air and support the gigantic stone." Thereupon King Solomon commanded Ephippas to become flat, and the flask to appear as if depleted of air. He then placed it under the stone, and behold, the demon lifted up the stone on the top of the flask, and put it in its appointed place. And then the demon who presides over the Red Sea appeared and raised a column of air and the pillar remained in mid-air supporting the stone. King Solomon asked the spirit who had come up from the depth of the Red Sea to tell him who he was and what was his business. And the spirit replied: "I, O King Solomon, am called Abezithibod, and I once sat in the first heaven, being the descendant of an archangel. Fierce and winged I was, but I plotted against every spirit in Heaven. It was I who hardened the heart of Pharaoh, when Moses appeared before him; and also in the time of the exodus of the Children of Israel, it was I who excited the heart of Pharaoh and caused him and all the Egyptians to pursue the Children of Israel through the waves of the Red Sea. And it came to pass that when the Children of Israel had passed through the waves of the Red Sea, the waters came over the hosts of the Egyptians and hid them, and I, too, remained in the Sea." Thus spake the demon Abezithibod; and King Solomon wondered greatly, and praised the Lord.

CHAPTER X

Paradise, or the Abode of the Just

The two parks—Paradise in Heaven, and Paradise upon earth—Persian influence — Zoroastrian dualism — Egyptian and Greek doctrines — The realm of the dead, and the dog Anubis—Favourite persons visit Paradise and Hell during their lives upon earth—Orpheus and Ulysses—Enoch and the prophet Elijah—The three walls of Paradise—The just and pious men of the Gentiles—The sinners who repented—The seven compartments of Paradise—The tree of life—The river Jubal—Enoch-Metatron wanders through the city of the just—The Seat of Judgment—Description of Paradise in *Yalkut Rubeni*—The ten compartments—Rabbi Joshua ben Levi, the hero of a Jewish *Divina Commedia*—The angel of death leads Rabbi Joshua ben Levi to the gates of Paradise—The Rabbi enters Paradise alive —The complaint of the angel of death—Rabbi Joshua's description of Paradise—The reception of the just—The rivers of oil, balsam, wine and honey—The transformation of the Just—Childhood, adolescence, and old age—The thrones of gold and pearls—The purple covers woven by Eve— The compartment of the Messiah—Elijah comforts the Messiah—Rabbi Chanina and the angel of death—Moses visits Paradise and Hell—The thrones of the Patriarchs—The thrones of copper for the wicked whose sons are just and pious.

IN Rabbinic, Talmudic, and Midrashic literature, as well as in the apocryphal and pseudoepigraphic writings, the ideas with regard to Paradise and Hell, Garden of Eden, and Gehinnom, are numerous and varied. Some regarded Paradise as being on the earth itself, whilst for others it was in Heaven. Others again assumed two Paradises, one in Heaven for those who are perfect in holiness, and one on earth for those who are not quite perfect, or at least come short of perfection. There is no mention whatever of the myths of Paradise and Hell in the Holy Writ, in the Books of Moses or in the Prophets. The legislator promised his nation reward and punish-

ment in this world, and even the Prophets speak only of a
life here below.   The author of *Ecclesiastes* recognizes the
immortality of the soul,[1] but there is no question of Heaven,
Paradise, or Hell.

The majority of the Rabbis of the Talmud speak of the
immortality of the soul, but rarely indulge in descriptions of
Paradise or Hell.   The myths and legends about Paradise
and Hell all took their origin upon Persian soil.   Influenced
by Zoroastrian dualism, the Babylonian exiles applied it
in a truly Jewish spirit, that is in an ethical manner, not
only to the doctrines of angels and demons, but also to reward and punishment after death.   Foreign influence became
even more pronounced under the rule of the Seleucidæ and
the Ptolemies, when the Jews of Egypt came into close contact
with the ideas of Greece and Egypt.   From the Egyptians,
they learned the doctrine of the realm of the dead whither the
souls of the departed are led by the dog Anubis.   From the
Greeks they learned the existence of two realms, Elyseum,
where the pious and just dwell, and Tartarus where the shadows
of the wicked roam about.   The Jewish mythmakers of the
Persian and Hellenistic periods also created two cities, one
the abode of the just and the other the dwelling of the wicked,
whither the souls of the departed are taken by the angel
Dumah.[2]

And just as in Greek myth many favoured persons were
supposed to have visited Paradise and Hell during their lives
and to have become the heroes of a *Divina Commedia*, so
in Jewish myth, too, we meet with favoured personalities
who were translated to Paradise before they had " shuffled
off this mortal coil ".   Some of them, as we shall see later,
recorded their visions and gave a minute description of
Heaven and Paradise.   Rabbi Joshua ben Levi visited the
lower Paradise, that is Paradise upon earth.   Alexander the

---

[1] *Ecclesiastes*, 12, 7.   [2] Silence; see on *Dumah, Berachoth*, 18b; *Sanhedrin*, 94a.

Great knocked at its gates, but was not admitted. The Prophet Elijah and Enoch are supposed to have been translated into the lower Paradise, although in various places of the *Book of Enoch* the latter is described as having been carried to the upper Paradise, where also the Prophet Elijah dwells. But whilst in Greek myth living personalities are allowed to visit Hades and to return to the upper world, few, if any, persons in Jewish myth are supposed to have had a peep into Hell. Thus Orpheus goes down to Hades to fetch his wife Eurydice, and Ulysses undertakes the journey to consult the seer Tyresius. Moses was allowed to visit Hell; but it is only with difficulty that Rabbi Joshua, the son of Levi, obtained the permission to cast a glance upon the doings in Hell.

It is especially in Jewish mysticism, which is a more modern development of ancient mythology, that the descriptions of Paradise and Hell abound. Jewish mysticism teaches that there are two Paradises, one in Heaven and one upon earth. In the *Book of Enoch* and in the *Fourth Esra* both a lower Paradise and an upper Paradise are mentioned.[1] It is the garden of justice, or the city of the just, where the just and pious dwell. Various descriptions of both the upper and the lower Paradise are to be found in Midrashic lore. In one Midrash it is described as follows: The Garden of Eden has three walls all made of fire. The outer wall, of black fire, is visible and invisible, and a flaming sword is constantly turning round this wall. There are four gates in this wall at a distance of 120 yards one from the other. And the flaming sword, turning round and round night and day, never rests and devours all grass and everything that approaches the outer wall within one mile. And at a distance of 600 yards is the second wall. And there dwell the just and pious of the Gentiles and heathens, all the proselytes who were not sufficiently firm in their fear of the Lord. And every day at the

[1] R. H. Charles. *The Book of Enoch*. 65, 2; 106, 8; 77, 3; 60, 8; 87, 34; 89, 22.

time of the afternoon prayer the evil spirits and malignant angels assemble and endeavour to expel them and lead them straight into Hell. But they raise a loud cry, and the angel Azriel arrives and saves them from the clutches of the malignant spirits. Near that second outer wall dwell also all those who had given alms and done good deeds in the world publicly so as to gain fame, but not out of goodness of heart and for the sake of the Lord. Three times a day the malignant spirits and demons come to torture them, but the protecting angels save them from their hands. And all the sinners who had thought of repentance before leaving the earth are brought into the space between the two walls, and the angel, whose name is Mahariel, shows them from afar the abode of the just and of the blessed. The second wall is of green and red fire, and within that wall dwell all those who had striven to make their children study the law, although they did not succeed in their endeavour. Here also dwell those who, under the impulse of the moment, had performed a good deed. The light from the grace of the just shines upon them, but only for one moment when it is hidden again. The third wall consists of light mixed with darkness, and it is within the Garden of Eden, and within this wall is the abode of the just and of the blessed. And as soon as they enter this abode they become as light as air and part of it, and are robed in air as in a pure and holy garment. This garment resembles in shape and form the garments they had worn in the netherworld, so that they can recognize one another by it.[1] Another description runs as follows: The Garden of Eden forms the east of the world, and it measures æons, and therein dwell seven different kinds of the just and pious, and it contains houses built as dwellings for the just. The first house is the one wherein the prophets of justice have their abode. This house is built of the wood of cedars. In the second house the rafters are of cedar

[1] Jellinek, *Beth-Hamidrash*, Vol. III, pp. 131–132.

and the walls of silver, and therein dwell the sinners who repent
and who are purified of sin, even as silver is free from all spots.
And the third house is built of silver and fine gold, and ornamented with pearls and precious stones, and it is very vast,
and all that is good upon earth or in heaven is to be found
in this house, for all the delights and perfumes are planted
therein, and in its midst stands the tree of life. From the
tree issues the river Jubal dividing itself into four parts,
Gihon, Hiddekel, Pishon, and Phrat. And the fourth house
is built of olive wood, and therein dwell all those who
had suffered upon earth, but had not rebelled or grumbled
against Providence and the Creator, remaining humble, meek,
merciful, and just.[1]

Before being crowned by the Lord of the Universe, Enoch,
who afterwards became Metatron, wandered through the
celestial regions led by Michael. He made a circuit of the
heavens, wandering west and east, and saw the wonders of
Heaven, its secrets and delights. On the west he saw a great
and lofty mountain, a strong rock and four delightful places.
It was both deep and dark to behold, but internally it was
capacious and very smooth as if it had been rolled over. One
of the holy angels who was with him informed Enoch that
these were the places of delight where the spirits and souls
of the dead would be collected. All the souls of the sons of
men who were righteous would be collected in these delightful places formed for them. They would occupy these places
until the day of judgment, which will be long. But the spirits
of the dead are separated one from another. Three separa-
tions have been made between them, and they are separated
by a chasm, by water, and by light above it. And the sinners,
too, are separated one from another when they die and judgment has not overtaken them in their lifetime. Their souls
are separated in Heaven. Enoch-Metatron then went from

[1] *Midrash Konen*, Jellinek, *Beth-Hamidrash*, Vol. II, pp. 28–29.

thence to another place at the extremities of the earth towards
the west. Here he saw a fire blazing and running without
ceasing, continuing by day and night, never intermitting its
course. It was the fire of all the luminaries of Heaven. He
then proceeded to another place, there he saw a mountain
of fire flashing unceasingly by day and night. Approaching
a little nearer he saw seven splendid mountains all different
from each other. The stones of all the mountains were splendid
and brilliant to behold, and their surface was very beautiful.
Three of these mountains placed one upon another were
towards the east, whilst three others, equally placed one upon
another, were towards the south. The seventh mountain was
in the midst of them. Surrounded by delightfully smelling
trees, the mountains resembled the seat of a throne. And
among the delightfully smelling trees surrounding the mountains there was one tree of an unceasing smell, not even
among the trees which were in Eden was there a tree which
was so fragrant. Its fruit was beautiful to behold, and neither
bark, nor flower and leaf ever withered. Its fruit resembled
the cluster of a palm, it was pleasing to behold and a delight
to the eye. It was the mountain which will be the seat on
which shall sit the great and holy Lord of Glory, the Everlasting King, on the day when He shall come and descend to
visit the earth with goodness. And Enoch was informed by
the angels in whose company he was that on the day of judgment, when all shall be punished and consumed, the fruit of
this tree of an agreeable smell shall be bestowed on the elect,
the righteous and humble. Enoch then proceeded to the
middle of the earth, and here he beheld a happy and fertile
spot, containing branches continually sprouting from the
trees which were planted in it. There were two holy mountains and underneath them water flowed, and between them
there was a deep valley. It was the place where, on the day
of judgment, all who utter with their mouths unbecoming

language against God and speak harsh things of His glory will be collected.[1]

The *Yalkut Rubeni* gives the following description of the upper Paradise. Paradise consists of ten compartments, and they are inhabited by the souls of the departed pious and just, according to the degree of their respective piety. Here they dwell without being swayed by any of the passions which cause so much trouble to mortal man. Without food or drink, care-free they live happily, enjoying the Divine radiance, wisdom, and benevolence, having free access to the treasures of knowledge, and learning the secrets of nature. The first compartment is the seat of the simply pious souls, of those who upon earth kept the covenant, fought valiantly against every evil inclination, and scrupulously observed the law. This compartment is presided over by Joseph, the viceroy of Egypt, who is assisted by the angel-group known as *Erelim*. The second compartment is inhabited by the souls of the departed who, upon earth, have done more than strictly adhere to the law. The inmates of this compartment are presided over by Phinehas, the son of Eleazar, who is assisted by the angel-group known as *Hashmalim*. In the third compartment dwell pious men, a shade more perfect. They are presided over by the High-priest Eleazar, who is assisted by the angel-group known as *Tarshishim*. The fourth compartment is the abode of the really holy souls. Here celestial music is constantly heard, and the Divine radiance is often visible. The compartment is presided over by the High-priest Aaron, who is assisted by an angel-group known as *Seraphim*. The fifth compartment is the abode of the sinners who have repented. They enjoy special favours, and are esteemed even higher than the inmates of the fourth compartment, enjoying even more frequently the manifestation of Divine radiance. The president of this compartment is the King Manasseh, who

[1] R. H. Charles, *The Book of Enoch*.

has at his disposal an angel-group known as the *Ophanim*. In the sixth compartment dwell the souls of the innocent, early deceased children. Their president, guardian, and teacher, is the great angel-prince Metatron himself. Daily he visits these innocent souls, teaching and instructing them. The ministering angels of the children are the *Cherubim*.[1]

The hero of a Jewish *Divina Commedia*, and who frequently describes the life in Paradise and Inferno, was the famous Rabbi Joshua ben Levi, although he was not the only one who was allowed to have a peep into Paradise and Hell. He lived in the third century of our era, and has left a description of Paradise and Hell which occupies a prominent place in Jewish apocalyptic literature. He became the recorder, long before Dante started to write his *Divina Commedia*, of myths on Paradise and Hell.

The Story of the Angel of Death and Rabbi Joshua ben Levi

The legend of this Rabbi—who in his lifetime visited Hell and explored and entered Paradise where he remained alive, thus never tasting death and the power of the angel of death— runs as follows: He entered Paradise not by the door, but by leaping over the wall. When his earthly life was drawing to a close, the angel of death was instructed to visit the Rabbi, but to show deference to him and to respect all his wishes. And when Rabbi Joshua, the son of Levi, noticed how courteous and humble the angel of death showed himself, he asked the latter whether he would consent to do him a favour. " If it is in my power," replied the angel, " I will gladly grant thy petition." " Let me, before thou takest my life, contemplate from afar my place in Paradise." The request was granted by the angel of death, and he promised to let Rabbi Joshua

---

[1] Cf. Jellinek, *loc. cit.*, Vol. II, pp. 28–29; Vol. III, pp. 52–53.

have a glimpse of Paradise and point out to him the seat he was going to occupy there. As a proof of his good faith, he handed over to Rabbi Joshua his sword, which the Rabbi was allowed to keep during their journey and until they reached the gates of Paradise. Thus the two set out on the journey, and having travelled a long way finally halted before the gates of Paradise, outside that celestial city of the just, where the pious, after having shuffled off mortal coil, enjoy heavenly bliss. With the assistance of the angel of death Rabbi Joshua climbed up the wall of the celestial city, and peeped down into the abode of the blessed. The angel of death pointed out to him the place he was destined to occupy after death. Suddenly Rabbi Joshua ben Levi threw himself over the wall and was inside Paradise to the surprise and amazement of his companion, the angel of death. Seizing the Rabbi Joshua ben Levi by the skirt of his garment the angel of death urged him to return. But the Rabbi swore an oath that he would not return. Thereupon the angel of death ascended to Heaven where he complained before the tribunal of justice. And the heavenly decree was issued that as the Rabbi had never during his earthly career broken his word and much less his oath, and had never even sought to be relieved of the obligation of a promise or of an oath, he had deserved not to be compelled to commit perjury within the precincts of the city of the just. The angel of death had, therefore, to be content when the Rabbi returned unto him his sword, which he at first had declined to give up. He yielded only when a voice from Heaven ordered him immediately to restore the sword.[1]

The angel of death, greatly vexed, went to Rabbi Gamaliel and complained against Rabbi Joshua, the son of Levi, who had deceived him and taken his place in Paradise whilst alive.

[1] *Ketubot*, 77b; see Jellinek, *loc. cit.*, Vol. II, pp 48–51; Bacher, *loc. cit.*, I, 192–194; see also *Kol Bo*, fol., 136d–137a.

But Rabbi Gamaliel made answer: " Rabbi Joshua served thee quite right." Thereupon he asked the angel of death to go and request the Rabbi in his name to make a diligent search through Paradise and Hell, learn all its mysteries and send him a description. And the angel of death complied with the request of Rabbi Gamaliel and took his message to Rabbi Joshua who was now dwelling in Paradise. And Rabbi Joshua ben Levi gave the following description: Paradise has two gates of carbuncle, and sixty myriads of ministering angels are set to keep watch over them. And the lustre of the countenance of each angel is like the lustre of the firmament. And these angels are standing and waiting with crowns of gold and precious stones, and with myrtle wreaths in their hands, ready to welcome the righteous. And when a just man approaches the gates of Paradise, the ministering angels immediately divest him of the clothes in which he had been buried, and they array him with eight garments woven out of clouds of glory, and upon his head they place two crowns, one of precious stones and pearls, and the other of pure gold. Into his hands they place eight branches of myrtle, and they make him enter into the abode of the just, where eight rivers of water flow among eight hundred essences of rose and myrtle. And everyone of the just who enters the abode of the just has a canopy whence issue four rivers of oil, balsam, wine, and honey, and every canopy is overgrown by a vine of gold, thirty pearls hanging down from it. In every canopy there is a table of precious stones and pearls, and sixty angels minister to everyone of the just in the city of the just. And there is neither night nor day in the city of the just. The just also undergo three transformations, passing through the stages of childhood, adolescence, and old age. The just man is at first a child and enters the compartment of the children where he tastes the joys of childhood. He is thereupon changed into a youth, and the delights and pleasures of youth are his lot, which he is allowed to enjoy. He is then changed into an old man, and entering the compartment of aged people he is allowed to enjoy all the pleasures of mature age. And there are eighty myriads of trees in every corner of Paradise, and the smallest of these trees is more magnificent than a whole garden of spices. There are also sixty myriads of ministering angels in every corner of the Garden of Eden, who are singing with sweet and lovely voices. And in the middle of the Garden of Eden stands the tree of life, overshadowing the whole of the Paradise. The fruit of this tree has 500 thousand tastes, one taste being different from the other, and the perfumes thereof vary likewise. Seven clouds of glory hang over the tree of life, and its odours are wafted from one end of the world to the other. Underneath the tree sit the just and the scholars and explain the law.

And Rabbi Joshua went and searched through Paradise, and found therein seven compartments, each measuring both in width and length twelve myriads of miles. The first compartment is just opposite the first door of Paradise, and here dwell all the proselytes who have embraced Judaism not from compulsion but of their own free will. The walls of this compartment are of glass, and the wainscoting is of cedarwood. And when the Rabbi tried to measure it, the proselytes inhabiting this compartment arose and wanted to prevent him from doing so. But the prophet Obadjah, who presides over them, rebuked them, and they ultimately allowed the Rabbi to measure the compartment.

The second compartment facing the second door of Paradise is built of silver, and its wainscoting is of cedar, and here dwell all the sinners who repent, and Manasseh, the son of Ezekiah, presides over them.

The third compartment is facing the third door of Paradise, and is built of silver and gold; and here dwell Abraham, Isaac, and Jacob, and all the Israelites who came out of Egypt, and the generation that had lived in the desert. Here are also all the royal princes, with the exception of Absalom, and David and Solomon, and all the kings of Judah. And Moses and Aaron preside over the inmates of this compartment. And in this compartment Rabbi Joshua also saw precious vessels of silver and gold, and jewels and precious stones and pearls, and lamps of pure gold. And there were thrones, and canopies, and beds, all prepared for those who still dwell in the world of mortals, but who, after death, would obtain the merit of their good deeds.

And the fourth compartment, facing the fourth door of Paradise, is built beautifully, its walls being of glass and its wainscoting of olive wood. And here dwell all the just and perfect to whom life upon earth has been bitter even as olives.

And the fifth compartment of Paradise is of silver and re- fined gold, of crystal, and bdellium, and the river Gihon flows through its midst. The walls of this compartment are of silver and gold, and it is pervaded by delicious perfumes which are more exquisite and delightful than all the perfumes of Lebanon. There are beds of gold and silver with covers of purple and violet woven once by Eve, and they are mixed with scarlet made of hair of goats and woven by angels. In this compart- ment there dwell the Messiah and the prophet Elijah, seated under a canopy made of the wood of Lebanon. The pillars of this palanquin are of silver, the bottom of gold, and the seat is purple. And the prophet Elijah comforts the Messiah and assures him that the end draweth near. And the Patriarchs, too, and the fathers of the tribes, and Moses, and Aaron, and David, and Solomon all come to visit the Messiah and weep with him and comfort him, saying: " Rely upon the Creator, for the end draweth near."

And in the sixth compartment there dwell those who died because they performed a pious deed.

In the seventh compartment dwell those who died on account of the sins of Israel.[1]

But Rabbi Joshua was not the only one who was allowed to converse with the angel of death and to be shown his place in Paradise. Another Rabbi also enjoyed this privilege according to legend. His name was Rabbi Chanina, the son of Paffa, and he lived in the third century. When he was about to die, the angel of death was instructed in celestial regions to go and visit the pious Rabbi, and if necessary to render him a kindly service. The angel of death accordingly descended upon earth and made himself known unto Rabbi Chanina, the son of Paffa. " Leave me for thirty days," spoke the Rabbi to the angel, " until I have repeated all that I have studied here, for I am anxious to appear in the world above with all my studies of the Sacred Law in my hands, as it is said: ' Blessed is he who comes here with his studies in his hand '." And the angel of death, faithful to instructions received, granted the service which the Rabbi required of him. After thirty days he returned again, and the Rabbi now asked to be shown his place in Paradise while he was still alive. This, too, the angel of death consented to do. They accordingly set out on their journey. " Lend me thy sword," said Rabbi Chanina unto the angel of death, " that I may keep it until we reach Paradise, lest thou cheatest me on the road and dost deprive me of my expectation." But this the angel of death, remembering his experience with Rabbi Joshua ben Levi, refused to grant. " Dost thou mean to imitate the example of thy friend," he queried, and he did not entrust the sword to Rabbi Chanina, but he showed him his place in Paradise.[2]

But already before Rabbi Joshua ben Levi, Moses is supposed to have seen the two parks, Paradise and Hell, the city of the just, and the abode of the sinners. And Moses, modest

---

[1] Jellinek, *Beth-Hamidrash*, Vol. II, pp. 49–53; see also Gaster, *Journal of Royal Asiatic Society*, 1893, pp. 596–598.   [2] *Ketubot*, 77b.

as he was, exclaimed: " O Lord of the Universe, I am only flesh and blood, and am afraid to enter the blazing fire of Hell." But the Almighty God assured the son of Amram that he could tread the blazing fire of Hell and yet his feet would not be burned. When Moses entered the place of Hell, the fire drew back, and the master of Hell exclaimed: " Son of Amram, thy place is not here." But a voice from the Throne of Glory called out and commanded the master of Hell to show the son of Amram the horrors of Hell and the punishment of the sinners. And Moses heard Hell crying with a loud voice and clamouring for the sinners that it might destroy them. Moses then witnessed the punishment of the sinners who had committed murder, theft, and adultery; who were guilty of pride and slander; who had oppressed the poor and persecuted the orphan. And he saw how the wicked were punished by fire and snow and how they had no rest except on the Sabbath and festival days. And Moses prayed unto the Lord to save the sinners and forgive them.

And Moses again lifted up his eyes and beheld the angel Gabriel standing near him, who thus spoke unto him: " Come, O Son of Amram, and I will show thee Paradise." The angels watching at the gates of Paradise would not allow the son of Amram to enter the park created for the righteous. But a voice from the Throne of Glory commanded the ministering angels to open the gates of Paradise for the son of Amram who had come to witness the reward of the pious and the just. And when he entered Paradise Moses saw an angel sitting under the tree of life. He was the guardian of Paradise, and he thus addressed the son of Amram: " Why didst thou come hither?" " I have come," replied Moses, " to witness the reward of the pious in Paradise." Thereupon the guardian of Paradise, who was sitting under the tree of life, took Moses by the hand and led him through Paradise. He showed him the thrones of precious stones, of sapphires and emeralds, of diamonds and pearls, all surrounded by ministering angels who were guarding the thrones. They were the thrones of Abraham and of Isaac, and of other pious men. Thereupon Moses asked his guide to tell him for whom the thrones of pearls were prepared; and the guardian angel answered: " These thrones are for the scholars who study the law; the thrones of rubies are for the just; the thrones of precious stones are for the pious; and the thrones of gold are for the sinners who repent." He also beheld thrones of copper and asked the angel who accompanied him: " For whom are these thrones of copper?" And the angel replied: " These thrones of copper are for the wicked men whose sons are just and pious. Although they were wicked themselves and sinned, they obtain a portion of heavenly bliss through the merit of their sons who are just and pious, and God, in His mercy, grants them a modest place in Paradise." Moses thereupon beheld a spring of living water flowing from underneath the tree of life and dividing itself into four streams. And Moses felt great joy when he beheld all the pleasant things prepared for the pious in the city of the just.[1]

THE LEGEND OF RABBI BEN LEVI

Rabbi ben Levi, on the Sabbath, read
A volume of the Law, in which it said,
" No man shall look upon my face and live ".
And as he read, he prayed that God would give
His faithful servant grace with mortal eye
To look upon his face and yet not die.

Then fell a sudden shadow on the page,
And, lifting up his eyes, grown dim with age,
He saw the angel of death before him stand,
Holding a naked sword in his right hand.
Rabbi ben Levi was a righteous man,
Yet through his veins a chill of horror ran.

[1] *Journal of Royal Asiatic Society*, 1893.

With trembling voice he said: " What wilt thou here?"
The angel answered: " Lo! the time draws near
When thou must die; yet first, by God's decree,
Whate'er thou askest shall be granted thee."
Replied the Rabbi: " Let these living eyes
First look upon my place in Paradise."

Then said the Angel: " Come with me and look."
Rabbi ben Levi closed the sacred book,
And rising, and uplifting his grey head,
" Give me thy sword," he to the angel said,
" Lest thou shouldst fall upon me by the way."
The angel smiled and hastened to obey,
Then led him forth to the celestial town,
And set him on the wall, whence, gazing down,
Rabbi ben Levi, with his living eyes,
Might look upon his place in Paradise.

Then straight into the city of the Lord
The Rabbi leaped with the death-angel's sword,
And through the streets there swept a sudden breath
Of something there unknown, which men call death.
Meanwhile the angel stayed without and cried:
" Come back!"   To which the Rabbi's voice replied:
" No! in the name of God, whom I adore,
I swear that hence I will depart no more!"

Then all the angels cried: " O Holy One,
See what the son of Levi here has done!
The kingdom of Heaven he takes by violence,
And in Thy name refuses to go hence!"
The Lord replied: " My angels, be not wroth;
Did e'er the son of Levi break his oath?
Let him remain: for he with mortal eye
Shall look upon my face and yet not die."

Beyond the outer wall the angel of death
Heard the great voice, and said, with panting breath:
" Give back the sword, and let me go my way."
Whereat the Rabbi paused and answered: " Nay!

THE RABBI WITH THE DEATH ANGEL'S SWORD

Facing page 124, Vol. I

Anguish enough already has it caused
Among the sons of men." And, while he paused,
He heard the awful mandate of the Lord
Resounding through the air: " Give back the sword!"

The Rabbi bowed his head in silent prayer;
Then said he to the dreadful angel: " Swear,
No human eye shall look on it again;
But when thou takest away the souls of men,
Thyself unseen, and with an unseen sword,
Thou wilt perform the bidding of the Lord."

The angel took the sword again, and swore,
And walks on earth unseen for evermore.

H. W. Longfellow.

CHAPTER XI

Alexander the Great at the Gates of Paradise

Alexander the Great reaches the silent river—The agreeable taste of the salt fish—The entrance to the city of the blessed—The voice of the guardian of Paradise—The king is refused admittance—He asks for a gift—The fragment of a human skull—The king's disappointment—The advice of the learned man—The skull is weighed against gold and silver—It over-balances the gold—The socket of a human eye—It is covered with earth, and the scales containing the gold go down.

ALEXANDER THE GREAT is also supposed to have reached the gates of Paradise on earth. Alexander the Great was pursuing his journey through dreary deserts and uncultivated lands, when at last he came to a small rivulet, gliding peacefully between shelving banks. The smooth undisturbed surface of the waters was the image of peace and contentment. In their silence the waters seemed to say: " This is the city of peace, the abode of tranquillity." Nature was hushed, all was still and not a sound was heard. The waters seemed to murmur into the ear of the traveller: " Come and dwell here in this abode of peace and happiness and tranquillity, of forgetfulness and bliss, far from the turmoil of the world. Leave the valley of misery, the world where sin and crime are practised, where bloodshed and massacres, slaughter, and rapine reign supreme, and where men are inspired only by greed, ambition, and envy." Alexander, however, remained untouched by the beauty of the spot, by the peace and tranquillity which reigned in this abode of happiness. He marched on. Soon, however, overcome by fatigue

126

and hunger, he stopped and seated himself on one of the banks of the river flowing through this veritable abode of the blessed. Provided with salt fish he ordered some of it to be dipped in the waters of the peaceful river so as to take off the briny taste. And when the Macedonian conqueror tasted the fish, he was surprised to find that it had a finer and much more agreeable taste than on other occasions. He marvelled greatly and concluded that the river must flow from some very rich and luxuriant country. Thereupon he decided to explore and march to the place where the river took its origin. Onward he marched, following the course of the river. At last he arrived before the gates of Paradise. The gates being locked, the Macedonian conqueror knocked impetuously, demanding immediate admittance. At length a voice was heard from within the garden, asking: " Who is there?" " It is I, Alexander of Macedon, the great conqueror, the Lord of the Earth, the mighty ruler. Open the gates." But the voice replied: " This is the abode of the just, the city of peace; none but the just, those who have conquered their passions, may enter the abode of the blessed. We make no exceptions here for the conquerors of the earth, for the rulers of men, for the men who have been swayed by the will to power. Nations may have paid homage to thee, but thy soul is not worthy to be admitted within the gates of the abode of the just. Go thy ways, endeavour to cure thy soul, and learn more wisdom than thou hast done hitherto." Thus spake the voice from within the city of the just, the abode of the blessed, and all the great conqueror's pleading and insistence were of no avail. At last he asked the guardian of the city of the blessed to give him some gift, so that he might show it to the world, and prove that he, the great conqueror, had ventured as far as the abode of the blessed and been there where no mortal had ever been before. The guardian smiled and handed him something with the words: " Take this, may it prove useful unto thee, and teach thee wisdom, more wisdom than thou hast acquired during thy ambitious expeditions and pursuits." Alexander took the gift and returned to his tent. On examining the gift he found, however, that the guardian of the gates of Paradise had given him nothing but the fragment of a human skull. He was greatly disappointed and in a fit of rage threw it to the ground.

" This," he exclaimed, " this fragment of a human skull is all that they found worthy to offer to a mighty king like me, to the renowned conqueror, the Lord of the Earth!"

A learned man, however, who was present, thus addressed the king: " Mighty ruler! thou mayest be wrong to despise this gift, for, however despicable it may appear in thine eyes, it possesses nevertheless great qualities; order, please, that this fragment of human skull be weighed on the scales against gold and silver."

The king followed the advice of the learned man, and a pair of scales were brought before him. Thereupon the fragment of the human skull was placed in one, and a quantity of gold in the other. But lo! to the king's great astonishment and to the astonishment of all present, the fragment of the human skull overbalanced the gold. More gold was added and again more gold, but the more gold was put in the one scale, the lower sunk the other scale which contained the fragment of the human skull.

" This is truly strange," exclaimed the king, marvelling greatly. " It is strange indeed that so small an object should outweigh so much gold. Is there anything that would outweigh this small portion of matter handed to me by the guardian of the city of the just?"

" Yes, there is," said the learned man. " This fragment, great king, is the socket of a human eye which, though small in compass, is unbounded in desire. The more gold it has, the more it craves for and is never satisfied. But once it is laid in the grave, there is an end to its lust and ambition. If thou wilt order that a little earth be brought and the fragment of the skull, the socket of the human eye, be covered with it, then thou wilt see that the scale containing it will ascend." The king acted upon the advice of the learned man, and the socket of the human eye was covered with earth. And lo! the gold went down immediately and the scale containing the fragment of the skull ascended.[1]

[1] *Tamid*, 32*b*; see also Israel Levi, *La légende d'Alexandre dans le Talmud et le Midrash*, Paris, 1883.

CHAPTER XII

Hell, or the City of the Shadows

Jewish legends about Hell—Greek influence—The seven degrees of torment—Rabbi Joshua ben Levi describes the torments in Hell—The angels Komam and Kinor—The seven torments in Mohammedan tradition —Gehennom, Ladha, Hothama, Saïr, Sacar, Gehin, and Haoviath—The story of Enoch (Edris) in Mohammedan legend—Edris and Azrael, the angel of death—Edris visits Paradise—Ridhwan, the gatekeeper of Paradise —Persian and Indian influence—The description of Paradise in the *Mahabharata*—The description in the *Ardai-Viraf*—Paradise in Teutonic legend—The city of Asgard—Valhalla—The three fairies: Urda, Verandi, and Skulda.

WHILST the Holy Scripture, i.e. the Old Testament, only speaks of temporal reward and punishment for virtue and vice, of untimely and ignominious death, of cutting off, excommunication, of barrenness of land, captivity and slavery, the Talmud and later Rabbinic literature show clearly the belief in Hell obtained among them to a great extent. There is but little doubt that the Jews received these opinions round which so many myths and legends have gathered from the Greeks, when they became conversant with the latter. There are supposed to be seven degrees in Hell, for it is called by seven different names, and when the wicked are sent to this place of torment, they pass through a great diversity of suffering. No one is to remain for ever in this place of torment, for after one year in purgatory he is taken out and brought to the gates of the Garden of Eden. But three sorts of persons are condemned to eternal suffering in Tofet, or Hell. They who deny the existence of God, who deny the Divine authority of the Law, and who reject the resurrection of the dead. After a certain time, however, some souls of the wicked are annihilated altogether. Different torments are the lot of the wicked who are sent to Hell. Cold, heat, and despair are their lot. Hell is traversed by rivers of fire and of ice, and it is from the fire of Hell that the Creator took afterwards the fire which burnt down Sodom and the water with which the earth was overflowed at the deluge.

Rabbi Joshua, the son of Levi, is again the principal recorder of Hell. After visiting Paradise, he asked permission to look into Hell, but this permission was denied unto him, because the righteous are not allowed to behold Hell. He thereupon sent to the angel who is named Komam so that he might describe Hell unto him. But, as this angel could not go with him, he went afterwards with the angel named Kinor or Kipod who accompanied him to the gates of Hell which were open. He saw compartments ten miles in length and five in width, and they were full of mountains of fire and consuming the sinners. And in one compartment he saw ten nations from the heathens, and Absalom, the son of David, presides over them, and they say unto Absalom: " Our sin is because we have not accepted the Law, but what is thy sin and why art thou punished, seeing that thou and thy parents accepted the Law." And Absalom replied: " I am punished because I did not hearken to the commandments of my father." And after seeing this, the Rabbi returned to Paradise where he wrote a description of both Paradise and Hell and sent it to Rabbi Gamaliel, telling him what he had seen in Paradise and in Hell, and this is what he wrote about Hell: " I saw at the gates of Gehennom persons hung up by their noses, others by their hands. Some there were who were hung up by their tongues, whilst others were hung up by their eyelids or feet. I saw men devoured by worms but never dying, whilst at other places I saw some whose inner parts were burnt up

by coals of fire. There were some whose food was dust
which broke their teeth (because upon earth they had lived
on stolen goods); whilst others there were who were cast from
fire into ice and from ice into fire. And I saw angels appointed
to chastise each sin, and the three deadly sins are: adultery,
insulting a fellowman in public, and abusing the name of God.
And the faces of the inhabitants of Hell are black. But in the
midst of their sufferings, some of the Jewish sinners declared
that God, the Lord of the Universe, was a just God, and they
were forgiven and rescued after twelve months." [1]

Long before Dante visited the Inferno, the topic occupied
the mind of mythographers. The descriptions in Jewish myths
have their analogies in the traditions of other nations.

Just as Jewish myths and legends acknowledge seven
degrees of torments in Hell (and seven houses), so the Moslems,
too, speak of seven gates. These are: *Gehennom*, the first
degree of torment for Moslems; *Ladha*, for Christians; *Hothama*, for Jews; *Saïr*, for Sabians; *Sacar*, for Magians, or
Guebres; *Gehin*, for idolaters and pagans; *Haoviath*, the
seventh and deepest part of the abyss, is reserved for hypocrites, who, disguising their religion, conceal one in their hearts
different from the one they confess.

As for Paradise, a parallel to the story of Rabbi Joshua
ben Levi is also found in Mohammedan legend. There it is
told about Enoch who dwells in Paradise, whither he came
during his lifetime. He, too, in company of the angel of
death visited Paradise and Hell, and witnessed the bliss of
the righteous and the torments of the wicked. He is called
Edris by the Arabs, and is said to have been born in Hindostan,
and to have lived in Yemen, where he was an accomplished
tailor, author, and prophet. He knew how to sew, but also
wrote many books and prophesied in the name of Allah.

---

[1] Jellinek, *Beth-Hamidrash*, Vol. II, pp. 50–51; Vol. V, pp. 43–45; Gaster, *Journal of
Royal Asiatic Society*, 1893, pp. 572–620; *Jewish Quarterly Review*. VII, 596.

Men, in the days of Enoch-Edris, worshipped fire and many idols, and God sent Enoch to turn them from their wicked ways, and to induce them to abandon the worship of idols, but they would not listen unto him. There were indeed very few men in the days of Noah who worshipped the true and living God. Jared, the father of Enoch, had already fought the prince of evil, that is Iblis, captured him and led him about in chains. Now Enoch, seeing that men would not listen to him, began by first instructing them in various crafts and handiworks. He taught them the arts of tailoring and shoemaking; he showed them how to cut skins, sew them together and make garments and shoes, and men, being grateful to Enoch for this blessing and for the knowledge he had given them, were ready to listen to his books and to his words of wisdom. He thereupon read to them the books of Adam and his own books, and endeavoured to make them abandon idolatry and bring them back to the worship of the true and living, the only God. And when Enoch had passed many years in prayer, the angel of death appeared unto him, and thus he spake: " I am the angel of death and would fain be thy friend, Enoch, son of Jared. Thou mayest make a request unto me which I will for a certainty grant at once." " Take then my soul," said Enoch. " Thy time," replied the angel, " hath not yet come and I cannot take thy soul. It is not for this purpose that I have come to visit thee." " Take it away, then," said Enoch, " for a little while and restore it to me." " I cannot do this either," said Azrael, the angel of death, " without the consent of Allah." He thereupon presented Enoch's request to Allah, and having obtained the latter's permission took away for a short time the soul of Enoch which the Eternal at once restored to him. From that time the angel of death, having become a friend of Enoch, often came to visit him. One day, Enoch said again to the angel of death: " I have another request to make to thee." " If I can grant

it," said Azrael, " I am quite ready to do it." " I would visit
Hell," said Enoch, "for the sensations of death I already
know, having undergone it once, as thou dost well remember."
" I cannot grant thy request," replied the angel of death,
" without the special permission of the Eternal." But Allah
having granted the request of Enoch, the latter was borne
upon the wings of Azrael, who showed him Hell and its seven
stages. Enoch saw the torments inflicted upon sinners, and
was greatly impressed. After a while, he again requested
Azrael to show him Paradise. Once more Azrael had to obtain
the permission of Allah before granting Enoch's request.
The Almighty having replied that it should be even as his
faithful servant Enoch had desired, Azrael bore his friend
to the gates of Paradise. Here, however, Ridhwan, the gatekeeper refused to grant them admittance. " No man," said
he, " can enter Paradise, without having tasted death. Thou
canst therefore not enter Paradise as yet, Enoch, son of Jared."
Thus spake Ridhwan, the gatekeeper of Paradise. But Enoch
replied: " I have already tasted death, O Ridhwan; my soul
had left my body, but God hath resuscitated me." Ridhwan,
however, was obstinate, and refused to do what Enoch asked
him, without a higher authority. An order, thereupon, arrived
from Allah, bidding the gatekeeper to admit Enoch into Paradise. " Go in," said Ridhwan, " cast a glance upon Paradise,
but hurry back, for thou mayest not dwell there before the
Resurrection." Enoch promised to do so. He entered Paradise, viewed it, and speedily came out again. At the moment
of passing the threshold he said to Ridhwan: " I have left something in there, O Ridhwan, allow me to turn back and fetch it."

Ridhwan, however, refused to grant this request of Enoch,
and as the latter insisted, they began to quarrel. Enoch pretended that he was a prophet, and that Allah had promised
him Paradise. He had already tasted death and seen Hell,
and now that the gates of Paradise had been open to him

and that he had entered the place, he refused to leave it. The dispute between Enoch and Ridhwan was long, and was only put an end to by Allah who ordered the gatekeeper to reopen the gate of Paradise and readmit Enoch who still dwells there.[1]

The descriptions of Paradise and Hell in Jewish myth, which in a later age becomes mysticism, are also due to Persian and Indian influences. In the *Mahabharata* we find the following description of the heavens of Indra, Yama, and Varuna. These heavens recall the " Islands of the Blest " of Greece and the Celtic otherworld, where eternal summer reigns. They are also reminiscent of the Teutonic Valhalla.[2]

Narada spoke. " The celestial assembly-room of Shakra is full of lustre. It is full one hundred and fifty *yojanas* in length, and an hundred *yojanas* in breadth, and five *yojanas* in height. Dispelling weakness of age, grief, fatigue, and fear; auspicious and bestowing good fortune, furnished with rooms and seats, and adorned with celestial trees, it is delightful in the extreme. On an excellent seat there sitteth the lord of celestials, with his wife Shachi and with beauty and affluence embodied. Assuming a form incapable of description for its vagueness, with a crown on his head and bright bracelets on the upper arms, attired in robes of pure white, and decked in floral wreaths of many hues, here he sitteth with beauty, fame, and glory by his side. He is waited upon by the marutas, each leading the life of a householder in the bosom of his family. And the celestial Rishis, and the marutas of brilliant complexion and adorned in golden garlands, all wait upon the illustrious chief of the immortals, and the celestial Rishis also, all of pure souls, with sins completely washed off, and resplendent as the fire, and possessed of energy, and without sorrow of any kind, and freed from the fever of anxiety, also wait upon and worship Indra."

[1] *Tabari, loc. cit.,* I, Ch. 35.   [2] See Mackenzie, *Indian Myth and Legend,* p. 59.

The heaven of Yama is described as follows: Narada spoke: " The assembly-house of Yama is bright as burnished gold, and covers an area of much more than an hundred *yojanas*. Possessed of the splendour of the sun it yieldeth everything that one may desire. Neither very cool nor very hot, it delighteth the heart. There is neither grief nor weakness of age, neither hunger nor thirst. Every object of desire, celestial or human, is to be found in that mansion. And all kinds of enjoyable articles, as also of sweet, juicy, agreeable and delicious edibles are there in profusion, and are licked, sucked, and drunk. Of the most delicious fragrance are the floral wreaths in that mansion, and the trees that stand around it yield fruits that are desired of them. And there are both cold and hot waters and these are sweet and agreeable. And royal sages of great sanctity and Brahmana sages of great purity are in this mansion where they cheerfully wait upon and worship Yama, the son of Vivaswat.

The celestial Sabha of Varuna is also described by Narada who was capable of going into every world at will and at home in the celestial regions.

Said Narada: " The wells and arches of the celestial Sabha of Varuna are all of pure white. It is surrounded on all sides by many celestial trees made of gems and jewels, and yielding excellent fruit and flowers. And many plants with their weight and blossoms, blue and yellow and black and darkish, and white and red that stand there, form excellent bowers around. And within these bowers hundreds of thousands of birds of divers species, beautiful and variegated, always pour forth their melodies. And there are many rooms in the assembly-house of Varuna and many seats. Varuna, decked with jewels and golden ornaments and flowers, is throned there with his queen. The Nagas, or hooded snakes with human heads and arms, and the Daityas and Ianavas (the giants and demons) who have been rewarded with immortality, are there.

And so are the holy spirits of rivers and oceans, of lakes and springs, and the personified forms of the points of the heavens." [1]

And in the Persian book, entitled *Ardai-Viraf* (translated by Haugh and West), we read of the righteous man being allowed to glance at Heaven and Hell.

Heaven and Hell have three compartments, according to the three grades of good or bad thoughts, words, and actions. The uppermost heaven is full of light for the good God Ahuramazda; whilst there is also a nethermost and darkest hell for the bad spirit Ahriman and all his associate spirits. The three divisions of heaven are called the Sun, the Moon, and the Stars, and the dwelling place of Ahuramazda is above that of the Sun. We read also of the rivers of oil and wine which flow for the righteous, and of the terrible punishments meted out to the wicked. The lake of Tears is found in the Persian Inferno, and the lake Acheron, that great river of Hades which we meet in Greek mythology, is to be met with in the Sibyllines.[2] Another analogy to the Jewish myths about Paradise and Hell may also be found in Teutonic myth.

There exists in Heaven, near the city of Asgard, a vast room, called the Valhalla, where the courageous are received after their death. This room has 504 gates (or doors) through each of which eight dead warriors leave to engage in combat. These valiant dead shadows fight and then return to partake of a meal together. They drink of the milk of the goat Heidruma, which devours the leaves of the tree Loerada. This milk is in reality hydromel, and a jug is filled every day which the dead heroes drink and get drunk. They eat of the flesh of a marvellous boar which is cooked and eaten every morning, but is whole again in the evening to serve for the repast of the next day. There is also in Heaven the tree of Igdrasil, which

[1] *Mahabharata*, Sabha-Parva, Sections VII–X (Roy's Translation). See also D. A. Mackenzie, *Indian Myth and Legend*, pp. 57–59.
[2] Book I, 302; II, 341. See also *Jewish Quarterly Review*, Vol. VII, p. 605.

spreads over the whole world and has three roots; one in Heaven, one on earth, and one in Hell where it is gnawed by the infernal serpent. The tree is watered by three fairies: Urda, Verandi, and Skulda (past, present, and future). A beautiful squirrel constantly ascends and descends the tree to see what the serpent in Hell is doing, and then he tells it to the eagle of Heaven. Two black ravens daily report unto Odin all that they have seen in the world. After the death of Ymer the gods built Midgard, where later on they wish to erect a citadel against the giants.[1]

[1] Collin de Plancy, *Légendes de l'Ancien Testament*, 1861.

CHAPTER XIII

The Creation of our First Parents

The creation of man—The protest of the angels—Adam gives names to all the beasts—The dust from which Adam was created—Red, black, white, and yellow clay—The creation of man in Moslem legend—The protest of the earth—The angel Azrael brings seven handfuls of dust—The creation of man takes place slowly—Adam's stature—His head reaches the sky—God reduces him by a thousand cubits—The angels are ready to worship Adam—The impression produced upon the beasts of the earth—They come to worship Adam—Adam praises his Maker—He composes *Ps.* 104—The stature of Adam in Moslem legend—The angels, except Iblis, all admire the lifeless body of Adam—The breath of life enters the body of first man—The soul refuses to enter the body of Adam—It is enticed by the music of Gabriel—The angels do homage to Adam—Iblis alone refuses—The story of Adam in Christian works—*The Cave of Treasures*—The arrogance of the chief of the lower order of celestials—Satana, Sheda, and Daiwa—The angel Rasiel gives a book to Adam—The wisdom contained in the book—Adam knows all handicrafts—He makes a present of seventy years to David—The creation of Eve—Earth's protest—Why Eve was created from Adam's rib—The wedding of Adam and Eve—The banquet in Eden—Man created double, male and female—The story met with in the *Bundehesh*—Mashya and Mashyana—The story of primordial androgyns in the *Banquet* of Plato—The creation of Eve in Moslem legend—Adam's dream—He asks permission to take Hava as his wife.

WHEN the Creator wished to make man he consulted with the angels beforehand, and said unto them: " We will make a man in our image." The angels asked: " What is man that thou shouldst remember him, and what is his purpose?" " He will do justice," said the Lord. And the ministering angels were divided into groups. Some said: " Let man not be created." But others said: " Let him be created." Forgiveness said: " Let him be created, for he will be generous and benevolent." Truth said: " Let him not be created, for he will be a liar." Justice said: " Let him be created, for he will

139

bring justice into the world," whilst Peace objected and said:
" Let him not be created, for he will constantly wage wars."
The Creator hurled Truth from Heaven to earth, and in spite
of the protests of the ministering angels man was created.[1]
" His knowledge," said the Creator, " will excel yours, and
to-morrow you will see his wisdom." The Creator then gathered
all kinds of beasts before the ministering angels, the wild and
the tame beasts, as well as the birds, and the fowls of the
air, and asked the ministering angels to name them, but they
could not. " Now you will see the wisdom of man," spake
the Creator. " I will ask him and he will tell their names."
All the beasts and fowls of the air were then led before man,
and when asked he at once replied: " This is an ox, the other
an ass, yonder a horse or a camel." " And what is your own
name?" " I," replied man, " should be called Adam because
I have been created from *adamah*, or earth." [2]

The dust from which man was made was gathered from
various parts, for the whole earth is man's home, and earth
is the mother of man. The dust of Babylon, the earth of the
country of Israel, and the clay of other countries were all
employed to fashion the head, body, and limbs of man.[3] The
Creator, we read in the *Pirke de Rabbi Eliezer*,[4] commanded
His ministering angels to bring Him dust from all corners
of the earth, red, black, white, and yellow, out of which He
intended to fashion man, for the whole earth and all that
moves and lives upon it and its entrails will be subject to
man. The angel whose mission it was to bring the dust for
the creation of man took a handful from the place where the
Temple was once to stand, and some from other parts of the
world, and this dust the Creator mixed with drops from all
the waters of the world and fashioned man.[5]

---

[1] *Genesis Rabba*, 8.

[2] *Genesis Rabba*, 17; *Midrash Tehillim, Ps.* 8; see Geiger, *Was hat Mohammed aus dem Judentum genommen*, p. 99–100.   [3] *Sanhedrin*, 38b.

[4] *Pirke de Rabbi Eliezer*, Ch. 11 and 20.

[5] Gaster, *The Chronicles of Jerahmeel*, 6, 7; see also *Targum Jerushalmi, Genesis*, 2, 7.

First man was thus created from red, black, white, and yellow, or green clay. God fashioned the blood from the red dust, the entrails from the black, the bones from the white, and the body from the yellow dust. And the Creator thought: " A man might come from the east to the west, or from the west to the east, and his destiny would be to depart from the world. But the earth in that place shall not say: ' Return to the place whence thou wast created, I refuse to receive thee, for the dust of thy body was never taken from me.' But now, wherever man will go, to any place upon earth, and his hour will come to depart from the world, he will find the dust whence he was created and to which he will return.[1]

According to Moslem legend, God prepared, by rains of long continuance, the slime out of which He intended to fashion Adam. He then sent the angel Gabriel and commanded him to take a handful of earth from each of its seven layers. Gabriel obeyed and declared to the earth that he had received from the Creator the order to extract out of her entrails the substance out of which man was to be formed, man who would be monarch and ruler over her.[2] Amazed at such a proposition, the earth desired Gabriel to represent to All-Father her fears. One day, she maintained, the creature which was to be formed out of her bosom would disobey the commands of God, rebel against Him, and draw down upon herself the curse of the Creator. The angel Gabriel withdrew and reported to God earth's fears and remonstrances. God, having nevertheless resolved to execute His design, dispatched the angel Michael with the same commission, but Michael, too, was moved by earth's remonstrances, and returned empty-handed, reporting earth's excuses and her absolute refusal to contribute to the formation of man.

The Creator of the Universe then sent the angel Azrael

---

[1] *Pirke de Rabbi Eliezer*, Ch. 11.

[2] Abulfeda, *Historia Ante-Islamica*, p. 13; Weil, *Biblische Legenden der Muselmänner*, 1845, pp. 12–16.

to fetch a little mud. Once more the earth swore an oath that neither clay nor dust nor stone shall he take from her. But Azrael did not respect her oath and did not retire: " I must obey the command of God," said he, and violently tore out seven handfuls of dust out of seven different beds of earth. He carried off by force out of the mass belonging to earth the matter required for the formation of man. These seven handfuls, the angel Azrael carried away to a place in Arabia which is situated between Mecca and Taief. As a reward for his action, Azrael received the commission to separate the souls of men from their bodies, for which reason he is now called the angel of death.[1]

The creation of man took place slowly and by degrees.[2] At the first hour of the day the Creator collected the dust out of which he designed to compose the body of first man, and He so disposed it as to receive the form which he intended to give it. At the second hour Adam, or first man, stood upon his feet, at the third hour he gave names to the animals, the seventh hour was employed in the marriage of Adam and Eve, and at the tenth hour Adam sinned.[3] The form and stature of man were immense. He was so tall that his head reached to the sky. And when the ministering angels saw man and how tall he was they trembled and fled before him. " Lord of the world," they cried, " there seem to be two sovereigns, one in Heaven and one upon earth." [4] Then the Creator placed His hand upon the head of Adam and reduced him by a thousand cubits.[5]

Adam's body was beautiful and resplendent, and his spirit was unlike the spirit of all men who came after him. For all the souls and spirits and intelligences created before Adam and dwelling in Heaven, 600,000 in number, were

---

[1] Herbelot, *Bibl. Orientale, s.v. Adam.*
[2] *Pirke de Rabbi Eliezer,* Ch. 11. See also L. Ginzberg, *Die Haggada bei den Kirchenvätern,* p. 50; Kohut, *Z.D.M.G.,* XXV, pp. 59-94.
[3] *Midrash Tehillim, Ps.* 92; *Sanhedrin,* p. 38; *Abot de Rabbi Nathan,* Ch. 1.
[4] *Yalkut Shimeoni,* I, § 120.   [5] *Hagigah,* 12a; *Sanhedrin,* 38b.

THE CREATOR PLACES HIS HAND UPON THE HEAD OF ADAM

Facing page 142, Vol. I

all connected with the soul of Adam.[1] The aspect of man and his splendour brought awe and wonder into the hearts of all beings, celestial and terrestrial. When the ministering angels saw the splendour of man, made in the image of the All-Father, they quaked and were amazed. The sun, seeing the size and splendour of Adam, was filled with dismay; and the angels were frightened and prayed to God to remove the mighty being He had made. Some of the angels, however, were ready to worship Adam, and some even bowed before him whose face was brighter than the brightness of the sun, and said three times: " Holy." Thereupon God cast a deep sleep on man, and the ministering angels knew that he was only mortal and helpless, and they no longer feared him.[2]

In other sources we read that the angels, seeing Adam so mighty and great, and shining brighter than the sun, were all ready to worship him. Whereupon the Creator, in order to prove to them the weakness and helplessness of man, cast a deep sleep upon Adam, and during his sleep reduced him to smaller proportions. Great pieces of his flesh were cut off, and when Adam awoke and saw these pieces of flesh scattered round him, like the shavings in a carpenter's shop, he wailed and exclaimed: " O Lord of the Universe, how hast Thou robbed me." But God answered: " Take these pieces of thy flesh and carry them into all lands, and wherever thou wilt drop them and lay them in the earth, that land will I give to thy posterity."[3]

Profound was the impression produced by the aspect of Adam upon the beasts of the earth and the fowls of the air. They all came and fell down before him and desired to worship him. But Adam said to the beasts of the earth and to the fowls of the air: " Why have ye come to worship me who am only a creature of clay, fashioned by the Creator

---

[1] Isaac Luria, *Sepher Hagilgulim*, fol.1c; *Emek hamelekh*, fol. 171c.
[2] *Genesis Rabba*, 8; see *Midrash Tanchuma*, section *Pekkude*.
[3] *Sepher Chassidim*. See Eisenmenger, *Entdecktes Judentum*, Vol. I, p. 369.

of the Universe? Come ye and let us all clothe ourselves with power and glory, and let us praise the Lord and let us acknowledge Him as King over us, for He has created us. A people chooses a king, but a king does not appoint himself arbitrarily as monarch." Thus spoke Adam, and he chose God as King of all the world and as Ruler of the Universe. And all the beasts, fowls, and fishes listened to his word and did likewise.[1]

Thus the first act of Adam was to praise his Master and to acknowledge his Maker as King of the world. And when he witnessed the splendour of the world and all the creatures called into existence before him, he praised the Lord and said: " How wonderful are Thy works, O God."

The *Pirke de Rabbi Eliezer* [2] relates this incident as follows: Adam stood and gazed upwards to Heaven and downwards upon earth, and he beheld all the creatures which God had created. Wondering in his heart, he at once began to praise the Lord, to sing a hymn and to glorify the name of the Creator. He is said to have composed *Psalm* 104, which is a Psalm of creation. Thereupon all the creatures, seeing him adorned with the Divine image, came to prostrate themselves before him. But Adam said unto them: " Do not prostrate yourselves before me, but let us rather acclaim Him as our King." Thereupon he opened his mouth and acclaimed the Creator, and all the creatures answered after him and said: " The Lord reigneth and is apparelled in Majesty." [3]

Moslem tradition also knows of these legends relating to the creation of Adam. Adam's body, still lifeless, was stretched out and no one knew what he was. He was the object of the amazement and admiration of the ministering angels who passed the gates of Paradise where the lifeless body of man had been placed by the Creator, and where it remained for forty years.

---

[1] Eisenmenger, *loc. cit.*, Vol. I, p. 368.   [2] *Pirke de Rabbi Eliezer*, Ch. 11.
[3] *Ps.* 93, 1. Cf. *Rosh-ha-Shanah*, 31a.

But Iblis, who was jealous of man's beautiful face and figure and his intelligent and lovely countenance, said unto the angels: " How can you admire such a creature made of clay? Only weakness and frailty are the lot of such a creature." All the celestial inmates, however, with the exception of Iblis, admired in solemn silence the lifeless body of first man and praised the Creator. For man was so big that when he stood up his head reached to the first of the seven heavens.[1] Adam remained stretched out for another 120 years, when Allah gave him a soul and the breath of life. Before the breath of life had completely entered Adam's body, he tried to rise, but fell down, and when it entered his head he began to sneeze, and said: " Praise be unto Allah, the Lord of the worlds." [2]

Adam's soul had been created one thousand years before Adam, and it persistently refused to leave the heavenly regions and enter the body of man. Only through the music played by the angel Gabriel the soul, which had descended to listen, was enticed in a moment of ecstasy to enter the body of man. And because her union with the body of man was an involuntary one, it was decreed that she should leave it only reluctantly.[3] When Adam had received the breath of life blown into his nostrils by the Creator, God called all the creatures and living things, and taught him the names of all the beasts and fowls and insects and even the names of the fishes in the sea, and told him their natures and the purpose of their existence. Then the Father of All called the ministering angels and commanded them to bow before man, whom He had created in His image, for man was the most perfect of created beings. Israfil, one of the ministering angels, was the first to obey and to do the bidding of the Creator, and therefore he received as a reward the custody of the Book of Fate. All the other ministering angels followed the example of Israfil and bowed before man.

[1] Weil, *Biblische Legenden der Muselmänner*, p. 13.   [2] *Chronique de Tabari*, I, Ch. 22.
[3] See Collin de Plancy, *Légendes de l'Ancien Testament*, Paris, 1861, p. 55.

Iblis alone refused to do the bidding of his Maker. Arrogantly he spoke: " How can I, an angel made of fire, bow before a man, a creature fashioned of clay?" He was cast out from among the angels, and the gates of Paradise were forbidden unto him.[1]

When Iblis had been expelled, the angels stood before man in ten thousand ranks, and man spoke unto them and praised the omnipotence of the Creator and the wonders of His creation. And the angels were greatly amazed and saw that his knowledge by far excelled theirs, for he could name the beasts in seventy languages and knew all their names.[2]

The Syriac authors, too, know of these legends and refer to them. Thus in the work entitled *The Cave of Treasures*, the author of which belonged to the school of St. Ephrem, in the sixth century A.D., the creation of first man is related as follows: The ministering angels witnessed and saw how the Creator of All took a grain of dust from the entire earth, and a drop of water from the immensity of waters, and particles from the elements of air and fire, and fashioned man. And all the ministering angels saw how these four elements were combined and how out of them man was made. The Creator then took these four elements, so that all that is in the world should be subject to man; all the beings and natures that are in earth, water, air, and fire. When the ministering angels saw the glory of first man, and the beauty of his countenance and the brightness of his eyes, which was like the brightness of the sun, and the splendour of his body, which was like crystal, they were amazed and greatly moved. And all the wild and tame beasts, and the fowls of the air gathered before man and he gave them their names; they bowed their heads, worshipped man and served him. The ministering angels, too, bent their knees and worshipped man. And when the chief of the lower order of celestial beings saw what greatness

[1] Koran, *Sura*, 33, 70-85.   [2] Koran, *Sura*, 2, 29-36. See also Weil, *loc. cit.*, pp. 15-16.

had been given unto man, he was very jealous of him and refused
to bend his knee and to worship man. Turning to his hosts
he thus spake: " Do not worship man, and praise him not as
the other angels do. It is for him to worship me who am
fire and spirit, and not for me to bow before a creature of
dust." Disobedient and refusing to listen to the command of
the All-Father, the rebel was cast out of Heaven, he and his
hosts, in the second hour of the sixth day. He was divested
of his garments of glory and was named *Satana*, because
he had turned from God, and *Sheda*, because he had been
thrown down, and *Daiwa*, because he had lost his angelic
garment of glory. Then man was raised and brought into
Paradise in a fiery chariot, and angels sang before him, and
Seraphs sanctified him, and Cherubim blessed him.[1]

By means of the light created on the first day, man could
see from one end of the world to the other. But this light,
which in later days was only vouchsafed to the just and the
righteous, was hidden from the sinful.[2]

This Jewish legend finds a parallel in Moslem myths and
legends. As soon as the spirit which the Creator blew into
Adam reached his eyes, he opened them, and when it reached
his ears, he heard the celestial music and the song of the angels.
When at last the spirit of life reached the feet of man, he stood
up, but the light from the throne of the Creator, shining
directly upon man, blinded him and compelled him to shut
his eyes, for they could not bear the great light. Covering
his eyes with one hand and pointing to the throne with the
other, Adam asked: " What light is this?" And the Creator
made reply: " This is the light of a prophet who will spring
from thee and come into the world in later ages. I swear by
My splendour that the world has been created for him alone,
Ahmed, the much praised, is his name in Heaven, and by

---

[1] *The Cave of Treasures*, Ed. C. Bezold, 1888, pp. 3–4. See also M. Grünbaum, *Neue
Beiträge zur semitischen Sagenkunde*, 1893, pp. 57–58.
[2] *Hagigah*, 12a; *Yalkut Rubeni*, section *Ki-Tissa*.

the name of Mohammed he will once be known upon earth." [1]

Jewish legend further relates that, as soon as first man was created, the angel Rasiel handed him, at the command of the Creator, a book containing all divine and human wisdom. From this book Adam gathered knowledge; he learned the order of the world and of the planets, and the cause of their motion. This book contained 72 kinds of wisdom in 670 writings, and first man was thus enabled to receive 1500 keys to all the mysterious knowledge which was not given to all the inhabitants of Heaven. When the angels and spirits saw that first man was in possession of the keys to knowledge, which the Father of All had handed to him, they all gathered round, eager to listen and to be instructed. But Hadarniel, one of the ministering angels, came and warned first man. And thus he spake: " O man, the splendour of the Lord was hidden; it was not given to the ministering angels to know the mysteries but only to thee." Adam then took the book of wisdom and kept it hidden. He studied it daily and learned all the mysteries which the ministering angels were ignorant of. But when the day came on which he sinned, the book flew from him, and he wept bitterly. Raphael, however, brought the book back to Adam, and he studied it daily. On his death he left it to his son Seth. It was then handed from generation to generation, until it came into the hands of Enoch.[2] Adam also knew all handicrafts and had much knowledge.[3] He saw all his generations that would spring from him, and the history of man until the end of days.[4] He saw the generations of Israel and their rulers and preachers and kings. When David came before him, he saw that he was dead. Adam then asked: " O Lord! who is this man who has no life in him?" And the Master of the world replied:

[1] Weil, *loc. cit.*, p. 14.

[2] See Sepher Rasiel, *Zohar Genesis*. See also Jellinek. *Beth-Hamidrash*, Vol. III, pp. 155–160.   [3] *Genesis Rabba*, 24.

[4] *Sanhedrin*, 38b; *Abodah Zarah*, 5a; *Abot de Rabbi Nathan*, Ch. 31; *Exodus Rabba*, 40; *Midrash Tehillim*, Ps. 139.

" This is King David." When Adam saw that David was so created, he made him a present of seventy years to be taken off from his own life.[1]

Adam thereupon drew up a legal document of transfer, and sealed it with his own seal, and God and the angel Metatron signed the deed likewise. And thus Adam lived 930 years instead of one thousand.[2]

This legend is one of those taken over by Mohammed from Jewish lore. We are told by Tabari and Ibn el-Atir that God showed unto Adam all generations. He acquainted him with the names and fate of all his posterity. And when Adam learned that only thirty years had been allotted to David, he said: " How many years are allotted to me?" " One thousand," said God. " Then I make a present to David of seventy years," said Adam. A formal document of resignation was drawn up on parchment, and was signed by Adam and countersigned by Michael and Gabriel as witnesses.[3]

THE CREATION OF EVE

Now Adam walked about in the Garden of Eden at his leisure and like one of the ministering angels. But the Maker of the Universe said unto Himself: " It is not good for man to be alone. For he is alone in his world, just as I am alone in my world. And just as I have no companion, Adam has no companion, and the creatures, seeing that he does not propagate, will say to-morrow: ' Adam is surely our Creator, for there is no propagation in his life.' I will, therefore, make a helpmate for Adam." [4] But when the earth heard this decision of the Lord of the Universe, the earth quaked and shook and trembled, and thus it cried before the Creator: " Lord of the Universe! Sovereign of all the worlds! How

---

[1] *Book of Jubilees*, 4, 30; *Yalkut*, § 41; see also Friedlaender's edition of *Pirke de Rabbi Eliezer*, p. 128, Note 11.
[2] See Hugo Winckler, *Ex Oriente Lux*, p. 183 (15); Bin Gorion, *Die Sagen der Juden*, Vol. I, p. 253.   [3] Weil, *loc. cit.*, pp. 29–38.
[4] *Pirke de Rabbi Eliezer*, Ch. 12; Gaster, *The Chronicles of Jerahmeel*, VI, 13–15.

shall I be able to provide for the whole of humanity and feed all the multitudes that will issue from Adam? I have no power to feed all the multitudes!" Thus complained the earth. But the Lord of the Universe silenced the earth and replied:

" I and thou will feed together the multitudes that will issue from Adam and his wife." And God made a covenant with the earth, according to which the Creator of the Universe assists earth and waters it so that it yields fruit and thus provides food for all the creatures during the day. God also created the sleep of life, so that when man lies down and sleeps, he is strengthened, sustained, healed, and refreshed.[1]

Thereupon God created a helpmate for Adam. But He had pity upon man and, in order that he should not feel any pain, He caused a deep sleep to fall upon Adam, and during that deep slumber He took the thirteenth rib of man and flesh from his heart, fashioned woman and placed her before him.[2] Eve, however, was not created merely for the purpose of continuing the human species, for she enjoys a higher moral dignity. He, therefore, who remains single is without happiness, joy or blessing, peace and life. He is not called a man, and is like unto one who had committed murder.[3]

And when Adam awoke and saw Eve before him, his wonder and delight knew no bounds. He approached her and kissed her, and thus he spoke: " Blessed art thou before the Eternal. It is right and proper that thou shouldst be called Ishah (woman) for thou hast been taken from man (Ish)."

Jewish legend further relates that Eve was not created from the head of Adam, lest she should be vain; nor from his eyes, lest she should be wanton; nor from his mouth, lest she should be given to gossiping; nor from his ears, lest she should be an eavesdropper; nor from his hands, lest she

---

[1] *Pirke de Rabbi Eliezer*, Ch. 12; Gaster, *The Chronicles of Jerahmeel*, VI, 13–15.
[2] *Pirke de Rabbi Eliezer*, Ch. 12; *Targum Jerushalmi*, Genesis, 2, 21. See also *Lekach Tob*, Genesis, 2, 21. [3] *Jebamoth*, 63b; *Genesis Rabba*, 17.

should be meddlesome; nor from his feet, lest she should
be a gadabout; nor from his heart, lest she should be jealous.
She was drawn from man's rib, which is a hidden part, so
that she might be modest and retiring. And yet, notwithstanding all the precautions taken by the Creator, woman
has all the faults God wished to guard her against.[1]

Thereupon the Lord made ten wedding canopies for
Adam in the Garden of Eden, all of which were out of gold,
and pearls and precious stones. This was done in order to
bestow special honour upon our first parents. And angels
came into the Garden and played heavenly music. Then the
Holy One said unto His hosts and ministering angels: " Come
let us descend and do honour and render a loving service to
the first man, who hath been created in My image, and to
his helpmate, for it is only through loving kindness and the
service of loving kindness that the world will exist. It is love
and not burnt offerings that I will require of man." [2] And
the ministering angels descended into the Garden of Eden,
and walked before the bridal pair, the first man and his wife,
and guarded the wedding canopies, and the Holy One, blessed
be His name, blessed Adam and his helpmate.[3]

The Cabbalists give in glowing terms an imaginative
description of the marriage ceremony of Adam and Eve, and
of the banquet in Eden. Accompanied by myriads of ministering angels, who sang and played, Eve was brought to Adam.
The entire host of Heaven descended into the Garden of Eden.
Some of the ministering angels played upon harps, cymbals
and cithers, whilst the sun and the moon danced in honour
of Adam and Eve.[4] Here, we evidently see Babylonian astral
influences which the imagination of the Jews has made use
of in its own way.

[1] *Genesis Rabba*, 18.
[2] *Pirke de Rabbi Eliezer*, Ch. 12; Gaster, *The Chronicles of Jerahmeel*, XII. 1–2; *Menorath ha-Maor*, § 205.
[3] *Pirke de Rabbi Eliezer*, ibid.; *Midrash Tanchuma*, ed. Buber, I, 58b; cf. *Abot de Rabbi Nathan*, Ch. 1. [4] *Othioth de Rabbi Akiba*, Venice, 1546, fol. 6.

In some Jewish legends it is maintained that first man was created double with a woman at his back, and that God cut them apart. Adam was thus originally a male on the right side and a female on the left, but subsequently the Creator removed one half of him to make Eve.[1] The complete man thus consists of both sexes.

The idea that the first human pair had originally formed a single androgynous being with two faces, separated later into two personalities by the Creator, is met with in the myths and legends of other nations. It is found among the Indians, among the Greeks, and the Persians. Thus in the *Bundehesh*, a book written in the Pehlevi tongue and containing the exposition of a complete cosmogony, we read the following account of the creation of Mashya and Mashyana, the first man and the first woman.

His first act of creation Ahuramazda completed by producing simultaneously Gayômaretan or Gayômard, the typical man and the typical bull, two creatures of perfect purity. They lived 3000 years upon earth in a state of happiness, fearing no evil. But the time came when Angrômainyus, the evil principle, made his power felt in the world. Having struck the typical bull dead, useful plants and domestic animals sprung from his body. Thirty years later Gayômaretan, too, perished, struck by Angrômainyus. But at the end of forty years the seed of Gayômaretan, the typical man, shed upon the ground at the time of his death, germinated and brought forth a plant. A plant of reivas came forth from the ground and grew up. And in the centre of this plant a stalk rose up which had the form of a man and of a woman joined together at the back. They were divided by Ahuramazda, who endowed them with motion and activity. He placed within them an intelligent soul and bade them observe the law and be humble of heart, pure in thought, pure in speech, and pure in action.

---

[1] *Berachoth*, 61a; *Erubin*, 18a; see also *Genesis Rabba*, 7.

They were called Mashya and Mashyana, the human pair from whom all human beings are descended.[1]

Brahma, we read in Indian myth, engaged in the production of beings, saw Kaya divide itself into two parts, each part being a different sex, from whom the whole human race sprang.[2]

In the *Banquet* of Plato, Aristophanes relates the history of the primordial androgyns, who were subsequently separated by the Gods into man and woman. " In the beginning there were three sexes among men, not only two which we still find at this time, male and female, but yet a third, partaking of the nature of each, which has disappeared, only leaving its name behind. Filled with pride, this race attempted to scale Heaven. The Gods then decided to reduce their might and punish their temerity, and they were hewn asunder, so that each half had only left two arms and a pair of legs, one head and a single sex. They were made into male and female who desire to come together, in order to return to their primitive unity." [3]

The myths and legends about Adam and Eve were taken over from Jewish sources by the Moslems, and are related in different versions by the Arab commentators, such as Tabari and Masudi.[4] Thus Tabari relates that Adam was roaming through Paradise and eating from the fruit of the trees, when suddenly he fell fast asleep. When he opened his eyes he saw Eve before him and wondered at her presence. " Who art thou?" he asked. " I am thy wife," replied the lady; " God has created me out of thee and for thee, so that my heart might find repose." Then the angels said to Adam: " What thing is this, and what is her name?" To which Adam replied: " This is Eve." [5]

---

[1] See *Bundehesh*, trans. by West, in Sacred Books of the East, Vol. V, Chapters 1, 4, 14, and 15.
[2] *Bhagavat*, 3, 12, 51; Mackenzie, *Indian Myth and Legend*; F. Lenormant, *Les Origines de l'Histoire*, Ch. 1. [3] Plato's *Banquet*, Jowett's Transl.
[4] See Grünbaum, *Neue Beiträge zur semitischen Sagenkunde*, pp. 60–67; Weil, *Biblische Legenden der Muselmänner*; Geiger, *Was hat Mohammed aus dem Judentum genommen*, pp. 99–102. [5] *Chronique de Tabari*, I, Ch. 26.

Another Moslem version of the creation of Eve runs as
follows: As a reward for his having preached to the angels,
Adam received a bunch of grapes. Having eaten of the grapes,
he fell asleep, and whilst he slept God made Eve and placed
her beside Adam.[1] She resembled him exactly, but she was
more beautiful, her features were more delicate, her eyes
softer, her form more slender, her voice sweeter, and her
hair longer, being divided into seven hundred locks. Adam
had in the meantime been dreaming that he had a wife and
a helpmate, and great was his joy when, upon his waking,
he found his dream a reality. Putting forth his hand, Adam
tried to take hold of that of Hava, for that was the name God
had given her. The woman, however, withdrew hers, and
would not listen to Adam's words of love: " God is my master,"
she said, " and without His permission I cannot listen to thy
words of love, nor give my hand to thee. Besides, it is not
proper for a man to take a wife without first making her a
wedding present." Thereupon Adam dispatched the angel
Gabriel to go and ask for him God's permission to take
Hava as his wife. Soon Gabriel returned and informed Adam
that Hava had been created to be his wife and helpmate, but
that he was to treat her with love and kindness. Thereupon
Ridhwan, the gatekeeper of Paradise, brought to Adam the
winged horse called Meimun, and a lightfooted she-camel to
Eve. Helped by Gabriel, they mounted the animals and were
led into Paradise where they were greeted by the angels and
all the creatures with the words: " Hail, father and mother
of Mohammed." Then Adam and Eve were placed upon a
throne in a green silk tent supported on gold pillars. They
were then bathed in one of the rivers of Paradise and brought
into the presence of God, who bade them live happily in
Paradise which He had prepared for them as their home.[2]

[1] Weil, *Biblische Legenden der Muselmänner.* pp. 17–18,   [2] Weil, *loc. cit.*

ADAM IN PARADISE

God Warns Adam

Tunc figura vocet Adam propius, et attentius ei dicat:
Escote, Adam, e entent ma raison;
Io t'ai formé, or te doerai itel don:
Tot tens poez vivre, si tu tiens mon sermon,
E serras sains, nen sentiras friczion;
Jà n'avras faim, por bosoing ne beveras,
Jà n'averas frait, jà chalt ne sentiras;
Tu iers en joie, jà ne te lasseras
E en deduit, jà dolor ne savras.
Toute ta vie demeneras en joie;
Tut jors serras, n'en estrat pas poie.
Jo l'di à toi, e voil que Eva l'oie;
Se n'el entent, donc s'afoloie.
De tote terre avez la seignorie,
D'oisels, des bestes e d'altre manantie.
A petit vus soit qui vus porte en vie,
Car tot li mond vus iert encline.
En vostre cors vus met e bien e mal:
Ki ad tel dun n'est pas liez à pal.
Tut en balance ore pendiez par egal
Creez conseil que soiet vers mei leal,
Laisse le mal, e si te pren al bien,
Tun seignor aime e ovec lui te tien,
Por nul conseil ne gerpisez le mien.
Si tu le fais, ne peccheras de rien.

Adam, Drame Anglo-Normand du XIIe Siècle, publié par
Victor Luzarche (Tours, 1854), pp. 5–6.

CHAPTER XIV

The Plot of Sammael, or Paradise Lost

The plot of the angels—Sammael, the angel of light—His jealousy—
Sammael and the serpent—Sammael inspires the serpent—The sin of
Eve—The story of the bird Hol, or Milham (the Phœnix)—The story of the
fox and the weasel—Leviathan sends the large fishes to bring the fox—How
the fox cheated the fishes—The punishment of Adam and Eve—Sammael
is cursed—What Adam lost—He seeks shelter—The story of the Fall in the
Iggeret Baale Hayyim—Adam and the Sabbath—Paradise and the Peri.

WHEN the ministering angels saw the glory and power of
man, and how beloved he was by the Creator, they said unto
themselves, that they would never prevail against him, unless
they led him into temptation.[1] Foremost among the angels,
who were jealous of man and anxious to lead him into temptation, was Sammael, an angel of light, a Seraph with six wings.[2]
Sammael and the angels saw that man was powerful and
beloved by the Creator; they knew that only through a ruse
could they encompass his sin and bring about his perdition.
Then Sammael, accompanied by a host of rebels, descended
from his celestial abode and gathered all the living creatures.
None he found so wily as the serpent and so apt to do wicked
and evil deeds. Thereupon Sammael mounted the serpent
like a rider mounts a swift steed, inspired him with his spirit
and sent him to Eve, the first woman, and wife of Adam. "Man,"
said Sammael, "will not listen to thee, but woman will listen
unto thee, because she easily lends an ear to all creatures."[3]

[1] *Pirke de Rabbi Eliezer*, Ch. 13; Gaster, *The Chronicles of Jerahmeel*, 22, 1.
[2] *Hagigah*, 12b; *Yalkut, Genesis*, § 25.
[3] *Pirke de Rabbi Eliezer*, Ch. 13; *Midrash Haggadol* (ed. Schechter), col. 87; *Genesis
Rabba*, 17.

The serpent walked on two feet and was as erect as a reed.[1] It was superior to all other animals, and its physical strength and wisdom and intelligence were great. Had the serpent not been cursed, but retained its primeval shape and form and its intellectual powers and its power of speech, it would have rendered innumerable services to man. For like a camel the serpent would have fetched and carried and brought pearls and precious stones from the far East.[2]

And the serpent, too, was very jealous and envious of Adam. It harboured the plan of killing Adam and of marrying his widow and then of ruling over the world.[3] The serpent then came and sat down by the side of Eve and began to converse and thus it spoke: " The Creator has eaten from this tree (the tree of wisdom), and created the world, but He commanded you not to eat from this tree, for fear that you, too, might create new worlds. You should eat of the fruit of this tree, before He destroys you and creates new worlds.[4] If, as you tell me," the serpent continued, " the Creator has commanded ye not to touch this tree, then behold, I touch it, and yet I am alive, and you, too, will never die, if you touch it." Thus spoke the serpent. But the serpent was only a vessel, and it was Sammael who spoke through its mouth, having mounted it like a rider mounts a horse.[5] When Sammael mounted the serpent and rode upon it, the voice of justice (the voice of the law) cried out aloud: " It is wicked, O Sammael, now that the world has been created, to rebel against the omnipotent Creator, for He is omnipotent and omnipresent, and in His loving-kindness has He created the world and man to inhabit it."[6]

But Sammael inspired the serpent to go and argue with Eve and to lead her into temptation. Thereupon the serpent,

---

[1] *Genesis Rabba*, 19. [2] *Abot de Rabbi Nathan*, Ch. 1; *Sanhedrin*, 59b.
[3] *Abot de Rabbi Nathan*, Ch. 1. [4] *Midrash Debarim Rabba*, 5.
[5] *Pirke de Rabbi Eliezer*, Ch. 13; see also *Abot de Rabbi Nathan*, Ch. 1.
[6] *Pirke de Rabbi Eliezer*, Ch. 13.

who was more subtle than all other beasts in the field, went
to Eve, for he said unto himself: " Man is not so easily persuaded or swayed as is woman. Man is evil and churlish in
his doings.[1] I will, therefore, approach woman who is by
nature more kind hearted and simpler than man." [2] Then
Sammael rose and touched the tree with both hands and
feet and shook it. And the tree cried aloud and exclaimed:
" Touch me not, thou accursed one." [3] When Sammael saw
that Eve still hesitated to touch the tree he took hold of her
and threw her against the tree and she touched it. Then he
spoke: " Thou seest, just as thou hast not died when thou
didst touch the tree, so thou wilt not die when thou wilt eat
of its fruit." [4] But when Eve was persuaded and touched the
tree, she suddenly perceived the angel of death.[5] She was
greatly troubled in her heart, and said unto herself: " Now
I shall of a certainty die, and the Creator will fashion another
woman and give her to Adam as wife. I will, therefore, persuade my husband to eat of the fruit with me. If we die, we
die together, and if we live we shall live together, and he will
not take another woman to wife." Eve, therefore, after having
eaten of the fruit, took thereof and gave it to Adam and they
both ate. Then their eyes were opened and they saw that
they were naked, and their teeth were set on edge.[6]

Eve was very subtle and had easily prevailed upon Adam
to partake of the fruit of the forbidden tree. " Do not think,"
she argued, " that if I die the Creator will fashion another
wife for thee. Neither shouldst thou imagine that thou wilt
be allowed to remain a widower and inhabit the earth in
solitude. For the earth has been created to be peopled. If
I die, the Creator will destroy thee and fashion another man." [7]

[1] *I Samuel*, 25, 3.   [2] *Prov.* 9, 13.
[3] Menachem Recanati, *Commentary to the Pentateuch*, fol. 24b–25a; *Pirke de Rabbi Eliezer*,
Ch. 13; *Abot de Rabbi Nathan*, Ch. 1.
[4] *Genesis Rabba*, 19; *Midrash Haggadol, Genesis*, col. 88; *Pirke de Rabbi Eliezer*, Ch. 13.
[5] *Targum Jerushalmi, Genesis*, 3, 6; *Pirke de Rabbi Eliezer*, Ch. 13.
[6] Menachem Recanati, *loc. cit.*, fol. 24b–25a.   [7] *Genesis Rabba*, 19–20.

Eve was also jealous of all the beasts who were in
Eden. Having partaken of the forbidden fruit, she gave it
unto all the animals, to the tame and wild beasts and to
the fowls of the air. All the beasts and fowls obeyed her,
with the exception of one bird who is called *Hol*.

The Story of the Bird Hol, or Milham (The Phœnix)

All the animals and beasts in the field and fowls in the
air listened to the woman's voice, and ate of the fruit of knowledge, and were thus condemned to die. Eve then saw the
bird Hol, or Milham, and said unto it: " Eat thou, too, of
the fruit of which all the beasts in the field and the fowls of
the air have eaten." But the bird Milham said unto the woman:
" Is it not sufficient for you to have transgressed the command
of the Lord by eating of the fruit from the tree of knowledge
and to have caused all the animals and beasts in the field and
birds of the air to eat of it? Do you want to make me also
sin by transgressing the command of the Lord?" And the
bird Milham, who was very wise, did not listen to the voice
of the woman and alone of all the birds did not eat of the
fruit of the tree of knowledge.

Then a voice called from Heaven and resounded throughout creation and thus said unto Adam and Eve: " Ye received
My command not to partake of the fruit from the tree of
knowledge, but ye did not listen to My words and transgressed
My command and sinned. The bird Milham did not receive
My command, and yet it refused to listen to your voice and
it honoured My command. Henceforth of all living creatures
the bird Milham alone and its offspring in all eternity will
never die, but live for ever."

And the Creator, the Lord of the Universe, gave to the
angel of death power over all the living creatures. " All the
living creatures are in thy power," said the Lord, " but over
Milham alone thou shalt have no power, neither over it nor

over its offspring from now on unto all eternity." Then
the angel of death replied: " O! Lord of the Universe! Let
me separate this bird from all the living creatures, so that all
will know that Milham and its offspring are the just who will
never undergo the penalty of death or taste its bitterness."

The Lord of the Universe, the Creator and All - Father,
then commanded the angel of death to build a big town
and there to place the bird Milham and its offspring. And
the angel of death did as the Creator had commanded him.
He built a big town wherein he placed the bird Milham and
its offspring. He then sealed the gates of the big town and
said: " It is decreed from now unto all eternity that no
sword, neither mine nor that of any one else, shall have
power over the offspring of the bird Milham from now unto
all eternity. Never will the birds, the offspring of Milham,
taste the bitterness of death until the end of all generations."
And the bird Milham lives in the big town which the angel of
death had built at the command of the Lord of the Universe.
For one thousand years the bird Milham and its offspring
live, and they are fruitful and multiply like all other living
creatures. But every thousand years, when each bird grows
old, a fire is kindled in its nest and issues forth. It consumes
the bird and leaves only a part of it not bigger than an egg.
This egg then grows and changes into a new bird, and from
the ashes the bird rises rejuvenated and soars up like an eagle.
This is the bird Milham, or Hol, concerning which it has
been decreed by the Creator that it should never die.[1]

THE STORY OF THE FOX AND THE WEASEL

And it came to pass that when the angel of death had
closed and sealed the gates of the town he had built for the
bird Milham, the Lord of the Universe thus spake unto him:

---

[1] *Alphabetum Siracides* (ed.Steinschneider); see also Jellinek, *Beth-Hamidrash*, Vol. VI,
p. xii; *Monatsschrift*, 43, p. 219; *Genesis Rabba*, 19; *Midrash Samuel*, 12, 4; see also P. Cassel,
Der Phœnix und seine Aera.

" Throw into the sea a pair, male and female, from every species of the creatures I have created, and over all the others shalt thou have power." The angel of death obeyed and did as he had been commanded by the Lord of the Universe. He began to throw into the sea a pair from every species the Lord had created. When the fox—who was very wily—saw what was happening, he approached the angel of death and began to cry bitterly.

" Well, and why art thou crying so bitterly," asked the angel of death.

" I am weeping over my poor brother," replied the fox, " my brother whom thou hast just thrown into the sea."

" Where is thy brother?" inquired the angel of death.

The fox approached and came up to the water's edge, so that his image was reflected by the water, and pointing to his own image he said: " Here he is." When the angel of death saw the image of the fox in the water, he thought that he had already thrown one of the species into the sea. He therefore said: " As I have already thrown into the water one of thy species, thou canst go." And the fox ran away and was saved. On his way he met his friend the weasel, to whom he related what had happened and how he had cheated the angel of death and had escaped. The weasel greatly admired the cunning of the fox and did likewise. He, too, cheated the angel of death and was not thrown into the water.

Now it came to pass that after a time Leviathan, the king over all the creatures that live in the sea, gathered all his subjects round him, but he saw neither fox nor weasel among them. Greatly astonished, he asked the fishes why the fox and the weasel were absent and had not appeared in his presence. Then the fishes told Leviathan what had happened, how the fox and the weasel—who were both cunning and wily—had cheated the angel of death and been saved from the water. And Leviathan was very jealous of the fox and

envied him his cleverness and intelligence and cunning. He,
therefore, sent out the large fishes and commanded them to
go and fetch the fox and to use cunning so as to entice him
into the water and bring him before Leviathan. The large
fishes did the bidding of their King Leviathan, who is set
over all the fishes in the sea. They swam to the shore and
perceived the fox who was walking up and down along the
seashore. When the fox beheld the large fishes who had swum
up he wondered greatly.

"Who are you?" asked the fishes.

"I am the fox," he replied.

Then the fishes, who tried to be cunning, said: "Hail
King! Great honours await thee, for whose sake we have
come up to the surface of the waters and swum up to the
shore."

"How so," asked the fox. And the fishes replied:

"Our great King, Leviathan, who is the ruler of all the
creatures in the deep seas, is sick unto death. Feeling his end
near, he has decreed that none but thou shouldst succeed
him on his throne which will soon be vacant. He has
heard of thee and how clever and cunning thou art. And
he has dispatched us, the large fishes, to find and bring thee
before him that he might crown thee king and leave his
kingdom to thee for thou art cleverer than all the beasts of
the earth and all the fishes in the sea."

Thus spoke the fishes, and the fox was greatly flattered
and pleased to hear such tidings.

"But how can I go into the water," he said, "without
being drowned?"

"Do not trouble about this," said the large fishes. "We
will carry thee upon our backs, as befits a king. Right across
the waves and over the vast sea we will carry thee, until we
bring thee before our King Leviathan. And when thou wilt
have reached the abode of Leviathan thou wilt become king

over all of us, and thou wilt live happily for ever. For thy nourishment will be brought to thee daily, as it befits a king, and no longer wilt thou fear the wild beasts who are mightier and stronger than thyself."

And the fox listened to their voice and believed their words. He mounted upon the back of one of the large fishes who promised to carry him over the surface of the waters to the abode of Leviathan. But when the foam-crested waves began to beat mightily against him, the fox suddenly felt afraid; his heart fell and his ambition left him.

"Woe is unto me," he wailed. "What have I done? The fishes have deceived me and made a fool of me. I, who have deceived and misled other beasts, am now in their power, and who will save me?" And the fox thought deeply of means how to escape. Thereupon he addressed the fishes and said unto them:

"Tell me the truth, what is your purpose and what do you intend to do to me?" And the fishes said: "We will tell thee the real truth. Our King Leviathan, he who is the ruler over all the fishes in the deep seas, has heard of thee and how cunning thou art and he has said: 'I will cut open his body and swallow his heart, and be as wise and cunning as the fox.'"

Then the fox said unto the fishes: "Why did you not tell me the truth at once? I would then have taken my heart with me and offered it as a gift to the king. He would have honoured and loved me. But now evil will befall you, for your king will be angry, when he hears that you have brought me without my heart."

And the fishes marvelled greatly and said: "Is it really so that thy heart is not within thee and that thou hast come out leaving it behind?"

"Verily, it is so," replied the fox, "for such is the custom among us foxes. We leave our hearts behind us in a safe

place, and we walk about without any heart. When once we
need it, we go home and fetch it, but if we do not require it
our hearts remain at home in a safe place." Thus spoke the
fox. And when the fishes heard this, they were greatly troubled
and perplexed, and did not know what to do. But the fox
said unto them:

"My abode is on the shore of the sea, just where you met
me. If you will take me back to the water's edge, I will run
up and quickly fetch my heart where it is hidden. I will then
return with you to King Leviathan and offer him my heart
as a gift. He will be greatly pleased, and honour you and me.
But if you refuse and bring me to him without my heart,
he will be mightily angry with you and will swallow you up,
for you have failed to carry out his commands. As for myself,
I am not afraid, for I will tell him the truth. 'O Lord
Leviathan!' I will say, 'these fishes thou didst send out did
not tell me anything of thy desire. And when at last they
did tell me the reason of their errand, I urged them to
return and let me fetch my heart, but they refused, and so
I cannot offer thee my heart which I would fain do.'"

When the fishes heard these cunning words of the fox,
they said to one another: "Verily, he has spoken well."
They returned to the seashore and brought the fox to the dry
land. The fox immediately jumped upon the shore, threw
himself upon the sand and began to dance for joy.

"Hurry up," urged the fishes, "and fetch thy heart where
it is hidden, that we may return to King Leviathan."

But the fox laughed merrily and said: "Verily, you are
fools. Do not you know that if my heart had not been with
me I could not have gone with you upon the water and faced
the foam-crested waves? Is there a creature upon earth that
could walk about without a heart?"

And the fishes spoke: "Then thou hast deceived us." But
the fox only laughed and said: "If I have been clever enough

SAMMAEL AND HIS BAND OF ANGELS HURLED FROM HEAVEN

to cheat the angel of death, how much easier was it for me
to cheat you, stupid fishes." And so the fishes returned to
King Leviathan empty - handed and were greatly ashamed.
When Leviathan heard their story he said:

" Verily, the fox is very cunning, but you are very stupid
and deserve punishment." He, therefore, ate them all. And
ever since there are counterparts in the water of every species
of beasts upon earth, even the counterparts of man and of
woman, but there are none of either the fox or the weasel![1]

When Adam and Eve had eaten of the forbidden fruit,
their eyes were opened, and they saw themselves naked.[2]
Their glory then fled from them, for they lost their celestial
garments and angelic endowments. Only sensible matters
did they see and understand, but all divine and angelic wisdom
was taken from them. Stripped of his garment which was a
skin like finger nails, and a cloud of glory, man, after his
sin, stood naked. Then the voice of the Creator resounded,
calling upon Adam: " How art thou changed, O man!" And
Adam said: " O Creator of the world, Lord of the Universe!
I did not sin against Thee when I lived alone in Eden. The
woman thou hast given me enticed me." But the woman
replied that the serpent had beguiled her. And the voice of
the Creator resounded once more through the whole world,
and the mountains trembled and the earth quaked, and thus
He spoke·

" All three of you shall be punished, for you have sinned
and transgressed My commandment." And Sammael and
his band of angels who followed him were hurled from Heaven.
To the serpent the Creator spoke thus: " I made thee king
over all the beasts in the field, and thou didst walk erect like
a man. But now thou shalt drag thyself upon the ground
with thy belly, and dust shall henceforth be thy food." And

[1] *Alphabetum Siracidis* (ed. Steinschneider).
[2] *Pirke de Rabbi Eliezer*, Ch. 14; *Targum Jerushalmi, Genesis*, 3, 7.

the serpent was cursed above all the cattle and the living beasts. It was ordained that its feet be cut off, and that it should cast off its skin once in seven years and thereby suffer great pain.[1] And the Creator further spoke: " Thou didst harbour wicked thoughts in thy mind and evil in thy heart. Thou didst say unto thyself: ' I will kill Adam and take Eve to be my wife, and I shall be the Lord of creation and king of the world.' But now I will put death and poison in thy mouth, and a deadly venom, and will put hatred between thee and the woman and her children. Instead of being king of the world, walk erect and eat of all the agreeable and delightful food, thou shalt henceforth be cursed above all cattle, creep on thy belly and eat dust." [2] The Creator thereupon cursed Adam, and shortened his stature and took his glory from him. Six things were taken from Adam as a punishment for his sin, and these things were: his splendour, his stature, his life, the fruits of the trees, the fruits, and the heavenly lights. And he was to sow wheat and reap thistles, and earn his bread in anxiety, and his food by the sweat of his brow.[3]

When Adam heard his sentence, that the earth should produce thorns and thistles, his body trembled, tears welled up in his eyes, and sweat poured down his countenance, and thus he spoke before his Creator: " Lord of the Universe! shall I and my ass eat alike from the same crib?" But the Creator replied: " Since thou dost repent, and thy limbs did tremble and thou didst weep and sweat poured down thy countenance, thou wilt eat not grass, like the beasts in the field, but bread." [4]

Furthermore, in consequence of the sin of our first parents, the presence and splendour of the Creator (the Shekhina)

---

[1] *Targum Jerushalmi, Genesis*, 3, 14; *Yalkut Shimeoni*, § 27; *Pirke de Rabbi Eliezer*, Ch. 14; *Genesis Rabba*, 20.
[2] *Abot de Rabbi Nathan*, Ch. 1.   [3] Bin Gorion, *loc. cit.*, p. 111.
[4] *Pesachim*, 118a; *Genesis Rabba*, 24; *Abot de Rabbi Nathan*, Ch. 1.

which had manifested itself upon earth and dwelt in Eden, retired to the celestial regions.   As the future generations and the descendants of Adam sinned once more, it retired farther and farther from the inhabitants of earth.   Thus, after the fall of Adam, the Shekhina, or Divine presence, had retired to the first or lowest heavenly sphere.   It ascended to the second after the crime of Cain, to the third in the time of Enosh, to the fourth in the time of the deluge, to the fifth when the tower of Babel was being constructed, to the sixth in the age of Sodom, and to the seventh, that is the highest heavenly sphere, when Abraham visited the land of Egypt. But when the just and pious men arose, the Shekhina once more descended gradually to dwell among men.[1]

After his fall Adam wandered about begging the trees to give him shelter, but they all refused.   " Here is the thief," they said, " who has deceived his Maker."   The fig tree alone offered him shelter, for it is of the fruit of the fig tree that he had eaten.[2]

All this had happened on the first day of his creation, and Adam had not yet witnessed the sunset, nor the approach of night and darkness.   When he therefore suddenly noticed how the world was growing dark in the west, and the sun was disappearing upon the horizon, he was greatly perturbed and exclaimed: " Woe unto me!   On account of my sin the Creator is sending darkness upon earth, and is throwing creation back into chaos."   As yet, Adam was not aware that such was the course of the world, and he thought that it was death that was swiftly approaching.   But when on the following morning the sun once more arose in all its radiance in the east, he was mightily glad, built altars and praised the Creator.[3]

[1] *Genesis Rabba*, 19; *Midrash Haggadol*, col. 90.
[2] *Genesis Rabba*, 15; *Midrash Haggadol*, col. 90.
[3] *Abodah Zarah*, 8a; *Abot de Rabbi Nathan*, Ch. 1.

SAMMAEL, THE ANGEL OF LIGHT

In the *Iggeret Baale Hayyim*,[1] the story of the Fall is related as follows: When the Lord of the Universe had created man, He commanded the angels to pay homage to him, and they all obeyed the command of their Master. But Sammael alone, who was arrogant and obstinate, refused to obey. He was greatly grieved and very wroth, when he heard that his rule on earth had come to an end, and his wrath knew no bounds. He was loath to leave his throne and to obey another ruler and lord, where he had hitherto ruled supreme; to submit to the will of another, where hitherto all had submitted to his will. And the Creator commanded the angels to place man in the Garden of Eden, in a lovely spot on the top of the mountains, where the air is delicious, and where winter and summer, and day and night are alike. There are lovely streams and flowers and trees, pleasant to the eye, in abundance. And high upon the mountains Adam and Eve wandered. They walked by the river banks, among flowers and trees, beautiful to behold. They lived without care or sorrow, for they neither toiled nor laboured, but ate of the fruit of delight and listened to the song of the lovely birds. When Sammael saw the happiness of man, his envy and wrath increased, and he sought to seduce man, lead him into temptation and thus deprive him of his happiness. He came to him with smooth speech and thus he spoke: " Well enough do I know that the Creator has placed thee above all creatures and lent thee much wisdom. But if thou wouldst follow my advice and partake of the tree of life, thou wouldst never die, but live for ever and ever in all eternity. And Adam listened to the voice of Sammael, the seducer, and was greatly tempted. He ate of the tree of life and tasted its fruit. Scarcely had he eaten of the tree of life, when his body became black and his

[1] Trans. by Julius Landsberger, 1882.

countenance was changed. His garment of light fell from him and he was troubled by the heat of the sun. And all the animals, when they saw how greatly Adam had changed, no longer feared him.

And thus Adam and his helpmate did not remain long in the Garden of Eden. According to Rabbinic legend,[1] Adam entered Eden on Friday evening, and already at twilight on the next day, he was driven forth, and went out. He would have been sent out of Eden earlier, but he was saved by the Sabbath day which arrived and became the advocate for our first parent. The Sabbath day appeared before the Throne of Glory and thus it spoke: " Lord of the Universe, Sovereign of all the worlds, Thou hast blessed and sanctified the Sabbath day more than all the days of the week. No one has as yet been punished during the six days of creation, and shall this happen on the Sabbath day? Where is then my sanctity and where is Thy blessing?" And thus, by the merit of the Sabbath, Adam was saved from judgment on the Sabbath day.[2]

Thereupon Adam went forth outside the Garden of Eden, and he dwelt upon the Mount Moriah, which is near to the Garden of Eden.

PARADISE AND THE PERI

One morn a Peri at the gate
Of Eden stood disconsolate,
And as she listened to the springs
Of life within, like music flowing,
And caught the light upon her wings
Through the half-open portal glowing,
She wept to think her recreant race
Should e'er have lost that glorious place!

[1] *Pirke de Rabbi Eliezer*, Ch. 18; *Midrash Shokher Tob, Ps.* 92, 3; see, however, contradiction in *Pirke de Rabbi Eliezer*, Ch. 11.
[2] *Pirke de Rabbi Eliezer*, Ch. 19. See also *Midrash Shokher Tob, Ps.* 92, 3; cf. *Sabbath*, 118a.

" How happy," exclaimed this child of air,
" Are the Holy Spirits who wander there,
'Mid flowers that never shall fade or fall;
Though mine are the gardens of earth and sea
And the stars themselves have flowers for me,
One blossom of Heaven outblooms them all.

" Though sunny the lake of cool Cashmere
With its plane-tree isle reflected clear,
And sweetly the founts of that valley fall;
Though bright are the waters of Sing-su-Hay,
And the golden floods that thitherward stray,
Yet—Oh! 't is only the Blest can say
How the waters of Heaven outshine them all.

" Go, wing thy flight from star to star,
From world to luminous world, as far
As the universe spreads its flaming wall,
Take all the pleasure of all the spheres,
And multiply each through endless years,
One minute of Heaven is worth them all!"

The glorious angel, who was keeping
The Gates of Light, beheld her weeping;
And, as he nearer drew and listen'd
To her sad song, a tear-drop glistened
Within his eyelids, like the spray
From Eden's fountain, when it lies
On the blue flower, which—Brammissay—
Blooms nowhere but in Paradise.

" Nymph of a fair but erring line! "
Gently he said, " one hope is thine,
'T is written in the Book of Fate,
The Peri yet may be forgiven
Who brings to this Eternal Gate
The gift that is most dear to Heaven!
Go, seek it, and redeem thy sin—
'T is sweet to let the pardon'd in."

Thomas Moore (" Lalla Rookh ").

CHAPTER XV

In Exile

The prayer of Adam—The angel Rasiel brings the book back to Adam —Adam and Eve search after food—They decide to do penance—Eve goes to the Tigris and Adam to the Jordan—Eve is once more beguiled by Sammael—The story of Sammael's fall from Heaven—Eve gives birth to Cain— Her dream—Adam's sickness—His story of the Fall—Eve and Seth go to the Garden of Eden in search of the oil of life—Seth is bitten by the serpent —Eve's story of the Fall—The death of Adam—Angels come down to bury Adam—The death of Eve—The life of Adam in Moslem legend—The beasts show their pity—The locusts—Adam and Eve are forgiven—Iblis implores the grace of God—God makes a covenant with Adam.

ADAM AND EVE AFTER THE FALL

ADAM and Eve did not leave Paradise empty-handed. They carried with them various possessions, among these their garments, the rod which God had created on the eve of the Sabbath, and a book which the angel Rasiel gave them.[1]

When Adam was expelled from the Garden of Eden, he prayed unto the Creator and such was his prayer: " Eternal, Lord of the Universe! Thou didst create the whole world and all the creatures therein. Thy power is everlasting, and Thy glory goes from generation to generation. Nothing is hidden from Thee and nothing escapes Thine eye. Thou didst fashion me with Thine own hands and make me ruler over all Thy creatures. But the wily and cursed serpent seduced me and made me eat of the fruit from the tree of delight. And the wife of my bosom, she, too, seduced me. But Thou didst not inform me as to my fate and the fate of

[1] *Sepher Rasiel*, ed. Amsterdam, 1700.

my children after me, and as to what will happen to me and
to the generations who will come after me. I know that no
man is just before Thee, and who am I and what is my strength
that I should dare to resist Thee or rise up against Thee?
I dare not open my mouth to speak before Thee, or to raise
mine eyes, for I have sinned and transgressed Thy commandments and on account of my sin I am now driven forth and
expelled from Eden. And now I must plough and cultivate the
earth whence I have been taken. The inmates and inhabitants
of the earth no longer fear me nor do they tremble before me,
for since I have eaten of the fruit from the tree of knowledge
and transgressed Thy commandments my wisdom has been
taken from me, and I am a fool who knoweth not, and a stupid
who understandeth not what will happen and come to pass.
Now, merciful God, in Thy great mercy, turn to him who
is the chief and first of Thy creatures, to the spirit which
Thou didst breath into him and to the soul Thou didst give
him. Vouchsafe Thy mercy unto me, for Thou art gracious,
magnanimous, patient and rich in favour. May my prayer
ascend before the throne of Thy glory, and may my supplications reach the seat of Thy mercy, and mayest Thou be
merciful unto me. May the words of my mouth find favour
before Thee, and do not hide Thy countenance from me.
Thou who wast from the beginning and wilt be for ever,
Thou who didst reign and wilt continue to reign, have mercy
upon the work of Thine hands and let me understand and
know what will happen unto my offspring and to the generations
that will issue from me. Hide not from me the wisdom of
Thy help and the help of Thy ministering angels." [1]

Thus prayed Adam, and three days after he had thus
prayed, the angel Rasiel, who dwells near the river which
issues forth from the Garden of Eden, came to Adam and
manifested himself to him whilst the sun was hot. In his

[1] *Sepher Rasiel*, p. 3a; Jellinek, *Beth-Hamidrash*, Vol. III, p. 157.

hand the angel held a book and thus he spake unto Adam:
" Why art thou so troubled and why dost thou grieve?
Thy prayer and supplication have been heard, and I have
now come to teach thee the great wisdom through the words
of this holy book. Through it thou wilt know what will
befall thee until the day of thy death. And all thy offspring
and all those of thy children who will read and study this book
in humility of spirit and purity of flesh, and fulfil conscientiously all that is written within its pages, will know for a
certainty what will happen unto them and befall them every
month and between day and night. Everything will be manifested unto them, and they will understand and know whether
misfortune or hunger, rain or drought, good or bad harvests
will come; whether sinners will rule in the world and whether
locusts will plague men; whether wars will be waged and
much blood be shed among men; and whether diseases will
break out and death mow down the children of man. And
now, Adam, approach and lend thine ear and I will teach
thee the secrets of the book and its holiness." Adam approached
and lent his ear, and the angel Rasiel, he who dwells by the
river that issues forth from the Garden of Eden, read unto
him the secrets of the book.[1]

And it so happened that when Adam heard the words
of the holy book as they issued from the mouth of the angel
Rasiel, he fell down upon his face greatly trembling. But
the angel of the Presence spake unto Adam and said: " Rise
up, Adam, and take heart, fear not, neither do thou tremble,
but take this book from my hands and guard it carefully, for
from this book thou wilt learn much knowledge and from
its source thou wilt draw intelligence and understanding that
thou mayest impart this knowledge to all those who will be
worthy of it." [2]

And it so happened that when Adam took the book from

---

[1] Sepher Rasiel.   [2] Ibid.

the hands of the angel Rasiel, a fire broke out on the bank of the river, and in the flame the angel ascended to Heaven. Then Adam understood and knew that he had been face to face with an angel of the Presence, and that the book had been sent to him by order and command of the holy King and Ruler of the Universe. And he kept the book in sanctity and purity.[1]

Thereupon Adam and Eve constructed a hut where they passed seven days in sorrow and grief, in wailing and weeping. When seven days had elapsed, they began to feel the pangs of hunger, searched for food, but found none. Thereupon Eve said to Adam: " My lord, I am hungry, go and find some food for us that we may eat and live. And perhaps God in His mercy will bring us back where we were before." Then Adam went and searched for food seven days long, but found none such as they had enjoyed in the Garden of Eden. " My lord," said Eve, " if thou wouldst kill me, the Lord will perhaps have mercy upon thee and take thee back to Paradise, for it is solely on my account that He waxed wroth with thee. Kill me, and then thou wilt return to Paradise."

Said Adam: " Eve, do not speak foolishly; how can I lift my hand against my own flesh and blood. Let us rather wander about in the land, perchance we may find food and not die." [2] Thereupon they wandered about for nine days, but found only food fit for animals and beasts of the earth. And Adam said: " This is the food which the Lord has given to the beasts, whilst we partook of the food of the angels when we dwelt in Paradise.[3] Verily, the anger of God against us is great. Let us, therefore, repent of our sin and do penance, perchance He will have mercy upon us, forgive us and send us food that we may live and not die. Thou, my dear Eve, canst not do so much penance as I can, but do thou as much as thy health

---

[1] *Sepher Rasiel*; Jellinek, *Beth-Hamidrash*, Vol. III, p. 157.
[2] *Vita Adae et Evae*, ed. by W. Meyer in *Abhandlungen der bayrischen Akademie der Wissenschaften, Phil.-philos. Classe*, XIV, 3, 1878, pp. 185 ff.   [3] *Ps.* 78, 25.

will permit thee. I will fast for forty days, but go thou to the river Tigris and remain in the water up to thy neck. Do not open thy mouth for speech, for we are unworthy to address the Lord and beg His pardon. Thus thou shalt remain for thirty-seven days and not quit the water. And I will go to the Jordan and there remain up to my neck in the water for forty days and do penance, perchance the Lord will forgive us our sin and have mercy upon us." Thus spake Adam.

And Eve went to the Tigris and entered the water, whilst Adam was doing penance in the Jordan. " Mourn with me, O waters of the Jordan," said Adam, " for I have sinned; gather round me all the living things that are in the Jordan and let them mourn with me and help me to do penance." Whilst Adam and Eve were thus doing penance, Sammael, who is Satan, grew angry and cast about how he might bring to naught their decision to undergo penance.

He decided to frustrate the intention of our first parents. On the eighteenth day he took upon him the form of an angel of light and flew over the Tigris where he perceived Eve crying. Pretending that he was moved by her distress, Sammael began to cry aloud. And thus he spoke: " Quit the water of the Tigris, Eve, and cry no longer. Why art thou and thy spouse Adam still sad and unhappy? The Lord has heard your joint prayers and has accepted your penance. We angels of light have all prayed the Lord to forgive you, and the Almighty has sent me to fetch you out of the water and to bring you the food which you enjoyed in Paradise. Quit now the water, and I will lead thee to a place where thou wilt find food in abundance." And Eve listened to the speech of Sammael who had taken the form of an angel of light, and scrambled out of the water. Her body was trembling from cold like a blade of grass. She fell upon the ground exhausted, but Sammael lifted her up and led her to Adam. When Adam saw Eve following Sammael, he was filled with dismay, beat his breast and wept aloud. " Eve, Eve," he cried, "what has become of thy penance? How couldst thou once more listen to the voice of our enemy and be beguiled by his deception?"

When Eve heard these words, she perceived that indeed it had been their enemy Sammael who had taken the form of an angel of light. She fell down upon the ground in great despair and cried bitterly: " Woe unto thee, O Satan," she exclaimed, " why art thou seeking to destroy us? What have we done unto thee that thou art our enemy? Why dost thou hate us? Have we taken from thee thy splendour and glory? Why dost thou hate us so fiercely?" Thus cried Eve.

And Sammael, sighing aloud, replied: " Adam! all my enmity, envy, and jealousy are directed against thee, because it is on thy account that I lost the glory which I enjoyed in Heaven among the angels of light. It is on thy account that I was expelled from Heaven and hurled down to earth!"

" How am I guilty of thy fall?" asked Adam.

" Because," replied Sammael, " when thou wast created and God had breathed the spirit of life in thee and thou wast made in the image of God, the angel Michael brought thee among the celestials and commanded them to pay homage to thee. ' Worship the image of God,' he said, ' and prostrate yourselves before him.' Michael himself worshipped thee, and all the other angels followed his example. He thereupon called me and said: ' Worship the image of God!' But I replied: ' I will not worship Adam, for he is younger than I am and inferior to me. It is for him to worship me, for was I not created long before him?'[1] And when the other angels heard my words they, too, refused to worship thee. Thereupon Michael said: ' If thou wilt not worship Adam, the anger of the Lord will fall upon thee.' But I was arrogant

---

[1] Raimund Martin, *Pugio Fidei*, ed. Lips., p. 536, quoted from *Midrash of Rabbi Moses ha-Darshan.* See, however, Ginzberg, *Die Haggada bei den Kirchenvätern und in der apokryphischen Literatur, Monatsschrift*, Vol. 43, p. 151–152.

and exclaimed: ' If He will grow angry with me, I will raise my seat above the stars of Heaven and be like the Creator Himself.' Thereupon God grew angry with me and with all the angels who followed me, and expelled us from Heaven, from among the angels of light. And thus it was that on thy account we lost our former splendour and glory, and were expelled from Heaven. When we saw thee so happy, living in Eden, our envy and fury grew even stronger, and we decided to deprive thee of thy joy and glory. I, therefore, approached thy wife and persuaded her to partake of the forbidden fruit, so that thou, too, wast deprived of thy glory, as I had been deprived of mine." Thus spoke Sammael, and Adam, on hearing his words, wept aloud. " Lord of the Universe!" he prayed, " save me from this arch-enemy who is trying to lead my soul into perdition." Sammael vanished, and Adam continued to do his penance, remaining in the water for forty days.[1]

Thereupon Eve said to her spouse : " My lord, thou shalt remain alive, because thou didst not commit either the first or the second transgression, but I am very guilty and ought to die." And Eve went out towards the west where she mourned and wept. But her time came near to give birth to a child, and her suffering and pains were great, and she travailed much. She prayed to the Lord to have mercy upon her, but her prayers were not heard. " Who will bring the tidings to my spouse," thought Eve, in her distress. And she thus addressed the heavenly lights: " When ye travel east, bring the news to my husband and inform him of my distress." Adam heard Eve's lament and came to see her. " Thy arrival, my lord," said Eve, " has gladdened my heart, and now pray to the Lord that He may assuage my suffering." Adam was sorry in his heart and suffered much for her sake, and when he saw the strait in which Eve was, he arose and

---

[1] See *Pirke de Rabbi Eliezer*, Ch. 20, where it is said: "He went into the waters of Gihon and fasted seven weeks of days until his body became like a sieve." See also Ginzberg, p. 218. A similar legend is related by Tabari and Ibn el-Atir. See Grünbaum, *loc. cit.*, p. 66.

prayed to the Lord, and lo, twelve angels appeared and one of them, the angel Michael, touched Eve's face and said: "Blessed be thou, Eve, the prayers of thy spouse have found favour with the Most High and He has sent me to thee to bring thee out of thy distress." Thereupon Eve gave birth to a son whose countenance was radiant and shining. The child at once rose up and brought a reed to his mother, and they called his name Cain.[1] Adam then took his wife and child and travelled east. Soon the angel Michael came and brought different kinds of seeds to Adam, and taught him how to till the ground and cultivate the earth so that it should bear fruit. Then Eve bore another son whom they called Habel.

Now one day, Eve awoke and told Adam the dream she had, and said as follows: "My lord, I saw in a dream by night, that the blood of our son Habel was poured into the hand of our son Cain, which he drank and swallowed, and therefore I was sad at heart." When Adam heard this he said: "Woe unto us, I fear that Cain will slay Habel; let us therefore make Cain a tiller of the soil and Habel a shepherd, so that they may live apart." Thereupon Adam begat a son whom he named Seth, and many other sons.

When Adam was nine hundred and thirty years old he fell sick and he knew that his end was near. He called out and said: "Let all my sons gather round me so that I may behold them, speak to them and bless them before I die." All the sons of Adam gathered round their father near the place where they used to worship the Creator of the Universe. And they asked him and said: "O our father, how is it with thee and why dost thou lie upon thy bed?" Adam made answer: "My sons, I am sick and suffer greatly." Then Seth, his son, said unto him: "O my father, perhaps thou cravest for the delightful fruit of Paradise which thou didst

[1] *Kanah* in Hebrew means reed. See *Genesis*, 4, 1.

eat, and because of that craving thou art so sorrowful and sick. If this be so, tell me, my sire, and I will go near the gates of Paradise. I will place dust upon my head, and loudly lament before the Garden of Eden and beseech the Lord. Perchance the Lord will hear the prayer of His servant, and send His angel to give me of the fruit after which thy heart desires." But Adam made answer: " I do not crave for the fruit of Paradise, but great pains and weakness beset me." " And what is pain, O my father?" asked Seth; " I do not know it, so tell us about it and do not hide it from us."

Then Adam said unto his sons: " Hear me, my sons. When God created me and your mother Eve, he placed us in Paradise, and He gave me the command to taste, eat, and enjoy all the fruits of the garden, but of the tree of knowledge between good and evil He commanded me not to taste. It so happened that God had given one part of the garden to me and the other to your mother; the fruits of the eastern and northern corners He gave to me, but the fruits of the southern and western corners He gave to you mother. Then God, the Creator, set two angels as our guardians, but an hour came when the angels left us to go and render homage before the Creator. Seeing that the angels had departed, the enemy, Satan, availed himself of this opportunity and came and conversed with your mother, seduced her and made her eat of the forbidden tree. When she had eaten of it, God was angry with me, and He spoke to me and said: ' Forasmuch as thou hast transgressed My command and not listened to My words, I will bring upon thy flesh many woes, seventy in number, pains of the head and afflictions of the eyes and ears, and such woes will befall all thy members down to the soles of thy feet.' "

When Adam had said all this to his sons he was seized with great pains, and he called aloud and said: " What shall I do, who am beset with such pains and woes?" And when

Eve saw her sire cry, she, too, wept bitterly, and said unto
God: "O my God, give me all his woes and suffering, for
it is I who transgressed." To Adam she said: "My sire,
give me half of thy woes and suffering, for it is on my account
that thou hast fallen into guilt." But Adam said unto Eve:
"Do thou arise, my wife, and go with our son Seth near the
garden and cast dust upon your heads and prostrate yourselves before the Lord and lament and beseech. Perchance
He will have pity on me and send His angel to the tree of mercy
from which proceedeth the oil of life, and give some of it to
you that you may anoint my person therewith and that my
pains may cease."

Seth and his mother at once arose and went near the
garden. And when they were in the road, a beast suddenly appeared and beholding Seth it fell upon him and bit
him. This beast was the serpent. Eve wept bitterly and
said: "Woe to me, who am so unfortunate; I am cursed, for
I have disobeyed the commands of the Lord and not kept
the observance of His word." Looking at the serpent, she
said: "Cursed beast, art thou not afraid to wage war against
and throw thyself upon the image of God? Why did thy
teeth bite him?" Then the serpent called out and replied in
a human voice: "Eve, tell me why didst thou open thy mouth
to eat of the fruit of the tree, of which God commanded you
not to eat. Now thou canst not bear when I begin to accuse
thee, but it is not from me that there was the beginning of
evil." Thereupon Seth said to the beast: "Shut thy mouth
and be silent, thou cursed enemy of truth, thou seducer; hold
off from the image of God, until the day when the Lord will
call thee to judgment." But the wild beast said unto Seth:
"Behold, I stand aloof, as thou sayest, and hold off from the
image of God." Then the beast let Seth go.

Thereupon Seth and his mother Eve went nigh to Paradise for the oil of pity wherewith to anoint Adam who was

sick. When they reached the gates of Paradise they strewed dust upon their heads, prostrated themselves, and wept bitterly. They lamented and prayed to the Lord to have mercy upon Adam and to send His ministering angel who would give them oil from the tree of pity. Thus they remained for many hours, and lo, the angel Michael appeared and thus he spoke: "I have been sent by the Lord of the Universe, and I tell thee, Seth, to cease thy weeping and praying and not to worry concerning the oil from the tree of compassion wherewith to anoint thy father Adam. For I tell thee that in the present thou wilt not receive it. Go, therefore, Seth, to thy father, whose earthly life is now at an end. After six days his soul will leave his body; and when this will have happened thou shalt behold great wonders in Heaven and upon earth." When the angel of the Lord had said this, he left them and ascended to Heaven.

Then Eve and Seth returned to Adam who was lying sick. They told him of what had befallen them and how they had met the serpent who had bitten Seth. And Adam said to Eve: "What hast thou done unto me! Thou hast brought great suffering upon us and upon our whole race. Now when I am no more, tell our sons what thou hast done, for those who will come after us will curse us and say: ' Our first parents have brought all suffering upon us.' " When Eve heard this, she began to weep and lament bitterly.

EVE'S STORY OF THE FALL

Thereupon Eve said to her sons:

" Children, I will relate unto you how the enemy and adversary seduced us and robbed us of our bliss and delight and the Garden of Eden. When we dwelt in Paradise all the male animals were placed under you father's supervision in the north-eastern corner, whilst the female animals were under my supervision in the south-western corner. One day the

adversary, who is Satan, came into the domain of your father
where he found the serpent whom he approached, and thus
he spoke: ' I hear that thou art wiser than all the other
animals, and I will reveal unto thee what is in my mind. Thou
art greater and wiser than all the other animals and yet thou
dost worship one who is inferior to thee. Why dost thou
feed upon grass, whilst Adam and Eve are partaking of heavenly
food, and of the fruit of Paradise? Come, let us bring
about that Adam be driven out of Paradise on account of
his wife, even as we have been expelled from Heaven on his
account.'

" Said the serpent to Satan: ' I fear to do this thing, for
the Lord will be wroth with me.'

" ' Fear not,' said Satan, ' for thou wilt only be a vessel
unto me,[1] and it is I who will deceive them by thy mouth
through which I will speak and ensnare them.'

" Thereupon the serpent came and hung himself from the
wall of the garden. When the angels, our guardians, went
forth and ascended to Heaven to do homage to God, Satan
at once took the form of an angel of light, and sang songs of
praise. Looking up, I beheld him on the wall of the garden.
·He then said to me: ' Art thou Eve?' and I replied: ' Yes,
I am.' ' And what mayest thou be doing in Paradise?' he
asked. And I said to him: ' God placed us here to guard it
and to eat of the fruit of its trees.' He then said to me: ' Ye
do well, but ye do not eat of the trees which are in this garden.'
' It is not so,' I replied; ' for we eat of all the trees, except
of a single tree which is in the middle of the garden, concerning which God commanded us not to eat of it, lest we die
with death.' Thereupon the serpent said to me: ' Verily,
my soul is full of sorrow because of thee, Eve, for thou and
thy spouse are as ignorant as the cattle, and I will not leave
thee in ignorance. Come and eat of the fruit of this tree and

[1] Cf. *Pirke de Rabbi Eliezer*, Ch. 13.

thou wilt forthwith know the power and worth of this tree.'
Thus spake the serpent, but I replied: ' I fear lest the Lord
be wroth with me, even as He commanded us.' But the serpent
replied: ' Fear not, Eve, for when thou shalt eat of the fruit
of this tree, thine eyes shall be opened, and ye, thy spouse
and thyself, shall become like Gods, knowing what is good
and evil. God knew that ye shall become like God, if ye eat
of the fruit of this tree, and out of jealousy He forbade ye to
eat thereof.'[1] And I lifted up mine eyes and saw the glory
of the tree. ' It is pleasant to behold,' said I, ' but I fear to
partake of its fruit.'

" ' I will give it to thee,' replied the serpent. Thereupon
I opened the door of the garden of delight and the serpent
entered. He walked before me and I after him. After a little
while he turned to me and said: ' Swear unto me that when
thou hast eaten of the fruit of this tree, thou wilt also give to
thy husband to eat of the same.' ' I know not how to swear,'
I replied, ' but I will say whatsoever I know. On the Throne
of Glory, on the Cherubim, and on the tree of life, I swear to
thee that when I have eaten of the fruit of the tree, I will also
give to my husband to eat thereof.' And when the serpent
heard my oath he climbed up the tree and placed the poison
of his wickedness, that is desire, in the fruit.[2] He thereupon
bent the branches down to the earth, and I took of the fruit
and ate it. Mine eyes were at once opened, and I knew that
I was naked, divested of the righteousness with which I had
clad myself. Bitterly did I weep, saying unto the serpent:
' Why hast thou done this unto me, and thus deprived me of
my glory?' I also wept, because I remembered the oath I had
taken to give of the fruit to my husband. The serpent went
down from the tree and vanished, and I went about in the
garden to search for leaves wherewith to cover my shame.

[1] Cf. *Pirke de Rabbi Eliezer*, Ch. 13.
[2] See *Emek hamelekh*, fol. 23c—where it is said that on eating the fruit, Eve felt in herself
the poison of original sin, or *yezer hazā* (evil inclination).

There were none, for all the leaves upon the trees had disappeared, except those of the fig tree, and it was of the fruit of the fig tree that I had eaten.[1] I took the leaves and made a girdle to hide my nakedness. Thereupon I called your father and said : ' My lord, where art thou, come and I will show thee a wonderful thing and reveal unto thee a secret.' And I persuaded him to eat of the fruit of the tree, for Satan spoke out of my mouth. In the hour when your father had eaten the forbidden fruit, we heard the angel Michael sounding his trumpet and calling to all the angels: ' Come ye down, all angels, into the garden to hear the judgment by which the Lord will judge Adam.'

" Thereupon the Lord commanded His angels to drive us out of the garden. Your father then prayed to the Lord and said: ' O Lord of the Universe, remit unto me my transgressions and bestow on me of the fruit from the tree of life, that I may eat thereof before I go forth from the garden.' But the Lord replied: ' In the present thou shalt not receive of the fruit from the tree of life, for I have commanded the Cherubim with the flaming sword to guard the path and not allow thee to eat thereof and abide deathless for ever. But when, driven out of Paradise, thou wilt keep away from wickedness and be ready to die, when thy time comes, then, on the day of resurrection, I will raise thee up and give thee of the fruit from the tree of life and thou shalt abide deathless for ever.' We went forth from the garden and were placed on this earth."

Thus spoke Eve to her children, and wept bitterly, whilst Adam lay before them, afflicted in his sickness.

After six days, as the archangel Michael had foretold, Adam died. The sun and moon and stars lost their radiance and grew dark for seven days. Adam's soul was carried up in a fiery chariot, and angels went before the chariot. Then all

---

[1] Cf. *Genesis Rabba*, 15; *Midrash Haggadol, Genesis*, col. 90.

the angels prostrated themselves before the Throne of Glory, and beseeched the Lord to vouchsafe remission to Adam. "O Lord of the Universe," they prayed, "take pity on Adam who is Thine image and was fashioned by Thine own spotless hand."

And lo, the angel Michael appeared before the weeping Eve and the sorrowing Seth, and thus he spoke: "Arise now from the corpse of your father and husband, for God has taken pity on him who was fashioned in the image of the Lord." Thereupon one of the archangels blew his trumpet, and all the ministering angels called aloud: "Blessed is the glory of the Lord, for He has taken pity upon Adam." And Seth saw how God, having taken the soul of Adam, gave him into the hands of Michael saying: "Bear him unto the third heaven, and let him repose there until the great and terrible day, when I will change his suffering into joy."

Thereupon angels came down from Heaven and descended upon earth, and came to the spot where the body of Adam was lying. And the voice from the Throne of Glory called out: "O Adam, hadst thou not transgressed the commandment I gave unto thee, thine adversary, who has brought thee to such a state, would not rejoice now. But I say unto thee that I will turn the rejoicing of the enemy into sorrow, and thy sorrow into rejoicing." Then God commanded the angels Michael and Uriel to spread out fine linen cloths and enfold the body of Adam and to bury him, and the angels Michael and Uriel did as the Lord had commanded them. Thereupon they said unto Seth: "Thus shalt thou bury every man who shall die until the great day of the resurrection."

Six days after Adam's death, Eve, feeling that her end was near, gathered about her all her sons and daughters, and she prayed to the Lord not to separate her body from the body of Adam, her spouse, but to let her be near him, even as she had been together with him during their lives, and to let her be buried by the side of Adam from whose bones the Lord did fashion her. Thereupon she enjoined her children to erect two slabs of clay and stone, and write on them the names and history of herself and of Adam. " For I have been informed by the angel Michael," she said, " that God has decided to bring upon the world a destructive fire and a flood. These slabs of clay and stone alone will escape destruction." Thus spoke Eve and passed away six days after the death of Adam. The angels buried her by the side of Adam, in the neighbour- hood of Paradise. Then the angel Michael appeared to Seth and said: " Do not mourn more than six days for thy dead, and rest and rejoice on the seventh, for on that day, which is the symbol of resurrection, God and His angels will receive the soul freed from all earthly matter." [1]

In Moslem legend the story of Adam's life after his fall and his expulsion from Eden runs as follows: After Adam had fallen he was excessively grieved and penitent, and his beard grew. He was greatly perturbed at this growth of hair upon his chin, and a voice from Heaven called out and said: " Be not grieved, O Adam, for the beard is man's ornament upon earth where it distinguishes him from the weak woman." And Adam's tears flowed abundantly, and not only did beasts and birds drink freely, but the tears that dropped from his eyes, of him who had partaken of the fruit of Paradise, flowed into the earth, producing gum-bearing trees and fragrant plants. And Eve, too, shed many tears in her great sorrow. Her tears, when falling into the sea, were transformed into costly pearls, and into fragrant and beautiful flowers when they sank into earth. Both Adam and Eve wept bitterly over the loss of the Garden of Eden, and they wailed so loud that their cries were borne from one to the other on the wings of

---

[1] See for the above: *Vita Adae et Evae*, edit. W. Meyer; C. Fuchs, *Das Leben Adams und Evas*, in Kautzsch, *Die Apokryphen*, Vol. II, pp. 506 ff. Tischendorf. *Apocalypses Apocryphae, Apocalypsis Moses*, 1866; Conybeare, *On the Apocalypse of Moses*, *J.Q.R.*, Vol. VII, pp. 219 ff.

the east and west winds. And when they heard each other weep, their sorrow increased.[1]

Eve clasped her hands above her head, whilst Adam put his right hand under his beard. Then the tears poured afresh out of the eyes of our first parent that they formed two rivers, the tears out of the right eye the river Euphrates and the tears out of the left the river Tigris. And all nature wept with Adam, and the beasts and birds, who had hitherto shunned him on account of his sin, were moved by his wailing and his tears, and came to him to show him pity.

But the locusts were the first to arrive, because they had been created from the handful of earth left over after Adam had been created. The locusts, therefore, are privileged among other animals. There are seven thousand kinds of them in all colours and shapes, and they are ruled by a king whom God commands and sends out whenever He wishes to punish and destroy a sinful nation such as the Egyptians under Pharaoh. The black characters on the locusts' wings signify in Hebrew: God is one; He overcometh the mightiest; the locusts form a portion of His hosts which He frequently sends out against the wicked.

All nature was thus full of wailing and lamentation, for all nature wailed and lamented with Adam, from the smallest, almost invisible, insect to the angel who holds the earth in one hand. Thereupon God sent his angel Gabriel unto Adam, and he taught him how to cry and pray for forgiveness with a penitent heart. (He was to say: ' There is no God but Thou; forgive me for the sake of Mohammed, the great and last prophet, whose name is engraved on Thy throne.') When Adam had spoken these words with a penitent heart, the gates of Heaven opened, and the angel Gabriel cried out: " O Adam! God has accepted thy penitence; pray unto Him alone and He will grant thy prayers and give thee all

[1] Weil, *Biblische Legenden der Muselmänner*, pp. 29–38.

that thou desirest, even thy return to Paradise, after a certain time." And Adam prayed unto God and said: " O Lord, protect me from further intrigues of mine enemy Iblis." And a voice from Heaven answered him: " Speak continually the words: ' There is no God but God;' these words will wound Iblis even like a poisoned arrow." And Adam asked: " Lord, will not the food and drink provided for me by this earth lead me into sin?" And the voice from Heaven again replied: " Drink water and eat only clean beasts, beasts which have been killed in the name of God, and build mosques for thy dwellings, and then Iblis will have no power over thee." But Adam still continued to query; " And if Iblis torments me at night with evil thoughts and dreams?" " Rise from thy couch," was the answer, " and pray." " O Lord," Adam continued, " how shall I ever be able to distinguish between good and evil?" And the Eternal replied unto him: " I will vouchsafe unto thee My guidance, and two angels shall always dwell in thy heart; they will warn thee against evil and encourage thee to do good." And Adam once more prayed: " O Lord! assure me also of Thy grace against future sin!" But the Eternal replied: " That thou canst only obtain by good works. But this I can promise thee, however, that evil shall be punished one fold, good shall be rewarded ten fold." [1]

In the meantime the angel Michael was sent to Eve to announce to her the mercy and grace of God. And Eve asked the angel: " With what weapons shall I, who am feeble and frail, lacking strength of heart and mind, fight against sin?" Spake the archangel Michael: " God has endowed thee with shamefacedness which will serve thee as weapon. And just as man is able to restrain his passions by virtue of his faith, so thou mayest conquer them by this shamefacedness." " And what," queried Eve, " will protect me against the strength of man who is stronger and more vigorous than I am, both

---

[1] Weil, *loc. cit.*

in body and in mind, and who will, moreover, be always privileged by the laws made by man?" " I have placed in the heart of man," answered Michael, " love and the feeling of compassion, and these will protect thee in future against man's brute force."

When Iblis saw the mercy vouchsafed to Adam and to Eve by the Almighty, his courage grew and he dared to implore the grace of God for himself, and to entreat the Almighty to ameliorate his lot. And the Creator decreed that Iblis should not be tormented in Hell until the day of resurrection, and that he should exercise unlimited power over all the sinners and the wicked who should reject the word of God.

" And where, O Lord," queried Iblis, " shall I dwell in the meantime?"

" Among ruins, in tombs, and in many other unclean places shunned by men!"

" And what will be my nourishment?" asked Iblis.

" All that is killed in the name of idols."

" And what will I drink when I am thirsty?"

" Wine and other intoxicating liquors."

" And in my hours of idleness what will be my occupation?"

" Music, dancing, and song."

" And what is my destiny?"

" The curse of God until the day of judgment."

" And how," asked Iblis, " am I to fight against man who will have received Thy revelation and to whom Thou hast given two angels for his protection?"

" Thy offspring," was the reply, " will be more numerous than the offspring of man, for to every man born in this world, seven evil spirits will come into the world." [1]

And the Creator then made a covenant with the progeny of Adam. He touched Adam's back, and from it crept

[1] Weil, *loc. cit.*

out all the generations which were to be born until the end of days. They were about the size of ants, and they came and ranged themselves on his right and on his left. And God said unto Adam: " All the disobedient of thy children, if they remain obstinate, will be condemned to Hell, but the believers shall enjoy eternal bliss in Paradise." " So be it," said Adam. And thus shall it be on the day of resurrection, when Adam will call every one by his name and pass sentence according to merit. And then God again touched Adam's neck and all his posterity returned into it again.[1]

ADAM AND EVE DO PENANCE

Þanne seyde Adam wiþ ruful ble:
Eue, let swiche wordis be,
   Þat god vs eft noȝt werye!
Eue, þow were mad of me,
Þerfore in no wyse how it be
   Þe wile y noȝt derye.

Bote rys, and go we eft wiþ mod
For to seken vs sum fod,
   Þat we ne deye for mys!
Þeȝ souȝten aboute wiþ sory mynde,
Bote swich myȝte þeȝ, nowher fynde
   As hy hadden in paradys.

Bote þer þeȝ founden such mete
As bestis and briddes ete.
   Adam tolde Eue his þoȝte:
Þis mete god ȝaf bestis to.
Go we sorwen and nomen also
   In his siȝt þat vs wroȝte.

And for oure trespas do penaunce,
Fourty dayes wiþouten distaunce,
   And praye god, kyng of riȝt,

[1] Weil, *loc. cit.*

Gif he vs wolde forȝeuen his mod,
And granten vs som lyues fod,
  Wherwiþ we lyuen myȝt.

Þus to Adam þo seide Eue:
Tel me, lord, at wordis breue,
  What is penaunce to say?
And how mowe we penaunce do?
Þat we namore byholen him to
  Þan we fulfelle may:

In aunter ȝif oure god dere
Wile noȝt heren oure preyere
  Bote turne his face fro vs,
For þat we oure penaunce breke.
Þan anon gan Adam speke
  And seide to Eue riȝt þus:

Fourty dayes þow myȝt do,
And y rede þow do so,
  For oure synnes sake,
And y fourty and seuene wile fulfelle,
Gif god wile of his guod wille
  On vs eny mercy take:

For on þe seuende day god made ende,
Of his work guod and hende
  He restyde him þat day.
Þerfore rys and tak a stone,
To Tygre flod gynne þow gon,
  And do as y þe say:

Vppon þat ston loke þat þow stonde,
Vp to þe nekke in þe stronde,
  Til fourty dayes don be,
Of þy mouth let no word reke—
We be noȝt worþy to god to speke:
  Oure lippes vnclene be,

For þeʒ byten þe appel aʒens his steuene,
And y shel fourty dayes and seuene
  Be in þe fflom Jordon,
Gif ʒit oure lord aboue þe sky
On vs wile haue eny mercy
  For oure mochel mon.

Canticum Creatione, MS. Trin. Coll., Oxford, 57, fol. 156
    (written in 1375).   See C. Horstmann, *Sammlung
    altenglischer Legenden*, 1878, pp. 125–126.

CHAPTER XVI

The Quarrel of the Brothers

Cain and Abel—The jealousy of Cain—The twin sisters—The burial of Abel—The two ravens—The story of the fratricide in Christian and Mohammedan literature—Another version of the burial of Abel—The repentance of Cain—Cain is a son of Sammael—The death of Cain—His descendants—Cain was the first to build a city—Seth, into whom the soul of Abel passes—The Sethites and the Cainites—The sons of God and the daughters of man—The Nephilim, or the Fallen—The story of Seth in Christian and Mohammedan literature—Quotation from Suidas—Alexander the Great on the sepulchre of Cainan—God decides to destroy the world by water.

CAIN and Abel, the two sons of Adam and Eve, did not live in peace, but always quarrelled and never could agree, for whatever one brother had the other, too, wanted it at once. Abel, therefore, said unto his elder brother: " Let us divide our property, and thus we will live in peace, take thou the earth and all that is fixed, whilst I will take all the moveable property." But Cain was of a wicked disposition, and black envy and hatred always dwelt in his heart. He persistently persecuted his gentle brother and gave him no rest. " The earth is mine," he exclaimed one day, " and the plains are mine and I forbid thee to stand on my property." Greatly astonished at such a command from his brother, Abel meekly ran up the hills there to rest. But Cain called after him: " And the hills? Are not the hills mine too, for the whole earth belongs to me." [1] Thus the quarrel began.

One day the flock of Abel came to pasture near the ground

---

[1] See Bin Gorion, *loc. cit.* pp. 137 and 372; *Genesis Rabba*, 22.

which Cain was ploughing, and he bade his brother leave the spot at once. " But thou, too," said Abel, " art using my property. Hast thou not taken the skins of my sheep and the wool of their fleeces and used them for thy clothing? Have I ever grudged thee anything from my possessions?" But Cain grew even more furious at the gentle words of Abel and made up his mind to kill his brother.[1]

Cain, according to Rabbinic legend, was not the son of Adam, but the child of Sammael, the beautiful, the resplendent who had been hurled from Heaven into the region of darkness. He had seduced Eve, and the son she bore, Cain, was not like the earthly beings, but like unto the inmates of Heaven.[2]

Now Cain was jealous of his brother Abel, not only because the latter's offering had been accepted and his own abhorred, but because Abel's twin sister was the most beautiful of women, and Cain desired her in his heart. He, therefore, conceived the plan of slaying his brother Abel and of taking his twin sister from him.[3]

When the deed had been accomplished, Adam and Eve were sitting, mourning and weeping, in their great sadness and grief of having lost Abel, their son. But they were yet unaccustomed to burial, and did not know what to do with the body. The dog which had guarded Abel's flock was still guarding his master's dead body from all the beasts in the field and all the fowls of the heavens. Now the Lord decided to teach Adam what to do with the body. A raven had just fallen dead by the side of Adam, and behold, another raven came, took its fellow, dug it in the earth and buried it. And Adam watched and wondered and said unto himself: " I will act like this raven did act." [4] And he took the corpse of Abel, dug a hole in the earth and buried it. The ravens who had

---

[1] *Sepher Hajashar.*
[2] *Pirke de Rabbi Eliezer*, Ch. 21, and Ch. 22. See also *Targum Jerushalmi, Genesis* 4, 1; 5, 3; *Yalkut Shimeoni, Genesis*, § 29 and § 35.   [3] *Pirke de Rabbi Eliezer*, Ch. 21.
[4] *Pirke de Rabbi Eliezer*, Ch. 21, *Yalkut Shimeoni, Prov.* § 963.

done the bidding of the Lord and taught man how to bury his dead received a good reward from the Maker of the Universe, for when his young ones cry the Almighty provideth their sustenance without lack.[1]

The legends relating to the quarrel between the two brothers are also found in Christian as well as in Mohammedan sources. Thus Eutychius, Patriarch of Alexandria, relates in his *Annales* the following story: After their sin and disobedience to the command of God, Adam and Eve were expelled from Paradise on Friday at the ninth hour. They were sent to a mountain in India and commanded to produce children and increase and multiply upon the earth. Thus it came to pass that Eve bore a boy named Cain and his twin sister named Azrun. Sometime afterwards Eve again gave birth to twins, a boy named Abel and a girl named Owain, or in Greek Laphura. Azrun, Cain's twin sister, was much prettier than Owain, Abel's twin sister. Now when the children had grown up, Adam said to Eve: " Cain shall marry Owain who was born with Abel, and Abel shall marry Azrun who is Cain's twin sister, for they should not marry their own twin sisters." Thus spoke Adam, but Cain grew angry when he heard these words of his father: " I will marry my own twin sister," he said to his mother, " and Abel will marry his."

Thereupon Adam said to his sons: " Take of the fruit of the earth and of the young of the sheep, and ascend ye the top of this holy mountain, there to offer the best and choicest to God." The two brothers did as their father bade them, and Abel indeed offered the best and fattest of his first born lambs. But when they were ascending the top of the mountain, Sammael, or Satan, came and whispered to Cain to kill his brother, so as to get rid of him and thus be free to marry his own twin sister Azrun. As his oblation had not been

---

[1] *Pirke de Rabbi Eliezer*, Ch. 21; *Midrash Haggadol*, col. 117; *Genesis Rabba*, 22, where another story is given of Abel being buried by Cain himself.

accepted by God, Cain grew even more enraged against his brother and made up his mind to kill him.

When they were descending the mountain, he rushed upon his brother and hurling a stone at his head killed him. For one hundred years Adam and Eve bewailed the death of their son Abel, whilst Cain had been cast out into the land of Nod. He carried off, however, his sister Azrun with him.[1]

The same legend is told in Moslem tradition. Thus we read in the *Chronicle of Tabari* that Adam and Eve had many children, and that every time that Eve bore she bare twins, one male and the other female. Kabil, or Cain, and his twin sister were born when Adam and Eve still dwelt in Paradise, whilst Habil, or Abel, and his twin sister were born after the expulsion of Adam and Eve from Paradise. Now it was the wish of Adam that each of the brothers, when he was old enough to marry, should take to wife the twin sister of his brother. But the twin sister of Cain was of surpassing beauty, and Cain was dissatisfied. Thereupon Adam said to his sons: " Go ye, my sons, and sacrifice to the Lord, and he whose sacrifice is accepted, shall marry the beautiful girl."

Abel, being a shepherd, took the fattest of the sheep, bore it to the place of sacrifice and offered it to God. Cain, however, who was a tiller of the soil, took only the poorest sheaf of corn he could find and placed it upon the altar. Thereupon a fire descended from Heaven and consumed the offering of Abel, whilst the sheaf of corn offered by Cain remained untouched. Adam then gave the maiden to Abel as wife, and Cain was greatly vexed. He made up his mind to kill his brother, and one day, when Abel was asleep on the summit of a mountain, he took a stone and crushed his brother's head. He threw the corpse upon his back and walked about with it, not knowing what to do with it. One day, however, he saw two crows fighting and one killing the other. Thereupon the

---

[1] Eutychius, *Annales*, I, 14.

crow that had killed its companion dug a hole in the earth and buried the dead crow. When Cain saw this, he thought: " I, too, will lay the corpse of my brother in the ground and hide it." [1]

According to the *Pirke de Rabbi Eliezer*, it was Cain himself who had buried his brother's corpse, so as to hide what he had done from the eye of God, not knowing that God can see everything. And when the Lord accused Cain of the murder of his brother he exclaimed: " My iniquity is too great to be atoned for, except by my brother rising from the earth and slaying me, for my sin has no atonement." [2] And this utterance was reckoned to him as repentance. The Lord thereupon took one letter of the twenty-two letters of the alphabet and put it upon Cain's arm, so that he should not be killed. God had cursed Cain for his foul deed, but on account of his repentance and his contrition, the symbol of pardon was placed on his brow. Some say that it was a horn which grew out of the midst of his forehead. And when Adam met his son and seeing the token upon his brow, the symbol of pardon, he wondered greatly and asked: " How hast thou turned away the wrath of the Almighty?"

" By repentance and confession of my sin," replied Cain.

" Great is the virtue of repentance," cried Adam, " and I knew it not. Had I known it, I might have altered my lot." [3]

And Cain wandered over the face of the earth, accompanied by his wife, and at last settled in the land of Nod. But he did not mend his ways, for the spirit of Sammael was in him. He was not of Adam's seed, nor after his likeness, nor after his image.[4] His soul was from Sammael, his body alone from Eve. And all his children became demons of darkness, and all his offspring rebels against their Maker. Cain himself never changed his violent and passionate nature. He lived by

[1] *Chronique de Tabari*; Abulfeda, *Historia Ante-Islamica*, pp. 12–15. A similar story is told by Masudi and Yakubi. See Grünbaum, *loc. cit.*, p. 69.
[2] *Pirke de Rabbi Eliezer*, Ch. 21.   [3] *Genesis Rabba*, 22.   [4] *Pirke de Rabbi Eliezer*, Ch. 22.

robbery and rapine and encouraged his children to lead a similar life. They corrupted the primitive simplicity of men by introducing weights and measures, by placing boundaries and walling cities.[1] Cain was at last killed by Lamech who once exclaimed to his two wives Adah and Zillah: " For I have slain a man to my wounding, and a young man to my hurt." [2] Lamech, who belonged to the seventh generation after Cain, had two wives, named Adah and Zillah. Zillah was barren till in her old age she bare Tubal-Cain and his sister Naamah. Now it came to pass that Lamech became blind in his old age and was led about by his boy Tubal-Cain. One day Tubal-Cain saw in the distance their great ancestor Cain. From the horn upon the latter's forehead, the boy supposed that it was a wild beast and he hastily exclaimed: " Father, span thy bow and shoot the wild beast." Blind Lamech quickly complied with the boy's request, discharged his arrow and killed his great-ancestor Cain. When at last he was informed by Tubal-Cain of their error and that he had in reality slain his ancestor Cain, Lamech smote his hands together in his despair, and in so doing accidentally struck his own son and killed him. And his wives were very wroth with him.[3]

In this song of Lamech, in which some authors saw a song of triumph, others see a song of menace, and others again an expression of remorse and penitence, the blind man thus indicating his deed by which he had killed both Cain and Tubal-Cain.

This legend of the deed of Lamech was known to St. Jerome, who relates that in his day there existed a tradition among the Jews, accepted, too, by certain of the Christians, to the effect that Lamech had killed Cain by accident.[4]

[1] Josephus, *Antiquities*, 1, 2.   [2] *Genesis*, 4, 24.
[3] *Tanchuma* to *Genesis*, 4, 14; *Rashi* to *Genesis*, 4, 23; *Yalkut, Genesis*, § 38; *Sepher Haja-shar. Shalsheleth Hakkabbala*. See also Grünbaum, *Neue Beiträge zur semitischen Sagenkunde*, p. 70.
[4] St. Jerome, *Epist.* 26, *ad Damasum*. See also Lenormant, *Les Origines de l'Histoire*, I, p. 188.

The offspring of Cain were very wicked indeed, for from him descended all the generations who sin against the Lord and rebel against the commands of the Creator. And the sons and daughters who descended from Cain defiled themselves with immorality, and their wickedness was great on the earth. The daughters of the generations of Cain were walking about like harlots, having neither modesty nor shame, and with painted eyes and naked flesh they led astray not only mortal men, but also the angels who had fallen from Heaven and walked amongst men. They saw the daughters of man of the generations of Cain, that they were fair, and they went astray after them.

It is also related that Cain knew his wife Qualmana and she bore him a son named Enoch. He thereupon built a city and called it Enoch after the name of his son. Cain was thus the first to build a city, to surround it with a wall and to dig trenches.[1] He was the first to build a city and to surround it with a wall, because he was afraid of his enemies. To this city Cain used to entice people and there rob and plunder them. It has rightly been pointed out by Lenormant,[2] that the idea which associated the formation of a city with a fratricide is one of the ideas common to most nations, and may be traced almost everywhere. It begins with Cain and ends with Romulus, who laid the foundations of Rome in the blood of his brother Remus. This city became very corrupt, and its inhabitants were very wicked, as were all the descendants of Cain.

The Sethites and the Cainites

Now after the death of Abel Eve bore another son unto Adam, who was named Seth. Into the body of Seth passed the soul of the righteous Abel, and the same soul passed afterwards into Moses.[3] Seth, majestic in appearance and very

---

[1] Gaster, *The Chronicles of Jerahmeel*, p. 50, Ch. 24.   [2] *Loc. cit.* Ch. 4.
[3] *Shnee Loukhoth*, quoted by Eisenmenger, *Entdecktes Judentum*, Vol. I, p. 645.

handsome, was instructed by the angels who taught him much wisdom. He knew what would take place in the world, knew that men would be very wicked and their iniquity grow, so that they would, in the end, be destroyed by a flood.

It was revealed to him that the earth would be destroyed first by water then by fire. Thereupon Seth, lest those things revealed to him should perish from the memory of man, set up two pillars, one of brick and one of stone and wrote thereon all that he knew and all the science which he had acquired.[1] Seth married his twin sister named Azura, or, according to others, Noba, or Noraea.[2] He became the father of all the generations of the righteous. But the generations descended from Cain were all wicked. Among them were Tubal-Cain and his sister Naamah. Naamah became afterwards one of the wives of Sammael, or, according to others, of Shomron, and bare unto him the demon Ashmedai.[3] Naamah invented all kinds of instruments for weaving silk, and was the first to play upon musical instruments in honour of the idols.[4]

Now, as long as Adam was still alive, the sons of Seth had never intermarried with the daughters of Cain. The former dwelt in the mountains not far from the Garden of Eden, whilst the latter lived in the fields of Damascus. But when Adam had died, the children of Seth, who were called the Sons of God, or the children of Elohim, grew wicked. They looked upon the daughters of man, or the seed of Cain, took wives from among them and begat the giants who peopled the earth in the days of Noah. It is thus from the descendants of Seth and the descendants of Cain that the giants came forth; wicked, corrupt, and haughty of spirit, they were swept away by the waters of the flood, and were also called the Nephilim, or the Fallen.[5] It has been pointed out that Seth is the

---

[1] Josephus, *Antiquities*, 1, 2.   [2] *Book of Jubilees*, 4, 11.
[3] See Hamburger, *Real-encycplopædie für Bibel und Talmud*, Vol. II, *s.v. Ashmedai*.
[4] *Rashi to Genesis*, 4, 21; *Targum Jerushalmi to Genesis*, 4, 22.
[5] Gaster, *The Chronicles of Jerahmeel*, p. 52.

name of an Egyptian Sun deity, and subsequently identified
with Typhon. He was the chief god of the Hyksos or Shepherd
Kings.[1]   Some of the legends contained in Talmudic and
Midrashic lore concerning Seth may be traced back to Egyptian
influence, who regarded Seth as the giver of light and civilization.   Seth is also said to have dwelt in Heaven for forty
days and to have been instructed in the ethical law by the
angels.   It was he who invented the art of writing, who gave
names to the five planets and divided time into months, weeks,
and years.[2]

The legends concerning Seth and the Sethians, and Cain
and the Cainites, play an important rôle not only among the
Jews, but also among Moslems, Samaritans, and Gnostic
Christians.   Thus we read in Abulfaraj [3] that Seth discovered
letters and went to dwell upon Mount Hermon, where he
and his offspring served God and never associated with the
people of the land, abstaining to intermarry with them.   It
is for this reason that the Sethites, or descendants of Seth,
were called the Sons of God.

This same idea, which, as has been pointed out, occurs
in the *Chronicles of Jerahmeel*,[4] is found in Suidas, under the
heading *Seth*, and in Christian pseudoepigraphic literature.
Thus Suidas writes: " The Sons of God went unto the
daughters of men, that is to say, the sons of Seth intermarried
with the daughters of Cain. Seth was called God in those
days, because he had discovered Hebrew letters, and also
the names of the stars. He was especially called so on account
of his great piety, so that he was the first to bear the name
of God." [5]

In other Christian sources it is related that the sons and
descendants of Seth lived upon the holy mountain, where
they led a life of piety and abstinence, pleasing to God. There

---

[1] J. Braun, *Naturgeschichte der Sage*, Vol. I, p. 264.
[2] See Fabricius, *Codex Pseudoepigraphicus, Vet. Test.*, Vol. I, pp. 141–147.
[3] *Historia Dynastiarum*, p. 5.   [4] Ch. 24.   [5] Suidas, *Lexicon, s.v. Seth*.

they heard the voices of the angels and their heavenly music, and joined in their praises of the Lord of the Universe. Later, however, in the days of Jared, the descendants of Seth began to lend an ear to the alluring songs of the seductive daughters of Cain who dwelt in the plain, at the foot of the mountain. Seduced by the alluring women, drawn by their song, many of the Sethites left the sacred mountain and descended into the plain. Here they saw women, attractive and shameless, their eyes painted like harlots, beautiful and walking about with naked flesh. Their passions were kindled, they desired them in sinful love and went astray with them.[1]

The mountain where dwelt the Sethites was called Hermon, because there they had made a covenant and sworn one to another to take wives from among the daughters of Cain.[2] Whilst, according to the *Pirke de Rabbi Eliezer*, and generally in Jewish tradition, the giants are considered to be the children of angels, who intermarried with the daughters of man, in the *Chronicles of Jerahmeel* they are the offspring from the sons of Seth and the daughters of Cain.[3] Gedalya Ibn Yachia, in his book *Shalsheleth Hakkabbala* (Chain of Tradition), explains, however, the Sons of God as the descendants of Seth. This opinion is also mentioned by Ibn Ezra and by Nachmanides in his Commentary.[4]

In the *Chronique de Tabari* we read that Seth was the greatest of the sons of Adam, that every day he made a pilgrimage to the Kaaba and ruled the world with equity. He and his followers waged a perpetual war against the giants, the sons of Kabil, or Cain. The Sethites dwelt upon a mountain, the Cainites in the plain. The former were allured by the songs sung to the playing of musical instruments invented by the Cainites. In spite of the injunction they had received

---

[1] Malan, *The Christian Book of Adam*, pp. 82-93; Eutychius, *Annales*, Vol. I, pp. 21-26; Bezold, *Die Schatzhöhle* (Cave of Treasures), p. 10.

[2] *Cedrenus*, ed. Bonn, 1, 19 (also in Migne, *Patrologia*, Vols. 121-122). See Grünbaum, *Neue Beiträge*, p. 73.

[3] *Pirke de Rabbi Eliezer*, Ch. 22; *Yalkut, Genesis*, § 44.   [4] Grünbaum, *loc. cit.*, p. 75.

from Adam to keep away from the daughters of Cain, who were very attractive, enhancing their beauty by various artificial devices, but very shameless and wicked, the Sethites at last came down from their mountain and fell.[1]

Yakubi also relates that in the days of Jared, the Sethites broke their oath, came down into the plain and sinned with the daughters of Cain.[2]

In one of his espistles, sent to his teacher Aristotle, Alexander the Great also wrote that in a province of India he had found men and women who lived on raw fish, and spoke a language very much like Greek. They informed him that in the islands there was the sepulchre of a most ancient king named Cainan, son of Enos, who knew that God would bring a flood in the days of Noah, wherefore he engraved all that was to take place on stone tables. Therein he had written that the ocean would overflow a third part of the world, an event which took place in the days of Enos, the son of Seth.[3]

And after the Sethites had intermarried with the Cainites, the earth was full of wickedness, and the Lord decided to destroy it by water.

THE PRAYER OF ABEL

Oh God!
Who made us, and Who breathed the breath of life
Within our nostrils, Who hath blessed us,
And spared, despite our father's sin, to make
His children all lost, as they might have been,
Had not Thy justice been so temper'd with
The mercy which is Thy delight, as to
Accord a pardon like a Paradise,
Compared with our great crimes: sole Lord of light!
Of good, and glory, and eternity;
Without Whom all were evil, and with Whom

---

[1] *Chronique de Tabari*, I, Ch. 34.   [2] Grünbaum, *loc. cit.*, p. 77.
[3] *Josippon* (Josephus Gorionides), ed. Amsterdam, 1771, Ch. 11, p. 33a; Fabricius, *Codex Pseudoepigraphicus, Vet. Test.*, Vol I, p. 157.

Nothing can err, except to some good end
Of Thine omnipotent benevolence—
Inscrutable, but still to be fulfill'd—
Accept from out Thy humble first of shepherd's
First of the first-born flocks—an offering,
In itself nothing—as what offering can be
Aught unto Thee?—but yet accept it for
The thanksgiving of him who spreads it in
The face of Thy high heaven, bowing his own
Even to the dust, of which he is, in honour
Of Thee, and of Thy name, for evermore!

Lord Byron—Cain a mystery, Act III, Scene 1.

THE REPENTANCE OF CAIN

My hand! 't is all red, and with—
What?
Where am I? alone! Where 's Abel? Where
Cain? Can it be that I am he? My brother,
Awake! Why liest thou so on the green earth?
'T is not the hour of slumber—why so pale?
What, hast thou!—thou wert full of life this morn!
Abel! I pray thee, mock me not! I smote
Too fiercely, but not fatally. Ah, why
Wouldst thou oppose me? This is mockery;
And only done to daunt me: 't was a blow—
And but a blow. Stir—stir—nay, only stir!
Why, so—that's well! thou breath'st! breathe upon me!
      Oh, God! Oh, God!
The earth swims round me—What is this? 't is wet;
And yet there are no dews! 'T is blood—my blood—
My brother's and my own; and shed by me!
Then what have I further to do with life,
Since I have taken life from my own flesh?
But he cannot be dead!—Is silence death?
No, he will wake: then let me watch by him.
Life cannot be so slight, as to be quench'd
Thus quickly! he hath spoken to me since—

What shall I say to him?   My brother!—No;
He will not answer to that name, for brethren
Smite not each other.   Yet—yet—Speak to me;
Oh! for a word more of that gentle voice,
That I may bear to hear my own again.

Lord Byron—Cain, a mystery, Act III, Scene 1.

THE CURSE OF EVE

May all the curses
Of life be on him! and his agonies
Drive him forth over the wilderness, like us
From Eden, till his children do by him
As he did by his brother!   May the swords
And wings of fiery cherubim pursue him
By day and night—snakes spring up in his path—
Earth's fruits be ashes in his mouth—the leaves
On which he lays his head to sleep be strew'd
With scorpions!   May his dreams be of his victim!
His waking a continual dread of death!
May the clear rivers turn to blood as he
Stoops down to stain them with his raging lip!
May every element shun or change to him!
May he live in the pangs which others die with!
And death itself wax something worse than death
To him who first acquainted him with man!
Hence, fratricide, henceforth that word is *Cain*
Through all the coming myriads of mankind,
Who shall abhor thee, though thou wert their sire!
May the grass wither from thy feet! the woods
Deny thee shelter! earth a home! the dust
A grave!   The sun his light! and Heaven her God!

Lord Byron—Cain, a mystery, Act III, Scene 1.

THE DEATH OF CAIN

LAMECH MISTOOK CAIN FOR A DEER

Lamech ledde long lif til ðan
ðat he wurð bisne, and haued a man
ðat ledde him ofte wudes ner,
To scheten after ðe wilde der;
Al-so he mistagte, also he schet,
And cain in ðe wude is let;
His knaþe wende it were a der.

An lamech droge is arwe ner,
And letet flegen of ðe streng,
Cain unwar(n)de it under-feng,
Grusnende, and strekende, and starf wið-ðan.
Lamech wið wreðe is knaþe nam,

Vn-bente is boge, and bet, and slog,
Til he fel dun on deders sevog.
Twin-wifing ant twin-manslagt,
Of his soule beð mikel hagt.

The Story of Genesis and Exodus (Early English Text Society),
Edited by Richard Morris, 1865, p. 14, l. 471–486.

THE DEATH OF ABEL

The seducer, with triumph in his look, remained near the dead. Elate with pride, he stretched his gigantic form to its full height, and his countenance was not less dreadful than the black pillars of smoke, arising from the half-consumed lumber of a lonely cottage, is to the inhabitants, who, returning from their peaceful labours, find all their conveniences, all their riches, the prey of the devouring flames. The seducer followed the criminal with his eyes, while a ruthless smile spoke his exultation. He then cast on the bleeding body a look of complacency. " Pleasing sight!" said he, " I see, for the first time, this earth wet with human blood. The flow of the sacred springs of Heaven, before the fatal hour when the Master of the Universe precipitated us from the seats of bliss, never gave me half this pleasure.   Never did the harmonious harps of the archangels give me such delight, as the last sighs of a brother murdered by his brother. . . . His own brother has left him weltering in his blood. No! that honour is mine; I guided the arm of the fratricide.   It is by action, such as Satan himself would boast, I shall rise above the populace of Hell. I hasten to the foot of the infernal throne. The vast concave of the fiery gulf will reverberate my praises."

The Death of Abel, by Solomon Gessner (Transl. by Mary Collyer, 1810, p. 125–126).

CHAPTER XVII

The Righteous Man in his Generation

The angels are jealous of Noah, called Menahem, or comforter—Noah preaches to the sinners—He builds an ark during fifty-two years—The giants and the ark—They mock and rail at Noah—The giants are alarmed—The wonders in Heaven—The angels gather all the animals and bring them to the ark—The rhinoceros—The tip of its nose is admitted in the ark—God closes and seals the gates of the ark—The giants try to stop the waters with their hands and the soles of their feet—The regret of the sinners—Noah's reply—The giant Og climbs up on the roof of the ark—The story of Falsehood and Injustice who are admitted in the ark—The Patriarch and his sons are busy feeding the animals—The food of the grasshopper—The noise in the ark when the animals are fed—The bird Orsinia who is blessed with long life—The cat and the mouse—The story of Noah in Moslem legend—The oven of Noah's wife begins to boil—Canaan refuses to enter the ark—The story of Satan and the ass—Satan, or Iblis, catches hold of the tail of the ass—The pig and the cat—How they were created in the ark.

AND when the earth was filled with violence and wickedness, God resolved upon its destruction. Not only men, but also beasts were utterly wicked and demoralized.[1] Noah alone, who had found favour in the eyes of the Lord, he and his family, and one pair of all the beasts of the earth, were to be saved from the flood, whilst of every clean beast seven were to enter the ark.

Noah was the son of Lamech, born unto him by his wife Betenos, a daughter of Barakill. When Noah was born, his grandfather Methuselah said: " This son will comfort us for all our trouble and all our work." [2] By his grandfather the boy was called Noah, which signifies rest, because in his

---

[1] *Sanhedrin,* 108a.   [2] Charles, *The Book of Jubilees,* 4, 28.

days the land rested from the curse; but Lamech called his son Menahem, which means comforter.[1]

And the Lord said to Noah: " I have found thee alone a righteous man in this generation." But the angels were jealous of Noah and they asked the Lord of the Universe; " What is the virtue of Noah and what deed has he done that he has found favour in Thine eyes?" And the Creator replied: " When Enos, the son of Seth, was born, he was told to find sustenance for his old father, and he agreed to do so. But when he was told to feed also his grandfather Adam, he refused, saying: " I have enough to do to feed my father, and cannot trouble myself to find also sustenance for my grandfather." Cainan, too, and Mahalalel, Jared, Methuselah, and Lamech, none of them worked and fed anybody but their own fathers. When Noah came, he found sustenance for and worked and fed all his relatives."

Thus spoke the Lord, and when the angels heard this, they agreed that Noah was the most generous man of his generation. Thereupon the Lord said to Noah: " Go and speak unto all the men who have sinned and ask them to turn from their wicked ways and evil deeds and not to anger the Lord, lest He bring upon them the waters of the flood and destroy them all, and they perish from the face of the earth. If they repent and turn from their evil ways, I will refrain from bringing any punishment upon them."

Thus spoke the Lord to Noah. And Noah went and told Methuselah all that the Lord had spoken unto him. Thereupon these two righteous men, Noah and Methuselah, went out and preached to all the sinners, but none of them would repent. God then told Noah to build an ark, for in another hundred and twenty years a flood would come upon the earth. Noah did as the Lord bade him do, and he began to build the ark, making it during fifty-two years.[2] But the people

[1] *Sepher Hajashar.*   [2] *Pirke de Rabbi Eliezer,* Ch. 23.

and the giants mocked Noah and said: " If God brings from
Heaven the waters of the flood upon us, behold we are of
such high stature that the waters will not reach up to our
necks, and if He bring the waters of the depth against us,
behold, the soles of our feet can close up all the depths."
Thereupon they put forth the soles of their feet, and closed
up all the depths. But when the flood came, the waters of the
deep were hot, burned their flesh and pealed off their skin.[1]

When the giants saw that Noah was proceeding with the
building of the ark, they came again to watch and mock the
old man. " Repent ye of your sins," said Noah, " for God
is merciful and will listen to your prayers." But they only
mocked him and replied: " We fear not thy God, for if He
rains upon us fire, we will bathe our bodies in the blood of
the Salamander, and fire will have no power over us." [2] Thus
they spoke every day, and all mocked Noah and laughed at
his ark.

Now Noah had worked for fifty-two years upon the ark,
so as to give time to the wicked to repent of their ways,
but they did not repent. In other sources it is said that Noah
built the ark in 120 years.[3] When the days of the flood
approached, the men of Noah's generation began to be alarmed,
for they saw great wonders in Heaven and upon earth. The
sun rose in the west and set in the east. Now it happened
in those days that the virtuous Methuselah died, and all the
beasts and fowls of the air came to accompany him to his
last resting-place. Thereupon God said unto Noah: " Take
to thee seven and seven of every clean beast, and of the beasts
that are not clean two, the male and the female." [4] Then
Noah said to the Lord: " Sovereign of all the worlds, I have
never been a hunter in all my life, and I have not the strength

---

[1] *Pirke de Rabbi Eliezer*, Ch. 23.

[2] *Midrash Abkhir*, quoted in *Yalkut Shimeoni*, § 42; *Midrash Tanchuma*; *Pirke de Rabbi
Eliezer*, Ch. 22; *Sanhedrin*, 108b; *Sepher Hajashar*.

[3] *Midrash Lekach Tob*, ed. Luber, p. 36.   [4] *Genesis*, 7, 2.

to collect all the animals into the ark." The angels, however, appointed over each kind, came down and gathered all the animals and with them all their food, so that the animals came of their own accord.[1]

Among the beasts which Noah brought to the ark was also the rhinoceros. When Noah saw this animal, who was only one day old, he understood that he could not lodge it in his ark. Being very large, forty-four and a half miles long, it would swamp the whole ark. He therefore made an aperture in the ark, took in the head of the rhinoceros, whilst the animal swam behind the vessel. Others say that even the head and the neck of the rhinoceros, which are three and a half miles long, could not be lodged in the ark. It was only the tip of the nose of the rhinoceros which Noah admitted into the ark. He also tied the horn of the animal to the side of the vessel lest the beast should slip off when the vessel lurched and thus perish.[2]

Now when seven days had elapsed after the death of Methuselah, and still the sinners continued in their evil and wicked ways, God sent a rain upon earth, saying: " If they repent, this rain will become a rain of blessing, but if they do not repent, it will turn into a flood and destroy them." The men, however, did not repent, and the flood at last burst out. Thunder and lightning came, and the earth trembled and was tossed about like a ship in mid-ocean; the arteries of the earth broke and spirted out water. Thereupon Noah and his family entered the ark, and the Holy One, blessed be His name, closed and sealed with His own hand the gates of the ark.[3] When the sinners saw that the flood was increasing, they at first tried to stop the waters with their hands and with the soles of their feet, and then they threw their children into the abyss to close up all the depths. Their efforts were all

[1] *Sanhedrin*, 108b; *Midrash Abkhir*, in *Yalkut*, § 42; *Genesis Rabba*, 32; *Pirke de Rabbi Eliezer*, Ch. 23.   [2] *Zebachim*, 113b.   [3] *Pirke de Rabbi Eliezer*, Ch. 23.

in vain, for stronger and stronger the flood came and covered the earth. The people thereupon gathered round the ark and tried to enter it, but a fire came down from Heaven and burned their feet, so that they drew back.[1] The sinners now implored Noah to take them in and give them shelter in his ark. " We repent of our sins," they cried, " only take us in that we may not die." But Noah only replied: " Now it is too late, for I had warned ye." The men thereupon tried to take the ark by force, but God sent wild beasts who fell upon them and drove them away from the ark.

Thus all living things were destroyed, except Noah and those who were with him in the ark.[2]

Among those who came to ask admittance to the ark was the giant Og. He climbed up on the roof of the ark, and refused to leave. Others say that he sat down on a piece of wood under the gutter of the ark, or on a rung of one of the ladders. He swore to Noah that if he allowed him to remain on the roof of the ark he and his posterity would always be the slaves of Noah and of his sons. The Patriarch allowed him to remain, and daily passed him his food through an aperture bored in the side of the ark.[3] Thereupon Falsehood, too, came to the ark and asked to be admitted, but Noah refused. " I admit the animals only in pairs," replied Noah; " go thou and find thee a mate and then thou, too, wilt be admitted." Falsehood, refused admittance, went away in wrath, and met Injustice.

" Why art thou so sad?" queried Injustice.

" Noah has refused to admit me in the ark," replied Falsehood, speaking the truth for once, " until I have found a companion. Now, if I have found favour in thine eyes, come and be my companion, and the pair of us will be admitted in the ark." Thus spoke Falsehood, but Injustice answered:

[1] Berachoth, 59; Genesis Rabba, 32.   [2] Berachoth, 59; Sepher Hajashar.
[3] Pirke de Rabbi Eliezer, Ch. 23.

FALSEHOOD AND INJUSTICE GAIN ADMITTANCE TO THE ARK

Facing page 212, Vol. I

"And what will be my reward, if I agree to be thy companion? Thou knowest full well that never do I take companionship without prospect of gain."

"I will give thee all that I shall have earned through my lies," said Falsehood. Injustice agreed, and they both went to find Noah who had to admit the pair in his ark. Falsehood was very busy among the inmates of the ark and acquired much wealth by lying and cheating.

When the flood had ceased and all the beasts came out of the ark, Falsehood said to Injustice: "Where is all the plunder which I have acquired? I have done my work well, but I see no booty!"

"I have taken it," said Injustice. "Didst thou forget our agreement? Thou wast to spread the net and I to take the spoils."[1]

During the time of the flood the sun and moon had been locked up by the Lord, and did not shed their light upon the world. Noah, however, knew when it was day or night, because the pearls and precious stones which he had taken with him into the ark sparkled at night time, but lost their lustre during the day.[2] The Patriarch had to know when it was day and when night, on account of the animals. There were some animals who had to be fed during the day, whilst others, on the contrary, had their food only at night.[3]

During his sojourn in the ark Noah hardly ever slept, but was constantly busy feeding the animals. The Patriarch himself fed the beasts, Shem took care of the cattle, Ham of the birds, and Japheth of the insects, giving them their daily rations. God taught Noah not only what food he should give to each animal or bird, but at what hour to feed them and what quantity to offer. One day the Patriarch forgot to feed the lion, and the beast bit him in the leg, so that he became

---

[1] *Midrash Tehillim*, Ps. 7; see also *Monatsschrift*, Vol. 25, p. 449.
[2] *Pirke de Rabbi Eliezer*, Ch. 23.   [3] *Genesis Rabba*, 34.

lame.[1] Noah knew nothing at first what food to offer to the grasshopper. But one day, whilst cutting open a pomegranate, a little worm fell to the ground, and the grasshopper swallowed it. After that Noah soaked bran in water, and when the worms began to grow therein he gave them to the grasshopper to eat.[2]

When Noah went round to feed the beasts and birds, the noise that arose in the ark was tremendous. The inmates of the ark roared and neighed, bleated, mewed, and chirped in chorus, each calling for its daily ration. One day Noah noticed the bird Orsinia lying still in a corner of the ark and not chirping like the other birds. The Patriarch wondered greatly and asked: " Why art thou not asking for thy food?" But the bird Orsinia replied: " I saw how busy and hard worked thou art in feeding all the inmates of the ark, and I preferred to suffer the pangs of hunger rather than increase thy work." When Noah heard these words of the bird Orsinia, he said: " Since thou didst have pity with me and didst wish to spare me work, I will bless thee, and wish thee long life." And the Lord heard the prayer of Noah and gave the bird Orsinia long life.[3]

It is also related that the cat and the mouse were at first good friends and lived peacefully together in the ark, but the mouse was jealous and said: " There is not sufficient food for both of us." But the Lord said: " Thou wicked beast, thou dost slander thy friend, because thou wouldst fain eat the cat. Hast thou not learned a lesson from the case of the sun and the moon? Both were equal in size, but the moon having slandered the sun, I diminished her size. Thou, too, didst slander thy friend, and wast eager to devour the cat, therefore it is the cat that will devour thee." The mouse, however, rushed and bit the cat, and the cat killed and ate the mouse. And since that time, the mice tremble at the approach of the cat which devours them.[4]

[1] *Genesis Rabba*, 30.   [2] *Sanhedrin*, 108b.   [3] *Ibid.*; see also *Yalkut Rubeni, Genesis*.
[4] *Alphabetum Siracidis*, ed. Steinschneider.   Cf. Gaster, *Roumanian Bird Stories*.

In Moslem legend it is related that whilst Noah was building the ark, all the people came and mocked him. " Why art thou building this ark, thou stupid fool," they said. But Noah replied and said: " The day will come, ye sinners, when ye will regret your words, and it is I who will then rail at ye. Ye will then learn that God not only punishes the wicked in this world, but also in the next." [1]

Noah then built the ark according to the instructions given to him and with the assistance of the angels. He had planted a teak tree which grew to such a size in twenty years that he was able to build the whole ark out of it. [2] When the time of the flood arrived, the oven of Noah's wife began to boil, and water flowed out of it. Thereupon water flowed from all the arteries of the earth. [3] Noah thereupon embarked with his wife and his three sons, and their wives, the three daughters of Eliakim, the son of Methuselah, and he invited all those who dwelt on earth to embark with him in the name of the Lord. Noah then noticed that his grandson Canaan was not among those who had embarked and he called to him and said: " Come, embark, my child, do not remain with the sinners." But Canaan refused to come and replied: " I will ascend one of the mountains where I will be safe from the flood." " Thou canst never be saved except by the mercy of God," said Noah, but Canaan would not listen to him. A wave then came and submerged Canaan. Then all the animals that were to enter the ark were collected and wafted by the wind towards the vessel. Among those who came was also the ass. Satan, or Iblis, who wanted to enter the ark, caught hold of its tail just at the moment when the ass was about to enter the ark, so that it proceeded rather slowly. Noah, growing impatient, called out: " Come on, thou accursed one, come on quickly, even if Satan were with thee." Iblis at once entered the ark. When Noah beheld Satan, he exclaimed:

[1] The Koran, *Sura Hud.*   [2] *Chronique de Tabari.*   [3] Abulfeda, *loc. cit.*

" And what art thou doing here? By what right didst thou come?" " I came by thy own invitation," replied Iblis; " didst thou not say to the ass: ' Come on, even if Satan were with thee ' ?"

Two sorts of animals, however, left the ark without having entered it. They were the pig and the cat. God had created these animals in the ark for a special purpose. The vessel was becoming full of filth and human excrements, and the stench was such that it could no longer be endured. When the inmates of the ark complained to Noah, he passed his hand down the back of the elephant, and the pig issued forth and ate up all the filth that was in the ark. Thereupon the inhabitants of the ark once more came to Noah and complained against the rats who were busy in the ark and caused great annoyance. They ate up all the food, and plagued the travellers in many other ways. Noah thereupon passed his hand down the back of the lion. The king of beasts sneezed, and a cat leaped out of its nose. The cat at once ate all the rats, and the travellers had peace.[1]

AN ANGEL VISITS NOAH

It is an angel to thee sent,
Noah, to tell thee hard tiding:
For ever-ilk wight for-warks (him) wild,
And many [are] soiled in sin[n]is seir
And in felony fowly filed.
Therefore a ship thou dight to steer
With tree [and] timber, highly railed,
Of thirty cubits [hight], but feare.
Look that she draw, when she is drest,
And in her side thou shear a door
With fenesters full fifty fest,
And make chambers both less and more.

[1] Weil, *Biblische Legenden der Muselmänner.*

In earth [there] shall be such a flood,
That everylke life that is livand:
Beast and body with bone and blood,
They shall be stroied [in water and sand]
Al but thou, Noah, and thy brood,
[Thy wife] and their three wives in hand—
(For you are full righteous and good)
You shall be saved by sea and land.

> *Noah's Ark,* or, *The Shipwrights' Ancient Play or Dirge*—
> played at Newcastle-upon-Tyne. See *The History of
> Newcastle-upon-Tyne,* by Henry Bourne.

NOE

(19)

Lord, at your byddinge I am bayne,
sith non other grace will gayne,
hit will I fulfill fayne,
for gratious I thee fynde.

A 100 wynters and 20
this shipp making taried haue I,
if through amendment any mercye
wolde fall vnto mankinde.

(20)

Haue done, you men and women all!
hye you lest this water fall,
that each beast were in his stall,
and into the ship broughte.

Of cleane beastes seauen shalbe,
of vncleane two, this God bade me;
this floode is nye, well may we see,
therfore tary you noughte.

> The Chester Plays, *The Deluge* (p. 53), Early English Text
> Society, Extra Series, LXII. Part I (1892).

CHAPTER XVIII

The Foolish Shepherd, and the Planting of the Vine

The mission of the raven—The protest of the bird—The dove and the olive leaf—The usefulness of the raven—Noah is anxious to be delivered from prison—His prayer—The desolation of the world—God rebukes the Patriarch—The foolish shepherd—The planting of the vine—The story of Satan who immolates a lamb, a lion, an ape, and a pig—The version of Ibn Yahya—The story of Satan and the vine in Moslem legend—The angel Raphael hands a book to Noah—Noah on the Mount Lubar—The suffering and complaint of Noah's children—The prayer of the Patriarch—The binding of the spirits—Mastema, the chief of the spirits, and his plea—Noah, the first physician—The angel Raphael teaches him the science of medicine—The secrets of the trees of healing—The knowledge of medicine spreads among the wise men of the east—The journey of Asklepinos and the forty learned men—They find the trees of healing and the tree of life—They are burned to ashes.

THE flood covered the whole earth, except the land of Israel which remained dry.[1] Now when Noah wished to know the state of the waters, he addressed himself to the raven and thus he spoke: " Go thou and see whether the flood hath ceased." But the raven replied: " The Lord hates me, for hath He not said that of my kind and of that of other unclean beasts thou shouldst only bring two into the ark? and thou, too, dost hate me, for thou seekest my destruction by sending me from among all other animals out of the ark. Now the prince of cold or of heat will meet me and kill me, and the world will have no raven for evermore." But Noah replied: " The world will well exist without thee, for thou art only an unclean beast."[2] Thereupon the raven went out, but finding

[1] *Zebachim,* 113a; *Pirke de Rabbi Eliezer,* Ch. 23.   [2] *Sanhedrin,* 108b.

the carcass of a man cast upon the top of a mountain it settled and remained to devour it, and it did not return to Noah with its message. Noah, therefore, sent forth the dove. She departed and without tarrying returned, for she had found no resting-place for her feet. But the second time the dove flew as far as the land of Israel where she came to the gates of Paradise. Here she saw the wonderful fruit and smelt the pleasant perfumes, but she had an olive leaf in her mouth when she returned. The dove wished to indicate that it is preferable to accept food that is bitter from the hand of God, rather than nourishment sweet as honey given by the hand of flesh and blood.[1]

In the meantime the raven returned to Noah, but the latter refused to admit it. But God said unto Noah: " Admit the raven once more into the ark, for in days to come the bird will be useful."

" When will this be?" asked Noah. " In another 1359 years," said the Lord, " when it will happen that a just man will stop the heavens from sending any rain upon earth. He will be in great straits, and I will send the ravens to feed him."

Noah had remained in the ark for twelve months, that is, a solar year, or one lunar year and eleven days, for the flood began on the 27th of Marcheshvan and ended on the 27th of this month a year later. During his life in the ark, he had worked assiduously, feeding all the animals, and very rarely slept. He naturally felt the strain and prayed to the Lord to release him: " Sovereign of all the worlds!" he prayed, " bring me forth from this prison, my soul being faint, because of the dread of the lions and the stench of the animals. All the righteous will crown Thee through me with a crown of sovereignty, because Thou wilt have brought me forth from this prison." [2]

But when Noah left the ark and saw how the world had

[1] *Pirke de Rabbi Eliezer*, Ch. 23; *Sanhedrin*, 108b; *Genesis Rabba*, 33; *Midrash Agadah*, ed. Buber, Vol. I, p. 19.   [2] *Pirke de Rabbi Eliezer*, Ch. 33.

been destroyed, he began to cry and said to the Lord: " Sovereign of the Universe! If it was because of the sinners that Thou hast destroyed the world, why didst Thou create them? Thou shouldst never have created the world, or not created man! And now where should I and my children go! The earth has been cursed, and its inhabitants have disappeared." But the Lord said unto Noah: " The inhabitants of the earth have been destroyed, but thou and thy children have been saved, and ye will increase and multiply." [1] Thereupon Noah rebuilt the altar which Adam had once built at the time when he had been cast forth from the Garden of Eden and had offered an offering upon it. Upon this altar Cain and Abel had also offered their offerings.[2]

Another version runs as follows: When Noah came out of the ark, and saw the destruction and the desolation of the world, he began to weep, and thus he said: " Sovereign of all the worlds! Merciful art Thou, but why hast Thou not pitied Thy children?" " Thou art a foolish shepherd," said the Lord. " Thou dost implore my clemency now, but when I told thee that I would bring a flood on the world thou didst say nothing. Thou didst know that thou wouldst be rescued in the ark, and didst care but little for the world. Hadst thou implored my clemency then, it would not have come to pass." And Noah's punishment was that he became lame and was abused by his son Ham.[3]

Then the Lord swore to Noah that thenceforth He would never bring the waters of the flood upon the earth.

Noah thereupon began to cultivate the earth and was the first who began to plant. It is related that he found a vine which had been cast forth out of the Garden of Eden. It had clusters of berries with it, and Noah, having eaten of them, desired the fruit in his heart. He thereupon planted a vine-

---

[1] *Yalkut Rubeni, Genesis.*
[2] *Targum Jerushalmi, Genesis,* 8, 20; *Genesis Rabba,* 34; *Pirke de Rabbi Eliezer,* Ch. 33.
[3] *Zohar Chadash;* see Bin Gorion, *loc. cit.,* p. 226.

yard, and on the selfsame day the fruit ripened, and Noah drank the wine.[1]

Another legend runs as follows: Noah was working very hard to break the hard clods, for the purpose of planting the grape. Suddenly Satan appeared before the Patriarch and said to him: " What art thou planting here?" " It is a vineyard I am planting," said Noah. " And what fruit will it bring forth?" " The grape," replied the Patriarch, " which gives joy to man and gladdens his heart." " Then let us work together," said Satan. Noah consented. Thereupon Satan brought a lamb, slaughtered it and poured its blood over the clods of earth. He then caught a lion, slaughtered it and again poured out the blood, drenching the soil with it. Noah looked and wondered. Satan thereupon caught an ape, slew it and poured the blood upon the clods of earth. At last he brought a pig, slaughtered it and fertilized the ground with its blood. And thereby Satan wished to indicate to Noah the following lesson: after tasting of the juice of the grape, drinking the first cup of wine, man becomes as mild and soft-spirited as a lamb; after the second cup, he becomes courageous as a lion, boasts of his power and of his might; after the third cup, he becomes intoxicated, dances, leaps, and gambols like an ape, making a fool of himself; but when he has drunk four or more cups of wine, he is like a pig, bestial, filthy and degraded—he is like a hog that wallows in mud.[2]

Ibn Yahya, in his *Shalsheleth Hakkabbalah*,[3] gives a different version of this legend. The Patriarch saw a goat eating sour grapes, and, becoming intoxicated, it began to gambol and frisk. He thereupon took the root of the vine branch, washed it with the blood of a sheep, a lion, an ape, and a hog, and planted it, so that it brought forth sweet fruit.

---

[1] *Pirke de Rabbi Eliezer*, Ch. 33.
[2] *Midrash Abkhir*, in *Yalkut Shimeoni*; *Midrash Agadah*, Vol. I, 22; *Genesis Rabba*, 36.— This story is also related in the *Gesta Romanorum*, Ch. 159, where, however, it is wrongly attributed to Josephus.   [3] Ed. Amsterdam, 1697, p. 75a.

This legend is also found in Moslem tradition. Here we are told that it was Ham who planted the vine, and that Satan sprinkled the soil with the blood of a peacock, an ape, a lion, and a swine. And thence it happens that the first glass of wine makes a man to be like a peacock, red in colour and vivacious. He is like an ape, leaping and dancing, when the wine has risen to his head. When in an advanced stage of intoxication, man becomes furious like a lion; whilst in a state of complete drunkenness, he is like a swine, rolling in the gutter, soiling his clothes, and wallowing in mud.[1]

Before Noah had entered the ark, the angel Raphael, the holy prince, came to him and thus he spoke: " By the will of the Lord of the Universe I have been sent to thee to heal the earth and to proclaim the events which will happen, and to tell thee what thou art to do so that thou mayest be saved." And he handed unto Noah the holy book which had once been in the possession of Adam, and taught him how to study it and how to preserve and guard it in sanctity of spirit and in purity of flesh. " Lo," said the angel of the Presence, " I give to thee this book and from its holy pages thou wilt learn much wisdom, also how to find the wood of gopher and to build an ark, wherein to hide, thou and thy sons, and thy wife and the wives of thy sons." And when Noah studied the holy book and learned its secrets he gathered much knowledge. And before he entered the ark which he had built, he hid the book. When he had left the ark, Noah received another book on the mountain of Lubar, in the mountains of Ararat. For in those days the spirits of the bastards began to make an endeavour to tempt and lead into sin the sons of Noah. They also sent upon them all sorts of ills and diseases which bring suffering and death unto man. And then the children of Noah and his children's children came to the Patriarch and complained of their ills and sufferings. Noah was sore at heart and very

---

[1] Collin de Plancy, *Légendes Bibliques*, p. 121.

grieved. He knew that it was on account of their sins that they had been visited by all kinds of ills and diseases. And Noah prayed before God, his Lord, and thus he spoke: " God of the spirits who are in all flesh, Thou who hast shown mercy unto me and saved me and my children from the waters of the deluge and didst not let us perish, as Thou didst cause to perish the children of evil and perdition, for great hath been Thy grace towards me, and great hath been Thy mercy to my soul. May Thy grace be lifted up over my children and the children of my children, and let not the evil and the malignant spirits rule over them and destroy them from the earth. Bless me and my children, so that we may grow, increase and mul- tiply and fill the earth, and Thou dost know how Thy watchers who were the fathers of these spirits acted in my day; and I pray Thee to imprison the spirits which are living, and to hold them fast in a place of condemnation, so that they may not destroy the children of Thy servant. For verily, they are terrible and wicked and have been created to destroy. Thou alone knowest their strength, and let them not have power over the spirits of living men. Let them not have power over the just from now and for evermore." Thus did Noah pray, and the Lord of the Universe commanded His angels to bind the spirits. But Mastema, the chief of the spirits, came and thus he spoke: " O Lord of the Universe, Creator of the world, allow some of them to remain free before me, so that they may listen to my voice and do all that I may tell them. For if some of them are not left unto me how can I exercise the power and dominion of my will over the children of man? For verily, the wickedness of the sons of man is great." And then the Creator replied and decreed that a tenth part of the spirits remained before Mastema, but that nine parts descend into the place of condemnation.

And the Creator also commanded one of the angels of the Presence to teach Noah all the medicines, and he did the bidding of His Creator, the Lord of the Universe, and he taught Noah all the medicines of the diseases, and how he might heal them with the herbs of the earth. And the angels also did according to the words of the Lord, and bound all the malignant and wicked spirits and placed them in the place of condemnation, but one-tenth of them only they left upon earth where they might be subject unto Mastema who is called Satan.[1] The Creator of the Universe thereupon sent down the angel named Raphael who taught Noah all sorts of remedies, and how to prepare medicaments and physic from the trees of the earth and from the growth of the earth and roots. And he sent the princes of the spirits to teach unto Noah all the trees of healing and all the herbs and roots and seeds. And they taught him the secrets of all these trees and herbs and seeds, and the purpose for which they have been created and all their power to heal and give life. And Noah wrote all the words down into a book which he handed to Shem his eldest son.[2] It is from this book that the future sages studied medicine and the art of healing and wrote many books in various tongues. And thus the knowledge of medicine spread among the wise men of Hodus (India), of Greece, and Egypt. For the wise men of Hodus (India) travelled all over the world and studied the qualities of the healing trees and the balm trees, and the wise men of Aram discovered all kinds of herbs for healing purposes. The wise men of Greece began to heal men of various diseases; and the wise men of Egypt began to practise incantations, magic, and witchcraft by means of the images of the constellations and the stars. And they studied the books of the Chaldeans. And their wisdom was very vast, until one of the wise men of Greece, named Asklepinos (Asklepios) and forty learned men with him travelled far and wide, and went out to Hodus (India) and beyond it to the country which

---

[1] *Book of Jubilees*, Ch. 10; Kautzsch, *Die Apokryphen*, Vol. II, p. 58.
[2] *Midrash Noah*, Jellinek, *Beth-Hamidrash*, Vol. III, pp. 155-160.

lies east of Eden, there to find the trees of life, so that their glory and renown might increase and excel the glory and renown of the wise men of the land. And it so happened that when they arrived to the place east of Eden, they found the trees of healing and the wood of the tree of life. And they stretched out their hands to take it, but the flaming sword touched them, and they were all set aflame and were burned to ashes and none of them escaped. And thus the knowledge of physics and of medicine left the healers and physicians and rested for 630 years, until the days of another wise and learned man of Greece, whose name was Isppocrates (Hypocrates), and of other wise men, whose names were: Asaph, the Jew, and Dioscorides, and Galenos, the Kaphthorite, and many others who renewed the knowledge of medicine and the art of healing.[1]

DE INVENTIONE VINEARUM

Josephus in libro de causis rerum naturalium refert, quod Noe invenit vitam silvestrem, id est labruscam a labris terrae et viarum dictam. Que cum esset amara, tulit sanguinem quatuor animalium scilicet leonis, agni, porci et simee, quo terre mixto fecit fimum, quem ad radices labruscarum posuit. Sic ergo vinum lorum sanguine est dulceatum. Quo facto Noe postea de vino inebriabatur, et nudatus jacens a filio juniori derisus, qui omnibus filiis ejus congregatis dixit, se ideo sanguinem dictorum animalium posuisse hominibus pro doctrina.

Carissimi, per vinum multi facti sunt leones per iram, nec illo tempore habent discretionem, aliqui agni per verecundiam, aliqui sunt simee per curiositatem assumptam ineptamque leticiam; nam simea omnia coram se facta eciam facere proponit, sed destruit. Quam si capere nolueris, plumbeos calceos habeas, et dum te illos exuentem induentemque conspexerit et fortiter ligantem, similiter facit; que, cum currere temptat, torquetur gravedine et captitar; quod de multis hominibus est simile, qui dum singula temptant in ebrietatibus vix aliqua perficiunt, sed sicut simea destruunt et confundunt.

Gesta Romanorum, Ch. 159, p. 539. Edit. Oesterley, Berlin, 1872.

[1] *Midrash Noah*, Jellinek, *Beth-Hamidrash, ibidem.*

CHAPTER XIX

The Astrologers and the Boy in the Cave

The birth of Abraham—The banquet of Terah—The big star—The prediction of the astrologers—Nimrod sends for Terah—The boy in the cave —Nimrod reads the stars—The imprisonment of the pregnant women— The miracle in the case of Emtelai, the wife of Terah—The boy recognizes the existence of the Creator—The meeting of mother and son—The advice of Satan—Abraham is carried by the angel Gabriel to the gates of Babylon —The opinion of the magicians—Abraham warns Nimrod—The King sends away the boy unmolested.

IT happened in the year 1948, after the creation of the world, in the month of Nissan. On a fine starlit night, several high dignitaries of the court of the great and famous King Nimrod, among whom were many magicians and astrologers, were returning home from a banquet offered to them by their friend Terah, one of the commanders of Nimrod's armies. He had invited his friends to rejoice with him on the occasion of the birth of his son Abraham, whom his wife Emtelai, a daughter of Carnebo, had borne unto him.[1]

Late at night, the guests were returning home when they were struck by an unusual phenomenon. Yonder in the east they perceived a great star swiftly moving along in the firmament. And lo! this big and unusually bright star suddenly swallowed up four other stars, one after the other. Greatly marvelled the courtiers, magicians and soothsayers of Nimrod, in distant Mesopotamia, at this phenomenon.[2]

[1] *Sepher Hajashar; Pirke de Rabbi Eliezer*, Ch. 26; *Baba Batra*, 91a.
[2] *Sepher Hajashar.* See also Josephus, *Antiquities*, II, 9, 2.

" Verily," they said, " this can be interpreted only in one way. One day the newly born son of Terah will be great and mighty and will conquer the whole kingdom of Nimrod. He will dethrone all the princes and take their possessions, which will be inherited by the son of Terah and his offspring. His children will one day inherit the worlds below and above." [1] Thus spoke the courtiers, councillors, and soothsayers of Nimrod on that memorable night at Chur in Mesopotamia. On the following morning the councillors of King Nimrod, who had been the guests of Terah on the previous evening, hastened to the King and informed him of the events of last night and what they had read in the stars.

" And what am I to do?" asked the King, greatly perplexed. " Mighty King," replied the astrologers, " we advise thee to buy the newly born boy of Terah, and to kill the child immediately. Thus wilt thou have peace and continue to reign."

Nimrod listened to their advice, and at once sent for Terah to appear in his presence. And when Terah appeared in the presence of King Nimrod, the latter thus addressed the commander of his armies:

" I hear that thy wife Emtelai has borne a son unto thee. Now I will offer thee much gold and silver and vast treasures, if thou wilt hand over thy son unto me to do as I please."

" Great King," replied Terah, " thy word is law, and it is not for me, thy humble servant, to oppose thy royal wish, but may thy servant speak into thine royal ear?" [2]

" Speak," said Nimrod.

" Yesterday," said Terah, " a friend came to me offering a high price for the horse which thou hast once given me as a gift. I crave, therefore, thy permission to sell this horse to my friend."

When the King heard the request of Terah, the commander

---

[1] Jellinek, *Beth-Hamidrash*, II, 118.   [2] *Sepher Hajashar.*

of his armies, he waxed very wroth and exclaimed: " Art
thou then in such sore need of gold and silver that thou
wouldst fain sell this precious horse, a token of my
royal favour?"

" Great King," replied Terah, " be not angry with thy
servant. Even such a request thou makest now. Thou didst
offer me great treasures for my son who is a gift from Heaven.
What will the treasures avail me if I have no son to leave them
to? I would be like the man in the fable who allowed his horse
to be killed in exchange for a house full of oats." Thus spoke
Terah, greatly daring. On hearing such words from the
mouth of the commander of his armies, the King waxed mightily
wroth, and he commanded Terah to bring his son immediately.
The unhappy father agreed to do the bidding of the King,
but craved three days grace so as to prepare his wife for the
sad tidings. When three days had passed, the King sent his
servants to fetch the son of Terah. " If the boy is not delivered
unto our hands," the messengers informed the unhappy
father, " King Nimrod will wreak terrible vengeance and
destroy thy whole house and family." [1]

Thus threatened and yet unwilling to hand over his own
son, Terah took the newly born child of one of his slaves and
handed it over to the King's servants. Faithful to his royal
promise, King Nimrod bestowed upon Terah much wealth,
and bade his servants to slay the boy who had been brought
to him. Fearing, however, that one day Nimrod might learn
of the substitution, Terah sent his wife and her baby away
from home and concealed them in a cave.

Another version of this legend runs as follows:

Nimrod, the great King of Babylon, was a great astrologer
himself, and in the stars, which he constantly consulted, he
had read that a boy would be born in Mesopotamia who
would one day declare war unto the King and his religion

---

[1] *Sepher Hajashar.* Cf. Jellinek, *Beth-Hamidrash*, Vol. II, pp. 118–119.

and in the end come forth victorious.[1] Greatly troubled in his mind, Nimrod asked his councillors for advice. At the advice of the latter, he built a big house eighty yards in length and sixty in breadth, wherein all the women about to give birth to a child were kept and closely watched. The midwives and nurses were commanded to kill unhesitatingly every new born boy, but to bestow rich presents upon those women who would give birth to a girl. Thus 70,000 boys were massacred by order of the King Nimrod. Thereupon the angels in Heaven implored the Lord of the Universe, the God of Justice, to wreak vengeance upon Nimrod and to punish him for this massacre of the innocent babies. And the Lord of the Universe replied:

" I slumber not, neither do I sleep; in good time the cruel murderer will be punished and his deeds avenged."

Soon Emtelai, the wife of Terah, was about to give birth to a child, and was brought into custody by order of the King. But lo! a miracle happened and all the outward signs of her pregnancy disappeared, so that she was set free. And when the day of her delivery approached, she secretly left the town and concealed herself in a cave. Here she bore a son, Abraham, the radiance of whose countenance shed a brilliant light in the dark cave.[2] Wrapping the child in one of her garments, she left it there, relying upon the mercy of God Almighty. And when the Lord of the Universe heard the wailing of the boy, He sent His angel Gabriel into the cave to feed the baby. The angel Gabriel offered one finger of his right hand to the crying babe to suck, and lo! from the angelic finger milk flowed abundantly.[3]

When Abraham was thirteen[4] years, or, according to some,

[1] *Maasse Abraham*, Jellinek, *Beth-Hamidrash*, I, pp. 25–34; Weil, *Biblische Legenden der Muselmänner*, p. 68; Herbelot, *Bibliothèque Orientale, s.v. Abraham*.

[2] See *Exodus Rabba*, 1, and *Sotah*, 12a, where this incident is told of Moses.

[3] See also Weil, *loc. cit.*; and Herbelot, *loc. cit.*

[4] *Pirke de Rabbi Eliezer*, Ch. 26. See also *Sepher Hajashar*; and *Maasse Abraham*, Jellinek, *Beth-Hamidrash*, I, where it is said that Abraham was either three or ten years old, when he left the cave.

only ten days old, he left the cave. Perceiving the wide expanse of the firmaments he began to wonder where the firmaments and earth had come from and who was their Creator. It was soon after dawn, and at that moment the sun arose upon the horizon in its morning splendour; it tinted with orient hues the morning sky. This, thought the boy, must be the Creator of the Universe, and Abraham knelt and worshipped the sun. Thus he remained the whole day, when lo! the sun set in the west and twilight came. " This radiant orb," thought the boy, "which is changeable, cannot be the All-Father, the Creator of the Universe," and lifting up his eyes he perceived the moon in its pale glory, surrounded by myriads of stars twinkling in the firmaments. " This pale and radiant orb," thought the boy, "must be the Creator of the Universe, and the myriads of minor lights his servants." He prostrated himself before the moon and worshipped. But lo! the night passed and once more the sun rose in the east, the light of the moon having waned and disappeared.

" Neither the big nor the smaller heavenly lights," thought Abraham, " can be the Creators of the Universe. They both come and go and must be obeying an invisible ruler who alone is the Creator of all the Universe. Him alone will I henceforth worship and adore." [1]

Proceeding on his way, the boy met his mother, Emtelai. She had come to visit the cave where she had left her baby, and not finding it was greatly grieved. She wandered along the bank of the river, trying to discover where her child might be. Thus she met Abraham, but she knew him not, for he had already grown up and appeared to her as a boy.

" Knowest thou anything about a baby which I left in yonder cave?" she inquired.

" I am thy child whom thou seekest, Mother," replied Abraham.

[1] *Sepher Hajashar*; *Maasse Abraham*, Jellinek, *Beth-Hamidrash*, Vol. I.

His mother wondered greatly and would scarcely believe it.

" How is it possible," she exclaimed, " that thou shouldst speak and walk about, only ten days old?"

" Yes, Mother," replied the boy, " everything is possible for the living, eternal, and omnipotent God, the Creator of the world, the Ruler of the Universe. He dwelleth above in the heavens, but His glory filleth the whole earth. He sees and hears everything and nothing is hidden from him."

" Is there another God besides Nimrod?" queried Emtelai, Abraham's mother.

" Yes, Mother," replied Abraham. " He is the God of Heaven and earth, the God of the Universe, who is also the God of Nimrod. Go and tell Nimrod so." [1]

Emtelai, the wife of Terah, went and told her husband all that had happened unto their son and how miraculously he had been saved. And when Nimrod heard all about this wonder child, a great terror seized him and he summoned all his councillors, magicians, and soothsayers and asked them their opinion. " Great King," spoke the councillors and astrologers, " verily, a great and mighty king like Nimrod need not fear an infant, like the son of Terah. It will be easy for the King to bid one of his smallest army commanders to capture the boy and put him to death." But Satan, arrayed in the silken garments of one of the royal councillors, and mingling with them, opened his mouth and thus he spoke:

" Great King! I advise thee to summon thy best officers and to arm thy best regiments, and send them out to capture this boy who is a real danger unto thee and unto thy kingdom." And Nimrod did as Satan, arrayed in the garb of one of his councillors, had advised him. Thus a mighty legion of warriors was sent out in pursuit of Abraham. [2]

---

[1] *Sepher Hajashar*; see also Jellinek, *loc. cit.*
[2] *Maasse Abraham*, Jellinek, *Beth-Hamidrash*, Vol. I.

When the son of Terah heard what had happened and
knew that many legions had been dispatched to capture him,
and that a mighty host was drawn up in battle array, he prayed
unto God in this hour of his need to save and protect him
from the wrath and vengeance of Nimrod. And the Lord
of the Universe commanded His angel Gabriel to protect the
son of Terah. Gabriel thereupon sent clouds and thick mists
to envelop Abraham and render him invisible to the eyes of
his pursuers. The mists and clouds were so dense, and the
darkness so great, that the soldiers of Nimrod were greatly
frightened, gave up their pursuit, and returned to Babylon.
Carried on the shoulders of Gabriel, Abraham followed them,
reaching the gates of Babylon at the same time as the royal
soldiers.[1]

And opening his mouth Abraham cried to the inhabitants
of the city and thus he spoke:

" The Eternal is the true and only God, and there is no
one like Him. Worship God, the Lord of the Universe, all
ye men and women of Babylon, as I, Abraham, His servant,
am worshipping Him."

Abraham then went to his parents and admonished them
to worship the only and true God. But Terah, now greatly
frightened, hastened to Nimrod and informed him of all that
had occurred; how his son Abraham, whom the royal soldiers
had set out to capture, had travelled in such a short time over
a long distance, a journey of forty days. Hearing these words,
Nimrod was greatly frightened, and once more summoned his
councillors into his presence. The astrologers and magicians
thereupon advised the King to order a seven days festival, and
to command all his subjects to appear in the royal palace and
worship the king. But Nimrod, being anxious to behold the
wonder child Abraham, bade Terah to come before him
accompanied by his son.[2] Abraham now appeared in the pre-

---

[1] *Maasse Abraham*, Jellinek, *Beth-Hamidrash*, Vol. I; *Sepher Hajashar*.   [2] *Ibid*.

sence of Nimrod. He entered the vast throne room, thronged with all the mighty princes, magicians, and astrologers. Without fear or hesitation the boy approached the throne, seized it with his hand so that it shook and trembled, and called aloud:

"Woe unto Nimrod, the abominable blasphemer! Tremble, O Nimrod, before the living, only God, the Ruler of the Universe, who liveth for ever, who neither slumbereth nor sleepeth. Worship Him, Nimrod, even as I worship Him, for it is He who hath created the whole world, the heavens and the earth." Thus spake Abraham, and all the idols were immediately thrown to the ground by an invisible hand, so that Nimrod and his court were greatly frightened. Nimrod himself fell into a swoon which lasted two hours. When he recovered consciousness, the King asked Abraham:

"Was this thy voice, or the voice of thy God?"

"It was the voice of one of His humblest servants," replied Abraham.

"Then," said Nimrod, "thy God must verily be great and mighty and King of all the kings."

Nimrod allowed Terah and his son to depart unmolested, and they left his presence unharmed. Abraham, no longer fearing the wrath of Nimrod, dwelt for thirty-nine years with Noah and Shem, and studied the law and the wonders of the Creator.[1]

[1] *Maasse Abraham*, Jellinek, *Beth-Hamidrash*, Vol. I.

CHAPTER XX

The Mighty Tower of Babel, and the Iconoclast

Nimrod, the son of Kush—His garment—It was made for Adam—Stolen by Ham in the ark—The power of the garment—Esau covets the garment of Nimrod—Nimrod is worshipped as a god—The arrogance of the King—The mighty tower—Abraham preaches to the builders of the tower—The confusion of languages—The seventy nations—The relics of the tower—Terah, the seller of idols—Abraham smashes the idols of his father—The story of the poor woman who came to buy a nice god—Abraham before Nimrod—Another story relating how Abraham smashed the idols of his father—The story of the idols who refused to partake of the savoury meat—The Patriarch denounces idolatry—The illness of Terah—His son Haran sells a few idols—The story of the woman whose gods had been stolen—The conversion of the old woman.

AND in those days it came to pass that men still feared a recurrence of the flood which had visited the earth in the days of Noah.[1] Afraid, lest they would be destroyed and wiped out from the face of the earth, all men left the pleasant country of Palestine,[2] where Noah had dwelt and sacrificed unto the Lord,[3] and came to dwell in the valley of Shinnar. Here they no longer submitted to the wise rule of the God-fearing Shem,[4] the son of Noah, but paid homage unto Nimrod, the son of Kush,[5] the son of Ham, and Nimrod became very mighty indeed. He had been the darling of his father Kush, and the latter had bestowed upon him the garment which Adam had worn when he was expelled from the Garden of Eden. This garment Adam had left to Enoch, Enoch to Methuselah, and

---

[1] Josephus, *Antiquities*, I, 4, 1; *Pirke de Rabbi Eliezer*, Ch. 11.
[2] *Pirke de Rabbi Eliezer*, Ch. 24. [3] *Targum Jerushalmi, Genesis*, 7, 20.
[4] *Targum Jerushalmi, Genesis*, 10, 9. [5] *Pirke de Rabbi Eliezer*, Ch. 11 and Ch. 24.

Methuselah to Noah who took it with him into the ark. Here
Ham stole it and left it to his son Kush. It was in this garment
that Nimrod arrayed himself, thus becoming invulnerable
and invincible. He easily conquered all his enemies and
slew all the hostile armies. Arrayed in the clothes which
God had made for Adam and Eve, Nimrod was possessed of
great power. When he put on these garments all the animals,
the beasts in the fields and the animals in the air came at once
and prostrated themselves before him.[1] The sons of men,
thinking that this submission of the animals, beasts, and birds,
was due to Nimrod's power and might, made him king
over themselves. These coats of Nimrod were, however, in
the end the cause of his violent death. Esau, the son of Isaac,
who was also a mighty hunter, saw the coats which the Almighty
had once made for Adam and Eve, and he coveted them in
his heart. He was very anxious to make himself possessed of
this precious raiment, hoping thus to become a mighty and
powerful hunter and hero by means of these clothes. Esau,
therefore, slew Nimrod and took the raiment from him, and
was thus enabled to catch the animals and become a cunning
hunter.[2] The clothes were subsequently concealed in the earth
by Jacob, who said that none was worthy to wear them.[3]

Thus Nimrod had triumphed over the King of Babylon,
and he became a mighty ruler. And soon the whole earth and
all its inhabitants recognized his rule and became his humble
subjects:[4] they worshipped him as a ruler and as a god, for
Nimrod made men forget the love and worship of the true
God, the Creator of the Universe, and led them on the path
of sin and transgression. The longer Nimrod sat upon his
throne, the more arrogant he grew. And yet he was uneasy
in his mind, and in constant fear of losing his throne. He

[1] *Sepher Hajashar; Pirke de Rabbi Eliezer*, Ch. 24.
[2] *Genesis Rabba*, 65; *Targum Jerushalmi, Genesis*, 25, 27
[3] *Pirke de Rabbi Eliezer*, Ch. 24.
[4] *Targum Jerushalmi, Genesis*, 10, 9; *Pirke de Rabbi Eliezer*, Ch. 11.

had read in the stars that one day a man would arise who
would teach the world the knowledge of the true God, the
Ruler of the Universe, to whom alone belongs all power and
greatness. In order to prevent such an occurrence and to
turn men away entirely from the worship of the true God,[1]
Nimrod gathered his people and thus addressed them: " Come,
let us build a big city, where we can dwell so that we may not
be scattered all over the face of the earth. Let us further
erect in the midst of this city a high tower which will reach
into Heaven, so lofty that a flood may not reach its summit,
and so firm that a fire-flood will not destroy it. Let us then
ascend upon the summit of this tower and climb up to Heaven.[2]
With our axes we will cut open the firmament and let it empty
itself of all the waters contained therein, so that it may never be
a danger unto us. Thus will we also avenge our ancestors
who perished by water, the only weapon of our enemy. Let
us then wage war against the ruler who dwelleth upon the
firmament above our heads and hurl spears and arrows against
him. Never will he be able to resist our mighty hosts and our
spears and arrows. And upon the summit of the high tower
we will place an idol with a sword in his hand that he may
fight our battles and protect us. Thus our fame will be great
from one end of the earth to the other, and we will rule over
the whole world." [3]

Thus spoke Nimrod in his pride and arrogance, and although not all his subjects had faith in him and believed him
that he would truly conquer Heaven and establish his rule
there, yet they all gathered round him, determined to help
him carry out his design. Some of Nimrod's subjects believed
that a high and mighty tower in the valley of Shinnar would
indeed protect them against another deluge, whilst others

[1] *Pesachim*, 94*b*; *Hagigah*,13*a*; Josephus, *Antiquities*, I, 42; Herbelot, *Bibliothèque Orientale, s.v. Nimrod*; Weil, *Biblische Legenden der Muselmänner*. p. 77.

[2] *Sepher Hajashar*; *Pirke de Rabbi Eliezer*, Ch. 24; *Sanhedrin*, 109*a*. See also Josephus, *Antiquities*, I, 4, 1-2; Jellinek, *Beth-Hamidrash*, Vol. III, 46.

[3] *Sepher Hajashar*; *Sanhedrin*, 109*a*; *Genesis Rabba*, 38, *Targum Jerushalmi, Genesis*, 11, 4.

hoped thus to glorify their idols, the idols which they worshipped.[1]   Thereupon 600,000 [2] men gathered round Nimrod and among them were 1000 princes.   They started to build the mighty tower and never rested until the structure had reached a height of seven mils.[3]   As there were no stones wherewith to build the tower, they made bricks, and built up the tower to a height of fourteen thousand cubits, or seven mils, making ascents for the labourers on the east and the west side. Those who carried up the bricks went up on the eastern side, whilst those who descended had to go down on the western side.   The work and completion of the tower they valued very highly, but to the lives of the labourers they attached no importance.   If a workman fell down and died, they paid but little heed to it, but when a brick fell down and broke, they were grieved, and even shed tears.[4]   They now began to send their arrows against the firmament, and when the arrows fell down upon earth covered with blood, they shouted: " We have killed all those who dwell in Heaven." [5]

And it came to pass that Abraham, who was then in his 48th year, heard [6] of the mighty tower which was being built in the valley of Shinnar.   He travelled to the valley and endeavoured to make the builders desist from their sinful undertaking, but they refused to listen unto him.   Abraham thereupon prayed to the Lord of the Universe: " God Almighty," he prayed, " confuse their language and scatter them over the face of the earth."[7]

And the Lord called seventy of His ministering angels and bade them go and confuse the speech of the builders, so that one did no longer understand the speech of the other.   The Creator of the Universe called to the seventy ministering

---

[1] *Midrash Tanchuma, Genesis,* 1, 11; *Midrash Shokher Tob, Ps.* 1.   [2] *Sepher Hajashar.*
[3] *Pirke de Rabbi Eliezer,* Ch. 24.
[4] *Sepher Hajashar; Pirke de Rabbi Eliezer,* Ch. 24.
[5] *Sepher Hajashar.* See also Weil, *Biblische Legenden der Muselmänner,* p. 78.
[6] *Seder Olam,* Ch. 1.
[7] *Pirke de Rabbi Eliezer,* Ch. 24; *Genesis Rabba,* 61; *Midrash Shokher Tob, Ps.* 1; *Yalkut,* 2, § 703.

angels surrounding the Throne of Glory, and thus He said: " Let us go down and confuse their languages." The Lord then confused their languages, so that when the builders of the tower wished to speak one to another none understood the language of his fellow man. Thereupon they all seized their swords and fought one another, so that half the world fell by the sword, and the other half was scattered from the valley of Shinnar upon the face of the earth.[1]

They were thus compelled to give up the construction of the tower by means of which they had hoped in their arrogance to ascend to Heaven. And they were divided into seventy nations, each speaking a different tongue. Instead of being destroyed, even as the generation of the flood had been destroyed, the builders of the mighty tower were only scattered over the face of the earth. God had mercy upon them because, although they worshipped idols, they nevertheless lived peacefully among themselves and never robbed one another, whilst the generation of the flood had been addicted to robbery and discord.[2] As for the tower itself, one third, the uppermost, was destroyed by fire, one third by an earthquake, whilst one third remained.[3] But the worship of idols spread among men in those days. Not only Nimrod and his court, his councillors and magicians, but also Terah, the father of Abraham, worshipped idols. Terah had twelve idols, one for every month, whom he worshipped and to whom he sacrificed. He even manufactured many idols which he sold to strangers.

And it came to pass that Abraham, who had long studied in the school of Shem and Eber and was now fifty years old, returned to his parental home.[4] He was now intent upon showing how void and false this worship of the idols was, so as to make his father give it up and acknowledge the true God instead. And thus it happened one day, when he was alone in the shop

---

[1] *Sepher Hajashar.*   [2] *Genesis Rabba,* 38.
[3] *Sanhedrin,* 109a. See also Josephus, *Antiquities,* I, 4, 3. See also Beer, *Das Leben Abrahams,* p. 109, note 84.   [4] *Sepher Hajashar.*

where his father had left him to sell the idols to those who might ask for some, that he seized the opportunity to carry out his design. There were numbers of idols of various sizes. A strong and powerfully built man now came and asked for an idol, one that would be as strong as himself. Abraham took up an idol and handed it to him, but the purchaser expressed some doubt as to the strength of the idol.[1]

" If this idol did not possess great strength it would not have been placed above all the others and occupied the place of honour," said Abraham. " If thou wilt pay the price, thou canst carry away thy god and he himself will then speak unto thee."

The purchaser paid the price and was about to leave, when Abraham called him back: " And how old art thou?" he queried.

" I am seventy years old," replied the purchaser of the strong idol.

" And wilt thou prostrate thyself before the image or dost thou expect the idol to bow to thee?" further queried Abraham.[2]

" How canst thou ask?" said the stranger by way of a reply. " He is my god and I will prostrate myself before him and worship him."

" Then," rejoined Abraham, " thou art much older than the god thou hast just acquired, for he was only manufactured to-day." The disappointed purchaser threw away the idol he had just bought and asked his money back, which Abraham at once returned to him.

Thereupon a poor and scantily clad woman came and asked for a god who was as poor as she was herself. Abraham took up an idol which was very small in size and placed on the lowest shelf. " Here is a god as thou wouldst have."

" And will he not be exacting?" queried the poor woman. " I am a lonely and poor widow, and my poverty is very great,

---

[1] *Tana debe Eliahu*, 2, 25.   [2] *Ibid.*

so that I cannot satisfy gods who claim too much from their worshippers and whose claims only rich folk can satisfy."

" Dost thou not see," rejoined Abraham, " that this is a very modest god who will have compassion with thy poverty and not trouble thee overmuch?"

Well satisfied, the poor widow paid the price for her idol and was about to leave, when Abraham called her back. He pointed out to her that, however modest the god she had just acquired was, he was still inferior to herself, because he had only been manufactured this very morning. Greatly disappointed, the woman threw away the idol and went her way.[1]

Thereupon another woman brought a dishful of meal. " Place this dish," she said, " before the gods, so that they may eat and be satisfied." Thus she spoke and went her way.

Thereupon Abraham took up a stick and smashed all the idols with the exception of the biggest, into whose hands he placed the stick.[2] Now, when Terah, the father of Abraham, returned and saw how all the idols had been broken, his anger was great and he asked his son who it was that had wrought such havoc among the gods.

" Why should I withhold the truth from thee, O Father mine?" replied Abraham. " A woman came this morning bringing a dish full of fine meal to feed the gods with. I accordingly placed the dish before them to partake of it. But they began to quarrel among themselves, each wanting to have the entire dish for himself. Then the biggest among them took up yonder stick and broke them all."[3]

Thus spake Abraham. But Terah replied: " Dost thou mock me, boy? Have the idols power of speech and are they able to move and act?"

" O Father," said Abraham, " doth not thine ear hear what thy mouth is saying?"

---

[1] *Tana debe Eliahu*, 2, 25. See also *Genesis Rabba*, 38. Cf. Abulfeda, *Historia Ante-Islamica*.　　[2] *Genesis Rabba*, 38.　　[3] *Ibid.*

Terah, very angry on hearing these words, straightway went to report to Nimrod the conduct of his son. He moreover handed Abraham over to the King that he might punish him.

" If," said Nimrod to Abraham, " thou wilt not worship the gods of thy father, then worship at least fire!"

" Why," said Abraham, " should we worship fire rather than water? Is not water stronger than fire which it has the power to quench?"

" Well then," replied Nimrod, " prostrate thyself before water and worship it."

" But clouds," said Abraham, " are greater than water, for they contain in themselves this element."

" Well then, adore the clouds," said Nimrod.

" The wind," again said Abraham, " is more powerful than the clouds, for it disperses them. Why should we not worship the wind?"

" Well then, worship the wind," said Nimrod, growing impatient.

" Man," said Abraham, imperturbably, " is even stronger than wind, for he can fight against it. Why should we not worship man?"

Nimrod's patience, however, was at an end and he thus spoke unto Abraham: " Thou speakest idle words; fire is my god and I will throw thee into the fire and let thy God save thee if He can." [1]

Another version of this interview between Abraham and Nimrod runs as follows: One day, Abraham begged his father to show him the god who had created Heaven and earth and the whole Universe. Thereupon Terah led his son into an inner chamber where he showed him twelve big idols and a number of smaller ones, prostrated himself before them and went off.

Abraham at once ran to his mother Emtelai and thus

---

[1] *Genesis Rabba*, 38.

he spoke: "Mother dear, my father hath just shown unto me the gods who have created Heaven and earth and all the Universe. Now prithee, take a young kid from the goats and make it savoury meat for the gods, and let me bring it to them that they may eat and bless me."[1]

And Emtelai, the mother of Abraham, went and did as her son had asked her to. She fetched a young kid from the goats, made it savoury meat and placed it before the idols. As the idols neither moved nor did stir, Abraham said mockingly: "Perchance the meat is not savoury enough for the gods and the quantity too small. To-morrow they shall have a larger dish and meat that is even more savoury."

And indeed, on the following morning, Emtelai fetched from the flocks three of the best kids of the goats, made them savoury meat and placed the dish before the idols of Terah. But still the idols remained dumb and motionless. They never spoke, neither did they stir.

Thereupon Abraham exclaimed: "Woe unto those who worship idols, for they are vain and foolish." Straightway he seized an axe, smashed all the idols, with the exception of the biggest, and placed his axe in the hands of the latter.

Terah was just returning home, when he heard the noise of the smashing of his idols.[2] He hastened into the inner chamber and was amazed to see what had happened. All the idols, except the biggest, were no more; there was only a heap of splinters and stone.

"And who hath dared to do this?" called Terah in angry tones. In vain did Abraham try to make his father believe that the big idol had done this and had smashed all the smaller ones. "No," cried Terah, "this cannot be; the image could not have done such a deed, for he is only stone and wood, the result of mine own handiwork."

Thereupon Abraham told his father the truth and admon-

---

[1] *Sepher Hajashar.*   [2] *Ibid.*

ished him to give up his idolatry and acknowledge the true and only God, the Eternal and the Creator of the Universe.[1] As Terah, however, would not listen to his son's admonitions, Abraham seized the axe and cut the biggest idol too. And when Terah saw what Abraham had done, he grew very angry, hastened to Nimrod and related unto him what his own son had done to his gods.

Nimrod bade the daring god-smasher appear in his royal presence. Abraham repeated to the King what he had already said to his own father. He pointed out the stupidity of worshipping idols made by man, manufactured out of stone and wood. He reminded Nimrod of the flood of waters which the Eternal, the only God and Creator of the Universe, had brought upon the earth and destroyed all flesh because of the wickedness of man, and because all flesh had corrupted His way and the earth was filled with violence. He admonished Nimrod in fiery words to repent and to acknowledge the true God, the living Ruler of the Universe, lest he and his house should be destroyed, even as the generation of the flood had been destroyed from under Heaven. But Nimrod replied:

" I am a god myself; dost thou not know that I have created Heaven and earth with mine own hands?" [2]

" If thou art a god," replied Abraham, " then change the course of the sun, cause it to rise in the west and to set in the east. If thou canst do this I will worship and acknowledge thee as my god, but if thou art unable to accomplish this, I will refuse to obey thy commands. The God who lent me strength to destroy the idols will give me strength to fight against thee, O Nimrod."

" Do not be surprised," he continued, " to hear me speak thus unto thee. Thou art not the ruler of the Universe, but only a mortal man, the son of Kush. Hadst thou been a god

[1] *Sepher Hajashar*; Koran, *Sura*, 19, 43.
[2] *Tana debe Eliahu*; see also Herbelot, *Bibliothèque Orientale, s.v. Abraham.*

thine own father would not have died even like other men. And thou, too, wilt not escape death which will soon claim thee."[1]

Another version of the legend relating the scene between Abraham and Nimrod runs as follows: One day Terah fell ill and bade his sons Abraham and Haran to sell a few images so as to have the wherewithal to live upon. Haran at once did as his father had bidden him, sold the idols and brought his father the money he had received. Thereupon Abraham took a rope and dragging two of the idols into the streets offered them for sale, and thus he spake:

" For sale, two images, utterly useless; each idol hath a mouth but doth not speak; it hath eyes but cannot see; it hath feet but cannot stand; it hath ears but cannot hear."[2]

The people were amazed when they heard his words. Now an old woman came along and asked Abraham to sell her a fine beautiful image which she could cherish and worship properly. " Didst thou not buy an idol from my brother Haran?" asked Abraham.

" So I did," replied the old woman, " but thieves came and stole it while I was in the bath!"

" And how canst thou worship an idol which cannot protect itself from thieves?" queried Abraham. " Such an idol," he continued, " cannot protect thee."

" But whom shall I worship then?" asked the woman, " for I must have a god to worship in my old age, a god who will bless me."

" Worship the living God," said Abraham, " the God who is the Lord of the Universe, and who hath created Heaven and earth, the sea and all that is therein."[3]

" But what will it avail me," persisted the old woman, " if I worship thy God?"

---

[1] Beer, *Das Leben Abrahams*, p. 12, and note 102, p. 110.

[2] *Maasse Abraham*, Jellinek, *Beth-Hamidrash*, Vol. I.　See also Weil, *Biblische Legenden* p. 70.

[3] Jellinek, *Beth-Hamidrash*, Vol. I.

" Thou wilt recover thy lost property," replied Abraham; " and, moreover, thy soul will be saved from perdition."

And the old woman followed Abraham's advice and acknowledged the only living God, the Lord of the Universe. Soon afterwards the woman found the thieves and recovered her property. Then she dragged the idol she had once bought from Haran through the town and called aloud so that all the people could hear her:

" Woe unto the idols and woe unto those folks who worship stone and wood. Let all those who wish to save their souls acknowledge the God of Abraham who will give them protection and bless their handiwork."

Thus spoke the old woman, and the people listened unto her voice, and many among them abandoned their idols and acknowledged the God of Abraham.

When Nimrod heard of the doings of this old woman, he bade her appear in his presence, and commanded her to worship the idols and acknowledge himself as a god. This the woman refused to do, and she was beheaded at the command of Nimrod.[1]

[1] *Ibid.*

CHAPTER XXI

The Fiery Furnace and the Garden of Roses

The distinguished prisoner—He is fed by the angel Gabriel—The
fiery furnace—The conversion of the jailer—Abraham in the fiery
furnace—The prayer of the martyr—The whispering of Sammael—Emtelai
implores her son to give in—The terrible death of Haran—The garden of
roses—The Patriarch teaches men the knowledge of God—The marriage
of Abraham—Nimrod's strange dream—The man with the naked sword—
The egg that changed into a river—Anuko, one of Nimrod's astrologers,
interprets the dream of the King—Eliezer saves Abraham—Terah and his
family leave Mesopotamia.

WHEN Nimrod saw that Abraham had so many followers
among the people who were beginning to listen to his voice,
fear and terror seized him. At the advice of his councillors
and magicians he, therefore, commanded that a seven days
feast be held in the royal palace. All the idols, richly arrayed,
were brought to the palace, and the people were bidden to
assemble and witness the great splendour of the gods and
worship them. A great banquet was given in honour of the
gods, and Nimrod bade Terah bring his son Abraham, so that
he, too, might witness the splendour and power of the gods
and of Nimrod himself.[1] But Abraham refused to come to
court, and remained alone in his father's house, where he
broke all the idols, cutting them to pieces.

Nimrod thereupon bade his servants throw Abraham into
prison, where he was to remain without food and drink.
The servants of Nimrod did the bidding of their master, and

---

[1] Jellinek, *Beth-Hamidrash*, Vol. I, 25–34.

Abraham was thrown into a dungeon, where he remained a whole year. The walls of his prison opened, however, and a source of clear water issued forth, enabling Abraham to quench his thirst, whilst the angel Gabriel daily brought him food.[1]

Nimrod now assembled his councillors and magicians, and asked them to decide what was to be done with Abraham who had dared to declare war unto the gods of Nimrod.

" He is a blasphemer," said the councillors in one voice, " and deserves to be burned upon the stake." Accordingly Nimrod gave orders that after forty days Abraham should be thrown into a fiery furnace and burnt alive.[2] All the inhabitants were commanded to gather fuel for the furnace in which Abraham was to be burned.[3] An immense pile was lit, and the flames were so great that they reached up to the skies, sending fear and terror into the hearts of the people. All the people, rich and poor, high and low, men, women, and children, flocked to the place of execution in order to witness the burning of Abraham who had overthrown the idols. Multitudes of people thronged the roofs and towers, all waiting to see how the son of Terah would perish in the flames.

Nimrod now bade the jailer to lead Abraham forth from prison. " Mighty King," said the jailer, " how canst thou expect Abraham to be still alive, he who hath remained in prison for over a year without food or drink?"

Angrily Nimrod replied: " I command thee to bring forth Abraham, living or dead, so that his body may be thrown into the flames and the people witness the power of my gods." Thus spake Nimrod, and the prison-keeper went forth to fetch Abraham. Approaching the pit into which Abraham had been thrown a year ago he called aloud:

" Abraham, Abraham, art thou still alive?"

---

[1] Jellinek, Beth-Hamidrash, Vol. I, 25–34; see also Pirke de Rabbi Eliezer, Ch. 26; Baba Batra, 91a.

[2] Sepher Hajashar; Jellinek, Beth-Hamidrash, Vol. I, 25–34.

[3] Ibid; see also Weil, Biblische Legenden der Muselmänner, p. 72.

"Verily, I am still alive," [1] replied Abraham.

" But how can that be," asked the jailer, " who gave thee food and drink?"

" The Almighty," replied Abraham, " the God of the Universe, the Lord of Hosts who works miracles, He who is the God of Nimrod, of Terah, and of the whole world, He who feeds every living creature sent me meat and drink. He sees everything but is invisible Himself. He dwelleth in the Heavens above, but His majesty filleth the world." [2]

Thus spake Abraham, and the jailer was mightily impressed. He abandoned the worship of the idols and acknowledged the God of Abraham who had wrought such a miracle. Loudly he declared that the gods of Nimrod were useless idols and should be overthrown.

When the King heard what had happened, he bade his servants seize the prison-keeper and have him beheaded. But the sword, when it touched him, was blunted and broke in twain, so that he went unharmed. Now Nimrod's wrath knew no bounds; he commanded that Abraham be at once thrown into the flames, and the prisoner was led into the presence of the King.

When the soothsayers saw Abraham, they at once exclaimed: " This is the man of whose doings we read in the stars on the night of his birth. Terah, his father, hath deceived thee, O King.[3] It is he of whom it was written in the stars that he will be a great nation which will inherit the world."

" Who gave thee the advice to hand over to my messengers the son of thy slave in the place of thine own son?" asked Nimrod, addressing himself to Terah.

" It was Haran, my other son," said Terah. " It was he indeed who advised me to deceive the King."

Terah said so because he well knew that Haran was inclined to follow the teachings of his brother Abraham. He

---

[1] *Maasse Abraham*, Jellinek, *loc. cit.*   [2] *Ibid.*   [3] *Sepher Hajashar.*

had moreover read in the stars that Haran was destined to be burnt alive.[1]

"Well then," replied Nimrod, "Haran, too, shall die together with thy son Abraham." And the servants of Nimrod seized both Abraham and his brother Haran, and made ready to divest them of their garments, bind them with ropes and throw them into the flames. But lo! no sooner did they approach Abraham when they were themselves devoured by the flames.

And now Satan, in the shape of man, appeared before Nimrod and thus he spake:

"Great King, bid thy servants take a long spear and by means of it throw Abraham into the furnace, so that no one need approach him." And the King gave orders that it should be done so.[2]

Now Abraham raised his eyes to Heaven and prayed to God Almighty to save him from such a terrible death. Satan thereupon approached Abraham and whispered into his ear: "Verily, Abraham, thou art doomed to perish in the flames, and no one can save thee. Listen to my advice and acknowledge the god of Nimrod, thus wilt thou be saved." But Abraham knew the voice of the tempter and exclaimed: "Get thee hence, Satan, I will not listen unto thee."

Abraham's mother, Emtelai, fearing lest her beloved son perish in the flames, now fell upon his neck and with tears streaming down her face implored him to obey the command of the King and thus be saved from a terrible death.

But Abraham, firm in his faith, replied: "No, Mother dear, I cannot deny my God and forsake my faith. Water will extinguish the fire lit by Nimrod's servants, but the fires of the Lord burn everlastingly. Woe unto those who forsake the Lord." [3]

---

[1] *Midrash Shokhor Tob*, Ps. 118; *Sepher Hajashar.*
[2] *Maasse Abraham*, Jellinek, *Beth-Hamidrash*, Vol. I, 25–34; see also Weil, *loc. cit.*, p. 74.
[3] *Maasse Abraham*, Jellinek, *loc. cit.*

Encouraged by his fortitude, Emtelai herself began to hope that the God of Abraham would save her son from the flames.

Now, Haran was waiting to see whether the flames would devour his brother or not. " If Abraham is saved," he thought in his heart, " I will worship the God of my brother, but if he perisheth, then I will acknowledge the gods of Nimrod."

Haran, however, was seized first and thrown into the flames where his entrails were burnt at once.[1] He wailed and cried aloud that he was ready to prostrate himself before the gods of Nimrod, but it was too late. An angel appeared and threw his burnt body at the feet of Terah.[2]

When Abraham was thrown into the flames, they never touched him. The ropes with which he had been bound were burnt to ashes, but Abraham himself walked about in the midst of the flames for three days and three nights. All the slaves who had lit the fire and all those who approached the furnace became at once a prey to the flames and they died, suffering great torture.[3]

When Nimrod saw that the fire had no power over Abraham, he called out:

" Abraham, thou faithful servant of the God who dwelleth in Heaven, come out of the flames and appear before me." Abraham, accordingly, left the flames and stood before the King.

" Tell me," asked Nimrod, " how didst thou manage to escape the flames which none of my servants were able to withstand?"

" The Lord of the Universe, of the heavens and of the earth, who rules the world and in whom I had faith, he alone saved me from a terrible death and did not let his servant perish in the flames." [4]

---

[1] *Sepher Hajashar*; see also *Targum Jerushalmi*; *Genesis*, 11, 28.
[2] *Midrash Shokhor Tob, Ps.* 118. See also *Book of Jubilees*, 12, 12–14, and Josephus, *Antiquities*, I, 6, 5, who says that the tomb of Haran was to be seen at Ur, in Chaldea.
[3] *Sepher Hajashar*; see also Weil, *loc. cit.* p. 76.
[4] *Sepher Hajashar*; *Maasse Abraham*, Jellinek, *Beth-Hamidrash*, Vol. I, 25–34.

Thus spake Abraham. And lo! suddenly the flames were extinguished, and in the place where they had been a while ago a beautiful and lovely garden appeared. There were fruit bearing trees, lovely to behold, and angels were wandering about who received Abraham in their midst.[1]

When Nimrod beheld the scene, he exclaimed:

" This is only magic, and now I understand how Abraham was saved from the flames. He is a great magician and he knew well enough that the flames would not touch him."

But the magicians at Nimrod's court replied: " No, great King, the power of magic doth not go so far, and it is only the living God who hath saved Abraham from the flames."

Thereupon the people came and wanted to prostrate themselves before Abraham and pay him homage, but he rebuked them, saying: " Do not prostrate yourselves before me, but worship the true God, the Lord of the Universe. It is He who hath saved me from the flames, and He will save all those who have faith in Him." [2]

The King now bestowed many presents upon Abraham, and also made him a gift of two slaves whose names were Oni and Eliezer.[3] And the great ones of the realm also came, praised Abraham and bestowed gifts upon him, so that he grew very rich and went away in peace. Many of the people, seeing how his God had saved Abraham from the flames, brought their children to him and asked him to teach them the ways of the Lord.[4] Thus over 300 gathered round Abraham, and among them were many of the royal servants, who followed him to his father's house, listening unto his words. Thereupon Abraham took to wife the daughter of his brother Haran, whose name was Sarai (or Sarah) and also Jiska, that is the seeress, because she was so beautiful that everyone turned round to look at her.[5]

---

[1] *Maasse Abraham*, Jellinek, *Beth-Hamidrash*, Vol. I, 29–34. See also Weil, *loc. cit.*, p. 76.
[2] *Sepher Hajashar.*   [3] *Ibid.*   [4] *Ibid.*
[5] *Sepher Hajashar; Megilla,* 14a; *Sanhedrin,* 69b.

And it came to pass that at the end of two full years, Nimrod had a dream. And behold, in his dream he stood with his army on the very spot where once the fire had been kindled, and the furnace stood, into the flames of which Abraham had been cast. And behold, a man greatly resembling Abraham issued forth from the flames. In his hand he held a naked sword and thus advanced upon the King. When Nimrod recoiled, the man with the naked sword threw an egg at him; and behold, the egg was soon changed into a large river which drowned all the King's army. The King alone and three of his companions escaped with their lives. Nimrod now looked into the countenances of his companions, and he saw that they were all arrayed in royal garments and resembled himself. And behold, the stream suddenly became an egg once more, and out of it came a hen which sat upon the King's head and picked out one of his eyes.[1]

And it came to pass that when Nimrod awoke in the morning his spirit was greatly troubled. He sent and called for all the magicians and soothsayers of his land and the wise men thereof; and he told them his dream. Then rose up one of the magicians and interpreters of dreams, Anuko by name, and thus he spake:

" Know, O King, that thy dream can be interpreted only in one way. It foretells thee the misfortune which Abraham and his offspring will one day bring upon thee and thy house. A day will come when he will wage war against thee and destroy thine army. Thou alone wilt escape with three of thy companions, but one of Abraham's offspring will put thee to death. Well do I remember, O King, that fifty-two years ago, when Abraham was born, we read his destiny in the stars and we warned the King. As long as Abraham liveth, there will be no peace for Nimrod." [2]

Thus spake Anuko. And when Nimrod heard his words

---

[1] *Sepher Hajashar.*   [2] *Ibid.*

and the interpretation of the dream, he secretly sent out his servants, commanding them to seize Abraham and to kill him. But Eliezer, one of the servants whom Nimrod had given as a gift to Abraham, happened to be at court and knew of the danger threatening his new master.

He hied himself to Abraham, and even before the servants of Nimrod had arrived, Abraham knew of the danger awaiting him. He accordingly fled to the house of Noah and Shem, where he remained hidden for one month.

Now it came to pass that Terah came in secret to see his son, and Abraham thus addressed his father: " My father, Nimrod is once more threatening me with death, and who knows what he hath in mind against thee. Misfortune may await thee at any moment, and thine own life is not safe as long as thou dost remain in Nimrod's service. To-day he bestoweth gifts upon thee, but to-morrow he may take thy life. Listen unto my voice, O Father mine, and leave the service of Nimrod. Let us be off and journey to Canaan, where we shall be able to live in peace and serve the only living God."

Thus spoke Abraham, and both Noah and Shem approved his words. And Terah did listen unto the words of Abraham, because he now hated Chaldaea (or Mesopotamia) since the terrible death of his son Haran.[1] Terah, accordingly, took his son Abraham, and Sarah, his daughter-in-law, the wife of his son Abraham, and Lot, the son of Haran, his son's son, and all his household, and he went forth with them from Ur of the Chaldees, to go into the land of Canaan. But when they came to Haran and saw the land which was very fruitful and large, they dwelt there. And the inhabitants of Haran loved Abraham and listened to his words, because he walked in the path of God and of virtue, and he was beloved by God and men.[2]

[1] Josephus, *Antiquities*, I, 6, 5.
[2] *Sepher Hajashar*. See also *Abodah Zarah*, 9a; *Targum Jerushalmi, Genesis*, 12, 5.

CHAPTER XXII

The Journey to Egypt and the Battle of the Kings

The journey to Canaan—The visit to Haran—The return to Canaan—The great famine—The journey to Egypt—On the banks of the river Wadi-el-Arish—Sarah, the beautiful—At the Egyptian frontier—The mysterious chest and the custom-officers—The divine beauty of Sarah—She is brought before the Pharaoh of Egypt—The prayer of Sarah—The punishment of the King—The jealousy of the princes of Canaan—The attack upon Sodom —The news brought by Og, the giant—Og's love for Sarah, the beautiful —Abraham's instructions to his servants—The midnight battle—The spears which turned to earth, and the arrows which turned to straw—In the Kings' dale—The homage of the Kings—The modesty of the Patriarch —The venerable Shem—Melchizedek.

FOR three years Abraham remained in Haran, together with his family. And then the Lord commanded him to get out of his country and from his kindred, and from his father's house and to journey to Canaan. Abraham obeyed the command of the Lord and journeyed with his wife Sarah to Canaan, whilst Terah and Lot remained in Haran. When Abraham arrived in Canaan, he pitched his tent amidst the inhabitants of the land. He built an altar and proclaimed the name of the Lord. Fifteen years Abraham dwelt in the country, and when he reached his 70th year, he returned to Haran on a visit to his father and kindred.[1] He remained five years in Haran, but he disliked the idle and luxurious life of the inhabitants and yearned for the country of Canaan, the inhabitants of which were leading an agricultural and industrious life.[2]

[1] *Sepher Hajashar.*   [2] *Genesis Rabba,* 39.

254

And it came to pass that at the end of five years, the Lord once more spoke unto Abraham and thus He said:

"Twenty years ago I commanded thee to leave Haran and to go to Canaan; and now I again tell thee get thee out of this country, thou and thy wife and thy kindred. Take all thy substance and all the souls which thou hast gotten and all who have accepted thy faith. Fear not the troubles and hardships of thy journey, for I will strengthen thee and thy fame will be great. And I will make of thee a great nation,[1] and I will bless thee, and make thy name great. And I will bless all those who will bless thee, and I will turn into a blessing the curses of thine enemies."[2]

Thus spake the Lord, and Abraham replied: "O God Almighty! What will the folks say when they see me leave my old father alone?"

"Thy father," said the Lord, "is a worshipper of idols, but the mission with which thou art entrusted is sacred; thy duty to mankind is greater than that which thou owest to thy father."[3]

And Abraham did as the Lord had bidden him. He journeyed as far as Sichem, and as far as the plains between the mountains of Gerisim and Ebal. Here he builded altars and pitched his tents. He first made a tent for his wife Sarah and then one for himself.[4]

And it now came to pass that a famine came upon the land of Canaan. It was the third famine since the world had been created, and it was sent to try Abraham.[5] Abraham, without a murmur, left Canaan, accompanied by his wife and his servants, and went out to Egypt. When he reached Wadi-el-Arish, the river of Egypt, he rested a few days.

Here Abraham and Sarah walked along on the river's bank, and for the first time the Patriarch saw reflected in the

---

[1] *Genesis Rabba, 39; Midrash Tanchuma, Genesis, 12, 2.*   [2] *Genesis Rabba, 39.*
[3] *Ibid.* See also *Rashi to Genesis, 11, 32.*   [4] *Genesis Rabba, ibid.*   [5] *Genesis Rabba, 25*

water the extraordinary beauty of his wife.[1]   Never before
had he, in his great modesty, lifted up his eyes to her face,
and he knew not what she was like, until he saw her face
reflected in the water.[2]   He was now aware of the fact that
she was very beautiful indeed, and he therefore asked her to
pass as his sister in Egypt, for fear lest he should be slain.
When they approached the frontiers of Egypt, Abraham,
however, as a further precaution, shut up his wife in a chest.
The frontiers of Egypt were reached, and the custom officers
made the Patriarch pay heavy duty on all his goods.   They
insisted on his opening the chest wherein he had shut up
his wife.

"I will pay the customs due for the box," said Abraham,
"as if it contained not only silk or silver, but gold and costly
gems."

The custom-house officers, however, required that the
box should be opened, and Abraham's refusal to do so availed
him not.   The chest was violently broken open, and lo! in
it was seated one of the most beautiful women ever seen.[3]
The custom-house officers were struck by her divine beauty,
for her countenance illumined all the land of Egypt.   Speedily
they informed Pharaoh of the event.[4]   Abraham and Sarah
were thereupon taken before the ruler of Egypt.[5]   They were
sorely troubled and prayed to the Lord to protect them, and
an angel came down from Heaven to protect the Patriarch
and his beautiful wife.

"Fear not," said the angel to Sarah, "and be comforted,
for God has heard thy petitions."

"Who is the man," asked Pharaoh, when Sarah was
before him, "who accompanied thee to Egypt?"

"He is my brother," replied Sarah.

---

[1] *Sepher Hajashar*; *Midrash Tanchuma*, ed. Buber, pp. 65–66.
[2] *Targum Jerushalmi*, Genesis, 12, 11; *Baba Batra*, 16a.
[3] *Sepher Hajashar*; *Genesis Rabba*, 40; *Midrash Tanchuma*, ibid, p. 66; *Megilla* 15a.
See also Weil, *Biblische Legenden der Muselmänner*, p. 81.   [4] *Genesis Rabba, loc. cit.*
[5] *Sepher Hajashar*; see also Josephus, *De bello Judaico*, V, 9, 4.

" Who is this woman?" he asked Abraham.

" She is my sister," replied the latter. This lie of Abraham is called in legendary lore a justifiable falsehood.

Now Pharaoh's heart was filled with great love for Sarah, and he asked for her hand.

" I will give thee," he pleaded, " as my royal present for thy hand, all the gold and silver and slaves which I possess, and also the fair land of Goshen."

Sarah would not listen to his pleadings, and Pharaoh pressed his suit in an impetuous and vehement manner.[1] In her great trouble she cried to God and prayed for protection. Pharaoh was thereupon smitten with paralysis, and plagues afflicted all his servants.[2] And when he heard that Sarah was already married to Abraham, he sent for the latter and not only returned to him his wife but also dismissed him with many costly gifts. To Sarah, too, he gave many presents,[3] and also presented to her his daughter Hagar, by one of his concubines, to be the servant of Sarah.

" My daughter," said Pharaoh, " it is better to be a servant in a house which enjoys the special protection of God, than to command elsewhere." [4]

And it now came to pass that the fame of Abraham spread all over the land, and he was a blessing to the people. But the kings and rulers of men were jealous of him and said in their hearts:

" Let us kill Abraham and wipe out his name from the earth, so that our people will no longer talk of him and forget him." But one of the kings said:

" If we attack Abraham, his many friends will gather round him and protect him. Let us therefore go to Sodom and take captive his brother's son Lot and take all his sub-

---

[1] *Pirke de Rabbi Eliezer*, Ch. 26; *Sepher Hajashar*; *Midrash Tanchuma, ibid.*; *Genesis Rabba*, 41.   [2] *Pirke de Rabbi Eliezer*, Ch. 26; *Sepher Hajashar*; *Genesis Rabbi*, 41.
[3] *Pirke de Rabbi Eliezer*, Ch. 26.
[4] *Sepher Hajashar*; *Pirke de Rabbi Eliezer*, Ch. 26. See also Weil, *loc. cit.*, p. 82.

stance. When Abraham will learn that his kinsman is in our hands he will pursue us. It will then be easy for us to get him into our hands and do with him as we please." Thus spake one of the kings, and his words pleased his confederates. They accordingly went to Sodom and made captive many men, women, and children, and among them Lot, the son of Haran, the brother of Abraham.

Now Og the giant, one of whose descendants afterwards became king of Bashan, had long ago cast his eyes upon Sarah, the wife of Abraham, and coveted her for her great beauty. Og had been saved from perdition during the flood in the days of Noah and had been fighting in the ranks of the giants vanquished by King Amraphel, who was no other than Nimrod. Og escaped and hastened to Abraham, who at that time dwelt in the plain of Mamre the Amorite, and brought him the news of the captivity of Lot. "Abraham," thought Og in his heart, "is a mighty hunter and a great warrior, and if he hears that his brother's son has been taken captive, he will surely arm his trained servants and go out against the enemy to set Lot free. He will be killed in battle, and Sarah will no longer resist me and be mine." [1] Thus thought Og the giant.

When Abraham heard that his brother's son had been taken captive, he indeed grew angry. He gathered all his followers whom he was teaching the ways of the Lord, and asked them to follow and support him in his fight. But as few only would listen unto him, Abraham went out accompanied only by his faithful servant Eliezer and his trained servants.[2]

Then Abraham said unto his armed servants: "I know full well that ye will only think of booty and the goods to be taken in battle, but will pay little heed to the captives and make no effort to save them. I will therefore give everyone

---

[1] *Genesis Rabba*, 42; *Yalkut*, 1, § 42.　　　[2] *Genesis Rabba*, 43.

of you much silver and gold and precious stones, if ye will swear to me not to turn your attention to the booty, but only seek to deliver the captives, and above all the women and children, and try to save them from the hands of their captors." [1]

The armed servants of Abraham swore to do as they were bidden. Towards midnight, Abraham met the enemy. The angels hastened to Abraham's assistance, and the stars in Heaven fought for him.[2] When the enemy beheld Abraham and his armed servants from far, he prepared for battle. The kings threw their sharp spears at Abraham and his followers, but behold, the spears were turned to earth and did not harm the gallant Patriarch.[3] The kings then sent their arrows against Abraham, but the arrows turned to straw and fell to the ground, without causing any harm to either Abraham or his faithful followers. Greatly marvelling at this, the kings said: " Let us rush up and seize him quickly, for the angels in Heaven and the stars are fighting on his side." But no sooner did they make a step forward, when Abraham seized the earth and the straw, which had fallen at his feet, and threw both at the enemy. And behold, earth and straw turned again to spears and arrows and hit the advancing enemy.[4]

When the kings saw what had happened, they said: " Verily, Abraham is the beloved of God in Heaven." The Patriarch then smote the enemy, scattered the pursuers, and they hastily fled, leaving all the booty and captives behind. Abraham took all the goods and the captives and turned homewards.[5]

The kings, whom he had smitten and whose armies he had dispersed, met him in a valley called afterwards the Kings' dale. Here they had hastily constructed a throne, and when Abraham and his men approached, they thus addressed him: " We have seen thy strength and witnessed the wonders thou hast done; now we know that thou art in-

---

[1] Cf. *Midrash Tanchuma, ibid.*, p. 73.   [2] *Sanhedrin. 96a.*
[3] *Sanhedrin,* 108b; *Genesis Rabba,* 43; *Midrash Tanchuma,* ed. Buber, p. 76; *Midrash Shokhor Tob,* Ps. 110.   [4] *Ibid.*   [5] *Genesis Rabba,* 43.

deed the beloved of God. We, therefore, prostrate ourselves before thee and proclaim thee our king, our ruler, and our God." Thus spoke the kings in the dale of Kings.[1]

Thereupon Abraham replied:

" Far be it from me to be your king, much less your God! Know ye not that I am only a mortal man, like other men. It is not I, but the God in Heaven who has worked the wonders. If, however, I have found grace in your eyes, then go your ways, live peacefully together, wage no more wars, but be merciful and meek, and walk humbly before your God. Open your doors to the poor, the widow, the stranger, and the wanderer, and acknowledge the true God in Heaven and serve Him with all your heart." [2]

Thus spake Abraham, and taking leave of the kings he returned home. And yet Abraham was troubled in his mind, for he was thinking of that venerable old man, Shem, the son of Noah, in whose school he had studied for years and learnt to fear God and love men. " What will Shem think," thought Abraham, " will he not rebuke me for having drawn my sword against the sons of Elam, his grandchildren?" [3]

And behold, Shem, who was now priest of the most high God and ruled at Salem under the name of Melchizedek,[4] came to meet him, bringing forth bread and wine.

" What must Abraham have thought of me," said Shem in his heart, " when he learned that my own grandchildren with their wicked armies had invaded the peaceful valleys of the Jordan, plundered the inhabitants, and taken captives even the nearest kinsfolk of Abraham." Thus thought Shem, and aloud he spake thus:

" Blessed be thou, Abraham, and blessed be the most high God who hath delivered thine enemies into thy hands. It is indeed noble of thee to have delivered the captives and

---

[1] *Genesis Rabba*, 43.   [2] *Ibid.*   [3] *Genesis Rabba*, 44.
[4] *Genesis Rabba*, 44; *Midrash Shokhor Tob, Ps.* 76, 3; *Sanhedrin*, 108b.

restored unto them their goods, taking nought unto thyself, from a thread even to a shoe-latchet."

And Abraham gave thanks to the Lord, and thus he prayed:

"Lord of the Universe, it is not by the strength of my arm but by Thy power that I have been able to smite mine enemy and deliver the women and the children. Thou hast protected me and been my shield." Thus prayed the Patriarch and the angels in Heaven replied: "Blessed be the name of the Lord, the shield of Abraham." [1]

---

[1] *Midrash Shokhor Tob*, Ps. 106. See for the entire chapter, Jellinek, *Beth-Hamidrash*, Vol. I, pp. 25–34; Vol. II, pp. 118–119; Lewner, *Kol Agadoth*, Vol. I, pp. 63–65.

CHAPTER XXIII

The Sin of Sodom

The three travellers—The visit of the angels: Michael, Raphael, and Gabriel—The mission of the angels—The prosperity of Sodom—The cruelty of the people of Sodom—Charity is a crime—The thieves and the pitchers full of balsam—The perverted laws—The story of the poor boy who killed the cattle of the townspeople—The story of the stranger who had crossed the river—The claim of the inhabitants—The verdict of the judges—Eliezer visits the town—The bleeding judge—The banquet, and the flight of the guests—The empty house—The two beds—The story of the stranger, the ass, the carpet, and the greedy land-lord—The strange dream—The interpretation of the dream—The hungry maiden—The story of Peletith and the starving beggar—The cry of the poor girl that ascended to Heaven—The girl dipped in honey, and the bees—The worshippers of the sun, and the worshippers of the moon—The news of the terrible destruction—The Patriarch travels to the land of the Philistines.

IT was noon of the 15th of Nisan,[1] on the third day after Abraham's operation, and he was sitting in front of his tent. The heat was intense, for Hell had been let loose, so that the world might feel its heat, and also because the Lord wanted to test Abraham once more.[2] Abraham never thought of his suffering, for he was troubled in his mind on account of his inability on such a day to find an opportunity to practise his hospitality. No wanderer was to be seen on the dusty road. At first Abraham sent out his servant Eliezer to watch for any stranger that might happen to pass along, and invite him to his hospitable tent. Soon Eliezer returned and informed his master that, look as he might, no wanderer was to be seen. Abraham now raised his eyes, and behold, there were three

[1] *Midrash Tanchuma, Exodus*, 12, 41.
[2] *Baba Mezia, 86b; Midrash Tanchuma, Genesis*, 18.

strangers.[1] They seemed to be Arabs, Saracens or Naba-
thaeans, but in reality they were the angels Michael, Raphael,
and Gabriel, each entrusted with a separate message.[2] And
after Abraham had offered the three strangers his hospitality,
Michael informed him that his wife Sarai, or Sarah, would
bear a son. His mission accomplished, he spread out his
wings and returned to the celestial regions.

But Raphael and Gabriel had another mission. Gabriel
had been sent to overturn Sodom and Gomorrah, whilst
Raphael had been entrusted with the mission of saving Lot.
They both therefore wended their way towards Sodom, but
even after having accomplished their mission they remained
138 years upon earth, having no permission to return to the
celestial regions. This was their punishment for having
dared to announce to Lot that *they* would destroy the city,
thus speaking in their own name as if it was their own free
action and not a command they had received from the Most
High.

And in those days the sin of the men of Sodom was very
grevious.[3] The men of Sodom were very wealthy and prosperous, because their land was very rich and yielded good
harvests and plenty of fruit. There were moreover in Sodom
mines of gold, of silver, and of precious stones which the
inhabitants exploited. It often happened that when a master
said unto his servant: " Go and weed out the herbs in the
garden," the servant, in weeding out the herbs, would suddenly
discover a mine of gold.[4] Thus the men of Sodom waxed
rich, but forgot the name of the Lord who had sent them all
their wealth and made them prosperous and happy. They
worshipped the sun and the moon and all the stars in heaven,
and served them. Moreover, the inhabitants of Sodom never

---

[1] *Genesis Rabba*, 48.
[2] *Midrash Agadah*, ed. Buber, p. 39; *Yoma*, 37a; *Genesis Rabba*, 50; *Baba Mezia*, 86b.
[3] *Sepher Hajashar*; *Pirke de Rabbi Eliezer*, Ch. 25; *Sanhedrin*, 109b.
[4] *Pirke de Rabbi Eliezer*, Ch. 25; *Yalkut, Job*, § 915.

gave of their substance to the poor and the alien who came
to their city. They passed a law according to which all aliens
were to be expelled, and poor men seeking food never to
receive a piece of bread. Charity was a crime punished heavily
within the walls of the city of Sodom.[1] The men of Sodom
elected as their judges and rulers men of falsehood and wickedness, who mocked justice and equity, and committed evil
deeds.[2] Whenever a stranger happened to enter the city of
Sodom, the inhabitants at once took away his goods and
substance, divested him of his clothes, and sent him away
poor and naked. There was no use to appeal to the laws of
the city, for the judges themselves approved such deeds.

Thus the inhabitants of Sodom, who knew neither charity
nor human kindness, waxed rich and exceedingly prosperous,
and lived in peace. They even passed a law that whoever was
guilty of a charitable action, were it only the gift of a piece of
bread to a starving beggar, was to die.

Earthquakes and storms had several times disturbed the
peaceful lives of the inhabitants of Sodom, but they never
attributed such visitation to the wrath of the Lord and never
mended their ways, but continued to persevere in their deeds of
wickedness. When a wealthy man came to the city, they
placed him underneath a rickety structure or wall, and when
the wall fell down and killed him, they pretended that it was
an accident and took away all his possessions. They frequently
robbed one another too.

As the rich men jealously guarded their wealth in secret
vaults and chambers, men, seeking to rob them, acted as
follows: they would take pitchers full of balsam, and approaching the rich thus speak unto them: " Take these pitchers
full of precious oil and place them in your treasury, keeping
them for us." The rich man complied, took the pitchers full

---

[1] *Targum Jerushalmi, Genesis,* 17.
[2] *Sepher Hajashar; Sanhedrin,* 109ab; *Pirke de Rabbi Eliezer,* Ch. 25; *Genesis Rabba,* 50;
See also Homer, *Iliad,* 16, 386–389.

of balsam and placed them in his treasury. At night these hunters for gold and treasure went about, and like dogs smelt out the hiding-place, and made away with all the gold and silver hoarded up in the secret chambers.[1]

The judges who ruled in Sodom passed also the following laws. Whoever was the possessor of one ox was compelled to find pasture during one day for all the cattle of the town; but he who was poor and had none was compelled to find pasture for the cattle of the town for five days. All those who passed the river had to pay one *suz* (silver coin); but if anyone, to escape payment, chose to take a longer way without crossing the river, he was obliged to pay two *suz*. Whenever a man cut off the ear of another man's donkey, he was compelled to keep and feed the animal until the ear had healed.[2] Whenever one man in a quarrel with his neighbour, hurt the latter and caused him a wound, the judges made the wounded man pay a certain sum to his assailant for the service he had rendered him by bleeding him, which, they maintained, was a medical operation. Whenever one of the inhabitants of Sodom dared to invite a stranger to some festivity, he was immediately divested of his garments and thrown into the streets.

And it came to pass that one day the guardians of the town came to the son of a poor widow and thus they spoke: " Thou hast no ox and therefore we command thee to go and find pasture for two days for all the cattle of the town." The son of the widow seemingly complied with the request of the guardians, but when he was in the fields he rose up and slaughtered all the cattle. And when the men of Sodom, on hearing what had occurred, hastened to the fields, the boy said:

" Everyone who possessed one ox let him take one hide, but he who had none, because he was poor, let him take two hides." [3]

---

[1] *Sanhedrin*, 109b; *Sepher Hajashar*.
[2] See Beer, *Das Leben Abrahams*, p. 162, note 441.   [3] *Sanhedrin*, 109a.

" Thou art talking foolishly," said the men of Sodom; " didst thou not slaughter all our cattle, and now thou wouldst distribute their hides among the numerous poor beggars. This is not justice!"

" Talk ye of justice?" asked the boy. " Am I not acting even according to your own laws? Have not your judges decreed that he who was the possessor of one ox was to pasture the cattle of the town for one day, but he who possessed none shall be obliged to find pasture for all the cattle for two days?"

The men of Sodom had the good grace to feel confounded and ashamed, but they vented their wrath by spitting into the face of the boy, knowing that by their own perverted laws which they had passed he would go unscathed if brought before the judges.[1]

The peculiarity of Sodom was the fact that there was a semblance of order and justice, and that the men claimed always to be in the right and law-abiding, never doing any wrong. But their laws were perverted.

One day a stranger came to Sodom, having crossed the river. The men of the town at once gathered round him and said: " Pay four *suz* to the owner of the ferry."

" I never availed myself of the ferry," said the stranger, " but waded through the river."[2]

" If this be the case," replied the Sodomites, " then pay him eight *suz* for having tried to defraud him of four." And when the stranger refused to pay, saying that indeed he had no money and had therefore waded through the river, they fell upon him and beat him until blood oozed from his face. The stranger, unacquainted with the laws of Sodom, hastened before the judges and related how he had been beaten, and what treatment he had met with at the hands of the wicked inhabitants. But the judges severely replied:

" Stranger! thou art indeed unacquainted, as we see,

---

[1] *Sepher Hajashar.*   [2] *Sanhedrin,* 109b.

with the laws of Sodom. This, however, is no excuse, for every stranger who cometh to our town must abide by our excellent laws. Know then, O ignorant stranger, that the claims of the men of Sodom are justified. The men of our town never can do wrong, especially where a stranger is concerned. By the laws of our country, we condemn thee, therefore, to pay eight *suz* to the owner of the ferry, because wantonly thou didst try to defraud him of four. Moreover, thou wilt pay some money unto those men who have beaten thee and caused blood to issue from thy body, as we well perceive from thy bleeding countenance. Thou must pay them for their trouble in performing a medical operation upon thee."[1]

Thus spoke the judges with an air of severity and self complacency, for were they not the guardians of the law?

And it came to pass that Eliezer, the faithful servant of Abraham, one day came to Sodom, bringing a message to Lot from his uncle Abraham. Passing through the town, he perceived one of the inhabitants wrestling with a stranger and beating him. Eliezer—accustomed in the house of his new master Abraham to treat men with loving kindness, to practise charity and to espouse the cause of justice—interfered between the two combatants. "What wrong hath this man done unto thee, and why art thou ill-treating him?" asked Eliezer, addressing the man of Sodom.

"Because," replied the latter, "he is not law-abiding and refuseth to obey me. I did ask him according to the laws of our town, to divest himself of his clothes and hand them over to me, but he refuseth."[2]

"The laws of thy country are perverted indeed," replied Eliezer, "leave therefore this man alone and do him no harm."

But the man of Sodom, hearing such words from Eliezer, waxed wroth, and seizing a stone threw it at him, causing him a grievous wound. When he saw the blood on Eliezer's

---

[1] *Sanhedrin,* 109.   [2] *Sepher Hajashar.*

countenance, he took hold of him, saying: " Now thou wilt have to pay me money, for I have bled thee. Such indeed are the laws of our land."

" What," exclaimed Eliezer, " thou art talking foolishly; thou hast caused me a wound and now thou dost ask for money for having caused it."

" I see," replied the man of Sodom, " that thou art a stranger indeed and unacquainted with our excellent laws; let us betake ourselves before the judge."

And so before the judge they went. To Eliezer's great amazement, the judge spoke as follows:

" This man hath indeed bled thee, and by the laws of our country he who wounds another and causeth him a grievous wound must pay damages, for it is the weakest, the loser, who payeth. Besides, he had some trouble to draw thy blood."

Eliezer, amazed and angry, seized a stone and hurled it at the judge's head. " Now," he said, " I have a claim on thee, pay me and I will pay this man, or thou canst pay him thyself in my stead." [1] Thereupon Eliezer left the judge and betook himself to the river where he washed his face. He then entered a house and asked the inmates to sell him some food. But instead of food he received insults and harsh words; he fared not better at several other houses, where he repeated his request. No man of Sodom ever sold food to a stranger. Such were the laws of the land. And when Eliezer severely felt the pangs of hunger he entered a house where a banquet was being offered to the townspeople by one of the inhabitants, and calmly sat down at the end of the table. Some of the guests, perceiving that he was a stranger, asked him: " Who called thee hither?"

" The man by whose side I am sitting invited me hither."

But when the latter heard such words, terror seized him.

---

[1] See *Sepher Hajashar.*

THE WAYFARER IN SODOM IS STRETCHED TO FIT HIS BED

Facing page 268, Vol. I

He knew full well what awaited him, for his fellow citizens would soon divest him of his clothes for having dared to invite a stranger to a feast. They would, moreover, not believe his words, if he tried to deny Eliezer's statement. He, therefore, hastily rose up and fled. Eliezer thereupon sat down by the side of the next guest.

" Blessed be thou," he said, " for having invited me hither to partake of food, for I am hungry indeed." Hearing such words the guest was greatly frightened and he, too, hastily left the house. Eliezer now continued his stratagem by thus addressing all the guests, one after another. After a while they had all left the house whither they had been invited, and Eliezer, remaining alone, partook of food, left money behind in payment of what he had partaken, blessed the Lord, and left the house and the town of Sodom.[1]

In an open square of the town there were four beds for strangers to sleep in. Two of the beds were long ones and two very short ones. And when a stranger, unacquainted with the customs and doings of the town, came to Sodom, the inhabitants pretended to offer him hospitality.

" Choose any of these beds you prefer and sleep in peace," they spoke quite pleasantly. And when the unsuspecting stranger laid himself down upon one of the short beds, they cut off his feet, saying that the bed was too short for him and they would make it fit him properly. When, on the other hand, he laid himself down upon one of the long beds, six strong men immediately took hold of his head and feet, began to pull his head and limbs one way and the other, so as to stretch his body out and make it fit the long bed.[2] Now Eliezer, on leaving the house where he had managed to find food, passed the open square. The men of Sodom invited him to pass the night in one of the beds. Eliezer, however, very wary and not

---

[1] Lewner, *Kol Agadoth*, Vol. I, p. 75.

[2] *Sanhedrin*, 109a; *Sepher Hajashar*. Cf. The Story of the Bed of Procrustes; see also Introduction.

trusting the men of Sodom, replied to them: " I am greatly beholden unto you for your hospitality, but ever since the death of my mother I have vowed never in my life to sleep in a bed, but to pass the night on the ground."

And one day it came to pass that a stranger happened to visit Sodom, for many strangers, unacquainted with the customs and manners of the country and the wicked deeds of the inhabitants, frequently came thither. The stranger had an ass which he was leading by a long rope, and a costly carpet. He sat in the road, and no one invited him into the house. Thereupon a man, named Heydad, came along. Beholding the stranger, his ass and carpet, he went up to him and thus addressed him:

" Come, blessed of the Lord, why dost thou remain in the road? Follow me to my house and there thou wilt find food and shelter."

The stranger thanked the kindly host and followed him to his house. He passed the night under the seemingly hospitable roof of Heydad, and in the morning, thanking his host for his hospitality, made up his mind to continue his journey.

" Tarry awhile," said the host, " I will not let thee go until thou hast refreshed thyself." And he insisted so much that the man yielded.

Thereupon the stranger said: " Blessed be thou, mine host, for having taken me in and given me food and shelter, but now I must really be off."

" Nay," said the host; " why this hurry? The day is exceedingly hot; the heat of the sun is unbearable, and the roads are dusty. Wait until the sun sets and then thou wilt go thy way in the coolness of the night."

He begged and insisted so much that the stranger once more yielded to his entreaties and remained until after sunset. But when the night had come down and sent her shadows, Heydad once more refused to let him go.

" Dost thou not see that it is a very dark night, and no pale moon sends its rays of light to show thee the way. I am afraid lest something happen unto thee on the road and thou mayest meet with an accident." Thereupon he once more insisted upon the guest remaining under his roof another night. On the following morning, however, the stranger was firmly decided to leave the town, although Heydad still pressed him to remain a little longer.

" Nay," said he, " I have tarried too long and must really be off now."

Thereupon the wife of Heydad said unto her husband: " This man has remained in our house two nights, he has had food and drink and shelter, but has never paid us anything. Why art thou such a fool to throw away thy substance upon strangers?"

Thus spoke the wife of Heydad, but her husband bade her be quiet.

" Do not worry," he said, " I will make him pay."

Thereupon the stranger asked Heydad to hand him the rope by which he was leading his ass and also the costly carpet which he had given him on his arrival, so as to put it in a safe place.

" Rope and carpet!" said the host, in assumed amazement, " verily, thou hast had a strange dream, for thou hast only dreamed of the rope and of the beautiful carpet. I will, however, interpret the dream for thee. The rope means long years, whilst the carpet is surely a beautiful garden. The Lord loveth thee surely and hath shown thee in this dream that thou wilt live many years and possess a beautiful garden wherein thou wilt plant many trees, beautiful to behold."

" Why dost thou speak foolishly?" replied the stranger. " It is no dream I am speaking about, but of a real rope and carpet I handed over to thee. Hand it back to me that I may go my way." But Heydad imperturbably repeated that it was a dream.

" And now," he added, " pay me my fee for the interpretation of this dream." The stranger protested loudly and betook himself to the judge. Heydad went with him and once more claimed his fee for the interpretation of the dream.

" Pay him his fee," decided the judge. And when the stranger indignantly cried that the host had stolen his property, the judge added: " Throw this man out of the town."

The inhabitants came, insulted him and threw him out of the town.[1]

Now it also happened that two maidens of Sodom came to draw water at the well, and one of the maidens said to her friend:

" Why dost thou look so ill to-day?"

" Because," replied her friend, " I have had no food for two days, there is not a crust of bread in the house."

Taking pity upon her friend, the first maiden said:

" Tarry thou a moment here and await my return." She came back after a while and thus spoke to her friend:

" Take my pitcher and give me thine."

The hungry maiden did as her friend had bidden her, but when she came home she found that her friend had filled her pitcher with meal. She quickly kneaded a dough and made cakes. But when the deed of the first maiden became known to the people of the town, they took her and burned her on the stake, for charity was a great crime at Sodom.

Now it came to pass that one of Lot's daughters, Peletith [2] by name, was wedded to one of the great and mighty men of Sodom. One day she noticed in the street of the city a very poor man who was starving, and the sight of him touched her

---

[1] *Sepher Hajashar.*
[2] *Sanhedrin*, 109a; *Targum Jerushalmi, Genesis*, 18, 21; *Sepher Hajashar*; *Pirke de Rabbi Eliezer*, Ch. 25; cf. *Midrash Agadah*, ed. Buber, Vol. I, p. 42, where the name of the maiden is *Kalah.*

kind heart so that she was grieved on his account. Afraid
openly to strengthen his hand with a loaf of bread, she put
into her pitcher all sorts of provisions, and whenever she went
out to the well to draw water she handed the provisions to
the poor man and thus fed him daily.

The wicked men of Sodom, who would not themselves
strengthen the hand of this poor man with a loaf of bread,
wondered greatly and said: " How does this poor man
manage to live?"

They watched, ascertained the facts and at last knew that
it was Peletith, the daughter of Lot, who fed the hungry man.
They brought her out, according to their perverse laws, and
burnt her.

She cried unto the Lord and prayed: " Sovereign of all the
worlds, maker of the Universe, maintain my right and my
cause." Her cry ascended to Heaven, right to the Throne of
Glory. And the Lord said: " I will descend and see whether
the wicked men of Sodom have done according to the cry of this
woman." [1]

One day a maiden of Sodom met a stranger in the street.
" Whence hast thou come?" she asked him.

" I have come a long way from here, but the sun hath set
and I thought I would pass the night in this town and await
the dawn." He then asked the maiden for a piece of bread
and a drink of water, for he was very hungry and thirsty.

She gave him bread and water, and he ate and drank and
blessed her. But when her deed became known, the judges of
the town were very angry. They condemned her to be divested
of her clothes, be dipped in a cask of honey and placed near
a beehive. The bees gathered round her to suck the honey,
and the poor maiden, suffering greatly, cried unto the Lord.[2]

It was to such a town that the angels Gabriel and Raphael,

---

[1] *Pirke de Rabbi Eliezer*, Ch. 25; *Targum Jerushalmi, Genesis*, 18, 20.
[2] *Sanhedrin*, 109b. See also *Genesis Rabba*, 49–50; *Sepher Hajashar*.

upon leaving Abraham, wended their way, for they had been commanded by the Most High to destroy the town and its wicked inhabitants. And when at last the men of Sodom heard that the town would soon be destroyed, the worshippers of the sun said:

" If only the morning would come and the sun rise, the sun which we are worshipping will surely save us from perdition."

But the men who worshipped the moon said: " Let the sun never rise but the moon continue to cast its light, for it is the moon we are worshipping which will save us from any calamity." [1]

The Lord Almighty, however, destroyed their town when both the moon and the sun were visible upon the firmament. At the very moment He rained upon Sodom and Gomorrah brimstone and fire from Heaven, and the cities were overthrown, and all the plain and all the inhabitants perished, and all that which grew upon the ground. What had been prosperous towns and laughing verdant valleys were now a heap of ruins, and the smoke of the country which went up as the smoke of a furnace was seen far and wide.

The news of the destruction of the cities of Sodom and Gomorrah spread to distant lands, whilst the smoke was visible in the neighbouring towns. Fear and trembling seized the people, and no wanderer now wended his way to the places where once had stood prosperous cities. And as no strangers now passed the plain of Mamre, where Abraham had pitched his tent, the Patriarch no longer had an opportunity to offer hospitality as he had been accustomed to for some time. When many days passed and no one appeared at the door of his tent, Abraham was very troubled in his mind, and at last, in sheer despair, he left the lonely and desolate region and, travelling towards the south, he settled at Gerar, in the land of the Philistines. [2]

---

[1] *Genesis Rabba*, 50.

[2] *Genesis Rabba*, 52. See also for the entire chapter, Beer, *Das Leben Abrahams*; Bin Gorion, *Die Sagen der Juden*, Vol. II, pp. 209–237; Lewner, *loc. cit.*, pp. 72–79.

CHAPTER XXIV

The Hospitable Emir

Shem-Melchizedek, and the generous Patriarch—The feeding of the animals in the ark—Hospitality on a large scale—The palace with many doors—The tree that either spread out or raised its branches—The fame of the Patriarch—The charitable lady—Thank my master—The short blessing —The Patriarch as judge and arbitrator—The story of the two associates— Muddled accounts—The story of the obstinate old man—The anger of the host—The rebuke of God—The apology of Abraham.

" TELL me," said Abraham one day to Shem-Melchizedek, " what were the merits of thy father and of thy brothers in virtue of which you were all saved in the ark?"

" Our merit," replied Shem-Melchizedek, " consisted in our having practised charity and fed the needy."

" The needy?" queried Abraham, " but there were no needy in the ark, the inmates of which were only thy father and his household."

" There were also the dumb animals," replied Shem-Melchizedek, " the dumb animals whom we fed, giving them their daily food whenever they needed it. We never forgot to give them their daily ration, and even in the night we attended to their needs." [1]

Thus spake Shem-Melchizedek, and Abraham thought in his heart:

" If it was counted as a righteous deed to Noah and to his sons to feed the dumb animals, how much greater must be the merit of him who feeds man who is needy and hungry, man who has been created in the image of God!" [2]

[1] *Midrash Tanchuma, Genesis, 8, 16.*   [2] *Midrash Shokhor Tob, Ps. 37.*

275

And Abraham decided to practise hospitality on a very large scale, and to feed the needy and hungry wanderer and the tired traveller. Thereupon he planted a garden with vine, fig trees and other fruit-bearing trees, built a sumptuous palace, the doors of which were open to east, west, north, and south.[1] Here food and drink were offered in abundance to all passers-by, to all needy wanderers and tired travellers. And when a traveller, suffering from the heat of the sun, tired, hungry and thirsty passed by, he was invited to enter the hospitable place. Here he found food and shelter. He rested his weary limbs upon one of the couches, slaked his thirst and appeased his hunger. Beneath the shady trees he found protection against the burning sun of the east. And it came to pass that when a good man, believing in the God of Heaven, sat down under one of the trees, the tree immediately spread out its branches giving him protection. But when a worshipper of idols came, the tree raised its branches and he was exposed to the intense heat and the burning rays of the sun. Thus Abraham knew at once whether his guest was a believer in the God in Heaven or an idolater. And when Abraham knew that his guest was a worshipper of idols, he hastened to welcome him and to offer him refreshment.[2]

" Eat and drink, my friend," he said, " and bless the Lord who feeds the needy." He waited upon him as a servant waits upon his master, and spoke to him about the loving kindness of the Lord, of Him who had created Heaven and earth, and all its creatures. And he never left the worshipper of idols until the latter had opened his eyes and begun to understand the power and love of the Lord of the Universe.[3]

And the fame of Abraham the Hebrew spread far and wide, so that from all the corners of the earth men, women, and children, all the lowly and oppressed, the needy and miserable,

[1] *Sepher Hajashar; Midrash Shokhor Tob, Ps.* 37; *Abot de Rabbi Nathan,* Ch. 7.
[2] *Abot de Rabbi Nathan,* Ch. 7; *Sotah,* 10.　　[3] Cf. *Pirke de Rabbi Eliezer,* Ch. 25.

the suffering and the downtrodden, the hungry and the naked, came to him to seek solace and help. All of them Abraham received with open arms. He fed and clothed them, comforted and consoled them and wiped away their tears.

And Sarah, his wife, was sharing in the charitable work of her aged husband. Indefatigably she worked day and night. During the day she assisted her husband and waited upon the travellers, offering them food and drink; and during the night she worked assiduously and industriously, weaving, with her own hands, garments to cover the naked. Girding her loins with strength, she strengthened her arms; she laid her hand to the spindle, and her hands held the distaff. She sought wool and flax and worked willingly with her hands, she, the aged mate of the wealthy and prosperous oriental Emir, who owned fields and vineyards, slaves and cattle, and who was the friend and companion of potentates and princes. Her candle never went out at night, from Saturday to Saturday.

And the more Abraham and his wife Sarah worked and laboured for the benefit and in the interests of the poor and needy, the miserable, afflicted and suffering, the greater grew their fame, and the Lord blessed their work, and they became a blessing.

And it came to pass that when the guests who had found such hospitable treatment in the house of Abraham and his wife, such comfort and consolation, kissed his hands and thanked him for his help, Abraham used to reply:

" Nay, do not thank me, but my master who sendeth food to the hungry and help to the needy."

" And where is thy master?" asked the ignorant; " show him unto us that we may thank him and bless him."

" The Master, mine and yours, my friends," replied Abraham, " is the Lord of the Universe whose glory fills the whole world; it is He who feedeth all creatures in His great loving kindness and mercy." [1]

And Abraham's listeners wondered greatly, saying: " Verily, great and glorious is this master, the Lord of the Universe, but He is invisible and we know not how to thank and bless Him for His loving kindness; teach us how to thank Him daily for His mercies."

" My friends," replied Abraham, and his heart was full of joy, " say only a few words: ' Blessed be the Eternal, our Lord, from eternity to eternity.' It is a short blessing, but coming from the heart it is agreeable to God Almighty." [2]

But men came to Abraham not solely to ask his charity. They also came to seek his advice and judgment. Those who had some dispute, knocked at the gate of the famous hospitable Emir of Canaan saying: " We bring our difference before thee and ask thee to be our judge." Abraham, as a rule, patiently heard their claims and always endeavoured to bring about a reconciliation, so that the parties left his house not as enemies but as friends.

And it came to pass that one day two men came to Abraham laying their case before him. " For a long time," said the first of the disputants, " we traded together as associates, and now, having separated, I find that my former associate oweth me one hundred shekels, but he refuseth to pay me this sum."

Thereupon Abraham took out one hundred shekels from his own purse and, giving it to the claimant, said: " Here is thy money, but let us listen now to what thy former associate hath to say."

" My Lord," said the other, " he is mistaken, for instead of owing him such a sum, it is he who oweth me money." Thereupon the claimant brought witnesses to prove that he

---

[1] *Midrash Tanchuma, Genesis*, 15, 1.
[2] *Ibid.; Genesis Rabba*, 43 and 54; *Abot de Rabbi Nathan*, Ch. 7.

was right. Yet both associates persevered in their statement.

Abraham, therefore, sat down and examined all their business transactions, and found that they had both erred and that none owed the other anything. He proved their error unto them, and they were reconciled, blessed Abraham, and praised his wisdom.

" My brothers," said Abraham, " keep the hundred shekels I have given you and divide the sum between you. As my sole reward, I beg you to love one another, to live in peace, and never to quarrel." [1]

Sometimes, however, it happened that Abraham lost his patience, trying in vain to open the eyes of an obstinate worshipper of idols who persistently refused to acknowledge the God in Heaven, the Lord of the Universe. Thus one day an old man, tired and hungry, approached his gate. Abraham rose at once to meet him and invited him into his house.

" Come into my tent," said Abraham, " refresh thyself, and rest thy weary limbs upon a couch; pass the night in my tent, and when the sun riseth in the east thou wilt continue thy way." The old man at first refused, preferring to pass the night under one of the trees in the open, but Abraham insisted and begged him to accept his hospitality, until the old man yielded.

Abraham hastened to wait upon the old man, placing butter and milk and cakes before the traveller, who ate and was satisfied.

" Render thanks, my friend," said Abraham, " to God Almighty, and bless His name, for it is He who sendeth their food to all His creatures." But the traveller replied:

" I know not thy God, the God thou speakest of; I know my idols which I have made with my own hands, them do I worship and to them do I render thanks."

All Abraham's persuasions and pleadings were of no avail,

---

[1] *Abot de Rabbi Nathan*, Ch. 4.

for the old man obstinately persisted in his error, and angrily exclaimed: " Why dost thou endeavour to make me abandon my gods? Leave me alone that I may continue to worship the gods of my youth until I die." Hearing such words, Abraham waxed wroth and called to his guest:

" Woe unto thee, thou sinful and wicked old man; leave my house immediately, for I never wish to see thee again." Thus spake Abraham in his righteous indignation, and the old man left Abraham's house in the night and went out into the desert. But the Lord rebuked Abraham for his rashness and his treatment of the old man, whom he had driven out of his tent in the darkness of the night.

" Where is the weary wanderer," asked the Lord, " who came into thy tent?"

" I have sent him away," replied Abraham, " for he was very obstinate and would persist in his evil ways."

But the Lord replied:

" I have borne the sin of this old man for many years and have not waxed angry. In spite of his errors, I have given him food and clothes, magnanimously waiting until he had mended his ways. He came to thee and thou didst not bear with him even for one short night, but didst drive him out of thy tent, sending him away in the darkness of the night into the desert. Now, hasten and run after thy guest and beg his forgiveness."

Abraham repented of his rash act, and hastened out in search of the old man whom he had so inhospitably sent away from beneath his roof. He found him at last, and falling upon his knees he begged the old man's forgiveness. He implored him to return to his tent and there to pass the night.[1]

[1] Lewner, *Kol Agadoth*, Vol. I, pp. 90–91; see for the entire chapter, Beer, *Das Leben Abrahams*; Weil, *Biblische Legenden der Muselmänner*. Lewner, *Kol Agadoth*, Vol. I, pp. 86–91.

CHAPTER XXV

The Sacrifice of a Father

The sumptuous banquet—The royal guests—Sammael appears in the guise of a beggar—The accusation of Sammael—His challenge—The visit of the father—The angry wife—The message of the father—The threshold of the tent—The second visit of Abraham to Ishmael—Fatima, the good wife—The two sons—The virtuous Isaac—The tempter before the Throne of Glory—The accusing angels—Shaftiel, the accuser—The speech of Sammael—The sacrifice of the beloved son—The ruse of the Patriarch—The joyous meal—The preparations for the journey—A mother's sorrow—Another version of the story of the journey—The saddling of the ass—The hopes of Eliezer and of Ishmael—The anger of Sammael—The whisperings of the tempter—Sammael appears as a youth and tempts Isaac—The stream barring the way—The prayer of the father—Sammael's new effort—The holy mountain—Abraham addresses his son—The dutiful boy—A son's message to his mother—Isaac's vision of the heavens—The weeping angels—Their prayer—The ram that was created before sunset on the sixth day of Creation—Sammael, and the ram—The voice from the Throne of Glory—God's promise to the Patriarch.

IT was at Gerar that Abraham's son Isaac was born, and all the folks marvelled at the miracle God had wrought. When Isaac was weaned, Abraham made a great feast, " the same day that the child was weaned ".[1] And many were the guests invited to that splendid feast at which Abraham was happy to display his usual hospitality. Kings and princes and the great ones of the land gathered at the house of Abraham. There was Abi-Melech, the King of Gerar, and his suite, Og, the giant, envious in his heart and still brooding mischief, and all the princes of Canaan, with the commanders of their armies, sixty-two in all. And Og's friends mocked him and said:

[1] Cf. *Pirke de Rabbi Eliezer*, Ch. 29; *Midrash Shokhor Tob, Ps.* 112.

" Didst thou not laugh at Abraham, saying that he was even like a mule which hath no offspring? What sayest thou now?" But Og replied: " I could squash this imp of his with the little finger of my hand." [1]

At the feast arranged by Abraham on the day when his son was weaned, there were also present the venerable Shem and Eber, as well as Abraham's old father Terah and his brother Nahor.[2] They had all hastened to come and rejoice with Abraham in his great happiness. But Sammael, he who is also called Satan, was exceedingly jealous of the happy father, and black were his thoughts. He thereupon appeared at the feast in the guise of a beggar standing in the door. Abraham, too busy waiting upon his distinguished guests, never noticed the beggar standing in the door and did not invite him to sit down at the table. Satan, who had only come in search of some incident which he could bring up against the old man, was rejoiced at this neglect. Straightway he spread his wings and appeared before the Throne of Glory and thus he spoke:

" Lord of the Universe! Thou hast given unto Abraham all that his heart desireth; Thou hast heaped upon him wealth and prosperity, and, in his old age, Thou hast even given him a son. Now his heart is swelled with pride and his head is lifted high. No longer doth he care for the poor and the needy. To-day I did test him, standing at his once hospitable door in the guise of a beggar, but he never paid the slightest attention to me and never invited me to break bread at his table. Such is the frailty of man, and even the best and most God-fearing become arrogant in their days of happiness and prosperity." Thus spoke Satan, accusing Abraham before the Throne of Glory. But a voice from the Throne of Glory replied:

" There is no one so charitable as Abraham, and there

---

[1] *Sepher Hajashar*; *Yalkut*, 2, § 973; *Genesis Rabba*, 53; *Baba Mezia*, 86a.
[2] *Sepher Hajashar*.

is none so pious and so God-fearing.   Thou wilt see, Satan, accuser of men, that when I command Abraham to sacrifice his only son, born unto him in his old age, he will gladly and unhesitatingly obey My command."

But Satan only grinned and shook his head:

"Never," said he, "will a father, not even Abraham, obey such a command." [1]

Now it came to pass that after a while Abraham, urged by his wife Sarah, sent away from home his bondwoman Hagar, a daughter of the Pharaoh, or king, of Egypt, who had borne unto him a son named Ishmael.   Mother and son left the house of Abraham and dwelt in the desert of Paran, where Ishmael became an archer and a mighty hunter.

His mother then took him a wife out of Egypt.   Three years had thus passed, when Abraham felt a yearning for his son Ishmael and greatly wished to see him.   He thereupon spoke to his wife Sarah and thus he said: "Three years have now passed since Ishmael hath left my house and settled in the desert.   I will therefore go and visit him and see if he fareth well." [2]   Sarah agreed to this; and Abraham bade his servant saddle his camel, and he went off into the desert.

He arrived at noon before the tent of his son.   Neither Ishmael nor his mother Hagar were present, for they had gone to fetch dates and pomegranates.   Abraham saw his son's wife and her children, and gave them his greeting; but the woman never replied, nor even turned her head to take notice of him.

"Where is thy husband?" asked Abraham.

The woman, without even turning her head, replied in an angry tone: "My husband is away."

"My daughter," again spoke Abraham, "prithee, give me a drink of water, for I am very thirsty."

[1] *Sepher Hajashar.*
[2] *Sepher Hajashar*; *Pirke de Rabbi Eliezer*, Ch. 30; *Yalkut, Genesis*, § 95.   See also Weil, *Biblische Legenden der Muselmänner*, p. 90.

" I have neither drink nor food for thee," cried the woman, " go thy way."

Thereupon she entered the inner tent, and Abraham heard her curse and beat her children and also curse her husband.

Kindly and patiently Abraham called again to the wife of his son:

" My daughter, if I have found grace in thine eyes, hearken for a moment to what I have to say to thee."

The woman came out of the tent and with bad grace replied:

" Speak, old man, I am listening unto thee."

" When Ishmael, thy husband, returneth home, tell him this: an old man from the land of Canaan was here and inquired after thee; he also bade thee change the threshold of thy tent, for it is a bad one, and to put a better one in its place." [1]

Thus spoke Abraham and departed. When Ishmael came home, his wife told him what had happened and what message the old man from Canaan had left. Ishmael at once knew that his father had been to see him and that his wife had not found favour in the old man's eyes. He therefore bestowed gifts upon her, sent her back to her own people, and took unto himself another wife, Fatima by name, out of Egypt.

Again three years passed, and Abraham once more felt an urgent desire to visit his son Ishmael and to know how he fared. With the permission of his wife Sarah he once more travelled to the desert of Paran where his son dwelt. When he reached the tent of his son, Ishmael's wife came out and gave him friendly greeting.

" Where is thy husband, my daughter?" queried Abraham.

" He is away from home, hunting; but prithee, my Lord,

[1] *Pirke de Rabbi Eliezer*, Ch. 30.

come down from thy camel and honour me with thy presence in our humble tent. Rest awhile from the fatigue of thy journey and refresh thyself with food and drink. Thou wilt thus bestow a great favour upon thy servant."

Abraham at first declined, for he was in a hurry to return home before the sun set. But Fatima [1] insisted so much that he gave in. Dismounting his camel, he entered the tent and partook of refreshment which the woman had placed before him. He blessed her and prayed unto the Lord to send happiness and prosperity into this tent. Turning to Fatima he thus spoke:

" When thy husband, Ishmael, returns from his hunting, tell him this, my daughter: an old man from the land of the Philistines hath been here and inquired after thee. He also bade me say that he found the new threshold of thy tent a very good one. He bade thee keep it and cherish it."

Thereupon he took his departure.

And when Ishmael returned and heard what had happened, he knew that his father had been to visit him, and that he had approved of his new wife who had found grace in his eyes. [2]

Although he loved his son Ishmael, Abraham cherished his son Isaac, the son Sarah had borne unto him, much more. Isaac indeed deserved the love of his fond old father, for he was a God-fearing lad and walked in the ways of the Lord. He followed in the path of his pious parents, and his good deeds were many. His charity and generosity were boundless. If Abraham loved his son Isaac given to him in his old age, the boy endeared himself to his parents even more on account of his many virtues and his sweet disposition. He did more than his duty to his parents, and was zealous in the worship of God. But the Lord wanted to test Abraham. He decided to test the religious disposition of the Patriarch, and thus

---

[1] *Targum Jerushalmi, Genesis*, 21, 21; *Pirke de Rabbi Eliezer*, Ch. 30.
[2] *Pirke de Rabbi Eliezer*, Ch. 30; *Sepher Hajashar*; see also Weil, *Biblische Legenden der Muselmänner*, pp. 90–93.

show to the world to what an extent a pious man was able not only to fear but also to love his God.

Now there was a day when the sons of God came to present themselves before the Lord,[1] and among them were also Satan, he who is called Sammael, the tempter and accuser of men, and all the other accusing angels. And the Lord said unto them:

" Whence come ye?" And they answered and said: " From going to and fro in the earth, and from walking up and down in it." And the Lord said unto them: " What have ye to say concerning the actions of man?" And the accusing angels answered the Lord and said:

" Verily, we find that men only worship and serve Thee when they are in need of Thy help and have a favour to ask from Thee. Once Thou hast granted them this favour they at once forsake Thee."

The Lord then said unto the accusing angels:

" Have ye considered My servant Abraham, that there is none like him on earth, a perfect and an upright man, one that feareth God and loveth Him and escheweth evil, and still he holdeth fast his integrity. Ye moved Me against man, saying, when I once decided to create him in My image, that I would repent having done so. Now ye behold the righteousness of Abraham and the number of men he has converted to the knowledge of Me, teaching them to bless and glorify My name."

Thereupon Shaftiel, one of the accusing angels, came and stood before the Lord and thus he spake: " Verily, the good deeds of Thy servant Abraham are many, and there is none like him in the earth. But even Abraham will not obey Thee, O Lord, if Thou shouldst command him to sacrifice his own dear and beloved son."

---

[1] *Sepher Hajashar*; *Sanhedrin*; 89b; *Tana debe Eliahu*, Ch. 7. See also *The Book of Jubilees*, 3, 13.

Then Satan, he who is called Sammael, the accuser of man and the tempter, came and stood before the Lord, and thus he spoke: " Verily, it is not astonishing that Abraham worshipped Thee as long as he was childless. He builded altars, praised Thy name and spread Thy worship among men. But now, since Thou hast vouchsafed unto him Thy loving kindness, granted him his heart's desire and given him in his old age a son, he is already beginning to forsake Thee. He prepared a feast on the day when Isaac, his son, was weaned, but he paid no heed to a poor beggar who stood upon his threshold." [1]

But the Lord said unto Satan, who is called Sammael: " I know that there is none like Abraham in the earth, a perfect and an upright man, and even if I were to command him to take his son, his only son Isaac, whom he loveth, and offer him for a burnt offering upon one of the mountains, he would obey My command with a glad heart."

And Sammael said: " Do this, O Lord, and if Abraham obeys Thy command and offers his beloved son Isaac for a burnt offering upon one of the mountains, then I will know that indeed there is none like him on the earth."

Thereupon the Lord decided to test his servant Abraham and to show to Sammael that there was none so perfect as Abraham. The Lord therefore called unto Abraham and said: " I have a favour to ask of thee. I have bestowed many blessings upon thee and made thee superior to thine enemies. I have given thee a son in thy old age, thy son Isaac who is the cause of thy happiness, but now I require of thee to offer this son of thine as a sacrifice and a holy oblation." And the Lord accordingly commanded Abraham to carry his son to the mountain Moriah, to the country where mountains rise in the midst of dales, where once light and law and the fear of God were destined to dwell, and whence the light of wisdom and of the knowledge

---

[1] *Tana debe Eliahu*, Ch. 7; *Sepher Hajashar.*

of the true God will issue forth and cast its rays upon the world at large. He commanded Abraham to build an altar there and to offer Isaac as a burnt offering upon it.[1] " For thus," said the Lord, " thou wilt best manifest thy religious disposition towards Me, if thou wilt prefer what is pleasing to Me before the preservation even of thine own son."

Abraham listened to the voice of the Lord and thought in his heart that it was not right to disobey God in anything, and that he was indeed obliged to serve Him in every circumstance of life without asking any questions. " For do not," so thought Abraham, " all creatures that live enjoy life by divine providence and the kindness God bestoweth on them." He was, however, troubled in his mind about one thing and thought how he could best conceal this command of God from his dear wife Sarah.[2] " If I tell my wife of this command of the Lord," thought Abraham in his heart, " she will take the matter to heart and the loss of her beloved son will be such a blow to her in her old age that she will surely die of a broken heart. If again I take Isaac unbeknown to my wife, she will seek for him everywhere and not finding him will grieve greatly, and her sorrow and grief will bring her to the grave. I will, therefore, employ a ruse, so as to spare my dear wife and keep her in ignorance of what is about to happen." Thereupon Abraham, with joyous mien, although his own heart was very heavy in his breast, approached his wife and thus he spake:

" My dear one, prepare a special repast to-day that we may enjoy ourselves and make merry in our old age." Thus spoke Abraham, and Sarah asked in astonishment: " Why, dear husband mine, to-day of all days, and why this festivity?"

" To-day like every other day is a day of rejoicing for us when we remember the great loving kindness the Lord has

---

[1] *Sanhedrin*, 89b; *Midrash Tanchuma*, Section *Wayera*; *Genesis Rabba*, 39; *Pirke de Rabbi Eliezer*, Ch. 31.

[2] Josephus, *Antiquities*, I, 13, 2; *Sepher Hajashar*; *Yalkut*, I, § 98.

vouchsafed unto us, when He gave us such a precious gift in
our old age; when He bestowed upon us our beloved son
Isaac, who is indeed a blessing to his old and aged parents."
Sarah went and did as Abraham, her dear husband, had
bidden her, and prepared a festive meal.

When they were at table, Abraham said unto his wife:

" Hearken unto my words, wife of mine. Thou knowest
well that I was only three years old when I already acknowledged the true, living and only God, the Creator of the
Universe, and learned both to fear and to love Him. Now our
son Isaac is growing up and it is high time that he, too, should
learn the knowledge of God and the wonders He is working;
it is time to instruct Isaac and to educate him in the fear of
the Lord. I have therefore decided to take him to-day and
bring him to the school established by our near relatives Shem
and Eber.[1] There he will learn wisdom and knowledge and
the fear of the Lord."

Thus spoke Abraham, and his wife, always accustomed to
obey her husband, approved of his plan, although her heart
ached at the thought of being separated for a long time from
her beloved child. " Do this, husband mine," she said, " although thou knowest well that the boy is dearer unto me than
life itself." And she kissed and embraced her son and prepared
his festive garments and a headgear, but the tears were running
down her face when she thought of the separation.

The whole night Sarah was busy with the preparations for
the journey, and when dawn broke and the first rays of the
sun tinted with orient hues the sombre sky, she arrayed her
dear son in a costly garment, one of those garments which
Abi-Melech, King of Gerar, had once made a present unto her,
and placed upon his head a headgear ornamented with pearls
and precious stones. She fell upon the neck of her only son
and shed tears copiously. " Farewell, my beloved son," she

[1] *Sepher Hajashar*; *Midrash Tanchuma*, section *Wayera*.

said, " the Lord knoweth whether and when I shall behold
thy dear countenance again in this world, for I am old and my
years are numbered." [1]

In the meantime Abraham went out and with his own
hands, although he was a wealthy and slave-owning Emir,
saddled his ass, quite contrary to custom. Sarah prepared
food for the journey and accompanied by her maids escorted
her husband and her son part of the way. She once more
begged her husband to take care of her boy during the journey
and to minister to all his needs. Thereupon, she returned
home, and Abraham and his son Isaac continued their journey.

According to another version,[2] Sarah did not accompany
her husband and child. When Abraham saw her so greatly
upset and weeping so bitterly, he said unto her: " Hearken
unto my words, my dear, and lie down for a while and snatch
some sleep. Isaac, too, needs rest for our weary journey, for
we intend to leave with sunrise." Sarah listened to the advice
of her husband and lay down upon her couch, but she could
find no sleep, and cried all night; at dawn only she fell into
a troubled sleep. When Abraham saw her asleep, he seized
this opportunity to leave as speedily as possible before his
wife awoke, so that she might not hinder him in his enterprise
at the last moment.

Abraham thus rose up early in the morning, took with
him Ishmael, Eliezer, and Isaac, his son, and saddled his
ass. It was the offspring of that ass which had been created
during the twilight on the eve of the first Sabbath, in the week
of creation. The same ass was afterwards ridden by Moses when
he came to Egypt, and will be ridden upon in the future by
the son of David.[3]

On the way, a dispute arose between Eliezer and Ishmael.
" Abraham, my father," said Ishmael, " will now offer my

---

[1] *Sepher Hajashar.*   [2] *Midrash Tanchuma*, section *Wayera.*
[3] *Pirke de Rabbi Eliezer*, Ch. 31.

brother Isaac for a burnt offering, and I, his first born, will now inherit all his possessions."

" Thy father hath already once driven thee out and sent thee away into the wilderness. I, on the other hand, am his faithful servant, serving him by day and night, and I shall be his heir," [1] replied Eliezer.

Now Sammael waxed angry, when he realized how upright and God-fearing Abraham was and how he did not refuse to sacrifice and offer as a burnt offering his only begotten son, when God bade him do so. Sammael's whole aim now was to find means and ways how to prevent Abraham from accomplishing his journey and fulfilling the command of the Lord. He thereupon assumed the shape of an aged and broken man, bent with years, and in such disguise met Abraham and his companions: " Whither art thou going, venerable old man?" he queried.[2]

" To say my prayers to the Lord upon the mountains yonder," replied Abraham.

" But I see thee carrying fire and a knife in thine hand, and wood upon thy shoulders," said Satan, who is also called Sammael.

" I have provided myself," replied Abraham, " with all that we shall require on our journey. Should we be compelled to remain a few days, we can light a fire, kill an animal, and bake bread."

" Thou canst not deceive me, old man," cried Sammael, throwing off his disguise. " Was I not present when the Lord commanded thee to take thy beloved son and bring him for a burnt offering upon one of the mountains yonder? Verily, thou art a fool, and there is no fool like an old fool. Dost thou imagine that if thou dost bring for a burnt offering thy only begotten son, born unto thee at the age of a hundred

---

[1] *Sepher Hajashar*; *Genesis Rabba*, 56; *Pirke de Rabbi Eliezer*, Ch. 31; *Midrash Haggadol*, col. 320.

[2] *Genesis Rabba*, 56; *Midrash Tanchuma*, section *Wayera*, *Sepher Hajashar*.

years, thou wilt ever have another son? Besides, thou never didst hear the voice of the Lord who commanded thee to sacrifice thine own son. It was the voice of the tempter thou didst hear, the tempter who is endeavouring to lead thee to perdition. To-morrow the Lord will take thee to account for this wicked deed thou art about to perform. He will accuse thee of manslaughter, of the slaughter of thine own son whose blood thou didst not hesitate to shed, misled by the voice of the tempter. Could the Lord, who loveth thee so much, ever have asked thee to bring such a sacrifice and bid thee kill thine own son with thine own hands?[1] Verily, thy piety is exaggerated, and thou wilt soon have occasion to repent of it."[2]

Thus spake Sammael, trying to beguile Abraham and to make him waver. But Abraham held fast to his integrity.

" It was not the voice of the tempter I heard," said Abraham, " but the voice of the Lord, the Creator of Heaven and earth.[3] It is He who, indeed, commanded me to bring my son for a burnt offering, and it is not for man to question the ways of the Lord. His intentions are hidden from mortals, and we only have to obey and to have faith in Him who rules from eternity to eternity."

When Sammael saw that he could not move Abraham and make him waver in his purpose for even a fleeting moment, he tried to tempt Isaac and make him hearken to his words. Disguised as a youth, he suddenly appeared to the travellers,[4] and approaching the boy who was being led to the slaughter he thus addressed him:

" And whither mayest thou be travelling, young man?"

" To the school established by Shem and Eber, there to study wisdom and the fear of the Lord," replied Isaac.

" Art thou going to study this wisdom and the fear of the

---

[1] *Sanhedrin*, 89b. [2] Jellinek, *Beth-Hamidrash, Midrash Wayosha*, Vol. I, p. 36.
[3] *Sanhedrin*, 89b. [4] *Sepher Hajashar; Midrash Tanchuma*, ed. Buber, p. 114.

Lord," asked Sammael mockingly, "whilst thou art still among the living or after thy death?"

"Thou speakest foolishly," replied Isaac, "is there any study after death?"

Thereupon Sammael said: "Son of an unhappy sorrowing mother! Dost thou not know that thine own foolish father is leading thee like a lamb to the slaughter? Is it for this end that thy mother has wept and prayed and fasted and begged the Lord to send her a son in her old age? And now thou art going to die, and she will remain alone and desolate. Is not thy mother dear to thee?"

"She is dear to me, dearer than life itself," replied Isaac, "but I must obey the command of the Creator and that of my father."[1]

But in spite of his firmness Isaac was troubled in his mind, and related to his father what he had just heard from the youth who was none other than Sammael in disguise.[2]

"Hearken not unto him, my son," replied Abraham, "he is speaking with the voice of the tempter, who is trying to make us waver in our obedience to the commands of our Maker, our Father in Heaven."

They continued their way, and behold, there was a stream barring their way. They decided to wade through it and thus reach the opposite bank. The water soon reached to their knees, and when they were midways, it soon rose to their necks. Abraham, who knew the country well, was quite certain that he had never seen either stream or river in this region, and guessed right enough that it was the work of Satan. Lifting up his eyes to Heaven, he thus prayed unto his Maker:

"Lord of the Universe, thou didst manifest Thy glory unto me and didst say that none was like me in piety. Thou didst command me to bring my son Isaac as a burnt offering, and I never questioned Thy words, but whole-heartedly I

---

[1] Jellinek, *ibid*.   [2] *Tanchuma*, ed. Buber, p. 114.

obeyed Thy command, for through me Thy name shall be sanctified. But now, if we perish in these waters, how shall I be able to do Thy bidding and sanctify Thy name?" [1]

Thus prayed Abraham in his anguish, and behold, the stream suddenly disappeared, and Abraham and his companions were standing upon dry land.

Sammael, however, did not yet consider himself beaten. He tried again to prevent Abraham from doing the bidding of the Lord and to make him turn back. He once more appeared before the old man, and thus he spoke to him:

"Abraham, in vain dost thou continue this weary journey. A thing was secretly brought to me, and mine ear received a little thereof. I have heard it proclaimed in Heaven that the Almighty really desires a lamb as burnt offering, but not thy son."

"Even if it were so," said Abraham, "I would not believe thee now, for thou hast proved a liar too often." [2] And Abraham continued his way. Then, on the third day, Abraham lifted up his eyes and saw the place afar off. There was a wide valley before him surrounded by lofty mountains. And behold, all the mountains suddenly moved and, gathering together, became one immense mountain, and a pillar of fire came down from Heaven and hovered over the mountain and it reached up to Heaven. A cloud rose up and enveloped the mountain, and the glory of the Lord was visible unto Abraham. [3]

"What seest thou, my son?" asked Abraham, turning to Isaac.

"My Father," said Isaac, "I see a pillar of fire and a cloud."

"What do ye see?" asked Abraham of Ishmael and Eliezer who were accompanying them.

"We see mountains," replied both Eliezer and Ishmael.

---

[1] Jellinek, *ibid.*, pp. 36–37; see also *Midrash Tanchuma*, section *Wayera*.
[2] *Sanhedrin*, 109.　　　[3] *Pirke de Rabbi Eliezer*, Ch. 31; *Genesis Rabba*, 56.

And Abraham knew that it was not given to them to see the Glory of the Lord. He thereupon left them behind and proceeded on his way with his son Isaac.[1]

Isaac now understood that he was destined to be brought as a burnt offering, but he gladly and willingly accepted his lot. Abraham then opened his mouth and thus addressed his son:

" O my son! A vast number of prayers have I poured out that I might have thee for my son; when thou didst come into the world, there was nothing that could contribute to thy support for which I was not greatly solicitous, nor anything wherein I thought myself happier than to see thee grown up to a man's estate and that I might have thee at my death the successor of my dominions; but since it was by God's will that I became thy father, and it is now His will that I relinquish thee, bear this consecration to God with a generous mind, for I resign thee up to God who hath thought fit now to require this testimony of honour to Himself, on account of the favours He hath conferred on me in being to me a supporter and a defender. Accordingly, thou my son, wilt now die, not in any common way of going out of the world, but sent to God, the Father of all men, beforehand, by thy own father, in the nature of a sacrifice. I suppose He thinks thee worthy to get clear of this world, neither by disease, neither by war, nor by any other severe way, by which death usually comes upon men, but so that He will receive thy soul with prayers and holy offices of religion, and will place thee near to Himself, and thou wilt there be to me a succourer and supporter in my old age." Thus spoke Abraham to his son Isaac before bringing him as a burnt offering according to the will of God.[2] Now Isaac was of a very generous disposition, as indeed became the son of such a father, and he was pleased with his father's discourse.

---

[1] *Sepher Hajashar*; *Genesis Rabba*, 56. See also *Midrash Haggadol*, col. 320.
[2] Josephus, *Antiquities*, I, 13, 3.

" My Father," he said, " I was not worthy to be born at first, if I should reject the determination of God and of my father, and should not resign myself up readily to both your pleasures, since it would have been unjust if I had not obeyed, even if my father alone had so resolved." [1]

Thereupon Abraham builded an altar, laid the wood in order, bound Isaac his son, and laid him on the altar upon the wood. Well might Abraham's hand have shook a little, when he stretched it out to take the knife to slay his son. But Isaac, ready to be sacrificed, because such had been the will of his Maker, encouraged his father.

" My Father," said Isaac, " take heart, bare thy hand, bind my hands and feet, for I am a lad in all the strength of my youth, whilst thou art an old man. When I see the knife in thine hand, I may, against my own will, lose heart, seize thy arm to save myself. The instinct of self-preservation is deeply implanted in man and may prompt me to disobey thee. I implore thee, Father mine, fulfil as speedily as possible the will of the Lord. And when my body will have been burnt to ashes, take these ashes and place them in an urn in my mother's room that she may remember her son whenever she enters her room. But I tremble when I think what a hard task thou wilt have to break the news to my mother, and to inform her that her beloved son is no more, but has been brought as a burnt offering upon the altar of the Lord and of duty." [2]

Thus spoke Isaac and bared his throat. Tears were streaming down from Abraham's eyes, his hand trembled and shook, and the knife fell from his hand, for Satan was making a last desperate effort to make the old man waver in his purpose. The Patriarch pulled himself together and once more

---

[1] Josephus, *Antiquities*, I, 13, 3.
[2] *Pirke de Rabbi Eliezer*, Ch. 31; *Sepher Hajashar*; *Targum Jerushalmi, Genesis*, 22, 10; *Genesis Rabba*, 56; *Midrash Tanchuma*, ed. Buber, p. 114; Jellinek, *Beth-Hamidrash*, Vol. I, p. 37; cf. also Grünbaum, *loc. cit.*, pp. 112, 115-116.

seized the knife, his eyes looking deeply into the eyes of his
beloved son, as if to drink in remembrance. Isaac's eyes
were directed heavenwards, and he beheld the heavenly
hosts hastening to surround the Throne of Glory.[1] For, in
this supreme moment, nature was hushed, the radiance of
the sun was obscured, and fear and admiration seized the
heavenly hosts who were witnessing the old father ready to
slaughter his only son, and the son willing to accept his lot,
because the Lord had so ordained. The mighty spirits, the
beings of fire and flame, loudly lamented and cried:

" Behold! an extraordinary deed is being committed, a
father is sacrificing his son upon the altar of the Lord and of
duty." Bitterly wept the mild angels of peace[2], of love and mercy,
and their tears fell down upon the eyes of Isaac, so that in
old age his sight grew dim. And the heavenly hosts, the fiery
spirits, and the angels of mercy, of love and of peace, prostrated
themselves before the Throne of Glory and prayed to the
Creator of the Universe, and thus they said:

" Sovereign of all the worlds, Creator of the Universe,
merciful and compassionate art Thou called, Thy mercy
being upon all Thy works, have now mercy upon Isaac, who
is bound before Thee like an animal, he who is a human being
and the son of a human being. O Lord! Thy righteousness
is like the mighty mountains, and Thy judgments are like a
great deep. O Lord, Thou preservest man and beasts." [3]

Thus prayed the ministering angels, and the Most High
replied: " Now ye see, how man, whose creation ye once
opposed, can glorify and sanctify My name and how perfect
he can be." Thereupon He commanded the angel Michael
to call unto the pious old man, the loving father who would
not spare his own son, not to lay his hand upon the lad.
Michael immediately obeyed the command of his Master,

---

[1] *Genesis Rabba*, 56; *Pirke de Rabbi Eliezer*, Ch. 32.   [2] *Genesis Rabba*, 56.
[3] *Pirke de Rabbi Eliezer*, Ch. 31; *Sepher Hajashar*.

but Abraham would not listen to the voice of the arch-angel.[1]

"God alone," he replied, "commanded me to bring my son as a burnt offering, and Him alone will I obey but not his messengers." Thereupon the cloud dispersed, the mist lifted, and the heavenly spheres became visible to Abraham, and the voice from the Throne of Glory repeated the words of the archangel.[2]

And Abraham lifted up his eyes, and behold, behind him a ram was caught in a thicket by his horns. It was the ram which had been created before sunset on the sixth day of creation. It had dwelt in Paradise, under the tree of life, and had drunk the waters of the rivers of Paradise. One of the ministering angels had brought the ram down to be ready to take the place of Isaac.[3]

Now Sammael, black with envy and anger on seeing that all his efforts had been frustrated, tried to hide the ram from Abraham's sight,[4] but Abraham pursued it, and discovering it at last, he offered it as a burnt offering in the stead of his son. Abraham then prostrated himself before the Eternal and thus he prayed:

"Lord Almighty! Thou who knowest the innermost thoughts of man hast seen how ready I was to obey Thy commands. I did not withhold my only son, when Thou didst command me to bring him as a burnt offering. Remember my intentions, O Lord, and when one day the children of Isaac will sin against Thee and transgress Thy commands, let Thy mercy prevail against Thy just wrath. Have mercy upon them and forgive them their errors."[5]

And a voice from the Throne of Glory replied: "It was not out of a desire for human blood that thou wast commanded

---

[1] Jellinek, *loc. cit.*, p. 38.
[2] *Midrash Tanchuma*, ed. Buber, p. 115. Cf. Grünbaum, *loc. cit.*, p. 116; Weil, *loc. cit.*, pp. 86–89: see also *Pirke de Rabbi Eliezer*, Ch. 31.
[3] Beer, *Das Leben Abrahams*, p. 70.
[4] *Sepher Hajashar*; *Pirke de Rabbi Eliezer*, Ch. 31.   [5] Beer, *loc. cit.* p. 70.

SAMMAEL TRIES TO HIDE THE RAM FROM ABRAHAM'S SIGHT

Facing page 298, Vol. 1

to slay thy son, nor was I willing that thy son should be taken away from thee, for I am merciful. It was only to try the temper of thy mind, and to confound the tempter and accuser of man, whom I have created in My image. Since I am now satisfied as to thy alacrity and obedience even to such a command as the immolation of thy son, and the surprising readiness thou hast shown in this, thy piety, I will bestow blessings upon thee. Thou wilt leave an everlasting name, and thy family will increase into many nations." [1]

And now Abraham left the mount Moriah, and journeyed with Isaac to the schools once established by Shem and Eber, where the lad was to remain three years.[2]

ABRAHAM'S SACRIFICE

Angelus. Abraham, how! Abraham,
   Lyst and herke weylle onto me.
Abraham. Al redy, sere, here I am;
   Telle me your wylle what that it be.
Angelus. Almyghty God thus doth bydde the,—
   Ysaac this sone anon thou take,
And loke hym thou sclee anoon, lete se,
   And sacrifice to God hym make.

Thy welbelovyd childe thou must now kylle,
   To God thou offyr him, as I say,
Evyn upon yon hey hylle,
   That I the shewe here in the way,
Tarye not be nyght nor day,
   But smertly thi gate thou goo;
Upon yon hille thou knele and pray
   To God, and kylle the childe ther and scloo.

---

[1] *Pirke de Rabbi Eliezer*, Ch. 31.
[2] Cf. for this chapter also: Wünsche, *Aus Israels Lehrhallen*, Vol. I, pp. 49–58; Bin Gorion, *loc. cit.*, Vol. II, pp. 274—285; Lewner, *loc. cit.*, pp. 93–101; Beer, *Das Leben Abrahams*.

Abraham. Now Goddys commaundement must nedys
    be done,
  Alle his wyl is wourthy to be wrought;
But yitt the fadyr to sclee the sone,
  Grett care it causyth in my thought,
In byttyr bale now am I brought
  My swete childe with knyf to kylle;
But yit my sorwe avaylith ryght nowth,
  For nedys I must werke Goddys wylle.

With evy hert I walke and wende,
  My childys deth now for to be,
Now must the fadyr his swete sone schende
  Alas! for ruthe it is peté!
My swete sone, come hedyr to me:
  How, Isaac, my sone dere,
Com to thi ffadyr, my childe so fre,
  ffor we must wende to-gedyr in fere.

Isaac. Alle redy fadyr, evyn at your wylle,
  And at your byddyng I am yow by,
With zow to walk ovyr dale and hille,
  At youre callyng I am redy,
To the fadyr evyr mast comly,
  It ovyth the childe evyr batom to be;
I wyl obey, ful hertyly,
  To alle thyng that ye bydde me.

Abraham. Now, son, in thi necke this faget thou take,
  And this fyre here in thinne honde,
ffor we must now sacrefyse go make,
  Evyn aftyr the wylle of Goddys sonde.
Take this brennyng bronde,
  My swete childe, and lete us go;
Ther may no man that levyth in londe,
  Have more sorwe than I have wo.

Isaac. ffayr fadyr, ze go ryght stylle,
  I pray zow, ffadyr, speke onto me.

Abraham. Mi gode childe, what is thi wylle?
  Telle me thyn hert, I pray to the.

Isaac. ffadyr, fyre and wood here is plenté,
  But I kan se no sacryfice;
What ye xulde offre fayn wold I se,
  That it were don at the best anyse.

Abraham. God xal that ordeyn that sytt in hevynne,
  My swete sone, ffor this offryng,
A derrere sacryfice may no man nempne,
  Than this xal be, ny dere derlyng.

> *Ludus Coventriæ.* A collection of mysteries, formerly repre-
> sented at Coventry on the Feast of Corpus Christi;
> edited by J. O. Halliwell, London, 1841; pp. 51–53.

CHAPTER XXVI

A Mother's Broken Heart, or the Death of Sarah

Sammael and Sarah—A mother's fright—The tempter and the weeping mother—The terrible news—Another version of Sammael's efforts—The heartbroken mother seeks her son—The pity of Sammael—Joy kills the mother—The grief of husband and son—Their lamentations—The friend of the poor—The double cave—Ephron, the commoner, elected chief by the sons of Heth—The transfer of the land—The covenant with the sons of Heth—The engraving upon the pillars of brass—The city of Jebus—The funeral of Sarah—The protest of Adam and Eve—They return to their resting place—The fame of Isaac—His generosity—Abraham thanks the Lord—The old age of the Patriarch—His daughter Bakila—The Patriarch and the magicians of Egypt—He teaches them arithmetic and astronomy.

Now Sammael, when he saw that all his efforts and endeavours to make either Abraham or Isaac waver in their determination had been of no avail, grew black with anger. Neither father nor son would hearken unto his voice, his promptings and whisperings. In vain had he appeared to the pious pair in many disguises, in the shape of a man bent with age or in that of a youth. Even his sudden change into a mighty stream, barring Abraham's way, had not succeeded to prevent the latter from continuing his way. Sammael, therefore, even before Abraham had reached the mount Moriah, decided to turn to Sarah. "Woman," he thought, "is weaker than man, as I know from experience, when I once tempted Eve in the Garden of Eden and succeeded. Woman is always inclined to lend an ear to the whisperings of the tempter."

Straightaway Sammael spread out his wings and flew to Beer-Sheba. There he found Sarah who, after accompanying her husband and son for a distance, had returned to her tent, her heart full of grief and forebodings. Suddenly an old man, who was none other than Sammael in disguise, appeared before Sarah.

" Where is thy son?" queried the old man.

" He has left," replied the mother sadly, " for his father took him to the school once established by Shem and Eber, there to study wisdom and the fear of the Lord."

" Thou poor deceived mother," spoke the tempter, " my heart aches for thee, for thou wilt never see thy son alive, never wilt thou behold his countenance and feast thine eyes upon it. Thy foolish old husband hath indeed deceived thee, for not to the school of Shem and Eber hath he taken thy beloved son, but to the mount of Moriah, there to bring him as a burnt offering to his God."

When she heard this, Sarah was so frightened that a tremor seized her. She laid her head on the bosom of a slave and fainted.[1] Soon, however, she regained consciousness and thus replied to Sammael, disguised as an old man who seemed to pity her in her grief: " May the will of the Lord be done. What my dear husband doeth in obedience to the command of our Maker is well done."

Greatly disappointed, Sammael left the heroic mother. But when he knew that Abraham and Isaac had left mount Moriah where God had commanded the old man not to lay a hand upon the lad, he grew desperate, for all his efforts had been in vain.[2] Once more he appeared before the weeping mother and said: " Woe unto thee, bereaved mother, hast thou not yet heard what hath happened? I bring thee sad tidings indeed; my heart aches for thee, and mine eyes shed tears of grief and sorrow."

---

[1] *Yalkut*, 1, § 98.   [2] *Pirke de Rabbi Eliezer*, Ch. 32.

"What has happened?" cried Sarah piteously.

"The deed is done," said Sammael sadly. "Thy foolish husband, in his mistaken piety, hath indeed sacrificed thy son and brought him up as a burnt offering. Isaac is no more, and his ashes will be placed in an urn in thy room, so that thou mayest weep and mourn when thou wilt remember him who is no more. Greatly did thy poor son suffer. He wept and begged his hard-hearted father to have pity and spare him, but thy mistaken old husband lent not his ear to the prayers of thy son. He took his knife and slew him. It is a pity though that Abraham was so precipitate, for a voice from Heaven did indeed bid him stay his hand and not to lay it upon the lad, but it was too late. The deed had already been accomplished, that cruel deed which leaves thee a bereaved and sorrowing mother." [1]

Thus spoke Sammael. And when Sarah heard these words spoken by the tempter in a voice broken by sobbing, although there was no pity but rage in his black heart, the poor mother wept aloud. Bitterly she cried, until she fell down dead. Sammael cast a look of triumph upon her and went off.

Another version of this legend runs as follows:[2]

Whilst Abraham was busy sacrificing the ram, that ram which had been created for the purpose before sunset on the sixth day of creation, Sammael, disguised as an old man, came to Sarah and pretended to be greatly concerned in her sorrow. He told her in detail all that had occurred. "Abraham," he said, "had builded an altar upon mount Moriah, had bound his son, bared his throat and slain him with cruel hand. In vain did the lad wail and lament, begging his cruel father to spare him for the sake of his mother. His tears had been of no avail, and Isaac was now dead and burnt to ashes."

Sarah, who thought that the kindly, pitying old man was an acquaintance of her husband or of her son and to whom they

---

[1] *Midrash Tanchuma*, section *Wayera*.　　[2] *Sepher Hajashar*.

had perhaps once rendered a service, never doubted the words of Sammael. Convinced that what had been told her was true, she broke out into loud wailing, crying piteously: " O my son, my beloved son, could I have died in thy stead to-day. I have prayed for thee and wept over thee, and blessed the Lord when He sent me such a precious gift. I was ninety years of age when thou wast given unto me, but now thou hast been burnt to ashes. My only consolation is that thou, my son, didst obey the will of the Lord, and who durst question the commands of our Maker in whose hands are all living creatures. Just art Thou, O Lord of the Universe, and inscrutable are Thy ways. If my eyes weep for my beloved son, for I am only flesh and blood, my heart is grateful for the honour done unto my son."

Wearily Sarah laid her head upon the knees of her favourite maid and fainted. She awoke soon, however, and still clinging to the hope that her fears had perhaps been groundless and that the old man who had brought her the terrible news had been mistaken, she hurried with her servants to find out the truth. Accompanied by her faithful maids, she set off towards Hebron, there to find out where her husband and son were and whether the sad tidings about her beloved son's fate were true or false. In vain, however, did she question the inhabitants of Hebron, no one could answer her. Too weak and weary to proceed any farther, Sarah herself remained at Hebron, dispatching her slaves to go and make further inquiry. They went as far as the school of Shem and Eber, but none could inform them of the whereabouts of the well-known and highly respected Emir Abraham. Disappointed, the messengers returned to their mistress lying ill and exhausted at Hebron. And suddenly a spark of pity entered the heart of Sammael himself, when he heard the wailing and heart-rending cries of the weeping mother, sorely cast down and broken in spirit, and saw her agony. He decided to make an end to her suspense. He suddenly appeared to her, disguised as her beloved son Isaac,[1] rushing to embrace his mother. But the shock was too great for Sarah. She rose up, uttered a cry, fell down, and was dead. Joy had killed her.[2] The joy at the sight of her beloved son had been too great for the exhausted old woman, and uttering a loud cry she fell dead.

Sammael's efforts to prevent Abraham from doing the bidding of the Lord had been frustrated, but even when he tried to do a good action, it only had disastrous results.

Abraham was in the meantime hastening home to inform his wife of what had occurred. Great, however, was his astonishment when, on his arrival at Beer-Sheba, he found the doors of his tent locked and no one to welcome him. His heart told him that a misfortune had befallen him. He inquired of his neighbours whether they knew anything about his wife and her maids, and learned that Sarah had journeyed to Hebron.

" News," said the neighbours, " had been brought to thy wife that thy son Isaac had been brought up as a burnt offering, and in great distress she went off to Hebron to find out the truth." [3]

Hastily, therefore, Abraham went off to Hebron, where he found his wife whom he had only left a few days ago lying dead. Bitterly he cried and lamented the death of his dear wife, the companion of his youth and of his old age. " Closed," he cried, " are the eyes which shed such a light, casting looks of love upon all whom she met; stiff are the hands which were busy in distributing help to the poor and the needy and in wiping the tears from the countenances of the afflicted. Not I alone and our dear son will miss thee, my wife, but all the orphans and widows, whose friend and supporter thou hast always been."

---

[1] *Leviticus Rabba*, 20; *Ecclesiasticus Rabba*, 9, 1; cf. *Midrash Haggadol*.
[2] Beer, *Das Leben Abrahams*, p. 74.   [3] Beer, *loc. cit.*, p. 74.

The neighbours and townsfolk also wept at the death of Sarah, the generous and charitable lady they had known so well.

Abraham at once sent a messenger to his son Isaac to inform him of their sad bereavement. The son hastened to Hebron, there to pay the last respects to his beloved mother. He fell upon the dead and wept bitterly.

"Alas," he cried, "Mother dear, why hast thou forsaken me so suddenly? Why hast thou gone away? I had hoped to keep thee still for a long time and feast mine eyes upon thy countenance which was as radiant as the sun in its splendour. I was looking forward to hearing thy sweet voice and hoped to listen to thy words which were music in mine ears. But, alas, the sun of my life is now darkened, and my joy is gone." And Isaac wept bitterly, and all who were present joined in his lamentations.

All the people of Hebron, men, women, and children came to the house where the dead body of Sarah was lying. The townspeople had ceased work on that day in honour of the memory of the deceased lady, whose charity, generosity and good deeds were so well known.[1]

"The friend of the poor, of the suffering and of the afflicted is now dead," they said, "and we must be ready to pay her the last respects and accompany her in great numbers to her last resting-place."

As Abraham was bowing over the body of his dear wife, he heard the loud laugh of the angel of death who is none other than Sammael.[2] "Wherefore dost thou weep," mocked the angel of death. "The blame of her death is thine. For hadst thou not taken her son from her, she would certainly be alive now."

Abraham now rose from the body of his wife and set out to find a burying place for the dead. He approached the sons of Heth, the Hittites, and asked them to grant him a sepulchre

---

[1] *Midrash Tanchuma*, section *Hayé-Sarah*.   [2] *Genesis Rabba*, 58.

so that he might bury his dead. Thereupon the sons of Heth replied: " My Lord, take the choice of our sepulchres." Abraham bowed to the sons of Heth and said:

" If I have found grace in your eyes, then obtain for me the cave of Machpelah, the double cave which is in possession of Ephron, the son of Zohar, for it is this sepulchre that I have chosen there to bury my dead."

Now Abraham was rather anxious to buy this cave in possession of Ephron for the following reason. When he had gone out, sometime ago, after the calf which he slew for the three angels who came to him just before the destruction of Sodom, that calf had fled from him and entered the double cave. And when Abraham entered the cave, he found in an inner recess the bodies of Adam and Eve laid out. There were burning tapers round them, and there was the fragrance of incense in the air.[1]

When the sons of Heth heard Abraham's request, they said one to another: " Ephron is only a common person, let us hasten and elect him as our chief and prince, so that such a mighty and distinguished Emir like Abraham be not compelled to have dealings with an inferior, ordinary person."[2]

They therefore approached Ephron, the son of Zohar, saying unto him: " Wilt thou be our chief?" Greatly wondering at this unexpected honour, Ephron inquired after the reason, and was informed of the request of Abraham.

Thereupon Ephron hastened to meet the distinguished stranger, on whose account such great honour had been thrust upon him, and begged him to accept the field and the double cave as a gift. But Abraham refused to accept the place as a gift, and Ephron agreed to take four hundred shekels of silver from Abraham, which the latter weighed out in the current money of the land. A deed of sale was thereupon drawn up, duly signed and witnessed, and the field and cave became the

[1] *Pirke de Rabbi Eliezer*, Ch. 36.   [2] *Sepher Hajashar*.

property of Abraham. The transfer of the land and cave was signed by Amigal, son of Abishna, the Hittite, Elichoran, son of Essunass, the Hittite, Abdon son of Ahirah, the Gamorrhite, and Akdil, son of Abdis, the Sidonian.[1] The cave was called Machpelah, or the double cave, because it contained two chambers, or because Abraham paid double value for it. Some also say that it was so called, because it was doubly holy, or because Adam's body had to be doubled up so as to get it into the cave.[2]

Now the sons of Heth said one to another: " Days will come when the children and children's children of Abraham will take possession of the entire land and will inherit it. They will also conquer and take possession of our city of Jebus. Let us therefore make a covenant with Abraham that his offspring will never take possession by force of the town of Jebus and of the country and possessions of the Jebusites." The sons of Heth thereupon turned unto Abraham and thus addressed him:

" Thou shalt not bury thy dead before making a covenant with us that thy children and their children shall never take by force the possessions of the Jebusites." Abraham agreed to grant their request, and they brought their idols, engraved upon them the conditions of the covenant and placed them in the market-place of the town. There they remained until the days of David. When the Israelites conquered Canaan, they respected the covenant and left the Jebusites unmolested, so that they continued to dwell with them. And when David sought to take the stronghold of Jebus, the inhabitants said unto him: " Thou canst not storm our city, because of the covenant of Abraham which is engraven on the pillars of brass." David removed the pillars, but respecting the covenant, he *purchased* the city of Jebus.[3]

---

[1] *Sepher Hajashar.*   [2] *Erubin,* 53a; *Genesis Rabba,* 58.
[3] *Pirke de Rabbi Eliezer,* Ch. 26; *Midrash Haggadol,* Col. 350.

Thereupon Abraham buried his wife Sarah, and multitudes of people came to pay her the last respects. Shem and his son Eber came, and also Abi-Melech, King of Gerar, and all the great ones of the land. It was indeed a very great company which went to bury Sarah, the wife of Abraham, and all the people who followed the bier wailed and lamented. Abraham caused a great mourning to be made for seven days.

When he went into the cave to take off the stone which he had placed upon the grave he had digged for Sarah, Adam and Eve both arose and thus they spake unto him:

" How can we lie at rest in the same cave where thy wife Sarah will be buried? We have never ceased to repent and to be ashamed of our sin, the sin we committed and on account of which we have been expelled from the Garden of Eden. And now this perfect and righteous woman has come here, and we feel our shame even more." Thus spoke our first parents. But Abraham replied:

" Return to your resting place and sleep in peace, for I will pray on your behalf and ye will no longer need be ashamed of your transgression." Adam at once returned to his resting place, but Eve still protested, and her spirit would not be appeased. Abraham, however, begged her to return to her resting place and sleep in peace until she yielded to his entreaties. After the funeral Abraham sent his son Isaac to the school of Shem and Eber there to continue his studies.[1]

Isaac remained three years in the school of Shem and Eber, and there he learned wisdom and increased his knowledge greatly. He became learned and wise and God-fearing. He loved the poor and the needy and was their friend on every occasion, consoling the suffering, and wiping away the tears of the unhappy. He was beloved by all who came into contact with him, and he became a blessing to all who knew him. When Abraham heard how the fame of his beloved son was

[1] Cf. Lewner, *Kol Agadoth*, Vol. I, p. 106.

spreading far and wide, he was happy indeed. He thanked the Lord of the Universe for the favours he had bestowed on him.

" Almighty God!" he said, " great indeed is Thy loving kindness, for after many trials and afflictions, Thou hast blessed my old age and poured prosperity, wealth and fame upon me. I am honoured more than I indeed deserve, for kings and potentates come daily to inquire after my welfare. Thou knowest well, O Lord of the Universe, that my heart is not swelled with pride, for I am only like all the other mortals. But behold, Thou hast even sent me a blessing which is more than wealth, and fame, and life to me. Thou hast granted me the greatest joy of my life and a consolation in my old age, for Isaac, my beloved son, is as perfect as mortal man can be, and Thou hast given him a golden heart, full of pity for suffering humanity, and his deeds of kindness and generosity are numerous. This, O Lord, is the greatest blessing that Thou couldst have bestowed upon an aged father." [1]

Abraham's old age was indeed a happy one, for the Lord had blessed him in all things. Some say that Hagar, whom he had taken back, bore him a daughter named Bakila,[2] whilst others maintain that, on the contrary, his blessing was great and consisted in this that he had no daughters.[3] It would have caused the old man great worry to have a daughter in the midst of the dissolute and idol-worshipping inhabitants of Canaan, where he could not have found for her a fitting husband.

Abraham's fame as a reader of the stars was also very great, and the princes of both the East and the West constantly came to consult him. He conferred with the wise men of the land and always confuted the reasonings they made use of, when they refused to believe in the God whom Abraham taught them to love. But Abraham demonstrated

---

[1] *Ibid.*, pp. 107–108.   [2] *Baba Batra*, 16*b*, 141*a*; *Genesis Rabba*.   [3] *Genesis Rabba*, 59.

to them that their reasonings were vain and void of truth. He was therefore admired even by the readers of the stars and the magicians of Egypt and of Babylonia as a very wise man and one of great sagacity when he discoursed on any subject he undertook, and this not only in understanding it, but in persuading other men also to assent to him. It is said that Abraham communicated to the wise men of Egypt arithmetic, and delivered to them the science of astronomy. His presence was very magnetic, and it is said that the sick who approached him were at once healed.[1] Upon his breast he wore a precious stone, and the patient who gazed at it was at once cured from his disease. Thus Abraham's old age was indeed a happy one. He had only one desire left, and that was to see his son Isaac happily married, married to a mate worthy of him. This desire, too, was soon to be fulfilled.

ISAAC

Mon Dieu et mon souverain maistre,   10983
En quelle place ne quel estre
Est maintenant ma povre mère?
Hellas! j'ay aidé à la mettre
En terre!   Qui pourra congnoistre
Que j'en ay eu douleur amère?

O misère
Fière, austère,
A porter
Impropère,
Qui propère
Me advorter
Sans doubter!
Supporter

---

[1] Josephus, *Antiquities*, I, 8, 2. See also *Rashi, Yoma*, 28b.

A peine puis, c'est chose clère,
Tel douleur, qui desconforter
M'a fait si fort et tormenter
Que regarder n'ose mon père.

Aux champs m'en voys sçavoir se aucun confort
Me viendra point contre ce desconfort
Pour rapaiser mon pleur, qui est si fort,
Et repulser l'accez de mon mesaise,
Non obstant ce que je cuyde avoir tort,
Car arriver ne puis en aucun port
Ou il y ayt voix doulce ne accort
Armonieulx qui nullement me plaise.

Pleurs et souspirs sont mes gieux et mon ayse;
Au monde n'est rien qui ne me desplaise,
Considerant qu'il fauldra que je voyse,
Comme ma mère, par ung assault de mort,
Et ne sçay quant. O mort sure et mauvaise,
Tant ton fardeau pesant à porter poyse!
Nul ne le sçayt fors celuy qui le poyse.
Cruelle mort, tu as mauvais raport!

Le Mistère du Viel Testament. Edited by J. de Rothschild,
Paris, 1877, Tome II, pp. 95–96.

CHAPTER XXVII

A Rose among Thorns, or the Marriage of Isaac

The mission of Eliezer—The journey to Haran—The guardian angels—Eliezer's prayer—A rose among thorns—The beautiful and virtuous maiden—The generosity of Rebekah—The damsel at the well—The royal present—The greedy brother—The poisoned bowl—The death of the father—The speedy departure—A blessing but no dowry—The meeting of bride and bridegroom—The fall from the camel—The vision of Rebekah—The wife fills the place of the mother.

FOR three years Isaac had mourned the death of his mother,[1] but when this time had elapsed, Abraham called his faithful servant Eliezer and sent him to Mesopotamia, his own country, and to his own kindred there to take a wife for his son Isaac. Eliezer ventured to suggest his own daughter as a suitable mate for the son of his master, " For," said he, " peradventure the woman in thy own country and of thy own kindred will not be willing to accompany me unto this land of Canaan." Eliezer, however, being of the race of Ham, Abraham was not willing to allow his son to marry a daughter of Eliezer. Eliezer now did as his master had bidden him. Abraham signed a deed[2] wherein he declared that he left all his worldly possessions to his son Isaac and handing over this deed to Eliezer thus said to him:

" This deed thou wilt show to the father of the maiden thou wilt have chosen as a wife for my son."

[1] *Pirke de Rabbi Eliezer*, Ch. 32; *Midrash Haggadol*, col. 388.
[2] *Genesis Rabba*, 59; cf. *Baba Batra*, 130a.

314

And Eliezer, taking ten camels from the camels of his master, departed to Mesopotamia. The distance from Kirjath Arba or Hebron to Haran was a seventeen-days journey, but Eliezer and his suite reached Haran, their destination, in three hours, for the earth fled under the feet of his camels.[1] God called two of His ministering angels and commanded them to accompany Eliezer, the servant of Abraham, on his delicate errand.[2] One of the angels received as his mission to protect Eliezer on his way, whilst the other's mission was to cause Rebekah to be present at the well just at the moment when Eliezer arrived.

Eliezer had journeyed some distance when behold, he found himself already at the well in Haran. To have travelled such a long distance in such a short time was wonderful indeed, and Eliezer marvelled greatly and understood that the Lord had shortened the distance and wrought this miracle on his behalf. Thereupon he prayed unto the Lord, saying: " Lord of the Universe, show kindness unto my master Abraham and let me meet a damsel who is righteous and perfect, endowed with a kind and noble heart, who will thus be a suitable companion and mate for Isaac, the son of my master." [3] Thus spake Eliezer, and at that moment the second ministering angel arrived and caused Rebekah to leave her father's house and to go out to the well to draw water.

Rebekah, the daughter of Bethuel, the son of Nahor of Mesopotamia, was indeed like a rose among thorns. She had witnessed the sinful life and the wicked deeds of her father and brother, and had made up her mind not to follow in their ways. She was kind and generous and never missed an opportunity to practise charity. The poor who called at Bethuel's house found a kind helper in Rebekah, the beautiful and noble-hearted daughter of the house, who never allowed them to go away empty-handed. And

---

[1] *Ibid.*   [2] *Ibid.*   [3] Josephus, *Antiquities,* I, 16, 1.

although she had been brought up as it behoved the
daughter of a great, wealthy and influential man of the land,
although she had many slaves to serve her, she was never
idle, indulging in frivolous pursuits, but diligently looked
after the household. She was one of those women who eat
not the bread of idleness. She stretched out her hand to the
poor, yea, she reached forth her hand to the needy, not only
in her father's house but also in the town, going out among
the poor in search of opportunities to do good. Often, when
Rebekah saw the wicked deeds and the sinful conduct of the
men of her town, and the idle frivolous life led by those
oriental women-folk, she said in her heart: " I wish I could
leave this town and its wicked, idle, and frivolous life, useless
and purposeless!" [1]

All who knew Rebekah called her a rose among thorns.
But still, she was the daughter of a noble and distinguished
house, and was not in the habit of taking up the pitcher and
going out to the well to draw water.[2] But it was the angel
this time who prompted her to undertake this task to-day,
as it might give her an opportunity to do some kindness on
her way where she would meet the poorer classes of her townsfolk.

When Rebekah approached the well, carrying her pitcher,
the waters in the well rose by themselves,[3] and Eliezer,
noticing this, marvelled greatly. " I must watch this damsel,"
said Eliezer, " and see her conduct, for methinks that she is
the one appointed by the Lord to be the wife of the son of my
master. She is very fair to look upon, and if she showeth a
kind heart, I will speak unto her."

And Eliezer watched Rebekah for some time. He saw
her approach a child that was crying bitterly by the side of the

---

[1] Cf. Lewner, loc. cit., p. 107.

[2] Pirke de Rabbi Eliezer, Ch. 16; Midrash Haggadol, Genesis, col. 367; Yalkut, Genesis,
§ 109. In Pirke de Rabbi Eliezer we read: " A daughter of kings, who had never gone out to
draw water ".　　　　　[3] Genesis Rabba, 60.

well, and ask it to tell her the cause of its trouble. "I have hurt my foot," said the child, "and it is bleeding." Rebekah at once bathed and dressed the wound of the child and comforted it, sending it home to its mother. Thereupon, not far from the well, she met an old woman whose sight was dim. Rebekah took pity upon the aged woman and smilingly inquired: "Canst thou find thy way, Mother?"

"Sometimes," replied the old woman, "it happens that I lose my way home and am compelled to pass the night in the open." Rebekah asked her where she dwelt and accompanied the woman home. Thereupon she returned to the well, pitcher in hand, but being evidently tired she sat down upon a log to rest awhile. No sooner had she done so, than an old man, tired and travel stained, came along. She hastened up and offered him her seat to rest his weary limbs.[1]

When Eliezer saw her conduct and behaviour he said to himself: "This damsel hath a noble heart and a kind nature, and is, moreover, very fair to look upon. She will be a fitting companion and helpmate for my master's son." Thereupon he approached and asked her to give him some water to drink. He had previously addressed to all the other maidens a similar request, but one and all had refused, on pretence that they wanted it all at home and could spare none for him, and that the drawing of water was not an easy task. "We may not tarry," they replied, "for we must take the water home."[2] Rebekah complied with Eliezer's request with a kindness and grace which charmed him greatly.

Eliezer now began to hope that his journey would not have been in vain, and that his enterprise would succeed. But he still desired to know the truth and to learn the name of the damsel's father and the social position of her parents. He, therefore, commended her for her generosity and good nature, saying

[1] *Genesis Rabba*, 59, and 60; *Sanhedrin*, 110; *Yoma*, 28b: see also Lewner, *loc. cit.*, p. 107.
[2] Josephus, *Antiquities*, I, 16, 2.

that she did not hesitate to offer a sufficiency of water to those
who wanted it, though it cost her some pains to draw it.[1] He
then asked her who were her parents, and wished them joy of
such a daughter.   " And mayest thou be espoused," said he,
" to their satisfaction, into the family of an agreeable husband,
and bring him good children."

Rebekah did not disdain to satisfy Eliezer's inquiries, but told
him her family.   When he heard who she was, he was very glad
at what had happened, and at what she told him, for he perceived
that God had thus plainly directed his journey and crowned his
efforts with success. Producing some bracelets and some other
ornaments which it was esteemed in that country decent for
virgins to wear, Eliezer gave them to the damsel by way of ack-
nowledgment, and as a reward for her kindness in giving him
water to drink; saying it was but just that she should have them,
because she was so much more obliging than any of the rest.
Rebekah thanked him gracefully and said that she desired
that he would come and lodge with them, since the approach
of the night gave him no time to proceed farther.[2] Eliezer
replied that he might guess at the hospitality of her people
from the virtue he found in her. Moreover, he would not be
burdensome, for he was willing to pay the hire for his enter-
tainment, and spend his own money. To which the maiden
replied that he guessed quite right as to the hospitality of her
parents, but complained that he should think them so parsi-
monious as to take money from him. She further said that
she would run and inform her brother Laban, and would then
conduct him in.[3]

Rebekah thereupon quickly ran home and informed her
parents of all that had occurred. When her brother Laban,
a greedy youth, who was so called from the paleness of his
face,[4] or from the cowardice of his breast which made him

---

[1] Josephus, *Antiquities*, I, 16, 2.   [2] *Genesis Rabba*, 60.
[3] Josephus, *Antiquities*, I, 16, 2; cf. *Pirke de Rabbi Eliezer*, Ch. 16; *Genesis Rabba*, 59–60;
Sanhedrin, 110; *Yoma*, 286.   [4] *Genesis Rabba*, 60.

pale, saw the bracelets and other presents the stranger had made to his fair sister, he thought in his heart that the generous stranger must be a very wealthy man indeed, and decided to take his money from him by fair or foul means.[1] When Eliezer saw Laban coming, he at once knew that the youth was capable of any bad action. He, therefore, gave him proof of his strength. He lifted up the two camels as if they were toys, and Laban wondered and was greatly impressed.

" Come into the house," said Laban, very gracefully, " thou blessed of the Lord, for I have prepared the house and removed all the idols from within." [2]

Suddenly Eliezer heard the noise of running feet. He lifted up his eyes and saw men running to the well. Some of the inhabitants had already heard of the wealthy stranger and of his generosity, and had made up their minds to rob him. But when they came nearer and saw Eliezer lifting up the camels as if they were toys, they drew back duly impressed.[3] Eliezer thereupon followed the maiden and her brother into the house.

He was met by Bethuel and his wife who bade him welcome. Refreshments were placed upon the table, but the bowl of meat placed before Eliezer was poisoned, for Bethuel and Laban could not resist their innate greed and were intent upon robbing the wealthy stranger and taking possession of his money and valuables. But although there was meat before him, Eliezer said: " I will not eat until I have told my errand." He proceeded to do so, not touching the meat, and informed them who he was and what was his business in Mesopotamia. At that moment, one of the ministering angels who accompanied Eliezer and was there to protect him from any mishap, turned the table so that the poisoned bowl placed before Eliezer fell to the portion of Bethuel. And it came to pass that after he had finished his speech, Eliezer gave jewels of silver, and jewels of

---

[1] *Midrash Abkhir* quoted in *Yalkut*, 1, § 109.
[2] *Abot di Rabbi Nathan*, Ch. 8. [3] *Sanhedrin*, 105a.

gold, and raiment to Rebekah and also to her brother and to her mother, and then they did eat and drink and make merry. But no sooner had Bethuel partaken of the poisoned meat which he had intended for Eliezer, than he felt great pains and died in agony that same night.[1]

When they rose in the morning, Eliezer urged Rebekah's mother and brother to give him their answer. Eliezer now insisted upon a speedy decision.

" I must know at once," he said, " whether you agree to let your daughter go with me or not, otherwise I shall have to look for a wife for the son of my master among the daughters of Ishmael or Lot." [2] Rebekah's mother and brother, however, asked Eliezer to allow the maiden not only to abide with them the seven days of mourning for her father, but also to tarry another year or at least ten months, according to the usual custom, so that she could prepare her raiment. But Eliezer would brook no delay, and urged for a speedy departure. Thereupon they called the damsel and asked her opinion.

" Art thou willing," they said, " to go with this man to the house of Abraham, the uncle of thy father, and marry his son Isaac?"

Rebekah had already heard of Abraham, the mighty and generous Emir of Canaan who was so famed for his wisdom, his fear of the Lord and his many generous deeds and kind actions, and she declared her willingness to accompany Eliezer at once. But her mother still objected to such a speedy departure.

" How wilt thou go and thou hast not yet prepared thy raiment as is fitting for the daughter of our house?" But Rebekah replied: " Let not such trifles detain me." [3]

And when the mother of Rebekah and her brother Laban

---

[1] *Yalkut,* I, § 109; *Genesis Rabba,* 59; *Pirke de Rabbi Eliezer,* Ch. 16; cf. Lewner, *loc. cit.,* p. 112. [2] *Genesis Rabba,* 60. [3] *Genesis Rabba,* 60; *Sanhedrin,* 110.

THE PUNISHMENT OF TREACHERY: BETHUEL FALLS A VICTIM TO
THE POISONED BOWL

Facing page 320, Vol. I

saw that she was in such a hurry to leave them, they said unto themselves: " Well then, let her go, we will not give her any dowry but only our blessing."

Thus at noon of that day Eliezer and Rebekah, accompanied by her faithful and loving nurse Deborah, left Haran for Hebron. It was a long and weary journey from Mesopotamia to Canaan, but once more the journey was completed in three hours, for the earth fled under the feet of the camels.[1]

And it came to pass that at the same time Isaac was returning home from the school of Shem and Eber.[2] Rebekah saw him and was struck by his beauty and his noble appearance. She also saw that a guardian angel was accompanying him, and she wondered in her mind whether this distinguished stranger was the husband destined for her:

" Who is this man yonder," she asked Eliezer, " whose countenance is so radiant and whose bearing so noble?" " This is my master Isaac," said Eliezer, and in her confusion Rebekah fell off from the camel.[3] Some say that with prophetic vision Rebekah saw at that moment that she would become the mother of Esau, and that, therefore, she trembled and fell off the camel.[4] Eliezer related unto Isaac all that had occurred and all the wonders which the Lord had wrought.

Rebekah was duly married to Isaac, and once more the house of Abraham had a noble and generous mistress who took the place vacated by the noble-minded Sarah. The bride filled the vacated place with distinction, and once more the doors were opened to all the poor and the needy who flocked to the house to find help, comfort, and consolation.[5] The perpetual lamp was kindled again, and to Isaac it seemed that all the happiness —that had gone from his life when his mother died—had returned again with Rebekah. Isaac loved his wife dearly,

---

[1] *Targum Jerushalmi, Genesis*, 24, 61.
[2] He went out to say the afternoon prayer, say some Midrashim. See *Pirke de Rabbi Eliezer*, Ch. 16; *Midrash Haggadol*, col. 370.
[3] *Genesis Rabba*, 60; *Sanhedrin*, 110; see Lewner, *loc. cit.*, pp. 113-114.
[4] *Yalkut*, 1, § 109.   [5] *Genesis Rabba*, 60.

and he cherished her the more when he saw that she continued the traditions of his dear, never-to-be-forgotten mother.[1]

Abraham thanked Eliezer for his faithful services and the intelligence with which he had accomplished his delicate mission. In recognition of his services he set him entirely free, and it is said that he afterwards became King of Bashan.[2] Some say that Eliezer was one of the few who were taken into Paradise without having tasted death.[3]

[1] *Pirke de Rabbi Eliezer*, Ch. 32.   [2] *Ibid.*, Ch. 16.   [3] *Derekh Erez Sutta*, Ch. 1.

CHAPTER XXVIII

The Death of the Patriarch

Abraham's second wife—Keturah, the bondwoman—Ophren, the grandson of Keturah—The city with iron walls—Artificial lighting—Abraham exhorts his son Isaac—The archangel comes to prepare the Patriarch for the last journey—The sun-like splendour of the stranger—The tears that change into pearls—The pleading of the angel—Isaac's dream—The sun, the moon, and the stars—Abraham's request to be allowed to witness the wonders of creation, while yet in the body—The ride in the heavenly chariot—The wickedness of man—The Patriarch's indignation—A voice from heaven calls: Stop the ride—The visit to Paradise—The two roads and the two gates—Adam seated on a golden throne—His tears and his joy—The court of justice—The scales of justice—Abraham intercedes for a soul in distress—Michael refuses to take the soul of Abraham—The sixty-three thousand eight hundred and seventy-five days of Abraham's life bear witness to the perfection of the Patriarch—Abraham's vision of bliss in Paradise—Abraham's soul departs heavenwards—The funeral—Princes and potentates express their grief at the funeral of the Patriarch.

AND it came to pass that after having married his son Isaac, Abraham also took a wife named Keturah. Some say that Keturah was Hagar,[1] as the word signifies the Bondwoman, she having regarded herself as bound to Abraham.[2] To the sons of Keturah Abraham gave many gifts, and he also instructed them in the art of magic.[3] He settled them in colonies, and they afterwards took possession of Troglodytis and of the country of Arabia the Happy, as far as it reaches the Red Sea. One of the grandchildren of Keturah, named Ophren, made war against Libya and took it, and his grandchildren,

---

[1] *Baba Kama*, 92b; *Genesis Rabba*, 6o; *Midrash Tanchuma*. See also Josephus, *Antiquities*, I, 15-16.
[2] *Targum Jerushalmi*; *Yalkut*, 1, § 109; 2, 1073. Another explanation is that her name was Keturah, because she was perfumed with all kinds of scents.
[3] *Sanhedrin*, 91a; *Pirke de Rabbi Eliezer*, Ch. 30.

when they inhabited it, called the land from his name Africa. Abraham also built for the sons of Keturah and for her grand-children a city surrounded by iron walls, and as the walls were so high that the rays of the sun could not penetrate into the town, Abraham installed artificial lighting by means of disks made of pearls and precious stones, which shed a pale light upon the city.[1] Abraham was now one hundred and seventy-five years of age, and he felt his end approaching. He, therefore, called his son Isaac and thus spake unto him:

" Thou knowest, my son, that the Eternal is the only God, the Creator of Heaven and earth and of the Universe. He took me from my native land and from the house of my father, and brought me to this country of Canaan. In His loving kindness, which He vouchsafed unto me, He saved me from the furnace into which Nimrod had cast me, and wrought many wonders on my behalf, for great is His power. When I was cast into the fire by Nimrod's order, the flame turned into a bed of roses, on which I went to sleep. I therefore command thee, my son, to remain faithful to thy God and to serve Him with all thy heart all the days of thy life upon earth. Hearken unto His voice and have faith in His loving kindness and mercy. Be kind and charitable and generous to all thy fellowmen. Be a protector to the needy and comfort the afflicted. Never turn away a poor man from thy gate, but be ready to give food and shelter to those who require it and raiment to the naked. Comfort and console and wipe away the tears of the unhappy. The Lord will bless thee, and thou wilt be a blessing. Teach also thy children and thy children's children to love peace and mercy and to walk humbly before their God." [2] Thus spake Abraham, and Isaac promised faithfully to do as his beloved father had bidden him.

Now Abraham, not only the friend of God and the beloved

---

[1] *Tractate Sopherim*, Ch. 21; Josephus, *Antiquities*, I, 15.
[2] *Sepher Hajashar*; see also *The Book of Jubilees*.

of the Eternal, but also the friend of strangers, the hospitable and beneficent Emir, had reached the full measure of years allotted to him, and his time to die had arrived. God now sent His archangel Michael to prepare the Patriarch for the last journey.[1]

Disguised as a common traveller, seeking hospitality, the archangel appeared before the tent which Abraham had pitched in the plain of Mamre, that tent which was open to the four high-roads, and where all were welcomed as guests: rich and poor, beggars and kings. Abraham was not at home at that moment, for he was superintending his ploughing in the fields. Here the traveller met the old man who invited him home.[2] Abraham was struck by the radiance and the sun-like splendour of the stranger, and with his customary politeness and hospitality offered the guest one of his horses to ride home. The angel, however, refused the offer, and they walked home together. On their way home Abraham heard a huge tamarisk tree with its three hundred and thirty-one branches singing a song and whispering to him that God was about to summon him to himself.[3]

On their arrival home, Isaac hastened to bring water for his father to wash the feet of the guest as was customary. Abraham now had the presentiment that he was to perform the pious act for the last time, and tears came to his eyes. Isaac, too, cried. The archangel, knowing the nature of the tidings he was the bearer of, also shed tears which quickly changed into pearls. Now the archangel, before sitting down at a sumptuously prepared table, absented himself for a little while. Spreading out his wings, he rose speedily to Heaven there to join the choir of ministering angels who daily assemble before the Throne of Glory at sunset to sing the praises of the Eternal.[4] The archangel prostrated himself before the Throne of Glory and thus he spake:

[1] *Midrash Agadah*, Ed. Buber, p. 162.
[2] M. R. James, *The Testament of Abraham* in Robinson's Texts and Studies, II, 2, Cambridge, 1892, pp. 76–119.   [3] See *Succa*, 28a.   [4] *Yalkut, Genesis*, § 133.

" Lord of the Universe! how can I bring the sad message to the pious and generous old man, who has no equal in the world for goodness of heart? And how can I sit down at the sumptuous table prepared for me, unable as I am, being a celestial, to partake of food?"

Thus spake Michael, and the voice from the Throne of Glory replied: " Go thou and do My bidding. A dream will come upon Isaac, a prophetic dream which will announce to him the approaching death of his father. Thou wilt interpret the dream to him. I will furthermore send a spirit who will devour all that is placed upon the table for thee."

Michael thereupon descended upon earth and entering Abraham's tent, sat down at the table prepared for him.

After midnight, Isaac had a dream, seeing the death of Abraham. Greatly disturbed, he hastened to his father and roused the household.

" Tell me thy dream, O son," said Abraham, " that I may hear."

And Isaac thus spake: " In my dream, I saw the sun and the moon and the stars upon my head, giving me light. Thereupon a shining man, who was brighter than seven suns, came down from Heaven and prepared to take the sun from my head. I cried bitterly and asked him not to take the sun. And the moon and the stars also begged him not to take the sun away. The sun, too, implored him to give her a little time so that she might collect all her rays and leave none behind. But although I beseeched the shining man to leave the sun behind, he would not yield to my request. He only said: ' Grieve not, Isaac, for I am taking the sun from thee to carry it to the heavenly Father who is asking for it. I am taking it from sorrow to eternal joy and bliss.' Thus spake the shining one, and I awoke, greatly disturbed."

When Abraham heard what dream Isaac had dreamt, he wept

bitterly. Thereupon Michael, whose radiance was like the splendour of the sun, appeared before his hosts and, addressing Abraham, said: " The dream of thy son, Isaac, will come true. I am the shining man who hath come down from Heaven, and thou, Abraham, art the sun. I have come down to take thy soul and carry it up to the Father in Heaven, for thy time to die hath come. I am the prince of the Presence, the archangel Michael, who visited thee in the plain of Mamre, before the birth of thy son. I was one of the three strangers whom thou didst so hospitably invite to thy house." [1]

And when Abraham heard what message the angel had brought, he refused to give up his soul. Thereupon the archangel Michael spread out his wings and rose to Heaven to report the refusal of the perfect servant of God to give up his soul. But the Lord bade him go back to Abraham and tell him that all the offspring of Adam are doomed to die, and that none could escape.

Then the voice of the Lord spoke to Abraham and said: " My ministering angel Michael, the prince of the Presence, will lead thee from earth to the heavenly Paradise, and the angel of death will have no power to strike thee with his sword. Thou wilt be transferred from earth to a better world without suffering the pangs and agony of death."

Abraham now yielded, but asked yet a favour of God. " May I be allowed," he prayed, " while yet in the body, to witness the wonders of Thy creation, to see the world which Thou hast created by the word of Thy mouth; may I be allowed to see the world and all its inhabitants, and the heavenly order, that I may thereafter depart in peace."

Thus prayed Abraham, and Michael interceded for him before the Throne of Glory. The request of the old man, the perfect servant of the Lord, was granted.[2]

Thereupon Michael, at the bidding of the Lord, placed

[1] M. R. James, *The Testament of Abraham,* § VII.   [2] *Ibid,* § IX

Abraham in the heavenly chariot of the Cherubim, sixty
ministering angels surrounding it, and upon a cloud of light
carried him high above to Heaven, there to show him the
inhabited world and the wonders of creation. And thus the
Patriarch was allowed to see the whole world and to witness
the scenes of earthly existence, of human life and labour,
human joys and sorrows, human weal and woe, gladness and
grief, all the vicissitudes of man's life. He was also allowed
to see the actions of man, good and evil, beautiful and ugly,
and rejoice at the good deeds of man. A wave of righteous
indignation swept over the old man, when he saw the crimes
committed by men in every station of life. And he saw murderous swords raised by man against his brother, and by
nation against nation, and acts of violence committed everywhere. Beholding such evil-doers with swords in their hands,
ready to fall upon and slaughter their brethren, he called out
in agony, and prayed unto the Lord: " O Lord! Let Thy
wild beasts out of the forest come speedily forth and devour
these evil-doers who are about to commit murder." And
behold, at his prayer, wild beasts came out of the forest and
devoured the evil-doers about to commit murder.

Thereupon Abraham saw men and women who were
guilty of adultery, and once more in his righteous indignation
he prayed: " O Lord, may the earth open her mouth and
swallow them that they may not contaminate others." And
behold, the earth opened her mouth and swallowed up the
adulterers. Riding farther in the heavenly chariot, and upon
the cloud of light, surveying the world, Abraham beheld
thieves digging holes in houses and preparing to rob their
fellowmen and to carry off their possessions. " O Lord,"
he prayed, " let a fire come down from Heaven and consume
these thieves who are about to carry away the earnings of
hard-working men." And lo! a fire fell down from Heaven
and consumed the thieves. The archangel Michael had been

ordered to do whatever Abraham told him to do. And he thus smote with instant death all the malefactors whom Abraham, who had never sinned, condemned to death.[1]

But a voice from the Throne of Glory resounded and said: " Stop thy ride, Michael, and turn back the chariot, lest Abraham destroy all My creatures in his wrath and righteous indignation, for *all* live in wickedness. He hath no pity on sinners, for he hath never sinned. But I am the Maker of the Universe, and take no delight in destroying My creatures. I defer the death of the sinner, so that he may repent and live. Go thou now and direct the chariot to the eastern gate of Heaven, towards Paradise, and there show him the judgments and retributions.[2] He will then learn to have compassion upon the souls of the sinners he killed in his pious wrath." Thus spake the voice from the Throne of Glory. And Michael, doing the bidding of the Lord, turned the heavenly chariot and took Abraham to the first gate of Heaven.

And behold, there were two roads, one broad and one narrow, stretched out and leading to two gates or doors, a large door and a small door. Between the two doors there sat one upon a golden throne, a man of wondrous figure, whose appearance was terrible, like that of the Lord. Abraham beheld this wondrous figure upon the golden throne alternately weep and laugh, but his weeping was much more than his laughing, indeed his weeping was seven times as much as his laughing. Abraham then asked the angel Michael to explain unto him the meaning of the two doors, the large door and the small door, and to tell him who the wondrous figure was upon the golden throne.

Michael answered and thus he said: " The small door, the narrow one, leads to the path of life and to eternal bliss, but the large door, the wide one, leads to perdition and to

[1] M. R. James, *The Testament of Abraham*, § X.   [2] Cf. Charles, *The Book of Enoch*, 32.

destruction. The man who is seated upon the golden throne, and whose appearance is terrible like that of the Lord, is Adam, man's first parent. He is allowed by the Eternal to sit here and watch the procession of the souls which depart from their bodies and enter either by the narrow or by the wide gate. But he weepeth and grieveth when he witnesses the multitudes that go through the wide gate, and rejoiceth when a soul passeth through the narrow gate. But behold, his weeping is more than his laughing, for whilst multitudes of souls which go forth from their bodies and pass him enter by the wide gate, only few are allowed to enter through the narrow gate into eternal life. Against seven thousand walking on the wide road and entering by the wide gate, leading to perdition, very few walk on the narrow path of righteousness and thus enter through the narrow gate into bliss and life eternal. And because of this, Adam's weeping greatly exceeds his laughing." [1]

Thus spake the angel Michael, and Abraham looked and watched the procession of souls and witnessed the judgments awaiting them. And behold, he saw myriads of souls to whom the angel refused admittance through the narrow gate, so that they were compelled to enter through the wide gate which leads to destruction. Abraham also beheld two fiery angels driving with fiery thongs ten thousand souls through the wide gate to perdition and destruction, whilst one angel was leading a single soul. Then Abraham and Michael followed the multitudes through the gate, to see whether any would be saved.

There they beheld a man, whose countenance was as radiant as the sun, before a crystal table, upon which was spread out a book six cubits in thickness and ten cubits in breadth, whilst two angels were standing at his sides and officiating as recorders. The actions of man were weighed in

---

[1] *The Testament of Abraham*, § XI. The same legend is also found in Moslem tradition. See W. St. Clair Tisdall, *The Original Sources of the Quran*, 1905, pp. 206–207.

a balance by a fiery angel. The soul which Abraham had seen carried by one angel was now brought in. It asked for mercy, but its good actions and sins were looked out in the book, and it was found that its meritorious acts were outbalanced by its evil doings. The archangel Dokiel was holding the scales of justice, and Purael was holding the probing fire. Abel, the son of Adam, who was the judge, ordered the scrolls to be unrolled, and Enoch, the writer of righteousness, and the teacher of Heaven and earth, read out the account.[1] The soul was that of a woman who had murdered her own daughter, and although it protested of its innocence and pleaded not guilty, its crimes were proved and found recorded in the scrolls.

Loud did the soul lament: " Woe to me," cried the soul, " I have forgotten all my sins and crimes, but they are not forgotten here."

Another soul was then brought in, and her sins and good actions were weighed on the scales [2] and lo! it was found that her sins and righteous acts were exactly alike. It needed but one good deed to outweigh her sins, and the judge would neither condemn the soul for her sins nor grant her salvation, but decided that she must remain there until God, the judge of all, had decided her fate. Abraham had compassion upon that soul, which needed only one good deed to be saved. " What can we do for this poor soul?" he asked, and Michael replied that if she had one more meritorious deed she would be saved. Pitying that soul, Abraham interceded for her and prayed to the Lord of the Universe.[3] He was joined in his supplications by the angels themselves, by the judge and the recorder. And lo, the Lord of the Universe heard the righteous prayer of Abraham, and the soul was carried into Paradise by a shining angel.

[1] *Ibid.*, § XII–XIII. See also *Erubin,* 21a; *Hagigah,* 16a; *Targum Jerushalmi, Genesis,* 5, 24.
[2] *Ibid.,* § XIV. See also *Erubin,* 19a; *Hagigah,* 27a; *Rosh Hashana,* 17a. See also Koran, *Sura,* 7, 21.   [3] *Sotah,* 10b.

Thereupon Abraham saw the souls of those who had been destroyed by his prayer for their wickedness. Taking compassion upon them, he prayed to the Almighty to forgive them: " O Lord!" said Abraham, " I have been too precipitate in my wrath and have caused the death of the sinners, before they had time to repent. Forgive them now their sins or restore them to life again, so that they may be able to mend their ways and repent." And a voice from the Throne of Glory replied that the souls were forgiven, for they had suffered an uncommon mode of death.[1] Having witnessed the judgment in Heaven, Abraham was now taken back by the angel Michael to his home upon earth.[2]

" It is time," Michael said to the venerable old man, " to yield thy soul. Put thy house in order, and make thy will, for thou must now die."

But still the Patriarch refused to give up his soul.

And thereupon the archangel ascended to Heaven, and prostrating himself before the Throne of Glory thus he spoke: " O Lord of the Universe! I cannot lay hands upon Abraham and take his soul, for he was Thy friend, and there is none like him on earth."

And now the sixty-three thousand eight hundred and seventy-five days, during which Abraham had walked upon the face of the earth, appeared before the Throne of Glory and thus they spake: " We have come before Thee, O Lord of the Universe! to bear witness to the perfection and righteousness of Thy servant Abraham, that there is none so righteous and perfect in the land. On none of us," said the days of Abraham's life, " hath he done wrong or forgotten his duty, but hath always wrought good deeds, practised charity, and glorified Thy name."[3]

And suddenly Abraham felt himself carried upon wings

[1] Sanhedrin, 43b.   [2] M. R. James, The Testament of Abraham, § XV.
[3] Lewner, Kol Agadoth, p. 119.

high up to the celestial regions.   Higher and higher he was
carried, into regions of radiance and of splendour.   And behold,
he came to a place where there was a great light, and he could
perceive the whole world from end to end.   Thereupon two
gates made of precious stones were thrust open before him,
and he entered the city of the just.   Myriads of ministering
angels, whose countenances were as radiant as the splendour
of Heaven, hurried to his encounter and bade him welcome.
Divesting him of his raiment, they clothed him in clouds of
glory and he could smell the perfumes of the Garden of Eden
which sent a never-experienced feeling of bliss and delight
through his whole being.   And the ministering angels took
crowns made of precious stones and pearls and placed them
upon his head.   And eight branches of myrtle they put into
his hands, and their perfume filled the world.   They brought
Abraham to shores of lovely rivers, such as he had never seen
in his life, and there he saw roses and myrtles, whose perfume
filled his being with delight.   Thereupon the angels brought
him to a canopy prepared for him, and he beheld four rivers,
flowing from underneath it, and they were rivers of honey,
wine, oil, and balsam.[1]

Lifting up his eyes, he saw that his canopy was set in with
pearls, and precious stones sent out a dazzling light.   Beneath
the canopy, he beheld a table of pure gold, set in with precious
stones;   and ministering angels were standing around ready
to wait on him.   Whilst he was still wondering at the splendour
and radiance and delights surrounding him, behold, he felt
himself quite a young child, happy and careless.   He saw a
number of other children, of his own age, coming to meet him
and to play with him.   Happily he joined his little playmates,
and together they ran off to listen to the music of the spheres
and of the angels, gambolled and danced among the lovely

[1] Lewner, *loc. cit.* See also Gaster, *The Chronicles of Jerahmeel*, 18, 4; Jellinek, *Beth-
Hamidrash*, II, 52–53.

smelling trees, and rested under the shade of the tree of life.

And behold, the days of his childhood had passed, and Abraham felt himself a youth, full of life and the joy of life. The children, his playmates, had disappeared, but in their stead, happy and joyous and resplendent with health and beauty, youths, as young as himself, came to meet him, and he shared their joys and their pleasures. He beheld wonders without end and found delights innumerable. Youth and middle age passed swiftly away, and once more Abraham felt himself a venerable old man. He met other venerable and handsome old men, who came out to bid him welcome, and he enjoyed their talk and their company. They talked of justice, mercy and charity, and of the duties of man towards his Maker and towards his fellowmen. They talked of human life, of human suffering, and of the destiny of man.[1] The old and venerable men thereupon brought Abraham to the canopy prepared for him, and there he noticed a curtain made of lightning. He looked behind the curtain, and beheld three hundred and ten worlds spreading out before his gaze, wonderful worlds extending into infinity. The clouds of glory invaded the garden, and Abraham felt an indescribable delight, and he heard a voice calling to him and saying: " This is only a part of the delight and happiness which awaits thee in the next world."[2]

And then the Lord took the soul of Abraham from his body, never allowing the angel of death to touch his perfect and faithful servant.[3] The soul departed heavenwards to dwell in the celestial regions, among the angels and perfect souls. And at that moment the stone, which was hanging upon a chain on Abraham's breast, rose up, was carried heavenwards and placed in the sun.[4]

[1] Lewner, *loc. cit.* See also Gaster, *The Chronicles of Jerahmeel*, 18, 4; Jellinek, *Beth-Hamidrash*, II, 52–53. [2] *Ibid.* See also Lewner, *loc. cit.*, pp. 119–121.
[3] *Baba Batra*, 17a; see Weil, *loc. cit.*, p. 98. See, however, James, *loc. cit.*, § XX, where it is said that Abraham died because he had been induced to kiss the hand of the Angel of Death. [4] *Baba Batra*, 16b.

No sooner had the news of the death of the famous and generous Emir Abraham, the son of Terah, spread at Beer-Sheba, than loud lamentations and wailing filled the town. The news was carried to the neighbouring towns, and at once crowds of men, women, and children, flocked to Beer-Sheba, weeping and lamenting. They all came to bewail the death of the man who had been a friend of the poor and an adviser of the rich.

From distant Mesopotamia, from Haran and other places, men came to pay their last respects to the pious, generous, and famous Emir, to lament his death, in truly oriental fashion,[1] and to accompany to his last resting place this wise man of the East.

Abraham's son Isaac was greatly astonished, when he noticed among those who came to follow the procession many of the old and venerable men who had come to the funeral of his mother Sarah, thirty-eight years ago. " Were you not present, my friends," Isaac asked some of these old men, " at the funeral of my never-to-be-forgotten mother Sarah?"

" That is so," replied the old and venerable men, " but since that day the Creator of the Universe gave us a new lease of life and lent us strength, allowing us to live to this day, so that we might be able to accompany thy father to his resting place and pay him the last respects. Now we know that it is agreeable to the Lord that men pay the last respects to the dead." [2]

And Isaac placed his father upon a bier which was carried upon the shoulders of friends to the place of burial. Isaac and Ishmael, and the venerable relatives of the deceased, Shem and Eber, walked in front,[3] and men called out: " Make way for the bier of Abraham." When the people beheld the bier, they broke out into loud wailing, saying: " Woe unto

---

[1] Sepher Hajashar.   [2] Sepher Hajashar; Cf. Genesis Rabba, 62.   [3] Genesis Rabba, 64.

us, now that our father Abraham, the generous, our benefactor is dead and gone."

And the princes and potentates of Canaan, who had hastened to Beer-Sheba to follow the procession, asked the bearers
of the bier to wait a moment, so that they might give expression to their grief in suitable words. In a voice broken by
sobs, amidst the awed silence of the crowd, they cried:

" Woe unto the land which hath lost its leader, woe unto
mankind which hath lost the friend of peace, and woe also
unto us, the rulers of men, who have lost such an adviser and
a friend. Men have lost an instructor and a teacher, and the
poor their benefactor. We are all like a vessel which hath lost
its pilot, and like children whose father hath left them." [1]

Thus lamented the princes and potentates of Canaan, and
all the people wept loudly and shed copious tears. Thereupon
Ishmael and Isaac, and Shem and Eber, entered the cave of
Machpelah and laid Abraham to rest by the side of his wife
Sarah. [2]

[1] *Baba Batra*, 91a.   [2] Cf. Lewner, *loc. cit.*, pp. 121–122; Bin Gorion, *loc. cit.*, pp. 358–362.

CHAPTER XXIX

The Way of Life and the Way of Death, or the Twin Brothers

The prayers of Isaac and Rebekah—The struggle of the twins—They divide the two worlds—The contention of the angels—Michael and Sammael —The way of life and the way of death—Esau deceives his father— Rebekah's love for Jacob—Grandfather and grandson—Abraham's blessing —The death of Nimrod—The precious garment—The pottage of lentils The sword that had slain a thousand devils—A father's blessing—Wine from Paradise—The vision of Hell—Thoughts of revenge—The exile— Eliphaz, the robber—The quick journey—The quarrel of the stones.

AFTER his marriage, Isaac continued to live with his father Abraham in the land of Canaan. Rebekah was barren for twenty years and she said to her husband: " I have heard that thy mother, too, was barren and that thy father prayed unto the Lord and He sent her a son. Pray thou now on my behalf, and the Lord will listen to thy prayers." Thereupon Isaac took his wife Rebekah, and they went to mount Moriah, to the place where Isaac had been bound and offered as a burnt offering to the Lord. Isaac entreated the Lord and prayed on behalf of his wife, whilst Rebekah, too, prayed and implored the Sovereign of all the Worlds to bless her and to give her children. And God hearkened unto their prayer, and Rebekah conceived twins.[1]

Now the children were contending with one another in their mother's womb, like mighty warriors. When Rebekah

[1] *Jebamoth*, 64a; *Targum Jerushalmi, Genesis*, 25, 21; *Pirke de Rabbi Eliezer*, Ch. 32.

passed before an idol temple Esau made violent efforts to come forth, whilst whenever she went before a house of learning or a synagogue Jacob struggled and desired to escape into the world, so that he might attend the house of God. Rebekah suffered great agony, so that her soul was nigh unto death, on account of the pains.[1] It is also related that Jacob said unto Esau: " My brother, two worlds are before us, the world below and a world above, or a world to come. If it pleases thee, take thou this world, and I will take the other." Esau, however, denied the existence of a world to come and the resurrection of the dead. He, therefore, made a compact with his brother Jacob, giving over to him the right to the next world, whilst he himself took the right to this world.[2] Not only the children, but also the angels in Heaven contended one with another. Sammael, who is also the tutelary angel of Esau, wanted to kill Jacob already in his mother's womb, but Michael protected him. Some of the angels were on Sammael's side, whilst others supported Michael. But the Lord rebuked Sammael and his followers.[3]

Now when Rebekah was suffering great pains, she questioned all the other women whether anything similar had happened unto them, but they said that never had such a thing happened unto them. " Why should it only happen to me," said Rebekah, and she went to consult Shem and Eber, and begged them to intercede on her behalf before the Lord. She also asked Abraham to pray on her account to the Lord. And through Shem and Eber the Lord answered Rebekah that there were two nations in her womb. When the lads were born one was called Esau and the other Jacob.

The elder brother was called Esau, because he was hairy, having red hair all over his body, covering him like a garment. He was also called Edom, or Red, because before his birth he

---

[1] *Genesis Rabba*, 63; *Sepher Hajashar*.
[2] Bin Gorion, *Die Sagen der Juden*, Vol. II, p. 353.
[3] *Midrash Abkhir*, quoted in *Yalkut Shimeoni, Genesis*, § 110.

already sucked his mother's blood, and during his life he
frequently shed blood.[1]

The lads grew up, and Esau went the way of death, being
a cunning hunter, catching birds and beasts, and deceiving
and cheating men, whilst Jacob went the way of life, dwelling
in academies and in houses of learning, where he studied the
law all his days. He studied in the schools of Shem and Eber,
continuing to seek instruction and acquiring the knowledge
of God.[2]

Esau knew that his father was a holy man and that he whom
he would bless would be blessed indeed. He, therefore, endeavoured to find favour in the eyes of Isaac and never omitted
an opportunity to please him. Whenever he visited his father,
he came arrayed in his best garments and brought him the
best meat and wine, saying unto himself: " My father will
see how I honour him and will bless me." As Isaac, however,
paid but little attention to these things, the wily Esau changed
his tactics and decided to pretend to his father that he was a
man of justice and piety. One day Esau came to see his father
and thus he spoke:

" Father dear, I have been to listen to the words of God
in the house of learning, and I am now giving a tithe to the
poor from all that I earn. I have now come to ask thee how to
give tithe from salt and straw."

When Isaac heard these words he was very pleased with
the piety of the lad, and made up his mind to bless him before
he died. But the Lord decreed that the eyes of Isaac should
grow dim so that Jacob would be enabled to obtain the
blessing.[3]

But Isaac loved Esau, in whose mouth were words of
deceit, whilst both Abraham and Rebekah loved Jacob.
Abraham, indeed, saw the deeds of Esau and knew that

---

[1] See Eisenmenger, *Endecktes Judentum*, Vol. I, p. 646.
[2] *Pirke de Rabbi Eliezer*, Ch. 32; *Yalkut, Genesis*, § 110.
[3] See Lewner, *loc. cit.*, pp. 117-118.

they were wicked. He therefore called his daughter-in-law and thus he spoke unto her: " My daughter, watch over the boy Jacob, for it is he who will be in my stead on earth and a blessing among men. It is him whom the Lord will choose to be a people for possession unto Himself. It grieveth me to see that Isaac loveth Esau, but I am glad to notice that thou dost love Jacob. Therefore, my daughter, watch over the lad, for all the blessings wherewith the Lord hath blessed me and my seed shall belong to Jacob." And Abraham called Jacob and blessed him, and thus he said: " May the Lord give thee, my son, all the blessings wherewith He blessed Adam, and Enoch, Noah, and Shem, and may the spirits of Mastema never have any power over thee or over thy seed to turn thee from the Lord, who is thy God." [1]

Now it happened that on the day when Abraham died, Esau, as was his habit, went out to hunt. Nimrod, King of Babel, who was called Amraphel, also went out to hunt on that day. Being very jealous of Nimrod, Esau constantly sought for an opportunity to slay the King. Meeting Nimrod alone far away from his royal suite, he fell upon him, killed him and took away the coats of Nimrod, which the Holy One had once made for Adam and Eve.[2] On these garments the forms of all the wild beasts and birds which are on the face of the earth were embroidered in their proper colours. Suddenly Esau saw Nimrod's men approaching and he took to flight, carrying off the precious raiment, hurrying to conceal it in his father's house. Very weak and exhausted, he met Jacob and was surprised to see traces of tears upon his brother's countenance. " Why art thou crying, my brother," he asked, " and why hast thou dressed pottage of lentils to-day, which is food only fit for the poor?"

" Alas, dear brother," replied Jacob, " didst thou not know

[1] Charles, *Book of Jubilees*, 19, 15–29.
[2] *Targum Jerushalmi, Genesis*, 25, 27; *Midrash Agadah, Genesis*, 28, 13; *Midrash Lekach Tob, Genesis*; *Yalkut, Genesis*, § 115; *Pirke de Rabbi Eliezer*, Ch. 24; *Sepher Hajashar*.

that our dear grandfather Abraham died to-day? Lentil food is a sign of mourning and sorrow." [1] " If this pious old man," said Esau, " hath died like any other mortal, why should I believe in God and in punishment and reward? Now, my brother," he continued, " I am very faint, therefore let me taste some of thy red pottage."

Thereupon Jacob said: " Sell me to-day thy birthright." And Esau said: " I am going to die and I do not believe in another world; this birthright, therefore, hath no value in mine eyes." Jacob then wrote a deed of transfer upon a leaf, and Esau signed it, selling his birthright for a mess of lentils.

Esau thereupon laughed at Jacob, and mocked him, saying: " Thou fool, thou hast bought to-day something which is worthless." Esau indeed thought that he had had the better of Jacob, who, in addition to bread and pottage of lentils, had given him also the sword of Methuselah, wherewith the latter had slain a thousand devils. [2] And Esau went forth and told his friends of what had occurred, and they all laughed and mocked at Jacob. [3]

On the nightfall of the festive day of Passover, Isaac called Esau, his first born, and thus he spoke unto him: " To-night the treasuries of dew and blessing are opened, and the angels in Heaven utter songs and implore the Creator to bestow the blessing of dew upon the world. As it is a time of blessing, go thou, catch venison and make me savoury meat, that I may bless thee, whilst I am still alive. Take care, however, not to bring me anything stolen or robbed."

Esau went forth to catch venison but thought in his mind: " If I am not successful I will steal a lamb or a kid from my neighbours and make savoury meat for my father." Esau, however, had forgotten to take the garment of Nimrod and,

---

[1] *Pirke de Rabbi Eliezer*, Ch. 35.   [2] See Eisenmenger, *loc. cit.*, Vol. I, p. 651.
[3] For the entire passage see *Pirke de Rabbi Eliezer*, Ch. 35; *Targum Jerushalmi, Genesis*, 25, 29; *Genesis Rabba*, 63; *Baba Batra*, 16b; *Sepher Hajashar*.

not being successful in hunting as usually, was delayed.[1]

Now Rebekah had heard the words of her husband, and made up her mind to deprive Esau of his father's promised blessing for the benefit of Jacob. She called her younger son and thus she spoke to him:

" My son, on this night, the treasuries of the dew will be opened, and on this night, in the future, thy children will be redeemed from bondage and will utter a song.[2] Make thou, therefore, savoury meat for thy father that he may bless thee." But Jacob's heart dreaded the deceit, and he cried bitterly and said:

" O Mother dear, I cannot do such a thing." But his mother insisted, saying: " If it be a blessing may it come upon thee and upon thy seed, and if it be a curse, let it be upon me and upon my soul."[3] And Jacob did as his mother bade him, but wept copiously.

Rebekah dressed Jacob in the coats of Esau and sent him off to his father. When Jacob appeared before the latter, the room was suddenly filled with a fragrant smell, like the smell from Paradise. And Isaac ate of the meat his son had brought him, but he was thirsty, and an angel brought him from Paradise the juice of the grapes growing on the vine there.[4] Isaac blessed his son Jacob with ten blessings concerning the dews of Heaven and the corn of the earth, and Jacob left the presence of his father crowned like a bridegroom, on account of the blessing he had received. The dew which is destined to revive the dead came down from Heaven and descended upon him, and his bones were refreshed and became stronger, and he himself became a mighty man.[5]

But scarcely had Jacob left his father's presence, when Esau

---

[1] Lewner, *Kol Agadoth*, Vol. I, p. 128; *Pirke de Rabbi Eliezer*, Ch. 32; *Genesis Rabba*, 66; *Midrash Tanchuma*, section *Toledoth*.   [2] *Pirke de Rabbi Eliezer*, ibid.; *Sotah*, 12b.
[3] *Genesis Rabba*, 65, 66; *Midrash Tanchuma*, section *Toledoth*; *Targum Jerushalmi*; *Genesis*, 27, 13; see also Lewner, *loc. cit.*, pp. 128–130.
[4] *Genesis Rabba*, 66; *Midrash Tanchuma*, section *Toledoth*; Lewner, *loc. cit.*, p. 129. See also Eisenmenger, *loc. cit.*, Vol. II, p. 879, where Eisenmenger gives a wrong translation.
[5] *Pirke de Rabbi Eliezer*, Ch. 32.

returned. He entered Isaac's room with vehemence, and called aloud: " Arise, Father, and bless me." At that moment Isaac had a terrible vision. He saw Hell opened to him beneath his feet,[1] he saw an abyss of fire, and his son Esau standing over it and throwing fuel into it. Trembling at the sight, he asked in terror: " Who art thou?" And when he heard what had happened and that Jacob had bought the birthright from Esau he thought: " Now it is right that he should have my blessing." [2] But when he heard Esau crying, he blessed him too.

Esau now hated his brother and said unto himself: " If I kill my brother, I will be punished and my father will curse me. I will therefore go to my uncle Ishmael and marry one of his daughters. Then I will induce him to seek quarrel with Jacob, on account of my birthright; he will fight my brother and kill him. Then I will pretend to avenge the death of my brother, kill Ishmael and inherit the possessions of both my father and my uncle." Such were the wicked thoughts of Esau, but the Lord frustrated them.[3]

According to others, Esau said in his heart: " Cain made a mistake in killing his brother Abel whilst his parents were still alive, for his father afterwards begat Seth. I will wait until my father dies, then I will kill Jacob, and will thus be sole heir to all his possessions."

Afraid to meet his brother, Jacob went out only at night, hiding in the day. Jacob then fled and went to the school of Shem and Eber, where he remained for fourteen years, studying the law. After fourteen years he returned home, but found that his brother was still harbouring the thought of killing him. It was then that his mother advised him to go to Padan-Aram.

" Go thou to thy Uncle Laban," said Rebekah, " to my brother, the son of Bethuel. He is old and very wealthy.

---

[1] *Genesis Rabba*, 65 and 67.
[2] *Genesis Rabba*, 67; *Midrash Tanchuma*, section *Toledoth*: see also Lewner, *loc. cit.*, pp. 130-131.   [3] *Sotah*, 13; *Genesis Rabba*, 67.

Ask him to give thee one of his daughters as wife, and abide with him until the day when thy brother's anger will have abated."

And when Isaac heard what Esau was meditating, he called his son Jacob, and enjoined him not to marry any of the daughters of Canaan, but take to wife one of the daughters of Laban. He blessed his son and gave him gold and silver, as much as he could carry, to take with him.[1]

Now it happened that when Jacob set out on his way, Esau called Eliphaz, his first born, and thus spoke to him: " Take up thy sword, and hasten after Jacob who has just left and is carrying much wealth with him. Kill him and take away all his possessions."

Eliphaz, a nimble youth, clever in handling both the sword and the bow, hastened to comply with his father's request. He took ten of his followers with him, pursued his uncle Jacob and met him at the frontier of Canaan, near Sochem.

When Jacob saw Eliphaz and his men pursuing him, he stood still and awaited them.

" My father," said Eliphaz, when he came near, " has sent me to kill thee and to take away all thy possessions. Now prepare to die, for I must obey my father's command."

But Jacob begged his nephew to spare his life and not to commit such a sin before the Lord. " Take all the gold and silver I have," said he, " and leave me my life, so that the Lord will count it as a generous deed and bless thee." And God touched the heart of Eliphaz, so that he had pity with his uncle. He took, however, all the latter's possessions, leaving him quite poor, and· returned to his father to Beer-Sheba. When Esau heard what had happened, he was very angry with his son for having allowed Jacob to escape. He nevertheless took all the gold and silver which Eliphaz and his men had brought.[2]

---

[1] *Sepher Hajashar; Yalkut,* § 115.
[2] *Genesis Rabba,* 68; *Sepher Hajashar;* see Lewner, *loc. cit.,* p. 134.

Now when Eliphaz had left him, Jacob prayed to the Lord to help him in his misery: " When Eliezer, the steward of my grandfather Abraham, came to Haran, he showed all the signs of wealth and prosperity, whilst I am now poor and no one will take any notice of me." And then he lifted up his eyes and saw twelve stars shining brightly upon the firmament, and he marvelled greatly. " How is it," thought Jacob, " that I see stars shining during the day? No doubt, the Lord of the Universe, of whom my father and grandfather have told me, is beginning to show me His wonders." But this was not the only event which caused the Patriarch to wonder. Many miracles were wrought for him on that journey, when he went forth from Beer-Sheba. From Beer-Sheba to mount Moriah is a journey of two days, and yet in a few hours Jacob was there, arriving at midday. He therefore decided to continue his journey, but suddenly the hours of the day were shortened, and the sun went down before its time, because the Lord desired to speak to him and to reveal unto him the future.[1] And when Jacob saw that the sun had set in the west, he took twelve stones, of the stones of that altar on which his father had been bound, and placed them as a rampart against the prowling beasts, and the other stones he set as a pillow and went to sleep.

With regard to the stones, some say that Jacob took twelve stones, corresponding to the twelve tribes, whilst others relate that he took only three stones.[2] It is also related that the stones had been set up by Adam as an altar, and that on it Abel offered his sacrifice. After the deluge, Noah collected the scattered stones and offered his sacrifice upon the altar. Abraham once more reared the altar which had been overthrown, when he came to bind Isaac and to offer him as a burnt offering.[3]

[1] *Genesis Rabba*, 68; *Pirke de Rabbi Eliezer*, Ch. 35.
[2] *Pirke de Rabbi Eliezer*, Ch. 35; *Genesis Rabba*, 68; *Hullin*, 91a; *Sanhedrin*, 95b. see also *Midrash Shokher Tob*, Ps. 91.   [3] *Pirke de Rabbi Eliezer*, ibid.

But the stones began to quarrel among themselves, for each one said: " It is upon me that this pious man will lay his head." And the Lord said: " For many years Jacob did not sleep at nights, but studied the law, and now he has set stones for his pillow and they, too, quarrel." He therefore commanded the stones to merge into one stone and to be as soft as a cushion.[1]

THE STRUGGLE OF THE CHILDREN

Fra biginning o þe werld
O suilk a strijf o childir tuin
Þat lai þer moder wamb wit-in;
Þair strut it was vu-stern stith,
Wit wrathli wrestes aiþer writh,
Bituix vu-born a batel blind,
Suilk an was ferli to find.
He þat on þe right side lai
Þe toþer him wraisted oft away;
And he þat lay a-pon þe left
Þe toþer oft his sted him reft.
Þe leuedi was ful ferli drad,
Als womman þat ful hard was stad.
Bot oure lauerd o suthfastnes
Had don hir in to sikernes,
Thoru his werrai prophecie,
Quat suld be paa childer vie,
O þair weird and o þair lijf,
And quat for besening bar þe strijf.

Cursor Mundi, Edited by Richard Morris. Early English
Text Society, 1874–92. Part I, p. 206, ll. 3457–3476.

[1] *Genesis Rabba,* 68; *Midrash Tanchuma,* section *Wayeze; Hullin,* 91; *Pirke de Rabbi Eliezer,* Ch. 35.

CHAPTER XXX

Love, Hate, and Strife, or the Troubles of a Father

The wonderful dream—The four kingdoms—The vision of the future—The stone of foundation—Love at the well—The beautiful cousin—The greedy uncle—The patient shepherd—The deceit of Laban—The promise of the neighbours—The banquet and the pawned valuables—The Teraphim—Laban's message to Esau—The protecting angels—The consecration of Levi—The embarrassment of the angel—The heavenly songs—The High-Priest in Heaven—Sammael, the tutelary angel of Esau—A brotherly kiss and bite—The troubles of a father—The abandoned baby—The death of a mother—The hatred of a brother.

SLEEPING with his head on the pillow of stones, Jacob saw in his dream a ladder fixed in the earth, its summit reaching to the height of Heaven. And he beheld the angels who had accompanied him ascending to make known to the angels on high that Jacob, the pious, whose likeness was on the Throne of Glory, had arrived.

And in that night the Lord showed Jacob the four kingdoms, their dominion and subsequent destruction. He showed him the prince of the kingdom of Babylon ascending seventy rungs, and descending, and He also showed him the prince of the kingdom of Media ascending fifty-two rungs and descending. He then showed him the prince of the kingdom of Greece who ascended 180 rungs of the ladder and then descended. Jacob thereupon saw the prince of the kingdom of Edom ascending, but not descending, for he was saying to himself: " I will ascend above the heights of the clouds, and be like the Most High."

But the Glory of the Lord stood above Jacob, the seven heavens were opened, the world was filled with dazzling light, and the Lord spoke to Jacob: " Fear not the prince of Edom, for the land thou art lying upon I will give to thy children, who will be as many as the dust of the earth." And in that moment the whole land of Palestine folded up and placed itself under Jacob's head, so that in later days his children would have a right to conquer it. Thereupon Jacob had a vision of the future. He saw Mount Sinai surrounded by flames, and Moses receiving the Law. He saw the Temple in its glory, and Israel living in a land flowing with milk and honey. Suddenly the vision changed, and he saw Jerusalem burning, and the sack of the Temple. And once more he saw, gathering from the four corners of the earth, Israel returning from exile to rebuild the Temple and re-establish its glory.[1]

Jacob rose up early in the morning in great fear and said: " The House of the Lord is in this place." Thereupon he went to gather the stones, but found that they had turned into one stone. The Lord then planted His right foot on the stone and sank it to the bottom of the depths, making it the keystone of the earth. It is therefore called the foundation stone, for from it all the earth was evolved and upon it the Sanctuary of the Lord stands.[2]

Jacob now left Bethel and in a short time he was at Haran. There he saw a well in a field, and a great stone laid upon the mouth of the well; three flocks were lying near it. Jacob asked the shepherds whether they knew Laban, the son of Bethuel, at Haran, and they said: " We know him well. A plague had broken out among his sheep and only a few had been left, and he had therefore dismissed his shepherds, entrusting the remainder of the flock to his daughter Rachel who is tending them.[3] Behold," they added, " here the young

---

[1] *Genesis Rabba*, 68, 69; *Hullin*, 91a; *Pirke de Rabbi Eliezer*, Ch. 35; *Midrash Tanchuma*, section *Wayeze*.   [2] *Pirke de Eliezer*, Ch. 35; *Midrash Tanchuma*, *ibid*.
[3] *Pirke de Rabbi Eliezer*, Ch. 36: see also Lewner, *loc. cit.* pp. 140–141.

THE MEETING OF JACOB AND RACHEL

shepherdess cometh." Jacob hastened to roll away the stone
from the mouth of the well, and the water came up and spread
outside.[1] Jacob, when he saw Rachel coming, was glad indeed,
for she was beautiful. But he was also glad, because he knew
that he would now be prosperous. For whenever a man enters
a city and maidens come forth before him, his way is prosperous.
Thus it happened to Eliezer, the steward of Abraham; thus
it happened to Moses, when he came to Midian; thus it happened to Saul, when he acquired the sovereignty, and thus it
happened to Jacob.[2] And when Jacob had watered the sheep
of Laban, his uncle, he kissed Rachel and lifted up his voice
and wept. At that moment a prophetic vision came over him
and he knew that Rachel would die young, on the road, and
would not be buried in the double cave by his side.[3]

He thereupon told his cousin who he was, and that he had
come to stay with her father, and to marry one of his daughters.
" Thou canst not stay with my father," said Rachel, " for he
is cunning and deceitful." But Jacob assured her that the
Lord would be on his side and protect him against Laban.
The maiden thereupon went to inform her father of the arrival
of her cousin.

And when Laban heard the tidings of Jacob, how the
Lord had revealed Himself to him at Bethel, and what
power he had displayed at the well, rolling away the stone,
and how the water had risen and the well had overflowed,
he ran out, kissed and embraced him and led him into the
house.

Laban had also other reasons to rush out, embrace and
kiss his nephew. He said unto himself: " When Eliezer,
the steward of Abraham, came, he brought with him gold and
silver, pearls and precious stones, and now my nephew Jacob,
who is the favourite son of Rebekah, has come and no doubt

---

[1] *Tergum Jerushalmi Genesis*, 69, 10; *Genesis Rabba*, 70.
[2] *Pirke de Rabbi Eliezer*, Ch. 36. [3] *Genesis Rabba*, 70.

he does not come empty-handed."   When he noticed that
Jacob had arrived on foot and had neither camels nor servants
with him, Laban thought that perhaps all his wealth consisted
in precious stones concealed on his person.   He therefore
hugged him, thus having an opportunity of feeling his pockets.
But again he was disappointed.   At last he kissed his nephew,
thinking that perchance he had pearls and gems concealed
under his tongue.   Once more he was disappointed.   And when,
at last, Laban heard that Jacob had been robbed on his way
by his nephew Eliphaz and that he was poor indeed, his
enthusiasm abated, and he said to his nephew: " Stay with
me a few days." [1]

Now Jacob loved Rachel, because she was beautiful,
whilst the eyes of her elder sister Leah were weak and moist.
And Jacob was informed by the neighbours that Leah's eyes
were running because she had wept and prayed before the Lord
that He would not destine her to be the wife of Esau the wicked.
Jacob began to serve Laban seven years for his daughter
Rachel.   When seven years had passed, Laban gathered together all his neighbours, and thus he spoke to them: " My
friends, well do you know that the Lord has blessed us all on
account of Jacob.   Now his seven years are at end; he will
marry my daughter Rachel and leave this town, and then the
blessing of the Lord, which we enjoyed on his account, will
no longer be bestowed upon us and we will no longer prosper."
Thus spoke Laban, and his neighbours grew sad, and asked
anxiously:

" What shall we do, so as to prevent Jacob from leaving
our city?"   " I will tell you," said Laban; " I will deceive
Jacob, for in the place of Rachel I will give him Leah, so that
he will be obliged to serve me another seven years for Rachel."
When Laban's friends heard these words, they greatly rejoiced,
and approved his plan.

[1] *Genesis Rabba*, 70; *Pirke de Rabba Eliezer*, Ch. 36.

" Thou speakest well," they said.

" If such is your conviction," replied Laban, " then promise me that you will not reveal the secret to Jacob."

" We promise," said the men of the place.

But Laban, not content with their promise, asked them as a guarantee of their good faith to bring him valuables of gold and silver as a pledge that they would keep the secret until the morrow. The men of the town, not suspecting Laban's good faith, hastened to bring him their valuables as a pledge.

Laban at once pawned the things, bought wine and meat, and invited all the men of the town to a banquet and rejoicing. They ate and drank and rejoiced, making merry, singing songs, and shouting Ha-Lia-Ha-Lia (this is Lia), although Jacob never paid any attention to their allusions. When the neighbours came the next day to claim their valuables, Laban laughingly told them that they had enjoyed themselves last night at the banquet he had offered " on their account." The men of the town were compelled to redeem their possessions which Laban had pawned at the butcher's and the wine merchants and thus pay for the banquet. Henceforth, they called Laban no longer the son of Bethuel, but Laban the Deceiver.[1]

Jacob served another seven years for Rachel and six years for cattle which his father-in-law gave him, and then he fled to get away from Laban. On this occasion, his wife Rachel stole the image which Laban worshipped. This image, called Teraphim, was really the head of a man, a first born, which the worshipper had slain, pinched off his head and salted it with salt and balsam. The name of an unclean spirit and incantations were then written upon a plate of gold and placed under the tongue of this head. The head was then placed in the wall, lamps were lit in front of it, and the worshipper, bowing down before the head, asked it to tell him oracles.[2]

[1] *Genesis Rabba,* 70, 71.
[2] *Pirke de Rabbi Eliezer,* Ch. 36; *Sepher Hajashar; Yalkut, Genesis,* § 130; *Midrash Tanchuma,* section *Wayeze;* see also *Targum Jerushalmi, Genesis,* 31, 19.

As Laban had not been able to discover his Teraphim, he kissed his daughters and grandchildren and returned home. He was, however, far from reconciled, and still brooded mischief. On his arrival at Padan-Aram, he immediately dispatched his son Beor, accompanied by ten men, to his nephew Esau, with the following message: " Twenty years ago thy brother Jacob came to me naked and poor. I took him in, treated him well and gave him my two daughters as wives. He prospered exceedingly, thanks to my kindness and generosity, and he now possesses gold and silver, camels, asses, sheep, and oxen. But now he has left my house secretly, stealing my gods and never allowing me even to kiss my daughters and grandchildren before their departure. I advise thee, therefore, to go out with thy men against Jacob and slay him."

When Esau received this message, he remembered how Jacob had obtained his father's blessing, and his anger was very violent. He armed his followers and servants, and went out against Jacob at the head of an army of three hundred and forty men. But the messengers of Laban, upon leaving Esau, proceeded to Canaan and informed Rebekah of what had occurred. In haste the fond mother sent out seventy-two men to stand by Jacob in case of need.

They met Jacob and delivered to him the following message from his mother: " When thou wilt meet Esau, instead of waging war, offer him presents and beg him to make peace with thee. Perchance, he will be moved by thy prayers and presents." Jacob promised to listen to the words of his mother and to follow her advice. When he reached the ford of Jabbok, he saw 120,000 angels coming to meet him, and he sent out as many as he judged necessary to go to Esau's encounter.[1]

The nearer, however, Jacob came to Seir, the land of Esau, the greater became his fear that his brother's enmity and

[1] *Genesis Rabba*, 74; *Sepher Hajashar.*

anger had not yet abated. He prayed therefore to the Lord to protect him, and the Most High granted his prayer. The Creator of the Universe sent four angels to protect the Patriarch. At the head of one thousand horsemen each angel, in turn, met Esau and his men. Shouting aloud: " We are the servants of Jacob," they swept along, fell upon the troop that accompanied Esau, and dispersed it. Fear and trembling seized Esau, and he exclaimed:

" I am the brother of Jacob, and am hastening to meet my brother whom I have not seen for twenty years. Why are you thus treating me and my men?"

" Hadst thou not been the brother of Jacob, we would have destroyed thee long ago," replied the angels.[1]

In the meantime, Jacob, who was unaware of the help rendered to him by the celestials, prepared rich presents which he sent to his brother Esau, to appease his anger. Jacob was indeed like a man who had fled from a lion and was about to meet a bear.[2] The lion was Laban, and the bear was Esau. But Jacob prayed to the Lord and thus he said: " Sovereign of all the worlds! Thou didst say unto me ' Return unto the land of thy fathers, and I will be with thee.' And now my brother Esau has come ready to slay me and my house."

But the Lord sent down the angel Michael to protect and deliver Jacob, and he appeared to the Patriarch like a man. It happened at the ford of Jabbok. " Hast thou not promised once," said the angel to Jacob, " to give a tenth of all that thou dost possess to the Lord?" " I did," replied the Patriarch, and at once took all the cattle which he had brought from Padan-Aram and gave a tithe of them, amounting to 550 animals. Having done this, Jacob wished to cross the ford of Jabbok, but once more the angel Michael detained him, and thus he spoke: " Thou hast ten sons, but thou hast not given a tithe of them to the Lord." Again the Patriarch agreed.

---

[1] *Sepher Hajashar.*   [2] *Amos*, 5, 19.

He immediately set aside the four first born of the four mothers, and there remained eight children.[1] He thereupon counted from Simeon, finishing with Benjamin who was still in his mother's womb, and then started again to count from the beginning, so that Levi was the tenth. He accordingly set Levi aside as the tithe and consecrated him to the Lord.[2]

The angel Michael thereupon took up Levi and brought him up before the Lord and the Throne of Glory.[3] " Sovereign of all the worlds," said Michael, " this is Thy lot."

Thereupon the Lord of the Universe stretched out His right hand and blessed Levi, and thus He said: " Thy sons shall minister on earth before me, just as the angels are ministering in Heaven."

Michael then further spake and said: " Sovereign of all the worlds, Thou hast blessed Levi and his sons, but those who serve the king have no time to cultivate their fields and earn their sustenance."

And the Lord replied: " The sons of Levi will possess no land in the country which I shall give to the children of Israel, but provision of their food will be given to them, for they shall eat the offerings of the Lord, and all the tithes will be given to them." [4]

The angel was no longer able to hurt Jacob, but he wrestled with him until dawn broke, and the first rays of the sun tinted with orient hues the eastern sky.

Now Michael had been commanded not to leave Jacob until the latter had given him permission to do so. When day broke, the angel therefore asked Jacob to let him go, for the time had arrived when angels offer praise to the Most High and he must be there to lead the chant. As Jacob refused to grant his permission, Michael began to sing the praises from

---

[1] See Bechoroth, 53b, where it is said that the first born is excluded from the law of tithe.
[2] *Pirke de Rabbi Eliezer*, Ch. 37; *Genesis Rabba*, 70; *Book of Jubilees*, 32, 3.
[3] See *Testament of Twelve Patriarchs, Testament of Levi*, 2, 6.
[4] *Pirke de Rabbi Eliezer*, Ch. 37.

the earth.   Thereupon the angels from on high came down and bade Michael rise up to the Throne of Glory and chant the morning hymn, but Michael could not leave before Jacob had given him permission.   He blessed Jacob and changed his name from Jacob to Israel.[1] But the Lord rebuked his ministering angel for having touched the hollow of Jacob's thigh.

"Why didst thou hurt my ministering priest Jacob?" asked the Lord. "Sovereign of all the worlds," replied the angel, "am I not Thy High-Priest, ministering unto Thee?" "Thou art my High-Priest in Heaven," replied the Lord, "but Jacob is my High-Priest on earth." Thereupon Michael begged his colleague Raphael to heal Jacob, and Raphael complied with the request.[2] Although he had blessed him, the angel Michael refused to reveal unto the Patriarch the future. "If I do this," he said, "I shall be expelled from Heaven for 138 years, even as the angels who announced the destruction of Sodom had been expelled."[3]

Another version of this legend runs as follows: Sammael, he who is Satan, and not Michael, wrestled with Jacob at the ford of Jabbok. Sammael is the guardian angel of Esau and Edom, and he made up his mind to destroy Jacob on that night at the ford of Jabbok. He strove and contended with him, but could do the Patriarch no harm. The Patriarch had ferried over his wives and children and all his cattle, when he remembered that he had left behind some of his possessions. His servants had worked hard and were tired, and the Patriarch made up his mind to go over himself and fetch his possessions. Here he met the tutelary angel of Esau who appeared to him in the guise of a shepherd, and who tried to harm Jacob. The angel touched the hollow of his thigh, so that he halted afterwards. When dawn broke, Sammael begged the Patriarch to let him go, but Jacob refused until he had blessed him. "When

---

[1] *Pirke de Rabbi Eliezer*, Ch. 37. Cf. *Genesis Rabba*, 78. See Friedlaender's remark in his edition of *Pirke de Rabbi Eliezer*, p. 282.
[2] *Midrash Abkhir*, quoted in *Yalkut Shimeoni*.   [3] *Yalkut Rubeni; Genesis Rabba*, 78.

the angels came to visit my grandfather," said Jacob, " they never left him until they had blessed him." " Those angels," replied the tutelary angel of Edom, " were specially sent to bless thy grandfather, but I did not come to bless thee." [1]

Lifting up his eyes, Jacob saw his brother approaching with four hundred men of war. He divided his children and wives and went out before them, praying to the Lord, and bowing to the earth seven times, but it was to the Lord that he bowed.

Now when Esau perceived Jacob, his anger again rose up. Remembering, however, the defeat and humiliation inflicted upon him by the horsemen led by the angels, who proclaimed themselves the servants of Jacob, he said in his heart: " I will not try to slay Jacob with bow and arrows, but will bite him with my teeth, suck his blood and thus slay him." And then he ran up, embraced Jacob, and falling upon his neck, tried to bite him. Jacob's neck, however, became like marble, and as soon as Esau tried to bite Jacob, he broke his teeth. And he wept on the neck of Jacob, because of the pain of his teeth.[2] Esau pretended now to make peace with his brother, and the latter proceeded to Shechem.

Jacob never met Esau until the death of Isaac, when the sons came to bury the father. On this occasion, Jacob bought from Esau for a considerable sum his right to a burial place in the double cave of Machpelah, which Esau once more claimed at the funeral of his brother.[3]

Jacob and his family now settled at Shechem, where they prospered exceedingly. The Patriarch possessed over a million heads of cattle, and thousands of sheep-dogs. Some say that he had innumerable sheep and 600,000 sheep-dogs. He was not allowed, however, to end his days in peace at Shechem.

[1] Midrash Abkhir, quoted in Yalkut Shimeoni; Genesis Rabba, 78; Hullin, 91a.
[2] Sabbath, 30a; Genesis Rabba, 78; Midrash Tanchuma, section Wayishlach; cf. Midrash Haggadol, col. 517; Pirke de Rabbi Eliezer, Ch. 37.
[3] Sepher Hajashar; Tractate Sopherim, 21, 8.

His daughter Dinah was dishonoured by Shechem, the son of Hamor, and subsequently gave birth to a daughter who received the name of Asenath.

Jacob was greatly worried on account of this illegitimate child. Seeing that his sons hated her and wished to kill her, he wrote her name and the name of his family upon a gold plate, placed it on her neck and sent her away. Thereupon the angel Michael came down and led her to the frontier of Egypt. Potiphar, the captain of Pharaoh's guard, found her. As his wife Zuleika was barren, he adopted the baby and brought her up.[1] She subsequently married Joseph.

Sometime afterwards news was brought to Jacob that his mother Rebekah had died. Rebekah, at her own request, was buried very quietly at night, so that no one was present at her funeral. The reason of her request was that Jacob was away and only Esau near. People, thought the dying mother, would point to her son and say: " Here is the bier of the woman who bore the wicked Esau." [2] The clouds alone shed tears upon the mother's grave, and the night wind sighed and sobbed.

Jacob now decided to go and visit his old father Isaac at Hebron. On the road to Ephrath, Rachel died and was buried there. A prophetic vision had come over the Patriarch, and he knew that one day his descendants would be driven into captivity along that road. " When my children will pass this way," thought the Patriarch, " crying and lamenting, they will need Rachel's intercession. In her tomb she will hear their cries, implore the Lord's mercy and plead for the restoration of Israel."[3]

When he returned from Hebron, and again settled in Shechem, Jacob once more had to wage a long and terrible war against the princes of Canaan who were jealous of his

---

[1] *Midrash Abkhir*, quoted in *Yalkut Shimeoni*, § 146: see also *Sepher Rasiel*, p. 7*a*; *Pirke de Rabbi Eliezer*, Ch. 38.

[2] *Genesis Rabba*, 81: see Lewner, *loc. cit.*, pp. 166–167.

[3] *Yalkut Shimeoni*; *Genesis Rabba*, 82; *Midrash Agadah* to *Genesis*, 35, 19; *Midrash Threni*, § 25: see Lewner, *loc. cit.*, pp. 167–168.

power and prosperity. A long and weary war it was, wherein the sons of Jacob, and particularly Judah, gave proofs of their courage, bravery, and strength. Esau, too, was still brooding mischief and waiting for an opportunity to fall upon his brother. When he heard that Leah had died and that his brother and his sons were mourning their loss, he thought the moment propitious to carry out his plan. He came with a great army and attacked Jacob. In vain did the latter plead from the wall of his fortress, and not until Judah had hit Esau in his right loin with an arrow, did the latter's followers draw back. The greatest blow, however, came to the fond father when he suddenly lost his beloved son Joseph.[1]

[1] Cf. also for the entire chapter, Bin Gorion, *Die Sagen der Juden*, Vol. II, notes on pp. 430–432, sections XXXV–XLIV.

BIBLIOGRAPHY

I. WORKS IN HEBREW

Abot di Rabbi Nathan, ed. Schechter, Vienna, 1887.
Agadath Bereshith, ed. Buber, Cracow, 1903.
Alphabetum Siracidis, ed. Steinschneider, Berlin, 1858.
Bachja ben Asher, *Commentary to the Pentateuch*, Venice, 1549.
Ein Jacob, by Jacob Ibn Habib, Vilna.
Emek Hamelekh, Amsterdam, 1653.
Gedullath Moshe, Amsterdam, 1754.
Horovitz, Ch. M., *Agada Agadoth*, Berlin, 1881.
Jellinek, A., *Beth-Hamidrash*, 6 vols., Leipzig and Vienna, 1853-77.
Josippon (Josephus Gorionides), ed. Breithaupt, Halle, 1707; ed. Amsterdam, 1771.
Kalonymos ben Kalonymos, *Iggeret Baale Hayyim*, transl. by Julius Landsberger, 1882.
Kol Bo (*Sepher Halikkutim*), Venice, 1547.
Levita, Elia, *Tishbi*, Isny, 1541.
Luria, Isaac, *Sepher Hagilgulim*, Frankfurt a/M., 1684.
Menachem Recanati, *Commentary to the Pentateuch*, Venice 1545.
Menorath ha-Maor, Mantua, 1563.
Midrash Agada, ed. Buber, Vienna, 1894.
Midrash Bamidbar Rabba (*Numbers Rabba*).
Midrash Bereshith Rabba (*Genesis Rabba*).
Midrash Debarim Rabba (*Deuteronomy Rabba*).
Midrash Haggadol, ed. Schechter, Cambridge, 1902.
Midrash Koheleth Rabba (*Eccles. Rabba*).
Midrash Lekach Tob, ed. Buber, Vilna, 1884.
Midrash Shemuel (Samuel), ed. Buber, Cracow, 1893.
Midrash Shemoth Rabba (*Exodus Rabba*).
Midrash Shir Hashirim (*Song of Songs*).
Midrash Tanchuma (also called *Jelamdenu*), 1865.
Midrash Tanchuma, ed. Buber, 1865.
Midrash Tehillim, or *Shokher Tob*, ed. Buber, Vilna, 1891.
Nachmanides, *Commentary to the Pentateuch*, 1831.
Othioth de Rabbi Akiba, Venice, 1546.
Pirke de Rabbi Eliezer, Venice, 1544; and Lemberg, 1867.

Seder Olam Rabba, Vilna, 1897.
Sepher Hajashar, Prague, 1840. (French translation in Migne, *Dictionnaire des Apocryphes*, vol. 2.)
Sepher Rasiel, Amsterdam, 1700.
Shalsheleth Hakabbalah, by Gedalja Ibn Jachia, ed. Amsterdam, 1697.
Talmud Babli (Babylonian Talmud).

The Babylonian Talmud is classified under six orders or series:

I. *Seder Zeraim* (Seeds).
II. *Seder Moed* (Festivals).
III. *Seder Nashim* (Women).
IV. *Seder Nezikin* (Injuries).
V. *Seder Kodashin* (Holy Things).
VI. *Seder Taharot* (Purifications).

These sections, or *sedarim*, are divided into treatises or tractates (Massictot) of which there are seventy-one in all, including the minor treatises. Their order is as follows:

I. *Seder Zeraim.*

1. *Berachoth* (Blessings).
2. *Peah* (Corner).
3. *Demai* (Doubtful).
4. *Kilaiyim* (Heterogeneous).
5. *Shebiith* (Sabbatical Year).
6. *Terumot* (Offerings).
7. *Maaserot* (Tithes).
8. *Maaser Sheni* (Second Tithe).
9. *Hallah* (Cake).
10. *Orlah* (Foreskin of the trees).
11. *Bikkurim* (First Fruits).

II. *Moed.*

1. *Shabbat* (Sabbath).
2. *Erubin* (Mingling).
3. *Pesachim* (Passover Festivals).
4. *Bezah* (Egg).
5. *Hagigah* (Feasting).
6. *Moed Katan* (Half Feasts).
7. *Rosh-ha-Shanah* (New Year).
8. *Taanit* (Fasting).
9. *Yoma* (Day).
10. *Succah* (Booth).
11. *Shekalim* (Shekels).
12. *Megillah* (Esther Scroll).

III. *Nashim.*

1. *Yebamot* (Widows who are obliged to contract a Levirate marriage.)
2. *Ketubot* (Marriage Contracts).

3. *Kiddushin* (Betrothal).
4. *Gittin* (Documents).
5. *Nedarim* (Vows).
6. *Nazir* (Nazarite).
7. *Sotah* (Woman suspected of adultery).

IV. *Nezikin.*

1. *Baba Kamma* (First Gate).
2. *Baba Mezia* (Middle Gate).
3. *Baba Batra* (Last Gate).
4. *Abodah Zarah* (Idolatrous Worship).
5. *Sanhedrin* (Court of Law).
6. *Makkot* (Blows).
7. *Shebuot* (Oaths).
8. *Horayot* (Decisions).
9. *Eduyot* (Evidence).
10. *Abot*, or *Pirke Abot* (Sayings of the Fathers).

V. *Kodashin.*

1. *Zebahim* (Sacrifice).
2. *Menahot* (Meat Offerings).
3. *Bekorot* (First Born).
4. *Hullin* (Profane slaughtering of non-consecrated animals).
5. *Arakin* (Estimations).
6. *Temurah* (Exchange).
7. *Keritot* (Extirpations).
8. *Meilah* (Trespass).
9. *Kinnim* (Birds' Nests).
10. *Tamid* (Daily morning and evening burnt offering).
11. *Middot* (Measures).

VI. *Taharot.*

1. *Niddah* (Menstruous woman).
2. *Kelim* (Utensils).
3. *Oholot* (Tents).
4. *Negaïm* (Leprosy).
5. *Parah* (Red Heifer).
6. *Taharot* (Purities).
7. *Mikvaot* (Ritual Baths).
8. *Makshirin* (Predisposings).
9. *Zabim* (Sufferers from discharges).
10. *Tebulyom* (Ablutions of the day).
11. *Yadayim* (Hands).
12. *Okatzin* (Stalks).

In the editions of the Talmud after Abot usually follow Abot de Rabbi Nathan and the other minor treatises: *Sopherim* (Scribes); *Ebel Rabbati* (Great Mourning); also called *Semakhot* (Joy); *Kallah* (The Bride);

Derekh Eretz (The Way of the World); *Perek Hashalom* (A chapter on Peace);
Gerim (Proselytes); *Cuthim* (Cuthites); *Abadim* (Slaves).

Talmud Jerushalmi (Palestinian Talmud) Jitomir, 1860 – 1867 (Schwab's
transl., Paris, 1883–1889.)
Tana debe Eliahu, also called *Seder Eliahu Rabba*, ed. Friedmann, 1902.
Targum Jerushalmi (Palestinian Targum).
Wertheimer, S. A., *Bathe Midrashot*, Jerusalem, 1893.
Yalkut, also called *Yalkut Shimeoni*, Vilna, 1898.
Yalkut Reubeni, 1680.

II. OTHER WORKS

Abulfeda, *Historia Ante-Islamica*, ed. Fleischer, Leipzig, 1831.
Bacher, W., *Die Agada der Palestinensischen Amoräer*, 3 vols., 1892-1899.
——*Die Agada der Tanaiten*, 2 vols., 1884–1899.
Bartolocci, *Bibliotheca Magna Rabbinica*, 4 vols., Romae, 1675–1693.
Basnage, J., *Histoire des Juifs*, 15 vols., La Haye, 1716.
Beer, *Das Leben Abrahams*, Leipzig, 1859.
Bergel, J., *Mythologie der alten Hebräer*, 2 vols., Leipzig, 1882.
Bezold, C., *Die Schatzhöhle* (*The Cave of Treasures*), 1885.
Bin Gorion, *Die Sagen der Juden*, Vol. I, 1919.
Bischoff, E., *Babylonisch-Astrales, Ein Weltbild des Talmud und Midrash*,
Leipzig, 1907.
——*Die Elemente der Kabbalah*, 2 vols., Berlin, 1913.
Braun, J., *Naturgeschichte der Sage*, 2 vols., Leipzig, 1864–1865.
Bundehesh, The, transl. by West (Sacred Books of the East, Vol. V.).
Buxtorf, J., *Synagoga Judaica*, 1604.
Calmet, Dom Augustin, *Dictionary of the Holy Bible*, 5 vols., London, 1830.
Cassel, P., *Der Phœnix u. seine Aera*, Berlin.
Cedrenus, G., (in *Byzantinæ Hist. Scriptores*, ed. Paris, 1645–1711).
Charles, R. H., *The Book of Enoch*, Oxford, 1893.
—— *The Book of Jubilees*, Oxford, 1895, London, 1917.
—— *The Testaments of the Twelve Patriarchs*, Oxford, 1908. (See Trans-
lations of Early Documents, I, 5, London, 1917).
Charles and Morfill, *The Secrets of Enoch*.
Collin de Plancy, *Légendes de l'Ancien Testament*, Paris, 1861.
Edersheim, A., *The Life and Times of Jesus the Messiah*, 2 vols., London,
1883.
Eisenmenger, J. A., *Entdecktes Judentum*, 2 vols., 1700.
Eutychius, *Annales* (Chaplet of Pearls), Oxford, 1658.
Expository Times, The, 1895.
Fabricius, J. A., *Codex Pseudoepigraphicus, Vet. Test.*, 1722–1723.
Fleck, F. F., *Wissenschaftliche Reise durch d. südl. Deutschland*, Leipzig
1835–1838.
Frank, A., *La Kabbale*, Paris, 1843.
Frankels' Zeitschrift, 1846.
Friedlaender, G., *Pirke de Rabbi Eliezer*, London, 1916.
Fuchs, *Das Leben Adams und Evas* (in Kautzsch, *Apokryphen und Pseudoepi-
graphen* Vol. II.)

Gaster, M., *The Chronicles of Jerahmeel*, London, 1899.
—— *Roumanian Bird and Beast Stories*, London, 1915.
Gesta Romanorum, ed. Oesterley, Berlin, 1882.
Geiger, A., *Was hat Mohammed aus dem Judentum genommen*, Bonn, 1833.
Ginzberg, L., *Die Haggada bei den Kirchenvätern*, Berlin, 1900.
Görres, J., *Mythen-geschichte der asiatischen Welt*, 1810.
Graesse, J. G. T., *Gesta Romanorum*, Leipzig, 1905.
Grünbaum, M., *Gesammelte Aufsätze zur Sprache und Sagenkunde*, Berlin, 1901. (See also *Zeitschrift der Deutsch-Morgenländischen Gesellschaft*, Vol. 31).
—— *Neue Beiträge zur semistischen Sagenkunde*, Berlin, 1893.
Gunter, H., *Die Christliche Legende des Abendlandes*, 1910.
Hamburger, J., *Real-encyclopädie für Bibel und Talmud*, 5 vols., 1870–1892.
Hastings, *Dictionary of the Bible*, 5 vols., Edinburgh, 1898.
Herbelot de Molainville, *Bibliothèque Orientale*, 6 vols., Paris, 1781–1783.
Hershon, P. I., *Treasures of the Talmud*, London, 1882.
—— *A Talmudic Miscellany*, London, 1880.
James, M. R., *The Testament of Abraham* (in Robinson's *Texts and Studies*, Cambridge, 1892).
Jastrow, M., *Dictionary of the Targumim*, 2 vols., 1895.
Jeremias, A., *Das alte Testament im Lichte des alten Orients*, 1904.
Jewish Quarterly Review, Tomes VII, XI.
Journal of the Royal Asiatic Society, 1893.
Josephus, *Antiquities* (Whiston's).
Kautzsch, E., *Die Apokryphen und Pseudoepigraphen d. A. T.*, 2 vols, 1900.
Kazwini, *Cosmography* (Ethés' transl.).
Kohut, A., *Zur jüdischen Angelologie und Demonologie* (*Abhandlungen der D. M. G.*, 1886).
Koran, The.
Landesberger, J., *Iggeret Baale Hayyim*, 1882.
Lenormant, F., *Les Origines de l'Histoire*, 2 vols., Paris, 1882.
Mackenzie, D. A., *Indian Myth and Legend*, London.
Mahabharata, The (Roy's transl.).
Malan, S. C., *The Book of Adam and Eve*, London, 1882.
Meyer, W., *Vita Adae et Evae* (in *Abhandlungen der bayrischen Akademie der Wissenschaften*, Phil.-philosoph. Classe, XIV, 3, 1878).
Monatsschrift für Literatur und Wissenschaft des Judentums, vol. 43.
Proceedings of the Society of Biblical Archæology, Vol. 9.
Raymondus Martinus, *Pugio Fidei*, ed. Leipzig.
Robinson, *Texts and Studies*, Cambridge, 1892.
Rothschild, J. de (ed.), *Le Mistère du Viel Testament*, 6 vols., Paris, 1877.
Suidas, *Lexicon*, ed. 1854.
Tabari, *Chronique de*, by H. Zotenberg, Paris, 1867–1874.
Tischendorff, *Apocalypses Apocryphae*, 1866.
Tisdall, W. St. Clair, *The Original Sources of the Quran*, London, 1905.
Weil, G., *Biblische Legenden der Muselmänner*, Frankfurt a/M., 1845.
Zeitschrift der Deutsch-Morgenländischen Gesellschaft, Vols. 25 and 31.
Zeitschrift für Historische Theologie.

ANCIENT ISRAEL
Myths and Legends

Volume 2

ASENATH AND THE DIVINE MESSENGER
Page 114

Contents

VOLUME TWO

CHAPTER I

CHAPTER II

CHAPTER III

CHAPTER IV

CHAPTER V

CHAPTER VI

CHAPTER VII

CONTENTS

CONTENTS

CHAPTER XIX

CHAPTER XX

CHAPTER XXI

CHAPTER XXII

CHAPTER XXIII

CHAPTER XXIV

CHAPTER XXV

CHAPTER XXVI

CHAPTER XXVII

CHAPTER XXVIII

Plates

VOLUME TWO

PREFACE

In the first volume of this work the reader has been made acquainted with Jewish myths dealing with the origin of the world, angels and demons, paradise and hell, the creation of Adam and Eve, and also with some of the legends related of the Patriarchs Abraham and Isaac. The present volume deals exclusively with the legends clustering round Patriarchs, Prophets, and Priests, the friends and favourites of God, the Biblical personages like Jacob, Joseph, Moses, and Aaron. The reader is again introduced to the rich and abundant storehouse of Talmudical and post-Talmudical literature, to that vast legendary lore wherein the Jewish popular imagination has given full expression to its beliefs and ideals, its yearnings and hopes. Legendary lore, it must be remembered, is a branch of national literature; it is popular poetry, the poetic creation of the people, the anonymous work of the mind and soul of the people. The pious belief and the religious yearning of a people find their expression in the many legends clustering round the founder of the national religion and round the national heroes and saints.

Legendary lore has rightly been called the " religious heroic epic ", and the " popular religious philosophy of history ". Legends wander from generation to generation, from age to age, from nation to nation, and from country to country, but they always bear the traces of their origin, namely, the mind and soul of the *people*.

Israel has no saints in its history, but just as in the Christian legends the saints are glorified, and wonders are woven round their lives, so in the Jewish legends, too, the pious, the faithful servants of God, are endowed with supernatural gifts and are represented as supermen. Such supermen were the Patriarchs, were Joseph, Moses, and Aaron. For the sake of these pious men, the chosen of the Lord, His faithful servants and friends, the heavenly hosts are set in motion, the sun, the earth, and the constellations are bidden to alter their courses, time and space are reduced to relative values and conceptions, and the laws of nature are changed.

From the moment of his birth, nay, even long before it, to the day of his death, miracles innumerable are worked in favour of the pious man, miracles which tradition records and which the people delight in relating.

Created by the people, Jewish legends were handed down orally until the scholars and scribes, the Rabbis and preachers began to make use of them for the purpose of education and instruction. They collected the legends and tales, added new ones, and thus developed a popular and national literature which they infused with a spirit of grandeur and sublimity. By means of such legends and tales they managed to rivet the attention of their audiences, of the uneducated public, and were able to convey to them many moral lessons. The legends and tales served to point a moral and to adorn their discourses. The Rabbis and preachers, the scribes and scholars collected and edited the legends, and vast compilations were handed down to future generations. From this legendary lore the people could henceforth draw religious edification, moral instruction, consolation in days of oppression, and confidence in the Almighty in the hours of distress.

As in the first volume of this work so also in the present one comparative evidence has been provided, and the reader's attention has constantly been drawn to similar legends and tales related in oriental and European literature.

The comparison between Jewish and non-Jewish sources
(as pointed out in the Introduction to Vol. I) makes it clear that
whilst the Jewish legends bear traces of Egyptian, Indian,
Persian, and Mohammedan influences, the Jews, in their turn,
influenced Mohammedan tradition and Mediæval Christian
legendary lore.

Although the entire work is intended for the general reader,
we have everywhere indicated the original sources of the
legends and tales collected. We hope that these indications will
prove very useful to the more serious students.

ANGELO S. RAPPOPORT.

MYTH AND LEGEND
OF ANCIENT ISRAEL

VOLUME II

CHAPTER I

The Coat of Many Colours

The birth of a son—Joseph's ravishing beauty—The history of the son a repetition of that of his father—Joseph pays attention to his personal appearance—His talebearing—The brethren amputate the limb of a sick animal—Jacob sends for his sons and gives them instructions with regard to their conduct—The hatred of the brethren—The coat of many colours—*Passim*—The meaning of the initial letters—Joseph's dreams—He begs his brethren to listen to his dreams and interpret them—The Patriarch rebukes his son, but inscribes the dream in his book of records—Joseph in search of his brethren—A father's regret—The fatal place of Shechem—The meeting with an angel—Brethren prepare to set the dogs on their brother—Reuben's pleading and advice—Reuben's real intention—Cast into the pit—The violence of a brother and the forgiving spirit of another—In the depths of the pit—The snakes and scorpions creep away and hide in the holes of the pit—A cry for mercy—Grace after a meal—Judah's speech—Ishmaelites and Midianites—Preparing for battle—The rebellious slave—The bargain—A pair of shoes—The miraculous garment—An amulet extended by the angel Gabriel—The regret of the merchant-men—The pleasant scent of the merchandise carried by the traders—Sudden darkness.

Jacob's hope to enjoy life in tranquillity and to end his days in peace in his native land was frustrated. The loss of his beloved and favourite son Joseph was a terrible blow to the old man. He loved Joseph because he reminded him of his dear and never-to-be-forgotten wife, the beautiful Rachel. For six years Rachel had remained barren, and only in the

1

seventh year after her marriage, in the month of Tishri, the Lord remembered her, and her dearest wish was at last realized. On the first day of the month of Tammuz, in the year 2199, after the creation of the world, Rachel gave birth to a son. She called him Joseph, which means the increaser. The son had inherited the ravishing beauty of the mother, but he resembled also the father more than any of the brothers. Not only in appearance, however, did Joseph resemble his father Jacob, his whole history and the course of his life were a repetition of those of Jacob.

As Jacob's mother had remained barren for a long time, giving birth afterwards to the sons, so also did the mother of Joseph. Like Rebekah, Rachel, too, suffered great pains in giving birth to her son. Both the father and the son, although not the first-born, obtained the birthright. Jacob was hated by his brother Esau, and Joseph, in his turn, was hated by his brethren. Both the father and the son travelled to a foreign country, accompanied by protecting angels, and lived and died in a strange land, among strangers. Both the father and the son served masters who were blessed and prospered exceedingly on their account. But although father and son lived in a foreign country, their remains were carried to the Holy Land where they were buried. Jacob had undergone hardship and served a master for the sake of a woman, and it was a woman who was the cause of many of Joseph's sufferings.

Joseph was only eight years old when his mother died, but he found a foster-mother in the kind-hearted and noble Bilhah, his mother's handmaid, who lavished her love upon the handsome orphan, and treated him as if he were her own son.

Until his seventeenth year Joseph frequented the schools of learning, and his father imparted to him all the knowledge he himself had received from his distinguished masters Shem and Eber.

It was a great joy for the father, when he saw how eager and anxious the boy was to study and to acquire instruction. And yet, in many ways, Joseph was boyish. He, the young scholar, paid great attention to his personal appearance, dressed his hair, endeavoured to give his eyes a beautiful expression, and always walked with a light delicate step.

Although he acknowledged and frequently paid homage to the bravery and merits of his brethren, he nevertheless thought himself superior to his brethren. He was the favourite son of his father, and he knew it, but he was also a favourite with the sons of the handmaids who loved him. He acquired the habit of bearing tales to his father concerning the conduct of his brethren. His excuse was that the tales he bore to his father were not the result of his wish to calumniate his brethren, but so as to make his father preach to them and urge them to mend their ways. Indeed, feeling himself superior to his brethren in knowledge, Joseph often offered them counsel and tried to make them abandon their ways. In his zeal, however, he went too far.

Thus he informed his father that his brethren were paying little attention to the herds and were guilty of cruelty to the flock, tearing the limbs from living animals and eating the flesh. This charge was somewhat exaggerated, for indeed Joseph's brethren always observed the rules of the ritual and always slaughtered the animals before partaking of the flesh. One day Gad, who was keeping watch over the herd, snatched a kid from the jaws of a bear, and as the animal could no longer be kept alive, he slaughtered it. Sometimes also Joseph's brethren amputated the limb of a sick animal, so as to make it sound, a remedy often employed by the Arabs. For his exaggerated zeal and the tales he bore to his father, Joseph paid dearly and was punished. It is almost an irony of fate when one remembers that the kid into the blood of which Joseph's coat was dipped had not been cruelly tortured and slain, but killed according to the ritual prevalent among the sons of Jacob.

In his exaggerated sense of justice, the lad had charged his brethren with slighting the sons of the handmaids and treating them as slaves. He was punished for this too, for he was sold as a slave to Potiphar, and was very unhappy on account of the amorous advances of his mistress.

Soon Joseph's brethren learned of their brother's tale-bearing. One day Jacob sent one of his servants to call his sons from the fields. When they appeared in his presence the Patriarch thus addressed them: " My dear sons, I am growing old, and I know not when it will please the Lord to call me unto Himself. Hearken therefore unto my words. When I am dead and gone ye will inherit all my earthly possessions, my goods and chattels, my fields and vineyards, my sheep and cattle, my gold and silver. Ye will be very wealthy. Beware, however, my dear sons, of pride. Treat your step-brethren, the sons of the handmaids, Bilhah, and Zilpah, as your equals and your brothers, for you are all the sons of one father. Remember these my words, when I am no longer among you. Whenever ye eat meat, take care to slaughter the animals according to our ritual and do not let the animal suffer too much, for God hates those who are guilty of cruelty to animals. God, in His mercy, loves those who are kind and merciful to His creatures."

Thus spake Jacob, and his sons promised to take his words to heart. When they left their father's presence, however, they wondered greatly at the cause of his speech.

" Heaven grant our dear father long life," they said; " we hope that he will remain in our midst for many, many years, but it is rather surprising that he should have called us suddenly, without waiting for our return, and spoken to us as he did. Someone must have slandered us and borne tales to our father."

" Indeed, such is the case," said one of their slaves; " I have heard your brother Joseph one day charging you with cruelty to the animals and accusing you of slighting the sons of the handmaids."

When the sons of Jacob heard these words, they waxed wroth against Joseph and hated him. Their hatred increased when they noticed how Jacob constantly distinguished Joseph among his children, and saw the many tokens of their father's great love for the lad.

Among the tokens of Jacob's love for Joseph was a beautiful and costly coat of many colours, light and delicate, wonderful to behold. It was so light and of so fine a texture that it could be concealed in the palm of the hand. In Hebrew the garment was called *Passim*, and was symbolical of Joseph's subsequent fate. The four Hebrew letters constituting the word *Passim* (*P.S.I.M.*) were the initials of *Potiphar*, Joseph's master; *Socharim*, or merchantmen who bought the lad from the Ishmaelites; *Ishmaelites*, to whom he was sold, and *Medanites*, who obtained him from the Ishmaelites. *Passim* also means in Hebrew pieces and clefts, and in a prophetic vision Joseph's brethren foresaw that in days to come the Red Sea would be cleft in twain on account of Joseph's merits. The love of their father and the future glory of Joseph were cause enough to make the sons of Jacob hate their brother. Their hatred, however, was frank and open. They were fierce and cruel, these sons of Jacob, and were good haters, but there was nothing sneaky about them. They hated their brother, and he knew it, for openly they told him so. Joseph's dreams, which he never hesitated to communicate to his brothers, added fuel to their rage and increased their hatred. Joseph knew that his brothers hated him, but he nevertheless told them his dreams, so that they might interpret them, for a dream which is not interpreted is like an unread letter.

One day, when all the sons of Jacob were assembled together, Joseph thus addressed his brethren:

" As your prophets will one day beg your descendants to
listen to the word of God, so do I beg you now to give ear to
my words, and to interpret for me the dream sent to me by
God. In my dream, behold, we were all gathering fruit; your
fruit rotted, whilst mine remained sound."

The brothers knew well enough the meaning of the dream,
and that Joseph was destined for great things in the future,
that he would have power and dominion over them, but they
pretended that they knew not the interpretation of his dream
and gave it not. And yet they clearly showed what was in their
minds, when, swayed by envy and jealousy, they mockingly
replied: " Shalt thou really have dominion over us and reign
over us?"

Thus the Lord had put the right interpretation into their
mouths, and it was verified in the future in Joseph himself and
in his posterity, for kings and judges were among the descendants of Joseph and ruled over Israel.

Joseph told his dream also to his father, and the latter
kissed and blessed his son, for he knew that the dream would
come true.

Soon Joseph had another dream. He saw the sun, the
moon, and eleven stars bowing to him. He told his dream to
his father, and the latter was greatly rejoiced. Jacob knew that
the sun stood for himself, for when he had passed the night
upon the site of the Temple, he had heard the angels exclaim:
" The sun hath come." The moon stood for Joseph's mother,
and the stars for the brothers.

Jacob only wondered in his mind how Joseph knew that
he (Jacob) was called the Sun. He was greatly rejoiced, convinced as he was of the truth of his son's dream. In order,
however, to lessen the bad impression Joseph's dream would
produce upon his brethren, and in order to avert their envy
and hatred, Jacob rebuked his son, when the latter repeated
his dream to his brethren. In that tone of reproof in which

one day the Israelites were to forbid their prophets to speak
the truth, Jacob said to his son: " What is this dream that
thou hast dreamed? Will the resurrection of the dead take
place in our days, so that thy mother, who is dead, will rise
and return to earth?" The Patriarch did not know that the
moon stood for Joseph's foster-mother Bilhah, who had brought
him up. But even whilst he rebuked his son, Jacob had put the
right interpretation upon Joseph's dream, and the brethren
knew that it would one day be realized. Their hatred of Joseph
therefore increased. Jacob himself took his book of records
and therein inscribed all the circumstances of his son's dream,
the day, the hour, and the place, for the prophetic spirit called
his attention to these things which would surely come to
pass.

One day the brethren had led their flocks to the pasture
grounds of Shechem, where they intended to enjoy themselves
and to feed on the cattle of their father. As they were away
for a long time and no news of their whereabouts had reached
Jacob, he grew anxious about their fate. He feared that the
Hivites might have attacked them to wreak revenge for the
slaughter of Hamor and the inhabitants of Shechem.

He therefore decided to send Joseph out to find his brethren
and bring him word whether all was well with them, and also
to let him know about the flocks. Joseph knew that his brethren
hated him, and that he was exposed to danger in visiting them,
but, dutiful son that he was, he declared himself ready to do
his father's bidding. In later days Jacob remembered this
willingness of his son to obey his command, and his remorse
greatly increased his suffering. " My poor son," he would say,
" I knew that the brothers hated thee, and yet I let thee go out,
and thou, too, in filial reverence never didst demur."

" Go now," said the Patriarch to his favourite son, " and
find out whether all is well with thy brethren and with the
herds, and send me word. Travel only by daylight, for it is

right that one should enter and leave a place only by day, after the sun has risen and before it has set."

Joseph arrived safely at the fateful place of Shechem. Fateful indeed, and a place of ill omen the place of Shechem has always been to Jacob and to his descendants. It was at Shechem that Dinah was dishonoured by the son of Hamor; it was in the neighbourhood of Shechem that Joseph was cast into the pit and sold as a slave; and it was at Shechem where, in later days, the rebellion of Jeroboam took place, a great misfortune to the house of David. Not finding his brethren at the pasturing place of Shechem, Joseph continued his way, but lost himself in the wilderness. Three angels in human shape and form appeared to the lad, and one of them, the angel Gabriel, asked him what he was seeking. When Gabriel heard that Joseph was seeking his brethren, he replied: " Thy brethren have left this place, and in leaving it they have also given up the divine virtues which men should imitate: the virtues of brotherly love, kindness, and mercy. I have learned from behind the curtain " (*Pargod*) " that from to-day the Egyptian bondage of the Israelites will begin. Thy brethren have also had a prophetic vision that the Hivites would make war upon them. They have therefore left for the pasturing grounds of Dothan." And to Dothan Gabriel led Joseph.

From a distance Joseph's brethren saw him coming and prepared to set the dogs on him that would tear him to pieces.

Simeon and Levi, constant companions in deeds of violence, said: " Behold, the master of dreams cometh; let us slay him and see what becometh of his dreams."

But the Lord said: " Ye say, let us slay him, but I say, let us see what will become of his dreams, and the future will show whose word will prevail."

Reuben, however, when he learned the evil design of his brethren, did his best to dissuade them from their plan, and interceded on behalf of Joseph. He knew that, as the eldest brother, he would be held responsible by the father for Joseph's fate. He was also grateful to Joseph who, in spite of Reuben's disrespectful behaviour to his father, a conduct which made him feel unworthy of being a son of Jacob, nevertheless behaved respectfully to him. Reuben, therefore, did his best to restrain his brethren from their evil design, and attempted to save Joseph. Although Reuben's plan was frustrated, his intention was good, and his reward was that in later days Bezer—the first city of refuge, where those who were innocent of a crime they were charged with found shelter—was situated in the allotment of the tribe of Reuben. Eloquently did Reuben plead for Joseph, and thus he spoke:

" It is a heinous enterprise, my dear brethren, you are going about, and its nature is very horrid. Your action will appear wicked in the sight of God and impious before men. It is a sin to kill one even not related to us, but much more detestable is it to slay one's own brother. Have regard, my brethren, to your own consciences, and consider what mischief will betide ye upon the death of so good a child and your own brother. Fear God, who is both a witness and a spectator of the designs ye have against your brother. God will love ye if ye abstain from this act and yield to repentance and amendment, but, if ye proceed to do what ye have in mind, all sorts of punishments will overtake ye from God for this murder of your brother. Ye will be polluting God's providence which is present everywhere, and which does not overlook what is done, either in deserts or in cities, for wheresoever a man is, there ought he to suppose God is also. Your own consciences, my brethren, will be your enemies, if ye attempt to go through so wicked an enterprise. And even if the lad had injured ye, it would not be right to kill him, but rather forgive him and forget his actions even in things in which he might seem to have offended. But ye are going to kill your brother Joseph who is guilty of nothing that is really ill towards you. His young age, too, ought to move ye to mercy and pity. But, I know, that it is out of envy of Joseph's future prosperity that ye are determined to do away with him, and therefore the anger of God will be more severe upon ye. Ye will have slain one whom God has judged worthy of that prosperity, whilst by murdering the lad ye will make it impossible for God to bestow such prosperity upon him." Thus spoke Reuben, endeavouring to divert his brethren from the murder of their brother.

When Reuben, however, saw that his pleading was in vain, he begged his brethren to follow his advice in so far at least, as not to shed blood, but to cast the brother into one of the pits. He gave them this advice in the hope of being able later on to draw the lad from the pit, and restore him to his father, unbeknown to the others. The brethren agreed to Reuben's proposition.

In the meantime Joseph, rejoiced at finding his brethren, and not suspecting the fate in store for him, approached.

The brethren fell upon the lad, beat him, tore his garment, the coat of many colours, from him, stripped him bare of his other clothes, and Simeon seized and threw him into one of the pits, empty of water, but full of snakes and scorpions. Empty indeed of water was the pit, as the hearts of Joseph's brethren were empty at that moment of charity, piety, and Divine Law, which is compared to water, and severely enjoins the punishment of those who steal souls.

Simeon, who was the most violent and fierce of the brothers, bade them even throw stones at their brother.

Joseph learned afterwards of Simeon's advice, but he forgave him. For when he detained him as a hostage in Egypt, he treated him so well and provided him with such excellent food that he grew fat and looked like a leather-bottle. Such was the charitable and forgiving nature of Joseph.

When he was in the depths of the pit, surrounded by reptiles, a great terror seized the lad. But the snakes and scorpions did him no harm, for the Lord heard his cries, and the reptiles crept into the holes of the pit. In an agony of terror Joseph appealed to his brethren, and in cries of distress he begged them to have mercy upon him.

" My brethren," cried the poor and agonized lad, " what have I done unto you, and what is my transgression? Am I not flesh of your flesh and bone of your bone? Is not Jacob, your father, also my father? Are you not afraid to sin before God, in treating me so cruelly? What may be the cause of your action and how will you be able and have the courage to lift your countenances before our father Jacob?"

Thus cried Joseph and pleaded, but the brethren paid no heed to his cries.

" Judah, Reuben, Simeon, and Levi, my brothers," again cried Joseph, weeping bitterly, " have mercy upon me and deliver me from this terrible place, the pit into which ye have cast me. If I have sinned against you, you are the children of Abraham, Isaac, and Jacob, the generous men who always had compassion with orphans, fed the hungry and clothed the naked, never allowing the needy to go away empty-handed from their doors. Will you, their descendants, withhold pity and compassion from your own brother? For the sake of our father, listen to my prayers and have pity, although I may have sinned against you. If my father only knew how my brethren have spoken to me and how they are treating me!"

Thus wailed Joseph, but no heed did his brethren pay to his weeping. Afraid, however, that the lad's pitiful cries might at last move them to compassion, they left the pit and sat down at the distance of a bowshot.

They sat down to a meal, deliberating all the time whether to slay Joseph or restore him to his father. Almost unanimously they decided to fetch their brother from the pit into which they had cast him and to slay him, but before executing their design they attempted to say grace after their meal.

Judah, however, who had already on several occasions made his influence felt among the brethren, being their chief and king, arose and thus he spoke: " My brethren, we are going to commit the crime of fratricide, and yet we would bless God and are about to thank Him for what we have received. Are we not like the robber who blasphemes the Eternal even whilst he is praying?" (*Prov.* 10, 3). " What will it profit us if we slay our brother? Will not the punishment of God descend upon us? Hearken, therefore, to my words and to the good counsel I have to give you. Yonder do I see a caravan of Ishmaelites on their way to Egypt; let us follow the precedent established in the days by gone, when Canaan, the son of Ham, was cursed and made a slave, on account of his wicked deeds. Let our hand not be upon our brother, but let us sell him to the Ishmaelites who will carry him off to the end of the desert, where he will be lost among the people of the earth, and our father will never hear of him and his whereabouts." Thus spoke Judah, and the brethren agreed to sell Joseph into slavery.

But the Lord said: " At a meal ye sold your brother as a slave, and during a meal, in days to come, Haman will decree the destruction of your seed."

Before, however, the caravan of the Ishmaelites had approached, seven Midianitish merchantmen passed the pit wherein Joseph lay weeping and lamenting, and above which birds of prey were circling.

Being thirsty, looking for water, and assuming, on account of the birds they saw, that there was water in the pit, the Midianites halted in the hope of being able to refresh themselves. Suddenly they heard loud weeping and lamentations, and looking down into the pit beheld a comely youth of beautiful figure, stripped of his clothes.

"Who art thou?" asked the Midianites, "and who has cast thee into this pit?" Thereupon they dragged the lad up, took him along and continued their journey.

When they came near the brethren whom they had to pass, the latter exclaimed: "What right have ye to take along and carry off our slave whom we have thrown into the pit as a punishment for his disobedience? Return our slave immediately to us." Thus spoke the brethren of Joseph, but the Midianites only laughed at their words.

"We will pay no attention to your words," said the merchantmen, "for the lad is not your slave. His comely appearance and beautiful figure, by far excelling your own, proves the contrary, convincing us that more likely are you the slaves who have rebelled against your master. We found the lad in the pit and are going to take him along."

"If you do not immediately return to us our slave, you will feel the edge of our swords," threatened the brethren.

Their threats were of no avail, for the Midianites drew their swords and prepared for battle, uttering wild war whoops.

Thereupon Simeon jumped up, drew his sword and uttered a wild shout which resounded in the distance and caused the earth to tremble and reverberate. Terror seized the Midianites, when they heard that terrible voice, and in consternation they fell upon their countenances. And Simeon proceeded to address them: "I am Simeon, the son of Jacob the Hebrew. Alone and unaided, with my own hand, have I destroyed the town of Shechem, and together with my brethren have we annihilated the cities of the Amorites. If all your brethren, the Midianites, and all the kings of Canaan came to your assistance, you would never be able to hold out against me, for I am Simeon, the son of Jacob the Hebrew, whose name makes the inhabitants of Canaan quake. Now return our slave at once, or your flesh will soon be food for the birds of prey and the beasts of the fields."

Greatly frightened, the Midianites now spoke quite timidly: " Did ye not say that ye cast the lad into the pit on account of his disobedience and as a punishment for his conduct? What use is a rebellious slave to ye? Sell him rather to us who will pay you any price for him." The Midianites were anxious to buy Joseph on account of his comely appearance, but it was also the purpose of the Lord that they should buy him, so that the brethren might not slay him.

Having already made up their minds to sell their brother as a slave, the sons of Jacob accepted the offer of the merchant-men and sold them their brother for twenty pieces of silver.

The Midianites thus bought Joseph and carried him off, in spite of his prayers, his cries and lamentations. In vain did he implore his brethren to restore him to his father, begging them on his knees to have pity on him. The price of twenty silver pieces was very low, but the Midianites pointed out that the lad looked sickly and ill. The fear of the scorpions and snakes, and the terrible anguish the boy had endured in the pit, had driven all the blood from his face, and made him look ill and sickly indeed.

The brethren divided the twenty silver pieces among them, and each received just enough to buy himself a pair of shoes.

In days to come the Lord spoke through the mouth of his prophet, Amos. " For three transgressions and for four will I punish Israel; because they sold the righteous for silver, and the needy for a pair of shoes." (*Amos*, 2, 6.)

Now Joseph had been cast into the pit naked, for the brethren had stripped him of his clothes, and naked he would have had to travel with his masters, the Midianites. But the Lord would not suffer that such a pious and virtuous youth as Joseph should appear before men in such an unseemly condition. He therefore sent His angel Gabriel who extended an amulet suspended upon Joseph's neck, so that it became a garment covering the lad entirely. Scarcely had the brethren noticed that Joseph was clad, than they cried to the Midianites: " We sold you our slave naked and without any raiment; return therefore immediately his raiment unto us."

Joseph's new masters at first demurred and refused to comply with the request of the sons of Jacob, but they ultimately paid for the garment four pairs of shoes. Joseph was thus permitted to keep the garment made by an angelic hand, and wore it when he arrived in Egypt. He wore it as a slave, wore it in prison, appeared in it before Pharaoh, and wore it also when he ruled Egypt as Viceroy.

To Gilead the Midianites now journeyed, carrying their slave with them. On the way, however, they began to have some misgivings with regard to the statement made by the sons of Jacob. The latter's high-handed manner, the small price they had accepted, and their general conduct raised suspicions in the minds of the Midianites who feared that Joseph had been stolen. Afraid of being accused of man-theft, they were now anxious to get rid of the slave they had bought. They were pleased therefore when they suddenly beheld the company of Ishmaelites, whom the sons of Jacob had seen earlier in the day, and unanimously decided to sell the lad to the travelling company. Without losing the money they had paid for Joseph, they hoped to escape unpleasant consequences, should they be accused of man-theft. Thus Joseph quickly changed hands, the Ishmaelites buying him from the Midianites for twenty pieces of silver. Satisfied with their transaction, the Midianites continued their journey, whilst Joseph's new masters placed the lad upon one of their camels and journeyed to Egypt.

Now the merchandise the Ishmaelites were in the habit of carrying upon their camels were skins of beasts and pitch, unpleasant and ill-smelling, so that an ill smell also emanated from the merchantmen themselves. The Lord, however, had willed it that on this occasion the Ishmaelites, instead of such ill-smelling merchandise, had loaded their camels with aromatic substances and perfumery. Thus Joseph did not suffer from any unpleasant ill-smells wafted to him on his fateful journey to Egypt, but, on the contrary, inhaled the pleasant scent of perfumery and a sweet fragrance.

When the poor lad learned that his new masters were travelling to Egypt, and that he would thus be carried off so far away from his father in Canaan, he began to weep bitterly and to lament. One of Joseph's new masters, imagining that the cause of the lad's tears and lamentations was the discomfort he endured in riding upon the back of the camel, lifted him down and made him walk on foot. As the lad, however, continued to weep, unable to restrain his grief, the Ishmaelites began to beat him, and the more the lad wept the more cruelly they beat him, trying to silence him and to make him cease his wails and lamentations.

The Lord thereupon, seeing Joseph's distress, had pity upon him, and sent sudden darkness upon the men, so that they were seized with great terror, and their hands grew rigid whenever they raised them against the son of Jacob. Unaware that this was a punishment for their ill-treatment of Joseph, the men asked themselves in astonishment what this sudden darkness and terror could mean. They at last reached Ephrath, where Rachel, Joseph's mother, lay buried in her lonely grave.[1]

[1] Babylonian Talmud, *Rosh-hashana*, 11a; *Targum Pseudo-Jonathan, in loco*; *Genesis Rabba*, §§ 78, 84, 87, 91; *Midrash Tanchuma*, section *Vayesheb*; *Yalkut, Genesis* § 142 *Numbers Rabba*, § 14; *Midrash Lekach Tob, in loco*; *Book of Jubilees*, XXVIII; Josephus, *Antiquities*, II, 3; *Sepher Hajashar*; *Pirke de Rabbi Eliezer*, Ch. 38; Jellinek, *Beth-Hamidrash*, Vol. V, p. 157; Vol. VI, p. 120; Joseph Shabbethai Parhi, *Tokpo Shel Yosef*, Leghorn, 1846, see also Adolf Kurrein, *Traum und Wahrheit*, Regensburg, 1887; Lewner, *Kol-Agadoth*, Vol. I, pp. 186–194.

CHAPTER II

A Father's Grief

The remorse of the brethren—A solemn oath never to reveal the truth
—Reuben's return—His search for Joseph—His grief—Issachar's advice—
The torn coat—The blood of a lamb—A message to the father—The
Patriarch's grief—The mourning household—An unexpected visit from
Hebron—The blind Patriarch Isaac—The story of the speaking wolf—
The wolf's speech—A vague vision of the truth—The punishment of the
sons for having caused their father to rend his clothes—The torn covenant
—A faint hope—Isaac's knowledge of his grandson's whereabouts.

When the deed had been accomplished and Joseph carried
away, his brethren bitterly regretted their wicked deed. Their
hatred had abated, and they would gladly have undone the
past. It was too late, however, and they decided, binding one
another by a solemn oath, never to reveal the true state of affairs
to their father. In the meantime Reuben who had been absent,
having retired to the mountains to do penance, had returned.
According to another version he had gone home to wait upon
his father, as it was his day. He availed himself of the first
opportunity during the night to slip away to the pit with the
intention of dragging Joseph up and restoring him to his
father. He called the lad by name, but no answer came. Reuben
now feared that Joseph had died of anguish and fright or in
consequence of a snake bite. Hastily he let himself down into
the pit, but search as he might, there was no Joseph. He came
out of the pit, rent his clothes, in token of his great grief, and
hastened to rejoin his brethren whom he accused of the death
of Joseph. The brethren informed him of what had occurred;

17

how they had sold Joseph to a caravan of Midianites, and how they now greatly regretted their heinous deed.

" We must conceal the truth from our father," they said, " but we know not what plausible tale we could invent."

Issachar now proposed to tear Joseph's coat of many colours, dip it in the blood of a slaughtered lamb, as the blood of a lamb greatly resembles human blood, and send the coat to their father. The brethren agreed to Issachar's proposal, slew a lamb, dipped the coat of the unhappy Joseph in its blood, and sent it by the sons of the handmaids Bilhah and Zilpah to their father with the following message: " Pasturing our flocks, not far from Shechem, we found in the wilderness this garment covered with blood and dust."

It was a terrible blow to the Patriarch, when he recognized his favourite son's coat. Like a log he fell to the ground, remaining motionless in his great grief. Soon, however, he rose and gave vent to his sorrow in tears and lamentations. Jacob immediately dispatched one of his slaves to his sons, bidding them appear in his presence without delay.

In the evening the sons returned home, their clothes torn and ashes upon their heads in sign of mourning.

" Can ye explain the great misfortune which has befallen me to-day?" exclaimed Jacob. " Tell me everything and conceal nothing from me."

Thereupon the brethren related unto Jacob the story which they had made up beforehand.

" To-day," they said, " on the way leading to Shechem, in the wilderness, we found this coat, bloodstained and dusty. We recognized it at once as that belonging to our unhappy brother Joseph and sent it to thee, to see whether thou wouldst also recognize it."

" Alas," cried Jacob, " it is indeed the coat of my dear son, who has no doubt been devoured by a wild beast. I sent him this morning to see whether all was well with ye and also with the flocks, and to bring me word. Willingly he went to execute my command, and whilst I believed him safe in your midst this misfortune must have happened to him."

" He did not come to us," promptly lied the sons of Jacob, " and ever since we left thee have we neither heard from Joseph nor seen him."

When Jacob heard these words he broke out into fresh lamentations. He rent his garments, put on sackcloth and strewed ashes upon his head. Desperately he bewailed the untimely and violent death of his beloved son.

" Joseph, my son! My son Joseph," he cried, amidst tears, " I am the cause of thy death. How sweet was thy life unto me, but, oh, how bitter is thy death. How I suffer on account of thy death. It were a thousand times better that I had died in thy stead. Come back, my son, come back to me. Where art thou, Joseph? Where is thy soul? Come and count my tears and be a witness of my affliction; count the tears which are flowing from thy unhappy father's eyes. Gather them and bring them before the Throne of Glory, so that the Eternal may avert His wrath from us. Why didst thou die a death which should not have befallen a son of Adam? Thou didst fall a victim to a cruel and relentless enemy. I know, alas, that it is on account of my many sins that my beloved child has been taken from me. But it was God who gave me my darling son, and it is He who has taken him from me, and whatever the Lord doeth is well done and for the best."

Thus wept and lamented the unhappy and bereaved Patriarch.

When the sons of Jacob saw the great grief of their old father, they bitterly regretted their wicked deed and wept copiously. Judah lifted the head of the venerable old man from the ground, placed it upon his knees, wiped away his tears, and tried to comfort him. But Jacob remained motionless and rigid. Bitterly did Judah weep over the head of his

father, and he was joined by his brethren, and also by the
women and children and the servants of Jacob's household.
They had all assembled round the old man, trying to comfort
and to console him. Jacob, however, was plunged in his immeasurable grief, and would not listen to any words of consolation. Thereupon all the members of Jacob's household
arranged a great mourning for Joseph and his father's affliction.
The sad news soon reached the old and venerable Isaac. He
and his household also wept copiously and mourned over the
death of Joseph. Blind though he was, Isaac, accompanied
by his servants, journeyed from Hebron to Shechem to visit
his son and comfort him in his bereavement. But not even
from his old father would Jacob accept consolation.

After a while Jacob arose from the floor and amidst tears
he thus addressed his sons:

" Rise, my sons, take your bows and your arrows, gird
your swords, and go out into the fields. Make a search for the
body of my son, and if ye find it bring it to me that I may
bury it. Try also to catch the first beast of prey ye meet, perchance God will have pity upon me and upon my sorrow, and
let you catch the beast which has torn my Joseph, so that I
can take revenge upon it." Thus spake Jacob to his sons.

Early next morning the brethren set out, and when they
returned to the weeping father, they brought a wolf they had
caught.

" This is the first wild beast we encountered," said the
sons, " and we have brought it to thee, but we found no trace
of the body of thy son."

In the agony of his soul, weeping copiously and wailing,
the bereaved father seized the wolf and thus addressed him:
" Cursed beast, why didst thou devour my son Joseph, and
didst have no fear of God, the Lord of the Universe? Why
didst thou bring down such grief upon me by depriving so
suddenly my poor, innocent, and blameless son of his life,

who was guilty of no sin or transgression? But God punisheth every unjust action." Thus spoke Jacob in his agony of soul.

And the Lord had pity upon the sorrowing father, and in order to send him some consolation, He opened the mouth of the beast which thus spoke:

" By the living God who hath created me, and by thy life, my lord, I never saw thy son, nor did I tear him in pieces. From a far and distant land did I come here, in search of mine own son who seems to have suffered a fate similar to that of thy son. For my child, too, hath disappeared, and never did return to me. I know not whether he be dead or alive. I was searching for my lost child, when thy sons met me. They seized me and thus increasing my grief brought me hither to thee. I am in thy power now, O son of man, and thou canst deal with me as it pleaseth thee, but I swear once more by the living God, my creator, that I have never seen thy son, much less killed him, and that I have never in my life tasted human flesh."

Thus spoke the wolf, to Jacob's immense astonishment.

The Patriarch let the wolf go free without molesting the beast, but he continued to mourn for his lost son. And yet, Jacob had an inkling of the truth. The very fact that he remained inconsolable made him hope that Joseph was still alive. For whilst the heart of man is accessible to consolation when he has mourned and grieved for some time over the death of a dear one, the remembrance of the living can never be eradicated from the hearts of those who love.

A prophetic vision also came over Jacob and he said:

" Only vaguely do I foresee the future, but of one thing I seem to be sure and that is that no beast hath torn Joseph in pieces, nor hath he been killed by the hand of man. I see also that a wicked woman is the cause of his distress and that Judah is also responsible for his fate."

The brethren were the cause that Jacob had rent his

clothes on account of his lost son, and, as a punishment for
this, they were to rend their own clothes later on in Egypt.
Jacob himself—although in the innermost recesses of his heart
a hope lingered that Joseph was still alive—continued to mourn
for his son, putting sackcloth upon his loins, and this sign of
mourning, namely, the rending of the clothes and the sackcloth, was adopted in later days by his descendants, especially
by the kings and princes in Israel. Thus David, Ahab, Joram,
and Mordecai at Shushan, all rent their clothes and put on
sackcloth when a great misfortune had befallen them.[1] Twenty-
two years Jacob mourned for his son, just the same number
of years during which he had been absent from home, away
from his parents, and thus had never paid his respectful homage
which a son owes to his father and mother. Jacob was also
inconsolable for another reason and that was his lost hope of
seeing the twelve tribes established.

"The covenant concerning the twelve tribes," said Jacob,
"the covenant which God made with me, is now torn. My
great aim was to establish the twelve tribes of Israel with my
twelve sons, for all the works and creations of the Lord of the
Universe correspond to the number of twelve. Twelve is the
number of the planets" (signs of the Zodiac), "twelve months
hath the year, twelve hours the day, and twelve hours the
night: and twelve stones will be set in the breastplate of the
High-Priest."

To replace Joseph his lost son by another son, in con-
tracting a new marriage, never entered Jacob's mind. He had
once made a promise to Laban, his father-in-law, never to
take any other wives besides the latter's daughters.[2] And
although both Leah and Rachel were now dead, Jacob still
considered himself bound by his promise. But because a faint
hope that Joseph was alive somewhere continued to linger in
the Patriarch's heart, he would not be consoled or comforted,

---

[1] *I Chronicles*, 21, 16; *I Kings*, 21, 27; *II Kings*, 6, 30; *Esther*, 4, 1.   [2] *Genesis*, 31, 50.

THE WOLF SPEAKS TO THE SORROWING JACOB

accepting consolation from no one, not even from his own
father. As for Isaac, he wept and mourned with his son, when
he was in his presence, but as soon as he left him he ceased
manifesting any grief, for Isaac, being a prophet, knew that
Joseph was still alive. He did not, however, reveal this fact to
his son.

" As the Lord," said Isaac, " hath not acquainted my son
with the fate of Joseph, I do not feel justified in doing it."

Jacob also mourned the death of Joseph for another reason.
He was now no longer certain that he would not suffer the
torments of hell in the world to come. The Lord had once
assured him that if none of his sons died during his lifetime,
he could look upon the fact as a sure sign that he would not
taste the torments of hell in the world to come. This certainty
Jacob had now lost.[1]

---

[1] *Genesis Rabba*, §§ 84, 85; *Yalkut*, § 142; *Midrash Tanchuma, Genesis*; section *Vayesheb.*
Targum Pseudo-Jonathan, in loco; Pirke de Rabbi Eliezer, Ch. 38; *Sepher Hajashar*; see also
Lewner, *Kol-Agadoth*, Vol. I, pp. 200–202, and Adolf Kurrein, *loc. cit.*

CHAPTER III

Upon the Mother's Grave, or the Journey to Egypt

The lonely grave at Ephrath—A son's distress—He implores his mother's help—The voice from the grave—The cruel masters—Sudden darkness and raging storm—The terror of the Ishmaelites—The crouching beasts —Apology and forgiveness—The journey to Egypt—The new masters— Potiphar, the captain of the royal guard—His doubts—The story of the sale of Joseph as related in his Testament—The sacrifice of a brother— He admits being a slave, so as not to put his brethren to shame—The slave and the lucky shopkeeper—The Memphian woman—Punishment for man-theft—The advice of the Memphian woman—Joseph in prison—The fear of his masters—The new mistress—The dishonest eunuch—The story of the sale of Joseph in Moslem tradition—The fond great-aunt—The precious girdle—Accused of theft—The jealousy of the brethren—The Moon of Canaan—In the well—Saved from drowning by an angel—The caravan of Arabs—Melek-ben-Dohar and Buschra—The heavy bucket—The journey to Egypt—The dazzling light—The ladies of Egypt—Adopted as a son.

When Joseph beheld his mother's grave at Ephrath, he hastened and threw himself across the sepulchre, weeping loudly. Heartrending were the cries uttered by the poor lad.

"Mother, Mother," he cried, "thou who didst bear me, arise and behold thy son sold as a slave, heartlessly and piti-lessly. Come forth, Mother dear, look at me and weep with me over my misfortune and my suffering, and see how my brethren have treated me. Arise, Mother, from thy sleep, and help me to prepare for the conflict against my brethren who have torn me away from my father. Stripped of my gar-ments, they have sold me into slavery to strangers. Awake, Mother dear, from thy sleep and plead my cause before the throne of the Eternal. Accuse my brethren of their heinous

24

deed and learn His judgment. Awake, O Mother, for my
father's sake, and come to comfort and to console him, for his
heart is heavy with grief and sorrow." Thus the seventeen years
old lad, who was being dragged away into slavery, wept and
lamented upon his mother's grave, the lonely grave of Rachel
on the road to Ephrath.

Exhausted by grief and sorrow, he ceased at last and remained motionless upon the cherished grave. Suddenly
Joseph lifted up his head, listening intently. Was it a dream
or a fancy of his overworked and weary brain? But no, distinctly
he heard a voice. It was the voice of his mother speaking to
him from the depth of the grave.

"My son Joseph," said the voice, "my darling son, I hear
thy complaints and I see thy suffering, thy misery and affliction.
Greatly do I suffer for thy sake, and thy terrible state increases
the burden of my affliction. But, my dear son, put thy trust
in God and wait for His help. Fear not, my darling son, for
God is with thee and will deliver thee from distress in His
own time. Go, my son, with thy present masters to Egypt,
for God is with thee, and He will never forsake thee."

Such were the words uttered by the mother's voice, a voice
choked with tears and heavy with grief.

Silently and amazed Joseph had listened to the words
coming from the depth of his mother's grave, and when it
became silent, he broke out anew, weeping more violently.

One of the Ishmaelites, seeing the lad lying upon the grave
and weeping aloud, drove him away with kicks and curses.

"The lad is mad," said the merchantman to his companions; "to-day he calls a stone mother, and to-morrow he
will address a log of wood as father."

Joseph now begged his new masters to take him back and
restore him to his father Jacob, who would certainly reward
them richly, paying them a considerable sum for his lost son.

But the Ishmaelites only laughed at him, pointing out that

he could not be the son of a rich man, for else he would not have been sold into slavery for such a paltry sum. Thereupon they beat him more mercilessly, answering all his entreaties with more kicks and blows.

But the Lord who saw Joseph's distress had pity upon him, and once more sent darkness upon the earth. Lightning and heavy thunderbolts made the earth tremble, so that the Ishmaelites knew not whither to turn, for even the beasts and camels crouched upon the ground and refused to budge. In great despair the merchantmen asked one another why such a misfortune had come over them and what transgression they had committed to have thus brought down upon themselves the wrath of God.

" Perhaps," said one of the merchantmen, " we have committed a great sin by ill-treating the slave. Let us, therefore, entreat his forgiveness, and, if the storm passes, then we shall know on whose account we have suffered and the storm has raged."

Thus spoke one of the merchantmen, and his companions agreed.

Thereupon they all begged Joseph to forgive them.

" Forgive us," they said, " for we have sinned against thee, and therefore thy God is angry with us and hath sent down this raging storm. Pray, we beg thee, to thy God that He take away this storm from us."

Joseph forgave the Ishmaelites, and consented to pray to God on their behalf. The Lord heard his prayer; the storm abated, and once more the sky became clear. The sun once more appeared in its splendour, the beasts arose from their crouching position, and the merchantmen could continue their journey to Egypt. The men now knew that it was on Joseph's account that the storm had raged, and were now afraid to treat him harshly. They also took counsel together what to do with the slave.

"Let us take him back to his father, as he wishes," said one of the men. "His father is sure not only to return the price we have paid for him, but also to reward us handsomely."

"It is too late now," replied his companions, "to retrace our steps, for we have already travelled a long distance from Canaan, and we can no longer delay our journey. The best we can do now is to proceed to Egypt and there get rid of the lad by selling him at once." And thus the Ishmaelites continued their journey to Egypt, carrying Joseph with them.

When the merchantmen reached the borders of Egypt, they met four men from the descendants of Medan, a son of Abraham, and offered them Joseph for sale.

"We have a handsome slave," they said, "whom we wish to sell, and if he pleases you, we will take nine shekels for him." The Medanites, beholding Joseph who was very comely, agreed to pay the sum demanded and bought him. Satisfied with their transaction, the Ishmaelites continued their way to Egypt, and the Medanites also soon returned. They were already aware that Potiphar, the captain of Pharaoh's guard, was seeking a good slave, comely of appearance and wise, whom he could employ as the superintendent and steward of his household, and they therefore hastened to repair to the captain and to sell him the slave they had just acquired.

When Potiphar saw Joseph, the lad pleased him greatly, and he agreed to pay for him the high price demanded by the Medanites, namely four hundred pieces of silver (twenty shekels). He was, however, struck by the noble appearance of the lad, and suspected that he was not a slave by birth, but a noble youth stolen from his parents.

"This youth," said Potiphar, "does not seem to be a slave by birth, but a free man. Many free men are now being stolen from their parents and sold into slavery. I suspect that this lad, too, has been stolen from his father who may come and claim him from me. I therefore will consent to buy him from

you and pay the price of four hundred silver pieces, on condition
that ye bring the men from whom ye bought him."

The Medanites consented, brought the Ishmaelites from
whom they had bought Joseph, and the merchantmen maintained that Joseph was indeed a slave whom they had bought
in the land of Canaan. Satisfied now with his bargain, Potiphar paid the sum of four hundred silver pieces and took
Joseph into his house. And thus Joseph, the son of Jacob the
Hebrew, a powerful and wealthy man in Canaan, was sold into
slavery by the sons of slaves and bought by Potiphar, himself a
slave of Pharaoh. But it had been ordained by Divine Providence that Joseph should be brought to Egypt and in time
become the ruler of the country.[1]

In the *Testament of Joseph* the incident of Joseph's sale, his
arrival in Egypt, and his acquisition by Potiphar is related as
follows:

When the lad came with the Ishmaelites to the Indo-
Colpitæ, the latter asked him whether he was really a slave,
to which Joseph gave answer that he was a home-born slave.
He said so because he was anxious not to put his brethren to
shame. The chief of the Indo-Colpitæ then said to him:

" Thou art not a slave, for thy appearance is manifestly
not that of a slave," and he threatened to put him to death on
account of his lie.

Joseph, however, maintained that he was a slave, a slave
of those who had sold him.

When the merchants arrived in Egypt, each of them strove
to keep Joseph for himself. As they could not agree, they at
last decided to leave him in the meantime with one of their
merchants or shopkeepers until they returned again to Egypt,
bringing new merchandise.

Thus Joseph remained for three months and five days with

---

[1] *Targum Pseudo-Jonathan, in loco*; Babylonian Talmud, *Sotah*, 13b; *Genesis Rabba*,
§§ 84, 86, 87; *Book of Jubilees*, Ch. 34.

the shopkeeper. He found favour in the eyes of the latter who handed over to him his keys, entrusting unto him his entire house. And the Lord blessed the shopkeeper on Joseph's account, so that he prospered exceedingly.

Now it happened that at that time the wife of Potiphar arrived at Heliopolis, returning from Memphis. She heard from the eunuchs concerning Joseph, the Hebrew slave who was abiding with the shopkeeper, and she cast her eyes upon him. Thereupon she spoke unto her husband concerning the shopkeeper (merchant) who had grown rich through a young Hebrew slave. "They say," she added, "that the lad had been stolen out of the land of Canaan. Thou shouldst, therefore, call the shopkeeper to judgment, take the youth away from him and appoint him the steward of thy house; the God of the Hebrews will then bless thee, for the grace of Heaven is upon the lad." Thus spoke the wife of Potiphar, and her husband believed her words and sent for the merchant, calling him to judgment.

"I hear evil things concerning thee," said Potiphar, "for people tell me that thou stealest souls out of the land of Canaan and dost sell them as slaves."

The merchant fell upon his face and prostrated himself before Potiphar: "My Lord," said he, "I know not what thou sayest."

"Dost thou not?" replied Potiphar. "Whence then is the Hebrew slave in thy house?"

"My Lord," replied the merchant, "the Ishmaelites to whom he belongs entrusted him to me, and he is to abide with me until they should return."

Potiphar, however, did not give any credence to the assertion of the merchant, and commanded him to be stripped naked and beaten. Wailing and lamenting, the merchant still persisted in his assertions.

Potiphar, therefore, commanded that Joseph be brought in

his presence. When the lad was brought before Potiphar, who was the third in rank of the officers of the King, he prostrated himself. Potiphar took the lad apart and asked him: " Art thou a slave or a free-born man?"

" I am a slave," promptly replied the youth, for he wished to keep his real state secret, so as not to put his brethren to shame.

" Then whose slave art thou?" Potiphar continued to question him.

" I am the slave of the Ishmaelites," replied Joseph.

" And how didst thou become their slave?" again asked Potiphar.

" They bought me in the land of Canaan," said Joseph.

In spite, however, of Joseph's assertions that he really was a slave, Potiphar refused to believe him.

" Thou liest," he said, and ordered that he be stripped naked and beaten.

Now Potiphar's wife, who saw through the open door what was happening and how the handsome youth was being punished, sent to her husband and said:

" Unjust is thy judgment, for thou dost punish the free man who hath been stolen, as if he had transgressed."

As Joseph still persisted in calling himself a slave and refused to retract his statement, Potiphar ordered him to be sent to prison, there to remain until the Ishmaelites, his masters, should return.

But Potiphar's wife again remonstrated and said: " Thou art unjust! Why dost thou detain in bonds this youth, who is a captive but manifestly noble born? Thou shouldst set him free and take him into thy house and let him wait upon thee." She was anxious to have Joseph in her house, where she could see him daily, as she had fallen in love with him.

Her husband, however, replied: " We Egyptians are not allowed to take away the property which belongs to others before the truth is proved; I cannot take away the lad from the merchant, and it is best, therefore, that he abide in prison until his owners return."

And thus Joseph was sent to prison, where he remained for twenty-four days.

Now the Ishmaelites had in the meantime learned that Joseph was really the son of Jacob the Hebrew, a mighty and powerful man in Canaan, who was mourning for the lad in sackcloth and ashes. When they returned to Egypt they came to Joseph and said:

" Why didst thou tell us a lie; saying that thou art a slave? We have now learnt that thou art the son of a mighty man in Canaan and that thy father is still mourning for thee."

When Joseph heard them speak of his father and how he was mourning for him, he could scarcely keep back his tears, but he restrained himself, not wishing to put his brethren to shame.

" I know not what ye are saying," he replied. " I am a slave whom ye have bought."

The Ishmaelites thereupon decided to sell Joseph, so that he should not be found in their hands. They were greatly afraid lest Jacob should come and wreak terrible vengeance upon them, for they had heard that he was mighty with God and with men. And as the merchant was urging them to release him from the judgment of Potiphar, who had accused him of man-theft, they came to Joseph and bade him tell Potiphar that he had been really bought and not stolen.

" Thou wilt now say thou wast bought by us with money, and Potiphar will set us free."

When Potiphar's wife heard that the Ishmaelites were selling Joseph, she informed her husband that she intended to buy the lad, " For I hear," she added, " that the Ishmaelites are selling him."

Having obtained her husband's permission she sent one

of her eunuchs to the Ishmaelites, and offered to buy the
youth from them. But the eunuch returned and informed
his mistress that the price the owners had asked for the lad
was too high. The Memphian woman, as Potiphar's wife
is called, thereupon sent another eunuch with instructions
to buy the lad at any price.

" Do not spare gold," she said, " and even though they
ask two *minæ*, give it to them, only buy the lad and bring
him to me."

The eunuch then went and gave the Ishmaelites eighty
pieces of gold, telling his mistress that he had paid one hundred. Joseph knew of the eunuch's deceit, but he never said
a word, lest the eunuch be put to shame.[1]

In Moslem legend the story of how Joseph was sold and
how he arrived in Egypt is told somewhat differently, although
a good many incidents have been taken from Rabbinic literature both by Mohammed and the commentators of the Koran.

Joseph was the beloved son of his father Jacob, and the
old man was very unhappy when he was deprived of the sight
of his favourite son. The latter, after the death of his mother,
had been sent to his great-aunt, a sister of Isaac, who brought
him up. When Jacob claimed his son, the aunt, who loved
the lad dearly, would not think of parting with him. She
even went so far as to accuse Joseph of theft and to claim
him as a slave, so that he would be compelled to remain in
her house. The fond aunt took the family girdle—the one
which Abraham, her father, had worn when he went to offer
Isaac as a sacrifice, and which heirloom she had retained—
strapped it round the boy's waist, brought him before the
judge and accused him of theft. As a punishment for his
crime, the boy was made over to the fond aunt as a slave, and
had to remain in her house until her death, when he returned

---

[1] *Testaments of the Twelve Patriarchs, Joseph*, ed. by Sinker, Cambridge, 1869; Eng.
trans. in Anti-Nicene Library, Edinburgh, 1890, Ch. 1-10.

to his father Jacob. Here Joseph suffered greatly, in spite of the great love his father bore him, on account of the envy and jealousy of his brethren. They were jealous of him, not only on account of their father's fond love, but also on account of Joseph's great beauty of person. He was so beautiful that he was known by the name of the " Moon of Canaan ".

Enraged, at last, by his dreams which he constantly urged his brethren to listen to, the latter decided to drive their brother out of the country or kill him. " When Joseph is no more," they said, " we will repent of our deed, and the Lord is sure to forgive us."

And thus, one day, when they had Joseph in their power, the brethren stripped him naked and cast him into a well full of water. An angel, however, had thrown a stone into the well, and upon this Joseph stood so that he was above the surface of the water, else he would have been drowned.

" My brothers," cried the poor lad, " ye have taken away my clothes and stripped me naked, wherewith shall I cover my nakedness in the well?"

" Let the moon, the sun, and stars, who have adored thee in thy dreams bring thee clothes to cover thy nakedness," mocked the brothers.

For three days Joseph remained in the well. Judah secretly let him down food, whilst the angel Gabriel lit up the darkness of the pit by hanging up in it a precious stone which shed a light. Now on the third day a caravan of Arabs, passing near the well, stopped there for the purpose of drawing water to quench their thirst. Melek-ben-Dohar, the chief of the caravan, accompanied by Buschra, a freed Indian, carrying a rope and a bucket, approached the well and let down the bucket. To their great amazement they could not raise the bucket, pull it as they might, for Joseph had put his hand upon the bucket and kept it back. Melek looked down into the well and beheld Joseph, for his face illumined the well like a lamp.

" Who art thou?" asked Melek, amazed at the beauty of the lad in the well, " who art thou, what is thy name, and whence dost thou come?"

" From Canaan am I," replied Joseph, " and my brethren have cast me into this well for no guilt whatever."

Now when Melek saw Joseph he at once knew that he would fetch a high price in Egypt in the slave market. He therefore made up his mind not to permit the other members of the caravan to share the price which the lad would fetch, but divide it only with his companion Buschra.

" Hearken unto my words, Buschra," said Melek; " we need not tell all the members of the caravan that we found the handsome youth in a well and have drawn him out. If we tell the truth they will, no doubt, claim a share in him; rather will we say that we bought him from people at the well, and that he is therefore our sole property, mine and thine. When we arrive in Egypt we will sell him for a large sum of money, which we will share between us."

Thus spoke Melek, and Buschra consented to the compact. Joseph was then taken to the Arab caravan where he remained until they decided to continue their journey. But on the fourth day the sons of Jacob, seeing how their father was grieving and was even suspecting them of having done away with their brother, made up their minds to draw the lad out of the well and restore him to his father. Finding the pit into which they had cast him empty, they searched for him and at last discovered him in the Arab caravan. They claimed him as their property, a slave that had run away, and Melek offered the brethren much money for the lad and bought him from them.

Moslem legend also relates the incident of Joseph's outburst upon his mother's tomb, and Rachel's reply issuing from the depth of the grave.

It was near sunset when the caravan entered the chief city

of Egypt, which is Heliopolis, governed at that time by Rajjan, an Amalekite. But behold, Joseph's face, shining more radiantly than the midday sun, cast a new and dazzling light upon the city, so that everyone wondered, and the Egyptian ladies and damsels rushed to the windows to contemplate the radiant beauty of the Hebrew slave. Keen was the competition when on the following day Joseph was put up for sale before the royal palace, for all the noble and wealthy ladies of Heliopolis were anxious to acquire the radiantly beautiful slave. They sent either their husbands or their servants to bid for him, but Aziz, the King's Treasurer, bought the lad for a high price. As he was childless he made up his mind to adopt Joseph as his son and heir.[1]

SOLD INTO SLAVERY

(11) They said unto Jacob, O Father, why dost thou not entrust Joseph with us, since we are sincere well-wishers unto him? (12) Send him with us to-morrow into the field, that he may divert himself and sport, and we will be his guardians. (13) Jacob answered, It grieveth me that ye take him away; and I fear lest the wolf devour him while ye are negligent of him. (14) They said, Surely if the wolf devour him, when there are so many of us, we shall be weak indeed. (15) And when they had carried him with them, and agreed to set him at the bottom of the well, they executed their design: and we sent a revelation unto him saying, Thou shalt hereafter declare this their action unto them; and they shall not perceive thee to be Joseph. (16) And they came to their father at even, weeping, (17) And said, Father, we went and ran races with one another, and we left Joseph with our baggage, and the wolf hath devoured him; but thou wilt not believe us, although we speak the truth. (18) And they produced his inner garment stained with false blood. Jacob answered, Nay, but ye yourselves have contrived the thing for your own sakes: however, patience is most becoming, and God's assistance is to be implored to enable me to support the misfortune which ye relate. (19) And certain travellers came, and sent one to

[1] Koran, *Sura*, 12; Tabari, *Chronique*, I, pp. 213–214. Weil, *Biblische Legenden der Muselmänner*, 1845, pp. 100–105; cf. also Lewner, *Kol Agadoth*, Vol. I, pp. 194–197.

draw water for them; and he let down his bucket, and said, Good news! this is a youth. And they concealed him, that they might sell him as a piece of merchandise; but God knew that which they did. (20) And they sold him for a mean price, for a few pence and valued him lightly.

The Koran (Sale's translation), *Sura*, 12.

UPON HIS MOTHER'S GRAVE

And when the negro heeded not, that guarded him behind,
From off the camel Jusuf sprang, on which he rode confined,
And hastened with all speed, his mother's grave to find,
Where he knelt and pardon sought, to relieve his troubled mind.

He cried: " God's grace be with thee still, O Lady Mother dear!
O Mother, you would sorrow if you looked upon me here;
For my neck is bound with chains, and I live in grief and fear,
Like a traitor by my brethren sold, like a captive to the spear.

" They have sold me! they have sold me! though I never did them harm;
They have torn me from my father, from his strong and living arm,
By art and cunning they enticed me, and by falsehood's guilty charm,
And I go a base-bought captive, full of sorrow and alarm."

But now the negro looked about, and knew that he was gone,
For no man could be seen, and the camel came alone;
So he turned his sharpened ear, and caught the wailing tone,
Where Jusuf, by his mother's grave, lay making heavy moan.

And the negro hurried up, and gave him there a blow;
So quick and cruel was it, that it instant laid him low;
" A base-born wretch," he cried aloud, " a base-born thief art thou;
Thy masters, when we purchased thee, they told us it was so."

But Jusuf answered straight: " Nor thief nor wretch am I;
My mother's grave is this, and for pardon here I cry;

I cry to Allah's power, and send my prayer on high,
That, since I never wronged thee, his curse may on thee lie."

And then all night they travelled on, till dawned the coming day,
When the land was sore tormented with a whirlwind's furious sway;
The sun grew dark at noon, their hearts sunk in dismay,
And they knew not, with their merchandise, to seek or make their
    way.

               (*Poema de Josi*, *Poem of Joseph*, translated by G. Ticknor,
                  in his *History of Spanish Literature*, New York, 1849,
                  Vol. I, pp. 97-98.)

CHAPTER IV

The Perfect Servant and the
Passionate Mistress

A model servant—None of the characteristic traits of a slave—Joseph throws off his sadness—The silent prayer—The suspicious master—A magic spell—The God of Joseph—Potiphar is unable to gaze at the sun—The miraculous cup of hot water—Mixed vermuth—Absinthe and wine—Spiced wine—The blessing of God—Reconciled to his fate—The wild she-bear—Joseph's opportunity to show his virtue—The love-sick Zuleika—The astrologers and the horoscope—Zuleika endeavours to attract Joseph—Changing dresses three times—Zuleika flattering Joseph—The servant rebukes his mistress—The enchantress and the virtuous lad—The image of the Patriarch warning his son—The breastplate of the High-Priest—The would-be murderess—The veiled God—The dumb idol and the living Lord—The threats of the furious mistress—Her sickly appearance—The ladies of Egypt—The story of the oranges and the blood-stained hands—Zuleika's pleading—A storm of tears—The comb-like shackle—The fasting of Joseph—Zuleika promises to abandon her idols—The dish of food upon which a magic spell had been cast—The terrible man handing Joseph a sword—Zuleika threatens to commit suicide—The festival of the Nile—Zuleika the beautiful—The image of the father—The waves of the Red Sea will recede at the approach of Joseph's coffin—The story of the speaking infant in the cradle—The scene between Joseph and Zuleika as described by Josephus.

Potiphar, or Potiphera, as he was called, became the master of the free-born Joseph, but he could not fail to notice that his first suspicion had been right. Joseph had none of the characteristic traits of the slave. Slaves are always ready to devour and waste the substance of their masters, whilst Joseph, on the contrary, constantly endeavoured to increase his master's wealth, and the Lord blessed Potiphar and he prospered exceedingly ever since Joseph came into his house. Slaves, as a rule, are guilty of robbing their masters, stealing as much as they

38

can, but Joseph, on the contrary, economized and amassed great wealth for his master whom he served faithfully. Slaves are usually leading an immoral life, but Joseph remained pure and chaste, in spite of temptation.

And as the Lord protected Joseph, he found favour in the eyes of his master who put all his trust in him and appointed him chief steward of his entire household.

And Joseph thought in his heart: " I will now throw off my sadness, and cease my weeping, but do my best to give satisfaction to my master, serving him faithfully and conscientiously. The Lord will see how earnest, hardworking, and honest I am, and He will listen to my prayers and peradventure deliver me." Joseph, therefore, put his trust in God, and whilst serving his master he constantly prayed to the Eternal, and thus he spoke: " Lord of the Universe, be Thou my shield, for I have put my trust in Thee. May it be Thy will that I find favour in Thine eyes and in the eyes of my master, Potiphar."

One day, whilst Joseph was waiting upon his master, the latter noticed how Joseph's lips were moving silently, and he suspected his servant of being a magician and preparing to cast a spell upon his master.

" What is the meaning of this whispering," cried Potiphar, " dost thou intend to make use of occult arts against me, and to bring magic into Egypt, the land of magic and magicians?"

" Far be it from me," replied Joseph, " to do such a thing."

" Then why are thy lips moving silently?" asked Potiphar, still suspicious.

" I am praying to my God," said Joseph, " imploring Him to make me find favour in thine eyes."

" And where is thy God?" asked Potiphar. " Show Him to me that I may see Him."

" Lift up thine eyes to the heavens above and look at my God," replied Joseph.

Potiphar lifted up his eyes to the heavens above him, but soon had to turn away his gaze on account of the brilliance of the sun.

" My master," said Joseph, " only looked at one of the creations and servants of my God, and he has been dazzled by its splendour. How could he expect to behold the Creator of the Universe, and the Sovereign of all the worlds?"

Potiphar was convinced, especially when he saw that Joseph was always successful in his work and in whatever he undertook, that God was indeed with him. It happened that Potiphar once asked his perfect servant to bring him a cup of hot water, and Joseph hastened to comply with his master's request. Potiphar took the cup and said:

" I have made a mistake, for it is a cup of tepid water I really wanted."

And Joseph replied: " The water is tepid, as my master desires."

Potiphar dipped his finger in the water, and behold it was tepid indeed. Potiphar wondered greatly and made up his mind to test Joseph's powers even further.

" It is not water at all I wanted, but a glass of mixed vermuth."

" If my master will drink from the cup in his hand he will find that it contains mixed vermuth," said Joseph.

Potiphar drank, and to his amazement found that the cup really contained a delicious wine. Continuing to test Joseph he said again:

" I would rather have absinthe mixed with wine."

And Joseph replied: " My master has only to drink from the cup to find that it contains absinthe mixed with wine."

And indeed Potiphar convinced himself that the cup Joseph had brought him contained absinthe mixed with wine.

Continuing his test, Potiphar again said:

" It is spiced wine I would rather drink," and once more

he discovered that his cup contained spiced wine. And when
he saw that God was clearly on Joseph's side, and fulfilled all
his desires, he honoured him greatly, taught him all the liberal
arts, and placed before him better fare than the food offered to
the other slaves. He also placed the keys of all his possessions
and treasures in Joseph's hand, appointing him his chief steward.

Joseph now ruled over Potiphar's household, and all received
the necessary orders from him, for Potiphar " knew not aught
that was with him ". The blessing of God was the result of
Potiphar's action and of his treatment of Joseph, and he often
had occasion to say: " Blessed be the day on which I bought
Joseph." And when Joseph saw that his master was satisfied
with him and treated him no longer as a slave, but as a trusted
friend and companion, he was happy indeed, and thanked the
Lord for His protection. Feeling quite happy in his present
state, the lad reconciled himself to his fate.

Once more Joseph began to pay attention to his appearance.
He dressed his hair and walked elegantly, and in every respect
once more became the very image of his radiantly beautiful
mother, Rachel. With keen satisfaction he now remembered
the envy and hatred of his brethren and how they had made
him suffer, whenever he had received a token of love from his
father.

" I thank Thee, God Almighty," he said, " for the freedom and happiness Thou hast bestowed upon me."

Thus spoke Joseph who was not only quite happy to have
been removed from his brethren, but was also forgetting his
old father who was mourning for him in distant Canaan. For
this indifference he was soon to be punished, for the Lord
spoke:

" Thou art an egotist! In sackcloth and ashes thy old
father is mourning, bewailing thy loss, whilst thou art thinking
of thine own welfare, feeling happy in thy present state, and
paying careful attention to thy personal appearance. Thy

mistress, who is like a wild she-bear in her passion, will rise up against thee and bring affliction over thee."

Joseph, however, was glad when the trouble in store for him came. He had always wished for an opportunity to prove his piety, even as his fathers had proved their piety whenever it was tested. The Lord, therefore, whilst punishing the lad for his indifference with regard to his father, also wished to give Joseph his longed-for opportunity to show his virtue and his moral strength in the moment of temptation.

Joseph was exceedingly handsome, the very image of his mother Rachel who had been a ravishing beauty. No wonder, therefore, that the passionate Zuleika, the wife of his master Potiphar, cast her eyes upon Joseph. The more she had occasion to see the youth, the more violent became her love for him. Not venturing as yet to declare her love to her slave, Zuleika tried to attract his attention to her person. As it was customary in those days, especially in Egypt, she asked astrologers to cast her horoscope, and was informed that she was destined to have descendants through Joseph. This astrologic forecast was true in a certain sense, for Joseph later on married Potiphar's daughter Asenath who bore him children.

Zuleika, however, did not understand the prophecy and now hoped that her heart's desire would speedily be fulfilled. She did her best to seduce Joseph by feminine artifice and to enrapture the lad by her beauty. She omitted no occasion to enter into conversation with him, hoping thus to attract his attention. Several times during the day did she change her attire, arraying herself in beautiful and costly garments in the morning, at midday, and in the evening. But all her efforts and all her feminine artifices proved of no avail and had no effect upon the virtuous and chaste son of Jacob.

Under the pretence of visiting Joseph, Zuleika often came to him at night, pretending to regard him as her own son, for she had no male child. Joseph, thereupon, prayed to the Lord, and Zuleika gave birth to a son. But still she continued to visit him and to kiss and embrace him as if he were her own son.

In his innocence, Joseph did not recognize her deceit, and her evil and wanton thoughts. At last, however, his eyes were opened and he became aware of the Egyptian woman's criminal passion for him. When Joseph perceived what was in Zuleika's mind, he was very sad and grieved and lamented for her. He constantly persuaded her to turn away from her evil design and to eradicate from her heart her wanton passion for him.

When Zuleika saw that all her wanton efforts remained ineffectual, and that Joseph never, by either word or look, expressed his love for her, and steadfastly refused to look into her eyes shining with love, she decided to declare to him her love in undisguised terms. Joseph, she thought, is only timid and durst not raise his eyes to his beautiful mistress, but if I declare my love to him, he will be happy to reciprocate my passion. Thus thought Zuleika, reared in an Eastern harem and unable to understand the steadfastness and moral strength of her handsome slave. She now began to pursue him openly with her love and with her constant flattery.

" Fair is thy appearance," she said, " and comely is thy form, thou handsomest of all men. Never did I behold a slave who equalled thee in beauty."

But Joseph replied modestly:

" I am only the work of God who hath created and fashioned me, as He hath fashioned and created all men and women."

" Glorious and beautiful are thine eyes," continued Zuleika, " and no wonder that thou didst charm and stir up love in the hearts of all the ladies in Egypt."

" My eyes may be beautiful whilst I am alive," replied the son of Rachel, " but thou wilt recoil in horror when thou wilt behold their ghastly expression once I am dead and lying in the grave."

" Sweet and charming is thy voice," declared the woman

reared in the atmosphere of an Egyptian harem; " sweet is thy voice, and pleasant is thy speech, thou favoured of the Gods. Take up the harp which is lying idle in the house, play and sing to me, that I may hear thy voice and enjoy thy song."

" Pleasant and lovely are my words only when I proclaim the glory of the Eternal," replied Joseph.

But Zuleika would not be rebuked. Caressing the fair head of the beautiful Joseph, she exclaimed:

" Dost thou know that thy hair is exceedingly beautiful? I will comb it with my golden comb."

The amorous talk of the harem beauty made Joseph at last lose his patience. Disgusted with her wanton talk and her enticements, he exclaimed:

" How long, O woman, wilt thou thus speak to me, trying to seduce me? It would be better for thee to think of thy husband and to remember thy household duties."

" My household duties," laughed Zuleika. " There is nothing in the house I care for. Since I have seen thee," she added passionately, " there is nothing I can think of but thee and my love for thee."

The virtuous lad, unaccustomed to such amorous declarations and such wanton enticements, was shocked by the conduct of his mistress, and silently looked to the ground, never raising his eyes to his passionate mistress's face. The woman, however, did not consider herself beaten, but, on the contrary, continued her pursuit of the lad, practising her artifices in the hope of winning his love with her enticements and her harem tricks.

The more steadfast Joseph proved, the more deaf he seemed to be to her words of love, the more ineffectual Zuleika's blandishments seemed to be, the more violent became her passion. She forgot all womanly shame and decency, and in passionate words begged her handsome slave to yield to her desire.

The enchantress was beautiful, and the temptation was great, fraught with danger for a lad unequal to the fight against the enticements of an Egyptian passionate beauty, well versed in all feminine artifices and harem tricks. There were moments when his steadfastness threatened to forsake Joseph, and there was danger that he would not be able to resist the temptation. At such a moment of weakness, the image of his beloved father suddenly appeared before his mind's eye, and Joseph seemed to hear the voice of the latter warning him.

" A day will come," Jacob said, " when upon the breast-plate of the High-Priest the names of thy brethren will be engraven. Dost thou wish to forfeit this honour through thy sin of immoral conduct?" Thus spoke Jacob, and Joseph, on the point of yielding to the passion of the Egyptian woman, silenced the voice of temptation. In calm and sensible tones he tried to cure his mistress of her violent passion and to bring her back to her senses.

" The Lord," he said, " the Creator of the Universe, is in the habit of choosing among the favourite members of our house one whom He destines to be a sacrifice unto Himself. Should He desire to choose me as a sacrifice, I would make myself unfit for such an honour were I to commit the sin thou temptest me with. In visions of the night the Lord hath also frequently appeared to my worthy ancestors. Would He appear to me, if I were to defile myself with the sin of adultery? For a small transgression only Adam, our first parent, was expelled from the Garden of Eden and was heavily punished. How much greater will be my punishment, if I commit the grievous sin of adultery, and transgress the most sacred law of marriage? I also fear the wrath and punishment of my old father in Canaan. On account of a similar sin he deprived my eldest brother Reuben of his birthright and gave it to me. If I do thy desire, he would, with equal right, deprive me, too, of the gift of birthright. I also fear my master, thy husband, in whose eyes I have found grace and favour, and to the sin of adultery I would also add that of ingratitude, were I to fulfil thy wanton desire."

" My husband," stormed Zuleika, carried away by violent passion, " my husband, the hateful Egyptian, I will kill him, so that he will no longer be in the land of the living and stand in the way of our love."

" Murderess," cried Joseph in indignation, " wilt thou add the crime of murder to that of adultery? In thy violent wanton passion thou hast lost all womanly decency and shame, but dost thou not fear God who knows all and sees all?"

" God?" said the Egyptian woman, " come with me and I will show thee how I can hide our love from God." Thereupon she seized the reluctant lad by the hand, and dragged him from chamber to chamber until she reached her own quiet and secluded room. Above her bed an idol hung. Zuleika seized a cloth, and covering the idol thus spoke:

" See, I have covered the image of my god, and he will no longer be a witness to our sin, if sin it is, as thou sayest. He is a severe and revengeful god, but now our love will be hidden from him."

" Foolish woman," replied Joseph, " thou dost fear thy idol, whose face thou coverest, shall I not fear my God too? His face, however, thou canst not cover, for He is everywhere, and His eyes run through the whole earth. Now, I swear to thee, as the Lord, whom I worship, liveth, that I will never so far forget myself as to commit the sin thou biddest me do."

Joseph's constant refusal increased the more the woman's passion, especially since she hoped that he could not escape her. And thus she continued to pursue him with her amorous declarations, begging him daily to give her his love, or at least a friendly look. But still Joseph remained unshaken, refusing to give way. Unable to prevail upon the steadfast lad, Zuleika tried to threaten him.

" If thou refusest to do my will, I will have thee thrown into prison and have thee chastised," she said.

But Joseph only shrugged his shoulders and replied:

"The Lord who created man looseth the prisoners and He will also protect me and deliver me from thy punishment."

Zuleika's desire and her passion increased to such an extent, that Joseph's refusal to listen to her amorous talk and to accept her advances threw her into a sickness and she began to look very ill. Her husband had already noticed this before, but when he inquired after the cause of her illness, she only evasively replied that she had a pain in her heart. Now, her friends, the women of Egypt, came to visit her, and surprised at her wasted looks and sallow and sickly appearance, wondered greatly and asked:

" Whence cometh thy sickly appearance and wasted looks? It is impossible that the wife of such a great and esteemed prince of the realm as Potiphar is could lack anything that her heart desired. Tell us," they urged, " the cause of thy sickness and what it is that thy heart desireth?"

" To-day," replied Zuleika, " ye shall learn the cause of my secret grief."

She thereupon commanded her maidservants to prepare a festive meal for her friends, and a rich banquet was accordingly spread out before the ladies. Zuleika then bade Joseph appear before her, arrayed in his most beautiful and costly garments, and wait upon the noble ladies of Egypt. Zuleika had placed upon the table oranges and knives to peel them. She called Joseph in just at the very moment when the noble ladies were busy peeling the fragrant oranges with the knives in their hands. And so profound was the impression the startling and almost supernatural beauty of the son of Rachel had produced upon the Eastern ladies, that they could not turn their eyes away from him. Mechanically they continued to peel their oranges, but so enchanted were they with the lad's beauty, that they never noticed how they were cutting their hands with their knives, dyeing the red oranges redder still. With a start the enraptured ladies awoke from their enchantment, when in triumphant tones Zuleika suddenly exclaimed:

"What are ye doing? Ye are all cutting your own hands instead of peeling the oranges!"

"It is the fault of thy handsome slave," replied the ladies, "for his beauty is so great that we could not turn our eyes from him."

"Alas," sighed Zuleika, "well do I know to my misfortune the magic power of his supernatural beauty. Ye have only looked at him for one fleeting moment, and so enchanted were ye that ye could not resist the temptation of feasting your eyes upon his countenance. Now ye can understand my agony. Day after day and hour after hour I see him in the house and behold his countenance, and my heart yearneth for him. How can I refrain myself and not waste away and be sick to death?"

Thus spoke Zuleika, and her friends assured her with all the outward signs of pity that they were greatly sorry for her.

"We understand thy sickness now," said the noble ladies of Egypt. "No woman could control herself in the presence of such a man, and few indeed would remember either virtue or decency in such a case. And yet, we fail to understand the cause of thy suffering. He is thy slave, and it would be better for thee to tell him what thou desireth rather than waste away thy life."

"Ye know not Joseph," replied Zuleika. "I have already told him in unmistakable language what my heart desireth, I have begged and entreated, I have implored his love, but all in vain. All my enticements and all my promises remain without effect."

The woman's sickness increased daily, but neither her household nor her husband knew or even suspected the cause of her wasted appearance. Whenever her husband inquired after the cause of her fallen countenance and her wasted looks, Zuleika answered only evasively. But her lady friends now frequently came to visit her, and, as she had told them that her love for Joseph was the cause of her sickness, they advised her to try and entice the youth once more in secret, and persuade him to return her love so that she might not die of a broken heart. Zuleika, in her passionate unrequitted love for the handsome son of Rachel, was wasting away to a shadow, and her countenance looked sad and woebegone. She felt so ill that she could hardly stand.

Now it happened one day that Joseph came into the house to do his master's work. Zuleika suddenly appeared, threw her arms round him and in passionate language begged for his love. With all his strength Joseph warded her off. Thereupon Zuleika, woman-like, broke out into a storm of tears. She begged and entreated, pleaded and reproached the handsome youth who, in her harem imagination, ought to have been only too happy to accept the love of his mistress.

" Look at me," she cried in an agony of soul, and in a tone of wounded pride, " look at me! Hast thou ever seen or heard of another woman my equal in beauty, and much less of one whose beauty exceeds mine? Look at me," she cried passionately, " am I not beautiful and attractive? And yet daily do I try to persuade thee, to beg for thy love which thou dost refuse. My love for thee is wasting away my health, and I am grievously sick. Is it not an honour that I, one of the most beautiful and attractive women in Egypt, am conferring upon thee, and yet thou dost refuse to listen unto me. It is impossible that thou dost not love me, and only the fear of thy master refrains thee from hearkening unto my voice. But, as the king liveth, I swear unto thee that no harm will come to thee and

not a hair of thy head will be harmed on account of thy love
for me, for thy master will never know anything. Oh, my love,
hearken unto me at least for the sake of the honour I am conferring upon thee, or out of pity for my suffering. Take away
the certain death from me, for I shall surely die if thou dost
persist in thy refusal, and why should I die on account of thee?"

Thus begged and wailed Zuleika in a paroxysm of passion.
Her tears and supplications, her peerless beauty, her passionate
love for him made the lad waver for a moment. But once
more the image of his father appeared before his mind's eye,
and he triumphed over his momentary weakness. In spite
of her failures, the Egyptian was not discouraged, but constantly and unremittingly pursued her handsome slave with
her solicitations. She could not understand the lad's steadfastness, and it nearly drove her mad when she noticed that
he would not even look at her, for whenever she fell upon him,
he modestly cast his eyes upon the ground.

" I will compel thee," she cried, " to look into my beautiful
face, into my eyes shining with love." And she placed a comb-
like iron shackle under Joseph's chin, so that he was forced
to hold up his head and look into her countenance and read
her immeasurable love in her eyes. All her efforts, however,
remained ineffectual, and her amorous attacks recoiled from
the mail-coat of Joseph's moral strength and chastity.

On another occasion when Joseph, in a moment of weakness,
was almost on the point of giving way to Zuleika's attacks,
he was saved from sin by Divine interference. It seemed to
him that the Lord appeared to him, holding the stone of foundation in His hand and threatening him, if he committed the
sin, to cast away the stone of foundation and reduce the Universe to ruins.

Zuleika, as an Egyptian, bred and brought up in the atmosphere of a harem, was still convinced that Joseph's refusal
was due only to his fear of being discovered and punished

by his master. She therefore endeavoured to convince him that their love and relations would never be discovered.[1]

" I am a married woman," she would say, " and our relations will never be discovered."

" Foolish woman," replied Joseph, " a son of Jacob would defile himself even by his love for an unmarried daughter of the heathen, and much more so if he were to give his love to a married woman. I refuse to enjoy thy love in this world and to share thy punishment in the next."

When Zuleika saw that her enticements were of no avail, she frequently resorted to threats. She used to summon Joseph into her presence, and give him over to punishments, so as to make him comply with her request. Regretting, however, her harshness a moment later, she would call him back and once more supplicate him to fulfil her desire.

" My love," she would cry, " I am thine, and all that I possess is thine. Thou shalt be my lord and rule over me and over my house; thou shalt be my master, only give me thy love."

Joseph, however, remembered the words of his father, and retiring to his chamber wept and prayed to the Lord to save him from the shameless woman who was urging him to transgress and commit the sin of adultery.

He fasted for many days, although the Egyptians believed that he lived in plenty and even in luxury, so well did he look, for those who fast for the sake of God are made beautiful of face. He drank no wine, and for three days abstained from food, giving it away to the poor and to the sick. He prayed to the Lord to deliver him from the Egyptian woman who constantly pursued him.

[1] *Genesis Rabba*, §§ 86, 87; *Midrash Tanchuma*, section *Vayesheb*; *Yalkut*, §§ 145–146; *Midrash Abkhir* quoted in *Yalkut, Genesis*, § 146; *Midrash Lekach Tob, in loco*; *Targum Pseudo-Jonathan, in loco*; Josephus, *Antiquities*, II, 4; *Sepher Hajashar*; *Pirke de Rabbi Eliezer* Ch. 39; Babylonian Talmud, *Yoma*, 39; *Sotah*, 36b; *Gittin*, 7a; see also *Midrash Agadah*, ed. Buber, Vol. I, pp. 93–94; *Midrash Haggadol*, col. 579–594; Gaster, *The Chronicles of Jerahmeel*, pp. lxxxv and 94; A. Kurrein, *loc. cit.*

" Thou needst not fear the wrath of my husband, the hateful
Egyptian," she cried. " He thinks that thou art a holy man
and very chaste, for often have I spoken of thee to him, praising
thy conduct and lauding thy chastity. He is so persuaded of
thy chastity that he would never believe any tale concerning
thee. Thou art, therefore, safe, my friend, and having nothing
to fear, thou canst enjoy thy happiness."

Thus spoke the Egyptian, but Joseph brought up upon
the moral teaching of his father Jacob, put on sackcloth, slept
on the ground, and prayed to the Lord to deliver him from the
snares of the woman.

Zuleika never neglected any means by which she thought
she could endear herself to Joseph and win his love. One
day she came to him and thus addressed him: " If thou wilt
only give me thy love, I will abandon my idols. Instruct me
in the law of thy God, and we will walk in His ways. I will
also persuade the Egyptian " (meaning her husband) " to
abandon his idols. I am ready to do anything for thy sake,
only hearken unto my voice and give me thy love."

But Joseph only sadly shook his head and replied:

" The Lord hath no use in the reverence of those who live
in impurity, and He taketh no pleasure in those who commit
adultery." And again Joseph prayed to the Lord to deliver
him from the woman. Often Zuleika suggested to Joseph that
she would do away with her husband.

" I will kill the Egyptian," she cried, " and marry thee
lawfully." When Joseph heard these words and learned that
the woman was even ready to commit murder, he rent his
garments, and thus addressed her:

" Woman, if thou dost commit such a crime, I will proclaim
it to all men and accuse thee of the deed. Fear the Lord, therefore, for if thou dost commit such an evil deed thou wilt be
destroyed."

Zuleika, afraid lest Joseph would declare her device to her

husband, begged him never to breathe a word of what she had said in a moment of aberration. She went away and sent him many gifts, hoping thus to soothe him. Thereupon she sent Joseph a dish of food upon which she had cast a magic spell, hoping thus to beguile him and make him yield to her desire.

When the eunuch brought Joseph the dish, the boy suddenly beheld a terrible man who was handing him a sword together with the dish. Joseph knew that Zuleika's evil design was to seduce him and to lead his soul to perdition. When the eunuch had left, he wept and left the dish untasted. On the following day Zuleika came to visit him, and noticing the untasted food she asked:

" Why didst thou not partake of the food I sent thee?"

" Because," replied Joseph, " thou hast filled it with death. Didst thou not say thyself that I come not near to idols, but the Lord alone? Know then, that the God of my father hath sent unto me His angel and revealed unto me thy great wickedness. I have kept the dish so as to convict thee, so that thou mayest see it and repent. Think not, however, that I was afraid to partake of the food thou didst send me on account of thy magic spells, for they can have no power over me. Over them that fear God in chastity the wickedness of the ungodly hath no power."

Thus spoke Joseph, and praying to the God of his fathers and the angel of Abraham to be with him, he took up the dish and partook of the food in Zuleika's presence.

When the woman saw this, she fell upon her face at his feet and burst out in tears. He raised her up and gently admonished her, and she promised him not to commit this sin again.

Her love, however, for Joseph she could not eradicate from her heart. Again and again she would rush unto Joseph and plead and beg for his love. One day she appealed to his pity for her and to his kindness of heart.

" If thou wilt not love me," she cried, " I will take away my own life. I will hang myself, drown myself in the well, or jump from the top of the cliff." But Joseph prayed to the Lord to calm the storm that was raging in the woman's breast, and he himself gently addressed her and thus he spoke:

" Why art thou so excited and blinded by thy passion, that thou canst think of nought but thy sinful love? Remember that if thou dost kill thyself, Sethon, thy husband's concubine, and thy rival, will ill-treat and beat thy children and destroy thy very memory from off the earth." Thus spoke Joseph. But his words had a different effect upon Zuleika than he had expected.

" Then thou dost love me a little," she cried. " Thou dost love me a little, and it suffices me, for thou dost think and care for me and for my children. It proves to me that I am not indifferent to thee, and I now hope that thou wilt share the passion which is raging in my breast for thee."

Zuleika could not understand that Joseph had spoken thus only for the sake of the Lord. But the woman was so engrossed in her wanton desire and her wicked passion, and so enslaved by it that whatever kind word she heard and whatever good thing she noticed, she at once interpreted it as a sign that her heart's desire would soon be fulfilled. The passionate Egyptian, however, in whose breast the unholy fire of her criminal love was burning, never gave up hope.[1]

" I will wait for a favourable opportunity," she thought, " when I will resort to constraint and use force, should all my enticements and entreaties prove futile and ineffectual."

Such a longed-for opportunity at last came. On the day when the Nile overflowed its banks, Egypt celebrated an annual festival and a public holiday. On this festive occasion, accompanied by musicians who played on various instruments, Egypt's inhabitants, from the King and his princes to the

---

[1] *Testaments of the Twelve Patriarchs, Joseph*, Ch. 1–10.

lowest peasant, all repaired to the banks of the Nile. Men, women, and children thronged the river's banks.

Potiphar and his entire household went out to take part in the festival.

Joseph did not go, because as a Hebrew he did not share the Egyptian adoration of the River Nile.

As for Zuleika, she remained at home under the pretext of sickness. She hoped to make most of the absence of her husband and of the entire household, and that alone now with Joseph in the vast palace she would compel the reluctant slave to yield to her desire.

When she was alone, she arrayed herself in her most beautiful and costly garments, placed gold and silver ornaments and precious stones in her raven dark hair, employed the thousand and one means to which the ladies of the harem resort to beautify their faces and bodies, and perfumed the house with various perfumes calculated to excite the senses. Thereupon she sat down in the vestibule of the house where she knew Joseph had to pass.

She had not long to wait, for soon Joseph returned from the field to do his work which consisted in examining his master's books of account. Startled at the dazzling appearance of his mistress and divining her purpose, fearing also that his steadfastness might forsake him, the lad tried to slip away into another part of the house, where he would not behold the tempting beauty of his mistress. Zuleika noticed this quickly enough, and smilingly exclaimed:

" Why, Joseph, what prevents thee from passing to thy accustomed place to do thy master's work? See, I will make room for thee, so that thou mayest pass to thy place."

Pulling himself together, Joseph passed to his accustomed place in the house. But suddenly Zuleika, resplendent in her beauty, enhanced by her magnificent raiment, exhaling all the perfumes of Arabia which excite the senses, stood before

Joseph. The temptation was great indeed, and his senses entranced, the lad felt that his steadfastness was leaving him and that he no longer was able to resist the attractiveness of the Egyptian, versed in all the artifices of the harem. With triumph in her heart and her eyes shining with love, Zuleika threw her arms round Joseph. But suddenly he pushed her back, disengaging himself from her embrace. At this critical moment the images of his beloved father and of his never-to-be-forgotten mother appeared before Joseph's mind's eye. His rising passion cooled down, and he once more felt himself strong enough to resist the temptation.

"What aileth thee?" cried Zuleika, "Why dost thou suddenly hesitate and dost refuse to take thy happiness?"

"The vision of my father refrains me from committing a sin," replied Joseph, now completely sobered.

"Thy father?" asked the woman in astonishment. "This is idle talk, there is no one in the house besides ourselves!"

"And yet it is so;" persisted Joseph, "thy criminal desire and wild passion make thee blind so that thou dost perceive nothing, but I am one of the descendants of Abraham who are endowed with spiritual vision."

Mad with passion, wild at the thought that she was again being baulked in her desire, when she had thought herself so near happiness, Zuleika was beside herself. Seizing Joseph by his garment and swiftly drawing a sword which she had hidden under her dress, she pressed the weapon against his throat and cried vehemently:

"I will not be baulked in my desire. As the king liveth, fulfil my desire or thou diest."

With all the strength at his disposal, Joseph disengaged himself, pushed the woman back, and ran out of the room. In so doing, however, he left a piece of his garment in Zuleika's hands. The virtue of his ancestors, which Joseph constantly endeavoured to imitate, had saved him from sin, and it was on account of Joseph's virtue that the nation of Israel passed later on unharmed through the waves of the Red Sea.

" As thou didst fly from temptation," said the Lord, " so the waves of the Red Sea will recede at the approach of thy coffin."

As for Zuleika, in her mad passion for Joseph, she caressed and kissed the fragment of cloth which her beloved had left in her hand. Quickly, however, she perceived the danger of her position, and began to fear her husband's severe punishment, should he learn from Joseph of her sinful conduct.

In the meantime her friends, the noble ladies of Egypt, had returned from the festival, and, hearing of her sickness which they shrewdly suspected to have been only a pretext, came to visit her. Ostentatiously they came to inquire after her health, but secretly they hoped to hear the details and the result of Zuleika's efforts. To her intimate friends Zuleika confessed the truth, telling them all that had occurred, how she had failed and how she now feared the wrath of her husband and his punishment for her wanton conduct.

" Our advice," said the noble ladies of Egypt, " is to accuse thy slave of immorality before thy husband. He will give credence to thy words rather than to those of the slave, and will throw him into prison."

Zuleika promised to follow their advice, and implored her friends to support her.

" Ye, too, my friends, complain to your husbands against the Hebrew slave, and accuse him of having pursued you with his amorous proposals."

Her friends promised their help and departed. In the meantime Zuleika decided to resort to a ruse in her accusations of Joseph. Laying aside her magnificent garments and taking off all the ornaments with which she had beautified her person, she put on her ordinary clothes, and placed by her side the fragment torn from Joseph's garment which she still secretly covered with passionate kisses. Thereupon she called a little boy, one of her attendants, into the sick-room where she now remained, and ordered him to summon her household. When the men of her house appeared in her presence, she thus addressed them:

" See how the Hebrew slave, whom your master hath brought into the house, hath behaved towards me, his mistress. Scarcely had ye left the house, and gone away to the festival of the Nile, when he came into my room, and, knowing that I was alone in the house, he tried to force me and make me yield to his desire. I seized him by his garment, tore it and raised my voice. When he saw my indignation and heard me cry aloud, he became frightened and fled."

Thus spoke Zuleika, trying to save herself, should Joseph accuse her to her husband, and also because she wanted to wreak vengeance upon Joseph for having rejected her passion-ate amorous advances. The men of her household listened in silence to her story, and full of indignation went to their master, who had in the meantime returned, and informed him of what had occurred.

Potiphar, on hearing the report of his servant's immoral conduct from the lips of his men, hastened to the room of his wife, whom he found seemingly full of moral indignation against the daring slave who had made such a cowardly attempt against her honour. Bursting into tears, and pretending that she had been outraged in her feminine honour, she urged her husband, whom she received with many expressions of her unbounded love for him, to punish the wicked slave for his immoral conduct. Zuleika's friends kept their promise, and Potiphar heard from their husbands of Joseph's alleged be-haviour, and how he had pursued and annoyed them. He therefore believed his wife's story, and ordered his men to flog Joseph mercilessly. In his agony, when the blows fell upon him, the chaste and innocent son of Rachel prayed to the Lord, and thus he spoke:

"Sovereign of all the worlds, Thou knowest that I am innocent of the crime I am charged with, and why should I die to-day by the hands of these impious and unjust heathens, on account of lies and calumnies?" The more mercilessly the servants of Potiphar flogged him, the more heartrending became Joseph's cries which ascended to Heaven. And the Lord had mercy upon Joseph, the innocent victim of a wanton woman, furious because she had not succeeded in her criminal desire. God opened the mouth of an infant of eleven months which was lying in its cradle, and it thus addressed Potiphar's servants:

"Why are you punishing and mercilessly flogging this innocent man, for innocent is he of the guilt he is charged with by my mother? Lies did she tell you, and what did really happen differs greatly from the tale she told you." In detail the infant described the scene between Joseph and Zuleika, who had made desperate efforts to win Joseph's love. Potiphar himself and his men listened in great astonishment to the report of the child, which, its tale finished, spoke no word again. Ashamed of his injustice, the perplexed husband bade his men leave off flogging the innocent victim, and decided to make an inquiry and bring the matter before the priests and the judges of the land.

Joseph now appeared in court before the priests who asked him to tell his tale. He related to the judges what had really happened, and how he had rejected the lady's proposal. He swore that he was innocent, and that only in her fury, because she had been unsuccessful in her attempt, did his mistress now accuse him falsely.

The judges listened to his words, and ordered that this torn garment be brought for a minute examination. If the garment is torn on the front part, thought the judges, it will prove that it was the woman who had tried to hold him and that the man was innocent of the crime he is charged with. The garment was brought into court and examined by the judges who, from the nature of the tear, decided that the man was innocent. Joseph was freed from the penalty of death with which he had been threatened, but he was nevertheless condemned to prison, so as to silence the rumour which had spread concerning Zuleika's immoral conduct.

Potiphar himself was now convinced that Joseph was innocent and that his wanton wife had lied shamelessly. He had sufficient sense of justice to tell Joseph so, and to excuse himself for casting him into prison.

" I am convinced," spoke Potiphar, " of thy absolute innocence, and know too well, alas, that my wife's accusation against thee is only a ruse on her part, to save her own reputation. But I must cast thee into prison, lest my honour and my good name suffer, and my children bear the consequences of the stain upon their mother's honour."

Joseph was thus cast into prison, although innocent. It was his punishment to suffer, though innocent, the consequences of a trumped-up charge, and of calumny and slander, for having once calumniated his brethren and accused them before their father. As he had, however, refused to violate the laws of morality even in secret, and had thus sanctified the name of the Lord, he was rewarded for his chastity. One of the letters of the name of God, the letter " He " was added to his name, and henceforth the son of Rachel was called *Je-ho-seph*, and is always considered as the head of all the truly pious men.

Now Potiphar had grown so used to Joseph's services, that he could not spare them. Convinced of the lad's innocence, he obtained from the keeper of the prison permission for Joseph to spend some time in his master's house, where he could minister to the latter's needs. He cleaned the silver, dressed

"WHY ARE YOU MERCILESSLY FLOGGING THIS INNOCENT MAN?"

Facing page 60, Vol. II

the table, and made his master's bed, and executed other tasks. As for Zuleika, she still persisted in her pursuit of Joseph, and availed herself of the opportunity his presence in the house offered her to renew her proposals, and to make him yield to her wishes. She promised him release from prison, if he only gave her his love. But Joseph replied that he preferred to remain all his life in prison rather than to commit a crime against God. When her promises and enticements proved ineffectual, the wanton woman once more resorted to threats: " I will increase thy suffering and punishment," she cried in her fury. " I will use other means to make thee feel my power."

" God sends justice to the oppressed," replied Joseph.

" I will deprive thee of food," she threatened.

" God feedeth the hungry," Joseph replied.

" I will have thee cast into irons."

" God looseth the prisoners," replied Joseph.

" I will blind thine eyes," cried the woman in a rage.

" The Lord openeth the eyes of the blind," replied the steadfast youth.

" I will crush thy spirit and cause thy tall stature to be bent down."

" The Lord raiseth up them that are bowed," said Joseph.

" I will sell thee as a slave into a strange land," she cried.

" The Lord protects the strangers," replied Joseph.

When the lad was cast into prison, Zuleika suffered greatly, but Joseph praised the Lord in the house of darkness and joyfully, with glad voice, thanked Him Who had delivered him from the Egyptian woman. But even whilst Joseph was in prison, Zuleika did not give up hope. She would often send to him saying:

" If thou wilt consent to my wish, I will at once release thee from thy bonds, and set thee free from the darkness."

Often, although sick and oppressed with grief, she would

visit him at night, at unlooked for times, to persuade him or at least to listen to his voice. And when she heard him praying to the Lord, and glorifying the Creator, she went away groaning loudly. When Zuleika saw at last that all her efforts, her enticements, and her threats were of no avail, she gave up hope and let the youth alone.

Josephus describes the scene between Zuleika and Joseph as follows: When she had the opportunity for solitude and leisure, that she might entreat the lad again, the woman used more kind words to him than before.

" It was good of thee," she said, " to have yielded to my first solicitation, and to have given me no repulse, both because thou didst bear reverence to my dignity who am thy mistress, and also because of the vehemence of my passion. Although I am thy mistress, I am compelled on account of my vehement passion to condescend beneath my dignity." She assured him that it was only on his account that she had pretended sickness, so as to have an opportunity of declaring her love once more.

" If thou wilt comply with my request," she added, " thou mayest be sure of enjoying all the advantages thou already hast, but if thou dost reject me, I will make thee feel the consequences of my revenge and hatred."

But neither her tears nor her threats had any effect upon the chaste son of Rachel.[1]

---

[1] *Sepher Hajashar*; Adolf Kurrein, *loc. cit.*; see also note 1, p. 51; and Lewner, *Kol Agadoth*, Vol. I, pp. 202–208.

CHAPTER V

In Prison, or the Interpreter of Dreams

The favoured prisoner—Public attention diverted from Joseph—A new court scandal—The two court officers—The plot to poison the King—Joseph waits upon the chief butler and the chief baker—The strange dream—The story of Kimtom, the famous physician—Thirst for knowledge—The tramp and the physician—The dying boy and the incredulous father—Men are judged by their outward appearance—The skill of Kimtom—The bitter regret of a bereaved father—The dream of the chief butler—A prophecy concerning Israel's redemption—The meaning of the vine and the three branches—Joseph is punished for having put his trust in man—An unfavourable prophecy concerning Israel—The meaning of the three baskets—The three nations to whom Israel will once be made subject—The butler's plans to remember Joseph are frustrated by an angel—The Lord alone remembers Joseph.

The master of the prison soon noticed Joseph's zeal and his conscientiousness in executing all the tasks he set him. Charmed also by the youth's extraordinary beauty of person, the master of the prison conceived a great liking for Joseph, and did his best to make life easy for his prisoner. He took off his chains and ordered for him better food than the ordinary prison fare. And as he could find no wrong in the lad, for God was with Joseph in his misfortune, he found it unnecessary to keep a close watch over him as over the other prisoners. He even went so far as to place all his fellow-prisoners under the youth's command, bidding all obey Joseph's instructions.

Now, as people were constantly talking of Joseph's alleged misconduct, and of the accusation raised against him by a wanton and passionate woman, the Lord wanted to divert public attention from the innocent youth and make people think and talk of something else, and thus prepare the way for Joseph's future greatness.

Soon indeed the Egyptians found another *chronique scandaleuse* to talk about, for two high officers of state, the chief butler and the chief baker, accused of high treason and other crimes, were put in ward. The two officers were accused of having secretly conspired to poison Pharaoh, and thus remove him, so that one of the officers could marry the King's daughter. A fly had been discovered in the cup of wine which the chief butler had handed to the King of Egypt, whilst the bread served upon the royal table contained a pebble or a small piece of clay.

And thus, Divine Providence, by raising the wrath of the Pharaoh against the two officers, was paving the way for Joseph's future greatness and high honour.

The chief butler and the court baker were liable to the penalty of death, but God ordained that they should be first detained in prison for some time, before suffering the extreme punishment. They were put in ward in the house of the captain of the guard, but, in consideration of the exalted position they had occupied at court, Joseph was appointed to wait upon them. All this God had ordained for the sake of Joseph, so that the chief butler and the chief baker might in time be the cause of his deliverance.

For twelve months or, according to others, for ten years, the two distinguished court officials had been detained in prison and daily waited upon by the handsome son of Rachel, when they both dreamed a dream. Curiously enough, each of them dreamed a dream and at the same time saw the interpretation of his colleague's dream.

When Joseph, as was his custom, brought them in the morning their water for washing, he found them in low spirits, sad and dejected. Politely and in a wise manner the youth inquired after the cause of their depression and why they looked quite different on that day from other days. "We have both dreamed a dream this night," replied the prisoners, "and in spite of the difference between the dreams and certain details the two dreams seem to us to be one dream." "We are greatly troubled," they concluded, "because there is no one here who could interpret to us our dreams."

"Tell me your dreams," said Joseph, "and let me interpret them. It is God who granteth understanding to man to interpret dreams, but anyhow, my interpretation, if not useful to you, can do you no harm." Thus spoke Joseph, ascribing beforehand all merit and credit to God. And because he had done this, and on account of his modesty, he was raised to an exalted position.[1]

"We are sad and in low spirits," said the two court officials, "because we have dreamed a strange dream, and there is none here to interpret it to us. Go thou now and ask the master of the prison to send to us one of the magicians that he may interpret our dreams to us."

"What use is a magician to ye?" said Joseph. "Relate your dreams unto me, and the Lord may put wisdom in my heart so that I will be able to interpret your dreams."

When the chief butler heard these words from Joseph, he waxed very wroth and exclaimed: "Art thou not the slave of Potiphar? Then how durst thou pretend to be an interpreter of dreams? Is an ass able to read in the stars its future destiny?"

Joseph only smiled at the angry reply of the chief butler and calmly said:

"My lord, hast thou ever heard of the famous physician Kimtom?"

"I have heard of him," replied the chief butler, "and know that he was a very great physician indeed."

"Then may I tell my lord what once happened to the great Kimtom?"

"Thou mayest tell us the story," said the chief butler "and we will listen."

Then Joseph related to the two prisoners the following story: "Kimtom was a great physician, and his fame had travelled far and wide. In spite of his greatness and his vast knowledge, Kimtom, as befits a really learned man, was very modest, and his thirst for more knowledge was great. One day, therefore, he thought unto himself: 'I will travel into foreign countries, where I may perchance find physicians whose knowledge excelleth mine, and I may learn from them new remedies by which to heal the diseases of men.' Thus thought Kimtom, and having filled his knapsack with all sorts of drugs and medicines, he saddled his ass and set out upon his journey. He visited many foreign towns and countries and everywhere he healed the sick and cured them of their diseases, without asking any remuneration for his labours, for Kimtom was a benefactor of men and practised his art neither for fame nor for money. One day he halted outside a big city so as to give his ass a little rest and also to repose himself from the fatigues of a long and wearisome journey. Being very tired, he stretched himself out upon the ground and soon fell asleep. A tramp, unkempt, ragged and torn, happened to pass by and saw the sleeping stranger. Swiftly he took off his own rags, took Kimtom's dress from the sleeping physician, and stole away, riding upon Kimtom's ass. When the physician at last awoke, he was not a little amazed to see himself stripped naked and his ass gone. 'I have been robbed,' said the physician greatly vexed.

"There was nothing left for the great physician to do but to cover his nakedness with the miserable and dirty rags the tramp had left behind, and thus arrayed continue his journey on foot. Taking up his knapsack which the tramp had dis-

dained to take with him, Kimtom walked along until he reached
the town. Now it happened that when he was passing through
one of the streets he heard a loud wailing and weeping. Entering the house, the great physician, clad in dirty rags, perceived
three doctors bending over a couch on which lay a young
man on the point of death. The parents of the lad, sobbing
bitterly, entreated the men of science to save the life of their
only child, promising them high reward. Kimtom looked at
the face of the youth and knew that he could bring him back
to life and health. Forgetting that he had the appearance of
a low tramp, he boldly stepped forward and addressed the
weeping parents:

" ' Entrust the patient to me, and I promise you to make
him well again with the medicines I carry in my knapsack.'
The three doctors shrugged their shoulders and scornfully
said: ' This tramp is mad, imagining himself to be a doctor.'
The father of the boy, judging from Kimtom's miserable
appearance that he was a low thief, exclaimed: ' Get out
of the house, thou miserable wretch; hast thou come here to
mock me in my misery?' And seizing Kimtom by the collar
of his ragged coat he threw him out of the house. But when
the three doctors, declaring their patient to be past human
help, had left the house, the mother of the boy said to her
husband:

" ' Thou hast acted too hastily in sending away so unceremoniously the poor beggar, for who knows, he might perhaps
have been able to cure our child.'

" ' Why dost thou indulge in idle talk?' retorted her husband, ' didst thou not notice the miserable rags the man had
on his back? His knapsack, too, contained no medicines,
but, no doubt, a piece of dry bread and a pair of old torn
shoes. No, be sure that the man was only a madman who
had taken it into his muddled head that he was a skilled
physician.''

'Whilst the parents of the boy were thus talking among themselves, their son died, and they wept and lamented over him until they had no strength left to cry any more. In the meantime, Kimtom said unto himself: 'They did not know that I am Kimtom, the great physician, whose fame has travelled far and wide, and they would have had faith in me had I told them my name.' Kimtom, as it appears, was still ignorant of the fact that people are mostly judged by their clothes. He therefore walked through the streets of the town calling aloud: 'Let all those afflicted with any disease come to me and I will heal them, for I am Kimtom, the famous physician!' But the people only laughed at him, thinking that he was not right in his mind. When Kimtom saw that no one was inclined to believe him, he sat down in the market place, putting his various medicines in front of him. Attracted by the delightful smell of his pharmaceutic products, the people, somewhat astonished, gathered round the ragged physician, curiously examining his phials and bottles.

" 'If thou art indeed Kimtom,' asked one of the crowd, noticing that the tramp was anyhow talking quite sensibly, 'if thou art indeed Kimtom, why didst thou come among us clothed in rags?' Kimtom then told them his story, how he had been robbed and stripped naked.

" Thereupon one man, afflicted with a sore disease, decided to try the skill of him who pretended to be Kimtom. Great was the astonishment of the people when they saw that the beggar was indeed a great physician. They now believed his story, and crowds of patients gathered round him imploring his medical assistance. When the father of the youth who had died the day before heard what had occurred, he rent his clothes and wept bitterly. 'I alone am guilty of my son's death,' he cried; 'had I not scorned and despised the beggar because of his rags, my son would have been cured, and alive now. I now see that a man must never be judged by his clothes, but by his countenance, his deeds, his intelligence, and his merits.'

" This is the story of Kimtom, the great physician," concluded Joseph, " and to this I will add only a few words. Thou, my lord, dost look upon me as a slave, and as such thou dost despise me, not believing that a slave has knowledge and wisdom enough to interpret dreams, even like the magicians and interpreters of dreams in Egypt.   My lord is mistaken, for I am not a slave by birth, but the son of a noble, powerful, just, pious, and wise man, who has taught me wisdom and imparted unto me much knowledge.   I was stolen from my native country and sold into slavery, and even here I am guilty of no transgression, but have been cast into dungeon for no crime whatever." [1]

And when the chief butler and the chief baker heard Joseph's words, they believed him and told him their dreams.

When Joseph heard the details of the two dreams, he at once noticed that, apart from their importance and significance for the two dreamers, they contained a prophecy concerning the future of Israel.   Clearly did he see the recondite meaning of the three branches of which the chief butler had dreamed. He interpreted them as the three influential men who would arise in Israel and bring about the redemption of the nations, both in Palestine and in Babylon.   He also saw hope and consolation in the fact that, although in exile, three princes of the nations would offer protection and a refuge to Israel.   Joseph furthermore saw in the dream of the chief butler an image of the world.   The vine represented the world, the three branches were the three Patriarchs, Abraham, Isaac, and Jacob, and the three mothers of Israel, whilst the ripe berries stood for the tribes of the nation.   Joseph further interpreted the vine as the Holy Law, and the three branches as the three leaders and teachers of Israel, Moses, Aaron, and their sister Miriam.

[1] Joseph Shabbethai Farhi, *Tokpo shel Yosef*; see also Lewner, *loc. cit.*, pp. 209–213.

Rejoiced at the prophecy and the glad tidings announced to him in the dream of the chief butler, happy at the prophecy concerning the deliverance of Israel, Joseph exclaimed:

" Thy dream is full of great prophecies, and the interpretation I will give thee is a very favourable one. Be thou of good cheer, for in three days thou wilt be delivered from prison."

Josephus relates the incident as follows:

Having given a favourable interpretation to the dream of the chief butler, Joseph begged his fellow prisoner to remember him in his days of prosperity, and to liberate him from the dungeon into which he had been cast through the intrigues of a wanton woman.

Joseph had thus put his confidence in a man, in a mortal being, and had entirely forgotten his usual faith and confidence in God alone. He had entirely forgotten for the moment the words of the Lord: " Cursed is the man who trusteth in man, and maketh flesh his arm, and whose heart departeth from the Lord " (*Jeremiah*, 17, 5). And also the words: " Blessed is the man that trusteth in the Lord, and whose hope is God ".

Twice did Joseph ask the chief butler to remember him in his days of prosperity, twice calling his attention to the fact that he had been stolen from the land of the Hebrews and had committed no crime in Egypt. And because Joseph had twice put his confidence in mortal man, the Lord ordained that the chief butler should forget his promise to Joseph and the latter remain in prison another two years.

When the court baker heard Joseph's favourable interpretation of the butler's dream, he at once knew that the interpretation the youth had given was correct, for in his own dream he had also seen the interpretation of his friend's dream. He now related his own dream to Joseph who at once knew that the baker's dream, too, conveyed a prophecy with regard to Israel's future.

The prophecy was not a favourable one, for it announced the suffering of the nation. The three baskets which the chief baker had seen in his dream, Joseph interpreted as the three kingdoms to whom Israel would be made subject, whilst the uppermost basket stood for the fourth kingdom, destined to extend its sway over the nations of the earth, who would threaten Israel with annihilation. (The bird was the Messiah who would appear to redeem Israel.) The three baskets Joseph also interpreted as the three heavy tasks which the Pharaoh of Egypt would one day lay upon Israel. And as the dream of the chief baker contained nothing pleasant with regard to Israel, but, on the contrary, conveyed to Joseph the prophecy of Israel's suffering, he gave the baker an unfavourable interpretation of his dream, telling him that in three days he would be hanged.

And on the third day it really came to pass even as Joseph had foretold. A minute inquiry into the case of the two court officials who were languishing in prison had finally proved that the chief butler had taken no part in the alleged conspiracy against the life of the King. It was further discovered by the King's counsellors that through no fault of the butler had a fly dropped into the cup of wine he had presented to the Pharaoh. The butler was therefore declared free of guilt and restored to his former position. On the other hand, it was discovered that the chief baker had been really guilty of conspiring against the King's life, and it was therefore assumed that he had intentionally put the small pebble in the bread served upon the royal table. The chief baker was consequently condemned to death and promptly hanged, even as Joseph had foretold.

The butler had not forgotten Joseph and was constantly thinking of ways and means how, without causing any harm to himself, he could save the youth and deliver him from dungeon. But God had ordained that all the butler's plans should be frustrated, and an angel of the Lord always made him either forget his promise or miss the longed-for opportunity. In vain, therefore, had Joseph hoped for human interference, and in vain did he expect to be delivered from prison soon after the release of the butler. The Lord, however, had not forgotten Joseph in his distress, and in His own time He saved him. On account of his dreams Joseph had been sold into slavery, and through a dream, a dream dreamed by the Pharaoh of Egypt, he was liberated and raised to high honour and to the position of ruler of Egypt.[1]

[1] See note 1, p. 65; see also Lewner, *loc. cit.*, pp. 210–214.

CHAPTER VI

The Viceroy of Egypt

The royal dreams—The meaning of Pharaoh's dreams—The interpretations of the magicians and wise men of Egypt—The seven daughters—Seven rulers of Egypt—The conquest of seven fortified cities—The seven royal wives and their fourteen sons—The war of the brothers—The rebellion of seven princes of the realm—The King's anger—The decree to put to death all the wise men of Egypt—The speech of the chief butler—The Hebrew slave—The throne with seventy steps—An audience with the King—The knowledge of languages—Pharaoh puts Joseph to the test—The token of truth—The birth of a prince and the death of another—The King and his counsellors—The objection of the princes of Egypt—The angel Gabriel teaches Joseph all the seventy languages in one night—The additional letter " H "—Joseph ascends all the seventy steps of Pharaoh's throne—The King's secret—Joseph's promise—The new Viceroy—Virtue rewarded—The golden chain and the royal signet ring—Young in years but old in wisdom—Zaphnath Paaneah—The meaning of the letters—The revealer of secret things—The story of Asenath, the daughter of Dinah—The gifts of the ladies of Egypt—The mysterious amulet—Setirah, the hidden one—The great procession—The disappointed damsels—Joseph renders thanks to the Lord—The royal gifts—The sumptuous palace and the magnificent throne—The Viceroy's army—The war between the people of Tarshish and the Ishmaelites—The Viceroy's victory.

Pharaoh had dreamed a royal dream, the dream of a king in whose hands lies the destiny of nations. A worshipper of idols, he saw himself above the Nile, the river he worshipped as a god and from which, as he imagined, both abundant harvests and famines depended. In days of prosperity and of plenty, in days of happiness and abundant harvests, love and harmony reign supreme, and men live in peace and in unity, entertaining friendly relations among themselves. Such was the meaning of the seven fat kine who came up out of the river, keeping together. But in days of adversity, of famine and war and suffering, brotherly love and harmony among men are destroyed. Men turn away from each other and grow selfish and grasping, and such was the meaning of the seven ill-favoured, lean kine, who came up out of the Nile, each turning its back upon the others and finally swallowing the fat kine, but remaining lean for all that. Pharaoh awoke for a brief space of time, but soon fell asleep again. He dreamed another dream, and then finally awoke. In his dream, the king had also seen its interpretation, but this he forgot in the morning, and he was greatly distressed and sad.

Immediately, Pharaoh summoned all the wise men of Egypt, the magicians, with which Egypt abounded, and the interpreters of dreams. All endeavoured to find a plausible interpretation of their royal master's dreams, but none of them satisfied the perturbed King. Some of the wise men of Egypt interpreted the royal dreams as follows: " The seven fat kine," they said, " mean seven daughters to be born unto thee, O King, whilst the seven lean kine stand for seven daughters thou wilt bury. The seven rank and good ears of corn mean that thou wilt conquer seven provinces, whilst the seven blasted ears of corn stand for seven provinces which thou wilt lose."

Other interpreters explained the royal dreams differently. " Seven kings," they said, " will issue from thy house and will rule over Egypt, but in days to come seven other princes will rise up against them and destroy them." The interpreters also said that the seven fat kine stood for seven fortified cities which Pharaoh would build and which would ultimately be conquered by seven nations of Canaan who would wage war against Egypt. The seven ears of corn meant that the descendants of Pharaoh would in days to come reconquer the seven fortified cities and also capture seven fortified places in Canaan and subdue seven nations there, thus regaining sovereign authority.

Other interpreters again maintained that the royal dreams referred to his wives and male issue. " Seven wives will the King marry, but they will all die in his life-time, after having given birth to fourteen sons. Seven of these sons will wage war against their seven brethren and kill them in battle." Thus the strong sons would be destroyed by the weak sons, just as the rank ears of corn had been swallowed up by the withered ears of corn. Another interpretation of the royal dreams was as follows: " The seven fat kine betokened seven sons to be born unto Pharaoh. They will be killed by seven princes who will rise up against them, but seven other princes will then come and wage war against the usurpers. They will avenge the death of the sons of Pharaoh, and the sovereignty will ultimately remain in the house of Pharaoh."

None of these interpretations did satisfy the King, for God had ordained that the efforts of all the wise men of Egypt should meet with no success, but excite the wrath of their royal master. God had also ordained that the King should first narrate his dreams to the wise men of Egypt, so that they could not say afterwards: " Had the King narrated his dreams to us, we too, like Joseph, would have found the right interpretation." God had deprived Egypt's wise men of their wisdom and intelligence, so as to prepare the way for Joseph's greatness.

And so it came to pass that the King, little pleased with the numerous interpretations of his dreams, vexed and greatly distressed, was sick to the point of death. In his anger he decreed that all the magicians, wise men of Egypt and inter-preters of dreams, be put to death and none of them be left alive, since their much vaunted wisdom had left them. Already the princes of the royal guard began their preparations for the execution and the wholesale massacre, when the chief butler appeared before the King and asked permission to speak. He was greatly alarmed at the turn events had taken, and feared that the death of the King, who seemed to take matters so much to heart, would result in his own misfortune and loss of his influential post. A change of Government is always fatal to the safety of court dignitaries.

Prostrating himself before his royal master, the chief butler thus spoke: " Long live the King, great is his power upon earth. Loaded with the burden of two transgressions do I this day appear before my master. I saw thy distress, O King, on account of the wrong interpretation of thy dreams, and yet I did not remember the man who is able rightly to interpret dreams. I did not let thee know of the existence of this man. I am also guilty of the sin of ingratitude, for I have omitted to fulfil the promise I once gave this man to speak to my master on his behalf. Two years ago it pleased the Lord God that Pharaoh should be wroth with me and with his chief baker and cast us into prison. Now in the dungeon, where we were confined, there was also a young slave of the captain of the guard. He was a simple youth, this slave, and one of the despised race of the Hebrews, but he knew how to interpret our dreams, mine own and that of the chief baker, for his interpretation came to pass, and it so happened as he had foretold us. Let the King, therefore, not kill the wise men of Egypt, but summon the Hebrew slave to appear in his presence. He is still confined in dungeon, and will interpret the King's dreams rightly."

Thus spoke the butler who, although he now remembered Joseph, described him in contemptuous terms, calling the King's attention to the fact that Joseph was a slave and one of the despised race of the Hebrews. In his own interest the butler was urging the King to summon Joseph, but he was anxious to make it impossible for the son of Jacob, of whom he was already jealous, to attain a high post at court. A slave and a Hebrew, thought the chief butler, could never be raised to high dignities by the ruler of Egypt. In spite, however, of his chief butler's contemptuous description of Joseph, the King at once ordered that Joseph be summoned into his presence, and he revoked the decree of death issued against the wise men of Egypt. The King also ordered that Joseph be not excited and hustled, lest, in his confusion, he failed to interpret the royal dreams correctly.

The servants of the King hastened to execute their master's command, and brought Joseph out of prison. But before Joseph appeared in the presence of the ruler of Egypt, he insisted upon being allowed to cut his hair, and out of respect for majesty he put on fresh raiment, so that he could appear at court in fitting attire. It is said that an angel brought him his raiment from Paradise, whilst, according to others, Joseph wore the garment into which the amulet suspended upon his neck had once been extended by an angelic hand.

When Joseph was brought into Pharaoh's presence, the King was sitting upon his royal throne, arrayed in royal garments, and clad in a gold-worked robe. The crown upon Pharaoh's head sparkled and flashed with many precious stones and gems, so that Joseph stood amazed at the appearance of the King.[1]

It was customary in Egypt that when a prince or some other distinguished person came to have an audience with the King, the latter descended thirty-nine steps of the throne, after the person seeking an audience had mounted thirty-one steps. If, however, a man of the people came to seek an audience with the King, he was only allowed to mount three steps, and the King came down four steps, all in accordance with the ceremonial of Egypt. It was also the custom at the court of Egypt that those who knew all the seventy languages of the world were permitted to ascend all the steps of the royal throne

[1] *Genesis Rabba*, §§ 89, 90, 91; *Midrash Agadah*, ed. Buber, pp. 96–97; *Midrash Tanchuma*, section *Mikkez*; *Targum Pseudo-Jonathan, in loco*, Babylonian Talmud, *Sotah*, 36b; *Midrash Lekach Tob, in loco*; *Pirke de Rabbi Eliezer*, Ch. 39; *Sepher Hajashar*; *Zeenah Urenah, Genesis*. See also Adolf Kurrein, *loc. cit.*; Lewner, *loc. cit.*, pp. 219–221.

to the very top and there have speech with the King. Those
who could speak only a few languages were allowed to ascend
as many steps as they knew languages. The ruler of Egypt,
however, seated upon the throne of the country, had to know
all the seventy languages of the world. When Joseph appeared at
court, he bowed to the King and mounted three steps, whereupon the King descended four steps and spoke to Joseph:

" O young man! my servant spoke unto me concerning
thyself, declaring thee to be an excellent man and very discerning. Vouchsafe therefore unto me the same favourable
action as thou didst bestow on him, and tell me what events
my dreams are foreshadowing. Do not conceal the truth from
me, nor shalt thou, out of fear or a wish to please me, flatter
me with lying words, should the truth be sad. No one has
been able to interpret my dream, and thou alone, an adept
at interpreting dreams, mayest now endeavour to do so."
Thus spoke the ruler of Egypt, and Joseph modestly replied:

" To God alone all merit should be ascribed. Neither I
nor any other man are really adepts at interpreting dreams,
but through my mouth God will announce pleasant tidings
unto Pharaoh."

And a voice from Heaven exclaimed:

" Thou hast spoken well, Joseph, and as thou never didst
manifest pride at thy knowledge, thou shalt be rewarded with
greatness and the sovereignty over Egypt."

Pharaoh now began to narrate his dream to Joseph, but
in order to test the youth's intelligence and his powers, he
told only parts of his dream and not in such detail as he had
really seen them. Inspired by the Divine Spirit, Joseph cor-
rected the King's tale, supplementing the points omitted by
the King, or adding the correct details of the dreams exactly
as the King had seen them, so that the King was greatly
amazed. Joseph then gave the King the true interpretation of
the dreams that had visited him. Although greatly satisfied

with Joseph's interpretation of his dreams, Pharaoh still had some doubts, and asked for a token which would finally convince him of Joseph's prophetic powers. This Joseph did, saying: " This, O King, will be a token of the truth and of the correctness of my words and of my interpretation: The Queen, thy wife, will this day give birth to a son, and thou wilt greatly rejoice, but soon after the birth of this thy youngest son, thy eldest son, born unto thee two years ago, will suddenly die, and thou wilt find consolation in the newly-born prince." Thus spoke Joseph, bowed to the King, and withdrew from his presence.

Scarcely had Joseph withdrawn from the royal presence, when the events he had foretold really occurred, so that Pharaoh was now completely convinced of the truth of the interpretation Joseph had given him. He was now quite sure that his dream indicated seven years of plenty, and seven years of famine, and exclaimed: " As Joseph has been present at my dreams, he shall be set over my house." He thereupon summoned into his presence all his servants, the princes of Egypt, the governors of provinces, and the grandees of his realm, and thus addressed them:

" Ye have all heard the words of the Hebrew. The signs he has given have been accomplished, and ye will now admit that his interpretation of my dreams is the correct one. Advise me now whether a man of wisdom and understanding such as the Hebrew can be found in the entire land. Ye have heard the advice of the Hebrew, and his plan by which the land of Egypt can be saved from the consequences of the famine which threatens us, and I myself feel convinced that his is the only true and correct one." Thus spoke the King, and his princes and grandees unanimously replied:

" Excellent indeed is the advice of the young Hebrew, and thou, O King, hast the power to act in the country as thou pleasest."

" If we traversed the whole earth from one end to the other," said the King, " we could never find a man who, like Joseph, has received from God the spirit of prophecy. If ye are not opposed to my decision, I will set Joseph over the land of Egypt, that he may save us from destruction by his wisdom."

But the astrologers and princes of Egypt raised an objection to the King's proposition: " Dost thou intend, O King," they said, " to set over us as our master one who is a slave, and who was bought for twenty pieces of silver?"

" He is not a slave," maintained the Pharaoh, " for I perceived in him the bearing and manner of a king."

To this the princes again replied that, even were it so, Joseph could not be set to rule over Egypt: " It is a law of our country that none can be king or even viceroy if he does not know all the seventy languages of men. How could this Hebrew serve as viceroy and rule over us, considering that he does not even speak the language of our land, knowing none but his own tongue which is Hebrew? Let the King therefore have the young Hebrew fetched to court and examined in all things, and then he may decide as it seemeth right to him."

The King agreed to the advice of his grandees, and, promising to give his decision on the following day, after examining Joseph, dismissed them.

Joseph had in the meantime returned to prison, for his master, fearing his wife and no longer trusting her, would not allow his servant to stay overnight in his house. During the night, Joseph was roused from his sleep by the angel Gabriel who had been sent by God to teach Joseph all the seventy languages of the world. At first the youth had some difficulty in learning all the languages so quickly, but when the angel Gabriel had added one of the letters of the *Tetragrammaton*, or the Divine name, namely, the letter *HE*, to Joseph's own name, calling him *Jehoseph*, the youth acquired the knowledge very quickly.   Amazed at and overawed by the appearance of the divine messenger, Joseph went again to sleep until the morning, when he was once more awakened by the servants of the King who came to fetch him.

The next morning Joseph was brought into the presence of Pharaoh, surrounded by the princes of Egypt and the grandees of the realm.   As Joseph knew all the seventy languages of the world, he ascended all the seventy steps of the throne until he reached the top, where he took his seat by the side of the King.   Pharaoh and his nobles were greatly rejoiced to find that Joseph was really fit to occupy the high position of viceroy.   Joseph's knowledge of Hebrew, however, caused the King some temporary embarrassment, for when the son of Jacob addressed the Pharaoh in the sacred tongue, the latter did not understand him.

" What is this language thou art speaking?" asked the ruler of Egypt."

" It is Hebrew, the sacred tongue," replied Joseph.

The King had to admit that he did not know Hebrew.   He therefore said to Joseph: " If the princes of the realm and the people find out that I am ignorant of one language out of the seventy, and thus do not fulfil all the requirements needed by a King of Egypt, they may depose me.   Swear therefore to me that thou wilt never reveal this secret to my people."

Joseph took a solemn oath never to betray the King and make known to the people that he only knew sixty-nine languages.

Thereupon the King thus addressed Joseph: " Thou didst advise me to set a wise man over the land of Egypt that he may by his wisdom save the country from the ravages of the famine which is threatening us.   As I have found none wiser than thou, thou shalt henceforth be the viceroy of Egypt, and none but thou shall give me the kiss of homage.   According to thy word only the princes will occupy their high positions at court, and according to thy commands my people shall go in and out, only in the throne will I be greater than thee."

The King then bestowed upon Joseph high distinctions, which were the rewards granted to him by the Lord for his virtue. The mouth that had refused the kiss of adultery received the kiss of homage from the people of Egypt; the body that would not participate in sin was clothed in garments of byssus; the neck that steadfastly refused to bow unto the unlawful was adorned with a golden chain; the hand that did not stretch out to touch sin received the royal signet ring which Pharaoh had taken off from his own finger; the feet that refused to hurry towards an alluring woman ascended the steps of the royal chariot; and the mind of Joseph which had not been defiled by sin was publicly proclaimed as wisdom. " Young in years, but old in wisdom", Pharaoh said of Joseph.[1]

" I am Pharaoh," said the King, " but thou art my second, and without thee none shall raise his hand to take up arms; without thee none shall put his foot in the stirrup of a horse in the whole land of Egypt."

Pharaoh called Joseph *Zaphnath Paaneah*, or the revealer of secret things, he who can bring to light secret things with ease and understanding and thus pacify the minds and hearts of men. The title Zaphnath Paaneah has also a symbolical meaning, for, as in the case of *Passim*, each letter has a separate meaning being the initial of a word. The letter " Z " stands for *Zopheh*, or seer; the letter " P " stands for *Podeh*, or redeemer; the letter " N " for *Nabi*, or prophet; the letter " T " for *Tomekh*, or supporter; the letter " P " for *Poter*, or interpreter of dreams; the letter " A " for *Arum*, or clever; the letter " N " for *Nabon*, or discerning, wise; and the letter " H " for *Haham*, or wise.

Joseph was also called the revealer of secret things, be-

[1] *Sepher Hajashar.*

cause he had discovered the secret of Asenath's history and of her parentage, and had taken her to wife. Asenath, the daughter of Dinah, and Shechem, the son of Hamor, whom an angel had brought to the borders of Egypt, was the adopted daughter of Potiphar, Joseph's master. Joseph discovered her identity in the following manner: When the newly appointed viceroy, riding in the royal chariot, was being conducted in a brilliant procession through the streets of the metropolis, all the noble women and maidens of Egypt, who had heard of Joseph's supernatural beauty, rushed to their windows and balconies to gaze upon the handsome son of Rachel. Enchanted by his great beauty, and anxious to attract his attention, they threw into his carriage their valuables, golden chains, jewels, and rings. Asenath alone, as it happened, had nothing upon her person which she could offer to the viceroy in token of her admiration. Quickly therefore she took off the amulet suspended upon her neck, the amulet upon which the story of her parentage was engraved, and which her grandfather Jacob had once fastened round her neck, and threw it at the viceroy's feet. The efforts of the noble ladies remained ineffectual, for Joseph never raised his eyes to gaze upon the alluring beauties of Egypt. But the amulet which fell at his feet attracted his attention, and upon reading the words engraved upon the gold plate, he discovered the identity of the damsel. And thus he discovered her who was also called *Setirah*, or the hidden one, for on account of her extraordinary beauty Asenath was kept concealed by her parents. It is also related that it was Asenath who had saved Joseph from the penalty of death which Potiphar was about to inflict upon his slave for his alleged outrage of his mistress. When Joseph was being flogged by Potiphar's servants, the child hurried to her foster-father and informed him that the lad was being accused wrongly, for he was innocent of any guilt.

At the command of the King, Joseph was conducted

through the streets of the city in solemn procession. He rode in the royal chariot accompanied by two thousand musicians, striking cymbals and blowing flutes. Five thousand men with drawn swords preceded the procession, whilst twenty thousand men of the King's grandees with gold-embroidered belts marched at the right, and so many at the left of Joseph. Women and maidens mounted the roofs and the city walls, and thronged the thoroughfares, all anxious to feast their eyes upon the supernatural beauty of the Viceroy and his handsome and noble appearance. Never did the Viceroy look at them, and as reward God ordained that no evil eye could ever hurt either Joseph or any of his descendants. All the royal servants, marching in front or behind the chariot wherein sat Joseph, burnt incense and cassia and all sorts of spices, and strewed the path with myrrh and aloes.

Twenty heralds proclaimed: " See, this is the man whom the King hath appointed to be his second, and all affairs of state shall be administered by him. Whoever acts against his commands and whoever refuseth to bow to and prostrate himself before the Viceroy shall be condemned to death as a rebel against the King and his representative."

When the people of Egypt heard this proclamation, they prostrated themselves before Joseph and called:

" Long live the King, and long live his Viceroy."

From his seat in the royal chariot, the son of Jacob raised his eyes to Heaven and prayed to the Lord of the Universe. " Lord of Hosts," he said, " blessed is the man who placeth his trust in Thee, for Thou dost raise up the poor out of the dust, and dost lift up the needy from the dunghill."

Thus Joseph journeyed through the whole country of Egypt, accompanied by Pharaoh's servants and the princes of his realm, viewing the whole land and all the King's treasures, and on his return once more appeared before the King.

Then the King gave his Viceroy royal presents: fields and

vineyards, and also 3000 *kikars* of silver and gold, and precious stones, and many other costly presents. The King also commanded that every Egyptian, under penalty of death, give Joseph a gift. A platform was therefore erected in the open street, and costly cloths were spread out wherein everyone deposited his gift. The Egyptians, anxious to obey the command of the King, and also to show their own admiration for Joseph, vied with one another in generosity. They deposited golden rings, brooches, armlets, coins, gold and silver vessels, and also precious stones. The princes, too, and all the servants of the King offered Joseph many gifts and honoured him greatly, when they saw that the King had appointed him to be his deputy. Pharaoh was anxious that the Viceroy should live in accordance with his new dignity. He therefore made him a present of one hundred slaves to serve him, and Joseph himself acquired many more.

Near the royal residence a sumptuous palace was built for Joseph which contained a vast hall of state. In this hall of state a magnificent throne was erected, fashioned of gold and silver, inlaid with precious stones and with a representation of the whole land of Egypt and of the River Nile watering the country. Thus Joseph, whom his brethren had sold into slavery, sat upon a throne and ruled over Egypt, and God increased his wisdom, so that the people of Egypt, the royal servants, and the princes of the realm loved and honoured him. The blessing of the Lord accompanied Joseph everywhere, and the fame of his greatness spread in the land of Egypt and travelled far and wide.

Joseph also equipped an army consisting of 4600 men, well armed and ready to do his bidding. He provided his soldiers with shields, spears, bucklers, helmets, and slings, so that they were well prepared to fight the King's battles against hostile nations. This army was increased by the princes of the realm, the royal servants and many of the inhabitants of the country, who were all ready to render a service unto their king, and to fight for him and for the country. Soon Joseph had an opportunity to make use of the army he had equipped in a war against the people of Tarshish.

In those days it came to pass that the people of Tarshish made war upon the Ishmaelites whom they conquered, taking possession of their territory. The Ishmaelites, few in number in those days, were unable to resist the invasion of the enemy, valiantly though they fought, and in their need sent a deputation to the King of Egypt, entreating him to come to their assistance: " Great King," the deputation said, " send thy servants and army led by the princes, and help us to repel the men of Tarshish who are invading our country and are threatening us with destruction."

The King thereupon sent out Joseph at the head of his army and a host of heroes, who marched into the land of Havilah to help the Ishmaelites against their enemies, the men of Tarshish. Joining forces with the Ishmaelites, Joseph won a splendid victory over the men of Tarshish, conquered their land, and settled it with the Ishmaelites who henceforth inhabited it.

As for the routed and defeated men of Tarshish, whose land had thus been conquered, they fled and took refuge in the territory of their brethren, the Greeks. Covered with glory, Joseph and his host of heroes returned to Egypt, and not a man had they lost in the fight.[1]

[1] See note 1, p. 77; see also Lewner, *loc. cit.*. pp. 219–227.

CHAPTER VII

The Story of Joseph and Zuleika in Arabic, Syriac, Persian, Sanscrit, and Mediæval European Literature

The story of Joseph and Zuleika in Moslem tradition—The story of the camel from Canaan—Joseph in love with his mistress—The faithful nurse—Zuleika's confession—The nurse's advice—The festival of the Nile—Zuleika's sickness—The enchantress—The sudden flight of the lover—The neighbour's gossip—The story of the ladies who cut their hands—The story of the Greek ambassador—A plot to assassinate Rajjan—The old Greek woman—Kamra, the chief butler, comes to fetch Joseph from prison—Joseph refuses to leave his dungeon before his innocence had been proved—The ladies of Egypt confess their guilt—Zuleika's excuse—The Viceroy and the beggar-woman—Joseph marries Zuleika—Firdusi's poem—Food from Paradise—The speaking wolf—Yusuf and Zuleika by Jami—Adam marvels at the beauty of Joseph—*Kathakautukam* by Crivara—Ephrem Syrus—The story of Joseph and Zuleika described by Christian authors—Potiphar's complaint—Joseph's magnanimity—The *Poema de Jose el Patriarca*—The *Leyendas*—The story of the ladies and the oranges in mediæval European literature—The story of Joseph in mediæval drama—Purim plays.

The story of Joseph, and more particularly the incident between the son of Rachel and the wife of Potiphar, is a favourite subject of many Oriental and European authors. Mohammed devotes one of the most beautiful suras in the Koran to the history of Joseph. The Arabic commentators have borrowed many incidents from Jewish sources, although Jewish authors have also copied many details in their description of Joseph and Zuleika from Arabic works. In Moslem tradition the love affair of Joseph and Zuleika is described as follows:

Zuleika, the wife of Potiphar, or Aziz, conceived a violent

love for the handsome Hebrew slave. She gave him new clothes, a separate garden house, where he could live, and appointed him to tend the fruit and the flowers.

One day an Ishmaelite leading a camel passed Potiphar's gate. Joseph happened to be standing at the gate and behold, when the camel approached, it crouched at his feet, and shed tears over his feet. Pull and drag the beast as he might, the owner failed to make it budge. Amazed at the strange conduct of the camel, Joseph examined the beast and recognized it as one of the camels belonging to his father, a camel to which he had often given bread. Upon inquiry, he learned from the Ishmaelite that he had bought the beast from Jacob in Canaan.

Moslem legend continues to relate that Joseph, the seventeen years old lad, had also fallen in love with his beautiful mistress, but durst not hope that his love would be reciprocated. Now, although Zuleika had loved Joseph from the very first moment she had set eyes on him, she kept her passion a secret and was quite contented to look at Joseph from her window, whilst he was busy in Potiphar's garden. Gradually, however, her love for the handsome slave became so violent that Zuleika grew ill and began to waste away. Pale and haggard looking, she walked about the house, and no one knew or even guessed the cause of the suffering which was undermining her health and the secret yearning which consumed her whole being. Many physicians did Potiphar consult, but none of them seemed to be able to cure the love-sick lady. One day, however, Zuleika's faithful nurse thus addressed her pale and sickly-looking mistress:

" Well do I know, my dear, that it is not thy body, but thy soul that is in great pain. Confess the truth to thy faithful nurse, O Zuleika, and tell her the cause of thy secret grief which is gnawing at thy heart, undermining thy health and driving away the bloom of youth from thy cheeks. Confess, my dear, to thy nurse who has nurtured thee with her milk and taken the place of a mother since thy infancy."

Thus spoke the shrewd old nurse, and Zuleika was glad of being at last able to confide in a loving human being, and find some consolation in her suffering. Weeping bitterly, she threw herself into the arms of her faithful old nurse and told her the cause of her secret passion and suffering.

" For six long weary years," she sobbed, " have I loved the handsome Joseph, and for six years have I endeavoured and made vain efforts to conquer this love and eradicate from my heart the passion which is consuming me."

" Be of good cheer, my dear," said the old nurse. " Thou hast done thy best and fought valiantly against this passion, but considering that thy husband is old and feeble thou shouldst be excused for loving the handsome Hebrew. None of thy sex would have waited so long or tried so valiantly to conquer her passion. Now take care of thyself, try to regain thy health and beauty; eat and drink, and dress with care, as thou didst before. Joseph cannot but love thee when he sees thee in all thy alluring beauty. Besides," shrewdly added the old Egyptian, " he is thy slave and used to obey thy commands."

Zuleika felt her courage and hope revive. She followed the advice of her nurse, and soon she once more looked healthy and well, having regained all her former beauty and charm of person. She now only waited for an opportunity when she would find herself alone with Joseph who could surely not remain blind to her charms.

Now, one day, Zuleika's nurse came in and thus spoke to the wife of Potiphar: " To-morrow, my child, is the great festival of the Nile, on which all Egyptians, without distinction of sex, age, or rank, are visiting the temple. Pretend to-night that thou art sick, so that thou mayest remain at home to-morrow. Thou wilt thus be alone in the house with thy beloved

Joseph who, as a Hebrew, will take no part in our festival. Thou wilt then have the longed-for opportunity to reveal unto Joseph that thy heart is full of love for him. Beautiful and alluring as thou art, he will not resist thee."

Zuleika acted as her nurse had advised her, and the next day, when the house was empty, she invited her handsome slave into her private room. Now Joseph loved Zuleika as much as she loved him, for she was exceedingly beautiful, but in his modesty, and remembering his position, that of a slave to a noble and wealthy lady, he never dared to raise his eyes to Zuleika. When, therefore, on the day of the great festival, Potiphar and the entire household had gone to the banks of the Nile, and Zuleika invited Joseph to her private room, he joyfully obeyed his mistress's command.

Zuleika served wine and fruit, and invited the handsome youth to partake of the refreshments. Seated upon a soft couch, covered with silken cushions, sipping sweet wine, the Egyptian lady hinted at last to her slave that he had only to stretch out his arms for her to fall into them. The eyes of his mistress were shining with love and passion, and Joseph was rejoiced when he saw that his love was being reciprocated. Forgetting the fact that his lady-love was a married woman, and that it was a sin for the son of Jacob and of Rachel to love her, he was about to take her into his arms and to press her to his breast. Suddenly, however, Joseph drew back, to the astonishment and annoyance of the lady. He was brought to his senses by the sudden appearance of the image of his father. The love-sick youth saw his father standing in the door and warningly and reproachfully shaking his finger at him. Hastily, Joseph arose and rushed towards the door. Amazed at his sudden flight, Zuleika tried to detain him.

" Why this sudden haste, beloved of my heart," she cried, " why art thou growing so deathly pale? There is no one in the house and we are safe from detection."

"Never," replied Joseph, "will I commit a sin against my God and against my master."

Zuleika, her passion aroused, would not let Joseph go and tried to detain him by force. She subsequently brought false accusations against Joseph. He was mercilessly flogged by the outraged husband's servants, but was saved by the miraculous interference of an infant in its cradle which had witnessed the scene. One of Zuleika's neighbours, however, who, on account of sickness, had stayed at home instead of attending the festival of the Nile, had also seen all that had taken place, and naturally gossiped. Zuleika's conduct soon became common talk, and all the ladies of Egypt, in their virtuous indignation, blamed their beautiful and passionate friend. They blamed her guilty love, but more perhaps her subsequent hatred of the youth who had virtuously opposed her. It was only when Zuleika became aware of the town talk and of friends' gossip and criticism that she invited the ladies to a feast with a view to giving them a lesson. She would show them that no noble lady of Egypt could remain indifferent to the supernatural beauty of the son of Rachel. It was at that banquet that she placed the oranges before the beauties of Egypt who, absorbed in the contemplation of the handsome slave, cut their hands and deluged the table and their own dresses with blood.

"This is the handsome and steadfast youth," said Zuleika, "on whose account I have become the talk of the town and am criticized so severely by you. You see now that none of you, my friends, could help being amazed at and enchanted by his extraordinary and superhuman beauty. But, though I had loved him passionately before, he has hurt my woman's pride, and my love has turned to hate." And thus Joseph, although innocent, was cast into prison. The Lord, however, was with him, and his cell was illumined with a celestial light, whilst a fountain did spring up in the midst of it, and a fruit-bearing tree grew before the door.

Joseph had not been long in prison, when he was already well known and highly esteemed for his cleverness, his wisdom and his great ability in interpreting dreams.

And now it came to pass that in those days the King of Greece, who was waging war against the King of Egypt, sent a deputation to Rajjan, then Pharaoh of Egypt, with peace proposals. Officially, the Greek ambassador was supposed to have come for the purpose of concluding an honourable peace, but secretly he hoped to be able to find an opportunity how to assassinate the heroic King of Egypt. The Greek ambassador addressed himself to an old Greek woman who had lived for many years in Egypt, and asked her advice.

" I know of no other way," said the woman, " of carrying out thy plan, and of realizing the purpose thou hast come for, than that of bribing the chief butler or the cook of the King, paying them a large sum so that they poison the King."

The Greek ambassador was well pleased with the advice of the old woman, and acted accordingly. He made the acquaintance of both the royal butler and the royal baker, and bribed them with much money. At last he persuaded the baker to put poison in Pharaoh's bread. The ambassador then went to inform the old Greek woman that he had succeeded in his plan. But when he came to see her before his departure she was not alone, and he therefore could not tell her openly what he had accomplished. He simply said that he was well satisfied with his work in Egypt, as he had been very successful and had obtained the object he had come for.

These words were soon reported to Pharaoh, and, as they could not refer to the ambassador's peace negotiations which had been broken off, Pharaoh suspected that the Greek ambassador must have had some secret business in Egypt. The old Greek woman was sent for and questioned, and at last, under torture, she confessed the truth.

"Either the royal butler or the royal baker," she said, "has been bribed to poison the King."

Both officials were therefore cast into prison, pending a minute inquiry. In dungeon, the chief butler and chief baker made the acquaintance of Joseph who interpreted their dreams. Seven years after his liberation, the butler came to fetch Joseph to Pharaoh who had dreamed a strange dream and was greatly troubled. But Joseph, who had remained in prison another seven years, because Zuleika's friends had also lodged complaints against him, and, in order to support their friend, had pretended that the Hebrew had been annoying them, refused to leave his dungeon before his innocence had been proved. He informed the butler, whose name was Kamra, of what had occurred and how, though innocent of guilt, he had been cast into prison.

"The wife of my master," he said, "had confessed her wanton passion to her friends, making no secret of it. At a banquet to which she had invited all the noble ladies, whose names I can mention, she had confessed that she loved me. These ladies the King may call as witnesses, if he wishes to prove me innocent before I appear in his presence."

Thus spoke Joseph, and Kamra, the chief butler, hastened to the King and informed him of Joseph's reply. At the command of Pharaoh, Zuleika and all the ladies of Egypt who had attended her banquet were brought to court, and they confessed that they had indeed slandered Joseph. Zuleika herself fell upon her knees and confessed to the King that in her annoyance and vexation, because Joseph had rejected her love and taken no heed of her great passion, she had calumniated him and caused him to be cast into prison.

"My great love for him," she concluded, "is my only excuse."

The King thereupon sent a royal messenger to Joseph, informing him that his sentence was quashed and that he was free. Pharaoh moreover gave Joseph a document bearing the royal seal, wherein it was declared that the youth had been falsely accused and wrongly detained in dungeon.

Joseph now arrayed himself in the garments King Rajjan had sent him and betook himself to the royal palace, where the King, surrounded by his magnates and the princes of his realm, sat upon his throne. Well pleased with Joseph's interpretation of his dream, the King appointed Joseph to be his chief treasurer and manager of all his estates in the place of Potiphar, Joseph's former master. It was now Joseph's business to travel all over the country and to purchase all the corn which, on account of the superabundant harvest, could be had at a very low price, and to store it away in storehouses especially built for the purpose.

Now one day, when Joseph was riding out to view one of his magazines situated at some distance from the city, he noticed a beggar woman whose whole appearance was very miserable. The chief treasurer, moved to compassion, approached the beggar woman, and soon noticed that in spite of her present position, she still bore traces of former greatness and must have seen better days. He held out a handful of golden coins, and was surprised to notice the woman's hesitation to accept his gift.

Sobbing loudly, the woman said: " Great prophet of God! I am not worthy to receive thy gift! And yet, it was my fault and transgression which served thee as the ladder upon which thou didst ascend to thy present happy position." Amazed, Joseph looked more closely at the beggar and recognized in her his former mistress, Zuleika, the wife of Potiphar, who had loved him passionately and in her fury at being rejected had caused him to be cast into prison. Joseph inquired after Potiphar, and learned from Zuleika that after his loss of office her husband had suffered greatly and died in poverty and distress. She further told him that Potiphar had never been anything to her but a husband in name, and that she had been his wife only in so far that she had borne his name. When Joseph heard these words, he raised Zuleika and brought her to the house of a relative of the King, where she was treated well and taken care of as if she were his sister. Joseph had always loved Zuleika and only rejected her love because she was a married woman and he would not commit a sin.

Soon Zuleika regained her former beauty, and Joseph, with the permission of the King, took her to wife.[1]

In his religious-romantic poem *Yusuf and Zulaikha*, the Persian poet Firdusi, who is better known as the author of the *Shahnameh*, describes the love of Joseph and Zuleika and the entire history of Joseph. The poem begins with the acquisition of the birth-right by Jacob, his demand for the hand of Rachel, and ends with the death of Joseph in Egypt. The poet describes the scene of the sale of Joseph, how he is cast into the well, where he is received by the angel Gabriel, so that he is not hurt in his fall. The angel provided the lad with food from Paradise, and clothed him in a celestial garment. The poet further describes Jacob's lament and the legend concerning the speaking wolf. Jacob, who had examined the garment and noticed that it had not been torn, had expressed his doubts as to the truth of the story his sons had told him. They, therefore, pretended that they had caught the wolf who had devoured Joseph.

During his journey to Egypt, Joseph passes Ephrath where Rachel lies buried, and slipping away from his masters, he throws himself upon the grave of his mother, weeping and lamenting.

---

[1] Weil, *Biblische Legenden der Muselmänner*, 1845, pp. 115–126; Geiger, *Was hat Mohammed aus dem Judentum genommen*, 1833; Grünbaum, in *Z.D.M.G.*, Vol. XLIII, p. 1 *et seq.*; see also T. Schapiro, *Die haggadischen Elemente im erzählenden Teil des Korans*, Leipzig, 1907, pp. 33–53.

The love affair of Joseph and Zuleika is described with
many details, mostly following Moslem tradition. The story
of the ladies of Egypt who cut their hands whilst peeling the
oranges is not omitted. Many elements from the Haggada
are also interwoven in Firdusi's poem, although these incidents
in Jewish legendary lore may have been borrowed by Jewish
writers themselves from Arabic sources.[1]

Another Persian poem dealing with the history of Joseph
is that of Jami, entitled *Yusuf and Zulaikha.* Jami relates
how Adam saw in a dream all his posterity pass before him.
In the long procession he noticed Joseph, at the side of whom
beauty faded and the stars grew dim. Marvelling greatly at
the glorious beauty of this his descendant, he asked the Lord
who this radiant apparition might be, so perfect in beauty.
A voice from Heaven informed Adam that this was Joseph,
the son of Jacob, whose loveliness will excite the envy of everyone. Our first parent was then ordered to bestow upon this
beautiful " fair gazelle " all the natural and supernatural gifts
which the Lord had granted him. Adam thereupon bestowed
upon Joseph beauty and charm and also strength to keep him
pure in the face of temptation.[2]

A Sanscrit poem by Crivara, entitled *Kathakautukam*, based
upon the work of Jami, also relates the history of Joseph and
Zuleika.[3]

With regard to Joseph's treatment of his master, Ephrem
Syrus relates the following incident: When Potiphar, Joseph's
former master, heard and saw to what high dignity his slave
had been raised by the King, and what honour he was enjoying,
he came home and thus addressed his wife: " Joseph who was
once our slave is now our ruler and master; he to whom we
gave his raiment is now dressed in purple by Pharaoh; he

---

[1] Firdusi, *Yusuf and Zulaikha*, translated into German by Schlechta Wssehrd; see also
Z.D.M.G., Vol. XLI, p. 578.
[2] Translated into English by Ralph T. H. Griffith (Trübner's Oriental Series) 1882.
[3] Translated into German by Richard Schmidt, 1898.

whom we had driven out of our house is now riding in the
royal chariot, wearing a crown upon his head instead of iron
chains."

Thus spoke Potiphar, but his wife replied: " It is true that
I loved Joseph, dazzled and enchanted as I was by his extraordinary beauty, and out of love for him I treated him unjustly.
And yet, he owes his present greatness to us, for without us
he would never have attained such high honours." When
Potiphar subsequently appeared before Joseph, the latter forgave his former master his harsh treatment, for he knew that
such had been the will of the Lord.[1]

Some of the Christian authors tell the story of Joseph and
Zuleika as follows: Zuleika had fallen in love with the son of
Rachel, and offered to poison her husband so that she could be
married legally to Joseph. " As a rule," she said, " men make
love to women, but thou, being my slave, durst not open thy
lips to speak to me. And so I have condescended to reveal
unto thee the secret of my heart." When Joseph rejected her
love, she exclaimed: " Great is thy beauty, but small thy understanding, for whilst everyone is anxious to be free, thou art
content to remain a slave. If thou wilt hearken unto my words,
thou wilt be free and happy. Thou wilt be the master, and I
thy maidservant. If thou art afraid to commit a sin lest thy
God punish thee, then take gold and silver and distribute it
among the poor as an atonement for thy sin." Joseph refused,
and was cast into prison. When Potiphar heard what high post
his former slave was occupying at the court of Egypt, he was
greatly afraid. Bitterly did he reproach his wife for her conduct, for he was now convinced that it was Zuleika who
had conceived a wanton passion for Joseph and accused him
falsely.

" Thou hast put me to shame before the King and before
his magnates," he said. " Joseph, who was our slave and whom

[1] See Grünbaum in *Z.D.M.G.*, Vol. XLIII.

in consequence of thy wanton passion I had cast into prison,
is now father and ruler at the court of Pharaoh. How shall
I now dare stand before him and look up to him. I knew from
the very first that he was no slave, but a free-born man and
therefore I appointed him steward over my house. Joseph
had never committed any sin, but thou, in thy wanton mind,
didst cast an eye upon him, desiring his beauty."

But Potiphar's fears were unfounded, for in his magnanimity Joseph harboured no illfeeling towards his former master
and his wife. He sent them presents and splendid raiment, and
invited them to court. Arrayed in the costly garments Joseph
had sent them, Potiphar and his wife hastened to court to
Joseph, who received them very graciously.[1]

In a poem which Ticknor discovered in the National
Library at Madrid, written in Arabic characters, but composed
in Spanish, the history of Joseph is told with many legendary
additions. The poem, called *Poema de Jose el Patriarca*,
begins with a description of the jealousy of the brothers of
Joseph at his dreams, and describes in full the love of the fair
Zuleika, " who fills a space more ample than usual in the
fancies of the present poem ". The scene of Joseph's lamentation at his mother's grave is also described, varying from the
description given in Jewish and Arabic sources, and so is the
incident of the speaking wolf brought by the brethren as the
animal that had killed Joseph. In the description of Zuleika's
passion for Joseph, the story of the ladies of Memphis, who
were so enraptured with the lad's beauty that they cut their
fingers whilst peeling their oranges, is not omitted.[2]

Yusuf and Zuleika, the Moslem Song of Songs of Love, is
also the subject of a Spanish Arabic work called *Leyendas*,
written in Arabic characters and in the language of the Mori-

---

[1] M. Weinberg, *Die Geschichte Joseph's von Basilius dem Grossen aus Cäsarea*, Halle,
1893, pp. 34–35.
[2] Ticknor, *History of Spanish Literature*, New York, 1849, Vol. III, pp. 433–458, and
Vol. I, pp. 95–99; R. Kœhler, *Kleinere Schriften*, Berlin, 1900, Vol. II, p. 82; Grünbaum,
Z.D.M.G., Vol. XLIII, pp. 27–28.

scoes.[1] The contents resemble greatly those of the Moslem tradition and the poem of Firdusi.

The incident of the ladies of Memphis cutting their hands whilst peeling their oranges has passed not only into oriental but also into mediæval European literature. We have referred to the poem of Firdusi, *Yusuf and Zulaikha*, to Jami's *Yusuf and Zulaikha*, and to Crivara's *Kathakautukam*.

With regard to mediæval European literature, the incident is borrowed in *Olivier de Castille et Arthus d'Algarbe*, and in the *Romance of Blonde of Oxford and Jehan of Dammartin*, by Philippe de Reimes, a trouvère of the thirteenth century. It is also found in the German poem, *Spruch von aim Konig mit Namen Ezel*, and also in a Russian song about Eupraxia, wife of Vladimir.

The difference between Orient and Occident is interesting. Whilst in the Hebrew works, in the *Midrash Tanchuma*, the *Midrash Haggadol*, and the *Sepher Hajashar*, in the Persian poems and in the Koran, it is the ladies who are so absorbed in the contemplation of the beauty of the Hebrew slave that they cut their fingers, unaware that their blood is soiling their garments, in the mediæval poems it is the man who cuts his finger, absorbed as he is in the contemplation of his beloved. The Russian song, on the other hand, is oriental in its conception, and here, too, it is the lady who is casting glances of love upon the handsome hero.

In the romance of Olivier the story runs as follows: Olivier of Castille was in the service of Princess Helen of England, occupying the post of *premier écuyer tranchant*. He fell violently in love with the princess, and one day, whilst serving at table, he was so absorbed in the contemplation of the lady's beauty that he cut his thumb: " Elle n'avoit rien devant soi de tranché pour manger, pour ce lui dit-elle: Olivier, mon loyal ami, si mangerois-je bien si vous me donniez de

---

[1] *Z.D.M.G.*, Vol. XLIV, pp. 457–477.

quoi; et lui, tout honteux, commença à la servir: mais comme celui-ci n'avoit pas son entendement bien présent, il se coupa le pouce presque tout jusqu'à l'os ".[1]

A similar story is told of Jehan of Dammartin who was in the service of the Count of Oxford, and fell violently in love with the earl's daughter Blonde. One day, whilst waiting at table, he is so absorbed in the contemplation of Blonde's beauty that he cuts his finger.[2]

In German literature the incident is related of King Ezel. At the palace of King Ezel a beautiful maid once appeared, whilst the King and his heroes were at table. All were so enchanted by the extraordinary beauty of the maid that they cut their fingers instead of their meat.[3]

In the Russian song, on the contrary, it is Eupraxia, wife of Vladimir, who is so struck by the handsome appearance of Tshurillo that she can hardly take her eyes off him. Absorbed in the contemplation of the hero's beauty, the lady cuts her hand, like the ladies of Memphis. Turning to her women, she then said: " Wonder not that I have cut my hand, I am losing my head, and my senses are disturbed as soon as I perceive the handsome Tshurillo." [4] At his sight, " her reason grew dark and dim, and madness possessed her for the love of him ".

The history of Joseph is also the subject of numerous dramatic works. During the Middle Ages, religious subjects were dramatized in Spain, France, and England, and one of the most favourable themes was the history of Joseph, wherein many elements from the Haggada were interwoven.

In the *Mistère du Viel Testament* [5] which appeared towards the end of the fifteenth century, the history of Joseph is treated fully, and many incidents directly remind us of the legendary

[1] See Kœhler, *loc. cit.*, p. 80.
[2] Edited by Leroux Lincy, and printed for the Camden Society in 1858; see also Kœhler, *loc. cit.*, p. 84.
[3] *Erzählungen aus altdeutschen Handschriften*, Gesammelt durch Adelbert von Keller.
[4] A. Rambaud, *La Russie Epique*, Paris, 1876, p. 97.
[5] Edited by J. de Rothschild, Paris, 1881.

history of Joseph as related in Talmud and Midrash. As in
the Jewish legend, Potiphar's wife excuses herself from attending the public festival to which the entire household went.
She thus has the longed-for opportunity of remaining alone
in the house with Joseph. Whilst, however, according to the
Haggada, it was the annual festival of the Nile, in the *Mistère
du Viel Testament*, the occasion is a public festival in honour
of the King, on the occasion of his miraculous escape, for the
chief baker and the chief butler had planned to poison him.
In the majority of mediæval passion-plays a parallel is drawn
between Joseph, the just and pious, and the person of the
Saviour. Besides the passion-plays,[1] there are also independent dramatic productions, some of them even written in the
dialect called Yiddish (Jewish jargon). One of these plays,
which were produced at the *Purim* festival, is reproduced by
Schudt,[2] and another by Ave Lallemant, in his great work
Das deutsche Gaunertum (Vol. III, p. 491). These plays were
acted by strolling players, going from house to house, on the
festival called *Purim*, the day on which, according to the *Book
of Esther*, the Jews were saved from the plot of Haman.[3]

In the majority of cases, the play, enacted on that day, was
a dramatic production containing the history of Esther, but
the drama of the sale and greatness of Joseph was also frequently played. It may be remarked, *en passant*, that Goethe
wrote a Joseph drama in his youth.[4] In the majority of the
dramas composed on the history of Joseph during the sixteenth
century, the lady endeavouring to win the love of Joseph is
called Zenobia,[5] Berenica, Moscha, or Seraphim, but never
Zuleika. There also exists a Hebrew drama entitled *Joseph and
Asenath*, by Susskind Raschkow (1817), and Joseph is the
subject of a novel by Grimelshausen.

[1] Weilen, *Der aegyptische Joseph im Drama des 16ten Jahrhunderts*, Wien, 1887.
[2] *Jüdische Merkwürdigkeiten.*
[3] See also Landau, *Hebrew-German Romances and Tales*, in *Teutonia*, Heft 21, Leipzig,
1912, p. xxx.
[4] Weilen, *loc. cit.*, p. 189.   [5] Cassel, *Mischle Sindbad*, pp. 23-24.

THE LADIES OF EGYPT

(30) And certain women said publicly in the city, The noble-man's wife asked her servant to lie with her; he hath inflamed her breast with his love; and we perceive her to be in manifest error. (31) And when she heard of their subtle behaviour, she sent unto them and prepared a banquet for them, and she gave to each of them a knife; and she said unto Joseph, Come forth unto them. And when they saw him they praised him greatly, and they cut their own hands, and said, O God! this is not a mortal; he is no other than an angel, deserving the highest respect.

The Koran (Sale's translation), Sura, 12.

THE WOMEN OF MEMPHIS AND THE ORANGES

Like a bed of roses in perfect bloom
That secret treasure appeared in the room.
The women of Memphis beheld him, and took,
From that garden of glory, the rose of a look.

One glance at his beauty o'erpowered each soul,
And drew from their fingers the reins of control.
Each lady would cut through the orange she held,
As she gazed on that beauty unparalleled.
But she wounded her finger, so moved in her heart,
That she knew not her hand and the orange part.

One made a pen of her finger to write
On her soul his name who had ravished her sight.
A reed which, struck with the point of the knife,
Poured out a red flood from each joint in the strife.

One scored a calendar's line in red,
On the silver sheet of her palm outspread,
And each column, marked with the blood drops, showed,
Like a brook when the stream o'er the bank has flowed.

When they saw youth in his beauty's pride,
" No mortal is he," in amazement they cried,

" No clay and water composed his frame,
But, a holy angel, from heaven he came."

Yusuf and Zulaikha, a poem by Jami, translated by Ralph
  T. H. Griffith (Trübner's Oriental Series), London, 1882
  (p. 229).

THE SERVANT AND HIS MISTRESS

La Dame

Or ne sçay je par quelle voye
De son amour Joseph tempter,
De peur que esconduite ne soye;
C'est cella qui me faict doubter
S'il me veult de luy debouter,
Et, on le sçait, je suis infame.
D'autre part, c'est honte que femme
Prie l'homme de villenie,
Principallement une dame
Comme moy; je suis esbahye,
Je considère ma follye,
Mais, bref, amour me contrainct tant
Qu'il sera force que je prie
Joseph pour estre mon amant,
Et le prieray que en ce dormant
Avecques moy seulement couche.

Putiphar

Veez cy jour solemnel et hault
Que tout s'esbat et se delicte
Selon la manière d'Egipte;
Mesmement ad ce jour les dames
Viennent avecques autres femmes
Pour la feste solemnizer,
Et pour tant je vueil adviser
Ma femme de ce mettre a point,
Affin qu'elle n'y faille point
Plus que les autres de la terre.

La Dame

Amour, tant tu me fais de guerre,
Amour, tant tu me maine grief,
Amour, tant tu me tiens en serre,
Se je ne jouys de Joseph!
J'é le cueur aussi froid que nef,
Aucunes fois, et, l'autre, ardant
Comme feu en le regardant,
Tant suis de son amour esprise.

Putiphar

M'amye, ma femme, je advise
Que au jour d'huy la solemnité
Se faict en la communité;
Preparez vous honnestement
Pour venir a l'esbatement
Et y veoir les choses nouvelles,
Comme les autres damoyselles
Qui y prendront plaisir et joye.

La Dame

Mon amy, voulentiers je iroye;
Mais, je vous pry, ne vous desplaise
Reposer vueil, mais qu'il vous plaise
Tant que les esbas on fera.

Putiphar

Faictes ainsi qu'il vous plaira,
Car ce n'est pas ma voulenté
Que ne gardez vostre santé
Plus que autre femme naturelle.

La Dame

Il m'est pris une douleur telle
Que je ne le puis exposer.

Putiphar

Je vous lesse donc reposer,
Et vois a la solemnité.

Le Mistère du Viel Testament, Ed. by J. de Rothschild, Paris,
1881, Tome III, pp. 67–69, v. 18732–18789.

JOSEPH'S PRAYER

Vray Dieu puissant, souverain roy des roys,
De qui je vueil garder les sainctes loix
Sans fraction, et le commandement,
La mauvaistié de ceste femme vois;
Preserve moy et garde en touz endroiz
De luy donner aucun consentement.
Je congnois bien son faulx entendement,
Son fol desir, son villain pensement,
Ou, se Dieu plaist, je ne m'accorderay.
S'elle me veult donner empeschement,
Elle ne peult, sinon tant seulement
De mon manteau qui luy est demouré.
  S'on me faict mal, j'endureray;
  S'on me tance, je me tairay;
  S'on me impose vice ne blasme,
  Tant doulcement m'excuseray,
  Et a tesmoing appelleray
  Dieu qui gard mon corps et mon ame.

Ibid., pp. 73–74, v. 18897–18914.

BLONDE OF OXFORD

Blonde, qui si le voit penser,
De cel penser le veut tenser;
Si li dist que il pense tost,
Mais il ne l'entent pas si tost.
Puis li redist: " Jehan, trenchiés!
Dormés-vous chi, ou vous songiés?

S'il vous plaist, donés m'à mengier;
Ne ne welliés or plus songier."
A cel mot Jehans l'entendi;
S'est tressalis tout autressi
Com cil qui en soursaut s'esveille.
De s'aventure s'esmerveille.
Tous abaubis tint son contel,
Et qui da trenchier bien et bel;
Mais de penser est si destrois
Que il s'est trenciés en ij dois;
Si sans en saut et il se liève.

Blonde of Oxford and Jehan of Dammartin, by Philippe de
Reimes (see Kœhler, *loc. cit.*, pp. 84–85).

CHAPTER VIII

The Romance of Asenath, or the Marriage of the Viceroy

Asenath supposed to have been the daughter of Dinah and Hamor—Joseph and Asenath, a novel of the Middle Ages—The journey of the Viceroy—The proud beauty—Fit to be queen of Egypt—The son of a Canaanitish herdsman—The damsel at the window of her palace—Asenath's regret—The proud virgin who never looked at men—The humble salute—A kiss refused—The blessing of a brother—The disappointment of the maid—Asenath's conversion—Sackcloth and ashes—The visit of the angel—The city of refuge—Honey from Paradise—The seven virgins—Eleven columns of the city of refuge—The fiery chariot—The arrival of the Viceroy—The kiss of betrothal—" Let me wash thy feet, my lord "—The overjoyed parents—Marriage postponed—The royal gift—A seven days feast.

Joseph is said in *Genesis* to have married Asenath, daughter of Potiphera, priest of On. Legend was busy inventing incidents which would whitewash the son of Rachel from the sin of having married a heathen. Asenath, therefore, is represented as the daughter of Dinah, and consequently Joseph's niece, whose identity he had discovered.

Legend relates that Asenath, the daughter of Dinah and Shechem, was deposited at the frontier of Egypt by the angel Gabriel (or Michael), carried there by a flood, or brought to the borders of the country by a travelling caravan. Here she was adopted by Potiphera, and subsequently married Joseph.[1] This legend is also repeated by certain Syriac authors, whilst it is criticized by Samaritan and Caraite writers.[2]

[1] *Midrash Abkhir*, quoted in *Yalkut, Genesis*, § 146; *Pirke de Rabbi Eliezer*, Ch. 38; Tractate *Soferim*, 21, 8; see also *Revue des Etudes Juives*, Vol. XXI, pp. 87–92.
[2] See Payne Smith, *Thesaurus, s.v. Dinah.*

According to Moslem tradition, Joseph married, by command of the King, Zuleika, the wife of his former master, who was now a widow. (See D'Herbelot, *Bibliothèque Orientale, s.v. Yussuf.*)

Another version of the story of the viceroy's marriage to Asenath is contained in an apocryphal work called *Joseph and Asenath*, a novel well known during the Middle Ages.[1] The romantic story of Joseph's love and marriage runs as follows:

In the course of the second year of Joseph's rule in Egypt, his prophecies were confirmed, for the seven years of plenty, even as the new Viceroy had foretold, began. God had ordained that the famine which was to visit Egypt should last fourteen years, but Joseph had prayed to the Lord and his prayer was heard, so that the fourteen years were reduced to seven. During the years of plenty, the Viceroy gathered up all the grain in the country, laying up the produce of each district in the city situated in the middle of the district. He ordered that ashes and earth from the very soil on which the corn had grown be strewn on the collected grain to be preserved. These precautions were taken in order to preserve the food from rot. For the purpose of garnering food, collecting the produce and preserving it against the need of the years of famine, Joseph frequently journeyed through the land of Egypt, visiting many cities. It was during one of these journeys that he met and married his wife Asenath.

Asenath was the proud daughter of Potiphera, the mighty prince and priest of Heliopolis and a counsellor of Pharaoh. She excelled in beauty all the comely maidens of Egypt whom she did not resemble. She was more like Sarah, Rebekah, and Rachel, being tall like Sarah, comely like Rebekah, and

---

[1] *Life and Confession,* or *Prayer of Asenath,* published (Greek and Latin) by P. Batiffol, in *Studia Patristica,* Paris, 1889–1890; see also Oppenheim, *Fabula Josephi et Asenathae Apocrypha,* Berlin, 1886—Fragments of this novel appeared in Fabricius, *Codex Pseudo-epigraphicus Vet. Test.,* II, 85–102, and an abridged Latin translation was published by Vincent de Beauvais in his *Speculum Historiale,* Ch. 118–124. See also the article in *Jewish Encyclopedia, s.v. Asenath.*

beautiful like Rachel.   The fame of her beauty spread far
and wide, and many were her admirers and suitors for her
hand.   But Asenath disdained them all.   A proud beauty,
reared in luxury, she inhabited a magnificent castle where
she was waited upon by seven virgins.   Brought up in the
religion of Egypt, she worshipped innumerable idols, whose
golden and silver images filled her rooms, and whose names
were engraven upon the gems of her necklace.

The offers of all the suitors for her hand she disdainfully
refused, for only the son of Pharaoh would she marry.   The
King, however, forbade this union.   Potiphera, too, was rather
in favour of his daughter marrying Joseph, the Viceroy of
Egypt, the mighty man of God.   When Potiphera expressed
his wish that his daughter should marry the mighty man of
God, as he called Joseph, who would soon honour him with
a visit, Asenath scornfully replied:

" I am fit to be the wife of the son of Pharaoh and sit
on the throne of Egypt.   How canst thou expect me to marry
a former slave, the son of a shepherd in Canaan?"

Thus spoke Asenath in her indignation.   But she knew
not Joseph and had never contemplated his divine beauty,
which made all the ladies of Egypt fall in love with him.

Now it happened that in the first year of plenty Joseph was
journeying through Egypt to collect corn.   He was expected
to visit also Heliopolis, and he sent word to Potiphera that
he would put up at his house.   Potiphera was very glad at
this, for he now hoped to be able to arrange a marriage between Joseph and his daughter Asenath.

But when he informed his daughter of the visit of the
Viceroy, telling her that it would be his dearest wish to see
her become Joseph's wife, the girl once more scornfully refused
to entertain such a proposal, as it was only the King's son
she would marry.

The next day Joseph arrived, seated in the royal chariot, all of gold, and drawn by four snow-white horses. He was radiantly beautiful, dressed in a magnificent tunic with gold embroidery, and from his shoulders hung a crimson robe woven with gold. A circlet of gold was round his temples, and he carried an olive branch in his hand. No lady of Egypt could see Joseph and remain indifferent, for no woman had ever given birth to a son who could be compared to the son of Rachel, the radiantly beautiful, or, as the Egyptian ladies called him, the son of God. Joseph was received by Potiphera and his wife in the hall of state, and they paid him due homage.

Although Asenath had spoken angry words of Joseph, and scornfully refused to listen to her father's proposal, her feminine curiosity nevertheless made her look out of her window when the Viceroy arrived. When she beheld the ruler of Egypt, she bitterly regretted her harsh words.

" He is not a slave," she said, " nor is he the son of a shepherd, but the son of God, for only the son of God could be so radiantly beautiful."

Bitterly did Asenath now regret her scorn of Joseph. Ah, how gladly would she now consent to marry him whom she had so disdainfully called a slave, if he would only consent to take her to wife. Not his wife, but his slave and handmaiden would she be only to be near his enchanting personality. Thus mused Asenath, looking out of the window of her apartments, unable to turn her eyes away from the glorious and radiant son of Rachel.

Joseph, in the meantime, had noticed the proud beauty looking out of the window, and he requested Potiphera that she be ordered away, for he did not permit women to look at him so insistently. The Viceroy was indeed weary of the advances of the Egyptian ladies who constantly pursued him and gave him no respite.

" My lord," said Potiphera, the priest of On, " this is my daughter, a proud virgin who never looks at men and keeps aloof from them. She is very modest and retiring, and until this day she hath seen no man save myself, for she dwells in her own apartment, waited upon by seven virgins. If it please thee, my lord," added Potiphera, "she shall come down and salute thee."

When Joseph heard that Asenath hated the sight of men, he asked Potiphera to have her brought down, so that he might treat her as his sister. Quickly did the proud Asenath now obey her father's request, and hurried down into the hall of state to salute him whom she had only recently called a contemptible slave. She came down and greeted the son of Jacob with the words:

"Hail, my lord, blessed of the most High God."

And Joseph replied:

"May the Lord who vivifies all bless thee." Thereupon Potiphera bade his daughter kiss Joseph.

"Go, my daughter," he said, "and kiss thy brother."

Asenath advanced to do the bidding of her father, but Joseph warded her off.

"It is not meet," said he, "for one who blesses with his mouth the living God, who eats of the blessed bread of life, who drinks out of the blessed cup of incorruptibility, to kiss a strange woman who blesses dumb idols, eats bread from their table, and anoints herself with the oil of corruption."

Joseph's speech and action produced a deep impression upon Asenath who grew very sad, her eyes filling with tears. When Joseph saw her tears, he had compassion on the poor maiden. Laying his hand upon her head he thus spoke:

"Lord of my father Israel, Thou who didst create light out of darkness, truth out of error, and life out of death, bless this maiden, quicken her and renew her with Thy spirit, that she may eat of the bread of life and drink out of the cup of blessing. Number her days with the days of Thy people whom Thou hast chosen in the days before the world ever was, so that she may enter Thy rest which Thou hast prepared for Thy elect, and dwell in Thy eternal life until eternity."

Thus Joseph blessed the weeping Asenath. Thereupon he departed, announcing, however, that he would soon return.

Asenath, glad and happy at the blessing Joseph had bestowed upon her, but sad and grieved at her former scornful words, retired to her apartments. Divesting herself of her resplendent raiment, she put on dress of mourning, cast the idols she had worshipped out of the window and began to do penance, sitting in sackcloth and ashes, praying and weeping for seven days and seven nights. Thus she remained alone, shut up in her apartment, for even the seven virgins, her constant companions, were not allowed to come near her. And Asenath prayed to the living God, the God of Joseph, to forgive her her sins and to pardon her former idolatrous life.

"Lord of the Universe," she prayed, "I have now done with the dead and profitless idols of Egypt. I no longer honour them, but have flung them away from me. Here am I now, an orphan, repulsed by my people, I the daughter of a great and powerful lord of Heliopolis. Only a short time ago, in my arrogance and pride, I rejected the offers of my many suitors, but now I come before Thee, O Lord, humbled and penitent, and, like a frightened child, I seek Thy protection. Forgive me, O Lord, for having spoken scornfully of my lord Joseph, whom I have treated as the son of a Canaanitish herdsman. I did not know, unfortunate sinner that I am, who he was, but now I love him with all my heart and all my soul, and am ready to be his handmaiden and slave all the days of my life."

Thus Asenath wept and prayed and did penance for seven days. At dawn of the eighth day she arose, for she knew that God had hearkened to her prayers. And indeed, she saw the morning star arise and the sky rent with a great light; and a man, a divine messenger, radiant with light, appeared before the girl.

" Arise, Asenath," he called.

" Who calleth me?" queried the maiden.

" I am a prince of the house of God," replied the voice, " and a prince of the army of the Lord."

Asenath arose and beheld before her a man who greatly resembled Joseph. He was radiantly beautiful, and his eyes sparkled and shone like the rays of the sun. Upon his head he wore a crown and in his hand he held a royal staff. Overawed and frightened, Asenath began to tremble, but the man before her said:

" Be not afraid, Asenath, but cast off thy garments of mourning, thy black robe and thy sackcloth; remove the ashes from thy head and rejoice. Thy name is now written in the book of the living, and never will it be blotted out. Thou hast been newly born and quickened, and now thou shalt eat of the bread of life and of blessing, drink out of the cup of incorruptibility and be anointed with the holy unctions. This day I have given thee as a spouse to Joseph, and thy name shall no longer be Asenath, but the ' pillar of refuge ', for Penitence, which is the daughter of the Most High and is a virgin modest and mirthful, has prayed for thee before the Eternal Throne."

And Asenath said:

" If I have found grace in thine eyes, my lord, sit down upon my couch, upon which no man has ever sat down, and I will dress the table, bring bread and wine that thou mayest refresh thyself before departing."

The divine messenger accepted the invitation of the hospitable maid, but when she had brought bread and wine and placed the refreshments upon the table, the angel produced a honeycomb.

" This honeycomb," said he, " hath been made by the bees in Paradise and from the dew of the roses there. Of this heavenly food the angels partake, and those who approach the Lord in repentance shall also eat of it." And the angel placed a portion of the honeycomb upon Asenath's lips, bidding her eat it.

Asenath ate, and the divine messenger thereupon said:

" Now thou hast eaten of the bread of life, drunk out of the cup of immortality, and hast been anointed with the holy unction of incorruptibility."

Thereupon Asenath said to the angel:

" My Lord, I have seven companions, virgins born with me on the same day; and if I have found favour in thine eyes, I would fain call them so that thou mayest bestow thy blessing upon these seven maidens who are unto me like sisters."

Having obtained the divine messenger's permission, Asenath called the seven virgins, her companions, and the angel bestowed upon them the blessing of eternal life, calling them the seven columns of the city of refuge. Thereupon her visitor departed, and Asenath saw him rise heavenwards in a fiery chariot, drawn by four horses who were like lightning.

Asenath now understood that she had been conversing not with mortal man, but with an angel from Heaven, and she thanked the Lord who had vouchsafed unto her such grace. Whilst she was thus uttering her prayers and thanking the Lord, one of Potiphera's maid-servants came to announce to her young mistress the arrival of Joseph. Quickly Asenath washed her face to prepare for the reception of her beloved. The reflection of her face in the water filled her with amazement, so changed was she, and so great was now her beauty. And indeed, so dazzling was the maiden's beauty that when Joseph, whom she hastened to greet, beheld her face, he failed to recognize her.

" Who art thou?" asked the Viceroy in great astonishment.

" I am Asenath, thy slave," replied the maid; " Asenath who hath cast away her dumb and useless idols. This day an angel from Heaven came to visit me and gave me heavenly food to eat. He also said unto me: ' This day I have given thee as a spouse unto Joseph, thy bridegroom, and he will be thy rightful husband into all eternity '. The angel further said that no longer will my name be Asenath, but the city of refuge, for through me many nations will find refuge under the protection of the Most High. The angel informed me, my lord, that he had thus spoken to thee this day concerning thy humble servant, and now thou knowest whether the angel did visit thee."

Thus spoke Asenath, her eyes shining with profound love for Joseph, and Joseph replied:

" Blessed be thou by the Most High, and blessed be thy name in all eternity, for the Lord God hath indeed sent unto me His angel and he hath spoken to me concerning thee. And now approach, my beautiful and beloved maid, why dost thou stand at such a distance from me?"

Bashfully Asenath approached, and they kissed each other. Thereupon Asenath said:

" My Lord, come into the house and let me wash thy feet."

Joseph at first objected to this service being performed by his bride-elect.

" Is there no other maid in the house," asked the Viceroy, " who could perform this service?"

But Asenath insisted upon being permitted to perform this act of love.

" No, my lord," she replied, " it is for me to perform this act of love and hospitality, for thou art my master and I am thy loving maid. And why should, as thou sayest, another maid wash thy feet? Thy feet are mine, and thy hands are mine, and thy soul is mine."

Thereupon the parents of Asenath arrived and were greatly amazed at their daughter's beauty. When they heard what had occurred they rejoiced exceedingly. A banquet was spread, and the parents and relatives of Asenath partook of the meal and blessed the Lord. Thereupon Potiphera, the priest of On, said unto Joseph:

"I will now invite all the high officials and courtiers of Pharaoh and also the princes of Egypt to a sumptuous wedding feast, at which thou wilt take to wife my daughter Asenath."

But Joseph declined this offer.

"No," said the Viceroy, "I could not accept this offer of thine, of giving the wedding feast here in thy house. I must first proceed to Pharaoh, the King of Egypt, who is my father here; I will inform him of my choice and ask him to give me to wife thy daughter Asenath."

Thus spoke Joseph, and Potiphera agreed that he had spoken wisely.

"Go in peace," said he, "and do as thou thinkest right."

When Pharaoh was informed of Joseph's choice and heard his Viceroy's request, he immediately sent for Potiphera, the priest of Heliopolis, and for his daughter Asenath. The King greatly admired the maiden's beauty and placed upon their heads golden crowns, the most beautiful that were in the house of the Pharaohs. Laying his hands upon their heads, he blessed them, saying:

"May the Most High bless you and glorify you for ever." Thereupon he made Joseph and Asenath kiss each other. The King then ordered a seven days feast to be held to which all the princes of Egypt were invited. The feast was also proclaimed a public and national holiday, for under penalty of death, by order of Pharaoh, no one was allowed to do any work during the nuptial festivities of Joseph and Asenath.[1]

[1] See Batiffol, *loc. cit.*

CHAPTER IX

The Visit of the Brethren

The greedy king and the generous Viceroy—The famine in the land of Canaan—Jacob's stores—An opportunity to search for the lost brother—" Ye are spies "—The hero of Shechem—The valiant men who broke their teeth—" A blow worthy of one of my family "—Joseph's uncanny knowledge—The grandchildren cry for bread—A touching scene—The powerful ruler of Egypt—Judah's pleading—The Patriarch's letter to the ruler of Egypt—Prayers and veiled threats—The magic cup—The astrolabe—Benjamin's astonishment—The long-lost brother—The sons of Jacob are put to the test—Benjamin insulted by his brethren—Thief and son of a thief—The reward of the meek—The punishment of Manasseh for having caused the sons of Jacob to rend their clothes—A private audience—The anger of the Viceroy—" The rope followed the bucket ".

When the famine, even as Joseph had foretold, broke in upon the inhabitants of Egypt, they were at once compelled to apply to Joseph. They had put aside some grain saved from the superabundant harvest, but when they opened their stores, they found that the grain had rotted. The Egyptians went to Pharaoh and cried: " Give us bread, so that we may live, for all our grain is unfit for food, because Joseph willed it so."

When Pharaoh heard that his people had no food whatever, he was greatly troubled in his mind. " If I command Joseph," he thought, " to feed all the inhabitants of the land, little will remain for myself and my family." Pharaoh therefore sent word to Joseph to conceal in a safe place all the grain he had gathered in the royal granaries, and let the Egyptians manage as well as they could.

Joseph, however, took no notice of the King's command, but fed all the hungry inhabitants of Egypt who blessed him for it. The Viceroy had been secretly hoping that the famine would soon bring his brethren to Egypt to buy corn. And indeed, his hope was realized, for the famine soon spread to Arabia, Phœnicia, and Palestine. " It is quite possible, however," thought Joseph, " that my father will send some of his slaves to Egypt to buy corn, and I will miss the opportunity of seeing my brethren." He therefore issued a decree enacting that anyone who desired to buy grain in Egypt could not entrust his slaves with the business, but would have either to come himself or send his sons. Joseph also placed guards at the gates of the city, commanding them not to permit anyone to enter the city unless he had given his name, and the name of his father and of his grandfather. " When you will have taken down the names of the visitors," said Joseph, " you will submit the lists to my son Manasseh."

Jacob was not yet exactly in want, and he still had grain in his stores, for he had known long ago that a famine would break out, but he advised his sons to go down to Egypt for the purpose of buying corn. " Go down to Egypt, my sons, and buy corn, for otherwise we will arouse the envy of the sons of Esau and of Ishmael and of the other inhabitants of Canaan who will say: ' Jacob is in a comfortable state and his stores are full of corn.' They will fall upon us, kill us, and seize all we possess."

Thus spoke the Patriarch, and his sons were ready to go down to Egypt, because having long repented their unbrotherly treatment of Joseph, they hoped to find him on the banks of the Nile.

The sons of Jacob were therefore glad of the opportunity to search for their brother and redeem him from slavery.

" If we find Joseph," they said, " we will ransom him, however high a price his master should demand. Should Joseph's master refuse to sell him, we will use force."

Thus the brethren of Joseph came to Egypt, and, obeying

the instruction of their father, they entered the city through different gates so as not to attract the attention of the people by their heroic stature and their handsome appearance. They searched the town for three days, hoping to find Joseph.

The latter, who had in the meantime been informed of the arrival of his brethren, had them seized and brought into his presence. He accused them of being spies, and ultimately permitted them to depart only if they left Simeon as hostage. Joseph said unto himself that if he detained both Simeon and Levi the two of them might destroy the whole city, as they had once destroyed the city of Shechem. Besides, Levi was a great favourite with the brothers, whilst Simeon was not. The brethren, Joseph feared, would sooner wage war against the whole city rather than depart without Levi. It was not an easy matter though to seize Simeon and put him in dungeon.

When Joseph ordered his men to seize the hero of Shechem, the brethren gathered round him, ready to defend him, but Simeon waved them back.

" Stand aside," he exclaimed, " I do not need your assistance, for I can fight these slaves single-handed."

Joseph thereupon sent a messenger to Pharaoh and asked him for seventy valiant men to help him arrest robbers who had been caught, and to cast them into prison.

When the valiant men appeared, Joseph commanded them to seize Simeon and cast him into prison. Scarcely, however, had the Egyptians approached the hero of Shechem and made an attempt to lay hands on him, when he uttered such a loud cry that they fell to the floor and broke their teeth. All the other servants who stood around fled in a great fright, so that only Joseph and his son Manasseh remained.

Joseph thereupon bade his son seize Simeon and cast him into prison. Manasseh then dealt Simeon such a mighty blow on the back of his neck that it nearly stunned him. Simeon was amazed to find such strength in a mere youth, whom he took to be an Egyptian. " It is strange," said he to his brethren, " that this Egyptian youth should be endowed with such heroic strength. His blow, I assure you, was one which any member of our family might be proud of. In fact, I could have taken my oath on it that the blow was dealt by one of our family."

Simeon was bound and cast into prison, but as soon as the brethren had left Joseph gave orders that he should be treated kindly. He sent one of his servants to minister to all his wants, and to set before him the best meat and drink.

When Joseph's brethren returned to Canaan and told the Patriarch all that had occurred, and that the ruler of Egypt had commanded them to bring their youngest brother with them when they came again, the old man was greatly grieved. He suspected his sons of being guilty, not only of Joseph's disappearance, but also of Simeon's detention. As for Benjamin's going to Egypt, the Patriarch would not hear of it. " Wherefore," he reproached his sons, " did ye tell the man in Egypt that ye had another brother?"

" Your reproach, Father, is undeserved," replied one of the brothers; " we were not such fools as to acquaint the ruler of Egypt with our family history, but his knowledge is something uncanny. He seemed to know all our family relations to the smallest detail, down to our babies and the very wood out of which their cradles are fashioned." For the moment, however, Jacob remained adamant, firmly resolved not to let Benjamin out of his sight.[1]

A day, however, arrived when the supplies of corn came to an end, and the family began to suffer hunger. When the

---

[1] *Genesis Rabba*, §§ 91, 92, 93; *Midrash Tanchuma*, section *Mikkez* and *Vayigash*; *Yalkut*, § 150; *Midrash Abkhir*, quoted in *Yalkut Shimeoni*, section *Mikkez*; *Midrash Agadah*, ed. Buber, pp. 98–100; *Targum Pseudo-Jonathan, in loco*; *Midrash Lekach Tob, in loco*; *Midrash Haggadol*, col. 637; Babylonian Talmud, *Baba Mezia*, 39; *Taanit*, 9a, 10b; *Pirke de Rabbi Eliezer*, Ch. 39; *Sepher Hajashar*; see also *Tokpo shel Yosef*; Kurrein, *loc. cit.*; Lewner, *loc. cit.*; Schapiro, *loc. cit.*, pp. 54–56.

provisions bought in Egypt were exhausted, the sons of Jacob sent their children to the old man to ask him for bread.

One morning, therefore, the sons of Reuben, Judah, and Issachar appeared before the Patriarch and cried: " Grandfather, give us bread, for we are dying of hunger, and our fathers say they have no bread to give us."

" What can I do," replied Jacob; " I am old and feeble, and am compelled to remain at home. Go and ask your fathers to journey to Egypt and buy us corn."

And whilst he was thus talking to his grandchildren, there arrived the sons of Levi dressed for a long journey, their knapsacks upon their backs and their staffs in their hands. " We have come to say good-bye, Grandfather, for we are going on a long journey. Pray for us to the Eternal to protect us on our way."

" And whither are you going, my children?" asked the Patriarch.

" We are going to Egypt," replied the youngsters. " We asked our father for bread, but he had none to give us and advised us to go to Egypt. ' Go to Egypt,' he said, ' where you will join my brother Simeon, who has been cast into prison. You, too, will no doubt be arrested and detained in dungeon, but, at least, you will be fed there and not lack bread.' Thus spoke our father Levi, and we are taking his advice, for it is better to be a prisoner than die of hunger."

Thereupon Yemuel, Yemin, and Chad, the sons of Simeon, arrived, their sticks in their hands. They fell upon Jacob's servants and slaves and drove them out of the house.

" What is the meaning of your action?" asked the Patriarch; " wherefore did ye ill-treat these faithful servants and drive them out of the house?"

" Because," replied the boys, " we are anxious to take their place. As thy servants thou art feeding them, and so we thought of offering ourselves to thee as slaves, and take the place of the strangers so that thou wilt feed us. Our father who provided for us is no longer here, being a prisoner in a distant land, and we shall soon be compelled to sell ourselves to some master. It is better, therefore, that thou shouldst buy us as thy slaves rather than some strange master."[1]

These scenes moved the old man greatly. He summoned his sons and bade them go down to Egypt and buy some provisions.

But Judah replied that they could not go unless Benjamin accompanied them. "Thou shouldst know, Father," he said, "that there is none equal to this King of Egypt, either in power or in wisdom. We, who have beheld many kings of the earth, know of none who could be compared to this King of Egypt. Thou hast seen, O Father, that the greatest and most powerful among the kings of Canaan is Abimelech, but know that even Abimelech cannot be compared to one of the ministers of the King of Egypt. We have been surprised, O Father, by the magnificence of his palace and of his throne, and by his many servants. We have beheld him amidst all the royal pomp and splendour, and our eyes have been dazzled by the grace and wisdom with which the Lord hath favoured his person. Thou shouldst have heard, O Father, the words of wisdom, prudence, and sagacity which the Lord hath placed in his mouth when he did converse with us. He knows all that has happened unto us from the very beginning, and he asked us with great concern: 'Your aged father, is he well?' No one addresses himself unto Pharaoh, because all orders are given by the Viceroy. When he did accuse us of being spies we waxed wroth indeed, and were on the point of dealing with Egypt as we have dealt with the city of the Amorites. But the ruler of Egypt inspired us with such awe and respect that we dared not give vent to our anger. I therefore pray thee, O Father, to confide the lad to me, and I promise thee faithfully to bring

[1] *Tokpo shel Yosef.*

him back to thee. Have pity upon the little ones who are crying for bread, and have also faith in the Lord."

Thus pleaded Judah, and the Patriarch finally consented. With tears in his eyes, he now bade them travel to Egypt.

" Take Benjamin with ye," he said, " as ye cannot appear without him before the ruler of Egypt." He handed over Benjamin to Judah who promised on his happiness in the next world, which he offered as surety, to bring the lad back.

" Now," said the old man, " take some presents with ye for the ruler of Egypt, and here is money; do ye require anything else?"

" Yes," said his sons, " we require thy blessing and a prayer to the Lord on our behalf."

Jacob was well pleased with their reply, and thus prayed to the Lord on behalf of his sons:

" Sovereign of all the worlds! Thou who at the moment of creation didst call ' Enough ' to Heaven and to Earth, when they were stretching themselves out into infinity, say ' Enough ' also to my sufferings. And may it be Thy will that my sons find mercy before the ruler of Egypt that he may release unto them my missing sons."

Jacob also wrote a long letter to the ruler of Egypt and put it into the hands of Judah. And thus the Patriarch wrote in his letter:

" To the Royal Majesty and wisdom of Zaphnath Paaneah, the King of Egypt, from thy servant Jacob, the son of Isaac, the son of Abraham the Hebrew, peace. My lord, the King of Egypt, is no doubt well aware that the famine is very heavy in the land of Canaan. I am compelled therefore to send my sons to thee to buy food for our sustenance. I have already once sent my sons to Egypt in order to obtain some provisions from thee, and to buy food for our sustenance. Numerous are my descendants in whose midst I dwell, and I am surrounded by seventy children and grandchildren. But I am old myself

and cannot see with mine eyes, which have grown dim, both
on account of my advanced age as on account of my constant
tears shed for my lost son Joseph. It was I who commanded
my sons not to enter the city all together through one gate, so
as not to attract the attention of the people of Egypt. It was I
also who charged them to go about in the city and to look
round, as perchance they might find their lost brother Joseph.
Thou didst, however, accuse them of being spies, although
thy wisdom, the report of which has spread abroad, ought
to have made thee know from their looks that they were not
spies. Thou art famous, in consequence of thy interpretation
of Pharaoh's dreams, for telling the coming of the famine, and
it is strange that a man possessing great wisdom should have
made such a mistake regarding the appearance and character
of my sons and take them for spies. My Lord and King!
as thou didst command, I am sending unto thee my son
Benjamin, and I implore thee to have an eye on him until
thou dost send him back to me with his brethren. As a reward
for thy action, the Lord will take care of thee and have His
eye on thee and on thy kingdom. Thou hast no doubt heard
what our God once did unto a Pharaoh when, against all right,
he wanted to take to wife my grandmother Sarah, and also
what happened unto Abimelech on her account. Hast thou
not heard that our father Abraham, followed by a few men,
conquered and killed the seven kings of Elam, and that two of
my own sons, Simeon and Levi, destroyed eight towns of the
Amorites to avenge the wrong done to their sister? Now the
presence of Benjamin has somewhat consoled them for the
loss of Joseph, and thou canst easily imagine to what excesses
they will go if one of thy people so much as raised his hand
against their brother or tried to snatch him away from them.
Thou shouldst also know, O King of Egypt, that the mighty
help of our God is always with us, and that the Lord always
hearkens unto our prayers and never abandons us. When my

sons told me how thou didst treat them, accusing them of being
spies, I had only to call upon my God, and long before the
arrival of Benjamin thou and all thy people would have been
destroyed. But I refrained from calling upon God to punish
thee, because at this moment my son Simeon is in thy house
and perhaps thou art being kind unto him, treating him well.
Now my son Benjamin cometh to thee, together with his
brethren, and I appeal to thee to treat the lad well, and direct
thine eye upon him. Thou wilt be rewarded for this, for the
Lord will also direct His eye upon thee and upon thy kingdom.
All that is in my heart I have now said, and I ask thee once more
to grant entire liberty to my sons, whilst they are abiding with
thee, and to permit them to depart in peace."

This letter the Patriarch handed over to Judah for delivery
to the ruler of Egypt.

When the sons of Jacob arrived in Egypt and presented
themselves at the palace of the Viceroy, they were invited by
Manasseh, the steward of Joseph's house, to dinner. It was a
Sabbath meal, for Joseph observed the Sabbath even before
the Israelites were bidden in the law to observe the seventh
day. The steward also brought out Simeon unto them, and
the brethren were not a little astonished to notice how well
the prisoner looked.

Simeon told his brethren how well he had been treated
during their absence. " Scarcely had you left the city," said
the hero of Shechem, " when I was released from prison and
treated like a distinguished guest in the Viceroy's house."

Joseph now appeared, and Judah, leading Benjamin by the
hand, presented the lad to the ruler of Egypt, to whom he
also handed his father's letter. When he beheld the hand-
writing of his aged father in distant Canaan, the Viceroy was
deeply moved. Unable to restrain his tears, he withdrew into
an inner apartment to weep freely.

He soon returned, and was overjoyed to see how closely

Benjamin resembled his father, being the very image and counterpart of the Patriarch. He summoned his brother to approach and entered into conversation with him. During the meal Joseph made Benjamin take his place at his own table, pretending to consult his magic cup for all the seating arrangements. Taking up his famous magic cup, whence he drew his knowledge, the Viceroy thus addressed his brethren: " My cup tells me that Judah is king among you, and he will therefore sit at the head of your table, whilst Reuben, who is the firstborn, will sit next to him. Simeon, Levi, Issachar, and Zebulun, being the sons of one mother, will sit together on one side; and Gad and Asher, Dan and Naphtali on the other. Now my cup further tells me that Benjamin lost both his mother and brother, and he is like me who have neither mother nor brother. He may therefore take his seat at my own table, by the side of my wife and sons."

For twenty-two years neither Joseph nor his brethren had tasted any wine, having led the life of Nazarites, but at this meal of reunion, although only Joseph was aware of the fact, they all partook of wine. During the meal Joseph continued to converse with Benjamin, asking him many questions, and afterwards led him into his private apartment. Thereupon he bade one of his servants bring his magic astrolabe, whereby he was enabled to read future events.

" I have heard," he said to Benjamin, " that the Hebrews are well versed in all wisdom, and I wonder whether thou dost know anything about the signs of astrology."

Benjamin smiled.

" My father," he replied, " has imparted much knowledge to me and taught me many things; thy servant is therefore quite at home in many sciences, including that of astrology."

" Then take up this astrolabe," said Joseph, " read in it and find out whether thy brother Joseph, who as you all pretend was taken to Egypt, is to be found in this country."

Benjamin took up the astrolabe and examined it carefully. Thereupon he divided the sky of Egypt into four astrological regions, and suddenly stood up amazed. He had read in the astrolabe that he who was sitting upon a throne before him was none other than his lost brother Joseph.

Joseph, noticing Benjamin's astonishment, asked him: " What hast thou read in the astrolabe that thou seemest so moved and excited?"

Pointing to the instrument, Benjamin replied: " I have read here that my lost brother Joseph is facing me, seated upon a throne."

" This is quite true," replied Joseph, " for I am thy brother. It is true," continued Joseph, " I am thy brother Joseph, the son of Rachel who died on the way to Ephrath." Thereupon he embraced his younger brother and kissed him, and both shed tears of joy at the happy reunion.

" And now, my dear brother," said the Viceroy, " I will ask thee to keep our secret for some time, for I wish to put my brethren to the test and find out whether they have repented of their sin against me."

Thereupon he told Benjamin how he had been sold into slavery, and what suffering he had endured until the Lord had released him and raised him to such a high position. " But tell me, brother mine, what tale did my brothers bring to my father and how did they account for my disappearance?"

" They dipped thy coat in blood," replied the lad, " and said that a wild beast had torn thee. Our old father rent his clothes and has mourned ever since."

" It was a cruel deed," said the Viceroy, " although God had willed it so. Now I am going to put my brethren to the test to see if they have repented of their sin. I will send you all away to Canaan, but I will give instructions that before you have travelled a long distance, you all be stopped and accused of having stolen my magic cup. It will be found in thy sack, and you will all be arrested and brought back. I will claim thee as my bondman, and then I will see how our brethren behave and what attitude they take up. If they are ready to fight for thee and take thee away by force, risking their lives in thy defence, then I will know that they have repented of their cruelty to me, and that thou art dear to them. I will then make known to them my identity, and they will rejoice. Should they, however, consent to thy becoming my bondman and be ready to leave thee behind, then I will fight them and take my revenge, but thou wilt abide with me for ever. And now," he concluded, " return to our brethren, but never breathe a word concerning our secret."

In blithe spirits Benjamin joined his brethren who wondered at his evident happiness and smiling countenance. " The Viceroy," explained the lad, " has promised me to find out the whereabouts of our brother Joseph."

The brethren only shrugged their shoulders, for they had now given up all hope of ever discovering among the living the brother whom they had sold into slavery.

With the break of dawn the brethren left the city on their homeward journey, because Joseph had so arranged that they should travel by day. " By day only," he thought, " these fierce, powerful and courageous men can be compelled by my servants to return to Egypt. In the night, however, an encounter with them is dangerous, for when roused they are like wild beasts which no one can resist in the darkness. Rightly has Judah been called a lion, Dan a serpent on the road, and Naphtali swift as a running hare." The brethren, on the other hand, also remembered the instructions of their father to leave a city after sunrise and to enter it before sunset.

The sons of Jacob had scarcely left the city, when they were followed by Joseph's messengers who accused them of having stolen the Viceroy's magic cup. Their sacks were searched, and, to the amazement and vexation of the brethren, the cup was discovered in Benjamin's sack. The fury of the brethren was great, and turning to their youngest brother they thus addressed him: " Now we understand the reason of thy contentment and happiness last night. Thou art a thief and the son of a thief, for thy mother once stole the Teraphim of our grandfather Laban. Thou shameless thief, thou hast brought shame upon us, even as thy mother, the thief, once brought the blush of shame to the cheek of our father, when the Teraphim were discovered in her possession."

Thus they hurled abuse and even blows upon Benjamin who bore it all in patience and humility. He was rewarded for his conduct in later days, for the Holy Temple was situated in the allotment of the tribe of Benjamin, and the Glory of God dwelt between his shoulders (*Deuteron.*, 33, 12).

The brethren then rent their clothes in sign of grief, and because they had been compelled to do so on account of Benjamin, one of his descendants, Mordecai, was destined to rend his clothes on account of the children of Israel. On the other hand, if the sons of Jacob now rent their clothes it was a Divine punishment for the crime they had committed in causing their old father to rend his clothes at the loss of his son.

Manasseh, too, who, at the head of Joseph's servants, had searched the sacks of his kinsmen and inflicted upon them such humiliation, did not escape Divine retribution. In later days the allotment of the tribe of Manasseh was " torn " into two parts, situated on the two banks of the River Jordan. As for Joseph, who had caused his brethren to rend their clothes, one of his descendants, Joshua, rent his clothes after the defeat of Ai (*Joshua*, 7, 6). Thus, sooner or later, Divine Providence metes out retribution for every reprehensible act.

Without raising any protest, the brethren followed Manasseh and his men back to the city, and were brought into the presence of Joseph.

The Viceroy received them in his private apartments, for, in order to spare his brethren shame in public, he had announced that he would hold no court on that day. Outwardly calm, but inwardly boiling with rage, Judah and his brethren were already contemplating the eventuality of using force, should Joseph insist upon detaining Benjamin in bondage.

The capital of Egypt was a big city, but to the heroic sons of Jacob it appeared only like a small hamlet with ten inhabitants which they could easily destroy, if driven to extremes. Judah, however, who was king among Jacob's sons, and their spokesman, decided to plead at first, before resorting to force. Brought into the presence of the apparently furious ruler of Egypt, the eleven brethren fell to the earth and prostrated themselves before Joseph, thus realizing and making true the dream of the latter. In apparent rage, Joseph thus addressed them:

"Why did ye steal my magic cup? No doubt, ye were anxious to practise magic, and with the help of the cup discover the whereabouts of your lost brother."

"My Lord," replied Judah, "we are not guilty of the crime we are charged with, and cannot acknowledge ourselves as thieves, because we are innocent. Appearances, however, are against us, for the cup hath been found in the sack of our brother. God hath found out our iniquity, and it is His will to punish us. Now although the cup was found in the sack of our youngest brother, we, who were in the company of the supposed thief, are all equally responsible."

Shaking his purple mantle in royal dignity, Joseph replied: "It is not worthy of a king to punish the innocent. I am not accusing ye all of the theft committed, but only your youngest brother, who will be punished accordingly. Ye may, therefore, return to your old father in peace, whilst this young man will remain as my bondman." And mockingly Joseph added: "If ye are worried concerning the report ye will have to give to your old father, to whom ye must account for the disappearance of this your brother, ye can easily invent some plausible story. When this lad's brother, who was no thief, had disappeared years ago, ye did not hesitate to inform your father that a wild beast had torn him. It will be easy for ye now to separate yourselves from a brother who is a thief and tell your father that ' The rope has followed after the bucket.' Benjamin, therefore, remains here, and ye all may return to Canaan in peace!"

" Thou mayest call it peace," replied Judah, " but we call it war, for the foundations of peace will have been destroyed if Benjamin is separated from us."

Without deigning to reply, Joseph waved his hand, indicating that the audience was at an end, carried Benjamin off, and locked him up in a chamber. Losing all hope of rescuing Benjamin, the brethren were on the point of giving in and of abandoning their youngest brother, who, they thought, had really stolen the cup. Judah, however, who had stood surety for the lad, was determined to liberate the lad at all costs. Should further arguments, pleadings, and entreaties fail, I will use force, thought the heroic son of Jacob.[1]

---

[1] See note 1, p. 120; see also *Midrash Haggadol*, col. 661–663; Schapiro, *loc. cit.*, pp. 56–74.

CHAPTER X

The Lion, the Bull, and the Wolf

The dispute of two kings—The roaring lion—The penalty for theft—
Benjamin's grandmother—The strength of Manasseh—Judah's argument
—His responsibility—His towering rage—Tears of blood—Hushim the
deaf jumps from Canaan to Egypt—The terrific noise—The rage of Jacob's
son—The broken marble pillar—Naphtali counts the streets of the city—
A stone crushed to dust—The fire of Shechem and the fire kindled to burn
Tamar—The expert dyers—A brother's tears and his forgiveness—Why
Joseph wept upon the neck of Benjamin—The destruction of the two temples
—The happy return to Canaan—Serah the beautiful maid and clever musician
—The glad tidings—" Uncle Joseph liveth "—Jacob blesses Serah and
bestows upon her eternal life—The joy of the Patriarch—A banquet offered
to the kings of Canaan—The cedars once planted by Abraham—Pharaoh
lends his royal crown to Joseph—The Viceroy makes ready his chariot—
—The meeting of father and son—The Patriarch would not interrupt his
prayers—The joy of Egypt—The low door—The miracle of a raised door
—Og the giant's astonishment—Joseph's treasures—Their hiding places.

Judah is called a lion, Joseph a bull, and Benjamin a wolf,
and a mighty contest now ensued between the bull and the
lion concerning the wolf. Joseph knew him to be innocent
of guilt, but accused him of theft, whilst Judah thought him
guilty, but did his best to liberate him. Two kings stood
facing one another, and the brethren listened in silence, not
venturing to interfere. It was a mighty contest, a fight at
which even the angels in Heaven did not disdain to be spec-
tators.

" Let us descend," said the angels, " and witness the fight
of the bull against the lion. As a rule the bull fears the lion
whom he recognizes as his master, but here the two combatants are equal in strength. Their present combat is only

the beginning of a long and mighty contest which will continue for ages between the descendants of these two, until the day when the Messiah arrives."

Roaring like a lion, Judah had approached the locked door, broken it, and in a threatening attitude was now standing before the ruler of Egypt. Outwardly calm, but inwardly boiling with suppressed fury, he decided to plead at first and to resort to argument, and he thus addressed Joseph:

" My Lord, according to our laws, a thief is sold into slavery only when he has no money to make restitution. Benjamin, however, can make restitution and pay, according to our laws, double the value of the object he has stolen. Therefore, I request that Benjamin be set free. Besides, if it is a slave thou dost require, take me as thy bondman in the place of the lad, for I am stronger than he and will be more useful to thee both for military service and for manual tasks. Let also the words I am about to address unto thee find entrance into thine ear. Know that years ago the Pharaoh of Egypt and his entire household were stricken with plagues because the King had detained in his palace the grandmother of Benjamin for one night against her will. Know further that two of us once destroyed the town of Shechem, to avenge the honour of our sister, and we will do more to set free our brother in whose allotment the Holy Temple will once be situated. I warn thee, my lord, that I can destroy the whole of Egypt, for I have only to utter a word in this thy palace, and pestilence will be the result outside, carrying destruction as far as the city of No. Thou didst say that thou dost fear God, but methinks thou art like Pharaoh who maketh promises but doth not keep them. In thy country Pharaoh is the first and thou art the second, but in *our* country of Canaan my father is the first and I am his representative. If I but draw my sword, I will kill thee first and then Pharaoh."

When Joseph heard these threats uttered by his brother,

and knowing full well that he was quite capable of carrying them out, he made a sign to his son Manasseh, and the latter stamped his foot on the ground with such force that the whole palace shook and trembled.

"This young Egyptian," muttered Judah, "seems to be endowed with extraordinary strength which, strange enough, equals that of our own family." He wondered greatly at the strength and stamping of Manasseh, whom he took to be a young Egyptian of the race of Ham.

Mitigating his tone, Judah spoke again: "Why, my lord, did thy reception of us differ so greatly from the reception accorded to all the men who came to Egypt from different countries for the purpose of buying corn? Why didst thou single us out from among all the other visitors, inquiring into all the details of our family affairs, as if we had come here not to buy corn but to ask the hand of thy daughter in marriage? Or was it, perhaps, because thou didst have the intention of taking our sister to wife, and wast, therefore, anxious to learn all about our family? From the very beginning thou didst try to find quarrel with us, accusing us first of being spies, and now charging us with theft."

"Thou art a clever and impressive talker," said Joseph, "but I really have very little time to stand here, listening to thy eloquence. Tell me, though, why art thou alone among all thy brethren pouring out this eloquence, whilst some of them are older than thou?"

"Because," replied Judah, "I alone am responsible for the lad, having stood surety for him to my father."

"And wherein did thy surety consist?" queried Joseph; "if it was gold and silver, I will pay it for thee."

"There is no question of gold and silver," replied Judah, contemptuously. "I promised my father to bring Benjamin back, otherwise I lose my happiness and my portion in the world to come. It is for this reason that I so insist upon setting

Benjamin free, and upon remaining here in his stead as thy bondman. Besides, I could never return to my father without the lad, for I could not witness the old man's grief over his youngest son."

" Thou wast not so much concerned for thy father's grief on another occasion, and didst not venture to be surety for the other brother whom ye sold into slavery for twenty pieces of silver. Then thou *couldst* witness the grief of thy old father, telling him that a wild beast had devoured his favourite son. And that brother of yours had done thee no wrong, whilst Benjamin hath brought shame upon thee, because he hath committed theft. It will be easy for thee to tell thy father that the rope has followed the bucket."

Thus spoke Joseph, still resolved to put his brethren to the test, and to see whether they would really fight for Benjamin, and risk their lives in an attempt to set him free.

Breaking out into sobs, Judah cried: "What shall I say to my father when I return without the lad?"

" I have already told thee to say the rope has followed the bucket."

When Judah saw that his entreaties and arguments remained without effect, his towering rage once more broke out. He seized a piece of brass, bit it with his teeth and spat it out as fine powder. He roared like a lion, and his voice carried four hundred parasangs; it was heard by Hushim, the son of Dan, in distant Canaan. With one bound Hushim jumped from distant Canaan to Egypt and stood beside his uncle, joining his voice with that of the heroic son of Jacob.

Egypt trembled from their joint noise; two cities, Pithom and Ramses, which the Jews were afterwards forced to rebuild, collapsed and fell into ruins. Joseph's valiant men were hurled to the ground by the terrific noise and lost their teeth. Judah's brethren, too, fell into a rage, assumed a threatening attitude,

and stamped upon the ground with such force that the dust
rose high, and the ground looked as if deep furrows had been
made in it by a ploughshare. The towering rage of Judah
rose higher and higher. His right eye shed tears of blood,
and the hairs upon his chest bristled and grew stiff, piercing
the five garments he wore.

Joseph knew well enough these signs of his brother's
rage, foreboding mischief, and he began to fear for his life
and for the safety of the country. In order to impress his
brethren, and to show that he, too, was a powerfully strong
man, he pushed with his foot against the marble pillar he was
seated upon so that it broke into splinters.

Judah was amazed to notice that the ruler of Egypt was his
equal in strength. He made an attempt to draw his sword,
but it would not move from the scabbard, and he concluded
that the man facing him was not only a hero like himself, but
a God-fearing man, too. He dispatched his brother Naphtali,
who was as swift as a hart, to run out and count the streets
of the city. Simeon, however, exclaimed: " I will go up to the
mountain, seize a huge stone, hurl it over the city and kill
all its inhabitants." Naphtali soon returned and reported that
the city was divided into twelve quarters.

" Now," said Judah to his brethren, " I have done with
argument, and it is war. We are going to destroy the city.
I myself will undertake to destroy three quarters, whilst each
of you will deal with one of the remaining quarters."

" Egypt though," remarked the brethren, " is not like
Shechem; if Egypt were now to be destroyed, the whole world
would suffer, for it is this country that is providing food for
the whole world."

Joseph, who understood their talk, was well pleased with
these sentiments they had expressed.

Judah once more turned to Joseph and cried: " I swear
to thee that I alone, even without the help of my brethren,

am capable of destroying the whole country. I have only to draw my sword, and rase the country to the ground."

" I will break thy sword upon thine own head, and crush thy arm," replied Joseph.

" I will raise my voice, and Egypt will fall into ruins," cried Judah.

" I will shut thy mouth with a stone," replied Joseph.

Judah at once seized a huge stone with one hand, hurled it into the air, caught it up again and sitting down upon it crushed it to dust.

Joseph was little impressed by this feat of strength, for at a sign from him his son Manasseh did the same with another stone. Joseph remained inexorable.

" Thy judgment is wrong and unjust," cried Judah.

" Not so unjust as the sale of a brother who had done no wrong," replied the Viceroy.

" Verily," thundered Judah, in a paroxysm of rage, " the fire of Shechem is burning in my heart."

" I may be able to cool thy fire," replied Joseph. " Perhaps the remembrance of the fire which threatened to burn Tamar, thy daughter-in-law, may cool and even extinguish the fire in thy heart."

" I will dye Egypt red," thundered Judah.

" I am not surprised," mocked Joseph, " ye were always expert dyers, for did ye not dye your brother's coat red, dipping it in the blood of a kid, and telling your father that a wild beast had devoured his son."

The shaft went home and increased Judah's wrath. He made now serious preparations to destroy the city of Egypt. He would risk his life in the struggle sooner than return to his father without Benjamin.

Joseph now realized that things had gone far enough. He was satisfied with his test, convinced that Judah would lay down his life in his attempt to set Benjamin free, ready

to atone for his sin against Joseph. There was no necessity to
see Egypt laid in ruins. The Viceroy, therefore, made up his
mind to make himself known to his brethren. This scene,
however, during which his brethren would be put to shame,
should not be witnessed by strangers, and the Viceroy accordingly bade all his servants and valiant men leave him.

Addressing his brethren in more gentle tones, he said:
" Ye told me that the brother of Benjamin is dead, but this
is a lie, for he was sold into slavery and I bought him. I will
bid him come hither and appear in the presence of his brethren."
Raising his voice, he then called aloud: " Joseph! Joseph,
son of Jacob, come hither and speak to thy brethren who
once sold thee into slavery."

Abashed, the sons of Jacob looked round, turning their
eyes to the four corners of the room, but they saw no Joseph
coming forward.

" Why do ye look hither and thither?" cried Joseph.
" Your brother is here, he is standing before ye, for I, the
ruler of Egypt, am Joseph whom ye did sell into slavery!"

At these words, the brethren were so abashed that their
souls fled from them and they remained lifeless. But God
wrought a miracle and sent them new life. They would not
believe Joseph at first, for he had changed so greatly. The
bearded, handsome ruler of Egypt, arrayed in royal robes,
clad in purple and wearing a crown upon his head, could
not possibly be the smooth-faced, beardless youth they had
once cast into the pit and afterwards sold into slavery. They
were, however, convinced at last that the ruler of Egypt
was their lost brother, and then the sons of Jacob were both
ashamed and afraid. They were ashamed of their sins and of
their former heartless cruelty towards a brother, and afraid
lest this brother, now a powerful ruler, wreak now his revenge.
Judah raised such an outcry, that the walls of the city of Egypt
tumbled down, pregnant women miscarried, and both Pharaoh

and Joseph rolled from their seats. Three hundred of Joseph's heroes fell to the ground, knocking out their teeth. Others who had turned their heads to look round and find out the cause of the tumult, became immobile and their heads thus remained forever facing backwards.

Joseph, seeing his brethren's shame and fear, calmed them and gently called them to come nearer and kiss him. They yielded at last, timidly approached the ruler of Egypt who fell upon their necks and wept. He wept for joy, but he also wept in sorrow, for in a prophetic vision he foresaw that their descendants would be enslaved by the nations of the earth. He wept upon Benjamin's neck even more, because the two holy temples, situated in the allotment of the tribe of Benjamin, would be destroyed. Benjamin, too, wept upon Joseph's neck, because he foresaw that the sanctuary of Shiloh, situated in Joseph's allotment of territory, would also be destroyed. Tears were shed at Joseph's reconciliation with his brethren, and tears will be shed when Israel is once more redeemed by the Lord. (*Jerem.*, 31, 9.)

Pharaoh, who had wondered at the noise and tumult going on in the Viceroy's palace, was informed of the quarrel between Joseph and the Hebrews. He was well pleased when he heard the news of the reconciliation, for he had feared for the safety of the country. He now sent his servants to Joseph to rejoice with him, and all the magnates of the realm too came to take part in their Viceroy's joy. An invitation was extended to the brethren of Joseph to come now with their families to Egypt and to dwell in the country of Goshen, where they could take up their abode. The country of Goshen belonged to them by right, for it had once been made a present of to Sarah by the Pharaoh of the time.

Richly laden with presents for themselves and their families, such as embroidered clothes, gold and silver apparel, costly raiment, jewels and precious stones, the brethren left Egypt.

They travelled in wagons placed at their disposal by Joseph, who also sent the chariot wherein he had ridden on his appointment as Viceroy for his father's use. Joseph himself accompanied his brethren to the frontier of Egypt, and insisted upon their speedy return.

"Tell my father," he said, "should he hesitate to believe your words, that when I took leave of him he had been teaching me the section dealing with the law of the heifer whose neck had been broken in the valley."

The return of the sons of Jacob to Canaan was a happy one, and in high spirits they travelled home. But when they approached the boundary of Canaan they said to each other: "If we come to our father and suddenly inform him of what has happened, the glad tidings may frighten him and he may also refuse to give credence to our words." Not far from Hebron, however, they caught sight of Serah, the daughter of Asher, who had come out to meet them. The sight of the little maiden, who was as beautiful as she was clever, gave them an idea. Serah was a clever musician and could sing sweetly, accompanying herself upon the harp. When she came up and kissed her father and her uncles, they told her the great news. Thereupon they gave her a harp and instructed her to go and play to her grandfather.

"Go now, little one," they said, "into thy grandfather's tent and sing and play to him, and in thy song tell him the glad tidings, how his son Joseph liveth and is ruler of Egypt."

The little maiden took the harp and hurried into her grandfather's tent. She was a great favourite with the Patriarch, who loved to listen to her singing and playing. Serah sat down beside the old man and began to sing the following song:

> "My Uncle Joseph is not dead,
>   For he liveth all the while;
> A crown he weareth on his head,
>   As King of Egypt by the Nile."

Her melodious sweet voice, her soft music, soothed the old man, and he was pleasantly thrilled.

" Play again, child," he said, " for thy singing has put new life into me."

Serah repeated her words again and again, and peace entered Jacob's heart. A wave of joy swept over his whole being, and in that moment the spirit of prophecy came over him, and he knew that the words of his granddaughter were true.

Approaching the child, Jacob laid his hand upon the comely head and blessed the little maid: " My dear," said the Patriarch who had mourned for his beloved son twenty-two years, " may death in all eternity never have power over thee, because thou hast brought joy to my afflicted heart. Repeat this song often to me, for it is balm to my wounds and brings joy to me."

And whilst Jacob was still blessing his granddaughter his sons arrived, happy and radiant. The Patriarch lifted up his eyes and was amazed at beholding his sons arrayed in costly and magnificent garments, riding in royal chariots, and servants running before them. He would not believe them at first, when they communicated to him the glad tidings, for he dared not give credence to their words that Joseph was not only alive, but also ruler of Egypt. The presents, however, the chariots, the servants, the jewels and raiment, were real and not a dream, and he was soon convinced of the truth. Great was his joy when he heard from his sons that honours, power, and wealth had not made his son swerve from the path of virtue, and that he was constant in his piety.

" Joseph," said the brethren, " as ruler of Egypt, is beloved and blessed by all, for he feeds the hungry and metes out justice to the oppressed. There is none so generous and magnanimous like Joseph." These words brought great joy to the heart of the old man. He was even more happy to hear of his son's piety and noble deeds than of his power, wealth, and honours. Rising from his seat and lifting up his eyes to Heaven, he gave thanks to the Lord:

" Blessed art Thou, the God of my fathers, who hast given strength to my son to withstand all the sufferings, and hast enabled him to remain steadfast in his piety. My son," continued Jacob, " is even more constant in his piety than I, for did I not say ' My sufferings seem to be hidden from the Lord ', and yet, the Lord has bestowed many gifts and blessings upon me. He saved me from Esau and from Laban, and from the Canaanites who did pursue me. I have hoped to receive more benefits, but never did I hope for this joy. Now I am convinced that the Lord will bestow even greater blessings upon me."

Thereupon Jacob and the members of his household put on the costly garments Joseph had sent them, and rejoiced exceedingly. All the kings and magnates of Canaan came to visit Jacob and rejoiced with him. The Patriarch prepared a banquet for his noble guests and thus addressed them:

" Ye know that I had lost my favourite and beloved son Joseph, and mourned for him these twenty-two years, but now my sorrow hath been turned into joy, for my son liveth and is ruler of Egypt. What gladdens my heart most is the fact that, although ruler of a great country before whom nations bow down, Joseph is still steadfast in his piety, is charitable and generous, feeds the hungry, clothes the naked, and comforts the afflicted. Let this be a proof to ye, my noble guests, that the living God whom I worship, even as did before me my grandfather Abraham, and my father Isaac, never abandons those who put their trust in Him. A day cometh when He comforteth the afflicted, rewardeth the pious, and punisheth the wicked and the hypocrites."

The Patriarch had now decided to travel to Egypt and see

his son, but then to return to Canaan, as he would not dwell in a country like Egypt where there was no fear of God, and where idols were worshipped. But a divine vision came to him, and the Lord bade him go down to Egypt and remain there:

"Go down to Egypt," said the Lord, "and do not fear, for I shall be with thee and with thy descendants who will become a great nation."

But before leaving Canaan, his native land, Jacob first went to Beer-Sheba. A prophetic vision had descended upon the Patriarch and he knew that his descendants would one day build the Tabernacle. He therefore went to Beer-Sheba to hew down the cedars once planted by Abraham. "These cedars," he said, "my sons will plant in Egypt, and hew them down afterwards to carry them into the desert and build the Tabernacle."

Judah was sent ahead to inform Joseph of his father's arrival. "Our father is coming," said Judah, "and he bade thee erect dwellings for him and for his household, but, first of all, construct a house of learning and a school where he can continue to impart to his children the knowledge of the Lord, and teach them the laws of justice and of loving-kindness." Thus spoke Judah, and Joseph rejoiced exceedingly, and gave orders that his father's request be carried out. The Viceroy now made all necessary preparations to meet his father, and all the nobles and magnates of Egypt decided to accompany their Viceroy.

"Let us go out," they said, "to meet the pious man from Canaan, and pay homage to the father of such a generous and just man as is our present ruler."

Pharaoh sent unto Joseph his royal crown and bade him wear it for this occasion.

"Wear this crown," said the King, "in honour of thy father."

Crowds of nobles and magnates, all the valiant men and heroes of Egypt, musicians and players upon all sorts of instruments, gathered round Joseph, ready to follow the procession and greet the grand old man from Canaan.

Joseph himself, arrayed in purple, went down to make ready his chariot with his own hands. Amazed were the nobles and magnates of the land, when they saw their Viceroy dragging out the chariot and harnessing the horses with his own hands, although numerous slaves were standing about, ready to do their master's bidding.

" I am going out to meet my father, whom I have not seen for twenty years," said Joseph, " and I cannot permit anyone to perform this loving action in making ready my chariot." The Egyptians wondered at his words and praised their Viceroy who thus honoured his father. To the sound of music, of cymbals and timbrels, the great procession, headed by nobles, arrayed in byssus and purple, by valiant men and heroes in warlike attire, marched on. Flowers, myrrh, and aloes were strewn on the way, and the women and maidens of Egypt ascended the roofs and walls of the city to greet Jacob upon his arrival. At a distance of about 50 ells from his father, Joseph descended from his chariot, walking on foot the rest of the way, and all the nobles of Egypt, riding in chariots or on horseback, followed the example of the Viceroy. When the Patriarch beheld the splendid procession which had come out to meet him, and saw among them a man arrayed in purple and wearing a crown upon his head, he bowed down, thinking it was the King.

" Who is this man," he asked his son Judah, " the Egyptian in royal attire, wearing purple upon his shoulders and a crown upon his head? He has just left his chariot and is coming towards us on foot?"

" It is thy son, Joseph," replied Judah.

And because Joseph had allowed his father to bow to him,

JOSEPH AND HIS FATHER MEET AGAIN IN EGYPT

he was punished afterwards, for he died before his other brothers.

In the meantime Joseph had approached, bowed low to his old father and then fell upon his neck, kissed him and wept. Jacob, too, wept for great joy and happiness, but he did not yet kiss his son. At that moment, the Patriarch was praying to the Lord, rendering thanks to God for the benefits bestowed upon him, and the pious old man would not be interrupted in his prayer. He was just reciting the words: " And thou shalt love the Lord, thy God, with all thy heart and all thy might." When he had finished his prayers, Jacob said: " Were I to die now, I would be comforted, for my death will only be in this world and not in the world to come."

The procession now returned to Egypt, and the whole country reverberated from the shouts of joy and from the sounds of music. Joseph thereupon took his father and set him before Pharaoh.

Now the door through which one entered into the royal palace of the Pharaohs of Egypt was very low, so that all the visitors were compelled to bow and bend their heads before the idol standing in the entrance. When Jacob came to visit Pharaoh, an angel appeared and raised the door so that the Patriarch could pass without stooping.

Pharaoh marvelled greatly at this wonder, and thought that it was Abraham who was standing before him.

" Years ago," said Pharaoh, " such a miracle occurred at this very door, when Abraham the Hebrew came to visit one of my predecessors. Is it possible that the famous Patriarch Abraham is still alive?"

It is also related that at that moment Og happened to be with Pharaoh, and the giant, who had known Abraham well, was so struck by the resemblance of Jacob with his grandfather that he actually believed it was Abraham who was standing there. Therefore Pharaoh asked Jacob: " How old art thou?"

to which the Patriarch replied: " Few and evil have been the days of my life."

Thereupon Jacob blessed Pharaoh, saying: " May the waters of the Nile rise at thy approach, overflow their banks and water and fructify the land of Egypt." And the Lord blessed the country on account of the pious Patriarch, for the famine soon came to an end.

The Egyptians now came to Joseph and said: " Give us seed, O our ruler, that we may cultivate the land and sow." Joseph granted their request, but he did not permit them to remain in their native districts. He gave them fields and seed and settled them in other cities, thus making them aliens everywhere. " The Egyptians," said Joseph, " will now no longer be able to speak of my brethren as aliens and exiles in the country, for they, too, having changed their dwelling places, are aliens and exiles."

Jacob and his family were now settled in the country of Goshen, and Joseph provided for them very generously, giving them food, drink, and even clothing, whilst the Patriarch and his sons took their meals daily at the Viceroy's table. Joseph also gathered much treasure, gold, silver, and precious stones which the Egyptians gave in exchange for the grain he sold them, whilst Pharaoh was keeping his stores for his own use and would not part with them. His possessions and treasures Joseph divided into four parts, burying them in the desert, near the Red Sea, on the banks of the River Euphrates, and in the desert near Persia and Media. The remainder he gave partly to his brethren and partly to Pharaoh who put it into his treasury. But Joseph also gathered the treasures of other nations besides the treasures of Egypt, for money from various parts of the world flowed into the country. These treasures the Jews took along with them in the time of the exodus. As for the treasures which Joseph had hidden in different spots, one part was discovered by Korah, the other by the Emperor

Antonine, the son of Severus, whilst the remaining two hiding places are still unknown, the treasures being reserved for the pious, among whom they will be distributed in the days of the Messiah.[1]

[1] *Genesis Rabba*, §§ 93, 94; *Targum Pseudo-Jonathan, in loco*; *Midrash Tanchuma*, section *Vayigash*; *Midrash Agadah*, ed. Buber, pp. 102–105; *Yalkut*, §§ 151, 152; *Midrash Haggadol*, col. 661–663; Babylonian Talmud, *Pesachim*, 119a; *Pirke de Rabbi Eliezer*, Ch. 39; *Sepher Hajashar*; see also Schapiro, *loc. cit.*, pp. 56–74.

CHAPTER XI

The Lovesick Prince and the Jealous Brethren

Asenath visits the Patriarch at Goshen—The wonderful old man—
The affection of the sons of Leah and the jealousy of the sons of the handmaids—The lovesick prince—A plot to assassinate Joseph—The loyal
brothers—The heroes of Shechem draw their swords—The frightened
prince—The heir to the throne and the sons of the handmaids—A false
accusation—The treachery of the stepbrothers—The jealousy of Dan and
the hatred of Gad—Naphtali's visions—The ship of Jacob—In ambush
in the ravine—The king passes a sleepless night—The disappointment of
the son who would assassinate his father—The attack—Benjamin jumps
from the chariot and wounds the prince with a pebble—Simeon and Levi
appear upon the scene—The fight for Asenath—Her forgiving nature—
The death of the prince.

Immediately upon Jacob's arrival in Egypt, Asenath came to
see him.[1] " I will go to Goshen and pay a visit to thy father,"
said Asenath unto Joseph, " because thy Father Israel is like
a God unto me."

And Joseph replied: " Come with me and thou wilt see
my father."

When Asenath arrived at Goshen and beheld the Patriarch,
she was greatly impressed by his beauty and nobility of appearance. Although a very old man, Jacob nevertheless resembled
a vigorous youth. His hair was snow white, and his long
white beard covered his chest, his eyes were shining brightly,
and had lost none of their powerful youthful expression,
whilst his arms and shoulders were powerful, and his legs and

[1] For the entire episode see *The Life and Confession*, or *Prayer of Asenath* (Part II),
published (Greek and Latin) by P. Batiffol, *Studia Patristica*, Paris, 1889–1890.

148

feet were those of a giant. Greatly impressed by the appearance of the Patriarch, Asenath bowed low and bade him greeting.

" Is this thy spouse?" asked Jacob, addressing Joseph.

" She is," replied Joseph. Thereupon Jacob blessed her, and bidding her come near kissed her. " May the Eternal bless thee," said the Patriarch, " for thus is welcomed the warrior who hath escaped the dangers of the battle-field and returneth home." [1]

The sons of Leah took a great liking for their sister-in-law, but not the sons of Zilpah and Bilhah, the handmaids, who seemed to have been jealous of Joseph's greatness and happiness, and also of the favour Asenath had found in the eyes of their father and of the blessing the latter had bestowed upon his daughter-in-law.

Joseph and Asenath left Goshen and returned home, accompanied by Levi, so that Joseph was on the left of his wife and Levi on her right. Asenath had conceived a great respect and liking for Levi, for he was a very intelligent man. But Levi was more than an intelligent man. He was a saint and a prophet, could read the heavenly writings, and instructed Asenath in them. Levi also, during his ascension to Heaven, had seen in the highest Heaven the place destined for Asenath in the next world.

Now, on their journey home, Joseph and Asenath had to pass the royal residence, and the eldest son of Pharaoh, beholding the beautiful wife of the Viceroy, fell in love with her. He made up his mind to kill Joseph, and to take his widow to wife, but he knew that unaided he could never get his rival out of the way. The Prince therefore sent for Simeon and Levi, and thus addressed them:

" I know that you two are powerful and brave men, and

---

[1] In his Introduction Batiffol points out that in these words Jacob probably refers to Asenath as his granddaughter who had joined the family.

that by your hands the town of Shechem was destroyed and the inhabitants exterminated. I know that your swords send terror into the hearts of brave and warlike men. Now if you are willing to stand by me and help me in what I am about to carry out, great will be your reward. I will give you great treasure, much gold and silver, man servants and maid servants, asses and camels. I hate your brother Joseph, because he took Asenath to wife, the maiden who ought to have been betrothed to me. If you will help me to kill Joseph by the sword, so that I can marry Asenath, you will always be unto me like my brothers and trusted friends. Should you, however, refuse to fulfil my request, you will certainly regret it."

"We are God-fearing men," replied the brothers, "and our father is a servant of the Lord, and our brother, too, is a God-fearing man. We will commit a great sin before the Lord, if we consent to accomplish such a wicked deed. Shouldst thou, however, persist in thy design, know that we will fight for our brother and if needs be die fighting." Saying this, the brothers drew their swords from their scabbards, saying: "These are the swords with which we destroyed the city of Shechem, when we came to avenge our sister's dishonour. The same swords will serve us to defend our brother's life, and to avenge his death, should some coward attempt to take it. Now, thou art warned," concluded the two heroes of Shechem.

When the son of Pharaoh heard these words and saw the drawn swords of the brothers, he was greatly frightened and nearly fainted.

Although afraid of Joseph and of his brethren, the heir to the throne nevertheless persisted in his desire to kill Joseph, so as to marry his widow. He was torn between his deep passion and his abject fear.

Thereupon his faithful servants, when they saw their master in such affliction and so perturbed in spirit, said unto him:

" The sons of the handmaids will no doubt be persuaded to listen to thy words and do thy bidding, for they are hostile to and jealous of the sons of Leah and Rachel."

The son of Pharaoh listened to the advice of his servants, sent for the sons of Bilhah and Zilpah, and thus addressed them: " Either blessing or death await ye soon, O sons of Bilhah and Zilpah, and I advise ye to choose blessing rather than death. I have heard your brother Joseph speak to my father Pharaoh concerning ye, and thus he said: ' They are only sons of the handmaids, and not my real brothers. I will wait for the death of my father and then I will destroy them and all their seed, so that they may not inherit with us. I also have a grudge against these sons of slaves, because they were guilty of my having been sold into slavery to the Ishmaelites. I will, therefore, punish them for their treatment of me, and repay hatred with hatred.'

" My father, Pharaoh," continued the heir to the throne, " applauded your brother's words and promised to help him in the execution of his deed." Thus spoke the son of Pharaoh, inventing a falsehood, so as to excite the hatred against and fear of Joseph in the hearts of the sons of Bilhah and Zilpah.[1]

Now the sons of the handmaids knew in their hearts that they had been guilty of deep hatred against Joseph, and had resolved on his death on that fatal day when the future ruler of Egypt was thrown into the pit.

Dan had been very jealous of Joseph, and more than once the evil spirit had stirred him up to take his sword and slay Joseph, crush him as a leopard crusheth a kid. He regretted it deeply afterwards, and, on his death-bed, he exhorted his children to keep away from anger and wrath, and never be moved to anger, even if any one spoke evil against them.

Gad, too, confessed on his death-bed that he had hated

[1] See note 1, p. 148.

Joseph in his early youth, on account of the latter's talebearing.
Very valiant in keeping the flocks, it was Gad's duty to guard
them at night. When a lion, wolf, or any other wild beast came,
he used to pursue the beast, and seizing its foot with one hand
hurl it about until he killed it. One day, he succeeded in delivering a lamb, snatched and carried away by a bear. The
lamb, however, had been grievously hurt and could no longer
live, and the brethren, therefore, slew it and ate its flesh.
Now Joseph had been with the flock for thirty days until he
had fallen sick on account of the heat. On his return home to
his father, he told the latter that the sons of Bilhah and Zilpah
were slaying the best of the flock and eating them without
asking the permission of either Reuben or Judah. Gad, therefore, hated Joseph from his heart, and often wished to kill
him, to " lick him out of the land of the living, even as an ox
licketh up the grass of the field ". No wonder, therefore, that
Dan and Gad, who felt guilty of their former treatment of
Joseph, were afraid of the powerful ruler's revenge and gave
credence to the story told them by the son of Pharaoh.[1]

" And what shall we do, my lord?" asked Gad and Dan.

" My plan," replied the Prince of Egypt, " is as follows:
This night I will kill my father, the King of Egypt, for he is
unto Joseph like a father and loves him greatly, whilst ye will
kill your brother Joseph, the Viceroy. Thereupon I will take
me to wife Asenath and ye will be to me like my brethren, and
inherit everything with me."

Thus spake the son of Pharaoh, and Dan and Gad agreed
to his plan, whilst Naphtali and Asher demurred.

Naphtali had been greatly loved by Joseph's mother,
Rachel, who constantly used to kiss him and to wish for a son
from her own womb like Naphtali. And when Joseph was
born he was like Naphtali in all things. Naphtali, too, saw

---

[1] R. H. Charles, *The Testaments of the Twelve Patriarchs*, London, 1917 (*Testament of Gad*, pp. 82–83).

visions, and also used to dream dreams which he told to his father who replied that the things he saw would be fulfilled in due season.

Naphtali had once seen a vision or dreamed a dream, wherein he beheld his father standing by the shore of the sea of Jamnia. Thereupon a ship, without either sailors or pilot, came sailing by, and upon the ship was written: " The ship of Jacob ". The Patriarch then said to his sons: " Come, let us embark on our ship." This they did, and Jacob took the helm. But, lo, a mighty storm arose, and a terrible tempest raged, the ship being tossed about by the angry waters. It was ultimately broken up. Jacob departed from his sons, Joseph fled away upon a little boat, whilst the other brethren held fast to nine planks, until they were scattered to all the corners of the earth. But Levi prayed for them all to the Lord, the storm ceased, and the ship reached the shore. Thereupon Jacob returned, and they were all re-united.

Naphtali and Asher, therefore, tried to dissuade their brothers from committing the wicked deed, but in the end they followed them.[1]

" We know," said Dan and Gad, " that to-morrow Asenath is going down to the country and will be accompanied by an escort of six hundred valiant men, whilst Joseph will go to town to sell corn. Now, if my lord will send with us a greater number of warriors, we will start this night, lie in ambush in the ravine, and hide in the thicket, whilst thou wilt precede us with a vanguard of fifty spearmen. When our sister-in-law approacheth our hiding-place, we will fall upon her escort, kill all the men, and let Asenath escape, so that in her flight she will fall into thy hands for thee to do unto her as thou pleasest."

Thus spoke Dan and Gad, and the son of Pharaoh, on hearing their words, was greatly pleased, and put 2000 men

[1] Charles, *loc. cit.*, p. 80.

at the disposal of the brothers who started at once on their errand.

During the night the prince made an attempt to penetrate into the royal apartments, but the guards on duty would not allow him to pass.

" Thy father," they said, " having suffered from an acute headache, passed a sleepless night, and is now resting awhile. He has, therefore, given orders that no one be allowed to pass and enter his room, not even his eldest son."

Greatly disappointed, the prince, unsuccessful in his parricidal design, went out to capture Asenath, taking with him five hundred spearmen. He stationed himself not far from the place where Dan and Gad were lying in ambush.

Early the next morning Asenath left town for the country. " I am going," she said, " but it grieves me greatly to leave thee, my beloved."

" Have no fear, my dear," replied Joseph, " and put thy trust in God who will guard thee and protect thee. I cannot accompany thee, as I am bound to go to the storehouse, there to distribute corn to the hungry."

They separated, and Asenath, accompanied by a bodyguard of six hundred valiant men, proceeded on her journey. Scarcely had they reached the place where the prince's forces led by the sons of Bilhah and Zilpah were lying in ambush, when the latter came forth from their hiding-place and attacked Asenath's bodyguard. When Asenath perceived Pharaoh's son, she called upon the Lord to help her and fled from her chariot. Benjamin, too, who was accompanying his sister-in-law, leaped from the chariot and prepared to face the enemy.

Gathering small pebbles from the ravine, he hurled them at the son of Pharaoh, hitting him in the forehead and inflicting a severe wound, so that the prince fell down from his horse, like one dead. Supplied with pebbles by the charioteer,

Benjamin, who resembled a lion in power, continued to cast his stones against the prince's spearmen, killing fifty of them.

In the meantime one of Asenath's bodyguard had escaped, carrying the news of the attack to the other brethren of Joseph, although Levi already knew what was happening, thanks to his prophetic gifts. Simeon and Levi soon appeared upon the scene and set the spearmen in flight.

The sons of the handmaids meanwhile made an attempt to fall with drawn swords upon their sister-in-law, but she prayed to the Lord and the swords of her assailants turned to ashes. They now regretted their crime, and falling upon their knees implored Asenath's forgiveness and her protection against the wrath of Simeon and Levi. She readily forgave them their murderous attempt, advising them to hide behind the thicket until she had succeeded in appeasing the anger of Simeon and of Levi.

When the latter returned from their pursuit of the prince's spearmen, they looked round for the sons of the handmaids, having decided to punish them as they deserved. To their surprise they found in Asenath an advocate of the criminals.

" Do not kill them, O sons of Jacob," she pleaded, " for they are your brethren, the sons of your father. If ye kill your brethren ye will commit a heinous deed, cause deep sorrow to your old father, and be shunned by men."

The brethren forgave the sons of the handmaids, and Levi even washed the wounds of the prince. The heir to the throne died, however, soon afterwards, and Pharaoh grieved greatly.[1]

[1] See note 1, p. 148.

CHAPTER XII

A Father's Blessing, or the Death and Burial of the Patriarch

The Patriarch's last request—His reasons for wishing to be buried in Canaan—The dead who will roll through the hollowed earth—Jacob's humiliation before his death—Ephraim brings the sad tidings—The prophetic spirit forsakes the Patriarch—Joseph's prayer—The Patriarch adopts the sons of Joseph—The discontent of the sons of Jacob—He who hath to him it is given—Blessings enough for all of ye—Reuben deprived of birthright, kingship, and priesthood—Simeon and Levi rebuked—It is not the destiny of Israel to draw the sword and commit deeds of violence—The offspring of Judah—Merchant princes will issue from Zebulun and scholars from Issachar—The fair daughters of Asher—The Patriarch's last instructions—The order in which his sons are commanded to carry his bier—The couch upon which reposed the body of the Patriarch—The guard of honour—The Queen intercedes on behalf of Joseph—The royal secret—Pharaoh is compelled to grant Joseph leave of absence—The golden bier of the Patriarch—He has the appearance of a living king—The funeral procession—The perfumed carpet—The kings and magnates of Canaan join the procession—Disarmament in honour of Jacob, the man of peace—The thirty-six crowns suspended from Jacob's bier—The arrival of Esau—The lord of Seïr claims his portion of the family tomb—The deed of sale—The disputed document—Naphtali runs to Egypt—The anger of Hushim the deaf—He knocks his great uncle's head off—The head of Esau is buried in the cave of Machpelah—The fight for the headless body of Esau—The capture of Zepho, son of Eliphaz—The return to Egypt.

For seventeen years Jacob had dwelt in Goshen, when he felt his end approach. Seventeen years of peace were granted to the Patriarch as a reward for the seventeen years which he had devoted to the bringing up and education of Joseph. When Jacob knew that his end was near, he summoned his favourite son, the ruler of Egypt, and thus addressed him:

" If I have found grace in thine eyes, O my son, do not bury me in the land of Egypt, but carry my remains to the land of Canaan, the land which the Lord did promise to give to my descendants. A day will come, my son, when the dead will awaken and come to life again, but those buried in the Holy Land will rise first to new life, whilst the dead buried in other places of the world will roll through the hollowed earth until they reach Canaan. Besides, the Egyptians, who look upon me as a saint, might turn my grave, if I were to be interred in this country, into an object of idolatrous worship. A day will also come when the country will be visited by ten plagues, one of them vermin with which the soil of Egypt will swarm. My grave will thus be desecrated, and my corpse exposed to uncleanness. I am also anxious, even as my fathers were before me, to lie in the Holy Land, for the Lord once promised me to give it to my descendants. ' The land where-on thou liest,' He said, ' I will give it to thee and to thy seed.' If I have, therefore, found grace in thine eyes, carry my remains to the Holy Land for burial, but take with thee some of the earth of Egypt upon which my corpse will have lain to strew it over my dead body. Swear to me, my son, that thou wilt carry out my request."

When Joseph promised to do his father's bidding and to carry out his request, the Patriarch bowed low before his own son, who was the ruler of Egypt, so as to let come true Joseph's dream wherein he had seen the sun (his father) bowing low before him. But Jacob also bowed low to the Majesty of God (which had appeared at the head of his bed), thanking the Lord for the blessing He had vouchsafed unto him in giving him such a son. Jacob had nevertheless humiliated himself before his own son, both in repeating his request three times and asking a favour and a service of Joseph, and in bowing low to him. Just as death in itself is a humiliation for man, just as Moses and David had to experience this humiliation

(*Numbers*, 25, 7; *Kings*, 2, 1) so Jacob also humiliated himself before his death.

" And where shall I bury thee in Canaan?" asked Joseph.

" Bury me in the double cave which I bought from my brother Esau," replied Jacob.

Some time afterwards, Ephraim, the son of Joseph, who was constantly with his grandfather who instructed him in the knowledge of God, came over from Goshen and informed his father that the Patriarch was grievously sick. The Viceroy at once hastened to his father's bedside, taking with him, at the urgent request of his wife Asenath, his two sons, so that the pious Patriarch might bless them.

When Jacob raised his hands to bless his grandsons, he suddenly saw in a prophetic vision that Jeroboam, the son of Nebat, and Ahab, the son of Omri, their descendants, would introduce idolatry in Israel. He saw crowds worshipping idols, and the Holy Spirit forsaking him, he could not bestow his blessing upon Ephraim and Manasseh.

" I cannot bless thy sons," he said unto Joseph, " for they seem to be unworthy of it. Who are they? Whose sons are they? Are they the offspring of a worthy mother whom thou didst marry according to the law?"

" Whoever they are," replied Joseph, " they are my sons, and I did marry their mother Asenath according to the law, and here is the marriage contract."

Joseph also prayed unto the Lord to have mercy on him and his sons and permit his father to bless them. " Do not put me to shame to-day," he prayed, " O Lord of the Universe, and may Thy Holy Spirit once more descend upon my father so that he may bless my sons who are innocent of the sin to be committed one day by their descendants."

Thus prayed Joseph in the agony of his soul, and the Lord hearkened unto the prayer of Joseph the Just. The Holy Spirit once more descended upon Jacob, and he blessed his grand-

sons, giving the birth-right to Ephraim from whom would issue
Joshua, the son of Nun, who was to lead Israel into the land
of Canaan. Joshua, Jacob saw, would work wonders in the
presence of Israel, for he would one day bid the sun and the
moon stand still and wait until he had brought to a successful
issue the war he was waging.

"May the Lord protect ye," said the Patriarch, "against
all evil, and may ye grow and multiply like the fishes in the
sea, and may the evil eye have no power over ye for the sake
of the merits of your father Joseph."

Happy and in blithe spirits, Joseph left his father who had
bestowed his last blessing upon his sons. When the brethren
beheld Joseph's radiant countenance, they murmured: "Such
is the way of the world: he who hath, to him it is given, and
a favourite of fortune is favoured and loved by all. Joseph is
king and ruler of Egypt, and therefore our father, too, hath
bestowed his blessing upon him and his sons, and left none
for us."

When Jacob heard these words, he said to his sons: "It
is not so. I have blessed Joseph and his sons not because
your brother is more powerful than ye, but because he is just,
pious, and generous. As for ye, fear the Lord, practise justice,
and be pious and generous, and ye will never want anything,
for those who honour the Lord are blessed. I will bless ye
too, my sons, for I have blessings enough for all my sons."
Thereupon the Patriarch summoned all his sons and bestowed
his last blessing upon each of them separately.

He rebuked Reuben for the sin he had once committed
with regard to Bilhah, pointing out that one sin committed
makes a man lose many privileges and benefits. "Thou art
my first-born, the beginning of my strength, and the crowns of
birth-right, priesthood, and kingship ought therefore to have
been thy share. But the birth-right is given to Joseph, the
priesthood to Levi, and the kingship to Judah. I bless thee,

however, my son, and from thee will issue priests to the Lord, heroes and kings."

Jacob also rebuked Simeon and Levi, because they had been the first to draw their swords, and had thus imitated the example of their uncle, Esau, who lived by his sword. " Know, my sons, he said, that it is not the destiny of Israel to draw the sword and to commit deeds of violence. It is not seemly for the sons of Jacob to shed blood and for Israel to wage wars. Our prayers are our weapons, and our supplications are our arrows."

When Judah heard these rebukes, he was greatly alarmed and feared his father's reproaches, which he knew he well deserved. " I will slip away and not be put to shame by my father's reproaches," thought Judah. But the Patriarch called him back and spoke gently to him:

" Thou, my son, didst once confess thy sin publicly in the case of thy daughter-in-law Tamar; thou also didst save the life of thy brother Joseph. Thy brethren, therefore, will praise thee, and the nation will be called after thee and known as Judæans (Jews) from Judah, and not as Reubenites, Simeonites, or Levites. From thee will issue kings, rulers and teachers of the law, judges and prophets."

The Patriarch thereupon blessed Zebulun and Issachar, Dan, Naphtali, Gad, and Asher. The descendants of Zebulun will be distinguished by their commercial careers, for merchant princes and business magnates will issue from him, and they will grow prosperous. They will inherit the sea-coasts, and their merchant ships will ply the high seas. With their abundant wealth they will support the sons of Issachar, whose descendants are destined to devote themselves to the study of the law, giving issue to great scholars and members of legal assemblies.

In blessing Dan, the Patriarch saw in a prophetic vision the hero Samson who would issue from him, Samson who would redeem Israel from their oppressors the Philistines. But he saw Samson standing between the two pillars in the temple of the Philistines, blind and defeated, and he knew that although he would bring victory to Israel, Samson was not the redeemer of Israel.

To Naphtali he said: " Thou wast always as swift as a hart to do my bidding; in thy domain will be the plain of Gennesaret, famous for its gardens and its delicious fruit, which will ripen quickly and be served upon royal tables.

" From Gad famous heroes and warriors will issue, and the descendants of Asher will be famous for the beauty of their women, and kings and high-priests will seek their wives among the daughters of Asher."

When Joseph's turn came the Patriarch thus addressed him: " Thou art mighty and powerful, my son, and thou hast been strong in life; thou art like the vine planted at the edge of the water, its roots being in the depth of the earth and its branches surpassing and excelling all the other trees. Thy wisdom excelleth the wisdom of the magicians of Egypt, and thy pious deeds conquered them all. When Pharaoh placed thee in his chariot and men called out before thee: ' Long live the ruler of Egypt, old in wisdom but young in years!' the daughters of kings and princes rushed to their windows, casting their eyes upon thee. They threw down gold and silver ornaments, trying to draw thy attention to them, but thou didst not look at them nor wast thou enticed by their beauty. The instruction thou didst receive from thy father has rendered thee worthy of being the feeder of men. May the blessing thy father now bestoweth upon thee and the blessing which his fathers, Abraham and Isaac, gave him—and which the great ones of the earth, Ishmael, Esau, and the sons of Keturah envied—rest upon thee and be a crown upon thy head. Mayest thou enjoy their fruits in this world and in the next."

To Benjamin Jacob foretold that the first King of Israel

would issue from his tribe and that the Holy Temple would
be built in his allotment.

The Patriarch was on the point of revealing the future to
his sons, but the Holy Spirit left him, and he was unable to
communicate to his sons the mysteries of the future of the
nation.

" Be united, my sons," said the Patriarch, " for union will
be your strength, and will bring about the redemption of Israel,
who will be driven into exile twice." Thereupon the Patriarch
commanded all his sons to abstain from idolatry and to love
truth, peace, and justice. His sons faithfully promised to obey
his commands. He then gave them instructions how to bear
his body and transport his bier from Egypt to Canaan.

" No stranger shall help to bear my body, and not even
your sons, for some among you did marry heathen wives.
The order ye will observe shall be as follows: Judah, Issachar,
and Zebulun shall march to the east, in front; Reuben, Simeon,
and Gad to the right of the bier, or the south; Dan, Asher,
Naphtali to the left, or the north; and Ephraim, Manasseh,
and Benjamin behind, or to the west."

It was the same order in which the tribes were afterwards
to march through the desert, bearing their standards.

Joseph and Levi were rather astonished at the instructions
their father had given them with regard to the order in which
they were to transport his bier.

" Why, Father," they complained, " didst thou exclude us
from the last honour to be paid unto thee?"

" Thou, my son Joseph," replied the Patriarch, " art the
ruler of Egypt, and it is not seemly that thou shouldst help
bear my bier, whilst Levi is destined one day to carry the ark
of the Lord. Therefore, he too shall not carry the bier containing my dead body.

" Know, my sons," concluded the Patriarch, " that great
suffering will be your lot in this land of Egypt, but if you serve

the Lord and teach your children to walk in His ways, He will send you a redeemer who will deliver you from bondage and lead you into the Holy Land which the Lord promised to your fathers. A day will come when this redeemer will bless the tribes of Israel, but his blessing will only be bestowed upon you when you will observe the commands written in his law."

When the Patriarch had finished blessing his sons and giving them his last instructions, he breathed his last, dying gently as if sent to sleep by Divinity, his soul lured from his body by a Divine kiss.

The brethren rent their garments, girded their loins with sackcloth and strewed dust upon their heads in sign of mourning. They wept and lamented the death of their pious father.

When the news of Jacob's death became known in the land, the great ones of the realm and the women of Egypt came to weep over the Patriarch.

The sons immediately began to make preparations for the burial. Joseph gave orders to his physicians to embalm the corpse of his father, an operation to which they devoted forty days. But Joseph's command displeased the Lord, who alone preserves the corpses of the pious from corruption.

Jacob's body was placed upon a couch made of cedar wood, covered with gold and set with gems and precious stones. A drapery of purple was hung over the couch, fragrant wine was poured out at the side, and aromatic spices and perfumes were burnt. A guard of honour stood round the bier of Jacob, among them being heroes of the house of Esau, and heroes of the house of Ishmael, and also Judah, the bravest hero among the sons of Jacob.

For seventy days the Egyptians mourned over the death of the Patriarch. " Come," they said, " let us mourn the pious man on account of whose merits the famine in our land has been reduced from forty-two to two years."

Joseph now made the necessary preparations to transport

the body of his father from Egypt to Canaan. First, however, he had to obtain Pharaoh's permission to absent himself from the country. As he did not wish to appear at court during the time of mourning, he decided to address himself to the queen, asking her to put his petition before Pharaoh and to intercede on his behalf. He sent for the governess of the royal children and asked her to put his petition before the queen, so that she might speak favourably to the King and influence him to grant the required permission.

"I have given a solemn oath to my father," said Joseph, "to carry his body up to Canaan, and I must, therefore, absent myself from the country for some time."

Pharaoh was at first not inclined to grant the permission Joseph craved, and advised the Viceroy to obtain an absolution from his oath from the wise men of Egypt.

Joseph thereupon sent to Pharaoh the following reply:

"If I seek absolution from the oath I have given my father, I will also seek absolution from the oath I once swore unto thee, never to reveal thy secret. I will now be free to inform the princes of thy realm and thy people that thou art ignorant of Hebrew, and dost not fulfil the condition under which only a man who was supposed to know all the seventy languages could be appointed ruler of Egypt."

When Pharaoh heard these words, he trembled greatly, for if the secret were to be betrayed, the people might depose him and raise Joseph to the vacant throne. Pharaoh, therefore, speedily granted Joseph his request, permitting him to carry the body of his father from Egypt to Canaan. The funeral procession consequently started for Canaan.

In a bier, made of pure gold, inlaid with onyx and bdellium, reposed the body of the Patriarch. An artistically woven cover of gold, fastened to the bier with hooks of onyx and bdellium, covered it. Upon the head of the Patriarch, Joseph placed a golden crown, and in his hand he put a golden sceptre, so that even in his death the Patriarch had the appearance of a living king. The bier was borne by Jacob's sons, but first came the valiant men of Pharaoh and the valiant men of Joseph, in warlike attire and brilliantly arrayed. The rest of the inhabitants, all in coats of mail and girt with swords, walked behind, at some distance from the bier, accompanied by weepers and mourners. Close behind the bier walked Joseph and his household, with bare feet and weeping, accompanied by servants in splendid warlike attire. Fifty of Joseph's servants walked in front of the bier, strewing, as they passed along, myrrh and aloes and aromatic spices, so that the sons of Jacob carrying the bier walked upon a perfumed carpet. Thus the procession moved on until it reached the boundary of Canaan and halted at *Goren Heatad*, the threshing floor of Atad, beyond the Jordan, where " they lamented with a very great and sore lamentation ".

When the kings of Canaan heard the tidings of Jacob's death, they ordered their servants to saddle their horses, mules, and asses, spreading black cloth over them, and came out to join the procession, and to show their respect to Jacob the Hebrew. Before approaching the bier, the kings loosed the girdles of their garments and bared their shoulders in sign of grief and mourning. They also took off their weapons and laid them down upon the ground, not daring to approach the bier of Jacob, the man of peace, in their accoutrements and with their weapons of war which he had abhorred. When they saw Joseph's golden crown suspended from the bier of the Patriarch, the kings of Canaan also took off their crowns and placed them round the bier, so that thirty-six crowns were attached to it.

The news of Jacob's death had also reached his brother Esau at Seïr, who, accompanied by his sons and numerous followers, hastened to the threshing floor of Atad to meet and join the procession.

Joseph and his brethren now proceeded to Hebron, there to bury the Patriarch in the Double Cave, or the Cave of

Machpelah. But scarcely had they reached the burial place, when Esau came forward and made an effort to prevent the burial of his brother in the cave.

" I will not permit you," said Esau, " to bury my brother Jacob in this cave, for the only place available in it belongs to me by right."

" How so?" queried Joseph, angry at his uncle's aggressive attitude.

" Thou knowest," replied Esau, " that there is room in this cave for eight people only. Now, Adam and Eve, Abraham and Sarah, Isaac and Rebekah, lie buried here, and thus only two places remained, one for Jacob and one for me, the sons of Isaac. Thy father Jacob, however, buried his wife Leah in his place, and the remaining vacant place therefore is my portion."

Thus spoke Esau, but Joseph waxed wroth and replied:

" This is idle talk, for thou hast forfeited thy portion in the family tomb. Twenty-five years ago, when my grandfather Isaac died, my father offered thee to choose between a heap of gold and silver and thy portion in the family tomb. Thou didst choose the gold, resigning thy portion in the family tomb. My father acquired it from thee in a legal way, and a bill of sale was made out. I know all this, although I was not in Canaan at that time, for the bill of sale, duly signed, is in Egypt."

Esau, however, denied that any such document existed. " Produce the document," he replied, " and I will comply with thy request to permit thy father to be buried here in this cave."

Joseph, therefore, speedily dispatched his brother Naphtali, the swift runner, to Egypt, bidding him hurry and fetch the disputed document. Swift as a hart, Naphtali hurried away, running up-hill and down-hill, over dales and mounts, on his way from Canaan to Egypt.

When Esau saw that Naphtali had been dispatched to fetch the bill of sale which he well knew did exist, he summoned his sons and all his followers to prepare for battle against Joseph and his brethren.

In the meantime Hushim, the son of Dan, who was deaf, wondered at the tumult and the evident dispute which he did not understand. He endeavoured to find out the cause of the altercation, and the reason why they did not proceed with the burial of Jacob. By signs it was made clear to Hushim that the hairy man yonder was the cause of all the trouble. He would not permit the Patriarch to be buried in the cave, and they would have to await Naphtali's return from Egypt. When Hushim grasped the facts his indignation knew no bounds.

" What?" cried he, " shall my grandfather lie here dishonoured awaiting burial?" Seizing a club, he rushed into the midst of Esau's men and with one vigorous blow knocked the hairy one's head off. Esau died, and his eyes fell upon Jacob's knees.

Esau being dead, his sons and followers no longer dared interfere with the sons of Jacob who buried their father in the cave of Machpelah. The head of Esau, however, rolled into the cave and dropped into the lap of his father Isaac where it remained.

Joseph and his brethren mourned for seven days and then prepared to return to Egypt. But as soon as the period of seven days had elapsed, a war broke out between the sons of Esau and the sons of Jacob for the body of the lord of Seïr, which still lay unburied on the field of Machpelah. The sons of Esau were defeated, loosing eighty men, and Joseph captured Zepho, the son of Eliphaz, the son of Esau, and fifty of their men whom he sent down as prisoners to Egypt. The remaining men of the house of Esau took to flight, carrying with them the body of their chief, which they buried on Mount Seïr. The sons of Jacob pursued the enemy, but slew none of them out

of respect for the headless corpse of their Uncle Esau. They
returned to Hebron, but on the third day were once more
attacked by the enemy. The sons of Esau had gathered all the
inhabitants of Seïr and the children of the East and led a
mighty army against Joseph and his brethren, marching right
down into Egypt. Joseph, however, at the head of the heroes
of Egypt, met the enemy on the way and a fierce battle was
waged. The sons of Seïr and the children of the East suffered
a great defeat, their entire army being destroyed. Joseph and
his brethren pursued them as far as Succoth, and then returned
to Egypt.[1]

[1] *Genesis Rabba*, §§ 96–100; *Targum Pseudo-Jonathan, in loco*; *Midrash Tanchuma*, section
Vaichi; *Midrash Agadah*, ed. Buber, pp. 105–117; *Midrash Lekach Tob, in loco*; *Yalkut
Shimeoni, in loco*; *Numbers Rabba*, section *Nassoh*; Babylonian Talmud, *Sotah*, 13a, 36b; *Pirke
de Rabbi Eliezer*, Ch. 39; *Sepher Hajashar*; see also Gaster, *The Chronicles of Jerahmeel,*
p. 95 (XL, 3); Adolf Kurrein, *loc. cit.*; Lewner, *Kol Agadoth*, pp. 254–270.

CHAPTER XIII

Joseph's Magnanimity, and the Wars of the Cousins

Joseph no longer invites his brethren to have their meals at his table—His reasons for doing so—The fear of the brethren—Bilhah's message—Joseph's reply—His love and affection for his brethren—His gratitude to the sons of Jacob—He cannot act against the decrees of Providence—The death of Pharaoh—King Magron—Joseph the actual ruler of the country—The quarrel of the sons of Esau and the sons of Seïr—King Agnias of Africa—The war between the sons of Esau and the sons of Seïr—The victory of the sons of Esau—The election of a king—Bela, the son of Beor—The sons of Esau make war upon Egypt—Joseph's victory—Jobab, King of Edom—The escape of Zepho—At the court of Agnias, King of Africa—'Uzi of Pozimana—The fair Yaniah—The people of Kittim—The suitors for the hand of Yaniah—Turnus, King of Benevento—The reply of the men of Kittim—Lucus, King of Sardinia—The war between Agnias and Turnus—In the plain of Campania—The death of Neblus, son of Lucus—The golden statue and the two graves—Zepho's plan of revenge—The campaign against Egypt—Balaam, the magician—The wax figures—Zepho's flight to Kittim—The monster in the cave—The festival of Zepho—The sickness of Yaniah—The waters of Africa and Kittim—The waters of Forma for Queen Yaniah—Zepho is elected King of Kittim.

Since their return to Egypt, Joseph had ceased to invite his brethren to take their meals at his table and to entertain them, as he had been in the habit of doing for seventeen years whilst the Patriarch was still alive. Joseph's attitude, however, was not the result of any altered feeling on his part, but was dictated by a sentiment of justice. " So long as my father was alive," thought the Viceroy, " I used to sit at the head of the table, obeying therein my father's command. Now, however, it is not seemly, and I have no right to do so, for Reuben is after all the first-born, whilst kings will issue from Judah.

And yet, being the ruler of Egypt, I cannot allow anyone to sit at the head of the table."

For this reason Joseph hesitated to invite again his brethren to take their daily meals at his table. The brethren, however, unaware of Joseph's motives and of his fine scruples, attributed his changed attitude to a change of feelings. They now feared greatly that Joseph hated them and would avail himself of the first opportunity to wreak his vengeance. What he had not dared to do whilst the Patriarch was still alive he would not hesitate now to accomplish. Thus thought the brethren, and decided to ascertain what was in the Viceroy's mind and whether he intended to do harm unto them.[1]

They sent Bilhah as their deputy to Joseph with an invented message, and informed the Viceroy of their father's last wish, conjuring him in the name of Jacob to condone the brethren's former aim.

When Joseph heard Bilhah's words and knew that his brethren still suspected him of harbouring hostile feelings towards them, he wept copiously and was greatly grieved. He hastened to assure his brethren of his love and affection, and consoled them as well as he could.

" If I did no longer invite you to sit at my table, the Lord knoweth my reason and that my action was dictated by my respect for you. Fear not," said the Viceroy, " for why should I repay you evil for good? You have rendered me a great service when you came to Egypt. Before your arrival in the country the Egyptians looked upon me as a slave, the son of an obscure shepherd, who was released from prison and became their ruler. They never would believe that I was really of noble birth and the scion of a great house. By your advent here you have proved to all Egypt that I am a man of noble birth. I am therefore grateful to you, and will not forget what

---

[1] *Midrash Tanchuma; Genesis Rabba,* § 100; *Targum Pseudo-Jonathan; Midrash Agadah; Yalkut Shimeoni.*

I owe unto you. Besides, it is in my own interest to treat you well and to show you every mark of love and affection. Were I to act otherwise, were I to kill you, then my proofs of being the scion of a noble house would at once no longer hold good. The Egyptians would say: ' Either this man is devoid of all brotherly feelings, and doth not keep faith with his own kith and kin and is not to be trusted, or he is a deceiver. He induced a gang of young men to come down to Egypt and give themselves out as his brothers, but now that they have served his purpose and have become rather troublesome he quickly found a pretext to get rid of them.' I beg you, therefore, my brethren, to banish all suspicion from your hearts, for I harbour no evil thoughts against you, and be convinced of my brotherly love and affection. Besides, are ye not like the dust of the earth, the sand on the seashore, and the beasts of the field? Could they all be exterminated, leaving no trace? Have ye not seen that ten stars were unable to do ought against one? Then how could one star destroy ten? I could not act against the decrees of Providence and the laws of nature. The day hath twelve hours, and twelve hours hath the night. Twelve months hath the year, twelve is the number of the constellations, and twelve tribes are we. I am the head, whilst ye represent the body, but the head cannot continue to live without the body. Go therefore home in peace, my brethren, and remember our father's last words and his instructions. The Lord will then be with ye, and ye need fear no man." Thus spoke Joseph, and the brethren were greatly relieved and consoled.[1]

Now when Joseph was seventy-one years of age—it was thirty-two years after the arrival of his brethren in Egypt—Pharaoh died, and his son Magron ruled in his place.

Before departing this life Pharaoh called Joseph and thus he spoke to him: " I beg thee to guide my son Magron with thy counsel and be a father unto him."

[1] *Ibid.*

The Egyptians, who loved their Viceroy greatly, for he had found favour in their eyes, were well pleased with Pharaoh's last injunctions, and they made Joseph the actual ruler and regent of the land, whilst Magron bore the royal title and was called Pharaoh, as is the custom in Egypt to call the kings. Magron, however, left all the affairs of the state to be administered by Joseph's hand, who was thus the real ruler of the country.[1]

As regent and actual ruler of Egypt, the son of Jacob was just and generous as before. He was also as modest and humble on the throne as he had been years ago, when a slave in the house of Potiphar. The Lord was therefore with Joseph, and he was successful in all his undertakings. He was well beloved by all his subjects, and his fame travelled far and wide. He also extended his rule over the land of the Philistines, of Canaan and Sidon, and the land east of the Jordan, and the inhabitants of these countries sent rich presents to the ruler of Egypt and brought him a yearly tribute. The sons of Jacob dwelt in Goshen, happy and peaceful, and served the Lord as they had been commanded by the Patriarch before he died. They did not mix with the Egyptians, who worshipped idols, and cherished their own tongue, the Hebrew language.

Now when the sons of Esau and the sons of Seïr had returned to their own country after their campaign, they began to quarrel among themselves: " It is because of you," said the sons of Seïr, " that we were forced to wage a war against the sons of Jacob. And now you have brought misfortune upon us, for we have suffered a great defeat and have lost all our valiant men, none having remained who know the art of war. Leave, therefore, our territory and go to Canaan, the home of your ancestors. Why should your children possess this country together with our own descendants?"

Thus spoke the sons of Seïr, wishing to get rid of the sons

[1] *Sepher Hajashar*; *Exodus Rabba*, § 1; *Pirke de Rabbi Eliezer*, Ch. 48.

of Esau. As the latter refused to leave the country, the sons
of Seïr decided to expel by force those whom they called *aliens*
in their midst. The sons of Esau, however, secretly sent a
deputation to Agnias, King of Denaba, in Africa, asking him
for help.

" The children of Seïr," they informed Agnias, " have
decided to expel us from their country, and we therefore
urgently beseech thee to send us armed assistance that we may
be able to resist our enemy."

Agnias, who at that time was favourably disposed towards
the sons of Esau, immediately sent 500 foot soldiers and
800 mounted men.

The sons of Seïr had in the meantime addressed themselves
to the children of the East and to the Madianites for help.

" You have seen," they wrote, " what misfortune the sons
of Esau have brought down upon us. Against our will they
involved us in a war with the sons of Jacob in which all our
valiant men have perished. Now, we want to get rid of the
sons of Esau who are dwelling in our midst. Come therefore
to our aid and help us expel them from our land and to revenge
the death of our brethren of which the sons of Esau are the
cause."

The sons of the East granted the request of the sons of
Seïr, and immediately sent them 800 men well versed in the
art of war.

The two hostile armies met in the desert of Paran, where
a fierce battle was waged. The battle ended with a complete
defeat of the sons of Esau, who lost 200 men. On the following
day they once more gathered their forces and returned to the
charge. This time, too, the God of battles was against them,
and they lost heavily. Twenty-eight men of the army of Agnias
had also been killed, and many of the sons of Esau deserted
their brethren, joining the ranks of the enemy. On the third
day, the sons of Esau thus spoke to each other:

" What shall we do unto our brethren who have forsaken us in our hour of need?"

Thereupon they once more sent a messenger to Agnias, requesting him to send them fresh support.

" Twice," they wrote, " have we suffered a defeat at the hands of the sons of Seïr, who are superior to us in number."

Agnias once more put at their disposal an army of 600 valiant men to help the sons of Esau in their need. Ten days later, the latter again attacked the enemy in the desert of Paran and this time gained a decisive victory. The hostile forces were routed, all the valiant men, 2000 in number, fell in the combat.

The children of the East and the Madianites were put to flight, and were pursued by the sons of Esau who slew another 250 men. The sons of Esau themselves had only lost thirty men slain by their own brethren, who had joined the hostile army.

On their return to Seïr, the sons of Esau slew all the women and children who had remained behind, sparing only fifty boys whom they made slaves, and fifty maidens whom they took to wives. They thereupon divided among themselves all the possessions of the sons of Seïr, all the land and the cattle. They also divided the whole land into five districts, according to the number of the sons of Esau.

Some time afterwards the sons of Esau determined to elect a king who would rule the country and command the army in times of war. They swore, however, that never would a son of their own people rule over them, for ever since the treachery of their brethren during the wars with the sons of Seïr they had no faith in their own people, and every one suspected his brother, his son, or his friend.

There was among the officers sent to them by King Agnias, King of Denaba, a warrior named Bela, son of Beor. He was a gallant soldier, handsome and well made, comely of person, well versed in all the sciences, and of good counsel. There was none like him among the officers of King Agnias. The choice of the sons of Esau fell upon Bela, whom they chose as their ruler. They proclaimed him King, prostrated themselves before him, and cried aloud: " Long live the King!" Thereupon they spread out a carpet whereupon all deposited their gifts, consisting of precious ornaments and gold and silver pieces, so that the King became very rich, possessing much gold, silver, and precious stones, and lived in opulence. The sons of Esau also constructed a throne for their King, set a golden crown upon his head, and built for him a sumptuous palace as his royal residence. Bela reigned over the sons of Esau for thirty years. The valiant men of Agnias thereupon returned to their own country, after having been well paid for their services by the sons of Esau.[1]

Many years had passed, when the sons of Esau, who had grown mighty during the reign of their King Bela, and had recovered from the defeat they had once suffered, again decided to wage war against the sons of Jacob and the Egyptians. Their purpose was to take their revenge for the defeat they had once suffered and also to deliver Zepho, the son of Eliphaz, and the other prisoners who were still being detained in Egypt.

Thereupon the sons of Esau concluded an alliance with all the sons of the East, and also with the sons of Ishmael, and a mighty army numbering 800,000 men, infantry and cavalry, gathered before the town of Raamses.

At the head of a company of 600 men, Joseph marched against the mighty host of the enemy, and, aided by his brethren, the heroic sons of Jacob, won a splendid victory. Over 200,000 slain of the enemy's army covered the battle-field, among them being King Bela. The remainder of the army took to flight, and were pursued by Joseph and his valiant soldiers. Joseph only lost twelve men, all Egyptians.

[1] *Sepher Hajashar.*

On his return, the Regent of Egypt put Zepho and the other prisoners in fetters, and made their captivity even more bitter than it had been before.

After the death of Bela, the sons of Esau appointed a new king to rule over them in his place. They elected Jobab, son of Zara of Bozrah, who reigned for ten years, but desisted from making any war upon the sons of Jacob. As for the sons of Esau, they were now convinced that it would be futile to fight against any of the heroic sons of the Patriarch. They therefore abstained from waging any new wars against Joseph and his brethren, but their hatred of their cousins increased and grew fiercer from generation to generation.

Jobab, King of Edom, was succeeded by Husham of Theman, who ruled over the sons of Esau for twenty years. It was during his reign, seventy-two years after the arrival of the children of Israel in Egypt, that Zepho, who had been a prisoner in Egypt for many years, managed to escape with his fellow prisoners. They sought refuge at the court of Agnias, King of Africa, who received them very kindly, and appointed Zepho Commander-in-Chief of his armies.

Zepho, having found favour in the eyes of King Agnias and of his people, availed himself of his influence and endeavoured to persuade his sovereign to declare a war on Egypt and the sons of Jacob. He was anxious to induce the King and his nobles to gather an army and invade Egypt, so that he could revenge the death of his brethren. But King Agnias and his nobles, in spite of Zepho's constant arguments, refused to listen to him.

King Agnias was only too well acquainted with the strength of the sons of Jacob, and he still remembered how they had dealt with his army on a former occasion.

In these days it happened that a man named 'Uzi, who lived in the city of Pozimana, in the land of Kittim, and whom his countrymen venerated as a god, died. He left a daughter

named Yaniah, and Agnias, who had heard from his men of
the wisdom and beauty of the damsel, sent messengers to
Kittim to sue for her hand. His request was readily granted
by the people of Kittim, but scarcely had the messengers of
King Agnias left the country taking with them the promise
that Yaniah should become the wife of Agnias, when a new
deputation arrived. Turnus, King of Benevento, had also
heard of the fair and wise Yaniah, and was anxious to take
her to wife, but his request was rejected.

" We have already promised the hand of Yaniah," said
the men of Kittim, " to Agnias, King of Africa, and we cannot
break our promise, for we fear Agnias who will come down
with an army and exterminate us. Your King Turnus," they
continued, " will not be able to protect us against the mighty
King Agnias."

Thus spoke the men of Kittim, and the ambassadors of
Turnus returned to their King who, on hearing their words,
swore to take his revenge. Thereupon the men of Kittim sent
a message to Agnias, King of Africa, wherein they informed
him of what had occurred.

" We have refused the hand of Yaniah to Turnus," wrote
the men of Kittim, " but we now learn that he has gathered
a mighty army and is determined to invade thy country. His
design is first to invade Sardinia, and make war upon thy
brother Lucus, and after having defeated him, to march
against thee."

When Agnias read the message from the men of Kittim,
he waxed very wroth, gathered a great army and hastened
to Sardinia to the assistance of his brother Lucus. Neblus,
son of Lucus, hearing of the arrival of his uncle, came out
with a numerous suite to meet him, welcoming him very
warmly. He begged his uncle to intercede on his behalf with
his father that the latter might appoint him commander
of his armies. The request of Neblus was granted, for his

father appointed him Commander-in-Chief of the Sardinian troops.

The two armies of Agnias and Lucus crossed the sea and arrived in the region of the Asthores. They met Turnus and his army in the plain of Campania, where a fierce battle was fought. The encounter was at first fatal to Lucus and to his army, for he lost nearly all his men, and his own son Neblus was among the slain. But Agnias once more engaged in battle, and came out victorious. He slew Turnus with his own hand, and the latter's entire army was routed. Those who had not been slain fled, closely pursued by Agnias and Lucus, as far as the cross road between Rome and Albano. Thus Agnias revenged the death of his nephew Neblus, and the destruction of his brother's army.

The King thereupon commanded his men to construct a golden statue, and to put the body of Neblus inside of it. The statue was put in a bronze coffin and buried on the cross road between Rome and Albano, and over the grave of the slain General Neblus a high tower was erected. The body of Turnus, the slain King of Benevento, was also buried here, and the two graves are opposite each other, on the cross road between Rome and Albano, and a marble pavement runs between them.

After the burial of Neblus and Turnus, King Lucus, with the remainder of his army, returned to Sardinia, whilst King Agnias proceeded to Benevento, the capital of Turnus.

When the inhabitants of the city heard of the approach of the victorious king, they came out to meet him, and amidst tears and supplications, begged him to have mercy upon them and not to put them to death, and also to spare their city. Agnias granted the request of the inhabitants of Benevento, for the city was considered at that time as belonging to the federation of the children of Kittim. But thenceforth frequent incursions were made into the land of Kittim by soldiers from the army of the King of Africa, sometimes led by General Zepho, and sometimes by the King himself. Now and again the bands came to pillage these provinces, carrying off rich booty.

From Benevento Agnias proceeded to Pozimana where he married Yaniah the daughter of 'Uzi, taking her to his capital in Africa.[1]

Zepho, the Commander-in-Chief of the African armies, had never given up his plans of revenge. Continually he urged King Agnias to invade Egypt and to attack the sons of Jacob, but he always met with a refusal on the part of the King who, knowing the strength and the courage of the sons of Jacob, feared to meet them in the open field. At last, however, a day came when Agnias was persuaded by his general and granted the latter's request. A vast army, as numerous as the sand on the seashore, was equipped, ready to march and invade Egypt, and attack the sons of Jacob.

Now it happened that among the servants (shield-bearers) of Agnias, there was a youth called Balaam, the fifteen years old son of Beor. He was a very clever lad and well versed in the science of magic. Agnias, knowing that Balaam, the son of Beor, was an adept in magic, said to the lad:

"Try to ascertain by virtue of thy magic what will be the issue of the battle and who will be victorious in the war we are about to wage, we or the sons of Jacob." Thus spoke King Agnias, and Balaam, the young son of Beor, had wax brought to him out of which he moulded and fashioned the figures of men on horseback, and war chariots, and he so disposed the wax figures as to represent two hostile armies facing each other. He thereupon plunged the wax figures into magic water, and, holding a palm branch in hand, he practised incantations. He saw the figures representing the army of Agnias subdued by those representing the sons of

---

[1] *Sepher Hajashar*; *Josippon*, ed. Venice, p. 1a; Gaster, *The Chronicles of Jerahmeel*, p. 96.

Jacob. This vision he communicated to the King who grew frightened, lost his courage, and dared not proceed with the war.

Zepho, thereupon, seeing that Agnias had definitely given up the Egyptian campaign, and being now quite convinced that he would never succeed in persuading the King to invade Egypt, gave up his post, fled the country and went to the land of Kittim.

He was received with open arms by the men of Kittim who offered him rich presents and invited him to stay with them and conduct their wars.

The troops of Agnias were still continuing to make incursions into the land of Kittim, and the inhabitants were compelled to take refuge on the mountain of Koptizah (or Kophitra).

One day Zepho went out in search of an ox he had lost, and he discovered at the foot of the mountain a spacious cave, the entrance to which was barred by a huge stone. He broke the stone to pieces, and entering the cave perceived a strange animal devouring his ox. The upper part of the monster was that of a man whilst the lower part was formed like a quadruped. Zepho killed the monster with his sword.

When the men of Kittim learned of Zepho's deed, they rejoiced greatly and said:

" What honours shall we show unto this man who has killed the monster which had for a long time been devouring our cattle?"

They unanimously decided to set aside one day of the year and call it the festival of Zepho. And every year, out of gratitude to their deliverer, they offered sacrifices in honour of Zepho, and brought him many presents.

Now it came to pass in these days that Yaniah, the daughter of 'Uzi and wife of Agnias, fell into a sickness, and the King and his courtiers were greatly grieved. Agnias consulted the physicians, asking them to find a remedy for his wife's sickness and to make her recover her health.

"Great King," replied the physicians, "the climate and the water of our land are not suitable for the Queen and not so good as the climate and waters of her native land of Kittim. Both the climate and the water of Africa are the cause of her sickness, for even in her native land the Queen was accustomed to drink the water of Forma (Firmium) which her parents had caused to be drawn to the house by means of an aqueduct."

When Agnias heard these words, he commanded his servants to fetch water from Forma (Firmium) in a vessel, and the water being weighed was found to be lighter than the water of Africa. Agnias thereupon commanded his officers to gather stone-cutters by thousands and myriads and employed them to hew a vast number of stones for building. He then gathered a great number of stone-masons and ordered them to build a huge aqueduct by means of which the waters of Forma were drawn to Africa. The water was for the sole use of Queen Yaniah who employed it for drinking and cooking, for her baths and even for the washing of her linen. She even made use of it to water her plants and fruit trees. The King also had earth and stones brought in ships from Kittim to Africa, and the architects built a palace for the Queen, who soon regained her former health.[1]

In the course of the next year the African troops once more invaded the land of Kittim for the purpose of pillage as in the past. Zepho, now in command of the army of Kittim, marched against the enemy and won a decisive victory. The hostile armies were put to flight, and the country was saved from their depredations. Out of gratitude for their heroic commander and admiration for his valour, the men of Kittim chose Zepho as their king. His first act as ruler of the country was to undertake a campaign against the sons of Tubal, to subdue

---

[1] *Sepher Hajashar*; Gaster, *The Chronicles of Jerahmeel*, pp. 97–98; *Josippon*, p. 2a–b.

them and to take possession of the neighbouring islands. He was very successful, and on his return the men of Kittim once more confirmed Zepho in his kingship and built for him a great palace. The King also built a throne for himself, and reigned over the land of Kittim and the whole country of Italy for fifty years.[1]

[1] *Sepher Hajashar*; Gaster, *The Chronicles of Jerahmeel*, pp. 97–98; *Josippon*, p. 2a–b.

CHAPTER XIV

The Death of the Regent

Joseph's early death—His punishment—The oath of the sons of Jacob
—Joseph exhorts his sons—Love and forgiveness—The death of Joseph—
The advice of the magicians—The royal tomb and the magic dogs—The
iron coffin in the Nile—The redemption of Israel—The search for the bones
of Joseph—Moses on the banks of the Nile—His perplexity—Serah, the
daughter of Asher—The swimming iron coffin—The wanderings of Israel—
The two shrines—Joseph's reward—The shrine of the living God, and the
shrine of the dead—The burial of Joseph.

Joseph had lived in Egypt ninety-three years, and for eighty
years had ruled the country, when he felt his end approach. He
was 110 years of age, and his end came ten years sooner than
it ought to have come. This was a punishment for his having
permitted his brethren to repeat ten times the words: " Our
father, thy servant," and because he had also given orders
to have the dead body of his father embalmed by the physicians
of Egypt. He had not had faith enough in the Lord who
preserves the bodies of the just, as it is promised by the prophets.
When he felt his end near, Joseph sent for his brethren and
his entire household and thus addressed them:

" I am soon going to die, but the Lord will remember ye
and redeem ye from bondage in this country and lead ye
into the land He has promised as an inheritance to our fore-
fathers. He will never forsake ye, either here, or in the midst
of the waves of the sea, on the banks of the rivers of Arnon,
or in the desert, in this world or in the next. Now promise
me that when the Lord will send the Redeemer to lead ye
into the promised land, ye and your descendants will carry
my body with ye to bury it in the Holy Land. Swear also

unto me that neither yourselves nor your descendants will
ever try to force the hand of Providence and make an attempt
to shake off the yoke of the Egyptians who will put heavy
tasks upon ye. Swear unto me that ye will patiently await
the moment when the Lord Himself will send unto ye His
Redeemer to lead ye out of bondage, as He hath promised.
My father of his free will came out to Egypt, but I carried
his body to Canaan for burial. Me, however, ye have stolen
from the land of the Hebrews, therefore, swear unto me that
ye will return my body to the land whence I had been dragged
away against my will." [1]

Joseph made only his brethren take an oath, but not his
own sons, for fear that the Egyptians might not grant to them
the permission to carry the body of their father to Canaan.
Joseph also reminded his children and all his household of
the great things he had endured, because he had refused to
put his brethren to shame. He exhorted them to love one
another and to hide one another's faults, for the Lord delighteth
in the unity of brethren and in the hearts that take pleasure
in love. He thereupon exhorted them to walk in the ways of
the Lord and to obey His commandments, and if they did so
the Lord would exalt them and bless them with good things
for ever, and ever.

And Joseph further said unto his sons:

" After my death, the Egyptians will change their love for
ye into hatred and will afflict ye and your seed. But in His
own time the Lord will send you a Redeemer and lead ye
out of bondage into the land which He promised unto your
fathers. Carry therefore my bones with ye, for when my
bones will be taken up to the Holy Land the Lord shall be
with ye in light, whilst the Egyptians shall be in darkness
with Beliar."

---

[1] *Sepher Hajashar*; *Mekhilta*, 13, 9; *Targum Pseudo-Jonathan*; Babylonian Talmud,
Sotah, 13b.

He also enjoined them to carry up their mother Asenath and to bury her near Rachel.[1]

Soon afterwards Joseph died, and his body was embalmed by the physicians of Egypt. Thereupon the counsellors of Pharaoh came and thus spoke to the King:

" We have heard that the brethren of Joseph and all their descendants are bound by a solemn oath never to leave this country without taking with them the body of the Viceroy. Now we advise thee, O King, to order that the bones of Joseph be placed in a heavy iron coffin and sunk into the Nile, so that no one will ever be able to find his burial place. The sons of Israel will then be compelled to remain in Egypt for ever and serve us. The King may also order that the body of Joseph be buried in the royal tomb, and we will place golden dogs in front of it. By virtue of our magic art, we will so contrive that these dogs will raise a terrible howling whenever a stranger will attempt to approach the royal tomb." Thus spoke the wise men of Egypt, but Pharaoh replied:

" Ye had better make an iron coffin and sink the body of Joseph into the Nile. Thus, on the one hand, the waters of the river will be blessed on account of the merits of Joseph, will water the land and fructify it, whilst, on the other, the burial place of the son of Jacob will never be discovered. The Israelites, this industrious and wise people, will therefore remain our slaves for ever."

Thus spoke Pharaoh, and the coffin wherein the body of Joseph had been placed was consequently sunk into the Nile.[2] Joseph's wish to have his body carried to the Holy Land was fulfilled after many years, at the moment when the nation of Israel was redeemed from bondage and led by Moses out of Egypt. It was Moses himself, the great leader, who thought of the oath once taken by the sons of Jacob. And whilst the

[1] R. C. Charles, *The Testaments of the Twelve Patriarchs, Testament of Joseph*, XX, p. 101.
[2] *Exodus Rabba*, § 20; Babylonian Talmud, *Sotah*, 13b.

Israelites were busy amassing wealth and carrying with them out of Egypt as much booty as they could as a reward and compensation for the many years of slavery and for the heavy labour they had accomplished, Moses himself was thinking of the oath once taken by the sons of Jacob, and made every effort to discover the coffin wherein reposed the body of Joseph.

" Verily," said the Lord unto Moses, " in thee are fulfilled the words: ' The labour of the righteous tendeth to life '." (*Proverbs*, 10, 16.)

" As a son of Jacob, it was once Joseph's duty to bury his father, but thou art a stranger to him, and it is not incumbent upon thee to render him this service. As a reward for thy service, when thy own time arrives to die, I myself will bury thy body and render thee a similar service."

But Moses was greatly perplexed, for he knew not the place where the coffin of Joseph could be discovered. He was not even quite sure whether it had really been sunk into the Nile or placed in the royal tomb.

Plunged in meditation, Moses stood on the banks of the River Nile when Serah, the aged daughter of Asher, who, in consequence of the blessing bestowed upon her by Jacob, was never to taste death, approached him.

" Man of God," she spoke, " the coffin of Joseph was sunk into the Nile, so that its waters may be blessed on his account, and also in order to make impossible the exodus of the Israelites."

Moses thereupon wrote the words " Arise, O *Shor* " (bull) upon a piece of clay and thrust it into the Nile. He then called aloud: " Joseph, the time hath come when the Lord is at last redeeming his children from bondage. For thy sake, and on account of the oath once taken, the majesty of the Lord is detained in Egypt, and the redemption of Israel is being delayed. Reveal unto us thy resting-place, so that we may carry out our duty and fulfil thy last wish."

Thus spoke Moses, and lo, the waters of the Nile suddenly stirred and to the surface rose up the coffin of Joseph.

For forty years during the wanderings of the Israelites in the desert, the coffin of Joseph was carried in their midst. It was Joseph's reward for his promise to his brethren to nourish them and to take care of them. And the Lord said: " For forty years the Israelites will take care of thy bones and carry thy coffin in their midst." Thus two shrines were carried by Israel in the desert: one contained the Ark of the Covenant, and the other the bones of Joseph. It was Joseph's reward for his virtues, and a great distinction vouchsafed unto him. For whilst the coffin containing the remains of Jacob had been accompanied by Joseph, the servants of Pharaoh, the nobles of the land, and all the inhabitants of Egypt, Joseph's coffin was surrounded by the Divine Majesty and the pillars of cloud and accompanied by priests and by Levites.

And the nations, when meeting the two shrines, wondered and asked: " What is the meaning of these two shrines, one containing the dead and the other the Law of the living God?"

And the answer was given unto them:

" The dead whose body reposes in one shrine fulfilled the commandments written in the Law enshrined in the Ark. In the Law it is written, ' I am the Lord, thy God ', and he said: ' Am I in the place of God?' In the Law it is written, ' Thou shalt have no other gods before My face ', and he said: ' I fear the Lord '. In the Law it is written: ' Thou shalt not take the name of the Lord in vain ', and he, therefore, said: ' By the name of Pharaoh ', abstaining from swearing by God. In the Law it is written: ' Remember the Sabbath ', and he commanded his overseer to ' make ready everything ' on the day before the Sabbath. In the Law it is written: ' Honour thy father and thy mother ', and he honoured his father and obeyed his commands even when the latter sent him on a perilous mission. In the Law it is written: ' Thou shalt not

commit adultery ', and he refused to sin and commit adultery
with the wife of Potiphar. In the Law it is written: ' Thou
shalt not steal ', and he never stole any of Pharaoh's treasures.
In the Law it is written: ' Thou shalt not bear false witness ',
and he never informed his father of the cruel treatment he
had met at the hands of his brethren. In the Law it is
written: ' Thou shalt not covet thy neighbour's wife ', and
he never did covet the wife of his master Potiphar. In the
Law it is written: ' Thou shalt not hate ', and he never hated
his brethren, but comforted them. In the Law it is written:
' Thou shalt not take revenge ', and he never revenged himself upon his brethren, but nourished them and took care of
them."

The work which Moses had begun, namely that of carrying the bones of Joseph to Canaan, he was unable to complete,
for he died on Mount Nebo. But on their arrival in the Holy
Land the Israelites buried the bones of Joseph at Shechem,
for from Shechem Joseph had once been stolen, and unto
Shechem he was returned and buried there.[1]

[1] *Mekhilta*, 13, 9; *Yalkut*, § 227; see also A. Kurrein, *Traum und Wahrheit*, pp. 178–182;
cf. also Grünbaum, *Neue Beiträge*, pp. 149–152.

THE COFFIN OF JOSEPH RISES TO THE SURFACE OF THE NILE

CHAPTER XV

The Egyptian Bondage

Joseph and King Magron—The rule of the foreigner—The Hebrews in Egypt are deprived of their former privileges—Anti-Semitism in Egypt—The death of Levi—The oppression of the aliens—The effeminate Egyptians and the industrious Hebrews—The fear of the Egyptians—King Melol—The heavy tasks—The invasion of Egypt and the war of liberation—The war between Zepho, King of Kittim, and Agnias, King of Africa—Zepho's message to Hadad, King of Edom—The reply of the sons of Esau—Their refusal to help Zepho—The prayer of Zepho to the God of his fathers—The command of King Agnias to the inhabitants of Africa—The victory of Zepho—The arrival of Balaam at Kittim—The royal banquet—Zepho's plan of revenge—The Egyptian campaign—Zepho's message to the sons of Esau—The Egyptian volunteers—The Hebrew regiment—The natives mistrust the aliens—The failure of Balaam's magic—The defeat of the Egyptians—The assistance and victory of the Hebrews—The ingratitude of the Egyptians—The counsellors of Pharaoh—The fear of the aliens—The advice of Pharaoh—The fortresses of Pithom and Raamses—National work—The decree of Melol—The royal proclamation—Patriotic Hebrews—The example set by the King—Basket and trowel—The production of bricks—The toil of the Hebrews—Their enormous tasks—The labour of the women—The bitter life—Pharaoh *Meror*—The sons of Levi are exempted from doing national work—Semla of Masreca, King of Edom—The threat of a new war—The Egyptian taskmasters, and the voice from Heaven—The noble women of Israel—Words of comfort.

With soft and hypocritical words the descendants of Jacob were drawn into servitude soon after the death of the Patriarch. During the life of Joseph, however, the position of the Israelites in Egypt was a favourable one, for the Viceroy had found favour in the eyes of Magron, the successor of the Pharaoh who had once raised the son of Rachel to high dignities. Joseph was not only the first counsellor of the King, but the actual ruler of the country, Magron having left to him the administration of all affairs of state, retaining only the royal title. The majority

189

of the inhabitants of Egypt all loved Joseph, and only a few
raised their voices and murmured against the ruler, dissatisfied
that a foreigner should exercise such extensive powers in the
country. Things, however, changed soon after the death of
Joseph, and half a century later the Hebrews were gradually
deprived of their former privileges, and the apparent love of
the Egyptians for Israel disappeared. The hostility towards
the aliens and foreigners became open, and the hatred implacable. The more the descendants of Jacob were endeavouring
to assimilate themselves with the inhabitants of the land—
learning their ways, imitating their manners and customs,
speaking their language, and even abandoning the sacred rite
of circumcision—the more the Egyptians repulsed them and
looked askance at them as intruders and aliens. What is called
in modern times Anti-Semitism was prevalent in Egypt. God
had so ordained that the love of the Egyptians for the children
of Israel should be changed into hatred, so that they should
turn to the Lord. Oppression of the Israelites now began.
Heavy taxes were laid upon them, from which they had been
hitherto exempt as free-born strangers in the country. Soon
the King issued a decree commanding his people to build him
a sumptuous palace. The Hebrews, too, were compelled to
give their labour without receiving any pay, and even to erect
the castle at their own cost.[1]

Levi was the son of Jacob who had outlived all his brethren,
and he died twenty-two years after Joseph. And now all consideration for the descendants of Jacob disappeared completely. The strangers and aliens were oppressed and enslaved.
Their property was confiscated, the fields, vineyards, and houses
which Joseph had given his brethren soon after the death of
his father were claimed and appropriated by native Egyptians.
The latter hated work, were effeminate and fond of pleasure,

---

[1] *Midrash Tanchuma*, section *Shemot*; *Midrash Agadah*, section *Shemot*; *Sepher Hajashar*;
see also Beer, *Das Leben Mosis*, in *Jahrbuch für die Geschichte der Juden*, 1863, Vol. III, p. 11.

and formed a contrast to the industrious and clean-living Hebrews, whose prosperity they envied. Leading a moral and virtuous life, the Hebrews were thriving exceedingly in Goshen, and their numbers increased daily, for the Hebrews' wives bore sometimes six, twelve, and even sixty infants at a birth. All the children were strong and healthy, and by virtue of industry, thrift, and energy, the Israelites acquired wealth and position in the land. The native Egyptians began to fear lest the Hebrews should increase and become a danger to the native population. They might seize the power in the land and enslave all Egyptians. In vain, however, did the Egyptians urge their King to enslave the Hebrews completely.

" Ye fools," said the Pharaoh, " hitherto the Hebrews have nourished us and ye want me to enslave them! Had it not been for Joseph, we would not have been alive to-day, but died during the years of famine."

But his words were of no avail. The King was deposed from his throne and imprisoned, and only when he had given way to the demands of his people was he reinstalled in his dignity.

Nine years afterwards the King of Egypt died, and a new ruler, named Melol, was proclaimed. The heroes and magnates of Egypt of the generation of Joseph and his brethren had all died, and the new generation no longer remembered the sons of Jacob nor the services they had rendered to the country on many occasions. The Egyptians now laid heavy tasks upon the Israelites and oppressed them, ignoring or forgetting the fact that Joseph and his family had saved Egypt in her hour of need. Melol was twenty-six years of age when he ascended to the throne, and he reigned ninety-four years. He took the title of Pharaoh, as it was the long established custom of the country. In those days Egypt was once more invaded by a hostile army. A fierce war ensued, and although the Israelites had done their best to assist the Egyptians in the

war of liberation, sparing neither blood nor money, their help
was soon forgotten. On the contrary, their position became
worse, as soon as the war had been terminated. The new
enemy who had threatened the country was none other than
Zepho, King of the land of Kittim. For many years the grandson
of Esau had been ruling over his country, undisturbed by the
incursions of the African troops, but now it came to pass that
the peace of Kittim was once more disturbed by a new invasion
of the soldiers of Agnias. Zepho, who had ruled for thirteen
years over the country, at once marched to their encounter
and mowed them down so that none was left to carry the sad
tidings to King Agnias. When the latter at last heard of the
annihilation of his troops to the last man, he was greatly
alarmed, and assembled all the men of Africa, a mighty host as
numerous as the sand on the seashore. He also sent a message
to his brother Lucus, asking him to hasten to his assistance with
all the men at his disposal.

"Come at once," he wrote, "and help me to defeat Zepho
and the men of the land of Kittim who have exterminated
my entire army."

Lucus immediately hastened to join his brother with a
great host.

When Zepho and the men of Kittim heard of these preparations, they were greatly alarmed and their hearts were agitated
by fear and despair. The King wrote therefore to Hadad, son
of Badad, King of Edom, and to all the sons of Esau, his
brethren, and thus he said: "I am informed that Agnias, King
of Africa, and his brother Lucus are marching against me at
the head of a mighty army, and we are greatly afraid. Now,
my brethren, if you would not have us perish altogether and
be exterminated by the enemy, come to our assistance and
help us repulse the soldiers of Agnias."

The children of Esau, however, replied to Zepho as follows:
"We cannot take up arms against Agnias and his people,

for already in the days of King Bela, the son of Beor, we concluded an alliance with the ruler of Africa. There is also friendship between us and this King since the days of Joseph, son of Jacob, the ruler of Egypt, against whom we fought beyond the Jordan, when he came to bury his father. We are therefore compelled to refuse thy request."

Thus wrote the sons of Seïr, and Zepho, abandoned by his brethren, the sons of Esau, who refused to come to his aid, was in great despair, but he determined to face the enemy alone and unaided.

In the meantime, Agnias and his brother Lucus, having organized their vast army which consisted of 800,000 men, reached the territory of Kittim. Zepho, mustering only a small company of 3000 men, all that he could gather, went out to face the mighty host. Then the people of Kittim spoke to their King, and thus they said:

" Pray for us unto the Lord and invoke the help of the God of thy ancestors. Perchance He will protect us against Agnias and his people, for we have heard that He is a mighty God and protects those who put their trust in Him."

Thereupon Zepho prayed unto the Lord and thus he said: " O Lord, God of Abraham and Isaac, my fathers, may it be known to-day that Thou art the true God, and that the gods of the nations are all vain and false. I pray Thee to remember this day unto me Thy covenant with Abraham, our father, which our ancestors have transmitted unto us. For the sake of Abraham and of Isaac, our fathers, be gracious unto me this day and save me and the sons of Kittim from the hands of the King of Africa."

And the Lord hearkened unto the prayer of Zepho for the sake of Abraham and Isaac, his ancestors.

Zepho now engaged in battle, and the Lord delivered into his hand the army of Agnias and of Lucus, so that by the end of the first day 400,000 men were slain.

Agnias, having lost his entire army, sent a decree to his
people and commanded that all males of the land who had
attained their tenth year were to join immediately the army.
Whoever would disobey and not hasten to fight for King and
country would be punished by death and his property confiscated.

Frightened by the threat of the King, all the males of
Africa, men and boys to the number of 3,000,000, hastened
to join their King and to swell the ranks of the soldiers he still
commanded. After ten days the King engaged in a new battle
against Zepho and the men of Kittim, but in spite of his new
accessions he was beaten and lost a great number of men,
among the slain being his general Sosipater. The remainder
of the soldiers, at their head Agnias, his son Asdrubal, and
his brother Lucus, saved themselves by flight, pursued by
Zepho and his men. Discouraged, they arrived in Africa, and
henceforth never dared to invade the land of Kittim or to
wage any new wars against Zepho.

Balaam, the son of Beor, the great adept of magic, had
accompanied Agnias on his expedition. But when the young
magician saw his King defeated, he forsook him and betook
himself to the land of Kittim. He was received with great
honours by Zepho and his people, who had heard of Balaam's
great ability as a magician and of his deep wisdom. Balaam
fixed his abode at the court of Zepho who gave him rich presents and attached him to his service.

Now, on his return from the war, Zepho summoned all
the sons of Kittim whom he had led, and he found that not
one was missing. Great was his joy, for such a splendid victory
strengthened his kingship and his power, and he offered a
great banquet unto all those who had served him and helped
him to win the war. But he never remembered the Lord who
had protected him and helped him in his hour of need, saving
him and his people from the hand of the King of Africa.

Zepho continued to walk in the wicked ways of the people of Kittim and of the sons of Esau, serving idols and strange gods as he had been taught by his brethren, the sons of Esau. As the proverb rightly saith: " Out of the wicked cometh forth wickedness ".

Having won such a splendid victory, Zepho now took counsel with the sons of Kittim and determined to march upon Egypt and to make war against the posterity of Jacob and against Pharaoh. He knew that not only all the valiant men of Egypt and all the heroes of Pharaoh, but also Joseph and his brethren had long ago been gathered to their fathers and were sleeping their last sleep. Now was the time, thought Zepho, to revenge his brethren, the sons of Esau, whom Joseph, with the help of the Egyptians, had slain, when he came to Hebron to bury his father Jacob.

Thereupon Zepho dispatched a message to Hadad, son of Badad, King of Edom, and to all the sons of Esau, his brethren, and thus he wrote:

" You said that having concluded an alliance with Agnias, King of Africa, you could not take up arms against him. I was therefore compelled to face his mighty host with a small band and I won a splendid victory. Now I have determined to invade the land of Egypt and to make war against the posterity of Jacob who dwell in the land. Thus will I revenge the death of mine and your brethren, the sons of Esau, and repay the sons of Jacob for the harm their fathers had done unto us, the sons of Esau, when they came to Hebron to bury the Patriarch Jacob. Come, therefore, to my assistance and together let us revenge the death of our brethren."

This time the sons of Esau granted the request of Zepho, their kinsman, and joined him in great numbers. Zepho also sent messengers to the sons of the East and to the sons of Ishmael, and they all answered to his call, so that a mighty army was gathered and covered the space of a three-days' journey. They marched against Egypt and camped in the valley of Pathros, near Daphé.

When the news of the approaching host reached the Egyptians, there came from all parts of the country men ready for battle to the number of 3,000,000. At the request of the Egyptians, some of the posterity of Jacob came from Goshen, to the number of 150, and joined the ranks of the natives. The Egyptian army marched to the encounter of the enemy, but the natives mistrusted the Hebrews, and would not allow them to proceed beyond a certain spot. The Israelites were to remain in the rear, and only to take part in the fight when the need arose and the Egyptians were losing.

" The sons of Esau and the sons of Ishmael," said the Egyptians, " are of the same blood as the Hebrews, and a defection is greatly to be feared on the part of our allies, who might deliver us into the hands of their kinsmen." They therefore bade the Israelites remain in the rear and only come forward when they were urgently needed.

" Should the enemy be getting the upper hand and prove stronger than we, then you will hasten to our assistance." Thus spoke the Egyptians, and went out to meet the enemy without having a single Hebrew in their ranks.

Now Balaam, the son of Beor, had accompanied Zepho on his expedition, and the King asked him to find out by means of his magic art who would be victorious in the battle that was to take place. Balaam at once prepared to learn the outcome of the combat and made magic exercises and incantations, but his repeated attempts to divine the future failed, and it remained closed to him. In despair Balaam gave up his attempts, for the Lord had chained up all the impure spirits and withheld all knowledge from the magician, so that Zepho's army would fall into the hands of the Israelites who were praying to the God of their fathers and putting their trust in Him.

Thus the Egyptians marched against Zepho and his mighty host, without taking any of the Israelites with them. But the issue of the battle was fatal to the Egyptians. They lost 180 men, whilst of the troops of the enemy only thirty were slain. Put to flight, the Egyptians, who had been driven back upon the camp of the Hebrews, appealed to the latter for help. Although they were only a small company, the Hebrews hastened to the assistance of the nation in whose midst they were dwelling. Courageously they fought and defeated the mighty army of Zepho and his allies.

The Lord was with the Israelites, and the hostile army, thrown into confusion, was routed. The Hebrews pursued the fugitives to the confines of Ethiopia, slaying many thousands of the enemy, whilst they themselves had not lost one man. Great, however, was their astonishment when they discovered that their allies, the Egyptians, to whose assistance they had rushed, had fled and deserted them, hiding like cowards and leaving the Israelites to fight the battle alone. Full of wrath and cursing the Egyptians for their ingratitude, they returned to Goshen.[1]

Thereupon the counsellors of Pharaoh and the elders of Egypt appeared before the King, and prostrating themselves thus they spoke: " Verily the children of Israel constitute a nation within a nation, they are stronger and mightier than we, and thou knowest well, O King, how courageously they have fought during the last war. Only a handful of them defeated a mighty army, and had there been more of them they would have entirely exterminated the armies of our enemy. They are a danger to us, the natives, for if they are permitted to increase in numbers, they will soon be a constant menace unto us, and may one day resolve upon seizing the power in this land. During the next war they may join the enemy and fight against us. They may then either exterminate us or drive

[1] *Sepher Hajashar*; Beer, *loc. cit.*, pp. 12–15.

us out of the country. Give us therefore an advice, O King, and tell us how we can best exterminate the Hebrews slowly."

Thus spoke the counsellors of the King, and Pharaoh replied: "Hearken ye to my advice and act upon it. The cities of Pithom and of Raamses are not strong enough to withstand a foe for any length of time, and must therefore be strengthened. It is therefore incumbent upon all the inhabitants of the land to strengthen these places by ramparts and make them impregnable fortresses which could withstand the attacks of our foes. Now I will issue a decree commanding all the inhabitants of Egypt and of Goshen, both Hebrews and Egyptians without distinction, to come forward and help to build the new fortresses. At first ye, too, will work, so as to set the Hebrews an example, frequently repeating my proclamation so as to stimulate their ardour and their patriotism. Ye will also pay them their daily wages. After a time ye will gradually cease work, leaving the Hebrews to the task, and after a time ye Egyptians will be appointed as overseers, officers, and commissaries, and as such ye will use force and compel the Israelites to work hard, and finally pay them no wages. We shall thus gain two advantages; the cities of Pithom and of Raamses will be strengthened, and the Israelites will be weakened."

Thus spoke Melol, the Pharaoh of Egypt, and the Egyptians were well pleased with his advice. A royal decree was accordingly issued, and it went forth over all the land of Egypt and Goshen. "O men, inhabitants of Egypt, of Goshen, and of Pathros," it said, " ye know that the children of Esau and the children of Ishmael have made an incursion into this country and have tried to invade our territory. In order to protect ourselves against new incursions of hostile powers and to be able to withstand our foes, the King commands all the inhabitants to come forward, build ramparts and walls, and strengthen the places of Pithom and of Raamses. All of ye, Egyptians or Hebrews, who will enlist and help to build will receive their daily wages."

The decree was proclaimed throughout the land, in Egypt and in Goshen, and in all neighbouring towns. The King thereupon called the Israelites and appealed to their sense of honour and their patriotism, and invited them to participate in the great national work of strengthening the fortresses of Pithom and of Raamses. The King himself set an example, put a brick mould on his neck, took basket and trowel in hand, and started to work. No one, of course, could be a slacker if the King himself worked so hard, and everybody hastened to imitate the noble activity of Pharaoh. Numerous Egyptians, and all the children of Israel, joined the ranks of the labourers. The nobles of Egypt and the high officers of Pharaoh also pretended to be working with the Israelites, who were paid their wages regularly. Energetically the Israelites went to work, and at the close of the first day, working conscientiously and assiduously, they had produced a respectable number of bricks. This number was at once fixed as their normal amount, and subsequently exacted as their daily task. A month had scarcely passed when the Egyptians were gradually withdrawn from the work and the Hebrews alone left to toil on, though they were still being paid their wages. But when a year and four months had elapsed, all the Egyptians who had been making bricks had been withdrawn, whilst the Hebrews were kept to their tasks. The harshest and most cruel Egyptians were appointed as overseers, officers, and commissaries, who relentlessly compelled the Hebrews to toil on, finally stopping their wages. Other Egyptians were appointed as tax collectors, and they exacted from the Israelites heavy sums, taking from them in dues the wages which they had previously earned by their hard work. Whenever one of the Hebrews dared to claim his wages or refused to work unless he was paid, or maintained that he could not work on account of weakness or sickness,

he was cruelly punished, beaten, or laid in fetters. Gradually
the Hebrews were compelled to strengthen the whole land of
Egypt. They were forced to build storehouses and pyramids,
to construct canals for the Nile, and to surround the cities with
dykes, so that the water should not overflow and form swamps.
This work had to be done over and over again, as the con-
structions frequently tumbled down or were carried away by
the inrushing waters.

The Israelites were thus compelled to undertake tasks
beyond their strength, and had not only to make bricks and
build, but also to do all sorts of work in the field, to plough,
dig, and prune the trees. They were also forced to learn various
arts and crafts and trades, so as to become used to hard work
of any kind. Neither were the Hebrew women spared. They,
too, were employed to do all sorts of work, and forced to
accomplish tasks which are only fit for men. They carried
water, hewed down trees, gardened and pruned the fruit
trees. As for the men, after the completion of their day's work,
they were not permitted to take any rest, but were employed
in housework, such as kneading, baking, and so on. Neither
rest nor proper sleep were they allowed to take, but were
forced to sleep in the open air upon the bare ground. The
Egyptian taskmasters and overseers pretended that the Hebrews would lose too much time if they were to go backwards
and forwards from their work to their houses. Thus the Egyptians hoped to separate the Hebrews from their wives. The
Israelites were also forced to put aside all signs in their outward appearance that could remind them of their origin. Bitter
indeed became the life of the Hebrews in Egypt during the
reign of the Pharaoh Melol, and they consequently called
him *Meror*, or the bitter one, instead of Melol, because he
had embittered their life.

It was not enough, however, and soon matters grew worse.
The only people who were exempt from the forced labour

and the hard tasks were the sons of Levi. They had kept aloof when the royal invitation was issued to come forward and to help in building the fortresses. They refrained from enlisting in the labour battalions, for they suspected that there was guile in the hearts of the King and of his counsellors. And as they had kept away from the labour which was represented as of national importance, the Egyptians left them in peace for the future.[1]

In the meantime Hadad, son of Badad, King of Edom, had died, and was succeeded by Semla of Masreca who reigned for eighteen years. The new king gathered a mighty army and decided to make war upon Zepho and the men of Kittim, because they had attacked Agnias, King of Africa and Edom's ally, and exterminated his armies. But the sons of Esau said to their King: " We cannot make war upon Zepho, son of Eliphaz, because he is our kinsman." And the King of Edom renounced his plan to make war upon Kittim. There was danger now that the King of Edom, who had raised a considerable army, would make use of it elsewhere and probably invade Egypt.[2] When the Egyptians heard of the danger threatening them, they availed themselves of the opportunity to lay still heavier tasks upon the Hebrews, appealing, however, all the time, to their patriotism and duty:

" Hurry and complete the fortresses you are building," they urged, " for the sons of Esau may surprise us and fall upon us unawares. It behoves you to do the work diligently, for if the sons of Esau invade the country, it will be solely on your account."

Thus spoke the Egyptians, anxious to let no opportunity pass which gave them a chance to weaken the Hebrews and to diminish their numbers. And whilst their Egyptian taskmasters were constantly endeavouring to exterminate the

---

[1] *Sepher Hajashar*; *Exodus Rabba*, § 1; *Midrash Agadah*, section *Shemot*; *Midrash Tanchuma*, section *Shemot*; Babylonian Talmud, *Sotah*, 12*b*; see also Beer, *loc. cit.*, pp. 15–18.

[2] *Sepher Hajashar*.

Hebrew race, diminish its numbers and crush its spirit, a voice was heard from Heaven, saying: " In spite of your oppression this race will increase and multiply."

This heavenly voice gave hope and courage to the long-suffering Hebrews. They were also comforted by their wives who proved noble and faithful companions in hours of need and misfortune. These faithful women were ever ready to labour for their husbands, to relieve and strengthen them, whenever the latter felt exhausted after their unspeakable sufferings, and their daily tasks. Whenever the women saw their husbands tired out, bodily and mentally, losing courage and falling into gloomy brooding, they sustained them with words of comfort and hope. Daily they hastened to the springs, there to draw pure water for their husbands to drink. And the Lord in His mercy ordained that the pitchers of the women of Israel contained each time half water and half fish. The noble, gentle, and faithful women dressed the fish, and prepared it with loving hands, bringing the food and other tastefully prepared meats to their hard-working husbands. They looked after the men, took care of them and were not only anxious for their bodily welfare, but also cheered up the minds of the oppressed with gentle words of encouragement.

" Be of good cheer," they said, " for these sufferings cannot be for ever, and the day will soon come when the Lord will have mercy upon us and redeem us from bondage." Thus spoke the faithful women of Israel, and the loving care of their wives and their constant gentle attention moved the men, soothed their hearts, and gave them fresh hope and courage to live and to suffer. In vain was the calculation of the Egyptians to diminish the number of the Israelites, for their posterity increased and multiplied.[1]

[1] See note 1, p. 201.

CHAPTER XVI

The Fate of the Innocents

The wise men of Egypt and the King—The advice of Job of Uz—
The command to the midwives to kill the babes—Jochebed and Miriam—
The heroic midwives—Shifrah and Puah—The indignation of Miriam—
Persuasion and threats—Pharaoh's dream—The old man and his balance—
The sucking lamb and the inhabitants of Egypt—The interpretation of
Balaam—The Hebrew child that will destroy Egypt—The national calamity
—The three members of the Privy Council—Jethro the Midianite—His
advice and plea for Israel—Jethro's disgrace and his flight to Midian—The
silence of Job—The advice of Balaam—Destroy Israel by water—Fire and
sword will not prevail against them—The God of Israel protected Abraham,
Isaac, and Jacob—Heavy tasks will not crush the spirit of Israel—The
drowning of the Innocents—The Egyptian spies—The heroic women of
Israel — Angels attend mothers and new-born babes — The miraculous
preservation of the babes—The polished pebbles full of milk and honey—
The earth hides the babies and vomits them out—The drowned children
rejected alive upon the river's banks—The prediction of the soothsayers—
The child whose death will be caused by water—The new decree of Pharaoh.

It now came to pass that when 125 years since the arrival
of Jacob in Egypt, and fifty-four years after the death of Joseph,
had elapsed, the elders and wise men of Egypt presented
themselves before Pharaoh, and thus they spoke:

" Long live the King! Thou didst give us an advice the
result of which has had consequences contrary to our expectations, for the children of Israel are increasing and multiplying,
and the land is full of them. Now give us a new advice, O
King, in thy wisdom."

" Well," said the King, turning to his counsellors, " find
ye now some means by which we could gain our purpose."

Thereupon one of the King's counsellors, a young officer

named Job of Uz, in Mesopotamia, rose up and thus he spoke:

"Long live the King! and may it please his Majesty to listen to my words. Excellent and to the purpose was the advice given by the King to lay heavy tasks upon the shoulders of the Hebrews, but something more should now be done, for this device is not sufficient. Whilst it is necessary to continue enslaving the Hebrews by laying heavier and heavier tasks upon them, new means ought to be devised how to diminish their numbers more effectively. I therefore make so bold as to suggest to his Majesty the following plan. May the King issue a decree to all midwives and nurses and command them to kill every Hebrew male child as soon as it is born. If his Majesty will issue such a decree and have it recorded in the Statute Book and incorporated in the Code of Laws of Egypt, so that it becomes obligatory and has force of law, the number of the Israelites will surely diminish, and they will no longer constitute a danger to us in case of war."

Thus spoke Job of Uz, in Mesopotamia, who was one of the counsellors of Pharaoh, and his counsel pleased well the King and also the other counsellors and wise men of Egypt. Pharaoh thereupon summoned into his presence the two Hebrew midwives and commanded them to kill all Hebrew male children at their birth. The two midwives were mother and daughter, and their names were Jochebed and Miriam, the mother and sister of Moses. According to others, they were mother-in-law and daughter-in-law, and their names were Jochebed and Elisheba, whilst another version makes them two pious Egyptian proselytes. Miriam was only five years old, but already she was of considerable assistance to her mother, to whom she lent a helping hand in her difficult calling. Both mother and daughter showed great kindness to and gently nursed the new-born babes. They washed and dressed the little ones, soothed them with cheerful sounds, strengthened

the mothers with cordials and draughts, and in every possible
way furthered the growth and development of the children.
Thanks to the loving care of these two kind and energetic
midwives, Israel could boast of a vigorous, flourishing and
speedily increasing posterity. The people, out of gratitude,
called the two midwives *Shifrah* (or the beautifier and the
soother) and *Puah* (or the caller and the sprinkler). To these
two noble, gentle, kind-hearted but energetic ladies Pharaoh
issued his command to kill the new-born babes of Israel.
The mother, more experienced in the ways of the world,
remained silent for a while, but a wave of moral indignation
swept over young Miriam's frame. With flashing eye and
flushed face, she raised her hand, and pointing to the tyrant
on the throne called out:

" Woe unto this man when the day of retribution comes and
God punishes him for his evil deed." They were daring words
uttered by the future prophetess, and Pharaoh was on the
point of ordering his executioner to put to death the precocious
and troublesome maid for her audacity. Her mother hastened
to implore the King's pardon and to soothe his anger.

" Forgive her, O King," she begged, " and pay no attention
to her words, for she is still a foolish child who talks idly and
without understanding."

Pharaoh consented to forgive the audacious child, and
assuming a more gentle tone he explained to the evidently
more reasonable elder lady that all the newly born *daughters*
of Israel were to be saved, and that it was only the *male* children
that he wanted put to death. " This deed," he added, " you
can accomplish quietly without letting the mother know
anything or guess the cause of her baby's death." The King
at first tried to gain the consent of the midwives by gentle
words and promises, making even amorous proposals to the
younger one, which, however, she indignantly rejected. Pharaoh
finally threatened them with death, if they refused to obey his

commands. " I will have you and your houses consumed by fire if you refuse to do my bidding." [1]

Five years had elapsed, and it was the year 130 since the arrival of Jacob in Egypt, when Pharaoh dreamed a dream. In his dream he saw himself seated on his throne and before him stood an old man, holding a balance in his hand and in the act of hanging it up. Thereupon the old man seized all the princes and nobles and elders of Egypt, and all the inhabitants of the land, men, women, and children, bound them together and put them into one scale. He then took a sucking lamb and put it into the other scale, and lo, the scale containing the sucking lamb outweighed all that the other scale contained. Pharaoh marvelled greatly and failed to understand the reason of this strange phenomenon, a sucking lamb weighing more than all the inhabitants of Egypt. When he awoke, he at once summoned all the wise men, magicians, and soothsayers of Egypt, related his dream in their ears and asked them to interpret it. Thereupon Balaam, the son of Beor, who, together with his sons Jannes and Jambres, was now dwelling at the court of Egypt, rose up and thus he spoke.

" Long live the King! this dream, O King, signifies a great misfortune which will break upon this land of Egypt. A male child shall be born among the Hebrews who, when he grows up, shall lay waste our land, weaken the power of the Egyptians, but raise up the Hebrews, and with a strong hand bring them out of the land. The virtues of this male child will excel those of all men, and its name will for ever be gloriously remembered. And now, O King, our master, we must devise means how to destroy all the children of Israel and crush their hope. It is only thus that we shall be able to avert a great misfortune from Egypt."

Thus spoke Balaam, the son of Beor, and the King, greatly

---

[1] *Exodus Rabba*, section *Shemot* (I, 17); *Sepher Hajashar, Sotah,* 11*b*; see also Beer, *loc. cit.*, pp. 19–21.

dismayed, asked: " What shall we do? All that we have done
hitherto and all that we have devised has failed, and this people
is, on the contrary, increasing and multiplying. Give thou now
an advice, Balaam, and tell us what means we should devise
in order to diminish the number of the children of Israel.

And Balaam replied: " May the King first hear the advice of
his other two principal counsellors, then will I speak and give
my opinion."

The other two counsellors of Pharaoh, besides Balaam,
the son of Beor, were Job of Uz, and Reuel, called also Jethro,
the Midianite. Invited by the King to give his opinion,
Reuel, the Midianite, thus spoke:

" May the King live for ever! If it pleases the King to
hearken unto my words, this is the advice I give. Give up thy
plan of persecution. Leave the people of Israel in peace and
do them no harm. They are the chosen of the Lord, and His
possession, and He has preferred them to all other nations and
to all the Kings of the earth. Whoever oppresses them is
punished. Is there anyone who resisted them and was not
brought to destruction? Whoever has raised his hand against
them was speedily destroyed by the Lord. Hast thou not heard
how one of thine ancestors, the Pharaoh of Egypt, was visited
by plagues, because he had dared to usurp Sarah, the wife of
Abraham, who had come to Egypt to seek hospitality? Abimelech, King of Gerar, met with a similar fate, for the God of
Abraham appeared to the King in a dream, and the King
speedily returned his wife to the Patriarch and gave him many
presents. Another of their ancestors, Jacob, was saved from
the hands of his brother, and the Aramæan Laban could not
prevail against him. Thou knowest also, O King," continued
Reuel, " that the King of this land, thy grandfather, the Pharaoh
of former days, found it necessary to raise Joseph the Hebrew
to high dignities, because he had discerned the wisdom of the
son of Jacob, and the inhabitants of Egypt were thus saved

from famine. And as Egypt was indebted to the Hebrews for its salvation, the latter were invited to dwell in the land of Goshen in peace and tranquillity, Goshen being apportioned unto them as their *legally assured home*. My advice, therefore, O King, is to leave off oppressing the Hebrews and let them live in peace and security. If their presence in this country doth not please thee and it is not thy will that they dwell here, then permit them to go forth from here in peace and to return to Canaan, the home of their ancestors, where they sojourned."

Thus spoke Reuel, or Jethro of Midian, but his advice pleased not the King who grew exceedingly wroth when he heard these words of his counsellor. Dismissed from the Privy Council, Reuel left the royal presence in disgrace and on the very day left Egypt for the land of Midian.

The King thereupon turned to Job of Uz, in Mesopotamia, and said: " Job, give us thy opinion now and tell us what we shall do with the Hebrews."

But Job never said a word, neither did he open his lips.

According to another version, Job's reply was very brief and non-committal. " Great King," said he, " are not all the inhabitants of Egypt in thy power? Do, therefore, with the Hebrews as it seemeth good in thine eyes."

It was now the turn of Balaam, the son of Beor, the third member of the Egyptian Privy Council, to speak. The great magician then rose and said:

" All the attempts made hitherto to destroy the Israelites have failed, and they will all fail if the King doth not follow my advice. It will be useless to try and diminish the number of the Israelites by fire, for their God will deliver them from the fire. Thou wilt never prevail against them, for their God once saved their father Abraham from the furnace into which he had been thrown by Nimrod at Ur, in Chaldæa. Neither wilt thou, O King, prevail against the Hebrews, if thou thinkest to try the sword against them and destroy them. Knowest thou not that their ancestor Isaac was saved from death by the sword at the very moment when he was about to be slaughtered? When the knife was raised, Isaac was delivered by an angel from Heaven, and a ram was sacrificed in his place. No, iron and steel will never destroy Israel, nor diminish the numbers of this people. Think not, O King, of crushing their spirit and exterminating them by hard work, forced labour and heavy tasks, for the hardest labour will not break the resistance of this people. It hath already been tried without effect by Laban against their father Jacob. He was forced to accomplish heavy tasks and do all manner of hard work, and yet he prospered exceedingly. One way only remains of proving the Israelites, a way which hath not yet been tried against them or any of their ancestors. None of the Israelites hath been saved from water, and by water thou mayest hope to exterminate the Hebrews and wipe them out from the face of the earth. If, therefore, it please the King, let him hearken unto my advice and decree that all the male children born unto the Hebrews be cast into the river. Do not fear to incur any harm thyself and to be punished for this deed, for God always pays measure for measure, and He hath sworn once, as tradition tells us, never to bring a flood again upon men, nor to destroy the human race by water. Thou art, therefore, perfectly safe from the wrath of the God of Israel, and canst destroy the Israelites by water."

Thus spoke Balaam, the son of Beor, the great magician and counsellor of the King of Egypt, and his advice was accepted by Melol, the Pharaoh of Egypt, and by all the Egyptians, for it pleased them well. The King did not hesitate to issue a decree commanding that all the new-born sons of Israel be cast into the river. In order to secure the faithful execution of his decree, the King also decreed that only Egyptian midwives should assist the wives of the Israelites at a birth. They were instructed to watch carefully and find out the exact time when the women of Israel expected to be delivered, and to report whenever a male child was born. Egyptian children were also sent to the baths frequented by the women of Israel, so as to observe the Hebrew women and give precise information as to the probable time of their delivery. Whoever dared to evade the law and to hide a newborn male child, and thus save it from drowning, would be put to death with his whole posterity.[1]

Terrible was the effect the new decree produced upon the Hebrews, who were thus threatened with complete extermination. Many of the Israelites at once separated themselves from their wives and kept away from them; but others put their trust in God, hoping that He would not permit their race to be destroyed and wiped off from the face of the earth.

The women of Israel behaved heroically in those days of oppression. When the time of their delivery arrived, they used to go out into the fields and there, in distant solitude, in secluded spots, under the shadow of the fruit trees, they went to sleep, putting their trust in God. They were delivered during their sleep, and the Lord, who had made a covenant with Abraham, and sworn to multiply his seed, looked upon the mothers and remembered His covenant. He sent down his ministering angels from the heavenly heights to attend the mothers and new-born infants of Israel. The angels washed and dressed and anointed the babes and swathed them in pretty garments. They also placed in the hands of the babes two polished pebbles, out of which the little ones sucked milk and honey, or they smeared their hands with butter and honey so that they could lick them.

The Lord also caused another miracle to happen. The hair of the babes grew at once until it reached their knees, and thus kept them covered and well protected.

And when the mothers awoke and beheld the wonders

---

[1] *Sepher Hajashar*; *Exodus Rabba*, section *Shemot*; Jellinek, *Beth-Hamidrash*, Vol. II, pp. 1–11; see also Beer, *loc. cit.*, pp. 22–24.

of the Almighty, they exclaimed: " Blessed be Thy name, O God of the Universe, who art omnipresent, and dost not forsake the seed of Abraham. Into Thy hands do we commit our offspring, and may Thy will be done, O Lord."

But the servants of Pharaoh and his emissaries, who were constantly spying upon the women of the Hebrews, used to follow them about everywhere. It was almost impossible to escape the vigilance of these emissaries, who came to seize the newly-born infants and drown them.

But once more the Lord did not forsake those who had put their trust in Him. Obeying the will of the Almighty, the earth suddenly opened her mouth and swallowed up the babes, receiving them in subterranean caves and hiding them there until they had grown up.

The Egyptians, who witnessed the miracle, and saw how the little infants vanished, hastened home and brought out their yokes of oxen. They then ploughed up the earth at the spot where the babes had disappeared, thus hoping to destroy them. But their efforts were in vain, and they could not harm those whom God protected.

When the babies, fed all the while by angels' hands, were grown up, the earth once more opened her mouth and vomited them out, returning them to the light of day. Like the herbs of the fields and the grass of the forests, one could see these young, vigorous, and healthy Hebrew boys sprouting from the soil, and unhesitatingly walking away to their homes.

Thus Balaam's advice and all Pharaoh's attempts to diminish the numbers of the Hebrews and gradually exterminate the entire seed of Abraham proved futile, for the Hebrews in Egypt increased and multiplied exceedingly.

In the meantime Pharaoh's emissaries were constantly visiting Goshen, where the children of Israel dwelt, and whenever they discovered a male infant at its mother's breast, they tore it away by force from the weeping mother's arms, and

cast it into the river. Some say that about 10,000 were thrust
into the Nile, whilst according to others, their number reached
600,000. But even those who were cast into the Nile, the Lord
did not forsake, for alive they were rejected upon the river's
banks. And here milk and honey flowed from the rocks to
feed the babes, and oil to anoint them until they had grown up.
Thus the persecution of the Israelites continued for three
years and four months, and the decree of Pharaoh to kill the
innocents by drowning still persisted, when one morning, on
the seventh day of the month of Adar, the soothsayers and
astrologers presented themselves before Pharaoh and informed
him of an important event.

" This day," spoke the astrologers, " this day, O King, will
be born the boy foretold by thy dreams, the boy who will
deliver Israel from bondage. Not only this have we read in
the stars, but also the fact that the death of this child will be
caused by water. We do not know, however, whether this
child to be born be of the race of the Hebrews or of the Egyptians, for the stars are silent respecting this." Thus spoke the
soothsayers and astrologers of Egypt, and Pharaoh immediately
decreed that henceforth *all* male children, whether of Egyptian or Hebrew origin shall be cast into the river until the day
when the fate of the future redeemer of Israel will have been
settled.[1]

---

[1] *Sepher Hajashar*; *Exodus Rabba*; *Midrash Agadah*; Babylonian Talmud, *Sotah*; 11b;
Jellinek, *loc. cit.*; see also Beer, *loc. cit.*, pp. 25-26.

CHAPTER XVII

The Birth of the Redeemer

Adina, the graceful—The saintly Amram—Jochebed, the daughter of
Levi—The birth of Miriam and Aaron—Amram divorces his wife—
Miriam's prophecy—She rebukes her father—Amram takes back his wife—
Miriam and Aaron dance at the wedding—Amram's prayer—His vision—
The birth of Moses—Miracles accompany his birth—The cries of the Egyp-
tian and Hebrew babies—The ark of bulrushes—The wonder of the angels
—The voice from the Throne of Glory—Melol, the King of Egypt and his
daughter Thermutis—The scorching heat and the baths in the Nile—The
princess and her maids—The angel Gabriel punishes the Egyptian servants
—The lengthened arm of Thermutis—The radiantly beautiful baby—
The angel Gabriel gives Moses a blow and causes him to cry—The baby
refuses to take the milk of the Egyptian women—The prediction of the
astrologers—The waters of Meribah—The new-born babes of Israel are
saved from drowning—The merits of Moses—Shemaiah ben Nethanel—
The baby at the royal palace—Bithia, the daughter of God—The pretence
of Bithia—The education of Moses—The wonder-child—His loveliness and
understanding—Bithia's confession—Pharaoh kisses the wonder-child—
Moses tramples the royal crown under his feet—The advice of Balaam—
The Hebrews always endeavour to rule over kings and nations—The conduct of the Patriarchs—The angel Gabriel appears among the royal counsellors—The advice of the disguised angel—The live coals and the precious
stones—Moses burns his fingers—He becomes slow of lips and slow of
tongue—The masters of Moses—He is looked upon as the future sovereign.

Now it came to pass that Amram, who belonged to the tribe
of Levi and enjoyed the high esteem of his brethren, decided
to divorce his wife. He loved her dearly, but as soon as Pharaoh's
decree to drown all the male children born unto the Hebrews
became known, he thought it best to separate from his wife.
Amram was the son of Kohath, the son of Levi, the son of
Jacob. Levi's wife Adina (the graceful), a daughter of Jobab,
the son of Joktan, the son of Eber, had borne unto him in

Canaan three sons, Gerson, Kohath, and Merari, and on their way to Egypt she gave birth to a daughter, who was named Jochebed. Amram excelled all his ancestors in piety and saintliness. So saintly indeed was he that on his account and for his merits the Glory of Divine Majesty, which after the fall of our first parents had ascended to Heaven and refused to dwell among men, came down again. Amram had no equal in knowledge, gentleness, and modesty, and he was free from sin and so saintly that, had it not been for the Divine decree that all the children of Adam are doomed to die, death could not have touched him. He married Jochebed, and she bore him a daughter called Miriam (or bitterness), because it was at the time of the maiden's birth that the Egyptians began to embitter the life of the Hebrews. Four years later Jochebed bore a son whose name the parents called Aaron, from *hara*, to conceive, because Pharaoh's command to the midwives to kill all the Israelitish children was issued during the months before Aaron's birth.

Amram enjoyed the high esteem of his brethren and was appointed head of the Hebrew Council. When he learned of Pharaoh's intention to slay all the Hebrew male children he suggested to his brethren that under such circumstances it would be better for the Hebrews to live separated from their wives. He was the first to set an example and to thrust away his wife, and his example was naturally followed by many other Hebrews.[1]

Three years had elapsed when the spirit of prophecy came over Miriam, the daughter of Amram and Jochebed, and she said:

"Another son shall be born unto my parents; he shall redeem Israel from bondage and deliver them out of the hands of the Egyptians." Turning to her father she thus spoke to him:

[1] *Sepher Hajashar.*

" Woe, my father, what hast thou done? Thy decision is even more cruel than the decree of Pharaoh, for he hath only in mind the destruction of the male children, whilst the result of *thy* decision will be to deprive the Hebrew nation of all posterity. By his decree, Pharaoh is anxious to kill the new-born sons of Israel and to deprive them of life, but he can only deprive them of life in this world and not in the next, whilst thou and the other Israelites will deprive them even of future life by not allowing them to be born. It is doubtful whether the wicked and cruel decree of Pharaoh will prevail against Israel, but *thy* decree, Father, will be upheld, for thou art a pious and just man, and thy enactments will be executed." [1] Thus spoke the youthful Miriam, reproving her father for having sent away his wife, because he would spare her the sorrow of seeing her male child drowned.

Amram listened to his daughter's reproof and unhesitatingly decided to take back his banished wife. Once more he led his wife Jochebed under the wedding canopy, accompanied by the Angel Gabriel and encouraged by a voice from Heaven.

Miriam and Aaron danced about it, whilst the angels in Heaven sang joyfully: " Thus rejoiceth the mother of the children " (*Psalms*, 113, 9).

Amram's example was soon followed by other men in Israel, who now took back their divorced wives.[2]

Jochebed was 130 years of age, but once more she became resplendent in her beauty as in the days of her youth, when she was still unmarried and known simply as the daughter of Levi.

Soon Jochebed became pregnant, and Amram, remembering the royal decree, was greatly concerned about his wife's state. He prayed to the Lord and thus he said:

---

[1] *Sotah*, 11b; 12a; *Megillah*, 14a; *Exodus Rabba*, section *Shemot*; *Sepher Hajashar*; Josephus, *Antiquities*, II, 9, 3; Beer, *loc. cit.*, p. 29.

[2] *Sotah*, 12a; Jellinek, *Beth-Hamidrash*, Vol. II, pp. 1–11.

" Lord of the Universe! Have compassion upon thy people of Israel, upon those who are worshipping Thy name, and deliver them at last from their misery. Frustrate the hope of the Egyptians, their enemies, to destroy the nation of Israel."

The Lord hearkened unto the pious Amram's prayer, and in a dream He appeared to him, exhorting him not to despair of the future.

" I will remember thy piety," said the Lord, " and reward ye for it, even as I have vouchsafed my favour unto your fore-fathers. I granted my favours unto Abraham who came to Canaan from Mesopotamia. His wife bore him a son in her old age, and I have also blessed his son Ishmael to whom I have given the land of Arabia, while the sons of Ketura received the land of the Troglodytes. To Isaac, however, I have given Canaan which will be the inheritance of his seed. With 70 souls Jacob came to Egypt, and now ye number more than 600,000. With loving care I shall prepare the welfare of Israel, and thy own fame, O Amram, son of Kohath, will be great. For thy wife, Jochebed, will bear unto thee that child whom the Egyptians so greatly dread, and for whose sake they have doomed to death all the children of Israel. Concealed he will remain and be brought up in a miraculous way. He shall then redeem Israel from bondage, and his memory will be ever-lasting, not only among the Hebrews, his own nation, but also among the other nations who will reverence him for ever. Such favour will I grant unto thee and unto thy posterity, for his brother, too, will be great and obtain the priesthood for himself and for his posterity for ever."

Thus spoke the Lord to Amram, who told his vision to Jochebed, his wife.[1]

Soon the prophetic vision of Amram was realized, for after six months Jochebed gave birth to a son and she suffered no pain, either during the time of pregnancy or in the moment

---

[1] Beer, *loc. cit.*, p. 31.

of her delivery. And when Moses, the future redeemer of
Israel, who was to lead the sons of Israel from the brick-
fields of Egypt to the Promised Land of Canaan, was born,
the whole house was filled with a radiance like the dazzling
splendour of sun and moon. Great was the joy of the mother
when she beheld the lovely angelic appearance of her child,
and from the miracles which accompanied his birth she knew
that he was destined for great things.[1] The parents called the
child *Tobia*, God is good, and Amram kissed his daughter
Miriam, saying: " Now I see that thy prophecy will be accomplished."

For three months the mother kept her infant concealed,
for the emissaries of Pharaoh had not expected her delivery
for another three months, but at the end of this time she could
no longer conceal her babe from the spying Egyptians. The
latter had devised a means by which they could discover the
Hebrew new-born babes kept hidden. They used to send their
women carrying their own babies into the houses of the Hebrews
where they thought an infant might be concealed. Babies
usually join the cries of other babies or respond to their cooing.
The Egyptian infants were made to cry out, and immediately
the Hebrew infants that were kept hidden also raised their
voices and betrayed their place of concealment.[2]

" It is better," said Amram, " to expose the child and entrust
its fate to Providence, than let our secret be discovered and
the boy seized and put to death. The ways of the Lord are
many, and He, in His mercy, will protect the child and fulfil
the prophecy concerning him." Thus the future redeemer
of Israel was exposed in an ark of bulrushes on the waters of
the Nile.

This happened on the twenty-first day of the month of
Nisan, on the day on which later on Moses and Israel were

---

[1] *Sepher Hajashar; Pirke de Rabbi Eliezer*, ch. 48; *Sotah*, 12a.
[2] Jellinek, *loc. cit.;* Beer, *loc. cit.*, p. 32

to sing a hymn of praise to God for their redemption from the waves of the Red Sea.

Greatly wondered the angels, and, appearing before the Throne of Glory, thus they spoke: " Need we remind Thee that the child who, on this day of Nisan, is to sing a song of praise unto Thee for rescuing Israel from the waves of the Red Sea, hath to-day been exposed on the waters? Shall he find his death to-day in the sea?"[1]

According to another version it was the sixth day of the month of Sivan on which the ark of bulrushes containing the infant redeemer was exposed, the day on which the Law was to be revealed on Mount Sinai. And the ministering angels appearing before the Lord thus spoke: " Lord of the Universe, shall the great mortal who is to reveal Thy Law on Mount Sinai perish to-day in the sea?"

But a voice from the Throne of Glory replied: " Ye know well that I see everything! What hath been decided in My counsel, the efforts and contrivings of men will never alter. Those who lead others to perdition for the sake of their own safety, using malice and intrigues, never prevail, nor do they attain their end. But those who put their trust in Me in the hour of peril are saved whenever they least expect it, and their distress is speedily changed into sudden and unlooked-for happiness. My omnipotence will reveal itself in the fate and fortunes of the infant now floating on the waves."[2]

Thus spoke the Lord, and He sent one of his numerous agents to rescue the future redeemer of Israel from the waves of the sea.

Melol, the King of Egypt, had only one daughter named Thermutis or Therbutis, known also as Bithia or Bathia, the daughter of God, and whom he loved greatly. The princess was childless and always yearned for a son who could one day inherit the throne of her father. Of a pious disposition, Ther-

---

[1] Beer, *loc. cit.*, pp. 33–34.　　　[2] *Ibid.*

mutis also suffered greatly on account of the idol worship that
prevailed at the court of Egypt, and she frequently sought an
occasion to escape from her father's palace, so as not to be a
witness to the impurity and wicked ways practised by the King
and his suite.

Now it came to pass that in those days the Lord sent an
unbearable scorching heat upon Egypt, so that all the inhabitants suffered with leprosy and boils.   They all sought relief
from their pains in a bath in the Nile.   Thermutis, too, was
among the sufferers, but having found no relief in the warm
baths prepared in her apartments, she decided to try the baths
in the Nile.[1] Accompanied by her maids, the princess was
walking along the banks of the Nile, suffering both mentally
and physically, when she beheld the little ark, wherein lay the
future redeemer of Israel, floating on the surface of the waters.
Thermutis naturally supposed that the ark contained one of the
children exposed at the royal command, and sent one of her
maids to fetch it.   The maids protested, pointing out that the
princess at least ought to observe the royal decree, even if it
was unheeded by others.   Scarcely, however, had these Egyptian
maids raised their voices in protest, than the angel Gabriel
appeared and punished them.   The earth opened her mouth,
swallowed them up, and they all disappeared from the surface,
one maid alone, faithful to the princess, remaining for her
service.[2]

The princess now stretched out her arm to take the little
ark, and in a miraculous manner her arm was lengthened to
such an extent that she succeeded in grasping the little ark
swimming at a distance of 60 ells.   As soon as Thermutis had
touched the ark, her affliction departed from her, her leprosy
disappeared, and she was suddenly restored to health.[3]

On opening the ark and beholding the radiantly beautiful

---

[1] Jellinek, *Beth-Hamidrash*, Vol. II; Josephus, *loc. cit.*; *Book of Jubilees*, XLVII, 4.
[2] *Sotah*, 12b; *Exodus Rabba*, section *Shemot*.
[3] *Exodus Rabba, ibid.*; *Targum Pseudo-Jonathan, Exodus*, 2, 10.

baby, she felt as if she were looking upon the radiance of Divine Glory.[1] Knowing that the babe was one of the Hebrew children and suddenly remembering her father's decree, the princess was on the point of throwing the ark back into the Nile and of abandoning the infant to his fate. But at this moment the angel Gabriel once more appeared, gave the child a blow and caused it to cry aloud and to continue weeping piteously.

The heart of Thermutis was touched; a wave of compassion for the little innocent swept over her, and even a feeling of motherly tenderness stirred in the bosom of the childless princess.[2]

Deciding to save the child, in spite of her father's cruel decree, she called one of the Egyptian women to nurse the boy. The future redeemer of Israel, however, who was to speak face to face with the Lord, refused to take milk from any of the Egyptian women. The Lord had so ordained it that none of the women of Egypt could boast afterwards of having been the nurse of the Elect of the Eternal.[3]

It was at this moment that Miriam, who had been watching the scene from a distance, stepped forward, and with the permission of the princess called Jochebed, the child's own mother. And thus the rescued child was returned to his mother's arms, and Jochebed, one of the midwives who had disobeyed the cruel decree of Pharaoh, was rewarded by the Lord for her heroic action, for the Lord never forgets the merits of those who put their trust in Him.

On the very day on which the babe who was one day to redeem Israel from bondage was rescued, the astrologers appeared before Pharaoh, and thus they spoke:

" Long live the King! We bring thee glad tidings, for we have read in the stars that the boy destined to redeem Israel

---

[1] Philo, *De Vita Mosis*, II.
[2] *Midrash Abkhir*, in *Yalkut*, § 166; *Exodus Rabba, ibid.*
[3] *Sepher Hajashar*; *Sotah*, 12b; see also Jellinek, *Beth-Hamidrash*, Vol. II, pp. 1–11, and Vol. I, pp. 35–57.

and to bring calamity upon Egypt has met his fate in water. No longer needst thou fear him, O great King."

Thus spoke the astrologers who had been misled by a vague vision, for they had read in the stars that Moses was to die one day on account of water, and it meant that his death was decreed because he had disobeyed the command of the Lord with reference to the waters of Meribah. Pharaoh, however, satisfied with the tidings brought to him by his astrologers, recalled his decree, and the new-born babes of Israel were saved from drowning.[1]

It was on account of the merits of Moses that all the male children begotten on the same day with him were saved from drowning, and it was no vain boast on the part of the redeemer of Israel, when he afterwards said: " The people that went forth out of the water on account of my merits are six hundred thousand men ".[2]

Moses remained with his parents for two years. His father called him Heber, and his mother Jekuthiel, whilst the people of Israel called him Shemaiah ben Nethanel. All Israel knew that the child was destined to deliver them from bondage, and that in his days the Lord would listen to their prayers, and through Moses give them the Law.[3]

When two years had elapsed, Jochebed brought the child to the royal palace and handed it over to the daughter of Pharaoh.

Thermutis, attracted by the supernatural beauty of the boy she had rescued, grew greatly attached to him and conferred upon him the name of Moses, not only because she had drawn him out of the water, but because one day he was destined to draw Israel out of Egypt, and a voice from Heaven called and said to the pious princess:

" Daughter of Pharaoh! Because thou didst have compassion

---

[1] *Exodus Rabba, ibid.; Sotah, ibid. Pirke de Rabbi Eliezer*, ch. 48; see also Grünbaum, *loc. cit.*, p. 154.   [2] *Numbers*, 11, 21.

[3] Jellinek, *Beth-Hamidrash*, Vol. II, pp. 1–11; *Sepher Hajashar, Megillah*, 13a.

upon a child not thine own, and didst call it *thy* son, thou art henceforth *My* daughter, and thy name shall be Bithia (or Bathia), daughter of God."

Her reward for rescuing Moses was great, for Bithia never tasted death, being one of those who entered Paradise alive.[1] In order to be able to maintain that the child was her own son, Bithia had even pretended for some time previously that she was pregnant, and on the day on which the child had been brought to her from his parents' house, it was announced that the princess had been delivered.

Moses was educated and brought up with the royal princes, and his foster-mother, who had adopted him as her own son, constantly kissed and caressed him, never letting him leave the palace or allowing him to be out of her sight. His loveliness was so great, and his beauty so attractive, that all were desirous of seeing him, and whoever set eyes on the boy could not turn their gaze away. Those who met him when he was being carried along on the road would turn and gaze at the wondrous child, feasting their eyes on its supernatural beauty and loveliness. Not only physically, but also mentally was Moses a wonder-child, for his understanding was beyond his years, and in his infancy he already proved that once grown to manhood he would perform great deeds.

Delighted with the extraordinary beauty and gifts of her foster-son, the princess could no longer keep her secret from her father.[2] When Moses was in his third year, she brought the child to the King, and thus she spoke:

" My royal Father! before thy assembled court I confess that this child of such wondrous beauty and noble mind is not my own son. Through the bounty of the River Nile I have received him as a precious gift, and I have adopted him as my son, so that he may one day inherit thy throne

---

[1] *Leviticus Rabba; Yalkut,* § 166; see *Pirke de Rabbi Eliezer*, ch. 48; Grünbaum, *loc. cit.*, p. 154.   [2] *Sepher Hajashar.*

and kingdom." Thus speaking, Bithia, or Thermutis, put the infant in her father's arms.

Pharaoh loved his daughter greatly and would not contradict her wishes, but he was also attracted by the magnetic beauty of Moses, so that he took the child, kissed and hugged it, keeping it close to his breast. Moses thus became the recognized heir to the throne of Egypt.

Now it happened one day, when Moses was three years old, that Pharaoh was seated at the royal table. To his right sat his Queen Alpharanith, and to his left his daughter Bithia with the child in her lap. The princes of the realm and all the royal counsellors, among them Balaam, the son of Beor, and his two sons, stood about the King. Then Moses stretched out his hand, caught the royal crown and placed it on his own head. He thereupon threw it on the ground and alighting from his foster-mother's knee trampled it under his feet.[1] Great was the dismay of the King and his counsellors. Such an action on the part of the child could only augur evil to the King and to the safety of the realm.

" What is your opinion, O my counsellors," said the King, " and what shall be done to this evil child who has taken the royal crown from our head and trampled it under foot?"

Thus spoke Pharaoh, and immediately, Balaam, the son of Beor, rose up, and thus he spoke: " Long live my Lord and King! Dost thou not remember thy dream which thou hast once dreamed, and the interpretation thereof of thy servant? Remember, O King, that this child is one of the Hebrew race, and, endowed with more wisdom and cunning than other children of his age, he has acted with deliberation and purposely. His great aim is, when he is old enough, to take the crown from thy head, to tread thy power under his feet, and to bring Egypt under the sway and dominion of the

---

[1] *Sepher Hajashar*; *Yalkut*, § 166; Jellinek, *Beth-Hamidrash*, Vol. II, pp. 1–11, and Vol. I, pp. 35–57; see also Beer, *loc. cit.*, p. 39; Grünbaum, *loc. cit.*, pp. 156–158; Josephus, *Antiquities*, II.

Hebrews. His ancestors already have constantly endeavoured to rule over kings and nations and have realized their efforts by intrigues and cunning. Thus Abraham defeated the armies of Nimrod and conquered a portion of his kingdom which was the land of Canaan. Isaac became more powerful than the King of the Philistines, whilst Jacob took from his brother Esau his birthright and blessing, and grew rich at the expense of Laban. As for Joseph, he arrived in this land of Egypt as a slave, and was cast into prison by his master, but he subsequently rose to the highest dignities and became the actual ruler of Egypt. He invited his father and brethren to come over and dwell in the land of Goshen. He gave them the best of this land and kept them at the expense of the country. We may expect a similar attitude on the part of this child who is already treating the royal crown and the royal dignity with contempt. The day will come, O King, when this evil child will tear the crown from thy head and enslave thy people. My advice, therefore, is to slay him at once and thus save Egypt from perdition."[1]

Thus spoke Balaam who had read in the stars that Moses would one day cause the downfall of Pharaoh and the misfortune of the country, but Pharaoh still hesitated to put the child to death.

" Before I decide what shall be done with this child," said Pharaoh, " I will summon all the nobles of my realm and all the wise men of Egypt, and take their counsel."

Thereupon the nobles and counsellors and wise men of Egypt were summoned into the royal presence. The King related unto them what had happened and also what advice had been given by Balaam.

Many nobles agreed with Balaam, some advising that the child be slain with the sword, whilst others were of opinion that he be burnt with fire. Thereupon the Lord sent his angel

[1] See note. p. 227.

Gabriel, who took the shape and form of an old man and mingled with the counsellors of Pharaoh.[1]

According to another version, it was not the angel Gabriel, but Jethro, a member of the royal Privy Council, who was still in Egypt, who prevented the execution of Moses.

" Do not listen, O King," said the angel Gabriel, " to the advice of thy counsellors to slay the child. It will be innocent blood that thou wilt shed, for this child is still young and without discerning. He knows not what he is doing. Before thou dost sentence so young a child to death, it is only just that thou shouldst prove whether his understanding and wisdom are really so great as Balaam, the son of Beor, pretends, and whether his action is the result of design. May it therefore please the King to command that two bowls be brought here, one filled with gold and precious stones, and the other full of live coals. We shall then see whether the child is wiser than befits his age. If he stretches out his hand and takes the gold and precious stones, then he is certainly endowed with wisdom and understanding beyond his years and must have acted with design. He therefore deserves death, but if he grasps the live coals, then it is evident that he is devoid of reason and discerns not between good and evil. His action therefore was only the result of a childish fancy and he is innocent of purpose."

Thus spoke the angel Gabriel, disguised as an old man and one of the wise men of Egypt, and his advice pleased the King greatly. Orders were immediately given that two basins be brought, one full of gold and precious stones, and the other full of live coals.

When the bowls were brought in and placed before Moses, he stretched out his hand and was on the point of taking hold of the jewels, but Gabriel, who had become invisible, caught his hand and directed it towards the live coals. Moses burnt

[1] Jellinek, *Beth-Hamidrash*, Vol. II.

his fingers, and putting them into his mouth burnt his tongue and lips, so that he became slow of lips and slow of tongue (*Exodus*, 4, 11).[1]

The King and his counsellors, now convinced that the child had acted without design when he thrust Pharaoh's crown upon the ground and trampled upon it, decided that no harm should be done unto Moses. Bithia, Pharaoh's daughter, henceforth took great care that her beloved foster-son was kept far away from those who constantly tried to harm him. Moses was educated with love and care in the royal palace, in Bithia's private apartments, and the Lord inspired Pharaoh with love and affection for the son of Amram and Jochebed, so that he always refused to listen to those of his counsellors who strove to destroy the future redeemer of Israel.

Bithia spared no costs to have her foster-son educated as befitted a royal prince. Masters were brought from neighbouring lands who taught the child all sciences and instructed him in the vast learning and wisdom of the Egyptians, so that the boy soon surpassed all his masters in learning and knowledge. It is said that the sons of Balaam, Jannes and Jambres, were his tutors in his early age.[2] Moses acquired knowledge so easily that it seemed as if he were only recalling to his mind instruction which he had already learned before. And so the boy Moses was highly respected by the court of Pharaoh, and the people looked upon him as their future sovereign.[3]

THE JEWELS AND THE LIVE COALS

Quem dum quadam die Terimith obtulisset Pharaoni, ut et ipse eum adoptaret, admirans rex pueri venustatem, coronam, quam tunc forte gestabat, capiti illius imposuit. Erat autem in ea

---

[1] *Sepher Hajashar*; *Exodus Rabba*, section *Shemot*; Jellinek, *Beth-Hamidrash*, Vol. I and Vol. II; see also *Sotah*, 11a; *Sanhedrin*, 106; see also Grünbaum, *loc. cit.*, pp. 158–159.

[2] Abulfaraj, *Histor. Dynast.*

[3] See for the whole chapter, Lewner, *Kol Agadoth*, Vol. II, pp. 4–7.

Ammonis imago fabrefacta. Puer autem coronam projecit in terram, et fregit. Sacerdos autem Helipoleos a latere regis surgens, exclamavit: Hic est puer, quem nobis occidendum Deus monstravit, ut de caetero timore careamus, et voluit irruere in eum, sed auxilio regis liberatus est, et persuasione ejusdam sapientis qui per ignorantium hoc factum esse a puero asseruit. In cujus rei argumentum cum prunas allatas puero obtulisset, puer eas ori suo opposuit, et linguae suae summitatem igne corrupit. Unde et Hebraei impeditionis linguae eum fuisse autumant.

> Comestor, *Historia Scholastica, Exodus*, Cap. V (see Migne, *Patrologia*, Vol. 198, p. 1144).

THE ROYAL CROWN AND THE BURNING COALS

An time after ðat ðis was don,
  She brogte him bi-foren pharaon,
And ðis king wurð him in herte mild,
So swide faiger was ðis child;
And he toc him on sunes stede,
And his corune on his heued he dede,
And let it stonden ayne stund;
ðhe child it warð dun to de grund.
Hamonel likenes was ðor-on;
ðis crune is broken, ðis is misdon.
    Bissop Eliopoleos
  Sag ðis timing, and up he ros;
" If ðis child," quad he, " mote ðen,
He sal egyptes bale ben."
If ðor ne wore helpe twen lopen,
ðis child adde ðan sone be dropen;
ðe king wið-stod and an wis man,
He seide, " ðe child doð als he can;
We sulen nu witen for it dede
ðis witterlike, or in child-hede;"
He bad ðis child brennen to colen
And he toc is hu migt he it ðolen,
And in hise muth so depe he is dede
His tunges ende is brent ðor-mide;

ðor-fore seide de ebru witterlike
ðat he spac siðen miserlike;

The Story of Genesis and Exodus, Edited by Richard Morris,
London, 1865. Early English Text Society, Vol. VII,
p. 75, ll. 2633–2658.

MOSES AND THE GLEAMING COALS

CORDELAMOR

Je prens grant plaisir et lyesse
A voir cest enfant gracieux.

LA FILLE

Aussi est il gent et joyeux
Et de rien qui soit ne s'estonne.

LE ROY CORDELAMOR

Je luy vueil mettre ma couronne
Sur le chef, ou le dieu Hamon
Est figuré, que tant aymon.
En signe d'amour je luy mets.
> [*Icy Moyse prent la couronne et la jecte
> contre terre, et la ront en piéces.*

LE PREMIER MEDECIN

Sire, ne me croyez jamais
Se cest enfant que voyez cy
Ne met toute Egipte en soucy;
C'est celuy, tresredoubté sire,
Que Dieu nous demonstra occire,
Et si doit le régne abesser
D'Egipte, detruire et casser.
Par quoy plus endurer n'en puis,
Et de fait deliberé suis
Le mettre tout soudain a mort.

Le Second Medecin

De l'occire auriez grant tort.
S'il a mal faict, c'est ignorance;
Ce qu'il a faict luy vient d'enfance,
Tout clérement le prouveray.

Le Premier Medecin

Par noz haulx Dieux je le tueray,
Car autrement il regnera
Et toute Egipte destruira;
Brief de le tuer ay envye.

Moyse

Ma dame, sauvez moy la vie;
Vela qui me veult mettre a mort.

Cordelamor

Si ne vous vueil je pas permettre
De luy faire aucun desplaisir.

Therimit

Entre mes bras le vueil saisir,
Affin que on ne luy face mal.

Le Premier Medecin

Ung jour sera le principal
Des Ebrieux, je le vous dis franc,
Et sera respandu le sang
Des Egiptiens de sa main.

Le Second Medecin

Si vous debatez vous en vain;
Je vous ay ja dit en substance:
Ce qu'il a faict ce n'est qu'enfance.
Qu'i soit vray, je le prouveray.
Des charbons luy presenteray

Tous ardens, et puis on verra
Que c'est que des charbons fera.
Esprouvons ung petit ce point.

CORDELAMOR

Or sus donc, ne differez point.
A charbons vifz luy presenter.
[*Il fault des charbons vifz et qu'il y en ait ung faint.*

LE SECOND MEDECIN

Moyse, il fault diligenter
De vous venir ung peu esbatre.

MOYSE

A cela je ne vueil debatre;
Tous jeux nouveaux me semblent bons.
Et que sont ce icy?

LE SECOND MEDECIN

          Des charbons
Que j'ay icy faiz arrenger.

MOYSE

J'en vueil taster, j'en vueil manger;
Ilz me semblent beaux, par mon ame.
    [*Icy met le charbon en sa bouche, et puis dit en
      plurant:*
Helas! m'amye, helas! madame,
J'ay la bouche toute affolée.

THERIMIT

Qu'esse?

MOYSE

        J'ay la langue bruslée.
En me jouant, en m'esbatant
Je me suis bruslé.

THERIMIT

Mon enfant,
Ton enfance tu monstres bien.

J. de Rothschild, *Le Mistère du Viel Testament*, Tome III,
p. 251, ll. 22958–23017.

MOSES AND THE GLEAMING COALS

De Moyse autem parvulo dicunt Hebrei quod coronam quam
Pharao in capite ejus posuit in terra projecit videns in ea ymaginem
Jovis, et voluit Pharao interficere eum eo quod sapientes Egypti
dixerunt regi quod puer ille destrueret Egyptum. Quidam autem
liberavit eum dicens. Videamus si ex infantia fecit; et allatis car-
bonibus incensis, posuit in ore suo et lingua ejus lesa est unde impe-
dite linguae factus est ad loquendum.

The Exempla of Jacques de Vitry, Edited by Th. F. Crane
London, 1890, p. 131, CCCXIII.

CHAPTER XVIII

The Youth and Education of Moses

The virtuous prince—Moses conquers his passions—He avoids pleasure and sin—His visits to Goshen—The golden chain and the family ties—Love and gratitude—The toiling Hebrews—The sad prince—His animosity towards Balaam—His sympathy with the labourers—Moses comforts the Hebrews—Everything is liable to change—The escape of the wizard and his sons—The office of Moses—His request to the King—A day of rest for the labourers—The Sabbath—The gift of Moses—A new decree—The toll of bricks and the babies built in the wall—The cruel taskmasters and the weeping mothers—The beautiful Salomith and the Egyptian taskmaster—The dishonoured wife—The anger of the husband—The righteous indignation of Moses and his hesitation to mete out justice—The heavenly court and the voice from the Throne of Glory—The Ineffable Name, and the death of the Egyptian criminal—The silent sand on the seashore—A secret divulged—The repudiated wife, and the talk of the neighbours—The quarrelsome brothers—The sin of Israel: tale-bearing and back-sliding—The complaint of the nobles of Egypt—The arrest of Moses—The appeal of the angels—The promise of the Lord—The miracle at the scaffold—The ivory neck—Gabriel beheads the executioner—The King's guards stricken with blindness and dumbness—The escape of Moses.

Moses had now grown up, and as he advanced in years, and his knowledge, wisdom, and understanding increased, he constantly strove to conquer all his passions and evil inclinations and to lead a life of virtue and purity. The luxurious life at the court of Egypt offered the young foster-son of the princess many temptations, but Moses persistently refused to be lured by pleasures and sin. Upon his brow he wore the royal diadem, but his heart was full of noble and pure sentiments, and great thoughts filled his mind. He conquered all the passions to which idle youth, reared in opulence and luxury, will easily fall a prey, so that all his friends wondered

232

greatly at his conduct and readily believed that the soul of the young Hebrew was not human, but divine, and that even his body was composed of divine elements. Moses never lived or acted like other mortals, for he excelled all men in noble and elevated sentiments. He spoke what he thought, and acted according to his words.

As the adopted son of Princess Bithia, as the acknowledged heir to the throne of Egypt and successor of Pharaoh, he had reached the summit of earthly greatness, for he was everywhere considered as the heir-apparent, and often called the young king. But Moses was not dazzled by his brilliant prospects and never forgot his extraction, his race, and his ancestors. From his mother Jochebed, whom he was in the habit of visiting, he had learned his true origin, and he knew that he was not an Egyptian, but a Hebrew who had been saved miraculously from the waters, and that the princess was only his foster-mother. He knew that Amram and Jochebed were his real parents, Aaron and Miriam, his brother and sister, and the toiling Hebrews, his brethren. Upon his white brow he wore the diadem, the sign of Egyptian royalty, but in his heart he harboured deep affection and love for his own kith and kin, for the suffering slaves and the toilers in the brick-fields of Egypt. The bond which attached the young prince to his own family and people was stronger than the golden chains and necklace he wore as Prince of Egypt and which were the symbol of his close relation to the throne. And yet Moses was too noble to forget his benefactors, or to diminish the love and gratitude he owed them. Loving his real parents, he was yet deeply attached to Pharaoh, and especially to his foster-mother Bithia, whose love he never forgot, even in those moments when, in the interest of his people, he was compelled to declare war on Pharaoh. His sentiments of gratitude towards Pharaoh, and even his affection for the ruler of Egypt, would scarcely have undergone a change had it not been for the fact that his eyes were opened, when he beheld the oppression of the Hebrews.[1]

Daily Moses went out to Goshen to visit his parents and relations, and he was surprised to notice how the Hebrews were groaning under the heavy yoke which was being pressed on their necks, and how they were being compelled by their cruel taskmasters to labour without a respite. Moses asked the reason of this cruel oppression and learned that it was the result of the advice given to Pharaoh by Balaam. He learned how it had come to pass that the Hebrews were now groaning under such heavy burdens, and also how Balaam had sought to destroy Moses himself when he was still in his infancy. This was news indeed for Moses who had been ignorant of these facts. The information filled his heart with indignation and sadness. He felt sad to find himself unable to love Pharaoh as he had loved him before, and could not forgive him his cruel treatment of his brethren. As for Balaam, Moses' indignation and his animosity towards the wizard knew no bounds, but greater still were his sufferings when he saw the toiling labourers and felt that he was not strong enough to rescue them from bondage or even to take them under his protection and at least ease their burden. " Alas," he cried bitterly, " I had rather die than witness the affliction of my brethren."

He took off the golden chain which he wore round his neck, the sign of his princely position, and mingling with the toilers tried to help them and lighten their burden. He noticed how feeble old men and even women were groaning under loads too heavy for them, and he took the loads and placed them on the shoulders of the young and strong, thus making each labour and toil according to his strength, which was already a step towards lightening the sufferings of the slaves. To the Egyptian overseers and taskmasters it seemed, however, as if Moses was acting thus in the interests of the King, so as

---

[1] *Sepher Hajashar*; *Exodus Rabba*, section *Shemot*; Beer, *loc. cit.*, pp. 42–43.

to have the work of building executed sooner. Moses availed himself of his influence over the overseers to diminish their cruelty towards the slaving Hebrews. As for the latter, he tried to comfort and console them.

" My dear brethren," he said, " bear your present hard lot, but be of good cheer and lose not your courage. Better times will soon follow upon the gloomy days of the present, and then suffering and sorrow will change into joy. The world is always full of change, a blue sky follows black clouds, and the storm is succeeded by fair weather."

Thus spoke Moses, doing his best to cheer up his brethren by words of encouragement and consolation, but in his own heart he desponded and could neither forget nor forgive the cruel oppression of his brethren. Balaam he considered as the real culprit and author of the cruel oppression and suffering of his people, and he meditated how he could prevail against this wicked counsellor of Pharaoh.

The magician evidently noticed Moses' change of attitude towards himself, and knew what was in the Hebrew's mind. Fearing the influence of the adopted grandson of the King, who was influential enough to do him harm, Balaam, accompanied by his sons, Jannes and Jambres, left the court of Egypt and escaped to Ethiopia.

Moses in the meantime rose higher and higher in the favour of the King who appointed the lad to the office of introducing distinguished and illustrious foreigners into the royal presence. The whole aim, however, of the future redeemer of Israel was to relieve his people from their terrible burden and suffering and redeem them if possible from bondage. As yet, he was an outsider, for he had not thrown in his lot with his people; but he made use of his influence at the court of Pharaoh to lighten the intolerable burden of his brethren.

One day Moses appeared before Pharaoh and said: " Long

live the King! I have a small favour to ask from your Majesty, will it be granted unto me?" and Pharaoh answered:

" Speak, my son, for I am ready to grant thee any request."

" Sire," said Moses, " it is well known that even the slaves, condemned to constant labour, are granted at least one day in the week on which they are allowed to rest, so that their strength may not be exhausted and their work may not become unsatisfactory and even useless. Now I have noticed during one of my inspections in the land of Goshen that the Hebrews toiling there are given no day of rest. All the week, from dawn till dusk, they work incessantly and know no rest. Such a forced labour, O King, is not profitable to thee, for their strength being exhausted they proceed rather slowly with the building and their work is inferior. Grant, therefore, my request, O King, and give them a day of rest on which they may be able to recruit their strength and, refreshed, start their labour on the following week."

Thus spoke Moses, and Pharaoh replied:

" Thou has spoken well, my son, and I readily grant thee thy request. Which day dost thou think is the best to be given to the Israelites as a day of rest?"

" The seventh day of the week is the most appropriate day of rest, for on this day, consecrated to the planet Saturn, work is anyhow not crowned with success."

" Thy wish is granted," said the King, " and thou mayest inform all the overseers and taskmasters of my royal wish, and make known unto them that henceforth the Hebrews are to cease work on the seventh day, which will be their weekly day of rest."

In blithe spirits Moses left the royal presence and hurried to Goshen to announce the glad tidings to his brethren. Great was the gratitude of the children of Israel for this noble deed of Moses, who had obtained for them at least one day of rest in every week, and they never forgot this boon. The seventh day of the week, the Sabbath, is still praised after many centuries as the " Gift of Moses ".[1]

In the meantime, however, the number of the Hebrews increased considerably, for the decree of Pharaoh to cast all the new-born children of the Hebrews into the Nile had been withdrawn soon after the birth of Moses. This fact once more raised the fear of the Egyptians and of their ruler, so that Pharaoh issued a new law calculated to put a stop to the increase of the subject nation.

It was decreed that every Hebrew had to deliver by sunset a number of bricks imposed upon him by the Egyptian taskmasters. If even one brick was short, then the youngest child of the Hebrew labourer who had not made up his toll of bricks was seized and built into the wall in the place of bricks. Such a cruel decree was executed by the Egyptian taskmasters with great alacrity, and they no longer respected the most sacred bonds of the Hebrew families. It often happened that one of the Hebrew slaves, labouring in the brick-fields, could not make up the toll of bricks imposed upon him, and then the ruthless overseers penetrated into his house and snatched away his beloved child from the arms of the weeping and desperate mother. Alive the child was built into the walls.

The Hebrew labourers were furthermore arranged in groups, each group of ten placed under one Hebrew overseer, and ten such overseers were controlled by one Egyptian taskmaster. It was the duty of the Hebrew overseers to wake the men placed under their control early before dawn and to bring them to their work. Whenever one man was missing, the Egyptian taskmaster called at once the Hebrew overseer and bade him produce the man not at his post without delay.

Now it happened that one of these Hebrew overseers had a wife, Salomith by name, the daughter of Dibri from the

---

[1] *Exodus Rabba*, section *Shemot*; *Sepher Hajashar*; Beer, *loc. cit.*, pp. 43-45; see also Lewner, *loc. cit.*, pp. 8-9.

tribe of Dan, who was beautiful of face and figure and faultless in body. The Egyptian taskmaster had long noticed her beauty and a wild passion entered his heart. He thought of means how to possess this beautiful Hebrew woman. One morning therefore, before dawn, the Egyptian taskmaster appeared at the house of the Hebrew overseer and bade him arise and call the men under his control. Not suspecting any guile, the husband of the beautiful Salomith quickly arose and went out to wake and call his men. The Egyptian taskmaster had in the meantime concealed himself in a dark corner, and as soon as the husband had left the house he re-entered and took the place of the husband by the side of the beautiful woman. After a while the Hebrew overseer, having called his men, returned, and was surprised to see his taskmaster coming out of his house.[1]

"With what intent had this Egyptian come back here in my absence?" he asked his wife, who was still sunk in slumber.

In great dismay Salomith exclaimed: "Woe unto me! What is it thou sayest, my husband? The taskmaster has been here, and in thy absence? I thought that thou hast never left this room."

Thus lamented the poor woman, and her husband knew that the Egyptian had dishonoured his unsuspecting wife. During the morning he cast furious glances at his Egyptian tormentor, and the latter guessed that the Hebrew had found out the truth. He therefore was more cruel than usual towards the man he had sinned against, and not only laid heavier tasks upon him, but subjected him to more than one bastinado during the day.

Now it happened that Moses drew nigh at this moment. The Hebrew, perceiving Moses, the heir to the Egyptian throne,

---

[1] *Exodus Rabba*, section *Shemot*; *Midrash Agadah*, ed. Buber, Vol. I, p. 125; see Beer, *loc. cit.*, pp. 46-47.

whom he knew to be merciful and just and always ready to take up the cause of his toiling and suffering brethren, hastened and complained to him of the cruel treatment of the Egyptian taskmaster. He also related unto Moses how his tormentor had dishonoured his wife. Moses' anger was kindled against the Egyptian, but a wave of pity and compassion for the Hebrew filled his heart.

"Lord of the Universe," he cried, "where is Thy promise to Abraham that his children will be as many as the stars in Heaven? They are now being slowly tortured and put to death by their tormentors." He looked round to see whether any other labourer would come forth, and in a moment of righteous indignation avenge the misdeed and cruel injustice of the Egyptian. But none came forward, for the suffering labourers no longer dared to protest, however cruel the conduct of their oppressors had become. Burning with indignation, and swayed by a deep sense of justice, Moses raised a spade and was on the point of smiting the Egyptian on the head, when he suddenly hesitated.

"Lord of the Universe," he said, within himself, "I am about to kill this man, and yet what right have I to take his life? He is a criminal just now who deserves severe punishment, but how do I know whether he will not repent one day and atone for his wicked ways by just and pious deeds? Have I read the future to know that this man will not bring forth children who will walk in the ways of the Lord, be merciful and just? and even if it were not so, who am I to dare force the arm of Providence, to punish when vengeance is the Lord's alone?" Thus thought Moses within himself, and lo! the heavenly heights were suddenly revealed unto Moses, the heavens opened before him, and his eyes witnessed the mysteries of the world below and of the worlds above. He saw the ministering angels surrounding the Throne of Glory and the heavenly court was sitting in judgment over man.

And Moses heard a heavenly voice calling unto him: " Thy scruples, O Moses, just as they are and inspired by noble sentiments, are out of place in this case. Justice should take its course. Know that this Egyptian who has committed adultery and manslaughter many a time and was on the point of slaying the man against whom he has sinned, will never repent, but persist in his evil ways. Neither he nor his children will ever do righteously, but only work evil. Wert thou even to give him now his life until the end of days, none of his seed will ever commit any just and meritorious deed which would wipe out his wickedness. The future is an open book to the omniscience of the Almighty. This man has deserved death, and thou, Moses, hast been called hither to execute the decree of Providence."

No longer did Moses now hesitate to slay the Egyptian, so as to save the Hebrew from a certain death which would sooner or later be his fate. But before raising his hand to smite the Egyptian, Moses called on the name of the Most High, so as to strengthen himself in his purpose. Scarcely had the Ineffable Name left his lips and the sound reached the ears of the Egyptian, when the latter fell down to the ground and died, even before the hand of Moses had touched him. Not with his hand but with a word of his mouth did Moses kill the Egyptian criminal.[1]

Moses, however, knew that his deed, although morally justified, would be legally condemned in Egypt, and that were it to be bruited abroad he would incur the wrath of the King, and the consequences would be fatal. He therefore decided to conceal the deed. Turning to the Hebrews, who alone were present and had crowded round their comrade whom Moses had thus rescued, the future redeemer of Israel thus spoke unto them:

---

[1] *Exodus Rabba*, section *Shemot*; Beer, *loc. cit.*, pp. 46–48; see *Sepher Hajashar*; Jellinek, *loc. cit.*, Vol. II, pp. 1–11; see also *Pirke de Rabbi Eliezer*, Ch. 48; Grünbaum, *loc. cit.*, p. 160.

" My brethren, remember the promise once made by the Lord unto your forefathers: *Ye shall be like the sand on the seashore.* Just as the sand falls and makes no sound and is silent when it is pressed by the foot of man, so may ye be silent and make no sound concerning this deed which shall remain a secret never to be divulged."

Unfortunately, however, the deed remained not long a secret. It was bruited abroad, and Moses soon found that his deed was known not only to his own people, but also to the Egyptians. He had returned to the palace, whilst the Hebrew whom he had rescued went home to inform his wife that according to an old Hebrew custom he was compelled to separate from her and to send her away, as another man had approached her. The poor woman hurried to her relatives and asked them to intercede on her behalf. In vain, however, did the latter plead and even threaten, for the husband remained adamant. The matter was thus being talked about, and so the whole story in all its details, including Moses' punishment of the Egyptian, became known to all the Hebrews. Thus Dathan and Abiram, two brothers, the sons of Pallu, of the tribe of Reuben, who were known for their quarrelsome character and their contentiousness, learned of what had occurred. On the following day the Hebrews began to talk on the event of the previous day, some of them maintaining that the husband had acted wisely in repudiating his wife, whilst others blamed him. Dathan and Abiram began to discuss the matter, and a scuffle ensued.

Moses was just approaching when he saw Dathan raise his hand to deal Abiram a deathly blow, and he exclaimed:

" Why art thou acting so wickedly as to lift up thy hand against thy brother? He is no better than thou, but thou art a villain to deal him a blow!"

Insolently Dathan turned against Moses and cried:

" And what business hast thou, beardless youth, to inter-

fere! Dost thou imagine because thou art the foster-son of the
Princess that thou hast a right to be a judge over us and command us? We know that thou art the son of Jochebed and hast
no right to rule over us. We will make known what thou didst
do unto the Egyptian whom thou didst slay with the sword of
thy mouth, by pronouncing the name of God. Dost thou intend
to slay us, too, in the same manner?"

Thus spoke Dathan, and Moses was greatly affected by
his taunts. " Alas," he cried, " it is now clear to me why such
heavy burdens have been laid upon the shoulders of my people.
I have wondered in my heart what crime my brethren could
have committed to be punished thus and be oppressed so
mercilessly. Now I know that their great sin is tale-bearing
and back-sliding."

His rebuke, however, had no effect upon the wicked pair,
Dathan and Abiram. They betook themselves to the King
and informed him of what had happened and how Moses had
slain the Egyptian and buried his body in the sand.

Their words made an impression upon Pharaoh and kindled
his wrath. It was not so much that the adopted son of his
daughter had slain an Egyptian, as the fact that the young man
seemed to be opposed to his wishes and to disregard his decrees.
For some time already the nobles of the land had been com-
plaining against Moses, pointing out to Pharaoh that the
acknowledged heir to the throne was an enemy of the King and
of the country. " The friends of the King," they said, " are
not his friends, and he associates with the enemies of his
Majesty. He hates the men whom the King honours and loves,
and befriends those whom the King hates. Such conduct,"
urged the magnates, " only proves that the young man harbours
evil thoughts and is only waiting for a suitable opportunity to
do away with the King and seize the power." Pharaoh, who had
always been favourably disposed to Moses, now made up his
mind to get rid of him, and he issued an order to arrest the

foster-son of Bithia. Accused of homicide, Moses was condemned to death by the sword.[1]

At that moment the ministering angels appeared before the Throne of God and thus they spoke: " Lord of the Universe! Moses, whom Thou didst called the familiar of Thy house, is lying under restraint, awaiting death by the executioner's hand! He is on the point of being led to the scaffold!"

But the Lord replied:

" Be assured, my angels, that I will espouse the cause of my faithful servant and that no harm will be done unto him who is to redeem my people from bondage." [2]

Thus spoke the Lord, and indeed a miracle happened when the son of Amram was led to the place of execution and mounted the scaffold. The sharp sword was set ten times upon his neck, but every time it slipped away, for the neck of Moses had become as hard as ivory. Thereupon the Lord sent down the angel Gabriel who assumed the shape and form of the Royal Executioner, whilst the latter was changed into the form of Moses. Gabriel, seizing the sword destined to slay Moses, beheaded the executioner, whilst Moses escaped.

In vain did Pharaoh, who soon perceived that the intended victim had escaped, order the pursuit of Moses. The King's guard were momentarily stricken with blindness and dumbness, so that they could neither see his flight, give information about his abiding-place, nor get at him.

An angel had in the meantime carried away Moses to a spot far away from Egypt, at a distance of a forty days' journey, so that he was safe from pursuit and out of reach of the wrath of Pharaoh.[3]

[1] *Exodus Rabba*, section *Shemot*; see also Beer, *loc. cit.*, pp. 48–50; Lewner, *loc. cit.*, pp. 9–10.   [2] Beer, *loc. cit.*, p. 51.
[3] *Sepher Hajashar*; see also Jellinek, *loc. cit.*, Vols. I and II; Lewner, *loc. cit.*, p. 10.

CHAPTER XIX

The King of Ethiopia

The war between Ethiopia and Aram—Kikanos, King of Ethiopia—
Balaam is appointed Regent—The treachery of the wizard—The impregnable city—The poisonous serpents—The return of Kikanos—The long
siege—The arrival of Moses—The majestic stranger—Moses is appointed
Commander-in-Chief of the Ethiopian army—The death of Kikanos—The
new king—The men of Ethiopia, and the counsel of Moses—The story of
the serpents and the storks—The triumphant entry into the capital—
Adoniah, the wife of Moses—The rebellion of the men of Aram—Moses
rules over Ethiopia—The jealous nobles—The speech of the Queen—A
neglected wife—Monarchos, the son of Kikanos—The dethroned king—
Moses leaves Ethiopia.

Now it happened in those days that a war had broken out
between the King of Ethiopia and the children of the East and of
Aram. Kikanos, the King of Ethiopia, went out at the head of a
mighty army against the enemy whose hosts were as numerous
as the sand of the sea shore. Before leaving his capital city
of Saba, or Meroe, Kikanos entrusted the country to Balaam
and appointed the magician and his two sons as regents during
his absence.

The wily wizard, however, powerful magician that he was,
succeeded in bewitching the people by his enchantments and
persuaded them to forget their allegiance to the King. The
inhabitants deposed Kikanos and chose Balaam as their King,
appointing his two sons as Commanders-in-Chief of the
armies.

The city of Saba was already almost impregnable, surrounded as it was by the Nile and Astopus, or Astaboras, but

Balaam took steps to make the city absolutely unapproach-able, so as to prevent Kikanos from entering it on his return. He raised the walls of the city on two sides, and dug numerous canals on the third side, between the city and the Nile. Into these canals he let run the waters of the rivers, so that none could approach the city of Saba even after crossing the rivers. As for the fourth side, Balaam, thanks to his magic power and his enchantments, assembled poisonous serpents which were very numerous on the roads between Egypt and Ethiopia.

In the meantime Kikanos, having subjugated the nations of the East, returned to Ethiopia. Great was his surprise, when he found the new city walls and ramparts and the barred gates.

" No doubt," said he, " the inhabitants have raised these walls and fortified them so as to protect themselves against an attack by the Kings of Canaan."

Soon, however, he found that such was not the case. The guards refused to open the gates to him and to his army. " Balaam," they replied, " is now our rightful king, and we have instructions not to open the gates to King Kikanos and his army."

In vain did Kikanos make several attempts to enter his capital by force. The vessels and rafts transporting his men were submerged by the wild rushing and swirling waters of the canals, and he lost many men. His attempts to enter the city from the side protected by the snakes and scorpions also failed, for the reptiles killed a great number of his men. Nothing remained for the King to do but to lay siege to his own city, and for nine years he surrounded it, so that none could either leave or enter it.

It was at this time that Moses, a fugitive from Egyptian justice, appeared in the camp of King Kikanos. His majestic and noble appearance, his radiant beauty, and his extraordinary strength struck Kikanos and his men and exercised a great attraction upon them. Gladly they received Moses in their midst, and soon afterwards the King, in whose eyes Moses had found favour, appointed the son of Amram as his counsellor and Commander-in-Chief of his armies.[1]

The siege had lasted nine years, when Kikanos fell sick and died after a seven days' illness. The men of Ethiopia, weary of the long siege and despairing of ever taking the city and entering their homes, were now at a loss what to do. They decided to set a king over themselves who would counsel them and decide their conduct in the future. None was found more fit to occupy the vacant throne than Moses, the handsome and majestic stranger from Egypt. Stripping off their upper garments, the men of Ethiopia made a sort of throne and set Moses upon it. The trumpets were blown, and Moses was proclaimed King of Ethiopia, Adoniah, the widow of Kikanos being chosen as his wife. This happened 157 years after the arrival of Jacob and his sons in Egypt, when Moses was twenty-seven years of age.

On the seventh day after the proclamation, the people and the nobles appeared before their new king, and thus they spoke: " We have come, O King, to ask thy counsel. Tell us how to proceed so as to hasten the fall of the city which we have been besieging for many years."

Thus spoke the people and nobles of Ethiopia, and Moses replied: " For nine years ye have been besieging this city, but ye will never take it unless ye hearken unto my words. Now this is my counsel, and if ye do my bidding, the city will soon be delivered into our hands, and we will enter its gates triumphantly.

" Make it known in the camp," continued Moses, " that the King commands each man to go to the forest and there to fetch a fledgling from the nests of the storks. He who will not

[1] *Sepher Hajashar*; Jellinek, *loc. cit.*, Vol. II, pp. 1–11; cf. Gaster, *The Chronicles of Jerahmeel*.

obey the King's command shall die, and all his belongings shall be taken by the King."

The men of Ethiopia did as they had been bidden, and each man brought a young stork. Moses thereupon bade them rear the fledglings until they had grown up, and then ordered his men to starve the birds for three days. On the third day, he led his army, prepared for battle, against the city, each man holding his trained stork in his hand. When they had reached the spot which Balaam had filled with poisonous serpents and snakes, Moses ordered his men to send forth the storks upon the reptiles. The trained and hungry birds swooped down upon the snakes and destroyed them, so that the way to the city became clear. The Ethiopian army, led by Moses, thereupon rushed the city, and subdued it. They killed all those who offered any resistance, whilst none of Moses' men died. Balaam, his two sons, Jannes and Jambres, and his eight brothers, managed to escape, thanks to their magic art. They flew through the air and betook themselves once more to Egypt, where Balaam took service at the court of Pharaoh.

Moses had thus delivered the city and the Ethiopian army, and led them to victory. Great was the gratitude of the people to their king who had saved them from destruction, thanks to his good counsel and courage. They confirmed him in his kingship, set the royal crown upon his head, and gave him the widow of Kikanos as wife, the lady willingly offering her hand to the handsome king. Even as King of Ethiopia, Moses continued to fear and love the God of his fathers and never strayed from the path of virtue and righteousness, either to the right or to the left.[1]

The children of the East and the men of Aram, having heard of the death of King Kikanos, made an attempt to shake off the Ethiopian yoke, but Moses went forth with a mighty army

[1] *Ibid*; see also Beer, *loc. cit.*, pp. 51–54; Lewner, *loc. cit.*, pp. 11–14.

and quickly subdued the rebellious nations. Thus Moses ruled over Ethiopia for forty years. The whole country honoured and loved the King, the pillars of whose throne were right, integrity, and justice.

There were some nobles, however, who could not forget that their King was not of their own race, but a stranger and an alien in their midst, and a party was formed for the purpose of deposing Moses. They succeeded in gaining the ear of Queen Adoniah, who was Moses' wife only in name, for never had he approached the heathen woman, nor turned his eyes towards her. One day, therefore, in the fortieth year of his reign, when Moses was seated upon his throne, his wife before him, and all the nobles surrounding him, the Queen rose up and thus she spoke:

" Men of Ethiopia! Forty years have now elapsed since ye appointed this husband of mine as your King and ruler. Great are his merits and the services he has rendered to our country. But know ye, people and nobles of Ethiopia, that he is a stranger in our midst. Never has he worshipped the gods of the Ethiopians, and never has he approached me, his lawful wife. I therefore think that it will be more seemly and right to appoint my son Menacham (or Monarchos), who has now grown up, as your rightful king. He is the son of Kikanos, one of your own race, and not a stranger, a subject of the King of Egypt."[1]

Thus spoke the Queen, and in silence the people and nobles listened to her words. Their attachment to their ancient royal house, to the memory of Kikanos and his seed, was deep, but their love and veneration for Moses prevented them from paying immediate heed to the words of their Queen. A popular assembly was at last convened, and the question of the abdication of the King and the crowning of Monarchos was discussed. The counsels of the partisans of Monarchos at last

[1] *Ibid.*

prevailed, and he was crowned King, Moses being invited to abdicate in favour of the son of Kikanos.

Willingly did the son of Amram yield to the wishes of the people, and without regret he left the country and the men of Ethiopia, who dismissed him with great honour and rich presents.[1]

[1] *Ibid.*

CHAPTER XX

At the Well of Midian, or the Marriage of Moses

The weary traveller—The high-priest of Midian—The futility of idol worship—The abdication of the high-priest—The anger of the Midianites against Jethro, or Reuel—The ban—The rude shepherds and the daughters of the high-priest—A scene of violence—Moses interferes—The gallant Egyptian—The gratitude of the modest maidens—Zipporah falls in love with the handsome stranger—Reuel is afraid of trouble—Moses is cast into a pit—The kindness of Zipporah—Her stratagem—She remains at home and takes care of the house—The prosperity of Jethro, or Reuel—The numerous suitors—The wonderful staff in the garden—The story of the sapphire rod—Zipporah reminds her father of the prisoner—With God all things are possible—Moses is set free—His prayer in the garden—He uproots the staff in the garden—The amazement of Jethro—A prince in Israel—Another version of the marriage of Moses and Zipporah—The maiden's confession—The test of the suitors—The devouring tree—Moses asks the hand of Zipporah—The test—The wonderful rod and the anger of Jethro—Moses set free after seven years—Jethro kisses Moses and blesses the Lord—The united lovers—The faithful shepherd—The story of the white wolf—The story of the dove and the hawk—Angels in disguise—The thirsty kid and the loving shepherd—" Thou shalt pasture the flock of God "—The story of the three travellers and the dropped money-bag—The murder of the innocent—The amazement of Moses—His prayer to God—The reply of the Lord—The mysterious workings of Providence—Divine justice—The ways of the Lord are inscrutable—A Jewish legend in European literature—A poem by Jami—Gellert's " Das Schicksal "—Parnell's " Hermit "—The *Gesta Romanorum*.

Sixty-seven years of age was the future redeemer of Israel, when he journeyed through the desert towards Midian, not daring to return to Egypt. It was a hot day when, towards noon, Moses reached a well outside Midian, where he sat down to rest from the fatigues of his weary journey. It was here that he met the daughters of Jethro, or Reuel, and among them Zipporah, his future wife.

Jethro, or Reuel, who had returned to Midian after leaving the court of Pharaoh, had risen to the dignity of high-priest and prince of the country. Soon, however, he became convinced of the futility and vanity of idol worship, and his priestly dignity became repugnant to him. He decided to give up his office and ask the people to entrust it to someone else. He dared not, however, confess his hidden motives to the people, and therefore pretended that only old age compelled him to give up his sacred duties.

" I am old," said Jethro to the representatives of the people, " and can no longer fulfil my duties. Choose, therefore, someone in my place." Thus speaking, he handed over to the representatives of Midian all the holy vessels appertaining to the idol worship, and divested himself of his sacred garments.

The people appointed a new high-priest, but they suspected Jethro of heretic views. In great fury they pronounced the ban against their former high-priest and decreed that none should render him any service, pasture his flocks, or help him in any way.

Jethro, whose entire wealth consisted in flocks, was greatly embarrassed when all the shepherds left his service. There was nothing for him to do but to bid his seven daughters undertake the task of pasturing his flocks, and of leading them daily to the watering troughs.

Water was scarce in those regions, and the maidens, afraid of being prevented by the shepherds from watering their flocks, hastened to the watering troughs early before the other shepherds had made their appearance. Scarcely, however, had the daughters of Jethro filled the troughs, than the shepherds appeared, and unceremoniously drove away the feeble shepherdesses, watering their own flocks from the troughs the latter had filled with great trouble.

It was such a scene of rudeness and violence that Moses witnessed on the day he had reached the well outside Midian. Full of indignation, the former King of Ethiopia rose up and hastened to the protection of the maidens, whom the shepherds had thrown into the water, intending to kill them. Burning with righteous anger, Moses interfered, rebuking the shepherds for their rudeness and violence.

" In the name of Divine justice," he cried, " which is exercised even in the desert, and in the name of the Almighty who has sent me to deliver these innocent maidens, I swear unto you that I will not permit you to do them any harm."

The shepherds, both afraid and ashamed, drew back.

Moses thereupon dragged the daughters of Jethro out of the water, filled the troughs and gave first the herds of the maidens to drink, and then the flocks of the shepherds. When Moses let down the pitcher to draw the water and fill the troughs, the water leaped up and flowed in such abundance that one bucketful was sufficient to water the herds of Jethro and also of the other shepherds. It was the same well at which Jacob had once met Rachel, and which had been created in the twilight of the first Sabbath eve.[1]

Although reared in modesty, the daughters of Jethro did not hesitate to address the stranger and to thank him for his kind assistance. " Do not thank *me*," said Moses, " but thank that Egyptian whom I killed and on account of whom I had to flee from Egypt."

Great was the astonishment of Reuel, or Jethro, when he saw his daughters return so soon on that day, and when he heard their tale he bade them go and invite the stranger to their house. Zipporah, who had at once attracted the attention of Moses, and who, in her turn, had also fallen in love with the handsome stranger, hastened to do her father's bidding. Amazed at the handsome appearance and majestic bearing of the

---

[1] *Pirke de Rabbi Eliezer*, Ch. 40.

stranger, Reuel asked him whence he came. " My daughters tell me that thou art an Egyptian." Moses, without admitting that he was an Egyptian, but also without asserting that he was of the Hebrew race, related unto Reuel that he hailed from Egypt, and that he had been compelled to leave the country. " I have since been King of Ethiopia," he added, " but was compelled to abdicate."

Reuel began to consider the matter, and wondered why his guest had been forced to leave both Egypt and Ethiopia. " He may have been guilty," thought the ex-high-priest of Midian, " of an act of high treason, and if I give him shelter and protection, I may find myself in trouble and embroil myself with Pharaoh and with the men of Ethiopia who have wrested the kingdom from him. Besides, I may incur the further displeasure of my own countrymen, the men of Midian, who are already hostile unto me, if I venture to harbour this somewhat mysterious stranger. I will not deliver him unto the King of Egypt, but I will put him in prison." And thus Reuel bound Moses with chains and cast him into a dungeon.[1]

Soon Reuel, who was constantly thinking of reconciliation with his countrymen, forgot all about Moses, who would have perished in the pit had it not been for the love the gentle and fair Zipporah bore him. She had loved Moses from the very moment she had set eyes upon him, and could never forget his kindness to herself and to her sisters, when he saved them from the shepherds of Midian. She thought of ways and means how to provide the prisoner, not only with food and drink, but also with various dainties and to lighten his confinement. One day Zipporah came to her father and thus she spoke to him:

" Thou hast no wife, but seven daughters, and if we all go out to pasture and water thy flock there remains none at

---

[1] Jellinek, *Beth-Hamidrash*, Vol. II, pp. 1–11; *Sepher Hajashar*; see also Beer, *loc. cit.*, pp. 56–59; Lewner, *loc. cit.*, pp. 16–17.

home to look after thy house. If it were thy will to hearken
to my voice, then I would advise thee to send out my sisters
to tend the herds and I will remain at home and take care of
thy house. If not, then let me go abroad and tend the flock,
whilst my sisters remain at home and take care of thy house."

And Reuel replied: " Thou hast spoken well, my daughter,
and henceforth thy sisters shall go abroad and tend the herds,
whilst thou wilt remain in the house and take care of it."

And thus Zipporah remained at home, and could find many
an opportunity to provide Moses with food and drink and even
with all sorts of dainties. In return for which the prisoner,
who knew that she was his destined wife, instructed her in the
law of the Most High.

Thus seven years, and according to others ten years, had
passed. Reuel had long forgotten the existence of Moses
whom he had once cast into the dungeon. He had reconciled
himself with his countrymen, and had been restored to his
former rank and position.

He had grown prosperous, and princes and magnates came
to ask his daughters in marriage. It was especially the noble
and fair Zipporah who had many suitors for her hand. She
loved Moses in secret, but she dared not confess it to her
father, for fear that, remembering the existence of the stranger,
he would put him to death. Zipporah was therefore happy
when she heard on what condition her father had promised
to grant the hand of his daughter.

There was a tree in Jethro's garden, a staff he had once
planted there and which no one could pluck up or even touch.
The story of this staff runs as follows: It was a staff made of
sapphire which the Almighty had created in the twilight of
the first Sabbath eve.[1] When Adam was driven out of the
Garden of Eden, he carried this staff with him, as one of the
gifts he had received from the Creator. He handed it to Enoch,

---

[1] *Pirke de Rabbi Eliezer*, Ch. 40; *Abot di Rabbi Nathan*, ed. Schechter, p. 48a.

ZIPPORAH BRINGS SUCCOUR TO MOSES IN THE PIT

Facing page 254, Vol. II

who transmitted it to Noah, who again handed it to Shem. The staff reached Abraham, who transmitted it to his son Isaac. The latter gave it to Jacob, who brought it with him to Egypt and handed it to his son Joseph. When the Viceroy died, the Egyptians pillaged his house and took away this sapphire rod which they brought to Pharaoh. Reuel, who was one of the counsellors of Pharaoh, saw this rod and made up his mind to possess it. His desire was so great that he did not hesitate to steal it and carry it away when he left Egypt. He planted the rod in his garden, and no one could uproot it or even approach it.

Now Jethro, or Reuel, made it known all over the country of Midian that he who could pluck up this staff would take Zipporah to wife.

Thereupon the strong chiefs of Midian, the sons of Keni and all the mighty men of Ethiopia whom the fame of Zipporah's beauty had reached, and who were anxious to win her, came and tried to uproot the staff, but without avail.[1] Thus the staff remained in Jethro's garden, whilst his fair daughter was free from the importunities of her numerous suitors.

It was time, however, she thought, to liberate Moses from prison and perchance her father would give her to him to wife. One day therefore she approached Reuel and thus she spoke unto him:

" Many years ago thou didst cast into dungeon a stranger who hailed from the land of Egypt. Wilt thou not seek and inquire for him? He is crying and praying to his God, and there is a sin upon thee. Now wilt thou send forth and fetch him?" Thus spoke Zipporah, but Reuel replied:

" Whoever has heard that a man who has been without food or drink for so many years could still be alive?"

Zipporah, however, said that with God all things were possible.

[1] *Pirke de Rabbi Eliezer* Ch. 40; *Yalkut*, §§ 168 and 173.

" Hast thou not heard, my father, that the God of the Hebrews is great and powerful, and that at all times He works many wonders in favour of his people? He delivered Abraham the Hebrew from the furnace of the Chaldæans, and Isaac from the knife of his father. He protected Jacob when he wrestled with the angel at the brook of Jabbok, and He has done many wonders even for this man whom thou didst cast into prison, for He saved him from the river of Egypt and from the swords of Pharaoh and of the children of Cush. Could He not also have saved him from death by hunger and delivered him from the dungeon in which he lieth?"

Thus spoke Zipporah, and Reuel was at last persuaded and consented to go and see whether Moses was still alive. He was surprised to find Moses not only alive, but standing erect and praying to the Almighty. Immediately he set him free, cut his hair, gave him a change of garment, and set food before him.

Moses thereupon went out into Reuel's garden, which was at the back of the house, to pray to the Lord and to give thanks to Him for the many wonders He had done unto him. Then he lifted up his eyes and suddenly beheld the sapphire staff planted in the ex-high-priest's garden. Approaching this wonderful staff he saw that the Ineffable Name, the name of the Most High, was engraved upon it, and he stretched out his hand to take it. Moses uprooted the staff as easily as one lifts up a branch in a dense forest, and it became a rod in his hand. When Reuel came into the garden and saw the staff in Moses' hand, he was amazed, for none had hitherto been able to uproot or even to touch it.

" This man," said Jethro, " is called upon to be a great man and a prince in Israel." He immediately gave him his daughter Zipporah to wife, whose secret wish had thus been fulfilled.[1]

[1] *Sepher Hajashar*; Jellinek, *Beth-Hamidrash*, Vol. II, pp. 1–11; Gaster, *The Chronicles of Jerahmeel*, pp. 120–121; see also Grünbaum, *Neue Beiträge*, p. 163; Beer, *loc. cit.*, pp. 60–62.

The story of the marriage of Moses and Zipporah and of the rod of Moses is told somewhat differently in the *Midrash Vayosha*. It is Moses himself who relates the story to the children of Israel, after giving an account of his birth, of his upbringing, his escape from Egypt and sojourn in Ethiopia. When he arrived at the well of Midian and had saved the seven daughters of Reuel from the cruel shepherds and watered their flocks, he saw Zipporah and noticed her modest and pious demeanour. He then knew that she was different from all the others. He spoke to her and proposed marriage unto her. Zipporah, struck by the appearance of the handsome and majestic stranger, however, replied:

" Alas, noble stranger, I cannot be thy wife, for never wilt thou be able, in spite of thy eourage and thy strength, to carry out the condition imposed by my father and to stand the test by which he tests all the suitors for my hand. In his garden he has a tree, and he asks every suitor for my hand to uproot it, but none has as yet been able to do so. As soon as a would-be suitor approaches this tree and touches it, it devours him."

Moses asked the maiden whence her father had this wonderful tree, to which Zipporah replied that it was really the rod which the Lord had once created and given to Adam. Reuel, who had been one of the astrologers of Pharaoh, had seen the staff, stolen it and brought it to Midian. Upon this staff was engraved the Ineffable Name and also the ten plagues which the Lord was one day to bring upon Egypt. For many days and years the wonderful staff had remained in Reuel's house, when one day he took it into his hand, went out into his garden and there stuck it into the ground for a while. When he returned to fetch it, he found that his attempt to draw it out again failed. The staff had sprouted and was bringing forth blossoms. Thus the staff remained in Reuel's garden and he tested with it all those who came to marry one of his daughters. He insisted upon their pulling the staff out of the ground, but everyone fell a victim to the devouring tree.

All this Zipporah, in great distress, related unto Moses, for she would willingly have become then and there the affianced wife of Moses. The maidens thereupon went home, and Moses accompanied them. Their father, astonished at their speedy return from the well, asked them the cause. They replied that an Egyptian had delivered them from the rude and cruel shepherds, and had watered their flocks.

"I heard them describe me as an Egyptian," Moses is supposed to have said afterwards to the children of Israel; "I heard them calling me an Egyptian, and yet I did not step forward and loudly proclaim my Hebrew birth. God has punished me for this, and I am not permitted to enter the Holy Land." Because he had not protested when he was described as an Egyptian, he had to die outside of Canaan.

And when the daughters of Reuel informed their father that a kind Egyptian had saved them on that day, the ex-high-priest of Midian said unto them: "Go and call the man, who has done to you such a valuable service, to come into our house that he may eat bread at our table."

And when Moses had entered Reuel's home and partaken of food, he spoke to his host at once on the subject of Zipporah whom he wished to take to wife.

Reuel replied: "I will give her to thee, if thou wilt uproot the rod which is in my garden, and bring it to me."

Moses went out into the garden, found the sapphire rod, and, having easily pulled it out, brought it to Reuel. When the latter saw the rod in Moses' hand, he at once knew that he was that man, the great Prophet of whom it had been prophesied by the wise men of Egypt that he would one day arise and destroy the whole land of Egypt. His wrath was kindled against Moses and he seized him and cast him into a pit in his garden, where he expected he would find his death.

But Zipporah loved Moses and said unto herself: " How can I allow this just and perfect man to die such a death?" and she thought of a way how to save him. She therefore approached her father and thus spoke unto him. " Would it be thy will, my Father, to hearken unto my advice. Thou art a man who has no wife but seven daughters who are compelled to tend thy flocks. Now, if thou dost desire that my sisters preside over thy household, then I shall go with the herds, otherwise let my sisters go abroad with the herds and I will take care of the house."

And Reuel replied: " Thou hast spoken well, my daughter, and henceforth thou shalt remain at home and take care of my house and of all that there is therein."

And from that day Zipporah was able to provide Moses with food and drink and even with all sorts of dainties. Thus seven years had passed, and then Zipporah again spoke to her father: " Dost thou remember that once upon a time thou didst cast into the pit a stranger who came to our house and uprooted the staff in thy garden? Now thou didst commit a great sin, and would it were thy will to open the pit and see whether the man be still alive or dead. If he is dead after these many years, then throw his corpse away so that it does not rot in thy house. Should he, however, be still alive, then thou must know that he is a perfect saint."

And Reuel said unto Zipporah: " My daughter, thou hast spoken well, but dost thou remember the name of that man?"

" His name," replied Zipporah, " was Moses, the son of Amram."

Thereupon Reuel went out and uncovering the pit called aloud: " Moses! Moses, son of Amram!" and Moses replied: " Here am I." Thereupon Jethro drew him up, kissed him upon the head and thus he spoke: " Blessed be the Lord who hath guarded thee in the pit for seven years. I now acknowledge that He is the Lord who slayeth and reviveth, and I also acknowledge that thou art one of the perfect and just men. Through thy hand Egypt will one day be destroyed, and through thy hand the Lord will redeem Israel from Egypt and drown in the sea Pharaoh and his army."

Thus spoke Jethro and he gave Zipporah to Moses as wife.[1] Moses was now tending the flocks of his father-in-law Jethro, and very true and faithful was he in the discharge of his duties. One day, when pasturing his herd in the desert of Midian, an angel suddenly appeared to him in the disguise of a white wolf.

" Peace unto thee, O man of God," said the white wolf.

In amazement the future redeemer of Israel looked up and contemplated the speaking beast.

" Man of God," continued the white wolf, " I am hungry and no food has passed my mouth for many days. Give me one of thy lambs that I may appease my hunger and not die."

Having somewhat recovered from his first fright Moses said: " How is it that thou art able to speak with a human tongue? The beasts have not been endowed with speech by the Creator of the Universe!"

To which the white wolf replied: " Dost thou wonder that an animal speaketh? One day the Law will be given through thee, and thou wilt thyself relate the story of the golden calf which will open its mouth and speak, and the story of the speaking ass of Balaam. I wonder at thy asking me such a question. Hasten now to give me one of thy lambs that I may appease my hunger and then go my way to fulfil the will of my Maker."

Thus spoke the white wolf, but Moses replied: " I am only a hired labourer and have no right to dispose of the property of my master. The flocks belong to my father-in-law,

[1] *Midrash Vayosha* (Jellinek, *Beth-Hamidrash*, Vol. I, pp. 35–57); see also Wünsche, *Ex Oriente Lux*, Vol. II, p. 43; cf. Lewner, *loc. cit.*, pp. 21–22.

Jethro, and without his permission I cannot give thee even the smallest lamb, however great thy hunger. When the Patriarch Jacob tended the flocks of his father-in-law Laban, he served him faithfully and watched over his herds with such loving care that none was ever lost. He was devoured by heat during the day and suffered from cold during the night." (*Genesis*, 31, 40.)

The white wolf seemed to grow impatient. " Have I come here," he replied, " to listen to thy arguments? If thou dost refuse to give me one of the lambs wherewith I may appease my hunger, without first consulting thy father-in-law, then hasten and ask his permission."

" I cannot grant thy request," replied Moses, " for I am only a hired labourer and have no right to leave my work without the consent of my master. If I leave the herds, who will look after them and protect them from the wild beasts of the desert: lions, panthers, and wolves, dumb or speaking? There are many such beasts of prey around here besides thee."

But the wolf replied: " Fear not for thy flocks, I will look after them and protect them against any beasts of prey. As for myself, I swear unto thee by the living God that I will devour none of them. Should I be guilty of any robbery, thou mayest call me one belonging to the tenth generation which is more wicked than the generation of the flood, or that of the tower of Babel."

Thus spoke the white wolf, and Moses had compassion with him and hastened to find his father-in-law, to whom he related all that had occurred.

And Jethro said: " Give the hungry white wolf one of my best sheep, that he may appease his hunger."

In blithe spirits, Moses returned to announce the glad news to the waiting beast, whom he beheld from a distance patiently guarding the flock.

" Take one of the best lambs," said Moses, " and appease

thy hunger." But scarcely had he spoken these words, than
the white wolf suddenly disappeared.[1]

A similar story, wherein, however, the animal appealing to
the sense of pity of the future redeemer of Israel is a hawk, is
told in the *Tuti-Nameh*.

One day a dove suddenly came flying to Moses, imploring
his protection. " O prophet of God," cried the dove, " a fierce
enemy is pursuing me and would that it were thy will to give
me protection."

Touched by this pitiful appeal, Moses offered a refuge to
the homeless bird, taking it under his garment.

Suddenly the pursuing hawk appeared, and thus spoke unto
Moses: " O Moses, I am tormented by the gnawing pangs of
hunger, and in vain am I searching for food. Hast thou any
right to deprive me of my rightful prey and thus increase my
torments? Man of God, hand over unto me the dove thou hast
taken to thy bosom, and let me appease my hunger."

But Moses replied: " Is it food in general, any food, thou
seekest, or just this dove? If it is food thou art after, then I
will do my best to give thee satisfaction, but if it is this dove
thou wishest to devour, then I will not let the bird go. It is
under my protection, and under no condition will I betray its
trust."

Thus spoke Moses, and the hawk replied: " Man of God!
It is only food I am seeking, no matter whether it be this dove
or anything else that will appease my hunger." Thereupon the
future redeemer of Israel cut from his holy limbs a piece of
flesh, equivalent in weight to that of the dove, and gave it to
the hawk saying: " Here is thy nourishment."

" O prophet of God," said the hawk, " I am no hawk at
all but the angel Michael, and the dove thou hast so lovingly
taken care of is the angel Gabriel. We have only come to

---

[1] *Hagoren*, Vol. VIII, p. 21 (*Maasse al dor haassiri*); *Jewish Quarterly Review*, New Series,
Vol. II, pp. 339–364; see also Bin Gorion, *Der Born Juda's*, Vol. III, pp. 16–17.

test thee and to make manifest thy generosity, noble mind, and magnanimity." Thus speaking, both hawk and dove disappeared.[1]

Another time it happened that a kid had left the flock and escaped over valley and hill. It finally stopped at a mountain stream and drank to appease its thirst.

" Poor little kid," said Moses, " so it was thirst that made thee run so swiftly in search of a water course. Poor, tired little one, I knew it not when thou didst run away from me. And now thou must be weary and tired out from thy long run."

Thereupon Moses, the kind and loving shepherd, took the little kid, laid it upon his shoulders and carried it back to the flock.

And the Lord said: " Thou hast patience and forbearance with a little kid, and hast shown compassion with the flock belonging to a man. Thou shalt therefore pasture the sheep of God and be the shepherd of Israel, My flock." [2]

At the Well

Another legend of Moses runs as follows: He was in the habit of roaming about in the country, and, whilst feeding his flock, he gave free play to his meditation, for his mind was busy with great thoughts and with his impending mission to redeem Israel from bondage, to lead them from the brick-fields of Egypt to the land flowing with milk and honey. Moses preferred solitary places where, undisturbed, he could meditate over the ways of God and the laws of nature, and where the spirit of the Lord of the Universe often came over him. One day, the prophet had reached such a spot and sat down under a tree not far away from a well which he could overlook. He was ruminating and meditating in his usual manner, when

---

[1] *Tuti-Nameh*, German transl. by G. Rosen, 1858, Vol. II, pp. 32–33; see also Bin Gorion, *loc. cit.*, pp. 244–245.
[2] *Exodus Rabba*, section *Shemot*.

suddenly he saw a man approaching the well, drinking from it and then continuing his way. The traveller had not noticed that he had dropped a money-bag whilst drinking from the well. Soon afterwards another traveller appeared who likewise approached the well and slaked his thirst. He noticed the money-bag, picked it up and departed joyfully. Thereupon a third traveller appeared, quenched his thirst at the well and lay down to rest.

In the meantime, the first traveller had found out his loss and thought that he had no doubt dropped his money-bag at the well. He hurried back to the well where he found the resting man.

" Didst thou find a money-bag here, which I dropped whilst bending down to drink from the well?"

" I have seen no money-bag," replied the traveller, " I came here, quenched my thirst, had some food, and am now resting awhile before continuing my way, but never have I set eyes upon any money-bags."

" If thou hast been resting here for a little while," said the first traveller, " then thou must surely have found my money-bag which I lost here."

" My friend," replied the other, " I found *no* money, and thou must have lost thy bag somewhere else or perhaps didst not lose it at all."

" Thou art a thief," cried the first traveller in a rage, " and I command thee immediately to return my money."

Accused of theft, whilst knowing himself to be innocent, the third traveller waxed wroth and in angry tones repudiated the accusation of the stranger. From high words the two men soon came to blows, and a mighty quarrel ensued.

Moses, awaking from his meditations, hastened to the spot to pacify the men, to explain how matters stood and to exculpate the innocent man. But the prophet came too late. In his fury the man who had lost his money killed the third traveller whom he accused of theft, but realizing what he had done, he took to flight.

Compassion filled the heart of the future redeemer of Israel, and tormenting thoughts crowded his brain. Raising his hands to Heaven, he called in his agony to the Lord and entreated the Most High to explain unto him the mysterious workings of fate and why a benevolent God had permitted such unjust deeds to take place.

" Lord of the Universe," spoke Moses, " can it be Thy will to punish the innocent and let prosper the guilty? The man who hath stolen the money-bag is enjoying wealth which is not his, whilst the innocent man hath been slain. The owner of the money, too, hath not only lost his property, but his loss hath been the cause of his becoming a murderer. I fail to understand the ways of Providence and workings of Divine justice. O Almighty, reveal unto me Thy hidden ways that I may understand."

Thus prayed Moses in the agony of his soul, and a voice from Heaven replied: " Thou deemest My decrees unjust, and canst not understand My ways, but the human mind cannot always conceive the Divine measures and the mysterious workings of Providence. Know then, O Moses, that the man who lost the money-bag, though God-fearing and pious himself, had inherited the money from his father who had robbed it from the father of the man who found it now. The finder hath thus come into his own again, and regained his property. The man who was slain, although not guilty of theft, was only apparently an innocent man. In years gone by, he had slain the brother of the man who has killed him now. He was never punished because none had witnessed the bloody deed. The blood of the victim, crying for vengeance, hath now been avenged. Know then, O Moses, that I ordained it that the murderer should be put to death by the brother of the victim, whilst the son should find the money of which his father had once been robbed. My ways are inscrutable, and often the human mind wonders why the innocent suffer and the wicked prosper." [1]

This legend, which is of Jewish origin, is referred to in a somewhat different version in an article in *The Spectator*, where " a Jewish tradition " concerning Moses is related:

" That great Prophet, it is said, was called up by a voice from Heaven to the top of a mountain; where, in a conference with the Supreme Being, he was permitted to propose to Him some questions concerning His administration of the universe. In the midst of this Divine colloquy he was commanded to look down on the plain below. At the foot of the mountain there issued out a clear spring of water, at which a soldier alighted from his horse to drink. He was no sooner gone than a little boy came to the same place and, finding a purse of gold which the soldier had dropped, took it up and went away with it. Immediately after this came an infirm old man, weary with age and travelling, and having quenched his thirst, sat down to rest himself by the side of the spring. The soldier, missing his purse, returns to search for it, and demands it of the old man, who affirms he had not seen it, and appeals to Heaven in witness of his innocence. The soldier, not believing his protestations, kills him. Moses fell on his face with horror and amazement, when the Divine Voice thus prevented his expostulations:

" ' Be not surprised, Moses, nor ask why the Judge of the whole earth has suffered this thing to come to pass. The child is the occasion that the blood of the old man is spilt; but know that the old man whom thou sawest was the murderer of the child's father.' " [2]

This legend forms the subject of a graceful poem by Gellert

---

[1] *Megillath Esther*, in *Zeena Urena*, quoted by Grünbaum, in his *Judisch-Deutsche Chrestomathie*. Leipzig, 1882, pp. 215–218; see also *Jewish Quarterly Review*, *loc. cit.*, pp. 350–351; Bin Gorion, *loc. cit.*, pp. 23–25.

[2] *The Spectator*, No. 237.

entitled " Das Schicksal ". It has been pointed out [1] that the fable is of Oriental origin, and that it bears a striking resemblance to one written by the Persian poet Jami, contained in his *Subhat ul Abrar*. Jami's poem was translated into English and published in the *Journal of the Asiatic Society of Bengal*.[2] Whether Gellert derived his story from *The Spectator* or not is of secondary interest to us. What is more important is the fact that this Oriental legend has made its way into European literature, such as Gellert's " Das Schicksal " and Thomas Parnell's " Hermit ".

> The Maker justly claims that world He made,
> In this the right of Providence is laid;
> Its sacred majesty through all depends
> On using second means to work his ends:
> 'T is thus, withdrawn in state from human eye,
> The power exerts his attributes on high,
> Your actions uses, nor controls your will,
> And bids the doubting sons of men be still.
> What strange events can strike with more surprise,
> Than those which lately struck thy wondering eyes?
> Yet, taught by these, confess the Almighty just,
> And where you can't unriddle, learn to trust.
>
> *Thomas Parnell*, " The Hermit ".[3]

The legend is also found in *Thousand and One Nights* [4] and in the *Gesta Romanorum*,[5] and Thomas Parnell most probably based his poem upon the story in this Latin collection.[6]

---

[1] *Z.D.M.G.*, 1860.   [2] 1860, pp. 13–15.
[3] S. Johnson, *English Poets*, 1790, Vol. XXVII, p. 81.   [4] Lane, II, 577–578.
[5] *Gesta Romanorum*, ed. Oesterley, Berlin, 1872, Ch. 80 (72), p. 396; see also Ch. 127.
[6] See also Gaston Paris, " L'Ange et l'Ermite, étude sur une légende religieuse " in *La Poésie du Moyen Age*, Paris, 1885, pp. 151–187; cf., however, Vol. III of the present work, chapter on the Prophet Elijah.

DIVINE JUSTICE

One day spake Moses in his secret converse with God,
" Oh thou all-merciful Lord of the World,
Open a window of wisdom to my heart,
Show me thy justice under its guise of wrong."
God answered, " While the light of truth is not in thee,
Thou hast no power to behold the mystery."
Then Moses prayed, " O God, give me that light,
Leave me not exiled far away from truth's beams."
" Then take thou thy station near yonder fountain,
And watch there, as from ambush, the counsels of my power."
Thither went the prophet, and sat him down concealed,
He drew his foot beneath his garment, and waited what would be.
Lo from the road there came a horseman,
Who stopped like the prophet Khizr by the fountain.
He stripped off his clokes and plunged into the stream,
He bathed and came in haste from the water.
He put on his clothes and pursued his journey,
Wending his way to mansion and gardens;
But he left behind on the ground a purse of gold,
Filled fuller with lucre than a miser's heart.
And after him a stripling came by the road,
And his eye, as he passed, fell on the purse;
He glanced to right and to left, but none was in sight;
And he snatched it up and hastened to his home.
Then again the prophet looked, and lo! a blind old man
Who tottered to the fountain, leaning on his staff,
He stopped by its edge and performed his needful ablutions,
And pilgrim-like bound on him the sacred robe of prayer.
Suddenly came up he who had left the purse,
And left with it his wits and his senses too,
—Up he came, and, when he found not the purse he sought,
He hastened to make question of the blind old man.
The old man answered in rude speech to the questioner,
And in passion the horseman struck him with his sword and slew
    him.

When the prophet beheld this dreadful scene,
He cried, " Oh Thou whose throne is highest heaven,
It was one man who stole the purse of gold,
And another who bears the blow of the sword.
Why to that the purse and to this the wound?
This award, methinks, is wrong in the eye of reason or of law."
Then came the Divine Voice, " Oh thou censurer of my ways,
Square not these doings of mine with thy rule.
That young boy had once a father,
Who worked for hire and so gained his bread;
He wrought for that horseman and built him his house,
Long he wrought in that house for hire,
But ere he received his due, he fell down and died,
And in that purse was the hire which the youth carried away.
Again, that blind old man in his young days of sight.
Had spilt the blood of his murderer's father;
The son by the law of retaliation slays him to-day,
And gives him release from the price of blood in the day of retri-
bution.

> Jami, in *Subhat ul Abrar*, translated from the Persian by
> G. B. Cowell, in *Journal of the Asiatic Society of Bengal*,
> 1860, pp. 13–15).

CHAPTER XXI

The Divine Mission, or the Humble Shepherd

Heavy tasks are laid upon the Hebrews—Moses at Horeb—The burning bush—Moses remembers his duties—The voice of Amram—The modesty of Moses—Elohim, Zebaoth, and Adonai—The honour of the elders—Punishment for slander—Believers and sons of believers—Jethro's consent—Satan in the guise of a serpent—Zipporah and Eliezer—The meeting of the brothers—Aaron's reward—The anniversary of the King of Egypt—The royal palace—The lions gambolling like dogs—The amazement of the kings —The message of the sons of Amram—The Chronicles of Egypt—The names of the gods—The living among the dead—How old is your god? —The strength of the Lord—Balaam's advice—Brine to Spain and fish to Accho—Straw to Ephraim—Moses and the magicians—The miraculous rod —Pharaoh's terror—The sheep between the wolf and the shepherd—The cry of Moses—The faith of the Patriarchs—The ten plagues—The first Passover—The slaying of the first-born—Pharaoh in search of Moses—The pleading of Bithia—Children of Israel, you are your own masters—The march towards a new destiny.

In the meantime the children of Israel were sighing under their heavy yoke in Egypt, for the new King, instead of lightening their toil, had put new and heavier tasks upon their shoulders. The Lord now remembered His covenant and decided to hasten the hour of redemption.

Now one day, when he was guarding the flocks of his father-in-law Jethro and wandering through the desert, Moses came to Mount Horeb. Moses always used to lead his sheep to open places, so as to prevent them from pasturing in private property. It was thus that he came in his wanderings to Mount Horeb. Here a wonderful sight was offered to his gaze. Mount Horeb began to move at his approach, coming to meet him, and only stood still when Moses placed his foot on it. He further saw a blazing flame enveloping the upper part of a bush, but never consuming it.

Moses looked at the thorn bush and its low appearance, and he said to himself: " The thorn bush is like Israel, whose symbol it is, for like the bush Israel, as compared with other nations, is lowly indeed, being in exile."

And whilst such thoughts were crowding the brain of the Prophet, and his heart was aching for his people, lo! a blazing flame enveloped the upper part of the bush, but neither did it consume it nor did it prevent it from bearing blossoms.[1]

Moses approached the bush and he heard a voice saying: " Just as the fire hath not consumed the bush, so Israel will never be destroyed, for the fire which will threaten it will be extinguished, and suffering and oppression will never put an end to this nation."

Suddenly Moses remembered his duties and turned from the wonderful sight, little inclined to be interrupted in his work for which he received wages. The sight offered to his gaze became, however, more wonderful, so that it startled him completely, and he decided to investigate it more closely. It was then that the Lord spoke to him again.[2]

Not wishing to startle Moses, who was still unused to the appearance of God and to prophetic missions, the voice addressing him sounded like the voice of his father Amram.

It called: " Moses, Moses!"

" Here am I, my father," he said. But the voice replied:

" I am not thy father, I am the God of thy father, the God of Abraham, Isaac, and Jacob."

Great was the joy of the son to hear his father mentioned together with the Patriarchs, and even first, but he covered his

---

[1] *Exodus Rabba*, section *Shemot*.   [2] *Ibid.*

face before the Divine glory to which he was not yet accustomed.

" Who am I," said he, " to dare look at the Divine Glory?"

And the Lord said: " Because thou hast been so meek and modest, therefore wilt thou dwell forty days and forty nights on the mountain, and thy face will so shine that men will fear to look at thee."[1]

The Lord had appeared to Moses in the midst of a thorn bush also for another reason. The thorn bush is the symbol of sorrow and of distress, and it was fitting that He should convey His message there, because He saw how Israel dwelt in sorrow and distress, and He dwelt with them.[2]

" Come," said the Lord, " I will send thee unto Pharaoh to deliver the people of Israel."

But Moses replied: " Lord of the Universe! Who am I to go to Pharaoh, and how can I accomplish such a mission as to bring the children of Israel out of Egypt? How could I alone minister to the people? Where shall I take food and drink for them? How shall I be able to protect them against the heat of the scorching sun, against storm, hail, and rain? How shall I be able to provide for the pregnant women, the women in child-birth, the new-born babes, and the little children?"

But the Lord replied: " I will be with thee, and will provide the little ones with food."

" But how can I go to Pharaoh," said Moses, " who is mine enemy and seeketh to hurt me, lying in wait to take my life?"

But the Lord said: " There is no need for thee to fear any man, either Pharaoh or anyone else, for I shall be at thy side."

Moses still objected and declined his mission. " Lord of the Universe!" he said, " when I come to the children of

---

[1] *Exodus Rabba*, section *Shemot*; *Berachoth*, 8; cf. Lewner, *loc. cit.*, pp. 22–24.
[2] *Pirke de Rabbi Eliezer*, Ch. 40; *Midrash Tanchuma, Exodus*, § 14; *Yalkut, Psalms*, § 843; *Exodus Rabba*, section *Shemot*.

Israel, and they will ask me: 'Who sent thee?' what can I say? I shall not be able to tell them Thy name."

"Dost thou desire to know My name?" said the Lord. "Know then that My name is according to My acts. *Elohim* is My name when I judge My creatures; and I am the Lord of Hosts, *Zebaoth*, when I lend strength to men in battle, enabling them to rise and conquer their enemies; I am *Yahveh* or *Adonai*, when I have mercy upon My creatures; and I am *El Shaddai*, when I am the Lord of all strength and power. But unto the children of Israel thou wilt say: 'The Lord who hath saved you from evil in the past, will deliver you from Pharaoh, redeem you from the Egyptian bondage and also from the suffering which will be your lot in days to come.'"

"I know," said Moses, "that everything is possible to Thee, but how can I reveal unto Israel their future suffering, when they are still sighing under the yoke of Egypt?"

"Thou hast spoken well," replied the Lord, "and thou needst not tell them this, but say to them that I will redeem them from their present bondage[1] Assemble first the elders of Israel, for the honour of the elders of a people is great in Mine eyes, and they will listen unto thee. Pharaoh will be obdurate, but do not fear, for in the end he will let the people go, and they will not leave the country empty-handed."[2]

"But the Israelites will not believe me," again pleaded Moses.

"No," replied the Lord, "thou art mistaken, for the children of Israel are great believers, the sons of believers; they are the sons of Abraham who was a great believer, and they will believe thee too."

God then bade Moses cast his rod upon the ground, and it became a serpent, and then He bade him put his hand in his bosom, and it became leprous, as white as snow. This was to

---

[1] *Exodus Rabba*, section *Shemot*; cf. Lewner, *loc. cit.*, pp. 24–25.
[2] *Exodus Rabba*, ibid.; *Berachoth*, 10.

indicate to the Prophet that because he had slandered the children of Israel, accusing them of lack of faith, he deserved to be punished with leprosy, even as the serpent had once been punished for being slanderous.[1]

" Lord of the Universe!" once more pleaded Moses, " when Lot was made a captive, Thou didst send one of Thy angels to save him, whilst in the case of Hagar, Abraham's bond-woman, five angels came to rescue her. Do the children of Abraham deserve less? Why shouldst Thou not send Thy angels to redeem them, instead of sending me who am only a poor mortal? And even if it is Thy will to send a man who will be the redeemer of Israel, my brother Aaron is greater than myself, and more worthy to be chosen as Thy messenger."

" Thy brother Aaron will be thy companion," replied the Lord, " and he will never be jealous of the honour vouchsafed unto thee." [2]

Meek and humble though he was, Moses yielded at last to the command of the Most High, and accepted the great mission, still feeling in his heart that he was unworthy to undertake it. He now hastened to acquaint his father-in-law with his purpose, for he had promised never to leave Midian without the latter's permission. Jethro at first objected to Moses taking his wife and children with him.

" The suffering of those who are in Egypt is already great, and God is sending thee to redeem them; why then shouldst thou take more hither?"

Thus spoke Jethro, but Moses replied:

" Should my wife and sons remain in Midian and not hear the voice of God on Mount Sinai, when the Lord will come to give the Holy Law?" Jethro then gave his consent, and Moses, taking his wife and children with him, went forth on his return journey to Egypt.[3]

---

[1] *Exodus Rabba*, 3; cf. also *Pirke de Rabbi Eliezer*, Ch. 40.
[2] *Ibid.*   [3] *Exodus Rabba*, 4.

He mounted the ass which had once borne Abraham when he rode to Mount Moriah, there to sacrifice his son Isaac, and upon which the Messiah will one day ride when he appears at the end of days.[1]

His faith, however, and enthusiasm were not great at this moment. He was still afraid lest he would be scorned by the Israelites who would not believe in him and in his mission. For this lack of faith in the Lord, Moses was punished. On the road to Egypt, Satan appeared to him in the guise of a serpent and swallowed up his body down to his feet, but he was saved by his faithful wife Zipporah. She knew that this was a punishment because their second son had not yet been circumcised, Jethro having made it a condition that one half of the children should be Israelitish and the other Egyptian. Swiftly Zipporah took a sharp flint stone, circumcised their son Eliezer and touched the feet of her husband with the blood of circumcision. Immediately a heavenly voice called out: " Spew him out," and the serpent obeyed.[2]

On the very day on which Moses was travelling through the desert, accompanied by his wife and children, the voice of the Lord fell upon the ears of Aaron the Levite in distant Egypt. Aaron was walking along on the banks of the Nile, when the Lord appeared to him and bade him go out and meet his brother. He hastened to obey the will of the Lord, and the meeting of the brothers was a happy one. After embracing his brother, Aaron lifted up his eyes and saw Zipporah and her children.

" Who are these?" he asked.

" They are my wife and my sons," replied Moses.

At this Aaron was displeased, and advised his brother to send them back to Midian.

" Our sorrow is already great enough, on account of those

---

[1] *Pirke de Rabbi Eliezer*, Ch. 2.
[2] *Exodus Rabba*, 5; Jellinek, *Beth-Hamidrash*, Vol. I, pp. 35–37; *Nedarim*, 31b–32a; see also *Book of Jubilees*, XLVIII, 2.

who are in Egypt, why dost thou bring more to the land?"
Thus spoke Aaron who realized that the mission Moses was
engaged upon would be both long and perilous, and he wanted
him to be care-free and not bothered by the presence of wife
and children. Moses subsequently sent his wife and children
back to the house of his father-in-law where they remained till
the day when Israel was delivered from the hand of Pharaoh.[1]

And because Aaron had not been envious of the honour
and distinction vouchsafed unto Moses, his younger brother,
who had been elected to be the redeemer of Israel, the Lord
rewarded him afterwards by placing upon his breast the *Urim*
and *Thummim*, and raising him to the dignity of High-Priest.

Arrived in Egypt, the brothers immediately assembled the
elders of Israel and announced to them the glad tidings. With
the elders came the aged daughter of Asher, Serah, whom
Jacob had once blessed with life eternal. She knew the very
words which the redeemer coming to deliver Israel would use,
as the secret had been revealed unto her by her father. When
she heard the words Moses spoke, she knew at once that he
was indeed the redeemer sent by God.[2]

Moses and Aaron now invited all the elders of Israel to
accompany them to Pharaoh. The elders started out with the
leaders, but stealthily, on their way, they dropped off, one by
one, and two by two, so that when at last the sons of Aaron
reached the palace, they were alone.

And the Lord said: " Since ye have acted thus and abandoned my messengers, ye will be punished."

When the hour, therefore, came for Moses to receive the
Law on Mount Sinai, the elders of Israel were not permitted
to accompany him, and to ascend the holy mountain, for they
were told to tarry at the foot of the mountain and to wait until
Moses returned.[3]

---

[1] *Mekhilta Yitro*, ed. Venice, p. 22a; *Midrash Agadah*, ed. Buber, Vol. I, p. 150; see
also *Exodus Rabba*, 4, where Jethro raises the same objection.   [2] *Exodus Rabba*, 5.
[3] *Ibid.*, and *Midrash Tanchuma*, ed. Buber, *Exodus*, p. 13; cf. Lewner, *loc. cit.*, pp. 28–29.

The day on which Moses and Aaron first appeared in the presence of Pharaoh happened to be the anniversary of the King. All the kings of the earth came on this occasion to do homage to Pharaoh and to bring him crowns, for he was the ruler of the whole world. Now the servants of the King came and announced that two old men were standing outside asking to be admitted.[1] The palace of Pharaoh had 400 doors, 100 on each side, and each door was guarded by 60,000 valiant soldiers. But Moses and Aaron penetrated into the palace, led by the angel Gabriel, who brought them in, unobserved by the guards. When the two leaders of Israel explained to Pharaoh their Divine mission, he not only drove them out of his presence, but was furious against the guards who had admitted them. They were severely punished, some slain, and others scourged. New guards were put in their place, receiving the instruction not to admit the two old men. The next morning Moses and Aaron were once more in the presence of Pharaoh, and none of the new guards could explain how they had been able to effect their entrance.[2]

Another version of the appearance of Moses and Aaron before Pharaoh runs as follows: At the gate of the royal palace there were stationed two lions, and no one durst approach the door, for fear of being torn to pieces. Only when the magicians came and led the beasts away, could a visitor penetrate into the palace.

When the keepers heard that Moses and Aaron were coming, they let the beasts loose, as they had been advised by Balaam and the other magicians of Egypt, so that the lions might devour the two brothers. But when the sons of Amram approached the gate, Moses raised his rod, and the lions joyously bounded towards him and his brother, gambolling round them like dogs round their masters, and followed them wherever they went.[3] When the brothers came into the presence of

---

[1] *Yalkut, Exodus,* § 181; *Exodus Rabba,* 5.   [2] *Sepher Hajashar.*
[3] Jellinek, *Beth-Hamidrash,* Vol. II, pp. 1-11.

Pharaoh, the kings and magnates and sacred scribes trembled exceedingly and started up in awe. Moses and Aaron resembled the ministering angels, their stature was like that of the cedars of Lebanon, the pupils of their eyes were like the spheres of the morning star, their beards were like palm branches, and the radiance of their countenances was like the splendour of the sun. In his hand Moses held the wonderful sapphire rod, and the speech of the sons of Amram was like fiery flame.

Great was the awe of all present, and the kings took off their crowns and prostrated themselves before Moses and Aaron. Pharaoh sat and waited for the two to speak. " Perchance they have brought me gifts or a crown," thought he. " Who are you," he queried, " and what is your request?"

" We are the messengers of the Most High; the God of the Hebrews hath met us and He requests thee to let His people go a three-days' journey into the wilderness to sacrifice unto Him."

When Pharaoh heard these words, he waxed wroth and said: " Who is your God that I should listen unto Him? Hath He sent me a crown or a present? Ye have only come to me with words! I know not your God, and I will not grant His request."

Thereupon Pharaoh ordered the chronicles to be fetched from the royal archives so as to find out whether the name of the God of the Hebrews was recorded among the names of the gods of other nations. And the scribe read unto him: " The God of Moab, the God of Ammon, the God of Zidon," but he could not find the God of the Hebrews recorded in the chronicles of Egypt. He could not find the name of the Lord, of the God of the Hebrews, among the other gods recorded in the book of chronicles, for he was seeking for the living among the dead, the Eternal among the perishable.

But Pharaoh said:

" I do not find the name of your God in my books. Tell

me, is He young or old? How old is He? How many cities hath
He captured? How many countries hath He made subject to
Himself? How many nations hath He subdued? How long is
it since He ascended His throne?"

And Moses and Aaron replied: " The strength and power
of our Lord fill the whole world. He was before the world was
created, and He will be till the end of days. He created thee
and breathed into thee the spirit of life."

" And what is His occupation?" asked Pharaoh, whereto
Moses and Aaron replied:

" He stretched out the heavens and laid the foundations
of the earth; His voice heweth out flames of fire; He uproots
mountains and breaks rocks. His bow is fire, and His arrows
are flames. His spear is a torch, His shield a cloud, and His
sword a lightning flash. He created the hills and the mountains
and covered the earth with grass. He sends down dew and
rain upon earth, causes plants to grow, and sustains life. He
forms the embryo in the womb of the mother and sends it
forth as a living being."

" Ye lie," cried Pharaoh, " when ye say that your God
created me, for I am the master of the Universe and I created
myself, and also the River Nile." [1]

Then Pharaoh said unto his wise men: " Have ye ever
heard the name of the God of these people?"

And the wise men of Egypt replied: "We have heard of Him
that He is the son of wise men and the son of ancient kings."

And the King of Egypt said unto Moses: " I know not
your God, and I will not send away your people." [2]

Thereupon Pharaoh sent for the magicians of Egypt and
related unto them what had occurred, and how Moses and
Aaron had penetrated into the palace in spite of the lions,
and what request they had made.

[1] *Exodus Rabba*, 5; *Yalkut*, § 181; *Midrash Tanchuma*. ed. Buber, *Exodus*, p. 19; *Midrash Agadah*, ed. Buber, Vol. I, p. 133; *Sepher Hajashar*; cf. Lewner, *loc. cit.*, pp. 29–31.
[2] *Exodus Rabba*, 5; *Yalkut*, § 181.

"How could these men," asked Balaam, "enter the palace without being torn by the lions?"

"The beasts," replied the King, "did do them no harm, but fawned upon them and gambolled like so many dogs joyously running to meet their masters."

"Then they must be magicians like myself and the other wizards of Egypt," said Balaam, "and, if it please the King, let these men be fetched again, and we will test their powers."

Moses and Aaron were summoned before the King, now surrounded by Balaam and the other magicians of Egypt. In his hand Moses carried the rod of God.

Pharaoh then said unto them: "Who will believe ye, that ye are sent by the God of the Hebrews? Show us a miracle."

Then Aaron cast his rod and it became a serpent.

Pharaoh then called his magicians and they did likewise. Then the King laughed aloud and mocked them.

"Verily," he said, "this is but little proof of the greatness and power of your God. This is but poor magic for Egypt, a country steeped in the art of magic. Our little children can do this."

He then ordered little children to come before him, and also his own wife came, and they all cast their rods which turned to serpents.

"It is customary," continued the King, "to bring to a place merchandise of which it is in need, but you seem to bring brine to Spain and fish to Accho."

Then Jannes and Jambres, the two magicians, mocked Moses and Aaron and said: "Are you carrying straw to Ephraim?"

But Moses replied: "One carries vegetables to a place of many vegetables."[1]

Thereupon the serpent of Aaron swallowed up all the other

---

[1] *Exodus Rabba*, 9; Jellinek, *loc. cit.*, Vol. II, pp. 1–11; *Sepher Hajashar*; cf. Lewner, *loc. cit.*, pp. 33–34; Bialik, *Sepher Haagadah*, Vol. I, pp. 55–57.

serpents. This miracle, too, produced but a small impression upon the Egyptians.

" It is only natural," said Balaam, " that a living thing should devour another living thing, and one serpent swallow other serpents. If thou wishest us to admit that the spirit of God is in thee, then cast thy rod upon the ground, and whilst it is still wood, let it swallow up our rods of wood."

Aaron did as he had been bidden, and his rod of wood swallowed up the wooden rods of the Egyptians. The bulk of the rod, however, remained as before.[1]

When Pharaoh saw this miracle, terror seized him, and he was afraid lest Aaron's rod would swallow him up too. But in spite of his fear, he remained obdurate.[2] The result of the request made by Moses and Aaron to Pharaoh was that he made the lot of Israel even heavier, and that their suffering increased. This extreme suffering of his people distressed the Prophet greatly, and his heart grew heavy. It was then that he took his wife and children back to Midian, so as to be free to devote all his time to the work of redeeming his people. On his return to Egypt, he still found that his people were sighing under a reign of terror, and his spirit almost rebelled. His people were like a sheep that had been carried away by a wolf. The shepherd rushed after the wolf to snatch the sheep and save it from the jaws of the beast of prey; he pulled it one way, whilst the wolf pulled it the other way, and thus the poor sheep was torn to pieces. Such was the position of Israel between Moses and Pharaoh, and two of the Israelitish officers, Dathan and Abiram, did not hesitate to tell Moses so, when he returned to Egypt from Midian.[3] Moses' spirit almost rebelled, and he uttered words which were a challenge to the Most High.

" Lord of the Universe," he cried, " why is the nation of Israel suffering more than all the other nations in the world?

[1] Jellinek, loc. cit.
[2] Exodus Rabba, 9; Midrash Agadah, ed. Buber, p. 136; cf. Lewner, loc. cit., pp. 33–34.
[3] Exodus Rabba, 5.

Is it really because Abraham had once asked for a sign and said: 'Whereby shall I know that I shall inherit the land?' and had thus been guilty of a lack of faith? Is it for this that Thou hast decreed that his seed shall be a stranger in a land which is not theirs and be in bondage there? Then, why hast Thou compassion with the children of Esau and of Ishmael, who are also of the seed of Abraham? Why are *they* not in bondage, but are living peacefully in their own lands and are not aliens and slaves among strangers? And now the position of Israel is desperate, and its sufferings are cruel to the extreme, 'for living children are immured in the walls of the buildings'."

Thus cried Moses, in the agony of his soul, and at that moment the angel of Justice approached and said: " Lord of the Universe! for such audacious words Moses deserves to be punished."

But the Lord forgave Moses, for He knew that only out of his great love for his people and his compassion with the sufferers had he uttered such words.[1]

The Lord nevertheless rebuked Moses and said: " Alas for the departed and who no longer are here! Many a time did I appear and manifest myself to Abraham, Isaac, and Jacob, under my name of *El Shaddai*, but never did they venture to question My acts, or ask for My name.

" I spake unto Abraham: ' Walk throughout this land, for unto thee will I give it ', but when the time came for him to bury his wife Sarah, he found no resting place for her until he had bought and paid for it four hundred silver shekels. And yet he never questioned My words or promise.

" I said unto Isaac: ' Dwell in this land, and I will be with thee and bless thee'. When his herdsmen required water they found none but had to strive for it. And yet he did not question My words, nor did he find fault with me.

" I spake unto Jacob: ' The land whereon thou liest, to

---

[1] *Exodus Rabba*, 5–6.

thee will I give it ', but when he looked for a piece of ground where to pitch his tent, he found none and had to buy it for a hundred pieces of silver. And yet he never questioned My acts nor did he find fault with Me. None of them ever asked to know My name. Thou alone didst at first ask to know My name, and now thou sayest: ' Thou hast not saved Israel '. Well, now thou shalt see what I will do unto Pharaoh. Thou wilt witness the war against Pharaoh and his punishment, but thou wilt not be permitted to witness and be present at the war of the thirty-one kings of Canaan."[1]

Ten plagues did the Lord bring over the land of Egypt, but Pharaoh remained obdurate until the Lord slew the first-born. It was midnight, when Pharaoh awoke from his sleep and heard the commotion and tumult. Cries and wailing filled the air, and pale and haggard his servants came to inform the King of the calamity that had befallen the country.

Pharaoh arose, and, accompanied by his daughter Bithia and his servants, went forth to seek Moses and Aaron. He did not expect Moses to come again to him, for he knew that the latter had never uttered an untruth, and had he not said: " I will see thy face again no more "? With great difficulty did Pharaoh find the abode of the son of Amram, the leader of the Israelites who was to deliver them from bondage, for neither in palace nor in mansion did the son of Amram, the redeemer of Israel, dwell, but humbly among his people. And when Pharaoh at last discovered the dwelling place of Moses, he knocked at the door and called aloud: " Moses, Moses, my friend, pray to the Lord on our behalf."

Moses and Aaron were at that moment celebrating the first Passover, and when they heard the voice of Pharaoh, Moses asked: " Who art thou and what is thy name?"

" I am Pharaoh," replied the King, " Pharaoh who stands here in humiliation."

[1] *Sanhedrin*, 111a.

"Why dost thou come thyself?" again asked Moses. "It is not the custom of kings to come to the doors of common people."

"I entreat thee, my lord," said Pharaoh, "come and pray for us, intercede on our behalf, for the whole population of Egypt will soon be dead."

"I cannot leave the house," said Moses, "for the Lord hath commanded us not to go out until the morning."

"Then step up to the window, and speak to me," pleaded Pharaoh." [1]

Moses stepped up to the window, and saw Pharaoh and his daughter Bithia who began to reproach him for his ingratitude.

"Why hast thou brought this evil upon us?" she cried. "I have brought thee up and been kind to thee and saved thy life many a time!" Thus cried Bithia, whereto Moses replied:

"Ten plagues did the Lord bring upon Egypt; hath any of these affected thee? Thou hast been spared, because the Lord remembered thy great merit and thy good deeds."

Bithia acknowledged that no evil had accrued to her personally, but she could witness no longer the great calamity that had befallen the country and the plight her people were in.

"I warned thy father," said Moses, "but he would not hearken unto my words." [2]

Thereupon Pharaoh stepped nearer and said: "Thou didst say yesterday that all the first-born in the land of Egypt shall die, but now nine-tenths of the people are already dead."

And Moses said: "Thou art a first-born thyself, but thou wilt be spared and not die, and in spite of all that has happened, I will teach thee something and thou wilt learn. Raise thy voice and shout aloud: 'Children of Israel! Ye are henceforth your own masters, arise and depart from among my people.

---

[1] Jellinek, *Beth-Hamidrash*, Vol. I, pp. 35–57.
[2] *Sepher Hajashar; Midrash Shokher Tob, Ps.*, 68.

Hitherto ye were the slaves of Pharaoh, but now ye are in the power of the Eternal. Go and serve the Lord, your God!' "

Pharaoh obeyed, and, raising his voice, repeated three times the words Moses had dictated to him. And the Lord caused the voice of Pharaoh to be heard all over the land of Egypt.[1] The people heard and knew that the hour of redemption was at hand. Then Pharaoh insisted upon the Israelites leaving at once, in the darkness of the night, but Moses replied:

" Are we thieves or burglars that we should sneak away under cover of darkness? The Lord hath commanded us not to leave our houses until the morning, and we will depart from the country, holding our heads high, and before the whole of Egypt.[2] But why dost thou so insist upon our leaving at once?" he asked.

" Because I am a first-born myself," replied Pharaoh, " and I fear lest I, too, will die."

" I told thee already," said Moses, " that thou needst not fear for thy life, for thou art destined for greater things. Thou wilt live to manifest to the greatness of God." [3]

And thus the slaves, the labourers in the brickfields of Egypt, left the country, redeemed from bondage, and began their long march towards their new destiny.

[1] Jellinek, *loc. cit.*

[2] *Midrash Tanchuma*, ed. Buber, p. 52; *Midrash Agadah*, ed. Buber, p. 142, cf. Bialik *loc. cit.*, p. 61.

[3] Jellinek, *loc. cit.*; cf. also Lewner, *loc. cit.*, pp. 40–42.

CHAPTER XXII

The Redemption, or the Passage through the Red Sea

Uzza, the tutelary angel of Egypt—His contention with Michael—Michael's reply—The Lord espouses the cause of Israel—The situation of the people—The four parties—The prayer of Moses—Moses and the disobedient sea—The tribes of Benjamin and Judah enter the cleft sea—Their reward—Gabriel and the turbulent waters—The twelve channels—Food out of the water-walls—The pillar of cloud and the pillar of fire—Uzza pleads for the Egyptians—The heavenly judges—Uzza and Gabriel—The brick wherein a Hebrew child had been immured—The Lord upon His Throne of Justice—Pharaoh in the waves of the sea—Gabriel tortures him for fifty days—Pharaoh as King of Nineveh—Pharaoh at the gates of hell—The fear of the Hebrews—The Egyptians floating on the surface of the waters—The quarrel between the sea and the earth—The Israelites intone a song of praise—The angels are commanded to wait—The precedence of the women of Israel—The wealth of the Egyptians.

When the Israelites had left Egypt, Uzza, the tutelary angel of the Egyptians, appeared before the Lord and thus he spoke: " Thou didst decree and foretell unto Abraham that his descendants, the people of Israel, shall be held in bondage for a period of four hundred years. Now my people, the Egyptians, have had dominion over the nation of Israel only for eighty-six years. The Israelites are therefore still bound to serve the Egyptians for another three hundred and fourteen years."

Thus spake Uzza, the tutelary angel of the Egyptians, and the Lord called unto Michael, the tutelary angel of Israel, and said unto him: " Contend with Uzza, answer his arguments, and save Israel from his hands."

Michael replied: " Israel has never sinned, either to thee

286

or to thy nation, and has been condemned to serve the Egyptians only because Abraham had once uttered the words: ' Whereby shall I know that my children shall inherit the land?' On account of the Patriarch's lack of faith, the duty of serving thy nation was laid upon my people. But the Lord only said: ' Thy seed shall be strangers in a country which is not their own.' And they have indeed been strangers in Egypt ever since the date of Isaac's birth, and the period of four hundred years has now elapsed." Thus spoke Michael in defence of Israel.

When Uzza heard these words, he found no answer and was silent.[1]

In the *Midrash Vayosha* a somewhat different version is given: Uzza said that he had a suit with the nation of Israel, and if it seemed well to the Lord, let Him summon Michael to contend with him. Michael knew not how to contradict the words of the tutelary angel of Egypt, and the Lord Himself pleaded and espoused the cause of Israel, bringing Uzza to silence.[2]

When the Israelites saw the mighty hosts of Pharaoh and the detachments of the Egyptian army approaching, they were greatly afraid. Great terror seized them, and they said unto Moses: " What have we done? Now Pharaoh will wreak terrible vengeance upon us for the death of the first-born. If we march into the desert, we shall be torn by wild beasts; if we advance into the sea, we shall be drowned; and if we return to Egypt, our sufferings will now be greater than ever."

Desperate indeed was the situation of the people. The sea was in front of them, the desert, full of wild beasts of prey, to the right and to the left, and the advancing army of Egypt behind them. They were contending among themselves what it would be best to do and were divided into four opinions.

One party, the tribes of Reuben, Simeon, and Isachar, said:

---

[1] *Midrash Abkhir*, quoted in *Yalkut*, § 241.
[2] Jellinek, *Beth-Hamidrash*, Vol. I, pp. 35–57.

" It is better to be drowned in the sea than return and fall into
the hands of the Egyptians, our implacable enemies and oppressors, who will now deal with us mercilessly." Another party,
the tribes of Zebulun, Benjamin, and Naphtali, were in favour
of returning to Egypt and trusting in the Lord. A third set,
the tribes of Judah and Joseph, advised an open battle with
the Egyptians; whilst the fourth party, the tribes of Dan, Gad,
and Asher, said unto Moses: " Let us shout and raise a great
clamour and noise and thus intimidate the Egyptians and
frighten them."

But Moses silenced all the parties.

" Ye will see the Salvation of the Lord to-day," he said,
" but the Egyptians ye will see to-day for the last time and
never again. As for fighting, the Lord will fight for ye, whilst
ye yourselves shall hold your peace, pray to the Lord and
glorify Him."

And the Israelites remembered the words of Jacob, when
he blest his sons: " It is not for Israel to fight and use weapons
of war. Prayers are its swords, and supplications its bows."

Then the people uttered a loud prayer to God, and cried:
" Lord of the Universe! Help us!" And the Lord hearkened
unto their prayers. Moses, too, cried to the Lord and prayed:
" Lord of the Universe! Succour the people whom Thou hast
led out of Egypt and let them not fall into the hands of their
pursuers."

But the Lord replied: " Do not pray now, but command
the people to advance towards the sea."

Moses was amazed: " How can they pass the sea?" he cried.
" They will be drowned."

" Thou hast little faith," replied the Lord. " Have I not
once commanded the waters to gather in one place, and the
dry land to appear, and all for one man, Adam? Should I
not do the same for the sake of this multitude, the seed of
Abraham, Isaac, and Jacob?"

At the command of God, Moses lifted up his rod and stretched his hand over the sea, commanding it to divide. But the sea asked: " Who art thou that hast come to cleave my waters?"

" I am the messenger of God," replied Moses, " and I command thee to do my bidding."

Still the waters refused to obey and divide.

Moses lifted up his rod and said: " Look at the rod in my hand, the rod given to me by the Almighty."

The sea, however, still continued to be perverse and refused to obey.

Thereupon the strength of the Lord appeared at the right hand of Moses, and immediately terror seized the sea and it began to skip and flee.

" For hours," said Moses, " have I been bidding thee to divide, but thou didst not hearken to my command, and now thou art suddenly running away."

" I am not fleeing before thee, son of Amram," replied the sea, " but before God, the Lord of the Universe, the Master of all created things." [1]

Israel now approached the cleft sea and stood before it. When the people saw the black mud at the bottom of the sea, they hesitated to enter it.

The men of the tribe of Reuben said: " In Egypt we used to sink in mud, and now Moses has brought us here to enter the sea and to sink again in black mud."

The tribe of Simeon, too, refused to enter the sea, and none of the other tribes showed any readiness to venture upon the muddy soil.

But the tribe of Benjamin sprang into the sea, followed by the tribe of Judah, and all the other tribes followed their example.

---

[1] *Exodus Rabba*, 21; *Sepher Hajashar*; *Mekhilta*, ed. Venice, p. 12*b*; quoted in *Yalkut* § 234.

And the Lord said: " As the tribes of Benjamin and Judah have shown their trust in Me, therefore shall they be rewarded. In the allotment of Benjamin, the Temple will once stand, and from Judah will issue kings who will rule over Israel."[1]

Another version runs as follows: When Moses commanded his people to advance, they approached the sea, but suddenly fear seized them, and they turned backwards, afraid lest the waters would swallow them up. But the tribe of Judah sanctified the Lord and entered the waters first, led by Nachshon, the son of Judah, and all Israel followed them.[2]

In the meantime the Egyptians approached and saw Moses, his rod in his hand, and the Israelites passing the cleft sea.

Although the waters had divided at the command of God, they were still rather turbulent and ready to sweep over Israel and to drown the nation, but Gabriel preceded the tribes and held back the waters. Turning to the wall of water on the left, the angel said: " Do not touch Israel, and beware of attempting to destroy them, for in times to come, they will wind the phylacteries about their left hand." He then turned to the wall of water on the right and said: " Beware of touching Israel who are going to receive the law which will be given unto them by the right hand of the Holy Lord."

And the waters obeyed and kept back.

But Sammael, who is Satan, was busy raising accusations against Israel. He appeared before the Lord, and said: " Lord and Judge of the Universe! the people of Israel have worshipped idols in Egypt "; but the Lord replied:

" If they have done so, they did it involuntarily and because heavy tasks had been laid upon their necks, and I have forgiven them."[3]

---

[1] *Exodus Rabba*, 27; *Mekhilta, ibid.*; quoted in *Yalkut*, § 234; Jellinek, *loc. cit.*, Vol. I, pp. 35–57; cf. Lewner, *loc. cit.*, pp. 47–48.
[2] *Pirke de Rabbi Eliezer*, Ch. 42; see also *Sotah*, 36b–37a; *Midrash Shokher Tob, Ps.*, 76, 1.
[3] *Midrash Abhkir*; *Exodus Rabba*, 21; cf. Lewner, *loc. cit.*, pp. 48–49.

GABRIEL PROTECTS THE TRIBES DURING THEIR PASSAGE
THROUGH THE RED SEA

Facing page 290, Vol II.

Many miracles were wrought for Israel during their passage through the Red Sea. The waters were congealed and made into twelve channels or valleys, one for each of the tribes who walked along them. There were walls of water between the different paths, but the water was clear and transparent as glass, so that each tribe could see the others. Whatever their hearts desired, the Israelites found in the middle of the sea. There was sweet water to slake their thirst, and delicious food grew on the water walls. The Hebrew women were following their husbands, carrying their children in their arms, and when a child cried, the mother had only to stretch out her hand and pluck an apple, a pomegranate, or any other fruit to quiet the crying babe.[1]

The Egyptians, seeing the Israelites passing through the cleft sea, prepared to follow them, but suddenly turned back, afraid lest the waters would swallow them up. Thereupon an angel of the Lord appeared before them in the shape of a man riding on a mare, and the horse on which Pharaoh rode neighed, ran and entered the sea, and the Egyptians immediately followed their king.[2]

The Lord then fought against the pursuing Egyptians with a pillar of fire and a pillar of cloud. The pillar of cloud turned the soil and clay into mire, whilst the pillar of fire heated this mire so that the hoofs of Pharaoh's horses dropped off, and the wheels of his chariots fell off and were burnt to ashes.

And when Uzza, the tutelary angel of the Egyptians, saw the great distress his nation was in, and how his people were on the point of being drowned in the sea, he came before the Lord, ready to defend the Egyptians and to plead their cause.

" Lord of the Universe," he pleaded, " Thou art called up-

---

[1] *Exodus Rabba*, 21; *Pirke de Rabbi Eliezer*, Ch. 42; *Yalkut* to 2 *Samuel*, 20, § 152; cf. also Grünbaum, *Neue Beiträge*, p. 167, and see Friedlaender's edition of *Pirke de Rabbi Eliezer*, p. 331, note 6.

[2] *Pirke de Rabbi Eliezer*, Ch. 42; *Abot di Rabbi Nathan*, ed. Schechter, Ch. 27, p. 42a; see also Jellinek, *loc. cit.*, Vol. I, pp. 35–57; Gaster, *The Chronicles of Jerahmeel*, p. 160 (LIV, 9); Grünbaum, *Neue Beiträge zur semitischen Sagenkunde*, p. 166.

right and just in Thy judgment; there is no wrong before Thee, no bribery, and no respect for persons. Why then dost Thou judge my children to-day not according to their actions, for they do not deserve the punishment of drowning? Have my children drowned any of Thine? Have they massacred or slaughtered them? All that the Egyptians did was merely to impose slavery upon the children of Israel, and the latter have received their wages for this work, for they carried away with them the silver and golden vessels of the Egyptians."

Thus pleaded Uzza, and the Lord bade all the heavenly judges and members of the celestial court assemble in His presence. " Judge," said the Lord, " between me and the angel Uzza, the tutelary angel of the Egyptians, who hath come to plead the cause of his nation. There was a famine in Egypt in days gone by, and I sent Joseph to the country. He came and saved the people from death by hunger and ruled over them; and all the Egyptians swore allegiance to Joseph and were his slaves. Now when my children came down to Egypt, the Egyptians soon forgot their benefactor Joseph and laid heavy tasks upon his kith and kin, condemning them to such hard labour that in their agony they cried unto Me, and their prayers have ascended to Heaven. I heard their bitter groans, and I sent my faithful servants, Moses and Aaron, who asked Pharaoh, in My name, to let the people of Israel go. He refused to do so, but was compelled to let them go, when I sent ten plagues upon him. And now he is pursuing my children, ready to destroy them." Thus spake the Lord, and the members of the celestial court replied unanimously: " Just is the Lord in all His ways, and the Egyptians deserve to perish in the sea."

But Uzza still continued to plead the cause of the Egyptian: " I know and admit," he said, " that my nation hath deserved heavy punishment, but Thou, Lord of the Universe, art merciful and full of pity for Thy creatures; may it be Thy

will to deal with the Egyptians according to Thy mercy."
Thus pleaded Uzza, the tutelary angel of Egypt, and the
Lord was almost on the point of letting mercy prevail.

But Michael spread his wings and swiftly flew to Egypt
whence he fetched a brick wherein a Hebrew child had been
immured. He held up this brick and thus he spoke: " Lord
of the Universe! Wilt Thou have mercy upon this nation which
has been cruel, torturing and massacring the innocents?"

Uzza saw the incriminating brick in Michael's hands,
heard his words, and he was silent.

Thereupon the angel Shaftiel came up and thus he spoke:
" Lord of the Universe! Wilt Thou have compassion upon
such a nation?"

The Lord then seated Himself upon the throne of judgment
and allowed justice to have its course, and it was decreed that
the Egyptians should receive their well-deserved punishment.
The waters surged upon the army of Pharaoh, the sea began
to seethe, black clouds gathered under the sky, the stars were
darkened, and the Egyptians began to sink.[1] They all perished,
with the exception of Pharaoh.

Pharaoh was being tossed about in the waves of the sea,
when he heard the children of Israel raise their voices to praise
the Lord, rendering thanks to Him for His great wonders. " I
believe in Thee, O God," he cried. " Thou art righteous, and
I and my people are sinners. I acknowledge that there is no
God beside Thee in all the world."

Gabriel immediately descended, laid an iron chain upon
Pharaoh's neck, and thus he spoke unto him: " Thou art a
sinner! Yesterday only thou didst deny the Lord, and didst
say: ' Who is the Lord that I should hearken unto Him?'
But to-day, tossed about on the waves of the sea, thou art ready
to repent!" Thereupon the angel let Pharaoh drop into the

---

[1] *Exodus Rabba*, 22–23; *Midrash Abhkir*; quoted in *Yalkut*, § 241; cf. *Pirke de Rabbi Eliezer*, Ch. 43: *Targum Pseudo-Jonathan* to *Exodus*, 24, 10; Jellinek, *loc. cit.*, Vol. I, pp. 35–57; see also Bialik, *loc. cit.*, pp. 63–64, and Lewner, *loc. cit.*, pp. 49–51.

depth of the sea where he kept him securely, torturing him for fifty days. At the end of the time, Gabriel carried Pharaoh to the city of Nineveh where he became King. He ruled over Nineveh 500 years, and was King when Jonah came to announce the overthrow of the city on account of the wickedness of the inhabitants. It was Pharaoh, then King of Nineveh, who covered himself with sackcloth and ashes and proclaimed once more that there is no God beside the Lord, whose judgments are faithful and whose words are true.

Pharaoh never died, for it had been decreed that he should live eternally. His station is at the gates of hell, where he receives the kings and rulers of the nations whom he rebukes for their wickedness and their lack of knowledge of the Lord:

" Ye ought to have learned wisdom from me," he says unto them. " I, too, once denied the Lord and would not hearken unto His voice. He sent ten plagues upon me and upon my country, and hurled me to the bottom of the sea. He kept me there for fifty days, at the end of which He released me, so that I was compelled to believe in him." [1]

Although they had miraculously escaped danger, the Israelites were still afraid that the Egyptians, having passed the sea like themselves, were still alive. Pharaoh, they feared, would soon be upon them again. But the Lord commanded the sea, and it cast out the corpses of the enemy who were floating on the surface of the waters like skin bottles. Then a north wind blew and cast them out opposite the camp of Israel who recognized all the officials of Pharaoh. " These were the officials," they said, " and these the taskmasters who laid the heavy burdens upon us." [2]

With regard to the corpses of the Egyptians, there ensued a mighty quarrel between the sea and the earth. The sea said:

---

[1] Jellinek, *loc. cit.*, Vol. I, pp. 35–57; Vol. II, pp. 1–11; see also Gaster, *The Chronicles of Jerahmeel*, p. 128 (XLVIII, 12) and p. 37 (XVI, 5).
[2] *Pirke de Rabbi Eliezer*, Ch. 42.

" I will wash ashore all these corpses so that they might not defile my waters," and it cast them upon the shore.

But the earth replied: " I will not take all these corpses, for when I once sucked up the blood of Abel, a terrible curse was pronounced against me by the Lord. I tremble when I think of the curse that will fall on me if I receive all these slain." Thus spoke the earth, and cast the dead Egyptians back into the sea.

But the Lord, remembering Pharaoh's repentance and his words wherein he acknowledged God and His justice, decided that as a reward for this the Egyptians should not remain un-buried. He bade the earth swallow up all the corpses of the Egyptians and grant them burial.[1]

When the Israelites were quite convinced that the Egyptians had been drowned and that they had been indeed delivered from bondage, they prepared to sing a song to the Lord and to sound His praises. All the angels then assembled, ready to intone their song, too, but the Lord bade them wait.

" Let Israel sing first," He said.

And the spirit of the Lord came over the children of Israel, so that sucklings dropped their mothers breasts, raised their eyes to heaven, opened their mouths, lifted up their voices, joined in the song and sounded the praises of God. When the men had completed their song, the angels once more wanted to raise their voices, but God once more bade them tarry awhile. " It is the turn of the women of Israel now," he said.

The angels began to murmur. " Is it not enough that the men have come before us? Shall also the women precede us?"

But the Lord replied: " Let the children of man sing first, for they are mortal and may die before having completed their song; ye are eternal and will have many an opportunity to intone a song." [2]

[1] *Mekhilta*; see Jellinek, *loc. cit.*, Vol. I, pp. 35–57; *Pirke de Rabbi Eliezer*, Ch. 42.
[2] *Sotah*, 30b; *Exodus Rabba*, 23; *Yalkut*, § 241; *Midrash Tanchuma*, ed. Buber, p. 61; cf. Lewner, *loc. cit.*, p. 52.

The sea had not only cast out all the Egyptians, but also their horses, and plenty were the jewels and pearls upon the men and the beasts. Not only all these ornaments, but also the treasures it contained did the sea cast out upon the shore. The liberated slaves collected vast wealth, but with the wealth their greed also increased. When Moses urged them to proceed now, they would not listen unto him, unable to tear themselves away from the seashore. Moses, whose great aim was to lead his people to Sinai, there to receive the Divine law, and hence bring them to the Promised Land where they could practise it, lost patience.

"Do you imagine," he cried, "that the sea will for ever cast out upon the shore precious stones, gems, and pearls?" [1]

[1] *Exodus Rabba*, 24; *Midrash Agadah*, ed. Buber, p. 63; see Lewner, *loc. cit.*, pp. 52-53.

CHAPTER XXIII

From the Red Sea to Sinai

In the wilderness of Shur—The miraculous food—The angels grinding the mills—The tables of congealed dew—The rivers running through the land of the heathen nations—The wonderful flavour and taste of the manna —The perfume and fragrance—The heavenly food helps to settle doubtful points—The disputed slave—At Rephidim—Amalek, the first enemy of Israel—The jealousy of the nations—The Lord rebukes them—Eliphaz and Amalek—The hatred of Esau—An army of magicians—The faithful leader of the people—A stone as a seat—Jethro's letter to Moses—Zipporah's regret—Her reward—The sanctification of the nation—They become physically and mentally perfect—The Lord offers the Torah to the heathen nations—Their refusal—The quarrel of the mountains—Mount Sinai chosen as the holy spot on account of its humility—The Torah and the women of Israel—The bondsmen of Israel—The Patriarchs and the little children—The wonders accompanying the Revelation—The Divine voice —The fear of the people—The dead revived—The Torah and the dew of life—The heathen kings and Balaam—Moses in Heaven—Kemuel, the heavenly porter—Hadarniel and Sandalphon—The murmur of the angels— Moses contends with them—What avails the Torah to you?—The laws of the Torah for men and not for angels—The Law written in black fire— Moses and Rabbi Akiba—The martyrdom of the learned Rabbi—Satan and the Torah—Earth, sea, and abyss—The modesty of Moses—The Law of Moses—Satan and the Israelites—The bier of Moses between heaven and earth—The sin of Israel—Jannes and Jambres—Aaron and Hur—The jewellery of the women—The women refuse to deprive themselves of their ornaments—The magic golden plate—Sammael and the golden calf—Get thee down from thy greatness—Moses and the angel Yefefiyah—The anger of the prophet—The punishment of the sinners—The golden lips—The five angels of destruction—Peor and the burial place of Moses.

Into the wilderness of Shur the people now followed Moses. The wilderness was full of serpents and scorpions, but the pillar of cloud made the way of the people even, and the snakes and scorpions not only did them no harm but fled at the approach of the Israelites, hiding in holes. The wonders and

miracles wrought in favour of the Chosen Race during their
life in the wilderness were many. They fed on heavenly food
called manna.

Miraculous was its origin, miraculous the manner in which
it came down from Heaven, and miraculous its taste and flavour.
Created on the second day of creation, manna, or the food of
the angels, is ground by the angels in mills standing in the
third heaven called *Shekhakim*. Moses saw the mills and the
angels grinding the manna, when he ascended to Heaven to
receive the Law. Before the manna descended upon earth,
a north wind used to pass over the desert, sweeping it of the
dust, whilst a rain immediately came and washed the ground
clear. Then a dew came down which the wind turned into a
hard substance, forming tables two ells high. The sun, casting
its rays upon these tables of congealed dew, made them glisten
and sparkle, wonderful to behold, and upon these tables the
manna then descended. Then the dew again came down,
forming a sort of cover for the manna to protect it from
dust.

For two hours the manna, or food of the angels, lasted every
day, and after that time it melted away and streams of it ran
through the desert into the lands of the nations.

The heathen nations made attempts to drink out of these
rivers, but the water tasted bitter unto them. Whenever they
caught a roe that had drunk out of these streams, killed it and
partook of its flesh, it had a delicious flavour, so that they
exclaimed: " Happy are the people that are in such a case."[1]
The flavour of the manna was not less miraculous, for this
heavenly food had the taste of milk and honey and of cakes
made of fine flour, dipped in oil and honey. But there was
more in it. The manna had the flavour of any dish a man
desired to eat, and when he partook of the manna it tasted

---

[1] *Yoma*, 75a; *Midrash Agadah*, ed. Buber, p. 148; *Midrash Tanchuma*, ed. Buber, p. 67;
Midrash Abkhir, quoted in *Yalkut*, § 258.

exactly like the food he fancied, so that he felt as if he were partaking of that particular food. When children partook of the manna, it tasted to them like milk, and they exclaimed: " How delicious the milk we have drunk to-day!" whilst the youths said: " How delightful the honey to-day!" Old men used to say: "We have never eaten such excellent bread in all our lives." When men wished to eat meat, or a bird, then manna tasted like meat to them.

The perfume and fragrance of the manna were wonderful, but on the Sabbath, when a double portion came down on the preceding day, its taste, flavour, and fragrance were even a thousand times more wonderful. It was no trouble whatever to gather the manna, and those who were too lazy to go out, found it at the entrance of their tents, and even whilst lying upon their beds, they had only to stretch out their hands, take the manna, and eat it.[1] The manna came down in such abundance that it would have been sufficient for many nations to feed on it, and yet, when the Israelites measured it, it only contained the measure required for each individual.

Another peculiarity of this heavenly food was that it served to settle sometimes doubtful points, as, for instance, to prove the truth or falsehood of a statement.

One day two men came before Moses: " My neighbour," said the first, " has stolen my slave."

" This is a lie," cried the other, " I never did steal thy slave, I bought him from thee."

" Return to your tents," replied Moses, " and to-morrow I will give judgment."

On the morrow they counted the measures of the daily ration of manna required for each household, and lo, the daily ration required for the disputed slave came down before his first master's tent. It was a clear proof that the slave still belonged to him and had never been sold. Moses consequently

[1] *Yalkut*, § 258.

commanded the thief to return the property to the rightful owner.[1]

At Rephidim the first enemy of Israel moved against them with armed forces. The heathen nations saw from afar the manna descending and rising to great heights, and they witnessed the great miracle the Lord had wrought for Israel by sending down to them heavenly food.

The kings and people grew jealous, and said in their hearts: " Let us go out, meet Israel, destroy the nation and wipe out its very name."

But the Lord replied: " Ye are jealous of my children! Many of you are living in peace and prosperity in your own countries, and Israel never envies you nor does she grow angry. Scarcely, however, have ye noticed that the slaves of yesterday have been set free, that the labourers in the brickfields of Egypt are advancing towards Canaan, the land promised to their ancestors as their national home, than ye already envy this nation its possible peace and prosperity. Ye already hate Israel and are thinking of means how to destroy the people oppressed."

Thus spoke the Lord, but, on account of Israel's lack of faith at Rephidim, He turned Amalek against them. Amalek was the son of Eliphaz, the son of Esau, and when he saw the great favours bestowed upon his kinsmen, the seed of Jacob, he grew jealous. His father Eliphaz advised him to make friends with this favoured nation and to go out into the wilderness and render them services, but Amalek only waxed wroth with his father. He sent messengers to many heathen nations and invited them to join him in his expedition and fight Israel. The heathen nations, however, declined to make war upon Israel, for whom the Lord had wrought so many miracles. And so Amalek went out alone, rapidly moving in one night over a distance of 400 parasangs.[2]

---

[1] *Yoma*, 75a; *Midrash Agadah*, ed. Buber, p. 148; cf. Lewner, *loc. cit.*, pp. 55–56.

[2] *Yoma*, 75a; *Mekhilta*, ed. Venice, p. 20b; *Midrash Tanchuma*, section *Ki-Teze*; *Pirke de Rabbi Eliezer*, Ch. 44.

Whilst the other nations were afraid to wage war against Israel who had been chosen by the Lord, Amalek, who had inherited the hatred of his grandfather Esau for the seed of Jacob, marched against them. He acted treacherously before openly attacking them. From the archives of Egypt he had procured himself the list of the tribes, and, acquainted with their names, he stationed himself with his men before the camp of Israel and invited them by their names to come and do business with him. Suspecting no guile, many Israelites answered the call and were treacherously slain by Amalek.[1]

Being a magician himself and accompanied by a vast army of wizards and enchanters, Amalek knew exactly the hour of death of each individual and attacked them accordingly.[2] He also mutilated the bodies of the Israelites and jeered and mocked at and made sport of the covenant of Abraham.[3]

Amalek was defeated in battle by Joshua, the son of Nun, but only with the aid of Moses, who lifted up his hands heavenwards and prayed to the Lord. Unable to stand all the while with raised arms, Moses was compelled to sit down for a while. At that moment his servant came and offered to bring him a cushion or a comfortable seat, but Moses waved him away. He would not sit down upon a comfortable seat, he, the leader, whilst Israel, his people, were in distress and fighting a desperate foe.

" Bring me a stone," he said, " and thereupon will I sit and pray."[4]

When Jethro, the father-in-law of Moses, heard of all that had occurred, how the Israelites had been led out of the land of Egypt, and passed the Red Sea, he decided to set out for the desert. He sent a messenger to Moses, announcing his

---

[1] *Midrash Tanchuma*, section *Ki-Teze*; *Pesikta* (1868), 3, p. 26*b*; *Pesikta Rabbati*, ed. Friedmann, 52*a*.

[2] *Yalkut Reubeni*; see also, Gaster, *The Chronicles of Jerahmeel*, XLIII, 13.

[3] *Pesikta*, 3, 27*b*.

[4] *Midrash Tanchuma*; *Taanith*, 11; *Mekhilta*, ed. Venice, p. 21; *Yalkut*, § 265; *Midrash Agadah*, ed. Buber, p. 149; cf. Lewner, *loc. cit.*, pp. 56–59; Bialik, *loc. cit.*, pp. 66–67.

arrival. Some say that he arrived at the camp of Israel but
could not enter it, because it was surrounded by a pillar of
cloud. He then wrote a letter to Moses, tied it to an arrow and
shot it into the camp. In his letter he begged Moses to come
out and meet him.

" If I am unworthy of this honour," wrote Jethro, " then
come out for the sake of thy wife Zipporah and thy two sons
whom I have brought with me."

And the Lord said unto Moses: " Go out and meet Jethro
and treat him kindly, for Israel should be kind to and love
strangers and aliens, even as I do."

Moses, accompanied by Aaron, Nadab, Abihu, and seventy
elders, came out to meet Jethro and did him honour.

When Jethro heard all the miracles, he rejoiced, but he was
also grieved at the destruction of his former co-religionists
the Egyptians, and felt a sting in his flesh. He blessed, however,
and praised the Lord, and acknowledged His greatness.

As for Zipporah, when she heard how the women of Israel
had intoned a song and sounded the praises of God, she was
sorry not to have been present on this occasion and joined the
women of Israel. And the Lord said: " As Zipporah has been
grieved on this account, she shall be rewarded and her soul
will one day be in Deborah, the prophetess, who will sing a
song of salvation and redemption." [1]

The great day was now approaching, the day on which the
Lord was to give the Law to Israel on Mount Sinai.

The Law was not proclaimed to Israel immediately after
the exodus and their deliverance from Egypt, because they
were still steeped in idol worship. The Lord, therefore, waited
until the bricklayers of Egypt had grown accustomed to liberty
and divine miracles.

They had partaken of heavenly food, witnessed the miracles

[1] *Exodus Rabba*, 27; *Midrash Tanchuma*, ed. Buber, p. 73; *Midrash Agadah*, ed. Buber,
p. 150; *Mekhilta*, ed. Venice, p. 22b; *Yalkut*, § 268; see also *Seder Hadorot*.

of God, shaken off the materialism of Egypt, and become more worthy of receiving spiritual nourishment. The manna, the quails, and the well were gifts bestowed upon Israel as a preliminary to the great treasure to be handed to them at the foot of Sinai.[1]

Mentally and physically the people became more worthy of receiving the Law. At the time of the exodus there were many mutilated, sick, maimed, and lame persons among the Israelites, in consequence of their hard labour in Egypt and the accidents connected with such work. But the Lord commanded the ministering angels, and they descended upon earth, healed all the sick and made whole all the halt. The whole nation became perfect, physically and mentally.

Before, however, giving the Torah to Israel, the Lord at first offered it to the Gentiles who unanimously refused it. The Lord did act thus, so that the heathens might not pretend hereafter that they would have accepted the Law had it only been offered unto them.

God, therefore, approached the sons of Esau and said to them: " Will ye accept the Law?"

But they asked by way of a reply: " What is written in this Law?"

" It is written therein," said the Lord, " 'Thou shalt do no murder '."

And the sons of Esau replied: " We cannot accept Thy Law, for when Isaac once blessed our father Esau, he said: ' By the sword shalt thou live!' We are men of war and live by our swords, killing our enemies and robbing them. If we accept the Torah, we shall thus have to abandon the blessing bestowed upon us."

The Lord thereupon turned to the sons of Ammon and Moab.

" Will ye accept the Law?" he said.

[1] *Midrash Echa Rabba*; cf. Bialik, *loc. cit.*, pp. 67–68.

" And what is written therein?" they asked.

" It is written in the Law: ' Thou shalt not commit unchastity '."

But the sons of Ammon and Moab replied: " We owe our very origin to unchastity, and we cannot accept Thy Law."

The Lord thereupon approached the sons of Ishmael and said unto them: " Will ye accept the Law?"

But the sons of Ishmael replied: " What is written therein?"

" It is written in the Law," replied the Lord: ' Thou shalt not steal '."

When the sons of Ishmael heard these words, they replied: " We cannot give up the laws and customs of our fathers who have always lived and thriven on theft and robbery. Did they not once steal Joseph out of the land of the Hebrews and sell him to Egypt? We cannot accept Thy Law."

The Lord thereupon offered the Torah to the Canaanites, and they, too, asked: " What is written in this Torah?"

" It is written therein," replied the Lord: " ' Thou shalt have a right measure and a right weight '."

But the Canaanites refused the Law which contained such injunctions.

The Lord thereupon sent messengers to all the heathen nations of the world, offering them the Torah, but all refused it.

Then the Lord revealed himself to the people of Israel, and they replied: " All that the Lord hath spoken, we will do and be obedient."[1]

And at that moment sixty myriads of ministering angels came down and crowned each Israelite with two crowns, one for the words: " We will do ", and the other for the words: " We will be obedient."[2]

Before giving the Torah to the Israelites, the Lord also

[1] *Midrash Shir-Hashirim*; *Mekhilta*, ed. Venice, p. 25a–b; *Yalkut*, § 286; *Exodus Rabba*, 27; *Pesikta Rabbati*, ed. Friedmann, 21. p. 99b; cf. Lewner, *loc. cit.*, pp. 60–61.
[2] *Sabbath*, 88.

said unto Moses: " Go and speak to the daughters of Israel, make known to them the contents of the Torah and ask them whether they will accept it." Thus the women were asked first, because, as a rule, men follow the counsel of women.[1]

And when the mountains heard that God intended to reveal the Law upon one of them, they began to quarrel among themselves and to contest for the great honour. Each was anxious to be chosen as the spot where the Glory of the Lord would be revealed. Mounts Tabor, Hermon, and Carmel, all rushed forward and claimed the honour. A mighty dispute thus ensued between the contesting mountains, a dispute settled only by God Himself.

" Do not quarrel," said the voice from Heaven, " for Mount Sinai has been chosen as the spot for the delivery of the Law. I have measured all the mountains and My choice hath fallen on Mount Sinai, because it is lower than all of ye, and humbler, and the Lord loves humility. Upon all ye proud mountains, on account of your height, idols have been worshipped, and ye are unworthy to be the holy spot where the Law will be delivered. Upon Sinai alone the feet of idol worshippers have never trodden, and no heathen sanctuaries have been erected there." [2]

Now Moses sanctified Israel and bade them prepare for the Revelation. At first, however, as he had been requested by the Most High, he assembled the women of Israel and with kindly words explained to them the contents of the Law. " Men, as a rule, hearken to the counsel of women," said the Lord, " and if the women accept My commandments, they will not be able to imitate their mother Eve who, when she sinned, excused herself with the words: ' The commandment had not been given to me, but to my husband alone.' The women, too, will instruct their children in the Law."

---

[1] *Pirke de Rabbi Eliezer*, Ch. 41; *Exodus Rabba*, 28; *Sabbath*, 87a; *Mekhilta*.
[2] *Genesis Rabba*, 99; *Sotah*, 5a; *Leviticus Rabba*, 23; *Numbers Rabba*, 13.

Thereupon the Lord asked Israel to furnish Him with a guarantee and bring him bondsmen who would stand surety for them that they would observe the Law.

" Who will be your bondsmen?" asked the Lord.

" Our ancestors, Abraham, Isaac, and Jacob, are our bondsmen, and will stand surety for us," replied the Israelites.

But the Lord replied: " And who will stand surety for your forefathers? They lacked faith sometimes, and are moreover already in my debt. I want better bondsmen than these."

" Our children shall be our bondsmen," cried Israel.

The Lord accepted their offer, and thus the children at the mothers' breast and those yet unborn became the bondsmen for Israel that they would observe the Law, and it is the children that God calls to judgment, when the sons of Israel abandon the Law.[1]

Great were the wonders and miracles accompanying the Revelation on Sinai. Mount Sinai rose from the earth and became taller than all the mountains of the world. The heavens opened, and the summit of the holy mount towered into the opening.[2] Nature was hushed, the whole universe stood still, and no creature uttered any sound. Birds did not sing, nor did oxen low; the sea ceased her roaring, the Ophanim their motion, and the Seraphim no longer uttered their " Holy ". A breathless silence prevailed, and there was a stillness never witnessed before and never to occur again. And in the midst of this solemn and supernatural silence, the voice of the Lord resounded, calling: " I am the Lord, your God." The Divine voice travelled from one end of the world to the other, and was heard by all the inhabitants of the earth, by old and young, by the aged and the suckling, by the youth and the maiden. And the Divine voice divided itself into seventy tongues and travelled from one end of the world to the other, so that all

---

[1] *Midrash Chasit*; *Exodus Rabba*, 28; cf. Lewner, *loc. cit.*, pp. 62–63.
[2] *Pirke de Rabbi Eliezer*, Ch. 41; *Exodus Rabba*, 28.

could understand it. Each individual understood it in his own way, according to his individuality and his intelligence. Scarcely had the words been uttered, when they became flame and visible to the whole nation.

When the people heard the Divine voice and the Divine words, they trembled greatly and were alarmed. They rushed forward to the south, for it seemed to them that the voice was coming from the south, and then it seemed to them again as if the voice had come from the north. Then they heard the voice coming forth from all corners of the world, and also from heaven and from earth, and they called out: " Now we know that the glory of the Lord fills the whole universe."

Thereupon the angels of the Lord came down, two angels for each Israelite, brought unto them the Invisible Word and explained unto them its sanctity, and the reward and punishment awaiting every one who will either observe or disobey the Word. The angels thereupon having warned each Israelite, asked everyone separately: " Wilt thou accept the word of God?" and each answered: " Yea." Thereupon the angels kissed each Israelite, and the word returned to the Lord who engraved it upon the Tables.[1]

When the first commandment was uttered, and the flames, thunder and lightning increased, the people were so alarmed and so frightened that their souls fled from them. Immediately, the Torah appeared before the Lord and said: " Lord of the Universe, Thou hast given me to the living and not to the dead. Thou hast given me to man that he may live and prolong his days upon earth, and behold! they are all dead. Restore them to life, and give them strength to listen to Thy word." Thus spake the Torah, and for the sake of the Torah, the Lord let fall upon the Israelites the dew of Heaven, the dew that is destined to revive the dead, and their souls returned unto them and they came to life again.[2]

[1] *Exodus Rabba*, 29; *Midrash Shir-Hashirim.*   [2] *Exodus Rabba*, 29.

The great light, thereupon, emanating from Mount Sinai, filled the whole world, and the Voice was heard by all the inhabitants. And when the heathen nations heard that Voice, the kings trembled upon their thrones, and came to Balaam to ask for an explanation. " What is that awful voice we hear, those rumblings and peals of thunder that accompany it? Is it possible that God is bringing another flood upon the world?"

" No," replied the wizard, " the Lord has once promised that He would never visit the world with a flood."

" Perchance," said the kings, " He intends to destroy the world by fire?"

But Balaam replied: " Such is not the case. The light ye see, and the voice ye hear are the result of another cause and of a great event. The Lord is bestowing His Torah upon the people of Israel."

And when the kings of the heathen nations heard these words, they were quietened, and returned each to his country and to his kingdom.[1]

Now Israel withdrew from Mount Sinai, as they could no longer stand the awful vision, and implored Moses to receive himself the Law and to communicate it to them afterwards. Their wish was granted, and Moses alone ascended the holy mountain, where he remained for forty days.

For seven days Moses remained on the mountain, and then he ascended to Heaven, there to receive the Law. At that moment a cloud appeared before him, but he knew not whether to ride on it or only to take hold of it. Whilst he was thus deliberating, the cloud suddenly opened and Moses having entered it, it carried him aloft. He thereupon walked along on the firmament, even as a man walks upon earth. Suddenly the angel Kemuel, the heavenly porter who is appointed over 12,000 angels guarding the gates and portals of Heaven.

---

[1] *Yalkut*, § 286; *Mekhilta*, p. 25a; *Zebachim*, p. 116a.

approached him and harshly inquired: " What dost thou here, son of woman, and how darest thou walk among the angels, and art not afraid of their consuming fire?"

" I am the son of Amram," replied Moses, " and have come here by the command of the Most High to receive the Law."

But Kemuel wanted to destroy Moses, and the Prophet called upon the Name of God. Immediately a great fear seized the angel Kemuel and he fled from Moses a distance of 13,000 parasangs (according to another version, Moses destroyed Kemuel and wiped him out of existence).

The cloud then carried Moses higher up until he reached the angel Hadarniel, an angel from whose mouth issue 12,000 flashes of lightning with every word he utters. When Moses beheld Hadarniel, a terrible fear seized him and he could not utter a word, tears only flowing from his eyes. But the Lord had mercy upon Moses and rebuked Hadarniel. The angel thereupon said unto Moses: " I will go before thee, O son of Amram, and show thee the way, even as a pupil goes before his master." He led the son of Amram until he reached the spot where stood the angel Sandalphon, and then he spoke to Moses, saying: " I cannot go farther lest I be consumed by the fire of Sandalphon."

When Moses heard these words and beheld the angel Sandalphon, he was greatly frightened, and tears once more flowed from his eyes. He prayed to the Lord and besought his mercy, and God had compassion upon Moses and stood before him till he had passed the fire of Sandalphon. Moses then came to the river of fire called Rigyon, but the Lord took Moses, drew him across the river of fire and brought him into the vicinity of the angels who surround the Throne of Glory and who are mightier and stronger than all the other ministering angels. They wished to scorch Moses with their fiery breath, but God spread the radiance of His Glory upon Moses and strengthened him, so that the fiery breath of the angels could not harm him.[1]

As soon as the angels became aware that Moses had ascended to Heaven to receive the Law, they murmured and complained at this.

But the Lord said to Moses: " Answer them and prove unto them that the Torah avails them not."

" How can I answer them?" cried Moses. " They will consume me with their fiery breath."

" Take hold of My Throne of Glory," replied the Lord, " hold on tight to it and answer them."

Thus strengthened, Moses argued with the angels and said: " What avails the Torah to you? In the Torah it is written: ' I am the Eternal, thy Lord, that hath led thee out of the land of Egypt and out of the house of bondage.' Have you ever been slaves in Egypt and redeemed?

" It is again written in the Torah: ' Thou shalt have no other Gods beside Me.' Are you dwelling among the heathen nations and are there idolaters among you, you who witness the Glory of God, His greatness, and strength?

" It is written in the Torah: ' Thou shalt not utter the name of the Eternal in vain '. Are you engaged in business that you have to be taught concerning oaths?

" It is written in the Torah," Moses continued: " ' Remember to keep the Sabbath holy '; now is there work among you that you need rest?

" It is written in the Torah: ' Honour thy father and mother '. Have you any parents to honour?

" It is further written in the Torah: ' Thou shalt not kill, thou shalt not commit adultery, thou shalt not steal, thou shalt not covet '. Are there murderers among you, are there women among you, is there money in heaven or private pro-

---

[1] *Exodus Rabba*, 28; Gaster, *The Chronicles of Jerahmeel*, pp. 144–147 (LII, 1–8), and *Journal of the Royal Asiatic Society*, 1893, pp. 588–590.

perty? Are there houses or fields or vineyards in Heaven which you might covet, if you are not taught by the Torah that it is a sin?"

Thus argued Moses, and when the angels heard his words, they agreed that the Lord was right in deciding to deliver the Law to Israel, and they called out unanimously: " Eternal, our Lord, how mighty is Thy name in all the earth! Thou who hast extended Thy glory over the heavens." [1]

When Moses reached Heaven, he beheld the Law written in black fire upon skins of white fire, and he also beheld the Lord seated upon the Throne of Glory and occupied in adding and ornamenting the letters of the Torah with crowns. He asked:

" Why art Thou now adding these crown-like ornamentations to the letters?" Whereto the Lord replied:

" In days to come there will be born a man named Rabbi Akiba, a scholar in Israel, full of knowledge and wisdom, to whom the secret of these dots and ornamentations will be revealed. He will interpret them, basing upon their inter‹ pretation numerous laws and injunctions."

" If it is Thy will," said Moses, " may I be permitted to behold this wise man?"

" Look behind thee," said the Lord.

Moses did as he was bidden, and lo, he saw a house full of students, sitting at the feet of a master who was explaining unto them the secrets and mysteries of the Torah. Moses heard their discussions, but could not follow them and was greatly grieved. Thereupon he heard the disciples asking their master: " Whence dost thou know this, O our master?" and Rabbi Akiba replied: " What I have told you has already been explained to Moses, the son of Amram on Mount Sinai." When Moses heard these words, he was content.

In his modesty, however, the Prophet turned to God, saying:

---

[1] *Sabbath*, 88b–89a; Gaster, *loc. cit.*, p. 147 (LIII, 9).

" Lord of the Universe! Thou wilt one day create a man like Rabbi Akiba who will excel me in knowledge and wisdom; why dost Thou not give the Torah to Israel through him instead of me?"

But the Lord replied: " Such is my decree."

" Lord of the Universe," said Moses again: " Thou hast shown me this man and I have beheld his great learning, may I also be permitted to see the reward awaiting him?"

And the Lord replied: " Look behind thee."

Moses looked, and horror seized him. He saw cruel men seizing the erudite and holy Rabbi and tearing his flesh from his body with sharp iron instruments. In the agony of his soul, Moses cried: " Lord of the Universe! Is this the reward meted out to the holy man for his great erudition?"

The Lord answered: " Be silent, for such is my decree; but as thou hast shown thy modesty, thou shalt be rewarded, and I will make thee excel in wisdom all other men." The Lord then opened the treasures of wisdom and bestowed upon the son of Amram forty-nine parts, one part only remaining for the rest of the world, so that the Prophet became wiser than all other men. And all the mysteries of creation were revealed unto Moses, and he read in the future as in an open book.[1]

When Moses had received the Torah and was about to descend upon earth, Satan appeared before the Throne of Glory and thus he said: " Lord of the Universe, where is the Torah?"

" I gave the Torah to earth," replied the Lord.

Immediately Satan betook himself to earth and asked: " Where are the whereabouts of the Torah?"

Whereto earth replied: " The Lord knows of its course. He looketh to the end of the earth and seeth under the whole heaven."

---

[1] *Menachot*, 29b; *Leviticus Rabba*, 26; *Exodus Rabba*, 41; cf. Lewner, *loc. cit.*, pp. 69–71.

Satan then betook himself to the sea, and asked for the Torah, but the sea replied: " It is not with me."

He turned to the abyss, but the abyss only replied: " The Torah is not with me."

Satan returned to God and said: " Everywhere have I searched for the Torah, but found it not."

" Go and ask the son of Amram," replied the Lord.

And to Moses Satan at once betook himself.

" Where is the Torah, O son of Amram," asked Satan, " the Torah which God hath given thee?"

" Who am I," answered Moses, " that the Lord should make me a present of the Torah?"

" Moses," said God, " thou art uttering a falsehood."

" Lord of the Universe," replied Moses, " Thou dost possess a rare treasure which delights Thee daily; have I any right to claim it now as my own because Thou didst teach me its contents?"

" Since thou hast been so humble," replied the Lord, " the Torah shall henceforth be named after thee, and shall be known as the Law of Moses." [1]

In the meantime the Israelites were waiting for the return of Moses from the Mount. Satan, now anxious to accuse Israel and to make them forget the first commandment, did his best to lead them astray. Moses had promised the Israelites to come down from Mount Sinai after forty days, and at noon of the fortieth day he had not yet returned. Satan, always eager to lead men astray, and particularly jealous of Israel at that moment, came to the Israelites and asked: " Where is your law-giver, Moses, the son of Amram?"

" He has ascended to Heaven," replied the Israelites.

When Satan saw that they would not listen to his insinuations, he said to the people: " Look up and behold your leader who is dead."

---

[1] *Sabbath*, 89a.

And indeed, midway between heaven and earth, the Israelites beheld a heavy cloud, and on it a black bier on which lay stretched out dead their leader Moses.

Thereupon the rabble, 40,000 in number, who had come out of Egypt with the sons of Israel, led by the two magicians, Jannes and Jambres, came up to Aaron and Hur and thus they said: " The Egyptians among whom we dwelt were in the habit of carrying their gods about with them, uttering hymns and singing before them, and they saw their gods before them. Now Moses is dead, and we ask thee to make unto us a god like the gods of the Egyptians, that we may see it before us." Thus spoke the mixed multitude to Aaron and Hur.

" Tarry awhile," said Aaron and Hur, " Moses will soon come down from the Mount."

But the rabble, led by the magicians Jannes and Jambres, would not listen to them.[1]

Then Hur, the son of Miriam, whose name was also Ephrath, because she was of noble birth, rebuked them, and spoke harsh words unto them: " Ye stiff-necked people," he cried, " have ye already forgotten all the miracles the Lord hath wrought on your behalf?"

Then they rose up and slew Hur.[2] They then turned to Aaron and said: " If thou wilt make us a god, it is well, otherwise we will do unto thee as we have done unto Hur."

When Aaron saw that Hur was dead, he was afraid lest Israel would commit another great sin by killing him, too, and he preferred to grant them their wish, still hoping that in the meantime Moses would return. But Aaron thought: " If I ask the Israelites to bring me gold and silver, they will do so immediately. I will therefore ask them to bring me the jewellery of their wives and their daughters, and as the latter will no doubt refuse to deprive themselves of their ornaments, the

---

[1] *Midrash Tanchuma*, section *Ki-Tissa*; *Midrash Agadah*, ed. Buber, p. 181; *Sabbath*, p. 89a; *Pirke de Rabbi Eliezer*, Ch. 45.   [2] *Ibid.*

matter will be delayed or fail altogether." Thus thought Aaron, and he bade the people bring him the ornaments and earrings of their wives and daughters.

The men approached the women, but the latter refused to give up their ornaments, saying: "Heaven forbid that we should give our ornaments to make a graven image and thus deny the Lord who has wrought such miracles on our behalf." Thus spoke the women of Israel, and the men at once broke off their own earrings which were in their ears after the fashion of the Egyptians and the Arabs, and brought them unto Aaron.[1]

When Aaron saw that his plan had failed, he raised his eyes to Heaven and said: "Lord of the Universe, Thou knowest my innermost thoughts and the reason why I am doing this." He thereupon cast the ornaments into the fire.

Now, among the ornaments was a golden plate upon which the name of God was written, and upon it was also engraven the figure of a calf. This plate a man named Micah cast into the furnace, and a calf came out.[2] Into this calf Sammael immediately entered, so that it ran about like a living beast and lowed like one.[3]

Aaron was amazed and sorely grieved, when he saw this, and he said unto the Israelites: "Why are you in a hurry to worship your god? I will build an altar unto it, and to-morrow will be a great festival." Aaron thus still cherished the hope of delaying the sin of idol worship, as Moses would certainly return in the meantime. His hope, however, was frustrated, for on the morrow Moses had not yet returned, and the people began to worship the golden calf.[4]

Then the Lord said to Moses who was still in Heaven: "Get thee down from thy greatness, for it is only for Israel's sake that I gave thee greatness and cast honour upon thee. Now that Israel hath sinned and become disloyal to Me, I

---

[1] *Ibid.*   [2] *Midrash Tanchuma*, section *Ki-Tissa*.   [3] *Pirke de Rabbi Eliezer*, Ch. 45.
[4] *Sabbath*, 89; *Midrash Tanchuma*, section *Ki-Tissa*.

have no use in thee and there is no reason why I should distinguish thee.[1] Thy people," the Lord said, " whom thou didst lead out of Egypt, have sinned."

And when Moses was allowed to descend from Heaven, he had once more to pass the angels of Fear and of Sweat, of Trembling and Quaking, and he was so filled with horror that he forgot all that he had learned. God then called the angel Yefefiyah, who brought back remembrance to him and handed to him the Torah. Armed with the Law, Moses passed the ranks of all the angels, and they became his friends, giving him presents and revealing to him mysteries. They taught him the secret of the Holy Names, and the angel of Death taught him a remedy against Death.[2]

Moses descended from Heaven, carrying the tables of the Law. The tables carried their own weight so long as the celestial writing was upon them, but when Moses came down and beheld the cymbals, the dances and the calf, he suddenly became aware of the enormous weight of the tables and felt that he could not carry both himself and the tables. He noticed at the same time how all the letters upon the tables were vanishing, so that no celestial writing remained upon them. Amazed, the law-giver stood still contemplating two almost meaningless heavy stones in his hand, uselessly burdening him. He cast them from him and broke them.[3]

Moses' anger was great. He burned the calf, powdered it like the dust of the earth and cast it upon the water. He thereupon made the Israelites drink this water, and the lips of all those who had worshipped the calf and kissed it became golden, so that they could be distinguished from those who had not sinned.[4] The sinners were punished, and Moses ultimately succeeded in appeasing the anger of God.

[1] Berachoth, 32a.　　　　　　　[2] Yalkut Reubeni, fol. 107c.
[3] Pirke de Rabbi Eliezer, Ch. 45; Abbot de Rabbi Nathan, p. 67a; Targum Pseudo-Jonathan; Exodus, 32, 19; see Yalkut, § 293; cf. Lewner, loc. cit., pp. 76–79.
[4] Pirke de Rabbi Eliezer, Ch. 45.

MOSES CASTS FROM HIM THE TABLES OF THE LAW

The Lord had sent down five angels to destroy Israel, they were Wrath, Anger, Temper, Destruction, and Glow of Anger, but Moses hastened to the Cave of Machpelah and there invoked the Patriarchs on behalf of Israel: " If ye are children of future life," he cried, " then stand by me now, in this hour of need, for your children are like sheep given over to slaughter."

The Patriarchs arose and also invoked God who had once promised to multiply their seed as the stars of heaven. God took into consideration the merits of the Patriarchs, and the three angels, *Kezef*, *Af*, and *Hemah* were at once called away, but two of them, Mashit and Haron remained.

Thereupon Moses once more prayed to God, and He held back the angel *Mashit* (Destruction), and *Haron* (Glow of Anger) alone remained. Moses, however, conquered even this last angel. He cast Haron down into the earth and buried him in a spot in the possession of the tribe of Gad, where he remained bound and kept in check by the Prophet. The name of this angel is also *Peor*, for every time when Israel sinned, he tried to rise from the earth, open his mouth and destroy Israel with his breath. But Moses had only to pronounce the name of God, and Haron was at once drawn down beneath the earth.

When Moses died, God buried him opposite to the place where Peor is kept a prisoner. Every time that Israel sins, Peor rises to the upper world, ready to destroy the nation with his breath, but no sooner does he behold the burial place of Moses than he falls back terror-stricken, returning to the depths of the earth.[1]

[1] *Pirke de Rabbi Eliezer*, Ch. 45; *Exodus Rabba*, 41; *Midrash Shokher Tob*, Ps., 7; *Yalkut*, Ps., 7, § 673; see also *Sabbath*, 55a; *Nedarim*, 32a.

CHAPTER XXIV

In the Wilderness

The revolt of Korah—His ambition—Korah and his wife—The Levites —Moses speaks kind words to the rebels—The parable of the poor widow and her orphaned daughters—The exigencies of the priests—The heavy taxes—The punishment of Korah and his company—On, the son of Peleth— A clever woman—The lady with the streaming hair—The reproach of the Israelites—The plague—The secret taught unto Moses by the angel of death—Death and incense—The foes of Israel—False friends—Amalek and the sons of Esau—The prayer of Israel—The Amorites—The valley of Arnon—The enemy in hiding—The jutting rocks and the caves—The two lepers, Eth and Hav—The miracle of the well—Sihon, King of Heshbon— The offer of peace—Og, the giant—Og and the ark—Og and Sarah the beautiful—The giant's thigh-bone and the gravedigger—Og, a former slave of Abraham—The wonderful bed—The giant's food and drink—The mysterious wall—The mountain and the ants—The leap into the air—The death of Og—The Moabites—Balak and Balaam—The magicians' advice —The seductive maidens—Linen garments and unchastity—Simri and Cozbi—Phinehas the zealot—The war against the Midianites—The flying magician—The death of Balaam.

During the sojourn of the children of Israel in the desert, Moses had much trouble with them, and many revolts embittered his life. Such was the revolt of Korah who, jealous of the greatness of the son of Amram, revolted against him, and incited many of the people. According to Jewish legend it was his wife that excited Korah to revolt against Moses. Korah was of the tribe of Levi, and when Moses commanded the Levites to " cause a razor to pass over all their flesh ",[1] Korah was also compelled to cut his hair and shave. Thereupon his wife said unto him:

" How long will Moses, thy kinsman, laugh and mock at

[1] *Numbers*, 8, 7.

318

thee? He himself is King, and Aaron, his brother, he has raised to be High-Priest. Not only the children of Israel are compelled to give tithe to the priests, but also the Levites. And now he is humiliating you, treating you as if you had been sheep, commanding you to cut off the hair of your head and to shave, and also to offer you as a wave offering as if you were animals." [1]

Now Korah was an exceedingly wealthy man, possessing vast treasures, gold and silver and precious stones; and being very wealthy he desired also honour.

He thought in his heart: " Am I not the son of Izhar, the son of Kehath, who was the father also of Amram? My father Izhar was a younger brother of Amram, and I am a cousin of Moses and of Aaron. Moses is King, Aaron is High-Priest, and I had always hoped that I would be appointed the Prince of my tribe. But no, Moses has raised to this dignity Eliphaz the son of Usiel, who was a younger brother of my father. He has evidently made up his mind to slight me, and is holding me in contempt, although I am the possessor of vast treasures. I will therefore raise a revolt against Moses and upset all his plans." [2]

Thereupon Korah went from tent to tent and incited two hundred and fifty princes of the congregation, " called to the assembly, men of renown ".

When Moses heard that a conspiracy had been formed against him, he went himself to the tent of Korah and spoke kindly to the rebels.

" My brethren," said he, " I have heard that ye are not satisfied with me, and are accusing me of pride and arrogance. Have you forgotten that I went from Midian to Egypt for your sake, but never asked any reward for all my trouble and my labours? If I am now supposed to be ruling over you, it is not

---

[1] *Numbers*, 8, 11.
[2] *Yalkut*, § 750; *Midrash Tanchuma*, section *Korah*; *Midrash Mishle (Proverbs)* 11.

because I have sought greatness and been ambitious. It is the Lord who has commanded me to be your leader, and I have never done anything except what the Lord has commanded me to do."

Thus spoke Moses, but Korah replied:

" Thou hast done but little for us. Thou hast taken us out of Egypt, where we lived in plenty, but hast not brought us to Canaan, the land thou didst promise to give us."

And when the followers of Korah heard his words, they rose against Moses and were almost on the point of stoning him.

The Prophet was sorely grieved, not because they wanted to stone him, but because they were thus committing a grievous sin against the Lord.[1]

Thereupon Korah went out to the tents of Israel, endeavouring to find followers and partisans for his conspiracy among the people.

" What wrong has Moses done unto thee that thou art so angry with him?" asked the children of Israel. To this Korah replied hypocritically:

" Had it only been a question of myself, of my honour and of my thwarted ambitions, or of the wrong he has done unto me, I would never have said a word and borne all offences silently, without a murmur, but Moses has wronged the whole congregation. He has laid upon all the children of Israel heavy burdens and given them laws which are very severe. Let me tell you what cruel treatment a poor widow living in my neighbourhood has met at the hands of Moses."

" Tell us the story of the poor widow," said the children of Israel, and Korah told them as follows:

" There was a poor man dwelling in my neighbourhood, a man whose days were full of misery, for he suffered great want. When the man died, his widow and her two orphan

[1] *Yalkut, ibid.; Midrash Tanchuma, ibid.*

daughters had only one small field in their possession. This
the widow decided to cultivate so as to find sustenance for
herself and for her children. But when she started to plough
her field, Moses came and said:

"'Thou shalt not plough thy field with an ox and an ass
together.'[1]

"The woman hired an ass only and ploughed her field.
When she started to sow, Moses again came and said:

"'Thou shalt not sow thy field with two kinds of seed.'[2]
When she had finished sowing and her field had borne fruit,
and the time came to reap, Moses came again and told her
not to reap wholly the corners of the field, not to gather the
gleanings but to leave them for the poor.

"She obeyed his instructions and brought the harvest into
her barn. When the woman was about to thrash the grain,
Moses again came and said: 'Give me the heave-offering,
the first and the second tithes for the priests.'

"And the poor woman said unto herself:

"'There is very little to be got out of the field, and it will
scarcely yield anything for myself and my two daughters, if
I am to pay such heavy taxes and give away a large portion to
the priests. I will sell my field and buy unto me two ewes
whose milk will nourish us, my two daughters and myself,
and out of their wool we shall make clothes unto ourselves.'
Thus thought the woman. She sold her field and bought
two sheep. When her sheep brought forth young, Aaron, the
High-Priest, came and said:

"'Give me the first-born of thy sheep, for they belong to
me, according to the Law, as it is said: "All the firstlings, males
that are born of thy herd and thy flock, thou shalt sanctify unto
the Lord thy God".'[3]

"The poor woman handed over the firstlings to the High-
Priest. When the time of shearing came and she hoped to be

---

[1] *Deuteron.*, 22, 10.   [2] *Leviticus*, 19, 19.   [3] *Deuteron.*, 15, 19.

able to weave out of the wool garments for herself and her daughters, Aaron came again and demanded his share of the shearing:

" ' Give me the first of the fleece of thy sheep which is the priest's due according to the Law, for it is written: " And the first of the fleece of thy sheep shalt thou give unto him ".' [1] The poor widow did as she was bidden, but she was sorely grieved and said in her heart:

" ' This priest is robbing me constantly and leaves me but little for myself and my children. I will slaughter the two sheep and eat their meat, and the priest will cease to rob me.'

" Thus thought the poor widow in her heart, but scarcely had she slaughtered her two sheep, her only property, than Aaron once more appeared and demanded the shoulder, the two cheeks and the maw as his share.

" ' This is the Law,' he said, ' for it is written: " And this shall be the priest's due from the people, whether it be the ox or sheep, that they shall give unto the priest the shoulder, and the two cheeks, and the maw ".' [2]

" When the poor widow heard these words, she exclaimed:

" ' Woe unto me! I had hoped never to see again the face of this priest who has been robbing me all my life, but lo! he has come again.' In her anger she said in her heart:

" ' I will contrive that neither I nor he shall have anything of the meat of my sheep.' Turning to Aaron, she said:

" ' I cannot give thee the share thou art claiming, for I have devoted the slaughtered sheep to God.' But Aaron replied:

' " If such is the case, then *all* is mine, for everything devoted in Israel belongs to the priest.[3] Such is the Law.' Thus speaking, he seized the two slaughtered sheep and walked away, leaving the widow and her orphan daughters weeping bitterly.

" Thus," concluded Korah, " the priests are always acting,

[1] *Deuteron.*, 18, 4.   [2] *Deuteron.*, 18, 3.   [3] *Numbers*, 18, 14.

despoiling the poor, the widows, and the orphans. When the children of Israel are asking them: why are ye acting thus? they reply: because such is the Law!"

When the people heard these words spoken by Korah, they were very wroth against Moses and Aaron.[1]

Korah and his partisans rebelled against Moses and Aaron, the Prophets of the Most High, but swift punishment was meted out to them. The ground clave asunder, the earth opened her mouth and swallowed up Korah, his followers and their households, and all the men that appertained unto Korah, and all their goods.[2]

One man, however, had a lucky escape, owing his salvation to his wife. His name was On, the son of Peleth. His wife was a clever woman, and when she saw Korah talking to her husband and persuading him to rebel against Moses and Aaron and depose them from both leadership and priesthood, she did not approve of the plot. On had given his promise to Korah to join him, but when the leader of the rebellion had left, and On was discussing the matter with his wife, the latter said to him:

" I do not approve of this plot, and as for thyself, my dear husband, no benefit will ever accrue to thee from the rebellion, whether it be successful or not. If Moses gains the victory and is master, thou wilt be subject to him, and if Korah is successful, thou wilt be subject to him."

" Thou art right," admitted On, struck by the truth of his wife's argument, " but what can I do now? I have given an oath to Korah to join him when he comes to our tent to fetch me, and it is incumbent upon me to keep my oath."

" Do not thou worry," said On's wife, " and leave the matter to me. I will contrive it so that neither Korah nor his followers will dare approach the tent to fetch thee." [3]

---

[1] *Yalkut*, § 750; *Midrash Shokher Tob*; *Midrash Agadah*, ed. Buber, Vol. II, pp. 116–117.
[2] *Numbers*, 16, 32.   [3] *Sanhedrin*, 109b; *Midrash Tanchuma, ibid.*

Thereupon she gave wine to drink to her husband, so that he became intoxicated and fell into a deep sleep. When Korah and his company came to fetch On, the latter's wife uncovered her hair, and, letting her long tresses stream loose, appeared at the door of the tent. None of Korah's company dared approach a woman with uncovered head and streaming hair, and they at once drew back. In vain did they make several attempts to get at On, the son of Peleth, but every time when they saw the woman in this condition they started back.

On awoke from his sleep at the very moment when Korah and his company were being swallowed up by the earth. He heard a tremendous noise and loud clamour, and the bed upon which he slept began to rock. Greatly frightened, he asked his wife what it meant.

" It is the punishment meted out to Korah and to his company for their sin in plotting a rebellion against Moses and Aaron," replied his wife.[1]

When On heard these words, he thanked the Lord who had sent him a righteous and clever wife, to whom apply the words:

" Every wise woman buildeth her house; but the foolish plucketh it down with her own hands." [2]

The sons of Korah, too, had been saved.

The death and destruction of Korah and his company ought to have convinced the children of Israel that Moses was only acting according to the will of God, that he had never usurped the power for himself or arbitrarily invested his brother Aaron with the priesthood. The conviction may have been brought home to the children of Israel, but still they persisted in seeking quarrel with Moses. They now accused him of being responsible for the death of many noble men in Israel.

" Had Moses not excited the revengefulness of the Lord," they said, " the men would not have perished."

[1] *Sanhedrin*, 110a; *Pesikta* (*Sutarta*), section *Korah*.   [2] *Proverbs*, 14, 1.

These words of the children of Israel brought upon them the anger of the Lord.

The wrath went out from the Lord, and the plague began. At this critical moment, Moses remembered the remedy against death which the angel of death had once taught him. When he ascended to Heaven to receive the Torah, the angels had at first objected to Moses' presence in the celestial regions, and had looked upon him as an intruder. In the end, however, they became his friends, bestowed gifts upon him, and taught him many secrets. The angel of death, too, had taught him a remedy how to stay death, and this was to burn incense.

Turning now to Aaron, Moses commanded him to take holy fire from the altar, put incense upon it, and go quickly among the congregation. Unaware of the secret remedy taught unto Moses by the angel of death Aaron was surprised.

"My brother," he said, "hast thou in view my death? Dost thou not remember that my two sons, Nadab and Abihu, died because they had put strange fire into the censers, and now thou commandest me to carry holy fire outside."

"Know, my brother," said Moses, "that whilst thou art thus talking, the children of Israel are dying. Go and do quickly as thou art bidden."

"If such is the case," said Aaron, "and the lives of the children of Israel are at stake, I will carry out thy command, for it is better that I or a thousand like me should be burned, but that Israel might be saved."

Aaron hurried out and stayed the angel of death.[1]

During their wandering in the wilderness the Israelites had to contend with many foes, Edomites, Amorites, and Moabites, Og, King of Bashan, and Balak, King of Moab, all of whom were jealous of the strength of the children of Israel, and sought to harm them.

When Aaron died, the clouds of glory which for forty years

---

[1] *Pesikta Sutarta*, section *Korah*; *Sabbath*, 89a; cf. *Midrash Agadah*, p. 118.

had covered the site of the camp, vanished, and their disappearance brought terror to the hearts of Israel.

"Now that we are no longer protected by the clouds of glory," they said, "the clouds which made it impossible for our enemies to approach our camp, we shall be harassed by our foes." And indeed, thus it really soon came to pass.

The first foe who now once more came to wage war upon Israel, though not an open but an underhand war, was Amalek, the grandson of Esau. The other sons of Esau, as soon as they learned that Aaron was dead and that the clouds of glory had disappeared, rejoiced greatly and sent word to Amalek requesting him to wage war upon Israel. Amalek was ready to appear once more in the field, especially since Israel seemed to have stumbled and sinned before the Lord. Remembering, however, past experiences, Amalek decided not to go in open warfare against the sons of Israel, but to use craft. His men, therefore, disguised themselves as Canaanites, donned Canaanite costume, and learned to speak the speech of the Canaanites.

"The Lord," said Amalek, "hearkens unto the prayers of Israel and always answers them. Now, when the Israelites will see us and take us for Canaanites they will, no doubt, implore the Lord to come to their assistance against the Canaanites and not against the Amalekites, and we shall thus be saved and will slay them."

Amalek's men, disguised as Canaanites, now concealed their swords in their garments and appeared in Israel's camp.

"We are Canaanites," they said, "and have come to condole with you, for we have heard that a great calamity has befallen you on your way, and that your High-Priest Aaron is dead." Thus spoke the Amalekites, making use of the speech of Canaan, and suddenly fell upon the children of Israel.

But when the latter saw these men dressed like Canaanites and speaking the speech of Canaan, but whose countenances

denounced them as Amalekites, descendants of Esau, they
prayed unto the Lord as follows: " Lord of the Universe!
strange are these men with whom we are now waging war, and
strange are their deeds, we do not know whether they are of
the nation of Canaan or of Amalek. We pray therefore unto
Thee to visit punishment upon them to whichsoever nation
they belong."

The Lord hearkened unto the prayers of the children of
Israel, stood by them and delivered Amalek into their hands.[1]

One of Israel's foes were the Amorites. When they heard
that the children of Israel would soon have to pass through the
valley of Arnon, they said to each other:

" Let us go to that valley and there lie in wait for Israel."
Now the valley of Arnon was enclosed by two lofty mountains
that lay very close together. The Amorites hurried to the
valley and hid in the numerous caves on the slopes of the
mountains. " When the Israelites," they said, " will penetrate
into the narrow defile between the two mountains, we will
sally forth, attack them suddenly and thus easily destroy
them."

The plan of the Amorites was, however, frustrated by the
Lord. Before Israel went the ark which levelled the mountains
and smoothed the rough places.

When Israel had reached the valley of Arnon, ascended
one mountain and intended to descend into the defile, the two
mountains were by a Divine miracle moved so close together
that the Amorites were crushed. One mountain was full of
caves wherein the Amorites were hiding, whilst the other
consisted of pointed, jutting rocks. When the rocks entered
into the caves, the Amorites concealed in them were all crushed,
and Israel was thus delivered from a dangerous foe.

The Israelites passed on and would never have known what
a miracle had just been performed for them by the hand of

[1] *Midrash Tanchuma*, section *Chukath*; *Yalkut*, § 764; cf. *Midrash Agadah*, p. 127.

God. But there were two lepers among the Israelites, Eth and Hav, who, according to custom, were following the camp. These two suddenly saw blood flowing from under the mountains and they hurried and informed the people of what had occurred.[1]

According to another source the Israelites learned the fate of the Amorites through the well. The Lord bade the well to flow past the caves and wash out the corpses of the Amorites, and it was thus that the children of Israel discovered the miracle the Lord had wrought for them.[2]

When the Israelites had passed the valley of Arnon, the Lord commanded Moses to wage war against Sihon, King of Heshbon, the Amorite. Before, however, waging war against Sihon, Moses sent him messengers of peace. " The Lord," he said in his heart, " has commanded me to contend in battle against Sihon, but I know that He loves peace and will not be angry with me if I first send messengers of peace to the Amorite." Moses was following the example of the Lord who had sent him to Pharaoh with words of peace before punishing the Egyptians and compelling them to let Israel go.

Sihon, King of Heshbon, refused the peace proposals of the leader of Israel, but the Lord was well pleased with the conduct of His servant.

" Thou hast acted well," He said, " in offering peace before waging war, and in future thou shalt never declare war upon a city, but first urge the inhabitants to surrender in peace."

Another redoubtable enemy of Israel was Og, King of Bashan. Og was one of the giants who had been saved during the flood by clambering upon the roof of Noah's ark.[3] It was he also who had hurried to bring news to Abraham concerning Lot's bondage. Og's motive was not a disinterested one. He

---

[1] *Berachoth*, 54b; *Yalkut*, § 764; cf. *Midrash Agadah*, pp. 128–129.
[2] See *Midrash Tanchuma*, section *Chukath*; *Num*, Rabba, 79.
[3] See Vol. I, Ch. 17.

hoped that Abraham would hasten to the rescue of his kinsman, be killed in battle, and thus would he, Og, be able to get possession of Sarah the beautiful.[1] Og was of a gigantic build, and his strength was enormous. His thigh bone alone is said to have measured more than three miles (parasangs). " I was once a gravedigger," relates one Rabbi in the Talmud, " and I hunted a stag that fled into the thigh bone of a dead man. For three miles did I run after the stag without either catching it or reaching the end of the thigh bone. I made inquiries afterwards and found out that it was the thigh bone of Og, King of Bashan."[2] Og is said to have been a slave of Abraham who subsequently gave him his freedom. One day, when Abraham rebuked him, Og was frightened, and one of his teeth fell out. Out of this Abraham fashioned a bed in which the giant used to sleep.[3] The giant's food and drink were in accordance with his size and strength. He devoured daily a thousand oxen and as many other animals, and his daily drink was a thousand measures of liquid. Such was the giant Og, and it was quite natural that Moses should have hesitated to wage war against him, but the Lord told him not to fear the giant.

Now when Og heard what had happened to Sihon, King of Heshbon, he said unto himself: " It will be easy for me to destroy Moses and the whole camp of Israel." He went up and sat upon the wall of the city with his feet touching the ground.

Moses approached the place of Edrei, reaching the outskirts at nightfall. " Let us pass here the night," he said, " and in the morning we shall attack the city."

Next morning, when Moses looked towards the city, he was amazed.

" Is it possible," he cried, " that during the night the men of Edrei could have built such a high wall?" But when Moses

---

[1] See Vol. I, Ch. 22.   [2] *Niddah*, 24b.   [3] *Yalkut Chadash*, 16b.

looked more closely he saw that it was not a second wall, but Og sitting upon the first wall and darkening the sun with his giant stature.[1]

Og then said in his heart:

" I see that the camp of Israel is three parasangs in circumference. I will therefore tear up a mountain three parasangs wide, lay it upon my head and then hurl it upon Moses and the Israelites and thus crush them." Thus thought Og and carried out his plan.

" Fear not," said the Lord to Moses, " for he is in thy hand."

A miracle now happened which caused Og's death. Ants came and perforated the mountain and it sank over the giant's head. He made an effort to shake it off, but his teeth suddenly grew into tusks, pushed and thrust through the mountain so that the giant, in spite of his efforts, could not draw his head out.

Now Moses was ten cubits in height, and he took a hatchet ten cubits long, leaped into the air ten cubits and hit Og on the ankle. The giant fell down, and Moses was able to slay him.[2]

Moses and the Israelites had also to fight against the Moabites. Balak, King of Moab, a great magician himself, having noticed that the Israelites were conquering their enemies by supernatural strength, decided to call upon Balaam to curse the people of Israel.

Accompanied by his two sons, the famous wizards Jannes and Jambres, Balaam, after some hesitation, set out to curse the people of God. His magic power, however, had no effect on Israel, the nation being protected by the merits of the Patriarchs and by angels. The heathen prophet's curses turned to blessings. Unable to fulfil Balak's wish to curse Israel, the

---

[1] *Deuter. Rabba*, 1; cf. Eisenmenger, *loc. cit.*, Vol. I, p. 389.
[2] *Berachoth*, 54b; *Sepher Hajashar.*

magician gave the King of Moab an advice, counselling him
to resort to seduction.

"The God of this people," said Balaam, "hates lewdness
and unchastity. Select thou, therefore, pretty women, the
handsomest daughters of Moab, and send them out to seduce
the sons of Israel to unchastity and then to idolatry. The God
of this people will then punish them for their sin."

Thus spoke Balaam, the wicked magician, and Balak, acting
upon his advice, proceeded in the following manner. He
pitched tents, at the entrance of which old women were offering
linen garments for sale.

When the Israelites came to buy the garments, the old
women showed them some samples of the goods which they
were selling at a cheap price, but invited the men into the
interior of the tents where, they said, they would find more
beautiful wares. The unsuspecting purchasers, anxious to
buy linen garments, went inside, where they were received
by young and beautiful women, wearing splendid and costly
robes and well perfumed. The sirens of Moab employed all
their blandishments and allurements and seduced the men
to unchastity and then to idolatry, making them worship the
idol of Peor. It was thus that Israel sinned at Shittim in consequence of the wicked counsel of Balaam the magician.

The heathen prophet, however, was very soon punished
for the harm he had thus done to Israel. When Phinehas,
the son of Eleazar, had slain Simri, the prince of the tribe of
Simeon, and Cozbi, the woman with whom he had sinned,
and who was a daughter of Balak himself, the Israelites were
commanded to wage war against the Midianites. Balaam was
with that nation helping them against Israel. Resorting to
witchcraft, he flew in the air, but Phinehas held up the pure
gold plate upon which was engraved the ineffable name, and
Balaam fell to the ground. In vain did the magician plead for
his life. "Thou dost deserve death," said Phinehas, "for in

addition to thy evil deeds in the past, as one of Pharaoh's counsellors, thou art responsible for the death of 24,000 Israelites who had been lured to sin by thy wicked counsel." Thus the great magician, who is supposed to have been none other than Laban, met his death.[1]

[1] *Targum Pseudo-Jonathan, Numbers*, 22, 22; 23, 9, 10, 23; 24, 25; 31, 8; *Numbers Rabba*, 20; *Midrash Tanchuma*, section *Balak*; *Sanhedrin*, 106b; *Sepher Hajashar*; Philo, *De Vita Moysis*, I, 48; 54–56; Josephus, *Antiq.*, IV, 6, 2; 6–9; see also *The Samaritan Book of Joshua*, Ch. 3 and 4; Hamburger, *Real-Encyklopädia, s.v. Balaam*; cf. for the whole chapter, Lewner, *Kol Agadoth*. Vol. II, pp. 98–110; 120–130.

CHAPTER XXV

The Death of Aaron, or Aaron the Peacemaker

Moses is commanded to prepare Aaron for his death—The grief of Moses—He changes his usual custom—The difficult passages of the Law —The book of *Genesis*—The wonders of the Creator—The sin of Adam— The sentence of death—Human destiny—Moses talks of death—The walk to Mount Hor—Aaron is honoured—The joy of the children of Israel— The popular High-Priest—Aaron the Peacemaker—Nabal the son of Bir-shah—The women praise Aaron—On Mount Hor—The light of God— Moses is embarrassed—The mysterious cave—The couch spread out by celestial hands—Aaron mentions the word of death—Moses consoles his brother—The soul lured away by a Divine kiss—The return of Moses and Eleazar—The anger of the children of Israel—Satan among the people— The prayer of Moses—The bier of Aaron is carried in mid-air by angels— The grief of the people—The disappearance of the clouds of glory—The sun and the moon reappear.

When the day arrived for Aaron to die, the Lord said unto Moses:

" The time has now come for thy brother Aaron to be gathered to his people. Go thou now and tell him to prepare for death. Console him, however, and say that even if he is doomed to die, his sons will inherit his High-Priesthood." Moses was sorely grieved when he heard these words, and he wept passionately all the night. When dawn broke, he betook himself to Aaron and called: " Aaron, Aaron, come out."

The High-Priest hurried out of his tent and was astonished to see his brother standing at the door. It had been the custom for Aaron and the elders to appear every morning before Moses to give him greeting. Aaron was therefore surprised to see his brother making a change in the usual custom.

"I have studied the Holy Law all the night," said Moses, "and finding some difficult passages I came hither to ask thee to elucidate them, perchance thou wilt be able to explain them unto me."

"Tell me what it is about?"

"I have not tasted any sleep this night," said Moses, "and I no longer remember the difficult passages, but I do know that they are in the book of *Genesis*."

Aaron fetched the book of *Genesis* and they began to read it. They read the section relating the creation of the world, and both exclaimed:

"How wonderful are the works of the Lord and how great His wisdom with which He created the Universe!"

When they came to the section relating the creation of Adam, Moses said:

"What can I say with regard to Adam who brought death into the world?"

"Such is the will of the Lord," said Aaron. "God had placed Adam and his wife in the Garden of Eden and bestowed upon them benefits such as He has not bestowed upon mortal man ever since, but as they sinned, they were expelled from the Garden of Eden, and death was decreed upon man. Such is the end of man."

"And such will be our end," added Moses, "although I carried off a victory over the ministering angels, and thou didst ward off death and stay the hand of the angel of death. How long have we still to live? A few years, perhaps." Thereupon Moses began to speak about death.

Aaron listened and wondered.

"Moses," he said, "why art thou talking so much about death to-day?"

Moses did not reply, but when Aaron insisted, he answered evasively:

"The Lord has bidden me to make a communication to

thee: let us therefore ascend the mountain of Hor, and there I will communicate unto thee the word of the Lord." [1]

In other sources we read that when the Lord commanded Moses to inform Aaron of his approaching death, the Prophet exclaimed:

" Lord of the Universe! Thou art the Lord of the world and the Master over all the creatures that Thou hast created in the world. They are in Thy hand, and in Thy hand it lies to do with them as it pleases Thy sovereign will. But how can I go to my brother and announce to him the sentence of death? I am not fit to repeat Thy commission, for my brother is older than I. How shall I presume to go to him and tell him to ascend the mountain of Hor and die there?"

" There is no need for thee, Moses," said the Lord, " to utter the word of death with thy lips, or to tell thy brother that he is to be gathered to his people. Take thou Aaron and Eleazar, his son, and bring them up unto Mount Hor. There thou wilt speak to thy brother soothing words, gentle and sweet, and he will understand what awaits him, and that his time has come to die. Thereupon wilt thou strip Aaron of his priestly garments and put them upon Eleazar, his son, who will inherit the High-Priesthood."

Thus spake the Lord, and Moses was sorely grieved and there was a great tumult in his heart, and he knew not what to do. He wept all night, until the cock crew, and in the early morning he summoned Eleazar and the elders of the congregation, and they all proceeded to Aaron's tent.

Astonished to find Moses so early at the door of his tent, and so contrary to the usual custom, Aaron inquired after the cause.

" The Lord," said Moses, " has bidden me to communicate something to thee."

" Speak," said Aaron.

[1] *Yalkut*, § 764; Jellinek, *Beth-Hamidrash*, Vol. I, pp. 91–95.

But Moses replied: " Wait until we are out of doors."

Aaron thereupon put on his priestly garments, and they all proceeded to Mount Hor.[1] And that was the manner in which they were walking along. Aaron was walking in the centre, Moses at his right hand, and Joshua at his left, the princes of the congregation were at the right hand of Moses, and the elders at Joshua's left.

When the children of Israel saw Aaron walking in the centre, thus occupying the place of honour, they rejoiced greatly, for Aaron was well beloved by and popular with the people. " Blessed be the Lord," they exclaimed, " who has vouchsafed such honour unto Aaron, the man of peace."

When the group arrived at the Tabernacle, Aaron wanted to enter, but Moses held him back and said: " No, we shall go beyond the camp."

When the children of Israel saw Aaron, accompanied by Moses, Joshua, the princes, and the elders, approaching Mount Hor, they began to speak of his many good deeds and acts of kindness and peace, praising the noble disposition and kindness of heart of the popular High-Priest.

" Do you know," said one of the children of Israel, " do you know Nabal, the son of Birshah?"

" We know him well," said the others. " He used to be a wicked man, very quarrelsome and hard-hearted. He embittered the lives of his kinsfolk and was despised and shunned by all his acquaintances. What has happened to him?"

"Nabal, the son of Birshah," replied the first speaker, "has now mended his ways; there is no one like him in the whole camp, so single-hearted and loving peace and justice so much."

" How did his conversion come about?" asked the astonished hearers.

" His conversion was brought about by Aaron, the man of peace. When the High-Priest heard how wicked Nabal the son

---

[1] Jellinek, *loc. cit.*

of Birshah was and how evil were his ways, he sought him out, visited him daily and became his close friend, even like a brother unto him. Nabal was proud and pleased at the honour of being such a close friend of Aaron the High-Priest. He then said in his heart: ' I must mend my evil ways, be kind and merciful, and love peace and justice, even as Aaron does, for if he hears of my evil ways he will no longer associate with me, and I will be deprived of his friendship.' Thus Nabal became a man of peace and of justice, kind, merciful, and forgiving, and Aaron praised and blessed him."

Many women now joined the group and they, too, extolled the virtues of Aaron the Peacemaker.

" Our husbands," they said, " used to seek us quarrel, and our lives were so embittered that many a time during the day did we pray for death. When this became known unto Aaron, he began to visit our tents and to speak kind words to our husbands, pointing out to them the advantages of peace, of justice and loving kindness. At first our husbands would not lend an ear to the noble words of the High-Priest, but he never lost patience and continued to pursue his work of reconciliation. He did not leave our tents until our husbands had promised him to mend their ways. A few days passed, during which our husbands did not seek us any quarrel but treated us kindly, and when they noticed how happy our lives had become since peace was reigning supreme in our families, they exclaimed: ' There is no greater blessing for men than peace.' Our hearts are now full of gratitude to the High-Priest, and daily do we bless Aaron the Peacemaker." [1]

When Moses, Aaron, Joshua, and the elders reached the mountain of Hor, Moses said unto them:

" Stay ye here until we return to you. Aaron, Eleazar, and myself will go up to the top of the mountain."

---

[1] See *Midrash Agadah*, ed. Buber, p. 126; *Abot di Rabbi Nathan*, Ch. 12; cf. Lewner, *loc. cit.*, pp. 115-117; see also Bialik, *Sephar Haagadah*, Vol. I, pp. 80-81.

The three of them went up to the summit, but Moses knew not how to communicate the sad tidings to his elder brother, and tell him of his impending death.

" Aaron," he began, " has the Lord given anything into thy charge?"

" Yes," said the High-Priest. " He has given into my keeping the altar, the table, and the showbreads."

" Is that all?" asked Moses. " The Lord has also entrusted unto thee a light, and He may now command thee to return unto him all the treasures he has entrusted unto thee."

" Not one light," said Aaron, " but the seven lights which now burn in the sanctuary has the Lord entrusted to me."

Moses saw that his brother did not yet understand what light he was alluding to.

" I was not speaking of the lights which are the handiwork of man," he said, " but of the light of God, the soul of man which is likened to a light, as it is written: ' The spirit of man is the lamp of the Lord '." [1]

Aaron, who was a simple-hearted, innocent man, at last understood the allusion. He trembled greatly and exclaimed: " The fear of death is seizing me."

Whilst they were thus conversing, behold, a cave opened before them.

" Aaron, my brother," said Moses, " let us enter this cave." He was anxious to strip Aaron of his priestly garments, but knew not how to effect this or even how to mention the subject to Aaron. At last he spoke and thus he said:

" The cave seems to be attractive, but it is not proper for thee to enter it whilst wearing the holy garments of priesthood. The cave may be unclean and perchance there are old graves therein, and thy garments might be defiled. Take them off therefore and hand them over to thy son Eleazar until we return."

[1] *Proverbs, 20, 27.*

" Thou hast spoken well," said Aaron, and he permitted his brother to strip him of four of his priestly garments which were those distinguishing the High-Priest from the ordinary priests.

Eleazar put on his father's garments and remained outside, whilst the brothers entered the cave.

Here they beheld a couch spread out by celestial hands, a table prepared, and a lighted candle on it. Ministering angels were surrounding the couch.

" Moses," said Aaron, " wilt thou now tell me at last what it is that the Lord has spoken unto thee concerning me and what is the commission He has entrusted to thee? Let me hear it now, whether it be good or bad news, whether it be about my life or even my death." Thus spoke Aaron, and Moses replied:

" My brother, as thou hast thyself pronounced the word of death, then I can tell thee now that it is concerning thy death that the Lord has spoken unto me. Thy time to depart from the earth has come. I have been very grieved over the news, and could not bring it over myself to tell thee about it. Thy death, however, is not like the death of other mortals. Ministering angels have come to stand by thee in thy last hour. See thou now, my brother. When our sister Miriam died, we, thou and I, stood about her bier, wept for her and buried her. When thou wilt now die, thy son Eleazar and I will show thee the last marks of honour, weep for thee and bury thee, but who will bury me? I have no brother to perform this pious act. Thy lot is more envious than mine. When thou art dead, thy sons will inherit thy dignity, but when I die, strangers will take my place."

Thus spoke Moses, uttering soothing and comforting words so as to make his brother Aaron reconciled to his fate, and look forward to his hour of parting with equanimity. Moses thereupon invited the High-Priest to lie down upon the couch prepared by celestial hands. Aaron did as he was bidden, and at the request of Moses he folded his hands upon his breast and shut his eyes.

Immediately the Lord lured away the soul of Aaron by a Divine kiss. And clouds of glory came down and enveloped the body of the High-Priest.

As soon as Moses left the cave it immediately vanished.

When Eleazar saw his Uncle Moses reappear again without his father, he asked:

" Master, where is my father?"

" He has entered into the house of eternity," replied Moses. Both now descended from the mountain of Hor into the camp.[1]

The children of Israel were watching the descent of Moses and Eleazar, and noticed with astonishment and concern that their favourite, Aaron the Peacemaker, was not with them. Immediately Satan mixed among the people and kindled their anger against Moses and Eleazar. " Moses and Eleazar," he whispered into their ears, " are descending the mount of Hor, but the High-Priest is not with them! What has become of him? What have his brother and son done to him?"

Some at once suggested that Moses, jealous of Aaron's popularity, had put his brother to death, whilst others thought that it was Eleazar who had done the deed, anxious to inherit the High-Priesthood. Others, however, thought that Aaron had been translated to Heaven.

When Moses came down, the people rushed at him and loudly clamoured for Aaron.

" Where is Aaron?" they demanded fiercely. " What have ye, thou and Eleazar, done unto him, he who was a man of peace and our friend?"

Bursting into tears, Moses replied:

[1] Jellinek, *loc. cit.*

" Aaron, my brother, has entered the house of eternity."

" Dost thou mean to say," queried the children of Israel, " that he died?"

" So it is," replied Moses.

" How can that be?" said the people. " How could the man who had overcome and set to flight the angel of death and stayed the hand of death die? We do not believe thee. Either thou or Eleazar put him to death. Show us the High-Priest, either living or dead."

Incited by Satan, the people wanted to stone Moses and Eleazar.

Moses thereupon prayed unto the Lord and thus he said: " I am not afraid to meet death at their hands and be stoned, but I am grieved at the sin they will thus commit. I also fear that if the people are not convinced of Aaron's death but think him still alive, they may worship him as a god, for they loved and admired him much. I pray therefore unto Thee to show to the people the couch whereupon lies the body of my brother."

Thereupon the Lord beckoned to His ministering angels, and they immediately opened the cave, lifted up and carried on high the couch whereupon Aaron lay. The children of Israel saw the couch floating in the air; they saw and knew that Aaron the Peacemaker, their friend, was indeed dead, and they wept and mourned for him thirty days.[1]

When the children of Israel turned to the camp they perceived that the clouds of glory had vanished. Now the generation which was born in the desert had never seen either the sun or the moon, for these heavenly bodies had always been hidden by the clouds of glory. When the men of this generation, owing to the departure of the clouds of glory, now perceived the sun and moon for the first time, they were ready to prostrate

---

[1] *Midrash Agadah*, p. 126; Jellinek, *loc. cit.*; *Yalkut*, § 764; cf. *Midrash Tanchuma*, section *Chukath*.

themselves, and to worship the heavenly bodies. But the Lord rebuked them.

" Have I not commanded you," he said, " not to be drawn away and worship the sun and the moon, when you lift up your eyes to heaven and see the sun and the moon and the stars, even all the host of heaven?" [1]

---

[1] *Deuteron.*, 4, 19; see Jellinek, *loc. cit.*; cf. for the whole chapter, Lewner, *loc. cit.*, pp. 113–120; Grünbaum, *loc. cit.*, pp. 174–176.

THE CHILDREN OF ISRAEL SEE AARON'S COUCH FLOATING IN
THE AIR

CHAPTER XXVI

The Death of Moses

Moses refuses to die—His pleading—Adam and all the Patriarchs had died—If his life were to be spared, the children of Israel would worship him as a god—Moses pretends that he is worthier than Adam and the Patriarchs—The two oaths of the Lord—The prayer that slashes and tears like a sword—The heavenly windows are locked so that the prayer of Moses may not ascend to Heaven—Moses asks to be changed into a bird or a fish and be permitted to enter the Promised Land—Sun and moon intercede for the son of Amram—The Lord rebukes them—Moses implores heaven and earth, the mountains and the sea, and the whole nature to pray for him —The Lord consoles Moses—Moses serves Joshua and shows him honour —When Moses is dead there will be no one to plead for Israel—The triumph of Sammael, the angel of death—Michael and Zagzagel refuse to take the soul of Moses—Sammael and Moses—The Prophet triumphs over the angel of death—Sammael acknowledges his inability to take the soul of Moses—He is set to flight and blinded by the Prophet—Moses blesses the children of Israel—The Lord, accompanied by the angels Michael, Gabriel, and Zagzagel, comes to take the soul of Moses—The soul of the Prophet refuses to leave his body—Lured away by a Divine kiss—The lamentations of the ministering angels, of the stars and constellations, of heaven and earth—The King of Aram and the sepulchre of Moses—The elusive tomb— The reason why the sepulchre of Moses is unknown—Joshua's lack of modesty—He is unable to answer the questions put to him.

When the day approached on which Moses was to depart from earth, the Lord said unto him: " Behold thy days approach that thou must die." [1]

Moses replied: " Lord of the Universe! After all the trouble I have had, Thou sayest unto me that I must die. I refuse to die for I want to live."

But the Lord said: " Enough! Thus far shalt thou go and not farther; call thou Joshua that I may give him My instructions, and appoint him as thy successor."

[1] *Deuteron.*, 31, 14.

343

Thereupon Moses began to plead before the Lord, and thus he said: " Lord of the Universe! What sin have I committed that I should die?"

But the Lord replied: " Thou must die, because death has been decreed upon the first man."

" Was it in vain then," pleaded Moses, " that my foot trod the clouds and that I did run before the children of Israel like a horse?"

" Even Adam did die," said the Lord.

" Adam," said Moses, " had received only one command that he could have easily obeyed and even this he disobeyed, whilst I have not transgressed any of Thy commandments."

" Abraham, too," said the Lord, " had to die."

" He was the father of Ishmael who did evil deeds," said Moses, " and his descendants arouse Thy anger."

" Isaac, his son," replied the Lord, " did not hesitate to bare his throat, when I commanded his father to offer him as a sacrifice."

" From Isaac," replied Moses, " issued the wicked Esau who will destroy Thy Temple."

" Twelve tribes," answered the Lord, " issued from Jacob, and they did not anger me."

But Moses still continued to plead.

" Lord of the Universe," he said: " none of the Patriarchs did ascend to Heaven and their feet did not tread the clouds. Besides, the future generations will say that had Moses not perchance been found guilty, the Lord would not have taken him out of this world. Lord of the Universe, let me enter the land of Israel and live there at least two or three years! If I have sinned, forgive me. How often did it happen that the children of Israel have sinned, but when I prayed unto Thee Thou didst forgive them, dealing with them according to Thy quality of mercy, whilst me Thou wilt not vouchsafe forgiveness, even for one single sin. Let me live that I may proclaim Thy glory to the future generations and sound Thy praises unto the inhabitants of the earth. Thou didst manifest Thyself unto me in the burning bush; through me Thou didst cleave the seas and give the Law to the children of Israel. Let me live so that I may be able to tell to the future generations how Thou didst rain manna from Heaven for the children of Israel and bring forth water from the rock. Let me live, Lord of the Universe, that I may tell all this to the future generations and to the children of Israel."

" If thy life were to be spared," said the Lord, " the children of Israel will look upon thee as a god and worship thee as such."

" Thou didst already test me," said Moses, " when the children of Israel sinned in the matter of the golden calf."

" Whose son art thou, Moses?" asked the Lord.

" I am the son of Amram," replied Moses.

" And whose son was he?"

" The son of Jizhar."

" And he?"

" The son of Kehath."

" And he?"

" The son of Levi."

" And did any one of thy ancestors remain alive and not die?"

" They all died," said Moses.

" Then why shouldst thou remain alive? Art thou more just than Adam? Art thou worthier than Noah? Art thou greater than Abraham, whom I tested with ten tests? Art thou worthier than Isaac?"

" Lord of the Universe!" pleaded Moses, " Adam and Eve stole the forbidden fruit from the Garden of Eden and ate of it against Thy command. Did I ever steal aught from Thee?" ' My servant Moses who is faithful in all mine house ', Thou Thyself didst write of me. Adam and Eve were seduced by

the serpent, but I called the dead back to life through a serpent.
Thou didst send the waters of the Flood upon Noah and his
generation, but he never begged Thy mercy for the sinners in
his generation, whilst I prayed unto Thee and said: ' Yet now,
if Thou wilt forgive their sin; and if not, blot me, I pray
Thee, out of Thy book which Thou hast written!' [1] Ishmael
is a son of Abraham, and his children will once destroy Thy
children. Esau is a son of Isaac, and one day his children will
burn down Thy sanctuary and destroy Thy children, Thy
priests, and Thy Levites!"

" Didst thou not kill the Egyptian?" said the Lord; " Did
I perchance counsel thee to kill him?"

" Lord of the Universe!" pleaded Moses, " Thou didst
slay all the first-born of Egypt, and should I die because I
slew one single Egyptian?"

" Art thou my equal?" replied the Lord. " I slay and I
restore to life; canst thou call back to life him that thou didst
slay? But enough, I showed thee great honour and made
thee great, but thou must share the fate of all men and die."

" Lord of the Universe, I am aware that Thou didst set me
on high and I am unable to enumerate the many benefits
Thou didst bestow upon me, but now I am asking of Thee
only one thing: let me pass the Jordan into the land of
Israel."

" Moses," said the Lord, " I swore two oaths, one was that
thou shouldst not enter the Promised Land, and the other
was that I will never destroy the children of Israel. If it is
thy wish that I should break the first oath, then I may also break
the other and destroy the children of Israel."

" Lord of the Universe," cried Moses, " may Moses die
and a thousand others like him, but let not one soul of the
children of Israel be destroyed. But what will Thy creatures
say? Will they not say: ' The feet that trod upon the clouds,

----
[1] *Exodus*, 32, 32.

the hands which received the Holy Law, the mouth which
spoke to the Almighty, should die!'?''

Moses' pleading was in vain, and the Lord refused to grant
his request. Moses thereupon put on sackcloth, threw ashes
upon his head and stood in prayer, so that heaven and earth
and all forms of creation trembled and said: '' Perchance it is
the will of the Lord to destroy this world and create a new one.''

Moses drew a circle about himself, stood in the centre of it,
and said: '' I will not move from this spot until judgment shall
have been suspended.''

Thereupon the Creator of the Universe bade the angels
proclaim in Heaven and make known to all the heavenly courts
of justice His command not to admit or accept the prayer of
Moses, and that no angel was to carry the prayer of the Prophet
before the Throne of Glory. And the Creator of the Universe
called the angel princes and all the angels of the Presence and
commanded them to descend at once and lock all the heavenly
gates and windows so that the prayer of Moses might not
ascend.

At that moment heaven and earth, all the foundations
thereof and all creation trembled and quaked, on account of
the prayer of Moses which was like a sharp sword that slashes
and rends. His prayer was like unto the Ineffable Name which
he had learned from the mouth of his teacher, the angel Zagzagel. Five hundred and fifteen prayers did Moses utter and
he said:

'' Lord of the Universe: remember how much trouble I
had to take with the children of Israel and how much I had to
bear until I gave them the Law and made them accept Thy
commandments, and I had hoped that even as I had suffered
pain with them shall I also behold their joy and good fortune.
And now, when the moment is near for Israel to enter the
Promised Land, I am to die and am not allowed to cross the
Jordan. Will not people say that Thou givest the lie to Thy

Torah? Didst Thou not say of the labourer: ' In his day thou shalt give him his hire '? [1] Is this my reward for my labours during forty years? For forty years I have suffered and laboured for the sake of Thy children in Egypt and in the desert, and now I may not even cross the Jordan?"

But the Lord replied: " Such is My decree."

Moses, however, pleaded again: " If I am not permitted to enter the Holy Land alive, let me enter it whilst I am dead."

But the Lord replied: " When Joseph came to Egypt, he never denied his origin, but proudly proclaimed ' I was stolen away out of the land of the Hebrews ', whilst thou didst give thyself out as an Egyptian, when thou camest to the land of Midian."

And Moses continued:

" Lord of the Universe! If I am not permitted to enter the Holy Land, let me be like one of the beasts in the field who feed on grass but are free to roam about and to see the world."

But the Lord would not grant his request.

" Lord of the Universe," Moses continued to plead, " let me fly like a bird in the air, that flies in the four directions of the world, gathers its food and at eve returns to its nest. Let me fly like a bird so that I may enter and see the Holy Land."

But the Lord refused to grant his request. And Moses pleaded again: " Let me be like a fish that I may spread my arms like two fins, leap over the Jordan and see the Holy Land! Carry me upon the pinions of the clouds, three parasangs above the Jordan, so that the clouds will be below me and I above, so that I may see the Land of Israel." [2]

But the Lord replied: " Speak no more unto Me of this matter."

---

[1] *Deuteron.*, 24, 15.
[2] *Deuteron. Rabba*, 9–11; *Midrash Tanchuma*, section *Vaethanan*, ed. Verona, p. 86a–b; *Yalkut*, § 819–821 and § 940; Jellinek, *Beth-Hamidrash*, Vol. I, pp. 115–119; see also *Proceedings of the Bibl. Arch. Soc.*, Vol. IX (1886–1887), pp. 40–47.

" Cut me into pieces, throw me over the Jordan and revive me there," pleaded Moses.

But the Lord refused to grant his request.

" Then let me at least cast a glance upon the Land of Israel," said Moses. In this point, the Lord complied with his wish.

Thereupon the sun and the moon left the Rakia and entered the heaven called Zebhoul and thus they pleaded before the Throne of Glory: " Lord of the Universe: if Thou wilt grant the request of the son of Amram we will continue to shed our light, but if Thou wilt refuse, we shall no longer shed our light upon the world."

And the Lord replied: " Every day men are worshipping you and yet you continue to shed your light. Ye care not for My honour, but ye show concern for the honour of a mortal man." [1]

When Moses saw that God lent no ear to his prayers, he tried to find someone to plead for him. He turned to heaven and to earth and implored them to plead for him.

Heaven and earth however replied: " Who are we that we should intercede for thee? Before imploring God's mercy for thee, we must first pray for ourselves, for is it not written: ' For the heavens shall vanish away like smoke, and the earth shall wax old like a garment '?" [2]

Moses then addressed himself to the sun and moon and cried: " Intercede for me!"

But sun and moon replied: " We have enough to do in praying for ourselves, for is it not written: ' Then the moon shall be confounded and the sun ashamed!'?" [3]

Moses then betook himself to the stars and the constellations. " Plead and pray for me," he cried.

But the stars and the constellations replied: " Before we plead for thee, we must plead and pray for ourselves, for is it not written: ' And all the host of heaven shall be dissolved '?" [4]

---

[1] *Nedarim*, 39b.   [2] *Isaiah*, 51b.   [3] *Ibid.*, 24, 23.   [4] *Ibid.*, 34, 4.

Moses then went to the hills and the mountains and beseeched them: " Pray for me!"

But the hills and the mountains replied: " We are too busy praying for ourselves, for is it not written: ' For the mountains shall depart, and the hills be removed '?" [1]

In vain did Moses betake himself to Mount Sinai, to the rivers, deserts, and all the elements of nature, none would intercede for him.

He then went to the sea and cried: " Pray and plead for me."

When the sea heard these words it trembled and quaked at the approach of the son of Amram: " Son of Amram," called the sea, " what has happened to thee, what ails thee, and why art thou different to-day? Art thou not the son of Amram who once came to me with a rod in his hand, beat me and clove me into twelve parts? I could not resist thee and was powerless against thee, because the Divine Majesty was at thy right hand. And now—what has come to thee, that thou art weeping and lamenting?"

When Moses was thus reminded by the sea of his past greatness, and the miracles he had performed, he burst into tears and cried aloud: " Oh, that I were as in the months of old.[2] When I came upon thee, O Sea, I was King of the world, but now I am prostrating myself and no one will hearken unto me or pay attention to me." [3]

Thereupon Moses went to the angel of the Face and begged him to intercede on his behalf, but the angel of the Face said: " Why dost thou exert thyself in vain? I have heard from behind the curtain that thy request in this instance will not be granted."

Then Moses put his hands upon his head and wept bitterly: " To whom," he cried, " shall I now go and beg him that he might implore God's mercy for me?"

[1] *Isaiah*, 54, 10.　　　[2] *Job*, 29, 2.　　　[3] *Yalkut*, § 821.

The Lord consoled Moses and said: " Moses, my son, why art thou so much aggrieved? Great honours await thee in the future world, for thou wilt enjoy and take part in all the delights of Paradise as it is written: ' That I may cause those that love me to inherit substance, and that I may fill their treasuries '.[1] Three hundred and ten worlds wilt thou inherit in the world to come." [2]

When Moses saw that the Lord had determined to carry out His sentence, he said: " If I am to die, only because the time has come for Joshua to be honoured and lead Israel into the Holy Land, then I am ready to retire, relinquish the leadership to Joshua and remain alive." Moses then went and stood before Joshua and called him Master.

Joshua was greatly frightened and said: " Dost thou call me Master?"

" Joshua," said Moses, " wouldst thou have me live and not die?"

" It is so," replied Joshua.

" Then submit that I should show honour unto thee even as thou didst show honour unto me. As long as I am alive I will be able to explain unto thee the difficult passages in the Torah."

" My Master," said Joshua, " I will submit to whatever thou mayest decide so that I may not be deprived of thy countenance."

Moses then began to show to Joshua due honour and served him as a pupil does serve his master.

When the children of Israel came to the tent of Moses they were informed that Moses, their teacher, had betaken himself to the tent of Joshua. When they saw Joshua sitting and Moses standing, they exclaimed in surprise: " Joshua! How canst thou allow Moses to stand, whilst thou art sitting?"

And when Joshua raised his eyes and beheld Moses, he

---

[1] *Proverbs*, 8, 21.   [2] Jellinek, *loc. cit.*

tore his clothes and cried: " Master, Master, Father, Father!"

Thereupon the children of Israel said unto Moses: " Moses our Master! Teach us the Law," but Moses replied:

" I have no right now!"

They insisted, however, and a voice called from Heaven: " Let Joshua teach you now God's word!"

Thereupon Joshua sat at the head and Moses was on his right and the sons of Aaron on his left. And when they entered the tent of assembly a pillar of cloud came down and separated Joshua from Moses.

" What did the Lord tell thee?" Moses asked of Joshua.

" Was I informed," replied Joshua, " with regard to the words of the Lord when He did speak unto thee?"

At that moment Moses cried: " Better a hundred deaths rather than jealousy. Lord of the Universe! Hitherto I have asked for life, but now I am ready to die." [1]

And as soon as Moses had thus expressed his readiness to die, the Lord called:

" Who will rise up for me against the evil-doers?" [2]

At that moment Metatron, the angel of the Presence, came and prostrated himself before the Throne of Glory: " Lord of the Universe!" he cried, " Moses was Thine in life, and is Thine in death."

But the Lord replied: " I will explain it unto thee. To what is it like? It is like to a king who had an only son. Every day this son angered him, and he would have put him to death had not his son's mother interceded on his behalf. After a time the mother died, and the king was grieved, both on her account and on account of his son. ' Many a time,' he said, ' did my son anger me, and I should have put him to death had not his mother pleaded for him, but now who will intercede for him?' Thus," said the Lord to Metatron, " I am not crying for the sake of Moses, but for the sake of Israel. Who will now plead

[1] *Deuteron. Rabba*, 9; *Yalkut*, §§ 821 and 940.   [2] *Psalms*, 94, 16.

for the children of Israel, when My anger is roused against them?"[1]

From the first day of the eleventh month to the sixth day of the twelfth month, that is the day before his death, Moses paid homage to Joshua, waiting upon him as a disciple would wait on his master, thus showing to the people of Israel that Joshua had now assumed the reins of government and that Moses had resigned his position.

All the Israelites were seized with sorrow and trembling, and Joshua himself wept and said: " How cometh such greatness and such honour unto me?"

Now a voice came from Heaven and called: " Moses, thou hast only five more hours to live."

Thereupon Moses desired Joshua to sit before the people like a king, wearing a crown studded with pearls, and a helmet of royalty and a garment of purple. And the face of Moses was radiant and lustrous like the sun, and the face of Joshua shone like the moon. Thereupon Moses set forth the Law, and Joshua expounded it.

And whilst they were thus instructing the people, a voice from Heaven was once more heard, and it called: " Moses, thou hast only four hours to live!"

In reply to Moses' new appeal, a Divine voice said: " Thou shalt see the land from afar."

And Moses beheld 400 parasangs of the Promised Land reduced into a small scale. And he beheld all that is concealed and hidden, and all that is far and near.

" Thou hast only three hours more to live," a Divine voice once more called.

When his parting hour came, Moses called Joshua and thus he spoke to him: " My son, to thee I deliver up the people of Israel, the people of the Lord. Innocent and untaught are as yet their babes, say therefore nothing before

[1] *Deuteron. Rabba*, 11; Jellinek, *loc. cit.*

them that is not fitting to be said in the presence of God's children." [1]

When it was announced that Moses' life was now measured by seconds, he took a scroll and wrote upon it the Ineffable Name, and the book of *Yashar*. He handed the scroll to Joshua upon whose head he placed his hands.

Joshua's eyes became dimmed with tears, so that he could not behold his master.

Moses lost the power of teaching, and a voice from Heaven exclaimed: " Henceforth Joshua is your leader! Take instruction from him and from him carry the instruction further!"

When the hour of Moses' death came near, the wicked Sammael, head of the Satans, was rejoicing and waiting for the moment when he would be allowed to take the soul of Moses.

The angel Michael was crying, but Sammael was laughing and triumphing.

And when the moment came for Moses to give up his soul, the Lord said unto Michael (according to others it was Gabriel who was commissioned): " Go and fetch the soul of Moses."

But Michael replied: " Lord of the Universe! How could I presume to approach Moses and take the soul of him who outweighs 60 myriads of other mortals?" And thus saying, Michael wept.

Thereupon the Lord said unto Zagzagel: " Go and fetch the soul of Moses."

But Zagzagel replied: " Lord of the Universe! I was his teacher and Moses was my pupil; how then can I go and take his soul?"

Thereupon Sammael came and stood before the Lord and thus he spoke: " Lord of the World! Is Moses, the teacher of the children of Israel, greater than Adam, the first man, whom Thou didst create in Thine own image and Thy likeness? Is he greater than Abraham, Thy faithful servant, who permitted

[1] *Yalkut*, § 941; cf. Lewner, *loc. cit.*, pp. 136–137.

himself to be cast into the fiery furnace so as to glorify Thy name? Is Moses greater than Isaac who lay bound upon the altar, ready to be slaughtered as a sacrifice to Thee? Is he greater than Jacob, or than the fathers of the twelve tribes? Nothing can save him from my hand, if Thou wilt only give me permission to take his soul!" Thus spoke Sammael, and the Lord replied:

" Not one of these is like unto Moses, and how, too, canst thou take his soul? Wilt thou take it from his countenance, he with whom I have spoken face to face? Wilt thou take it from his hands? His hands have received the Torah and carried the Tables of the Law! Wilt Thou take it through his feet? His feet have trodden upon the clouds! Thou canst not approach him and hast no power over any of his limbs."

But Sammael said: " Lord of the Universe! This may be so, but still I pray Thee to grant me permission to take the soul of Moses."

" Well then," said the Lord, " Thou hast my consent and I grant thee permission to take the soul of Moses."

Full of joy and in great glee, Sammael spread out his wings and betook himself to Moses. He took his sword, girded himself with his cruelty and appeared before the son of Amram. He found the Prophet writing the Ineffable Name; darts of fire shot from his mouth, his countenance was as radiant as the sun, and he looked like an angel of the Lord of Hosts. Fear and trembling seized Sammael, and he quaked and was unable to utter a word.

Moses now lifted his eyes and saw Sammael, for he knew that he would come to him. The eyes of Sammael grew dim before the radiance emanating from the countenance of Moses, and he fell upon his face and was seized with pains; he suffered like a woman giving birth. Thereupon Moses spoke: "'No peace,' saith the Lord, ' to the wicked.' [1] Why art thou here?"

---

[1] *Isaiah*, 57, 21.

" Thy time," replied Sammael, " has come to leave this world. Give me thy soul!"

" Who sent thee to me?" asked Moses.

" He who has created the world and all the creatures therein."

" I will not yield my soul unto thee," replied Moses.

" Ever since the creation of the world, all souls have been put into my power, and the souls are delivered into my hand." Thus spoke Sammael, but Moses replied:

" I have more power than all the inhabitants of the world, for I came circumcised out of my mother's womb, and on the day on which I was born, I spoke to my father and to my mother. I took no milk even from my mother until she received her pay for it. I prophesied when I was only three years old, for I was from the beginning destined to receive the Holy Law, and I took the crown from the head of Pharaoh. When I was eighty years old I performed many miracles and led sixty myriads of the children of Israel out of Egypt, cleaving the sea into twelve parts and leading Israel through the waters. The bitter waters I changed into sweet, and I ascended to Heaven, conquered the heavenly family, and spoke face to face with the Lord of the Universe. I received the Torah and wrote down from the mouth of the Most High the 613 commandments which I taught unto the children of Israel. I waged war against two kings, the descendants of Anak, who were so tall that in the days of the flood the waters did not even reach to their ankles. Sun and moon stood still at my command! Is there anyone like me among mortals? Wicked one, get thee hence!"

And when Sammael saw the soul of Moses pure and resplendent, he fled. He appeared before the Throne of Glory and thus he said: " Lord of the Universe! I cannot prevail against Moses. If Thou wouldst bid me go to Gehenna and turn hell undermost to uppermost, I could do it, but the son of Amram I cannot touch. I am even unable to abide in his presence, for the radiance of his countenance is like that of the Seraphim, and darts of fire issue forth from his mouth. Do not, therefore, send me to him to take his soul."

But God's wrath against Sammael was kindled and He said: " Thou hast been created out of the fire of hell and to the fire of hell thou shalt return. Thou didst set out in great joy to take the soul of Moses, but now that thou didst behold his greatness, thou comest back ashamed! Go thou therefore now, I command thee, and fetch me the soul of Moses."

What did Sammael do? He drew his sword out of its sheath and once more appeared before Moses.

When the son of Amram again beheld Sammael, the angel of death, standing before him and holding in his hand his naked sword, he rose up in great anger, took up his staff, the staff upon which was engraved the Ineffable Name, and with all his strength pushed Sammael back and threatened him, until he fled. Moses pursued him, struck him with his staff, and blinded him with the radiance of his countenance.

Thereupon a voice came from Heaven and exclaimed: " Moses, the moment of thy death is nigh."

But Moses once more began to pray: " Lord of the Universe!" he cried, " Thou didst manifest Thyself unto me in the burning bush, and Thou didst make me ascend into Heaven where I remained for forty days and forty nights, where I partook of neither food nor drink. Merciful God, remember this, and do not deliver me to Sammael." Thus prayed Moses, and the Lord replied:

" I have heard thy prayer, O Moses, and I myself shall take thy soul." [1]

Thereupon Moses said: " Lord of the Universe! Let me bless the children of Israel before I die. During my life they were not pleased with me, for I constantly rebuked and

---

[1] Jellinek, *loc. cit.*; *Deuteron. Rabba*, 11; *Yalkut*, §§ 940–941; *Midrash Tanchuma*, section *Vesot Habracha*; see also *Abot di Rabbi Nathan*, Ch. 12.

censured them, but now that I am going to die, I will bless them." He called all the tribes and began to bless each tribe separately, but when he saw that time was short, he blessed them all together. " My children!" he said, " I have rebuked you all my life, and admonished you to fear God and observe the Law and the commandments, but now forgive me if I have been too severe with you."

And the children of Israel cried: " Our Master! Thou art forgiven, but we, too, beg thy forgiveness, for often have we caused thee grief and given thee trouble. Forgive us, our Master!"

And Moses replied: " I forgive you my children with all my heart!"

Thereupon a voice came from Heaven and called: " Moses, thou hast only one moment more to live, thy time to depart from this world has come."

" Blessed be the Name of the Lord who is Eternal," said Moses. Turning to the children of Israel, he added: " When you enter the Holy Land remember my body and my bones."

" Woe unto the son of Amram," said the children of Israel, " he who has been running before us like a horse and whose bones are now to lie in the desert."

" Thou hast now only half a moment more to live," called a voice from Heaven, and Moses, laying his hands upon his heart, said to the children of Israel: " See ye, such is the end of mortal man."

Thereupon Moses sanctified himself, as do the angels of the Presence and the Seraphim, and the Lord, accompanied by the three angels, Michael, Gabriel, and Zagzagel, revealed Himself unto Moses and descended from Heaven to take the soul of the Prophet. Gabriel arranged Moses' couch, Michael spread upon it a purple garment, and Zagzagel placed a woollen pillow for his head. Zagzagel then stationed himself at his feet, Michael to his right, and Gabriel to his left. And the

Lord said to him: " Close thine eyes, and fold thy hands and lay them upon thy breast." Moses did so.[1]

Thereupon the Lord called to the soul of Moses and said: " My daughter! One hundred and twenty years have I allowed thee to dwell in the body of this righteous man, but the moment to leave it has come, do not hesitate!"

The soul of Moses replied: " Lord of the Universe, Thou art omniscient, and in Thy hand are the souls of all living. Thou didst create me and put me into the body of this righteous man. Is there in the world a body that is so pure and so holy as his? I will not leave it, but dwell in it for ever." Thus spoke the soul of Moses, and the Lord replied:

" My daughter! Do not hesitate, and I will take thee up to the highest Heaven where thou wilt dwell under the Throne of Glory, like the Seraphim, Ophanim, and Cherubim."

" Lord of the Universe," cried the soul of Moses, " I prefer to remain in the body of Moses, the righteous man. When the angels Aza and Azael descended from Heaven to earth they corrupted their ways, and loved the daughters of the earth so that Thou didst suspend them between heaven and earth, but Moses, who was only flesh and blood, lived apart from his wife ever since the day when Thou didst speak to him in the burning bush. Let me dwell in him for ever." [2]

But the Lord drew the soul of Moses by a Divine kiss. And the Lord himself lamented over the Prophet and said: " Who will rise up for me against the evil-doers? Who will stand up for me against the workers of iniquity?" [3]

And the ministering angels wept aloud and said: " Where shall wisdom be found?" [4] The heavens cried and said: " The godly man is perished out of the earth," [5] and the earth wept and said: " And there is none upright among men." [6]

The stars and constellations, the sun and the moon cried

---

[1] Jellinek, *loc. cit.* [2] Jellinek, *loc. cit.*; *Deuteron. Rabba*, 11.
[3] *Psalms*, 94, 16. [4] *Job*, 28, 12. [5] *Micah*, 7, 2. [6] *Ibid.*

aloud and said: " And there hath not arisen a prophet since in Israel like unto Moses." [1]

And the children of Israel wept aloud and lamented. " He executed the justice of the Lord," they cried, " and his judgments with Israel." [2] And all said: " He entereth into peace, they rest in their beds, each one that walketh in his uprightness." [3]

Joshua looked for Moses, his master, but found him not, for the Lord had taken him. He died in the land of Moab, and angels buried him in the valley of the land of Moab over against Beth-Peor.

And the news of the death of Moses spread far and wide among all the nations. The King of Aram thereupon sent his messengers to the master of Beth-Peor and thus they said: " We have heard that Moses has died in the land of Moab and has been buried over against Beth-Peor. Show us now the grave of Moses!" Thus spoke the messengers from the King of Aram.

And the ruler of Beth-Peor stood up and went with the messengers from the King of Aram and ascended the mountain of Nebo. They beheld the grave of Moses at the foot of the mountain, but when they came down, they suddenly saw it at the top of Nebo.

They wondered greatly and said: " Let us divide, half of us ascending the mountain, and half of us standing at its foot."

They did so, and those who were standing upon the top called out: " We see the grave of Moses at the foot of the mountain."

" No," replied those who were standing at the foot of the mountain, " it is on the top of Nebo that we see the grave of Moses."

---

[1] *Deuteron.*, 34, 10.　　　　[2] *Deuteron.*, 33, 21.
[3] *Isaiah*, 57, 2; see Jellinek, *loc. cit.*, *Deuteron. Rabba*, *loc. cit.*; cf. *Targum Pseudo-Jonathan*, Deut. 34, 5; *Baba Batra*, 17a; *Abot di Rabbi Nathan*, Ch. 12; see also *Midrash Shir-Hashirim*.

Thereupon the messengers from the King of Aram returned home and said: " It is true that Moses is dead, but no man knoweth of his sepulchre." [1]

The sepulchre of Moses remained unknown so that men could not go and pray before it. The Lord foresaw that on the day on which the Temple will be destroyed, and the children of Israel driven into exile, they would hurry to the sepulchre of the Prophet, weep and lament and ask him to plead for them. " Moses, our Master," they would cry, " rise up and pray for us." He would then rise up and by his prayer annul the decree against Israel, for the righteous men are more powerful and beloved by God after their death than what they were whilst alive.[2]

Before Moses died he had spoken unto Joshua and thus said to him: " If there are any passages in the Law that have remained obscure to thee, ask me now and I will explain them to thee before I die. If thou hast any doubts, mention them and I will settle these."

But Joshua had replied: " I have never left thee all my life, and I have never been away from thee for a single moment. I know all that the Lord has spoken to thee, and I am acquainted with all His commandments." This lack of modesty on the part of Joshua did not please the Lord, and Joshua at once forgot three hundred laws, and seven hundred doubts arose in his mind.[3]

As soon as Moses was dead, the manna ceased to come down from Heaven. The children of Israel came to Joshua, and told him what had happened.

But Joshua consoled them and said: " Do not grieve over this, for the Lord will send you food until you enter the Holy Land and eat of its fruit."

Thereupon the children of Israel came to Joshua to study the Law under his guidance, but Joshua had forgotten the

[1] *Sotah*, 14a. [2] *Deuteron. Rabba*, 11. [3] *Temurah*, 16a.

meaning of many passages, and he could not answer the questions put to him. The children of Israel were angry with him, and he prayed to the Lord.

The Lord replied: " If I teach thee all that thou hast forgotten, thou wilt not be able to remember it, and if I do not, the people will worry thee. Tell them, therefore, to prepare themselves to cross the Jordan and to take possession of the Holy Land." [1]

[1] *Ibid*; see for the entire chapter, Lewner, *loc. cit.*, pp. 137–144, 161–166; Bialik, *loc. cit.*, pp. 88–93; Grünbaum, *loc. cit.*, pp. 182–184. See also Meyer Abraham, *Légendes Juives Apocryphes sur la Vie de Moïse*, Paris, 1925, pp. 28–43, and pp. 93–113.

CHAPTER XXVII

The Birth and Education of Moses in Hellenistic, Syriac, and Arabic Literature

Josephus acquainted with Talmudic legends—Thermutis on the banks of the River Nile—Moses tramples upon the royal diadem—The advice of the sacred scribe—The expedition to Ethiopia—Tharbis, the daughter of the King of Ethiopia—The love-sick princess—The peace treaty followed by a marriage—Artapanus, quoted by Eusebius—The jealousy of Chenephres, King of Upper Egypt—Moses built the city of Hermopolis—The *Book of the Bee*—The story of the rod—Adam cut a branch from a fig tree in Paradise—The staff in the possession of Phinehas—It is buried in the desert—It served as one of the planks in the Cross of Christ—Moses in Moslem tradition—Pharaoh's dream—Queen Asia riding on a winged horse—The wise men of Egypt interpret the royal dream—Grand vizier Haman—The angel Gabriel brings Jochebed to Amram—The heavenly voice—The search in all the Hebrew houses—The child in the oven—The miraculous escape from the flames—The soldier swallowed up by the earth—Iblis in the shape of a serpent—The basket on the waves—The seven daughters of Pharaoh—The miraculous cure—The beautiful maidens and the happy father—Moses kicks the royal throne—The anger of Pharaoh—The burning coal and the ruby—Moses and the Egyptian priest—The punishment of the traitor—Moses and Samiri—The flight of the Prophet—The angel disguised as a Beduin—At the well of Midian—Moses refuses to accept a reward for services rendered—The hospitality to shy guests—Safuria and the wonderful rod—The staff returns seven times to Moses' hand.

According to Josephus, who was evidently acquainted with the Talmudic legends, it was Pharaoh's daughter Thermutis who, whilst diverting herself by the banks of the river, saw a cradle borne along by the current. She sent some of her maids that could swim, and bid them bring the cradle. When she saw the little child in it, she was greatly in love with it on account of its largeness and beauty; for God had taken such great care in the formation of Moses, that He caused him to be thought

worthy of bringing up, and providing for, by all those who
had taken the most fatal resolution, on account of the dread
of his nativity, for the destruction of the rest of the Hebrew
nation. Thermutis, when she perceived Moses to be so remarkable a child, adopted him for her son, having no child of her
own.

One day the princess carried the child to her father and
thus spoke to him: " I have brought up a child who is of a
Divine form and of a generous mind; and as I have received
him from the river in a wonderful manner, I thought proper to
adopt him for my son and the heir of thy kingdom." And
when she had said this, she put the infant into her father's
hands, and Pharaoh took him and hugged him close to his
breast.

On his daughter's account, in a pleasant way, Pharaoh
put his diadem upon the child's head, but Moses threw it
down to the ground, and, in a puerile mood, he wreathed it
round, and trod upon it with his feet; which seemed to bring
along with it an evil presage concerning the kingdom of Egypt.

Then the sacred scribe, who had already foretold that the
Hebrew child about to be born would bring low the dominion
and power of Egypt, cried out in a frightful manner, when he
saw what the child had done. " This, O King," he said, " is
the child whom the Gods have told us to kill, so as to ward off
the danger threatening us. If we kill him, we shall be in no
danger. He himself now bears witness to the prophecy, for he
has put thy sovereignty under his foot and is trampling upon
thy diadem. Slay him therefore, O King, and deliver thy
people, the Egyptians, from their fears." Thus spoke the
sacred scribe, but Thermutis snatched the child away, and
the King declined to follow the advice of the sacred scribe, for
God had inclined his heart to spare Moses.

Now, when Moses had grown up, it happened that the
Ethiopians, close neighbours of the Egyptians upon the south,

had invaded the country and defeated the Egyptians in battle,
The Egyptians betook themselves to their shrines and oracles,
and they were told to make use of the Hebrew, by which was
meant Moses. The Hebrew was accordingly appointed Commander-in-Chief of the Egyptian army, and the sacred scribes
of both nations were glad. The Egyptians hoped that thanks
to the skill, valour, and courage of Moses, they would easily
overcome their enemies, but that at the same time their general
would be slain, whilst the Hebrews were glad to have Moses
as their general instead of an Egyptian. Moses led his troops
into the enemies' country and by importing ibises into Ethiopia
he got rid of the numerous serpents which prevented his army
from advancing. He laid siege to the capital of Ethiopia, Saba,
but found it difficult to take the city.

Tharbis, however, daughter of the King of Ethiopia, happened to see Moses as he led his army near to the walls of the
city, and, greatly attracted by his deeds of valour, she fell in
love with him. Upon the prevalency of that passion she sent
one of her most trusted servants to the Egyptian general
offering him her hand in marriage.

Moses accepted her offer, on condition that she would
bring about the delivering up of the city. He gave her the
assurance of an oath that as soon as the city had been surrendered he would take her to wife. Tharbis, therefore, persuaded her father to come to terms with Moses and to conclude
a treaty with him, on condition that he make Tharbis his wife.
The agreement was made and took effect immediately, Moses
celebrating his marriage with Tharbis, Princess of Ethiopia,
and soon leading his army back to Egypt.[1]

According to Artapanus, Moses, whom he identifies with
Musaeus, the teacher of Orpheus, was adopted by Merris,
wife of Chenephres, King of Upper Egypt, who was childless.
Pretending to have given birth to a child, she brought Moses

---

[1] Josephus, *Antiquities*, Ch. 2, 7-11.

up as her own son. Moses, when he grew up, was so wise, learned, and skilled, that Chenephres became jealous of his qualities. He therefore decided to send him out on a military expedition at the head of troops who were very inadequately equipped and unskilled in the art of war. In spite, however, of these disadvantages, Moses won a splendid victory in his expedition against Ethiopia. Thereupon he built the city of Hermopolis, and taught the people how to utilize the ibis in protecting themselves against the serpents, the bird thus becoming the sacred guardian spirit of the city.

On his return to Memphis from his Ethiopian expedition, Moses taught the people the art of agriculture. Threatened once more by the King, he fled to Arabia, where he married one of Reuel's daughters.[1]

In the *Book of the Bee* it is related that Jethro invited Moses to go into the house and to select a shepherd's staff, and that at the command of the Lord one of the staffs left its place and moved towards Moses. The story of the rod of Moses is related as follows:

When Adam was driven out of Paradise, he cut a branch from the fig tree which was the tree of knowledge, and this branch served him as staff all his life. This staff he left to his son, and it was transmitted from generation to generation till it came into the possession of Abraham. It was with this staff that the Patriarch smashed the idols of his father Terah. Jacob used the staff when he tended the flocks of Laban, and his son Judah gave it as a pledge to his daughter-in-law Tamar. The staff was subsequently concealed by an angel in the cave of treasures, in the mountains of Moab. When the pious Jethro was pasturing his flocks, he found the staff and used it henceforth. When Jethro had grown old, he asked Moses to go into the house and fetch this staff. Scarcely had the prophet passed the threshold of the house, when the staff moved towards

[1] Quoted by Eusebius in his *Præparatio Evangelica*, IX, 27.

him. It was this staff which afterwards swallowed up the rod of the Egyptian witch Posdi. The staff then came into the possession of Phinehas, who buried it in the desert. It belonged to Joseph, the husband of Mary, at the moment of the birth of the Saviour, and it served afterwards as one of the planks in the Cross of Christ.

The early life of Moses is the subject of many legends in Mohammedan tradition. The birth and upbringing of the Prophet is told in many sources.

When the time came for the Lord to send a new prophet upon earth, Pharaoh had three dreams in one night. At first he heard a voice calling unto him: " Pharaoh, repent, for the end of thy rule approacheth; a youth from a foreign race will put thee and thy people to shame before the whole world."

Greatly disturbed by this ominous dream, the King awoke, but soon fell asleep again, and once more saw a strange dream:

A roaring lion was attacking a man whose only weapon was the staff he was holding in his hand. But scarcely had the king of beasts approached the defenceless youth than the latter dealt him one blow with his staff, killed him, and threw the body into the Nile.

Once more Pharaoh awoke, greatly perturbed. For a long time he lay awake, and only when dawn was already breaking, he once more fell into a troubled sleep. Scarcely had he closed his eyes than he beheld his virtuous spouse, Asia, riding heavenwards on a winged horse, and waving a farewell to her astonished husband. Pharaoh was following with his eyes his flying and swiftly disappearing queen, when suddenly the earth at his feet opened and he was swallowed up.

When Pharaoh at last awoke from his troubled sleep, he summoned into his presence Haman, his grand vizier, and commanded him to assemble all the wizards, magicians, astrologers, and interpreters of dreams. Several thousand of these wise men of Egypt soon thronged the audience chamber of the King, and with trembling voice Pharaoh related unto them his three dreams. One of the interpreters thereupon informed the King that one of the Hebrew women would in the course of the year give birth to a child who would bring disaster upon the King and his country. Great was the King's distress when he heard those words and he wept bitterly, all those present also shedding tears, when they witnessed their royal master's distress.

Haman, however, the grand vizier, stepped forward, and thus he spoke: " My lord and master! Forgive thy slave if he venture to blame thy despair and to offer an advice to thy wisdom. There is still time to ward off the calamity threatening our country. Thou hast only to issue a decree and order that all pregnant Hebrew women and all newly-born Hebrew babes be put to death."

Thus spoke Haman, and his words pleased the King well. Pharaoh acted upon the advice of his grand vizier, and 7000 innocent Hebrew babes were massacred by order of the King, whilst many pregnant women were drowned in the Nile. The Hebrews were also forbidden, under penalty of death, to approach their wives.

Now it came to pass that Amram the Hebrew, one of Pharaoh's viziers, was keeping guard one night in the royal chamber, when suddenly the angel Gabriel appeared unto him carrying upon his wings Jochebed, the wife of Amram.

" The time has come," said the angel Gabriel, " for the Redeemer of Israel to be born, and I have brought thy spouse unto thee."

Thus, in spite of all the precautions taken by the royal servants, in spite of the stringent decrees of the King and the orders of Haman keeping the Hebrew men away from their wives, the birth of Moses was brought about.

Nine months passed, and Jochebed gave birth to a male

child and never suffered the slightest pain at the time of her delivery. Great, however, was her grief when she thought of the destiny awaiting that handsome babe, whose countenance was as radiant as the full moon. But Moses opened his mouth and said: " Fear not, Mother, for the God of Abraham will not forsake us."

During the night in which Moses was born, all the idols in the temples of Egypt fell to the ground, and Pharaoh once more heard a terrible voice calling unto him: " Repent, O wicked King, and acknowledge the living God, the Creator of Heaven and Earth, otherwise thy doom will come swiftly."

Pharaoh awoke, and his spirit was greatly perturbed. Once more he summoned all his wise men, astrologers, wizards, and interpreters of dreams into his presence, and they all informed him that the child who would bring about the destruction of Egypt had been born. Thereupon Haman gave orders to make a thorough search in all Hebrew houses including that of Jochebed.

Although Amram, on duty in the Royal palace, had been separated from his wife for many months, Haman was afraid that another Hebrew woman might have concealed her son in the house of Amram.

When the servants and spies of Pharaoh came to the house of Jochebed, she was out. She had previously concealed the baby in the oven, and piled wood in front of it.

Haman, not finding any child in the house, put fire to the wood and then went forth. " If there is a baby in the oven," thought the wicked vizier, " it will perish in the flames."

According to another version, it was Jochebed herself who, losing her presence of mind, had put Moses into the burning oven, and finding the oven full of fire wept bitterly, but Moses called to her from the flames not to despair, for at the command of the Lord the flames had no power over him.

Fearing, however, Haman's repeated visits, Jochebed decided to put her trust in God and to expose Moses upon the waves of the Nile.

In the silence of the night she was carrying the basket in which lay Moses, when she came upon one of the spies of Pharaoh who stopped her and inquired what she was carrying. Scarcely, however, had the soldier addressed his question to Jochebed than the earth at his feet opened and swallowed him up to his neck. A voice thereupon coming from the depth of the earth commanded the imprisoned soldier, under the penalty of death, to let the woman go undisturbed and never to utter a word betraying what he had seen. When Jochebed had gone, the earth at once vomited out the soldier. When the unhappy mother reached the bank of the Nile she suddenly beheld a big black serpent; it was Iblis who had taken the shape of a reptile so as to make the mother waver in her decision. But Moses called out from the basket. " Be not afraid, Mother, continue thy way, for my presence alone will cause this venomous reptile to creep away." And lo, hearing these words, Iblis disappeared. Thereupon Jochebed opened the basket and kissed and hugged her baby before setting it upon the waves of the Nile. In her innermost heart, the fond mother hoped that some kind-hearted Egyptian woman would find her baby, take it home and adopt it. And when, weeping bitterly, she was leaving the water's edge, a heavenly voice called out: " Be of good cheer, wife of Amram, for thy son will be restored unto thee, having been chosen as the Divine messenger."

As soon as Jochebed had abandoned the basket with the little Moses in it, the Lord commanded the angel appointed over the waters to drive this basket into the canal connecting the palace of Pharaoh with the Nile. This canal had been constructed in order to bring the waters from the Nile into the royal palace for the benefit of Pharaoh's seven leprous daughters who used to bathe therein.

The eldest of the princesses was the first to perceive the

basket with the child. Scarcely, however, had she raised the lid of the basket and looked upon the infant than she was dazzled by such a radiant light that she hurriedly covered the baby with her veil. At the same moment, her own face became so radiantly beautiful, shining like the purest moon, that her sisters were amazed.

" How is it that thou hast been so suddenly cured of thy disease?" they asked.

" My sudden recovery," replied the princess, " is due to the wonderful power of this infant. The radiance emanating from his face, when I first contemplated it, has caused all impurity to vanish from my body, even as the sun drives away darkness."

Thus spoke the eldest of Pharaoh's daughters, and her sisters hastened to lift the veil she had thrown over the infant's countenance and to gaze upon it. All of them became in turn beautiful as the full moon and as pure as driven snow.

Thereupon the eldest daughter of Pharaoh put the basket upon her head and carried it to her mother Asia, to whom she related what had occurred. Asia took the infant Moses into her arms, and, accompanied by her seven daughters, hurried to the King's apartments. Great was Pharaoh's astonishment when he beheld the seven maidens who now had no equal in beauty.

" Who are these maidens?" queried the King; " are they beautiful slaves whom some subject prince has made me a present of?"

" These maidens," replied Asia, " are thy own daughters, and here in my arms lies the physician who has worked this wonderful cure."

She thereupon related unto her husband what had occurred. At first Pharaoh was overjoyed at the news, but soon gloom overspread his countenance.

" This boy must not live," he spoke to his wife Asia; " his

mother may be one of the Hebrew women, and he himself may be the very child of whom my soothsayers and stargazers have prophesied so many calamities."

Thus spoke Pharaoh, but Asia rebuked him for his superstitious fear and reminded him that by his orders all pregnant women of the Hebrews and all newly-born babes had been put to death.

" Besides," added the pious and virtuous queen, " this frail infant will always be in thy power to do with him as thou pleasest. Take it only for the present and let it remain in thy palace out of gratitude for the wonderful cure he has worked upon thy seven daughters."

The seven princesses joined in their mother's request, and Pharaoh at last gave way. Thus Moses was educated in the royal palace.

When the child was four years old, the incident with the crown, and the test by means of two bowls full of gems and live coals occurred.

When Moses was six years old, Pharaoh teased him one day so much, that the child, in its anger, kicked with such force the royal throne, that the throne fell down and Pharaoh rolled to the ground. Bleeding from mouth and nose, the King arose in a fury and, drawing his sword, was on the point of killing Moses.

In vain did Asia and her seven daughters plead, but suddenly a white cock appeared, calling aloud: " Pharaoh, if thou dost shed the blood of this innocent child, thy daughters will become even more leprous than they had been before."

Casting a glance at the princesses and beholding their countenances which had already grown yellow out of fear, the King gave up his murderous design upon Moses.[1]

Tabari gives the following version of this legend in his

---

[1] Weil, *Biblische Legenden der Muselmänner*, pp. 126-144; see also, Zamahsari and Baidawi, Commentaries to *Sura*, 7, 124, and 28, 3; Grünbaum, *Neue Beiträge*, p. 159 ff.

commentary to *Sura*, 20, verse 28: *And loose the knot of my tongue.*

Pharaoh was one day carrying Moses in his arms, when the latter suddenly laid hold of his beard, and plucked it in a very rough manner, which put the King into such a passion that he ordered him to be put to death. Aishia, his wife, representing to him that Moses was but a child, who could not distinguish between a burning coal and a ruby, he ordered the experiment to be made. A live coal and a ruby being set before Moses, he took the coal and put it into his mouth and burnt his tongue, and thereupon he was pardoned.[1]

One day Moses was standing on the banks of the Nile and praying.

An Egyptian priest saw him and asked: " Whom art thou worshipping?"

Moses first completed his prayers which he would not interrupt, and then replied: " I worship my master."

" Thy master?" said the priest, " thou dost mean, no doubt, thy father, the King!"

" May God punish thee and all those who look upon Pharaoh as a God," replied the future redeemer of Israel."

" For this blasphemy and curse thou shalt pay the penalty of death," cried the priest; " I will now betake me to the King and inform him of thy sin."

Thereupon Moses prayed unto the Lord and thus he spoke: " Lord of the waters! Thou who didst once destroy by water the whole race of man, excepting Noah and Audj, may it be Thy will to command the waters of the Nile to swallow up this wicked and blaspheming priest."

Scarcely had Moses spoken these words, when lo! the waters of the Nile rose up, and waves, rushing and roaring, discharged themselves upon the banks and swept away the priest. In his agony the Egyptian cried for mercy: " Moses,"

[1] See E. M. Wherry, *A Comprehensive Commentary on the Quran*, Vol. III, p. 120, note.

he begged, " have mercy upon me, and I swear unto thee that never will I reveal thy secret."

" And what will happen if thou dost break thine oath?" asked Moses.

" Then may my tongue be cut from my mouth," promptly replied the trembling priest."

Moses waved his hand, the waters retreated, and the priest was saved. Scarcely, however, had Moses reached the royal palace than he was summoned into Pharaoh's presence where he found the lying priest who had preceded him.

" Whom dost thou worship?" asked Pharaoh, turning to Moses.

" I worship my master," replied Moses, " my master who feeds, sustains, and clothes me."

Moses, of course, meant the only God, the Creator of the Universe, but Pharaoh applied the answer to himself and was well pleased. He therefore ordered the priest to have his tongue torn out and then be hanged in front of the palace.[1]

One day, when visiting the camps of the Hebrews and the brickfields wherein they were labouring, Moses rebuked an Israelite named Samiri, who had raised his hand against his companion.

Samiri thereupon denounced Moses to the King and informed the latter that his adopted son had killed an Egyptian.

Pharaoh condemned Moses to death, but informed by one of his friends of the fate awaiting him, the future redeemer of Israel managed to escape.

For several days Moses wandered about in the desert, but the Lord sent one of his angels disguised as a Beduin who brought the exile to Midian, to the priest Shueib.

At a well outside Midian, Moses met Lija and Safuria, the two daughters of Shueib, to whom he rendered a service by watering their flocks and protecting them against the hostile

[1] Weil, *loc. cit.*

shepherds. Invited to the house of Shueib, Moses at first refused to touch the meat and drink placed before him.

" Be seated and eat with us," said Shueib.

" I will not accept thy offer," replied Moses, " as a reward for the service which I have rendered to thy daughters. To do good without receiving a recompense for it is an inviolable law of my family."

" And it is my custom," answered Shueib, " and was that of my ancestors to give a kind reception to shy guests and to supply them with food.[1] I am offering thee hospitality because thou art a fugitive and a stranger, and not because thou hast rendered a service to my daughters. If thou wilt abide with me and tend my flock for eight or ten years, I will give thee Safuria as wife."

Moses accepted the offer and henceforth tended the flocks of Shueib. As he had left Egypt without taking his staff with him, Safuria brought him her father's wonderful rod which had formerly belonged to the prophets of the past.

Zamahsari, in his commentary to *Sura*, 28, 28, relates that there were many magic and prophetic rods in the house of Shueib, and that the latter invited Moses to select one of them. The future redeemer of Israel selected the rod which Adam had once carried away from Paradise, and Shueib asked Moses to select another staff. Seven times, however, the staff returned to Moses' hand, and so he knew that it was destined for him.[2]

SAFURIA AND MOSES

And one of them came unto him, walking bashfully, with the sleeve of her shift over her face, by reason of her abashment at him: she said, My father calleth thee, that he may recompense thee with the reward of thy having watered for us. And he assented to her call, disliking in his mind the receiving of the reward: but it seemeth that she intended the compensation if he were of such as desired it.

[1] Wherry, *loc. cit.*, p. 258 note.   [2] Grünbaum, *loc. cit.*, pp. 161–163.

And she walked before him; and the wind blew her garment, and her legs were discovered: so he said unto her, Walk behind me, and direct me in the way. And she did so, until she came unto her father, who was Sho'eyb, on whom be peace! And with him was (prepared) a supper. He said unto him, Sit, and sup. But he replied, I fear lest it be a compensation for my having watered for them, and we are a family who seek not a compensation for doing good. He said, Nay, it is my custom, and hath been the custom of my fathers, to entertain the guest, and to give food. So he ate; and acquainted him with his case. And when he had come unto him, and had related to him the story of his having killed the Egyptian, and their intention to kill him, and his fear of Pharaoh, he replied, Fear not: thou hast escaped from the unjust people. (For Pharaoh had no dominion over Medyen.) One of them (namely, of the women) said (and she was the one who had been sent), O my father, hire him to tend our sheep in our stead; for the best whom thou canst hire is the strong, the trustworthy. So he asked her respecting him, and she acquainted him with what hath been above related, his lifting up the stone of the well, and his saying unto her, Walk behind me; and moreover, that when she had come unto him, and he knew of her presence, he hung down his head, and raised it not. He therefore said, Verily I desire to marry thee unto one of these my two daughters, on the condition that thou shalt be hired servant to me, to tend my sheep, eight years; and if thou fulfil ten years, it shall be of thine own will; and I desire not to lay a difficulty upon thee by imposing as a condition the ten years; thou shalt find me, if God please, (one) of the just, who are faithful to their covenants. He replied, This (be the covenant) between me and thee: whichever of the two terms I fulfil, there shall be no injustice against me by demanding an addition thereto; and God is witness of what we say. And the marriage-contract was concluded according to this; and Sho'eyb ordered his daughter to give unto Moses a rod wherewith to drive away the wild beasts from his sheep: and the rods of the prophets were in his possession; and the rod of Adam, of the myrtle of Paradise, fell into her hand; and Moses took it, with the knowledge of Sho'eyb.

Koran, Ch. 28, 25–28, with commentary. P. W. Lane, *Selections from the Kur-an*, London, 1843, pp. 188–190.

CHAPTER XXVIII

The Later Life and Death of Moses in Moslem Tradition

The return to Egypt—Mount Thur and the light on its summit—Gabriel brings a glass full of old wine to Aaron—The meeting of the brothers—Aaron on the bank of the Nile—The mysterious horseman—Gabriel mounted on the fiery steed Heizam—Truth hath come and Falsehood hath disappeared—Moses before Pharaoh—The vizier Haman—Hiskil's advice—The great test—The conversion of the magicians—The fury of the King—Marchita, the daughter of Pharaoh, condemned to the flames—The death of Asia—Wife of Mohammed in Paradise—Pharaoh makes war against the God of the Hebrews—The great tower—The bloodstained javelin—The angel Gabriel and the treacherous servant—Pharaoh signs a document—The royal steed and the mare Ramka—Gabriel thrusts mire into Pharaoh's mouth—The spoil of the Egyptians—Samiri and the golden calf—The Israelites refuse to accept the Law—The threat of the rocks—Moses at the Persian Gulf—The fish in the basket—The Prophet El Khidr—The injured ship—El Khidr cuts a child's throat—The mended wall—The treasure beneath it—Karun and his wealth—His knowledge of chemistry—The wanton woman and her repentance—The punishment of Karun—The anger of God—Jalub Ibn Safun, King of Balka—Balaam and his wife—The sin of Israel—Phinehas and Zamri—The death of Aaron—The beautiful house on the top of the mountain—A couch prepared by the hands of the angels—The coffin with the mysterious inscription—I am for him, whom I fit—The popularity of Aaron—The death of Moses—The grief of Safuria—The cries of the orphans—The rebuke of the Lord—The worm under the black rock—The speech of the worm—Moses and the gravediggers—Moses and the angel of death—The apple from Paradise—The burial of the Prophet—The four angels.

Moses was forty years of age, when he made up his mind to return to Egypt and pay a visit to his relatives, friends, and co-religionists. It was a cold and rainy day when he arrived at the foot of Mount Thur. Noticing a fire burning on the mountain, he thought that travellers must be there whom he could ask for a brand wherewith to light a fire.

"Tarry thou awhile here," he said to his wife, "whilst I go to yonder mountain." When he approached the Mount Thur, Moses was surprised to notice the burning but never consumed bush. And behold, a voice called unto him and bade him go to Pharaoh and redeem Israel. Moses fell upon his face, and thus he spoke: "Lord of the Universe, how can I appear before Pharaoh? I have killed an Egyptian, and the King will surely put me to death if he beholds me." But God told him not to be afraid, and that his brother Aaron would speak for him.

Strengthened by several wonders which the angel Gabriel performed, Moses was now desirous of going back to his wife Safuria, and to travel with her to Egypt, but the angel Gabriel said to him: "Thou hast now higher duties, O Moses, to perform than that of looking after thy wife. At the command of God, I have already taken thy wife back to her father's house, so that thou canst now proceed alone on thy mission."

On the very night on which Moses entered Egypt, an angel appeared before Aaron, bearing a crystal glass full of the best old wine, and offering the glass to the brother of Moses, thus he spoke: "Drink of this wine, O Aaron, which the Lord is sending thee as a sign of glad tidings. Thy brother Moses hath returned to Egypt. God hath chosen him as His Prophet, and thee as his vizier. Arise, therefore, and go to meet him."

Aaron was at that moment one of the viziers of Pharaoh, occupying the post of his father Amram, who had died since, and was, therefore, keeping watch in the private apartments of the King. He arose, however, and hastened to the river bank, intending to cross the Nile at once.

He was looking round for a boat, when he suddenly perceived a light in the distance. Nearer and nearer it came, and then Aaron could distinguish a horseman who, swiftly as the wind, was riding straight upon him.

The horseman was none other than the angel Gabriel, mounted on the fiery steed Heizam, which shone like the brightest diamond, and whose neighings were hymns of praise. Aaron, however, ignorant of the fact that it was the angel Gabriel riding upon one of the Cherubim, supposed that he was being pursued by one of Pharaoh's men, and he was on the point of casting himself into the Nile.

Quickly, Gabriel declared who he was, and lifting Aaron up to the back of his fiery and winged horse, crossed the Nile to the other bank, where Moses was already waiting.

When the Prophet beheld his brother, he exclaimed: " Truth hath come, and Falsehood hath disappeared."

Gabriel now carried Moses to the house of his mother, whilst Aaron he brought back to the royal palace, so that when the King awoke, he found the son of Amram at his post.

Moses passed the night and the following day at his mother's house, and related unto her all that had befallen him ever since he had left Egypt.

The next day Moses appeared before Pharaoh. Aaron cast down the rod, and it became a serpent as big as a camel. Opening its jaws, the serpent took hold of the throne of the King and thus it spoke: " If God only commanded me, I could swallow up not only thee and thy throne, but all the people present, and the whole palace." Greatly frightened, Pharaoh jumped from his throne and entreated Moses, in the name of Queen Asia, who had once saved his life, to protect him against the monster. At the mention of the name of Asia, Moses was softened. He at once called the serpent back, and it became as tame as a lamb. Scarcely, however, had the King been saved from the peril threatening him than he once more hardened his heart, listening to the whisperings of Satan. Pharaoh's vizier, Haman, urged him to slay the two magicians, but Hiskil, the treasurer, exclaimed: " O King, follow not this advice, I pray thee. Remember how the nations once considered the prophets Noah, Hud, and Salih as magicians, till the wrath of God fell upon them, destroying them by water."

Now one of Haman's predecessors, a very old man who was 120 years of age, rose up, and thus he spoke: " O King of kings, suffer me to advise thee once more before I die. There is no king who has so many wizards as thou. It would be best therefore to summon all thy magicians and to name a day on which Moses and Aaron should meet, and strive with them. If the magicians of Egypt triumph over the Hebrews, then thou canst put them to death, but if, on the other hand, Moses and Aaron put to shame thy own magicians, then thou wilt know that they are indeed servants of a living God."

Thus spoke the old man, and his advice pleased Pharaoh greatly. A day was consequently appointed on which the great test between Aaron and Moses, on one side, and the magicians of Egypt, headed by Risam and Rijam, on the other, should take place. The magicians were put to shame, and when they saw the miracles wrought by Moses, they were converted. Prostrating themselves before Moses, they exclaimed: " We believe in the Lord of the Universe, in the God of Moses and of Aaron, who hath wrought such miracles."

Pharaoh's fury knew no bounds. " What," he cried, " ye dare to acknowledge another God, without my permission! If ye do not at once retract your blasphemy, I will cut off your hands and feet, and then hang you. Are you going to worship another God, only because his magicians are cleverer than you?"

Thus stormed Pharaoh, but the converted magicians refused to retract their words. Pharaoh, therefore, cut off their hands and feet, and put them to death. They died as martyrs, worshipping the true God. Even his own daughter, Marchita, the wife of Hiskil, Pharaoh did not spare, when he heard that she no longer worshipped her father as a god. She was condemned to the flames, and all her children were massacred before her very eyes. She bore the death by fire with fortitude. Even Asia, Pharaoh's wife, was now accused of being an apostate and was condemned to be burnt. The angel Gabriel, however, consoled her by telling her that she would become the wife of Mohammed in Paradise. The angel, thereupon, gave her a drink, so that after tasting it, she died without pain.

Pharaoh's heart was hardened, and he hearkened not to Moses. He gave orders to his vizier Haman to build a mighty tower for the purpose of making war against the God of the Hebrews. It was a tower which had no equal in the world. Not less than 50,000 men worked on this building, which was carried to such a height that none could stand on it. Pharaoh thereupon ascended the tower and threw a javelin towards heaven. The javelin fell down blood-stained, and Pharaoh boasted that he had slain the God of Moses. The Lord, however, sent the angel Gabriel who struck the tower with his wings, and it was demolished, falling down in three parts. One part fell upon Pharaoh's army, killing 1,000,000 men; another part fell into the sea, and the third towards the west, so that none of those who had taken part in the building of the tower remained alive.[1]

The Lord then brought the plagues over Egypt, during one of which everything throughout the land was turned to stone. All men were petrified and congealed to marble. Once more Pharaoh begged Moses to pray for him, but when, at the prayer of His servant, the Lord had revived the petrified men, Pharaoh again hardened his heart.

Thereupon the angel Gabriel assumed human shape, and appeared before the King. " One of my servants," he complained, " has assumed control over my house during my absence, giving himself out as the master. What punishment does he deserve, O King?"

" He deserves death," promptly replied the King, " death by drowning."

[1] Weil, *Biblische Legenden der Muselmänner*, pp. 147–164; see also Zamahsari, *Commentary to the Koran*; Grünbaum, *Neue Beiträge*, p. 164; E. W. Lane, *Selections from the Kur-an*, p. 199, note.

" Give me a written order, O King," said the Egyptian who was Gabriel in disguise.

Pharaoh did so, and signed an order to put to death by drowning the lying servant who had given himself out as the master. Thereupon Gabriel went to Moses and informed him that the time had now come for him to lead Israel out of Egypt.

When the Israelites reached the Red Sea, Moses smote it, and it at once divided into twelve heaps as big as mountains, with twelve ways between them for the twelve tribes to pass through. Marching through these ways, surrounded on both sides by walls of water, each tribe could not see the others and feared that they had been drowned. Thereupon Moses prayed to the Lord, and He wrought a miracle on his behalf. He made arches in the dividing watery walls, and windows through which the marching columns could see each other.[1]

When Pharaoh and his hosts pursuing the Israelites arrived at the water's edge, the King feared to enter the water. Some say that his steed of great beauty refused to go forward.

Thereupon Gabriel appeared, mounted upon the mare Ramka, and preceded him.

When Pharaoh's steed saw the mare Ramka, it plunged forward into the sea and went into one of the channels. Gabriel, who preceded the King, thereupon turned round and showed Pharaoh the deed which he had signed, and wherein he had sentenced the disobedient and arrogant servant to death.[2] Heaps of water were now overwhelming Pharaoh and threatening to drown him, and he exclaimed: " I now believe that there is no God but He in whom the children of Israel believe." [3] But Gabriel thrust into the King's mouth some of the mire of the sea, so as to prevent him from speaking again and from praying to God, who might have granted him mercy and pardoned him his wicked deeds. " Now," said Gabriel, " thou

[1] Grünbaum, *loc. cit.*, pp. 166–167; Commentaries of Zamahsari, Baidawi, and Ibn El Attir.   [2] Weil, *loc. cit.*, p. 168; Grünbaum, *loc. cit.*, p. 166.
[3] Koran, *Sura*, 10, 90–92.

believest, but hitherto thou hast been rebellious and art therefore numbered among the wicked." [1]

When Israel had reached the dry land they refused to believe that Pharaoh and his host had really been drowned.

" He will certainly reappear again and attack us," wailed the Hebrews.

Thereupon Moses prayed unto the Lord, and raising his miraculous rod, he once more clave the sea. And lo! the Hebrews perceived the dead bodies of 120,000 Egyptians at the bottom of the sea, all clad in their armour.

Among them they also saw the lifeless body of Pharaoh, armed with his coat of mail which was of gold, and by which they easily recognized him, and then the Israelites knew that the Lord had indeed redeemed them. [2] Moses forbade the Israelites to spoil the dead, and deprive them of their golden chains and bracelets. " For it is robbery," he said, " to strip the dead."

In spite of the many signs, however, the Israelites soon forgot the Lord. As long as Moses was with them, they never ventured to make idols and worship them. Scarcely, however, had their leader been summoned into the Mount to receive the Law than they came to Aaron and threateningly demanded that he should make a molten god to them.

It was a man named Samiri who, understanding the founder's art, cast all the golden rings and bracelets which the Israelites had borrowed from the Egyptians into a furnace, to melt them into one mass.

When the gold was melted, Samiri threw in a handful of sand which he had taken from under the hoof of Gabriel's horse. A calf came out and bellowed like a living one, born of a cow.

When Moses came down and saw what had happened and

---

[1] *Chronique de Tabari*, 1, p. 350; Grünbaum, *loc. cit.*, pp. 164–165.
[2] Tabari, *loc. cit.*, p. 355; Grünbaum, *loc. cit.*, p. 165.

was told by Aaron that Samiri had fashioned the golden calf which the Israelites had worshipped, he would have slain Samiri, but the Lord commanded him to spare his life, place him under ban and send him away. Like a wild beast Samiri is wandering ever since from one end of the earth to the other. Men shun and avoid him, and he himself, whenever he comes near men, exclaims: " Touch me not!" [1]

Moses then made the Jews drink the water mixed with the powder from the golden calf pounded to dust, and the faces of those who had worshipped the idol became yellow. They wailed and wept and piteously beseeched Moses to save them, for the golden calf was consuming their intestines. " Help us, Moses," they cried, " we are ready to repent and even to die, if only the Lord will pardon us." Moses prayed to God, and those who were really contrite were healed.[2]

Thereupon Moses went up again into the Mount, taking with him the seventy elders. When he read the Law to the Israelites, the Law wherein it is written that one should neither kill nor steal, the Israelites at first refused to accept it. Thereupon the Lord commanded the angel Gabriel to raise the Mount Sinai and hold it over the heads of the people, threatening them to hurl it upon their heads and destroy them. " Accept the Law," said Moses, " or Mount Sinai will fall on you and crush you." [3] And the rocks said: " Sons of Israel! The Lord hath redeemed ye from bondage and led ye out of Egypt, so that ye might receive and make known the Holy Law; if ye refuse, we will fall upon ye and ye will have to carry us until the day of Resurrection." [4] The Israelites then fell on their faces and accepted the Law.

For their stiff-neckedness and their constant rebellion, the Israelites were condemned to wander in the desert for forty years. Moses himself announced unto them that he would

---

[1] Weil, *loc. cit.*, p. 172.   [2] *Ibid.*, p. 173.
[3] Koran, *Sura*, 2, 60; 7, 170; Grünbaum, *loc. cit.*. p. 168.
[4] Weil, *loc. cit.*, p. 174.

travel over the whole earth from East to West and from North
to South, preaching and teaching the true faith.[1] One day he
boasted before his servant Joshua, who accompanied him, of
his great wisdom.

The Lord thereupon said unto him: " Go to the Persian
Gulf, where it joins the sea of the Greeks, and there thou
wilt meet one who surpasses even thee in wisdom."

" How will I recognize this wise man?" asked Moses.

" Take a fish into thy basket, and it will lead thee to My
faithful servant, whose wisdom excelleth the wisdom of all
men," replied the Lord.

Moses, accompanied by Joshua, now travelled to the place
indicated, always carrying the fish in his basket. Once he went
to sleep on the seashore, and when he awoke, it was late and
he hurriedly continued his journey. In their hurry, Moses and
Joshua had forgotten to take the basket with the fish, and
when they at last remembered it and returned to the place
where they had slept, they found the basket empty. Suddenly
they perceived a fish standing quite upright upon the surface
of the water and gliding along, instead of swimming in the
water like other fishes. Moses and Joshua recognized their
fish and followed it along the coast. They followed their
guide for a few hours, when it suddenly vanished in the
water.

" This must be the place," they said, " where the god-
fearing and wise man lives." And indeed, they soon perceived
a cave, over the entrance to which were inscribed the words:
" In the name of the All-powerful and merciful God ".

Entering the cave, Moses and Joshua found therein a man,
powerful and fresh like a youth of seventeen, but whose hair
was white and whose snow-white long beard descended to his
feet. This was the prophet El Khidr, the ever-young, venerable
old man.

[1] *Ibid.*, p. 176.

" Take me as thy disciple," said Moses, after greeting El Khidr, " permit me to accompany thee in all thy wanderings, so that I may admire the wisdom God has granted unto thee."

Thus spoke Moses, but El Khidr replied: " Thou wilt not be able always to comprehend the wisdom of the Lord, and thy stay with me will be short."

" Do not reject me," begged Moses, " for with the aid of God thou wilt find me patient and obedient."

" Thou mayest follow me in my wanderings," said El Khidr, " but promise me never to ask any questions and to wait patiently until I myself explain unto thee the reason of my often incomprehensible actions."

Moses promised never to ask any questions, and El Khidr took him to the seashore where a ship lay anchored. The ever-young prophet took a hatchet and cut two timbers out of the ship so that it foundered.

" Stop," cried Moses, " what art thou doing? The people on board of this ship will surely be drowned!"

" Did I not tell thee," quietly replied El Khidr, " that thy patience will be of short duration?"

" Thou didst," said Moses, " and I forgot my promise; pardon me for my hastiness."

They continued their journey, till they met a beautiful child playing with shells on the seashore. El Khidr took a knife hanging at his girdle and cut the child's throat.

Horror-struck, Moses exclaimed: " This is horrible! Why hast thou killed the innocent child?"

The ever-young prophet only shrugged his shoulders.

" I told thee," he replied, " that thou wilt not remain long in my company."

" Pardon me once more," begged Moses, " and thou mayest drive me away, should I again question thee."

They continued their journey for some time until they reached a big town. They were both tired and hungry, but

no one would give them food or shelter, unless they had paid
for it. Walking along, El Khidr noticed that the wall of a big
house, the inhabitants of which had driven them away from
their door, was menacing ruin. Unhesitatingly, he approached,
set the wall up firmly and made it solid. Once more, Moses
was greatly astonished at his companion's action.

" Thou hast done work which would have taken several
masons many days to perform. Why dost thou not at least
ask for a wage which would enable us to pay for our lodging
and for our food?"

" Now we must really part," replied El Khidr, " for thou
art asking too many questions. Before we separate, however,
I will satisfy thy thirst for knowledge and explain unto thee
the reasons of my incomprehensible actions. Know then, O
Moses, that the ship which I injured, but which can be easily
repaired, belongs to poor folks and is their only source of
revenue. Had I not injured it and it would have sailed, they
would have lost it. At that very moment the ships of a tyrannical
king were crossing the seas and capturing every good vessel
they could lay hands on. The poor fishers will now repair
their ship and retain their property.

" I killed a child," continued the Prophet, " but he had a
very bad and wicked disposition, and had he lived he would
have done evil and even corrupted his parents who are pious
people. God will now give them pious children in the place
of the one I have deprived them of.

" As for the wall I have repaired, the wall of the house
whence we had been driven away, the house belongs to two
orphans, the present inhabitant being only a tenant to whom
the owners have let their house. Under the wall there is buried
a treasure. Had I not mended the wall, it would have fallen
down, and the unworthy tenant discovered and certainly
appropriated the treasure. Now I have mended the wall, and
the treasure will remain hidden till the day when the orphans,

the rightful owners, come into the house. They will then find the treasure."

" Thou seest now," continued El Khidr, " that I have not acted blindly or been led by passion, but have obeyed the will of my Master."

Moses once more begged the Prophet to forgive him, but dared not ask to be allowed to accompany him farther.[1]

This story, which the Koran relates about Moses and El-Khidr, is told in Jewish legend of Rabbi Joshua Ben Levi and the prophet Elijah.[2]

When Moses returned to the Israelites, he found that many had died, and that Karun, who had married Moses' sister Kalthun, had not only grown very rich, but that his heart was lifted up with pride.

Karun had discovered a portion of the treasures once hidden by Joseph, but he had also learned chemistry from his wife Kalthun, and he was able to turn the base metals, lead and copper, into pure gold. He was so rich that he had raised golden walls round his gardens, and when he travelled, sixty mules were required to carry the keys of his treasury.[3]

During the absence of Moses, Karun had gained a great ascendancy over Israel and was not prepared to yield his power to Moses, now that the latter had returned. Karun, therefore, brooded evil and thought of means how to destroy Moses of whose influence and authority he was jealous. He bribed therefore a woman of bad character whom Moses had driven out of the camp, and promised her great reward, and even marriage, if she consented to bring false accusation against Moses.

The woman promised all that Karun had bidden her. When, however, she appeared before the elders and the congregation to bear witness to Karun's accusation, Moses turned

---

[1] Koran, *Sura*, 18; *Chronique de Tabari*, Ch. 76; Weil, *loc. cit.*, 176–181.
[2] See Vol. III of the present work, chapter on Elijah the Prophet.
[3] Koran, *Sura*, 28, 76; Weil, *loc. cit.*, p. 182; Grünbaum, *loc. cit.*, p. 172.

to her and said: " In the name of Him who did cleave the sea and give the Law through me, I charge thee to speak the truth and to tell the congregation whether Karun's accusation is correct."

The Lord, thereupon, sent fear into the heart of the false witness and caused her to speak the truth. She acknowledged her guilt and confessed the truth. " Karun," she said, " offered me a large bribe; he suborned me with gold and all sorts of promises, and made me come here to raise a false accusation against the Prophet."

Thereupon Moses fell upon his knees and prayed to the Lord, and thus he said: " O Lord of the Universe, if I am Thy messenger, protect me against such false accusations and prove my innocence before the assembled congregation." The Lord answered: " Command the earth whatever thou pleasest, and it will obey thee." And Moses called out: " Earth, swallow them up." Whereupon the earth seized Karun and his company and swallowed them up to their thighs.

Karun then cried: " O Moses, have mercy. For God's sake, tell the earth to release me."

But Moses repeated again: " Earth, swallow up him and his company."

And the earth swallowed them up to the waist.

Once more Karun begged Moses to have mercy and to release him, but Moses would not hearken, and again repeated: " Earth, swallow them up."

The earth, obeying the command of the Prophet, swallowed up Karun and his company up to their necks.

And once more Karun pleaded for his life, piteously entreating Moses to have mercy upon him and to save him.

But Moses remained adamant and stern in the execution of his justice. Once more he commanded the earth to swallow up Karun and all his company, and the earth swallowed them up and closed over them so that they were seen no more.

Four times Karun had pleaded for his life and cried out: "O Moses have mercy upon me," but four times Moses continued to say: "O earth, swallow them up," and the earth swallowed up Karun and his company and also his palace and all his riches.[1]

Moses now returned thanks to the Lord, but the Lord turned away His face and said: "They did ask thee several times to forgive them and to have mercy upon them, but thou didst not hearken unto them; had they cried but once to Me, I would have forgiven them."

The forty years during which Israel had been condemned to wander through the desert had now come to an end, and Moses led the nation to the frontiers of Canaan.

When Jalub Ibn Safun, King of Balka, heard of the approach of the Israelites, he invited the wizard Balaam, the son of Beor, to come and curse the people of Israel. An angel, however, appeared to the magician and told him not to go, and he decided to obey.

When the messengers of the King of Balka returned without Balaam, the King bought the most costly jewels and sent them as a present to Balaam's wife. She then gave her husband no peace till he finally consented to accompany the messengers.

Unable to curse the Israelites, he advised the King of Balka to lure Israel to sin, by sending beautiful women to seduce them. The advice was followed by the King of Balka, but the Lord sent the plague upon the Israelites and only when Phinehas had killed Zamri did the plague come to an end.[2]

The death of Aaron is told in Moslem tradition as follows: The Lord said to Moses: "The time hath come for Aaron to die. Ascend therefore the mountain of Hor." When Moses and Aaron had reached the top of the mountain, they saw a

---

[1] Koran, *Sura*, 28, 76–81; Abulfeda, *Historia Ante-Islamica*, p. 32; Weil, *loc. cit.*, pp. 181–183; Grünbaum, *loc. cit.*, pp. 172–173; see also Herbelot, *Bibl. Orient., s.v. Carun*; Lane, *loc. cit.*, p. 218, note.

[2] *Chronique de Tabari*, I, p. 398; Weil, *loc. cit.*, pp. 177–179; Grünbaum, *loc. cit.*, 177–179.

beautiful house surrounded by trees from which a balsamic perfume was wafted. Entering the house, they beheld a couch prepared by the hands of the angels.

" O Moses," said Aaron, " I am weary and should like to repose upon this couch."

" Do it, my brother," said Moses.

" But I am afraid that the master of the house may soon return and be angry with me."

" I will make excuses for thee," replied Moses.

Thereupon Aaron laid himself down upon the couch and suddenly felt death approaching him.

" Moses," he said, " thou hast deceived me," and thereupon he died. The bed with Aaron upon it was then carried by the angels up to Heaven.[1]

Another version is that Moses and Aaron ascended the mountain knowing that one of them was to die, but uncertain which. They found a cavern, wherein stood a coffin with the following inscription on it: " I am for him, whom I fit ". Moses first tried to lie down in it, but it was too short for him; then Aaron lay down and it fitted him exactly.[2]

When Moses returned to the camp without Aaron, the Israelites accused him of having murdered his brother, for they loved Aaron more than Moses. The High-Priest was always mild and amiable, whilst Moses was just and severe. Aaron was therefore more popular with the nation than Moses, and the people suspected Moses of having killed his brother out of jealousy. Moses now prayed to the Lord to prove his innocence to the people of Israel, and angels appeared carrying the death-bed on which lay Aaron, and he was dead. Everyone could thus see that Aaron had died, and a heavenly voice called out: " God hath taken him." [3]

The death of Moses is related as follows in Mohammedan

[1] *Ibid.*   [2] Weil, *loc. cit.*, p. 185.
[3] Abulfeda, *loc. cit.*, p. 32; Tabari, *loc. cit.*; Weil, *loc. cit.*, p. 186; Grünbaum, *loc. cit.*, p. 176.

tradition: When Gabriel came to Moses and informed him that his time to die had arrived, he hurried back to his tent, and knocked at the door. His wife Safuria opened the door for him and was not a little amazed to see her husband pale and trembling.

" What ails thee, Moses," she asked, " and who is pursuing thee that thou art running, pale and trembling? It looks as if thou wert running away from a creditor."

Whereto Moses replied: " There is no more powerful creditor than the Lord of the Universe, and no more implacable pursuer than the angel of death."

" Must then a man who has spoken face to face with the Lord, also die?" asked Safuria.

" Certainly," replied Moses. " Even the angels Gabriel, Michael, and Israfil are not exempt from the general law; God alone is Eternal."

Safuria cried bitterly till she swooned away. When she recovered her senses, Moses bade her go and wake their children so that he might bid them farewell. Safuria went and called her children.

" Arise, poor orphans," she cried, " arise and bid your father farewell! His last day in this world and his first in the world beyond has come."

In terror the children awoke and began to weep bitterly.

" Alas," they cried, " who will now pity us and protect us, now that we are fatherless?" Their tears moved Moses deeply, and he, too, began to cry.

Then the Lord said unto him: " Moses, what mean thy tears? Art thou afraid to die, or art thou reluctant to part from this world?"

" Lord of the Universe," replied Moses, " I fear not death, nor do I part reluctantly from this world, but I do lament these children who have already lost both their grandfather, Shueib, and their uncle, Aaron, and will now lose me, too."

" In whom," asked the Lord, " did thy mother put her trust when she cast thee in an ark into the waters of the Nile?"

" In thee, O Lord," replied Moses.

" And who protected thee, when thou didst appear before Pharaoh, and who gave thee the wonderful rod with which thou didst divide the sea?"

" Thou, O God," replied Moses.

" Then, go out once more to the sea, and extend thy rod over it, and thou wilt have a sign of My omnipotence."

Thus spoke the Lord, and Moses at once obeyed. He raised his rod, the sea divided, and he beheld in its midst a black rock. He approached the rock, and once more the Lord said unto him: " Smite it with thy rod." Moses did so and the rock divided, revealing to the astonished gaze of the Prophet a sort of cavity wherein lay a little worm, holding a little green leaf in its mouth, and the worm opened its mouth, lifted up its voice and said: " Praised be the Lord who doth not forget me in my loneliness; praised be the Lord who hath nourished me."

When the worm was silent, the Lord again spoke to Moses and said: " Thou seest, Moses, that I do not forget even the lonely worm under the rock, in the midst of the sea; how can I forget or abandon thy children who acknowledge Me and My Law?"

Ashamed of his lack of faith, Moses returned home, comforted his wife and children, and then went out alone into the mountain, where he met four men digging a grave.

" For whom are ye digging this grave?" asked the Prophet.

" For a man whom God will have with Him, in Heaven," replied the men.

" Will ye grant my request?" asked Moses, " and permit me to help ye dig the grave of such a pious man?" The request was readily granted, and Moses lent a hand to dig the grave of a holy man.

When the grave was ready, Moses asked: " Have ye taken the measure of the holy man who has died?"

" No," replied the men, " this we have forgotten to do, but the deceased was just of thy size and thy stature. Lie down, so that we may see whether the grave will suit him. God will reward thee for thy action." Moses did so.

Thereupon the angel of death appeared before him, and said: " Prophet of God! I am the angel of death, and have come to take thy soul!"

" How dost thou intend to take my soul?" asked Moses.

" From thy mouth," replied the angel of death.

" Thou canst not," said Moses, " for my mouth hath spoken with God."

" From thine eyes," said the angel of death.

" Thou canst not do it either," said Moses, " for my eyes have looked upon the Divine light."

" From thy ears, then," said the angel of death.

" Thou canst not," again objected Moses, " for my ears have heard the voice of God."

" From thy hands, then," said the embarrassed angel of death.

" Thou canst not do it either," said Moses, " for my hands have clasped and carried the diamond tables on which the Law of God was engraven."

Greatly perplexed, the angel of death returned to the Lord, and acknowledged his inability to take the soul of Moses. The Lord thereupon bade the angel of death address himself to Radhwan, the gatekeeper of Paradise, obtain from him an apple from the Garden of Paradise, and give it to Moses to smell. The angel of death handed the apple to Moses who smelt at it, and in this moment the soul of Moses was drawn from him through his nostrils.

Thus Moses, the Prophet of God, died, and his grave is known only to the angels Gabriel, Michael, Israfil, and Azrael, who were the four men in disguise digging the grave, and who buried him.[1]

According to Tabari, Moses had met several angels engaged in digging a grave which pleased him greatly.

" O angels of the Lord," asked the Prophet, " for whom are ye digging this grave?"

" O elect of the Lord," replied the Divine messengers, " we are digging this grave for a servant of God, whom the Lord intends to honour greatly."

" This servant of God," said Moses, " will indeed find here an excellent place of rest."

" Dost thou wish that this place of rest should be thine?"

" Yes," replied Moses. Whereto the angels replied:

" Then lie down in this grave, hold thy breath, and commend thy soul to God." Moses did so, and God took his soul.

According to another version, God sent the angel of death to fetch the soul of Moses, but the Prophet struck the angel a blow and sent him away. The angel of death then appeared before God, and thus he spoke: " Lord of the Universe! Thou hast sent me to Thy servant, but he hath no wish to die." Then the Lord sent the angel again to Moses, and the Prophet was compelled to yield to the Divine command.[2]

---

[1] Weil, *loc. cit.*, pp. 189-191.   [2] Grünbaum, *loc. cit.*, p. 184.

BIBLIOGRAPHY

I. WORKS IN HEBREW

Abot di Rabbi Nathan, ed. Schechter, Vienna, 1887.
Bialik and Ravnitzky, *Sepher Haaggadah*, Berlin.
Jellinek, *Beth-Hamidrash*, 6 vols., Leipzig and Vienna, 1853–1877.
Josippon (Josephus Gorionides), ed. Breithaupt, Halle, 1707; ed. Amsterdam, 1771.
Hagoren (Hebrew periodical), Vol. VIII.
Kol Bo (*Sepher Halikkutim*), Venice, 1547.
Lewner, *Kol-Agadoth*, Warsaw.
Mekhilta, ed. Venice; ed. A. H. Weiss, Vienna, 1865.
Midrash Abkhir, ed. Buber and Chones.
Midrash Agadah, ed. Buber, Vienna, 1894.
Midrash Bamidbar Rabba, Vilna, 1907.
Midrash Bereshith Rabba, Vilna, 1907.
Midrash Debarim Rabba, Vilna, 1909.
Midrash Haggadol, ed. Schechter, Cambridge, 1902.
Midrash Lekach Tob, ed. Buber, Vilna, 1884.
Midrash Shemoth Rabba, Vilna, 1902.
Midrash Shemuel, ed. Buber, Cracow, 1893.
Midrash Shir Hashirim, Vilna, 1907.
Midrash Tanchuma, ed. Buber, 1865.
Midrash Tanchuma (also called *Jelamdenu*), Stettin, 1865.
Midrash Tehillim, or *Shokher Tob*, ed. Buber, Vilna, 1891.
Parhi, Joseph Shabbethai, *Tokpo Shel Yosef*, Leghorn, 1846.
Pesikta Rabbati, ed. M. Friedmann, Vienna, 1880.
Pesikta Sutarta, ed. M. Friedmann.
Pirke de Rabbi Eliezer, ed. Venice, 1544; ed. Lemberg, 1867.
Sepher Hajashar, ed. Prague, 1840; (French translation in Migne, *Dictionnaire des Apocryphes*, Vol. 2).
Talmud Babli (Babylonian Talmud), see Bibliography to Vol. I of the present work.
Targum Pseudo-Jonathan, ed. Ginsburger, Berlin, 1899.
Yalkut (also called *Yalkut Shimeoni*), Vilna, 1898.

II. OTHER WORKS

Abraham, Meyer, *Légendes Juives apocryphes sur la vie de Moïse*, Paris, 1925.

Abulfeda, *Historia Ante-Islamica*, ed. Fleischer, Leipzig, 1831.

Bacher, W., *Die Agada der Palestinensischen Amoräer*, 3 vols., 1892–1899.

——*Die Agada der Tanaiten*, 2 vols., 1884–1899.

Batiffol, P., *Studia Patristica*, Paris, 1889–1890.

Beauvais, Vincent de, *Speculum Historiale*.

Beer, P., *Das Leben Mosis* (in *Jahrbuch für die Geschichte der Juden*, 1863, Vol. 3.)

Bergel, J., *Mythologie der alten Hebräer*, Leipzig, 1882.

Bin Gorion, *Die Sagen der Juden*, 3 vols., Frankfurt a/M., 1914–1919.

——*Der Born Judas*, 6 vols., Leipzig.

Cassel, S. P., *Mishle Sindbad*.

Charles, R. H., *The Book of Jubilees*, Oxford, 1895; London, 1917.

——*The Testaments of the Twelve Patriarchs*, Oxford, 1908; London, 1917.

Comestor, *Historia Scholastica* (Migne, *Patrol.*, Vol. 198).

Eisenmenger, J. A., *Entdecktes Judentum*, 2 vols., 1700.

Eusebius, *Praeparatio Evangelica*.

Fabricius, J. A., *Codex Pseudoepigraphicus*, *Vet. Test.*, 1722–1723.

Firdusi, *Yusuf and Zuleika*.

Friedlaender, G., *Pirke de Rabbi Eliezer*, London, 1916.

Gaster, M., *The Chronicles of Jerahmeel*, London, 1899.

Geiger, A., *Was hat Mohammed aus dem Judentum genommen*, Bonn, 1833.

Gesta Romanorum, ed. Oesterley, Berlin, 1882.

Grünbaum, M., *Gesammelte Aufsätze zur Sprache und Sagenkunde*, Berlin, 1901.

——*Neue Beiträge zur semitischen Sagenkunde*, Berlin, 1893.

——*Jüdisch-deutsche Chrestomathie*, Leipzig, 1882.

Hamburger, J., *Real-Encyclopädie für Bibel und Talmud*, 5 vols., 1870–1892.

Herbelot de Molainville, *Bibliothèque Orientale*, 6 vols., Paris, 1781–1783.

Jami, *Yusuf and Zulaikha*, translated by R. T. H. Griffith in Trübners' "Oriental Series", London, 1882.

Jewish Quarterly Review, New Series, Vol. II.

Johnson, S., *English Poets*, 1790, Vol. XXVII.

Josephus, *Antiquities* (Whiston's).

Journal of the Asiatic Society of Bengal, 1860.

Journal of the Royal Asiatic Society, London, 1893.

Keller, Adelbert von, *Erzählungen aus altdeutschen Handschriften*.

Koehler, R., *Kleinere Schriften*, Berlin, 1900.

Koran, The.

Kurrein, A., *Traum und Wahrheit*, Regensburg, 1887.

Lallemant, Are, *Das deutsche Gaunertum*.

Landau, *Hebrew-German Romances and Tales* (*Teutonia*, Heft 27), Leipzig, 1912.

Lane, P. W., *Selections from the Koran*, London, 1843.

Morris, Richard (ed.), *The Story of Genesis and Exodus* (" Early English Text Society," Vol. VII), London, 1865.

Neubauer, A., *Mediæval Jewish Chronicles*.

Oppenheim, G., *Fabula Josephi et Asenathae apocrypha*, Berlin, 1886.

Paris, Gaston, *La poésie épique du Moyen Age*, Paris, 1885.

Philo, *De Vita Moysis*.

Proceedings of the Biblical Archaeological Society, Vol. IX (1886–1887).

Rambaud, A., *La Russie épique*, Paris, 1876.

Revue des Études Juives, Vol. XXI.

Rosen, G., *Tutti Nameh* (German translation), 1858.

Rothschild, J. de (ed.), *Le Mistère du Viel Testament*, 6 vols., Paris, 1877.

Schapiro, T., *Die haggadischen Elemente im erzählenden Teil des Korans*, Leipzig, 1907.

Schmidt, R., *Kathakautukam*, by Crivera (German translation).

Schudt, *Jüdische Merkwürdigkeiten*.

Spectator, The, No. 237.

Tabari, *Chronique*, ed. by H. Zotenberg, Paris, 1867–1874.

Ticknor, G., *History of Spanish Literature*, New York, 1849.

Weil, G., *Biblische Legenden der Muselmänner*, Frankfurt a/M., 1845.

Weilen, *Der aegyptische Joseph im Drama des 16en Jahrhunderts*, Vienna, 1887.

Weinberg, M., *Die Geschichte Josephs von Basilius dem Grossen aus Cäsarea*, Halle, 1893.

Wherry, E. M., *A Comprehensive Commentary on the Quran*, Vol. III, London.

Wunsche, A., *Aus Israels Lehrhallen*.

——*Ex Oriente Lux*.

Zeitschrift der Deutsch-Morgenländischen Gesellschaft, Vols. 41, 43, and 44.

ANCIENT ISRAEL
Myths and Legends

Volume 3

SOLOMON SIGHTS THE MYSTERIOUS PALACE
Page 100

Frontispiece, Vol. III

Contents

VOLUME THREE

CHAPTER I

CHAPTER II

CHAPTER III

CHAPTER IV

CHAPTER V

CHAPTER VI

iii

CONTENTS

CONTENTS

CHAPTER XVIII

CHAPTER XIX

CHAPTER XX

Plates

VOLUME THREE

PREFACE

The present and last volume of the work on Myths and
Legends of Ancient Israel deals with the first three Kings of
Israel, Saul, David, and Solomon, and also with the Prophet
Elijah and Queen Esther. Both David and Solomon occupy
an important place in Jewish legendary lore. David is the
elect, the chosen of the Lord, not only during his mortal life
but also in Paradise where he will pronounce the blessing
over the cup of wine, an honour of which the Patriarchs and
even Moses and Aaron will deem themselves unworthy. As
for Solomon, who occupies an even larger space in Jewish
tradition than his father David, the opinions of the Rabbis
differ. Whereas the earlier school frequently criticizes the
actions of the famous King of Israel and dwells on his weak-
nesses and his downfall, the later school glorifies him as the
counterpart of his father David. He is represented as a pious
and wise ruler, the King of Israel *par excellence*, a Prophet
and Judge inspired by Divine wisdom.

In the present, as in the two preceding volumes, we have
once more related the legends not only of purely Jewish
origin, but also those found in Moslem tradition as well as
in occidental literature. In the tradition of the Mohammedans
King Solomon is represented as being far superior to his
father David. He is a Prophet of God, and long before the
birth of Mohammed he had already recognized and rendered
homage to the future messenger of Allah. In Jewish tradition

reference is made to Solomon's future life, but none to his
death, whilst in Moslem lore many legends are found which
relate the details of his death. The reader will also find in
this volume a chapter dealing with the mediæval literature
wherein Solomon is the central figure. In the chapters on
Elijah and Esther the reader's attention has also been drawn
to similar legends and tales related in Oriental and European
literature.

ANGELO S. RAPPOPORT.

MYTH AND LEGEND OF ANCIENT ISRAEL
VOLUME III

CHAPTER I

King Saul

Saul, the first King of the Jews—His handsome appearance—The welfare of the public—The lighted streets—Saul and the admiring maidens—The modest hero—Simple life—The Witch of Endor—The story of the King and the cocks—The familiar spirit—Samuel and the dead—Saul in Paradise—The burial of Saul—The famine in Palestine—David's investigations—The sins of the people—The royal coffin—Saul in Moslem legend—The spring in the desert—David and the five stones—Saul's jealousy of David—The suit of chain mail—Saul at the grave of his victims—The King and his twelve sons—The city of the giants—The crowing cocks.

SAUL, THE FIRST KING OF THE JEWS

In Jewish legendary lore King David and his son Solomon occupy a prominent place, but the aureole of legend and myth has also crowned the head of Israel's first King. There are, however, two distinct views in Jewish legend with regard to Saul. Whilst some of the Haggadists treat the first King of Israel with but little sympathy, others depict him in very glowing colours. He was chosen first King of Israel on account of his handsome appearance, his piety, his bravery, his military powers, his innocence and modesty. One of his ancestors, his grandfather Abiel, had received the promise that one of his descendants would ascend the throne of Israel. The merit of

1

this grandfather of Saul consisted in the care he took of the welfare of the public. He was in the habit of having the streets lighted so that people could go to the houses of study after dark.[1] But it was not only on account of the merits of his ancestors that Saul received the crown and was considered worthy to rule over Israel. His beauty was unusual, and when he asked the maidens about the seer and they told him concerning Samuel, these maidens did not seem to be in a hurry to shorten their conversation, but dragged it out so as to have an opportunity to contemplate his beauty as long as possible.[2] Saul, however, was far from noticing the admiring glances, and no pride swelled his pure and innocent heart, for he was as innocent as a babe and pure as a child, free from sin as a one-year child. He had never committed sin when he ascended the newly created throne of Israel.[3] He was a hero, too, for he had already carried off victories over the Philistines when he was called to the throne. And yet, ambition never entered his heart, and his modesty was as great as that of Moses, for he refused to accept the royal crown, and even after he had been anointed he would not accept it until the bright stones in the breastplate of the High Priest announced the decision of Providence. And even when he sat on the throne of Israel, Saul remained as modest as he had been before his election.

The Witch of Endor

After the death of Samuel Saul greatly missed the prophet and his advice. He soon found an opportunity to enter into communication with the departed prophet. When he told his servants to find him a necromancer, they wondered greatly. In legendary lore Saul is compared to a king who had given instructions that all cocks be put to death and then inquired of his servants whether there was any cock to wake him up with dawn.

[1] *Leviticus Rabba,* 9. [2] *Berachoth,* 48. [3] *Yoma,* 22b; *Leviticus Rabba.*

" Hast thou not given instructions to kill all the cocks in the land?" asked his servant.[1]

Thus Saul, who had removed the witches and necromancers from the land, once more loved what he had formerly hated. Thereupon he went to En-Dor, where dwelt Abner's mother, the witch of En-Dor, wife of Zephaniah. Saul inquired of her for himself by the familiar spirit, and the woman brought Samuel, whose figure appeared upright before them. Then the woman knew that the man who had come to visit her was the King, as for an ordinary mortal the spirit raised from the dead would have appeared feet in the air and head downwards.

Samuel was not alone, for many dead who thought that the day of resurrection had come accompanied Samuel. When the woman beheld the number of dead by the side of Samuel, she became very much confused.[2] Then Samuel, whose voice the witch could not hear, said unto Saul: " If thou wilt accept the judgment of God, to-morrow thou wilt be with me and thy lot shall be with me in the place where I abide, that is in Paradise." [3]

Thereupon the Lord summoned His angels and said: " When a man is invited to a banquet he usually leaves his children at home for fear of an evil eye, but Saul goes out to battle and yet takes his sons with him. He knows that he will meet his death, but he gladly accepts for himself and for his sons the Divine judgment."

And thus Saul died with his sons so that his portion might be with Samuel in the future life and that he might dwell in the prophet's division in heaven.[4]

---

[1] *Midrash Tanchuma*, ed. Buber, III, p. 42a; *Midrash Samuel*; Grünbaum, *Neue Beiträge*, p. 188.

[2] *Leviticus Rabba*, 26; *Midrash Samuel*, 24; *Pirke de Rabbi Eliezer*, Ch. 33.

[3] *Midrash Tanchuma*, ed. Buber, III, p. 42a; *Midrash Samuel*, 24; *Leviticus Rabba*, 26.

[4] *Berachoth*, 12b; *Leviticus Rabba*, ibid.; *Pirke de Rabbi Eliezer*, ibid.

The Burial of Saul

The remains of Saul and his sons were interred at Jabesh Gilead, outside the land of Israel. Now in the days of David a famine arose in the land, lasting three years, year after year.

In the first year of the famine the King said to his people: " Are there some among ye who worship idols?" And he caused an investigation to be made so as to discover whether any idolatry was being practised in the land.

During the second year that the famine prevailed, David said unto his people: " Are there perchance some among ye who are leading immoral lives?" And he again caused investigations to be made for the purpose of finding out whether the punishment had been inflicted upon the people for the sin of lewdness. Investigations, however, proved that such a sin did not prevail in the land.

During the third year that the famine prevailed, David asked himself whether the people were perhaps punished because they had committed the sin of shedding blood. Once more the investigations yielded no result.

Thereupon David prayed to the Lord, and God answered: " It is for Saul. Saul was anointed with the oil of consecration; he abolished idolatry and he dwells in Paradise together with the Prophet Samuel. Yet, ye are in the land of Israel, while he and his sons are buried outside of the Holy Land."

When David heard these words of the Lord, he gathered together all the elders of Israel, all the nobles and scholars, and they all betook themselves to Jabesh Gilead, where they found the bones of Saul and of his son Jonathan. The procession crossed the Jordan, and the coffin containing the bones of the disinterred King was brought to the borders of each tribe. All Israel showed respect to the remains of the dead King, and they were laid to rest in the land of Benjamin. The

THE SPIRIT OF SAMUEL APPEARS TO SAUL

Facing page 4, Vol. III

Lord, seeing the respect paid by the people of Israel to the memory of Saul, had compassion, sent rain upon the land, and the famine ceased.[1]

SAUL IN MOSLEM LEGEND

In Mohammedan tradition Saul is the subject of many legends, the majority of which have been borrowed from the Jews. When Thalut was made King of Israel, he summoned all his fighting men, who numbered seventy thousand, and he led them against the Philistines. Saul started with his army, and his way led through the desert. One day the men had no water, and the heat was great in the wilderness. The soldiers began to murmur against Saul and Samuel. Thereupon the Prophet prayed to the Lord and a miracle happened. Out of the rocky, stony ground a spring suddenly bubbled up, and its water was as fresh as snow, as sweet as honey, and as white as milk. Thereupon Samuel spoke to the soldiers who came hurrying up, anxious to slake their thirst:

" Ye have murmured and been discontent and have thus sinned against the Lord and your King. Abstain therefore from drinking of this water so as to expiate your fault by your abstinence."

Thus spoke Samuel, but the soldiers paid no heed to the words of the Prophet and disregarded his advice. Three hundred and thirteen men were only found who had strength enough to control themselves and not to drink but just a little out of the hollow of their hands, all the others drinking greedily. When Thalut saw this, he dismissed his army and went out with the small number who had had sufficient control over themselves. Among them were also the six sons of a virtuous man of the name of Isa, his seventh son, by name of David, having remained at home to attend to his father. Saul

[1] *Pirke de Rabbi Eliezer*, Ch. 17; see also *Yalkut, Samuel,* § 154; *Midrash Samuel,* 28; *Jebamoth,* 78b; *Jerushalmi Kiddushin,* IV, I, 65b–c; *Taanith* III, 3, 66c; *Numer. Rabba,* 8, 4.

set his army in array, but none of his men dared advance to
fight in single combat the giant Djalut, the King of the Philistines. Thereupon Isa sent also his seventh son to the battle-
field to take provisions to his brethren and to inquire after
their welfare. The boy was not dressed as a warrior but like
a simple shepherd, carrying his pouch and a staff in his hand.
On his way he suddenly heard the voice of a stone that was
calling to him, and thus it spoke: " Pick me up and take me
with thee, for I am the stone wherewith the Prophet Abraham
had once driven away Satan." David stooped, picked up the
stone, and placed it in his pouch. When he had taken a few
paces, another stone addressed him, and thus it spoke: " Pick
me up and take me with thee, for I am the stone on which the
foot of the angel Gabriel once rested when he caused a fountain to be opened in the desert for Ishmael, the son of Hagar."
Once more the boy stooped down, and picking up the speaking
stone placed it in his pouch.

And when he had taken a few more paces he heard the
voice of the third stone, and thus it spoke: " Pick me up, for
I am the very stone wherewith Jacob once strove against the
angel whom his brother Esau had sent against him." For the
third time David stooped down and picked up the stone.

When he reached the army, he heard the voice of a herald,
making the following proclamation: " He who will kill the
giant Djalut shall marry Thalut's daughter and become his
successor upon the throne."

David tried to persuade his brethren to wrestle with the
giant, not on account of the promised reward, but so as to
wipe out the shame and disgrace thus cast upon the name of
the Israelites. As his brothers, however, lacked the courage to
meet the enemy in single combat, he went himself to Thalut
and offered to fight the giant.

SAUL'S JEALOUSY OF THE YOUNG HERO

Now Thalut grew very jealous of the young and now popular hero, and although he had promised to give him his daughter to wife, he refused to do so until David had brought him a hundred more heads of giants. And the greater David's heroism, the more intense Thalut's jealousy grew, for the boy's praise was in everybody's mouth.

One day Thalut came to visit his daughter in her husband's absence, and thus spoke to her: " Introduce me to-night into thy husband's chamber so that I can slay him with my own hand."

When his wife informed him of the promise she had been compelled to give her father, David calmly bade her be comforted, and do as she had promised: " The God of my Fathers," said he, " will deliver me from the sword of thy father and make his weapon harmless, even as he made harmless the knife of Abraham when he raised it to slaughter Ishmael." Thereupon David went into his smithy, where he fashioned for himself a suit of chain mail that was to cover his whole body. This suit of chain mail was as fine and thin as hair, and fitted his body as if it had been made of wool; it also resisted the thrust of every weapon.

David went to bed and slept, but was awakened at midnight when his father-in-law began to stab him in his sleep. He awoke, and wresting the sword from Thalut's hands broke it as if it had been a piece of cake.

David thereupon escaped and was pursued by his father-in-law. One night Thalut and his soldiers lodged in a cave. David was in another near by, but his pursuers knew it not. In the middle of the night he carried off the seal-ring of the King and also his sword and his banner and went forth out of the cave, which had a double issue. On the following morning he appeared on the top of a mountain, opposite the camp of the

Israelites. Girt with the King's long sword and waving the royal banner, he stretched out his hand so that all could perceive the royal seal-ring on his finger. Great was Thalut's astonishment, and he admired not only David's pluck and courage but also his generosity. His jealousy and envy abated, and he reconciled himself with his son-in-law. Henceforth they lived in peace and unity until Thalut was killed in the battle against the Philistines.[1]

The story of the Witch of Endor and the death of Saul is related as follows in Mohammedan tradition:

When Saul went out in pursuit of David, the future King of Israel, the wise and learned men of Israel came and reproached the King for the sin he was committing in trying to kill the anointed of the Lord. Thereupon Saul waxed wroth and slew them. Of all the people who had interfered and remonstrated with the King only one escaped and remained alive, and she was a wise woman. The vizier had not only spared her life but also taken her into his house, where she henceforth lived.

Now it happened that some time afterwards King Saul had a dream wherein he was reproached for the sin he had committed in slaying the wise men of Israel. When he awoke in the morning, he was full of grief and remorse. He went to his vizier and thus he spoke:

" I have put to death all the wise men in Israel and now I am full of remorse and would fain atone for my crime. Has none of the wise men escaped so that I might ask counsel and learn how to expiate my sin?"

Thereupon the vizier made reply: " There remains only one, and she is a woman."

" Bring her to me," said Saul.

And when the wise woman was brought into the presence of the King, the latter said unto her: " I am greatly troubled

[1] Weil, *Biblische Legenden der Muselmänner*, pp. 200-7.

in my mind and I want thee to tell me how I could best make atonement for my crime."

To this the wise woman made reply: " Take me to the tomb of a prophet where I will pray. Perchance God will permit him to speak and let thee know His will."

Thereupon Saul led her to the tomb of the Prophet Samuel, where the wise woman prayed.

And suddenly the voice of Samuel coming from the sepulchre was heard, and thus he spoke: " Let the King and his sons go down to the city of the giants and there they shall fall."

Saul then called his twelve sons and related unto them what had occurred. They all declared themselves ready to go to the city of the giants. They fought valiantly and fell all in one day.[1]

Tabari relates the story of the Witch of Endor somewhat differently. Saul had caused all the wise men of Israel to be put to death, and only one woman had escaped because she knew the Ineffable name of God. Thereupon Saul commanded a giant to kill this woman, but the giant had pity on her and let her escape. Later on, however, Saul repented of his sin and wept and lamented. Every night he went out to the graves where lay the victims he had slain, and thus he spoke: " I conjure you, in the name of God, if you know a way how I can expiate my crime, tell me."

And one night a voice from the grave answered him, and thus it spoke: " O Thalut, is it not enough that thou didst put an end to our lives that thou must come now and worry us when we are dead?"

When Thalut heard these words he was sorely grieved, and the giant, who had pity on him, inquired after the cause of his suffering.

" Dost thou know," said Thalut, " any wise man in the

---

[1] Weil, *Biblische Legenden der Muselmänner*, pp, 200–7.

land who could tell me how I can expiate my sin and thus obtain the forgiveness of the Lord?"

To this the giant made answer: " Dost thou know, O King, to whom thou art to be compared? To the King who had caused all the cocks to be killed. One day, being on a journey, he reached a town and heard a cock crow. Considering the cock's chant as a bad omen, he gave instructions for all the cocks in the town to be killed. When it was time for him to go to bed, he ordered his servant to wake him up with the crowing of the cock, but his servant replied: " All the cocks have been killed and there is none left to crow. Thou, Thalut, hast killed all the wise men in Israel, and there is none whom thou canst consult."

When he saw, however, how grieved Thalut was, he said: " There is one wise woman in the land whose life I did spare."

Thalut visited the wise woman, and she led him to the grave of Joshua the son of Nun. He came out of his grave and asked: " What has happened? Has the day of resurrection come?"

" No," replied the woman, " but Thalut wants to know how he could expiate his crime?"

" Let him resign his power," answered Joshua the son of Nun, " and go out with his sons and fight until they all fall in battle in the defence of the true faith."

Thalut informed his sons of what had occurred, and they were all ready to go out and seek death on the battlefield.[1]

---

[1] Tabari, I, p. 324; Grünbaum, *loc. cit.*, pp. 186–7.

CHAPTER II

The Birth of the Shepherd

David before his birth—Three hours only allotted to him—Adam's
gift—The piety of Jesse—Ruth, the ancestress of David—Nazbath, the
mother of David—Jesse and his beautiful slave—The wife's ruse—David's
life in the desert—Tender care of young lambs—The sleeping rhinoceros
—David's vow to build the Temple—The visit of Samuel—The red-
haired youngster—The anointment of David—Miraculous tall stature—
The flowing horn—The honey jars—David's cleverness—The gold pieces
in the honey jars—The thief detected—The blaspheming giant—Orpah,
the sister-in-law of Ruth—Forty steps—Saul's armour—Goliath's in-
coherent speech—Uriah's request—The promised wife—Why Goliath fell
face downwards—The descendants of the clans of Perez and Zerah—
David pursued—The advantages of lunacy—Ahish, King of Gath—The
wasp and the water-bottle.

KING DAVID—HIS BIRTH AND YOUTH

Long before his birth David is supposed to have played
an important rôle, for the whole world, according to Jewish
legendary lore, is said to have been created only for the
sake and merits of David. He was the goal and purpose of
creation, for his Psalms give expression to the complete development of the human soul. Three hours, says a Midrash,[1]
were only allotted to David when he was born, and he would
have died immediately had not Adam made him a present of
70 years. His ancestors are compared in Midrashic lore with
worthless sand wherein a king on his travels had once lost
a precious jewel from his crown.[2] David's father, however,
Jesse, forms an exception, for he is said to have been one of

---

[1] *Yalkut*, I, § 41; see also Vol. I of this work.   [2] *Genesis Rabba*, 39.

the four men who were absolutely without sin. The other
three were Benjamin, the son of Jacob, Amram, the father of
Moses, and Kilab, the son of David. Had not the Almighty
ordained, in consequence of the fall of Adam, that all men
must die, the Angel of Death would never have had any power
over these four pious men.

Among David's ancestresses are mentioned Thamar, the
daughter-in-law of Judah, Miriam, the sister of Moses,[1] and
Ruth, the Moabite. She was called Ruth because she had a
great happiness to count among her descendants David, who
was destined to offer unto the Lord his songs and praises.[2]
David's mother's name was Nazbath, the daughter of Adiel,
although he was at first supposed to have been the son of a
slave.[3]

It happened as follows: In spite of his great piety, Jesse
was not quite free from temptation. He possessed a beautiful
slave upon whom he had cast his eyes, and one day he made
up his mind to set the slave free and marry her. He would
have carried out his design, had not his wife frustrated it.
Nazbath disguised herself as the slave, and was thus married
to her husband for the second time. The fruit of this union
was David, and hence his words: " Behold, I was shapen
in wickedness and in sin did my mother conceive me "
(Psalms, li, 5).

Although Jesse afterwards discovered the deception, he
esteemed David but lightly, and the supposed son of a slave
was not educated with the other sons. David was sent to tend
the sheep and was practically the servant of his brethren.
When Samuel came to anoint one of the sons of Jesse as King
of Israel, the father brought before the Prophet his twelve
sons except David, the despised boy who was accustomed to
do the menial work and to pasture the sheep. He was twenty-
eight when Samuel appeared upon the scene and anointed the

---

[1] Sotah, 11b.   [2] Berachoth, 7b.   [3] Yalkut Makhiri, ed. Buber, II, 214.

lad as King of Israel. Hitherto David had led a life of hardship in the desert. Here the future King of Israel had grown accustomed to a life of privation, but he also developed his physical strength and had many an opportunity to give proofs both of his nobility of character and his courage. Like Moses, when he tended the flocks of his father-in-law Jethro, David treated the sheep entrusted to him with such loving care and such tenderness that the Lord said: " David tends his father's sheep with gentleness and loving care and therefore he shall one day be the shepherd of my flock Israel." [1] David used to separate the sheep from the young lambs. At first he led the young lambs and let them feed on the tender grass and the heads of the herbs, then he guided the older sheep to feed on the less juicy grass, and finally he led the strong sturdy young rams and let them devour the tough roots and weeds.[2]

More than once the future King of Israel had an opportunity to show his physical strength and courage in the wilderness where he passed almost his entire existence. He is supposed to have killed in one day three lions and two bears.[3] One story, which also shows David's anxiety to build a temple to the Lord, runs as follows:

One day David was wandering in the desert, seeking pasture for his flock, when he suddenly came upon a reem (rhinoceros) asleep. David, unaware that it was a reem, took the gigantic animal for a big mountain and began to climb it, driving his flock up its back for the purpose of letting it feed on the grass which he supposed would grow on the mountain. Suddenly the rhinoceros (reem) awoke from his sleep and stood up. David was lifted up high into the air, up to the sky. Courageous though he was, the lad was seized with terror. He vowed then to the Lord that if God would save his life and bring him safely to the ground, he would build a

---

[1] *Exodus Rabba*, 2, 2; *Midrash Tehillim*, 78, 70.   [2] *Exodus Rabba*, 2.
[3] *Midrash Samuel*, 20, 5.

temple as high as the horns of the reem upon which he was
being lifted up, namely, one hundred cubits. David's vow was
heard, and the Lord sent a lion upon the scene. When the
reem beheld the lion he was awestruck, for all the animals,
even the biggest, are afraid of this king of all the beasts. The
reem at once lay down, and David could have descended with
his flock as fast as possible, but he was afraid of the lion. What
did the Lord do? He sent a deer which the lion immediately
pursued, so that David was saved both from the reem and the
lion.[1] David would have kept his promise and built the
temple of the Lord as he had vowed, but it was the Lord who
would not suffer him to do so.

Soon this lonely life of a shepherd in the desert was to
come to an end, for the supposed son of a slave was to be
anointed King of Israel by Samuel, the prophet of the Lord
and kingmaker. Originally David's eldest brother Eliab, had
been destined to become King, but on account of his violent
nature and his frequent ill-treatment of his brother David he
was not deemed worthy. That was the reason why Samuel
committed an error and assumed that God's choice had fallen
upon Eliab. David was red-haired, and when, at the request
of the Prophet, the despised son of a slave was fetched from the
field, Samuel, on beholding his red hair, was taken aback and
said: " He will shed blood even as Esau did." But the Lord
replied unto Samuel: " Fear not, for David will shed blood
only with the consent of the supreme tribunal, the Sanhedrin,
i.e. he will execute those whom the latter will have sentenced
to death." [2]

Thereupon Samuel proceeded to anoint David. He had
already tried to pour oil upon the heads of David's brothers,
but every time the oil remained in the vessel and would not
come forth. Scarcely, however, did he hold the vessel over
David's head, when the oil began to flow freely and of its own

---

[1] *Midrash Tehillim*, 22, 28.   [2] *Genesis Rabba*, 63, 8.

accord from the horn, which, nevertheless, remained as full as before.

Great was the astonishment of all present when they saw that the despised son of the slave was destined to become King in Israel. It was then that David's mother, Nazbath, came forward and related how she had frustrated her husband's intention and taken the place of the beautiful slave, and that David was consequently her own son.[1]

David was very small and short of stature, but as soon as Samuel had poured the Holy Oil over him he became very tall. It is said that when he later on went out to fight the giant Goliath and put on Saul's armour, it fitted him perfectly, although King Saul was a head and shoulder taller than every man in Israel.[2]

Soon after his anointment David came to the court of King Saul. The latter had already had occasion one day to make the acquaintance of the lad and to admire his cleverness under the following circumstances:

The Money and the Honey Jars

There was a certain man in the days of King Saul, the King of Israel, who had a very beautiful and fascinating wife. He also possessed great wealth. He was very old and felt that the time was drawing near when he would have to depart from this world. Now the governor of the town had cast his eyes upon the young woman and wanted to take her as his concubine. The young woman refused to listen to the governor's proposal, and was consequently in great fear. She therefore took all the gold she possessed, placed it in jars, and poured on the top of it a quantity of honey. Thereupon she went to a friend of her husband, and in the presence of witnesses besought him to take care of these jars of honey until her

[1] *Yalkut Makhiri, ibid.*
[2] *Yalkut Makhiri, ibid.; Midrash Tanchuma*, ed. Buber, III, 84.

return. The woman then left the country so as to escape the
wrath of the governor. Now one day the friend to whom the
jars containing the gold had been entrusted married his son
and required some honey for the banquet. He accordingly
sent his servant to open one of the jars in his keeping and to
take a little honey. Great was the servant's surprise when, on
opening one jar, he discovered the gold underneath the honey.
He informed his master of his discovery, and the latter examined all the other jars. They were full of gold. The man did
not hesitate to abstract the gold, and on the following day he
procured a quantity of honey and filled all the jars.

Some time afterwards the governor of the town died, and
the woman returned to her home. She immediately claimed
the jars wherein she had concealed the gold, but great was
her amazement and distress when she found all the gold gone
and the jars filled with honey. She went to the judge and
complained of the theft of her fortune, but the judge asked
her whether she could bring any witnesses or produce some
other evidence to prove the theft committed by her friend.

" Alas," replied the woman, " no one knew of the gold
concealed in the jars."

" Then I cannot help thee," said the judge, " and I can
only advise thee to appeal to King Saul. He may be able to
render thee justice."

The woman betook herself to the royal palace and begged
the King to help her in her distress. But neither the King nor
his councillors dared give judgment in favour of the poor
woman, as her friend persistently denied having received any
gold from her, and his faithlessness could not be proved.
Thus the poor woman left the royal palace sorely grieved.
On her way she met young David, the future King of Israel,
who was a child then and playing with his companions. When
he noticed the dejection of the woman and learned the cause
of her distress, David thus said to her: " Go and desire the

King to allow me to deal with this matter, and I promise thee that I will prove the truth."

Thereupon the woman returned to King Saul, and thus she spoke to him: " My Lord, I have met a clever boy who maintains that he can prove the truth of my assertions. I desire thee, O King, in the name of justice, to let that boy deal with the matter."

Saul gave his permission, and when young David was brought into his presence, he authorized him to deal with the matter and to prove if he could that the woman had spoken the truth.

" With the help of God," said David, " I will try to let the truth prevail." Thereupon he had the honey jars wherein the woman had concealed her fortune brought, and caused them to be emptied completely and then broken in the presence of the accused and all the court. And lo, one or two gold pieces were found to have stuck to the bottom and the inner side of the jars. In his greed and eagerness to refill the jars with honey and thus hide his theft, the dishonest friend had overlooked the gold pieces adhering to the jars. He had to admit his guilt, and was ordered to restore her fortune to the woman he had cheated.[1]

DAVID AND GOLIATH

Soon afterwards David was called upon to meet the giant Goliath whom he slew in battle. Goliath was the son of Orpah, the Moabite, the sister-in-law of Ruth, who was the ancestress of David. For forty days this giant was allowed to come and jeer at the children of Israel because his mother Orpah had accompanied her mother-in-law Naomi forty steps.[2]

[1] Jellineck, *Beth-Hamidrash*, IV, pp. 150–1; *Hibbur Maassiot*; Wünsche, *Aus Israel's Lehrhallen*, II, pp, 22–24; cf. *Monatsschrift*, XXII, pp. 121–2; *Hebraische Bibliographie*, XVIII, p. 40. [2] See Rosner, *David's Leben u. Character*.

Thereupon Jesse, David's father, said unto his son: " Now is the time for thee, my son, to redeem the pledge once given by thy ancestor Judah, the son of Jacob, who had pledged himself for the safety of Benjamin, the ancestor of Saul." [1]

Saul himself being unable to go out and fight with Goliath, David obeyed his father and went out to wrestle with the giant. In spite of the attractive and alluring promises of the King, none of the Israelites was willing to go out and encounter the terrible giant, whilst the King himself, hero though he was, was prevented by his malady from fighting Goliath. David therefore obeyed his father and declared his willingness to meet the giant in single combat.

Saul now offered the lad his armour, and though David was only of slight build and Saul very tall, the armour fitted the young hero perfectly.[2]   Saul at once recognized that the boy had been chosen by the Lord for the encounter with the giant, but he nevertheless grew pale for jealousy. David, noticing it, at once asked the King to allow him to fight the giant in his ordinary shepherd's array. On his way five stones came to meet him on their own accord, and all five turned into one stone when David touched them.[3]

David was full of misgiving when he began to move towards the redoubtable giant, but when he heard the latter blaspheming Israel, his fear disappeared completely.[4]   When he came face to face with his foe, David noticed that confusion had come over Goliath and that he was terror struck.[5]   Goliath was so confused that he uttered foolish words that had no sense: " I will cast thy flesh to the cattle of the fields."

" He seems to have lost his senses," thought David, " for he is talking foolishly, as if cattle ate flesh."

Goliath had cause for confusion and fear, for he suddenly felt that he was rooted to the ground and could not move.

---

[1] *Midrash Tanchuma*, section *Vayigash*.   [2] *Midrash Tanchuma*, section *Emor*.
[3] See Rosner, *loc. cit.*   [4] *Midrash Tehillim*, 36, 2.   [5] *Midrash Samuel*, 21, 3.

Two hundred and forty-eight chains enchained the limbs of the giant's body.[1]

David was now sure of victory. Throwing a pebble, he struck the giant on his forehead. The latter fell to the ground face downwards and not on his back, for two reasons. It was first for the sake of David, so that he should not have to walk a long way to cut off the head of the giant. Another reason why Goliath fell face downwards was because he was wearing the image of the idol Dagon on his breast, and the latter thus came to shame.[2]

David now approached and tried to cut off the head of Goliath, but he did not know how to remove his armours. At that moment Uriah the Hittite came up and offered to show David how Goliath's armours were fastened at his heels.

" I will help thee," said Uriah, " but promise me that thou wilt assist me in finding a wife among the daughters of Israel." David promised, and Uriah showed him how the armour was fastened by bands across the giant's feet. The Lord, however, was not pleased with David because he had not hesitated to promise the hand of a Jewess to the Hittite. " I will give him her who had been destined to be thy own wife," said the Lord. And thus Bath-Sheba, who had been predestined from the day of creation to be the wife of David married Uriah, and later on was the cause of David's sin.[3] His victory over Goliath made David famous, and his praises were sung in Israel. Saul grew even more jealous. He knew that the boy was of the tribe of Judah, but he caused inquiries to be made whether he was of the clan of Perez or Zerah, because he was aware that the descendants of Perez were destined to be kings in Israel.[4]

David's enemy, Doeg, informed King Saul that David

---

[1] *Midrash Samuel*, 21, 3; *Pesikta de Rab Kahana*, Piska, 27.
[2] *Midrash Tehillim*, 18, 32; *Midrash Shir Hashirim Rabba*, 4, 4.
[3] *Alshech*, I, Samuel, 17, 50.
[4] *Jebamot*, 76b–77a; *Midrash Ruth Rabba*, 4, 4: *Midrash Samuel*, 22.

practically had no right at all to be considered a member of the Jewish community, for he was a descendant of the Moabitess Ruth.[1]   Soon after he had defeated Goliath David was compelled to flee from the court of Saul on account of the King's jealousy.   Saul had promised David as a reward of his great victory over Goliath the hand of his daughter, but he tried to break his promise.   David fled to Samuel, and even in his days of storm and stress assiduously studied the Law and glorified the Lord with his praises.   During his wanderings he received more than one lesson in humility, and found out the wisdom of God and acknowledged His just rule and guidance of the World.

Thus one day David said unto God: " All that Thou hast created is beautiful, and wisdom is more beautiful than anything in the World.   Lunacy, however, Thou shouldst not have created, for it is useless in the World and has no place in the plan of Thy harmonious and beautiful Universe.   Is it beautiful or does it serve any purpose to see some lunatic running through the streets, tearing his garments and being pursued by mocking children and a hooting mob?"

Thus spoke David, to which the Lord replied: " Thou dost not approve of lunacy which I have created, but the day will soon come when thou thyself wilt take recourse to it and find it useful.   Thou wilt supplicate me to afflict thee with madness."

Now it soon happened that David, fleeing from Saul, came to Ahish, King of the Philistines, who dwelt in Gath.   The brothers of Goliath, whom David had killed in battle and whose sword he still carried, were in King Ahish's bodyguard.   " Our Lord and King," said the brothers of Goliath, " the earth is still wet with the blood of our brother slain by David, and we therefore demand that his murderer, who is now in Gath, be executed as he well deserves."   But King

[1] *Jebamot*, 76b–77a; *Midrash Ruth Rabba*, 4, 4; *Midrash Samuel*, 22.

Ahish took David's defence and tried to save his life: " He has killed your brother," said the King, " in open battle. Moreover, it was Goliath who had challenged the Jews to combat, and he was slain according to the conditions of an open and honest combat."

Thus spoke Ahish, who was a pious heathen and wished to save David's life, but the brothers of Goliath replied: " If such be the case, then according to those conditions of the combat thou shouldst now give up thy throne to David and let us be his servants." David's position was desperate, and he was in great distress. He therefore prayed to the Lord to let him appear in the eyes of King Ahish as if he had been afflicted with lunacy. The Lord granted his prayer and lent him strength to appear a madman in the eyes of the King. David now went about in the streets of Gath and wrote upon the doors: " King Ahish owes me one hundred myriads and his wife fifty." Now it happened that both Ahish's wife and his daughter were insane and caused a terrible tumult in the palace within, whilst David did likewise in front of the royal palace. And it was on account of this that the King exclaimed: " Do I lack madmen that ye have brought this fellow here?" Thus David was saved from death, thanks to his pretence of lunacy, and he admitted that even madness served some purpose and was not out of place in the harmony of creation. He composed Psalm 34, where he began his praise with the words: " I will bless the Lord at all times." His son Solomon said afterwards: " Everything hath He beautifully created in its proper time." [1]

One day, when he was being pursued by King Saul, David, having surprised his enemies while they were asleep, made up his mind to carry off Abner's water-flask, which was standing between this giant's feet. Now Abner's knees were at first drawn, and David could pass beneath them quite easily.

---

[1] *Midrash Tehillim*, 34, 1; cf. Bialik, *Sepher Haaggadah*, Vol. I, pp. 99-100.

Suddenly, however, Abner moved in his sleep, and stretching out his feet pinned down David with his legs as with two solid pillars. In that moment David prayed to the Lord for help, and God sent a wasp to sting Abner. The giant in his sleep once more moved his feet and drew up his knees so that David could escape. This was another instructive lesson for David, who had once doubted the usefulness of wasps and wondered why the Lord had ever created them.[1]

It was when he was being pursued by Saul that David once cut off the skirt of Saul's robe, and for this sin he was afterwards punished. He expiated his fault in his old age, when he found no warmth in his clothes wherewith he wrapped himself.[2]

Long and hot were the pursuits of Saul, and endless the sufferings of David, who had been anointed and destined to succeed Saul upon the throne of Israel. News at last reached David of the tragic death of his enemy. He uttered his famous funeral oration, cursing the mounts of Gilboa, but it is only natural to expect him to have felt some relief at the death of his bitter enemy. The way to the throne now stood open, and David is said to have composed Psalm 18 on that occasion. He was rebuked by the Lord, who reminded him of Saul's many virtues.[3]

[1] *Alphabetum Siracidis*, ed. Venice; Bialik, *Sepher Haaggadah*, Vol. I, p. 100,
[2] *Berachoth*, 62b.   [3] Rosner, *David's Leben*, p. 48.

CHAPTER III

The Pious King

The conquest of Jerusalem—The claims of the Jebusites—Abraham's covenant with the heathen—The brass monuments—Joab and the tall cypress—In the valley of the giants—The tutelary angel of the Philistines —The rustling treetops—A scrap of paper and a piece of bronze—The bridle of a mule—Laban's Mazebot—David's piety—The wonderful harp —David rebuked by a frog—The power to call down rain—David's coins —The modesty of the King—The beautiful Bath-Sheba—David is tempted —Satan in the shape of a bird—The beauty behind the wicker screen— David's penance—The King afflicted with leprosy—The rebellious son— The visit to Hebron—The giant Ishbi Benob—David hunting a deer —The water that turned to blood—The moaning dove—The royal mule —Abishai and Orpah—The spindle of Orpah—A story in the *Ramayana*— Rama and the demon Mârica—The ruse of the demon—The rape of Sita— Stories told in mediæval literature—Joab the son of Zeruya—The capture of Kinsali—The broken sword—Blood issuing from underneath the gates —The crown of the Amalekite King—The father and his twelve sons— The love of a father.

As soon as David had ascended the throne and been recognized as King by the whole nation of Israel, he made up his mind to subdue the remaining part of the land which the Israelites had not yet conquered. He also decided to capture the ancient city of Jerusalem, which was in the possession of the heathen Jebusites. He advanced with his army against the heathen possessors of the city which was destined to become the centre of Israel's greatness and religion. The Jebusites, however, laughed at David. In the burgh of Zion they felt quite safe, not only because the city was surrounded by a high wall, but also because they could appeal to a covenant once made by Abraham with their ancestors.[1]

[1] *Pirke de Rabbi Eliezer*, Ch. 36; see Vol. I of the present work.

When Abraham came to acquire the Cave of Machpelah from the Hittites, the latter consented to sell him the cave only under certain conditions. They insisted that the Patriarch should make a covenant with them according to which his descendants, when they came to conquer Palestine, would never wrest the city from the Jebusites. Thereupon the Jebusites had erected in their market place brass monuments upon which the conditions of the covenant were engraved. To these monuments the Jebusites now pointed when David approached their city.

" You cannot enter our city," the Jebusites said, " before you have destroyed these monuments."

David could, of course, have pointed out that the Jebusites had already attacked the Jews in the time of Joshua, but he determined to buy the city from them.

At first, however, he decided to enter the city so as to show the heathen possessors that he feared neither their power nor their high wall, but respected the promise once given by the Patriarch Abraham. His commander Joab now devised a plan how to enter the city. He took a flourishing tall cypress tree, planted it near the wall, and then bent the tree downwards, giving it to David to hold. Standing on David's head, Joab grasped the tip of the tree, and when it rebounded he sat high above the wall. He jumped into the city and here destroyed the brass monuments. The wall in the meantime miraculously lowered itself and David could enter the city.[1]

Jerusalem was now in his possession, but David wanted to indemnify the Jebusites and offered them 600 shekels, that is, 50 shekels for each of the twelve tribes of Israel.[2] The descendants of the sons of Heth took the money even as their ancestors had accepted the shekels from the Patriarch Abraham for the Cave of Machpelah. Thus Jerusalem was not only captured but bought by David, King of Israel.

[1] *Midrash Tehillim*, 18.   [2] *Pirke de Rabbi Eliezer, ibid.*

David now prepared for battle with the Philistines whom he met in the valley of Rephaim, or the Giants. Now God commanded David not to attack the enemy until he heard the treetops move. The tutelary angel of the Philistines was namely pleading the cause of the nation under his protection, and the Lord decided to pass judgment first on the tutelary angel of the Philistines and then to hand over the nation to David.

The two armies were facing one another, and the distance between them was only four ells. The Israelites were anxious to throw themselves upon the enemy, but David forbade them to move. He even had to make use of his royal authority to refrain his heroes from giving battle. " I will not disobey the will of the Lord," said David, " and I prefer to be killed by the Philistines and die a pious man rather than be victorious and disobedient to the will of the Almighty." Thus spoke David, and lo, suddenly a rustling noise was heard, and the treetops moved. The tutelary angel of the Philistines had been judged, and David was thus commanded by the Lord to attack the enemy. Thereupon the Lord said unto his angels: " Behold the difference between Saul and David." [1]

This was not the only occasion on which David obeyed the will of the Lord before going to war. Moreover, he carefully considered his right to make war and attack the enemy. To break a covenant made by his ancestors, to disregard a scrap of paper, or rather a piece of stone or brass which contained such a covenant, never entered his mind. His jurisconsults, the Sanhedrin, were instructed to investigate the causes of the war and the possible claims of the enemy. Thus before going out to war against the Philistines, David instructed the Sanhedrin to investigate certain claims the enemy had raised. The Philistines pretended that David had no right to wage a war against them because Isaac had once concluded

[1] *Midrash Tehillim,* 27.

a covenant with their King Abimelech, and the nation still possessed a pledge which consisted in the bridle of a mule which the Patriarch had given to the King of the Philistines.

A modern king, Frederick II of Prussia, is supposed to have said: " Let us first take Silesia, we shall easily find a jurisconsult afterwards who will prove our right to it." David, according to Jewish legend, acted in a different manner. He instructed the Sanhedrin carefully to investigate the claims of the Philistines. The Court decided that the claim of this nation was unfounded. Isaac had indeed concluded an alliance with Abimelech, but the present-day Philistines were in no way the descendants of the ancient inhabitants of the country. They had come to Palestine at a later date, immigrating from Caphtor.[1]

A somewhat similar claim to an alliance was raised by the Aramaeans. This nation pretended that David had no right to wage war against them because the Patriarch Jacob had once concluded a treaty with Laban, and they pointed to those *Mazebot* once erected as a sign and in memory of the alliance between the countries of Aram and Canaan. Again David consulted the Sanhedrin, and the latter declared that the Aramaeans themselves were the first to break the ancient covenant, for did they not make war against Israel in the days of Moses and Joshua? [2]

DAVID'S PIETY

David was not only a hero and a great ruler, but also a pious man, a poet, and a Psalmist. He judged his people by day and occupied himself with affairs of State, devoting the nights to study and prayer, and tasting but little sleep. " Sixty winks " of sleep did Israel's King enjoy, and the alarm-clock which awakened him was worthy of the poet and Psalmist.

---

[1] *Pirke de Rabbi Eliezer*, Ch. 36; *Midrash Tehillim*, 60.   [2] *Ibid.*

He had hung up a wonderful harp over his head, and the strings of that harp had been made of the gut of that ram which Abraham had once sacrificed on Mount Moriah. At midnight the cool night breeze blowing from the north through the open window whispered and stirred the strings of the royal harp, and they began to vibrate, giving forth sweet and harmonious sounds, and immediately the King arose and began to study and to sing his Psalms. Once only did the royal singer forget his modesty and boast that no creature praised the Lord as much as he did. Immediately a croaking frog appeared and informed David that it had uttered more praises to the Creator than he ever did. It was then that David sang Psalms 119 and 57 (119, 62; 57, 9).[1]

It is said that David's piety was so great that he had the power to call down the rain, the tempest, and the hail. These things were formerly stored up in heaven, but to David, on account of his great piety, was granted the power to make them descend on the earth. David showed his modesty even in the manner in which he had his coins struck. They contained not his own effigy, as is and was the custom of modern and ancient rulers, but the tower of David on one side and a shepherd's pouch on the other.[2]

BATH-SHEBA

Even the sin David had committed when he took to wife the beautiful Bath-Sheba, the widow of Uriah the Hittite, is explained in Haggadic lore as a punishment sent to him for his self-confidence and his boast that he had the power to resist temptation, even like the three Patriarchs.

One day David himself besought the Lord to lead him into temptation. "Lord of the Universe," he prayed, "why

[1] *Berachoth, 3b; Midrash Tehillim,* 22, 8; 37, 4; *Midrash Ruth,* 6, 1; *Succah, 26b; Pirke de Rabbi Eliezer,* Ch. 21; *Yalkut,* II, § 889; *Sotah,* 10b; cf. Lewner, *Kol Aggadoth,* Vol. III, pp. 265–268.   [2] *Genesis Rabba,* 39.

art Thou called the God of Abraham, Isaac, and Jacob, and not the God of David?"

"Because," replied the Creator, "I have proved these pious men, but thee I have not yet proved."

"Then try me, too, O Lord," prayed David. God granted his request, and even warned him beforehand, a privilege never vouchsafed to the Patriarchs, that he would be tempted and tried by a woman.

One day Satan appeared in the disguise of a bird, and David shot an arrow at the bird. It had perched on a beehive or wicker screen behind which the beautiful Bath-Sheba was combing her long tresses. The shot, instead of hitting the bird, threw over the wicker screen, and the King suddenly beheld the dazzling beauty of Bath-Sheba. David fell in love with her and took her to wife. In legendary lore, however, it is explained that the royal lover never really committed any sin in marrying Bath-Sheba. Uriah the Hittite had left for the wars and, as it was customary, had given his wife a bill of divorce.[1]

Whatever his sin, David repented of it and strove to expiate it. He did penance for twenty-two years, and accepted with pious resignation and even joy the punishments and sorrows the Lord sent him.[2] It is said that David was afflicted with leprosy for six months and was cast out and separated from his people, his court, and even the Sanhedrin.[3]

The greatest blow to David was perhaps the rebellion of his son Absalom. David's friends reproached him for having married a captive of war, the woman who bore him Absalom, the rebellious son. The latter had cunningly obtained from his father a written permission to select two distinguished men who would accompany him on his visit to Hebron. Thereupon he travelled all over Palestine, showing his father's letter in every town, and thus induced two of the most distinguished

---

[1] *Sanhedrin*, 107a; *Sabbath*, 56a.   [2] *Tana debe Eliahu Rabba*, II.   [3] *Sanhedrin*, 107a.

and influential men to accompany him. He thus succeeded in
gathering two hundred men round him whom his faithful
followers tried to win over to his cause during a banquet he
offered them at Hebron.[1]

DAVID AND ISHBI BENOB

David repented of his sins, and he gladly accepted the
numerous sufferings that were sent upon him, but his sins
were not so easily forgiven. He was responsible for the murder
of the priests of Nob, and for the death of many others who
had perished through him (or been punished by him).

One day the Lord said unto him: " Choose now, what
dost thou prefer, to see thy posterity destroyed or to fall into
the hands of the enemy." And David replied: " Lord of the
Universe, deliver me into the hands of my enemy, but let not
my house be doomed to destruction."

Now it happened that war had again broken out between
Israel and the Philistines.

One day David went out hunting when Satan appeared to
him in the disguise of a deer. David chased the animal and was
thus enticed into the land of the enemy. He was suddenly
recognized by Ishbi Benob, a brother of the giant Goliath,
who exclaimed: " Here is the man who has slain my brother;
he is now in my power, and I will take my revenge." Thereupon Ishbi Benob seized King David, chained him, and cast
him down and laid a wine-press upon him. David might have
been crushed and life squeezed out of him, but a miracle
happened which saved his life. God caused the earth underneath the prisoner to soften and sink so that it yielded to the
weight of David's body, and the King was saved from death.
All this happened on a Sabbath eve. At this moment Abishai,
the son of Zeruyah, was just preparing for the incoming

---

[1] *Sanhedrin*, 107a; *Jerushalmi, Sotah*, I, 5; *Midrash Tanchuma*, section *Vayetze*, 17.

Sabbath and was washing his head in four basins of water. Suddenly he perceived drops of blood in the water. Raising up his head, he beheld a dove, and was startled by the moaning and plaining of the bird. " The dove," thought Abishai, " is the symbol of the people of Israel, and I presume that this bird has come to apprise me that the King is in danger." Thereupon Abishai hurried to the royal palace and searched for the King. Not finding David at home, he made up his mind to mount the swiftest animal he could find and hurry out in search of the King. Now the swiftest animal at Abishai's disposal was the royal mule, the one David himself was wont to ride. Abishai, however, hesitated to mount the royal mule without an express permission of the doctors learned in the law. He knew that the law forbade the subject to ride the King's horse, mount his throne, or grasp his sceptre.[1] This, however, was a case of emergency, and time was pressing.

Abishai therefore went to the sages and obtained their permission. On account of the impending danger, the sages permitted him to avail himself of the mule used by the King. Abishai now mounted the animal and swiftly rode out into the desert. A miracle, however, happened, and the earth flew under him. He had scarcely left Jerusalem when he already found himself in the land of the Philistines and in front of Ishbi's house. Here Abishai met Orpah, the mother of the giant, who was sitting without the door spinning. The mother of the giant, on perceiving the new arrival, broke her thread and flung the spindle at him with intent to kill him. Abishai picked up the spindle and hurled it at Orpah with such force that it struck her on her brow and killed her.

When Ishbi saw what had happened, he said unto himself: " Now there are two of them here and they will kill me." Thereupon he drew David from under the wine-press and, hurling him up in the air, held his lance up in the hope that David would

[1] *Sanhedrin, 22a.*

fall upon it and be transfixed. Abishai, however, quickly
uttered the Ineffable name of God, which had the effect of
arresting David in his fall and keeping him suspended between
Heaven and Earth. Thereupon Abishai questioned David as
to how he had come to be in such a sore plight, and the King
acquainted his cousin with the question the Lord had asked
him and with the answer he himself had made. Abishai, however, persuaded the King to change his mind. This courtier,
had he lived centuries later, would have approved of the
famous saying: *Après nous le déluge*.

" What dost thou care," said Abishai to his royal master,
" what happens to thy descendants? Let them sell wax if they
like, as long as thou art left in peace! Follow my advice and
reverse thy prayer, plead for thyself rather, and let thy descendants take care of themselves."

David was persuaded, and the two now joined their prayers
and pleaded to the Lord to avert David's doom and to save
him from the hands of the Philistine. Thereupon Abishai
once more spoke the Ineffable name, and David gradually
came down to earth at some distance from the lance of the giant.
The two now at first swiftly ran away from the giant, but
suddenly changing their minds offered resistance. When they
reminded Ishbi of his mother's death, his strength and courage
forsook him and he was slain by David and Abishai.[1]

This story is told in a different version in another place,
where it is given as an illustration of the words of the Prophet:
" Let not the strong boast of his strength." (*Jeremiah*, 9, 22.)
David was namely beginning to be proud of his strength, for
it is said that he could transfix 800 men with one throw of his
spear. The Lord wanted to show him that without divine
assistance he was a weak, helpless mortal.[2]

There is a story in the *Ramayana* which closely resembles

---

[1] *Sanhedrin*, 95a; cf, Lewner, *l.c.* 286–291.
[2] Jellinek, *Beth-Hamidrash*, IV, p. 140; VI, pp. 106–108; *Midrash Tanchuma*, section
Vayetze; *Midrash Tehillim*, 18, 30.

this Talmudical legend of David and Ishbi Benob. Rama was living in the forest of Dandaka together with the beautiful Sita and his brother Lakshmana. Single-handed he had destroyed fourteen thousand giants and demons who were infesting the forest where he had chosen his abode. Now Ravana, King of the Rakshasas, heard of the massacre of his people, and was also informed of Sita's supernatural beauty. To wreak revenge on Rama he decided to carry off Sita, and for that purpose sent to the forest one of his faithful serving spirits, the demon Mârica. The latter assumed a disguise and appeared to Rama as a deer, dazzling like gold.

When Sita beheld the glorious animal, she expressed the desire to possess its brilliant fur and to spread it on her couch. Rama thereupon left Sita with his brother whilst he himself went out in pursuit of the deer. The disguised demon enticed Rama to the very outskirts of the forest. Rama at last loosed an arrow, and Mârica was hit. But even whilst feeling himself on the point of death the demon remained faithful to his King, and by a ruse tried to help him. He uttered a terrible cry, shouting: " It is I, Rama, help, my brother!"

Sita heard the cry and, thinking that Rama was in danger of death, dispatched Lakshmana to her husband. Thereupon Ravana, who had been lying in wait, availed himself of the absence of the two heroes, and captured Sita.

The situation is, of course, different in the Talmudical legend and in the tale in the *Ramayana*, but in both it is a demon in the disguise of a deer who is enticing the hunter, leading him into danger. Are we entitled to conclude that the Talmudical legend is of Indian origin and that the Rabbis of the Talmud had received the story from Persian sources? [1]

In addition, however, to the demon assuming the disguise of a deer and enticing the hunter, the above legend also contains another motive, namely that of the water changing into

[1] *Revue des Études Juives*, II, p. 302.

blood which is supposed to have informed Abishai that David was in distress. This motive is found not only in an Egyptian legend of the fourteenth century B.C., but also in a Serbian tale; in the famous mediæval French novel *Histoire d'Olivier de Castille et d'Artus d'Algarbe*, where the water, as a sign of danger, turns black; in a Russian popular tale,[1] and in many other European folk-tales.[2]

There are numerous examples in folk-lore where a metal object is changing colour at the moment the person who is dear to us is in danger or distress. We find it in the Talmud in the case of the friends of Job who knew of his distress because they had each a crown on which were engraven the portraits of the other three friends. When one of them was in danger, the aspect of his portrait was suddenly changed.[3] We find this trait in a story of *Thousand and One Nights* (the story of the two sisters who were jealous of the younger sister), in a tale of the *Pentameron*, and in the French novel *Floire et Blanchefleur*.[4]

We see no reason whatever why the Talmudical legend should have been borrowed from a Persian source. It must be borne in mind that the tale is an interpretation, as the majority of Talmudical legends are, of the Biblical passage *II Sam.* 21, 16–17, " and Ishbi Benob who was of the descendants of Harapha ". It is quite possible that the Talmudical legend is an adaptation from the Persian, but then it has exercised its influence (as we have pointed out in the Introduction to Vol. I) upon mediæval folk-lore.

---

[1] A. Rambaud, *La Russie épique*, p. 378.
[2] Cosquin, *Contes populaires de Lorraine*, Vol. I, pp. lxv, ff; *Revue des Études Juives*, XVII, p. 204.
[3] *Baba Batra*, 16b.
[4] Cosquin, *loc. cit.*; Israël Lévi, in *Revue des Études Juives*, XVII, 204.

JOAB THE SON OF ZERUYA. THE CAPTURE OF KINSALI

One of David's most famous chieftains was the hero Joab, whose achievements in the field were very great. The occasion on which he gave proof of his heroism in the most remarkable manner was when he captured single-handed the Amalekite capital Kinsali.

In the days of David, King of Israel, it happened that Joab, the son of Zeruya, betook himself to Kinsali, the Amalekite capital, which he wanted to take. The children of Israel laid siege to the town. When six months had elapsed, the heroes assembled, and thus they spoke unto Joab, their general.

" We can no longer remain here, for it is such a long time since we left our villages, and it is high time that we returned to our homes, our wives, and our children."

Thereupon Joab said to them: " If ye return home the King will be displeased, and moreover, all the other nations will hear of this and will be greatly encouraged to unite and make war against us. I now propose unto ye to make a sling and to hurl me into the city."

Thereupon Joab took 1000 pieces of silver and his sword, and he was hurled into the city. Before leaving his men he thus spoke to them: " Wait another forty days, and when ye see blood flow from underneath the gates of the city then know ye that I am still alive, otherwise ye may conclude that I am dead and ye can return to your houses."

Thus Joab was cast into the city, and he fell into the courtyard of a widow who also had a married daughter. The young woman, on going out into the courtyard, found Joab lying there in a faint. She called her mother and her husband, and the three brought him into the house, where they revived him. When he had regained consciousness, they asked him who he was and how he had come into the courtyard.

" I am an Amalekite," said Joab, " and was taken prisoner by the Israelites. They brought me into the presence of their King, who ordered his soldiers to hurl me into this city. I beg you, therefore, to spare my life." Thereupon he handed them ten silver pieces, and they received him kindly and gave him hospitality.

Joab remained in the house for ten days and then asked permission to go out into the town.

" Thou canst not go out," said his hosts, " in thy present apparel." They gave him an Amalekite garb, and he went out into the town.

There were 140 squares in the town, one larger than the other, and each had two entrances. Joab immediately went to an armourer and, showing him his broken sword, asked the Amalekite to forge him another like the weapon he had broken. When the armourer saw Joab's broken sword he was amazed, for he had never seen such a weapon in all his life. He forged a new sword, but Joab snapped it in two, and he did likewise with the second sword. The third sword the armourer had fashioned Joab shook but did not break. Grasping the sword, he asked the armourer whom he ought to slay with it, to which the latter unhesitatingly replied: " Joab, the general of the King of Israel."

" Let us suppose that I am he," said Joab, and then added: " Look behind thee." The smith turned his head, and Joab ran him through and threw aside his body. Thereupon he went out into one of the squares and killed 500 warriors, and none of them remained alive. He sheathed his sword and returned to the house where he had found hospitality.

In the meantime the rumour had spread in the town that Ashmedai, King of the demons, had slain 500 warriors. When his hosts inquired of Joab whether he had heard the rumour, he said that he had not heard anything about it. Once more Joab took out some money and dispensed it among his hosts.

On the following day he went out for the second time, slew another 500 Amalekites, and returned to his lodgings. As his hand was tired from so much action and his sword clave to it, he asked his young hostess to bring him some warm water to wash his hand and to take the sword out of it.

"Thou eatest and drinkest with us," cried the young woman, "and yet thou slayest our warriors." He immediately slew the woman, afraid lest she betray him. His hand became immediately free, and he once more sallied forth. He heard a herald proclaiming that the King had commanded that anybody who sheltered a guest in his house should bring the stranger immediately. Joab slew the herald and did likewise to everyone whom he met.

Thereupon he opened the gates of the city and blood issued forth. When the Israelites, who had mourned Joab as dead and made up their minds to return to their homes, saw the blood they knew that their general was alive, and they cried out with one accord: "Hear, O Israel, the Eternal is our God, the Eternal is One."

Thereupon Joab mounted upon the tower, so that the children of Israel could see him, and called aloud: "The Lord will not forget His people for the sake of His great name, and ye, Israelites, assault the city and capture it."

They slew all the inhabitants and destroyed the heathen temples. The Amalekite King, however, whom Joab had left alive, he brought before David. And he took the crown which was of pure gold and set in with a wonderful gem from the head of the heathen King and placed it upon that of David, the King of Israel.[1]

[1] Jellinek, *Beth-Hamidrash*, V, pp. 146-148.

The Father who would not Sell his Son

Although a warrior, a blunt soldier, Joab was not dis-
inclined to study and even to argue with David on moral
questions. Now when he heard the King utter the words,
" Like as a father pitieth his children, so the Lord pitieth
them that fear him ", he felt rather surprised, and thus he spoke
unto himself: " Should the love of a father for his child be
used for the comparison and not the love of a mother for her
child? Is it not the mother who loves the child more, who is
looking after it and is taking care of it? How can my royal
master utter such words? I will keep my eyes open, observe
the conduct and behaviour of the people, and endeavour to
find out whether the words of David are really true to fact."

And Joab roamed about in the land of Israel. On one of
his journeys he came to a place where he happened to meet
an old man who was rather poor but had twelve children.
All day long the old man toiled hard to support his twelve
children, and when evening came he bought with the money
he had earned a loaf of bread, and thus he supported his
family with his scanty earnings. Though he was old and feeble,
none of his children had to work, for the father supported
them and worked for them. When the man came home in the
evening, it was his habit to cut his loaf into fourteen parts,
two for himself and his wife, and twelve for his twelve children.

When Joab saw this man and the hard life he was compelled to lead, he said unto himself: " I will try my first experiment with this man." Thereupon he approached the man
when he was about to begin his work in the field, and thus he
spoke to him: " How strange is thy conduct! Thou art an
old man and yet dost thou work hard in order to support thy
children. Would it not be more just if thy children were to
work for thee and support thee in thine old age? Anyhow, I
propose unto thee to sell one of thy children to the King, my

royal master. Thou wilt thus have one less to support, whilst the money thou wilt realize thou canst apply to the support of thy other children."

Thus spoke Joab, but the old man angrily rejected the proposition. No, he would not sell any of his children.

Joab now decided to approach the mother and to make the same proposal to her. He visited her in the absence of her husband and thus spoke to her: " Thou and thy husband are both old and ye have brought up twelve children, and whilst ye are working they are living on the labour of your hands and your daily toil." Thus spoke Joab, to which the woman replied: " What can we do? Such is the way of the world that parents work for and take care of their children."

" That may be true," replied Joab, " but I wish to lessen your burden, and I therefore offer thee a hundred gold pieces if thou wilt sell me one of thy sons. The money will be enough for you to end your days in peace and plenty."

The woman soon yielded to his persuasions, but she was afraid of her husband. " If my husband," she said, " becomes aware of the fact that I have sold one of our sons, he will surely kill me."

" He will not miss one son out of so many," said Joab, " but should he do so, then I will give thee back thy son."

The woman accepted the offer, took the hundred gold pieces, and sold one of her sons. When the old man returned home in the evening, he cut his bread, as was his daily custom, into fourteen portions, and when he saw that one piece of bread had remained, he missed one of his children. He inquired after the missing child, and insisted so long until the woman told him the truth. " I have sold the child," said the mother, " to the stranger who called here before, and here are the hundred gold pieces he gave me."

When the father heard what had occurred, he was greatly grieved and would take neither food nor drink. Impatiently

he waited for the next morning, when he immediately set out
to find Joab and to claim his child. He took with him the
hundred gold pieces and a weapon, firmly decided to return
the money to the stranger, but to slay him should he refuse to
give up the child.

Joab was in the meantime waiting on the road to see what
would happen. When the old man beheld Joab he angrily
exclaimed: " Here is thy money, and give me back my child."

" Thy wife sold me thy son," replied Joab, " and she had
a right to do so." But the father waxed very wroth and
threateningly said: " I will not parley with thee; if thou wilt
return my child it is well, otherwise I will fight thee to the
death and either kill thee or be killed myself." Joab smiled
and finally surrendered the child to the loving father.

" David was right," he exclaimed, " when he uttered his
words: ' Like as a father pitieth his children, so the Lord
pitieth them that fear him '. He did not say ' Like as a mother
pitieth her children ', for here have I met a mother who was
ready to sell one of her sons, although she had not to work
for the child's maintenance. The father, on the contrary, who
has to support the twelve children, was ready to lay down his
life rather than part with one of them." [1]

---

[1] Jellinek, *loc. cit.*, V, pp. 52–53; cf. pp. xxii–xxiv, and VI, pp. xvi–xvii; *Ozar Midrashim*,
I, pp. 213a–214a; Bin Gorion, *loc. cit.*, Vol. III, pp. 87–90.

CHAPTER IV

The Dead Lion, or King David
after his Death

The death of a king—The measure of his days—David's request—The Lord's refusal—David destined to die on a Saturday—The angel of death and the study of the Torah—The angel's ruse—The noise in the garden —The broken stairs—The removal of the corpse—The barking dogs— Solomon's perplexity—The decision of the Sanhedrin—A living dog is better than a dead lion—David is still alive—Messiah the son of David— The messianic banquet—The cup of blessing—The royal tomb—The pious washerwoman—Her miraculous escape—The sword of the pasha—The kadi's advice—The Rabbi of Jerusalem—The pious beadle—What he saw in the royal tomb.

THE DEATH OF A KING

A Living Dog is better than a Dead Lion

David had frequently prayed to the Lord " to inform him as to his end, and the measure of his days " (*Psalms*, 39, 4), that is, to tell him when his life would run out. The Lord, however, refused to grant David's prayer, for it was an inalterable decree that such information be hidden from man, and no man (with the exception of Hezekiah) was to foreknow his end. David thereupon begged to be informed on what day of the week his life would come to an end, and it was revealed to him that this would happen on a Sabbath.

" Lord of the Universe," prayed David, " let the day of my death be postponed for one day, and may I be permitted to die on the Sunday following." This request was not vouch-safed unto him. " The reign of Solomon," said the Lord, " will begin on that Saturday, the day of thy death, and no reign should overlap even by one moment the reign of another."

Thereupon David besought the Lord to permit him to die on the Friday, the day before. Once more the Lord denied his request. God delighted in the study of the Law, rather than in holocausts. " One day," said the Lord, " spent by thee in the study of the Torah is better than a thousand burnt offerings which thy son Solomon will bring upon the altar in the Temple " (*Psalms*, 84, 10).

Now the angel of death has no power over a man when he is engaged upon the study of the Torah. Henceforth David spent every Sabbath in the study of the Torah, never per-mitting himself any pause. He thus hoped to foil the angel of death. When David's life had actually run out and the angel of death presented himself to take the pious king's soul, he was greatly embarrassed, for David never for a moment interrupted his study.

Weary of waiting, the angel of death at last had resort to a ruse. There was a garden behind the royal palace, and the angel of death went and shook one of the trees, making a tre-mendous noise. Greatly astonished, David rose up and went out to ascertain the cause of the strange noise. He interrupted his study for a moment and descended a stairway leading into the garden. This was an opportunity which the angel of death immediately seized. One of the steps gave way, and David fell down and was killed.

Now the body of David was exposed to the scorching sun, and Solomon doubted whether he could remove it on the Sabbath. The dogs, too, had not been fed the day before and were barking fiercely. Solomon therefore sent word to the Sanhedrin and asked the assembly's advice.

" My father is dead," said Solomon, " and exposed to the scorching sun, and the dogs have not been fed and are growing fierce. What can I do in the matter without desecrating the Sabbath?" Promptly came the decision of the Sanhedrin: " Put a loaf of bread or a child upon the body of thy father and then remove it, so that it will appear as if the loaf or the child were *really* moved. As for the dogs, cut a carcass and throw it before them, for it is permitted to profane the Sabbath for the purpose of feeding a living creature."

When Solomon heard this decision of the Sanhedrin, he exclaimed: " A living dog is better than a dead lion." [1]

According to another version, the day on which David died was both a Sabbath and the first day of Pentecost. As the body of the dead King could not be moved, Solomon, who had sway of beasts and birds, summoned the eagles and commanded them to guard the body of his father with their wings.[2]

David, however, the King of Israel, is supposed to be still alive. His death was merely a removal from his earthly scene of action. He dwells in Paradise among the elect, his brilliant crown upon his head.[3] He is the ancestor of the Redeemer who will put an end to Israel's suffering and who is referred to as " Messiah, the son of David ".

According to several Haggadic passages in the Talmud, it is not one of his descendants but King David himself who will be the Messiah. He will reappear and assume the rule over Israel. He ruled in the past and he will rule in the future, in this world and in the world to come.[4]

King David enjoys great distinction among the elect and the just who dwell in Paradise. According to Talmudic legend, a great distinction and honour will be vouchsafed unto

---

[1] *Sabbath*, 30a–b. [2] *Ruth Rabba*, I, 17; cf. Lewner, *l.c.* Vol. III, pp. 303–305.
[3] Jellinek, *Beth-Hamidrash*, V, p. 168; VI, pp. 25–26.
[4] *Midrash Tehillim*, 5, 4; 18, 27; 57, 3; *Midrash Samuel*, 19, 6; see also A. Rosner, *David's Leben*, 1908, p. iii.

him on the day of the Last Judgment. On the day on which
the Lord will have redeemed His people and accomplished
His loving kindness to the seed of Isaac, He will make a banquet for the righteous. The throne of David will be placed
by the side of the Throne of Glory. At the end of the banquet
a blessing will have to be said over a cup of wine. This cup
will be offered at first to the Patriarch Abraham. Abraham,
however, will decline the honour: " I am not worthy," he
will say, " to pronounce the blessing over the cup of wine,
because I begot Ishmael whose descendants do not walk in
the ways of the Lord."

The cup of blessing will then be offered to Isaac, but he,
too, will decline the honour. " I am not worthy to pronounce
the blessing," he will say, " because I am the father of Esau."
Jacob, too, will refuse to say the blessing because he had
married two sisters simultaneously, which the Torah afterwards prohibited.

" Moses," the Lord will say, " speak thou the blessing
over the cup of wine," but he who led the Israelites out of
bondage will decline the honour. " I am not worthy of it,"
he will say, " since I was not counted worthy to enter the
Holy Land."

Joshua, too, to whom the cup will be offered, will refuse
the honour on the ground that he was not deemed worthy to
have a son. The cup will then be offered unto David, who
will accept the honour of saying the blessing.

" I will pronounce the blessing," the King of Israel will
say, " and I will not decline the honour. I will take the cup
of salvation and call upon the Name of the Lord." [1]

[1] *Pesachim,* 119b.

The Royal Tomb

Many wonderful stories are told in post-Talmudical literature of the tomb of David and the miracles which happened in connection with it. The two following tales are a good example.

The Pious Washerwoman

There once lived in Jerusalem a righteous woman who had lost her husband and children. She was earning her living by the toil of her hands, washing the clothes of her neighbours. Among her customers was also the keeper of the tomb of David, peace be upon him.

One day when she brought to this man his linen, white as snow, he thus spoke unto her: " Thou art a good and pious woman, and my soul is yearning to give thee a great joy. Thou wouldst no doubt be happy to visit the tomb of the King, which no Jew has hitherto been allowed to enter."

" I should indeed be most happy," replied the woman, " to be deemed worthy of such an honour."

" Then come with me," said the keeper of the tomb. He led her to a gate which he bade her pass, but scarcely had she entered the passage when he closed and locked the gate, leaving the poor woman alone in the darkness. Thereupon he ran to the *kadi* and informed him that a Jewess had had the audacity to enter the tomb of David, and that as soon as he had noticed it he had immediately locked the gate.

When the kadi heard this he was greatly incensed, and exclaimed: " By the Prophet, this woman deserves death. Lead her out, and she will be condemned to be burnt alive."

The poor woman, in the meantime, realized the fact that she had been betrayed by the keeper and that her life was in danger. She fell upon her knees and prayed to the Lord to have pity on her for the sake of His servant David. As she was thus weeping and praying, a great light suddenly rent the darkness of the tomb, and she beheld a white-haired old man with a shining and benevolent countenance. Taking the trembling woman by the hand, he led her through tortuous and winding subterranean passages until they reached the open. Thereupon the old man said to her: " Run swiftly to thy house, and there start thy work at the wash-tub without confiding to anyone what has occurred." The woman opened her mouth to thank the wonderful old man, but he had already vanished.

In the meantime the kadi, accompanied by his officials, arrived before the gate of the tomb, and orders were given to seize the woman and lead her to the place of execution. In vain, however, did the kadi and his servants search the tomb, for no trace of the woman was to be found. Greatly astonished, the kadi accused the keeper of having mocked him, but the latter swore by the Prophet that the woman had really entered the tomb. The kadi thereupon sent his servants to the home of the washerwoman, and the messengers soon returned informing their master that they had found the accused in front of her washing-tub.

The keeper was now accused of perjury, and by the order of the kadi he was seized and burnt. The pious washerwoman never divulged to anyone the miracle which had happened to her in the tomb of David. On her deathbed only she acquainted the community of Jerusalem with her secret.[1]

The Sword of the Pasha

Another miraculous story about the tomb of David runs as follows: It happened one day that a pasha, standing in front of the tomb of David and looking through a window of the mausoleum, let fall his sword. The weapon, ornamented with

[1] *Maasse Nissim*, § 3; see *Midr. Abot*, 44*b*; Bin Gorion, *Der Born Judas*, Vol. V, pp. 63–66.

pearls and diamonds, dropped into the interior of the cave. The pasha was anxious to recover his sword, and an Ishmaelite, or Mohammedan, was lowered on a cord through the window. When the man was drawn up again he was dead. A second, a third, and a fourth Mohammedan met with the same fate.

The pasha declared that he was determined to have his sword, even if all the inhabitants of Jerusalem were to perish in the search after it.

Thereupon the kadi approached, and thus he spoke: " My Lord, may it please unto thee to spare the lives of the faithful and to listen to the advice of thy servant. Send thy messenger to the house of the Jewish Rabbi, the Haham Basha, and command him to send one of his co-religionists to be lowered into the tomb. King David is of the Jewish race, and he will not harm any one of the children of Israel."

Thus spoke the kadi, and the pasha acted upon his advice. He informed the Rabbi of Jerusalem that should he refuse to send one of his community to fetch the weapon, all the Jews of Jerusalem would suffer.

Great was the distress of the Rabbi when he saw himself placed between the alternative of either desecrating the tomb of King David or of letting his people suffer. For three days he and his community fasted and prayed at the grave of Rachel, and on the fourth day he decided to cast lots as to who should dare descend into the tomb of David. The beadle of the Synagogue, a pious and righteous man, was designated as the messenger. He accepted the mission, purified his soul, and made ready for the perilous descent. In an attitude of prayer, with tearful eyes, he betook himself to the mausoleum containing the royal tombs of the Kings of Israel. He was lowered down through the window, and both Jews and Mohammedans breathlessly waited for the result. After a while, a feeble voice was heard calling from the tomb: " Draw me up."

Soon the beadle, deathly pale, but holding the pasha's

THE RECOVERY OF THE PASHA'S SWORD

sword in his trembling hand, came up. The people present fell upon their faces and exclaimed, " Blessed be the Lord, the God of Israel," and the Jews of Jerusalem manifested great joy. The beadle refused to reveal to anyone what he had seen in the tomb. He told the Rabbi, however, that when he entered the tomb he saw a great light, and then a venerable old man suddenly stood before him and handed him the sword he had come to fetch.[1]

[1] *Maasse Nissim*, § 2; see Bin Gorion, *loc. cit.*, Vol. V, pp. 61–63.

CHAPTER V

King Solomon's Judgments

SOLOMON'S PRAYER

The Lord appeared to Solomon in Gibeon in a dream by night and said unto him: " Ask what I should give unto thee;" and Solomon thought in his heart: " What shall I ask from the Lord? Gold and silver? Power over my enemies? The Lord will surely grant my request, but then I will only be like the other Kings of the earth. I will therefore ask some gift besides which everything else is as nought." And he asked from the Lord to bestow upon him wisdom and understanding which will enable him to distinguish between right and wrong and help him to judge the children of Israel. And when the Lord saw that Solomon did not ask for wisdom so that it might enable him to make war and conquer many lands, but for the purpose of judging the children of Israel with justice and equity, He granted his request.[1] Solomon was greater in wisdom than the wisest men before him and after him. He gave many proofs of his early wisdom, as the following stories told of the famous. King will show.

THE TRUE SON

A certain man who lived in the days of King David had acquired great wealth and had vast possessions and slaves. He had only one son, to whom he gave much gold and merchandise, and sent him to distant lands to traffic and do business. The son boarded a ship and sailed to Africa, where he prospered exceedingly. In the meantime his father had died and left all his gold and his possessions in the hands of one of his servants. The latter now began to ill-treat all the other servants so that they all ran away. The servant now appropriated unto himself all the gold and possessions his master had left, and began to behave as if he were the rightful heir and owner of the vast wealth. After a lapse of time the son returned from distant lands, and when he heard that his father was dead he wished to come into his inheritance. But the servant beat him and drove him out of the house.

" I am the rightful son and heir," he cried, " and thou art only a lying slave who wishes to take the place of his master." In his despair the rightful son went to King David and submitted the matter to him.

" Hast thou any witnesses who could prove that thou art the son of the deceased and his rightful heir?" asked King David.

" I have been away for many years," replied the son, " and all the people who knew me are dead. I have no witnesses who could prove my identity."

[1] *Midrash Tanchuma*, section *Houkat*; see Lewner, *Kol Aggadoth*, Vol. III. p. 307, No. 304.

When King David heard these words, he said: " If thou canst not produce any witnesses then I cannot give judgment in thy favour."

The cries and lamentations of the son deprived of his rightful inheritance availed him not until Solomon, who was then only a child, came to his rescue. The young Prince called the son aside and thus said unto him: " Go thou again before the King and ask him to pronounce judgment in thy favour, but if he be perplexed, beg him to allow me to deal with the matter, for I can bring it to a just end."

The man followed Solomon's advice, and King David consented and allowed his son to act as judge. Solomon now called the servant who had usurped the place of his master and asked him whether he knew the place where his father was buried.

" I do," replied the usurper.

" Then go and cut off one of his fingers and bring it to me," said Solomon.

The usurper did as he was bidden. When the finger of the dead man was brought, Solomon commanded both the rightful son and the pretender to cut their flesh and let their blood run into separate vessels. He then commanded that the dead man's finger be dipped into the blood of the servant. This was done, but the blood had no effect upon the dead bone, and it remained as white as if the blood had been water. The finger was then dipped into the blood of the son, and lo, the bone was at once dyed red, having sucked in all the blood.

" He is the son of the deceased," said Solomon, " and the rightful owner of his wealth." Lifting up the dead man's finger, he said: " See that this bone and this blood are related, for this man is flesh of the flesh and bone of the bone of the deceased. He has proved himself to be the son and rightful owner, and the other is only an usurper." Solomon accordingly gave judgment in favour of the son.[1]

Another version of this story runs as follows:

A certain man had three sons, but entertained some doubts as to their being all legitimates and in reality his sons. He believed, moreover, that only one of the three sons was his. What did he do? When his time to die came near, he made a will, in which he bequeathed all his money to him who was his legitimate son. After their father's death, the three sons naturally began to quarrel among themselves, each maintaining that he and not the others was the legitimate son and entitled to the inheritance. As they could not agree, they at last determined to go to King Solomon and to submit the matter to him.

As no witnesses could be produced in favour of any of the sons able to prove that he and not the others was the legitimate son, King Solomon ordered the corpse of the dead man to be disinterred and brought into his presence. He thereupon commanded his servants to tie the corpse to a tree. Turning to the three sons, he thus addressed them:

" It is impossible to say which of you is the legitimate son and the rightful heir to the wealth your father has left, and I have therefore decided to give the inheritance to him who will have proved the best shot of the three. Take ye, therefore, your bows and arrows and loose an arrow at the corpse of your father."

The first son immediately took up his bow and aiming at his father's corpse pierced his hand, whilst the second shot it through the forehead. When it was the turn of the third son to shoot, he at first took up his bow and prepared to follow the example of his brothers, but suddenly he realized what an impious act he was about to commit. Casting his bow and

[1] Jellinek, *Beth-Hamidrash*, IV, pp. 145–146; Wünsche, *Aus Israel's Lehrhallen*, Vol. II, pp. 13–14; *Hibbur Hamaassiot Vehamidrashot*, ed. Venice; Bin Gorion, *Der Born Judas*, Vol. III, p. 61; *Hebr. Bibliographie*, XVIII, p. 39.

arrow to the ground, he exclaimed: " I prefer to give up my
claim to my father's inheritance rather than treat his body
in such an unfilial manner unworthy of his son."

" Thou art indeed the deceased man's son," cried the King,
" for thou alone hast shown thy filial affection and respect
for thy deceased parent. By his will, thou art therefore the
heir of his wealth." [1]

This tale is told differently in the *Sepher Hassidim*, where
it runs as follows:

It happened in the days of the Gaon Saadya ben Joseph
the wise. There was a man who went on a journey, leaving at
home his wife in a state of pregnancy. He had taken with him
much wealth and was accompanied by his servant. Now it
happened that the master suddenly died, leaving a considerable
amount of property behind. The slave now appropriated all
the wealth and passed himself off as the deceased man's son
and rightful heir. In the meantime the son to whom the widow
of the deceased had given birth grew up, and when he learned
of his father's death he went to the slave and claimed his
property. The usurper, however, had in the meantime established high connections and was related to the mighty in the
land, so that the rightful heir was afraid to press his claim lest
he lose it and come to harm besides. He therefore went to
the Gaon Saadya, to whom he told the entire story.

" My advice," said the Gaon, " is that thou seek redress
from the King."

This the son accordingly did. The King now sent for the
Gaon and asked him to give judgment in the matter. Thereupon the Gaon gave orders for both the son and the slave to be
bled and their blood collected in separate vessels. He then
caused some bones to be brought from the disinterred body of
the deceased merchant. He dipped the bone of the dead man
first into the blood of the slave, but the blood was not absorbed

by the bone; he then dipped the bone into the blood of the
son, and at once the blood was absorbed by the bone, for the
two were one body and flesh. Thereupon the Gaon restored
the property to the rightful heir.[1]

THE JUDGMENT OF SOLOMON, OR THE TRUE HEIR

This incident, in a naturally different version, is told by
Barbazan in his *Fabliaux*, under the title of *Le Jugement de
Solomon*. The story runs as follows:

After the death of their father, two princes quarrelled about
the inheritance. Solomon, who was King of Christendom, was
appealed to and gave judgment. He ordered the father's
corpse to be disinterred and fastened to an upright stake. He
then declared that he of the two brothers who would drive his
spear farthest into the body should be declared the right heir.
The elder brother immediately seized his spear and struck
home, but the young brother refused to commit an impious
act and mangle the corpse of his father.

" I prefer to lose all my share in my father's inheritance,"
he said, " rather than dishonour the body of my father."
He was declared the rightful heir by consent of all the Barons
and put into possession of the principality. Thus by resorting
to the test of natural affection, Solomon managed to solve the
difficulty.[2]

In the *Gesta Romanorum* the story is somewhat similar to
that related in the Midrash. It is told of the sons of a King,
and the judgment is pronounced by a knight of the late King.

There was once a certain King who had a beloved but not
loving wife. He also had four sons, only one of whom was
legitimate. After the King's death, the sons quarrelled about
the succession, and at last decided to refer the matter to an

---

[1] *Sepher Hassidim*, ed. Bologna, § 232. See also Salzberger, *Die Salomon Sage in der
semitischen Literatur.*
[2] Barbazan, *Fabliaux*, Paris, 1808, Vol. II, p. 440; cf. Kemble, *The Dialogue of Solomon
and Saturn*, 1848, p. 106.

honourable knight of the late King. The knight bade them
draw out the body of their father from his sepulchre and set
it upright as a mark for their arrows.

" Whosoever of you," he declared, " will succeed in trans-
fixing the heart of your father shall succeed to the throne and
be King."

The four sons agreed. Three of them took up their bows
and drove their arrows, one wounding the father's hand, the
second sending his arrow into his father's head, whilst the third
nearly pierced the father's heart. The fourth son, however,
refused to drive an arrow into the dead king's body, and would
rather give up his claim to the kingdom than commit an impious act. He was therefore declared to be the true son and
proclaimed King.[1]

Very little attention seems to have been attached to a
legend in the Talmud where the following incident is told:

One day a man overheard his wife conversing with her
daughter and boasting that although she had ten sons only one
of them was by her husband. What did the man do? He left
a will wherein he bequeathed all his property to one son, the
one that was his legitimate child. As no name was mentioned,
the sons naturally quarrelled among themselves, each pretending that he was the legitimate son. At last the sons decided
to put the matter before Rabbi Benaiah and ask him to arbitrate.

" As you do not know to whom your father intended to
bequeath his property, you will be well advised to go and beat
at your father's grave until he rises up and tells you whom he
meant to be his heir."

Although somewhat puzzled, the sons went and did as the
Rabbi had advised them to. One son only refused to beat
at his father's grave and show such marked unfilial behaviour. He preferred to lose the property rather than show
disrespect to his father's grave, and because he alone of the

---

[1] *Gesta Romanorum*, ed. Graesse, No. 45.

ten brothers had shown respect for his father's memory and affection for his dead parent, the Rabbi decided that he was the rightful owner, and that it was to him that his father had bequeathed the property.[1]

The blood-test story related of Solomon is, in our opinion, of a purely Jewish origin.

There are many superstitions among the Jews connected with blood, blood having always been considered as an object of sacred and religious awe, and nothing is more preposterous than the ritual blood-accusation raised against the Jews from time to time.

The Bible already considers the blood to be the seat of the soul, and the Talmud considerably intensifies the commands and prohibition against partaking of blood. In folk-lore blood plays a prominent part, and it is employed not only for the binding of compacts and sealing of kingships, but also for various superstitions as well as judicial purposes.[2]

It has been proved by Hermann Strack that the Jews have never practised the blood-rite, and that the sacred awe they had for blood prevented them from the practice of the blood-rite, but also from covenanting by blood and applying it for the purposes in vogue among other nations. There are, however, many superstitions among the Jews connected with the power of blood, some of which, although they may be traced to the Talmud, did not originate among the Jews. One of these superstitions is the accusing power of blood, which has given rise to many superstitions and folk-tales. We read in the Talmud [3] that the blood of the Prophet Zechariah, whom the Jews had killed, could never be stilled, and continued to flow even when Nebuchadnezzar had killed many innocents and caused their blood to mingle with that of the Prophet.

[1] Hershon, *A Talmudical Miscellany* p. 142, § 29; *Revue des Études Juives*, Vol. XXXIII, pp. 233–234; see also Clouston, *Popular Tales*, Vol. I, p. 14.

[2] Cf. P. Cassel, *Die Symbolik des Blutes und der Arme Heinrich von Hartmann von der Ane*, Berlin, 1882; H. C. Trumbull, *The Blood Covenant*, Philadelphia, 1893.

[3] See Hershon, *loc. cit.*, 110, 275, 276.

It is upon this story that is based the legend of John the Baptist, who is supposed to wander through the world, his blood boiling and bubbling, and of the miracle of St. Januarius.[1]

Another passage in the Talmud relates that when Cain had killed his brother Abel, the earth refused to absorb the blood of the victim until the assassin had been punished.[2]

Now, although the Jews, as a rule, are opposed to any covenanting by blood, and considered the so-called ordeals and trials such as the ordeal of water as a heathen custom, they seem to have believed during the Middle Ages in the trial by blood. Some superstitions and ceremonies ascribed to the Jews are pure inventions, whilst others did not in any case originate among the Jews. Curiously enough, the Jews seem to have shared the belief in the accusing power of blood, namely, that the blood of a murdered man is crying aloud for vengeance, and when the murderer is touching the inanimate body the blood will begin to flow afresh. Thus mediæval Jewish writers, such as the author of the famous *Sepher Hassidim*, by Joseph Hahn (1630), and even Manasseh ben Israel (1604–1657), write that the body of a murdered man will break out bleeding afresh whenever the murderer comes near it, or if it is approached with a knife.[3] This popular belief gave rise to several Jewish folk-tales, one of which clusters round Solomon and which has been related above.

It is this old superstition of discovering blood kinship by means of the blood itself which attributed the story to King Solomon and afterwards to the Gaon Saadya.[4] The story is quoted by Strack from the *Sepher Hassidim*, and is also referred to by Hartland.

"The bond of blood," writes Hartland, "has always proved stronger than any other force that can sway human

---

[1] Grünbaum, *Neue Beiträge*, pp. 237–240.   [2] *Gittin*, 57b.

[3] See *Sepher Hassidim;* Manasseh ben Israel, *Nishmat Chayim*, Amsterdam, 1651, III, 3.

[4] *Sepher Hassidim*, ed. Bologna, 1538, § 232; see H. Strack, *Der Blutaberglaube*, 1891, p. 37; cf. Steinschreider, *Hebraische Bibliographie*, XIII, p. 134; *Germania*, No. XVIII, pp. 363, 365.

nature, until it encounters the overmastering energy of one of the great world religions, or becomes distracted and spent amid the complexities of modern life. Weakened as it is in Europe nowadays, it is yet not entirely dissipated. Its claims are put forth more timidly but they are still within certain limits respected. To the utmost of those limits they are still efficient instruments in the hands of the poet, the playwright and the novelist,—and not only on the moral side, where we are accustomed to appeals founded upon kinship, but also upon what I may call the physical side. The involuntary recognition of the same blood is a convention not yet wholly discarded by the writers who thus aim at affecting our emotions." [1]

The Three Travellers and the Theft of Gold

On another occasion Solomon gave proof of great wisdom by detecting a clever thief, compelling him to confess his guilt.

In the days of Solomon it happened that three youths were travelling together on the eve of Sabbath. Not wishing to carry any money about them on the day of rest, they said to each other: " Let us go and conceal our gold in one place," and this they accordingly did.

In the middle of the night one of the three travellers arose, stole all the gold, and concealed it in another place. On the night following the Sabbath the three travellers went to the place where they had concealed the gold, but, to their great surprise, found that it had gone. They accused each other of the thefts, saying one to the other: " Thou hast stolen it." They finally went to King Solomon and laid the matter before him, each accusing the other two of the theft.

King Solomon then said: " To-morrow will I decide the matter and give judgment." But he was greatly embarrassed and perplexed, thinking within himself: " If I do not elucidate the truth and decide the matter, my people will say that

[1] Hartland, *The Legend of Perseus*, Vol. II, p. 423.

Solomon's wisdom has been overrated, and they will laugh at me."

What did he do? He sat and pondered and thought of means how to make the thief confess the truth. " If I command them to take an oath, two of them will have sworn for no purpose, whilst the thief will have committed perjury. I must therefore try and ensnare them in their own talk and answers."

When the three travellers appeared before him on the following morning, the King thus addressed them: " I have heard of ye that ye are great merchants, wise men, and capable judges of affairs. I would therefore ask your opinion on a matter which has been submitted to me by a king of Rome. It happened thus: There dwelt in a certain place in his kingdom a youth and a maiden. They lived in one house and from their earliest childhood had loved each other. One day the youth said to the maiden: ' If I can manage to be betrothed to thee before a certain day, then it is well, otherwise promise me that thou wilt not marry any other man unless I have given my consent.' The maiden promised him to do so, and they confirmed their agreement with an oath. After a time, the maiden was betrothed to another man, but when the bridegroom wished to marry her and take her to wife, she told him of the agreement she had made with her friend, and the oath she had sworn.

" ' I cannot be thy wife,' she said, ' unless my friend give his consent.'

" When her betrothed heard these words, he said: ' Let us go to this man and ask him to set thee free.'

" They accordingly took much gold and silver, and went to the house of the friend and begged him to set the maiden free.

" ' I have been faithful to my oath,' said the maiden, ' and I have now come to ask thee to set me free and consent to my marrying this man.'

" When the friend of her early childhood heard these words, he said unto the maiden: ' Since thou hast been faithful to thy oath and hast kept our agreement, I will not stand in the way of thy happiness and I set thee free. Go ye both in peace and be happy, but I will take no gold for setting thee free.' So the maiden departed with her betrothed.

" On their way homewards, they were attacked by robbers. One of the brigands, an old man, took all the gold and silver they carried and all the jewels of the maiden, and also wished to take her to wife against her will and without her consent.

" ' I beg thee,' said the maiden, ' to wait a little until I have acquainted thee with my history.' Thereupon she told him all that happened.

" ' If this man, my friend, who is a youth, has acted so nobly, curbed his passion and refused to take my gold, thou, who art an old man, and venerable, shouldst be God-fearing, curb thy passion, and let me go in peace with my betrothed.'

" When the old robber heard these words, he took them to heart and said: ' I am old and will soon die, and will not commit such a wicked deed.' He had pity on the maiden, gave her back all her gold and silver and jewels, and let her go in peace with her betrothed.'

" This," continued King Solomon, " is the matter submitted to me by the King of Rome. He has asked me how to decide and to tell him who of all these people has acted most nobly. Tell me now your opinion and declare which was the most praiseworthy." Thus spoke King Solomon.

Thereupon the first of the travellers said: " I praise the betrothed who had respected the oath of the maiden and would not marry her until she had been set free." The second traveller answered: " No, I praise the maiden who had been faithful to the oath she had sworn."

" And what sayest thou?" asked the King, turning to the third traveller.

" I praise them both," replied the man, " but I think that the first young man, though he acted nobly, is a fool to have refused to take the gold offered to him."

When King Solomon heard his reply, he said:

" If thy thoughts turn to the gold which thou hast *not* seen, and thou art prompted to call the youth a fool because he refused to accept what was offered to him, how much more must thou have coveted the gold which thou *didst* see. Now thou art the thief and hast stolen the gold of thy travelling companions."

Thereupon the King ordered him to be bound and put in prison, and he confessed the truth and indicated the place where he had concealed the gold he had stolen. And the people saw that the wisdom of God was in Solomon, and no one ever dared to put forth his hand and take what did not belong to him.[1]

Another version of this tale runs somewhat differently:

When King Solomon asked the three travellers to tell him whom they considered to be the most praiseworthy, the first man answered that he praised the maiden, whilst the second was of the opinion that the betrothed was the most praiseworthy; the third man, however, answered: " I praise the old robber, he had the maiden in his power, and he also possessed himself of her gold and silver and jewels. It was quite noble of him to let the maiden go in peace and not compel her to become his wife, but there was no need for him to return also her gold. He is therefore the most praiseworthy of the three."[2]

There is a similar tale in *Thousand and One Nights*, told of the Sultan Akshid, and another in the Persian *Tutti Nameh*. The contents of the latter are briefly as follows:

---

[1] *Hibbur Yafeh*, p. 38a–b.

[2] *Hibbur Hamaassiot-ve-Hamidrashot*, ed. Venice; Jellinek, *Beth-Hamidrash*, Vol. I, p. 86; Wünsche, *Midrash Ruth Rabba Anhang*, p, 81; *Hebr. Bibliographie*, XVIII, p. 40; cf. Benfey, *Orient and Occident*, II, p. 316; Grünbaum, *Neue Beiträge*, p. 236.

A husbandman once discovered a precious stone in his field the like of which no man had ever seen before. No one could tell him the value of the stone, and his friends advised him to offer the gem as a present to the Sultan of Rum.

"No one," said the peasant's friends, "will be able to pay thee the money the precious stone is worth; besides, should the king hear of thy find, he will take the gem away from thee by force. On the other hand, the Sultan of Rum will reward thee richly for the present thou wilt bring him."

The peasant acted upon this advice and set out on his journey. On the road he met three travellers with whom he struck up an acquaintance and continued his journey in their company. They stopped the night at a wayside inn and during the night, when the peasant, tired from tramping all day, was fast asleep, the travellers, who had learned of the existence of the precious stone, stole it. When the peasant awoke in the morning he missed the gem, but thought it wiser to say nothing about it, lest the thieves take his life.

On reaching the capital of the realm of Rum, he immediately sent a petition to the Sultan wherein he accused his fellow-travellers of the theft. The Sultan summoned the accused into his presence and commanded them to restore the jewel, but the thieves protested their innocence and swore that they had never seen the stone. As the peasant could not prove his accusation, the Sultan was greatly perplexed, for he was anxious to let justice prevail—without punishing the innocent.

Now the Sultan had a daughter whose name was Mihr-i-Shah-Banoh, and whose beauty was only equalled by her wisdom and intelligence. When she learned the cause of her father's evident perplexity she craved permission to deal with the matter. The Sultan readily granted her request. Thereupon the princess betook herself to the house where the thieves were lodging and thus she spoke to them:

"My august father was on the point of committing an

injustice, for, without further proof, he was about to punish you for a theft you have never committed. I have made inquiries and learned that the ' garment of your honesty has never been soiled by such a crime, nor has the breath of theft dimmed the brightness of your innocence '. But as ye are travelled men and no doubt have gathered much wisdom on your journeys, it will give me pleasure to see ye often in my home and learn wisdom from such men as ye." Highly flattered, the thieves consented to visit the princess and to tell her their experiences. One day she asked them to solve a riddle for her, and told them the following story:

" There was once a beautiful maid, the daughter of a very wealthy merchant at Damascus. One day Dilefruz, such was the name of the damsel, saw a wonderful rose in her father's garden and asked her maidservants to fetch it for her. The maidservants were unable to pluck the rose, and in her impatience Dilefruz promised to grant any wish to whomsoever would bring her the beautiful rose. The gardener heard her words and swiftly ran and brought the rose to his mistress.

" ' What is thy request?' asked the happy Dilefruz.

" ' My desire ', replied the gardener, ' is that on the eve of thy marriage thou comest to see me here.' The maiden consented to keep her promise.

" Soon afterwards her father found a husband for her and on the eve of her marriage she told him of the promise she had given to the gardener. ' Thou must keep thy word,' said her affianced husband; ' go and visit the gardener, but beware of sin.'

" Arrayed in costly garments and decked out with jewels, Dilefruz hurried to the abode of the gardener. On her way she was attacked by a wolf, but when she told him her story he let her go. A robber, springing from the thicket, then fell upon her, but he, too, had compassion on her and allowed her to continue on her way without taking any of her jewels.

When she reached the abode of the gardener, the young man was overjoyed to see his mistress. Praising her loyalty and faithfulness to her given word, he assured her that his intentions were pure. Thereupon he led her back to her husband.

" ' Such ', continued Princess Mihr-i-Shah, ' is the story of the beautiful maid of Damascus. And now, ye who are men of great experience, tell me, who in your opinion acted most nobly: the husband, the wolf, the robber, or the gardener?"

The travellers, without any hesitation, replied that all the four were big fools to let go a prize they actually had in their possession. When the princess heard these words she knew that they were guilty of the theft of the precious gem, even as the peasant had accused them. Thereupon the Sultan put the three travellers in prison and they were compelled to confess their guilt and to produce the stolen gem.[1]

A similar tale is told by Campbell of a farmer and his three sons.

THE INHERITANCE

There was once a farmer who was well off. He had three sons. When his time to die came, he called his three sons and informed them that in a certain drawer he had left a sum of gold. " This," he said, "ye will divide fairly and honestly amongst ye."

After his death, the sons went to seek for the gold, but found the drawer empty, for one of the sons had stolen the money.

" There has perhaps never been any money in this drawer," said the brother who had stolen it."

" No," replied the others, " our father never told a lie, and wherever the money is now, it surely was in this drawer."

Thereupon they went to an old man who had been a great friend of their father, and asked for his advice.

---

[1] *Tutti Nameh*, German translation by G. Rosen, Leipzig, 1858, Vol. II, pp. 243–258.

" Abide with me," said the old man, " and I will think this matter over." And so the three brothers stayed with him for ten days. When ten days had passed, he sent for the three young lads and made them sit down beside him and told them the following story:

" There was once a young lad, and he was poor; he took love for the daughter of a rich neighbour, and she took love for him. But because he was so poor, there could be no wedding. So at last they pledged themselves to each other, and the young man went away and stayed in his own house. After a time there came another suitor, and because he was well off, the girl's father made her promise to marry him, and after a time they were married. But when the bridegroom came to her, he found her weeping and wailing; and he said: ' What ails thee?' When she told him that she was pledged to another man, he told her to dress herself and to follow him. He took her upon his horse and brought her to the other man, where he left her.

" When the other man got up and fetched a light and saw the bride, he asked her who had brought her. She told him that her husband had done this because she had told him of their pledge. When the man heard these words, he took the horse, rode to the priest, and brought him to the house, and before the priest he loosed the woman from the pledge she had given, and gave her a line of writing that she was free.

" So the bride rode away, but in a thick forest, which she had to cross on her journey homewards, she was stopped and seized by three robbers.

" 'Let me go,' she said, ' let me go; the man I was pledged to has let me go. Here are ten pounds in gold, take them and let me go,' and she told them her story. One of the robbers, who was of a better nature, had compassion on her and took her home, refusing to take even a penny from her.

" ' Take thou the money,' she said, but the robber replied:

' I will not take a penny.' The other two robbers, however, said: ' Give us the money,' and they took the ten pounds. The disinterested robber brought her home, where she showed to her husband the line of writing the other had given her." This is the story which the old man told the three sons.

" Now," said he, " which of all these do you think did best?"

So the eldest said: " I think the man that sent the woman to him to whom she was pledged was the honest, generous man; he did well."

The second said: " Yes, but the man to whom she was pledged, did still better when he sent her to her husband."

The youngest said: " I do not know myself, but perhaps the wisest of all were the robbers who got the money."

Then the old man rose up and said: " Thou hast thy father's gold and silver. I know your father never told a lie, and thou hast stolen the money." [1]

THE TWO-HEADED MAN, OR SEVEN THAT ARE EIGHT

One day Ashmedai, King of the demons, came to King Solomon, and thus he spoke: " Art thou of whom it is said that he is the wisest of all men?"

" So it is," replied the King. Ashmedai then said: " If thou wilt allow me, I can show thee something the like of which thou hast never seen."

" Be it so," said the King.

Thereupon Ashmedai stretched out his hand, and from the entrails of the earth he brought forth a man with two heads and four eyes. Fear and terror seized the King at this sight, and he said: " Bring him into my own apartment." He then sent for Benaiah, the son of Jehoiada, who immediately appeared in the royal presence.

[1] J. F. Campbell, *Popular Tales of the West Highlands*, 1890, Vol. II, pp. 24–27. No. 29.

" Dost thou believe," asked the King, " that there are men living under us in the entrails of the earth?"

" By the life of my soul, my Lord King," replied Benaiah, " if I know it. But I have heard it said by Achitophel, thy father's counsellor and teacher, that there are indeed men living under us."

" What wilt thou say now," replied Solomon, " if I show thee one of these men?"

" How canst thou do such a thing?" asked Benaiah, " and bring up one of these men from the depth of the earth which is at a distance of five hundred years' journey, and the distance between our earth and the next is again a five hundred years' journey?"

Thereupon Solomon commanded that the two-headed man be brought into his presence. When Benaiah saw this inhabitant of another planet, he fell upon his face and said: " Blessed be Thou Eternal, our God, King of the Universe, who hast preserved me alive to this day."

Thereupon he asked the man: " Whose son art thou?"

" I am the son of men," replied the two-headed one, " and of the descendants of Cain."

" Where dost thou dwell?" Benaiah continued.

" In an inhabited world," replied the man.

" Are there sun and moon in your world?"

" Yes. We also plough, and reap, and possess sheep and other cattle."

" And on which side does the sun rise in your world?" queried Benaiah.

" It rises in the West and sets in the East."

" Do ye pray?" asked Benaiah.

" So we do," the two-headed one made answer.

" And what prayer do ye utter?"

" How manifold are Thy works, O Lord; in wisdom hast Thou made them all " (*Psalms*, civ, 24).

" If thou wilt," said Benaiah, " we will send thee back to thine own land."

" May it please ye to send me back to my own land." replied the man.

King Solomon thereupon summoned Ashmedai and commanded him to bring the man back to his own country. To this Ashmedai answered: " That I cannot do, O King; I cannot bring this man home."

When the man saw his position, he married a wife and settled. He had seven sons by his wife, six of whom resembled the mother, whilst the seventh was like his father, for he had two heads. The stranger now bought land, ploughed and reaped, and soon became a wealthy man, one of the rich in the land. Many years passed and the man died, leaving his possessions to his sons. Now the six sons who were like their mother said among themselves: " We are seven brethren and will divide our father's property into seven equal parts." The son, however, who had two heads said: " We are eight, for I am entitled to two portions of our father's inheritance."

So all the sons went to King Solomon, and thus they said to him: " Our Lord the King, we are seven, but our brother here, he with two heads, pretends that we are eight. He desires us to divide our father's inheritance into eight parts, and he himself claims two portions." When Solomon heard this matter it was somewhat hidden from him. He therefore summoned the Sanhedrin, and said to the members of this Court: " What say ye to this matter?"

Now the members of the Sanhedrin thought within themselves: " If we say that the man with two heads is one and is entitled only to one portion, the King will perhaps say that he is two and should consequently receive two portions." So they kept silent.

Thereupon Solomon said: " To-morrow will I give judgment."

At midnight he went into the Temple and stood in prayer before the Lord.

"Lord of the Universe," he prayed, "when Thou didst manifest Thyself unto me at Gibeon, Thou didst say unto me, 'Ask whatever thy heart doth desire,' and I asked neither silver nor gold but wisdom, so as to be able to judge Thy people."

And the Lord hearkened unto Solomon's prayer and assured him that on the morrow He would send him wisdom.

The next morning the King summoned the Court of the Sanhedrin, and when all the members were assembled he said to them: "Let now the man with the two heads come before me." The two-headed man was accordingly brought in. The King then said: "If the one head knows what I am doing to the other, then the man is one person, but otherwise he is two persons."

Thereupon he commanded to bring him hot water, old wine, and linen cloths. When the hot water, old wine, and linen cloths were brought, Solomon ordered the two-headed man to be laid upon his face and blindfolded, and then he poured out the hot water and old wine on *one* head. The man called out: "My Lord King! We die, we die, we are only *one* person and not two."

"Did ye not say," replied the King, "that ye were two?"

When the Israelites saw the wisdom of the King and his judgment, they were filled with wonder, but they also trembled before him and feared him. Therefore it is written: And he was wiser than all men.[1]

---

[1] Jellinek, *loc. cit.*, IV, pp. 151, 152; *Hibbur Maassiot.* Wünsche, *Aus Israel's Lehrhallen*, Vol. II, pp. 24–26; cf. *Hebraische Bibliographie*, XVIII, 61; *Revue des Études Juives*, XLV, pp. 305–308; see Bin Gorion, *loc. cit.*, Vol. III, p. 73; Bialik, *loc. cit.*, Vol. I, p. 103.

CHAPTER VI

Solomon's Wisdom, or Solomon
and the Animals and Birds

One man in a thousand—Solomon and the Sanhedrin—The upright man and his beautiful wife—The offer of the king—The sleeping wife and her babes—The kind-hearted husband—The beautiful woman—The temptation—The tin sword—The treachery of woman—The indignant husband—In the presence of the King—The dead men and their shrouds —Solomon and the King of Egypt—The artists who were destined to die within the year—Solomon's wisdom—His letter to the King of Egypt— The quarrel of the organs of the body—The King of Persia and his physician —The milk of a lioness—Benaiah's ruse—The physician's dream—The superiority of the tongue—The three brothers—Solomon's three counsels —The success of the youngest brother—The false accusation—His condemnation and escape—The man and the snake—The jug of milk and the snake's promise—The cock's advice—The language of birds and animals —The ox and the ass—The laughing husband—The curious wife—The grief of the dog—The cock's advice—The game of chess—The cheating of Benaiah—The two thieves—The ruse of Solomon.

ONE MAN IN A THOUSAND HAVE I FOUND

Solomon had a thousand wives, and Oriental potentate that he was, his opinion of them was not very high. He uttered many wise sayings containing severe criticisms of women, whom he was wont to accuse of falsehood, inconstancy, and treachery. In this connection the following story is told, where the King is said to have convinced his court of the truth of his psychological analysis.

One day the members of the Sanhedrin asked King Solomon to explain unto them the meaning of his words: " One man among a thousand have I found; but a woman among all those I have not found " (*Ecclesiastes*, vii, 28).

" Are there not," argued the members of the Sanhedrin, ' many women in the world who are faithful and worthy?"

" I will prove to you," replied the King, " that my words are true."

Thereupon he commanded his servants to seek out in the land a man who was upright and righteous, and who had a beautiful wife who was apparently as upright and righteous as her husband. The servants of King Solomon sought all over the land and informed their master that they had indeed found such a man who was upright and righteous and who also had a very beautiful wife.

" Bring the man before me," commanded the King.

When the man appeared in the royal presence, Solomon thus addressed him: " I have heard of thy righteousness and uprightness and thy understanding, and I desire to honour thee and to make thee great. I will give thee my daughter to wife and raise thee above all the princes of my realm."

The man said: " Who am I that I should marry the daughter of my master the King?" But the King replied: " Thy modesty only shows thy worth and thy wisdom. If thou wilt therefore slay thy wife to-night and bring me her head, to-morrow I will do as I have said. I will give thee my daughter to wife and make thee great."

When the man heard these words, he replied: " I will do as the King doth command me." Thereupon he went home, but he was sore grieved and thought in his heart: " How can I slay my wife who is so beautiful, upright, and righteous, and is the mother of my little children."

When his wife saw how sad he was, she asked him: " Why art thou so downcast and so troubled?"

" My heart is afflicted with sorrow," he replied.

She placed before him food and drink, but he could neither eat nor drink, and she ate and drank herself, and went to bed with her little children and soon fell asleep.

The man sat deep in thought, greatly troubled, and thought within himself: " How can I commit such a crime and sin before God?" and he made up his mind to despise the honour and the gifts the King had promised him. But once more he remembered the King's words and thought within himself: " If I slay her I shall become the King's son-in-law, rich and honoured." He took his sword and approached his wife, but when he saw her sleeping with her children, one child on her breast and the other in her arms, he let his sword fall from his hands and said: " How can I slay my wife and children and lose my portion in the next world? The Lord rebuke thee, Satan," he added. He returned his sword to its sheath and went and sat down. But evil thoughts once more crowded his brain, and the tempter stirred ambition in his heart. Thereupon he once more drew his sword and approached the bed upon which lay his wife and her children. He found that her hair had fallen over the child that lay at her breast, covering it, and it touched his heart, and he was overcome with pity.

" No," he cried, " I cannot do such a deed. I despise all the honours the King has promised me, and even the hand of his daughter, for they are like nought." Thereupon he sheathed his sword once more and lay down upon his bed.

On the following morning there came the messengers of the King and said: " Come with us before the King, for he waiteth for thee."

When the man was brought into the King's presence, Solomon said unto him:

" Where is the head of thy wife which thou didst promise to bring me? What hast thou done?"

" May it please unto the King," said the man, " to have pity on me and not to ask me to do such a deed."

Thereupon he related unto the King all that happened.

" Twice," he said, " during the night, I made an attempt

to obey the King's command. Twice did I draw my sword and approach the bed upon which lay my wife and children, but overcome with pity I could not find it in my heart to slay her. I pray the King not to be wroth with me."

Thus spoke the man, and King Solomon smiled. Turning to the members of the Sanhedrin, he said: " One man among a thousand have I found." To the man he said: " Go thou home; I did desire to honour thee, but thou didst not know how to avail thyself of the opportunity."

The man, however, went home happy and content.

When thirty days had elapsed, Solomon sent again his servants and summoned the wife into his presence. When the woman was brought before him, he said unto her: " I have heard of thy beauty and of thy wisdom, and I have a great desire to take thee to wife. I will set thee above all my wives and exalt thee above all my Kingdom, I will deck thee with gold and array thee in royal garments and place a golden crown upon thy head."

When the woman heard these words, she bowed low and said: "My Lord the King, I am thine, and thou canst do with me as thou pleasest."

" I cannot, however, marry thee," continued the King, " as long as thou hast a husband and he stands between us. Go thou, therefore, home and slay thy husband, and thou wilt be free. I will then take thee to wife and exalt thee above all in the Kingdom."

" I will do as the King doth command," replied the woman, " and to-morrow I will bring to my Lord the King the head of my husband."

Thus spoke the woman, ready to do the bidding of the King. And the King thought in his heart: " If I do not prevent this woman, she will certainly have no pity upon her husband and shed innocent blood. I will therefore give her a sword which can do no harm." And he had a sword of tin brought to him and gave it to the woman, saying unto her: "Take this sharp sword and slay thy husband with it. Strike once with it and thou wilt cut his neck."

The woman took the sword, not knowing that it was made of tin, hid it in her garments, and returned to her house.

When the husband came home in the evening, she hastened to meet him, kissed and hugged him, and placed food and drink before him. She gave him wine to drink, and he drank until he was intoxicated and fell down into a deep sleep. Thereupon the woman drew the sword which the King had given her and struck at her husband's neck with it. The sword, however, only bent, and the husband awoke from his sleep. When he saw his wife standing before him with a bent sword in her hand, as if ready to slay him, he waxed very wroth and said: "Who gave thee this sword, and why didst thou intend to slay me? Tell me the truth and hide nothing from me, for otherwise I will cut thee into little pieces."

Greatly embarrassed and ashamed, the woman confessed the truth and related all that had occurred, and how the King had given her the sword to slay her husband with it.

In the morning the messengers of the King came and brought the man and his wife before Solomon and the Sanhedrin. When the King saw them he broke out into loud laughter and said: "Tell me what hath befallen ye during the night?" And the man related what had occurred.

"My Lord King," he said, "when I awoke in the night, I saw my wife standing before me with this tin sword in her hand. Had not the sword been made of tin, she would surely have killed me and had no pity on me even as I had pity on her."

"I knew," said the King, "that thy wife would have had no pity on thee, therefore I gave her this sword of tin so as to prevent her from shedding innocent blood."

And when the members of the Sanhedrin heard this, they admitted that Solomon's words were true when he said: " One man among a thousand have I found; but a woman among all those have I not found." [1]

THE DEAD MEN AND THEIR SHROUDS

Many a time did Solomon have occasion to impress foreign rulers with his wisdom, which was greater even than that of the Egyptians renowned for their manifold knowledge. When the Lord had commanded Solomon to build the temple, the King wrote to Pharaoh, King of Egypt, and asked him for help. " Send me, I beg of you," he wrote to the King of Egypt, " master-artisans and artists who can do all the work I require, and stipulate their fees, which I will gladly pay."

Pharaoh thereupon sent for his astrologers and commanded them to determine which among his artists were destined to die within the year. The astrologers did as they had been commanded by their royal master. Thereupon Pharaoh took all the men destined to die within a year and sent them to Jerusalem.

" Here are the men," he wrote, " that thou dost require."

But when King Solomon looked at the artists from Egypt, he at once knew that their days were numbered, and that Egypt's King had played a trick upon him. He therefore commanded his servants to provide every one of the Egyptians with a shroud and a coffin, and to send them back to their native country. To Pharaoh he sent word:

" Is it because thou hast no graves or shrouds in Egypt that thou didst send the men to me? I return them to thee with their coffins and shrouds, and in future there is really no need for thee to send the men themselves to the land of the Hebrews to be measured for shrouds and coffins. You have

[1] *Hibbur Yafeh*, pp. 14a–15a; Jellinek, *Beth-Hamidrash*, IV, pp. 146–148; Wünsche, *Aus Israel's Lehrhallen*, Vol. II, pp. 16–19.

only to send their measurements, and all they require will be forwarded."

And when the King of Egypt read these words he was greatly astonished and exclaimed: " Verily, the wisdom of the Lord is dwelling in Solomon, King of Israel." [1]

The Quarrel of the Organs of the Body

On another occasion it was the King of Persia who turned to Solomon for advice.

There was once a King of Persia who fell very ill, suffering from consumption. The physicians who were treating him told him that there was only one way to save the King. His disease could be cured only by the milk of a lioness, and the King would surely become well again if he were to drink such milk. Thereupon the King of Persia sent his physician to King Solomon, who was reputed for his great wisdom, and begged him to help him obtain lion's milk.

Solomon sent for his faithful chancellor Benaiah and gave him instructions to obtain lion's milk. Benaiah knew a lion's den in the neighbourhood of Jerusalem, and thither he repaired with his servants, taking with them ten young kids. Every day he threw a young kid to the lioness, and each time he came a little nearer to the den, until on the tenth day he became quite familiar with the beast and could play with her. Thereupon he came quite close to her, touched her udders, and then drew some milk. He returned to Solomon and handed the lioness's milk to the foreign physician, who went away well content to have succeeded in his errand. On his way back to his native land of Persia, the physician fell asleep and dreamed that the organs of his body were quarrelling among themselves. The feet said that had they not carried him to King Solomon he would never have been able to obtain the

[1] *Numer. Rabba*, 19.

lioness's milk. The hands argued that had not Benaiah's hands
touched the udders of the beast there would not have been
any milk. The mouth and the eyes, in their turn, pretended
that the greatest credit in procuring the remedy for the King
of Persia belonged to them.

Thereupon the tongue said: " You are all wrong; the
greatest share of credit belongs to me, for had there been no
language you would all have been useless." The other organs,
however, upbraided the tongue and said: " How durst thou
compare thyself to us, and much more pretend that thy own
contribution to the service which has just been rendered is
superior to ours? Thou art only flesh without bone, and thou
dost dwell in darkness." The tongue thereupon replied:
" To-day even ye shall know that I am your master."

The physician awoke from his sleep and remembered his
dream. When he appeared in presence of his royal master, he
thus spoke to him: " Here is the dog's milk which I have
obtained for your Majesty; drink it." Greatly enraged, the
King gave orders for his physician to be hanged. When he
was being led to the place of execution, all the members and
organs of the condemned man's body began to tremble violently.
Thereupon the tongue thus addressed all the other limbs:

" I told ye that without me you were all useless; now will
ye admit my superiority and acknowledge me as your master
if I promise to save ye even now from death?"

The organs of the body readily promised, and the physician's
tongue spoke to the executioner, requesting him to lead him
once more before the King. Brought into the presence of his
royal master, the physician asked him why he had ordered
him to be hanged.

" Because," said the King, " thou didst not obey my instruction, and didst bring me dog's milk instead of that of a
lioness."

" And what does it matter if it is a remedy and will cure

thee of thy disease? Besides, we often call a lioness a bitch. I beg now your Majesty to drink of the milk I have brought."

The King granted the physician's request, drank of the milk, and soon recovered. He thereupon set the physician free and dismissed him in peace.

The members and organs of the body then said to the tongue: " Now we see that thou art really master over all the organs of the human body, and we readily acknowledge thee as such."

Therefore Solomon said: " Death and life are in the power of the tongue " (*Proverbs*, xviii, 21).[1]

THE THREE BROTHERS

The fame of Solomon's wisdom spread far and wide, and from all parts of the world men came to his court to learn wisdom from the King of Israel.

One day three brothers came to King Solomon to learn from him wisdom and instruction in the Law.

" Abide with me," said the King, " and serve me, and I will teach ye as ye desire." He appointed them as officers in his court, and they spent thirteen years with him. At the end of that time one of the brothers said to the others: " What have we done? It is thirteen years now since we left our houses and all that belongs to us and came hither to learn wisdom and to study the Law. We have served the King faithfully, but he has taught us nothing. Come, let us take leave of him and return to our homes."

Thereupon they appeared before the King, and thus they spoke:

" Thirteen years have now passed, O King, since we quitted our houses and came to thee to study the Law and

[1] *Midrash Tehillim*, 39; *Sepher Hamaassiot*, pp. 38b–39a; cf. *Monatsschrift*, Vol. XXXIX, pp. 107–110.

learn wisdom. Grant us now thy permission to return to our homes and to our families."

On hearing this, King Solomon commanded his treasurer to bring three hundred pieces of gold, and thus he spoke to the brothers: " Choose whatever ye prefer. Either will I give unto each of ye three wise counsels or a hundred pieces of gold." They consulted with one another, chose the gold, and departed.

When they had gone a little way on their journey, a distance of four *mils* from the town, the youngest of the brothers suddenly said: " What have we done? Was it for the sake of gold that we came hither or for the purpose of learning wisdom from the King? If ye are willing to listen to my advice and be guided by me, I propose that we return the gold to the King and rather learn wisdom from Solomon and good counsel instead."

Thus spoke the youngest, but his brothers replied: " If thou art anxious to restore the gold to the King and learn wisdom instead, do as thou pleasest. We, however, are not going to retrace our steps and acquire wise counsel for gold."

Thereupon the youngest of the three brothers returned to King Solomon, and thus he spoke: " My Lord! I did not come to thy court for the sake of gold, and I beg thee to take it back and teach me wisdom and wise counsel instead."

" My son," said the King, " I will take back the pieces of gold and give thee three wise counsels instead.

" Whenever thou hast occasion to go on a journey, start with dawn and be careful to go to rest ere sunset. That is the first counsel. Whenever thou comest to a river in flood, beware of crossing it, but wait until the waters have subsided and the river has returned to its bed. That is the second counsel. Never entrust a secret to a woman, be she even thine own wife. That is the third counsel."

Thus spoke the King. The disciple took his leave, mounted

his horse, and departed, hastening after his brothers. When he had caught up with them, they asked him: " And what hast thou learned from the King?" " The wisdom I have acquired," replied the youngest brother, " I have acquired for myself."

After riding for nine hours, the travellers came to a beautiful spot which seemed to be suitable for rest.

" Methinks," said the youngest brother, he who had learned wisdom from King Solomon, " that this spot is excellent and well suited for camping. We can pass the night here, for here we have trees and water and grass for our horses. If ye are willing, let us remain here overnight and repose, and to-morrow morning at dawn, if God spares our lives, we will set out again on our journey."

" Thou art a fool!" replied the others. " It seems to us that since thou hast restored the gold to King Solomon, so as to acquire wisdom instead, thou hast no wisdom whatever but folly. We can travel at least another eight miles ere night falls, and thou dost counsel us to camp here for the night."

" Do as ye please," replied the youngest brother. " As for me, I am not going to stir from this spot but abide here alone."

Thereupon the two elder brothers continued their journey, the youngest remaining behind. He cut down wood and made a fire, and also built a booth to shelter himself and his beast. He let his horse graze until night fell, then gave it barley and also took his own meal, whereupon he made ready to go to rest.

The other two brothers had in the meantime continued their journey until night had fallen. In vain, however, did they look for wood and water for themselves and pasture for their beasts. Then a snowstorm arose and snow began to fall heavily. Many wanderers succumbed to the bitter cold, but the young man who had remained behind suffered neither from the snow nor from the cold, because he was sheltered in the booth he had built unto himself. He also had fire, food, and drink.

With the break of day the young man arose, made ready for the journey, mounted his horse, and hastened after his brothers. He did not search long for them, but found them on the road frozen to death. When he saw his brothers lying dead, he threw himself upon them weeping aloud. Thereupon he took the gold which his brothers had with them, buried their bodies, and continued on his journey. The sun had in the meantime risen high, shining warmly; it caused the snow to melt and the rivers to swell. When the young man came to a river, the latter was in flood, and the traveller refrained from crossing it. He dismounted and prepared to wait until the waters had subsided.

Whilst he was walking up and down on the bank, he saw two servants of King Solomon approach, leading two animals laden with gold. They asked him: " Why art thou not crossing the river?" He replied: " Because I am waiting until the waters subside." The servants of King Solomon were not afraid of the high water. They made an attempt to cross the river, were carried away by the flood, and perished. The young man, however, who had patiently waited until the waters had subsided, crossed the river in safety. He took with him the gold which the servants of the King were carrying and returned to his home.

Now the wives of his brothers came to see him on his return, and inquired after their husbands. " They have remained behind to learn wisdom," replied the young man. He then began to purchase fields and vineyards, to build houses, and to acquire many possessions.

One day his wife said unto him: " My Lord, tell me, whence hast thou this gold?" On hearing this question, he waxed very wroth and began to beat her. He said: " Never ask again this question, and try not to discover the secret."

His wife, nevertheless, did not abate in her curiosity, and wearied him so often with her question that at last he told her all. One day, when he was hotly disputing with his wife, she cried out aloud and said: " Thou hast not only slain thy two brothers, but now thou wouldst slay me too." When his sisters-in-law heard these words and learned of the death of their husbands, they hastened to King Solomon and accused the young man of having murdered his brothers. The King thereupon commanded that the accused be brought into his presence, and he sentenced him to death.

When the condemned man was being led to the place of execution, he said to the soldiers accompanying him: " I beg you to grant my last request; lead me once more into the presence of the King that I may once more speak and relate unto him the true story."

When he found himself in the presence of the King, the condemned man fell upon his face, and thus he spoke: " My Lord the King, I am one of the three brothers who once came to thee to learn wisdom and who served thee thirteen years. I am the youngest of the three who alone, as thou wilt remember, O King, came to restore the gold pieces unto thee so as to acquire wise counsel instead. It seems, however, that the wisdom I have acquired has proved my misfortune."

The King immediately recognized the truth, and thus he said: " Fear not, the gold thou hast taken from thy brothers and from my servants is thine, and the wisdom which thou hast acquired has saved thee from death and from these women. Now go in peace."

And in this hour King Solomon said: " How much better is it to get wisdom than gold " (*Proverbs*, xvi, 16).[1]

---

[1] Jellinek, *loc. cit.*, Vol. IV, pp. 148–150; Lewner, *l.c.* 349–354; Wünsche, *loc. cit.*, pp. 19–21; *Hebr. Bibliographie*, XVIII, pp. 39–40; cf. *Revue des Études Juives*, Vol. XI, pp. 224–228.

The Man and the Snake

One day a man carrying a jug of milk in his hand was crossing a field. Suddenly he perceived a snake wailing and lamenting for thirst.

"Why art thou wailing so pitifully?" the man asked the snake, to which the latter replied:

"I am wailing because I am tortured with thirst. And what art thou carrying in that jug?" the snake further asked.

"It is milk that I have in the jug," replied the man.

Thereupon the snake begged the man to let it drink of the milk. "If thou wilt let me drink of the milk, I will show unto thee a place where a great treasure lies hidden." The man was moved to pity, and gave the milk to the snake to slake its thirst. Thereupon the snake led the man to a place where a great rock was lying.

"Here, underneath this rock," said the snake, "a big treasure is hidden." The man rolled aside the rock, found the treasure, and prepared to carry it home, when suddenly the snake sprang up and coiled itself round its benefactor's neck.

"And what is the meaning of this?" asked the man, greatly frightened.

"It means," replied the snake, "that I am going to kill thee because thou art taking away all my wealth."

"Well," said the man, "I suggest that we put our case before King Solomon, and let him judge who of us is right and who is wrong."

The snake consented, and the two betook themselves before King Solomon. When they had explained the case, the King asked of the snake: "What is it that thou dost demand of the man?"

"I want to kill him," was the snake's answer, "because

Scripture commands me to do it, for it says: ' And thou shalt bruise the heel of man '." [1]

" Thou art quite right," said the King, " but first of all release thy hold of the man. You are both now standing before the judge, and before judgment has been given none of the litigants should hold fast the other party and thus enjoy an advantage."

The snake obeyed, released its hold upon the man, and uncoiling itself from the latter's neck glided down.

Thereupon King Solomon said unto the snake: " Now explain thy case and what it is thou dost want of the man." The snake repeated its words: " I want to kill this man because Scripture commands me to do it."

Thereupon Solomon turned to the man and said: " And thee, too, the Lord commanded ' to bruise the head of the snake '; [2] why dost thou not do it?" The man immediately raised his foot and crushed the snake's head. [3]

The King's Disciple and Friend, or the Cock's Advice

King Solomon had a friend and disciple who lived in a distant land and annually came to visit the King and to learn wisdom from him. Before his friend departed home, the King was in the habit of bestowing some gifts upon him and giving him also presents to carry home for his family. One day the friend brought Solomon some precious gift, and when he was about to depart the King wanted to give him some costly present. The man, however, refused the gift, and thus he spoke:

" My Lord and Master, I have no desire for wealth and riches. Thanks to the Almighty and to thy generosity, I have all that a man might desire, and I want nothing. If I have,

---

[1] *Genesis*, iii, 15.   [2] *Ibid.*
[3] *Midrash Tehillim*; see Bialik, *loc. cit.*, Vol. I, pp. 104–105; Cf. Grünbaum, *Neue Beiträge zur semitischen Sagenkunde*, p. 236.

however, found favour in thine eyes, bestow another gift
upon me and teach me the language of birds and animals."

Thereupon King Solomon said unto his friend: " I will
not refuse thy request and teach thee the language of the birds
and animals, but I must warn thee that such a knowledge is not
without great danger and that it must remain a dead secret.
Shouldst thou one day reveal to others what thou hearest
from some animal, then thou wilt surely die; no expiation will
save thee from death." Thus spoke King Solomon, but his
friend, nevertheless, insisted upon his request.

" If I can only acquire a part of thy wisdom, I will do as
thou dost advise me." And when the King saw how anxious
his friend was to learn the language of birds and animals, he
granted his request and instructed him in the art. The man
then went home full of joy.

Now it happened one day that this man and his wife were
sitting in front of their house when the ox was brought home
from the field. The animal was attached to a crib full of fodder
and placed side by side with the ass that had remained at
home all that day, as it had given itself out to be sick. And
the friend of King Solomon, who now understood the language
of animals, overheard the ass address the ox as follows:

" Friend, how dost thou fare in this house?"

" Alas, friend," the ox replied, " by day and night I know
nothing but hard toil and labour." Then the ass said:

" I am well disposed towards thee, wishing thee relief and
rest, and I can give thee good advice how to get rid of thy
misery and hard work."

" Brother," said the ox, " thou hast pity on me; may thy
heart always be with me. I will obey thy words and follow
thy advice implicitly."

Thereupon the ass said: " Heaven alone knows that I am
speaking in the sincerity of my heart and the purity of my
thoughts; my advice is that thou shalt devour neither straw

nor fodder this night. When our master notices that thou hast not eaten anything, he will conclude that thou art sick and relieve thee from burdensome work and painful toil. Thou wilt then enjoy a good rest like me."

Thus spoke the ass, and his words pleased the ox very much. He followed the advice of his companion and touched neither straw nor fodder. Before dawn the master, who had overheard the conversation, went down to the stable, and he saw how the ass was devouring the fodder belonging to the ox, whilst the latter was asleep. Remembering the conversation he had overheard and understanding now the ruse of the ass, he laughed aloud. His wife heard him and wondered greatly what it was that had made her husband suddenly burst out into loud laughter. When he re-entered the house, she insisted upon knowing the reason of his merry outburst.

" Oh, it was nothing," replied the husband evasively; " I just remembered a ludicrous incident which once happened to me, and I could not help laughing out aloud." On the following morning the master of the house instructed the stable-boy to relieve the ox from work on that day. " The ox," he said, " shall do no work to-day; harness the ass instead, and let him do to-day the work for himself and the ox." In the evening the ass returned to the stable tired and exhausted.

" Brother," asked the ox, " hast thou heard the heartless children of man speak concerning me?" To which the ass promptly replied: " I heard our master saying that should the ox continue to abstain from fodder then he would have him slaughtered and use his flesh as food."

When the ox heard these words he was greatly frightened, and like a lion upon his prey he threw himself upon his manger full of fodder. He never lifted his head until he had devoured his fodder to the last mouthful. The master, who had again overheard the conversation between the two animals, burst out into loud uproarious laughter, and his wife, who heard him, insisted upon knowing the cause of his merriment.

" Yesterday," she said, " you laughed aloud, and I thought it was by accident. Now you have again been moved to an uproarious laughter for no evident reason, no stranger being present to have given you cause for merriment. You are no doubt laughing at me, perceiving something ridiculous and ludicrous in my person. I swear that I will not allow you to come near me until you will have revealed unto me the reason of your merriment."

Thereupon the husband, who loved his wife dearly, begged and implored her not to insist upon knowing the cause of his laughter.

" Be quiet, my dear," he said, " do not urge me, for I am not allowed to reveal the secret unto thee." The woman, however, remained obstinate.

" I have taken an oath," she replied, " not to live with thee, and thou shalt not behold my face again until thou hast told me the truth."

" I know that if I reveal the secret unto thee," said her husband, " I will suffer death."

" And I know," retorted the woman, " that I will not partake of either food or drink, but sooner die unless thou dost tell me the truth."

Thereupon the man said: " I am ready to sacrifice my life and give my soul rather than see thee suffer; I prefer death than life without thee, for what is my life without thee?" He loved her so devotedly that he was willing to lose his life, and made up his mind to tell her his secret.

" Now," he said, addressing his wife, " I will go and put my house in order, and then I will tell thee all thou dost wish to know."

Now the unhappy man had a dog who was very grieved when he became aware of the fate that awaited his master.

"YOU ARE NO DOUBT LAUGHING AT ME"

Facing page 86, Vol. III

Sadly did the faithful beast run about all over the house, refusing to touch some bread and meat that had been put before him.

Thereupon the cock came along and appropriated the bread and meat which the dog had disdained to touch, and he and his wife joyfully and with great predilection devoured it. The dog was shocked at the conduct of the cock and waxed very wroth.

" Thou heartless, impious fellow," he barked, " how great is thy greed and how insignificant thy modesty. Thy master is hovering between life and death like a poor miserable sinner, and thou gorgest thyself and doest thee well in his own house."

Thereupon the cock made reply: " Well, is it my fault that thy master is such a fool, lacking understanding? Look at me, I have ten wives, and I rule over them; none of them would dare do anything that is contrary to my wish. Thy master has only one companion, and even her he is unable to command, control, and punish!" And aloud the cock shouted: " Is there any greater evil than that of being caught in the meshes of one's wife? Now prick thine ears, my friend dog, and learn wisdom from the mouth of a cock!"

" Then what ought my master to do? how is he to treat his wife?"

" Do, treat?" said the cock contemptuously; " let thy master simply take up a stick and belabour his wife with it properly. I warrant thee, friend dog, that the lady will scream and beg for mercy, and never again will she dare worry her husband and induce him to reveal his secrets unto her."

Now the master of the house, who was preparing to die, had overheard the conversation, and found the words of the cock wise.

He followed his advice and thus escaped destruction. There is a similar story in the *Tutti Nameh*.[1]

[1] *Ben Hamelech ve-Hanazir*, pp. 71b–73a; see Bin Gorion, *loc. cit.*, pp. 105–109; Lewner, *loc. cit.*, Vol. III, pp. 362–370; cf. Meinhof, *Afrikanische Märchen*, p. 81. *Tutti Nameh*, Vol. II, pp. 236–241

The Court of Solomon. A Game of Chess

Among the courtiers of King Solomon the most famous was Benaiah ben Jehoiada. Now King Solomon's most favourite pastime was a game of chess. One day he was playing with his chancellor Benaiah, and the latter was, as usually, on the point of losing, for no one was a match for Solomon in the game of chess. Suddenly a noise of a street fight between two drunken men made the King look up and then approach the window to see what was the matter. Benaiah availed himself of the absence of the King to remove one of the latter's chess-men, and the King consequently lost the game. Solomon did not at first notice the absence of one of his chess-men, and Benaiah, who was always in the habit of being the loser, won the game.

The King was both annoyed and surprised that he had lost his game, and tried to find out where he had made a mistake. Replacing the chess-men just as they had been when he had left the table, he began to play the game over again. He found out that one of the chess-men was missing, and soon came to the conclusion that the chancellor had removed a figure.

" He cheated me," thought the King, " when I was looking out of the window. Now I am not going to tell him openly that he had dealt dishonestly with me and thus put him to shame, but arrange it in such a way that he will be compelled to confess the truth of his own free will." Some time afterwards the King found an opportunity how to elicit the truth from his chancellor.

One day Solomon was leaning out of the window of his palace and noticed two suspicious individuals, carrying sacks on their shoulders, passing in front of the palace and whispering between themselves. An idea at once occurred to him. Disguising himself as one of the royal servants, he hurried down into the street, where he joined the two suspicious individuals. He had rightly guessed that the two were out to commit some act of burglary, and he now proposed unto them to rob the royal palace. " Greeting unto you, my friends," said the King, " I, too, am one of your profession, and my fingers have learned the art of burglary. Look, here is the key to the royal apartments where the King's treasures are hidden. I have planned the robbery, but dare not undertake it alone. If you are willing, then come with me and together we will carry away precious booty."

Thus spoke the King, and the two thieves, suspecting no guile, readily accepted his proposal.

" We are quite ready to follow thee," they said; " show us the way and we will soon do the job."

They decided to wait till midnight, when the palace would be wrapt in darkness and all its inmates asleep. Thereupon Solomon took his companions to the palace, and leading them through several rooms full of valuables brought them to a chamber which contained many precious stones and gems.

" Take as much as you like," said the King, " and whilst you two are filling your pockets, I will go out and keep watch lest we be surprised and taken unawares." Thereupon Solomon went out and locked the door behind him. He then put on his royal garments and roused his servants."

" There are thieves in my treasure house," he said; " catch them and take them into custody, let none of them escape." The thieves were accordingly caught and secured.

The next morning Solomon convened his supreme tribunal of justice presided over by Benaiah.

" Tell me," said the King, " ye truth-loving and learned judges, what punishment deserves the thief who has been caught in the act of robbing the King?" When Benaiah heard these words he began to tremble, for he felt sure that the King had invented the story of the two thieves whom his servants had apprehended, and had only used it for the purpose of punishing him for having dealt dishonestly with his royal master.

" The King," thought the chancellor, " has surely found out that I had cheated him at the game of chess, and he will have me convicted and condemned as a thief. If I keep silent and wait until the sentence is pronounced, I will be doubly disgraced. It is better, therefore, for me to confess and to beg my master's forgiveness."

Thereupon Benaiah fell at the feet of the King, confessed his guilt, and begged his royal master's pardon.

" I am the thief, your gracious Majesty," said Benaiah, " for at our last game of chess I stole one of the chess-men and thus won the game. I frankly confess my guilt and humbly beg your Majesty's pardon."

Solomon heard his chancellor's confession, and smilingly replied: " Do not worry, my friend, I harbour no evil thoughts against thee, for I have long forgotten the incident and readily forgiven thee for having dealt dishonestly with me. I assure thee, my friend, that to-day I have convened the supreme tribunal in order to judge two delinquents, for two thieves have really broken into my treasury this night, and have been caught in the act of robbing me. Now, gentlemen judges, pronounce your sentence."

The tribunal examined the case and condemned the two thieves to death. Solomon, however, was greatly pleased to have thus compelled Benaiah to confess his guilt. His chancellor's confession thus confirmed his supposition that Benaiah had cheated him, and that he had in reality not lost the game.[1]

[1] Jellinek, *Beth-Hamidrash*, Vol. VI, pp. 124-126.

CHAPTER VII

Solomon's Wisdom (*Continued*)

The charitable woman—The three loaves of bread—The shipwrecked stranger—The hungry prisoner—The empty sack—The gust of wind—The woman's complaint—The wealthy merchants—The leak in the boat—The miracle—The merchants' vow and prayer—Seven thousand gold pieces—The leaking vessel—The sack of flour—The Lord never forsakes those who walk in His ways—The borrowed egg—The promise of the borrower—The revenue derived from an egg—Solomon's advice—Boiled beans—The surprised soldiers—Boiled beans and boiled eggs.

THE CHARITABLE WOMAN

In the days of King Solomon, peace be upon him, there lived a charitable woman who was always ready to do good. Although not rich herself, she constantly gave away of her possessions to others. Every day she baked three loaves of bread, two of which she distributed among the poor, keeping the third loaf for herself. One day a stranger knocked at her door, and thus he spoke: " I was sailing in a vessel with all my possessions when a storm arose and broke my craft. All my companions and the pilot perished and I alone escaped, thrown on the shore by the waves. I am tired and exhausted, as I have not tasted any food for three days."

When the charitable woman heard these words, she immediately fetched one of the loaves she had baked and offered it to the hungry stranger. Thereupon she sat down and prepared to consume the second loaf herself, when another stranger appeared on her threshold. " My dear lady," he said, " I was kept a prisoner by enemies but managed to escape three days ago. I have not tasted any food ever since, and I implore thee to have pity on me and give me a piece of bread so that I may appease my hunger and not die." The woman immediately handed the stranger the second loaf and praised the Lord, who had afforded her the opportunity of bestowing charity upon the needy and the hungry.

Thereupon she produced the third loaf and prepared to make a meal, when a third beggar suddenly appeared and asked for bread. " On the road," said he, " I was caught by robbers, but I escaped into the forest. For three days I have lived on roots and herbs, and I have forgotten the taste of bread. Have pity on me and give me some to appease the pangs of my hunger."

Unhesitatingly the charitable woman offered him the third loaf, leaving none for herself. Thereupon she said unto herself: " I will see whether I can find some more flour in the sack and bake another loaf for myself. The sack, however, was quite empty, and the woman went out into the fields to gather a few grains of wheat. She collected a handful of grains, carried them to the mill, and had them ground to flour. Carrying her small sack upon her head, she was walking home when suddenly a gust of wind came from the sea and snatching the small sack, hurled it away into the distance. The woman's hopes were thus frustrated, and she remained without bread for the day. Bitterly did she cry, exclaiming in her despair: " Lord of the Universe! What sin have I committed that I should thus be punished?"

She went to King Solomon to complain of her misfortune. On that day the High Council had been convened by the King of Israel, and the woman thus addressed the members of the Sanhedrin:

" Ye judges in Israel, tell me why hath the Lord punished me thus that I, who have given of my substance to the hungry, am compelled to suffer the pangs of hunger myself?"

Whilst she was thus speaking, three merchants who had landed from their boat entered the judgment hall. " Our Lord and King," said the merchants, " take these seven thousand gold pieces and distribute them among the noble and deserving poor." Said King Solomon: " What has happened to ye that ye are so willingly giving away in charity so much gold?"

Thereupon the merchants told their story: " We were sailing in our vessel, which was laden with costly merchandise, and were already approaching the shore, when we suddenly noticed that the boat had a leak. We looked round for something to stop the hole but found nothing suitable. The boat was about to sink, and we seemed to be doomed to drown with all our belongings. In our dire distress we prayed to the Lord, and thus we said: " Lord of the Universe! If we reach the shore safely then we will give away to the poor the tenth part of the costly merchandise which we are carrying in our vessel. Thereupon we fell upon our faces and in silent prayer awaited a miracle or death. And so great was our distress that our senses were troubled, and we never noticed that our vessel had in the meantime safely reached the shore. Thereupon we calculated the value of our merchandise and found that the tenth part of it was exactly seven thousand gold pieces. This money, faithful to our vow, we have now brought to thee, and beg thee to distribute it among the poor."

Thereupon Solomon, the wise King of Israel, asked the merchants: " Know ye the exact spot where your vessel did leak, and did ye notice how the hole was stopped?" to which the merchants replied: " This we know not, for in our joy and our anxiety to come here we never investigated the matter."

" Then go and examine your vessel," said the King, who had already guessed the truth. The merchants went away and soon returned with a small sack of flour.

" This sack," they said, " had, unbeknown to us, stopped the hole in our vessel."

Turning to the pious and charitable woman, Solomon asked: " Dost thou recognize this sack of flour?"

" I do," replied the woman; " it is the very sack I was carrying on my head when the gust of wind snatched it away and hurled it into the distance."

Thereupon King Solomon said: " The seven thousand gold pieces are thine; it is for thy sake that the Lord wrought this miracle. The Lord never forsakes those who walk in His ways." Thus spoke King Solomon, and the members of the High Council and all present admired the wisdom of the King of Israel.[1]

The Borrowed Egg

One day the servants of David were partaking of a meal, and boiled eggs were served unto them. One of the boys, being more hungry than the others, had quickly eaten up his portion, and when his friends began to take their food he felt rather ashamed to see his plate empty. He therefore said unto his neighbour at table: " Lend me one of thy eggs."

" I will gladly do it," said his comrade, " if thou wilt promise me before witnesses that whenever I ask thee for the egg thou wilt return it to me together with the full amount it would have yielded to me during the time that will have elapsed." The boy accepted the bargain and promised before all present to fulfil the conditions.

A long time had passed, when the lender asked for repayment. " Thou hast lent me an egg," said the borrower, " and I will return thee another." But the lender asked for a large sum of money, which he pretended the egg would have brought him in during the time. They went to King David and submitted their case to him. Before the gate of the royal palace the youths met the boy Solomon, who was in the habit of asking all the litigants coming to see his father after the nature

---

[1] *Maassim Tobim*, § 13; see also Bin Gorion, *Der Born Judas*, Vol. III, pp. 67–70.

of their respective cases. When the two boys appeared, Solomon asked them to acquaint him with their case, and they did so. Thereupon Solomon said: " Submit your case to my father and then tell me what judgment he has given."

The litigants went before the King, and the plaintiff brought his witnesses, who confirmed his story of the bargain. He claimed from the borrower the entire amount which the egg would have brought him in during the time since he had lent it. Thereupon King David said to the borrower: " Thou must pay thy debt."

" Your Majesty," replied the youth, " I do not know how much the amount is."

The lender now explained to King David how much he claimed. " In the course of one year," he said, " the egg would have produced a chicken, next year this chicken would have given birth to eighteen other chickens, and in the third year these would have given birth each to another eighteen chickens, and so on. He thus claimed for the one egg he had lent an enormous sum, the equivalent of hundreds of chickens. The borrower of the egg left the hall of justice greatly distressed.

At the gate of the royal mansion Solomon once more addressed the two litigants, inquiring what judgment his father had given. " I am compelled," replied the borrower of the egg, " to pay an enormous sum which my friend, as he pretends, could have realized from the egg he had once lent me." Thereupon young Solomon said: " Listen unto me and I will give thee good advice."

" Long mayest thou live," replied the poor youth.

Said Solomon: " Go thou out into the fields and busy thyself at a ploughed plot of ground—where the regiments of the King are daily passing by. When thou dost perceive the warriors coming along, take a handful of boiled beans and throw them upon the ground. Should they ask thee what thou art doing, then say: ' I am sowing boiled beans.' And when they mock thee and ask: ' Who has ever heard of boiled beans bringing forth any fruit?' then reply: ' And who has heard of a boiled egg bringing forth a chicken?' "

The boy did as Solomon had advised him to. When the soldiers inquired what he was doing, he replied that he was sowing boiled beans. " Who has ever heard of such a thing?" asked the astonished soldiers, " that a boiled thing should take root and bring forth fruit?"

" And who has ever heard of a boiled egg producing a chicken?" retorted the boy.

Every regiment that passed asked the same question and received the same answer. The news of the strange conduct of the boy at last reached King David, who immediately summoned him into his presence.

" Who was it that advised thee to act as thou didst?" asked the King.

" It was my own idea," replied the boy.

" No," said the King, " I recognize the hand of Solomon in it." Thereupon the youth confessed the truth and admitted that it was indeed Solomon who had commanded him to act as he had done. David now summoned his son Solomon and asked him to give judgment in the case.

" How can the boy," asked the Prince, " be responsible for things which cannot be looked upon as really existing? An egg boiled in hot water can never be considered as a potential chicken."

David admitted the justice of Solomon's words and ordered the youth to pay his friend the value of one egg and not more.[1]

---

[1] *Revue des Études Juives*, XXXV, pp. 65–67, §{IX; see also *Ozar Midrashim*, I, pp. 347–348; cf. Bin Gorion, *loc. cit.*, pp. 64–67.

CHAPTER VIII

The Magic Carpet and the Mysterious Palace

The magic carpet—The four princes—The travel in the air—A morning
meal at Damascus and an evening meal in Media—Solomon's boast—
Rukh's retort—In the valley of the ants—The black ant—Solomon's question and the ant's answers—The ant rebukes the King—The mysterious
palace—The three old eagles—The entrance to the palace—The four
doors—The inscriptions—The idol—The tablet on its neck—The mysterious writing—Solomon's trouble—The young man from the wilderness
—Sheddad, son of Od—King over ten thousand provinces—Nothing
remains but a good name.

IN THE VALLEY OF THE ANTS, OR A LESSON IN HUMILITY

This is what happened in the days of Solomon, King of
Israel. When the Holy One gave Solomon, the son of David,
the Kingdom of Israel, and made him the ruler over all sorts
of wild and tame animals, over man and all the creatures in the
world, over the beasts in the field and the birds in the air, in
a word, over all the creatures that the Lord had created, He
also gave him a great carpet to sit upon.

This carpet was made of yellow-green silk, interwoven
with fine gold and embroidered with all sorts of images. It
was sixty mils in length and sixty mils in breadth. Solomon
had also four princes to serve him: one prince was of the sons
of men, the other of the demons, the third of the wild beasts,
and the fourth of the birds. The prince of the sons of men
was Asaf, the son of Berechiah, the prince who was of the

demons was Ramirath, whilst the two princes who were of the wild beasts and the birds were a lion and an eagle respectively. When he travelled, Solomon only did so upon the wings of the wind, and he would have his morning meal in Damascus and his evening meal in Media, that is in the East and in the West.

Now it happened one day that Solomon was boasting himself and saying: " There is none like me in the world, for the Lord hath given me wisdom and understanding, knowledge and intelligence, and hath made me ruler over all His creatures." Immediately the wind moved away and 40,000 men fell off from the carpet. When Solomon saw this, he cried to the wind and said: "Return, Rukh! Rukh! I command thee to return." Then the wind replied: " If thou, O Solomon, wilt return to thy God and not boast thyself any more, then will I return to thee!" And in that hour Solomon was put to shame by the words of the wind.

One day, whilst travelling on his carpet and on the wings of the wind, Solomon was passing over a valley in which there were ants. He suddenly heard the voice of a black ant saying to the other ants: " Go into your houses, lest the hosts of King Solomon crush you."

When King Solomon heard these words, he grew very angry and at once commanded the wind to descend upon the earth. The wind obeyed, and King Solomon sent for the ants and said unto them: " Which of you said: ' Go into your houses, lest the hosts of King Solomon crush you?' " And the black ant that had spoken answered and said: " It was I who had thus spoken to my companions."

" Why didst thou speak thus?" asked King Solomon.

" Because," replied the ant, " I feared that they might feel inclined to go out and look upon thy hosts, and would thus interrupt their praises with which they constantly praise the Lord, and then the anger of the Holy One might be kindled against us and He would destroy us."

Thereupon King Solomon asked: " Why didst thou alone speak amongst all the ants thy companions?"

" Because," replied the black ant, " I am their queen."

" And what is thy name?" asked King Solomon.

" Machshamah is my name," replied the ant.

Then Solomon said to the ant: " I wish to ask thee a question."

She answered: " It is not fitting that he who is asking questions should be on high, whilst the one that is being asked should be below."

Solomon lifted the ant up to him, but she again said: " It is not fitting that the one who asks should be seated on his throne, whilst the one who is being asked should be standing on the ground; take me, therefore, into thy hand, and I will answer thee."

Thereupon Solomon took the ant into his hand, but she remained facing him and said: " Now ask thy question."

" Is there in the world anyone greater than I?" he asked.

" There is," said the ant.

" Who is it?" asked Solomon.

" It is I," replied the ant.

" And how art thou greater than I?" asked Solomon, greatly astonished.

" Because," said the ant, " had I not been greater than thou, then the Lord would not have sent thee to me to take me into thy hand."

When Solomon heard these words of the ant, his anger was kindled, and he cast her down upon the ground.

" Ant," he cried, " knowest thou not who I am? I am Solomon, son of King David, peace be upon him."

But the ant said: " Dost thou know that thou art sprung from a vile and evil-smelling clot and shouldst not boast thyself?"

In that hour Solomon fell on his face, and was ashamed

on account of the words of the ant. Turning to the wind, he commanded: " Lift up the carpet and let us go." When the wind lifted up the carpet, the ant cried after Solomon: " Go, but do not forget the name of the Lord, and do not boast thyself exceedingly." [1]

THE MYSTERIOUS PALACE

The wind now set itself into motion, rising higher and higher, and lifted up Solomon between heaven and earth, where he passed ten days and ten nights. One day the King perceived from a distance a lofty palace built of fine gold. " I have never seen anything in the world like this lofty palace," said Solomon to his princes. In that hour Solomon said to the wind: " Descend." The wind immediately obeyed, and Solomon and his prince Asaf, the son of Berechiah, went forth and walked round and round the palace, and the scent of the herbage wafted into their nostrils was like the scent of Paradise. As they could not, however, discover any entrance or gate by which to enter the palace, they wondered greatly at this and asked themselves how they could enter the palace.

While they were thus engaged, the prince of the demons approached, and thus he spoke: " My Lord, why art thou so troubled?"

" I am troubled," replied Solomon, " on account of this palace which has no gate, and I do not know how to enter it or what to do." But the prince of the demons said: " My Lord the King! I will at once command the demons to mount upon the roof of the palace, where they will perhaps find something, a man or a bird, or some other living creature."

Solomon at once commanded the demons to hasten and mount up to the roof of the palace and to see whether they could find aught. The demons obeyed and mounted up to the roof of the palace, but they soon descended again and said:

[1] Jellinek, *loc. cit.*, Vol. V, pp. 22–26; see also *Ozar Hamidrashim*, II. pp. 534–536.

" Our Lord! We have seen no man on the roof of the palace, only a great bird, an eagle, sitting upon his young ones."

Thus spoke the demons, and Solomon at once called the prince of the demons and commanded him to bring the eagle to him. The vulture went immediately, and brought the eagle to King Solomon, upon whom be peace.

Thereupon the eagle opened his mouth in songs and praises to the Holy One, the King over all the Kings of Kings, and then he saluted King Solomon.

" What is thy name?" asked Solomon.

" Alanad," answered the eagle.

" And how old art thou?" asked the King.

" Seven hundred years," replied the eagle.

" Hast thou ever seen, or known, or heard," asked Solomon, " that this palace had an entrance or a gate?"

" By thy life, my lord the King," replied the eagle, " and by the life of thy head, I know it not; but I have a brother who is older than myself by two hundred years; he has knowledge and understanding, and he dwells in the second storey."

Said Solomon to the vulture: " Take back this eagle to his place and bring me at once his brother who is older than himself." And the vulture at once disappeared and returned after a time to Solomon, bringing with him another eagle greater than the first. The eagle opened his mouth in praises to his Creator and then saluted the King.

" What is thy name?" asked King Solomon.

" Elof is my name," answered the eagle.

" And how old art thou?" asked Solomon.

" Nine hundred years," answered the eagle.

" Dost thou know or hast thou heard that there is an entrance or a gate to this palace?"

" By thy life, my lord the King," answered the eagle, " by thy life and by the life of thy head, I know it not; but I have a brother who is older than myself by four hundred years, and he may know; he has knowledge and understanding, and he lives in the third storey."

Thereupon Solomon said to the prince of the birds: " Take back this eagle to his place and bring me his brother who is older than himself." The prince of the birds obeyed and disappeared. He returned after a time and brought the greatest eagle. He was very old and could not fly, and had to be carried by the birds on their wings, who set him before King Solomon. The eagle at once opened his mouth in praises to the Creator and then saluted the King.

" What is thy name?" asked Solomon.

" Altamar," replied the eagle.

" And how old art thou?"

" Thirteen hundred years."

" Dost thou perhaps know, or hast thou heard, whether this palace has a gate or an entrance?" asked Solomon.

" By thy life, my lord," answered the eagle, " I know it not; but my father told me that once there was an entrance to this palace on the western side. In the course of the number of years that had passed the dust had covered it up. If thou wilt command the wind to blow away the dust that has been heaped up round the house, then the entrance will reappear."

Thereupon Solomon commanded the wind to sweep away the dust which had gathered round the house, and the wind immediately began to blow and swept away all the dust so that the entrance was disclosed. There was a big iron gate, but owing to the lapse of time it looked as though it had been consumed and was mouldering.

There was a lock on it upon which were written the words: " Sons of men, be it known unto ye that for many years we dwelt in this palace in delight and prosperity. When famine came upon us we ground pearls *under the wheat*, but it profited us not, and we therefore left the palace to the eagle and laid us down on the ground. We thus said to the eagles: If any man asks ye concerning this palace, then say unto him: We found it ready built."

There was also written: " No man shall dare enter into this house unless he be a Prophet or a King. If he desires to enter this palace, let him dig on the right side of the entrance, where he will find a chest made of glass; let him break this open and he will find therein the keys. When he will open the entrance gate, he will find a door of gold. Let him open this and enter. He will then find a second door; let him open this and enter. He will then find a third door, and when he will have opened this and entered he will perceive a magnificent building, and therein he will see a hall set with Odem, Pitdah, and Bareket, ruby, topaz, emerald, and pearl (*Exodus*, xxviii, 17). He will also see a room adorned with all kinds of pearls, and also many chambers and courts paved with bricks of silver and gold. Let him then look on the ground, and he will behold the figure of scorpion which is of silver. Let him remove the figure, and he will find a room underground full of pearls without number, and silver and gold. Farther down he will find another door and a lock on it, and upon the door is written: ' The Lord of this palace was once highly honoured and mighty, and even lions and bears dreaded him and trembled before his power and majesty. In prosperity and delight did he dwell in this palace where he sat upon his throne and reigned.'

" His hour to die came, however, upon him, and he was taken away before his due time, and the crown fell from his head. Wanderer, enter into the palace and thou shalt behold wonders."

Solomon then opened the door and entered, and he beheld a third gateway on which was written that the inhabitants of the palace had dwelt in riches and honour, they had died, and the ills of time had passed over them. Their treasures alone had remained after them, but they themselves had departed to their graves, and not a trace of them had remained upon earth.

And Solomon unlocked the gate and found himself in a hall of precious stones, and on the wall was written: " How mighty was I who once dwelt in this palace! I possessed great wealth, how I ate and drank, and what beautiful apparel I did wear! How I was feared and how I, in my turn, had to fear!"

Solomon went farther and entered a beautiful mansion of precious stones which had three exits. On the first door the following lines were written: " Son of man, let fortune never deceive thee; thou, too, wilt waste and wither away and depart from thy place, and lie in the end beneath the ground!"

On the second door the following lines were written: " Be not in a hurry, for small only is thy share; be circumspect, for the world is given from one to another."

On the third gate was written as follows: " Take provision for thy journey, and provide thyself with food while it is yet day, for thou shalt not be left upon earth and the day of thy death is hidden from thee."

Solomon then opened the door, crossed the threshold, and entered. He saw the image of a man in sitting posture, and anyone that looked upon the image would have thought that it was alive, and it was surrounded by numerous idols. And when Solomon went up and drew near, the image quaked and cried aloud: " Help! Come hither, ye sons of Satan, for King Solomon has come to destroy you."

Thus cried the image, and fire and smoke issued forth from its nostrils. Then a tremendous noise arose among the demons who raved and shouted, causing earthquake and thunder.

Then Solomon cried out loudly unto them: " Do ye intend to affright me? Know ye not that I am King Solomon, who reigns over all the creatures that the Almighty has created, and that they are subject unto me? I will chastise ye because ye dare rebel against me."

Thereupon King Solomon uttered the Ineffable name of the Lord, and all the demons immediately became motionless, and none of them could utter a word. The images and idols all fell to the ground, and the sons of Satan fled and threw themselves into the waves of the great sea, that they might not fall into the hands of Solomon, the son of David.

Thereupon Solomon drew near to the image and, putting his hand into its mouth, withdrew a silver tablet. On that tablet all that concerned the palace was written, but Solomon could not read the words. He was greatly grieved at this, and turning to the princes who accompanied him he said: " Ye know how much trouble I have taken in order to reach this image, and now that I am in possession of this tablet, I am unable to read the words engraved upon it!"

And while he was considering the matter and asking himself what to do, he suddenly beheld a young man who had come from the wilderness. The youth came up and, bending low to the King, thus addressed him: " Why art thou so grieved, O King Solomon, son of David?" And Solomon answered: " I am grieved on account of this tablet, because I cannot read the words written on it."

Thereupon the young man said: " Give the tablet to me and I will read it for thee. I was sitting in my place, but when the Lord Almighty saw how grieved thou wast, He sent me to read the writing to thee."

Solomon handed over to the young man the tablet he had taken from the neck of the image, and the youth looked at it and his face expressed surprise, and he began to weep. Thereupon he addressed the King, and thus he spoke: " O Solomon! the writing upon this plate is in the Greek tongue, and that is what it says: ' I Sheddad, son of Ad, reigned over ten thousand provinces, and I rode on ten thousand horses; ten thousand

Kings were subject to me. Ten thousand heroes and warriors have I slain, but in the hour when the Angel of Death came to me I could not withstand him.'

" There is further written as follows: ' Whoever doth read this writing, let him give up troubling greatly about this world, for the destiny and end of all men is to die, and nothing remains of man but his good name.' "

And this is what came over King Solomon in this world.[1]

---

[1] *Ibid.*; see also Lewner, *loc. cit.*, pp. 371–375; see *Miscellany of Hebrew Literature*, ed. by A. Lowy, London, 1877, Vol. II, pp. 135–141.

CHAPTER IX

The Royal Marriage and the Exiled Princess

The Egyptian princess—Solomon's love for Bathya—The consecration of the Temple—The royal marriage—Great rejoicings—The angel Michael inserts a reed in the sea—The power of Rome—The destruction of Jerusalem —The thousand songs of the Egyptian princess—The wonderful canopy— The starlike gems—Solomon oversleeps himself—The morning sacrifice— A mother's rebuke—The exiled princess—The deserted island—The high tower—The young man from Akko—The strange shelter—The carcass of an ox and the enormous bird—A ride in the air—The miraculous escape— The amazed princess—The lovers—The contract written in blood—The eunuch's discovery—The arrival of the King—Solomon's amazement—It is vain for mortal man to try and prevent the decrees of Providence.

The Egyptian Princess

Solomon, who is renowned for his severe criticism of the fair sex, loved many foreign women. His love affairs were numerous, but he loved most of all Bathya, the daughter of Pharaoh Necho, whom he married soon after the death of his teacher, Shimei ben Gera. The King loved the Egyptian princess more than all the other women, and she, more than all his wives, made him commit many sins.[1]

Solomon married Bathya on the very day on which the building of the temple had been completed. Great joy reigned in Jerusalem, on account of the consecration of the sanctuary, but in the royal palace there were two joys, and the rejoicing over the royal marriage and the revelry were greater than the

[1] *Sifré*, ed. Friedmann, p. 86a.

rejoicings of the people over the consecration of the Temple. All were paying flattery to the King, and he was induced to forget the fear of God. The Lord thereupon decided then and there to destroy Jerusalem and the holy Temple.[1]

On that very night on which Solomon took to wife the Egyptian princess, the angel Michael (according to others it was Gabriel) came down upon earth and inserted a reed in the sea. In the course of time earth gathered round the reed, and a sandbank was formed which became an island. A dense forest grew on it, and on its site one day Rome was built, that mighty empire which was destined to cause the destruction of Jerusalem.[2]

It seems that the Egyptian princess, well versed in allurements and harem tricks, knew how to hold the King in the power of her many charms. From her native home she had brought to Palestine a thousand musical instruments, and she knew a thousand sweet songs. She played and sang to the King on the nuptial night, and at each song she pronounced the name of the idol to which the song was dedicated. The Egyptian woman did more. Above the nuptial couch she spread out a wonderful canopy studded with gems which shone and sparkled like so many stars. When Solomon opened his eyes and wanted to rise, he beheld the starlike gems and, thinking that it was still night, he continued to sleep. He thus slept on until the fourth hour, that is, ten o'clock. As the keys to the Temple were under the King's pillow, the morning sacrifice could not be offered. The people were greatly distressed, but none dared to go and wake the King. They therefore approached the Queen-mother, Bath-Sheba, who came and rebuked her son. " People will say," she complained, " that it is my fault if my son is forsaking the Lord. And yet, I am not to be blamed. Unlike your father's other wives, I

---

[1] *Numer. Rabba*, 10, 8; *Midrash Mishle*, 31; *Leviticus Rabba*, 12, 4.
[2] *Sanhedrin*, 21b; *Jerushalmi Aboda Zara*, 1, 2; *Sabbath*, 56b.

never prayed to the Lord to give me a son worthy to reign, but for one who would be pious, learned, and virtuous.[1]

KING SOLOMON AND HIS DAUGHTER

THE PRINCESS AND THE HANDSOME BUT POOR LAD FROM AKKO

King Solomon had a daughter named Kaziah who was of peerless beauty and whom the King loved dearly. Once he read in the stars that his daughter would marry a poor and destitute lad of the children of Israel. Greatly grieved at this, King Solomon made up his mind to prevent the occurrence of such an event, and in order to do so he sent his daughter away from Jerusalem.

He commanded his trusted servants to erect a high tower on one of the distant islands out in the sea, and to this tower he sent his daughter. The builders of the tower and the seamen who brought her to the island were all sworn to secrecy. Seventy eunuchs were thereupon commanded to accumulate provisions for the girl and to guard her in this place of seclusion, and not to allow anyone to penetrate into the tower.

Now it happened that the poor lad who was destined to be the husband of the princess, and who lived with his parents at Akko, had made up his mind to go out into the world in order to earn his living and make his way. Journeying on one cold night, he was surprised by the falling darkness in an open field, and he knew not where to hide himself and find shelter. At last he perceived the torn carcass of an ox, and he crept into it so as to warm himself and pass the night therein. He soon fell asleep in his strange place of shelter.

Now an enormous bird came along and, seeing the carcass of the ox, swooped down, seized it, and carried it off in his talons to some place where he could devour it undisturbed.

---

[1] *Sanhedrin*, 21b; see Faerber, *König Salomon in der Tradition*, 1902, pp. 49–61.

As fate would have it, the bird bore the dead ox with the youth inside it to the roof of the very tower where the daughter of King Solomon was kept in seclusion. The bird devoured the flesh of the ox and went off.

On the following morning the princess as usual went upon the roof of the tower for a walk, and great was her surprise when she beheld the young man.

" Who art thou?" she asked the youth, not less astonished than herself, " and how comest thou hither upon the roof of this high tower?"

" I am from the town of Akko," replied the lad, " and my name is Reuben."

He thereupon told her all that had occurred and how he had been carried here by an enormous bird.

The princess had compassion on the lad and brought him to her apartment, where she set food and drink before him. Thereupon she conducted him to a room where he could bathe and anoint himself and put on other robes. When he again appeared before the princess, she saw that he was very handsome. She talked to him, and soon discovered that he was not only of marvellous beauty but also very learned.

" Thou canst not leave this high tower," said the princess, " nor wilt thou be able to cross the sea, for no ship ever passes this island. Abide thou, therefore, here until the day when my father will come to fetch me, as he promised me on the day when he sent me hither."

Thus the handsome poor lad of Akko, he who was destined to be the husband of King Solomon's daughter, remained with her upon the island. The princess fell in love with the boy of surpassing beauty, of great learning and intelligence, and she wished to marry him.

One day she asked the lad to take her to wife, and as he, too, was burning in love for her, he was only too happy to yield to her request.

Thereupon they plighted their troth, and the lad took a small knife, opened a vein, and, dipping a quill in his blood, wrote the marriage contract according to the law, taking God and two angels as their witnesses. Thus the princess became the wife of the poor and handsome lad from Akko.

A year elapsed, and the eunuchs discovered the truth. They immediately sent word to King Solomon and acquainted him with the true state of affairs. Greatly astonished, the King decided to visit his daughter and to find out how she could have found a man on that distant island and in spite of all the care he had taken.

He journeyed to the place where his daughter was imprisoned, and marvelled greatly when he heard how the lad had been carried by an enormous bird to the very tower where his daughter dwelt. When Solomon saw the lad, beheld his marvellous beauty, and convinced himself that he was wise and learned, he knew that he was indeed the husband concerning whom he had read in the stars. He now understood that it was vain for mortal man to try and prevent the decrees of Providence. He was also overjoyed to find that the lad was indeed a husband not unworthy of his daughter, and he praised God.[1]

This story, which is referred to by Hartland in his *Legend of Perseus*[2], reminds us of the prince borne by the enchanted horse in the *Arabian Nights*.

---

[1] Buber, Introduction to *Midrash Tanchuma*; Grünbaum, *loc. cit.*, p. 234; *Salzburger loc cit.*, p. 80.

[2] Pp. 100–101, quoted from Koehler in *Academy*, 21st March, 1891

CHAPTER X

Solomon's Throne and Temple

Solomon's throne—Description of the throne according to Targum
Sheni—The fame of Solomon's throne—The Kings of the nations come to
admire the throne of the King of Israel—The fate of Solomon's throne—
Nebuchadnezzar, Shishak, King of Egypt, Antiochus Epiphanes, and Cyrus
—Ahasuerus, King of Shushan—David tries to build the Temple—The
waters of the deep—The jealousy of Achitophel—His advice—The artisans
who built the Temple—The master and his chaste wife—The talisman—
The glimming coal and the piece of cotton—Solomon's surprise—The
two youths who came to tempt the virtuous woman—Solomon in disguise
—The dish of boiled eggs differently painted—The rebuke of the virtuous
woman—The finding of the Shamir—The gates refuse to open—The
merits of David.

It is said in Scripture that Solomon made a great throne of
ivory and overlaid it with gold. There were six steps to the
throne, with a footstool of gold, which were fastened to the
throne, and steps on either side of the sitting place, and two
lions standing beside the steps: and twelve lions stood there
on the one side and on the other upon the six steps.[1] Legend
is very busy in describing the magnificence and glory of the
King's throne. It is related as follows in the *Second Targum to
Esther*.

One day King Solomon sent for Hiram, the artificer from
Tyre, and thus he spoke unto him: " I know that thou art a great
artificer and very clever, and I have sent for thee so that thou
shouldst make a throne for me which will surpass in magnificence the thrones of all the Kings in the world. And Hiram

---

[1] *1 Kings*, x, 18; *2 Chronicles*, ix, 17.

from Tyre made answer: " If the King will place at my disposal gold and silver and gems and precious stones, I will construct a throne the like of which has never been seen. Thereupon King Solomon gave instructions that his treasure-stores be opened to Hiram. And such was the throne which the artificer from Tyre made for King Solomon. There were six steps, and twelve lions of gold stood upon them and twelve eagles of gold faced them. The right paw of a golden lion was directed towards the left wing of each golden eagle, and the left wing of the golden eagle was towards the right paw of each golden lion. There were seventy-two golden lions and as many golden eagles. The top of the throne where the King's seat was, was round-shaped, and it had six steps. Upon the first step there lay a golden lion and facing it was a golden ox. Upon the second step there crouched a golden wolf and opposite to it was a golden lamb. Upon the third step there was a golden panther and opposite to it lay a golden camel. Upon the fourth step there lay a golden eagle and facing it was a golden peacock. Upon the fifth step lay a golden cat and opposite to it was a golden hen. Upon the sixth step lay a golden hawk and opposite to it was a golden dove. On the top of the throne was a golden dove holding in its claws a golden hawk. There was also a candlestick made of pure gold with its lamps, ashpans, and snuffers. And seven pipes issued from it on which were engraven the images of the seven Patriarchs, the work of a clever artificer. The names of the seven Patriarchs are: Adam, Noah, Shem, Abraham, Isaac, Jacob, and Job. On the other side of the candlestick were seven other pipes upon which were engraven the images of the seven pious and just men of the world, who are: Levi, Kehat, Amram, Moses, Aaron, Eldad, and Medad. A golden jar filled with the purest olive oil stood on the top of the candlestick for the purpose of supplying the lamps in the Holy Temple. Underneath the candlestick was a vessel of pure gold filled with the purest olive oil, supplying the lamps, and upon it was engraven the image of Eli the High Priest. And two branches proceeded from the vessel upon which were portrayed the images of the two sons of Eli the High Priest, Hophni and Phinehas. Two pipes proceeded from the two branches, and upon them were again portrayed the images of two sons of Aaron the High Priest, Nadab and Abihu. Twenty-four vines of gold were placed on the upper side of the throne so as to give a shade to the King.

Whenever Solomon wished to ascend his throne and set his foot on the first step, the golden ox at once raised him to the second step, the golden bear to the third step, the golden panther to the fourth step, and so on until the King reached the sixth step. Then the golden eagles took him up and seated him on the throne. Whenever he ascended the throne and sat down, an eagle came and placed the crown upon his head. Thereupon a golden dove descended from one pillar and opened a cabinet. It took out the Holy Law and placed it in the hands of the King. The throne moved upon wheels and there was a silver serpent round about the wheels. Wherever Solomon wished to go the throne moved with him, and rivers of spices flowed wherever he went. On either side of the throne sat the elders of Israel to judge the people, and no one could bear false witness before them. Whenever a man came before the King and the elders and harboured in his heart the intention of bearing false witness, he was immediately denounced. At the approach of the would-be perjurer the wheels of the throne began to move, the oxen to low, the bears to growl, and the lions to roar. The panthers yelled, the owls hooted, and the lambs bleated; the peacocks shrieked, the cocks crowed, and the cats mewed; the birds chirped, and the hawks screamed. And terror seized those who intended to bear false witness so that they were greatly afraid and spoke the truth. " Let us speak the truth," they said, " and only the truth, for otherwise the world may be destroyed because of us." [1]

The fame of Solomon's throne spread far and wide among all the Kings of the nations. They gathered themselves together and came to visit Solomon and to see with their own eyes the magnificence of his throne and its wonders.

When they came to Jerusalem and beheld the wonderful throne they were dazzled by its great splendour, and falling to the ground, they prostrated themselves before Solomon in his Glory and did him homage. " Never," exclaimed the Kings of the nations, " have we beheld such a throne, for never has such a throne been made for another King and never will its like be made." They coveted the glorious throne in their hearts and envied the King of Israel.

Solomon's throne was later on taken from Jerusalem and carried to strange lands, but none of the rulers of Babylon, Egypt, or Greece was ever allowed to ascend and sit on the throne of the son of David. When Nebuchadnezzar captured Jerusalem and destroyed the Temple, he took the throne with him and it formed part of his plunder. He carried the throne to Babylon and desired to seat himself upon it, but he was punished for his presumption. Ignorant of the mechanism of the throne and the particular manner in which it could only be ascended, Nebuchadnezzar set his foot upon the first step, and the lion stretched out its paw. Instead, however, of raising the ruler of Babylon to the second step, it smote him upon the left foot, and Nebuchadnezzar was lame for the remainder of his life. Afterwards Alexander the Great brought the throne to Egypt, where Shishak, the Pharaoh of Egypt, admired its beauty and glory. He, too, desired to seat himself upon it, but met with the same fate as did Nebuchadnezzar. The lion, stretching out its paw, wounded him, and he remained lame

---

[1] *Targum Sheni*, ed. M. David, Berlin, 1898, and P. Cassel, Leipzig and Berlin, 1885; see also P. Cassel, *Kaiser u. Königsthrone*, Berlin, 1874; Jellinek, *Beth-Hamidrash*, V, pp. 34 ff; Vol. III, pp. 83 ff; Salzberger, *Salomons Tempelbau u. Thron*, Berlin, 1912, pp. 74–99.

until the end of his days. He was therefore called Pharaoh Necho, or the lame Pharaoh. Afterwards Antiochus Epiphanes took the famous throne away from Egypt and put it on board ship, but a leg of it was broken. The King summoned and brought together all the artificers and goldsmiths of the world, but none of them was able to repair the broken leg of Solomon's throne. The throne afterwards came into the hands of the Persian King Cyrus, who had brought about the downfall of the Kingdom of Antiochus. And because Cyrus had rebuilt the Temple of Jerusalem he was rewarded for his noble deed and was granted the distinction of being allowed to ascend the throne of Solomon and to seat himself upon it. The throne was thereafter in the possession of King Ahasuerus, and he sat on it in Shushan the palace.[1]

THE TEMPLE

David had vowed to build a Temple to the Lord, and he actually began the work. He instructed the labourers to dig the foundations, and in the course of their labours they came down to the waters of the deep. Immediately the waters surged up tumultuously, threatening to flood Jerusalem and the whole world as in the days of Noah. Great was the despair of David, and he turned to Achitophel for advice. Achitophel was jealous of David and thought to himself: " David will now be drowned and I shall be King in his place." David, however, turned to him and said: " Whoever knows how to stop the waters of the deep and refuses to do it, will one day throttle himself." Then Achitophel was compelled to tell the King what to do.

He counselled David to take a stone and engrave upon it the Ineffable Name, the Tetragrammaton, and set it in the orifice through which the waters were surging. David followed

---

[1] *Yalkut Esther*, § 1046; Salzberger, *loc. cit.*, pp. 60–62, 64–70; *Midrash Abba Gorion*; Jellinek, *Beth-Hamidrash*, Vol. I, pp. 1–18; see also chap. XIX of this vol.

Achitophel's advice, and immediately the waters of the deep subsided, and Jerusalem and the whole world were saved from the danger that threatened them. In the end Achitophel, nevertheless, committed suicide by hanging himself.[1] The digging proceeded, but David was not allowed to build the Temple on account of his having been a man of blood.[2] When Solomon ascended the throne of his father David, he carried on the work and built the Temple of Jerusalem with the help of Hiram, King of Tyre, Sidon, and Phœnicia. He also wrote to many kings and princes and asked them to send him artisans and architects to help in the building of the Temple.

In connection with the masters and artists who came to Jerusalem from foreign lands the following story is told, according to which Solomon had to admit that not all women were worthless.

The Master and his Faithful Wife

King Solomon had uttered many harsh words concerning women, of whose faithfulness he had but a poor opinion. Once, however, he met a true and good woman as is related in the following story.

When the King was about to build the Temple in Jerusalem, he dispatched messengers to the kings and princes of other countries and asked them to send to the land of Israel their cleverest artisans, to whom he promised high remuneration for their work. The kings and princes complied with Solomon's request and sent their best artisans to Jerusalem.

Now in a certain place there lived a clever master who always refused to betake himself to another town, even when high remuneration was offered to him for his work. This master artisan namely had a very beautiful and charming wife,

---

[1] *Jerushalmi Sanhedrin*, X, 29a; *Succah*, 52b–53a.
[2] G. Salzberger, *Salomons Tempelbau und Thron*, p. 7; *Folklore*, Vol. XVI, p. 422.

and he was afraid to leave her alone lest sinful men come and
lead her astray from the path of virtue.

Now when King Solomon's messengers arrived in the
town where dwelt the master artisan and his beautiful wife and
made known the request of the King of Israel, the Prince of
the locality summoned into his presence the master artisan.
The latter came and, prostrating himself before his King, said:
" What is the command of my Lord to his servant?"

" My command," said the King, " is that thou shouldst
immediately travel to Jerusalem and there help to build the
Temple for King Solomon. He is a mighty ruler, and I dare
not disobey his request."

Greatly perturbed and sad at heart, the master returned to
his home. When his wife inquired after the cause of his grief,
he told her what had occurred. Thereupon the woman said:
" If it is on my account that thou art so grieved, then be of
good cheer. I will give thee a talisman, and as long as it remains unchanged thou mayest consider it as a sure sign of my
innocence and purity. Obey the command of the King and
go to Jerusalem, there to work among the other artisans. Have
no fear and be sure that I shall remain pure and faithful unto
thee."

In the morning the woman gave her husband a tiny glass
bulb which contained a small piece of cotton and a glimming
coal. " See," she said, " as long as this piece of cotton does
not catch fire, thou mayest be sure that the flame of sinful
passion has not entered my heart."

The master attached the glass bulb to a chain which he
put round his neck, embraced his wife, and proceeded to
Jerusalem. Arrived in the holy city, he offered his services to
the King and helped in the building of the Temple. Now King
Solomon daily came to visit the artisans to see what progress
they were making. Well content, he promised to double their
wages. One day he raised his eyes and perceived the strange

talisman on the neck of the master. Greatly astonished, he summoned the latter and asked him to explain the meaning of the glass bulb. The master related unto the King what had occurred and how his wife had given him the talisman.

Now what did Solomon do? He summoned two handsome youths and commanded them to travel to the town where the beautiful woman dwelt, to abide in her house and to seduce her. When the youths arrived in the town, they took lodging in the woman's house and made themselves agreeable to her. The woman offered the two strangers hospitality and invited them to dine with her. When night came she took them to a room she had prepared for them. Scarcely, however, had the youths entered the chamber when she locked the door and thus kept them prisoners for a whole month.

Every day King Solomon watched the talisman on the master's neck, but lo! the piece of cotton never caught fire. Greatly astonished, Solomon said in his heart: " I will go myself to that city and try to tempt the woman." Disguising himself as an ordinary traveller and accompanied by two servants, he proceeded on his journey. Arrived in the city where dwelt the chaste woman, he took lodging in her house. The woman, who at once guessed that he was Solomon, received him with great honour and prepared a meal worthy of a king. She offered him many dishes, but the last she placed upon the table contained boiled eggs, every one of which was painted with another colour.

" Taste these eggs, my Lord and King," she said.

" Whom dost thou call King?" asked Solomon, to which the woman replied: " The royal dignity and majesty are visible in thine eyes and upon thy countenance. I am only thy humble handmaiden, and I beg thee to partake of these eggs and to tell me how they taste."

King Solomon ate a little of every egg in the dish and said: " These eggs taste all alike."

" Such is the case with us women," replied the chaste wife
of the master; "we are only differently painted. It was not
worth thy while to travel such a long distance for the sake of
a smooth face. I am thy humble servant and thou canst of
course do with me as thou wishest, but know that all earthly
desires are vain and sinful."

Thus spoke the charming and chaste woman, and Solomon
replied: " Blessed be thou unto the Lord and blessed be thy
noble and chaste heart." He asked her to be as a sister to him,
gave her a costly gift, and returned to Jerusalem. Here he
related unto the master what had occurred and sent him home
in peace. He paid him his wages a tenfold and bidding him
farewell said: " Go back to thy chaste wife and be happy in
the possession of such a jewel." The master returned to his
wife, and when she related unto him how she had acted, he
kissed her upon the head and honoured and loved her even
more than he had done before his departure. Everlasting
friendship existed henceforth between the pair and King
Solomon.[1]

There is a similar story in *Thousand and One Nights* about
the King and the wife of his vizier,[2] and one in the *Tutti
Nameh* about the Indian Prince and the wife of the warrior.[3]

The story of the finding of the Shamir which Solomon
required for the building of the Temple has been told at
length in the first volume of this work.[4] It is said that during
the building of the Temple none of the artisans died or even
fell sick; none of them ever broke his shovel or pickaxe or
lost his shoelaces.[5] When the Temple was at last completed
and Solomon wished to bring the ark into the Sanctuary, the
gates suddenly refused to open. The King recited twenty-four

---

[1] Isr. bar Sason, *Likkute Maassioth*, Jerusalem, pp. 11b–15a; cf. Bin Gorion, *loc. cit.*
pp. 109–113.
[2] *Thousand and One Nights*, 10th Night.
[3] *Tutti Nameh*, German translation by G. Rosen, Leipzig, 1858, Vol. I, pp. 83–87.
[4] Vol. I, pp. 80–86; see also Introduction to Vol. I, pp. xxxvi–xl.
[5] *Pesikta Rabbati*, ed. Friedmann, Wien, 1880; see Salzberger, *Tempelbau*, pp. 17–18.

prayers, but still the gates remained shut until Solomon cried out, " O Lord, remember the love Thou didst bear unto Thy servant David," and immediately the gates opened.[1] When at last the ark was brought into the Temple, all the cedars and trees in the courtyard of the Lord began to blossom and bear fruit.[2]

[1] *Sanhedrin*, 107*b*; *Sabbath*, 30*a*; *Yalkut*, § 698; *Moed Katton*, 9*a*; cf. Salzberger, *loc. cit.*, p. 22.
[2] *Midrash Tanchuma*, ed. Buber; cf. Salzberger, *ibid.* p. 21.

CHAPTER XI

Solomon and the Queen of Sheba

Solomon master over beasts and birds—The royal guests—The missing hoopoe—The city of Kitor in the East—The wonderful country—The Queen of Sheba—The hoopoe's plan—The letter of King Solomon—The frightened Queen—The royal gifts—The visit of the Queen of Sheba—The beauty of Benaiah—The lion and his lair—The house of glass—The bare legs of the Queen—The riddles of the Queen of Sheba—A tube of cosmetic—Naphtha—Flax—The nineteen riddles—The sawn trunk of a cedar tree.

One day, when Solomon was of good cheer and his heart was gladdened on account of wine, he invited the Kings and princes of the neighbouring countries, and they dwelt in his royal palaces. He thereupon commanded his court-musicians to play upon the cymbals and violins which his father David used to play upon. As he was master over beasts and birds, demons and spirits, he summoned before him the birds of the air, the beasts of the field, the creeping reptiles, the *sheddim*, spirits and ghosts, so as to impress his guests, the Kings of the neighbouring countries, with his greatness. The royal scribes called the beasts and birds by name, and they all came of their own accord, neither bound nor fettered, no human being guiding them. Now it happened that the King was examining the birds but found the hoopoe missing from among them. The bird could nowhere be found, and the King waxed wroth and commanded his servants to find the hoopoe and chastise him. The hoopoe, however, appeared of his own accord, and thus he spoke: "Hearken unto me, O Lord of the World, and

may my words find entrance in thine ear. Three months have
now elapsed since I took a certain resolution, having first taken
counsel with myself. No food have I eaten and no water have
I drunk, for I said unto myself: ' I will fly about all over the
world and see whether there is a country or a realm which is
not subject to my lord the King.' And I have discovered a
realm the capital of which is the city of Kitor in the East.
The dust in that city is more valuable than gold, and the silver
is like mud in the streets. The trees in that land are from the
days of creation, and are being watered by the waters from the
Garden of Eden. Crowds of men, wearing crowns upon their
heads, inhabit that city. They know not the art of war, nor
do they know how to use the bow or shoot an arrow. I have
also noticed that a woman is ruling over the men in that city
of Kitor, and her name is Queen of Sheba. If it now please
thee, my lord and King, I shall gird my loins like a hero and
fly to the city of Kitor, in the country of Sheba. I shall fetter
their Kings with chains and their rulers with iron bands, and
I will bring them all before my lord the King."

This plan and advice of the hoopoe pleased the King
greatly. The royal scribes were immediately summoned, and
a letter was written and bound to the hoopoe's wing. Thereupon the hoopoe rose up and flew skyward. He flew high up
among the other birds, who followed him to the city of Kitor,
in the land of Sheba. Now it happened that in the morning
the Queen of Sheba went forth from her palace to pay worship
to the sun, and lo! the birds that had just arrived had darkened
the light of the sun. The Queen immediately raised her hand
and rent her garment, wondering and greatly perturbed.
Then the hoopoe alighted, and she perceived that a letter was
tied to his wing. She loosed it and read its contents, and this
is what was written in it:

" From me, King Solomon, who sends greeting, peace
unto thee, Queen of Sheba, and unto thy nobles! Ye are no

doubt aware that the Lord of the Universe has appointed me King over the beasts in the field, the birds in the air, the *sheddim*, spirits and ghosts, and that all the Kings of the East and the West, of the North and the South, are coming to bring me greeting and pay homage unto me. Now if ye will come and pay homage unto me I will honour thee more than I honour all the other Kings who are attending me. But if ye refuse and will not appear before me, salute and pay homage unto me, I shall send out against ye Kings and legions and riders. Ye ask who are these Kings, legions, and riders of King Solomon? Know then that the beasts in the field are my Kings, the birds of the air my riders, the spirits, *sheddim*, and ghosts my legions. They will throttle ye in your beds, the beasts of the field will slay ye in the fields, and the birds of the air will consume your flesh."

And when the Queen of Sheba read these words she once more took hold of her garments and rent them. Thereupon she summoned her elders and princes and said unto them: " Know ye not that King Solomon has written to me?"

But they replied: " We know not King Solomon and care not for his dominion."

The Queen, however, trusted not their words, nor did she incline her ear unto them. She sent word and assembled all the ships in the land and loaded them with presents, the finest wood, pearls, and precious stones. She also sent the King six thousand youths and maidens, born in the same year, in the same month, on the same day, in the same hour—all of the same stature and nature and all of them clad in purple garments. And she wrote a letter which she gave them to bear unto King Solomon, and this is what she wrote: " From the city of Kitor to the land of Israel is a journey of seven years, but I will hasten my journey and be in Jerusalem to visit thee at the end of three years."

At the end of the appointed time the Queen of Sheba

KING SOLOMON AND THE QUEEN OF SHEBA

Facing page 124, Vol. III

came to visit Solomon, and when the King heard of her arrival he sent out Benaiah, the son of Jehoiada, to meet her. He was of great beauty, and his countenance shone like the dawn of morn in the sky and like Venus, the bright evening star that outshines all other stars, and like a rose that is growing by the waterbrook. When the Queen of Sheba beheld Benaiah, the son of Jehoiada, she descended from her chariot. Benaiah asked her why she had left her chariot, and she made answer:

" Art thou not King Solomon?" to which Benaiah replied: " I am not King Solomon, but only one of his servants attending him and standing in his presence."

The Queen then turned to her nobles and the princes accompanying her and said to them: " If you have not seen the lion, then you may at least behold his lair; if you have not seen King Solomon, then behold at least the beauty of the man who is standing in his presence."

Thereupon Benaiah brought the Queen into the presence of his royal master. Solomon had gone to sit in a house of glass to receive her, and when the Queen of Sheba approached she was deceived, thinking that Solomon was sitting in water. She consequently raised her garments in order to cross the water, and thus bared her legs so that the King noticed the hair on her bare feet. Thereupon King Solomon said: " Thy beauty is the beauty of a woman, but thy hair is the hair of a man; it is an ornament to a man, but it is ugly in a woman."

THE RIDDLES OF THE QUEEN OF SHEBA

Then the Queen of Sheba addressed King Solomon, and thus she spoke: " My lord and King, I will put to thee three riddles, and if thou wilt solve them I will know that thou art wise indeed, but if not, then I will conclude that thou art like other mortals.

"What is it?" she said. "A wooden well and an iron bucket; it draws stones but pours out water."

"It is a tube of cosmetic," replied the King.

Said again the Queen of Sheba: "It comes as dust from the earth and dust is its food, it is poured out like water, but it lights the house. What is it?"

"Naphtha," replied the King.

And the Queen further asked: "It walks in front of all things, it raises a loud and bitter wailing and crying; it bends its head like a reed, is the glory of the nobles and the disgrace of the poor, the glory of the dead and the disgrace of the living; it is a delight unto the birds, but a distress unto the fishes. What is it?"

"It is flax," answered the King.[1]

The riddles of the Queen of Sheba are enumerated in the second *Targum to Esther* (I, 2) and in the *Midrash Mishle*, or *Midrash to the Proverbs*.[2] The first source contains the above-mentioned three riddles, whilst the second mentions four.

The Queen's meeting with Solomon is related as follows: The Queen said to him:

"Art thou Solomon of whom I have heard so much?"

"Yes."

Then she asked further: "Wilt thou reply to my questions?" to which Solomon made answer:

"The Lord will lend wisdom."

Then she asked the somewhat unseemly questions for a woman:

"What is it? Seven depart and nine enter; two pour out the draught and one only drinks."

Said he: "Seven are the days of woman's defilement, and nine the months of her pregnancy; two breasts nourish the child, and one drinks."

---

[1] *Targum Sheni to the Book of Esther*, ed. P. Cassel, Leipzig, 1885; ed. E. David, Berlin, 1898.

[2] *Midrash Mishle*, ed. S. Buber, Vilna, 1893; A. Wünsche, *Midrash Mishle*, Leipzig, 1885.

Said she: " I will ask thee another question. A woman once said unto her son: Thy father is my father, thy grandfather my husband; thou art my son but I am thy sister."

To which Solomon made answer: " It must surely have been one of Lot's daughters who thus spoke to her son." [1]

Thereupon she called boys and girls all of the same stature and wearing the same garb, and said unto the King: " Distinguish between the males and females."

He immediately beckoned to his eunuchs, and they brought nuts and roasted ears of corn, which he distributed among them. The boys, who were not bashful, received them in their laps, lifting up their dresses; the girls took them in the veils which served them as headgear. Whereupon King Solomon said: " These are the boys and these the girls."

She thereupon brought to him a number of boys, some circumcised and others uncircumcised, and she said to him: " Distinguish between the circumcised and uncircumcised."

Solomon immediately made a sign to the High Priest and commanded him to open the ark of the covenant. The persons who were circumcised immediately bowed their bodies to half their height, and the radiance of the *skekhinah* shone upon their countenances, but the uncircumcised ones prostrated themselves and fell upon their faces.

" These are circumcised," said Solomon, " and these are uncircumcised."

" Thou art wise indeed," said the Queen of Sheba.[2]

The *Midrash Hachefez*,[3] however, contains nineteen riddles. The first four coincide, with only a slight difference, with those given in the *Midrash Mishle*, and we shall therefore only give here the following fifteen:

5. She put other questions to him and said: " Who is he

---

[1] *Midrash Mishle*; see J. Lightfoot, *Horæ Hebraicæ*, Rotterdam, 1686, II, 527; see also *Yalkut*, II, § 1085.
[2] *Midrash Mishle*.
[3] *Midrash Hachefez*, ed. and translated by S. Schechter, *Folklore*, No. 1, pp. 349-358.

who neither was born nor has died?" to which Solomon replied: " It is the Lord of the Universe, blessed be He."

6. She asked again: " What land is that which has seen
the sun but once?"

" It is the land on which the waters of creation were
gathered and the bottom of the sea on the day when the waters
were divided for the Israelites to pass."

7. She asked again: " What is it? An enclosure with ten
doors; when one is open, nine are shut, and when nine are
open, one is shut."

Said he: " The enclosure is the womb, and the ten doors
are the ten orifices of man, namely his eyes, his ears, his nostrils,
his mouth, the apertures for the discharge of excreta and urine,
and the navel. When the child is still in its mother's womb, the
navel is open but all the other apertures are shut, but when
the child issues from the womb, the navel is closed and all the
other orifices are opened."

8. She further asked: " What is it? It never moves when
it is living, but when its head has been cut off it moves."

" It is a ship in the sea (made of trees that have been cut
down)."

9. " Who are the three," she asked, " who neither ate,
nor did they drink, nor has ever a soul been put into them, and
yet they saved three lives from death?"

Said he: " They are the seal, the thread, and .the staff
(which Judah gave unto Thamar), for they saved the lives of
Thamar, Pharez, and Zarah."

10. " What is it?" she asked. " Three entered a cave and
five issued from it."

" It is Lot, his two daughters and their two children," said he.

11. " What is it?" she asked again. " The dead lived, the
grave moved, and the dead prayed."

Said he: " The dead that lived was Jonah, who lived and
prayed, and the grave that moved was the fish."

12. " Who were the three," she further asked, " who ate and drank on the earth, but were never born of male and female?"

Said he: " They were the three angels who came to visit Abraham."

13. " What is it?" she asked. " Four entered a place expecting to die and came forth alive, and two entered a place of life and came forth dead."

Said he: " The four were Daniel, Hananiah, Mishael, and Azariah, and the two were Nadab and Abihu."

14. " Who is he," she asked, " who was born but did not die?"

" Elijah and the Messiah," he replied.

15. " What is it that was never born but to which life was given?"

Said he: " It is the golden calf."

16. " What is it? It is produced from the earth but man produces it, and its food is the fruit of the earth."

" It is a wick," said he.

17. " What is it?" she asked. " A woman was married to two husbands and bore two sons, but all these four had one father."

" It is Thamar," he said, " who was married by Or and Onan and bore two sons, Pharez and Zarah, and the four had one father, Judah."

18. " What is it? A house full of dead; no dead came among them nor any living came forth from them."

" It is Samson and the Philistines."

19. The Queen of Sheba thereupon ordered that the sawn trunk of a cedar tree be brought, and then she asked Solomon to tell her at which end the root had been and at which end the branches.

Solomon ordered the trunk to be cast into the water, and one end sank, whilst the other floated on the surface of the water. Then he said unto her: " The part which sank was the root, and that which floated on the surface was the end containing the branches."

Thereupon the Queen of Sheba said unto Solomon: " Thou dost exceed in wisdom and goodness thy great fame; blessed be thy God." [1]

[1] Cf. Perles, *Zur Rabbinischen Sprach und Sagenkunde,* 1873; Delitzsch, *Iris,* 1889; see also Bialik, *Sepher Haaggadah,* Vol. I, pp. 108–110.

CHAPTER XII

The Beggar King

Solomon's pride—The transgressed commandment—The King has multiplied wives—The complaint of the commandment—The Lord summons Ashmedai—The King in exile—I, Koheleth, *was* King over Israel—The sufferings of Solomon—The two hosts—Solomon's grief and tears—The consolation of the poor man—Better is a dinner of herbs where love is than a stalled ox and hatred therewith—The charitable old woman—Solomon's confession—Naamah, the daughter of the King of Ammon—The exiled monarch and the royal head cook—Solomon as a kitchen boy—The delicious food—The enamoured princess—The anger of the King—The exiled lovers—The fish and the signet-ring—The King of Ammon visits Jerusalem—Solomon introduces his wife—The joy of the parents—The behaviour of Ashmedai—The indignant wife—The amazed Queen-mother—Benaiah and the exiled King—The Sanhedrin fight Ashmedai—The Divine voice.

The incident describing the circumstances under which Solomon was temporarily deprived of his crown and had to wander, an exile in foreign lands, has been related in broad outlines in Vol. I of this work. A more detailed version of the King's exile runs as follows:

Seated upon his magnificent throne and wielding great power over men, beasts, birds, demons, and spirits of the air, Solomon's heart was filled with great pride and presumption.

" No one," he spoke in his heart, " is as wise as I."

In his pride and arrogance he transgressed and broke the commandment which forbids the King to multiply wives unto himself.[1] He took a thousand wives unto himself who led him astray, and he declined from the right way.

[1] *Deuteronomy*, xvii, 16, 17.

Thereupon the commandment flew up straight to heaven and thus complained before the Lord: " Lord of the Universe," spoke the commandment which Solomon had trodden down, " is there any law in Thy Holy Torah which is superfluous and for no purpose?"

And the Lord replied: " There is none."

" Ruler of the world," spoke the commandment, " Solomon has transgressed me, for he has taken unto himself seven hundred wives and three hundred concubines, who are leading him astray and making him deviate from the right path. He is treading under foot Thy Holy Law."

The Holy One replied: " Thy claim shall be considered and justice rendered unto thee."

Thereupon the Holy One summoned Ashmedai, prince of the demons, unto His presence, and thus He spoke to him: " Descend immediately into the palace of King Solomon, take the signet-ring from his finger, assume his likeness, and seat thyself upon his throne." The Evil One gladly obeyed the command of the Ruler of the universe and took the place of the King.

Snatching up the King, Ashmedai swallowed him up, then he stretched out his wings, so that one touched heaven and the other the earth, and vomited out the King of Israel in a distant land, four hundred miles away. Ashmedai then gave himself out as King Solomon and took his place, whilst the King himself was far away in a strange country and obliged to beg his bread from door to door. He wandered for many years until he came back to Jerusalem, where he claimed his right to the throne. " I, the preacher, was King over Israel in Jerusalem," he repeated every day, but the members of the Sanhedrin thought that he was mad, and would not believe him.[1]

For three years the exiled King wandered through cities

[1] *Gittin,* 68b; Jellinek, *Beth-Hamidrash,* Vol. II, pp. 86–87.

and villages from door to door, crying aloud: " I, Koheleth, *was* King over Israel in Jerusalem," but no one would believe him, and he was treated with derision.

" Thou art a fool," they mocked him, " for our King is seated upon his throne in Jerusalem, and thou dost pretend that thou art the King."

Great were the sufferings of the exiled King, who was compelled to beg his daily bread from door to door. One day, during his wanderings, Solomon met a rich man who actually recognized him, but failed to understand the reason of the King's predicament. He invited him to his house, where he prepared a banquet for the dethroned monarch and placed delicious food upon the table. Thereupon the host began to speak of the past glories of the King.

" Dost thou remember," he said, " the deeds thou didst accomplish when thou wast King? Great was the splendour which I once witnessed at thy brilliant court."

These reminiscences made the exiled monarch shed bitter tears, and he left the rich man's house in sorrow and grief.

On the following day Solomon met another acquaintance who was a poor man, and whom the beggar-king implored for alms.

" My Lord," said the poor man, " wilt thou honour me with thy presence in my poor dwelling and partake of my hospitality?"

" Gladly will I come and break bread under thy roof," replied the sorely tried monarch, " but promise me that thou wilt not move me to tears by speaking continually of my past glories and the splendour of my court."

" My Lord," said the host, " I am but a poor man and can offer thee only a meagre meal, but I will assuage thy grief and do my best to console thee."

Thereupon he led the King under his humble roof, where he placed a dish of greens before Israel's exiled King. He consoled, however, the once mighty ruler, and assured him that the Lord would not break the oath He had once sworn to David, and would surely restore his son to his kingdom.

" Such are the ways of the Lord," said the kind host. " He punishes and deals severely with us, but, in due course, He vouchsafes unto us His grace. Whom God loves He punishes, but His punishments are those of a father who loves His children." Thus the host comforted his royal guest, and Solomon left the humble dwelling with hope in his heart. And it was then that the exiled King spoke the wise words: " Better is a dinner of herbs where love is than a stalled ox and hatred therewith." [1]

In the course of his wanderings, which had now lasted three years, Solomon came to the house of an old but charitable woman. Tired and exhausted, the King was sorely grieved, and he wept from even till morn. The kind hostess asked her guest to unburden his heart and to tell her why he was so sore grieved and shedding such bitter tears. To this the wanderer replied:

" I am ashamed to tell thee the cause of my sorrow and the story of my misfortunes, for thou wilt never give credence to my words."

But the woman insisted on his unburdening his heart to her. Thereupon the dethroned monarch said:

" Know then that I, a beggar and a wanderer, am in reality Solomon, King of Israel."

" And how didst thou lose thy kingdom and throne?" asked the woman, and Solomon told her.

" One day," he said, " I was playing with my signet-ring when suddenly the prince of demons appeared, and snatching it from my hand hurled it into the sea."

" This is a strange story thou art telling me," said the

---

[1] *Proverbs*, xv, 17; see *Midrash Mishle*; *Yalkut Shimeoni*, II, § 953; Bialik, *Sepher Haaggadah*, Vol. I, p. 112; Lewner, *Kol Aggadoth*, Vol. III, p. 383–385.

SOLOMON'S SIGNET RING IS RESTORED TO HIM

Facing page 134, Vol. III

woman, " but it happens that yesterday I bought a big fish in the market, and when I cut it open I found a ring in its belly. Wilt thou see the ring? Perchance it is thy own signet-ring."

Thus spoke the woman and produced the ring.

When Solomon beheld his ring he immediately recognized it. It sparkled and shed a brilliant light in the room.

Once more the dethroned King wept, but this time they were tears of joy which he shed. The woman put the ring upon Solomon's finger, and immediately an angel appeared and carried the dethroned monarch to the very gates of Jerusalem.[1]

The Exiled King and the Enamoured Princess

The story of the ring is told in a more romantic manner in another source. It relates the miraculous restoration of the ring and the love affair of Solomon and Princess Naamah.

He was a dethroned monarch, exiled and begging from door to door, and she was a beautiful princess, the daughter of a mighty king. Solomon had been wandering in strange lands for three years, when the Lord had pity on him and decided to restore him to his kingdom for the sake of the merits of his father David. And because it had been decreed that the Messiah should issue from Naamah, the Ammonite Princess, Solomon was led to the court of the Princess's father. Thus the wandering beggar-king came to Mesichmem, the capital of the land of Ammon.

One day the exiled monarch, sad and weary, was standing in the street of the capital, when the royal head cook passed by. He was carrying baskets laden with all sorts of food which he had bought in the market for the royal table, and he asked the poor, tattered, strange youth to carry them home for him. As the strange youth had found favour in his eyes, the cook engaged his services, and Solomon helped him in the kitchen.

---

[1] *Midrash Shir-ha Shirim*, ed. Grünhut, III, 7, pp. 29a–30a; see also Grünbaum, *Neue Beiträge*, pp. 222–226.

One day Israel's dethroned King begged the cook to permit him to prepare the royal meal, for he was an expert cook himself. The cook granted his request, and Solomon prepared a sumptuous repast. When the dishes were placed upon the royal table and the ruler of Ammon had tasted the food which Solomon had cooked, the King was greatly surprised.

" Never," said he, " have I tasted such delicious food."

He summoned the head cook and asked him how it happened that the food he had tasted to-day was so excellent. The head cook confessed the truth, and related to the King his meeting with the ragged youth. Ammon's King thereupon summoned Solomon into his presence and appointed him head cook.

Now it happened one day that Naamah, the daughter of the King of Ammon, was looking out of a window of the royal palace and beheld Solomon. She fell violently in love with him and informed her mother that she desired to be wedded to her father's cook.

The astonished Queen waxed very wroth and exclaimed: " In thy father's kingdom there are many noble princes from among whom thou mayest choose a husband. How canst thou, a royal princess, so forget thyself as to think of a union with a mean cook, a menial in thy father's service?"

But the charming and headstrong Princess remained firm. " Him will I marry," she said, " and none other."

Thereupon the Queen informed her royal spouse of their daughter's strange infatuation. Ammon's King waxed very wroth and decided to put the lovers to death sooner than give his consent to such a dishonourable union between his daughter and a poor cook. The Lord, however, did not permit the destruction of Solomon and Princess Naamah, and He softened the heart of the King.

" I will not shed their blood," said Ammon's ruler, " but will cast them out and let them meet their doom." He accordingly summoned his servants and bade them take the Princess and her lover to the desert.

Now Solomon and Princess Naamah wandered for a long time in the desert until they reached a town on the seashore. Weary and exhausted, the exiled King was walking along the shore when he saw some fishermen offering for sale the fish they had caught. He bought one fish and brought it to Naamah to clean and prepare it for their evening meal. Great was the astonishment of the Princess when she opened the fish and found within a ring upon which was engraved the Ineffable Name. Naamah handed the ring to her lover, who immediately recognized it as his own signet-ring. He slipped it on his finger, and immediately he was a changed man, no longer a meek and humble tramp, but a King used to rule and command.

Accompanied by the Ammonite Princess, he wended his way to Jerusalem, where he defeated and set to flight Ashmedai, the usurper. He once more placed the royal crown upon his own head and seated himself upon the throne of his father David.

Thereupon Solomon sent word to the King of Ammon and invited him and his Queen to Jerusalem. When Ammon's ruler arrived, Solomon thus addressed him: " Why didst thou put to death two innocent people, the cook who served thee and thy own daughter?"

On hearing these words, the King of Ammon was greatly frightened. He swore that he had never killed the two but sent them away into the desert, and he did not know what had become of them.

" Wouldst thou recognize thy daughter's lover?" asked Solomon.

Ammon's King replied that he would. Solomon smiled and summoned the Princess, and the latter, arrayed in royal garments, soon appeared before her amazed parents.

" Know then," said Israel's King, " that I, Solomon, King of

Jerusalem, am the cook who once served thee, and the charming and faithful Naamah, thy daughter, is my lawful wife."

Naamah kissed the hands of her parents, who were over-joyed at her great fortune. Happy and content, they returned to their own country.[1]

In other sources the *dénouement* and the manner in which the exiled King regained his throne is related differently:

In the semblance of King Solomon, Ashmedai had sat on the throne for three years, and during this time he behaved rather strangely. He visited the ladies in the harem during the days of separation, as prescribed by the Law. One day, one of his wives rebuked him and said: " Solomon, why art thou behaving so strangely and so contrary to thy custom?" The demon kept silence, and the woman suddenly exclaimed: " Thou art not Solomon, but some demon in disguise."

Ashmedai thereupon went to Bath - Sheba, the Queen-mother, and made a certain request to her. Greatly surprised, the old Queen cried: " Is it possible that thou my son shouldst make such a request to thine own mother who bore thee? By my life, thou art not my son."

Thereupon Bath-Sheba sent for the chancellor Benaiah and related unto him what had occurred. Benaiah rent his clothes and tore his hair in sign of despair and said: " This cannot be Solomon, the son of David. He is surely Ashmedai in the semblance of the King. The youth who is wandering about in the streets of Jerusalem may be right when he pretends to be the King. He must indeed be the true Solomon."

Thereupon Benaiah sent for the youth who was wandering hither and thither and thus addressed him:

" My son, tell me in truth, who art thou?"

" I am Solomon, son of David and King of Israel," replied the youth.

[1] Jellinek, *Beth-Hamidrash*, II, pp. 86–87; *Emek-Hamelech*, ed. Amsterdam; Wünsche, *Aus Israel's Lehrhallen*, II, pp. 9–12; cf. Steinschneider, *Hebräische Bibliographie*, XIII, pp. 57–58.

" And how," Benaiah further questioned, " did it happen that thou didst lose thy throne?"

And the youth replied: " I will tell thee. One day when I was sitting on my throne there suddenly came a great gust of wind which seized me and hurled me away out of my palace. From that day I have been as one bereft of his senses and understanding, and I have been wandering about all over the country."

Then Benaiah, the son of Jehoiada, said: " Canst thou give me some proof that thou art really Solomon, the son of David?"

The exiled King replied: " This I can do. On the day of my coronation my father David placed one of my hands in thine and the other in that of the Prophet Nathan. Then my mother, who stood near, kissed my father's head."

On hearing these words, which Benaiah knew to be true, he immediately summoned the members of the Sanhedrin and instructed them to write the Ineffable Name of the Lord upon pieces of parchment and put it over their hearts.

" We are afraid of Ashmedai," said the members of the Sanhedrin, " because he is wearing over his heart the Name of the Most High."

" Should seventy fear one?" asked Benaiah. " Is not the grace of God with ye?"

Thereupon Benaiah, accompanied by the members of the Sanhedrin, appeared before Ashmedai, and dealt him a blow. He tore the signet-ring from his finger, and was about to kill him when a heavenly voice bade him to desist. " Kill him not," it cried, " for it was the Divine command he had obeyed. Solomon was punished because he had trodden under foot one of My Holy Commandments." Thereupon Benaiah handed his signet-ring to the dethroned monarch, who resumed his crown and was restored to his throne and kingdom.[1]

[1] Jellinek, *Beth-Hamidrash*, VI, pp. 106–107; see also Bin Gorion, *Der Born Judas*, Vol. III, p. 291, notes.

CHAPTER XIII

The Dethroned King in Mediæval Lore

Solomon in mediæval legend—The legend of Merlin—Rulers guilty of pride and arrogance—The magnificat of pride—The Emperor Jovinianus—The naked Emperor—The usurper—The distress of Jovinianus—The gatekeeper and the Emperor—The repentant ruler and the hermit—The tutelary angel—*Der hochfertig Keiser*—The *Dit du Magnificat*—*Robert Cycyl*—Der Stricker—Herrand de Wildonie—*Von dem nackten Kaiser*—Giovanni Sercambi—The *Gesta Romanorum* and the *Jerushalmi Talmud*—An Indian tale—King Vikramaditya—The magician Samadra-Pala—The art of divesting oneself of one's own body and entering another—The magician enters the vacated body of the King—King Mukunda of Lilavati and the hunchback—Demons and angels—The legend of Solomon of purely Jewish origin—Lesson in humility—Solomon and Nebuchadnezzar—The *Historia Scholastica*—The *Disciplina Clericalis*—The version of the Jerusalem *Talmud*—*Robert of Cisyle*—Longfellow's poem *King Robert of Sicily*.

We shall deal in a subsequent chapter with the Solomon legends in Mohammedan traditions and in mediæval and popular European lore. In all these traditions the name of Solomon has been retained, and all the legends cluster round the King of Israel, although he is often represented as a follower of the true faith or as a good Christian. There are, however, many mediæval legends where the name of Solomon has been entirely omitted, but which are nevertheless based upon a Solomon legend as it is related in Talmud and Midrash. With regard, for instance, to the tale of Merlin, Professor Vesselovsky already pointed out that " there can be no doubt that the whole legend of Merlin is based upon the apocryphal history of Solomon ". " The legend of Merlin," he goes on to say, " is more archaic than the German poem of Solomon and Morolf, and more nearly approaches the Talmudic-Slavonic legend.[1]

Vortigern, King of Britain, having determined to erect an impregnable castle, sent for artificers, carpenters, and stone-masons, and collected all the materials requisite to building. When the materials collected repeatedly vanished during the night, Vortigern inquired of his wise men and astronomers the cause of this. The wise men thereupon advised the King to find a child born without a father, put him to death, and sprinkle with his blood the ground on which the castle was to be built. Vortigern's messengers, searching throughout Britain for a child born without a father, found Merlin, whom they decided to bring alive to the King. On their way they passed a market town, the streets of which were crowded with merchants. Merlin suddenly burst out into a violent fit of laughter. On being questioned about the cause of his mirth, Merlin pointed out a young man who was bargaining for a pair of shoes. "See you not that young man," he said, that has shoon bought, and strong leather to mend them?" The young man, Merlin swore, would be dead before he entered his gate. And so it really happened.

" In Vortigern and Merlin," writes Gaster, " we have the counterpart of that famous Talmudical legend of Solomon and Ashmedai." [2]

We find many tales and legends in Eastern and Western literature where a ruler, guilty of some transgression and particularly of arrogance and pride, is dethroned and his place occupied either by an angel, a demon, or a sorcerer. These tales and legends have been rightly called the *magnificat of pride*, and appear in numerous mediæval and modern versions dating from the thirteenth century to modern times.

---

[1] See Vesselovsky, *Iz istorii literaturnavo obshtshenia vostoka i zapada*, St. Petersburg, 1872; see also Dunlop, *History of Prose Fiction*, Vol. I, pp. 458–459.

[2] M. Gaster, *Jewish Sources of and Parallels to the Early English Metrical Romances of King Arthur and Merlin*, in Papers read at the Anglo-Jewish Historical Exhibition, London, 1888, p. 247.

Let us briefly enumerate the legends which in one way or
another are known in mediæval and modern literature. The
most popular and probably most ancient version is that contained in the *Gesta Romanorum*. It is told of the Roman
Emperor Jovinianus.

One day, when the Emperor Jovinianus was reposing on
his couch, his heart was filled with pride, and he spoke in his
heart: " Is there another God besides me?" His blasphemy
soon met with the punishment it so well deserved. On the
following day he went out hunting, accompanied by his
warriors. The day being very hot, he made up his mind to
seek coolness in the waters of a river that was flowing past.
Scarcely had the Emperor undressed and entered the water,
when another man, closely resembling Jovinianus, appeared
and dressed himself in the garments Jovinianus had left on
the river bank. Thus arrayed, the usurper, accompanied by
the Imperial suite, returned to the palace. Jovinianus, not
finding his clothes, returned naked to the palace, knocked at
the gate, and demanded admittance, but no one recognized
him. When he informed the gatekeeper that he was the Emperor, the indignant servant insulted him, calling him a liar
and a deceiver. He had himself seen with his own eyes the
Emperor entering the palace. As the naked Emperor still
insisted, the gate-keeper led him before him whom he believed
to be the real Emperor. The usurper gave instructions to have
the imposter beaten and thrown out of the palace. In his distress Jovinianus addressed himself to the Duke, his former
trusted adviser, but the Duke, too, did not know him. Jovinianus was at last thrown into prison, where he was compelled
for some time to live on bread and water; he was then chastised
and ordered to leave the city.

Once more Jovinianus went to the palace and asked the
gate-keeper to inform the Empress of his distress. He asked
his wife to send him some clothes, for he was her true husband.

To prove his words, he reminded her of certain intimate occurrences which were known only to herself and her husband. On hearing these words, the Empress was greatly astonished, for how could the mad beggar know what had happened in her intimate conjugal life?

The pretender was once more brought into the presence of the new Emperor and the Empress. Scarcely, however, had Jovinianus entered the hall when a dog which had been very devoted to him caught him by the throat, whilst his favourite falcon hurriedly flew out of the room. The Empress and the entire court solemnly declared that they knew him not, had never set eyes on him, and that he was an impostor.

The new Emperor threatened Jovinianus with a shameful death should he ever dare again appear in his presence with his ridiculous claim. In his distress the dethroned ruler now remembered his confessor, a hermit who lived in the neighbourhood, and hoped that the latter would recognize him. When, however, he told the hermit that he was the real Emperor, the latter bade him go, accusing him of being the devil in person.

It was now that Jovinianus thought of his former arrogance, and, prostrating himself in humility, repented his sin and confessed all to the hermit. The hermit now recognized him as the real Emperor, gave him absolution, and provided him with garments. Once more Jovinianus returned to the Imperial palace, where the gate-keeper immediately saluted him as the Emperor. Brought into the palace, he was also recognized by the entire court and the Empress. The usurper now informed all present that the Emperor had been punished for his arrogance and presumption, and that he himself who, in Jovinianus' semblance, had assumed the crown was his tutelary angel who had come to teach the Emperor a lesson in humility.[1]

[1] *Gesta Romanorum*, ed. Oesterley, p. 722; ed. Graesse, p. 263; see also Graesse, *Literärgeschichte*, III, p. 964.

Numerous are the mediæval and modern productions based on this legend. Thus in 1549 Hans Sachs wrote a poem entitled *Der hochfertig Keiser*, and a comedy, *Julianus der Keyser*, in 1556. The trouvère Jehan de Condé, who lived in the fourteenth century, treated the subject in his *Dit du Magnificat*, and an unknown English poet, a contemporary of Jehan de Condé, wrote a poem on the subject, wherein King Robert of Sicily went to sleep after having declared the *magnificat* as stupid.[1] An English morality play, *Robert Cycyl*, was performed at Chester in 1529.[2] A French morality play, entitled *L'orgueil et présomption de l'empereur Jovinian*, appeared in 1581. During the first half of the thirteenth century a poet known as *der Stricker* wrote a poem entitled *Der König im Bade*, whilst another poet living during the second half of the same century, Herrand von Wildonie, dealt with the subject in a poem entitled *Von dem nackten Kaiser*.[3] All these European stories of the proud and arrogant King have forgotten the name of Solomon, substituting another personality for him, such as Jovinian, Robert, Gorneus, or Nimrod. Giovanni Sercambi, who lived in the second half of the fourteenth century and in the first half of the fifteenth, deals with the subject in one of his legends, where the name of the punished King is Anibretto of Navarre.[4]

Another similar story in Oriental lore is related in *Thousand and One Nights* (17th night), and also in the *Forty Viziers* of the Sheikh Shehabeddin. It runs as follows:

An Egyptian Sultan refused to believe that in the course of a few seconds the Prophet had been able to visit the seven heavens, the hells and Paradise, and to have exchanged with Allah ninety thousand words. He could not admit that all this had taken place in such a short span of time so that when

---

[1] Horstmann, *Sammlung Altenglischer Legenden*, 1878, p. 209; see also Ellis, *Specimens*, ed. Halliwell, p. 474.
[2] Collier, *The History of English Dramatic Poetry*, II, pp. 128, 415.
[3] Von der Hagen, *Gerammtabenteuer*, III, p. cxv.
[4] D'Ancona, *Novelle di Giovanni Sercambi*, Bologna, 1871, p. 235.

the Prophet returned to the bed he had so hastily left, he found it still warm and that the water had not entirely run out of a jug he had overturned in his hurry. In vain did the wise men at his court try to convince the Sultan of the truth of the assertions in the Koran.

Now one day there appeared in the palace the famous Sheikh Shehabeddin, who had heard of the Sultan's unbelief. After giving the Sultan some proof of his wonder-working powers, he gave instructions for a tub full of water to be brought in, and then invited the Prince to undress, enter the bath, and then submerge his head under the water. The Sultan, curious to see the results, obeyed. Scarcely, however, had he submerged his head under the water when he found himself at the seashore, at the foot of a barren and lonely mountain. A few woodcutters whom he met provided him with some clothes and directed him to the nearest town.

Here fortune favoured him, for he met and married a beautiful and wealthy woman, with whom he lived seven years and who bore him several children. When the wife's money was all exhausted, the Sultan was compelled to earn his living, and he became a carrier. One day he came to the seashore, and as he had to perform some ablutions, he undressed and entered the water and submerged his head. When he raised it up again, he was in his own palace, seated in the bath he had entered seven years ago.

When he beheld the Sheikh and his courtiers all standing round, he waxed wroth, but the Sheikh thus addressed him:

"Why art thou so angry, O Sultan? Thou hast submerged thy head only once and immediately raised it up again; if thou dost not believe my words, ask thy servants." The latter all said: "It is true," but the Sultan exclaimed:

"What do ye know? I tell ye that I have been away from throne and crown, wandering as a stranger over the world, for seven years!" Then the Sheikh said: "Why shouldst thou

be angry with me on this account, O Sultan? Look, I, too, will
enter the bath and submerge my head under the water."
Saying this, the Sheikh entered the bath. The Sultan then
beckoned to his executioner and commanded him to cut off
the Sheikh's head the moment he raised it again to the surface.
But when the Sheikh had submerged his head he at once
became invisible and found himself at Damascus. From that
city he sent a letter to the Sultan in which he wrote: " You
and I, O Sultan, are God's, the exalted One's, creatures;
He, who had created the whole world in one moment in which
He said, " Let it be," showed thee in one brief moment
seven years. He has also shown to His beloved Prophet 18,000
worlds in such a short span of time that when the latter returned to the earth he found his bed still warm. And because
thou didst refuse to believe this I performed the deed on
thee." [1]

In *Old Deccan Days*, or *Hindoo Fairy Legends*, collected
by M. Frere, a similar story is told under the title of *The
Wanderings of Vicram Maharajah.*

Vicram learned wisdom from the Hindu God of Wisdom,
Gunputti, but it happened that near the palace there lived the
son of a carpenter who was very cunning. When he heard that
the Rajah went to the temple to learn wisdom, he determined
to go and see if he could not learn it also. Each day, when
Gunputti gave Vicram Maharajah instructions, the carpenter's
son would hide close behind the temple and overhear all
their conversation; so that he also became very wise.

One day Gunputti said to the Rajah: " Vicram, what gift
dost thou choose?" And Vicram replied: " Most wise, give
me the power to leave my own body when I will, and translate
my soul, and sense, and thinking powers, into any other body
that I may choose, either of man, or bird, or beast—whether
for a day, or a year, or for twelve years, or as long as I like."

---

[1] Behrnauer, *Die Vierzig Viziere*, Leipzig, 1851, p. 16 ff; see also *Germania*, II, pp. 432–434.

His request was granted, and he was instructed by what means he should translate his soul into another body, and he also received something which, being placed within his own body when he left it, would preserve it from decay until his return. The carpenter's son, who had been listening outside the temple, heard and learnt the spell whereby Gunputti gave Vicram Maharajah power to enter into another body; but he could not see nor find out what was given to the Rajah to place within his own body when he left it, to preserve it; so that he was master only of half the secret.

Vicram transported himself into the body of a parrot and flew to the Pomegranate country, and brought the little Queen Anar Ranee whom he married. He thereupon decided once more to make use of the gift bestowed upon him, and to fly all over the world in the shape of a parrot. Scarcely, however, had he left his own body when the carpenter's son entered it, giving himself out to be the Rajah. The secret was discovered by the Rajah's vizier, Butti, and he so contrived it that the pretender's life was made rather miserable. He would gladly have returned to his own body, but alas! having no power to preserve it, his spirit had no sooner left it than it began to decay, and at the end of three days it was quite destroyed; so that the unhappy man had no alternative but to remain where he was. After many vicissitudes Vicram returned into his own body, the pretender having escaped it to enter that of a ram which Butti, however, soon killed.[1]

In the *Peregrinaggio de tre figliuoli del Re di Serendippo*, as well as in the French imitation *Les Soirées Bretonnes*, there is told the story of an eastern King who possessed the power of animating a dead body by flinging his own soul into it, but having incautiously shot himself into the carcass of a fawn, which he had killed while hunting, his favourite vizier, to whom he had confided the secret whereby the transmigration was

[1] Mary Frere, *Old Deccan Days*, pp. 103–106.

accomplished, occupied the royal corpse, which had been thus left vacant, and returned to the palace, where he personated the master. At last the King had an opportunity of passing into the remains of a parrot, in which shape he allowed himself to be taken captive and presented to the Queen. The vizier afterwards, in order to gratify Her Majesty by a display of his mysterious science, animated the carcass of a favourite bird which had died. Thereupon the King seized the opportunity of re-entering his own body, which the vizier had now abandoned, and instantly he twisted off the neck of his treacherous minister.[1]

The legend of the punishment meted out to the proud and arrogant King forms also the subject of Longfellow's famous poem, *King Robert of Sicily*, and of a Danish poem, *Den forvandlede Konge* (The changed King).[2]

Now the legends told respectively in the *Gesta Romanorum* and in the above-mentioned mediæval poems are based upon the tale of Solomon as told in the Talmudic and particularly upon the version given in the *Jerushalmi Talmud*. It has been pointed out that the Jews themselves have been influenced by the literature of India. " Legends told of Vikramaditya," wrote Benfey, " have been applied to Solomon. This legend, with insignificant alterations, was taken over by the Mohammedans, who brought it to Europe, where it gave rise to the legend told of Emperor Jovinianus, or of King Robert of Sicily. It is changed in a Christian sense, and the usurper is not a demon but an angel, the tutelary angel of the ruler."[3] This theory of Benfey has been adopted by Varnhagen.[4] According to this author, India was the cradle of all the imaginative tales, of myths and legends which delighted the mediæval ages and have been handed down to modern times. The legend of Solomon which has been applied to other

[1] See Dunlop, *loc. cit.*, Vol. II, p. 504; *The Spectator*, No. 578; L'Oiseleur Deslongchamps, *Essai sur les Fables Indiennes*, p. 175, note 5.
[2] Varnhagen, *Ein Indisches Märchen*, Berlin, 1882, p. 73; see also Vesselovsky, *loc. cit.*, p. 558.   [3] *Panschatantra*, I, pp. 129–130.   [4] *loc. cit.*

personalities is traced back to an Indian *Märchen*. It is told of King Vikramaditya.

This sovereign had ruled for a long time over his people, but with advanced age had grown feeble and impotent. The magician Samadra-Pala, who knew the art how to divest himself of his own body and to enter another, taught his Sovereign this art, and one day he thus spoke to him: " I will teach thee the art how to divest thyself of thy own body, and then thou canst choose another, more vigorous body of a young man as thy abode." The King listened to the advice of the magician, and when he had been instructed by the latter in the wonderful art, he divested himself of his own feeble body, and his soul entered that of a young man who had recently died. Immediately the soul of the magician entered the vacated body of the King, killed the deceived ruler, and ascended the throne.

According to another version, the magician did not put to death his royal master, and the latter, after many sufferings, regained his throne and crown. It is told of King Mukunda, who lived in the city of Lilavati, into whose vacated body the soul of a hunchback clown enters.[1]

According to these theories, the story of the King who had lost his throne originated in India, whence by way of Persia it travelled to the Jews, who turned it into a legend told of their wise King Solomon. The legend was then taken over by the Arabs, who combined it with another version. From the Arabs the legend migrated to Byzantium, whence it was brought to the West. The hero is alternatively Vikramaditya, Nanda, Mukunda, Solomon, Nebuchadnezzar, the Roman Emperors Jovinianus, Julianus or Gorneus, Anibretto, King of Navarre, or Robert, King of Sicily, whilst the usurper is either a magician, the demon Ashmedai, Sakhr among the Arabs, or an angel.[2]

[1] Benfey, *loc. cit.*, pp. 125–127.
[2] Cf. M. Landau, *Die Quellen des Dekameron*, 1884, p. 72; Von der Hagen, *loc. cit.*, cxv–cxx; Jellinek, *Beth-Hamidrash*, VI, p. xxvi; cf. Grünbaum, *ZDMG*, Vol. XXXI, pp. 214–224.

Now there is not the slightest doubt that Egyptian, Persian, Babylonian, and Indian civilizations have left their traces upon Judaism, and that Jewish myths and legends are subject to foreign influences. To maintain, however, with Benfey, that India is the sole cradle of all Jewish and mediæval legends appears to us to be an exaggeration. Such may be the case with many Midrashic and Haggadic tales and legends, but the legend of Solomon, dethroned and exiled, wandering as a tramp and a beggar all over the cities and villages of Palestine, is of purely Jewish origin. It must be borne in mind that the entire legend not only clusters round a Biblical personage, Israel's great King, but is based upon a passage in *Ecclesiastes*, i, 12: " I, Koheleth, the Son of David, *was* King of Israel in Jerusalem ". The Rabbis were struck by the verb used in the past tense. If Solomon said that he *was* King of Israel, then he evidently had lost the throne, and yet no mention of this fact is made in the *Book of Kings*. The Rabbis therefore imagined that Solomon had been dethroned and that someone who had taken his semblance was reigning in his stead. The incident of Solomon's sin, of his arrogance and presumption, and the subsequent punishment meted out to him as a lesson in humility and as explained in the Haggada, is also based upon the Biblical text. This legend of Solomon's exile and sufferings also explains his fear and terror during the later part of his life.

Paulus Cassel, in his essay entitled *Schamir*, derives the story in the *Gesta Romanorum* from Jewish sources. " Holy Scripture," writes Cassel, " relates of the errors into which Solomon had fallen, and Jewish legendary lore explains the discrepancies and contradictions by the story of Ashmedai who had deprived Solomon of his signet-ring and taken his semblance. This legend has roots in the old Iranian tale of Jemshid who, like Solomon, after reigning wisely for a long time, had grown arrogant and deviated from the right

path. It has analogies with the legend told about Emperor
Jovinianus." [1]

It must also be pointed out that there is a difference between the Jewish and the subsequent Christian legends and
the Indian tale. Both Solomon and the Christian arrogant
King remain in their own bodies, whilst Ashmedai, or the
angel, assume their semblance and take their places. In
the Indian tale the King's soul wanders into another body,
whilst his own vacated body is occupied by the soul of his
rival. [2]

In the majority of Haggadic legends imagination certainly
plays a part, but this imagination is based upon a Biblical text,
inspired by some etymological derivation, and usually follows
some Biblical narrative. Now a Biblical narrative resembling
to some extent the legend of Solomon's exile is found in the
story of Nebuchadnezzar [3] who, on account of his arrogance,
was deprived of his throne. There is no reason whatever, in
our opinion, to maintain that the entire legend was borrowed
from India. [4]

On the other hand, it seems to us that although the Arabs
borrowed the legend of Solomon's exile from the Jews and
transmitted it to the Byzantines, it is not the latter but the Jews
themselves who brought it to the West. Peter Comestor's
work *Historia Scholastica* is full of passages borrowed from
Midrash and Talmud; Petrus Alphonsus, author of *Disciplina
Clericalis*, and John of Capua, two converted Jews, acquainted
mediæval Europe with the legendary lore of the East, and
Eisenmenger and Raymondus Martinus have collected a great
number of texts from Jewish legendary lore. There is therefore but little doubt that many other works compiled either
by such converted Jews or by priests who had a close acquain-

---

[1] P. Cassel, *Schamir*, p. 53.
[2] Koehler, in *Archiv für Litteraturgeschichte*, Vol. XI, p. 582; A. D'Ancona, *loc. cit.*,
p. 293 and *Sacre Rappresentazioni*, Firenze, 1872, III, 175; see also *Lemke's Jahrbuch*,
XII, 407.   [3] *Daniel*, vi, 22–36.
[4] See also Israel Lévi in *Revue des Études Juives*, Vol. XVII, pp. 58–65.

tance with learned Jews must have existed during the early Middle Ages.[1]

Indeed the legends related in the *Gesta Romanorum* and in the other European works mentioned above closely resemble not the Arab version of the story but that given in the Talmud of Jerusalem, where it is not a demon but an angel who takes the place of Solomon, an angel sent from heaven to punish the King for his pride and arrogance and to teach him a lesson in humility.

The version of the Jerusalem Talmud runs as follows: Solomon boasted of having trodden under foot the three commandments given to the King.

Thereupon the Lord said unto him: " What is the crown which thou art wearing doing upon thy head? Get thee down from my throne." Then an *angel* came down from heaven and casting Solomon from his throne seated himself upon it. As for the King, he wandered from town to town, and at the doors of the synagogues and schools called aloud: " I, Koheleth, was King over Israel in Jerusalem." Then the people mocked him and said: " The King is seated upon his throne, and thou sayest that thou art Koheleth, the son of David." And they beat him and gave him a dish of ground beans to eat.[2]

Rightly writes Professor Vesselovsky: " I do not see why Benfey thought it necessary to assume that the Arabic version must have served as the intermediary between the original Talmudical legend and its European imitations. There is no need for such an assumption, and in the case of the Slavonic version it is right down impossible." [3] The European legends of the proud King have forgotten the name of Solomon, substituting for it those of Jovinian, Robert, Gorneus, Nimrod, or Anibretto, the punishment of the Emperor is everywhere

---

[1] See also Israel Lévi in *Revue des Études Juives*, Vol. XVII, p. 65.

[2] *Leviticus Rabba*, XIX; *Shir ha-Shirim Rabba*, V, 9; *Eccles Rabba*, II, 2; *Pesikta de Rab Kahana*, pp. 168b–169a; *Midrash Tanchuma*, ed. Buber, III, p. 28.

[3] *Archiv für Slavische Philologie*, Vol. VI, p. 556.

considered as a trial, *but* the demon is changed into an angel.
Now this coincides with the version given in the Talmud of
Jerusalem, where it is an angel and not a demon who takes the
place of the King.[1]

ROBERD OF CISYLE

Princes proude þat beþ in pres,
I wil ȝou telle þing nobles.
In Cisyle was a noble kyng,
Fair and strong and sumdel ȝyng.
He hadde a broþer in grete Rome,   5
Pope of all Cristendome;
Anoþer broþer in Almayne,
Emperour, þat Sarzins wrouȝte payne,
Þe kyng was hote Kyng Roberd;
Neuer man wiste him ferd;   10
He was kyng of gret honour,
For þat he was Conquerour;
In all þe worlde nas his per,
Kyng ne prince, fer no ner.
And for he was of chiualrye flour,   15
His broþer was mad Emperour,
His oþer broþer Godes vikere,
Pope of Rome, as I seide ere.
Þe pope was hote Pope Vrban:
He was good to God and man;   20
Þe emperour was hote Valemounde:
A strengur werreour was non founde
After his broþer of Cisyle,
Of whom þat I schal telle a while.
Þe kyng þouȝte he hadde no per   25
In all þe worlde, fer no ner;
And in his þouȝt he hadde pride,
For he was nounper in ech a side.

[1] See also Vogt, *Die deutschen Dichtungen von Salomon und Markolf*, Halle, 1880, p. 213;
Revue des Études Juives, Vol. VIII, p. 204.

At midsomer, a seynt Jones niȝt
Þe kyng to cherche com ful riȝt,   30
Forto heren his euensong.
Him þouȝte he dwelled þer ful long:
He þouȝte more in worldes honour
Þan on Crist, oure saueour.
In Magnificat he herde a vers: 35
He made a clerk hit him rehers
In langage of his owne tonge—
In latyn he niste what þei songe.
Þe vers was þis, I tele þe:
Deposuit potentes de sede   40
Et exaltauit humiles—
Þis was þe vers, wiþouten les.
Þe clerk seide anon riȝt:
" Sire, such is Godes miȝt
Þat he may make heyȝe lowe,   45
And lowe heyȝe, in litel þrowe.
God may do, wiþoute lyȝe,
His wille in twynkling of an eiȝe.'
Þe kyng seide wiþ herte vnstable:
" Al ȝoure song is fals and fable.   50
What man haþ such pouwer
Me to bringe lowe in daunger?
I am flour of chiualrye,
Min enemys I may distrye,
Noman liueþ in no londe   55
Þat me may wiþstonde:
Þan is þis a song of nouȝt."
Þis errour he hadde in þouȝt.
And in his þouȝt a slep him tok
In his pulpit, as seiþ þe bok   60
Whan þat euensong was al don,
A kyng ylich him out gan gon,
And alle men wiþ him gan wende—
Kyng Roberd lefte out of mynde.
Þe newe kyng was, I ȝou telle,   65
Godes angel, his pride to felle.

Þe angel in halle joye made,
And alle men of him were glade.
Þe kyng waked, þat lay in cherche:
His men he þouȝte wo to werche   70
For he was left þer alon
And derk niȝt him fel vppon.

．　　　．　　　．　　　．　　　．

Þe angel seide to kyng Roberd: 141
" Þou art a fol, þat art nouȝt ferd
Mi men to do such vileynye;
Þi gult þou most nede abye.
What art þou?" seide þe angel.   145
Quaþ Roberd: " Þou schalt wite wel:
I am kyng, and kyng wil be;
Wiþ wronge þou hast mi dignite.
Þe pope of Rome is mi broþer,
And þe emperour min oþer;   150
Þei wil me wreke, for soþ to telle,
I wot þei nille nouȝt longe dwelle."
" Þou art mi fol," seide þe angel,
" Þou schalt be schore euerichdel
Lich a fol, a fol to be—   155
Wher is now þi dignite?
Þi counseyler schal ben an ape,
And o cloþyng ȝou worþ yschape:
I schal him cloþen as þi broþer
Of o cloþyng—hit nis non oþer;   160
He schal be þin owne fere—
Sum wit of him þou miȝt lere.
Houndes, how so hit falle,
Schulen ete wiþ þe in halle;
Þou schalt eten on þe ground,   165
Þin assayour schal ben an hound
To assaye þi mete bifore þe.
Wher is now þi dignite?"

．　　　．　　　．　　　．　　　．

" I am an angel of renoun,   405
Sent to kepe þi regioun.

More joye me schal falle
In heuene among mi feren alle
In an oure of a day,
Þan in erþe, I þe say,   410
In an hundred þousend ȝer,
Þeiȝ al þe world fer and ner
Were min at mi likyng.
I am an angel, þou art kyng."
He went in twynklyng of an eȝe.
No more of him þer nas seȝe.

C. HORSTMANN, *Sammlung Altenglischer Legenden*,
1878, pp. 209–219 (*Roberd of Cisyle*).

THE SICILIAN'S TALE

KING ROBERT OF SICILY

Robert of Sicily, brother of Pope Urbane
And Valmond, Emperor of Allemaine,
Apparelled in magnificent attire,
With retinue of many a knight and squire,
On St. John's even, at vespers, proudly sat
And heard the priests chant the Magnificat
And as he listened, o'er and o'er again
Repeated, like a burden or refrain,
He caught the words, " Deposuit potentes
De sede, et exaltavit humiles;"
And slowly lifting up his kingly head
He to a learned clerk beside him said,
" What mean these words?"   The clerk made answer meet,
" He has put down the mighty from their seat
And has exalted them of low degree."
Thereat King Robert muttered scornfully,
" 'T is well that such seditious words are sung
Only by priests and in the Latin tongue;
For unto priests and people be it known,
There is no power can push me from my throne!"
And leaning back, he yawned and fell asleep,
Lulled by the chant monotonous and deep.

When he awoke, it was already night;
The church was empty, and there was no light,
Save where the lamps, that glimmered few and faint,
Lighted a little space before some saint.
He started from his seat and gazed around,
But saw no living thing and heard no sound.
He groped towards the door, but it was locked;
He cried aloud, and listened, and then knocked;
And uttered awful threatenings and complaints,
And imprecations upon men and saints.
The sounds reëchoed from the roof and walls
As if dead priests were laughing in their stalls.
At length the sexton, hearing from without
The tumult of the knocking and the shout,
And thinking thieves were in the house of prayer,
Came with his lantern, asking " Who is there?"
Half choked with rage, King Robert fiercely said,
" Open: 't is I, the King!   Art thou afraid?"
The frightened sexton, muttering, with a curse,
" This is some drunken vagabond, or worse!"
Turned the great key and flung the portal wide;
A man rushed by him at a single stride,
Haggard, half naked, without hat or cloak,
Who neither turned, nor looked at him, nor spoke,
But leaped into the blackness of the night,
And vanished like a spectre from his sight.
Robert of Sicily, brother of Pope Urbane
And Valmond, Emperor of Allemaine,
Despoiled of his magnificent attire,
Bareheaded, breathless, and besprent with mire,
With sense of wrong and outrage desperate,
Strode on and thundered at the palace gate;
Rushed through the courtyard, thrusting in his rage
To right and left each seneschal and page,
And hurried up the broad and sounding stair,
His white face ghastly in the torches' glare.
From hall to hall he passed with breathless speed;
Voices and cries he heard, but did not heed,

Until at last he reached the banquet-room,
Blazing with light, and breathing with perfume.

There on the dais sat another king,
Wearing his robes, his crown, his signet-ring,
King Robert's self in features, form, and height,
But all transfigured with angelic light!
It was an Angel; and his presence there
With a divine effulgence filled the air,
An exaltation, piercing the disguise,
Though none the hidden Angel recognize.

A moment speechless, motionless, amazed,
The throneless monarch on the Angel gazed,
Who met his look of anger and surprise
With the divine compassion of his eyes;
Then said, " Who art thou? and why com'st thou here?"
To which King Robert answered with a sneer,
" I am the King, and come to claim my own
From an impostor, who usurps my throne!"
And suddenly, at these audacious words,
Up sprang the angry guests, and drew their swords;
The Angel answered, with unruffled brow,
" Nay, not the King, but the King's Jester, thou
Henceforth shalt wear the bells and scalloped cape,
And for thy counsellor shalt lead an ape;
Thou shalt obey my servants when they call,
And wait upon my henchmen in the hall!"

Deaf to King Robert's threats and cries and prayers,
They thrust him from the hall and down the stairs;
A group of tittering pages ran before,
And as they opened wide the folding-door,
His heart failed, for he heard, with strange alarms,
The boisterous laughter of the men-at-arms,
And all the vaulted chamber roar and ring
With the mock plaudits of " Long live the King!"

Next morning, waking with the day's first beam,
He said within himself, " It was a dream!"
But the straw rustled as he turned his head,
There were the cap and bells beside his bed,
Around him rose the bare, discoloured walls,
Close by, the steeds were champing in their stalls,
And in the corner, a revolting shape,
Shivering and chattering sat the wretched ape.
It was no dream, the world he loved so much
Had turned to dust and ashes at his touch!

Days came and went; and now returned again
To Sicily the old Saturnian reign;
Under the Angel's governance benign
The happy island danced with corn and wine,
And deep within the mountain's burning breast
Enceladus, the giant, was at rest.

Meanwhile King Robert yielded to his fate,
Sullen and silent and disconsolate.
Dressed in the motley garb that Jesters wear,
With look bewildered and a vacant stare,
Close shaven above the ears, as monks are shorn,
By courtiers mocked, by pages laughed to scorn,
His only friend the ape, his only food
What others left,—he still was unsubdued.
And when the Angel met him on his way,
And half in earnest, half in jest, would say,
Sternly, though tenderly, that he might feel
The velvet scabbard held a sword of steel,
" Art thou the King?" the passion of his woe
Burst from him in resistless overflow,
And lifting high his forehead, he would fling
The haughty answer back " I am, I am the King!"

Almost three years were ended; when there came
Ambassadors of great repute and name
From Valmond, Emperor of Allemaine,

Unto King Robert, saying that Pope Urbane
By letter summoned them forthwith to come
On Holy Thursday to his city of Rome.
The Angel with great joy received his guests,
And gave them presents of embroidered vests,
And velvet mantles with rich ermine lined,
And rings and jewels of the rarest kind.
Then he departed with them o'er the sea
Into the lovely land of Italy,
Whose loveliness was more resplendent made
By the mere passing of that cavalcade,
With plumes, and cloaks, and housings, and the stir
Of jewelled bridle and of golden spur.
And lo! among the menials, in mock state,
Upon a piebald steed, with shambling gait,
His cloak of fox-tails flapping in the wind,
The solemn ape demurely perched behind,
King Robert rode, making huge merriment
In all the country towns through which they went.

The Pope received them with great pomp and blare
Of bannered trumpets, on Saint Peter's square,
Giving his benediction and embrace,
Fervent, and full of apostolic grace.
While with congratulations and with prayers
He entertained the Angel unawares,
Robert, the Jester, bursting through the crowd,
Into the presence rushed, and cried aloud,
" I am the King! Look, and behold in me
Robert, your brother, King of Sicily!
This man who wears my semblance to your eyes,
Is an impostor in a king's disguise.
Do you not know me? does no voice within
Answer my cry, and say we are akin?"
The Pope in silence, but with troubled mien,
Gazed at the Angel's countenance serene;
The Emperor, laughing, said, " It is strange sport
To keep a madman for thy Fool at court!"

And the poor, baffled Jester in disgrace
Was hustled back among the populace.

In solemn state the Holy Week went by,
And Easter Sunday gleamed upon the sky;
The presence of the Angel, with its light,
Before the sun rose, made the city bright,
And with new fervor filled the hearts of men,
Who felt that Christ indeed had risen again.
Even the Jester, on his bed of straw,
With haggard eyes the unwonted splendor saw,
He felt within a power unfelt before,
And, kneeling humbly on his chamber floor,
He heard the rushing garments of the Lord
Sweep through the silent air, ascending heavenward.

And now the visit ending, and once more
Valmond returning to the Danube's shore,
Homeward the Angel journeyed, and again
The land was made resplendent with his train,
Flashing along the towns of Italy
Unto Salerno, and from thence by sea.
And when once more within Palermo's wall,
And, seated on the throne in his great hall,
He heard the Angelus from convent towers,
As if the better world conversed with ours,
He beckoned to King Robert to draw nigher,
And with a gesture bade the rest retire;
And when they were alone, the Angel said,
" Art thou the King?"   Then, bowing down his head,
King Robert crossed both hands upon his breast,
And meekly answered him: " Thou knowest best!
My sins as scarlet are; let me go hence,
And in some cloister's school of penitence,
Across those stones, that pave the way to heaven
Walk barefoot, till my guilty soul be shriven!"
The Angel smiled, and from his radiant face
A holy light illumined all the place,

And through the open window, loud and clear,
They heard the monks chant in the chapel near,
Above the stir and tumult of the street:
" He has put down the mighty from their seat,
And has exalted them of low degree!"
And through the chant a second melody
Rose like the throbbing of a single string:
" I am an Angel, and thou art the King!"

King Robert, who was standing near the throne,
Lifted his eyes, and lo! he was alone!
But all apparelled as in days of old,
With ermined mantle and with cloth of gold;
And when his courtiers came, they found him there
Kneeling upon the floor, absorbed in silent prayer.

LONGFELLOW, *King Robert of Sicily*.[1]

[1] There is no need to assume that Longfellow borrowed the contents of his poem from
Leigh Hunt's story told in " A Jar of Honey from Mount Hybla " (*Ainsworth's Magazine*,
1844). If he was unacquainted with the Hebrew and Oriental sources, then he must have
probably availed himself of the Anglo-Saxon poem.

CHAPTER XIV

Solomon and Marcolf, or Salman and Morolf

It does not enter within the scope of this work to relate all the legends clustering round Solomon found in European lore, but it will be interesting to deal here with the famous dialogues of Solomon and Marcolf.

" There are two dialogues," writes Stopford A. Brooke, " between Solomon and Saturn with which we may close the poetry of the ninth century. The oldest is the second in the MS. Saturn had wandered through all the East, and Solomon asks him about ' the land where none may walk '. Saturn

answers. Then Solomon answers and Saturn begins his
questions. Their wits are set over one against the other.
Solomon stands as the representative of Christian wisdom,
Saturn of the heathen wisdom of the East. The other poem,
although it begins the MS., is the later of the two. Saturn
asks Solomon to explain to him the power of the Paternoster.
The answer takes up the whole poem, and in the course of
it many interesting examples of folk-lore and superstitions
occur.[1] Now these Solomon dialogues have become common
in Western literature under the title of Dialogues of Solomon
and Marcolf. Marcolf does not play the grave part of Saturn,
the Eastern sage, but that of the peasant or mechanic full of
uneducated mother-wit and rough humour. It suited the
mediæval temper, a little in rebellion against the predominance
of Church, noble and King."[2] The contents of the Dialogues
of Solomon and Marcolf are briefly as follows:

SOLOMON AND MOROLF

Sitting in all his glory upon the throne of his father David,
Solomon one day saw a misshapen, coarse, and clownish man
come into his presence, accompanied by a foul sluttish woman,
his wife, in every way answering to himself. This was Morolf.
When he mentioned his name, he was immediately recognized
by the King as a person quite famous for his shrewdness and
wit. Solomon now challenged him to a trial of wisdom, promising him great rewards, should he prove victorious. Solomon
begins the contest, uttering at first some moral common-
places or reciting some of his own Biblical proverbs. These
are immediately paralleled or contradicted by Morolf, who
ridicules the King's sayings in the very coarsest terms.
Moreover, Morolf always draws his illustrations from the most
common events of homely life, expressing himself in popular

---

[1] Stopford A. Brooke, *English Literature from the Beginning to the Norman Conquest,*
1898, pp. 210–211.   [2] *Ibid.,* p. 210, note 1.

proverbs. Solomon is at last exhausted and wishes to discontinue the contest, but Morolf is ready to go on. He calls on the King to declare himself beaten and give him the promised rewards. Solomon, refusing to listen to his councillors who urge him to drive Morolf out of court, keeps his promises and dismisses Morolf with many gifts. Morolf leaves the court, uttering the words: " Where there is no law, there is no King."

One day, whilst out hunting, Solomon suddenly comes upon Morolf's hut. He calls upon him and receives a number of enigmatic answers which foil him completely. The King, unable to find the solution of the riddles, is compelled to have recourse to Morolf. He leaves his hut, but desires him to come to court the next day and to bring with him a pail of fresh milk and curds from the cow. Morolf does this on the next day, but on the road he grows hungry, eats the curds, and covers up the milk with cow-dung. When he appears before Solomon, the latter, not seeing the curds, asks him what he had done with them. Morolf answers that he had eaten them, but that the dung he had used to cover up the milk was also curd from the cow. Now Solomon condemns Morolf to sit up all night in his company, and should he fall asleep he would be put to death in the morning. Morolf submits, sits down, and begins to snore aloud. Solomon asks him whether he is asleep, to which Morolf replies that he is *thinking*.

" And what art thou thinking about?" asks Solomon.

" I am thinking," replied Morolf, " that there are as many vertebræ in a hare's tail as there are in his backbone."

The King imagines that Morolf will not be able to prove his assertion, and quickly says:

" If thou canst not prove this thou shalt die in the morning."

Morolf now again begins to snore and is frequently awakened by Solomon. He informs the King every time that he is thinking. He asserts that there are as many white as black feathers in a magpie, that milk is not whiter than daylight, that nothing can be entrusted to a woman, and that nature is stronger than education. All these assertions he is to prove in the morning, otherwise he is to die.

Solomon now becomes sleepy and Morolf leaves him. He runs to his sister Fudasa, and under the seal of secrecy informs her that he had been so badly treated by the King that he had made up his mind to kill him. Taking up a knife, he hides it ostentatiously in his bosom. Fudasa swears to her brother to respect his secret, and Morolf returns to the King and is present at the latter's waking. Then a magpie and a hare are brought, and Morolf proves that he was right. In the meantime he placed a pan of milk in a dark closet and suddenly called the King to him. Solomon, on entering the closet, stepped into the milk, splashed his clothes, and nearly fell on his face. He turns to Morolf in a rage and asks him what he meant by it.

" Merely to show to your Majesty," calmly replies Morolf, " that milk is not whiter than daylight."

Now Solomon sits down on his throne and Morolf cites his sister Fudasa before him, accusing her of various crimes. The astonished woman immediately reveals the secret her brother had entrusted to her, that he intended to murder the King. Morolf thus proves to the much amused King that a woman could not keep a secret.

The King now commands Morolf to prove his last assertion, that nature is stronger than education, and the latter promises to do this at supper-time.

Now it happened that Solomon had a cat which had been trained to sit upon the table and to hold up in its paws a lighted candle whilst the King was having his supper. When all were seated at supper and the cat had taken up her post, Morolf suddenly threw a mouse at her feet. The cat did not budge,

THE CAT AND THE CANDLE

but when a second mouse was thrown the candle began to tremble in the cat's paws, and when at last a third mouse was let loose the cat could no longer resist, threw down the lighted candle, and gave chase to the mouse.[1]

Instead of rewarding Morolf, the King, however, commands him to be thrown out of the palace and that the dogs be set on him should he ever dare to return. The next day Morolf provided himself with a live hare, threw it to the dogs, and appeared in the presence of the King. Solomon does not punish him, but merely warns him not to commit any impropriety in the hall of audience and not to spit, except on some bare spot. Unfortunately the only bare spot in the audience hall is the bald head of one of the nobles. In the meantime the two women arrive and the famous judgment is given. Morolf is all the while sneering, and he frequently abuses womankind in general. An altercation between the King and Morolf follows, and the latter remarks to the King: "You praise women now, but I assure you that I shall live to hear you abuse them with all your heart."

The King now orders him out of the palace, and Morolf immediately sets out to find the two harlots, whom he informs that the King had decreed that every man shall have seven wives. Such an arrangement, Morolf endeavoured to prove to the women, would only result in great mischief. The news spread all over the city, and soon the women of Jerusalem congregated under the windows of the palace, vociferated against the royal decree, and abused the King in no measured terms. The King, who was quite unaware of the cause of this feminine outburst, tried to pacify the assailing women, but was received with a tempest of abuse. He now lost patience and burst out into a most furious diatribe against women. Morolf, who was standing by, was delighted and sneeringly approached

---

[1] Cf. for a similar incident in a story by Marie de France; C. A. Robert, *Fables Inédites*, I, 155; cf. also R. Koehler, *Kleinere Schriften*, II, p. 640, where other passages are quoted.

to thank the King, who had taken such trouble to prove the truth of his assertions. Solomon now becomes aware of the trick played upon him, pacifies the infuriated ladies, and orders Morolf to be turned out. " Never," added the King, " let me see thy ugly face again."

Some time afterwards, on a snowy night, Morolf made an extraordinary track, and in the morning managed to allure the King and his courtiers to follow him into the forest. The King is thus led to a hollow tree wherein Morolf had so placed himself that the King is unable to look him in the face. Solomon now gives orders to have Morolf hanged, but the latter implores the King to allow him at least to choose his own tree. The request is granted, and Morolf, accompanied by his guards, sets out to find a tree to his own liking. He is naturally in no hurry, and leads the guards backwards and forwards all over Palestine. In the end the guards are so wearied out that they let him go, dismissing him with his life, upon his promising never to show his face at the court.[1]

This wit combat or Dialogue of Solomon and Morolf is preceded by another poem wherein the story of Solomon and his wife Salomé is related.

Solomon's wife has bestowed her love on a heathen with whom she corresponds. She is anxious to be united to him, and for that purpose feigns to be sick. The heathen King, whom she has managed to inform of her design, sends two minstrels to her who are also well versed in the art of magic. They pretend to be hailing from Greece and to be able to cure sick folk with their songs and music. They are admitted to the presence of the Queen. They place an herb under her tongue which has the power to throw her into a death-like sleep, although her colour never changes.

[1] Kemble, *The Dialogues of Solomon and Saturn*, pp. 25–30; Von der Hagen, *Deutsche Gedichte des Mittelalters*, Berlin, 1808, Vol. I (Salman and Morolf), pp. 44–64; see also Dr. P. Piper, *Die Spielmannsdichtung* (in J. Kürschner's *Deutsche Nationallitteratur*, II, 1, pp. 206–209).

When the news of the Queen's death becomes known, no one will believe that she is really dead since her mouth is still so red. Morolf or Marcolf should advise in the matter, but he is nowhere to be found, since he is in hiding. He is at last brought to court by a ruse. When he hears what has happened, he immediately suspects foul play and is quite convinced that the Queen is not really dead. He tries to make the Queen show some sign of life by pouring molten lead into the palm of her hand. All in vain, the beautiful Salomé remains to all appearance dead, and all are convinced of her death except Morolf. In the third night the minstrels manage to carry off the dead Queen to their master, the heathen King.

The King now entreats Morolf in strict confidence to advise him, and Morolf declares himself ready to set forth to find the Queen. He traverses many lands until he at last learns the whereabouts of the Queen. He immediately returns and informs Solomon of the place where his wife is living. Accompanied by an armed force, Solomon and Morolf go to the castle where the Queen is dwelling. Whilst Morolf and the armed force remain hidden in the adjoining wood, Solomon, disguised as a pilgrim, goes alone to the castle, where he begs for food. His companions, it is arranged, are only to come to his rescue when they hear him blow his horn. Now when the faithless wife sees Solomon she immediately recognizes him, in spite of his disguise, and informs the heathen of his presence. The heathen is overjoyed when he hears the news that Solomon is now in his tower. " Now," said the heathen, " what should be my death, were I in thy hands?"

Solomon sighs and replies: " I wish to God it were so, for I would take thee to the nearest wood and there let thee choose a tree and hang thee on it."

" Then such shall also be thy death," replies the heathen.

Accompanied by his entire suite, he took Solomon to the nearest wood and bade him choose his tree. Solomon, remind-

ing the heathen that he is of kingly strain, asks as a special
boon to be allowed to blow his horn three times before he dies.
In spite of the objections of the Queen, who fears some ruse
on the part of Morolf, the heathen grants Solomon's request.
The latter blows his horn, and immediately Morolf arrives
with Solomon's men. The heathen King is strung up, his
men are all slain, and the Queen is taken back to the land of
the Jews, where, at Morolf's advice, she is put to death by
opening her veins in a bath.[1]

A longer version of this legend, where Morolf is Solomon's
brother, runs as follows:

Solomon, King of Jerusalem and Emperor of all Christendom, has abducted Salomé, the beautiful daughter of Cyprian,
King of India, and compelled her to embrace Christianity.
Beyond the seas, on the shores of the Mediterranean, there
ruled a mighty heathen King named Fore, or Faro, the son of
Memerolt. One day, when he asked his heroes to find him a
wife, the latter called his attention to the beautiful Salomé,
wife of Solomon, of whose beauty they had heard. Faro decides to do battle for her and to take her by force from her
husband. Faro lands with 40 ships and an army of 15,000
heroes before Jerusalem, and a fierce battle is waged. Faro
and his whole host are defeated, and the King is made prisoner.
Morolf advises Solomon to put the heathen King to death,
but the King of Jerusalem spares his enemy's life and com-
mits him to the keeping of the Empress. In vain does Morolf
warn Solomon, pointing out to him that it is dangerous to
put temptation in the Empress's way and to give her an opportunity of thus becoming familiar with the heathen King.
Solomon ignores the arguments of Morolf, having implicit
faith in Salomé. Soon, however, he has cause to regret his
rash conduct.

[1] Von der Hagen, *loc. cit.*, pp. 62–64, verses 1605–1875; Vogt, *Salman und Morolf*, pp.
lxi–lxii; Piper, *loc. cit.*, pp. 209–210; F. J. Child, *The English and Scottish Ballads*, Vol. IX,
pp. 3–5.

Thereupon Faro received a magical ring from his nephew, the sorcerer Elias, and of which he made a present to the Empress. Scarcely had the latter put the ring on her finger than she fell violently in love with the heathen King. The lady helped the prisoner to escape, and even promised him to leave her husband and rejoin him. When half a year had elapsed, Faro sent Salomé, through a heathen minstrel, a magical root which she placed under her tongue. Immediately she fell down dead, although her beautiful colour remained unchanged. Morolf pretended that the Queen was still alive, and endeavoured to bring her back to life by pouring molten gold into her hands. To all appearance, however, the Empress remained dead, and Morolf was only rebuked by his brother Solomon.

The Empress was laid in a golden coffin and buried, but within a few hours the minstrel carried her off to his master Faro. Morolf now decides to seek the Empress. He kills an old Jew named Berman, takes off his skin, which he puts on, and thus disguised begs money from the King, to whom he afterwards reveals his true identity. Solomon now consents to his going out in search of Salomé, and Morolf, after seven years' wandering, discovers the whereabouts of the faithless Empress and enters her palace. He is immediately recognized by Salomé and condemned to death. After having intoxicated the guards and clipped their hair, he manages to escape to Jerusalem under water by means of a long leather tube which made it possible for him to breathe from the surface.

Solomon now arms a large host and, accompanied by Morolf, sets out to recover his wife. Whilst Morolf and Solomon's men are hiding in a wood near by, Solomon, disguised as a pilgrim, enters Fore's city. He is brought before the Empress, who immediately recognizes him. In vain does Solomon now try to recall his wife to her duty. She informs him, however, that she loved Fore and would stick to him.

Solomon is put in a side room where he can hear how tenderly Fore, who had in the meantime returned, is embraced by Salomé.

When the two sit down to their meal, Salomé informs Fore of the arrival of the handsome pilgrim, and that Solomon, King of Jerusalem, was now in his power. Solomon, led into the presence of Fore, is asked by the latter what he would do with *him* were he in Jerusalem, to which he replied that he would keep him a prisoner till the morning and then hang him. Fore declares that such shall be Solomon's own doom.

Solomon, however, has found a friend in Fore's beautiful sister, who had been smitten with a violent love for the pilgrim. She now intercedes on Solomon's behalf, and ultimately persuades Fore to commit the prisoner to her custody till the morning. She takes him into a sumptuous room, relieves him of his chains, and sets food and drink before him. Solomon listens to the lays of a famous minstrel, and himself, forgetting all care and the doom awaiting him, plays the harp, to the delight of the beautiful heathen maid. The latter urges him to escape, but he loyally refuses to do so, assuring her that his angels in the wood would save him in the morning. In the morning Solomon is led to the place of execution, and under the gallows he asks as a last favour to be allowed to blow his horn thrice. He alleges that he wishes to do this so as to give notice to St. Michael and the angels to come and take his soul in charge. Salomé objects, but Fore gives his permission to Solomon's request. Morolf had in the meantime divided his army into three divisions, a black, a white, and a pale. When Solomon sounds his horn, Morolf and his army burst from their ambush and slay the heathen host. Faro is hanged upon the gallows which had been erected for Solomon. The latter, accompanied by Salomé and the beautiful sister of Faro, now returns to Jerusalem, where Morolf persuades the heathen maid to become a Christian, promising her that should Salomé die, Solomon would take her to wife.

Seven years again elapse, and once more the Empress runs away. This time it is Prince Princian of Ackers, another heathen King who had heard of Salomé's beauty, who makes up his mind to capture her. He sends the Empress a magical ring, and the lady falls in love with him and once more elopes with the heathen Prince. Once more Morolf is asked to go out in search of the Empress. He promises to do so, but not until Solomon has given him his promise that should he recover the flighty Empress he could deal with her at his pleasure. Morolf discovers the whereabouts of the Empress, but when he returns Solomon is not anxious to expose his own life. Morolf, therefore, accompanied by a great host, sets out himself and invades King Princian's land. With the help of a mermaid and dwarfs, he slays the King and carries the Empress back to Jerusalem, where, however, he puts her to death in a bath. Solomon then marries the beautiful heathen maid, the sister of Fore, who had been baptized and who reigned as Empress in Jerusalem for thirty years.[1]

An imitation of the Morolf legend is told in Little Russian literature.

The tsar Solomon took to wife the daughter of a heathen tsar; she hated him, and refused to go to Church. At last she concerted an elopement with a heathen tsarevitch, and pretended to be dead. Solomon burned her hands through and through with a red-hot iron. The lady, however, uttered no sound, and was consequently buried in the evening. She was immediately disinterred and carried off by her lover. Now Solomon went to the house of the tsarevitch attended by three armies, a black, a white, and a red, but which were lying in ambush in a neighbouring wood. The tsarevitch recognizes

---

[1] Vogt., *loc. cit.*, pp. xxi–xxxiii; Vincenti, *Die altenglischen Dialoge von Salomon und Marcolf*, pp. 18–19; Kemble, *loc. cit.*, pp. 17–20; Child, *loc. cit.*, p. 4; (cf. *The Scottish Ballad John Thomson and the Turk, ibid.*, Vol. IX, p. 9).

Solomon and has a gallows set up, but Solomon craves the permission to play on his three pipes before dying. The request is granted, and the sound of the first pipe brings out the red army, that of the second the white, and that of the third the black. The tsarevitch is hanged, whilst the tsaritsa is dragged at a horse's tail.[1]

From the East the legend of Solomon wandered to the West. According to Vogt, the oldest version is the Greeko-Byzantine, which developed directly from the Oriental sources and gave rise to the Russian versions.[2]

The tale of the capture of Solomon's wife and the revenge taken by him is related as follows in the *bylini*, or ballads:

A certain Emperor Vassilj Okulyeviez is feasting with his nobles. When he is of good cheer, he asks his heroes to find him a wife who shall be a match to him in stature, beauty, and wit. One of the company, a certain Ivashka, undertakes to get for his master the wife of Solomon, the beautiful Salamaniya. He manages it by making use of a ruse. In a fine ship full of beautiful things Ivashka and his company set out and sail to Jerusalem. Solomon is just away from his capital, and the wily Ivashka, after having presented the Empress with costly gifts, manages to entice her on board the ship, where she is promised even finer things. Here she is made drunk and falls asleep. The ship immediately sails away, carrying the lady off to the Emperor Vassilj, with whom she lives for three years. Solomon, attended by a large army of winged horsemen, sets out to retrieve his wife, hides his men in a grove, whilst he presents himself, disguised as a pilgrim, at the palace of the Emperor. He is recognized by his wife, who shuts him up in an iron cage.

When the Emperor returns to the palace from hunting, the

[1] Dragomanov, *Popular Traditions and Tales*, 1876, p. 103; *Revue des Traditions Populaires*, Vol. II, pp. 518–520.

[2] Vogt, *loc. cit.*; Vincenti, *loc. cit.*, p. 13; see also Vesselovsky in *Archiv für Slavische Philologie*, Vol. VI, pp. 405–410, and 554 ff; Dunlop, *loc. cit.*, p. 637; Varnhagen, *loc. cit.*, p. 48; Gaster, *Literatura populara Romana*, 1883, p. 332.

lady informs him of what had occurred and advises him to
put Solomon to death. The execution is decided upon, and, at
his own request, Solomon is to be hanged instead of beheaded.
Under the gallows he begs permission to be allowed to blow
his horn. In spite of the objection of the Empress, his request
is granted. At the first sound of Solomon's horn all the animals
and birds gather round him, and Solomon explains that they
have come to be present at his execution. At the second sound
of his horn all the trees in the forest tremble, and the roar of
all the seas is heard. At the third sound Solomon's winged
horsemen appear. Ivashka, who had carried off the wife of
Solomon, the Emperor Vassilj, and Salamaniya are all hanged
in the three nooses which, at Solomon's request, had been
provided.[1]

In addition to the popular ballads or *bylini*, there are also
Russian prose versions of the same legend. Here the wife of
Solomon is stolen from him not by the Emperor Vassilj but
by Solomon's own brother Kitovras, who, during the day,
ruled over men, and during the night, changed into an animal,
ruled over the animal world. Kitovras sends to his brother a
magician disguised as a merchant, who offers for sale to the
King a magnificent purple robe. Solomon buys the robe and
invites the merchant magician to his table. After enveloping
the King and his people in darkness, the magician brings a
heavy sleep upon the Queen, and thus carries her off to his
master Kitovras.

When Solomon learns that his wife is in the possession of
his brother King Kitovras, he sets out with an army in order
to retrieve his wife. He instructs his men to come forward
when they hear him sound his horn thrice. As an old beggar,
he proceeds to his brother's castle and enters the garden. Here
he meets a girl who is going to draw water with a golden cup,
and asks her to allow him to drink from this cup. The girl at

[1] Vogt, *loc. cit.*, pp. xlii–xliii; Vincenti, *loc. cit.*, p. 14; Child, *loc. cit.*, p. 2.

first refuses, but in the end grants his request, induced by the gift of a golden ring. When the Queen notices the ring on the girl's finger, she asks who gave it to her.

" An old pilgrim, or beggar," replies the girl.

" No," retorts the Queen, " it is not an old pilgrim, but my husband Solomon."

She now gives instructions to have Solomon brought into her presence, and asks him what he had come for.

" I have come to put you to death," says Solomon, to which the Queen rejoins: " It is you who will die, you will be hanged." She sends for Kitovras, who pronounces Solomon's doom.

" You will neither see your wife back in your house nor go away alive from here," says Kitovras. Solomon now begs his brother to allow him at least to die in regal style. Kitovras, the Queen, and the whole court, with all the people in the city, should attend the execution, ample food and drink should be provided, and under the gallows there should be a feast. His request is granted. He furthermore begged that three nooses should be provided, one of bast, another of red silk, and a third of yellow. This request was also granted.

Under the gallows Solomon once more reminds Kitovras of their brotherhood, and implores him to grant him, as his brother, the permission to blow his horn. The whim is complied with, and upon the third blast Solomon's army appears. Kitovras, the Queen, and the magician are all hanged, the first two in the red and yellow silken nooses and the magician in the bast.[1]

---

[1] Vogt, *loc. cit.*, pp. xliii–xliv; Jagic, *Archiv für Slavische Philologie*, Vol. I, p. 110 ff; Vesselovsky, *ibid.*; Vincenti, *loc. cit.*, pp. 14–15; Child, *loc. cit.*, pp. 2–3.

CHAPTER XV

David in Mohammedan Tradition

David's melodious voice—The chapel in the mountain—The birds and beasts come to listen to the King's voice—The merits of David and Abraham—David's request—God grants his prayer—The beautiful bird—David is fascinated—The secluded lake—The beautiful woman—Saya, daughter of Josu—David falls in love—The angels in disguise—David's punishment—His tears and repentance—The reed of iron and the little bell—The pearl in the stick—The silent bell—The reed and bell are taken away from David—David's companion in Paradise—The King wanders over Palestine—The old man carrying a bundle of faggots—The cave in the mountains—The hermit reciting his prayers—Mata, the God-fearing stranger—The wet patch on the summit of the mountain peak—David's surprise—The mysterious stranger—Mata's prayer—David and the angel of death—The death of David and the angel Gabriel.

David was not only a great warrior and a wise ruler, but also a great Prophet. God revealed unto him seventy psalms, and endowed him with a voice such as had never been vouchsafed to any mortal man. No other human voice had ever equalled his in power and sweetness. His voice was as loud as the deafening peal of thunder or the roaring of the lion, and as sweet as the warble of the nightingale. There was no musician or singer in Israel like David. Every third day he sang in a chapel hewn in a mountain, and when he sang not only men gathered to hear him, but also birds and beasts came from a distance to listen to his wonderful song.

He divided his time into three parts, devoting one part of it to affairs of State, one to the service of God, and the third to his wives, of whom he had ninety-nine, besides his concubines. One day, as David was returning home from prayer, he heard two of his subjects discussing his merits and comparing him with Abraham.

" Was Abraham or David the greater Prophet?" the men
were asking.

" Was not Abraham," said the first man, " saved from the
fiery furnace?"

" Didst not David," asked the other, " slay the giant
Goliath?"

" But what has David done," retorted the first speaker,
" that can be compared with the obedience of Abraham when
he was ready to offer his only son as a sacrifice?"

When David reached home he fell on his face before God,
and thus he prayed: " Lord, Thou who didst put to the test
in the pyre the faithfulness and obedience of Abraham, grant
me, too, an opportunity wherein I may be able to prove to my
people that my love for Thee can resist temptation."

God granted David's prayer. When on the third day David
was singing psalms before the congregation, he suddenly beheld
a bird that was so beautiful that it attracted all his attention.
David was greatly perturbed, and the sight of the beautiful
bird fascinated him in a strange manner. He followed its
movements and sang less psalms on that day than usual.
He could scarcely sing when the bird disappeared from his
view, and his voice became very soft and melodious whenever
the beautiful bird once more came in sight.

To the great surprise of the congregation the King concluded the recitation of his psalms earlier than usual, and
immediately went out alone in pursuit of the beautiful bird.
From bush to bush and from tree to tree did the beautiful
bird fly, leading the King onwards until towards sunset it
brought him to the bank of a secluded lake. Here the bird
vanished in the water, and David soon forgot it, for in its place
there emerged out of the water a beautiful woman who dazzled
the King like the midday sun. Anxious not to startle the bath-
ing woman, David hid behind the bushes and waited until
she was dressed, then he approached and asked her name.

" My name," replied the woman, " is Saya, the daughter of Josu, and I am the wife of Uriah Ibn Hanan, who is with the army." David went home, but his passion was so violently inflamed that he immediately sent instructions to the captain of his hosts to set Uriah in the most dangerous place in battle. The King's command was obeyed, and soon Uriah was killed in battle. Thereupon the King married the widow.

On the day after his marriage the angels Michael and Gabriel appeared in human form before David at his court, and Gabriel thus said to the King: " The man thou seest here possesses ninety-nine sheep, whilst I have only one, and yet he is pursuing me constantly and claiming my ewe lamb."

" This is unfair, and shows an evil and unbelieving heart and a bad nature," replied David.

" There are plenty of noble and learned believers," Gabriel interrupted the King, " who permit themselves worse things."

David now understood that the man was alluding to his own conduct with regard to Uriah, and his wrath was kindled. Seizing his sword, he wanted to pierce Gabriel, when Michael suddenly burst out into loud laughter. Both angels, now rising up on their wings, exclaimed:

" Thou hast given judgment against thyself, and hast declared thine own action to be that of a wicked unbeliever. Therefore God has decided that the power He had intended to give thee will only be granted to one of thy sons. Thy sin is the more heinous because thou thyself didst ask God to put thy piety to the test and to give thee a trial, but when the opportunity was afforded thee thou wast too weak to resist temptation." Thus spoke the angels and vanished, and David felt now the greatness of his sin. He tore his golden crown from his head and his royal purple robe from his body, and clad in rough woollen clothes went out into the desert, where he shed tears and repented of his sin. Thus he wandered about in the desert for three years, and the angels in heaven had pity on the repentant King and prayed to God to forgive him. After three years David heard a heavenly voice which informed him that the all-merciful God had opened unto him the Gates of Grace.

David was now consoled and returned home, where he soon regained his physical strength.[1]

According to other sources, David only wept and repented for forty days and forty nights, praying to the Lord for forgiveness. He shed more tears during these forty days and nights than all the men in the world have ever shed. He had written the history of his sin upon the palm of his hand, and whenever he looked at it his hand trembled. For shame David never dared lift his eyes to heaven, until, after the expiration of forty days, God bade him lift up his head, for his sin had been forgiven.

Thereupon David said: " O Lord, Thou art a just judge; when on the day of Resurrection Uriah, blood soiled, will appear before Thy Throne and say: ' Lord, ask this man why he did slay me,' what wilt Thou reply?"

And God answered: " I will ask him to forgive thee, and as his reward I will give a great inheritance in Paradise." Thereupon David said: " Now I know that I am pardoned." [2]

Although David was now again being loved and honoured by his people, he never dared, remembering the incident with the two angels, to give sentence in cases brought before him. He had already appointed a judge to give sentence in his place, when one day the angel Gabriel brought him a reed of iron and a little bell, and thus said unto him: " God has seen thy humility and is pleased with it, and He therefore sends thee this reed of iron and this little bell, which will enable thee to give judgment and to uphold right and justice in Israel. Place this reed in thy judgment hall and hang up the bell in

---

[1] Weil, *Biblische Legenden der Muselmänner*, pp. 208–212.
[2] Grünbaum, *Neue Breitäge zur semitischen Sagenkunde*, p. 197.

the middle. When a case is brought before thee, place the accuser on one side and the accused on the other, and always give sentence in favour of him who will cause the bell to tinkle when he touches the reed."

Thus spoke Gabriel, and David was greatly pleased with the gift which enabled him to give righteous judgment. Henceforth men feared to commit evil or do wrong, because they were certain to be discovered by the tinkling of the bell.

Now one day two men came before David, and one accused the other that he had left in the charge of his friend a costly pearl, but when he claimed it back the accused denied it to him. The latter swore that he had indeed returned the pearl. David, as usual, bade the men each to lay his hand on the reed, but the bell remained silent in both cases, so that David knew not which of the two had spoken the truth, and he began to doubt the power of the reed. He bade the men try again, but the result was the same. When he had made them try several times, he noticed that whenever the defendant went up to the reed to lay his hand on it he gave his stick to the plaintiff to hold. David's suspicion was aroused, and he made the men try again, but when the defendant went up to the reed to lay his hand on it David took the stick himself, and lo! when the accuser touched the reed the bell began to tinkle. David now examined the stick and found that it was hollow and the pearl was concealed in it, so that the accused had really spoken the truth when, after giving his stick to the plaintiff to hold, he maintained that he had returned the pearl to him. But because David had doubted the power of the heavenly gift, God was displeased with him, and the reed and bell were taken from him and returned to heaven whence they had come. After that David often erred in his judgment until his son Solomon, whom Saya had borne unto him, gave him the benefit of his wise counsel.[1]

[1] Weil, *loc. cit.*, pp. 213-215.

David and Mata

When the time of his death was approaching, David prayed to the Lord to let him see the man who was destined to be his companion in Paradise. His prayer was granted, and a voice fell from heaven and bade him give up his royal power and go forth as a poor pilgrim and wander about until he found the man who was to be his friend and comrade in the abode of the Blessed.

David immediately appointed Solomon as Regent to rule in his absence, whilst he himself, arrayed in pilgrim's garb and staff in hand, went forth in search of the man who was to be his companion in Paradise. From city to city and from village to village did the King of Israel wander, and everywhere he inquired after the pious and God-fearing men and made their acquaintance. For weeks, however, he had already wandered all over Palestine without finding a man whom he could deem worthy of being his companion in Paradise.

One day he reached a village on the shores of the Mediterranean Sea and met a man who was walking alongside of him. Poorly dressed, the old man was carrying on his head a very heavy load consisting of a bundle of faggots. The man was very old, and looked so reverend that David was interested and followed him to see where he lived. The old man walked on, but never entered any house in the village. He sold his bundle of faggots, and then gave away half the amount of the money he had received to a poor person who begged him for alms. Thereupon he bought bread for his money and retired from the town, wending his way to the mountains whence he had come. David followed him. He saw the old man break his bread in half and give a big portion to a blind woman whom he met on the way. " This man," thought David, " is worthy to be my companion and comrade in Paradise, for he is old and reverend and his actions prove him to be very pious and charitable. I must try and become more closely acquainted with him."

At some distance, therefore, David followed the old man, who was walking for several hours until he reached a cave among the rocky mountains which was lighted by a rent above. David remained at the entrance of the cave and heard the old man recite his prayers, then read the Thora and the Psalms till the sun had set. He then lighted a lamp and recited his evening prayers, and then only he drew forth his piece of bread and ate about half of it. David, who had not ventured to interrupt the old man in his devotions, now approached, entered the cave, and saluted the hermit.

"Who art thou?" asked the pious hermit, after returning the salute of David. "I have seen no human being in these mountains except the God-fearing Mata Ibn Juhana, who is destined to be King David's companion in Paradise."

David now revealed his identity to the hermit, and asked him to give him information where he could find this Mata. But the hermit replied: "I am not permitted to tell thee where he dwells, but if thou wilt go over these mountains, search very carefully and observe everything well, thou canst not miss the place where thou wilt meet Mata."

David continued his search, and wandered about for a long time without, however, noticing any trace of a human foot. He was just abandoning hope, and had made up his mind to return to the hermit and ask him for more precise information, when suddenly on the summit of a rugged mountain peak he noticed a spot that was wet and soft. David was surprised.

"It is rather strange," thought he, "that just on the summit of this rugged mountain peak the ground should be so soft and sloppy; it is impossible that there should be a spring here."

And whilst he was thus musing and wondering at this

strange patch of soft ground, an old man came up from the other side of the mountain. He resembled an angel rather than a mortal man, and his eyes were depressed to the earth, so that he did not notice the presence of David. He stood still on the wet patch and began to pray with such fervour that the tears flowed from his eyes like two rivulets. David now understood why the ground on the topmost peak of the rocky mountain was so wet and sloppy, and he thought in his heart: " A man who can pray to the Lord with such fervour, shedding tears in such abundance, well deserves to be my companion and comrade in Paradise."

He did not venture, however, to interrupt the pious and God-fearing Mata until he heard him pray as follows: " O my God! Forgive King David his sins and let him not be led into temptation and save him from further trespass; be merciful to him for my sake, since Thou hast destined me to be his comrade in the life to come!"

David now ran towards the old man, but when he reached him Mata was dead. David dug into the soft ground with his staff, washed the body, and laid it in the grave, reciting the funeral prayer. He then covered the grave and returned to his capital. In his harem he found the angel of Death awaiting for him. The latter greeted the King with the following words:

" The Lord has granted thy request, but now thy life has reached its end."

" The Lord's will be done," said David, fell to the ground, and expired.

Thereupon the angel Gabriel came down to console Solomon, and brought him a heavenly shroud wherein to wrap his father. All Israel followed the bier of David to the entrance of the cave of Machpelah, where lies buried the Patriarch Abraham.[1]

[1] *Ibid.,* pp. 220–224.

CHAPTER XVI

Solomon in Mohammedan Legend

SOLOMON'S SIGNET-RING

When he had shown to his father David the last offices,
Solomon, having sat down to rest in a valley between Hebron
and Jerusalem, fell asleep. Awaking from his sleep, he suddenly
beheld eight angels standing before him. Each had countless

wings of various shapes and colours and bowed three times before the King.

"Who are ye?" queried Solomon, his eyes still half closed.

"We are the angels appointed to rule over the light winds, and the Lord, our and thy creator, has sent us to pay homage unto thee and to give thee the dominion and power over us and over the winds which are subject to our command. Henceforth, at thy command, the winds will be either stormy or mild, blowing from the side to which thou wilt turn thy back. At thy command, too, the winds will rise up and bear thee above the highest mountains."

Thus spoke the angels, and the greatest of them gave Solomon a jewel inscribed with the words, "To God belong power and greatness". "Whenever thou hast a command for us," said the angel, "then raise this stone towards heaven, and at once we shall appear before thee as thy servants." Thus spoke the greatest angel, and they all departed.

Thereupon four other angels appeared, each greatly differing from the others. One had the shape of an immense whale, the second that of an eagle, the third was like a lion, and the fourth like a serpent. They bowed before Solomon and said: "We rule over all the living creatures that move on the earth and in the water, and have come at the command of God to pay homage unto thee and to give thee dominion over us. Command us according to thy wish, and we will grant unto thee and thy friends all the good which the Lord has placed in our power, and will use all the evil against thine enemies."

Thereupon the angel who ruled over the winged fowls handed to Solomon a precious stone inscribed with the words, "All creatures praise the Lord". "Raise this stone," they said, "above thy head, and by virtue of it thou canst call us at any moment to thy assistance and give us thy commands."

Solomon immediately decided to test the power of the stone and ordered the angels to bring him a pair of every living creature that moved and lived in the water, upon earth, or in the air. The angels vanished, and in an instant there were assembled before Solomon all sorts of creatures, from the elephant to the smallest worm, and also all sorts of fishes and birds. Solomon conversed with them and was instructed in all their different habits. He also listened to their complaints and rectified many abuses and evil customs amongst the beasts, birds, and fishes. It was, however, with the birds that he entertained himself longest, both on account of their beautiful and melodious speech, which he understood as well as the language of man, and the sentences full of wisdom which they uttered.

Translated into the speech of man, the cry of the peacock signified: " As thou judgest others, so shalt thou thyself be judged." The song of the nightingale, expressed in human speech, signified: " Contentment is the greatest happiness." The call of the turtle-dove meant: " It were better for some created things that they had never been created." The piping of the peewit signified: " He who hath no mercy will never find mercy himself," whilst the bird *syrdar* called: " Return to the Lord, ye sinners." The swallow said: " Do good, and one day ye shall receive your reward." The pelican said: " Praised be the Lord in heaven and upon earth." The dove said: " Everything in the world passeth away, God alone remaineth eternal," whilst the *kata* uttered: " He who is silent will certainly pass through." The eagle's cry signified: " May our life be ever so long, it inevitably ends in death." The raven croaked: " The farther I am from man, the better I feel." The cock crowed: " Remember the Creator, ye thoughtless men."

Solomon then chose the cock and peewit to be his constant companions, the first on account of the wise sentence it uttered, the second because it is able to see through earth as through a crystal, and therefore could indicate to him on his travels the place where a fountain of water was to be found, so that he would never lack water either to drink or for his ritual ablutions. He thereupon stroked the dove and bade it dwell in the Temple which he was about to build. In a few years this pair of doves, on account of the touch of Solomon, multiplied to such an extent that all those who came to visit the Temple moved from the farthest part of the town under the shadow of the wings of the doves.

When Solomon was again alone, there appeared an angel whose upper half was like earth, whilst his lower half was like water. Bowing very low before Solomon, he said: " I was created by God to do His will both on dry land and in the water. He has now sent me to do thy bidding, and through me thou canst rule over earth and water. The highest mountains will disappear at thy command, and others will rise up on level land. At thy command, rivers and seas will dry up, whilst fertile dry land will be changed into sea and ocean." Thereupon the angel gave unto Solomon a precious stone inscribed with the following words: " Heaven and earth serve God ".

Finally another angel brought the King a fourth precious stone inscribed with the words: " There is no God save the one God, and Mohammed is His messenger ". " By virtue of this stone," said the angel, " thou shalt have dominion and rule over the whole world of spirits, which is much greater and vaster than the world of men and beasts, for it occupies the entire space between earth and heaven. A portion of these spirits," continued the angel, " is faithful, worshipping the one and only God, whilst another portion is unfaithful. Some of the last adore fire, others worship the sun, the stars, the planets, or water. The first, who are the good spirits, always hover round the true believers, protecting them from evil and also from sin, whilst the evil spirits are always trying to injure and plague men, or to lead them into temptation.

Being invisible, and able to assume any shape they like, they often succeed in their endeavour."

Solomon now asked to be allowed to see the Jinns in their original and natural shape, and his request was granted. Like a column of flame the angel immediately shot up into heaven, and an instant later he returned accompanied by a host of Satans and Jinns. In spite of the power and dominion he had over them, Solomon shuddered when he beheld their horrible appearance. Never had he imagined that such loathsome beings existed in the world. He saw human heads attached to the necks of horses whose feet were those of an ass; he saw the wings of eagles attached to the humps of dromedaries, and the horns of gazelles upon the heads of peacocks. He asked the angel to explain the cause of such a strange mixture, to which the latter replied that it was the result of a sinful and shameless life.[1]

The Building of the Temple

When Solomon returned home, he gave instructions to have the four stones the angels had made him a gift of set in a signet-ring, so that he might at any moment make use of his power and dominion over the beasts and spirits, the earth and the wind. His first care was to subject the Jinns. He summoned them all in his presence, with the exception of the mighty Sakhr, who had concealed himself upon an unknown island in the ocean, and of Eblis, the master of all the evil spirits, to whom God had given complete independence and liberty until the day of the last Judgment. When all the Jinns had assembled before him, Solomon at once pressed his seal upon their necks, thus marking them as his slaves. Thereupon he commanded the male Jinns to construct many buildings, and especially the great temple similar to that of Mecca, but much greater. The female Jinns Solomon bade cook, bake, wash,

[1] Weil, *Biblische Legenden der Muselmänner*, pp. 225-231.

weave, carry water, and do all sorts of work. All that they produced he distributed among the poor. All the food they cooked
was placed on tables which covered an area of one square mile.
Thirty thousand oxen, and so many sheep, besides many birds
and fishes, were devoured daily. The Jinns and Satans sat at
iron tables, the poor at tables of wood, the heads of the people
and the commanders of the army at silver tables, whilst the
learned, the wise, and the pious sat at tables of gold. Solomon
himself in person served the latter.[1]

When Solomon returned to Jerusalem, he heard a mighty
noise of the hammers and other instruments of the Jinns who
were constructing the Temple. The noise they made was so
great that the inhabitants of Jerusalem could not hear one
another speak. Solomon therefore commanded the Jinns to
cease their work, and asked them whether any one of them
knew of a means whereby the various metals could be cut
without making such a tremendous noise. Thereupon one of
the Jinns stepped forth and said that the means was known
only to the mighty Sakhr, who had hitherto escaped the King's
authority.

" And could not this Sakhr be captured?" asked Solomon.

" Sakhr," replied the Jinn, " is mightier and stronger than
all the Jinns together, and he is superior to all of us both in
strength and in speed. I know, however, that once a month
he goes to the land of Hidjir, there to slake his thirst at a
fountain. Thou mayest thus, O wise King, subdue him and
bring him under thy sceptre."

Solomon immediately commanded a number of swift Jinns
to fly to the land of Hidjir, to empty the fountain, and to fill
it with strong wine. Some of the Jinns he bade remain in
ambush by the side of the fountain and see what would happen.
The Jinns accordingly emptied the source of water, filled it
with wine, and hid themselves nearby behind trees. Soon

[1] Weil, *loc. cit.*, pp. 231–232.

Sakhr appeared, and smelling the wine, exclaimed: " O wine, thou art delicious, but thou dost deprive one of intelligence, makest stupid the wise, and causest regret." He left the source without having drunk out of it. On the third day, being tormented by thirst, he returned. " I cannot escape," he exclaimed, " the fate which God has decided to bring upon me." Thereupon he drank his fill, made a few steps, but fell down. From all sides the Jinns and Ifrits now appeared, hurried to the spot where Sakhr lay intoxicated, and put him in chains, whilst flames were issuing forth from his mouth and nostrils.[1] One day, when Solomon was standing on the terrace of his palace, he saw a Jinn flying swifter than the wind from the direction of Hidjir. " Great King," he said, " Sakhr lies drunk by the side of the fountain, securely bound with chains as thick as the pillars of the Temple, but when he will have slept off the wine he will snap them as if they were the hair of a maiden."

Solomon at once mounted the winged Jinn and in less than an hour was transported to the land of Hidjir. He was just in time, for Sakhr was already opening his eyes and awakening from his drunken sleep. Solomon had just time to press the signet-ring upon the demon's neck. Sakhr uttered such a cry that the whole earth rocked and trembled.

" Be without fear, mighty Jinn," said Solomon; " I will restore unto thee thy liberty as soon as thou wilt tell me how I can cut the hardest metals without making a noise."

" I know no means," replied Sakhr, " but the raven can certainly advise thee. Take thou now the eggs out of the raven's nest, cover them with a crystal globe, and then thou shalt see how the raven will break the glass."

Solomon did as Sakhr had advised him. When the raven came, he fluttered round the crystal globe but could not reach the eggs. He vanished, and soon returned carrying in his beak

---

[1] Grünbaum, *Neue Beiträge zur semitischen Sagenkunde*, pp. 227–228.

a stone called Samur, and with this stone he cut the crystal globe.

"Whence hast thou taken this stone?" asked Solomon.

"From the mountain in the Far West," replied the raven.

Solomon now commanded some of the Jinns to fly to that mountain and fetch more of these stones. Sakhr, however, he released, as he had promised. When the chains were taken off the demon, he uttered a loud cry of joy, but which sounded in Solomon's ears like mocking laughter.

The Jinns had in the meantime returned with the Samur stones, and Solomon was borne back to Jerusalem. Here he distributed the stones among the working Jinns, who were now able to continue their work without making the slightest noise.[1]

Solomon also built a great and splendid palace unto himself with vast riches in gold, silver, and precious stones as no other King before him had ever possessed. Some of the halls in the Temple had crystal floors and ceilings. He also built a throne for himself of sandalwood, set in with gold and precious stones.[2]

SOLOMON AND THE ANTS

Whilst the Jinns were building the Temple, Solomon undertook a journey to Damascus. He was borne on the back of a Jinn or, according to others, transported on his magic carpet. He was carried over a precipitous valley surrounded on all sides by craggy mountains with sharp peaks, so that no man had ever ventured to visit the spot. It was the valley of ants. When Solomon looked down he beheld a host of ants as large as wolves. They had grey eyes and grey feet, and from a distance looked like a cloud. When the Queen of the ants, who had never beheld a mortal man before, saw Solomon, she was filled with amazement and fear. She immediately com-

[1] Weil, *loc. cit.*, pp. 234–237; Grünbaum, *loc. cit.*, p. 229; Salzberger, *Tempelbau.* p. 47.
[2] Weil, *loc. cit.*, p. 237.

manded her army to fly and conceal themselves in their hiding-places. God, however, commanded the Queen of the ants not to fear but to summon all her subjects and do homage unto Solomon as King of all the insects.

From a distance of many miles Solomon heard the command of God and the answer of the Queen of the ants borne to him upon the wind. Gently he descended into the valley, and taking the Queen of the ants upon his hand, he began to converse with her.

" Why didst thou fear me?" he asked. " Art thou not surrounded by such a mighty host?"

" I did not fear thee," replied the ant, " for I fear God alone. Should any danger threaten my subjects then, at a sign from me, seven times as many would appear in an instant."

" Then why didst thou command thy subjects to run to their hiding-places?"

" Because I feared that they would look on thee with wonder and amazement, and thus forget for a moment to praise their Creator."

" Is my power greater than thine?" asked the King.

" No," replied the ant, " I am greater than thou, for thy throne is only a metal one, whilst I am now reposing in the palm of the hand of a mighty King."

" And hast thou any request to make unto me before I release thee?" asked Solomon.

" No," replied the ant, " I ask nothing of thee, but I will give thee some advice. Beware of acting on any occasion so as to have to be ashamed of thy name which signifies The Blameless. Moreover, never give the ring from thy finger before saying first, ' In the name of God the all merciful '."

" Lord," exclaimed Solomon, " Thy Kingdom is greater and by far exceeds mine." Thereupon he bade farewell to the Queen of the ants and departed.

On his return journey Solomon commanded the Jinn to

take another direction, as he did not wish to disturb the ants in their devotions. When he reached the borders of Palestine, he heard the piteous cry of someone exclaiming: " O God, Thou who didst choose Abraham as Thy friend, release me from this miserable life."

Solomon followed in the direction of the voice and descended. He beheld a very old man bent with age and trembling in all his limbs.

" Who art thou?" asked Solomon.

" I am an Israelite from the tribe of Judah."

" And how old art thou?"

" This God alone knows. I reckoned my years until they numbered three hundred, but then I ceased, and another fifty or sixty may have passed over me."

" And how came it," asked Solomon, " that thou hast attained an age that has not fallen to the lot of man since Abraham?"

" Because," replied the old Israelite, " I once prayed to God to be allowed to behold the greatest of all the Prophets before I died."

" Thy wish is now fulfilled," said Solomon, " for I am that Prophet. I am Solomon, King and Prophet, unto whom God has given power and dominion such as was never given to any man before. Thou hast now reached thy goal, and now prepare to die."

Hardly had Solomon uttered these words, when the angel of Death appeared in human shape and took the soul of the old man.

" Thou must have been very near," exclaimed Solomon, " to have been able to appear with such speed."

" Thou dost greatly err," replied the angel of Death. " Know that I rest upon the shoulders of an angel whose head reaches ten thousand years' journey above the seventh heaven, whilst his feet are five hundred years' journey beneath the earth. He is so strong that if God only gave him permission he would have destroyed the earth and all that it contains. It is he who tells me when I must fetch a soul. His eyes are always fixed on the tree Sidrat-Almuntaha, which has as many leaves as there are men in the world. Every time that a child is born a new leaf shoots forth on which its name is inscribed; and every time that a man is about to die the leaf withers and falls off. Then I come and fetch the soul."

" And what dost thou to the souls and whither dost thou lead them?"

" When a believer dies, Gabriel accompanies me. He wraps the soul in green silk, and a green bird carries it to Paradise, where it remains till the end of time. As for the souls of the sinners, I carry them myself in a tarred cloth to the gates of hell, where they wander about in misery until the day of Judgment.

Solomon thanked the angel for the information, and asked him, when his time came, to keep his death secret. Thereupon he washed the body of the old man, buried it, and prayed for his soul that it might be eased of the pains it would have to undergo during its purgation by the angels Ankir and Munkir.[1]

This journey on the backs of the Jinns had exhausted Solomon, and on his return to Jerusalem he ordered his serving Jinns and demons to weave a carpet of stout silk which could transport him and his entire household from one place to another. When he made up his mind to go on a journey he ordered the winds to blow, and they immediately wafted him whither he wanted to travel. One night the Patriarch Abraham appeared to him in a dream and commanded him to visit the city of Jathrib or Medina, where the greatest of Prophets will one day find shelter, and also the city of Mecca, where he will be born. The King was accompanied on his journey by such

---

[1] Weil, *ibid.*; pp. 237–242; Tabari, *Chronique*, Vol. I, pp. 457–459; Mirkhond, *Rauzat-us-Safa*, ed. Rehatsek, Part I, Vol. II, p. 82; Migne, *Dictionnaire des Apocryphes*, Vol. II, col. 856.

a great number of pilgrims that he ordered the Jinns to weave
a new carpet of vast dimensions on which the whole caravan,
the camels and the oxen, could be accommodated. When all
was ready, Solomon ordered the winds to blow and to waft
the carpets to Medina. In the vicinity of the city, at a sign
from Solomon, the winds abated, and slowly the carpets sank
to earth. He visited the spot where Mohammed was once to
build a mosque and then returned to the carpet. Through the
air the King and his suite then sailed to Mecca, where Solomon
offered sacrifices and preached a sermon in the Kaaba, prophe-
sying the birth of Mohammed. Three days Solomon, his suite,
and all the pilgrims remained at Mecca and then returned to
Jerusalem.

When Solomon remounted his throne on the carpet and
the birds accompanying him spread out their wings, he noticed
a ray of the sun piercing the ranks of the birds, and he knew
that one bird had deserted its place. He immediately bade the
eagle to ascertain which was the missing bird. When the eagle
informed Solomon that it was the peewit who had deserted its
place, the King commanded him to find and bring the run-
away. The peewit, trembling in every limb, was brought
before Solomon, and excused his absence by the news he had
obtained of a land and a Queen whose names the King had
never heard. It was the land of Sheba, and the name of the
Queen was Balkis. A lapwing of that country had told the
peewit that the name of King Solomon was absolutely unknown in his native land.[1]

THE QUEEN OF SHEBA

The peewit now related unto Solomon what he had learned
of the land of Sheba and its Queen. Sheba was the name of
the King who had founded the kingdom, and Sheba was also

---

[1] Weil, *loc. cit.*, pp. 242–247; Tabari, *loc. cit.*, pp. 436–438; Grünbaum, *loc. cit.*, pp.
211–217.

the name of the capital. King Sheba was succeeded by a number of rulers the last of whom was Scharabel, a tyrant of dissolute habits. He had a vizier of such extraordinary beauty that all the daughters of the Jinns fell in love with him, and even transformed themselves into gazelles so that they might walk alongside of him and admire his exquisite beauty. One of these damsels once appeared to the vizier and offered him her hand. Dazzled by the marvellous beauty of Umeira—such was the name of the daughter of the Jinns—the vizier was only too happy to marry her. She gave birth to a daughter whom they called Balkis. Now the vizier had promised his wife never to inquire after her origin, but one day he forgot himself and asked her to what race she belonged. Immediately the lady-Jinn uttered a wail of sorrow and vanished.

The vizier now lived in seclusion with his daughter Balkis, who grew up to be a maiden of extraordinary beauty. One day King Scharabel saw her, and the licentious ruler fell violently in love with her. Balkis consented to give him her hand, and the marriage was celebrated with great pomp. On the bridal night, however, the bride-elect plied the King with drink and then stabbed him to the heart with a dagger. As the people of Sheba were already furious against the licentious monster, they received the news of the tyrant's death with a shout of joy, and unanimously elected Balkis as their Queen and sole ruler. " Thus," concluded the peewit, " Balkis rules over Sheba, and the country is prosperous, but, like her predecessors, the queen is a worshipper of the sun." [1]

" We shall soon see," said Solomon, " whether thou hast spoken the truth or not."

He wrote a letter, sealed it with his ring, and bade the peewit carry the missive immediately to Queen Balkis. Like an arrow the bird flew away and arrived at Sheba on the following morning.

[1] Weil, *loc. cit.*, pp. 247–258; Grünbaum, *loc. cit.*, pp. 217–219.

And this is what Solomon wrote to Queen Balkis: " Solomon, the son of David, and servant of God, the most Merciful, sendeth greeting to Balkis, Queen of Sheba. In the name of the most merciful God, peace be to those who walk in His ways. Do what I bid thee and submit immediately to my power."

The Queen read this letter to her counsellors, and they told her to do as seemed best to her, but assured her of their fidelity. The Queen decided to propitiate Solomon with gifts. " If he accepts these gifts," said the Queen, " he is not above or greater than other kings, but if he refuseth them, then he is indeed a Prophet, and we must yield to his sway and do what he commandeth us." Thereupon she had five hundred boys dressed as girls and five hundred maidens dressed in men's clothes. She also sent Solomon as presents a thousand carpets of gold and silver tissue, a crown set with pearls and precious stones, and a box containing a pearl, a diamond cut in zigzags, and a crystal goblet. Then she sent a letter to Solomon, and this is what she wrote: " If thou art a Prophet, thou wilt be able to distinguish the boys from the girls and also guess the contents of the box."

Balkis handed the letter to her ambassadors and gave them the following instructions: " When ye arrive near the palace of Solomon, request him to separate the males from the females, because if he be a Prophet, this will not be difficult for him to do. Ask him further to guess the contents of the box, to pierce the pearl, to thread the diamond, and fill the goblet with water which has come neither from heaven nor from earth. If he speaks and acts righteously, then leave these gifts with him, otherwise bring them back to me. If Solomon looks at ye with haughtiness and pride, then know that he is a King and not a Prophet, and ye need not fear his power and bravery. But if he receives ye graciously, meeting ye with affability and kindness, then be on your guard, for he is indeed a Prophet."

The peewit had remained all the time by the side of the Queen, watching the proceedings and listening to her injunctions. Thereupon he flew back to Solomon and acquainted the King with all that had occurred. When the messengers from Queen Balkis arrived and beheld the magnificence of Solomon, they were greatly astonished. Terror seized them when they set foot on a carpet the end of which they could not see, and had to pass between ranks of demons and Jinns, princes, nobles, and soldiers. They were confused and ashamed of the poverty of their own gifts when they beheld the floor of gold and silver and the great magnificence of the King. Solomon received them with a gracious smile, and when they presented to him the letter of their Queen, he told them its contents without opening it.

When the ambassadors offered the box, Solomon guessed its contents. He drilled a hole in the pearl by means of the worm Shamir and threaded the diamond. A Jinn brought him a worm, and Solomon put the end of a silken thread in its mouth and inserted it in the diamond. The worm crept through the winding passage and appeared at the other end. The diamond was threaded. Solomon was anxious to express his gratitude to the worm, and asked it what reward it desired. The worm asked for a tree from which it could draw for ever its nourishment, and Solomon gave to the little creature the mulberry tree, and therefore the silkworm always dwells on the mulberry tree. The King then proceeded to fill the goblet with water that came neither from heaven nor from earth. He summoned a huge and heavy negro slave and commanded him to mount a fiery young horse and gallop it about the plain until it streamed with sweat. When the horse returned, Solomon easily filled the goblet with the sweat pouring down its flanks.

He next bade his servants bring a thousand silver basins filled with water, and commanded the disguised youths and

maidens to wash their hands after their journey. He watched
intently and saw that the girls washed their faces with both
hands, whilst the boys dipped their hands in the water and
rubbed their faces only with one hand. He thus distinguished
the males from the females.

Having accomplished these tasks, Solomon now turned to
the ambassadors and thus addressed them: " Ye have seen
that I have answered the riddles set to me by your Queen.
Take now back your presents, for ye cannot augment my
possessions. What God the magnificent and glorious has bestowed upon me is better than anything ye are able to offer.
Return and tell your Queen to submit to my power and profess
the Faith, or else I shall come with an army to which she will
be unable to offer resistance. I will take possession of her
country and lead her into captivity."

The messengers returned to Sheba and informed their
Queen of all they had seen and heard. The Queen swore that
Solomon was not only a sovereign but a Prophet, and made
up her mind to go to him and do him homage. She prepared
for her journey and set out at the head of twelve thousand
generals and all her army.

When Balkis was a league away from Jerusalem, Solomon
summoned a demon of hideous appearance and commanded
him to bring the throne of Queen Balkis which the latter had
locked up in a hall in her own palace. The Jinn promised to
fetch the throne before noon, but Solomon would not wait,
for the Queen was already approaching Jerusalem. Thereupon
Asaph, the son of Berachiah, stepped forward and thus addressed the King: " Lift up thine eyes to heaven, O King,
and before thou canst lower them to earth again the throne
of Balkis will be here." Asaph knew the Ineffable Name of
God, and by its power he was able to accomplish what he had
promised. When the King lowered his gaze, the throne of
Balkis stood before him. Although portions of the throne had

been quickly changed by Solomon's servants, Balkis recognized it on her arrival. When Solomon asked her if she knew the throne, she replied prudently: "It looks as though it were mine." [1]

Now Solomon fell in love with Balkis and wanted to marry her. The Jinns, however, were envious of the Queen, and spread a rumour that her beauty was far from peerless because she had the feet of an ass, or ass's legs.[2] According to Mirkhond, the rumour had been spread not by Jinns but, what is more likely, by the ladies of Solomon's harem. When Solomon became aware of the intelligence of Balkis, he sent her to live with his sister who apprised him, after the expiration of forty days, of the noble virtues, exquisite qualities, and exalted disposition of her guest. Solomon then determined to "string this royal pearl of the diadem of sovereignty upon the thread of matrimony". At this news the ladies of Solomon's harem became distressed and, for the purpose of causing the noble prophetic mind to get disgusted with Balkis, enviously spread the rumour that her legs were extremely hairy.[3] The King, anxious to convince himself with his own eyes of the truth of this report, bade the Jinns build a palace with a crystal floor on the surface of the water, so that it should appear to the beholder as if it were also of water. He then called Balkis to himself, and when she reached the edge of the palace and imagined it to be all of water, she raised her garments and bared her legs. Solomon then saw that the lady had been maligned, and that there were only three goat's hairs on her legs. These Solomon was able to remove, thanks to a cure invented by the demons, which consisted in the use of mortar or some other depilatory preparation.

When the Queen approached Solomon she offered him two wreaths of flowers, one natural and the other artificial,

[1] Weil, *loc. cit.*, pp. 258–266; Tabari, *loc. cit.*, pp. 439–441; Mirkhond, *loc. cit.*, pp. 83–91; Grünbaum, *loc. cit.*, pp. 217–219.
[2] Tabari, *loc. cit.*, p. 441; Weil, *loc. cit.*, p. 267.   [3] Mirkhond, *loc. cit.*, p. 91.

and Solomon was rather embarrassed, for he could not distinguish one from the other. He then opened the window and let a swarm of bees fluttering outside enter the room. The insects immediately settled on the wreath of natural flowers, and Solomon chose the latter.[1] Thereupon Solomon married Balkis, and she bore him a son.[2]

According to Mirkhond, Solomon had a throne of gold constructed for Balkis which was surrounded by four lions, invented by the acuteness of those who excelled in talismanic art. The lions were near the supports of the throne, but inside, and vomited fire from their throats. Two vultures were perched on the back of each lion, and their eyes were of rubies and their teeth of pearls. Whenever Solomon ascended this throne and sat on it with Balkis, two eagles came and poured rosewater upon them. On the two upper extremities of this couch a pair of birds were stationed, which so spread their wings around the throne that whenever Solomon desired with Balkis to be seen by no one, they were completely screened. At the sides of the throne four peacocks were erected, whose beaks constantly exhaled a perfume of ambergris.[3]

Queen Balkis went back to her own land, where she bore a son from her union with Solomon.

When Balkis died, Solomon had her body conveyed to the city of Tadmor in the desert, where she was buried. Until the days of the Calif Walid her grave remained unknown. One day, however, in consequence of prolonged rains, the walls of Tadmor fell, and there was found an iron sarcophagus sixty ells long and forty ells wide, on which was engraved the following inscription: " Here lies buried the devout Balkis, Queen of Sheba, wife of the Prophet Solomon, son of David. Converted to the true faith in the thirteenth year of the reign

---

[1] Weil, *loc. cit.*, p. 267; Tabari, *loc. cit.*, pp. 441–442.　　　[2] Weil, *ibid.*; Tabari, *ibid.*
[3] Mirkhond, *loc. cit.*, p. 92; cf. Salzberger, *Tempelbau*, pp. 99–109.

of Solomon, she married him in the fourteenth year, and died in the twenty-third year of his reign."

The son of the Calif had the lid of the coffin raised, and he beheld the body of a woman which was as fresh as if she had just been buried. The Prince announced his discovery to his father, and Walid ordered him to leave the tomb undisturbed, and to pile great blocks of marble over it so as to conceal it from the gaze of man.[1]

SOLOMON AND PRINCESS DJARADA

Balkis had a rival for Solomon's affections in the person of Djarada, daughter of the Indian King Nubara. Solomon had heard that on one of the islands in the Indian Sea there lived a mighty King. Mounting his carpet, he at once marched against this King, whom he defeated and slew. In the royal palace he found the Princess Djarada, who was distinguished by elegance and beauty, surpassing not only all the wives of Solomon but even Balkis. Solomon made a prisoner of the Princess and forced her to mount the carpet. Love for the fair Princess was kindled in the heart of the King, and he forced her to adopt his faith and marry him. The Princess, however, " passed her days in grief and her nights in burning pain ", and led a sad life ever since she had been separated from her father. In Solomon she saw the murderer of the latter, and she recoiled from his embrace.

One day the King asked Djarada what he could do for her which might console her, give her comfort, and reconcile her to her fate. The lady immediately asked him to have a statue of her father made by the Jinns and placed in her chamber, so that by looking at it in the morning and evening her sorrowful mind might be comforted. Moved by compassion, Solomon ordered the Jinns to make the statue and set it up in Djarada's apartment. When this was done Djarada, who had been a

[1] Weil, *loc. cit.*, p. 274; Migne, *loc. cit.*, col. 869.

worshipper of idols before she associated with Solomon, began to worship the statue like an idol in the company of her maid-servants. Daily she prostrated herself before it and offered incense. This continued for forty days without Solomon being aware of it. Then the rumour spread among the people that the Princess was worshipping an idol, and the case was reported to Asaph. Thereupon Asaph preached a sermon before the King and all the people, and narrated in an eloquent manner the history of the virtues and noble acts of every Prophet of past times. Turning to Solomon, he praised his wisdom and piety during the first years of his reign, and only mentioned the acts the King had performed in his youth before the decease of his father David. Solomon was amazed and displeased at this brevity and open rebuke, and summoning Asaph into his presence, asked him to explain why he had thus rebuked him before all the people. Asaph replied: " I cannot laud or praise a man who has suffered his passions to blind him so that idolatry is practised in his house since forty days."

" In my house?" queried Solomon.

" Yes, in thy house," replied Asaph, and narrated what was taking place.

" We all belong to Allah and to him we shall return," said Solomon, and immediately hastened to Djarada's apartment. Finding her in prayer before the image of her father, he smashed the idol and punished Djarada. Thereupon he put on his garment of purity, which had been woven and sewn by virgins, strewed ashes on his head, and went out into the desert to bewail and repent of his sin. Thus he wept and fasted for forty days, and God forgave him.[1]

[1] Weil, *loc. cit.*, pp. 269–271; Grünbaum, *loc. cit.*, pp. 221–222; Tabari, *loc. cit.*, pp. 450–451; Mirkhond, *loc. cit.*, pp. 95–97.

The Lost Ring

Solomon had a female slave Amina, and every time when he went to perform his devotions or ritual ablutions he gave his signet-ring into her charge. One day, when he had entrusted the ring to this female slave (according to Mirkhond the girl's name was Jarada, and Solomon was going to answer a call of nature), one of the Jinns, Haritsu by name (according to Mirkhond it was the mighty Sakhr), took advantage of the King's act. Assuming the dress and guise of Solomon, he went to the girl, obtained the ring from her, and flung it into the sea. He then took Solomon's seat on the throne, whereon genii and men girded their loins in obedience to him. When Solomon returned and claimed his signet-ring from the girl, she exclaimed:

" I have already given it to thee! Thou art not the King," she cried, " but an impostor who has assumed the shape of Solomon for evil purposes. The King is at this moment in his judgment hall."

Whilst he was expostulating with the girl about the ring, Solomon threw a glance into the judgment hall and beheld an individual sitting on his throne. He became convinced that the Lord was angry with him and had therefore wrested the reins of power from him. He no longer asked for the ring, but put on poor clothing, took a staff in his hand, and went forth.

He wandered about as a mendicant, and when people asked him who he was, he replied: " I am Solomon." The people accused him of folly, threw dust at his blessed head and face, and said: " Thou madman art Solomon? Behold the King sitting on his throne in pomp and glory!—Look at this fool," they cried, " who pretends to be Solomon, the son of David." [1]

During his wanderings the exiled monarch came to the

[1] Grünbaum. *loc. cit.*, p. 223; Mirkhond, *loc. cit.*, pp. 97–98.

land of King Hiram of Tyre, who was just building a great
palace. According to one source it was to the land of the
King of Yram that Solomon came. He asked for employment
and obtained it from the overseer, who set him to draw water
from a cistern. One day, when he was reposing in the shadow
of a tower belonging to the palace, the Princess, standing at
the window, saw him asleep. For several days she watched
the handsome youth, and with amazement saw that one day
two lions came down from the mountains and, placing themselves by the side of the sleeper, kept away the flies from him
with their tails. On the next day two eagles came who fanned
him with their wings. Whenever Solomon awoke, he exclaimed: " Extolled be God the only one." The Princess
asked him who the God whom he extolled was, and Solomon
replied:

" To Him belong all things in heaven and earth, in the air
and under the earth."

Then the maiden said: " I have heard it said that all things
obey Solomon; art thou perchance Solomon?" And when he
answered in the affirmative the Princess exclaimed: " Then,
O Prophet of God, I have a request to make thee; take me as
thy wife, I will renounce my former belief and learn of thy
God. My father," she continued, " has long ago promised
me to allow me to marry whomever I will."

The King of Yram kept his promise, but bade his daughter
leave the palace and go forth without her beautiful robes and
her jewels. He left her only two copper dineros. Thus the
pair set out on their wanderings. Solomon bought bread and
oil for one coin, and some fishermen made him a present of
two fish. These he brought to his wife to clean, and she found
within one of them the ring which the demon Haritsu had
thrown into the sea. Solomon took the ring and exclaimed:
" There is no power or might except with God, the great, the
exalted." Thereupon he placed the ring upon his finger, and

immediately Jinns laden with costly robes and rich food came through the air. They reared a palace, and Solomon and his wife arrayed themselves in costly garments. The King summoned the fishermen who had given him the fish and bade them eat of the rich food to their heart's content. Then he sent for the King of Yram, and when the latter arrived and saw the great wealth and power, he begged his daughter's pardon and confessed the true faith. Thereupon Solomon commanded a cloud to approach, and he and his wife and the King of Yram were immediately conveyed to Jerusalem.[1]

When Solomon returned to his capital, he ordered the Jinns to find Sakhr and to bring him to his presence. They obeyed, and Solomon fettered and shackled the demon with his adherents and cast them all into the sea. According to another version the demon was riding in the sea. Then a troop of female Jinns or Peris came and began to lament in a loud voice: " Solomon is dead." Suspecting nothing, the Jinn came out, and the Peris seized him and brought him to Solomon. At the command of the King, the Jinn was bound between a piece of iron and a stone and cast into the sea.[2]

THE DEATH OF SOLOMON

Solomon knew that the end of his life was approaching, and he was anxious to see the building of the Temple completed. He was sure that if he died and the Jinns knew of it they would at once leave off building, for the demons were only kept at labour by the power of the King's signet-ring. The King was now in the habit of visiting the unfinished Temple very frequently, and he often remained there for one or two months, plunged in prayer. He even took his food in the Temple. When people saw him in a humble attitude before God, with his head bowed, neither man nor Jinn dared

---

[1] Grünbaum, *loc. cit.*, pp. 223–224 and 273–276; Mirkhond, *loc. cit.*, p. 100.
[2] Tabari, *loc. cit.*, p. 453.

approach him; if a Jinn ventured to draw near, then fire fell from heaven and destroyed him.

Now in the garden of Solomon each day a tree grew which was unknown to him. Solomon used to ask each tree what its name was and for what purpose it had been created, and the tree would reply. One day he saw a new tree and he asked: " What is thy name, and what purpose dost thou serve?"

Then the tree gave the following answer: " I serve for the destruction of the Temple, make me into a staff and lean upon me!" This answer puzzled Solomon.

" No one can destroy the Temple as long as I am alive," he said, and he understood that the tree had warned him of his approaching death. He accordingly cut the tree and made a staff out of it, and henceforth, when he prayed, he used to lean upon the staff.

Solomon now prayed to God and said:

" O Lord, let my death be unknown to the Jinns, that they may finish the work of the Temple."

God granted Solomon's request, for when the angel took away his soul his body remained leaning on his staff with his head bowed in adoration. Those who saw him thus thought that he was alive, and never dared to come near him. He thus remained for a whole year. The Jinns, therefore, continued to work day and night until the Temple was completed.

God, however, had sent a white ant on the day on which Solomon's soul was taken, and commanded it to gnaw the inside of the staff. The white ant gnawed a little every day, and at the end of a year the staff was eaten up and crumbled under the weight of the King, and then all knew that he was dead.[1]

The sages then took the ant and enclosed it in a box with a piece of wood, and thus kept it for twenty-four hours. Comparing the amount that was eaten up in that time with the

---

[1] Tabari, *loc. cit.*, p. 455; Weil, *loc. cit.*, p. 279.

length of the staff, they could ascertain how long it had taken the ant to gnaw through the entire staff.[1] According to Mirkhond, the Ifrits themselves found out that Solomon was dead. When the stay of the King had become protracted beyond all reasonable expectations, one of the Jinns entered the Temple by one window and left it by another, but, contrary to his previous experience, failed to hear the voice of Solomon reading. He therefore said to the other Jinns: " It is my opinion that Solomon has departed from this world." Thereupon the Jinns, who were anxious to obtain certainty on the subject, procured a beetle whose nourishment is water and earth and made it gnaw the staff on which Solomon was leaning. When the staff broke down, the Jinns were convinced of the King's death and spread the information in the world.[2]

[1] Weil, *loc. cit.*, p. 279.   [2] Mirkhond, *loc. cit.*, p. 103.

CHAPTER XVII

The Prophet Elijah

The Prophet Elijah and his many disguises—Elijah and Rabbi Shila—
Rabbi Kahana and the Roman lady—Death preferable to sin—Elijah travels
over a distance of four hundred parasangs—Rabbi Bar Abbuha and Elijah—
The leaves growing in Paradise—The fragrant mantle—Nahum of Gimso—
The present for the Emperor—The precious casket and the thieves—The
piety of Rabbi Nahum—The casket full of common dust—The anger of the
Emperor—Elijah disguised as a Roman—The virtues of the dust in the
casket—The earth turns to bows and arrows—The disappointed thieves—
Rabbi Akiba and the daughter of Kalba Shebua—The distress of the lovers
—The bundle of straw—A knock at the door—Elijah disguised as a beggar
—The seven years of happiness—Elijah disguised as an Arab—Seven years
of prosperity—Charity and good deeds, or good use made of wealth—
Elijah as an architect—The pious poor man and his starving family—Elijah
sold as a slave—The wonderful palace built overnight—Elijah rebukes the
scholars—The master who thinks first of his own needs and then of those
of his servants—Elijah and the farmer—The man who refused to say:
"Please God"—The loss of money—The lesson learned—Rabbi Joshua and
Ulla ben Kishar—The punishment of the informer—Rabbi Baroka and
Elijah—Judge not by appearances—The man who was destined to occupy
a place in Paradise—Good deeds performed unostentatiously—The two
men whose purpose in life was to cheer up those who were a prey to sorrow—
The lawsuit and the gift of fish—Rabbi Anan and Elijah—The Prophet's
rebuke—The Prophet Elijah and the angel of death—Rabbi Reuben and
his son—The angel of death at the wedding dinner—The pleading of the
bride—The compassion of the angel of death—Another version of the
story—The bride and her three husbands—The book of *Tobit*—The story
of Savitri and Satyavan in the *Mahabharata*.

Among the later Kings of Israel one of the most well-known
rulers was Ahab, the husband of Jezebel. Legends cluster
round this royal pair not only on account of their wickedness,
but because during their reign the famous prophet Elijah
the Tishbite arose. The latter waged a continual war against
Ahab and idol-worship, which had spread in Israel. In the

following two chapters we shall relate some of the many legends told of the Tishbite.

Many prophets arose in Israel after Moses, but the most popular prophet, round whom cluster numerous legends, was Elijah the Tishbite. The prophet Elijah is represented in Jewish legend as the protector of the innocent, as the guardian angel bringing help to people in distress. He is ubiquitous, and neither time nor space are obstacles when he is engaged upon his mission of bringing succour to the pious, and especially to the students of the Law and to the scholars. The prophet is supposed to employ various means and to adopt many disguises. In the Talmudic legends we see him disguised as an Arab,[1] as a rider upon horseback,[2] or arrayed in the Roman toga. He appears as a Roman dignitary, especially when he is called upon to revoke an unfavourable law passed against Israel.[3] One day, legend relates, Rabbi Shila was denounced to the government and accused of administering the law in accordance with Jewish legislature. The Rabbi was in great distress, but Elijah, disguised as one of the court officials, suddenly came and bore witness in favour of Rabbi Shila and against the informer, so that the Rabbi was saved.[4]

Another Rabbi whom Elijah saved from death was Kahana. He was very poor and earned his living by peddling about with household goods. A great lady, at whose house he used to sell his wares, cast an eye on him, and one day decided to force him to commit an immoral act. Rabbi Kahana, preferring death to sin, threw himself out of the window, but the Prophet Elijah appeared just in the nick of time and caught up the Rabbi before he had reached the ground.

" Thou hast compelled me," said Elijah, " to hasten to thee over a distance of four hundred parasangs so as to be in time to save thee from death."

---

[1] *Berachoth*, 6b.   [2] *Sabbath*, 109b.   [3] *Abodah Zarah*, 17b.
[4] *Berachoth*, 58b; see also *Abodah Zarah*, 17b.

" I prefer death," said the Rabbi, " to a life of misery and a trade beset with perils wherein I am always running the danger of committing a sin."

The prophet gave Rabbi Kahana means which enabled him to change his occupation.[1]

Rabbi Bar Abbuha was another student of the law who suffered great poverty. One day he met the Prophet Elijah and complained to him that his poverty was so great and his worries so constant that he had no time to study the law as he should like to.

" Come with me," said Elijah, and he led the Rabbi straight to Paradise where he told him to spread out his mantle and gather the leaves growing in the abode of the blessed, which he could sell on earth at a high price.

The Rabbi did as he was bidden, and was about to depart with his precious load, when he heard a heavenly voice calling out:

" Rabbi Bar Abbuha is already anticipating his reward in the world to come by taking his share during his earthly life!"

When the Rabbi heard these words, he hastily emptied his garment of the celestial leaves he had gathered. He nevertheless sold his mantle afterwards at a high price on account of the wonderful fragrance it had acquired from the leaves of Paradise. The sum he thus realized enabled him to live free of care and to devote his leisure to the study of the law.[2]

As a guardian angel hurrying to save him from certain death and thus bring him help in his hour of need, the Prophet Elijah appeared to the famous Rabbi Nahum of Gimso. This pious Rabbi was one day sent by his co-religionists to Rome on a political mission. As a gift to the Emperor, the Rabbi was carrying a casket full of diamonds and precious stones. He had to pass the night in an inn, where thieves found out

---

[1] *Kiddushin*, 40a.   [2] *Baba Mezia*, 114b.

how precious were the contents of the casket. They robbed
the Rabbi of the jewels, replacing the abstracted gems with
common earth. Unaware of the substitution, Nahum continued his journey. When he arrived in Rome he offered his
gift to the Emperor. The casket was opened, and the anger of
the Emperor knew no bounds when it was discovered that it
contained nothing but common earth.

" Do the Jews perchance wish to mock me?" he exclaimed.
" Let their delegate be put to death at once."

The pious Rabbi never lost faith in God, but, as was his
usual custom, said:

" This, too, is for the best."

But behold, suddenly the Prophet Elijah appeared, wearing
the Roman toga and disguised as a court official.

" Your Majesty would do well," said the supposed court
official, " to test the qualities and the virtues of this earth.
It may be the same earth which their ancestor, the Patriarch
Abraham, once hurled against his enemies and which turned
to bows and swords. Your Majesty can test the virtues of this
earth against the enemy with whom the Romans are now at
war." Thus spoke the Prophet Elijah, and the Emperor
decided to follow his advice.

In vain had the Romans been besieging one city which was
still resisting their onslaughts. The Emperor ordered some of
the soldiers to throw a handful of earth from the casket against
the besieged city, and lo, the earth turned to swords and bows
which worked havoc among the enemy.

Convinced of the great value of the casket and its contents
which worked such wonders and were more efficacious than
Roman valour and Roman weapons, the Emperor loaded the
pious Rabbi Nahum with gifts and treasures and dismissed
him in honour.

When the thieves heard what had occurred, they filled
another casket with the same earth and brought it to the

Emperor as a gift. " Here is more of the earth which the Jew has offered to Your Majesty," they said.

The Emperor gave instructions to test the virtue of the earth the thieves had brought him, but it naturally proved to be ordinary dust, and they were put to death.[1]

When the Prophet Elijah does not immediately bring help to pious scholars in need, he at least inspires them with hope and confidence, making them look at life from a brighter point of view. Thus it happened in the case of Rabbi Akiba, whose romantic marriage to the daughter of a very rich man will be told elsewhere. Before he became a great Rabbi, Akiba had married the daughter of Kalba Shebua. As his daughter had married Akiba against his will, Kalba Shebua refused to have anything to do with the pair, and they consequently lived in great poverty. Once, on a very cold night, Akiba had managed to gather a little straw which he could offer to his wife as a bed to sleep upon.

" My dear," he said, " you have been brought up in luxury and comfort, and now I have neither food nor clothing to offer you, and only a little straw to lie down upon. I wish I were rich and I would place a golden crown upon your head. Be assured, however, that my love for you is great and that you are very dear to me. The privations you are undergoing for my sake are immense, but it will be my constant endeavour to prove myself worthy of your noble love."

Thus spoke Akiba, when suddenly there was a knock at the door. He opened the door of their miserable hut and beheld a poor beggar who was none other than Elijah in disguise.

" My friends," he cried pitifully, " my wife has been delivered of a child, and I have not even a bundle of straw in my hut to make a bed for her. For God's sake give me some straw if you can spare it."

---

[1] *Sanhedrin*, 108b–109a; see also *Hibbur Yafeh*, by Rabbi Nissim, p. 8b.

Turning to his wife, Akiba, who had been full of despair a moment ago, said:

"You see, my dear, there is even greater misery than ours in the world, and we must not lose heart."

He thus consoled himself and his wife, and their courage revived, which was exactly the end Elijah had wished to attain.[1]

The deserving and worthy poor to whom Elijah is supposed to offer his help are not always scholars or rabbis. The Prophet appears even to ordinary folk in the hour of dire distress, as long as they are pious and deserving.

THE SEVEN YEARS OF HAPPINESS

It happened once that a rich man had lost all his wealth and become so poor that he was compelled to hire himself out as a labourer so as to earn his bread for his wife and child. One day, when he was working in the field, the Prophet Elijah appeared to him, disguised as an Arab, and thus he spoke:

"My friend! It has been decreed that thou shalt enjoy seven years of happiness, wealth, and comfort, and thou hast only to tell me whether thou dost want these good years now or at the end of thy existence, as the seven closing years of thy life."

Thus spoke Elijah, but the poor man, taking him for an Arab sorcerer, replied:

"Go thy way, I have nothing to offer thee for thy witchcraft."

Elijah went away but came again three times and repeated the same question.

"I require nothing from thee," he said, "tell me only when thou dost wish these seven good years to come to thee."

At last the man replied:

[1] *Nedarim*, 50a; *Ketubot*, 62b.

" I will talk the matter over with my wife and ask her advice."

Elijah consented to wait for his reply till to-morrow. The poor man now went and told his wife of what had happened.

" Tell the man," said the woman, " to send us the good years at once, for the near is preferable to the far off."

The poor man followed his wife's advice, and when Elijah again appeared and repeated his question, the man replied:

" Let the seven good years come to us at once."

" So it shall be," declared the Prophet. " Go thou home and before thou reachest the gate of thy house the Lord will have blessed thee and sent thee good fortune."

The man went home and, to his great surprise, found that the Prophet's prediction had come true. His children had just informed their mother that whilst digging the ground they had found a treasure, and his wife was coming to meet him and tell him the happy news. The man thanked the Lord for the treasure he had sent them, and he also praised his wife for her excellent advice.

His wife now said unto him:

" We are sure of the grace of God for seven years, let us therefore practise charity all these years, feed the hungry and befriend the poor, perchance the Lord will continue His grace towards us when the seven years are over and send us further wealth or allow us to keep in our possession to the end of our days what he Has given us now."

Thus spoke the pious and good woman, and the husband approved her words. They practised much charity, and whenever they heard of a case where they could do some good they hurried at once to offer their help. Whatever they gave to the poor the woman made her little son write down in a book. Seven years passed, and once more Elijah appeared and thus he spoke:

" The time has now come for thee to return the gift I gave thee."

" My Lord," said the pious man, " when I accepted thy blessing I did so with the consent of my wife. Suffer me now, before I return the gift thou didst bestow upon us, to consult with my wife and to acquaint her with thy request."

Elijah gave his permission, and the man who was about to lose again his fortune went to tell his wife that the old man had come to take away what he had given them.

" Tell our benefactor," replied the woman, " that if he has really found people who are more faithful than we, who will guard better the treasure entrusted to them and make a better use of it, then we are quite ready to return the pledge entrusted to us."

The Lord hearkened to the words of the pious woman, and saw that she and her husband had performed good deeds and made a proper use of the wealth entrusted to them. He therefore continued to bestow His grace upon the worthy people, and allowed them to keep in their possession till the end of their days the wealth He had sent them through Elijah.[1]

THE PROPHET ELIJAH AS AN ARCHITECT

There was once a pious man, the father of five children, who was very poor. One day, when his distress was very great, for he had no food to give to his family, his wife said to him: " Go into the market, perhaps the Lord will send thee some help so that we may live and not die."

" How can I go?" said the poor man; " I have no friend to whom I can address myself in my need."

But the children, being hungry, wept and cried for bread.

" Go into the street," said the wife, " canst thou sit here and see how thy children are dying of hunger?"

[1] *Midrash Sutta, Ruth*, 4, 11; *Seder Elijahu Rabba*, p. 28; see also Kuttner, *Jüdische Legenden*, 2, pp. 31–33; Bin Gorion, *Der Born Judas*, Vol. II, pp. 225–226.

" I am almost naked," replied the man, " how can I go out into the street?"

Thereupon the poor woman took her own torn garment, threw it over her husband, and sent him out into the street. The poor man, not used to begging, stood in a corner and, lifting up his eyes to heaven, thus he prayed:

" Lord of the Universe! Thou knowest that I have no friend and have no one to whom I could tell my tale of distress and ask him to have pity upon me and my children. I have neither brother nor friend, and my starving children are crying with hunger. Have Thou therefore pity upon us and send us Thy mercy, and if not, be compassionate and take us away, so that we need no longer suffer."

Thus prayed the poor man, and God hearkened unto his prayers, and suddenly the Prophet Elijah appeared before him.

" Why art thou crying?" he asked of the poor man. The latter told him of his misery and distress and acquainted the Prophet with his tale of woe.

" Cry no more," said Elijah, " but come with me and do as I will tell thee. Take me into the market and sell me as a slave, and the money thou wilt thus receive will suffice for thy needs."

The poor man refused to accept such a sacrifice.

" Master," said he, " how can I do such a thing? Besides, the people here know that I am very poor and they will never believe that I am thy master, but will say that I am the slave and thou the master."

" Be not afraid," replied Elijah, " but do as I am telling thee."

The poor man, thinking of his starving wife and children, gave in and went with the Prophet to the market-place. The people at first thought that Elijah was the master and the poor man his slave, but the Prophet informed them that such was not the case. Thereupon one of the servants of the King passed, saw the slave offered for sale, liked his appearance, and decided to purchase him for his master. He paid eighty *dinars* for the Prophet and took him away.

" Take the money thou hast received for me," said Elijah to his supposed master, " go to thy starving wife and children and feed them; mayest thou never know either want or suffering; and may distress and misery never visit thee."

Full of joy the poor man hurried back to his wife and children to whom he brought food and drink. God blessed him, and he amassed a great fortune which he enjoyed to the end of his days. And neither he nor his children ever knew poverty or want.

In the meantime the Prophet followed the King's servant who brought the slave he had purchased before his master. The King had made up his mind to build a palace, and he was buying many slaves whom he employed to hew and carry stones and cut down trees and prepare everything for the structure.

" What canst thou do?" he asked Elijah.

" I am an architect," replied the Prophet, " and I can build thy palace."

The King rejoiced when he heard these words.

" If thou canst build me this palace, as I wish it to be built, within six months, thou shalt be free then, and I will reward thee royally," said the King. Elijah promised to give his new master satisfaction.

During the night the Prophet offered a prayer to God that He might let the palace be built instantaneously. Before dawn broke, a wonderful palace stood quite ready and complete. Great was the King's amazement when he saw the palace finished. but in vain did he seek for his slave to reward him. Elijah had disappeared. The King realized that it must have been an angel from Heaven who had constructed such a wonderful palace overnight.

Elijah now met the poor man whom he had helped in his need and told him what had occurred.

" I have accomplished," said the Prophet, " what the King had asked me to do. I built him a palace which is worth a thousand times more than the sum which he paid thee for me. I have thus enriched him, as I did not wish to cheat him when I let him purchase me."

The pious man, who was now no longer poor, praised the Prophet and thanked him for his timely help.

" Thou hast given back life to me, to my wife, and to my children," said he.

" Praise the Lord who showed thee grace," replied the Prophet.[1]

This legend has entered the Jewish liturgy, and under the title of *Ish-Hasid* (a pious man) is sung on Sabbath evening.[2]

Another characteristic trait of the Tishbite is his rigour practised towards all those he has relations with. He not only punishes the arrogant, the misers, and evil-doers, but he often rebukes his friends, the scholars, if they fail to come up to his standard of morality. Thus Elijah was in the habit of visiting a pious man. One day the man built a vestibule, constructing it in such a way that the supplications of the needy could be heard only faintly in the house, and immediately the Prophet ceased to be a visitor at the house.

Another story runs as follows: There were two brothers, one of whom was in the habit of attending first to the needs of his guests and servants and then to his own, whilst the other brother first looked after himself and only when his own needs were satisfied did he think of his guests and servants. Elijah frequently visited the first brother, but never honoured the second with his presence.[3]

In another instance he preferred one of two brothers who

---

[1] *Hibbur Yafeh*, pp. 24a–25a; Jellinek, *Beth-Hamidrash*, Vol. V, pp. 140–141; *Seder Elijahu Rabba*, p. 30; see also Bin Gorion, *loc. cit.*, Vol. II, p. 355.
[2] See Bin Gorion, *loc. cit.*, p. 363. [3] *Ketubot*, 61a.

was in the habit of providing for his servants as for his own family, permitting them to eat of all the courses served at his own table. He did not, however, consider worthy of his visit the other brother who allowed his servants to eat abundantly only of the first course and only the remnants of the others.[1]

Just as he is in the habit of helping the pious and needy in their hour of distress, Elijah never hesitates to give a lesson, to rebuke, and even to punish severely the arrogant and the greedy, as the following story will show.

ELIJAH AND THE FARMER

There was once a rich farmer who possessed vast tracts of land and many fields, but required cattle to work his fields. Putting a considerable sum of money in his pocket, about 100 *dinars*, he set out to a cattle sale in the neighbouring town with the intention of buying oxen and cows. On the road he was accosted by Elijah.

" Whither art thou going?" the prophet inquired of the farmer.

" I am going to the town to buy cattle," said the farmer, who was not aware that the stranger was none other than the Prophet Elijah.

" If it please God, you should add," said Elijah.

But the farmer arrogantly replied:

" If it please God or not, it makes no difference. I have money in my pocket and I can do what I like with it."

" Quite true," replied Elijah, " but without luck." Saying this he went his way.

Arrived at the market town, the farmer selected the cattle he intended to buy, but when he put his hand into his pocket he discovered to his annoyance that he had lost his purse. He was compelled to return home and provide himself with other money. Remembering the stranger he had met and who

[1] *Ketubot,* 61a,

seemed to have brought him ill-luck, he went to another town and by another road so as not to meet the man. On the road, however, he again met Elijah disguised as an old man, and once more the stranger inquired of him whither he was going.

" I am going to buy cattle," replied the rich farmer.

" Say, if it please God," again said Elijah.

" What has it to do with God?" angrily replied the farmer. " I have money in my pocket and I will buy the cattle I require."

He had walked some distance when he suddenly felt rather tired. He sat down to rest awhile, fell asleep, and when he awoke his purse had disappeared. Amazed at his repeated ill-luck, he returned home to provide himself once more with money. For the third time he set forth on his journey, and for the third time he met a stranger who was none other than Elijah.

" Whither art thou going?" asked the Prophet.

" To buy cattle, if it please God," replied the farmer, who had now learned his lesson.

" Go in peace, and may thy journey prove successful." Thus spoke Elijah, slipping into his pocket the two purses the man had lost on his previous trips. When the farmer arrived at the market town he found two fine red cows which he decided to buy. When he inquired after the price, he was told that it was two hundred *dinars*.

" I have not so much money about my person," said the farmer. Thereupon he put his hand into his pocket to take his purse, and, to his amazement, he discovered the other two hundred *dinars* he had lost. He bought the two cows and also an ox, and later on sold the cattle to the King for a thousand *dinars*.[1]

The Prophet Elijah is supposed to be even more severe in

---

[1] See *Alphabetum Siracidis*, ed. Steinschneider, p. 17; Bin Gorion, *loc. cit.*, Vol II, p. 248, and notes, p. 356.

the case of the scholars and sages whom he censures or dissolves intimacy with them, as soon as they fail to come up to his own moral standard. In the Prophet's opinion it is not enough for the scholars and students of the law to obey literally the commandments of the law. They must also listen to the categorical imperative of their conscience and do more than merely follow the letter of the law. None of the Rabbis could boast of such intimacy with the Prophet as Rabbi Joshua ben Levi, and none did the Tishbite esteem so highly. During his life-time he led the Rabbi into Paradise and showed him the place he would once occupy among the blessed.[1] When Rabbi Joshua, after the close of his earthly life, came to the abode of the blessed in Paradise, it was Elijah himself who announced to the inmates the advent of the new-comer. He went before him calling out:

" Make room for the son of Levi." [2]

And yet, when the Rabbi failed to come up to the moral standard Elijah had set up, he at once ceased to visit him. It happened thus:

The Punishment of the Informer

A man named Ulla ben Kishar, being sought by the officers of the law, escaped to Lydda and took refuge in the house of Rabbi Joshua. His whereabouts became known to the officers of the law; they came to Lydda but failed to discover Ulla's place of concealment. They demanded his surrender and threatened to wreak vengeance upon the whole city of Lydda if Ulla was not delivered to them. Rabbi Joshua now urged the fugitive to give himself up to justice.

" It is better," he said, " that one man should die than all the inhabitants of the city run the danger of being put to the sword."

Ulla listened to these arguments and allowed the Rabbi

[1] *Sanhedrin,* 98a.   [2] *Ketubot,* 77b.

to hand him over to the officers of the law. After that event Elijah ceased to visit the Rabbi.

Greatly affected by the absence of the Tishbite, Rabbi Joshua fasted many days, and when at last Elijah once more appeared to him, he inquired after the reason of his absence.

" Why has my lord not honoured me with a visit for such a long time?" asked Rabbi Joshua.

" Because," replied the Prophet, " I will have nothing to do with informers."

The Rabbi quoted a passage from the *Mishnah* in justification of his conduct, but Elijah was not satisfied.

" This is the letter of the Law," he said, " enough for the ordinary man, but the really pious must do more, and thou shouldst have acted otherwise.[1]

A similar rebuke the Prophet made to Rabbi Baroka, to whom he proved that it is wrong for men to go by appearances. One day Rabbi Baroka was walking in the crowded market-place when he met Elijah. The Prophet revealed to the Rabbi his identity and they conversed together.

" Is there one among this crowd," asked Rabbi Baroka, " who is destined to occupy a place in Paradise?"

" Not one in this throng," replied the Prophet, " will occupy a place in Paradise." He had hardly spoken these words when a man, whose dress did not at all indicate a pious man, hurried by.

" This one," said the Prophet, pointing to the passer-by, " is destined to occupy a place in Paradise."

Greatly astonished, Rabbi Baroka accosted the man and entered into a conversation with him. He questioned him about his occupation and life, and the man replied:

" I am a prison guard, and I take great care to keep apart the men and women detained in jail, so that no opportunity is offered to them to violate the laws of chastity. I sleep myself

[1] *Talmud Jerushalmi, Terumot,* 8; *Genesis Rabba,* 94.

between the two rooms wherein the prisoners are kept, and I am particularly careful when a Jewess is brought to prison."

" How is it," asked Rabbi Baroka, " that thy dress is not that of a pious man and that thou dost not wear the *zizith* prescribed by the Law?"

" On account of my occupation," said the man, " I often have business with the authorities and I am a frequent visitor at court. It is better that they should remain ignorant of my origin and unaware that I am a Jew. I am thus able to find out whenever new and hostile laws against the Jews are planned. I immediately convey the information to the wise men and leaders of Israel, and they are enabled to take steps to make the authorities in power favourably disposed towards the Jews and to avert misfortune. At the present moment, I am hurrying to court, because I have heard that a council of the princes has been convened and that new and hard laws against the Jews are being planned." Thus spoke the man and hurried away.

Rabbi Baroka then understood that in spite of his appearance this man was doing a great deal of good quietly and unostentatiously and that he was worthy to occupy a place in the abode of the blessed and the pious.[1]

The Rabbi soon again met Elijah and once more conversed with him. Two men were just passing, and the Prophet, pointing to the passers-by, said: " These men, too, will occupy an honourable place in Paradise."

Curious to know the merits of the future occupants of Eden, the Rabbi took leave of the Prophet and hurried after the strangers. He questioned them and found out that their purpose in life was to cheer up and console all those who were a prey to despair and sorrow.

" We visit all those who are sighing and weeping," said the men, " those who are a prey to hopelessness or are suffering

[1] *Hibbur Yafeh.*

from illness. We cheer them up, console and encourage them, and make them look upon the brighter side of life. We make them forget what has occurred, the sorrow that is gnawing at their hearts, the despair that is gripping their souls, and the fear that is paralysing their thoughts and actions. With our comforting words and even jokes we drive away the shadows and call forth brighter visions." Thus spoke the men, and Rabbi Baroka once more understood that it is also possible to do good in a humble station, and even more perhaps than in an exalted one.[1]

The Lawsuit and the Gift of Fish

The Prophet Elijah was very severe in the case of Rabbi Anan. One day someone brought the Rabbi little fishes as a present. The Rabbi accepted the gift and asked the donor: " What can I do for thee?"

" I should like to bring a case before thee and would ask thee to act as judge in my lawsuit," replied the man.

" This I can no longer do," replied the Rabbi. " I cannot act as judge in a lawsuit thou art interested in since I have accepted a gift from thee."

" Well then," replied the litigant, " I no longer ask thee to serve as judge in my case. Take the fish, for a gift offered to a scholar is as meritorious as the firstlings given to the priest, and assign one of thy colleagues to act as judge."

Rabbi Anan sent the applicant to his colleague Rabbi Nachmann, requesting his friend to act for him, as he himself was not allowed, according to Talmudic law, to serve as judge. Rabbi Nachmann now imagined that the reason why his colleague was incapacitated from serving as judge was that of the litigant being a relation of his.

Although strictly just, he nevertheless treated the litigant with some consideration and felt favourably disposed towards

---

[1] *Hibbur Yafeh*; see also *Taanith*, 22a; cf. Bin Gorion, *loc. cit.*, Vol. II, p. 384.

him. The other party, noticing Rabbi Nachmann's friendly treatment of the opponent, felt somewhat intimidated and failed to plead as convincingly as he might have done under different circumstances. He lost the case as a result of Rabbi Anan's carelessness, although unintentional, both in sending a message to his legal friend and in not explaining fully the reasons why he could not serve as judge.

From that moment the Prophet Elijah, who had been both a friend and a teacher of Rabbi Anan, shunned him and refused to come near him for a long time.[1]

Elijah and the Angel of Death

In several cases the Prophet, by his interference and advice, saved a pious man from the angel of death.

Once upon a time, there lived a pious scholar whose name was Rabbi Reuben. He had a son who was as pious and saintly as himself. One day the angel of death appeared to Rabbi Reuben and informed him that his son would soon have to die.

" Such is the fate of man," said the pious father, " and no mortal can do anything against it. If, however, I have found favour in thy eyes, and thou canst grant my request, allow my son thirty days respite so that I might have the happiness of seeing him under the canopy and married."

The angel of death consented to wait thirty days.

When the appointed time had drawn near, Rabbi Reuben arranged the wedding feast of his son for the thirtieth day.

On that very day, the son, who was on his way to invite the guests to the wedding feast, met the Prophet Elijah:

" Whither art thou going?" the Prophet asked the bridegroom.

" I am going to invite the guests to my wedding feast," replied the bridegroom.

---

[1] *Ketubot*, 105b; *Sanhedrin*, 113a; *Makkot*, 11a.

" Dost thou know," queried the Prophet, " that the time
of thy death is approaching?"

" If such is the decree of the Lord," replied the pious son
of a pious father, " I cannot oppose it. Am I greater than
Moses, Abraham, Isaac, and Jacob, who, too, had to die?"

" My son," said Elijah, " I will give thee an advice. When
the guests will arrive and you will all be seated at the wedding
dinner, do thou not taste anything but watch the door. As soon
as thou wilt perceive one disguised as a beggar, ragged, dirty,
and dishevelled, know thou that it is the angel of death. Hasten
to run and meet him, greet him in a very friendly manner, and,
seating him beside thee, set at once food and drink before him.
If he refuses, insist upon his partaking of refreshment." Thus
spoke the Prophet Elijah and went his way, whilst the would-be
bridegroom returned home.

He never said a word of what had happened, or of his
encounter with the Prophet Elijah, but when he sat at the
wedding dinner among the guests, a dirty and ragged beggar
suddenly stood in the door. Immediately the bridegroom rose
up, greeted him in the kindliest manner and insisted upon his
sitting down and partaking of food and drink.

The angel of death, for it was none other, at first refused,
but soon was prevailed upon to take a seat. He seemed to be
eating and drinking like the other guests, and when he had
finished he said to the bridegroom:

" I am the angel of death, and the messenger of God who
has sent me to fetch thy soul. It had been lent to thee for a
time, and now the Master claims it." Thus spoke the angel of
death, revealing his identity.

" Grant me permission," said the son, " to inform my
parents, and bid them farewell."

Rabbi Reuben thereupon came and began to supplicate
the angel of death and to implore him to spare his son's life,
whilst the son was weeping and kissing his father and mother.

THE YOUNG BRIDE AND THE ANGEL OF DEATH

Facing page 228, Vol. III

But the angel of death remained adamant, although his heart had been somewhat softened.

" Let me go and bid farewell to my newly-wedded wife," begged the son.

The angel of death gave his permission, and the young husband hurried to his young wife, kissed her and informed her of what had happened.

" The angel of death has come to fetch my soul," he said. Fear and terror seized the young bride, but she was determined to plead and argue and fight for her spouse.

" Wait thou here," she said, " and let me go out and speak to the angel of death."

" Is it true," she asked the latter, " that thou hast come to take the soul of my husband?"

" So it is," replied the angel of death.

" Dost thou not know," asked the young wife, " what is written in the Law with regard to the newly-wed? It is written that he who marries a young wife is exempt from military and other duties, and is to remain at home a whole year so as to enjoy himself and be happy in the company of his young wife. Wilt thou now take the life of my husband, and give the lie to the Torah?"

Thus argued the young bride, for love and despair gave her courage and cunning. Somewhat taken by surprise, the angel of death, who had already been moved by the tears and supplications of the parents and had been touched by the kind treatment of the son, replied:

" I will go before the throne of God and present the matter to Him. He may have pity upon thy husband and grant him a new lease of life."

Spreading out his wings, the angel of death ascended to Heaven, where he found the angels Gabriel and Michael, and other ministering angels, praying the Lord to have mercy upon Rabbi Reuben, and to leave this son. The angel of death now presented the petition of the young bride, and the Lord had compassion upon her and upon the unhappy parents, and bade the angel of death annul the decree of death against the son of Rabbi Reuben. God then added seventy years to his life, as against the seven days of the wedding festivities.[1]

THE MAIDEN AND HER THREE HUSBANDS

A similar story is told in the *Midrash Tanchuma*. Here it is related of a pious and rich man who had a beautiful daughter. She had already been married to three husbands, but every time, on the day of her wedding, she lost them. She had made up her mind never to marry again, when one day a cousin of hers came to their house from a distant land. He fell in love with his beautiful cousin and wished to marry her. The arguments of his uncle, who acquainted him with the terrible fate of his predecessors, had no effect upon him, and the wedding accordingly took place. Whilst he was standing under the wedding canopy, the Prophet Elijah appeared to him and gave him the advice to receive in a friendly manner the ragged and dirty beggar who would soon appear and who would be none other than the angel of death. The bridegroom did as the prophet had advised him, and the result was that the pleading, arguments, and tears of the young bride, who had already suffered so much, touched even the angel of death. He himself went up to Heaven and presented the petition, pleading for mercy for the newly wedded pair. The Lord had compassion and granted the request of the pious wife.[2]

This legend, to some extent, resembles the story of Sarah in the book of *Tobit*, where, however, it is the power of Ashmedai that is broken by some magic means and not by the efficacy of prayer. The two tales again remind us not only of *Thousand*

---

[1] *Hibbur Hamassiot Ve-Hamidrashot Ve-Haagadot*, Venice, p. 1; see Bin Gorion, *loc. cit.*; see also *Mélusine*, Vol. II, col. 573–574, French translation by Israel Lévi.

[2] *Midrash Tanchuma*, section *Haazinu; Kav Hajashar;* see also Tendlau, *Die Sagen der Juden*, p. 108 ff., No. 28; cf. Bin Gorion, *loc. cit.*

and One Nights,[1] but also of the famous story of Savitri and Satyavan; one of the most beautiful episodes in the *Mahabharata*.

SAVITRI AND SATYAVAN

And hearing these words, Yama said: " The words that thou utterest, O fair lady, I have not heard from anyone save thee; I am highly pleased with this speech of thine. Except the life of Satyavan, solicit thou, therefore, a fourth boon, and then go thy way!"

Savitri then said: " Both of me and Satyavan's loins, begotten by both of us, let there be a century of sons possessed of strength and prowess and capable of perpetuating our race! Even this is the fourth boon that I would beg of thee!"

Hearing these words of hers, Yama replied: " Thou shalt, O lady, obtain a century of sons, possessed of strength and prowess and causing thee great delight. O daughter of a king, let no more weariness be thine! Do thou desist! Thou hast already come too far!"

Thus addressed, Savitri said: " They that are righteous always practise eternal morality! And the communion of the pious with the pious is never fruitless! Nor is there any danger to the pious from those that are pious. And verily it is the righteous who by their truth make the sun move in the heaven. And it is the righteous that support the earth by their austerities! And, O King, it is the righteous upon whom both the past and the future depend! Therefore, they that are righteous are never cheerless in the company of the righteous. Knowing this to be the eternal practice of the good and righteous, they that are righteous continue to do good to others without expecting any benefit in return. A good office is never thrown away on the good and virtuous. Neither interest nor dignity suffereth any injury by such an act. And since such conduct ever adheres to the righteous, the righteous often become the protectors of all."

Hearing these words of hers, Yama replied: " The more thou utterest such speeches that are pregnant with great import, full of honeyed phrases, instinct with morality, and agreeable to mind, the more is the respect that I feel for thee! O thou that art so devoted to thy Lord, ask for some incomparable boon!"

---

[1] Cf. Perles, *Monatsschrift*, Vol. XXIII, p. 123; Chauvin, V., *La Recension égyptienne des Mille et une Nuits*, Bruxelles, 1899, pp. 59–60; 116–118.

Thus addressed, Savitri said: " O bestower of honours, the boon thou hast already given me is incapable of accomplishment without union with my husband. Therefore, among other boons, I ask for this, may this Satyavan be restored to life! Deprived of my husband, I am as one dead! Without my husband, I do not wish for happiness. Without my husband, I do not wish for Heaven itself. Without my husband, I do not wish for prosperity. Without my husband, I cannot make up my mind to live. Thou thyself hast bestowed on me the boon, namely of a century of sons. Yet, thou takest away my husband! I ask for this boon: may Satyavan be restored to life, for by that thy words will be made true!"

" So be it," said Yama, the dispenser of justice, untied his noose, and with cheerful heart said these words to Savitri: " Thus, O auspicious and chaste lady, is thy husband freed by me! Thou wilt be able to take him back free from disease, and he will attain to success. And along with thee, he will attain a life of four hundred years. And celebrating sacrifices with due rites, he will achieve great fame in this world. And upon thee Satyavan will also beget a century of sons."

The Mahabharata (*Vanaparvan*, 49, 297; Roy's translation).

CHAPTER XVIII

The Prophet Elijah in the Kabbalah and in Moslem Tradition

The Prophet Elijah in Jewish mysticism—An angel descended from Heaven—Sandalphon-Elijah—The mission of Elijah—Elijah and John the Baptist—Elijah identical with Phinehas, the son of Aaron—The angel of the covenant—The chair of Elijah at the ceremony of the rite of circumcision—The forerunner of the Messiah—Armilaos and the Anti-Christ—Elijah in Christian legend—*The Book of the Bee*—Elijah in Mohammedan tradition—Elijah and El Khidr, the ever-young—The source of eternal life—Rabbi Joshua ben Levi and Elijah—The Prophet Elijah and the wandering Jew—The origin of this legend.

Whilst, however, the Haggadists consider Elijah as a man who had attained immortality, the teachers of the Kabbalah and of Jewish mysticism look upon him as a supernatural being who had never been born by woman. He is an angel descended from Heaven for the purpose of being useful to mankind.

When the Creator of the Universe made up his mind to create man, Elijah, one of the ministering angels, approached the Throne of Glory and thus he spoke: " Lord of the Universe! If it be pleasing in Thine eyes, let me descend to earth where I can be of service to the sons of men." Thus spake Elijah, whose name was really Sandalphon, or, according to other teachers of mysticism, Metatron.

The Lord thereupon changed the angel's name to Elijah, but some time elapsed before this benefactor of humanity was permitted to descend from the regions celestial, assume the shape of mortal man, and abide on earth. This happened in the days of King Ahab.

When Elijah had converted the world to the true faith and belief in the Eternal, God took him again to Heaven and thus He spoke to him: " Be thou now the protector and guardian spirit of My children and spread the knowledge of Me and the belief in Me in the whole world." [1]

This belief is derived from the fact that neither the father nor the mother of Elijah are mentioned in Holy Writ and that he ascended to Heaven, which had never happened to mortal man before.[2]

In the Talmud already Elijah is identified with Phinehas, just as in the New Testament John the Baptist was held to be Elijah.[3] In Mohammedan legend, too, Elijah is identical with Phinehas, the grandson of Aaron, the High-Priest.

In Kabbalistic and mystic lore Elijah is represented as the angel of the covenant, and hence the custom prevalent among Jews to set aside a chair for the Prophet Elijah at the ceremony of the rite of circumcision.[4] He is also supposed to be the fore-runner of the Messiah. Before the advent of the Messiah, he will subdue Armilaos or Hermilaos, the Anti-Messiah who may be compared to the Anti-Christ of Christian legend, and then introduce the true Messiah, the son of David, to Israel. He will then perform the miracle of resurrection.[5] He will slay Sammael or Satan, and then the era of peace, the messianic time, will begin, the principle of evil having been eradi-cated.

From the Jews the myths and legends about Elijah were taken over by the Christians and the Mohammedans. In *The Book of the Bee* it is related that when Elijah was born, his father saw in a dream that one was born, and that they wrapped him in fire instead of swaddling bands, and gave him some of that fire to eat. He came to Jerusalem and told the priests the

---

[1] *Yalkut Rubeni, Genesis*, ed. Amst., p. 9*b*.   [2] *Ibid.*   [3] *Matthew*, 11, 14.
[4] *Pirke de Rabbi Eliezer*, ch. 29; see Friedlaender's translation, p. 214, notes.
[5] *Monatsschrift*, Vol. XII, p. 289; see also Jellinek, *Beth-Hamidrash*; Buttenwieser, *Die hebräische Eliasapokalypse*, 1897.

vision that he had seen. The learned among the people said to him: " Fear not, thy son is about to be a fire, and his word shall be like fire, and shall not fall to the ground; he will burn like fire with jealousy of sinners, and his zeal will be accepted before God." [1]

Mohammed, as we have already pointed out, borrowed largely from the Jews and very frequently applied the legends told of one Biblical personage to another. In Mohammedan tradition, the Prophet Elijah is that mysterious never dying being known as El Khidr, the ever-young. D'Herbelot[2] relates that in the distant and nebulous East there exists a source of eternal life and youth. Whoever drinks of this source is sure of immortality. Mighty kings and rulers travelled to those distant and mysterious regions, but never were they able to reach the spot where the source of eternal life and youth is bubbling. They all failed, and only El Khidr succeeded in reaching the spot. He drank from the source of life and enjoys eternal life and youth.[3] When the Arabs came into contact with the Jews and their legendary lore, and heard of the legends clustering round the person of the Tishbite who never dies, they identified him with El Khidr. All that the Jews told of Elijah, Islam relates of El Khidr, and all the myths and legends current in Mohammedanism and related of El Khidr are transferred to Elijah. El Khidr and Elijah are thus identical. Thus the story of Rabbi Joshua ben Levi and Elijah is told in the Koran of Moses and El Khidr.

RABBI JOSHUA BEN LEVI AND THE PROPHET ELIJAH

For many days did the pious Rabbi Joshua, the son of Levi, fast and pray to his Creator that He would grant him the sight of the prophet Elijah. And lo, one day, Elijah indeed

---

[1] E. W. Budge, *The Book of the Bee* (Aneed. Oxon. Sem. Series, Vol. I, Part 2), p. 70.
[2] *Bibliothèque Orientale*, s.v. *Ab Zendeghian*.
[3] See Wünsche, *Ex Oriente Lux*; J. Friedlaender, *Die Chadhirlegende und der Alexander-roman*, Leipzig, 1913.

appeared to him and thus he said: " Is there aught thou dost desire of me? Speak, and I will fulfill it."

And Rabbi Joshua, the son of Levi, replied: " I am anxious to accompany thee in thy wanderings, so that I may see thy works in the world and thus learn great wisdom from thee and profit."

But Elijah replied: " Thou wouldst not be able to endure all that thou wouldst see, and it would be a great worry and trouble to me to explain unto thee constantly the reasons of my conduct and actions."

Thus spoke the Prophet, whereto the pious Rabbi replied: " My Lord, I promise thee that I will never ask or inquire, nor will I weary thee with questions concerning thy deeds. All that I long for is to accompany thee and witness thy deeds."

And the prophet Elijah consented and permitted Rabbi Joshua to accompany him in his wanderings, on condition that he should never ask any questions concerning the reasons of his deeds, or the signs and wonders he might perform. Should he disobey, then they would at once part company.

The two sallied forth and wandered about until they came to the house of a poor and needy man, who had nothing but one cow which stood in the court of his house. When the man and his wife saw the travellers, they at once rushed out to meet them, saluted them and invited them to their house. They offered them the best room in their house, placed before them what meat and drink they happened to possess and made them eat and drink and remain the night under their roof. When it was morning, the Prophet and the Rabbi arose to go on their journey, but before leaving the hospitable roof, Elijah prayed concerning the cow, and she died, and then they went their way.

Greatly did Rabbi Joshua wonder at this deed and he was faint at heart. He said within himself: " All the reward this poor man has received for the honour he has shown us was to lose his cow, that has been killed, and he has no other." Unable to restrain himself, he said to the Prophet: " My Lord, why didst thou kill this poor man's cow, he being a worthy man who has shown us much honour?"

Thus spoke Rabbi Joshua, and Elijah made answer: " Remember the condition I made, that thou shouldst take heed but be silent, hold thy peace, and ask no questions. I am quite ready to give thee the reason of my action if thou art prepared to separate from me." Rabbi Joshua, afraid of being dismissed by the Prophet, was silent and spoke no further.

They continued their journey, and after travelling the whole day came towards evening to the house of a certain rich man. The host, however, never turned to them to do them honour, and the two travellers sat in his house without either meat or drink. Now in the house of this rich but un-generous man there was a wall that had fallen down, and he had to build it up again. In the morning Elijah prayed con-cerning the wall, and it was at once built up. Great was Rabbi Joshua's astonishment and trouble when he saw what Elijah had done. Remembering, however, the Prophet's rebuke, he restrained himself from asking any questions and kept his peace.

Thus they travelled all day, and towards evening came to a great synagogue. The seats therein were of pure gold and silver, and each man was sitting on his chair according to his rank and dignity. When they beheld the two wanderers, one of them said: " Who will give food and lodging to these two poor travellers?" Then another man answered: " There is no need; they will have enough with the bread and salt and water which they have brought with them hither."

The two waited for someone to invite them, but none of the men in the synagogue paid any attention to the weary wanderers. Thus they passed the night in the synagogue until the morning. When morning came the two travellers arose,

and Elijah said to the men: " May it be the will of the Lord
to make you all leaders and chief men of the community."

Thereupon the two continued their way, and Rabbi Joshua
greatly wondered and his trouble increased, but once more he
held his peace and said nothing. With sunset they reached
another town, where they were received with kindness, joy,
and cheerfulness. The two travellers were honoured, treated
with great courteousness, and lodged in the finest house in the
city. They ate and drank and passed the night in great honour.
When morning came Elijah prayed, and thus he said: " May
it be the will of the Almighty to make only one man among
you a leader of the community."

No longer could Rabbi Joshua restrain himself when he
heard these words uttered by Elijah.

" My Lord," he said, addressing the Prophet, " tell me
now, I pray thee, the reason of thy strange actions, and acquaint
me with the secret of all the works thou hast performed."

" As it appears to be in thy heart to separate from me,"
said the Prophet, " I will explain it all to thee and tell thee the
secret of my actions. Know then that with regard to the cow
of the poor man which I slew, I did it because it had been
decreed that on that very day his wife should die, and I prayed
to the Lord to accept the cow, his only possession, as a ransom.
Through the woman, I foresaw, great good and profit will
arise to the house and the man. As for the rich man whose
wall I built up, know that under the foundation of the tumbled-
down wall a great treasure lies hidden. Had I left the rich miser
to build up the wall himself, he would have laid bare the
foundation and discovered the treasure. The wall I have built
will soon tumble down and will never be rebuilt again.

" As for the hard-hearted men whom I wished and concerning whom I prayed that there should be many princes,
communal leaders, and chiefs among them, I did this because
this will turn out to be an evil thing for them. Whenever

there are many leaders there is a division in their counsels, and the place is destroyed and goes to ruin.

"It is for the same reason that I prayed concerning the just men who did us much honour that only one of them should be a chief man. It will be a benefit to them and their counsels and works will have unity, and they will be a happy people, for the spirit of division will not come among them; their counsels will not vary, and their plans will not be frustrated. Thus it is said in the proverbs: ' Through too many sailors the ships founder ', and ' Under the protection of one master a city stands firm '."

And Elijah continued: " I am now about to leave thee, but before parting I will tell thee something the knowledge of which will benefit thee. If ever thou seest a wicked man who prospers and upon whom the hour smiles, let not thine imagination entice thee, nor do thou wonder, but know that his fortune is for his hurt. If, on the other hand, thou seest a righteous and just man in trouble and in grief, pained and wearied, going about hungry, thirsty, naked, and lacking everything in this world, suffering greatly and visited by numerous afflictions, then again be neither angry nor provoked in spirit. Beware of letting thy imagination and thy heart delude thee to entertain the slightest doubt of thy Creator. Consider in thy heart and understanding that He is just and right, and that His judgment is right. His eyes are on the ways of men, and who shall say to Him: ' What doest Thou?' "

Thereupon Elijah bade farewell to Rabbi Joshua ben Levi and went on his way.[1]

Tabari relates the following story of Elijah:

Idolatry was general in the land of Israel when the Prophet Elijah appeared. The Lord had sent him to the city of Balbeck or Heliopolis for the purpose of persuading the inhabi-

---

[1] *Hibbur Jaffe*, pp. 4*b*–6*a*; Jellinek, *Beth-Hamidrash*, Vol. V, pp. 133–135; Vol. VI, pp. 131–133; *Seder Eliahu Rabba*, p. 36, § 4; *Serapeum*, XVII, 5; Wünsche, *Aus Israel's Lehrhallen*, Vol. I, pp. 127–130; see Zunz, *Gottesdienstliche Vorträge*, p. 138, note *a*.

tants to give up the worship of Baal, after whom the city was
called. The Prophet preached against idolatry, which had
spread among the Jews. The King of the Israelites, Ahab,
who had at first believed the Prophet and been induced to
reject Baal, soon returned to idol worship. Thereupon the
Prophet prayed to the Lord, and He sent a famine upon
the land which lasted three years. In those days none but
Elijah had bread and many men died. Whenever people
smelt the odour of bread, they said to each other: " The
Prophet Elijah hath passed this way."

One day Elijah came to the house of an old woman who
had a paralytic son named Elisha. Elijah gave bread to the old
woman and healed her son. Henceforth the boy accompanied
the Prophet. When the famine had lasted three years, Elijah
and his companion appeared before Ahab, King of Israel, and
thus he spoke: " For three years the famine has now lasted
in the land, and thou hast been without bread. If thy god
Baal can satisfy thy hunger it is well, but if not, worship the
God of Israel, and I will pray to Him that He send thee help
in thy distress." Ahab consented. Thereupon the idol of
Baal was taken out of the city, and the worshippers invoked
the heathen god. Their prayers, however, remained un-
answered. Thereupon Elijah prayed to the Lord, rain fell, and
the earth brought forth herb and corn. The people, however,
soon returned to idol worship, and Elijah prayed to the Lord
to take him away from the wicked generation. The Lord
granted the Prophet's prayer, but Elijah is not dead, for he
will live until the day when Israel shall sound the trumpet of
judgment.[1]

[1] Tabari. I, 84.

THE PROPHET ELIJAH AND THE WANDERING JEW

The legend of the Prophet Elijah, of his eternal wandering among men, may also have given rise to the legend of the wandering Jew. In Jewish legendary lore Elijah, the eternal wanderer, is active and benevolent. The messenger of peace, he encourages the irresolute, instructs those who are eager for knowledge, and brings succour to the needy. One day he will be the harbinger of salvation to the whole race of Israel. He has never tasted death, is omniscient and ubiquitous.

Mohammed, who drew very largely from Jewish sources, had heard of this legend of the eternal, immortal wanderer and represented him as a sage travelling since thousands of years, watching the eternal geological and social changes of the world and humanity, smiling at human ignorance and watching the march of events from the Pisgah heights of his age and travels. He is Khidr, the eternal-young. During the Middle Ages, the legend came to the Christians when it underwent a certain change. On the one hand, there was a constant desire of the Church to find as many witnesses as possible for the infallibility of the Church, whilst, on the other, hate of the Jews would not admit that the eternal wanderer is Elijah, particularly favourable to the Jewish race. He therefore became the wandering Jew, an eternal witness of Christianity. Called Cartaphilus, at first, he is soon changed to Ahasverus and condemned to bear witness to the Divinity of Christ.[1]

---

[1] See *Jüdische Zeitschrift*, Vol. V, p. 45–46.

CHAPTER XIX

The Romance of Esther, or the Jew-baiter and the Royal Favourite

The throne of Solomon—The King of Persia—Ahasuerus builds a new throne—The royal banquet—Great magnificence—The wealth of Ahasuerus—The copper vessels constructed by Nebuchadnezzar—The treasure at the bottom of the Euphrates—The holy utensils from the Temple—The royal gardens—The Jews as the guests of the King of Persia—The divine banquet in the future world—Customs at Persian drinking bouts—The huge beaker — New regulations introduced by Ahasuerus — The Lord waxes wroth—Beauty unadorned, or the disobedient queen—Jewish and Pagan feasts—The reasons of Vashti's refusal—The marks of leprosy—Punishment for her sin—The Queen's proud message—The advice of Daniel—Memuchan—The beautiful Jewess—Esther-Hadassa, origin of her name—The aged beauty—The portrait of Vashti—The conspiracy of the two Tarsians—The wealthy barber of Karzum—Haman becomes a soldier—The starving Haman and the generous Mordecai—Haman sells himself as a slave to the Jew—The sudden wealth of Haman—The ex-barber becomes vizier—Haman meets Mordecai—The image of an idol on Haman's breast—The bird who tried to dry up the ocean—The casting of lots—The days of the week plead in favour of Israel—The months of the year except the month of Adar unfavourable to Haman—The signs of the Zodiac—The Fishes alone are unfavourable to the Jews—Haman's denunciation—The objections of the King—The two cups of wine—The God of Israel has forsaken the nation—The royal decree—The St. Bartholomew Night of antiquity—Haman's arguments in favour of the annihilation of the Jews—The world will have peace only when the nation is destroyed—The indictment of Satan—The verses recited by the schoolchildren—The argument of Satan—The lament of the Torah—The weeping angels—The Prophet Elijah visits the graves of the Patriarchs—He implores Moses to intercede on behalf of Israel—Moses' advice.

THE ROYAL BANQUET

When Ahasuerus became king over Persia he gave instructions that the famous throne of Solomon be brought to him. Thereupon his counsellors and wise men said unto him:

" Why dost thou do such a thing, O King? Thou wilt surely not succeed."

Greatly surprised, Ahasuerus asked his wise men to tell him the reason of their fear.

" Know then, O mighty ruler," replied the wise men, " that one day Shishak, King of Egypt, captured Jerusalem and carried away the throne of Solomon, the son of David. The throne then came into the possession of Sennaherib, of Pharaoh Necho, and of Nebuchadnezzar, King of Babylon. But neither the kings of Ashur and Egypt nor the ruler of Babylon were ever allowed to seat themselves upon the throne of Solomon, for scarcely had they placed a foot upon the first step of the wonderful throne when the lion dealt them a blow. Thereupon Darius, thine own father, waged war against Babylon, and among the rich booty he carried away the famous throne and brought it to the city of Eilam in Media. Never, however, did thy father dare seat himself upon the throne of Solomon, the great King of Israel. Thy father, O King, was a wise ruler and a pious and god-fearing man, and if he was careful not to seat himself upon the throne of Solomon, why shouldst thou expose thyself to any danger?"

Thus spoke the wise men of King Ahasuerus. Thereupon the ruler of Persia sent for artificers from Tyre and Alexandria and bade them construct a throne similar to that of Solomon, King of Israel. This they did, but it took them three years to build the throne.

When the work of the throne was completed, Ahasuerus made a gorgeous feast for the hundred and twenty-seven rulers of the hundred and twenty-seven provinces of his mighty empire. All the grandees and nobles were seated upon couches of gold and silver set in with precious stones, and daily King Ahasuerus showed to his guests his vast treasures. The ruler of Persia boasted of his greatness and power and pretended that he himself had acquired all the vast wealth which was his personal possession. One day, however, one of the princes said unto his friends:

" In vain doth the King boast of his vast wealth, for it is not his personal property nor hath he himself acquired it. I will tell ye whence Ahasuerus hath his treasures. Ye know that Nebuchadnezzar, the mighty King of Babylon, had waged many wars, conquered many lands and carried away great booty and vast treasures. Now when Nebuchadnezzar felt his end draw near he was greatly reluctant to leave his possessions to his son Evil-Merodach. ' I will hide my treasures ', thought the miserly King of Babylon, ' rather than leave them to my son.' Now what did he do? He constructed vessels of copper wherein he placed his gold and silver and precious stones, and during the night sank the vessels into the River Euphrates. They remained at the bottom of the river until Cyrus came and gave permission to the Jews to rebuild their temple at Jerusalem. As a reward for his pious deed God allowed him to inherit and take possession of Nebuchadnezzar's vast wealth. One day, when Cyrus was crossing the River Euphrates, the waters suddenly separated and the King discovered the copper vessels containing Nebuchadnezzar's wealth. Such is the origin of the wealth of which Ahasuerus is now boasting."

The treasures which Ahasuerus was displaying to his guests were indeed immense, for the King of Persia was wealthier than all the kings of Persia and Media. Ahasuerus erected couches of silver and gold in the streets of his capital in order to let the whole world know how rich he was. All the vessels used at the feast of the King of Persia were not vessels of silver but of gold. When, however, Ahasuerus commanded that the utensils from the temple of Jerusalem be brought in, all the vessels in the palace changed in appearance; they became dim and lost their splendour, looking like lead when brought together with the sacred vessels of the temple. But not only to his princes did Ahasuerus offer a great feast. He also invited the inhabitants of his capital Shushan. The festivities took place in the royal gardens where wonderful trees bore delicious fruit and aromatic foliage wafted a fragrant smell. The pavement consisted of precious stones and pearls, and the guests were seated upon couches made of delicate draperies placed under the trees. Curtains of byssus and royal purple stretched from tree to tree, and servants hastened to do the bidding of the guests, for the King had commanded that every guest be allowed to follow his own inclinations. Walking through the royal gardens, Ahasuerus approached his Jewish guests, for whom separate tables had been set, and thus he said:

" Look at this wonderful scenery, at the golden couches, the pleasant trees and the aromatic foliage, and tell me whether your God will be able to offer you such a banquet in the future world?"

The Jews made no answer, for they thought in their hearts: " How stupid are the words of the King who does not realize the fact that all this scenery, the garden, the trees, the food and the wine are the handiwork of the Creator of the Universe." But when the King of Persia once more repeated his question, the Jews replied as follows:

" Know, O King, that the banquet which the Lord will prepare for the pious in the future world no eye hath seen it but God's. If the Lord, however, were to offer us a feast like thine, we should certainly feel ashamed and say: ' Such a banquet we have already partaken of at the table of Ahasuerus, King of Persia.' "

In spite of his vainglory and foolishness Ahasuerus was a tolerant monarch. He gave instructions to his servants to let every guest follow his inclinations in the matter of drink. Thus it was an old custom of Persia at drinking bouts to compel each guest to drain a huge beaker containing 15 eights and called *Pitka*. And when one of the guests said that he could not do it, the servants forced him to comply with the old custom, though he lost his reason over it or even died. The guests therefore at Persian wassails were in the habit of bribing the butler so as to permit them to drink only according to their respective capacities. The butler and other servants thus grew rich. Ahasuerus, however, gave instructions that the old Persian custom be ignored for once, and that each man should drink only as much as he could or wished to.

The King also commanded his officers never to use a cup more than once. The cups out of which the guests had drunk were also to be kept by them as a royal gift. Moreover the guests were to be served with drinks to which they had been accustomed from their youth.

When Ahasuerus issued his famous order " to do according to every man's pleasure " the Lord, however, waxed wroth. " Villain," said He, " how canst thou do every man's pleasure at once? This is only in the power of God to do. Tell me, what wilt thou do if two men came to thee who are in love with the same woman, both desiring to marry her? Canst thou do according to both these men's pleasure? Or suppose that two vessels are sailing from the port, one of them requiring a north wind and the other a south wind. Canst thou satisfy the two vessels at once and produce at the same time a wind that was both northern and southern?" The Lord alone can satisfy at one and the same moment the wills and pleasures of many men, as it is said: " He will fulfil the desires of them that fear him."[1]

Beauty Unadorned, or the Doom of Vashti

There is always a vast difference between the banquets and feasts of Jews and the carousals of the pagans. Whenever the former are gathered for the purpose of feasting on some momentous occasion, they discuss the Law, the Haggadah or the Halachah, or even a verse from the Scriptures. They sing

[1] *Psalm*, cxlv, 19.

hymns and praise the Lord. Not so the pagans, who indulge
in prurient talk whenever they are of good cheer. Thus it happened at the festive board of Ahasuerus. The conversation
began to turn on the subject of women, and Persians and
Medians began to praise the charms of their respective women.
Thereupon the " fool " Ahasuerus maintained that his own
wife, who was neither a Median nor a Persian but a Chaldæan,
excelled in beauty all the women in the world. In order to
prove the truth of his assertions the King, in his drunken
boast, consented to the request made by his boon companions.
Vashti, his queen, was to appear unadorned and without any
apparel before Persia's grandees and princes, so as to give them
the opportunity of judging whether in reality her charms were
such as described by her spouse, and whether she deserved the
palm of beauty.

The Queen of Persia was not such a prude as to feel shocked
at the order she received from her lord and master who had
forgotten all dignity in his drunken fit. To appear naked in the
company of men and to exhibit her charms to their gaze did
not at all offend the moral sense of that queen of pagan antiquity.
If the semi-nude is considered as *comme il faut* by the daughters
of Eve after twenty centuries of Christianity, why should the
nude have shocked the Queen of Persia, who, like her husband,
really revelled in carnal pleasures? According to Jewish
legendary lore, Vashti's refusal to obey His Majesty's command
was due to other reasons than that of an outraged moral sense.
When Vashti began to divest herself of her garments, ready to
walk into the banqueting hall, she suddenly noticed that marks of
leprosy and other diseases had become visible upon her forehead
and her body. No puff, powder, or perfume could remove the
marks of her disease, and Vashti was compelled to make a virtue
out of necessity. Unwilling to acquaint the King with the real
reason prompting her to disobey his command, she pretended
that her action was dictated by pride and a sense of decency.

Vashti's disease was a punishment meted out to her on account of her sins. She had been in the habit of forcing Jewish maidens to spin and weave on the Sabbath, and often would she strip the innocent girls of their clothing. It was for this sin that she was commanded to appear naked before the King and his drunken guests. Persia's queen would have obeyed the command of her royal spouse and gladly offered her beauty to the gaze of men, but the Lord sent His angel Gabriel, who struck Vashti with leprosy and other diseases.

Thereupon the proud beauty sent the following message to her husband: " I am Vashti, the daughter of Belshazzar, son of the great and mighty Nebuchadnezzar, the proud monarch who laughed at kings and princes. Thou hast never been deemed worthy even to run before my father's chariot. Had my father been alive now, I would never have been given to thee as wife. Even the criminals condemned to death by my father were never stripped of their clothes and led naked to the place of execution. Thou art only a fool and a madman who has lost his reason in consequence of too much drinking. I refuse to appear before thy boon companions stripped of my clothing, and I do it for thine own sake. Knowest thou not, thou fool, that if they are charmed with my beauty, they will kill thee and take possession of me, whilst if they remain indifferent they will simply say that thou art a liar and a boaster."

Such was the message which Vashti sent to King Ahasuerus. The great ladies of the Persian aristocracy, jealous of the queen's beauty, encouraged the latter in her refusal and advised her to persevere and disobey the command of the King. At the advice of the Memuchan—who was none other than Daniel —Vashti was thereupon condemned to death. The Queen was an enemy of Daniel and hated him, because he had once predicted her father's death. Daniel again was hostile to the Queen because it was she who prevented Ahasuerus from permitting the Jews to rebuild their temple at Jerusalem.

THE BEAUTIFUL JEWESS

The Persian court thereupon decided to find a new queen for Ahasuerus, and Esther was chosen. Esther was also called Hadassa, or Myrtle, on account of her good and pious deeds which spread her fame abroad even as the myrtle wafts its fragrance in the air. She was also like the myrtle because just as the myrtle has a pleasant scent but a bitter taste, so Esther was pleasant to her own people, but proved bitter to her people's enemy, the Jew-baiter Haman. She was called Esther, which means the mysterious one, because she jealously guarded the secret of her origin and descent from King and Court. Esther, according to Jewish legendary lore, was not really beautiful, but had grace and a bewitching charm, and all those who beheld her deemed her worthy of becoming Queen of Persia. According to some Jewish legends Esther was seventy-five years of age and it was really a miracle that such beauty was hers that even at an advanced age she charmed the mighty monarch, his court, and his people.

Ahasuerus, it seems, had been regretting his former wife Vashti, and for many years had her portrait in his chamber hung over his bed. None of the maidens brought to him equalled Vashti in beauty and he could not forget her, but when Esther came, Ahasuerus at once forgot the daughter of Belshazzar whom he had put to death.

THE CONSPIRACY

It was at that time that Mordecai, Esther's foster-father, discovered the conspiracy of two officials who had determined to poison the King. The two court-officials were Tarsians, and spoke in their native tongue, Tarsian, never suspecting that Mordecai, who was present, could understand them. They did not know that Mordecai was a member of the San-hedrin, and as such could converse in seventy languages. The two conspirators somehow got wind that their plot had been discovered, and they speedily removed the poison they had put in the King's cup. But a miracle happened, and when the King had the contents of the cup analysed, lo! it was found that it contained poison.

Haman the Jew-baiter of Antiquity, or the Wealthy Barber

Mordecai the Jew had thus saved his life, but Ahasuerus forgot the service the Jew had rendered him and acted most ungratefully. Instead of rewarding the man who had saved his life, he raised Haman, with whose feelings towards the Jews he was well acquainted, to the highest honours.

Haman was a man of very low origin, and owed his rapid advance and his rise to such high honours to his vast wealth. He was a *nouveau-riche* who became a prince for no other merit than that of having acquired a vast fortune. In Jewish legend the story of Haman's early life runs as follows.

In those days there came to Persia a man named Haman, son of Hamdata. He was a direct descendant of Eliphaz, the son of Esau, the brother of Jacob, and a barber by profession. For twenty-two years Haman exercised his craft in the village of Karzum, but when his family increased and he had ten sons, his small earnings no longer sufficed to provide his wife and children with bread. Thereupon Haman left his wife and children at Karzum, and taking up his staff set out from his village in search of some more lucrative occupation. Thus he journeyed from town to town until he heard that the commander of the King's army was asking for volunteers to whom he promised good pay. Haman immediately sold himself as a soldier and joined the army. A battle was waged, the commander was defeated and his army dispersed. Many soldiers, among them Haman, escaped into the desert, where for many days they suffered the pangs of hunger and the torture of thirst. In vain did Haman implore his brothers-in-arms for a crust of bread and a drop of water. None of them would part with the little he possessed.

One day the former barber came across a Jewish officer, Mordecai by name, who took pity on the starving son of Hamdata and gave him a morsel of bread and a drink of water, sharing with him the little he had himself. Great was the gratitude of Haman and thus he spoke to Mordecai: " Thou hast saved my life, for without thy generous help, I would at this hour have died of hunger and thirst. I shall now be thy slave for ever and serve thee faithfully." Thereupon Haman took a piece of old parchment and pricking his finger with a thorn, dipped a small stick in his blood and wrote out a deed wherein he solemnly declared himself to be the slave of Mordecai who had saved his life.

According to some sources Haman wrote the deed of sale upon Mordecai's knee. In the meantime the King sent out another army and the general defeated the enemy. The mercenaries were now disbanded and Haman returned to the village of Karzum.

" It would be best for us," said the son of Hamdata to his wife Zeresh, " to leave this village and betake ourselves to the capital where, perchance, we might be able to earn our living among the inhabitants. Zeresh agreed with her husband and the family journeyed to Shushan, the capital of Persia. On the way fortune smiled upon the barber, for he found a vast treasure and thus entered Shushan as a very wealthy man. He bought houses, fields, and vineyards, and acquired many friends who honoured him and paid him homage on account of his great wealth.

The fame of the ex-barber, the new-rich, increased, for he was reputed to be the wealthiest man in the land, and the King himself honoured him greatly. Ahasuerus raised Haman, in spite of his low origin, above all his princes and counsellors, and made him his vizier and Prime Minister. He also commanded all his subjects to pay homage to Haman, and to bow to him whenever they met him. Thereupon Haman put the image of an idol upon his breast and wherever he passed the people of Persia bowed low and prostrated themselves before the descendant of Agag.

One day Haman passed the gates of the royal palace and beheld old Mordecai, the generous Jewish officer who had once saved his life and to whom—in an outburst of gratitude —he had sold himself as a slave. The vizier immediately recognized his benefactor, but was annoyed at his discovery. " If the old Jew," thought Haman, " recognizes me and refuses to bow to me, looking upon me as his slave, then I will kill him." Mordecai indeed refused to bow to Haman and to prostrate himself before the vizier, not, however, because he claimed the former barber as his slave, for he had never expected any reward for his generosity. He refused to prostrate himself before Haman because the latter bore the image of an idol upon his breast.

" I would pay homage to and honour the man whom the King has set above all his princes," thought the pious and law-abiding Jew, " but never will I bow to and prostrate myself before the image of an idol and thus transgress the commandment of the Lord of the Universe." Thereupon the vizier determined not only to kill Mordecai, his former benefactor, the man who had shared with him his bread and water in an hour of need and thus saved his life, but also to exterminate the entire Jewish race. Haman's decision reminds us of the story of the stupid bird who had once made up its mind to dry up the ocean.

There was once a bird which had built its nest on the seashore. One day, when it returned after a flight in search of food, the bird found no trace of its nest and the young therein, for the waves of the ocean had destroyed the nest and swept it away. Great was the wrath of the bereaved bird and it vowed in its breast to wreak vengeance upon the cruel ocean.

" I will dry it up," cried the bird, and immediately set to work to carry out its design. Filling its tiny beak with water from the ocean it spat it out upon the sands and thus proceeded to empty the ocean. Night and day did the bird work, but, alas! perceived no progress. Then another bird came to the seashore and was mightily surprised to see its friend engaged upon a strange task.

" Tell me, sister," said the newcomer, " what is the task thou art engaged upon?"

" I have sworn," replied the first bird, " to empty the waters of the ocean, to turn the wide expanse of water to dry land and change the sands upon the seashore into an ocean."

" Thou stupid bird," laughed the newcomer, " it is an impossible task thou hast undertaken. Dost thou not know that if all the creatures in the world were to forgather and help thee in thy task, they would all perish in their enterprise, for never would they succeed to empty the ocean." Haman knew the story, but he spoke in his heart: " I am not a stupid bird, nor are the Jews the waters of the ocean. If only the King will give me permission, I will soon exterminate the entire race of Israel and wipe out its memory for ever."

The Casting of the Lots

Haman laid out his plan how to destroy the people of Israel, but being an astrologer he determined first to cast lots so as to find out the most favourable moment for his purpose. He began by casting lots with regard to the days of the week. Thereupon the seven days appeared before the Lord of the Universe and raised a protest. The first day said that it was the day on which heaven and earth had been created and these were to exist only as long as the nation of Israel existed. The second day pointed out that it was the day on which Rakia had been created and on which the Lord had separated the celestial from the terrestrial waters, even as Israel had been separated from the heathen nations. The third day protested against the destruction of Israel, because it was the day on which the trees had been created, and did not Israel offer the tenth part of all fruit, giving it to the widow and the orphan? It also praised the Lord with branches of palm trees during the Feast of Tabernacles. The fourth day refused to lend itself to the destruction of Israel, because it was the day on which the celestial luminaries, the sun, the moon, and the constellations had been created. " Hast Thou not sworn unto the Patriarchs," pleaded the fourth day of the week, " that their offspring will be as numerous as the stars in heaven?" Then the fifth day came and protested against the destruction of Israel, because it was the day on which the birds were created. " Israel," cried the day, " is in the habit of bringing offerings unto Thee, and who will do so when the nation will be destroyed?" Thereupon the sixth day raised its voice in protest and reminded the Lord that it was the day on which He had created the sheep, and Israel is called both sheep and man.[1] Finally the Sabbath came and objected to the destruction of Israel because it was the day called " a sign between Israel and God ".[2] " Destroy me first, O Lord," pleaded each of the seven days in turn, " and then Thou mayest destroy the nation of Israel."

The seven days of the week having thus refused to aid Haman in his plans, each, on the contrary, having pleaded in favour of Israel, the Jew-baiter of antiquity decided to find out which of the twelve months of the year would favour his undertaking. Once more, however, he was baffled in his design. The month of Nissan appeared before the Lord and thus it pleaded: " Lord of the Universe! I have found grace

---

[1] *Ezechiel*, xxxiv, 31.   [2] *Exodus*, xxxi, 17.

in Thine eyes, for in me the Children of Israel were redeemed from bondage, and now may it be Thy will to vouchsafe Thy favour unto me and not to turn the month of festivity into one of mourning." Thereupon the month of Jyar came and thus it spoke: " In me Thou didst send down heavenly food, Manna, to Israel in the desert and also hast subdued its enemy, Amalek." The month of Sivan protested against the destruction of Israel because it was the month in which the Law was given to the nation on Mount Sinai, the Torah in which it is written: " It is a tree of life for those who observe it." Thereupon the months of Tammuz and Ab came and pleaded in favour of Israel because the nation had already suffered enough during these two months. Ellul pointed out that it was the month in which the ruined wall of Jerusalem was rebuilt.[1] Thereupon the month of Tishri came and reminded the Lord that it was the month in which Israel celebrated the Day of Atonement and the Feast of Tabernacles. It was also the month in which Solomon once dedicated the Temple of Jerusalem. The month of Heshvan was favourable to Israel because it was the month in which the building of the Temple of Jerusalem was completed. In Heshvan also Sarah, the wife of Abraham, died, and the month implored the Lord to remember Israel for the sake of the merits of Sarah. The months of Kislev and Tebet pleaded that not only were they the months in which the Kings Sihon and Og were once defeated, but in which Israel celebrated the Feast of Lights, and in which Esra arose and performed good deeds. Thereupon the month of Shebat came and reminded the Lord that it was the month in which the Children of Israel once set out to punish the tribe of Benjamin for the misdeeds of Gibbah and the idol erected by Micah.

At last the turn of the month of Adar came, and the poor month found nothing to say either in its own favour or in the

---

[1] *Nehemiah*, vi, 15.

favour of the Jews. Curiously enough Adar proved to be the only month of the year in which nothing had happened that could be interpreted in favour of Israel. When Haman's lot fell upon the month of Adar, he rejoiced greatly, for it was a month of misfortune for Israel. Haman knew that during the month of Adar Moses died and Israel remained like a flock of sheep without a shepherd. What Haman, however, did not know was that in Adar Moses was born.

Thereupon the Jew-baiter once more cast lots so as to find out which of the twelve signs of the Zodiac would prove favourable to his plan and unfavourable to Israel. The constellation of the Ram said that Israel was a scattered nation and never would the heavenly Father consent to His son being offered to slaughter. The constellation of the Bull said that Joseph had been compared by his father Jacob to the firstling bullock. The constellation of the Twins said that twins did Tamar bear to Judah who both walked in the ways of the Lord. The constellation of the Crab recalled the merit of Jonah. The Lion said that God being called a lion was not likely to allow the fox to bite his children. It was also under the sign of the Lion that Daniel was cast into the den of lions. The sign of the Virgin said that Israel was often compared to a virgin. It recalled also the merits of Chananiah, Mishael, and Azariah. The constellation of the Balance claimed in favour of the Jews that they obeyed the Torah which forbade unjust balances. It also recalled the merits of Job. The Scorpion said that Israel was also called a scorpion, and it also recalled the merits of Ezechiel. The Archer said that the bows of the mighty men will be broken when directed against the sons of Judah who are masters of the bow. The Goat pointed out that it was a goat that once brought blessing to Jacob, whilst the Water-bearer said that Israel's dominion was like a bucket, and it also recalled the merits of Moses. The Fishes alone appeared to be favourable to Haman and unfavourable to the

Jews. Haman interpreted them as meaning that the Jews would be swallowed up like fishes.

Thereupon Haman urged King Ahasuerus to give his royal consent to a general massacre of the Jews. When Haman finished his long speech of accusation, Ahasuerus, who had listened very attentively, said: " Your advice to exterminate the Jews may be very good, and indeed it is good, but I am afraid lest their God destroy me even as He did destroy the Kings of old when they ventured to wage war against Israel."

" Your Majesty," replied Haman, " need not fear any longer the God of Israel, for He is old and weak, and His power is no longer what it used to be. Besides, the Children of Israel have sinned, and their God has abandoned them and no longer vouchsafes His favours unto them."

Many more objections did the ruler of Persia raise against Haman's arguments, but the Jew-baiter of old had a ready answer to everything.

" If Your Majesty," he said, " were to present to a Jew two cups of wine into one of which a fly had fallen, whilst the King himself had taken a sip out of the other, and bid the Jew drink out of one of the cups, then he would unhesitatingly choose the cup into which the fly had fallen rather than touch that out of which Your Majesty has drunk. Can Your Majesty have any pity with such a people?"

Ahasuerus still hesitated, for he feared the wrath of the Lord who had once destroyed the Kings Sihon and Og and all the rulers of Canaan. Thereupon the King summoned his counsellors and wise men and asked their opinion on the matter. The Persian grandees were inclined to dissuade Ahasuerus from following Haman's advice, for they, too, feared the anger of the Lord who would certainly wreak vengeance on the enemies of His chosen race.

" Chosen race!" mocked Haman, " had their God really loved the Jews, He would not have allowed the mighty Nebu-

chadnezzar to destroy the Temple of Jerusalem, and lead the
people into the Babylonian captivity. I tell ye, that ye need
no longer fear the anger of the God of Israel who has forsaken
the nation." Haman furthermore offered vast sums to the
King of Persia to compensate him for the loss of revenue
derived from taxes paid by the Jews. The heathen sages and
wise men ultimately agreed to Haman's plan, and the Persian
monarch yielded. He gave his signature to a sort of St. Bartholomew night of antiquity, allowing the massacre of the
Jews.

THE DECREE

Haman now called his scribes and dictated unto them a
decree which he issued to all the heads and princes of the
nation concerning the annihilation of the Jews. Among other
things the Jew-baiter informed the rulers of the provinces
that the world would have rest only when the whole of Israel
was destroyed, men, women, and children.

" The great eagle of Israel," ran the decree, " had stretched
out his pinions over the whole world, and neither bird nor
beast could withstand him. Then Nebuchadnezzar, the great
lion, dealt him a blow and plucked out his feathers, and the
world enjoyed rest for a while. We must not, however, permit
the eagle to let his feathers grow and to gather strength, but
lay snares to him and prevent him from returning to his eagle's
eyrie. It would be useless to destroy only the men, to carry
them into exile or to assign to them another land. If the world
wishes to enjoy tranquillity, then the entire nation of Israel
must be wiped out."

Another decree was sent out by Ahasuerus himself wherein
the King accused the Jews of being presumptuous, ungrateful,
and a stumbling-block in all times. In accordance, therefore,
with the consent of the Satraps and Princes, the King had
resolved to extirpate the Jews. The decree, declared the King

of Persia, was an irrevocable resolution according to the laws of the Persians and Medes.

THE INDICTMENT OF SATAN

Haman left the court full of jubilation, whilst Mordecai, who had learned all that had occurred, was in a state of despair. On his way Mordecai met three Jewish boys coming from school, and he asked them to tell him what verse from Scripture they had studied to-day.

The first of the children replied: " Be not afraid of sudden fear, neither of the desolation of the wicked, when it cometh."[1]

The second boy had studied the following verse: " Let them take counsel together, but it shall be brought to naught." [2]

The third boy had learnt the following verse: " And even to old age I am He." [3]

When Mordecai heard these verses recited by the school-children, he looked upon it as a good omen and was comforted.

" Good news has been announced to me by the school-children," he said to Haman when he met him.

" Is that so?" replied Haman; " then they shall be the first to feel my hand."

Mordecai's prayers almost induced the Lord to have mercy upon Israel, but Satan soared up before the Throne of God and indicted the Jews. When the Tempter saw that the Jews were repenting of their sins and praying to the Lord to save them from destruction, he rushed up to heaven, and standing before the Throne of Glory raised his voice of accusation against Israel.

" Lord of the Universe," argued the accuser, " do not be swayed and influenced by the prayers and lamentations of the nation of Israel, for such has always been their way. When they are left in peace they forsake Thee, but when a calamity

[1] *Prov.*. iii, 25.   [2] *Isaiah*, viii, 10.   [3] *Isaiah*, xlvi, 4.

threatens them they at once turn to Thee and plead for mercy. It is not out of love for Thee that they are now repenting and mending their ways, but because they are frightened of the doom that awaits them. It is not love of Thee but fear of Haman that has caused them to turn good and pious. Forty-eight prophets and seven prophetesses have in vain preached to that obstinate nation but it never heeded the words of wise counsel. Now that the Jews have suddenly been informed of the decree issued against them, they are turning to Thee and praying for mercy and divine intervention. Verily, such a nation does not deserve Thy divine mercy. Remember, O Lord, that thousands of these Jews never hesitated to feast at the table of Ahasuerus, although Mordecai had implored them to abstain."

" And who," replied the Lord, " will sing my praises, if I destroy the nation of Israel?"

" Heaven and earth, Thy creations, will praise Thee in all eternity," said Satan.

When the Torah saw that Israel was indeed doomed to destruction, she dressed in black, as a sign of mourning, and raised a bitter wail, and her lamentations resounded through the seven heavens. The angels in heaven, too, shed tears of pity and pleaded for Israel.

" Lord of the Universe," cried the angels of mercy, " if Thou dost destroy the nation of Israel, then destroy us too." And when the sun and the moon heard the bitter cries of the angels they grew dark and withheld their light from the world.

The loud wailings of the angels and the bitter cry of the Torah touched the heart of the Prophet Elijah. The Tishbite hastened to Hebron, where the Patriarchs lie buried, and he called aloud: " Awake, ye sleepers! know ye not that the sun and the moon, heaven and earth and the angels in heaven are weeping and lamenting because your children are to be exterminated? They have forfeited their life on account of their sins. How can ye sleep in peace and tranquillity! Arise, ye just and pious men, and intercede for Israel."

Elijah also hastened to the graves of the prophets and to that of Moses and cried in despair: " O faithful shepherd, an edict of annihilation has just been issued against thy flock!" Thereupon Moses asked:

" How has the decree been sealed, with wax or with blood?"

" With wax," replied Elijah.

" Then there is still hope," said the son of Amram.

Moses thereupon asked Elijah whether there were any saints in Israel in the present generation, to which the Tishbite replied that there was only one saint among them, namely Mordecai.

" Then go and tell Mordecai," said Moses, " to pray to the Lord, whilst the saints and just men who have departed will unite their prayers with his and thus avert the calamity that is threatening the nation." [1]

---

[1] The entire chapter is based on the following sources: *Babylonian Talmud, Megilla*, 10b ff.; *Pirke di Rabbi Eliezer*, Ch. 49; *Josippon*, ed. Breithaupt, Gotha, 1707, II, pp. 77–84; *Midrash Esther Rabba; Midrash Lekach Tob*, ed. Buber; *Midrash Abba Gorion*, Jellinek, *Beth-Hamidrash*, Vol. I, pp. 1–18; *Sifra d'Agadatha*, ed. Buber, 1880; *Targum Sheni to Esther*; cf. also M. Gaster, *The Oldest Version of Midrash Megillah*, in G. A. Kohut, *Semitic Studies*, p. 174 ff.; see also Lewner, *Kol Aggadot*, Vol. IV, pp. 87–104.

CHAPTER XX

Mordecai's Dream
and the Downfall of Haman

Mordecai's strange dream—The two dragons—the small nation—The
fountain separating the fighting dragons—Mordecai's dream as related in
the *Apocrypha*—Esther's prayer—Fast day and festival—Esther appears
before the King—Why Esther invited the King and Haman to her banquet
—The jealousy of the King—Haman and his friends—The advice of Zeresh
—The gallows for the Jews—A sleepless night—The despair of the Jews—
Esther has turned traitress to her people—Haman's threat to put the Jewish
infants to death—The suspicions of Ahasuerus—The book of records—
Shamshai, the confidential secretary—The mysterious voice—Mordecai's
reward—Haman's pleading—The vizier turns barber—The Jew-baiter's
daughter—Her suicide—The end of the vizier—Harbonah's denunciation
—The new decree of the King—The story of Haman in Mohammedan
legend—The Feast of Purim—Albiruni and Makrizi.

MORDECAI'S DREAM

When Esther heard from her attendants that her foster-
father had appeared in the streets of the capital in sackcloth
and ashes, she was greatly alarmed. She immediately sent
Hathach, who was none other than Daniel, to find out the
cause of Mordecai's mourning. Mordecai informed Esther of
what had taken place and of the impending calamity threatening the nation of Israel. He further said to Hathach, Esther's
messenger:

" Tell Esther to intercede on behalf of our people, for God
has already shown me the future in a dream, and I know that
the plan of our enemies will be frustrated if my foster-daughter
pleads before the King. If Esther asks thee what is that dream,
then answer her as follows:

" In the second year of the reign of Ahasuerus, in the capital of Shushan, Mordecai had a dream. And lo! there was a terrible earthquake and a mighty uproar and tumult in heaven and upon earth. And behold! in the uproar and tumult two dragons were fighting and the noise they made was terrible. And great fear and terror seized the nations of the earth, and they fled before the uproar and scattered themselves on all sides. And behold! there was a small people among the nations of the world, and all the other nations arose against that small people and tried to destroy it and to wipe out its memory from the land. And on that day there was darkness and obscurity for all the inhabitants of the earth, and the small nation was in dire distress. And it cried to the Eternal and prayed to God for its life. And the two dragons were fighting one against the other with great cruelty, but there was none to separate them. And behold! A small fountain issued forth from between the two dragons and separated them. And the fountain grew bigger and bigger until it became a mighty stream flooding the world and discharging its roaring waves over the earth even like the mighty ocean. Thereupon the sun rose up and shed its light over the whole world; then the small nation arose and became great, whereupon peace and truth reigned supreme upon earth and the world was at peace.

"Tell Esther," continued Mordecai, "that the interpretation of my dream is quite clear. The two dragons are Haman and myself, and the nations of the world have risen up to destroy Israel. The fountain of water is the fountain of help from which the people of Israel will draw as soon as it will repent and return to the Lord. The sun is Esther herself whom the King has taken to wife and made her queen in the place of Vashti. It is Esther's duty to go to the King and plead on behalf of her people." [1]

[1] *Esther Rabba*; *Yalkut Shimeoni, Esther*, Ch. 4; Jellinek, *Beth-Hamidrash*, Vol. V. pp. 1–8; Wünsche, *Aus Israels Lehrhallen*, Vol. I, pp. 149–160; see also E. Kautzsch, *Die Apocryphen und Pseudoepigraphen*, Tübingen, 1900, Vol. I, pp. 193–212, and Ryssel's Introduction, pp. 193–200; P. de Lagarde, *Hagiographa Chaldaice*, 1873, pp. 362–365; A. Merx, *Chrestomathia Targumica*, 1888, pp. 154–164.

It will be interesting to compare the Midrash relating Mordecai's dream with the additions found in the LXX, known as the *Apocrypha*.

2. In the second year of the reign of Artaxerxes the great, in the first day of the month Nisan, Mardocheus the son of Jairus, the son of Semei, the son of Cisai, of the tribe of Benjamin, had a dream;

3. who was a Jew, and dwelt in the city of Susa, a great man, being a servitor in the king's court.

4. He was also one of the captives, which Nabuchodonosor the king of Babylon carried from Jerusalem with Jechonias king of Judea; and this was his dream:

5. Behold a noise of a tumult, with thunder, and earthquakes, and uproar in the land:

6. and, behold, two great dragons came forth ready to fight, and their cry was great.

7. And at their cry all nations were prepared to battle, that they might fight against the righteous people.

8. And lo a day of darkness and obscurity, tribulation and anguish, affliction and great uproar, upon earth.

9. And the whole righteous nation was troubled, fearing their own evils, and were ready to perish.

10. Then they cried unto God, and upon their cry, as it were from a little fountain, was made a great flood, even much water.

11. The light and the sun rose up, and the lowly were exalted, and devoured the glorious.

12. Now when Mardocheus, who had seen this dream, and what God had determined to do, was awake, he bare this dream in mind, and until night by all means was desirous to know it.

Then Mardocheus said, God hath done these things

5. For I remember a dream which I saw concerning these matters, and nothing thereof hath failed.

6. A little fountain became a river, and there was light, and the sun, and much water: this river is Esther, whom the king married, and made queen:

7. and the two dragons are I and Aman.

8. And the nations were those that were assembled to destroy the name of the Jews:

9. and my nation is this Israel, which cried to God, and were saved: for the Lord hath saved his people, and the Lord hath delivered us from all those evils, and God hath wrought signs and great wonders, which have not been done among the Gentiles.

10. Therefore hath he made two lots, one for the people of God, and another for all the Gentiles.

11. And these two lots came at the hour, and time, and day of judgment, before God among all nations.

12. So God remembered his people, and justified his inheritance.

13. Therefore those days shall be unto them in the month Adar, the fourteenth and fifteenth day of the same month, with an assembly, and joy, and with gladness before God, according to the generations for ever among his people.[1]

ESTHER'S PRAYER

For a long time Esther resisted Mordecai's request urging her to intercede on behalf of Israel. Hathach had in the meantime been killed by Haman, and the archangels Michael and Gabriel came therefore to act as messengers from Mordecai to Esther and back again. Esther yielded in the end, but made a request to Mordecai to proclaim a fast on her behalf. Although it happened to be Passover, Mordecai consented and decided to transgress the law which forbids fasting on holidays and festivals.

[1] *The Apocrypha, Esther*, Ch. XI and Ch. X.

Arrayed in silken garments and decked out with diamonds and pearls, but with a heavy heart, Esther betook herself to the monarch of Persia to plead for her people. Before proceeding on her way, Esther uttered a long prayer to the God of her fathers.

" God of Abraham," she sobbed, " of Israel and Jacob, and God of my ancestor Benjamin, Thou art a great God. If I now dare to go and appear uninvited before that ' foolish ' monarch it is not because I consider myself to be without fault or blemish. I do this so that Israel may not be cut off from the world. The whole world has been created for the sake of Israel, and if this nation were to cease to exist, who will exclaim before Thee thrice daily ' Holy, Holy, Holy '? Thou who once didst save Chananiah, Mishael, and Azariah out of the burning furnace and Daniel out of the den of lions, save me from the wrath of that foolish King whom I am now going to approach. For the sake of Abraham protect now his beloved children and call Haman to account for the evil he intends to do unto us. I am now going to the King to plead for my people, but I implore Thee, O God, to send Thy angel of compassion with me and let Thy favour and grace be my companions. May it be Thy will to put the charm of Jacob into my mouth and the grace of Joseph upon my tongue. O Lord, Thou who art called merciful and gracious, lead us out of distress. For the sake of the Patriarchs, Abraham, Isaac, and Jacob, may it be Thy will that my request be not left unfulfilled nor my petition be turned aside."[1]

[1] Cf. Jellinek, *ibid.*; Kautzsch, *ibid.*; *Midrash Megillat Esther.*

Esther appears before the King

Thereupon Esther, accompanied by two of her faithful maids, betook herself to the royal palace. She entered the inner apartments and soon found herself, though uninvited, in the presence of the ruler of Persia. When Ahasuerus suddenly beheld Esther he waxed very wroth, for the Queen had thus acted against the etiquette of the Persian court, and according to the laws of the Persians and Medes she had incurred the penalty of death. Esther was greatly frightened when she noticed the anger of the King reflected upon his countenance, but the Lord had pity with the poor orphan and increased her grace and beauty so that she found favour in the eyes of Ahasuerus. The King hastily descended from his throne and hurried to meet his beloved wife.

"Esther," he called, "why art thou trembling? Art thou not my beloved wife? Woe unto the man who will dare to do thee harm." When the royal servants heard these words uttered by their master, they refrained from laying hands upon Esther, although she had transgressed the laws of Persia by appearing uninvited in the presence of the King.

Thereupon the King inquired after the cause which had prompted Esther to take such an unprecedented step, to which Esther replied that she had come to invite the King and Haman to a banquet she had prepared. Esther did this for several reasons. "When Haman hears," she said unto herself, "that he has been invited to my banquet together with the King, he will no longer think of speaking ill of my people, and of exciting the King's anger against Israel. He will also cease doing harm to my faithful servants even as he has put to death Hathach who served me as messenger, carrying my messages to Mordecai."

Esther also thought that when the Children of Israel will hear that all that the Queen had done for them was merely to invite the King and Haman to a banquet, they will lose faith in her and no longer expect anything from her intervention. " Esther has abandoned us," they will say, " and it will be best for us no longer to count upon the help of mortals but pray to the Lord to save us."

Esther had also another purpose in mind when she invited the King and Haman to her banquet. " When my royal husband sees," thought the Queen, " that I have invited only himself and Haman to my banquet, he will grow jealous of Haman.

" ' Why,' he will ask in his heart, ' did the Queen invite only Haman to her banquet? No doubt she is in love with him and wishes to see him near her. I will cast him down from his exalted position and then Esther will no longer love him.' " Such were Esther's reasons for asking the King and Haman to honour her with their presence at the banquet she had prepared.

During the banquet the King told Esther to ask him for whatever favour she liked except the permission to rebuild the Temple of Jerusalem, for he remembered the promise he had given to Geshem the Arab, Sanballat and Tobiah, never, to permit the Jews to rebuild their Temple. Esther, however, replied that she asked for nothing except the honour of seeing the King and Haman at another banquet which she would prepare for them on the morrow. Ahasuerus wondered greatly at the Queen's strange request, but he said nothing and promised to come.

Haman returned home greatly elated and in high spirits. He summoned his 365 friends and advisers, and his wife Zeresh, and boasted to them of his greatness and the many honours heaped upon him.

" Great is my wealth," proudly said the Jew-baiter of antiquity, " and all the princes of the Empire are paying homage unto me. All my sons are governors of provinces, whilst Shamshai, my son, is confidential secretary and private reader to our royal master. Even the Queen honours me above all the princes and grandees, for, besides the King himself, I am the only guest she has invited to her banquet." His only sorrow was to see Mordecai the Jew still alive. His friends wondered why he the mighty minister and favourite of the King did not simply kill the contemptible Jew.

Thereupon Zeresh said: " It is all very well for ye to say: ' Kill the Jew,' but have ye forgotten Mordecai's race and nationality? He is a son of that race whom neither water or fire, nor hunger or sword ever affect. Have you not heard what miracles the God of that people worked in favour of Chananiah, Mishael, and Azariah whom he saved out of the fiery furnace? Remember Daniel, whom the God of Israel saved out of the den of lions, and Joseph the son of Jacob whom he delivered from gaol and raised to be King over the land of Egypt. Remember their hero Samson who killed many more Philistines in the moment of his death than he had ever killed when he was alive. I advise thee therefore, O my husband, to decree death by hanging over Mordecai, for in all the history of the Jews I know of none of them whom their God had saved from such a death." Thus spoke Zeresh, and her advice pleased her husband well. Haman determined to put an end to Mordecai's life by hanging him on a tall tree. He immediately gave the necessary instructions to his servants, and during the night the gallows upon which Mordecai was to be strung up was speedily made ready.

A SLEEPLESS NIGHT

That night was a sleepless one for many people in Shushan, the capital of Persia. It was a sleepless night for Mordecai and his fellow Jews. They had heard of Esther's conduct and knew that she had merely invited the King and Haman to her banquet. Ignoring the real aim and purpose of the Queen, the Jews concluded that Esther had abandoned their cause and made friends with their enemy.

" Alas," they cried, " our hope has proved futile. We put our trust in our sister who is in an exalted position and hoped that she would plead for us and save us from destruction, but she has turned traitress."

Great was the distress of the Jews of Shushan, and they turned against Mordecai, accusing him of being the cause of their misfortune.

" Hadst thou not been so obstinate," they cried, " and consented to bow to Haman and pay him homage, our lives and the lives of our wives and children would at this moment not have been in danger."

It was a sleepless night for Esther, for with an aching heart she was busy preparing the banquet to which she had invited her royal spouse and Haman.

It was also a sleepless night for Haman. He remembered his threat, first to put to death the infants and little children of Israel, and decided to carry out this threat at once. Accompanied by a regiment of soldiers, he visited the Synagogue where the children were assembled, reading the Holy Law, weeping and praying. The Jew-baiter commanded his soldiers to count the children and there were twenty-two thousand of them. Haman gave instructions to put the innocent victims in irons and keep them prisoners until dawn when they would be led to the place of execution.

It was also a sleepless night for the King of Persia. Ahasuerus could not forget the fact that the Queen had invited no other guest to keep him company except Haman. He thought in his heart: " Who knows, Esther and her lover Haman are perhaps plotting to kill me and Haman hopes to become King in my place. I wonder whether there is one among my courtiers faithful enough to me to reveal unto me the conspiracy." Thereupon the King fell asleep and had a terrible

dream. He saw his vizier bending over him, holding a sword
in his hand and ready to kill him. Ahasuerus awoke with a
start and was greatly frightened. He thereupon commanded
his confidential secretary and reader to bring him the book of
records and read out aloud all the important events which had
occurred during his reign. The secretary was none other than
Shamshai, Haman's son, and he read aloud until he came to
the chapter relating the incident how Mordecai the Jew had
discovered a conspiracy and saved the King's life. Shamshai
was about to skip the pages, when lo! a miracle happened. The
writing was read aloud by some invisible person and a mysterious voice.

Mordecai's Reward

The Persian monarch decided to reward royally the man
who had saved his life. He summoned his vizier and asked
him to suggest some signal honour for a man who had saved
the King's life. Haman at first expressed it as his opinion that
the man whom the King wished to honour should not only
ride upon the King's horse, but also wear the royal crown
upon his head. Noticing, however, the great anger reflected
upon the King's countenance he wisely refrained from insisting
upon the wearing of the crown. " I am now firmly convinced,"
thought Ahasuerus in his heart, " that Haman is indeed plotting to kill me and to take my place."

When the King at last revealed unto Haman the identity
of the man whom he wished to honour, the vizier grew frightened. In vain did he advise Ahasuerus to heap other honours
upon Mordecai, in vain did he offer to the King to give the
Jew vast sums of money, to let his wife and children be his
servants if only the monarch would spare him the humiliation
of leading Mordecai riding upon the royal horse through the
streets of the capital. The more Haman pleaded the more
angry Ahasuerus grew.

" All that thou hast offered to give to the Jew thou wilt accomplish," cried the King of Persia, " but in addition to all this thou wilt instantly carry out my command. Hurry at once to Mordecai and array him in my royal robes and let him mount my horse which thou wilt lead through the streets of Shushan."

Haman was forced to do as the King commanded him, and humbly betook himself to Mordecai, to whom he communicated the royal wish.

" I cannot don the royal robes," replied the humble Jew, " for I must first bathe and anoint my body and trim my beard out of respect for His Majesty." Haman was in a great hurry to do the King's bidding, and delay was dangerous. Unable to find either a bather or a barber, he was perforce compelled to perform these functions himself. When the vizier was cutting Mordecai's hair and trimming his beard, he sighed heavily.

" Why art thou sighing?" asked the Jew.

" Is it not sad," replied Haman, " that I, the mighty vizier, should now be reduced to perform the humiliating functions of a bather and barber?" Mordecai smiled.

" Thou seemest to have a very short memory," he replied, " Hast thou forgotten that thou wast a barber in the village of Karzum in days bygone before thy sudden rise to power?"

Mordecai, having fasted for many days, was too weak and feeble to mount the royal horse, and Haman had to bend his knee and help his enemy into the saddle. When Haman was leading the Jew through the streets of Shushan, the vizier's daughter, looking down from the roof of her house, imagined that it was her father who was riding upon the royal horse, whilst Mordecai, the despised Jew, was running before him. Quickly she snatched up a vase full of dirt and excrements and emptied the contents upon her father's head. When she realized her mistake she threw herself down from the roof and was killed.

THE TRIUMPH OF MORDECAI

The End of the Jew-baiter

Swiftly now followed Haman's downfall. During the banquet the Queen revealed to her royal spouse his vizier's plans.

" The royal treasury," said Esther, " will suffer greatly in consequence of the annihilation of the Jews, for Haman has omitted to inform thee of the vast amount of revenue derived from the taxes paid by the Jews in the Empire."

Ahasuerus, who was already suspecting Haman of plotting to kill him, was glad of an opportunity to get rid of his vizier. Haman rose up to plead for his life and at that moment an invisible hand pushed him forward so that he fell upon the couch on which the Queen was seated. This increased the King's ire who was already suspecting Haman of being the Queen's lover.

Now Harbonah, one of the Persian courtiers, stepped forward and informed His Majesty that it was the vizier himself who had hired the two Tarsians to poison their royal master. Haman had thus hoped to become King himself, and when he heard that the plot had been frustrated thanks to Mordecai, his hatred of the Jew knew no bounds. The insinuations of Harbonah completely exasperated Ahasuerus and he gave orders to put the vizier and his sons to death.

Thereupon the monarch annulled the decree which he had issued commanding the wholesale massacre of the Jews. " For a long time," wrote Ahasuerus to the governors of his provinces, " I firmly believed that Haman, the son of Hamdata whom I had raised to the dignity of vizier, was my faithful servant and always acted in the interests of my Empire. I therefore listened to his words when he counselled the destruction of the Jews dwelling in my dominions. It has now, however, come to my knowledge that Haman was an enemy both of myself and the Empire, and was only inspired by an unjustifiable hatred of my peaceful subjects, the Jews. He even plotted to kill me and to take my place. A just punishment has been meted out to the traitor, who has been strung up on the gallows. It is now my royal wish and command that my loyal subjects, the Jews, be allowed to live unharmed and in peace in all my dominions." [1]

THE FEAST OF PURIM IN ARABIC LITERATURE

Several Mohammedan authors refer to the feast of Purim and the story of Haman and Mordecai. Thus Albiruni quotes the following passage:

" The Fasting of Alburi (Purim), i.e. casting of lots. The origin is this: once a man called Haman, a man of no importance, travelled to Tastar to undertake some office. But on the way thither he met with an obstacle which prevented him from reaching the end of his journey, and this happened on the identical day on which the offices (in Tastar) were bestowed. So he missed his opportunity and fell into utter distress. Now, he took his seat near the temples and demanded for every dead body (that was to be buried) $3\frac{1}{3}$ drachms. This went on until the daughter of King Ahashverosh died. When the people came with her body, he demanded something from the bearers, and on being refused, he did not allow them to pass, until they yielded and were willing to pay him what he asked for. But then he was not content with his first demand; he asked more and more, and they paid him more and more, till at last it reached an enormous sum. The King was informed of the matter, and he ordered them to grant his desire. But after a week he ordered him in his presence, and asked him:

" ' Who invested thee with such an office?'

" But Haman simply answered this: ' And who forbade me to do so?'

[1] See note on p. 261; cf. Lewner, *l. c.*, pp. 111–142.

" When the King repeated his question, Haman said: ' If I am now forbidden to do so, I shall cease and give it up, and I shall give you with the greatest pleasure so and so many ten thousand of denares.'

" The King was astonished at the great sum of money he mentioned, because he with all his supreme power had nothing like it, so he said:

" ' A man who has gathered so much money from the rule over the dead, is worthy to be made wazir and councillor.'

" So he entrusted him with all his affairs and ordered his subjects to obey him.

" This Haman was an enemy of the Jews. He asked the *Haruspices* and *Augures* which was the most unlucky time for the Jews. They said: ' In Adhâr their master Musa died, and the most unlucky time of this month is the 14th and 15th.'

" Now Haman wrote to all parts of the Empire, ordering people on that day to seize upon the Jews and to kill them. The Jews of the Empire prostrated themselves before him, and appeared before him, crossing their hands upon their breasts, except one man, Mordecai, the brother of Ester, the King's wife. Haman hated her and planned her destruction on that day, but the King's wife understood him.

" Now she received (in her palace) the King and his wazir, entertaining them during three days. On the fourth day she asked the King's permission to lay before him her wishes. And then she asked him to spare her life and that of her brother. The King said:

" ' And who dares to attempt anything against ye both?' She pointed to Haman.

" Now the King rose from his seat in great wrath: Haman dashed towards the Queen, prostrating himself before her, and then kissing her head, but she pushed him back. Now the King got the impression that he wanted to seduce her: so he turned towards him and said:

" ' Hast thou in thy impudence come so far as to raise thy desire to her?'

" So the King ordered him to be killed, and Ester asked him to have him crucified on the same tree which he had prepared for her brother. So the King did, and wrote to all parts of the Empire to kill the partisans of Haman. So they were killed on the same day on which he had intended to kill the Jews, i.e. on the 14th. Therefore there is great joy over the death of Haman on this day. This feast is also called the *Feast of Megilla*, and further Hâmân-Sur. For on this day they make figures which they beat and then burn, imitating the burning of Haman. The same they practise on the 15th." [1]

Another Arabic author, Makrizi, writes as follows with regard to the story of Haman and Mordecai: " The feast of Purim is of modern date and owes its origin to the following incident:

" When Nebuchadnezzar led away the Jews of Jerusalem into captivity and ruined the city, he led the captives to Irak where he settled them in the city of Djai, known to-day as Ispahan. When Ardeshir, the son of Babec, whom the Jews called Ahasveros, became master of the kingdom of Persia he had a vizier named Haimoun. The Jews had as their chief in those days Mordecai. Ardeshir having learned that the Jewish chief had a beautiful cousin, he took her to wife. She gained the favour of the King who raised his wife's cousin Mordecai to high honours.

" Now the vizier Haimoun grew very jealous of Mordecai and conceived the plan to destroy not only the Queen's cousin but all the Jews who lived in Ardeshir's dominions. He therefore arranged with his lieutenants and the governors of the provinces to massacre all the Jews living in their respective districts on a certain day which was the 13th of Adar. Mor-

---

[1] Albiruni, trnsl. by E. Sachau, quoted by Paul de Lagarde in *Purim, Abhandlungen der Königlichen Gesellschaft der Wissenschaften zu Göttingen*, 1887, Philologisch-historische Klasse Vol. 34, No. 3.

decai discovered the plot and speedily informed his cousin,
the favourite wife of Ardeshir. He urged her to use her influence with Ardeshir and thus save her people from destruction. The princess hastened to inform Ardeshir of the doings
of his minister and of the instructions he had sent out to all
the governors of the provinces to kill the Jews. She excited
the King against his vizier so that Ardeshir ordered Haimoun
and his family to be put to death.

" Thereupon Ardeshir granted the Jews many privileges,
and in consequence the Jews have established a feast which
they observe annually in memory of the event. They consecrate
this day to fasting and thanksgiving to God and the next two
days to merry-making, rejoicing, and giving presents one to
the other. They also make the figure of the vizier Haimoun
whom they call Haman, and after mocking this figure they
burn it."

¹ Silvestre de Sacy, *Chrestomathie Arabe*, I, 95; see also P. de Lagarde, *l. c.*, pp. 12–13.

BIBLIOGRAPHY

I. WORKS IN HEBREW

Alphabetum Siracidis, ed. Steinschneider, Berlin, 1858.
Babylonian Talmud (cf. Bibliography to Vol. I).
Ben Hamelech-ve-Hanazir, Hebrew edition of *Prince and Dervish*.
Bialik and Ravnitzky, *Sepher Haaggadah*, Berlin.
Emek-Hamelech, Amsterdam, 1653.
Exodus Rabba, Vilna, 1902.
Genesis Rabba, Vilna, 1907.
Hibbur Yafeh.
Hibbur Maassiot, ed. Verona.
Jellinek, *Beth-Hamidrash*, 6 vols., Leipzig and Vienna, 1853–1877.
Josippon (Josephus Gorionides), ed. Breithaupt, Halle, 1707, ed. Amster-
   dam, 1771.
Leviticus Rabba.
Lewner, *Kol Agadoth*, Warsaw.
Likkute Maassiot, by Israel bar Sason, Jerusalem.
Maasse Nissim.
Midrash Esther Rabba.
Midrash Lekach Tob, ed. Buber, Vilna, 1884.
Midrash Mishle, ed. Buber, Vilna, 1893.
Midrash Ruth Rabba.
Midrash Samuel, ed. Buber, Cracow, 1893.
Midrash Shir Hashirim Rabba, Vilna, 1907.
Midrash Tanchuma, ed. Buber, 1865.
—— Stettin, 1865.
Midrash Tehillim, ed. Buber, Vilna, 1891.
Nishmat Hayim, by Manasseh ben Israel, Amsterdam, 1651.
Numeri Rabba, Vilna, 1907.
Ozar Midrashim, ed. Wertheimer, Jerusalem.
Pesikta de Rabbi Kahana, ed. Buber, Lyck, 1868.
Pesikta Rabbati, ed. Friedmann, Vienna, 1880.
Pirke de Rabbi Eliezer, ed. Venice, 1544; ed. Lemberg, 1867.
Sepher Hassidim, ed. Bologna, 1538.
Sifre d'Agadatha, ed. Buber, 1886.
Tanna debe Eliahu (also called *Seder Eliahu Rabba*), ed. Friedmann, 1902.
Targum Pseudo-Jonathan, ed. Ginsburger, Berlin, 1899.
Targum Sheni to Esther, ed. Cassel, 1885.
—— ed. David, 1898.
Yalkut, Vilna, 1898.

II. OTHER WORKS

Academy, The, 1891.
Archiv für Literaturgeschichte, Vol. XI.
Archiv für Slavonische Philologie, Vols. I, VI.
Barbazan, *Fabliaux,* Paris, 1808.
Behrnauer, *Die vierzig Viziere,* Leipzig, 1851.
Benfey, Th., *Orient u. Occident.*
—— *Panschatantra.*
Bergmann, J., *Die Legenden der Juden,* Berlin, 1919.
Bin Gorion, *Der Born Judas,* 6 vols.
Brooke, Stopford A., *English Literature from the Beginning to the Norman Conquest,* London, 1898.
Budge, Sir E. A. W., *The Book of the Bee (Anecdota Oxoniensa, Sem. Series,* Vol. I, Part 2).
Buttenwieser, *Die Hebr. Eliasapokalypse,* 1897.
Campbell, J. F., *Popular Tales of the West Highlands,* London, 1890.
Cassel, P., *Die Symbolik des Blutes,* Berlin, 1882.
—— *Kaiser u. Königsthrone,* Berlin, 1874.
—— *Schamir,* in *Denkschrift der Kgl. Akademie,* Erfurt, 1854.
Chauvin, V., *La Recension égyptienne des Mille et une Nuits,* Bruxelles, 1899.
Child, F. J., The *English and Scottish Ballads,* Vol. IX.
Clouston, *Popular Tales.*
Collier, *The History of English Dramatic Poetry.*
Cosquin, *Contes populaires de Lorraine.*
D'Ancona, *Novelle di Giovanni Sercambi,* Bologna, 1871.
Dragomanow, *Popular Tales and Traditions,* 1876.
Dunlop, *History of Prose Fiction.*
Faerber, *König Salomon in der Tradition,* 1902.
Folklore, Vol. XVI.
Frere, Mary, *Old Deccan Days.*
Friedlaender, J., *Die Chadhirlegende und der Alexanderroman,* Leipzig, 1913.
Gaster, M., *Jewish Sources of and Parallels to the Early English Metrical Romances of King Arthur and Merlin,* 1888.
—— *Literatura Pop. Romana,* 1883.
—— *The Oldest Version of Midrash Megillah,* in G. A. Kohut, *Semitic Studies.*
Geiger, A., *Jüdische Zeitschrift,* Vol. V.
Germania, Vols. XVIII, XXV, XXVI.
Gesta Romanorum, ed. J. G. T. Graesse, Leipzig, 1905.
—— ed. Oesterley, Berlin, 1882.
Hartland, *The Legend of Perseus.*
Hebräische Bibliographie, No. XIII, XVIII.
Hershon, P. J., *A Talmudical Miscellany,* London, 1880.
—— *Treasures of the Talmud,* London, 1882.
Horstmann, *Sammlung Altenglischer Legenden,* 1878.
Kautzsch, E., *Die Apokryphen und Pseudoepigraphen d. A. T.,* 2 vols., 1900.
Kemble, *Anglo-Saxon Dialogues of Solomon and Saturn,* 1848.

Koehler, R., *Kleinere Schriften*, Berlin, 1900.
Kuttner, *Jüdische Legenden.*
Lagarde, P. de, *Hagiographa Chaldaice*, 1873.
Landau, M., *Die Quellen des Dekameron*, 1884.
—— *Hebrew-German Romances and Tales* (*Teutonia*, Heft 27), Leipzig, 1912.
Lemke's *Jahrbuch*, No. XII.
Lightfoot, J., *Horæ Hebraicæ*, Rotterdam, 1686.
Loewy, A., *Miscellany of Hebrew Literature*, London, 1877.
L'Oiseleur Deslongchamps, *Essai sur les Fables Indiennes.*
Longfellow, *Poetical Works.*
Mahabharata, The (Roy's transl.).
Merx, A., *Chrestomathia Targumica*, 1888.
Midrash Hachefetz, Schechter's transl.: *Folklore*, Vol. I.
Migne, *Dictionnaire des Apocryphes*, Vol. II.
Mirkhond, *Rouzat-us-Safa*, ed. Rehatsek, Part I, Vol. II.
Monatsschrift für Literatur und Wissenschaft des Judentums, Vols. 22, 39.
Perles, *Zur Rabbinischen Sprach- und Sagenkunde*, 1873.
Piper, Dr. P., *Die Spielmannsdichtung* (in J. Kurschner's *Deutsche National-litteratur*, II, 1.)
Rambaud, A., *La Russie épique*, Paris, 1876.
Revue des Études Juives, Vols. 2, 8, 11, 17, 25, 33, 45.
Revue des Traditions Populaires, No. 2.
Robert, C. A., *Fables Inédites.*
Rosner, *David's Leben und Charakter*, 1908.
Sacy, S. de, *Chrestomathie Arabe.*
Salzberger, G., *Die Salomon Sage in der semitischen Literatur.*
—— *Salomons Tempelbau und Thron*, Berlin, 1912.
Seymour, St. John D., *Tales of King Solomon*, 1924.
Spectator, The, No. 578.
Strack, H., *Der Blutaberglaube*, Berlin, 1891.
Tabari, *Chronique*, ed. by H. Zotenberg, Paris, 1867–1874.
Tendlau, A., *Das Buch der Sagen und Legenden*, Stuttgart, 1842.
Thousand and One Nights.
Trumbull, H. C., *The Blood Covenant*, Philadelphia, 1893.
Tutti Nameh, G. Rosen's transl., 1858.
Varnhagen, *Ein Indisches Märchen*, Berlin, 1882.
Vesselovsky, *Iz istorii, &c.*, St. Petersburg, 1872.
Vincenti, A. V., *Die altenglischen Dialoge von Salomon und Saturn.*
Vogt, Fr., *Die deutschen Dichtungen von Salomon und Markolf*, Halle, 1880.
Von der Hagen, *Deutsche Gedichte des Mittelalters*, Berlin, 1808, Vol. I.
—— *Gesammtabenteuer*, III.
Weil, G., *Biblische Legenden der Muselmänner*, Frankfurt a/M., 1845.
Wünsche, A., *Aus Israel's Lehrhallen.*
Zeitschrift der Deutsch-Morgenländischen Gesellschaft=ZDMG, Vol. 31.
Zunz, *Gottesdienstliche Vorträge.*

ICONOGRAPHY

A list of a few famous paintings, engravings and statues illustrating Biblical stories or Biblical characters, who form the subjects of the post-biblical legends related in this work.

(A) *Adam and Eve*:

1. Statue of Adam, in the Cathedral at Milan.
2. The Temptation, by Lucas Cranach, in the Uffizi at Florence.
3. The Fall, by Raphael, Loggie.
4. Adam and Eve hiding, by N. Pisano, at Orvieto.
5. Expulsion of Adam and Eve, by Raphael, Loggie.

(B) *Abraham*:

1. Abraham driving away Hagar, by Paolo Farinato (1524–1606) at the Historical Society, New York.
2. The Sacrifice of Abraham, by Andrea del Sarto (1486–1531) in the Gallery at Dresden.
3. The Sacrifice of Abraham, by Ghiberti, bas-relief in bronze, Nat. Mus., Florence.
4. Abraham journeying with Lot, by M. Corneille (1642–1708).
5. Abraham and the Angels, by A. van Diepenbeck (1599–1675), at Munich.
6. Arithmetic accompanied by Abraham, in the large group by Taddeo Gaddi in the Dominican Convent of Santa Maria Novella in Florence, painted in 1322.

(C) *Isaac*.

1. Isaac blessing Jacob, by Raphael, Loggie.
2. Eliezer and Rebecca, by Nicolas Poussin.

(D) *Jacob*:

1. Jacob and Esau, by A. M. Seitz (1811–1888).
2. Jacob and Rachel, by J. Führich (1800–1876).
3. Jacob wrestling with Angel, by M. Corneille.

(E) *Joseph*:

1. Joseph's Coat, by Velasquez (1599–1660) in the Escorial.
2. Joseph sold by his Brethren, by A. M. Seitz (1811–1888).
3. Joseph recognized by his Brethren, by Peter v. Cornelius, at the National Gallery, Berlin.

(F) *Israel*:

1. The Delivery of Israel, by Michelangelo on the walls of the Sistine Chapel (*c.* 1480).
2. Hebrews gathering Manna, by Nicolas Poussin (1594–1666).

(G) *Moses*:

1. The Life of Moses, on the walls of the Sistine Chapel.
2. Moses journeying to Egypt, fresco in the Sistine Chapel, by Pinturicchio (Bernardino di Betto) (1454–1513).
3. Moses rescued from the Waves (1647), by Nicolas Poussin.
4. Moses breaking the Tables of the Law, by Parmigiano (Francesco Mazzuola) (1504–1540).
5. The Finding of Moses, by A. M. Seitz (1811–1888).
6. Moses, scenes from his life, by Johann Schrandolph (1808–1879), frescoes in Church of All Saints at Munich.
7. Moses bringing down the Tables of the Law, by J. Rogers Herbert (1810–1890), in the House of Lords.
8. Moses striking the Rock, by Francisco Herrera the Elder (1576–1656), in the Archiepiscopal Palace at Madrid.
9. Moses, by Pinturicchio, in the Sistine Chapel, Rome.
10. Moses, by Philippe de Champagne, at Leningrad.
11. Moses, by Carlo Dolci, in the Pitti Palace at Florence.
12. Moses, statue by Michelangelo, Pietro in Vinculi, Rome.
13. Moses, life of, frescoes by Michelangelo.
14. Moses saved from the Waters, by Raphael, Loggie.
15. The Lord writes the Commandments upon the Tables of Stone, by Jos. Führich (1800–1876).
16. Moses striking the Rock, by J. A. von Gegenbauer (1800–1876), at Stuttgart.

(H) *Joshua*:

1. Joshua and the Destruction of Jericho, by Jos. Führich.

(J) *David*:

1. David, painting by Antonio Pollajuolo (1432–1498), in the Berlin Museum.
2. David (called the Zuccone, Baldheaded), by Donatello (1386–1466).
3. David in bronze, by Verocchio (1435–1488), National Museum, Florence.

(K) *Solomon*:

1. The Judgment of Solomon, by Nicolas Poussin (1649).
2. The Judgment of Solomon, by J. R. Herbert, in the House of Lords.
3. The Building of the Temple, by the same.
4. The Visit of the Queen of Sheba, by the same.

(L) *Mordecai and Esther*:

1. The Coronation of Esther.
2. Esther being presented to King Ahasuerus.
3. The Triumph of Mordecai, by Paul Veronese, in the Church San Sebastiano, at Venice.
4. Esther before Ahasuerus, by Hans Burckmair (1473–1531), at Munich.

INDEX

Aaron, dances at father's wedding, ii, 215; meets Moses, ii, 275; not envious of Moses, ii, 276; in presence of Pharaoh, ii, 277; resembles angel, ii, 278; and Balaam, ii, 280; celebrates Passover, ii, 283; and clouds of glory, ii, 325, 326; death of, ii, 333; as peacemaker, ii, 336, 337; soul lured away by Divine kiss, ii, 340; vizier of Pharaoh, ii, 378; death of, in Moslem legend, ii, 390.

Ab, mouth of, iii, 255.

Abel, story of, i, 193 *et seq.*; burial of, i, 194, 197; twin sister of, i, 195; " the prayer of ", a poem, i, 203; blood of, ii, 295.

Abiel, iii, 1.

Abihu, ii, 302; iii, 129.

Abimelech, ii, 207; iii, 26.

Abiram, ii, 241.

Abishai, iii, 29.

Abner, mother of, iii, 3; flask of, iii, 21.

Abraham, and Sammael, i, 68; death of, i, 69; birth of, i, 226 *et seq.*; leaves his cave, i, 230; before Nimrod, i, 232; sells idols, i, 239; in jail, i, 247; in fiery furnace, i, 250; in the King's dale, i, 259; hospitality of, i, 262; judges men, i, 278; visits Ishmael, i, 283 *et seq.*; tested by God, i, 287; covenant with Jebusites, i, 309; a reader of stars, i, 311; death of, i, 323 *et seq.*; installs artificial light, i, 324; refuses to give up his soul, i, 327; visits heaven, i, 329 *et seq.*; visits Paradise, i, 333; funeral of, i, 335; the ass of, ii, 275; and Og, ii, 329; covenant with the Jebusites, iii, 23.

Absalom, in hell, i, 131; rebellion of, iii, 28.

Academy, the heavenly, i, 8.

Achitophel, jealous of David, iii, 116.

Achseriel, i, 6.

Adam, creation of, i, 6; in nethermost earth, i, 24; and Lilith, i, 77; creation of, in Moslem legend, i, 141 *et seq.*; composes psalm, i, 144; and David, i, 148; marriage of, i, 151; penance of, i, 175 *et seq.*; death of, i, 178 *et seq.*; burial of, i, 185; life in Moslem legend, i, 186; and Iblis, i, 189; watches procession of souls, i, 330.

Adamah, i, 24.

Adar, month of, iii, 255; Moses born in, iii, 256.

Adares and Solomon, i, 105.

Adiel, iii, 12.

Adina, wife of Levi, ii, 213.

Adonai, ii, 273.

Adoniah, ii, 246, 248.

Advel, stone, i, 17.

Af, angel, ii, 317.

Agnias, ii, 173, 176, 179, 181, 192, 194, 195.

Agrath, i, 79.

Ahab, ii, 22; iii, 210, 240.

Ahasuerus, throne of Solomon, iii, 116, 243; and vessels from temple, iii, 244; banquet of, iii, 245; regrets Vashti, iii, 249; decree of, iii, 258; sleepless night of, iii, 270; jealous of Haman, iii, 273.

Ahasuerus, the wandering Jew, iii, 241.

Aheyya, i, 61.

Ahish, iii, 20.

Aishia, wife of Pharaoh, ii, 373.

Akatriel, i, 35.

Akher, i, 44.

Akiba, Rabbi, ii, 311; iii, 214.

Akko, the poor lad from, iii, 109.

Akshid, Sultan, tale of, iii, 60.

Alanad, iii, 101.

Alburi, Fasting of, iii, 274.

Alexander the Great, meets descendants of Cain, i, 203; carries off throne of Solomon, iii, 115.

Altamar, iii, 102.

Amalek, and Israel, ii, 300, 301, 326.

rebukes David, iii, 179; consoles Solomon, iii, 184; as messenger of Esther, iii, 265.
Gad, hated Joseph, ii, 52.
Galgaliel, angel, i, 36.
Gallizur, angel, i, 52.
Ge, i, 24.
Gellert, poem by, ii, 266.
Geshem the Arab, iii, 268.
Gesta Romanorum, tales from, ii, 267; iii, 53, 142, 152.
Gift of Moses, ii, 237.
Glow of Anger, angel, ii, 317.
Goat, constellation of, iii, 256.
God, in Jewish myth, i, 2, 4; of the Hebrews, ii, 278, 279.
Gods, of pagan antiquity, i, 3.
Goiel, i, 26.
Goliath, iii, 15; and David, iii, 17, 18; brothers of, iii, 20.
Grimelshausen, ii, 101.
Gunputti, iii, 146.

Hadad, son of Badad, ii, 192, 195, 201.
Hadarniel, i, 50; ii, 309.
Hadassa, iii, 249.
Hagar, a daughter of Pharaoh, i, 283; iii, 6.
Hahn, Joseph, iii, 56.
Haimoun, iii, 276 *et seq.*
Haman, vizier of Pharaoh, ii, 368 *et seq.*
Haman, and Mordecai, iii, 251 *et seq.*; speech of accusation, iii, 257; downfall of, iii, 262; in high spirits, iii, 268; sleepless night, iii, 270; and his daughter, iii, 272; performs function of barber, iii, 272.
Haman-Sur, iii, 276.
Hamdata, iii, 250.
Hans Sachs, poem by, iii, 144.
Haran, and Abraham, i, 244; death of, i, 250.
Harbonah, iii, 273.
Haritsu, demon, iii, 205.
Haron, angel, ii, 317.
Hartland, iii, 56, 111.
Harut, i, 64.
Hashmalim, i, 48.
Hathach, iii, 262.
Hav, the leper, ii, 328.
Heaven, description of, in *Mahabharata*, i, 135; two doors leading to, i, 329; refuses to plead for Moses, ii, 349.
Heavenly Court, i, 8.
Heavens, seven, i, 19, 20, 21, 22.
Heber, ii, 221.
Hebrews, moral life of, ii, 191; a danger to Egypt, ii, 197; sufferings of, ii, 202; God of the, ii, 278.
Hebron, iii, 260.
Heizam, fiery steed, ii, 378.
Helen of England, ii, 99.

Hell, description of, i, 131; in *Ardai-Viraf*, i, 137.
Hemah, angel ii, 317.
Hermilaos, iii, 234.
"Hermit, The", poem, ii, 267.
Hermon, Mount, ii, 305.
Herrand von Wildonie, iii, 144.
Heshbon, ii, 328.
Heshvan, month of, iii, 255.
Heydad, story of, i, 270.
Heyya, i, 61.
Hijja, i, 61.
Hills, refuse to plead for Moses, ii, 350.
Hindoo Fairy Legends, iii, 146.
Hiram of Tyre, iii, 112, 206.
Hiskil, ii, 379, 380.
Histoire d'Olivier de Castille, iii, 33.
Historia Scholastica, ii, 227; iii, 151.
Hiwwa, i, 61.
Hol, bird, i, 159.
Hoopoe, the, and Solomon, iii, 122.
Hor, Mount, ii, 336.
Horeb, Mount, ii, 270.
Hud, ii, 379.
Hur, ii, 314.
Husham of Theman, ii, 176.
Hushim, jumps to Egypt, ii, 135; kills Esau, ii, 137.

Iblis, i, 59; refuses to bow to Adam, i, 146, 189.
Igdrasil, tree, i, 137.
Iggeret Baale Hayyim, i, 168.
Injustice, in the Ark, i, 212.
Innocents, the fate of the, ii, 203.
Isa, ii, 5, 6.
Isaac, birth of, i, 281; sacrifice of, i, 290 *et seq.*; in the school of Shem, i, 310; meets Rebekah, i, 321; dream of, i, 326; consoles Jacob, ii, 20.
Ishbi Benob, iii, 29.
Ish-Hasrid, a hymn, iii, 220.
Ishim, i, 33.
Ishmael, i, 283 *et seq.*; iii, 6; sons of, refuse Torah, ii, 304.
Ishmaelites, ii, 15, 26, 31, 86.
Israel, myths of, i, 2; suffering of, ii, 281; accepts Torah, ii, 304; and Amalek, ii, 300; furnishes guarantee, ii, 306; in the desert, ii, 318; in valley of Arnon, ii, 327; and daughters of Moab, ii, 331; and dead Egyptians, ii, 383.
Israelites, servitude, ii, 189; assimilation, ii, 190; day of rest, ii, 236; leave Egypt, ii, 285; enter Red Sea, ii, 288; wonders worked for, ii, 297; fight Moabites, ii, 330; compelled to accept Torah, ii, 384.
Israfil, angel, i, 145; ii, 392, 394.
Istahar, i, 60.

(D 544)

70